JEWRY IN
ENGLAND

BOOKS FROM CLEMENS & BLAIR
— www.clemensandblair.com —

Jewry in France, by Telemachus Timayenis
Homilies Against the Jews, by John Chrysostom
A Plague on the World, by R. Ley and H.-G. Otto
Hitlerism, by Martin Friedrich
The International Jew, by Henry Ford
Hitler Avatāra, by Martin Friedrich
Sin Against the Blood, by Artur Dinter
Protocols of the Elders of Zion, edited by Thomas Dalton
The Riddle of the Jews' Success, by Theodor Fritsch
Triumph of the Truth, by Robert Penman
The Book of the Shulchan Aruch, by Erich Bischoff
For My Legionnaires, by Corneliu Codreanu
Myth and Sun, by Martin Friedrich
Unmasking Anne Frank, by Ikuo Suzuki
Pan-Judah! Political Cartoons of Der Stürmer, by Robert Penman
Passovers of Blood, by Ariel Toaff
The Poisonous Mushroom, by Ernst Hiemer
On the Jews and Their Lies, by Martin Luther
Mein Kampf, by Adolf Hitler
Mein Kampf (Dual English-German edition), by Adolf Hitler
The Essential Mein Kampf, by Adolf Hitler
The Myth of the 20th Century, by Alfred Rosenberg

BOOKS BY THOMAS DALTON
— www.thomasdaltonphd.com —

The Holocaust: 100 Questions and Answers
The Steep Climb: Essays on the Jewish Question
Classic Essays on the Jewish Question
Debating the Holocaust
The Holocaust: An Introduction
The Jewish Hand in the World Wars
Eternal Strangers: Critical Views of Jews and Judaism
Hitler on the Jews
Goebbels on the Jews
Streicher, Rosenberg, and the Jews: The Nuremberg Transcripts

JEWRY IN ENGLAND

A Thousand-Year History

by
Fritz Krueger

Translated by
William Penman

Edited by
Thomas Dalton, PhD

Clemens & Blair, LLC
— 2026 —

CLEMENS & BLAIR, LLC

Clemens & Blair, LLC, is a non-profit educational publisher.
www.clemensandblair.com

Library of Congress Cataloging-in-Publication Data

Krueger, Fritz P. H.
Jewry in England: A Thousand-Year History

From the German original: *Das Judentum in England* (1943)
Translated by William Penman

p. cm.
Includes bibliographical references

ISBN 978-1963-1436-07
(pbk.: alk. paper)

1. Jews and Judaism
2. History, Jews
3. History, England

Printing number: 9 8 7 6 5 4 3 2 1

Printed in the United States of America on acid-free paper.

CONTENTS

DEDICATIONS

Author's dedication: To my wife, with the deepest gratitude for her collaboration, without which this book could not have come into being.

Translator's dedication: This translation is dedicated to Kevin Mac-Donald and Ron Unz, two inspirational heroes of science. Because the truth shall set us all free.

EDITOR'S PREFACE

Say what you will about the Hitler era in Germany, but one thing is certain: it allowed detailed, precise, scholarly, and critical investigation into the long-standing Jewish Question for perhaps the first time in history. Jews, of course, had long been able to write their own history, but it was always from the Jewish perspective and thus always took a sympathetic eye to past events; difficult, problematic, or negative incidents were nearly always smoothed-over, if not ignored altogether, and those who found reason to clash with Jews or Jewish interests were nearly always portrayed as malevolent and dangerous outsiders. But with the coming of the Third Reich, an entirely new political atmosphere emerged, one in which non-Jews could undertake serious, state-sponsored research into Jewish history without fear of sanctions or recriminations. As a result, an entirely new assessment of Jewish history and Jewish influence was allowed to be written.

Among the more interesting of such works is the present study, *Jewry in England* (*Das Judentum in England*), written by a German lawyer from Hamburg named Fritz P. H. Krueger (or Krüger). Little is known of Krueger's life, and the few details that we do have come from suspect sources, so the following must be qualified as provisional background. Krueger was apparently born in 1905 or 1906, earned a doctorate in law, joined the National Socialist party in 1932, and married a woman named Lisa in 1934 or 1935.

In 1935, at the age of 29, Krueger and his wife moved to London in the quest to become proficient in English and to learn English law; Lisa worked at the Anglo-German Academic Bureau and was also employed by the German Press Agency. By 1936, Krueger had become interested in the Jewish Question in England and began researching the history, relying in good part on Jewish historians like Albert Hyamson, Heinrich Graetz, and H. S. Q. Henriques. By 1937, he was able to produce a small booklet, *The 30-Year Struggle of Jews for Admission to the English Parliament*, that was published under the name Dr. Peter Aldag; his British hosts were sensitive to any emerging 'anti-Semitism,' and thus Krueger surely found it more circumspect to use a pseudonym.

But his major work was soon to follow. Apparently aided in large part by his wife Lisa—who may have done the majority of the actual writing, based on her husband's accumulated factual data, research, and quotations—Krueger published the first edition of *Jewry in England* in 1939, evidently as a two-volume set. The book quickly appeared under other titles, including *Jews in England* and *The Jews and their Power in England*. The two volumes, which seem not to have been Krueger's doing, were individually named "Jews Conquer England" and "Jews Rule England." Krueger, rather, seems to have wanted a seven-volume collection of individual booklets, corresponding to different time periods in England, running from 669 AD up to (in the latest edition) 1942. These seven volumes we have here converted into individual chapters in a single large book.

In any case, the end result is an astonishing accomplishment. This book is a magisterial study of Jews in England, drawing from several established source books and supplemented by a substantial amount of material that Krueger acquired directly from the libraries in London. It is a detailed study, at times year-by-year and even day-by-day, examining precisely how Jews have operated in the past and how they came to acquire such wealth and power. There is a large amount of primary source material here, typically in the original old-English style of language, which has, for the most part, been left unaltered. This is in line with Krueger's stated goal: to present the facts, clear and simple, and to avoid extensive interpretation or commentary.

As the war progressed, Krueger seems to have published at least two more small books: *Dollar Imperialism* (1944) and *The Jew in the Plutocracies* (1944)—but neither garnered the attention of his primary work. After the war, he apparently stopped writing and lived a fairly low-key existence, serving as an attorney in Hamburg while managing a small export business. There are reports that he lived to the age of 74, dying in 1979; but again, nothing of this can be confirmed.

One thing, however, stands out for the perceptive reader of the present book. Despite the wide period of time covered here, and the many individual players involved, we are struck by a remarkable consistency in Jewish behavior across the ages: Jews are greedy money-grubbers; they are conniving liars; they seem to hold to no moral code other than self-interest; and they willfully corrupt others, and even destroy others, in their quest for wealth and power. Surely this does not apply to every individual Jew, but still, it seems to mark all the powerful Jews—those who influence kings and statesmen, and who affect entire national economies. For his part, Krueger stays carefully aloof, avoiding all polemics or critical assessment; clearly for him, the facts alone tell the story. And this is what makes this book such a valuable historical study.

The following translation was produced by an expert scholar, William Penman. He carefully went through all seven volumes/chapters, completed his accurate but readable translation, and then verified many of Krueger's citations. In the copious footnotes, all from Krueger but frequently supplemented by Penman ("Translator's note"), we find a detailed sourcing of all key facts and data, for those interested in verifying his claims. In many cases, Penman has been able to verify quotations from original sources, and these are marked as "QVOS" ("quotation verbatim from original source"). For the sake of readability, we have generally elected to combine all of Krueger's notes in a given paragraph into one longer note at the end.

All in all, this is a truly remarkable book; one might say, it is the proto-type for any such historical study. It is thorough, well-sourced, readable, and coherent. It is detailed without being trite, scholarly and yet accessible, im-portant and illuminating. Regarding the historical topic of Jews in England, I suspect that this work will never be surpassed.

—Thomas Dalton, PhD

TRANSLATOR'S FOREWORD

My decision to take a closer look at the obscure 1943 opus *Das Judentum in England* as a subject of serious intellectual consideration came after glancing through the various lists of chapter titles for its seven volumes. I had been intrigued to see if its author, Peter Aldag, aka Fritz Krueger, would provide solid evidence for Stephen Mitford Goodson's claim of Jewish involvement in the establishment of the Bank of England, as was made in the South African banker's infamous *A History of Central Banking* (2014). In fact, as I came to discover, not only did Aldag *not* support Goodson's assertion, he provided compelling evidence to the contrary. In a similar vein, when I looked to see if there had been a Jewish role in the fraud surrounding what latterly became known rather euphemistically as the South Sea Bubble (but which Aldag rendered more accurately in German as *der Südsee-Skandal*), I found the author telling his German readers that his investigations had yielded no evidence of Jewish involvement in the fraud, and he effectively berated a German contemporary for alleging Jewish misbehaviour without providing solid evidence. To me, this indicated that I was reading an author on the Jewish Question who cared about the truth over ethnic propaganda, the rarity of which immediately piqued my interest in the work.

Nevertheless, it would be disingenuous to suggest that this German lawyer, who updated his manuscript while his country was three years into a war with Britain, did not have a strong social identity which informed his work. Indeed, it is an open question to what extent the 'science' around group identity can ever truly be 'scientific,' or, as Professor Kevin MacDonald put it in his *Culture of Critique*: 'The truly doubtful proposition for an evolutionist is whether social science as a disinterested attempt to understand human behavior is at all possible.' All that a scientist can do is recognise, as MacDonald did, the potential biases and blind-spots in his own analysis, and state these openly, but not let the inexistence of a perfect vessel preclude the advancement of knowledge. As Professor MacDonald himself said in the same book: 'In the end, does it really matter if my motivation at this point is less than pristine? Isn't the only question whether I am right?' Being human, Aldag may have been a similarly less than pristine vessel, but he too cites his sources, the vast majority of which are impeccable.

In the spirit of ensuring maximum transparency and reliability, wherever possible, this translation returns to the original sources used by the author, not only to verify his assertions, but also to be able to accurately reproduce all original English-language quotations. Where additional evidence is available which indicates an element in the text to be needlessly ambiguous or misleading, or where there is an alternative viewpoint worthy of consideration, clearly marked translator commentary has been added into the footnotes, or less commonly, within the text itself. The resulting, one might say, *midrashic* presentation, in which many of the author's 2,896 footnotes have been extended by commentary, may deter all but the most determined from attempting this text, but my interest was to ensure that academically-inclined readers like myself had access to the relevant data (in all of its sometimes complex but accurate detail), to ensure that they could have confidence in what they were reading.

For those so minded to tackle such an extensive work, Aldag's stunning piece of scholarship should hopefully be an exciting and groundbreaking addition to the existing corpus of knowledge. Care should nevertheless be taken not confuse the text written by the author himself with later politicising additions to the text by the publisher, Nordland Verlag (Berlin). Even hostile critic C. C. Aronfeld, writing in the *Jewish Chronicle* of 7th February 1986, admits that the Hitler quotations bookending the author's Preface, and other less than 'scientific' elements of the book, were likely added post-hoc for political expediency, and were not the work of the author himself:

> The final touch—as regards form, not content—was added by more seasoned pens in the Ministry of Propaganda. They probably are responsible for parts of the Introduction and the equally militant epilogue, also for many of the more viciously violent turns of phrase.[1]

I would also suggest that the somewhat lurid title given to the spin-off publication of volumes 6 and 7, *Juden beherrschen England*, jars with the tone of the book itself. This would indicate that the choice of title was likewise a commercial publishing decision, as within his carefully written work the author regularly hedges his statements in the interests of accuracy.

For this reason, this is not a work simply for 'anti-Semites' looking to have their biases confirmed. While it is indeed true to say that this is a historiography from the Gentile perspective, a rare thing indeed at this point in Western history, it would be a mistake to presume that a Jewish and non-radical Gentile readership, able to stomach the anti-Jewish elements men-

---

[1] Not included in the present edition – editor.

tioned above, would not enjoy this work and take a lot from it. Indeed, the history of the Jews in England is very much the history of England, and those Englishmen who are uninterested in Jewish history but looking to gain insight into their own condition, will likewise benefit greatly from this study, as it is essentially a history of how money and power flows, often corruptly, through the country's various estates, institutions, and personages over the course of a millennium. Just as shadows throw the features of a subject into relief and makes them discernible, so the character of the English nation is inadvertently brought into focus through the telling of its relations with this formidable Other.

In an ideal world, in which the Jewish group evolutionary strategy and the historiography of Jewish-Gentile relations were just as open to scientific enquiry as the mechanisms of photosynthesis, the potential points of ethnic bias found in this book would be openly debated by Jewish and Gentile scholars alike, and where necessary, disproven or refined. Such open dialogue would also pave the way for a future in which we might be able to transcend the seemingly eternal tragic cycle of history, after which we could move towards the arguably more minor task of conquering inter-galactic space travel. But in the meantime, this book will hopefully spark the interest of the handful of fearless men who have put the quest for truth above the dangers of public defamation or dynamic silence. It is to two such men that I dedicate my translation, in the hope that the spirit of Aldag/Krueger is somehow able to see his great work make an impact in a new century.

—William Penman

JEWRY IN ENGLAND

CHAPTER 1
FROM THE EARLIEST YEARS TO EXPULSION (669-1290)

The Earliest Years

To this day, the beginnings of Jewish immigration to England are shrouded in complete darkness. Nevertheless—or perhaps because of this—much effort has been made to shed light on the matter.

It is probably due to clever inspiration from the Jews that many English writers are of the opinion that the Jews visited England for reasons of trade as early as the time of King Solomon. Indeed, even serious scholars, under the influence of this clever propaganda, have claimed that the British, prior to the immigration of the Angles and Saxons, were descendants of the so-called *Ten Lost Tribes of Israel*, who were led into captivity by the Assyrians.[1]

It may also be briefly mentioned that, according to the Jews and their allies, the word 'Britain' is of Semitic origin. Herodotus referred to the British Isles as '*Cassiterides*', which means 'Tin Islands.' The word '*Britannike*,' which was later used in the Greek language, was merely a mutilation of the Hebrew '*Barat Anach*' and must also be translated as Tin Islands. But all of this is likely nothing more than speculation, and it may indeed be the case that the wish is father to the thought that ancient England should have had such close connections with the original Jews.[2]

The first documentary evidence of the presence of Jews in England—most likely as permanent settlers—can be found in a statute from the year 669. This statute, named *Liber Poenitentialis Theodori Archiepiscopi Cantuariensis Ecclesiae*, was enacted by Theodore, the then-Archbishop of Canterbury, and included the provision that a Christian woman who accepted gifts from unbaptized Jews or who voluntarily sinned with them (e.g. extramarital intercourse), was to be excommunicated for a year, live in the worst conditions of poverty, and then do nine years of punishment. If, on the other hand, she got involved with a heathen, she would be punished for seven years.[3] What is particularly interesting here is that dealings with a Jew were punished more severely than dealings with a despised Gentile.

---

[1] Hyamson: *History*, p. 1 ff.; Hyamson: *Lost Tribes*; Margoliouth: *History*, Vol. I, p. 1 ff.; see especially the writers mentioned in Hyamson's *History* p. 6. & Hyamson: *History*, p. 3 and *Lost Tribes*, p. 673 ff.; Margoliouth: *History*, Vol. I, p. 22 ff.

[2] Margoliouth: *History*, Vol. I, p. 22 and Hyamson: *History*, p. 1.

[3] *Ancient Laws* p. 282; Liber Poenitentialis XVI § 35.

Another regulation stated that anyone who, contrary to the decision of the Council of Nicaea, used the Jewish calendar to celebrate Easter on the 14th day of the lunar month, was to be excommunicated if he did not repent. Furthermore, a Christian who accepted meat or unleavened bread from unbaptized Jews, or who drank with them and participated in their ungodliness, was to repent with bread and water for 40 days. Meanwhile, if a Christian sold another Christian—even if this person were his slave—to a Jew, he was said to be unworthy of living among Christians until he had bought the Christian back. If, for some reason, it was not possible for him to do so, he was to use the price he had received to redeem someone else from slavery, and abstain from all meat and wine for three years.[4] Finally, it was not permitted to celebrate mass in a place where Jews or other unbelievers were buried.[5]

Under Ecgbert, Archbishop of York, who lived from 735 to 766, references to Jews can also be found in a law he issued called Excerptiones Egberti Eboracensis Archiepiscopi. According to this law, it was determined that no Christian should dare to profess Judaism or take part in its festivals. It also stipulated that a Christian who sold another Christian to the Jews would be excommunicated from the church.[6]

Some people are of the opinion that these laws did not refer to Jews who were resident in England, but one cannot see why else the lawmakers of the time would find it necessary to draft such extensive legislation. Furthermore, the issues around Christian and Jewish co-existence must have needed to practically resolved because these laws feature in the official compendium *Ancient Laws and Institutes of England*, which evidences the need for permanent regulation.[7]

---

[4] *Ancient Laws* p. 295; *Liber Poenitentialis* XLII § 4. Translator's note: The 14th day of the lunar month is when the Jews sacrifice the lamb for Passover, and was used as the traditional way of calculating Easter, until a controversy arose due to this date sometimes falling on a weekday (known as the 'Easter Controversy'), and a change in this usage was formally decreed by the Council of Nicaea in 325 A.D. *Ancient Laws* p. 300; *Liber Poenitentialis* XVI § 1. *Ancient Laws* p. 300; *Liber Poenitentialis* XVI § 3.

[5] *Ancient Laws* p. 303; *Liber Poenitentialis* XVI § 1.

[6] *Ancient Laws* p. 340. Translator's note: Margoliouth [*Anglo-Hebrews*, p. 5] states that this law was promulgated in 740 A.D.

[7] Jacobs, *The Jews of Angevin England*, p. 3. Translator's note: Jacobs believed that that these ecclesiastical ordinances were made to regulate the 'passing intercourse with Gallo-Jewish slave dealers', the type to whom Pope Gregory I was referring when he complained about the sale of Christians to Jewish slave dealers in the north of Gaul (*ibid.*). We know that these Jewish slavers trafficked in English people, certainly in English children, thanks to the famous story about Pope Gregory spying two blond-haired slave children in Rome, asking their provenance, and on being told that they were Angles, replying '*Non Angli, sed angeli!*' [Not Angles, but angels!]. Jacobs (pp. 3-4) made the following disturbingly triumphalist remark on recalling the tale: 'Remembering that slaves have no nationality, I would suggest that if Gregory had stated the prosaic fact in his world-famous remarks about the chubby, blond-haired lads exposed for sale on the Roman slave-market,

In a Jewish book dating from 1575 [*Emek Habacha* by Joseph Cohen] there is a reference to the fact that, in the year 810, many Jews fled from Germany to England and Spain to escape persecution. It must be left open to debate whether this information is in fact correct.[8]

Finally, a law is said to have existed under Edward the Confessor (c. 1003-1066), according to which the Jews were considered the king's property and were therefore under his protection. Margoliouth is willing to recognize this assertion as valid, and it must be stated that this ordinance is also included in the official compendium of ancient laws.[9]

The First Wave of Immigration

In 1066, William the Conqueror landed in England, and not long afterwards the entirety of English life saw itself transformed. Until the conquest by William I, there had only been very loose connections with the European mainland, while relationships within the country itself barely extended beyond the individual counties. Trade was mainly by barter, and the circulation of money was therefore very limited.

William came from France and therefore laid the foundation for the subsequent close relations between these two countries. Under Norman rule, civilization in England also advanced, which in turn caused an increase in demand for goods and services. In the period that followed, difficulties were encountered in satisfying this demand through barter alone, which led to an increase in the need for liquid money.

In addition, as a result of the initial hostility of the English population after the conquest, William was forced to enlarge his standing army, for

---

he would have said, "*Non Angli nec angeli sed – Judaeorum servi.*"' [They are not Angles, nor angels, but slaves of the Jews.]

[8] Hyamson: *History*, p. 5; Jacobs, p. 4.

[9] Margoliouth: *History*, Vol. I, p. 49; *Anglo-Hebrews* p. 5. Translator's note: In the view of Jacobs (p. 3): 'The reference in the Laws of Edward the Confessor is an interpolation, *temp*. Hen. II.' & Jacobs: *The Jews of Angevin England*, p. 39; Gross: *Exchequer*, p. 172; Rigg, p. 10, Freeman, Vol. V, p. 818 ff. Also, this law is found in Latin and English on page 3 of William Romaine's 1753 *An Answer to a Pamphlet* [see Translator's Bibliography]. The English translation is as follows:

Be it known also, that all the Jews, wheresoever they be within the Realm, ought to be under the King's Guard and Protection, as his Vassals, neither can any one of them put himself under the Power of any rich Person, without the King's License: For the Jews and all they have belong to the King. And if any Person shall detain them, or their Money, the King may claim them (if he pleases) as his own Property.

which he again needed money, but which was not sufficiently available in the country. Even the barons who were called upon to finance the army could hardly raise the necessary funds, which made the desire for a money economy universal.

The Jews of that time controlled trade and finance to an almost greater extent than today. However, their number in England must not have been sufficient to cover demand. That fact soon became known in northern France, where there were large settlements of rich Jews.

Apparently these Jews turned to William the Conqueror and asked for permission to immigrate to England. Various writers are of the opinion that the Normandy Jews were even invited by William. Although these writers cannot provide documentary evidence for this assertion, they feel that it can reasonably be concluded from the country's economic situation.[10] Others argue that the Jews paid the king a sum of money for the right to immigrate to England.[11]

Most of them came from Rouen, France. After a short time, we find numerous Jews in the cities of England. The first larger Jewish colonies were probably founded in Oxford and Cambridge, as there is a note in a document made around 1075 in which the ancient writer found 'the Jews settled and their numbers great in Oxford', with a similar observation regarding Cambridge. The fact that Jewish immigration was considerable is evident from the fact that, as early as 1070, it was apparently deemed necessary to determine the legal status of the Jews by law. It was then stipulated that the Jews settled in the kingdom were under the protection of the king and were his property.[12]

Even at that time, one can notice the same signs of Jewish behavior which are familiar to us today. Until their expulsion from England, they were a people unto themselves. They remained true to their entire way of life, which was completely different from the English one. Without any coercion and of their own free will, they settled in a specific part of the city, and if possible, always near the market square. They never cared about the most honorable and important concern of a nation: the defense of the land. In those days of strict Christianity, they did not take the host population's values into account. They neither showed the necessary respect for the cross, nor allowed themselves to be deterred from carrying out their religious service with all the customs that were alien to the English. Deceased Jews were buried in special cemeteries, initially only in London. Their food and drink were also completely different from those of their Christian neighbors. They refused

---

[10] Jacobs: *The Jews of Angevin England*, p. 39; Gross: *Exchequer*, p. 172; Rigg, p. 10, Freeman, Vol. V, p. 818 ff, & Margoliouth: *History*, Vol. I, p. 50.

[11] Prynne, p. 2; B. B.: *Historical and Law Treatise*, p. 3.

[12] Jacobs, *The Jews...* pp. 4-5. Translator's note: QVOS. & Margoliouth: *History*, Vol. I, p. 52.

invitations to eat a meal prepared by a Christian in a Christian household. The animals for slaughter had to be killed under certain rites. It was not uncommon for the Jews to reject any spoiled food as inedible for themselves, but offer it for sale to Christians as perfectly good.[13] There were already many Christian maids and wet nurses in the Jewish household who reported horrific things about their habits.[14]

There are hardly any Jews of this period to be found in any craft. Although their rights as merchants were limited in certain respects by the regulations of the guilds, under a law of King John in 1201 they were generally free to buy whatever was brought to them, with the exception of certain church goods, and were allowed to sell the items pledged to them after a year and a day.[15]

Kings Favor the Jews

Such favorable treatment of the Jews can only be explained by their position in relation to the monarch of the time. As property of the king, they were subject only to his jurisdiction. They also had an exceptional position in that, unlike the English, they were allowed to charge interest on loans. Under the king's protection, the Jews almost exclusively practiced the business of lending money, and were even encouraged to do so by the king because he in turn demanded a certain percentage of the money, as a tax on their transactions. As a result, Jews were one of his largest sources of income. Given the size of their business and the level of interest, the Jews made large profits. No law stipulated a limit to the interest rate, and the floodgates were wide open to usury. Interest rates of 43.5% were considered standard and 50 to 80% were by no means uncommon. It is therefore not surprising that the wealth of the Jews was described as nothing short of incredible.[16]

---

[13] Abrahams, pp. 6-7; Hyamson: *History*, p. 10; Rigg, p. XI. & *Rogeri de Houedene*, Vol. II, p. 261; *Gesta Henrici*, Vol. I, p. 279. & *Gesta Henrici*, Vol. I, p. 182; *Rogeri de Houedene*, Vol. II, p. 137; William of Malmesbury, Vol. II, p. 371. & Abrahams, p. 6. & Jacobs, *The Jews of Angevin England*, pp. 54, 178. These references relate to kosher food and its preparation, implying that the English were sold food that was not kosher, rather than spoiled.

[14] *Gesta Henrici*, Vol. I, p. 230; *Rogeri de Houedene*, Vol. II, p. 180. Translator's note: Both references identically reproduce a decree from Pope Alexander III, made at the Third Lateran Council of 1179, while ruled, among other things, that Christians should not live with Jews (or Muslims), act as their wet nurses, or serve them in any capacity. The decree does not reference any complaint about Jewish behavior, although it may be argued that this decree came as a response to such complaints.

[15] Cunningham, p. 336 ff. & Hyamson: *History*, p. 9; Rigg, p. XII; *Select Civil Pleas*, Vol. I, p. 3 (Case 7).

[16] Rigg, p. XIII; Leonard, p. 104 ff. & Belloc, p. 218. Translator's note: It should be stated, however, that according to Rigg (*Select Pleas...*, p. xiii) that during the reign of Henry II

The Jews lived in the most magnificent (and at the same time most fortified) houses in the cities of that time, some of which were even able to
withstand a siege for a short period. The populace rightly looked down on
the Jews as intruders and a foreign body, especially since the individual Englishman was substantially in debt due to the high interest rates and consequently at the complete mercy of the Jews. It is therefore understandable that
feelings of enmity towards the Jews grew slowly but steadily, although it
was not openly shown, since the Jews enjoyed unlimited protection as the
property of the king. This even went so far that at the time of William the
Conqueror (1066-1087) and his successor William Rufus (1087-1100), the
Jews did not have to pay any special taxes, unlike the English. William
Rufus not only generally favored the Jews in every aspect of life, but he even
studied their doctrine and came to the decision to make his conversion to the
Jewish religion dependent on the outcome of a scholarly debate between
bishops and rabbis, which he attended as an observer. Some of the content of
this debate has been preserved and is very interesting as a contemporary
document. At that time, too, there was an argument about the value (or otherwise) of the Christian and Jewish religions, with both parties claiming victory in these learned discussions.[17]

In the last years of William Rufus' reign, the Jewish colony of Rouen
petitioned the king to prevent the Jews there from converting to Christianity.
Given that the Jews had supported their petition with a large sum of money,
William Rufus did not hesitate to comply with their request, and tried to
bring the baptized Jews back to the 'religion of [their] nation' by using the

---

the ordinary rate of lending was set at 43⅓ percent per annum, which in the thirteenth
century became recognized as the legal maximum, and compound interest was strictly
forbidden. Certainly, by the 1230s of Henry III's reign, the legislation for the above was
laid down (Stacey, 'The English Jews Under Henry III', p. 44, n.22), but certain loans
between Jews (which may have been a form of 'inter-bank lending') continued to go as high
as 4d per pound per week, or 87%, as evidenced by the documentation (*idem*, p. 48, n.44).

[17] Hyamson: *History*, p. 5 ff.; Belloc, p. 216; Prynne, p. 3. & Hyamson: *History*, p. 11.
Translator's note: Hyamson writes: 'From the first three Norman kings the Jews suffered
neither exaction nor annoyance. William Rufus and Henry I obtained by violence large
sums of money from their Christian subjects; but they spared the Jews. For instance, the
10,000 marks needed for the purchase of Normandy from Robert were raised with great
difficult, the abbeys, in some instances, having to melt down their plate in order to provide
their contributions; yet no levy was made on the Jews.' However, this honeymoon period
was not to last. & Margoliouth: *History*, Vol. I, p. 53. & Jacobs, *The Jews of Angevin
England*, pp. 7-12; Holinshed, Vol. III, p. 27 ff. Translator's note: Jonas Hanway [pp. 59-
60, see Translator's Bibliography] writing in 1735, reported that these disputations led to
some Jews openly deriding Christianity, which in turn caused many of them to have to
flee London in fear for their lives, and 'two hundred of them were converted to Christianity, in one day, at Dunstable'. However, given that Hanway does not give a source for this
tale, it may be that he was simply repeating a popular pro-Christian legend that had subsequently arisen after the real events of the religious disputations.

harshest threats. On one occasion, a single Jew offered the king sixty silver marks if the king would bring his son, who had converted to Christianity, back to Judaism. The king agreed to this deal and had the rich Jew's son brought before him. Despite the king's insult towards him ('thou dunghill knave') and threat of violence for non-compliance ('I shall cause thine eyes to be plucked out of thine head'), the young man stood firm and boldly explained to the king that he did not understand the king's attitude towards him, saying that if the king were really a Christian, it was his duty to bring his subjects *to* Christ, not to seek to separate them from Him. The king, confounded, then desisted from what he had begun. However, the convert's father was angry and demanded his money back, which the king refused. Only after lengthy arguments was it agreed to repay thirty silver marks. Prynne, a 17th-century historian recounting the deeds of the Jews, summed up the incident with the following words:[18]

> By this History we may perceive what a prevailing Engine the Jews money is, both to scrue them into Christian Kingdoms, though the most bitter, inveterate, professed Enemies of Christ himself, Christians and Christianity, and how their money can induce even Christian Princes to perpetrate the most unchristian, and antichristian actions; and enforce by threats and violence, even converted Christian Jews to renounce their Christianity, and apostatize to their former Jewish Errors which they had quite renounced. And do not they still work even by the self-same Money Engine?[19]

During the reign of Henry I (1100-1135) we hear next to nothing about the Jews, which may be a sign that they continued to pursue their trade and were able to accumulate wealth. The first extant documentary evidence of the presence of Jews in London occurs during this time. For the first time there is mention of a Jewish street in a document.[20]

In the first years of King Stephen's reign (1135-1154) the Jews continued to enjoy the favor of the royal family and were therefore able to accumulate more and more wealth through usury. However, everything was about to change.

---

[18] Hyamson: *History*, p. 11; Margoliouth: *History*, p. 54. Translator's note: The word 'colony' is the direct translation from the German original, which I have used to be true to the author, rather than opting for the preferred modern euphemism 'community'. It may be noted that the term 'colonization' was used unproblematically by scholar Joe Hillaby in his 2003 paper 'Jewish Colonization in the Twelfth Century' [ed. Skinner, *Jews in Medieval Britain*]. & Margoliouth: *History*, Vol. I, p. 56; Hyamson: *History*, p. 12; Prynne, p. 5.
[19] Prynne, p. 5-6. Translator's note: This quotation, along with other quoted elements earlier in the paragraph, are reproduced verbatim from the original source.
[20] Price, p. 17.

The Church Against the Jews

The church had initially been fairly indifferent to the Jews, but to some extent had favored their settlement in cities in the early years. As civilization increased, monetary transactions became increasingly necessary. Since Christians were forbidden by canon law to charge interest on loans, this business was left to the Jews, which spared the church from having to make changes to the canon law to conform with the needs of the time. In other words, economic development would have required the abolition of the ban on interest, but with the arrival of the Jews this became unnecessary because people preferred to leave the field to them. This church position meant that, not only were the Jews increasing their wealth on a daily basis through eye-watering usury, but the English themselves were being bled dry and were already completely indebted to them when Stephen ascended the throne. The Jews ruthlessly collected the claims when they were due and thus drove the English from their ancestral land. Although they were not allowed to be landowners, the king granted Jews the right to receive land as collateral from their debtors. The Jews were even able to appropriate half of the land until the debt was paid off. The church could not be indifferent to this impoverishment of the English if only for its own material interests, since under these circumstances it was hardly able to collect the tithes to which it was entitled.[21]

The church probably also secretly hoped to convert a large number of Jews to Christianity over time. However, around the year 1140 and even before that, the church must have realized that its expectations in this regard were not only mistaken, but that the Jews, in turn, had made successful attempts to convert the English to Judaism with the help of their money. This led to priests being sent into the cities which had a Jewish presence to preach forcefully against Jewish teachings.[22]

From all this, it is clear that the church now began to take an interest in the Jewish Question and to exploit the people's antipathy for its own purposes. Events that were taking place outside of England were also useful to this end.

From the end of the 11th century onwards, the Crusading movement began to spread over the European mainland, particularly in Germany and France. There too, the population was hostile to anything non-Christian and, as a result, the long-slumbering hatred towards the Jews awakened everywhere, not least because the Jews also played the role of usurer on the continent.

The first Norman kings were still too busy consolidating their power in England to pay much attention to the Crusading movement, but this was to

---

[21] Hyamson: *History*, p. 8 ff. & P. C. Webb: *The Question,* p. 10 ff.; Madox, Vol. I, p. 168.
[22] Hyamson: *History*, p. 22. Translator's note: Aldag apparently rests his assertion on Hyamson's phrase '...it appears that the Jews were at least as successful as the Christians in making converts'. Note that this phrase makes no mention of financial inducement, and might well be an ironic comment on the paucity of converts on either side.

change in the first years of Stephen's reign. It was also noticed that Stephen changed in his attitude towards the Jews, especially since the people's growing antipathy towards them could not remain hidden from him. Although Stephen did not initially take any major action, he made it clear that he would no longer stand in the way of the people's wishes. The king's change of heart resulted from the following event:

In 1240, a Jew was found guilty of manslaughter, although he denied the crime. However, the king was undeterred and sentenced the Jews residing in London to a total fine of £2,000, a huge sum for the time.[23] While this intervention by the king is significant, it should not be overlooked that England's kings of that period were to a considerable extent financially dependent on the Jews.

Ritual Murder

The sources inform us of the following incident from the year 1144: William, a twelve-year-old skinner's apprentice and son of the widow Elviva from Norwich, was abducted by the Jews (or, by other accounts, bought by the Jews) to be sacrificed in a mockery of the Christian feast of Easter. He was martyred and crucified like Jesus Christ. After the ritual was complete, the boy's tortured body was taken down from the wooden cross-beams which had served as a cross, and put in a sack. At daybreak, two of the Jews secretly set off for the forest on horseback, with the sack being held across the saddle bow of one of the horses. On the outskirts of the forest, they crossed paths with a prominent burgess of the city called Aelward Ded, who was on his way to St Leonard's church after visiting St Mary Magdalen church near the wood, and who recognized one of the Jews as the wealthy Eleazar. Knowing that it was strange to see Jews 'so far from home on a day when it was not the custom of the Jews to leave their house,' Aelward asked the Jews where they were going, and as he did so he laid his hand on the sack and perceived the nature of the gruesome burden within. The Jews, terrified, galloped off into the depths of the wood, then hung the body from one of the trees in a thicket.

---

[23] Margoliouth: *History*, Vol. I, p. 65. Translator's note: The German text says that several Jews were found guilty of being accomplices to the crime, but the original Margoliouth source only mentions the involvement of one person. I have therefore amended the text to be true to the source that Aldag has cited (Margoliouth himself not having given his source). However, if this 1240 judgement refers to the same homicide as that which reportedly took place in London in 1239 by 'a clan of Jews', and which caused a huge uproar among the common people [see Translator's Appendix II], it would appear that this may have been a premeditated murder (as opposed to an accidental killing, which Margoliouth's term 'manslaughter' implies), and a group enterprise, which is reflected in Aldag's text.

After returning to the city, they immediately rushed to John de Caineto, the sheriff, to whom they promised one hundred silver marks if he would protect them from the impending discovery of the murder. Luckily for them, the sheriff's protection was for sale. He sent for Aelward Ded and forced him to swear an oath of secrecy about what had happened. Out of fear of the sheriff, Aelward remained silent for another five years until, immediately before the Englishman's death, the boy appeared to him in spirit and asked him to confess everything because he was no longer bound by his oath [perhaps because the sheriff had died three years earlier]. The burgess did as he was told, giving a deathbed confession to the monk Wicheman and an unnamed priest of St Nicholas, and it was from these two religious men that the monk-chronicler Thomas of Monmouth heard the story [the doctrine of the Seal of Confession not being made canon law until the next century].[24]

In the meantime, a great commotion arose in the city after news spread about the body since discovered in the wood, which, despite being fully clothed, had been observed to exhibit a series of unusual stigmata-like wounds, a shaven head which was lacerated with thorn marks, and a wooden gag in its mouth. This, along with the fact that William had last been seen, by report of his cousin, going into a Jew's house on the Tuesday before Easter, led the populace to suspect the Jews. The sheriff tried to protect the Jews, but was powerless against the people's anger, and while a large number of Jews were killed, the rest fled.[25] Subsequently, the spot of William's burial place was found in Thorpe Wood, and the boy's body removed to the Monks' Cemetery, before he was eventually canonized by the local clergy.[26]

---

[24] Jacobs, *The Jews of Angevin England*, p. 19 ff.; *Chronica Jocelini de Brakelonda,* p. 114. & Rigg, p. XIV; Abrahams, p. 10; Hyamson, p. 20; Margoliouth: *History,* Vol. I, p. 65; Rye, p. 138 ff.; Prynne, p. 6; Brompton, col. 1048; Foxe, Vol. I, p. 302; Holinshed, Vol. III, p. 56. Translator's note: Note that it was the Anglo-Saxon Chronicle [Whitelock, p. 200] which alleged that William had been bought by the Jews, which is likely to have been the original source for this allegation. Thomas of Monmouth, the monk who wrote William's *Life* [see Jessopp and James] states that the child was abducted by a combination of deception and bribery.

[25] Translator's note: Thomas of Monmouth states that, fearing a clamor of the people, and facing demands for justice from Bishop Everard and the priest Godwin, not least given that the latter was William's uncle, the sheriff had the Jews moved into the castle for protection, where they remained safe until King Stephen issued an edict for their safety and the fuss from the people and the church died down. However, Thomas (Jessopp, p. 97) also states that the infamy of the charge caused many of the Jews to disperse to other parts, while those who remained eventually 'perished by visitation of sudden death, or were put an end to by the hands of the Christians'.

[26] Hyamson: *History,* p. 20. Translator's note: Additional details have been added from Jessopp and James for reader convenience. See also Translator's Appendices for further information. Note that the sheriff's family name is alternatively rendered 'de Querceto' (then later, de Caisnei/Chesney/Cheney) in official records. [Jessopp and James, p. xxxiii; Rubin, p. 211, note 43]. It appears providential that the evidence points to the fact that the

Many writers have doubted the truth of this story. Jacobs thinks it was invented by the church, because the child's canonization would have ensured the pilgrimage of many English people to Norwich every year, which would have brought the church a large income. However, he is unable to provide any evidence for his claim. Other authors say that the story was one that was only told to a simple populace, while it is often referred to as nothing but a legend. Be that as it may, old sources report this story perfectly, and other historical facts also seem to confirm the accusations made against the Jews in this respect. In mainland Europe, the Jews were also accused of similar acts, just as there was no lack of other related infamies in England. Other such murders were reported at Gloucester in 1168, at Bury St. Edmunds in 1181, at Winchester in 1191 and 1232, at London in 1244 and at Lincoln in 1255. The discoveries of the murders sparked great uproar in the cities concerned, and the Jews suffered greatly from the anger of the populace.[27]

Privileges Incur Resentment

Although the Jews still enjoyed the full protection of Henry II (1154-1189) he would still at times use force to make them pay special taxes, known as 'tallages.' In 1168 the Jews were ordered to raise 5,000 marks for the king, which a large part refused to pay until they saw that the king was serious enough in his demand to banish some of the rich Jews. As early as 1188 they had to pay the enormous sum of £60,000 to the king as a tallage.[28]

---

only surviving copy of William's *Life,* which was re-discovered in the late 19th century after some 350 years of absence from the record, had been copied in the Cistercian monastery in Sibton, Suffolk, a monastery was founded by Sheriff John's brother in 1850. Brother Thomas wrote that, after siding with the Jews and taking their bribe, Sheriff John fell soon gravely ill, and his health continued to decline until his death two years later. The parson Augustus Jessopp's description of the sheriff's fate as 'Divine Vengeance' may be infused with fin-de-siècle sardony ('St. William of Norwich', p. 756), but tradition does have it that Sheriff John vowed on his deathbed to arrange for the Cistercian abbey to be founded, to expiate 'the many ill deeds he committed while acting as sheriff, both in times of peace and times of war' (Rubin, p. lvi). If this is indeed true, then it is indirectly due to this sheriff's contrition that the full story of William of Norwich, as well as details of his own corrupt role in the event, is available to us today, almost 900 years later.

[27] Jacobs, *The Jews of Angevin England,* p. 21. & Rigg, p. XIV; Abrahams, p. 10. & Hyamson: *History,* p. 20 ff. & *Historia et Cartularium,* Vol. I, p. 20; Foxe, Vol. I, p. 302, col. II. & *Chronica Jocelini de Brakelonda* pp. 12, 113-4. & *Annales Monastici,* Vol. IV, p. 24. & *Annales Monastici,* Vol. II, p. 86. & Matthaei Parisiensis Vol. IV, p. 377. & *Annales Monastici,* Vol. I, p. 340; Foxe, Vol. I, p. 423, col. II. Translator's note: This martyr is known as 'Little Saint Hugh of Lincoln' in the historical sources. For a full list of the extant ritual murder allegations in England up until 1290, see Translator's Appendix II.

[28] *Chronicles of the Reigns of Stephen,* Vol. I, p. 280. & *Gervase of Canterbury,* Vol. I, p. 205. & *Gervase of Canterbury,* Vol. I, p. 422; *Radulphi de Diceto,* Vol. II, p. 4. Tovery, p. 14.

Since money will be discussed in greater detail in the next chapter, a comparison between the value of money then and now may be of interest. Jacobs made very long and detailed observations with reference to various experts and concluded that the values of that time are approximately thirty times as high today. He himself admitted to being not entirely sure, as was evidenced by the fact that he multiplied by fifty on at least one occasion.[29] Despite the aforementioned tax levies, the Jews not only continued to enjoy the king's protection, but he even granted them special legal privileges.

They were placed solely under the jurisdiction of the king and his judges and not, as the English in many cases were, under that of their respective feudal lord. In legal disputes between Jews, they were entitled to their own judges, they were allowed to take their oath on the Torah, and only Jewish law (not English law) was applied.[30]

In cases between Christians and Jews, the hearings took place before mixed courts made up of an equal number of Jews and Englishmen. Furthermore, the Jews had the crucial advantage over the English, namely: 'A Jew's oath was considered valid against the oaths of twelve Christians.' This different treatment and weighting of the oath is completely incomprehensible and can probably only be explained by the fact that the king gave considerable preference to the Jews in order to benefit financially from their usurious transactions.[31]

In addition, the Jew was advantaged in that in financial matters he only had to prove that the loan had been disbursed, while the defendant Christian had the full burden of proof for all questions that arose. The cases decided in favor of the Jews made the people ever more bitter, and resentment continued to grow in the population. The clergy also petitioned the king and complained about the Jews enjoying such privileges.[32]

In 1177, the king gave the Jews further favor by allowing them to bury their dead in various places in England, which up until that time had only applied to London. The historian Prynne expressed his surprise that this required the king's special permission. But as he observed:

---

[29] Jacobs, *The Jews of Angevin England*, p. 316 ff. Translator's note: Modern readers may find useful the National Archive's online currency converter, with the understanding that the earliest date of the converter is 1270: https://www.nationalarchives. gov.uk/currency-converter/#currency-result & Jacobs, ibid., p. 44.

[30] Henriques: *The Jews*, p. 54.

[31] Belloc, p. 218. & Hyamson: *History*, pp. 9, 27; Rigg, p. XII. Translator's note: QVOS [Hyamson, p. 9]. Translator's note: The resentment this caused among the gentiles of the courtroom can be seen in the fact that, in certain instances, gentile clerks drew 'grotesque caricatures of the Jews before them in the courtroom' in the margins of the court records [e.g. Bartlet, pp. 9, 71 – see Translator's Bibliography.].

[32] *Materials for the History of Thomas Becket*, Vol. IV, p. 148.

> It seems the Jews were then so odious to the whole Nation,
> that they would not permit them to bury their very dead corps
> in any *English* soyl, for fear of polluting it, nor near any Chris-
> tians bodies, without the Kings special License.[33]

But the Jews did not care about the hatred emanating from the population.
As long as they were under the king's protection, they could still successfully pursue their business of usury.

Aaron of Lincoln

The wealth of the Jews reached enormous proportions, especially under the
reign of Henry II. The richest and most famous Jew of that period was Aaron
of Lincoln (1125-1186).[34] Nothing is known of his early life. We only hear
about him in his last twenty years on earth. He is worth discussing in some
detail because from his business deals it can be shown how, even back then,
a single Jew controlled a significant part of the entire monetary economy of
England.[35]

Numerous Cistercian monasteries, such as those of Rievaulx, New
Minster, Kirkstead, Rufford, and Kirkstall were built with his money, as can
be seen indirectly from a contemporary chronicle. Thereafter, the aforementioned abbeys, along with others, owed Aaron large sums of money, which
must have been a significant part of the construction costs of the monasteries. After Aaron's death, this debt was escheated to the king, who forgave
the abbeys a substantial part of it. The debt was probably forgiven because a
large part of the overall claim consisted of accrued loan interest. In addition,
the cathedrals of St. Albans, Lincoln and Peterborough were built with Aaron's money, and we find him further mentioned in connection with the announcement that church property mortgaged to him had been redeemed.[36]

But the church not only played the role of borrower; it was also not
averse to doing business with Aaron, about which a particularly revealing
case has come down to us.

A certain William Fossard, near the monastery of Meaux, was in debt
to the Jews for an amount totaling £1,200. For this sum he had pledged part

---

[33] Prynne, p. 7. Translator's note: QVOS.

[34] Hyamson: *History*, p. 23 ff.

[35] Jacobs: *Aaron of Lincoln*, p. 157.

[36] *Memorials of the Abbey of St. Mary of Fountains*, Vol. II, p. 18, n 4. Translator's note:
The following are the other Cistercian monasteries listed as having been indebted to Aa-
ron, prior to King Richard I remitting their debts: Biddlesden Abbey, Revesby Abbey,
Roche Abbey and Louth Park Abbey. Note that the reproduced Latin charter has all of the
Cistercian debt forgiven, more than the 'substantial part' (*beträchtlichen Teil*) of Aldag's
text. & Hyamson: *History*, p. 23 ff. & *Giraldi Cambrensis Opera*, Vol. VII. p. 36.

of his property to them. Aaron bought this debt claim and was willing to forego almost a third of the entire debt if the abbot of the monastery in question took over the payment. William was not averse to this change of creditor, especially since his debts had increased to such an extent as a result of the huge interest that he was never able to pay it off. The trade was apparently quite favorable for the monastery, because in addition to the land, it also received two villages located there. This is how the deal came about; the monastery paid the debt, including interest, to Aaron, but William had lost his land.[37]

The existing document relating to this transaction shows that Aaron had bought up numerous claims against William from other Jews. As a result, his willingness to give up a third of the amount becomes clear. It is most likely that he bought the original claims totaling £1,200 from William's various creditors for far less than their book value, so that even with the aforementioned discount he would still have made a good deal.

Aaron had branches or agents in all parts of the country. A significant number of Jews were in his service as agents and most appear to have had business relationships with him.[38]

Among his many debtors were leading men of the time, including the Earls of Leicester and Chester, the Bishops of Bangor and Lincoln, and even the Archbishop of Canterbury. There is a careful list of Aaron's debtors and their debts compiled from old documents. The result is astonishing, and best shows Aaron's huge influence. The size of his fortune is also indicated the fact that when he died in 1186, a special department was set up in the royal treasury to manage his estate.[39]

Even as early as this period, we have an example of the way in which Jewish money was involved and interested in military matters. In 1170, a powerful liegeman of Henry II, Richard de Clare, raised an army and sailed to Ireland to conquer the Kingdom of Leinster without the king's knowledge or consent. According to some historians, the king was outraged because he viewed this conquest as the arbitrary act of a vassal. As a result, he imposed heavy fines on the Jews who, according to the reports he had received, had

---

[37] We find something similar reported in *Chronica Monasterii de Melsa*, Vol I, p. 306, 315. Translator's note: The source for this tale appears to be Jacobs: *Aaron of Lincoln*, pp. 163-4, which gives more particulars of the case.

[38] Hyamson: *History*, p. 23. & Jacobs: *Aaron of Lincoln*, pp. 166-7.

[39] Jacobs: *Aaron of Lincoln*, p. 169. & Jacobs: *Aaron of Lincoln*, p. 174 ff. [Appendix of Aaron's debts compiled by the Rev. S. Levy.] Translator's note: It must be borne in mind that this list of debtors and debts was compiled for the period corresponding to sixteen years after Aaron's death, that is to say, these are the debtors and debts that still remained outstanding after Aaron's business had formally ended sixteen years before. If a similar list could be compiled for the latter years of Aaron's life, we can only speculate as to how much bigger it would be. & Jacobs: *Aaron of Lincoln*, p. 168.

financed the military expedition. It was not possible to establish the facts underpinning this traditional history.[40]

People and Church in the Hands of the Usurers

We see the wealth of the Jews increasing and, as a result, their influence growing. This was offset by the poverty of the people, who could only helplessly stand by as they were exploited. It is not easy to get an idea of how much the debt had already grown by this time, so the best way to get a sense of the problem is by citing a few incidents.

The king's subjects were required to pay taxes and other state duties largely in cash. The money in circulation was still not very great, so the people usually had to turn to the Jews for such payments, who would give only too willingly. From one account we can see how a certain Richard of Anesty quickly fell into debt. Richard had borrowed the sum of £91.6s.8d and had to pay a usurious 60% interest rate on the loan. It need hardly be said that he was ruined in a very short time.

But it was not only the private individual who appears to have suffered from the usury of the Jews; the church was also particularly dependent on the Hebrews. When a natural son of King Henry II was appointed to succeed the Bishop of Lincoln in 1173, one of his first official acts was to 'redeem the ornaments of his church, which his predecessor had pledged to Aaron the Jew'.[41]

Another case sheds an even starker light on the conditions of the period. In 1175, Richard, Archbishop of Canterbury went to Peterborough Abbey to depose the local abbot, William of Walterville, because he had entered the monastery with the help of soldiers against the will of the monks and by force of arms had seized the bones of the saints that he had pledged to the Jews for money. What must have been the state of popular morale when even the highest dignitaries of the church committed such acts![42]

Around 1180, St. Edmunds Abbey [of the town of St. Edmunds, now Bury St. Edmunds] sank into a deplorable state. The woodlands were destroyed and the buildings had fallen into disrepair. There was therefore only one way out for the 'good and devout' Abbot Hugh: to borrow more money from the Jews. He had not been able to pay the interest for a long time.

---

[40] Hyamson: *History*, p. 26.

[41] *Giraldi Cambrensis Opera*, Vol. VII, p. 36.

[42] *Gesta Regis Henrici Secundi*, Vol. I, p. 106. Translator's note: Readers may be interested to know that among the saintly relics stolen was the arm of Saint Oswald, the 7th-century Northumbrian king famed for converting his kingdom to Christianity. The source also states that the abbot and his armed mercenaries inflicted mortal wounds on the monks and ministers of the church as these holy men tried to defend their relics.

When the debt fell due, the sum of the accrued interest was added to the capital and a new debt bond was drawn up. This repeated itself with each due date and the debt grew ever larger: 'In the last eight years of [the abbot's] life, sums of £100 or £200 were regularly added to the debt every Easter and Michaelmas.'

The individual monks who were abbey officials also believed that they could claim the same right for themselves as their abbot had for the abbey, and so it was not uncommon for them to borrow money from the Jews for personal purposes. Without the abbot's consent, they pledged 'silken copes, golden vessels and other church ornaments. The chronicler Jocelin of Brakelond recounts how he saw one debt bond for £1,040, in favor of William fitz Isabel [an important Christian financier], and another bond for £400, this time in favor of 'Isaac son of Rabbi Joce', without being able to fathom the circumstances that had led to the issuance of either document. Then he saw a third debt bond for £880, in favor of 'Benedict the Jew of Norwich', which had arisen for the following reason:

> Our treasury building was in a dilapidated condition, and William the sacrist was determined to restore it, come what may. He secretly borrowed 40 marks at interest from Benedict the Jew... When the sum owed had risen to £100, the Jew arrived with a letter from the king concerning the sacrist's debt, and in this way the secret was revealed to the abbot and convent. The abbot was furious, and would have deposed the sacrist, claiming that he had authority from the pope to dismiss him when he wished. But someone went to the abbot, and speaking on the sacrist's behalf, so deceived him that he allowed another bond to be made out for Benedict the Jew, this time for £400 to be paid at the end of four years. This was for the £100 already accumulated at interest and another £100 which the Jew lent the sacrist for the abbot's use...
>
> Four years later, when the obligation could not be met, a new bond was issued, for £880 to be paid off at fixed terms, at £80 per annum. The same Jew held several other bonds for smaller debts and one that was for fourteen years, so that altogether he was owed £1,200, excluding the compound interest.

The monk Jocelin also reports that the cellarer was also heavily indebted to the Jews:

> At that time the cellarer, like the other officials, borrowed money from Jurnet the Jew, without consulting the convent, in a bond sealed with the seal I mentioned previously [the con-

ventual seal]. But when the debt had grown to £60, the convent was summoned to pay the cellarer's debt. He was deposed, although he alleged that on the abbot's orders he had
for the last three years entertained in the guest-house, whether
the abbot was at home or not, all those guests who, according
to abbey custom, ought to have been entertained by the abbot
himself. Master Denis replaced him, and by careful management brought the debt of £60 down to £30... But still to this day
the Jew retains a bond for £26 capital and the cellarer's debt.[43]

When the tormented abbot Hugh finally closed his eyes forever in 1180,
William the sacrist had hopes for his position. The subsacrist Samson also
applied with him, but he was not acceptable to many others, both Christians
and Jews. The chronicler seems to understand the need to explain to a future
readership why a candidate for monastery abbot would require Jewish political support:

I should explain that the sacrist was referred to as the father
and patron of the Jews, for they enjoyed his protection. They
had free entrance and exit, and went everywhere throughout
the monastery, wandering by the altars and round the shrine
while Mass was being celebrated. Their money was deposited
in our treasury, in the sacrist's custody. Even more incongruous, during the troubles [of 1173-4], their wives and children
were sheltered in our pittancery.[44]

Despite having 'enemies and opponents' work against him, not least after he
put a mechanism in place to stop the embezzlement of church funds (which
others were doing, and which he himself was falsely accused of), Samson
was elected abbot. His first official act was to depose William as sacristan,
but William did not want to accept this and, in 1182, together with other dissatisfied monks, forged a plot against Samson. When Abbot Samson found
out about this:

... he resolved neither to remain completely silent nor to upset
the convent, so when he came into chapter the next day he

---

[43] *Chronica Jocelini de Brakelonda*, p. 1 ff. Translator's note: Aldag translated directly
from the Latin into German. To ensure reliability, all quotations and quoted elements used
in this chapter are therefore reproduced verbatim from the 1989 Oxford World Classics
translation [see Translator's Bibliography]; citations here are from pp. 3-4, 6-7.

[44] *Chronica Jocelini de Brakelonda*, p. 8. Translator's note: As footnote 79, quotation
from p. 10. Note that the original Latin '*Quod absurdius est...*' has been diplomatically
translated as 'Even more incongruous...'.

produced a bag full of cancelled charters [debt bonds], still bearing their seals, some in his predecessor's name, some in the prior's, some in the sacrist's, some the chamberlain's, and some in the names of other officials. The total of the capital involved was £3,052 and 1 mark, without the accumulated interest, whose real magnitude could never be known.

He had come to terms over all these debts within a year of his election, and he had paid them all off inside twelve years. 'Take a look at the wise policies of your sacrist William!' he said. 'Just see how many charters have been sealed by him without the convent's consent, pledging silk copes, dalmatics, silver thuribles, and volumes bound in gold, all of which I have repurchased and restored to you.' He went on to give further justification of his deposition of William, although he did not reveal the principal reason as he did not wish to cause him to stumble' (Mal. 2:8).

Then he appointed Samson the precentor to be sacrist in William's place, and thus everything was resolved peacefully, since Samson was superior in every way and was acceptable to us all. The abbot even ordered the sacrist's house in the cemetery to be completely demolished, as if it were not fit to stand upon the earth, on account of the frequent drinking sessions and other unmentionable activities of which he had been made painfully aware as subsacrist. Within a year he had it all razed to the ground: where a fine building had stood we saw beans pushing up their stems, and where wine barrels had been stored there grew a bed of nettles.[45]

These ancient chronicles are interesting not only because they show the general indebtedness to the Jews, but also because they teach us how their influence, with the help of their money, even penetrated the cloister.

Yes, the Jews even interfered in the affairs of the monastery, despite these places being completely alien to them. As we have seen, they found the choice of Samson unacceptable because he did not make common cause with them. And finally, this chronicle shows us the arrogance of the Jews: they dared to roam around the altar and St. Edmunds shrine during the solemnities of the Mass. It is no surprise then that as this Caesar worked to root out corruption and put the monastic house in order, morally and financially,

---

[45] *Chronica Jocelini de Brakelonda*, p. 22. Translator's note: Quotation reproduced from pp. 28-9 of the Oxford World Classics translation. It may interest readers to know that the upright Samson did not only succeed in routing out the corruption emanating from William's office – he also had the Jews expelled from the town of St. Edmunds in 1190 [pp. 41-2 in the Oxford text].

with a confiscation of the monastery's seals to prevent unauthorized borrowing that led to 33 seals being collected in total [p. 35], there was what appears to be an attempt on his life:

> One night, when he was staying at Warkton [Northants], he heard a voice speaking to him in his sleep, 'Samson, get up quickly', and then, 'Get up, you are too slow.' Astonished, he got up and looked around, and saw a light in the lavatory. It was a candle that was just about to fall on to some straw, carelessly left there by the monk Reiner. After he had snuffed out the candle, he went round the house and found the only door fastened in such a way that it could not be opened without a key and the windows tightly closed, so that if the fire had flared up, that would have been the end of him and all the people sleeping in that room, because there was no exit or escape route. [p. 29]

Meanwhile, the following anecdote from St. Albans monastery paints another frightening tableau of the times:

> But because no man on earth, not even a day-old infant, is without blemish, let us only briefly touch on the errors of this man [the abbot of St. Albans], for they are few in number compared to his good deeds. When he died, he left his abbey in debt of more than six hundred marks, which he owed to the Jews. This basic amount was burdened by an additional two hundred marks in debt interest. Hence Aaron the Jew, who kept us bound to him, appeared in St. Alban's House with great pride and boasting, as well as with threats, and used to brag that he had made the bier [i.e. the shrine] for our blessed Alban, and that he himself, out of hospitality, had housed the saint with his own money.
>
> [*Sed quia non vivit homo super terram, nec etiam infans unius diei, sine offendiculo, errores ipsius, quia respectu bonorum operum suorum breves, breviter transcurramus. Moriens, Abbathiam suam aere alieno obligatam plusquam secentis marcis contra Judaeos, sine aliis debitis, quae ad ducentarum marcarum et amplius summan excreverunt dereliquit. Unde Aaron Judaeus, qui nos tenuit sibi obligatos, ad Domum Sancti Albani, in superbia magna et jactantia, cum minis,*

*veniens, jactitabat se feretrum Beato Albano nostro fecisse, et
ipsi, dehospitato, hospitium de pecunia sua praeparasse.*].[46]

When Henry II died in 1189, the Jews not only expected his successor Richard, known as the Lionheart, to maintain the existing situation, but they even
hoped for improvements. When commenting on this, the historian Moses
Margoliouth then strangely goes on to say: 'They were encouraged in their
hopes by Richard's conduct, when, after returning from Normandy, he proclaimed liberty to all prisoners and captives, even to the greatest criminals.'[47]

Popular Anger Breaks Out

On 3 September 1189, Richard the Lionheart was crowned King of England,
a day that was extremely important for the history of the Jews in ancient
England. From that point on, they lost power and wealth until they were finally forced to leave the country. Subjects had flocked to London from all
parts of the Angevin Empire, including from the then English possessions in
France. The Jews had also sent their leaders to this event. For whatever reason
—some say superstition, others antipathy towards the Jews—the king, at the
instigation of Baldwin, Archbishop of Canterbury, passed a law prohibiting
Jews from entering Westminster Abbey or his palace during the coronation,
and they were forbidden on pain of death to enter during the banquet.

　　This order was publicly announced on the same day by heralds proclaiming it in the streets and posting notices of it in prominent places so that
everyone in the city knew about it in good time. A large crowd had gathered
near the church and the palace, including numerous Jews. These Jews carried
expensive gifts for the king and, despite the ban, were desirous to present
them to him that same day in homage. It is not entirely clear whether they
had only got as far as the gates of the palace or had already reached the king
when the 'foreigners,' or what other call 'the mob,' pounced on them.

---

[46] *Gesta Abbatum Monasterii Sancti Albani*, Vol. I, pp. 193-4. Translator's note: I have
reproduced the Latin original alongside this English translation for transparency, not only
because the text is open to interpretation, but also because readers familiar with Joseph
Jacobs' widely disseminated translation may wonder why the English version above does
not feature a window (presumably due to a confusion between *fenestram* and *feretrum*). In
one of his 'Provincial Letters', the Rev. Henry Beeching, later Dean of Norwich, was
scathing about this abbey incident, which he reproduced in Latin before explaining to
readers: 'He [Aaron] is said in the St. Alban's Chronicle to have ridden up to the gates of
that Abbey, which was deep in his debt, and to have boasted with threats that the shrine of
the Blessed Alban was built with his money and belonged to him. Probably the threat was
to take the shrine away unless his interest was more punctually paid.' From *The Cornhill
Magazine*, July 1901, (Vol. 11, No. 61), pp. 120-1.
[47] Margoliouth: *History*, Vol. I, p. 83. Translator's note: QVOS.

In any case, the crowd was outraged at the presumption of the Jews to disregard the king's decree. Margoliouth laments this outrage, the fact that 'the most loyal subjects, the most patriotic Englishmen, and the oldest settlers in the realm' had been driven back by brute force; for they could not have known anything about the decree that had been proclaimed just the day before. That this was not the majority view is evidenced by the behavior of the crowd, who themselves knew about the ban and were therefore upset by the behavior of the Jews. Threatening fists were brandished and soon blows began to rain down. The crowd became more and more agitated and finally attacked the Jews with sticks. Spectators standing at a greater distance saw and heard the commotion, believing that the king himself had ordered the Jews' expulsion because they had violated his ban.

By the time the Jews tried to escape, most of them had already been killed. False news spread like wildfire that the king himself had ordered the massacre. The population had been waiting for a long time for the king to give them a free hand, and now what had to come after all of the abuses finally happened: the people armed themselves and killed every Jew in sight unless he allowed himself to be baptized. Among those baptized was one of York's leading Jews, Benedict of York. When he was brought before the king a short time later, he again described himself as a Jew. He was allowed to live out of contempt for his fickleness and cowardice. The rioting in London continued into the day after the coronation. The king's attempts to suppress the riots were in vain given the anger of the people. The Jews withdrew into their fortified houses, which the English tried repeatedly to break into without success. Fires were then thrown onto the roofs, and the Jews burned to death in their homes. In some cases, the fire spread to English buildings nearby, and the tumult in London was indescribable.[48]

---

[48] *Grafton's Chronicle*, Vol. I, p. 219 ff. & *Chronicles of the Reign of Stephen*, Vol. 1. pp. 294-5; Margoliouth: *History*, Vol. 1, p. 86. Translator's note: The Jews were strongly associated with sorcery in the Middle Ages. To quote Margoliouth: 'The courtiers and the clergy – especially Baldwin, Archbishop of Canterbury – endeavored to make the king believe that the Jews were, in general, sorcerers, and might possibly bewitch him if they are allowed to be present at his coronation.' This association is also seen in the *Vita* of Christina of Markyate (?c. 1130s) in which, after the love potions of the local cunning woman failed, 'a Jewess was hired to bend Christina's will with spells more powerful than the others' [Furlong, p. 54, in Translator's Bibliography], while the 1240 Synod of Worcester decreed that Christians who consulted Jews for the purposes of magic should be brought before the bishop for punishment [Trachtenberg: *The Devil...*, p. 68]. Note that women were also banned from the event for the same reason [Margoliouth, p. 87]. & Rye, p. 8. & 'B. B.', p. 6. & W. H.: *Anglo-Judaeus*, p. 9. & *Chronicles of the Reign of Stephen*, Vol. I, p. 294 ff. & *The Metrical Chronicle of Robert of Gloucester*, Vol. II, p. 690 ff. & *Radulfi de Diceto*, Vol. II, p. 69. & *Rogeri de Houedene*, Vol. III, p. 12. & Margoliouth: *Anglo-Hebrews*, p. 12. Translator's note: QVOS. & *Radulphi de Coggeshall*, pp. 26-28; *Matthaei Parisiensis* [Matthew Paris], *Chronica Majora*, Vol. II, p. 350. Translator's note:

William of Newburgh, the late 12th-century chronicler, sees this outbreak of popular anger as the will of God, for the punishment of the haughty
and wicked Jews had been bound to come.[49]

Another chronicler of the same period, Richard of Devizes, a monk at
St. Swithun's Priory in Winchester, explains why his city of residence did
not take part in the anti-Jewish riots, and shares William's somewhat unchar-
itable view of Jews as a group:

> On the very day of the coronation, about that solemn hour in
> which the Son was immolated to the Father, a sacrifice of the
> Jews to their father the devil was commenced in the city of
> London, and so long was the duration of this famous mystery,
> that the holocaust could scarcely be accomplished the ensuing
> day. The other cities and towns of the kingdom emulated the
> faith of the Londoners, and with a like devotion dispatched
> their blood-suckers with blood to hell. In this commotion there
> was prepared, although unequally, some evil against the wick-
> ed everywhere throughout the realm, only Winchester alone,
> the people being prudent and circumspect, and the city always
> acting mildly, spared its vermin. It never did anything over-
> speedily; fearing nothing more than to repent, it considers the
> result of everything before the commencement. It was unwill-
> ing, unprepared, to cast up violently through the parts the indi-
> gestion by which it was oppressed to its bodily peril, and it
> was careful for its bowels, in the meantime temperately con-
> cealing its uneasiness, until it should be possible for it, at a
> convenient time for cure, to cast out the whole cause of the
> disease at once and once for all.

Although the king was very angry about the rioting, as it had happened on
his coronation day, he did very little against the people in relation to the incident. He had only three people involved in the tumult hanged: 'the one, for
that he had robbed a Christians house in this tumult, and the other two for
that they fired the houses, to the great danger of the city.'[50]

All future references to this famous work will be simply as *Chronica Majora. & Chronicles and Memorials of the Reign of Richard I*, Vol. I, p. 142. & *Gesta Regis Henrici Secundi*, Vol. II, p. 84; *Matthœi Pariensis, Historia Anglorum,* Vol. II. p. 9.

[49] *Chronicles of the Reigns of Stephen...*, Vol. I, p. 296. Translator's note: The subsequent
commentary from Richard of Devizes has been added by myself for reader interest, the
quotation being reproduced verbatim from the 1841 translation by Giles (pp. 5-6) [See
Translator's Bibliography].

[50] *Rogeri de Houdene*, Vol. III. p. 12; Foxe, Vol. I, pp. 304-305. Translator's note: Quotation reproduced verbatim from Foxe [p. 305].

A wave of anti-Jewish persecution swept throughout England. The people gave free rein to their long-held feelings. Wherever Jews were found and could be caught, they were killed. Many saved themselves and their valuable possessions by seeking refuge in the royal castles, which were largely granted to them by the king's officials. Particularly involved in the unrest were warriors who had followed Richard the Lionheart's call to go to Palestine. In Norwich, Lincoln, Stamford, and St. Edmunds [now Bury St Edmunds] the persecution was particularly severe and many Jews were killed.[51]

The reason for the 1190 persecution of Jews in King's Lynn is interesting. There a Jew had converted to Christianity, which enraged his Jewish brethren. When one day they came across the baptized Jew in the street, they tried to kill him, but he found refuge in a nearby church. The Jews did not stop pursuing him, but literally besieged the church and even tried to force open the church doors that had been closed by the refugee. Other Christians in the church, frightened, shouted on their fellow Christians outside for help, who came running to their aid and tried to drive away the frenzied Jews. However, the Jews did not give up and in the violence that broke out, many Jews were killed. The fleeing Jews were then pursued, their houses looted and burned down. The next day a distinguished Jewish doctor, well known in King's Lynn, insulted the people and prophesied vengeance. This incited the still furious population, who seized him and killed him.[52]

The persecutions were probably most intense in the north of England, but especially in York. Here the usury was worse than anywhere else, and nowhere were there more rich Jews than in that city. Their houses resembled palaces and their standard of living was royal for the time. And all of this was at the expense of the population. In no other place was there greater misery. The lowly people, the clergy and the nobility suffered equally. Anyone who had once borrowed money was hopelessly at the mercy of the Jews because of the enormous interest.

Various noblemen had already lost all of their property. Embittered, these peers gathered the equally dissatisfied common people to their side and waited for the day of reckoning. Crusading warriors passing through the city did the same, and one night, at the beginning of March 1190, an agitated mob stormed the house of one of the richest Jews—the aforementioned Benedict. Anyone found alive was beaten to death, while the house was looted and then set on fire. Most of the Jews of York reached the castle under cover of darkness, where the royal commander gave them refuge. When one day he left the castle for a short time, on his return the Jews refused to let him

---

[51] *Annales Monastici*, Vol. IV, p. 42 & *Radulphi de Diceto*, Vol. II, p. 75; *Rogeri de Wendover*, Vol. I, p. 176; *Chronica Jocelini de Brakelonda*, p. 33. & *Chronicles of the Reigns of Stephen...*, Vol. I, p. 312. & *Radulphi de Diceto*, Vol. II, p. 75; *Chronicles of the Reigns of Stephen...*, Vol. I, p. 310.
[52] *Chronicles of the Reigns of Stephen...*, Vol. I, p. 308.

back in. They had now made themselves masters of the castle. The commander summoned royal troops and, together with the angry citizens, stormed the castle. After the besieged Jews realized that their situation was hopeless, some of them killed themselves, while the rest surrendered, but were killed anyway by the embittered people.[53]

Immediately afterwards, the mob rushed to the cathedral [York Minster], where their debt bonds were kept. These debt bonds were seized and burned, an act which greatly angered the king, given that the Jews' debtors were now obligated to make their payments to him, by law their new creditor on the death of their Jewish usurer. With these debt bonds being the only proof of the debt to be recovered, the king had nothing in his hands to determine the deceased Jews' assets. He therefore sent a punitive expedition to York, but most of the rebels had already fled to Scotland. Of those who remained and had taken part in the trouble, 51 were sentenced to a total fine of £228.[54]

The never-ending series of riots, with the ensuing loss of debt bonds, apparently caused King Richard to pass a law to protect the Jews. The loss of these documents affected him personally, as the Jews' taxes to him were based on the assessed total of their wealth. The events in York probably accelerated the promulgation of the law, which took place at the end of March 1190. The Jews were then assured that they had the right to live in England. In addition, their assets were guaranteed, and it was also expressly confirmed that they could sell the items pledged to them after one year and one day. Finally, the law instituted the drastic measure, which had already been in practice previously and had caused endless bitterness among the population: 'that all Jews in England and Normandy should be free from Customs duties and taxes.' The statute ended on another solemn promise to protect all Jews.[55]

As is well known, Richard went off on Crusade in 1190 and did not return to England until 1194. His preparations for the Crusade had left him no time to adequately deal with the issues arising out of the Jewish Question.

Legal Status of the Jews

After his return from the Holy Land, Richard sent officials to the various cities where the persecution of Jews had taken place. He wanted to get an accurate picture of the number of Jews killed in order to determine the extent of their legacy. The investigations in York proved impracticable because a significant part of the Jews' wealth consisted of claims against Englishmen

---

[53] *Chronicles of the Reigns of Stephen...*, Vol. I, p. 313.
[54] *Chronicles of the Reigns of Stephen...*, Vol. I, p. 323. & *Chronicles of the Reigns of Stephen...*, Vol. I, p. 312 ff.; *Radulphi de Diceto*, Vol. II, pp.75-6. & *Chronicles of the Reigns of Stephen...*, Vol. I, p. 324.
[55] *Rymer's Fœdera*, Vol. I, p. 51. Translator's note: I was unable to find the information at the reference given, nor at the source pages which corresponded to the year 1190.

whose debt records had been burned by an embittered populace during the riots. This demonstrated to Richard that he had to take measures to avoid similar incidents, because he considered the Jews (and by extension their property) to be his property. Furthermore, according to the legal opinion of the time, he believed that Jews did not live for themselves but for others, and thus acquired material goods for those others.[56]

Abrahams concludes from this that the Jews were only serfs in their relationship to the king. A similar position is also taken by Rigg, Stokes and the writing duo Pollock and Maitland. However, Picciotto is of the opinion that this view of history must be rejected. He concludes this because, in his view, the Jews were entitled under the law to be property owners. However, given that this idea was very controversial right up until the first half of the 19th century, this Jewish writer's view is unlikely to have been the case [and may be an attempt to retcon history]. We too are of the opinion that the Jews were probably to be viewed as the king's serfs. When a Jew died, by law the deceased's estate passed to the king, who usually did not make use of his right but left the estate to the natural heirs and only levied a considerable inheritance tax. As a result, the king must always have felt at a disadvantage when he was unable to determine the exact amount of assets due to the lack of debt records. To remedy this situation, Richard had a law passed in September 1194, the year he returned to England, which contained a provision in which participation in anti-Jewish uprisings was to be punished and, additionally, all liabilities towards the Jews who had been killed had to be registered.[57]

Additionally, the section titled *Capitula Judaeorum,* which outlined the details of the new *archa* system for registering financial transactions, would have important repercussions for the future. It stipulated that from that point onwards, all claims, mortgages, houses, and other assets of the Jews should be registered. Any assets that the Jews did not honestly declare, whether tangible or financial, were to be considered forfeited. The new law stipulated that six or seven urban centers in the realm [which came to be known as

---

[56] Hyamson: *History*, p. 42. & *Henrici de Bracton*, p. 51. Translator's note: McCall provides a translation of this English jurist, who wrote (in Latin) at some point before 1256: 'A Jew cannot have anything of his own, because whatever he acquires, he acquires not for himself but for the king, because they do not live for themselves but for others and so they acquire for others and not for themselves.' [*The Medieval Underworld*, p. 272 – See Translator's Bibliography.]

[57] Abrahams, p. 13 ff. Translator's note: This was also the view of Thomas Aquinas, who in turn took this view from St. Bernard, so it might fairly be said that this was the traditional Christian view of Jewry in the medieval polity. McCall quotes Aquinas as saying 'since the Jews are the slaves of the Church, she can dispose of their possessions' and 'the Jews are the serfs of the Christian princes'. [*Idem*, pp. 271-2] & Rigg, p. XIII. & Stokes: *Relationship*, p. 161. & Pollock & Maitland, Vol. I, p. 471. & Picciotto, p. 70 ff. & *Rogeri de Houedene*, Vol. III, p. 263 [item IX].

archa towns] were to be the only places where debt contracts could be drawn up. This was to be done with the assistance of four notaries (two Englishmen and two Jews), two legal registrars, and other employees. The documents were to be issued in different copies, one of which remained in the Jew's possession, while a second was kept safe in the state depository. The chest [*archa,* pl. *archae*] intended for this purpose had three locks, for which the two Christians, the two Jews and the officials each had a key.

The issuance of these documents would continue to be subject to a type of stamp duty. For their legal validity it was necessary that they be completed in the presence of the persons mentioned. The same applied to any changes to the debt contract, such as an increase or decrease in the amount owed, or a change in the interest rate. An exact register of the payments made was also kept. At the end of the process, the Jews were again asked by the king to truthfully declare their assets so that these could be registered accordingly, and 'to report to him all contract forgers and coin clippers, as far as they were known'. If such orders proved necessary, there must have been quite a few cases of such crimes in which, as usual, Jews would be disproportionately involved.[58]

Incidentally, this appears to be the first extant documentary evidence, in this case a legal statute, in which Jews were linked to coin crimes in medieval England. We will see below how these Jewish crimes escalated to an ever-greater severity in the subsequent century and significantly contributed to the eventual expulsion of the Jewish people.

There can be no doubt that this law gradually gave rise to the so-called 'Exchequer of the Jews'. The basis for this government department was the public registration of debts and an existing department in the royal treasury that had been set up to manage Aaron of Lincoln's huge legacy. When Aaron died in 1186, King Henry II made full use of the right to confiscate his property, although the size of the estate necessitated the creation of a special treasury department. The exact year that this Jewish tax office was established is not known, but it certainly did not take place before the year 1194, when the aforementioned law was passed, nor after 1198, because in this latter year we find references to 'judges of the Jews' in contemporary documents.[59]

This 'Exchequer of the Jews', otherwise known as the *Saccarium Judaeorum* or *Thesauraria Judaeorum* in the historical record, had two main tasks to carry out, which were financial and judicial. On the one hand, the Exchequer as Jewish tax office handled all of the king's transactions with the Jews, e.g. the collection of a special inheritance tax, penny head tax, wealth tax, and confiscations. On the other hand, the Exchequer also administered

---

[58] *Rogeri de Houedene*, Vol. III, p. 266-7 [Item XXIV]; Twysden, p. 1258. Translator's note: To banish any reader doubt, the original Latin of the quotation, which is from *Rogeri de Houedene*, is 'retonsores denariorum', that is, 'coin clippers'.

[59] Hyamson: *History*, p. 43. & Madox: *Formulare Anglicanum*, p. 77.

justice, not only between the king and the Jews, but also between the king and the English, as far as Jewish business was concerned. Equally as important, it also made judgments in legal disputes between the English and the Jews. The entirety of the Exchequer's transactions were documented in the so-called 'Pipe Rolls' and are largely preserved today, giving a fairly accurate picture of the Jewish Exchequer's activities.[60]

The aforementioned first department of the Exchequer had to ensure that when a Jew died, his assets were determined and valued. This was not difficult after the 1194 law came into force, as there was normally reasonable documentary evidence to prove this. An inheritance tax of 33⅓ percent was generally levied on the estate.[61]

The so-called confiscations were a method of taxation which covered many aspects of life. Mainly they referred to taxes exacted when granting licenses of all kinds. Sometimes they were claimed when Jews entered into a marriage contract, and they were also included in the costs of litigation between creditors and debtors and vice versa.

Closely related to this method of taxation was the tallage [or mulct] on those who had committed capital crimes, such as the counterfeiting or clipping of coins, with capital punishment being carried out simultaneously. The amount of this latter type of tax was often considerable.[62]

However, the most profitable taxes for the king were the so-called poll taxes. They were regularly levied whenever the king's coffers were empty—a common predicament—and in the years 1194-1290 the Jews paid enormous sums in this way. To date, it has not yet been fully established how much these taxes generated for the king as an annual average. The renowned judge Coke speaks of around £50,000 a year, while Gross only wishes to consider £5,000-£10,000. The total will probably be somewhere between the two; but even if one accepts Gross's estimate, it was already significant in relation to the king's other income. King Edward I, of whom we will hear more below, only had an ordinary revenue of £65,000, so he had to rely largely on Jewish taxes. The poll tax was either levied on a per capita basis or a specific sum was set to be paid by the entire Jewry of England. How the tax burden was distributed among its individual members was then a matter

---

[60] Gross: *Exchequer*, p. 175. & Pollock & Maitland, Vol. I. p. 90. & Rigg: *Exchequer of the Jews*, Vol. III. p. XIII.

[61] Gross: *Exchequer*, p. 192; *Annales Monastici*, Vol. I, p. 340; Foxe, Vol. I, p. 423, col. II.

[62] Hyamson: *History*, p. 45; Gross: *Exchequer*, p. 193; Abrahams: *Expulsion*, p. 14. Translator's note: It may interest English-speaking readers to know that the German word used here for clipping [of coins] – *Beschneidung* – has the double meaning of circumcision. Note that there were instances where Jews were mulcted as a group for a criminal act (i.e. the fine was a form of collective punishment), regardless of whether or not the individual perpetrator(s) had been identified – as seen, for example, in the case of the apparent ritual infanticide in London, 1244.

for the Jews themselves. It was not uncommon for the richest Jews to be tasked with delivering the required sum, and it was up to them how they got the money together.[63]

This type of tax collection was only possible with the help of the Exchequer of the Jews, because the king could only determine the assets of the Jews and determine the amount of the poll tax to be paid based on the registers kept there. If the Jews were unable or unwilling to pay the sum imposed on them from their current income, the king quickly confiscated their debt claims and asserted them in his own name. A debtor's payment to the Jew after such a confiscation was not recognized. It was not uncommon for Jews to fail to pay the required poll taxes, resulting in all of their property being confiscated and even entire families being sent to the Tower as hostages.[64]

The Jew himself could never legally forgive a debt on his own, but required the consent of the Exchequer, just as he likewise had to obtain their approval for a legally valid assertion of a claim.[65]

In the course of the 13th century, another restriction was put in place, namely that Jews could only settle in places where there were branches of the Exchequer [symbolised by the *archa*]—a regulation of drastic importance, and the greatest regulatory change since Richard the Lionheart. According to Gross's careful research, there are likely to have been 26 such designated places [*archa* towns], including London, Bedford, Lincoln, Oxford, Cambridge, and York. Numerous cities had by this point even requested and received the royal privilege of being freed from any Jewish settlement. These included Derby, Leicester and Newcastle-upon-Tyne, among others. On the other hand, in exceptional cases, Jews were allowed to settle in cities where there was no *archa*.[66]

The aforementioned second department of the Jewish Exchequer functioned as a law court. Legal cases between Jews were not part of its jurisdiction, because as we have already explained, in such cases the Jews were granted complete jurisdiction, based on the existing legal provision. Only in a few criminal cases involving Jews was the Exchequer allowed to intervene. The jury in such cases consisted exclusively of Jews.[67]

---

[63] Coke, p. 506. & Gross: *Exchequer,* p. 195. & Stubbs, Vol. II, p. 595 ff. & Madox: *Exchequer,* Vol. I, p. 257; Prynne, Vol. II, p. 32. & Madox: *Exchequer,* Vol. I, p. 224; Prynne, Vol. II, pp. 32, 39, 76 ff.

[64] The documents from these events are still in the Record Office today. There are also numerous other documented sources, including: *Rymer's Fœdera,* Vol. I, pp. 337, p. 407; Prynne, Vol. II, pp. 51, 77, 86-7, 89, 104, 112. & *Chronica Majora,* Vol. V, p. 441; Madox: *Exchequer,* Vol. I, p. 230, 256; Prynne, Vol. II, p. 18. 40, 48, 75.

[65] Madox: *Exchequer,* Vol. I, p. 246. & Prynne, Vol. II, p. 64.

[66] *Rymer's Fœdera,* Vol. I, p. 634; Prynne, Vol. I, p. 39. & Gross: *Exchequer,* p. 187. & Gross: *Exchequer,* p. 190. & Gross: *Exchequer,* p. 189.

[67] Rigg: *Exchequer,* Vol. II, p. XV; Rigg: *Select Pleas,* p. XXI.

A mixed court was used in legal disputes between English and Jewish parties. Among the first four judges appointed for this category of case were two Jews, although it appears that this provision was abandoned at a later stage.[68]

The court of the Exchequer had to decide all cases which pertained to the laws passed for Jews, laws which the Jews themselves often ignored. The ecclesiastical courts, and even the king's own courts, were forbidden to pronounce justice on such matters. The fact that this was not always observed is evident from the king's warnings to the former not to concern themselves with such cases.[69]

The cases that arose as a result of disputes between English people as debtors and Jews as creditors are also likely to have been very common. And if the king had confiscated financial claims from Jews, he also sometimes appeared as a party in court.[70]

According to the historians we have surveyed, the activity of the judicial department was limited to the above matters. However, it seems necessary to point out that other functions were undoubtedly carried out by the judges in question. There are often instructions from the king to the judges to release certain English people from a debt and demand that the Jews return the debt bonds in their possession.[71] Regarding other identified activity, however, it is difficult to determine which of the two departments had competence in the matter.

One day, King Edward I learned that the Jews were oppressing a certain Robert Sturmy because he was unable to fulfil his obligations to them. He only got into this predicament because of the enormously usurious interest rates. The Jews apparently intended to take action against him with the help of the Jewish Exchequer, but the king ordered the judges to grant him a deferment.[72]

The king's motive for his order is clearly demonstrated, as he bases it on the fact that the debtor should be granted 'reasonable instalment payments in order to enable him to repay the debt without endangering his existence'. The king's forbearance is even more evident in another case in which

---

[68] Rigg: *Exchequer*, Vol. II p. XV; Rigg: *Select Pleas*, p. XX.

[69] Prynne, Vol. I, (2nd ed.), p. 34. Translator's note: Prynne gives examples of cases not to be dealt with by the ecclesiastical courts, but instead by the Jews' own 'proper delegated Judges'. These include: 'delinquency against an Ecclesiastical person', 'Sacrilege', 'laying violent hands upon a Clerk' and 'adultery with a Christian woman'.

[70] Gross: *Exchequer,* p. 204.

[71] *Rotuli Literarum Patentium* p. 31; *Rotuli de Liberate* p. 24, 34, 35, 38.

[72] Madox: *Exchequer*, Vol. I, p. 252. Translator's note: The verb 'oppress' is that used in the original source.

he demands that 'inquiries should be made to determine whether the debtor is able to pay without jeopardizing the maintenance of himself and his family'.[73]

The barrister James Macmullen Rigg has painstakingly and exhaustively researched the court proceedings of the juridical side of the Jewish Exchequer. His findings will be of particular interest to lawyers. For the purposes of this work, however, it will suffice to state that the regulations governing the hearings, service of lawsuits, etc. were fairly consistent with the general civil procedure rules of the time.[74]

The head office of the Jewish Exchequer was in Westminster, at that time a city near London. The highest officials were usually called '*Justiciarii ad custodiam Judaeorum assignati*', in other words, Justices assigned to the custody of the Jews. The number of these justices fluctuated continually. The posts must have been of particular importance because they were occupied by high-ranking Christian men of the time.[75] Their appointment was made by the king. They each had to report to the Accountant about all financial transactions in their department, and it was not uncommon for them to discover irregularities that were mainly due to bribes on the part of the Jews.[76]

There was also the so-called '*Presbyter omnium Judaeorum Angliae*' or '*Presbyter Judaeorum*', who was appointed by Richard the Lionheart's successor, King John. This 'Archpresbyter of all the Jews of England' was guaranteed very special protection, and all English people were told, under threat of punishment, to respect him because he was 'the royal Jew who had been employed in the king's service.' It almost seems like a joke that this archpriest of the Jews was appointed by the Archbishop of Canterbury. He was elected from among the leading Jews and was probably appointed for life, since we find only six holders of this office during the period 1200-1290. His rights and obligations are no longer known in detail. He probably advised the king on setting the poll tax, and helped the court with the translation and interpretation of Jewish contracts. The king as well as the Jews benefited greatly from the establishment of the Exchequer. Above all, the king could always determine the amount of the Jews' wealth from the registers and tax them accordingly. Furthermore, he always had a copy of the debt bonds, so that he was protected against their destruction, as in the York case.[77]

In addition, the taxation of individual transactions was made easier for him, as he could easily determine the transactions carried out from the doc-

---

[73] Madox: *Exchequer*, Vol. II, p. 209, footnote N. & Madox: *Exchequer*, Vol. II, p. 208, footnote L.

[74] Rigg: *Exchequer*, Vol. III, p. XXXI ff.

[75] Madox: *Formulare Anglicanum.*, p. 77; *Chronica Majora*, Vol. V, p. 261, 345; *Rymer's Fœdera*, Vol. I, p. 362; *Chronicles of Edward I*, Vol. I, p. 95; Prynne, Vol. II, pp. 80, 84, 98.

[76] Madox: *Exchequer*, Vol. I, p. 252 ff.

[77] *Rotuli Chartarum*, Vol. I, Part I, pp. 6-7. & *Rymer's Fœdera*, Vol. I, p. 95, 362, 591; Tovey, p. 59; Prynne, Vol. II, pp. 54, 80. & Prynne, Vol. II, p. 71.

uments and entries in the register. Apparently, the king levied a one-time tax of 10% when a deal was concluded, certainly a very worthwhile source of income. Meanwhile, the Exchequer provided legal guarantees to the Jews for their business of usury. The only people who suffered were the English people themselves. They had to pay loan interest either to the king or to the Jews, with the only difference being that the former sometimes exercised leniency.[78]

Population Figures

Before we discuss the reign of Richard the Lionheart's successor, let us make a few further observations about the Jewish population at the end of the 12th century.

Jacobs has gone to great pains to determine the number of Jews living in 12th-century England. His research involved going through the 12th-century Pipe Rolls and the other documents at the Record Office, and noting every Jewish name that was mentioned in some context. Using this method, he has drawn up a list containing about 750 names. He rightly notes that these refer to four generations, but only to the heads of the families. Thus, based on his findings, Jacobs comes to the conclusion that there were around 2,000 Jews in England at the end of the 12th century. To get to this figure, he also factored in that around 500 Jews were probably killed during the massacres of 1190. If it is now assumed that the English population at that time was around 1.5 million, then the Jewish population accounted for just under 1.5 percent of the total.[79]

The Jews Under King John

The already mentioned successor of Richard the Lionheart, King John (1199-1216) was initially fond of the Jews. After he appointed the archpresbyter of the Jews, straight after ascending the throne, he continued to be friendly towards them.

In the law, or 'charter', dated April 10th, 1201, John expressly confirmed to the Jews that their previous privileges would continue. They would remain exempt from Customs duties and taxes, and, like the king himself, would be exempt from all tolls, levies, and wine taxes, and were guaranteed every kind of protection. They were also allowed to accept as pawn or pledge all types of asset, with the exception of church goods [and any cloth 'stained with blood'], and to sell these assets after a year and a day of pos-

---

[78] *Rotuli de Oblatis et Finibus*, pp. 197, 202, 210, 231, 236.
[79] Jacobs, pp. 345-383. & Jacobs, p. 381.

session. In addition, they continued to have their own jurisdiction. The already de facto standard practice of not confiscating a Jew's estate when he or
she died, but instead levying a high inheritance tax, was enshrined in law.[80]

However, two important procedural innovations appear to have been
created. After this time, if an Englishman wanted to file a lawsuit against a
Jew, he had to consent to being tried by Jewish judges. These judges, namely
the rabbis, then basically spoke according to Talmudic law. In such a courtroom situation, the Englishman had little hope of prevailing, especially since
the law also stipulated that a Jew did not have to make any statement against
another and that the oath of a Jew was worth as much as the oaths of twelve
Christians.[81] As we read in Tovey [p. 62; the modern version from Pearl, p.
38, is substituted for clarity]:

> The Charter also decreed that if anyone took up a prosecution
> against a Jew without a witness, the Jew could be acquitted af-
> ter taking a single oath on his Scroll of the Law; and if the
> Crown took up litigation against a Jew, he would be likewise
> acquitted after taking an oath on the Rolls.

How could such a law have possibly benefitted the jurisprudence of the
time? Once again, it was only the people who suffered.

Of course, the king did not assent to this charter, which was so favorable to the Jews, for nothing—the Jews had to pay him £3,200, or 4,000
marks—but in the end it was the people who ultimately had to pay this sum
when the Jews raised the interest rates.[82]

This apparent favoritism caused large numbers of Jews to come to England from the European continent, a new wave of immigration which drove
the native English population to despair. The people rebelled, and riots broke
out in London in 1203. It is in this year that we find a proclamation from the
king to the people of London that he would not tolerate any excesses against
the Jews under any circumstances. He called on the burgesses [i.e. the free-
men] to defend the Jews, declaring that they would pay with their own blood
if harm befell any Jew. Apparently this strict decree had the intended effect,
for no more unrest against the Hebrews was heard of for a while.[83]

Surprisingly, the next few years saw a change in the king's attitude towards the Jews. Many Jewish historians conclude that King John was initially
friendly towards them only out of diabolical calculation. This may be so, but

---

[80] *Rotuli Chartarum*, Vol. I, Part I, p. 93.

[81] Margoliouth: *History*, Vol. I, p. 123. & *Select Civil Pleas*, Vol. I, p. 3.

[82] *Rotuli de Oblatis*, pp. 133, 402, 418.

[83] Hyamson: *History*, p. 48; Margoliouth: *History*, Vol. I, p. 124. & Hardy: *Descriptive
Catalogue*, p. 61; Tovey, pp. 67-8. Translator's note: I was unable to find any data with
this Hardy reference, having explored all volumes in the series.

it has not been proven. Rather, another explanation is at least equally worthy of consideration: that once again the Jews themselves were solely responsible for this turn of events due to their bad behavior. As always in history, they apparently could not tolerate the favor they received from the king and thus forfeited his goodwill, as can be seen from the following incidents.

A year after the London riots, on the death of his mother, King John issued an extremely far-reaching amnesty law in which all criminals, regardless of the type of crime they had committed, were to be released from prison. Only Jewish criminals were exempt from this benefit of the law, which was certainly due to the fact that Jewish criminality had got completely out of hand. The very next year, it became necessary to promulgate a special law that imposed a stricter penalty for coin clipping. The assumption of Jewish involvement is further reinforced by the legal ruling according to which, if there were coins found that had been devalued by clipping, the Jewish owner was to be viewed as the perpetrator from the outset until proven otherwise. It stands to reason that the Jews would often have used their monopoly on moneylending to force the coins that they themselves had devalued onto someone seeking a loan.[84]

The fact that this law did not have the intended effect can be seen from a new decree issued by the king in 1206, according to which the authorities were to carry out detailed investigations into the money-related crimes that had become common again. Even back then, strict laws were apparently not enough to deter Jews from committing serious crimes.[85]

These facts immediately suggest that it was not the king who lacked goodwill toward the Jews, but the other way around. He had greatly benefitted them with the charter of 1201, and it cannot therefore be assumed that he completely changed his attitude just three years later for the motives attributed to him. It is much more likely that it was solely the Jews who embittered the king through their behavior. Given this hypothesis, one should consider evaluating the following events from this perspective.

In 1210, all of the Jews were arrested and brought together into one place in Bristol. Apparently the king suspected that the debt entries in the registers were not true. In any case, immediately after the mass arrest he levied a poll tax of 66,000 marks, or around £53,000 (one mark then being equal to £0.8), and it took the most severe medieval torture to eventually collect this amount. This may confirm the suspicion that the registers were indeed in disorder, for in 1188 the Jews had paid the far larger sum of £60,000 easily and without the use of force. Since the year 1190, i.e. for 20 years, the Jews had been able to carry out their business of usury under the king's express protection. This must have given them enough time to extract

---

[84] *Rymer's Fœdera*, Vol. I, p. 90. & *Rotuli de Oblatis*, Vol. I, Part 1, p. 47.
[85] *Rotuli de Oblatis*, Vol. I, Part 1, p. 54.

a much larger sum from the people, as indicated by later payments, taking into account each individual period of time. The use of force appears to have been applied quite brutally. It is reported that a Jew from Bristol, who had refused to pay the sum of around £7,330, had a tooth pulled out every day that he refused to pay up, and that he only agreed to make the payment when he had a single tooth left. Indeed, the sum was paid quite quickly.[86]

A few years later the barons revolted against the king. The nobles were generally hostile to the Jews, to whom they were indebted. The war ended with the barons' victory and the subsequent promulgation of the famous Magna Carta, which laid the foundation for the free rights of the English. Given the barons' hatred of the Jews, it is not surprising that the charter in question included special provisions for protecting the English with regard to Jewish usurers. Among other things, the charter stipulated that a minor who inherited an estate that was burdened with debts to Jews did not have to pay any interest on the debt while he remained underage. Similarly, if a man died owing money to the Jews, his wife was to have her dowry and pay nothing towards the debt from it. If the indebted man had left underage children, their needs had first to be provided for, with the debt to the Jews (and any other creditors) to be paid out of the residue.[87]

However, the peace in England was to be short-lived. In January 1216, in the course of capturing Berwick from King Alexander II of Scotland during what later became known as the First Barons' War, King John had prisoners tortured to death in the cruelest way. A trustworthy source tells us that 'the king brought Jews with him to teach his people about this wickedness'. It is worth noting that, even at this time, the Jews already had the ingenuity required for such sadistic practices. Nothing has changed in this regard either, as their role in similar crimes in Red Spain and Russia is all too well documented.[88]

---

[86] Gervase of Canterbury, Vol. II, p. 105; Rogeri de Wendover, Vol. II, p. 54; *Chronica Majora* Vol. II. p. 528; Madox: *Exchequer*, Vol. I, p. 223. & *Roger de Wendover*, Vol. II, p. 54. *Chronica Majora*, Vol. II, p. 528. Translator's note: 'B. B.' (p.7) describes this man as 'Abraham of Bristol', while Rye (pp. 339-40) believes this unfortunate man to have been the magnate Isaac of Norwich. See also Adler (pp. 142-3) for a discussion of the event.

[87] *Magna Carta*, p. 2 ff. Translator's note: The points noted above are to be found in clauses 10 and 11 of the charter.

[88] *Chronica de Mailros*, p. 122 [page number for the 1835 Stevenson edition]. Translator's note: For those who wish to examine the original Latin: 'xviij. kalendas Februarii [Jan. 15] cepit Johannes rex Anglie villam et castellum de Berwic, ubi cum rutariis suis feroci supra modum et inhumana usus est tyrannide, utriusque enim sexus homines quoscunque satellites diaboli apprehendere potuerunt, alios per articulos manuum et pedum suspendentes, alios diversis suppliciis torquentes, nefandi questus intuitu immanissime cruciaverunt. Ibi etiam Judeos secum adduxisse et magistros malicie illos effecisse refertur.'

The opinion of the Jewish historian Hyamson is interesting. He claims that the Jews ended up in this position of executioner because the English refused to take part in such cruel tortures, which meant that the king then 'had recourse to his Jews, whom he compelled to act as the ministers of his barbarous designs.' However, despite diligent research, we were unable to find this perspective in the Melrose Chronicle, which Hyamson cites as the source for his assertion. Rather, only the excerpt cited above is found in the traditional history.[89]

Problems Continue to Ferment

King John died in 1216, and his nine-year-old son succeeded him to the throne as Henry III (1216-1272). The regency was led by men who abandoned the anti-Jewish policies of the final years of King John's reign and, by contrast, gave the Jews every protection. It can be seen that these regents repeatedly advocated for the well-being of the Jews through numerous decrees. The result, as always, was a greater increase in Jewish wealth and further Jewish immigration from the European mainland on the one hand, and the greater exploitation and deepening rancor of the English people on the other. The benevolence of these advisors went so far, that all Jews were released from prison after an amnesty law. In 1218, a law was promulgated requiring them to wear a badge identifying their race, consisting of two strips of white linen or parchment prominently placed on their clothing. Historians argue as to whether this law was to the advantage or disadvantage of Jewish interests. Whatever the case, there was undoubtedly a reason for the law's enactment that we can only guess at today.[90]

In 1208, it was necessary to sentence the Jew Isaac of Norwich to a fine of around £6,000. No further details are known about the reason. However, it was certainly due to a proven serious crime, since it is undisputed that the

---

[89] Hyamson: *History*, p. 50. Translator's note: QVOS.

[90] *Patent Rolls*, Vol. I, p. 23, 30, 59, 157. & Margoliouth: *History*, Vol. I, p. 133 ff. & Hyamson: *History*, p. 51. & *Rymer's Fœdera*, Vol. I, Part 1, p. 151. Translator's note: This law was evidently England's way of enacting the 68th Constitution (or Canon) of the Fourth Lateran Council of 1215, which demanded that Jews (and Muslims) were to be distinguishable from Christians by the character of their dress while in public in every Christian province at all times. & Tovey, p. 81 ff.; Hyamson: *History*, p. 52. Translator's note: William Prynne, in *The Second Part of a Short Demurrer* [pp. 21-22], reports from his study of the Close Rolls that King Henry had instructed the appointment of special justices for the Jews, 'for their custody and affaires' in every town where the Jews resided 'to protect them and theirs from injury'. To this end the Jewish badge was to be worn so that 'they might be manifestly distinguished from Christians, and the better known and secured from injury and violence by those their new Protectors'. & Margoliouth: *History*, Vol. I, p. 136; Rye, s. 152.

king or his regents showed every favor to the Jews at that time and this penalty cannot therefore have been caused by a general hostile attitude.[91]

Immigration to England must have continued to be significant. However, at a popular level there was clearly a desire to stop this influx, reflected in the fact that the Jews were often not allowed into the country by the wardens of the Cinque Ports, who seized them on arrival and threw them into prison. The royal protection, however, still prevailed, and as soon as the king heard of this treatment, he issued an order to all of the relevant port authorities that all foreign Jews should have freedom of entry. In order to incorporate the newcomers into the financial system of the Exchequer of the Jews, it was also stipulated that they had to report their name and whereabouts to the Exchequer judges, and they were also not allowed to leave the country without royal permission.[92]

The more Jews came into the country, the greater the growth in usury, and the more desperate the people's plight. However, knowing that the Jews enjoyed the protection of the king and his advisors, the English did not dare do anything. Unexpectedly, the church came to the aid of her flock, not least because—as has already been explained—the church also suffered greatly from Jewish usury. In addition, Jewish efforts to convert Christians to Jewish teachings continued unabated, and a deacon had even converted to the Jewish faith out of love for a Jewess. The church therefore believed that it had to act on its own initiative. At the 1222 Synod of Oxford, under the leadership of the Archbishop of Canterbury Stephen Langton, the renowned 'hero of Magna Charta', it was decreed:[93]

---

[91] Rye, p. 151.

[92] Hyamson: *History*, p. 52. & *Patent Rolls*, Vol. I, p. 180.

[93] *Annales Monastici*, Vol. IV, p. 62; *Chronica Majora* Vol. III, p. 71; *Chronica Minora*, Vol. II, p. 254. Translator's note: Rabbi Eli Brackman's 2024 online essay 'Haggai of Oxford', finds that there appears to have been two cases of Christian religious men converting to Judaism in the 12th century, which may account for some of the confusion between sources. Nevertheless, it does appear that deacon Robert of Reading converted to Judaism, a process which included undergoing circumcision and being renamed Haggai of Oxford, and then married a Jewess. As he refused to recant, the Oxford Synod of 1222, the same council described above, ordered that he be degraded and burnt at the stake. This execution took place on Sunday, April 17th, 1222, and is a reminder that Christians (not just Jews) were also very capable of killing their apostates. See: www.oxford-chabad.org/templates/blog/post.asp? aid=708481&PostID=124293&p=1 . In addition, F. W. Maitland's *The Deacon and the Jewess* and Chapter 6 of Horowitz [see Translator's Bibliography for both] provides an interesting background to the case. & Tovey, p. 81. & Leeming, p. 164 ff. Translator's note: Langton's decree is reproduced verbatim from page 53 of Hyamson's *History*, although it should be noted that Aldag in his gloss of the same reminded the reader that the church's order for a Jewish badge was simply a reiteration of the previous secular law passed in 1218. Hyamson (p. 68) also reminds us that it would not be until 1253 that the secular state took up the majority of the Synod's 1222 directives.

That Jews do not keep Christian slaves [servants]. And let the slaves be compelled by ecclesiastical censure to observe this; and the Jews by canonical punishment, or by some extraordinary penalty contrived by the Diocesans. Let them not be permitted to build any more synagogues, but be looked upon as debtors to the churches of the parishes wherein they reside, as to tithes and offerings. To prevent likewise the mixture of Jewish men and women with Christians of each sex, we charge, by authority of the General Council, that the Jews of both sexes wear a linen cloth, two inches broad and four fingers long, of a different color from their own clothes, on the upper garment, before their breast; and that they be compelled to this be ecclesiastical censure. And let them not presume to enter into any church, nor for that end lodge their goods there. If they do let them be corrected by the Bishop.

What must have been the prevailing conditions if these latter impositions were deemed necessary!

At the same time as this decree, the Archbishop of Canterbury and the Bishops of Lincoln and Norwich issued a decree prohibiting all Englishmen under their ecclesiastical jurisdiction from having any intercourse, least of all sexual, with Jews. In accordance with this regulation, it was also forbidden to buy anything from Jews or to provide them with food or other necessities for subsistence in return for payment.

However, the king viewed these measures as an infringement of his authority and apparently feared that the boycott demanded would lead to a gradual starvation of the Jews. As a result, he published a royal precept dissolving the church's injunctions, and directing the officers concerned to command all merchants and storekeepers to sell food and other necessities to Jews under pain of imprisonment, 'any spiritual inhibition notwithstanding'.[94]

In the years that followed, the Jews continued to enjoy the king's special protection. As long as the regent acting on his behalf, Hubert de Burgh, was still in office, this favor remained, but things changed immediately after his deposition. An outward sign of this was initially the levying of a poll tax of 4,000 marks (£3,200) in 1226, and soon afterwards another of 6,000 marks (£4,800) the latter of which was not paid until 1230. Tovey even claims, citing the monk Matthew Paris, that a third of the Jews' total wealth was confiscated by the king that year. However, this does not seem to be the case, because further poll taxes totaling 18,000 marks (£14,400) were levied

---

[94] Tovey, pp. 82-3. *Rotuli Litterarum Clauserum*, Vol. I, p. 567. Translator's note: Quoted element taken from Hyamson: *History*, p. 53. This event is also discussed, and the original Latin sources reproduced, in Prynne's *The Second Part of a Short Demurrer*, pp. 27-28.

in the years 1232-34. This much larger sum would have been impossible to collect if a third of the Jews' funds had already been taken from them in 1230, as this left the Jews insufficient time to make up their losses through usury.[95]

Naturally, the king gradually withdrew his favor from the Jews. It is therefore not surprising that, alongside the church, common people once more started to assert themselves against Jewish power. Leadership came from both the strengthening cities and the increasingly powerful barons.

The fact that the cities were the first in this fight is only too understandable, because it was only in these places that the Jews were allowed to reside (with exceptions), which meant that the burgesses not only had to endure the Jewish presence, but had also come to fear it, as it imperiled their newly won rights and freedoms. At the beginning of the 13th century, many cities had bought their self-government from the king or nobility at great expense and corresponding sacrifices. The freedoms consisted mainly in the fact that they were no longer subject to the royal courts, but only to their own. However, the Jews were expressly excluded from this and, as the king's property, were subject only to his jurisdiction. As a result, they also did not have to pay any taxes to the cities, which was always a strong reason for the people's bitterness. In principle, the king had no power within the city's boundaries. However, in various cities, such as London and Oxford, it had also been decreed that the Jews could use the king's sheriffs to collect their demands. As would be expected, such actions were most feared and rejected by the city's burgesses because they perceived an encroachment on their rights. When the king commanded his sheriffs and officers to elect burgesses to explicitly protect the Jews from all injury in order to avert riots in various cities, the people's resentment intensified.[96]

The beginning of 1234 sees the first attempts by the cities' burgesses to expel the Hebrews, who were an unwanted foreign body in their midst. When the king did not sufficiently accommodate these wishes, riots broke out. The Jews' houses in Norwich were looted and burned down. Hyamson reports that the Bishop of Norwich turned to the king's advisors to request action against the Jews, informing them that 'the well-founded complaints of the Christians against the Jews were becoming unbearable, and that the ex-

---

[95] *Rymer's Fœdera*, Vol. I, pp. 503, 634; Madox, Vol. I, p. 224, 260. & Tovey, p. 88; *Chronica Majora*, Vol. III, p. 194. & Rigg: *Select Pleas*, p. XXVI; Hyamson: *History*, p. 54.

[96] *Chronica Jocelini*, p. 2; *De Antiquis Legibus*, p. 16; Tovey p. 50. & Abrahams: *The Expulsion...*, p. 18. & *Patent Rolls*, Vol. 1281-1292, p. 15. Tovey, p. 77-79. Translator's note: Abrahams (p.19) notes that different cities had different orders of protection – in London, mayor and barons were to answer with their own lives if ill befell the Jews; in Worcester, York, Lincoln, Stamford, Bristol, Northampton and Winchester, the king's sheriffs were directly charged with Jewish protection, while in Gloucester and Hereford the burgesses were held personally responsible.

tortion, oppression and usury of the perfidious people... had reduced the people to a condition of exhaustion.' However, his appeal went unheeded and so the outraged people secured their own rights by forcibly removing the Jews from their midst. Something similar happened in Oxford in 1243. With the king's growing antipathy towards the Jews, we see that he granted more and more cities the right to refuse the settlement of Jews or to expel those who were already present. In 1245 he even passed a general law that forbade all Jews—except those who already had a special residence permit from the king—to settle anywhere other than where their co-religionists were already located.[97]

Violent anti-Semitism also appeared early on in the ranks of the barons, the first beginnings of which can be found in the second half of the 12th century. Even if the participation of the English knights in the Crusades was not as great as that of the Continent, we still find numerous nobles among them, especially in the time of Richard the Lionheart. However, such long expeditions turned out to require many purchases, which involved large expenditures of money. In addition, the crusaders had to carry a considerable amount of money with them in order to cover their living costs. They had hardly any liquid money of their own. They were ready to make any sacrifice to serve the great ideal. They therefore pledged their belongings, especially their land, without considering the enormous usurious interest rates. The Jews took advantage of this economic situation ruthlessly, and the foundation for a large part of their wealth was likely laid through such transactions. Repaying the debts was almost always impossible because their lands did not produce enough income to pay the usurious interest. Thus the barons were at the mercy of the Jews, or the king if he expropriated the Jews' claims.[98]

The barons therefore realized that they could only defend themselves against exploitation by forming a common front against the king and the Jews, which is why it is not surprising that they inserted the aforementioned clauses into the Magna Carta. However, circumstances had increasingly gone against their interests, and so, in the 1244 Great Council [or 'Parliament', as it was coming to be known], they petitioned the king for the right to be allowed to appoint one of the judges in the Jewish Exchequer. In this way, through the representative they had chosen, they not only had an insight into Jewish financial transactions, but also a share in their regulation. They had also realized that they could only be successful in their fight against the king for greater privileges if they simultaneously defeated the Jews, because

---

[97] Tovey, p. 101. & Hyamson, *History*, p. 54. Translator's note: QVOS. & Abrahams: *The Expulsion...*, p. 19. & *Annales Monastici*, Vol. IV, p. 91. & Prynne, Vol. II, p. 75; Madox: *Exchequer*, Vol. I, pp. 248-9. Abrahams, p. 20.

[98] Hyamson: *History*, p. 11; Gross: *Exchequer*, p. 173; Abrahams: *Expulsion*, p. 23.

the king was able to repeatedly fall back on the Jews' wealth for his military conflicts with the barons.[99]

The situation at this point in time was, then, that the people, nobility and church were all in one camp, which meant that all that remained was either to win over the king on the Jewish Question or force him to adopt their desired policy. It is astonishing to find that again and again in history, in times of severe distress and impending danger, the Jews worsen their own situation through acts of infamy that are obvious to everyone around them, and which almost exclusively contribute to their own downfall. This would also prove to be the case in the England of this period.

In Norwich in the year 1230, a Jew called Jacob abducted a five-year-old Christian boy called Odard, and with the help of others, forcibly circumcised him and held him captive. However, after a few days, the child escaped Jewish captivity and found refuge with a local Christian woman and her daughter, while a neighbor recognized the boy as the son of Benedict, the physician of Norwich. When the Jews managed to find the boy's location, they arrived at the woman's house in large numbers and tried to take him by force. When the English, including the boy's father who had arrived at the scene, refused to hand him over, the Jews even turned to the relevant authorities—the Constable and then the Bailiffs of Norwich—and asked for assistance in having him returned to them. But the authorities apparently refused to intervene, beyond checking on the well-being of the boy. There is no further information known about this event regarding this year.

It was not until some time later that the crime was processed by the authorities. Of the thirteen Jews finally indicted in 1234-1235, only ten appeared in court. The preliminary investigations ended with the burden of proof being sufficient to begin criminal proceedings and take the perpetrators into custody, who were then sent to London to be tried by the king's court. The king himself apparently presided over the trial, but in the presence of the Archbishop of Canterbury, as well as numerous nobles and bishops, he declared himself incompetent because, in his opinion, the case belonged before the ecclesiastical court.

After this decision, it was clear to the Jews that, given the well-known attitude of the clergy towards them, a harsh punishment was to be expected from the ecclesiastical court. They therefore, with the help of other Hebrews, turned to the king, asking him to delay the hearing and to refer the matter before a court specially provided under their charter, which was also achieved through numerous bribes. The court that was now appointed took no action, and nothing more is known about the case for several years.

---

[99] *Chronica Majora*, Vol. IV, p. 367. & Hyamson: *History*, pp. 62-3.

Suddenly, for unknown reasons, the king took up the criminal case again, and, despite previous and new bribes—as Hyamson complains—ordered the local justices of Norwich to try the crime as they thought best. In 1241 we hear that some of the Jews were executed. The Norfolk antiquarian Walter Rye has endeavored to irrefutably demonstrate that the Jews were innocent of the accusation that the circumcision was a prelude to ritual murder (as has been the common assertion of traditional historians), which he believes he can infer from 23 contemporary documents in particular. His detailed study of these documents is found in a dedicated article, which features the documents themselves in an appendix. However, his thesis that explains the Jews' actions—namely, that the boy was a child of baptized Jews—is neither convincing nor proven. Furthermore, Rye was also unable to refute the other contemporary sources.[100]

From the excellent chronicles of the monk Matthew Paris, the report on an incident which took place in Germany and other countries in 1241 is also extremely informative.[101]

---

[100] Hyamson: *History* p. 58-59. & *Historica Minora*, Vol. II, p. 375, Vol. III, p. 271; *Chronica Majora*, Vol. III, p. 543, Vol. IV, p. 30. & Rye: *Norfolk Miscellany*, Vol. I. p. 340. Translator's note: I feel that Aldag has rather unfairly represented Rye here, given that Rye's thesis does seem plausible. He had proved that Benedict was a local Jewish name of the time, and that physician was a common Jewish profession. In addition, the boy, whom the Jewish abductors had renamed Jurnepin, was told not to eat pork when in the Christian house by the Jews trying to regain possession of 'their Jew', suggesting that they were concerned about his continued Jewish identity and cleanliness – doubtful of the actions of a group of people wishing to crucify a Christian boy. Further, if they were related to the boy, this would explain the otherwise jaw-dropping *chutzpah* of trying to take him back from his 'own people' and even his own father, to the point of appealing to the authorities to do so. This 1230 event is also echoed by a later event in Jewish history in England: Prynne [Vol. II, p. 40] reports that in the 21st year of Henry III's reign (c. 1237), some Jews in Oxford had been imprisoned for abducting a baptized Jewish child. Less compelling is Rye's speculation that the four- to five-year delay in the indictment might be explained by the Benedict's *converso* reluctance not to proceed against his own people, being eventually pushed into doing so by an enthusiastic clergy; the obvious reason was simply that the next eyre was not due to take place in Norwich until 1234, there being up to a seven-year interval between eyres [Summerson, p. 322], and the king's coroner(s) had obviously determined to proceed with the case due to it being one of serious bodily harm [Gross, p. 662]. Whether or not this was a medieval Jewish version of the Mortara case, Aldag is nevertheless correct in his assertion that such egregious behavior (regardless of motive) would not endear the Jews to the host population. See Translator's Appendix II for a further discussion of this case.

[101] *Chronica Majora*, Vol. IV, p. 131-3; Prynne, Vol. I, p. 18 [2nd edition, p. 22]; B. B.: pp. 7-8 [p. 12-13 in 1720 edition]. Translator's note: Paris's long description of this incident is clearly the primary source for the other sources cited, and the quotation reproduced verbatim from Prynne is a summary of a much longer speech in *Chronica Majora*, in which the Jews are supposedly quoted as planning to use what is now called 'the Mongol Invasion of Europe' to achieve rule over Christendom.

At this time, there was fierce fighting in Eastern Europe against the Tartars and Cumans, who had invaded Europe from the East. The Jews, particularly those in Germany, believed that these nomadic warrior tribes from the Eurasian Steppes were descendants of the lost tribes of Israel, and, in Prynne's words 'believing, that the *Tartars* were of their own Nation, entered into a secret League with them, to destroy the Christians, and subdue the whole world to themselves'. As a first way of assisting the invaders, the Jews decided to purchase and send weapons. However, this could under no circumstance be allowed to become known to the Christian world, which is why the following plan was devised.

The rumor was spread, which was all too readily believed, that the Jews had received an order for wine from the Tartars, because, as the Tartars were Jews, they would only drink wine harvested by Jews. The Jews had agreed to deliver thirty casks of this wine. But in order to do the Christian world a service, they would poison it so that a large number of the Tartars would die as a result.

The Christian princes agreed, seeing nothing amiss with the Jews' stated plan. In fact, however, the Jews had secretly packed a large quantity of swords and knives into the hogsheads and it was only through the diligence of the German Customs officials that the crime was discovered and fittingly punished.

Given the circumstances described above, it is not surprising that the situation of the Jews in England became increasingly difficult due to their own actions. One poll tax replaced another. In 1236 they had to cede to the king around £13,000, and in 1239 a third of their assets, or, if they refused, they had to leave the country. They chose the first option. Despite being almost bled dry, they were able to raise taxes of around £15,000 and £44,000 in 1241 and 1244-1245 respectively. And even after these huge payments, they were still able to pay around £7,500 and £4,000 in 1246 and 1247 respectively, around £7,300 in 1249, and in 1250 part of their wealth was confiscated again, although the amount is not certain. For the period spanning 1251-1269, the Jews had to pay another £20,000. These sums can be determined from contemporary records with considerable certainty. The raising of these amounts, which to compare with today's purchasing power must be multiplied by at least 30, is hard to believe. But it was only possible because the Jews were charging interest of up to 86⅔ percent. In this way they were always able to make up for the ravages of royal taxation.[102]

---

[102] *Chronica Majora*, Vol. III, pp. 220, 292-6; Vol. IV, pp. 88, 260; Vol. V, pp. 115, 441, 487-8; *Rymer's Fœdera*, Vol. I, pp. 274, 293, 315; Prynne, Vol. II, p. 30 ff.; *De Antiques Legibus*, p. 19 ff.; Madox: *Exchequer*, Vol. I, pp. 224-61; Hyamson: *History*, p. 57; Margoliouth, Vol. I, p. 152 ff.; Rye, p. 155 ff. & Rye, p. 341. [Original source: *Palgrave's Rise and Progress of the English Commonwealth*, Vol. II, p. 9 ff.] Translator's note: Cf. footnote 29.

In the meantime, the king had created a supplementary institution to the Jewish Exchequer, which was briefly called the *Parliamentum Judaicum* or 'Jewish Parliament' [also known as the 'Worcester Parliament'].

An audit of the financial documents deposited in the various branches made the king decide to enact further measures to ensure that all Jewish assets were registered for tax purposes. To this end, in 1240 he appointed various officials who had to make a list of the Jews' assets in the individual cities. This must have been carried out relatively quickly, because the very next year the sheriffs of each county received a writ from the king, ordering them to send to Worcester six of the richest Jews from their county town, for negotiations regarding taxation. From towns with a very small Jewish population, only two representatives had to be chosen.[103]

The Jews, having endured long periods of heavy tallages from the king, therefore hoped that only good things would come from this gathering of their representatives. The content of the various writs to the sheriffs also gave reason to expect this, as the purpose of the meeting was stated: 'Negotiations with the king for his benefit and that of the Jews.' As soon as the 'parliament' met, however, it became clear that it was just a new method of collecting the Jews' taxes securely. The 'members' were obliged, as the king's representatives, to collect set sums from their ethnic kinsmen. They were solely responsible for their mission's success. In the event of failure, they were to expect the entirety of their wealth to be expropriated. Because their attendance was documented, it appears that the vast majority if not all of their names have been preserved; they were just over a hundred men.[104]

The 'members' of this 'parliament' also had to demonstrate their ability immediately, or face the consequences. In the first convocation of the 'parliament', they were given the task of collecting around £16,000 for the king. However, they did not raise this amount by the appointed time. The king therefore had the members' assets confiscated, while the members themselves, along with their families, were thrown into prison.

With a new ritual infanticide in London in 1244, the Jews did something else to turn the king, people, barons, and church against them. The marks found on the body left the judges in no doubt that it had been a Jewish ritual murder. The child was buried as a martyr near the high altar of [Old] St. Paul's Cathedral. A fine of 60,000 marks, or around £48,000, was imposed on the Jews.[105]

---

[103] *Close Rolls*, Vol. 1237-1242, p. 202 ff. & *Close Rolls*, Vol. 1237-1242, p. 346; Prynne, Vol. II, pp. 43-4. Translator's note: See also Tovey, p. 110.

[104] *Close Rolls*, Vol. 1237-1242, pp. 354-5.

[105] *Chronica Majora*, Vol. IV, p. 377. Translator's note: The marks on the child's body were perceived to be in the shape of Hebrew letters. For the full report on this incident, see Translator's Appendix II.

A short time later a new poll tax was demanded of the Jews. This time it was also threatened that if payment were not made, the Jews' families would be shipped to Ireland. In response, the Hebrews set about ensconcing their families in secluded corners of England. To counteract this, the king gave orders to the competent authorities that every Jewish family had to register in the area in which they lived, otherwise they would be declared outlaws and their assets would be confiscated.[106]

It may also interest the reader to know that in 1245 the Jews were asked to provide most of the money required for the renovation of Westminster Abbey.[107]

Scandals

An informative story about the behavior and morals of the Jews of that period has come down to us from the year 1250.[108] A rich Jew named Abraham of Berkhamsted was the declared favorite of the king's brother Richard, the Earl of Cornwall, and he had a wife called Flora who was very pretty and obedient. Abraham had a statue made of the Virgin Mary holding the baby Jesus. He took this statue into his privy and defecated on it day and night to symbolize his boundless contempt for Christianity. He also forced his wife to do the same. In the end, Flora not only refused to follow her husband's request, but is said to have cleaned the statue.

When Abraham noticed this, he strangled his wife. But the crime was discovered, and Abraham was arrested and promptly thrown into the Tower of London. However, he turned to his patron, Earl Richard, whom he paid 700 marks (around £500), to help him get released. Before this happened, however, his Jewish brethren accused Abraham of several crimes, particularly of 'Clipping the King's Coin', for which they said he deserved death. At the same time, they offered Earl Richard 1000 marks (around £800) if he would withdraw his support for Abraham. They justified their request by saying that they could no longer tolerate such a criminal in their ranks. In fact, they only wanted to have Abraham executed so that it would be impossible for him to turn king's evidence, and reveal their own numerous crimes in a bid to free himself. Apparently the Jews were unsuccessful in their ef-

---

[106] *Close Rolls*, Vol. 1242-1247, pp. 275, 339.

[107] *Chronica Majora*, Vol. IV, p. 427; *Patent Rolls*, Vol. 1232-1247, pp. 474, 478; Madox: *Exchequer*, Vol. II, p. 3; Margoliouth: *History*, Vol. I, pp. 175-6.

[108] *Chronica Majora*, Vol. V, p. 114 ff.; Tovey, p. 128; Prynne, Vol. I, p. 20 ff [2nd edition, p. 24 ff]. Translator's note: Quoted element reproduced from the Tovey account. For those wish to research the case, alternative versions of Abraham's toponymic are also rendered Berkhampstead/Berkhampsted/Berkhamstede/Berkame-stede/Berkamstude (etc). It is also likely that his wife's name, although rendered Flora in the traditional accounts, was actually Floria, in keeping with the fashion for Jewish women's names at that time.

forts, because Earl Richard continued to campaign for the murderer Abraham. The latter then fought back against his Jewish enemies and offered to bring the king proof that the Jews in England were the most notorious criminals and traitors. He apparently succeeded in this, for not only was he released, but immediately afterwards a detailed criminal investigation was carried out throughout the kingdom, which established the truth of his allegations and led to severe punishments.

But the very next year the Jews caused new scandals. Despite the recent harsh sentences, they had bribed Jewish Exchequer judges Philip Luvel [Lovell] and Nicholas of St. Albans to act against the interests of the Crown. Here too, everyone involved was severely punished.[109]

In 1252 a new incident occurred. The Jews accused a diligent official, who was in charge of handling Jewish affairs, of abusing his office towards them. Their accusation was so cleverly drafted that it was only after much effort that this official's friends were able to prove his innocence. Here too, the Jews' intentionally false report found its just atonement. It would appear that the Jews did not make the slightest effort to try to reduce popular anger, which was increasing daily, by behaving well. Just a year later, news of a nefarious plan spread throughout England: Jews in Northampton had been plotting to set fire to both that city and London. Fortunately, the conspiracy was discovered in time. William Hughes outlines the plot and reveals the harsh but just punishment that the plotters received:[110]

> And that which shewed their faithfulness sufficiently, and procured them hatred not in the least degree, was, that in the year 1253 at *Northampton* they combined together, and that for the destruction of that City, which first harbored them; preparing to set even the City of *London* on fire. This could not but enrage much; yet having entered such courses as rendered them more than odious, they are resolved to go on, though to their own destruction. But what they intended to do the City they suffer themselves, for many of them being taken in the same Town where they hatch their design, are themselves reduced to ashes, in the time of Lent.[111]

---

[109] *Chronica Majora*, Vol. V, p. 261; Tovey, p. 132; Prynne, Vol. I, p. 22 [2nd edition, p. 26].

[110] *Chronica Majora*, Vol. V, p. 345.

[111] 'W. H.': *Anglo-Judæus*, pp. 16-17. Translator's note: QVOS. The author 'B. B.' (*A Historical and Law Treatise*, p. 6) also puts the year of this plot as 1253, and states that 'around 40 Jews were Burnt'. This event is also reported in John Foxe's *Acts and Monuments*, which is the source cited by William Prynne (Vol. I, p. 24 [2nd ed. p. 28]). As we find in Foxe (1875 Cumming edition, Vol. I, p. 475): 'Of the Jews in Northampton, who had among themselves prepared wild-fire, to burn the city of London, for the which divers

Nuremberg Laws... in 1253

Apparently, after such events, King Henry III was no longer able to ignore the pressure coming from anti-Jewish circles, and issued drastic regulations. It is very interesting to note that this royal ordinance of 1253 has partly the same content as the Nuremberg Laws of 1935. As a result, it is reproduced verbatim below:

> MANDATE OF THE KING TO THE JUSTICES AS-SIGNED TO THE CUSTODY OF THE JEWS TOUCHING CERTAIN STATUTES RELATING TO THE JEWS IN ENGLAND WHICH ARE TO BE RIGOROUSLY OB-SERVED. THE THIRTY-SEVENTH YEAR OF KING HENRY. A.D. 1253.
>
> The King has provided and ordained etc.: That no Jew remain in England unless he do the King service, and that from the hour of birth every Jew, whether male or female, serve Us in some way. And that there be no synagogues of the Jews in England save in those places in which such synagogues were in the time of King John, the King's father. And that in their synagogues the Jews, one and all, subdue their voices in performing their ritual offices, that Christians may not hear them. And that all Jews answer to the rector of the church of the parish in which they dwell touching all dues parochial relating to their houses. And that no Christian nurse in future suckle or nourish the child of any Jew, nor any Christian man or woman serve any Jew or Jewess, or eat with them or tarry in their houses. And that no Jew or Jewess eat or buy meat in Lent. And that no Jew disparage the Christian Faith, or publicly dispute concerning the same. And that no Jew have secret familiar intercourse with any Christian woman, and no Christian man with a Jewess. And that every Jew wear his badge conspicuously on his breast. And that no Jew enter any church or chapel save for purpose of transit, or linger in them in dishonour of Christ. And that no Jew place any hindrance in the way of another Jew desirous of turning to the Christian Faith. And that no Jew be received in any town but by special license to the King, save only in those towns in which Jews have been wont to dwell.

---

of them were taken, and burned in the time of Lent, in the said city of Northampton, which was two years before, about the year of our Lord 1253.'

> And that the Justices assigned to the custody of the Jews are commanded that they cause these provisions to be carried into effect, and rigorously observed on pain of forfeiture of the chattels of the said Jews. Witness the King at Westminster, on the 31st day of January. By King and Council.[112]

As far as we can see, according to the evidence currently available, it is not known why the king issued this ordinance. However, it is very likely that it was for the same reasons that led us to publish the Nuremberg Laws.

Persecution of Jews

The people had only received partial protection against the Jews through the 1253 decree, because usury still weighed on them. As a result, major riots broke out again. Jewish historians pity their ethnic kinsmen and condemn the English. But it appears that these historians did not bother to investigate the underlying cause of the violence, otherwise they would certainly have come to the conclusion that the blame lay solely at the feet of the Jews.[113]

In 1254, the Jews sent a delegation led by their archpresbyter Elias to Earl Richard, whom the king had entrusted with the task of collecting a new tallage. They declared themselves unable to stay in England any longer and asked to be allowed to leave the country. They had placed all of their hopes in Earl Richard, as he had already shown them goodwill on several occasions. But even he rejected their petition, especially since France was now closed to Jews, from where they had been expelled in 1253 with a few exceptions.[114]

Just a year later they repeated their petition, but once again without success. Since the king was suffering from a great lack of money, in 1255 he leased the Jews to his brother, Earl Richard, for around £4,000 for 'some years', and in return Earl Richard agreed to collect about £13,000 from the Jews in order to settle their debt to the king. Despite everything, under Richard they had full protection and significantly recovered financially.[115]

---

[112] *Rymer's Fœdera*, Vol. I, p. 293; *Close Rolls*, Vol. 1234-1237, pp. 13-4. Translator's note: This English translation of the full royal mandate has been taken from Rigg: *Select Pleas...*, p. xlix, although 'male child' of the original translation has been substituted for 'child', given that Latin is a gendered language, and the masculine noun was likely used simply as the unmarked form. Careful readers will also note that most of the points listed above are the same as those promulgated by the 1222 Synod of Oxford, which itself took its inspiration from the Fourth Lateran Council of 1215. Thus, one could reasonably call this 1253 mandate a secular iteration of the 1222 religious decree.

[113] Hyamson: *History*, p. 64; Margoliouth, Vol. I, p. 181 ff.

[114] *Chronica Majora*, Vol. V, p. 441.

[115] *Chronica Majora*, Vol. V, pp. 487-8; Tovey, p. 135. Translator's note: Quoted element reproduced from Tovey, who had evidently translated Paris's *aliquot annos* (i.e. it is unclear how long the term of the lease was).

But in 1255, the Jews themselves were once again to initiate new punishments and disturb their own peace. They stole an eight-year-old boy, Hugh, from Lincoln, locked him in a room and fed him childish treats. Then they sent to all Jewish communities and requested their presence at the intended crucifixion of the boy. Jews flocked from all over England. The crucifixion then took place, and likewise with all the individual phases of Jesus Christ's suffering. The mother had desperately searched for the whereabouts of her child and learned that the boy had last been seen playing with Jewish children. During the course of house searches, the body was found buried under the floor of a Jewish house. A Jew then revealed the entire crime to the investigating judge and received exemption from punishment insofar as he had been involved.

The king was passing through Lincoln and took the case himself. Even though the Hebrews were directly subordinate to his brother after they had been leased, the power to punish was still in Henry's hands. Embittered by this new outrage, he immediately had the eighty to ninety Jews suspected of being involved in the murder arrested, the majority of whom were executed. Only some of them were later released. Since representatives from almost all of England's Jewish communities were present, persecutions broke out everywhere and, despite the protection of Earl Richard, the year 1255 was one of the hardest for Jews in medieval England.[116] The sufferings of the boy Hugh have provided the material for a number of folk songs and ballads in England, Scotland, and even Normandy in France.

As a result, times would get even worse for the Jews. The lower nobility were still indebted to Jewish usurers and it was only a matter of time before they would take the law into their own hands. A memorandum to the king around the year 1259 testifies to their growing restlessness, in which they complained that, as a result of usury, it was almost impossible to fulfil their current obligations. In addition, there was the still greater evil of the kingdom's grandees buying out the Jews' claims and driving the indebted landowners from their homes and farms in order to expropriate the land.[117]

Apparently this petition was unsuccessful. In any case, it was soon overtaken by domestic political events. Tensions between the king and the

---

[116] *Annales Monastici*, Vol. I, p. 340; Holinshed, Vol. III, p. 253; Foxe, Vol. I, p. 423, col II; *Royal and Historical Letters*, Vol. II, p. 110; *Chronica Majora*, Vol. V, p. 516 ff.; *De Antiquis Legibus*, p. 23. Translator's note: See Translator's Appendix II for more information on this incident, as there are many variations between historical versions that should be taken into account. For example, the vast majority of sources agree that the body was found in a well, although opinion varies as to whether this was the well at the house of accused Jew Copin, or a common well. And of the 91 Jews reportedly arrested after Copin's confession, the common consensus is that only 18 were eventually executed. & *Chronica Majora*, Vol. V, p. 553. & *Chronica Majora*, Vol. V. p. 537.

[117] Stubbs: *Select Charters*, p. 377; *Annales Monastici*, Vol. I, p. 442.

barons in 1262 led to the start of what later became known as the Second Barons' War. The king initially had to limit himself to defense and therefore had to give up parts of the country. The hatred against the Jews that had been simmering for decades suddenly boiled over. Wherever the barons had gained overall control, they took bitter revenge for the predations they had endured for years at the hands of the Hebrews, who were plundered and massacred by the hundred in London during the years 1262-64.

Regarding the events of 1264, the chronicler of the *Annales Monastici* states that the barons were particularly angry because the Jews had intended to set the city on fire. In terms of the dates, we could not determine with certainty whether this was a reference of the aforementioned attempt of 1253 or a separate incident. However, we find the same story from another historian regarding the year 1264, so it may safely be assumed that there were two separate attempts. The persecutions were repeated in other cities, such as Canterbury, Northampton, Cambridge, Worcester, Lincoln, and Winchester. Slaughtered Jews were found everywhere, and all of their property was confiscated by the barons. In Cambridge, the barons managed to seize the *archa* containing the debt records, which they then destroyed. The same thing was done in Lincoln. They publicly announced in the parts of the country they initially occupied that all debts to the Jews were to be regarded as settled. Such 'extreme' behavior can only be properly understood if one recognizes how the barons were gradually driven to these measures by usury.[118]

In the end, the power of the barons was broken and peace returned to the country, and similarly the Jews were left unmolested for a while. But the picture is always the same in history: during the good times, the Jew forgets his role as a guest and thus provokes new retaliatory measures against himself through his behavior. This was to prove just as true in England as elsewhere.

On the occasion of Ascension Day in 1268, a solemn procession took place in Oxford. The importance of the procession was marked by the presence of Crown Prince Edward and other high dignitaries. When the procession was reaching the spot where the sermon was due to take place, a Jew broke through the crowd of spectators, stopped the march of believers and tore

---

[118] *Annales Monastici*, Vol. II. p. 100. & *Florentii Wigorniensis Chronicon*, Vol. II, p. 192; *Chronicle of William of Rishanger,* pp. 24, 25, 126; *Annales Monastici*, Vol. III, p. 230; *Anglo-Judæus*, p. 20. Translator's note: Hyamson's *History* (p. 75) and 'B. B.' (p.6) state that 700 Jews were slain, with the latter alleging that this slaughter was the revenge for a Jewish plot to poison all of the barons in 1259, which was discovered when the poisonous liquor was found at the house of Jew named Elias, who apparently confessed his guilt before his execution. In Prynne's account (Vol 1, pp. 31-2; 2nd edition, pp. 34-35), the poison proved mortal to some of the noblemen, but Elias, surnamed Bishop, saved himself from punishment by converting, along with two others, to Christianity on Christmas Day. & *Annales Monastici*, Vol. II, pp. 101, 363, 371; Vol. IV, p. 142, 143, 448 ff.; *Liber de Antiquis Legibus*, p. 62; Holinshed, Vol. III, p. 267; *Chronicle of Pierre de Langtoft*, Vol. II, p. 150; Rigg: *Select Pleas*, p. XXXVII.

the crucifix that was being carried in the procession out of the bearer's hands. Before the astonished crowd could wrest it from him, he had trampled it under-foot. The heir apparent, who had witnessed this incident himself, reported it to the king. This event must have made a deep impression on the prince and like-ly guided his entire future policy towards the Jews. The people's anger was indescribable: they had expected a deterrent punishment, but were very disap-pointed by the extremely moderate retribution. All the Jews had to do was erect a valuable cross at the site of the incident and provide the university with another portable silver cross. The same or similar influences as those of the murderer Abraham were probably at work to prevent a just atonement.[119]

Harsh Laws

The common people, led by the barons and the church, could do nothing against the Jews at that point in time, but when they joined forces with Crown Prince Edward, his mother and the then Chancellor, Walter de Mer-ton, the anti-Jewish will of the people 'gathered irresistible force, and result-ed in most drastic measures'. Perhaps these measures would not have been taken if a common anti-Jewish front of people, nobility and church had not come together, the formation of which had been accelerated by the arrogant behavior of the Hebrews. Despite the fact that in individual cases they al-ready held land in pledge which had recently been taken away from them, they believed, in apparent complete obliviousness to how their situation in England had deteriorated, that the time had come to demand the privileges associated with land ownership for themselves. These privileges included the right of a landowner to exercise guardianship of the minors on his property, to grant permission for marriage, and to be the patron of a church. While the former two prerogatives were already confirmed by feudal law, the church recognized the latter as inseparable from land ownership.

When the Jews claimed these privileges, a storm of indignation arose among the people. The nobility and the church feared that the proposed measure would encroach on their monopoly position, and the population

---

[119] Rigg: *Select Pleas*, p. xxxvii; Leonard, p. 127. & Tovey, p. 168 ff.; Lyte, p. 67; Leon-ard, p. 127; Hyamson: *History*, p. 72; Rye, p. 165. Translator's note: For more on this incident, as well as additional reports, including from Jewish sources, of cross destruction and desecration, particularly by expectoration or urination, see Chapter 6 ('The Fascina-tion of the Abomination') of Elliott Horowitz's excellent *Reckless Rites* [in Translator's Bibliography]. Note that Lyte's version of events has a 'number of Jews' making an attack on the cross-bearer. William Prynne also reports on this story, and reproduces his Latin sources in his *Second Part of a Short Demurrer* (pp. 108-111). I should also state that, while my survey of the sources was not exhaustive, I found no reference to the popular mood regarding the punishment.

resentfully rejected Jewish patronage. Instead of being satisfied with their lot after the previous difficult years, the Jews believed that now, more than ever, they were entitled to special benefits. They made their demands formally to the Great Council, which would have to approve the legislation, and some of its members, who were probably connected to the Jews, did not seem averse to their demands. A Franciscan monk who somehow had access to the Council meeting in question spoke out vehemently against the proposal. He was followed by the Archbishop of York and the Bishops of Lichfield, Coventry and Worcester, who made it clear to the Jews that it was entirely by the king's grace that they were tolerated in England. It was impertinent to demand equality with English subjects and perhaps they would even claim nobility later. The anti-Jewish faction received decisive support from Crown Prince Edward. Not only were the Jews' demands rejected, but at the end of the session the following drastic law, *Provisiones de Judaismo liberatae ad Scaccarum* (1269), was drafted by the aforementioned Walter de Merton, in an attempt to force the Hebrews back into their proper place:[120]

> At the feast of St. Hilary in the fifty-third year of the reign of King Henry, son of King John, it is provided by the King himself, with the advice of the Lord Edward, his eldest son, and his other trusty lieges, for the better ordering of the land and the relief of the Christians from the burdens laid upon them by the Jewry of England: that all debts to Jews which are fees [i.e. debts that are based on or tied to fiefs (land estates)], and which are at present in the hands of the Jews and are not assigned or sold to Christians, provided that before this day they have been confirmed by the King or enrolled at the Exchequer, be quit to the Christians by whom they are owing, and to their heirs forever, with their arrears; and that the charters of the fee-debts aforesaid, wherever they shall be found, be returned to the Christians by whom the debts are owing, or to their heirs. And if perchance any such charter be hereafter placed or found in the Chest, let it be held of none. And let no Jew from this day forth take or make any such fee-debt.
>
> And in like manner it is provided that no Jew from this day forth sell any such fee to a Christian on pain of forfeiture of life and chattels, and that no Christian purchase it, on pain of forfeiture of his chattels and his inheritance.

---

[120] Rigg: *Select Pleas*, p. xxxvii. Translator's note: QVOS. & *Gesta Abbatum Monasterii S. Albani*, Vol. I, p. 401; *Liber de Antiquis Legibus*, p. 234 ff. & *Annales Monastici*, Vol. IV, p. 221.

And in the like manner it is provided by the aforementioned King, by the advice of the Lord Edward and the aforenamed trusty lieges, that no Jew hereafter may sell his debt, unless he have first obtained license of the King. And if a Christian purchase it by license of the King, let him have no more thereof than the King would have it the debt were in his hand; that is to say, the chattel that is found in the charter, without interest.[121]

The ageing king increasingly fell under the influence of his son Edward, who had a great dislike for the Jews, and it is therefore not surprising that just two years later, in 1271, the 55th year of Henry III's reign, a comprehensive law against the Jews was passed. At the beginning we find a preamble, so to speak, in which the populace's plight being caused by the Jews is given as the justification for the publication of the regulations:[122]

Know that for the honor of God and the Catholic Church, the better ordering and increased prosperity of our land, and the relief of the Christians from the losses and burdens, which they have sustained by reason of the freeholds which the Jews of our realm claimed to have in lands, tenements, fees, rents and other tenures; and lest mischief should grow therefrom in future to Us, or the people our realm, or the realm itself...

Firstly, it was ordained that from that point onwards 'no Jew do have a freehold in manors, lands, tenements, fees, rents or tenures of any kind whatsoever by charter, grant, feoffment, confirmation, or any other kind of obligation, or in any other manner'. However, the Jews were allowed to continue to dwell in the houses in which they presently lived, and if they had houses to let, 'they may lawfully let them to Jews alone, and not to Christians'. Under no circumstances was it permitted for Jews to purchase new houses in

---

[121] *Red Book of the Exchequer*, Vol. III, p. 978. Translator's note: This law has been reproduced in full for reader interest, with the English translation taken verbatim from Rigg: *Select Pleas...*, pp. xlix-li, as Aldag's original source is in Norman French only. This law, by returning the land to its rightful owners or stewards, may usefully be considered a permanent version of the biblical debt jubilee. Note also the final two paragraphs, evidently intended to prevent powerful Christians and Christian institutions (e.g. grandees and monasteries), from being able to use Jews as middlemen to get hold of coveted land, or to extort their Christian neighbors without the risk of obvious accusations of usury.

[122] *Rymer's Fœdera*, Vol. I, p. 489; *Liber de Antiquis Legibus*, Appendix, p. 234. Translator's note: For the full 1271 mandate, both in the original Latin and in English translation, see Rigg: *Select Pleas...* pp. l-liv. All quotations and quoted elements taken from this latter source.

the future. In addition, the law once again made clear, in great detail, that they could neither buy free property nor have it mortgaged.

In the penultimate paragraph, there also was a reiteration, with additional detail, of one of Henry III's earlier prohibitions, which featured in his ordinance of 1253:

> Touching persons in the employ of Jews as nurses of children,
> bakers, brewers, and cooks, since Jews and Christians differ in
> faith, We have provided and decreed, that no Christian man or
> woman presume to serve them in the said offices.

Immediately afterwards, the Jews were tallaged around £4,500 to enable Crown Prince Edward to go on Crusade. However, they only raised two thirds of the requested sum, the rest being paid by the Earl of Cornwall. As security for his loan, he received the free use of all Jews for a year. He died in 1272 before his claim expired. The Jews thus reverted back to being property of the king, who imposed on them a new tallage of around £3,600. A short time later, he too entered into his eternal rest.[123]

Edward I in the Fight Against Usury

After Henry III's death in 1272, his son Edward I ascended the throne *in absentia*, being on Crusade and not returning to England for his coronation until 1274. It would appear that nothing of importance happened during his absence, as far as the Jews were concerned. However, before we go into the years that followed, it would be instructive to dwell for a moment on Edward's character and his attitude towards the Hebrews.[124]

Edward I was the ideal king. He demanded nothing for himself, but subordinated his own wishes entirely to those of the nation. He was full of great plans, and was particularly keen to improve the impoverished lives of his people. His vision for the country was firmly fixed on the future. In order to achieve great goals for his country, he was ready to give up short-term advantages. He was also a pious man and tried to be a faithful son of the church. He enjoyed the goodwill of the common people and the lower nobility, groups who were particularly indebted to the Jews. The English people hoped that he would take measures against the Jews.[125] They did not

---

[123] *Gesta Abbatum Monasterii*, Vol. I, p. 400 ff.; *Rymer's Fœdera*, Vol. I, p. 409.

[124] Margoliouth: *History*, Vol. I, p. 239. Translator's note: Margoliouth reports that the country remained in the hands of the Archbishop of York, and the Earls of Cornwall and Chester during this interim period, and that life appears to have gone on peacefully and without remarkable incident.

[125] Abrahams, p. 28.

have to wait too long for this, because immediately after his return, Edward decided to tackle the problems that concerned him.

First of all, he needed a sound financial base from which to act. He did not want to create this by unilaterally using parts of the national wealth—as his ancestors had—but rather by harnessing the entire strength of the nation. He sought to achieve this through a strict feudal system. For this, however, it was necessary that as much land as possible in England was held in fiefdom [in fee] by the retainer for the overlord. At that time, however, there were considerable areas of land owned by monasteries or other spiritual corporations that were considered non-transferable and therefore unavailable to the feudal system. Edward hoped to fundamentally change this situation in the future in favor of the Crown, which he did with a law in 1279 [the Statute of Mortmain].

But the Jews still stood in the way of him achieving his goal: as soon as land was pledged to them, they took all the proceeds from it, and the king only received a fraction of what he would otherwise have been entitled to under the feudal system. In addition, it often happened that they gave up their rights to use the land pledged to them by monasteries in return for a certain sum. This land was no longer covered by the feudal system, but even if it did fall under it in principle, it was impossible for those entitled to it, even with the best of intentions, to fulfil their obligations as retainers when they were also burdened with paying usurious interest. Since in such cases they could always count on their master to be more understanding of their economic situation than on the Jews, the former often came up short in his demands. This was found to be the standard situation for the time, with property mortgaged to an unprecedented extent.[126]

The king, apart from his own interests in the feudal system, was deeply troubled by the people's indebtedness. The church was also still completely in debt. The situation had already reached an untenable level by the 12th century (as has been shown in previous chapters), and things had only gotten worse since then. The well-known chronicler Matthew Paris once observed that there was scarcely a person in all of England, especially the figure of the bishop, who was not entangled in the usurer's net. When the latterly famous John of Peckham travelled to Canterbury, he found that the cathedral had fallen into dilapidation because there was no money for repairs. All available funds were used to pay the loan interest. Glastonbury Abbey had such enormous debts that when the budget was reorganized, the exact number of meals the abbot would be served in his private rooms had to be calculated.

---

[126] *Rotuli Curiae Regis*, Vol. II, p. 62. & *Chronica Monasterii De Melsa*, Vol. I, pp. 173, 174, 306, 367; Vol. II. p. 116. & *Patent Rolls*, Vol, 1281-1292, p. 25; Madox: *Exchequer*. Vol. I, p. 227.

Urgent savings to pay off usurious debts made this necessary. The Bishop of Norwich no longer had the money for basic maintenance.

He therefore had to borrow £480 from the Archbishop of Canterbury. Newton's church was unable to retain a clergyman due to lack of funds. The Prior of Lewes asked permission to rent out the church for secular use in order to pay his pressing debts. In some cases, the indebted monks helped themselves by ruthlessly cutting down the forests belonging to the monasteries and turning the timber into money. The priory of St. Swithun in Winchester, which was otherwise rich in natural products and income, was also constantly in huge debt. The Bishop of Hereford even had to seek an intervention from King Henry III in order to obtain a moratorium from the Jews.[127] Similar conditions had also taken hold among the barons, which was why one of the most important points of Edward's program was to free his people from the shackles of usury.

In addition, the king was no longer dependent on financial assistance from the Jews. His father's heavy taxation of the English Jewry had greatly diminished their wealth and as a consequence, the royal income from this group had declined considerably.

The king's income had increased from around £35,000 to around £65,000 in later decades, but this was not due to the Jews, but rather to other sources of income. The value of the Jewish tallages had not only decreased relative to the king's income, but were also lower in absolute terms.[128]

Furthermore, the importance of Jews in the money market had also declined sharply. In 1235, Italian merchants and bankers called Caursini [also known as Cahorsins] came to England from Florence, Milan, Rome, and other Italian cities. They enjoyed the special protection of the Pope, who even concluded treaties with kings that obliged them to make use of these bankers. The Caursini were undoubtedly as astute in banking as the Jews. In the course of his diatribe against the Caursini, the chronicler Matthew Paris tells us of the perfect 'Christian' loan agreements that these Italian bankers set up when they disbursed funds.[129]

As Christians, they were not permitted by canon law to charge interest. On the other hand, of course, they wanted to make a profit from lending

---

[127] *Chronica Majora,* Vol. III, p. 328; Vol. V, p. 189. Translator's note: It should be noted that Matthew Paris's observation, which comes from Vol. III and corresponds to the year 1235, was in reference to the Caursini. & *Letters of John of Peckham,* Vol. I, p. 203. & *Letters of John of Peckham,* Vol. I, p. 261. & *Letters of John of Peckham,* Vol. I, pp. 177, 187. & *Letters of John of Peckham,* Vol. I, p. 194. & *Letters of John of Peckham,* Vol. I, p. 380. & *Letters of John of Peckham,* Vol. I, p. 244. & *Obedientiary Rolls of St. Swithins,* pp. 10, 18. & *Excerpta e Rotulis Finium,* Vol. II, p. 68.

[128] *Jewish Encyclopedia,* Vol. V, p. 165.

[129] Abrahams: *Expulsion,* pp. 35-6. & *Historia Minora,* Vol. III, p. 272; *Chronica Majora,* Vol. III, p. 328.

money. So they covered themselves by explicitly declaring that they would lend the money without interest. Now, if someone wanted a loan of £100 for six months, they agreed in a contract that the borrowed money would need to be returned within a period of three months. However, if the amount was not repaid within this timeframe, the lender would have to be paid some kind of compensation for not receiving the money back on time. This supposed 'compensation for damages' sometimes amounted to up to 50% and practically represented interest. These bankers from Italy soon became significant commercial rivals to the Jews, although the latter, enjoying the king's significant protection, capitalized on certain existing advantages such as the enforcement measures of the Jewish Exchequer. The Caursini likewise soon garnered the hatred of the population. King Henry III had already considered expelling them from the kingdom, but he feared the power of the Pope, their protector and sponsor, and therefore refrained from doing so. This is yet another example of the Catholic Church's policy of not only tolerating the circumvention of its laws, but even sometimes encouraging it.[130]

The Jewish historians are of the opinion that Edward relied solely on the financial help of the Caursini, which meant that he no longer needed the Jews, who now became his beleaguered victims.[131]

But they overlook and forget to mention that the Caursini also became 'victims of the king' the moment they charged usurious interest. Edward's measures were aimed indiscriminately against the usury from which his people had suffered so greatly. As a devout Christian, he could not countenance lightly setting aside the religious behests conferred on him, nor by any means bypassing them, as was done daily by the head of the Catholic Church itself, the Pope, even if this was to the detriment of the very Christendom he shepherded.

Edward's zeal was particularly seen when the 1274 Second Council of Lyons called out the ever-greater problem of usury. It may well be that the Pope at the time, Gregory X, was more sincere than his predecessor and truly wanted to fight usury when, as a result of the Council, he issued an edict banning all Christians from permitting usurers as tenants or residents on their land, with those already in that situation to be expelled within three months. Whatever the case was regarding the Pope, Edward was certainly determined with all his heart to put an end to usury in his kingdom. It is therefore unsurprising that by 1275, in obedience to the Pope's decree, Edward had ordered an inquiry to be made into the usury of the Italian bankers in his realm, with a view to its suppression.[132]

---

[130] Hyamson: *History*, p. 73, 74.

[131] See, among others, Hyamson: *History*, p. 73, 77; Abrahams, p. 36; Margoliouth: History, p. Vol. I, p. 241 ff.

[132] Abrahams: *Expulsion*, p. 34. Translator's note: As Abrahams explains, although Popes and Councils had declared usury accursed, churches and monasteries still had usurers as

It also appears that court hearings against the Caursini must have taken place in June 1275, January 1276 and July 1281, because according to available reports, a pardon was granted to them on condition that they no longer engaged in usurious practices. It can be seen from the fact that, when it came to people who took usurious interest from his subjects, Edward punished the miscreants equally, regardless of race or religion. This fact undermines the commonly believed assertion that only the poor Jews were made to suffer at the hands of this 'barbaric Edward' and that all of his actions were dictated by a blind hatred towards them as a people.[133]

However, it is correct to state that he flatly rejected association with Jews. He was influenced in this by his mother and in no small measure by the despicable incident in Oxford in 1268, which likely marked him for life. Despite everything, as his subsequent actions clearly show, he tried to use special legislation to encourage the Jews to live a life that was tolerable for the people and the realm. We shall see to what extent he was successful in this aim.

The relevant law was called the *Statute de la Jeuerie* or the *Statute de Judaismo*. It is extremely important and we shall therefore discuss it in detail.[134] The statute begins by explaining why Edward considered the prohibition of usury to be necessary, before following with the prohibition itself:

> Forasmuch as the King hath seen that divers Evils, and the disinheriting of the good Men of his Land have happened by the Usuries which the Jews have made in Time past, and that divers Sins have followed thereupon; albeit he and his Ancestors have received much benefit from the Jewish People in all time past; nevertheless for the Honor of God and the common benefit of the People, the King hath ordained and established, That from henceforth no Jew shall lend any Thing at Usury, either upon Land, or upon Rent, or upon other Thing; And that no Usuries shall run in Time coming from the Feast of Saint Edward [i.e. October 13th] last past. Notwithstanding, the Covenants before made shall be observed, saving that the Usu-

---

tenants on their estates, and sometimes even had whole ghettos as their property. & B. B.: Appendix. 13, Nr. 18 [?]; *Rymer's Fœdera*, Vol. I, Part 2, p. 539.

[133] *Patent Rolls*, Vol. 1272-1281, pp. 92, 93, 95, 128, 448; *Calendarum Rotulum Patentium*, p. 46 ff.

[134] *Statutes of the Realm*, Vol. I, p. 221; *Chronicle of Edward I und Edward II*, Vol. I, p. 96; *Florentii Wigorniens*, Vol. II. p. 214. Translator's note: It is commonly translated as 'Statute of the Jewry', but 'Statute of Jewry' or 'Statutes of Jewry' can also be found in English historical and academic texts. All English quotations of this Statute have been taken from pages 220-1 of the first volume of *The Statutes of the Realm* (1810), where the English translation is printed alongside the original Norman French.

ries shall cease [i.e. loans prior to this date will be legally binding, but only for the original capital borrowed].

Edward went on to order that all loans backed by pledges of moveable assets had to be settled by Easter, or these assets would be forfeited. He then made the following statement:

> And if any Jew shall lend at Usury contrary to this Ordinance, the King will not lend his Aid, neither by himself nor his Officers, for the recovering of his Loan; but will punish him at his discretion for the Offence, and will do justice to the Christian that he may obtain his Pledge again.

In making this statement, Edward had abandoned the policy of his ancestors, a policy that was more than two hundred years old. This break with the past was to benefit the people, but came at a cost to the Jews and the monarchy itself. From that point onwards, he as a monarch had to deal with the reality of no longer receiving any significant income from the Jews.

In pursuit of his anti-usury principle, Edward then ordered that the indebted English subject be given every protection against the ruthless exactions of the Jews:

> And that the Distresses for Debts due unto the Jews from henceforth shall not be so grievous, but that, the Moiety of the Lands and Chattels of the Christians shall remain for their Maintenance; and that no Distress shall be made for a Jewry Debt, upon the Heir of the Debtor named in the Jew's Deed, nor upon any other Person holding the Land that was the Debtor's, before that the Debt be put in Suit and allowed in Court.

Numerous protective measures are provided for this eventuality:

> And if the Sheriff or other Bailiff, by the King's Command hath to give Seisin [possession] to a Jew, be it one or more, for their Debt, of Chattels or Land to the Value of the Debt, the Chattels shall be valued by the Oaths of good Men, and be delivered to the Jew or Jews, or to their Proxy, to the Amount of the Debt; and if the Chattels be not sufficient, the Lands shall be extended by the same Oath before the Delivery of Seisin to the Jew or Jews, to each in his due Proportion; so that it may be certainly known that the Debt is quit, and the Christian may have his Land again; Saving always to the Christian the Moiety

of his Land and Chattels for his maintenance as aforesaid, and the Chief Mansion.

A review shows that this part of the law appears to be quite modern and is in a certain sense similar to our *Vollstreckungsschutzgesetz* [enforcement protection law]. The Jews were once again required to reside only in cities where the aforementioned *archae* were located.

It was also once more stipulated that all Jews over the age of seven had to wear the specifically designated badge on his outer clothing, which took the form of a six-by-three-inch patch of yellow felt in the shape of the two tablets of Moses [note the color change to yellow, from the white of the 1218 law]. And on turning 13 years of age, every Jew, regardless of sex, had to pay an annual poll tax of three pennies.

These regulations were intended to regulate the life of the Jews within the national body in a very specific way; indeed, with regard to the prohibition on usury and their dominance in this field, one can say that they had to completely change their ways. Now the efforts of this great English king, which were hopeless from the outset, were conceptualized in a bid to improve the character of the Jews in his kingdom. Through the issuance of legal regulations, he wanted to take away from the Jews the detestable profession of usurer, which is so detrimental to the people, and in its stead create a new, better existence for the Hebrews. But the king did not take into account the true character of the Jews. Because, for a person to improve himself, a sincere will of his own to want the change is required, and this has always been lacking among the Jews as a nation.

In the middle of his 1275 statute, the king gives the reason for his merciful stance, and sets out other reasonable protections for their right to thrive and prosper:

> And, Forasmuch as it is the will and sufferance of Holy Church, that they may live and be preserved, the King taketh them under his Protection, and granteth them his Peace; and willeth that they be safely preserved and defended by his Sheriffs and other Bailiffs, and by his Liege Men; and commandeth that none shall do them harm, or damage, or wrong, in their Bodies or in their Goods, moveable or immoveable; and that they shall neither plead nor be impleaded in any Court, nor be challenged or troubled in any Court, except in the Court of the King, whose Bond-men they are. And that none shall owe Obedience, or Service, or Rent, except to the King, or his Bailiffs in his Name; unless it be for their Dwellings which they now hold by paying Rent; saving the Right of Holy Church.

AND the King granteth unto them that they may gain their living by lawful Merchandise and their Labor; and that they may have Intercourse with Christians, in order to carry on lawful Trade by selling and buying. But that no Christian, for this Cause or any other, shall dwell among them. And the King willeth that they shall not by reason of their Merchandise be put to Lot or Scot ['Scot and Lot': local household taxes], nor [be considered] in Taxes with the Men of the Cities or Boroughs where they abide; for that they are taxable to the King as his Bondmen, and to none other but the King.

The extent to which the king has concern for his Jewish subjects can be seen from the last paragraph of the law:

Moreover the King granteth unto them that they may buy Houses and Curtilages [i.e. the accompanying enclosed land and outhouses], in the Cities and Boroughs where they abide, so that they hold them in chief of the King; saving unto the Lords of the Fee their Services due and accustomed. And that they may take and buy Farms or Land for the Term of Ten Years or less, without taking Homages or Fealties, or such sort of Obedience from Christians, and without having Advowsons of Churches; and that they may be able to gain their living in the World, if they have not the Means of Trading, or cannot Labor; and this License to take Lands to farm shall endure to them only for Fifteen Years from this Time forward.

The law did not change anything regarding the Jews' legal relationship to the king. They remained his property and as a result, despite having received express authorization to trade, etc., could not become burgesses [i.e. freemen] of the cities. At the same time, it was determined that they were not liable to pay taxes to the cities, but only to the king.

We will turn our attention onto whether or not the Jews made use of the opportunities that were given to them for an honorable profession. To put it bluntly: all of Edward I's efforts were in vain. The Jewish historians take great pains to prove in great detail that for various reasons the Jews were unable to make use of the king's benevolence and were thus driven to crime. It is most notably Barnett Lionel Abrahams who has most ably attempted to provide this proof. Since he is generally the source for the other historians, we will deal solely with his argument in order to make our own case.[135]

---

[135] Abrahams, p. 39 ff. & See, for example, Hyamson: *History*, p. 80.

Abrahams argues that it was impossible for Jews to engage in honest trade because the law prevented them from becoming burgesses [i.e. freemen] of a municipality. As a result, they were excluded from the so-called guilds and therefore from the merchant community, for which membership of a particular guild was a prerequisite.

This argument cannot be accepted for various reasons. In order to refute it, it is necessary to briefly discuss the legal nature of the guilds or, as they were also called, *Gilda Mercatoria*.

William the Conqueror not only brought orderly conditions to England, but trade and commerce also improved, closely linked to this new order of things. This led to the formation of guilds at the end of the 11th century, which were granted a range of special privileges by the king.[136]

It is difficult to find a general definition for the most recurring special rights of the guilds, since the latter almost never agree in their practical use of them. Charles Gross undertook to carefully compile the royal charters for each individual guild. From his study it was found that, in general, the members of a guild were free from municipal taxes and had a monopoly on a large part of the retail trade. However, almost nowhere was it forbidden to engage in wholesale trade without belonging to the guild; in fact, in various places on market days, strangers were usually allowed to sell goods on a small scale, and additionally, in some cities the monopoly in retail trade was only limited to products that were particularly important for urban traffic, such as furs, wool and dyed cloth.[137]

A wide range of commercial activities was still available to non-guild members, and as a result the Jews had great opportunities to develop business interests. The Jews already enjoyed the other fundamental advantage over guild members—freedom from municipal taxes—because under the aforementioned 1275 law, they were only liable to pay taxes to the king and not to the cities.

It can thus be seen that the guild members had little advantage over the Jews. With sufficient determination, the latter were easily able to make a decent living for themselves. Furthermore, we do not at all share Abrahams' view that the Jews could not become guild members because the 1275 law made it impossible for them to acquire burgess status in the cities.

Gross has now also shown that the guilds were not identical to the municipal governments, but rather only an important organ of the city admin-

---

[136] Gross: *Gilda Mercatoria*, p. 32. Translator's note: For his first assertion, Gross in his *Gild Merchant*. (p. 2). cites the Anglo-Saxon Chronicle: 'Among other things, is not to be forgotten the good peace that he (William the Conqueror) made in the land. It was such that a man... might go over the kingdom unhurt with his bosom full of gold.'

[137] Gross: *Gild Merchant*, Vol. I, p. 37 ff.; Vol. II, p. 16, 52, 110, 138, 175, 250, 358 etc. & Gross: *Gild Merchant*, Vol. I, p. 43 ff.; *Gilda Mercatoria*, pp. 54-5. Rigg (p. xi) also supports this view.

istration. From this, he has convincingly demonstrated that one could become a guild member without being a burgess of the city, and his argument is perfectly substantiated with documents. Accordingly, numerous people from neighboring towns, even complete strangers, were guild members in cities without possessing burgess status. Given these facts, Jews also had the opportunity to join the guilds. There is even a recorded case of a Jew becoming the member of a guild in 1268. This proves that if they had serious intentions the Jews were fully equal with the English in commerce.[138]

Incidentally, Abrahams' statements would be understood by an unwitting reader to mean that there were guilds all over England, which left nowhere for the Jews to trade.

Undoubtedly, there was not a single guild in the countryside, and likewise not all urban centers possessed a guild, only those that had received this privilege from the king. Again, it is thanks to Gross's research that we have a list of the towns and cities with guilds, but it only contains around 100 locations. The towns of Arundel, Colchester, Exeter, Huntingdon, Warwick, and others are missing. These are only selected from the number of non-guild cities because there were Jewish communities residing in them.[139] Even if Abrahams' argument were correct, there would still be enough places in England where the kingdom's 16,000 Jews could have traded.[140]

But his view is all the more astonishing given that he used documents to establish that the Jews actually did trade. He undertook an in-depth study of the documents in the Public Record Office and the British Museum to determine what lines of commerce were available to the Jews when they were expelled from England in 1290. The facts he published on the topic should easily confirm that the Jews enjoyed a good wholesale trade, mainly in grain and wool, which they could do even without joining the guilds. From his lists it emerges that the Jews in Bristol, Lincoln, Norwich, Oxford, but especially in Canterbury and Southampton, carried on a profitable trade in the above-mentioned commodities. And it is safe to say that much if not most of the documentation will have been lost, to which must be added the fact that some transactions will have taken place without being documented.[141] In any case, there can be no doubt that the Jews could have pursued honorable trade without any difficulty.

Abrahams further explains that there was little chance for the Jews to be able to make a living for themselves in agriculture, which was also granted to them under Edward's legislation. They were without any experience in

---

[138] Gross: *Gild Merchant*, Vol. I, pp. 36 ff.; 63, 64. & Gross: *Gild Merchant*, Vol. I, p. 66 ff.; *Gilda Mercatoria*, p. 56 ff. & Ochenkowski (p. 57) is of the same view.

[139] Gross: *Gild Merchant*, Vol. I, p. 9 ff.; *Gilda Mercatoria*, p. 37 ff. & Gross: *Gild Merchant*, Vol. I, p. 20; *Gilda Mercatoria*, p. 39. & Jacobs, pp. 373-385.

[140] Abrahams, *Expulsion*, p. 39.

[141] Abrahams: *Conditions of the Jews*, p. 85 ff. & Abrahams: *Conditions of the Jews*, p. 87 ff.

this sphere of production, and in particular they were unable to acquire any land because the oath of fealty had a Christian character, and as a result could not be taken by them. Abrahams is referring to an oath that ends with the words: 'So help me God and the Saints.' This version of the oath precluded Jews from being able to swear it. However, by looking at the passage quoted by Abrahams, it emerges that this oath could not have been enacted in law before the Jews' expulsion of 1290, which is fundamentally necessary for Abrahams to be able to use it as a valid argument. On the contrary, our own research showed that it was only introduced much later.[142]

In the source book *Liber Custumarum* cited by Abrahams, from pages 88-239 there are only laws after the year 1297, with one exception: most of them even date from after 1300. The aforementioned oath is recorded on page 215 of the collection, and is reproduced without specifying the date of the documentation in which it was found. The law preceding the oath's entry is from the year 1306; the one following it is from the year 1303. It is thus almost certain that the ordinance regarding the oath was also issued after the year 1300.

We have also discovered the aforementioned oath in another official collection of statutes. The accompanying footnote expressly states that this legal provision was enacted by Edward II in his 17th regnal year [i.e. 1323-1324].[143]

Both sources would indicate that the oath cited by Abrahams was only introduced long after the Jews had been expelled and could therefore not have represented an obstacle for them around the year 1276. As a result, there is no apparent reason why the Jews should not have sought a living in agriculture. The real reason, then as now, is likely to be that they had not the slightest inclination to put their hand to the plough; which would have been a welcome event, because it is only through a genuine peasantry that a nation finds its true source and regeneration.

Finally, Abrahams claims that there was no opportunity for Jews to become craftsmen. To justify his claim, he refers again to the aforementioned collection of laws and customs, from which he posits that there were special

---

[142] Abrahams: *Expulsion*, p. 40. Translator's note: Abrahams, of course, omit to mention the fact that, under classical Judaism from 800 A.D. onwards, in which the Babylonian Talmud is the acknowledged authority in all Jewish communities, the Jews 'developed a hatred and contempt for agriculture as an occupation and for peasants as a class, even more than for other Gentiles' and wherever Jewish society is to be found, in whatever form, 'it does not include peasants'. See Shahak, pp. 42, 53 [Translator's Bibliography]. Additionally, Edward I was not the only monarch to attempt (and fail) to get the Jews to give up parasitical financial functions in favour of honest labour – Aleksandr Solzhenitsyn's *Two Hundred Years Together* chronicles the failures of successive Tsars to turn the Jews into farmers [e.g. Vol I, Chapter 4].

[143] *The Statutes of the Realm* (1810), Vol. I. p. 227.

requirements for the craft professions. With the exception of two of the laws cited, all of the laws also date to the time after the Jewish expulsion. These first two laws are only really concerned with the days on which work was not permitted and the materials from which certain products had to be made. One also stipulates that the apprenticeship period for saddlers should be ten years. Neither law deals with restrictions that made it impossible for Jews to join the trades. Incidentally, it appears that, apart from everything else, it was only after the year 1300 that legal regulations regarding qualifications for craftsmen were made; because, for example, no relevant instructions for London are to be found for this time, but they have been found for later periods. Furthermore, while it is not even certain that there were special guilds in all cities, it was definitely possible to practice a craft in the open countryside. In fact, the craftsmen who gathered around a large country estate received certain land for their craft services. Apart from the difficulty of a certain number of years being required to master a craft profession, the Jews were also able to work as artisans.[144]

We have somewhat lingered on this topic because historians have almost unanimously taken the view that Edward I's law deprived the Jews of any opportunity to make a living after they could no longer practice their former business of usury. These previous historical claims should now be seen as sufficiently debunked. It seems really strange that, according to these historians, a king like Edward I—who is not wrongly called 'the English Justinian'—should have passed a law that remained largely only on paper because certain circumstances supposedly made its practical implementation impossible.

Judah Responds

It would soon become clear that the Jews did not have the slightest understanding of Edward I's efforts to make them honorable people. Rather, they saw everything as oppression. Although they did not dare to express their anger directly against the king, they nevertheless openly insulted the Christian religion. They claimed that Edward's law was against the principles of Christian doctrine: the same Christianity that the Jews allege is anti-Semitic at every other juncture, now had its doctrines receive an expedient Jewish interpretation for ethnic advantage. Thus, one can see how history repeats itself—only with the difference that today these Jewish interpretations of morality receive both applause and acceptance, especially in the Anglo-

---

[144] Abrahams: *Expulsion*, p. 40. & *Liber Custumarum*, pp. 78, 80-1, 101-2, 121, 124, 418-25. See also Riley, pp. 178-9. & *Liber Custumarum*, pp. 78, 101. & Riley, pp. 3-61. & Ochenkowski, p. 64. & Ochenkowski, p. 51 ff.

Saxon countries. In the England of the period, however, their argument apparently received very little attention. In their attacks, the Hebrews did not even stop at the person of Jesus Christ, and eventually their behavior, 'which vilified our *Savior*, and his Followers, with such scoffing *Blasphemy*', became so intolerable that the long-suffering king found himself obliged to put a stop to it by means of a special law of 1279 which meant that any Jew who dared to engage in such behavior did so at a risk to life and limb ('*sub periculo Vitae & Membrorum*').

In addition, Edward—apparently it had become necessary—once again strictly forbade Jews from employing Christian servants, whether male or female, and having them in their homes. It is striking that mention of this prohibition appears again and again throughout thirteenth-century records, which would indicate that certain critical incidents must have required its reiteration. However, the Jews did not stop at insults of the blasphemous kind mentioned. Rather, they resorted to actions that at times threatened the existence of the nation's administration, and one could even go as far to say the existence of the English economy.[145]

First of all, it was clear that the Hebrews paid little attention to Edward's statute of 1275 and continued to lend money at interest, despite the risk of harsh punishment for doing so. Few of them thought of acting honorably.[146]

Most of them, and quite possibly all of them, resorted to the worst crimes. Reports were made that they carried out highway robberies, committed burglaries and generally became a scourge on the country. However, their main occupation still seems to have been to ruin the country's currency. They clipped or ground the edges of the gold and silver coins, and while they kept the metal thus obtained for themselves, they passed on the debased coins at full face value.[147]

As early as 1248, it was mainly Jews who committed this crime, and only the harshest punishments were able to deter some of them. Indeed, the currency was so shaken by the problem of 'light coin' that foreign countries were loath to accept English money as payment, as reflected in the comment

---

[145] Tovey, pp. 207-8; *Rymer's Foedera*, Vol. I, Part 2, p. 570. Margoliouth: *History*, Vol. I, p. 250. Translator's note: Quoted elements reproduced verbatim from Tovey. Note that the same legislation also contained a ruling which ordered that Jewish women had to wear the Jewish badge alongside the men. This came in response to a complaint of 'malicious defamation' made to the king in 1288 by a certain Moses of Hereford and his wife Suetecota, who were aggrieved that she had been slandered a Christian [Prynne, Vol. II, p. 106]. The complaint and the king's response not only illustrate the Jews' tone-deafness to the deteriorating conditions in England at this time, but to the fact that this sixty-year-old regulation, like other legal restrictions on Jews which had been in place for decades, had obviously become routinely ignored in practice, and thus required regular reiteration from authority.

[146] Abrahams: *Expulsion*, p. 46 ff., Hyamson: *History*, p. 81.

[147] *Calendar of Patent Rolls*, Vol. 1281-1292, p. 98; Abrahams: *Expulsion*, p. 46 ff.

made by the monk Matthew Paris in his *Chronica Majora* that same year: 'No foreigner, let alone Englishman, could look on an English coin with a dry eye and an unbroken heart.'[148]

Shortly after Edward I's 1275 law was passed, the same evils were discovered—at first only on a small scale, but then gradually worsening until it reached an unprecedented level. In 1278, Edward was therefore forced to make the decision to confiscate all of the currency in circulation and have new coins minted. But first, he had to work to arrest the coin-clippers, so that they would not be able to ruin the currency again.

From the beginning, Edward's suspicions fell on the Jews because of what had happened in 1248. During the course of investigations, it was found that the Jews were in fact almost the sole perpetrators. In addition to the crime of coin clipping, they had smuggled in counterfeit coins from abroad, which did not appear to differ from the real English coins, but which were in fact only half the weight. It was found that the Hebrews had made a tremendous amount of profit from these activities, and had indulged in coin-tampering to such an extent that if it were to continue much longer, as one French manuscript noted, the English currency would soon be worth nothing.[149]

As soon as Edward I had enough evidence of the Jews' activities, he had them arrested throughout England one night in November 1278, and while the detainees were 'placed in safe custody in different castles throughout the country', their homes were carefully searched. A great deal of devalued and counterfeit money was discovered, along with special tools and equipment for committing the crimes in question.[150]

Court hearings then took place in all parts of the kingdom, which revealed, among other things, that a few Englishmen were also involved, but

---

[148] Tovey, p. 209-10. *Chronica Majora*, Vol. V, p. 15-16. Ruding, Vol. I, pp. 191-3. [English translation of Paris quotation taken from Abrahams: *Expulsion*, p. 47.]

[149] *Annales Monastici*, Vol. IV, p. 278; Tovey, pp. 209-10; Ruding, Vol. I, pp. 191-3. Translator's note: As Tovey (p. 210) tell us, some of the counterfeit coins were 'an artificial Mixture of Silver, Copper and Sulpher', while others appear to have been 'base Mettal, plated or scaled over with Silver'. & Tovey, p. 209.

[150] *Bartholomœi de Cotton*, p. 157; *Chronica Johannis de Oxenedes*, p. 253; *Chronica Monasterii S. Albani, Thomas Walsingham*, Vol. I, p. 18. & *Chronica Johannis de Oxenedes*, p. 252; *Annales Monastici*, Vol. II, p. 390; *Florentii Wigorniensis*, Vol. II, p. 220. Translator's note: Quoted element taken from Thomas Forester's 1854 translation of *Florentii Wigorniensis* [*Florence of Worcester*, p. 359, see Translator's Bibliography]. The same source also relates that goldsmiths were similarly arrested and their houses searched, which may explain the three Englishmen who were later hanged in London. According to the author 'B. B.', during the Jewish house searches 'several Barrels full of Clippings, above and under Ground, were Discovered, and all with the Clipping Instruments' [p. 8], while possession of silver plates and counterfeit silver plates (i.e. silvered base metal) was also seen as implication in the crime. See Rigg: *Select Pleas...* (pp. 120-1, 125-7) for cases of failed attempts by Jews to sell such silver plate.

that their participation was completely irrelevant compared to that of the Jews. Hundreds of Jews were sentenced to death. In London alone, 294 Jews were hanged or drowned, along with three Englishmen. Tovey's commentary [p. 210] is therefore vindicated when he says that King Edward 'was very jealous of every Thing that related to his Coin, (and is supposed to be the first of our Kings who fixed the Standard of it)'.[151] This put an end to this crime, from which the Jews had not only derived great material profits, but which had also severely beleaguered the king whom they so hated.

The Church Intervenes

One might have expected that the king would have been at best indifferent towards the fate of the Jews, given his bad experiences with them. But it is typical of his integrity that, in view of the people's outrage over these crimes, he passed special laws to protect the Jews. As before, he viewed them as his subjects and his property, and therefore forbade any harassment of them, as he similarly forbade any interference in their trade. Violations would result in punishment. How serious he was about this can be seen from the fact that in individual cases he issued numerous special decrees, as can be seen, for example, with the burgesses of Hereford who had apparently not observed the king's order.[152]

But all the king's measures to pacify the masses were unsuccessful because the people were too angry at Jewish behavior. One can therefore quite fairly conclude that it was the Jews themselves who contributed most to their own expulsion by means of their outrageous deeds, although there were other factors, such as Queen Eleanor's anti-Jewish stance, that must have played a role. The great bitterness of the people can best be seen from contemporary reports. In 1250, Matthew Paris wrote that no one pitied the Jews their fate [of having almost all of their money extorted from them by the king], 'as it was clearly proven that they were the ones who forged documents, seals and

---

[151] Holinshed, Vol. III, p. 277 ff; Tovey, p. 210; Prynne, Vol. I, p. 32, Vol. II, p. 81; *Chronicles of Edward I*, Vol. I, p. 88; *Annales Monastici*, Vol. IV, pp. 278-9. Translator's note: Note that the number of the Jews executed in London varies according to source – for example, *Florence of Worcester* (p. 360) gives 267, Prynne (Vol. II, p. 81) 294, Tovey (p. 210) 280, and 'B. B.' (p. 8) 207, variances which can surely only be partly attributable to scribal copying errors. Note also that these figures refer solely to London; according to numerous sources, 'great numbers' (Tovey) were also executed in other parts of England. Cf. Rokéah: *Money and the hangman* [in Translator's Bibliography].

[152] Prynne, Vol. II, p. 85. & Prynne, Vol. II, p. 100. Translator's note: The king had charged 24 burgesses of Hereford with the Jews' protection, advising them that if any of his Jews were molested in their goods or persons, those responsible would have their assets seized. Prynne also advises us that the king employed a similar strategy in other towns throughout England.

coins, crimes that needed greater punishment'. Even those in educated circles almost unanimously shared the view of the common people.[153]

The church was significantly involved in the fight against the Jews. Leading clergymen had tried in every way to keep contact between Jews and Christians to the bare minimum. The common people were still inhibited from freely expressing their feelings in public, because the king continued to protect the Jews in the hope that they might still improve as a people. However, he was only committed to this policy inasmuch as it could be reconciled to the overall welfare of society.[154]

Gradually the church became more politically active against the Jews. The Archbishop of Canterbury, John of Peckham, demanded that all synagogues in London, with one exception, be shut down. The Bishop of Hereford was utterly determined not to tolerate any intercourse between Jews and Christians. When he learned that Christians intended to be guests at an upcoming wedding celebration of rich Jews, he forbade their attendance under threat of excommunication. As a result, the English parishioners who disobeyed him were expelled from the church.[155]

In 1286, the English church received external support in this regard. The Pope sent a bull to the Archbishops of Canterbury and York in which he firmly opposed intercourse between Jews and Christians. If the church had previously tacitly tolerated such interaction, he condemned this laxity and demanded that it be stopped immediately. Furthermore, Christian wet nurses were to be removed from Jewish houses as quickly as possible, and the abuse of Christian men and women living under the same roof as Jews was to be ended. This was precisely why shameful things often happened in terms of Jewish men having sexual intercourse with Christian women and Christian men with Jewish women. He demanded that strict action be taken to resolve all aspects of the problem and a subsequent report drafted on the actions taken.[156] That the Jews still did not follow the king's command to wear a badge is indicated by yet another reference to the existing legal requirement in a special ordinance.

In 1278, immediately after the Jews were tried for the coin crimes, Edward set about putting England's currency back in order. He gradually re-

---

[153] *Annales Monastici*, Vol. II. p. 409. Translator's note: According to this chronicle (the Waverley Annals), it was Queen Eleanor who ordered the expulsion of the Jews from England. & *Historia Anglorum*, Vol. III, p. 76. & *Chronica Majora*, Vol. V, p. 517. Translator's note: This reference has to be incorrect, as it is Paris's account of the murder of Little St. Hugh of Lincoln in 1255, irrelevant here.

[154] *Letters of Bishop Grosseteste*, pp. 33, 318.

[155] *Johannes Peckham: Registrum Epistularum*, Vol. II, p. 407.

[156] *Richard de Swinfield*, Vol. II, pp. 100-1. Translator's note: This source has a short summary of the bull, lacking the detail given above, e.g. there is no mention of a report to be drafted, so Aldag may have used a second source.

moved all of the damaged coins from circulation that could be found, and replaced them with new ones. He also set a point in time, announced by public proclamation, at which the old coins would no longer be legal tender. At the end of the same year, the replacement of the coinage was considered complete.[157]

In 1282 the king started to receive complaints about the new coins being devalued. Counterfeit coins were also starting to reappear in the new circulation. The king set up a commission of enquiry with a decree dated 6 February 1283, and the investigators discovered that it was once more the work of the Jews. The guilty were certainly punished, although nothing is known about how.[158]

Apparently, however, all of the measures did not have the intended success in eradicating the problem, because the next year [15 September 1284] a new decree was issued for the commission to investigate and punish the Jews dealing in real and counterfeit silver plate, as made from coin clipping.[159]

Although hard to believe, even this new crackdown still did not produce the desired outcome. Some chroniclers speak of a general persecution of Jews in 1286 without, however, giving the reasons for it. Still others relate that in 1287 all of the Jews were thrown into prison because they had committed new money crimes, and were only released after paying a fine of £12,000.[160]

However, this operation may not have been completed until 1288, because King Edward again issued a decree on 26 January 1288, which indicated that the Jews were still active as coin clippers and counterfeiters [given that they were still buying and selling real and counterfeit silver plate]. As a result, the commissioners were ordered to take whatever action was deemed necessary to deal with the problem.[161]

Since 1286, the king had been in Gascony, then still an English possession, to carry out administrative reforms. In 1288 he issued a decree for this part of his realm which ordered the Jews to leave the province immediately, a decree which foreshadowed the measures which were to follow in England proper.[162]

---

[157] Holinshed, Vol. III, pp 279-280.

[158] Prynne, Vol. II, p. 102.

[159] Prynne, Vol. II, p. 105. Translator's note: Prynne notes that this commission, as well as the trials, were made up of both Christians and Jews, 'for the greater indifferency, and prevention of Injustice through malice or emulation'. This is seen by the Jewish judge Solomon of Rochester being named among the commissioners.

[160] *Chronica Johannis de Oxenedes*, p. 268. & *Florentii Wigorniensis*, Vol. II, p. 238. *Annales Monastici*, Vol. IV, p. 308. *Chronicles of Edward I*, Vol. I, p. 96.

[161] Prynne, Vol. II, p. 106.

[162] *Chronicle of Pierre de Langtoft*, Vol. II, p. 183. & *Gesta Abbatum Monasterii S. Albani*, Vol. II, p. 30.

The Expulsion of the Jews

When King Edward left Gascony for London in 1289, he was determined to expel the Jews from England as he had just done from the French duchy. But once back home, he first had to deal with some very unpleasant business that demanded his urgent attention. He was informed that a significant number of the judges had been bribed during his three-year absence and that there was no longer any assurance of an impeccable jurisprudence. This had already had the most undesirable consequences, and he was urged from all sides to take action against the 'seven corrupted judges'. The Jews were also involved in these corruptions to a significant extent—it would have been a miracle in Jewish history if this had not been the case. Edward immediately deposed the guilty judges, punished them, and replaced them with new men as quickly as possible. All in all, the purge of the judiciary took him until the beginning of 1290.[163]

Immediately after this matter was settled, he turned to the Jewish Question. The barons and the clergy had already petitioned Parliament to expel the Jews from the country. Their proposal became law in July 1290, according to which the Jews had to leave England over the next few months. Below is a contemporary report of the events which led up to this final decision:[164]

> To the treasurer and barons of the exchequer. Whereas the king in his parliament at Westminster at the quinzaine of Michaelmas, in the third year of his reign, ordained that no Jew of the realm should thenceforth lend anything in usury to any Christian upon lands, rents or other things, but should earn his living by trade and labor, and the Jews afterwards, maliciously deliberating amongst themselves, changed the kind of usury into a worse one, which they called 'courtesy' (*curiali-*

---

[163] *Annales Monastici*, Vol. IV, p. 318; *Chronicles of Edward I*, Vol. I, p. 97. & 'B. B.', p. 5. Translator's note: *Ibid:* 'by their Corruption and Briberies, most *Jews* escape Corporal Punishment; as it was Instanced by the Commitment and Judgement against seven Corrupted Judges, in the Reign of *Edward* I, who by their underhand Juggle with the *Jews*, and other foul Practices, were Discover'd and Committed to the *Fleet Prison*, where four of them paid Forty Thousand Marks Fine to the King, and more, besides Vessels of Gold and Silver, and the other three were Banished out of the Kingdom.' The author also cites his sources. & *Annales Monastici*, Vol. II, p. 408; Vol. III. p. 355, 356; Vol. IV, p. 319, 324; *Chronicles of Edward I*, Vol. I, p. 98; *Chronicles of Pierre de Langtoft*, Vol. II, pp. 184-5; *Flores Historiarum*, Vol. III, p. 70; Speed, p. 545.

[164] *Chronica Johannis de Oxenedes*, p. 277; *Bartholomæi de Cotton*, p. 178; *Flores Historiarum*, Vol. III, p. 70; *Annales Monastici*, Vol. II, p. 409; Vol. III, pp. 361-2; Vol. IV, pp. 326, 503; *Chronicles of Edward I*, Vol. I, p. 99, *Chronicles of Pierre de Langtoft*, Vol. II, p. 186; *Gervase of Canterbury*, Vol. II, p. 296; *Le Livere de Reis de Britanie*, p. 308; *Gesta Abbatum Monasterii S. Albani*, Vol. II, p. 31; *Richard de Swinfield*, p. 101.

tatem), and depressed the king's people under color of such, by an error double that of the previous one; wherefore the king, by reason of their errors and for the honor of Christ, has caused the Jews to leave his realm as perfidious men; the king, not wishing to be inconsistent with his previous ordinance, but rather to imitate it, has wholly annulled all manner of pains and usury and every sort thereof that may be exacted from any Christians of the realm for any reasons whatever by reason of Jewry for any times whatsoever, willing that nothing shall be exacted from the Christians except the principal debts that they received from the Jews [i.e. the capital only]; of which debts he wills that the amount shall be verified before the treasurer and barons by the oath of three Christians, and that they shall be then paid to the king at suitable terms to be appointed by the treasurer and barons.[165]

The content of this law clearly shows that the king was only ever prompted to take the actions he did because of the continual bad-faith behavior of the Jews. How little they were willing to do justice to the people's demands in the last two years of their stay can be seen from the fact that in 1289 all the Jews in London had to be thrown into prison and in 1290 a Jew even dared to publicly desecrate the host.[166]

The justification for the Edict of Expulsion also shows that, despite Edward's measures, usury must have continued to be a great problem. As a result, the living conditions of the common people were often horrifying, as some chroniclers inform us. How far the exploitation of the people had gone under the reign of Edward I was best summarized by great historian John Speed, who said that the Jews 'by their cruel usuries had...eaten his [Edward's] people to the bones'.[167]

The Jews were ordered to leave England by November 1st of that year. Any Jew who was still in England after that date would be punished with

---

[165] *Close Rolls of Edward I*, Vol. 1288-1296, p. 109. Translator's note: QVOS. It is unclear what 'courtesy' is here, but it may have been a form of commodity futures (see Abrahams: *Condition*, p 80).

[166] *Chronicles of Edward I*, Vol. I, p. 97. & *Annales Monastici*, Vol. IV, p. 503. Translator's note: This refers to the infamous Paris 1290 case of host desecration/eucharistic miracle involving a Jewish moneylender, which, despite taking place abroad, would still have influenced English public opinion. A frank discussion on the facticity of medieval host desecration reports can be found in Horowitz, pp. 172-4 [Translator's Bibliography].

[167] *Chronicon Domini Walteri...* Vol II, p. 20 ff.; Prynne, Vol. I, p. 40 ff.; Tovey, pp. 233-4; Daniel, p. 160. Translator's note: The Osney Annals [*Annales Monastici*, Vol IV, p. 327] reports of usury completely bankrupting people, reducing them to paupers who were forced to beg for food. & Speed, p. 545. Translator's note: QVOS.

death. They basically had to leave their property behind in England. However, they were able to take a large part of their movable property and money with them, as long as it was necessary for the journey to their new destination. All of their claims on loans against the English were escheated to the king. However, the wealth of the Jews was small compared to before and only amounted to around £10,000 in total. This therefore invalidates the argument that the king had the expulsion declared by Parliament in order to take possession of the Jews' vast wealth. Indeed, the Elizabethan historian Samuel Daniel wrote of Edward's 1290 Edict of Expulsion, which he saw as an act carried out for the benefit of the 'miserable People': 'the Justice of the Prince is more noted than any other Motive which may be for his Profit' (*Collection of the History of England*, p. 190).[168]

Edward I must have had the (justifiable) expectation that the populace, in their antipathy towards the Jews, would seize the opportunity to enact their own vengeance on their enemies. He therefore issued a writ ordering that the Jews and their belongings were to be given every possible protection by the authorities. The fact that these orders were not just on paper is evident from the fact that he imposed severe penalties for non-compliance, as can be seen from the following tragic case, when a large number of London Jews chartered a ship to take them to mainland Europe:[169]

> A sort of the richest of them being shipped with their Treasure in a mighty tall ship, which they had hired, when the same was under sail, and got down the *Thames* towards the mouth of the River beyond *Quinborow* [Queenborough]. The Master Mariner bethought him of a wile [came up with a devious trick]: and caused his men to cast anchor, and so rode at the same till the ship by ebbing of the stream remained on the dry sands. The Master herewith enticed the Jews to walk out with him on

---

[168] *Bartholomæi de Cotton*, p. 178. Translator's note: The Osney Annals [*Annales Monastici*, Vol IV, p. 327] affirms that death would be by hanging or beheading. & *Chronicles of Pierre de Langtoft*, Vol. II, p. 189; *Chronicon Domini Walteri*, Vol. II, p. 21. Translator's note: Prynne (Vol. I, p. 47), citing Holinshed, states that the king permitted the Jews to take all of their moveable property, including their gold and silver. & Abrahams: *Condition*, pp. 80-1. Translator's note: It should be noted that Abrahams bases his estimate on the extant *archae* records for 11 of the 17 towns in which the Jews resided, which total £9,100 (of which £4,000 is cash, the rest commodities), but appears to forget about the wealth of the six towns for which there are no records. This estimate also does not factor in the value of the Jews' own property, which he estimates is worth an additional £6,000. Nevertheless, these figures still represent a huge reduction in wealth when compared with the previous era. & For an example of this argument being used, see Margoliouth: *History*, Vol. I, p. 267 ff.

[169] *Close Rolls*, Vol. 1283-1296, pp. 95-6; Tovey, p. 240 ff.; *Calendar of Patent Rolls*, Vol. 1281-1292, pp. 378, 381, 382; *Rymer's Fœdera*, Vol. I, Part II, p. 736; Prynne, p. 240.

land for recreation: and at length, when he understood the tide to be coming in, he got himself back to the ship, whither he was drawn by a cord. The Jews made not so much haste as he did, because they were not aware of the danger. But when they perceived how the matter stood, they cried to him for help, Howbeit he told them, that they ought to cry rather unto *Moses*, by whose conduct their Fathers passed through the red Sea, and therefore if they would call to him for help, he was able enough to help them out of these raging floods, which now came in upon them: They cried indeed, but no succor appeared, and so they were swallowed up in the water.

The Master returned with the ship, and told the King how he had used the matter, and had both thanks and reward, as some have written. But others affirm, (and more truly as should seem) that diverse of those Mariners which dealt so wickedly against the Jews, were hanged for their wicked practice, and so received a just reward of their fraudulent and mischievous dealing.[170]

In the 1293 Close Rolls, we find an order to deliver a man for trial who had been in Sandwich prison for two years for failing to comply with the royal protection order regarding the Jews.[171]

The number of Jews who left England has been estimated at 15,000 to 16,000. They went mainly to France, Holland, and Belgium. Thus ended the Jews' first settlement in England.[172]

The history of these approximately 200 years has clearly demonstrated that the Jews, with or without the protection of the authorities, were never willing to take up an honorable profession, and that the laws essentially intended to force them to do so were also unsuccessful.

In good times and bad, they committed the greatest crimes, and despite the harshest punishments, continued to do so until the king was forced to expel them in the interest of the people and the maintenance of law and or-

---

[170] *Chronicon Domini Walteri*, Vol. II, pp. 21-2; *Annales Monastici*, Vol. III, p. 262; Vol. IV, p. 327; Prynne, p. 48. Translator's note: The quotation inserted here for reader interest has been reproduced verbatim from Prynne, with some spellings updated for comprehension. The Latin sources confirm that the sailors involved were hanged.

[171] *Close Rolls*, Vol. 1288-1296, p. 295. Translator's note: Given that this man, Henry Adrian, is in a Cinque Ports prison, and is charged with causing the death of Jews and committing trespasses against them 'in their passage to parts beyond the sea by him' outside of port jurisdiction, it may be that he was the ship captain of Prynne's tale.

[172] Prynne, Vol. I. p. 49; *Flores Historiarum*, Vol. III, 70; B. B., p. 11. Translator's note: Prynne rather implausibly gives the exact figure of 15,060 for the number of Jews who were expelled, while 'B. B.' gives that of 16,511.

der. All in all, another comment on modern times. Even then, it was the Jews with their shameful activities who, in violation of the hospitality granted to them, gradually forced the people and ultimately a great and just king to take action against them. So it was not a question of a nation's evil will to persecute poor, wandering Jews, but rather a healthy people with strong natural instincts, who took measures that were needed to maintain the purity of their customs and their decency. In other words, it was the Jews alone who brought about their expulsion.

Will the English people of today still have the strength to manage a feat similar to the one achieved by their vigorous ancestors under the leadership of their king?

CHAPTER 2

THE RETURN OF THE JEWS
UNDER CROMWELL (1290-1658)

England Without Jews

It has long been held that, after the expulsion of 1290, there were hardly any Jews in England for the next 300 years or so. Jewish historians have worked hard to prove the opposite. To summarize their findings, they actually found one or two Jews in England during this time, but larger numbers—such as Jewish communities—were completely missing. So this period is of little interest to us and will therefore only be touched upon briefly.[1]

It is often claimed that at that time the officials of the English Crown were not sufficiently trained to guarantee a complete cleansing of Jews from the country. This may be true, but it is likely that the Jews hardly dared to remain in England for fear of the threatened death penalty. Undoubtedly, any lack of orderly administration was made up for by the concern of the populace, who, because of the existing antipathy, made sure that the Jews—in the event that they did not emigrate—were reported.[2]

It may be that the odd Jew was baptized and still secretly followed his former religion, but this would have been of only minor importance, just as any mixing of these Jews with the English people was of no importance because the overall purity of the race at that time was not affected. In addition to these baptized Jews, perhaps one or two unbaptized Jews were in England during this period.

Under Queen Elizabeth we find two baptized Jews, John Immanuel Tremellius (1510-1580) and Philip Ferdinand (1555-1598), who were in her special favor. Both were Hebraists, with Tremellius becoming regius professor of Hebrew at Cambridge in 1549 and Ferdinand teaching Hebrew at both Oxford and Cambridge.[3] Another Jew named Joachim Gaunse, a metallur-

---

[1] See, for example, Wolf: *Middle Age*; Lee: *Jews in England before 1643*; Lee: *Elizabethan England and the Jews*. Translator's Note: See also Wolf's 'Jews in Tudor History' (in his *Essays*) and Roth's *Middle Period* [both found in Translator's Bibliography]. & Hyamson: *History*, p. 98.

[2] Wolf: *Middle Age*, p. 55

[3] *Idem*, pp. 65-6. Translator's note: Additional information from *Jewish Encyclopedia* (s.v. TREMELLIUS, JOHN IMMANUEL and FERDINAND, PHILIP) and *Dictionary of National Biography* (1899 ed., vol. LVII, pp. 186-7 and vol. XVIII, p. 333 respectively). For more on Ferdinand and his time in the state-run *Domus Conversorum*, the 'Convert's Inn' for Jewish converts to Christianity, see Adler and also Martin [Volume 1 Bibliography], the

gist and mining expert who converted to Christianity, rose to a certain prominence in England through the fact that, under his leadership, the smelting
process for copper was greatly improved.[4] All three were Hebrews who
were not born in England.

Rodrigo Lopez, Personal Physician to Queen Elizabeth

Queen Elizabeth placed the greatest trust in her *converso* doctor Rodrigo
[Ruy] Lopez, about whom much has been written and who was most likely
the model for Shylock in Shakespeare's *Merchant of Venice*.[5]

Lopez, born in Portugal, immigrated to England around 1559 after
spending a long time in Antwerp. He was one of the great schemers of his
time and had a burning desire to get rich as quickly as possible. He soon
managed to win the favor of Queen Elizabeth's then favorite, the Earl of
Leicester, and before long, had the reputation of being better at poisoning
than at healing. But his patron stood behind him to protect him, and so not
only was he able to reap great profits, but in 1586 he was even appointed
personal physician to the queen, whose special trust he enjoyed and who
used to initiate him into the most secret affairs of state.

With Elizabeth's knowledge, he came into contact with the Spanish
king, whom she deeply hated, and to whom he appeared to be working exclusively in his service. While he initially revealed unimportant things about
Spain to the queen, he deliberately concealed from her all the important matters that had become known to him. Later he went a step further and informed Spain about all sorts of details of events at the English court, and
even suggested to the king that he poison Elizabeth. He demanded fifty thousand gold escudos, or crowns [equivalent to £18,800 in the English pounds
of the day], for this villainous deed, which were to be deposited abroad before the crime. The King of Spain hesitated because of the enormity of the

---

latter including a facsimile of the receipt for Ferdinand's annual pension. After the initial pre-
1290 residents died out (or otherwise left), the Domus was virtually empty over the subsequent centuries but for the occasional entry of itinerant foreign Jews such as Ferdinand.

[4] Abrahams: *Joachim Gaunse*, p. 83 ff. Translator's note: In fact, as Abrahams attests,
while in England the Prague-born Gaunse [Gans] told Bristol magnates that he had never
been baptised a Christian, and that he was a Jew who did not believe in the divinity of
Jesus Christ or 'any Article of our Christian faithe for that he was not brought uppe therein' (p. 91). He was arrested for blasphemy, but although there is no record of how the
Queen's Privy Council dealt with his case, it is likely that he was dealt with leniently due
to his scientific talent not just having served oligarchic investments, but also English national security. He is also famed for being the first Jew in English America, having accompanied Raleigh on his 1585 expedition to the New World, where, among other things,
he smelted copper on Roanoke Island. See also Grassi [Translator's Bibliography] for
more on this fascinating figure.

[5] Lee: *Elizabethan England*, pp. 146 ff., 166; *Original of Shylock*, p. 195 ff.

sum; the plan was initially not carried out. Through interception of letters, the plot was uncovered in time and Lopez and two of his co-conspirators were arrested. After the accomplices confessed to their crime, Lopez, when faced with the weight of the evidence, had no choice but to confess his guilt. After a major criminal trial in London, Lopez and his aides were hanged.[6]

There are other Jews to be identified in the Elizabethan period, but they are of marginal interest. Wolf, who has dealt with this topic in more detail, has to admit that there were 'a large number of unworthy Jews' during what he designates the 'Middle Age' of Anglo-Jewish historiography, but he attributes this to the laws of the time.[7]

Return and Second Expulsion

No details could be found that would indicate a return of Jews to England in large numbers. But there can be little doubt that the first Marranos—as the baptized Jews from the Iberian Peninsula were usually called—came to the country around 1600. They must have behaved in such a way in England that James I was forced to officially expel them. Although we only have one piece of evidence to prove this, it seems to us to be completely sufficient. Sir Marmaduke Langdale, one of the bravest Royalist generals, who was born at the tail end of the 16th century and died in 1661, certainly heard about the King's ban on the Jews first-hand or at least heard about it from an older contemporary. In a letter dated 20 September 1655 to Sir Edward Nicholas,

---

[6] Dimock, p. 440. & Hume, p. 37; Lee p. 159. & Dimock, p. 441; Hyamson: *History*, p. 118. & Hume, pp. 39, 47. & *Calendar of State Papers of Edward IV*, Vol. 1591-1594, pp. 413, 434, 439, 445 ff., 455, 460, 482, 484; Hume, p. 50 ff.; Dimock p. 465 ff. Translator's note: It should be noted that this was far from a general witch-hunt against Lopez – as Dimock reports (pp. 459-460), the queen called the Earl of Essex a 'rash and temerarious youth' in front of the court when she found out that Essex was prosecuting Lopez. From Dimock: 'She charged him with bringing this ruinous accusation of high treason against her trusty servant from sheer malice, and told him that she knew Lopez to be innocent, and that her honor was at stake in seeing justice done.' Dimock then describes the violent scene at court before continuing: 'A point in favor of Lopez having a fair trial was that everyone else of weight and influence believed the hare-brained young earl was endeavoring to hunt an enemy to death with nothing substantial to go upon. Burghley and Cecil and Egerton and Coke, [the latter two] the attorney-general and solicitor-general, were inclined to favor the accused, both because of the accuser and of the manner of the accusation.'

[7] Wolf: *Jews in Elizabethan England*, p. 1 ff. & Wolf: *Middle Age*, p. 79. Translator's note: From the original source: 'Our survey has, I hope, not been altogether unpleasing. True, we have met with a large number of unworthy Jews: but it should be remembered that bad men are, to a great extent, the products of bad laws, and the Jews would have been something more than human had they all been able to resist the terrorism of the decree of outlawry, or the shameful bribery of the Domus Conversorum.'

Secretary of State to the fugitive Charles Stuart (the future King Charles II), he wrote the following:[8]

> If his Majesty could either have them [the Jews] or divert them
> from Cromwell, it were a very good service. I heard of this 3
> years agone, but hoped the Jewes, that understand the interest
> of all the princes in the world, had been too wise to adventure
> themselves and estates under Cromwell, where they may by
> his death or other alteracion in that kingdome runn the hazard
> of an absolute ruine; but they hate monarchy and are angry for
> the patent that was granted by King James to my Lord of Suf-
> folke for the discovery of them, which made most of the ablest
> of them fly out of England.[9]

Thus he unequivocally mentions the expulsion of the Jews under James I. We tried very hard to find the expulsion decree or any reference to it in the archives, and we especially looked for any documentary reference under the name of Thomas Howard, the first Earl of Suffolk. Howard lived from 1561 to 1626 and, with the exception of a short period during which he was disgraced for an embezzlement offence, held the highest offices in the kingdom until old age.

Henry Henriques is the only other scholar who appears to have dealt with this question. In his research, he reports coming across the appointment of the Earl of Suffolk as commissioner for the implementation of a law of expulsion of Jesuits and other subversive Catholics and is of the opinion that Sir Marmaduke's remark is based on this fact. This law applied not only to Jesuits and seminary priests, but also to 'other Preistes or Persons Ecclesiasticall or Religious whatsoever, made or ordained according to the Order or Rites of the Romishe Church, since the beginning of the Raign of the late Queene of famous Memory *Elizabeth late Queen of England,* being corrupted and brought upp seditiously beyond the Seas or elswhere'. These latter words are actually found in the aforementioned legal provision, and although in terms of sedition one could also say this of the Jews, there are nevertheless doubts as to whether Henriques' position is correct. He seems to have missed the fact that the Earl of Suffolk was often on commissions that had to take action against such subversive Catholics. We first find him on such a commission on 5 September 1604, which was probably connected to the law against '*Jhesuits, Semynaries and Preists*' of what sort soever' published on February 22nd of the same year.

---

[8] *Dictionary of National Biography* (1892), Vol. XXXII, pp. 95-7.

[9] *Nicholas Papers*, Vol. III, p. 51. Translator's note: QVOS (some spelling conventions updated to ensure reader comprehension). Also found at Henriques: *Return*, pp. 70-1.

However, as Henriques also mentions, this commission did not just in-clude the Earl of Suffolk with one or two dignitaries of the realm, but con-sisted of no fewer than 24 officials and members of the high nobility. The Earl of Suffolk was neither in the first place nor was he endowed with any special authority; he is only mentioned fifth in the list in question. In June 1610 and June 1618, new commissions were established to carry out the same task of banishment. On 20 April 1620, a long law of similar content was again passed, the implementation of which was entrusted to a commis-sion of 84 officials and members of the church and the nobility—ninth among them the Earl of Suffolk. Likewise, we see that on 20 April 1622 and in December 1624 new commissions were again established, and in these latter two cases without the Earl of Suffolk. Since the personage of the Earl of Suffolk is by no means particularly highlighted in any of this legislation, there was no reason for Sir Marmaduke to associate him with the expulsion of the Jews. Besides, Sir Marmaduke speaks of a patent from the king, while we have already demonstrated six such laws above.

There can be little reason, therefore, to believe that Sir Marmaduke, in his letter to Nicholas, meant all these laws when he speaks of the King's instruction to the Earl of Suffolk, and so we are forced to conclude that the Jews were again expelled from the country under James I. We can only try to guess the reasons for this banishment. But perhaps the law 'Proclamatio con-tra Exportationem Bullionis', passed on 11 June 1622 under James I, which strictly prohibited the export of gold and silver bullion due to the existing risk of currency collapse, is a hint to what happened. From the legislation: [10]

THE KINGES MOST EXCELLENT MAJESTY considering the scarcity of Money and Coyne of late Yeares growen with-in the Realm, occasioned partly by Transportation thereof out of this Kingdom, and partly by the unlawfull Consumption thereof within the Land, whereof many unsufferable Incon-veniences doe daily aryse, and more are like to ensue to the general hurt and damage of the whole Commonweale... many covetous and greedy Persons have and dailie doe with great Boldnes and Contempt contynue and proceed in those unlaw-ful and offensive Courses, tending to the exhausting of the

---

[10] *Dictionary of National Biography* (1891), Vol. XXVII, pp. 71-3. & Henriques: *Return*, p. 71. & Henriques cites as his sources *Calendar of State Papers, Domestic Series:* Vol. 1603-1610, p. 148; Vol. 1611-1618 p. 547. [Note that Aldag also references this series as *Domestic State Papers* in his notes.] & Rymer: *Foedera*, Vol. XVI, p. 597-8. Translator's note: QVOS. & Rymer: *Foedera*, Vol. XVI, pp. 572-3. Translator's note: QVOS. & Rymer: *Foedera*, Vol. XVI, p. 690; Vol. XVII, p. 92. & Rymer: *Foedera*, Vol. XVII, p. 200 ff. & Rymer: *Foedera*, Vol. XVII, pp. 367, 644.

Treasure of the Realme, and utter overthrow of Trade and Commerce within the same.

And therefore his Majestie, in his Princely Wisdome and upon necessitie of state, sees it fit that from henceforth all Care and Diligence in the Discoverie, and all Severitie in the Correction and Punishment of such Delinquents without favour to any shall be used... hereby straightly charging and commanding that no Person or Persons Alien, Denizen, or other Subject of what Estate Qualitie or Condition soever, doe at any tyme hereafter, without his *Majestie*'s Licence, transport carry or convey, or attempt or indeavour to transport carrie or convey out of this Realme any Gould or Silver, either in Coyne, Plate, Vessels, Jewels, Goldsmiths Worke, Bullion or other Masse, or otherwise howsoever, upon paine of his *Majestie*'s heavie Indignation and Displeasure...[11]

It is well known that even in Cromwell's time this trade was almost exclusively in Jewish hands. Given that around the year 1660—apparently as a result of the same cause—a currency crisis occurred again, and one that was severe enough to spark calls for the severe punishment and even expulsion of the Jews as the main participants, it is a reasonable conjecture that this was also a reason for James I to issue an order for the expulsion of the Hebrews.

We have no hesitation in presuming that the Jews were in fact expelled from England for a second time during the reign of James I. As a result, it is not surprising to find them later supporting the Parliamentarians, to whom they also gave every form of support, in the fight against the monarchy.

In order to understand what happened in England, we need to give a brief overview of the Jewish Question in the rest of the known world at the time.

The Jewish Question in the Seventeenth Century

In Spain, as is well known, the Jews exercised a tremendous influence on the economy and administration towards the end of the 15th century. Without exception, they dominated trade with the newly discovered parts of the world, from which they gained immense material advantages.

When in 1492 the call was issued to convert to the Catholic faith or leave the country, most of the Jews resumed their wandering, and largely poured out along the shores of the Mediterranean, where greater or smaller Jewish colonies emerged everywhere.[12]

---

[11] Rymer: *Foedera*, Vol. XVII, p. 376. Translator's note: QVOS.
[12] Roth: *History of the Marranos*, p. 54.

Nevertheless, their influence in Spain was hardly diminished, because the baptized Jews who remained there already represented the country's financial and economic power. Although these Jews attended Catholic services, they never seriously considered giving up their religion, which they continued to practice in secret. Despite their Jewish art of dissimulation, people soon discovered this fact and the Inquisition began to use the most ruthless means against these baptized Jews, or *Marranos*, as they were called. The word *Marrano* itself is of disputed origin.

The persecutions took place in Spain and Portugal at the beginning of the 16th century. As much as was possible, the Marranos fled, and a new wave of Jews flooded the world. Each new persecution resulted in a new wave of Jewish emigration. They took refuge in the newly founded colonies of their ethnic kin and increased their tribe's influence in the cities and countries concerned. The Marranos migrated in particularly large numbers to the European and Asian parts of Turkey. The Levantine trade was almost entirely in their hands, and they increasingly gained footholds in other areas. We even find that Sultan Suleiman had a Jewish personal physician [Moses Hamon], who also served as the ruler's advisor and who steered the sultan towards decisions that were favorable to the Jews. During this time, according to Graetz, Turkey was a haven for the Jews.[13]

The Marranos not only took refuge in places familiar to Europeans from ancient times, but they also went to India, Jakarta, and South America.[14]

Although their influence in Spain and Portugal diminished, it was not broken. The Jews knew how to regain their position in the usual way, and so in Spain we find a Marrano as secretary to the king, as well as Jews in the posts of finance minister and *mayordomo mayor* [head of the royal house-

---

[13] Wolf: *Menasseh ben Israel*, p. xii, note 2. Translator's note: Wolf's suggestion (from Graetz) is that the word comes from the Aramaic word *Maranatha*, used in the Catholic Church to signal excommunication. However, the Real Academia Española states that the word comes from the Arabic *muharram* ('declared anathema'). It may have been because of this association with the *haram* that the term Marrano became a term used for pig or pork (and by extension 'unclean'), and potentially from this meaning it developed its association with the crypto-Jews, given that the eating of pork, being anathema to the Jews, was a way of detecting crypto-Judaism in so-called New Christians. & Graetz, *Popular History,* Vol. IV, p. 366 ff. & Graetz, Vol. IV, p. 360 ff.; Roth: *History of the Marranos*, p. 63. Translator's note: It should be stated that with the 1492 Expulsion, large numbers of Spanish Jews fled to Turkey, so the Marranos who later emigrated there did so knowing that they live openly as Jews, and join the existing Sephardi colonies there, without fear of persecution. & Graetz, *Popular History,* Vol. IV, p. 406 ff. & Graetz, *Popular History,* Vol. IV, p. 421. Translator's note: 'Haven' is the word used by Graetz.

[14] Graetz, *Popular History,* Vol. IV, p. 366 ff.; Vol. V, pp. 54, 60, 67. Translator's note: Aldag may have meant the East and/or West Indies, given that I do not see India in the original sources, but if that were the case, this would make the listing of Jakarta and/or South America somewhat tautologous. I have therefore stated India [*Indien*], given that this is what is in the original text.

hold]. The trade in the gold imported from America was still primarily in the hands of the Marranos. The Spanish court, which now also ruled Portugal in a personal union, was in debt to the Marranos to the tune of 1,200,000 *cruzados*, an enormous sum for the time.[15]

In Rome, as Lucien Wolf admits, 'the Crypto-Jews commissioned a secret agent supplied with ample funds, who bribed the Cardinals, intrigued against the Holy Office, and frequently obtained the ear of the Pontiff.' Having influence over the Vatican was extremely important to the Marranos because they were formally considered 'New Christians' [*cristianos nuevos*], and the Inquisition's work against them could usually only be brought to a halt by means of a papal intervention.[16]

Amsterdam—Centre of International Jewry

It was not enough for the Marranos to have largely monopolized trade in southern Europe and in the other parts of the world that had recently been opened up to commerce; they also wanted to achieve the same in northern Europe. Despite their financially strong position in Spain and Portugal, a large part of the Marranos still preferred to settle in a country whose interests were opposed to those of Spain, where Spanish influence could not pursue them, and where there was an opportunity to carry out their plans of revenge. Their eyes therefore turned to the Dutch Republic, which had decades of experience of fighting the Spanish and where the Nordic spirit of endeavor was not only ready to send its ships to conquer and trade in all seas, but where it would soon come to dominate trade with new parts of the world in complete freedom.

The first negotiations between the Marranos and the Dutch can be seen around 1590, and a short time later the first Marranos were allowed to settle in Holland while maintaining their Jewish religion. Around the year 1593 we find evidence of the first arrivals in Amsterdam, which was later to become the center of the Marranos or, rather, of international Jewry itself. Jews from Spain and Portugal flocked to the new promised land, and soon there was a large Jewish colony in Amsterdam. They brought with them not only their enormous financial resources, but also, what was at least just as valuable, their global trading connections. These Marranos laid the foundation for Dutch supremacy in the East and West Indies, Jakarta, and South America.[17]

---

[15] Wolf: *Menasseh ben Israel*, p. xiii. & Graetz, *Popular History,* Vol. V, p. 56.

[16] Wolf: *Menasseh ben Israel*, p. xiii. Translator's note: QVOS.

[17] Graetz, *Popular History,* Vol. V, p. 50 ff.; Roth: *History of the Marranos*, p. 200. & Graetz, *Popular History,* Vol. V, p. 60 ff.

However, these Marranos not only received their fellow Sephardic refugees from the Iberian Peninsula, but also numerous co-religionists from Germany who had been driven out by the Thirty Years' War.[18]

Amsterdam had now become the center of international Jewry, where not only Marranos but also Jews from Turkey, North Africa, and other places came together. At times, a ship with Jews arrived every week. When they received legal authorization to settle and trade in 1615, they felt completely safe in the Dutch Republic. To their chagrin, however, at the same time as the law was passed, marriage between Christians and Jews was forbidden. The wealth of the Jews was indescribable. On one occasion, at a wedding in the Jewish community, the combined wealth of forty of the guests exceeded 40 million florins.[19]

The Hebrews soon felt strong enough to look for further settlements in Northern Europe. At Jewish instigation, the King of Denmark sent invitations to Amsterdam. He offered the Jews free exercise of religion and other privileges, and so, needless to say, they accepted. There were also successes in southern Europe, with similar offers made by the Dukes of Savoy and Modena that yielded the same result.

In addition to Amsterdam, Rotterdam also became a prominent Jewish center. The Jews also appeared in large numbers in Hamburg at the end of the 16th century. There, they first created, and subsequently monopolized, trade with the Iberian Peninsula. They were the sole importers of colonial products such as tobacco, cotton, and spices. When in 1619 the Bank of Hamburg was established, the Marranos took a prominent role in its founding and organization, and over forty of them were listed on its earliest roll of shareholders. The extensive trade between Hamburg and the Iberian Peninsula is due in part to their connections. One of the Jewish doctors who immigrated to Hamburg even later became the personal physician to Queen Christina of Sweden.[20]

However, the most important Jewish colony after Amsterdam was in Brazil, where the Portuguese were the first European colonizers. They had originally sent the Marranos there as a punishment, but after a short time they had resumed their trading activities. When the Dutch invaded Brazil around 1624, they found the greatest possible support in their campaign from the Marranos who lived there. After the Dutch conquered Brazil, the Marranos immediately established contact with their fellow 'Dutch' Jews and, like them, immediately openly reverted back to their own religion. Hundreds of Portuguese Jews left Amsterdam and sailed to Brazil. We find Jews in all of

---

[18] Graetz, *Popular History,* Vol. V, p. 63.

[19] Roth: *History of the Marranos*, pp. 242-3. & Roth: p. 244.

[20] Graetz, *Popular History,* Vol. V, p. 67. & Roth: *History of the Marranos*, p. 229. & Graetz, *Popular History,* Vol. V, p. 70-1.

the important places; their largest settlement was in Pernambuco. Trade and plantations were almost entirely in their hands, and in a short time they had accumulated great wealth. Amsterdam remained the center of trade and exchange, but more and more Jews moved to Brazil.[21]

In France, too, the Marranos managed to obtain great influence in trade and finance, but they were not allowed to practice their Judaism openly, instead having to appear entirely as Christians to the outside world.[22]

These migrations of the Marranos, their settlements, and their influence in the world of that time are so interesting that it would be worth writing an entire book about them. They laid the foundation for modern international Jewry.

It is not surprising that the Marranos also tried to gain a foothold in England. Since the expulsion of the Jews in 1290, England's economic structure had fundamentally changed. While England was more or less purely an agricultural state at the time of Edward I, the beginnings of its own significant industry can be seen under the rule of Queen Elizabeth. England's external power had also greatly increased. English ships plowed the seas all over the world. The preeminent position of Spain and Portugal, especially in the newly-discovered parts of the world, was in decline at the start of the 17th century, and England was increasingly proving herself to be one of Spain's most formidable opponents. All of this gave the Marranos a special incentive to settle in England.

Marranos in England

For a long time, it was unclear whether there was a large colony of Marranos in England at the beginning of the 17th century, but according to the latest research, this seems to be the case. First of all, it has already been indicated by James I's aforementioned expulsion law, but the work of the Jewish historian Lucien Wolf also shines a light on the situation. Wolf puts the earliest arrival of Marranos into England at 1493. To support this assertion, he refers to documentation in old state archives that allows the names of Jews to be identified.[23]

In England, however, the Marranos, even under the adopted cloak of Christianity, faced great difficulties in settling in larger numbers. The Marranos belonged to the Catholic Church. In England, however, due to ongoing issues with acceptance of the Reformation, certain laws had been passed to protect the new 'Church of England', which mainly fell into two categories. One punished the practice or propagation of a religious doctrine that was incompatible with the new Anglican dogma, the other punished non-

---

[21] Graetz, *Popular History,* Vol. V, p. 73-5.

[22] Graetz, *Popular History,* Vol. V, p. 75.

[23] Wolf: *Menasseh ben Israel,* p. xiv; *Crypto-Jews,* p. 57-8.

participation in Church of England services. The former provision was the Act of Supremacy of 1534 (renewed under Elizabeth I in 1558), the latter the Act of Uniformity of 1558.[24]

As Catholics, the Marranos were affected by both laws, and their outward display of Christianity was no longer of any use to them. However, after 1612, an infringement of the law against heresy no longer brought the same severe punishment. It must be said, nevertheless, that in those days one could never know whether some exceptional circumstance would lead to a stricter application of the law. In fact, this law can only truly be said to be toothless after it was amended by a special law in 1640 so that only clerical punishments could be imposed.[25]

The second category of law to enforce religious orthodoxy, the Act of Uniformity, is particularly interesting: in the event of non-compliance, or 'recusancy,' there was at first the risk of a moderate financial penalty, while later versions of the act brought a penalty of very severe fines [the Act of Persuasions 1581], or even imprisonment [the Popish Recusants Act 1592]. The Marranos neither desired nor were able to take part in the Church of England services, whether as Catholics or as Jews. But given that the laws applied to every person in England regardless of nationality, as long as said laws existed, the Marranos could not remain in England.[26]

In 1630, a peace treaty [commonly known today as the Treaty of Madrid (1630)] was concluded between England and Spain in a bid to settle their ongoing hostilities and to restore trade relations between the two nations. Among other things, the treaty stipulated a mutual obligation to fundamentally exempt from their respective religious laws nationals of the other's state who were in their country (or a third country) for the purposes of commerce. This secured access to England for the Marranos, and there can be little doubt that some of them settled in England shortly after the treaty came into force. It is perhaps not too bold to claim that the Marranos, with their great influence at the Spanish court, likely did everything they could to bring about this treaty between England and Spain, and perhaps initiated it themselves.

Our thesis regarding their influence may not even go as far as that of the Jewish historian Lucien Wolf, who claims that the Marranos 'played an important part in the story which culminated in the confusion of the Great Armada'. The Jewish historian Cecil Roth also states how a certain Jew, Hector Nunes [1520-1591], who served as a physician in England, who was well connected internationally due to his trading activities, and who enjoyed

---

[24] Henriques: *Return*, p. 17. Translator's note: I have added additional information to the text for clarity. Note that these 1558 Acts are sometimes referred to as 1559 Acts, as they were not signed into law until the following year.

[25] Henriques: *Return*, p. 17 ff.

[26] Henriques: *Return*, p. 29 ff. Translator's note: See also Hyamson: *History*, p. 128.

the complete confidence of both of Queen Elizabeth's great ministers, Burleigh and Walsingham, 'actually brought the latter the first news of the arrival of the Great Armada at Lisbon on its way to the English channel', thus enabling the English government to take countermeasures in good time.[27]

Although it is no longer possible to determine exactly when Marranos came to England in large numbers, it was probably not much later than 1635, given that, in 1655, the wealthiest and most influential of them, Antonio Fernandez Carvajal, was granted British residency by Cromwell. From Carvajal's surviving Patent of Denization, we learn that the Jewish merchant had 'for the space of twenties yeares and upwards been an Inhabitant in this nacon'.[28]

Antonio Fernandez Carvajal, the Rothschild of the Seventeenth Century

This chapter will be devoted to providing the reader with a detailed profile of the man known to posterity as Antonio Fernandez Carvajal, as the general history of the Jews in England up until the year 1655 can effectively be told in terms of the commercial dealings of this singular figure. Carvajal, known in his own community as Abraham Israel Carvajal, was also the first member of his people in England to assist the government in financial matters. Throughout the centuries that followed, we find other Jews, similar to Carvajal, being financial advisors to the English government and exercising considerable influence in government affairs of all kinds.

When he was young, Carvajal had lived in Fundão, one of the then commercial centers of Portugal with a large colony of Marranos. The persecution of the Inquisition caused him to leave Portugal and he apparently took refuge in the Canary Islands, where trade and the collection of taxes were then almost exclusively in the hands of the Marranos.[29] There is no precise information about the reason for his moving to England, but it can safely be assumed that it was to develop trade between England and Spain.

As is well known, in Spain the production of manufactured goods experienced an ever-greater decline due to the large quantities of gold and sil-

---

[27] Henriques: *Return*, pp. 31-32. & Wolf: *Menasseh ben Israel*, p. xv. Translator's note: QVOS. & Roth: *History of the Marranos*, p. 256. Translator's note: QVOS. Scholars today widely recognize Nunes' role as a diplomat and spy. As an interesting side note, Nunes illegally bought a black African to be his slave in London after the unfortunate man had been captured from the Spanish, and brought to England on an English ship. When the man refused to be Nunes' slave, the doctor attempted to bring a court case against him, but under English law he could not force the unnamed African man to 'tarry and serve' him. Nunes also had African female 'servants' working for him in his London home. See the following article by Miranda Kaufmann, specialist in Black British history, for further information: www.ourmigrationstory.org.uk/oms/african-freedom-in-tudor-england-dr-hector-nuness-request
[28] Wolf: *First English Jew*, p. 45. Translator's note: QVOS.
[29] Wolf: *First English Jew*, pp. 14-5; *Crypto-Jews*, p. 77 ff.

ver being imported from the newly discovered Americas, as the wealth that poured into the country caused interest in any kind of work to dwindle accordingly. England, on the other hand, was in the process of building up her industry and needed raw commodities such as wool and minerals, which she hoped to obtain from Spain. In a short time, lively trade relations were established between the two countries, and the English merchant made big profits from these transactions, with returns of up to 100% being by no means uncommon. On the Spanish side, business was mostly carried out by Marranos, while the English counter-party initially consisted almost entirely of Englishmen, who were later replaced more and more by Marranos until finally the trade was almost entirely in Marrano hands. Carvajal was probably induced by the promise of rich pickings to make his way to England.[30]

He must have experienced a rapid rise in England, because he soon had his own ships with which he traded not only in Spain, but also in the East and West Indies, Brazil, Syria, and all distant parts of the world wherever there was trade to be carried out and Marranos had settled. He had representatives in every major trading center on the European continent, and where he did not have his own agents, he found all of the necessary support from the Marranos who lived there.[31]

Apparently he was on good terms with the English government from the earliest days, because when a complaint was made against him in 1645 for 'recusancy', that is, failing to comply with the law regarding attendance of [Anglican] church services, not even a preliminary investigation was opened. And this despite the fact that, even if the previously described agreement with Spain existed, it was more than doubtful that this law also applied to Carvajal as a Portuguese national, especially since there was no express agreement to this effect. The complainant, Will Sherman, was even summoned to the House of Lords and roundly upbraided for his pains. This reaction by officialdom appears particularly unusual when one considers the conditions in England at the time, which were anything but favorable to foreigners. However, when one further learns that Carvajal had the closest relations with a government minister, it is not difficult to draw the necessary conclusions about the outcome of the criminal complaint and his connection to the government. The government's favoring of Carvajal in later times is quite blatant.[32]

In 1650, war broke out between England and Portugal. As a Portuguese subject, Carvajal was an enemy alien and there was nothing to stop the state from confiscating all of his assets. However, not only was he spared such a

---

[30] Baker, p. 3 ff.
[31] Wolf: *First English Jew*, p. 16.
[32] Henriques: *Return*, pp. 31-2. & Wolf: *Crypto-Jews*, p. 56; *Hist. Com Reports*, VI, p. 42. See also Hyamson: *History*, p. 136. & Wolf: *Crypto-Jews*, p. 56.

fate, but he was also assured by a State Council resolution of 4 September 1650 that he would not be troubled and that he could continue his trade. It is left to the reader to surmise how Carvajal came to receive such favor. Whatever the case, it is likely that his money played a significant role.[33]

Carvajal abused his special government-granted position by having goods from Portuguese—likely Jewish—merchants, who were friends of his and who as enemy aliens were no longer able to trade in England, entered under his name in the customs register. Apparently the government was informed of this and initiated extensive investigations against him. Wolf, who studied Carvajal's life in detail, could not discover the outcome of the criminal proceedings. In his opinion, the courts probably did not find anything incriminating against him, but this does not seem to entirely correlate with the documents we have seen. The remaining minutes of the Council of State clearly show that the confiscated goods were not released because of the strong suspicion against him. According to the minutes of 9 October 1650, a postponement apparently took place because the relevant witnesses were not present, but the main hearing took place on 11 October 1650. Carvajal was questioned closely by the Admiralty Committee, with the authorities particularly desirous to know whether the confiscated goods really belonged to him:[34]

> [A]nd upon examination, Fernandez would give no positive answer whether the bayes in question were his own proper goods, and whether he did not declare that, in case it should be proved that any other had an interest in them, his whole estate should be liable to confiscation; but at last confessed that he bought them with his own money, upon his own account, and that he intended to send 38 pieces of the bayes to Francisco Botelio Chacone and Thome Botelio Silveria, in Portugal, but on account of the troubles there, they ordered him last June to forbear doing so, and to remit the money to Holland. This, with the affidavit annexed, is all his answer.
>
> The committee further asking him whether 38 pieces of the bayes in question were shipped; he answered, no; also whether he shipped any for Lisbon in [to?] the Brazil merchant, to which he replied that 40 pieces were consigned to the parties aforesaid, and that the 38 pieces were to be consigned to the same parties, had he not received orders to the contrary. The committee therefore think that the said bayes still remain under suspicion and should not be delivered.[35]

---

[33] Wolf: *First English Jew*, p. 28; *Calendar of State Papers*, Vol. 1650, p. 558.

[34] *Calendar of State Papers*, Vol. 1650, p. 377. & Vol. 1650, p. 380.

[35] *Calendar of State Papers*, Vol. 1650, p. 380. Translator's note: QVOS.

The case mentioned was apparently not the only one. Already on 31 October of the same year, we find a report according to which Carvajal also claimed that another shipment of goods belonged to him and not to certain Portuguese merchants. Unfortunately, nothing can be determined about the outcome of this inquiry. However, given his relationship with the government, it was probably not too difficult for him to have the proceedings dropped, as in a much more serious criminal case in which he had still not been brought to justice after more than a year.

In 1658, a consignment of a hundred tons of West Indian logwood from the Canary Islands belonging to Carvajal, valued at around £15,000, was seized by customs authorities. The merchant was informed of the confiscation and informed that the logwood would only be delivered upon a specific declaratory document from the government. The report from the customs officer responsible, Timothy Whiting, shows that the seizure was due to a gross understatement of the timber's real value. Instead of dealing with the customs authorities, Carvajal filed a charge against the enforcement officer himself, causing him to be arrested. The merchant worked with a number of other Marranos and also Englishmen to do this, and so was able to ensure that the official in question was only allowed to go free if he provided security.

Seeing however that Whiting had managed to post bail, Carvajal then turned to the Admiralty court to get his foe out of the way. Here, based on forged evidence, he managed to get the officer arrested again and taken to an obscure place where he could not even get in touch with friends to tell them of his predicament. The poor man was only released after three days. In the meantime, Carvajal had used the help of confederates to break open the government warehouse and move all of the logwood to an unknown location.

From the official submission to Cromwell that has come down to us, we also see that the customs authorities demanded severe punishment. It was rightly pointed out that, if this punishment were not to take place, the most unpleasant consequences would result for future attempts at upholding the law. The petitioner, Timothy Whiting himself, stated that:

> [I]f such high Actings and misdemeanours of the sayd Ferdinando, and his Complices, shall goe unpunisht, it wil bee a great discouragement to the officers of your Highnes, in discharge of Their Dutys and, an emboldning to Merchants and others (as alredy it is) to withdraw their Customes, and Duty, and to committ the like outrages for the time to come.[36]

---

[36] *Calendar of State Papers*, Vol. 1658/1659, p. 116; Wolf: *First English Jew*, p. 38. Translator's note: QVOS (Wolf). Wolf (p. 23) also obliquely admits to Carvajal's guilt in the crime (or 'highhanded proceeding', to use Wolf's phrase), which by the author's slick presentation of events sounds like a cross between a jape and a fit of spleen: 'His nature was choleric even in old age, for in 1658, when he had a dispute with the Commissioners

Although this petition for justice was made on 19 August 1658, there is not
the slightest evidence of any punitive measure against Carvajal leading up to
the news of his death in November 1659. Hyamson claims that there was a
case pending under Richard Cromwell, Oliver Cromwell's son, but that it
was ended by the merchant's demise. However, he does not provide a source
for this claim. All in all, it is reasonable to assume that Carvajal prevented
consequences against himself due to his friends in high places. It is not even
known if he was forced to return the stolen logwood.[37]

Apparently Carvajal was not particularly ethical in his other business
dealings either, as shown by the following court case that has come down to
us. In 1642, a ship arrived in Southampton with a valuable cargo. Due to a
notification that the ship and cargo had been brought there without the owner's consent, the government initially seized the ship and cargo and later
handed them over to the recipients in return for a deposit of £500,000.

Part of the cargo, which actually belonged to the merchant de Lazon,
was sold by Carvajal as agent for a certain Diaz of Rouen, and the purchase
money received was supposedly sent to third parties in Spain. In any case, he
did everything he could to avoid giving justice to the real owner, who spent
three years trying to enforce his claims in England. It was bad enough that he
was left with nothing to live on—but then he was even thrown into prison
for a year because of debts that had arisen as a result of the delay in the trial.
It is not clear from the document why de Lazon was unable to enforce his
claims, but the official report leaves no doubt that he was badly wronged.[38]

In any event, based on the substance of the official account of this case,
de Lazon's ownership and the inexplicable treatment he received in this matter are perfectly clear. Then again, since Carvajal's involvement and his interests, which are undoubtedly contrary to de Lazon's claim, have also been
proven, de Lazon's claim that Carvajal made false representation is likely to
be correct. Perhaps it is also due to the latter's influence with the English authorities that de Lazon only gained what was rightfully his after three years.

It is interesting for Jewish historiography that this character flaw of the
so-called 'first English Jew' has not been properly discussed by such a diligent researcher as Wolf. Perhaps he was too embarrassed by these facts, especially since he makes the following leading statement about Carvajal's

---

of Customs over a cargo of logwood which had been seized by them, he collected a number of his friends, secured the Customs surveyor on board one of his ships, broke open the
Government warehouses, and carried off his merchandise. When he died, a special committee of the Council of State, which had originally been presided over Richard Cromwell,
was enquiring into this highhanded proceeding.'

[37] Wolf: *First English Jew*, p. 22. & Hyamson: *History*, p. 137. Translator's note: It is
likely that Hyamson used Wolf as his source (see note 63).

[38] See Wolf: *First English Jew*, Appendix, for a reproduction of the extant original documents of the case.

character: 'For the rest, his epitaph bears testimony to his hospitality, his generosity to the poor, his truthfulness, and his high sense of honor.'[39] The above statements are sufficient to show Carvajal's international connections and his influence on the English government.

In addition to Carvajal, it is also worth mentioning the singular personages of Simon [Jacob] de Caceres and Henrique Mendes da Costa. Caceres was born in Amsterdam and had travelled all over the world. He had seemingly unlimited trading connections, and his main interests lay not only in London and Hamburg, but also in the West Indies and South America. He later served as Cromwell's economic advisor on certain colonial matters and also served the king of Denmark and Queen Christine of Sweden in a similar capacity.[40]

Mendes was heavily involved in the Jewish banks of Lisbon and Antwerp, which formed a huge corporation and played the same role in Europe at the end of the 16th century as the Rothschild banking house did in the 19th and 20th centuries. One of Mendes' relatives, Joseph Nasi, conquered Cyprus for the Turks and was later made Duke of Naxos and Prince of the Cyclades. Mendes was also a close collaborator of Carvajal. Although there are still many wealthy Jews based in England with international connections who could be discussed, for the purposes of this study we shall limit ourselves to two: Antonio Rodrigues Robles and Augustin Coronel Chacon, who served as secret agents for the English Royalists during Cromwell's reign.[41]

After a great deal of research, the Jewish historian Lucien Wolf discovered that only about 26 male Marranos had settled in England by the year 1655.[42] We have no reason to reject this estimate, but in the course of our presentation of Jewish history under Cromwell we will show the level of influence that this colony of Jews, so small in number yet so powerful in

---

[39] Wolf: *First English Jew*, p. 23. Translator's note: QVOS. As for the author's supposition that Wolf was 'too embarrassed' to tell the truth, one should also consider the alternative suppositions: 1) ethnocentric self-deception, or 2) this was a cynical exercise in ethnic propaganda. The Jewish Hyamson (*History*, pp. 136-7) has the following apologia for Carvajal's criminal behaviour: 'Carvajal's character seems to have partaken more of the Spaniard than of the Jew.' (!)

[40] Wolf: *Crypto-Jews*, pp. 73-4; *American Elements*, p. 97; *Re-Settlement*, p. 5; Hyamson: *History*, p. 137.

[41] Wolf: *Re-Settlement*, p. 5. Hyamson: *History*, p. 137. & Wolf: *Crypto-Jews*, pp. 74-5.

[42] Wolf: *Crypto-Jews*, p. 67. Translator's note: It should be borne it mind that many, if not most, of these men would be heads of family, the rest of the family not being counted in this tally. In addition, elsewhere (*Re-Settlement*; *Jewish Chronicle*, 9/12/1887, p. 14) Wolf has said the following regarding Jewish numbers prior to the Cromwellian negotiations: 'How many more Jews there were in London at this time it is impossible to say. We many assume, however, that for everyone who can be identified there were at least two or three who baffle detection, and these, with their wives and children, would make a community of about two hundred souls.'

resources, had on the politics of England. Without the need for Wolf's careful research, it can be taken as a certainty that the Marranos secretly adhered to their Jewish faith and probably also had some kind of synagogue, because wherever there were Marranos in the world, they posed as Christians to wider society, while secretly observing the rites and ceremonies of Judaism.[43]

In conclusion, we can be sure that there was a small but powerful group of Marranos who had already settled in England at the start of the Jews' political maneuvering under Cromwell.

Philo-Semitic Puritanism

In 1652, civil war broke out in England, a war which led Charles I to the scaffold and Cromwell to power. It was mainly the Puritan faction among the Parliamentarians [also known as the Roundheads] to whom the revolution owed its victorious outcome. In the words of the Jewish historian Heinrich Graetz, who clearly sympathized with the Puritans:

> He [Cromwell] and his army fought for religious liberty for themselves and others. He and his officers were not bloodthirsty mercenaries in search of booty, but warriors filled with the spirit of God, who dreamed of establishing a theocracy and undertook its accomplishment. The Puritan warriors, like the Maccabeans of old, went to battle with the praise of God in their mouths and the sword in their hands. Cromwell and his soldiers read the Bible before and after an engagement.
>
> But the 'Roundheads' were inspired to courage and enthusiasm not by the New but solely by the Old Testament. The Christian Bible, with its Essenic, monkish forms, offered no model for warriors who had to declare war on a perjured king, a faithless aristocracy and unholy priests. Only the great heroic figures of the Old Testament who had the fear of God in their hearts while fighting, sword in hand, for their God and their nation could serve as a model for the Puritans; the judges who freed their people from the foreign yoke; Saul, David, Joab, who routed the enemies of their nation; Jehu, who exterminated an idolatrous and wicked dynasty—such were the favorite heroes of the Puritanic warriors. Each verse of the books of Joshua, Judges, Samuel, and Kings mirrored their own situation; each Psalm seemed peculiarly adapted to their own condition. Oliver Cromwell seemed another Gideon who, at first reluctant in obeying the voice of God, afterward routed the hea-

---

[43] Wolf: *Crypto-Jews*, p. 55 ff.

then hordes with heroic courage, or another Judas Maccabeus, who converted a handful of martyrs into a victorious army.[44]

Original English names were replaced by Jewish ones from the Old Testament, and the Lion of Judah was placed on the victorious banners of the Puritans. The period under Stuart rule was known as the 'Egyptian Bondage'. It was even seriously suggested that Saturday should replace Sunday as the real Sabbath. English people travelled the continent to have learned conversations with rabbis, and there were even Puritans who converted to Judaism. Given all of this, it is not surprising that in Puritan circles, which had become the dominant force in the English Commonwealth since 1649, there was a keen interest in the Jews living on the Continent.

All in all, there was little real difference between the Puritans and the Jews. In both we find the closest connection between business and religion and the rationalization of life. Both adhere to the principle that everything that is necessary for good business is also morally justified. Thus Werner Sombart came to the conclusion that 'Puritanism *is* Judaism'.[45]

With their admiration for the Jews, the Puritans could not imagine that the desired conversion of the Jews to Christianity, which was often sought after, was based on a lack of goodwill towards the Jews. Rather, they considered the previous methods used to attempt this to be wrongheaded. In their view, the Jews had been unjustly ill-treated at all times in history, as the scholar and politician John Sadler, who was close to Cromwell, publicly expressed. As a result, above all, kind treatment of the Jews was demanded. The Puritans viewed conversion attempts through missions and other efforts on the continent as inexpedient, and wanted the Jews to come to England in as large numbers as possible in order to make it clear to them with word and deed the necessity of converting to Christianity. As early as 1614, a certain Leonard Busher published an open letter to the king and Parliament, which largely dealt with this question. Persecution, he argued, would only make the Jews more obstinate:[46]

> ...because if persecution be not laid downe, and liberty of conscience set up, then cannot the Jewes, nor any strangers, nor others contrary mynded be ever converted in our Land: for so long as they know a fore hand, that they shal be forced to beleeve against their consciences, they wil never seeke to inhabit

---

[44] Graetz, Vol. V, pp. 102-3. Translator's note: QVOS.

[45] Hyamson: *History*, pp. 129-30. & Hyamson: *British Projects*, p. 1 ff. & Sombart, p. 249. Translator's note: QVOS.

[46] Sadler: *Rights of the Kingdom*, p. 74. Translator's note: There appears to be an error with this reference. & Godwin, Vol. IV, p. 245.

there: by which meanes you keep them from the Apostolic faith,
if the Apostolic faith bee onely taught where persecution is.[47]

These statements, which were not published until 1646, reinforced the Puritans' pro-Jewish stance. Sir Edward Spencer's optimistic treatise on the topic, published in 1650, also contributed strongly to this general attitude. In this member of Parliament's view, which he addressed to the Jewish activist Menasseh ben Israel, '...it will be a very glorious action, if wee can convert your Nation of the *Jewes* to the fulnesse of true beliefe. And indeed I beleeve we are the likelyest Nation under Heaven to doe it.'

This also reflects the Puritan belief, which is still widespread in England today, that the British are God's chosen people. Spencer formulated the conditions under which the Jews should come to England, many of which obviously amount to giving them advantages in the event of conversion. They were to be allowed to trade throughout England, but he proposed double taxation as long as they belonged to the Jewish religion. He did not want to allow Jewish fraternities or similar associations, just as marriages between Jews and Christians were to be banned. Even a large portion of the Puritan clergy supported Jewish readmission, as Hyamson points out and as we shall see later.[48]

In addition to all of these idealistic voices, as always in England, there were also pragmatic ones, and it was publicly admitted that the Jews had to be allowed back into England in order to improve trade. As well as business activity, the Jews were also expected to bring large amounts of capital into the country.[49]

Numerous pamphlets published in favor of the Jews' readmittance to England influenced public opinion then as now. Sometimes it seems as if the art of printing was invented for the Jews, because we all know to what extent they use this facility to serve their agenda. So from that point in history onwards, one sees rivers of printer's ink pour out in England whenever the Jews want to accomplish something. Since newspapers were still in their earliest infancy at that time, they were out of the question for reaching the people, and it was the pamphlets alone that made the no small contribution to the return of Jews to England.

Busher's aforementioned treatise of 1614, framed as an open letter, is probably the earliest of the form. Among other treatises, one worthy of men-

---

[47] Busher: *Religions Peace*, p 7. Translator's note: Quotation reproduced verbatim from original 1614 source.

[48] Spencer, p. 2. Translator's note: QVOS. & Hyamson: *History*, p. 131.

[49] Nicholas, p. 15. Translator's note: (quoted from source) 'That our receiving them again, and giving them all possible satisfaction, and restoring them to commerce in this kingdom, may be exemplary to other Nations that have done them, and continue to do them wrong...'

tion is the 1647 tract by Hugh Peters, *A Word for the Army, and Two Words to the Kingdom*. It is notable because of the author's close association with Cromwell. Peters was the army chaplain and more or less Cromwell's pastor. He played a significant role in the condemnation of Charles I, for which he was executed after the return of the Stuarts in 1660.[50]

In all of the various writings of that period, one should not forget the work published by pamphleteer Edward Nicholas in 1648. Nicholas' work is an incomprehensible screed, and excerpts such as the following are typical of its style:

> But the sin principally intended here, is, The strict and cruel Laws now in force against the most honorable Nation of the world, the Nation of the Jews, a people chosen by God, as appears by the many and large expressions of his favour to them, stiling them, *His Gems, his first-born, a precious people above all peoples of the earth, a kingdom of priests, an holy people unto himself*. And further saith, they are his own servants, and should not be in bondage to any, being onely to serve six years, and the seventh to go out free, and in the year of Jubile, every man was to return to his inheritance: But above all, that priviledge of theirs, the benefit whereof hath an influence on all the faithful, and redounds to their happiness, *That in thee and thy seed shall all the nations of the earth be blessed:* So strong an obligation are we bound in to them through Gods mercy.[51]

In his opinion, it was time to repeal the laws that were unfavorable to Jews. He hoped that men would soon arise in England who would put an end to such infamy. The author further believed that all the misery of the English civil wars of that time was God's vengeance for the persecution of His holy favorites. It would therefore be the duty of everyone to do everything in their power to atone for the innocently shed blood of the Jews and to bring about a close community and friendship with them.[52]

To this day, it is unclear who was behind the name 'Edward Nicholas.' Was it King Charles I's secretary, Sir Edward Nicholas, or was it a Marrano hiding behind this pseudonym? Some writers suspect that the man behind this pro-Jewish writing was the Jew Menasseh ben Israel, who is the subject

---

[50] Hyamson: *History*, p. 132.
[51] Nicholas, p. 4. Translator's note: QVOS.
[52] Nicholas, p. 6 ff.

of a later chapter. Although definitive evidence to prove the case is lacking, circumstantial evidence lends plausibility to the latter hypothesis.[53]

A book by Roger Williams, the famous Baptist, also caused a stir. Williams had already founded a community in America in which there was unrestricted freedom of belief and conscience. In his publications, he strongly advocated for the Jews. They might be heretics, he wrote, but that did not in itself mean that they could not become good citizens:

> For who knows not but that many seducing teachers, either of the paganish, Jewish, Turkish, or anti-Christian religion, may be clear and free from scandalous offences in their life, as also from disobedience to the civil laws of a state? Yea, the answerer himself hath elsewhere granted, that if the laws of a civil state be not broken, the peace is not broken.[54]

The remarks of the aforementioned scholar and politician John Sadler deserve particular interest. As a friend of Cromwell's, he may have had a considerable influence on the Lord Protector; his thoughts are more than strange to us. It is an extensive work that is difficult to read due to its incoherent structure. He may have been one of the first to claim that the English were descended from the Israelites, and he believes he can find many similarities between English and Israelite laws and customs. The constitutional arrangement under the previous English kings was that decisions about war and peace were more or less dependent on the decisions of the Great Council [*Magnum Concilium*], which could be compared with the power of the Sanhedrin. It is therefore not surprising that Sadler was extremely fond of the Jews and stood up for them.

It is strange that in England this doctrine about the ancestry of the British, known as 'British Israelism' or 'Anglo-Israelism,' was not simply dismissed as legend. Instead, scholars such as Rogers and Milner, Burt, Shirley Smith—to name a few—have written about the topic. People even go as far as to claim that the current British royal family is directly descended from the house of King David. Not only does this question haunt the minds of scholars, but even today there is an association in England founded to propagate this idea. Their speakers are still trying to convince their listeners of the correctness of this theory at the famous Speaker's Corner in Hyde Park, close to Marble Arch. Ancient and biblical prophesies, for example, the idea that the Jews should be scattered all over the world and that the sun should never set on the empire, are applied to Great Britain. One may smile at such

---

[53] Hyamson: *History*, p. 132, note 1.
[54] Williams, *The Bloudy Tenent*, p. 141. Translator's note: QVOS (1848 reproduction – see Bibliography).

teachings, but one thing is certain: the Jews welcome them, because they can only serve the Jewish cause in England. How much greater an impression must Sadler's book have made on the Puritans, who were favorable to the Jews, especially since they viewed themselves as God's chosen people.[55]

Of the large number of pro-Jewish pamphlets, it is worth mentioning the one written by John Dury, whose aim was to unite all of the different sects of Protestantism. For this purpose, he travelled all over Europe and tried to overcome the greatest difficulties. Because of this, he became very well known, and as a result many people paid attention to his statements on the Jewish Question. This overview of the abundant literature produced in the first half of the 17th century will suffice for our purposes.[56]

There were also pamphlets which were fundamentally in favor of allowing Jews to live in England, but which on the other hand openly pointed out the downsides to this. In his writing, John Weemse described to his compatriots the current despicable condition of the Jews, but believed that this could be positively influenced by baptism. The prerequisite, of course, was that the Christians themselves did not put too many obstacles in the way of the Jews. Later, Christians and Jews would only have one church, which wouldn't be difficult, especially since Jesus Christ himself was a Jew.[57]

We have seen that there was no lack of philo-Semitic literature, which gradually prepared the ground for Jewish endeavors. So it is not surprising that we see the following news at the end of 1648:

> Monday, Decem. 25.: Notice was given of what passed in the Councell of Mechanicke at Whitehall on Saturday, where they voted a toleration of all religions whatsoever, not excepting Turkes nor Papists nor Jewes.' *Pragmaticus*, Dec. 19-26.[58]

This decision was also endorsed by the Council of War.

On 5 January 1649, a formal petition for the readmission of the Jews was presented to Lord Fairfax and the General Council. It came from Johanna Cartwright, a widow, and her son Ebenezer, two Puritans who had settled in Amsterdam. They probably belonged to the aforementioned category of Puritans who revered the Jewish religion so much that they either converted to this faith themselves or lived completely under its spell. Given this and the fact that the large Jewish community in Amsterdam was the soul of the resettlement effort, one can assume that the request was made at the instigation of the Jews there. The Cartwrights did not just hand over the petition, but had it

---

[55] Sadler, p. 8 ff. & p. 47 ff.
[56] Levy, p. 76.
[57] Weemse, p. 295 ff. & p. 339 ff. & p. 370. & p. 378.
[58] Clarke Papers, Vol. II, p. 172, note A. Translator's note: QVOS. Note also the date of the event, evidencing the Puritan ban on Christmas.

printed and published [*The Petition of the Jews* (1649)], an additional factor which strongly indicates that the Jews had a hand in proceedings.[59]

In the aforementioned petition, the applicants complained of the 'intolerable cruelty of this our English nation' which had caused Jewish suffering prior to the Expulsion, suffering for which England should seek to appease the wrath of God for the 'innocent blood shed' by repealing 'the cruel, inhumane Statute of banishment' and readmitting the Jews to England 'under the Christian banner of charity and brotherly love'. This was especially important, given that the time of Second Coming 'draweth nigh', which would see the Jews 'come to know the Emanuell, the Lord of light, life and glory' and be given their promised land. In consequence, the petition hoped that, 'this nation of ENGLAND, with the inhabitants of the Nether-lands, shall be the first and readiest to transport IZRAELLS Sons & Daughters in their Ships to the Land promised to their fore-Fathers, ABRAHAM, ISAAC and JACOB, for an everlasting inheritance'.[60]

Contrary to expectations, the General Council's response was disappointing for the Jews and their fellow travelers. The Council agreed in principle to consider the petition favorably, 'with a promise to take it into speedy consideration when the present more publick affairs are dispatched'. Unfortunately for the petitioners, the situation at that time was extremely tense, with the ongoing proceedings against King Charles I, his subsequent execution, and the settlement of the state, all of which took up the totality of the government's energies for a long time.[61]

Perhaps the active assistance of the Jews in the above petition can also be inferred from the fact that they themselves submitted a similar application to the Council of War at almost the same time. In particular, they wanted the 1290 Edict of Expulsion to be repealed. The Jews did not ask permission for anything, but rather proposed a transactional arrangement, in which they would pay £500,000, an enormous sum for the time. However, this cash offer came with strings attached, namely, the almost incredible condition that St. Paul's Cathedral and the Bodleian Library in Oxford would be given to the Jews as their own property for their free use. As is well known, St. Paul's Cathedral is one of the largest English national shrines alongside Westminster Abbey, while the Bodleian Library is one of the five largest libraries in England. The Jews wanted to turn the cathedral into a synagogue and convert the library into a Jewish school.

---

[59] Wolf: *Re-Settlement*, p. 7.
[60] *Clarke Papers*, Vol. II. p. 172, note A; Wolf: *American Elements*, pp. 87-8. Translator's note: All quoted elements reproduced verbatim from Wolf, who reproduces the full petition as it was printed in the 1649 pamphlet.
[61] Hyamson: *History*, p. 134. Translator's note: Quoted element as per previous translator's note.

The negotiations of 1649 failed, although not because of a lack of willingness on the part of the English government. On the contrary, the government was only too willing to accept this deal in principle, the only sticking point being the price, which it considered too low, and a counter-offer was made for £700,000 or, according to another report, as much as £800,000. Perhaps there was no agreement on the price, or perhaps there was too much public indignation to allow the sale of these national shrines.[62]

In light of this information, the contemporary pamphlet *The last damnable Designe of Cromwell and Ireton and their Junto or Caball* is very revealing, as the following excerpt shows:

> Their next designe is, to Plunder, and Dis-arme the City of London, and all the Country round about; thereby to disable them to rise when the Army removes, but not to the use of the Souldiers, (although they greedily expect the first Week in *February* the time appointed) from whom they will redeeme the Plunder at an easie rate; and so sell it in bulk to the Jewes, whom they have lately admitted to set up their banks, and magazins of Trade amongst us, contrary to an Act of Parliament for their banishment; and these shall be their Merchants to buy off for ready money, (to maintain such Warres as their violent proceedings will inevitably bring upon them) not only all Sequestred, and Plundred goods, but also the very Bodies of Men, Women, and Children, whole Families taken Prisoners for sale, of whom these Jewish Merchants shall keep a constant traffique with the *Turks*, *Moores*, and other *Mahometans;* the *Barbadus*, and other *English* Plantations being already cloyed with *Welch*, *Scottish*, *Colchester* and other Prisoners imposed by way of sale upon the Adventurers...[63]

Quite apart from what the excerpt reveals about the callous venality of the Interregnum, the last sentence is of particular interest, because it indicates that the government of the time had no moral quandary about selling politically inconvenient families to the Jews, which meant that real human trafficking was going on. It is unfortunate that further information about this

---

[62] Walker, Vol. II, p. 60; Carte, Vol. I, p. 276; Tovey, p. 259; Blunt, p. 68; Menteith, p. 473; Picciotto, p. 25; *Hansard*, Vol. 125, p. 87 [Jewish Disabilities Bill (HC Debate 11 March 1853)]; *Hansard*, Vol. 141, p. 726 ff. [Oath of Abjuration Bill – HC Debate 9 April 1856]. Blunt also refers to a letter from Thurloe. His citation is correct except for the volume and page number. It is not Vol. III, p. 357, but Vol. I, p. 387. Translator's note: The sources (e.g. Menteith) also reveal that the Jews' purchase offer was solicited by Hugh Peters and Harry Marten, who acted as the Jews' brokers in the proposed deal.

[63] Walker, Vol. II, pp. 61-2. Translator's note: QVOS.

practice could not be found. However, based on the facts we know about modern trafficking in woman and girls [known historically as the 'white slave trade'], it is not surprising that it was the Jews who carried out this despicable commerce.

The pamphlet certainly had its impact on public opinion, which in turn contributed to the negotiations with the Jews being officially broken off, because the rise in popular indignation made further negotiations untenable. Apparently, however the negotiations never came to a complete standstill, because in the state papers of John Thurloe, the first secretary to the Council of State and head of intelligence under Oliver Cromwell, there is a letter dated 29 July 1653, intercepted while Thurloe was in the post of spymaster, according to which discussions on Jewish readmission were still ongoing at that time:

> There hath beene severall motions in the house, that all mariges since 1647 should be null; and that the Jews might bee admitted to trade as well as in Holland; and that all cathedrals should be forthwith pul'd downe; but there is nothing yet done therein, nor in many other things had in consultation, that may be very commodious for the commonwelth.[64]

In 1654, we hear of yet another official petition. On 16 October 1654, the French ambassador in Holland wrote to his colleague in London that 'a Jew of Amsterdam hath informed me for certain, that the three generals of the fleet have presented a petition to his highness the protector, to obtain, that their nation may be received in England, to draw the commerce hither'. Whether the Jew's statement was correct remains to be seen. In any case, it is interesting that the French ambassador received this communication from a Hebrew in Amsterdam, which shows that the Jews were aware of the plan of the English naval commanders and were therefore undoubtedly involved in this action, if not the actual authors of it.[65]

Oliver Cromwell

The year 1655 would see the greatest efforts of the Jews and their allies to gain admission to England. But before we deal with this history in detail, it is instructive to give the reader a rundown of the two leading men involved insofar as is relevant to the subject under discussion. It was Cromwell who threw his entire public reputation into the balance on behalf of the Jews and who sided with their leader Menasseh ben Israel.

---

[64] *State Papers of John Thurloe*, Vol. I, p. 387. Translator's note: QVOS.
[65] *State Papers of John Thurloe*, Vol. II, p. 652. Translator's note: QVOS.

Numerous works on the subject of Cromwell's character have come from both professional and non-professional sources, so we shall refrain from making a similar attempt here. Rather, we shall limit ourselves to examining the question of why Cromwell championed the Jewish cause.

As a Puritan, he was sympathetic towards the Jewish religion and not only felt a connection to it, but also a sense of reverence. Whether this is only out of idealism remains to be seen. He was probably one of those who hoped that the Jews would be won over to Christianity through hospitable treatment and religious freedom, especially since the teachings of the Puritans must have been attractive to Jews.[66]

He was inclined to grant the greatest freedom of religion as long as the religious community in question declared that it would never attempt to interfere in affairs of state. When Quaker patriarch George Fox met Cromwell, the first thing he had to do was sign a pledge 'not to take up a carnal Sword or Weapon against him or the Government, as it then was.' George Fox obliged and Cromwell even later became his friend.[67]

Based on his principle that the state is the highest authority in a country and that everyone can be saved in their own way, it is understandable that Cromwell had nothing against granting rights to the Jews in England. However, even his power as Lord Protector was not great enough to prevail over the will of the people on this issue.[68]

His pro-Jewish attitude was further strengthened by the fact that he had like-minded advisors around him. The latter included the aforementioned Thurloe, who, as his secretary, understandably had extensive influence on the Jewish negotiations, as can be seen from the content of his surviving letters. Cromwell's close associates also included the aforementioned Hugh Peters, his famous army chaplain who was very active in politics, Harry Marten, who was also a member of the Protector's Privy Council, and John Sadler, who is likely to have influenced Cromwell on the Jewish Question through his aforementioned book.[69] So one should not really be surprised that Cromwell turned out to be the greatest advocate for the Jews of the period, although other considerations may also have guided him towards this stance.

His main aim was to make England great and strong, which in his view required not only military power but also the supremacy of English trade in the world. When Cromwell came to power, this was out of the question because the Dutch Republic was the hegemon of global trade at that time. England had been financially depleted by its long and bloody civil wars and was

---

[66] Graetz, Vol. V, p. 112; Fletcher, p. 230; Godwin, Vol. IV, p. 245.

[67] Ranke: *History of England*, Vol. III, p. 151. Translator's note: QVOS.

[68] Ranke: *History of England*, Vol. III, pp. 151-2. Translator's note: As Ranke put it, Cromwell was tolerant of any religious doctrine so long as it 'put forward no claim to a share of political authority, and neither destroyed nor disturbed the public peace'.

[69] *State Papers of John Thurloe*, Vol. IV, pp. 308, 321. & Graetz, Vol. V, p. 113.

unable to achieve the success she desired on her own. It therefore seemed natural to Cromwell to look for foreign support, which he hoped to find among the Jews of the world. As has already been explained, even back then Judaism had a strong global trade network. The Spanish and Portuguese trade as well as the all-important Levant trade lay in Jewish hands, and both the Dutch East and West India Companies were largely controlled by Jews. The global trade in gold and silver bullion was almost completely controlled by the Hebrews, just as they also had major interests in the shipping of all countries.[70]

Cromwell was very well informed on all of these matters through contacts in the small Jewish community in London, as this community itself had important trading relationships with all of the major countries; in other words, even at this time there was hardly a branch of English international trade in which Jewish capital was not involved. However, Cromwell wanted increased Jewish immigration, especially from Holland, as he attributed Amsterdam's prosperity at least in part to the Jews. So if he moved the Jews from there to London, his hope was that levels of English trade would rise, just as levels of Dutch trade would correspondingly fall.[71]

Jewish historians cannot do enough to point out the role of Jews in the rise of England. Wolf comments on this as follows:

> Thus, at the very moment when Spain was on the threshold of a brilliant epoch of colonial expansion—which, if wisely managed, might have given her as wide a dominion as is enjoyed by Great Britain to-day—she had not only depleted herself of a numerous and valuable portion of her industrial population, but had raised up, both within and without her borders, many hundreds of thousands of embittered and insidious foes, who strove against her by every means in their power and who enjoyed peculiar facilities for gratifying their just enmity. And with every step in the extension of Iberian conquests, the Marranos extended their counteracting ramifications.
>
> The infatuation of the Inquisition assisted them in this by transporting to every new colony shiploads of suspected Jews, who subsequently acted as agents and correspondents of their kinsmen at home and in other countries. In this way, the net-

---

[70] Godwin, Vol. IV, p. 245. & Hyamson: *History*, p. 139. Wolf: *Menasseh*, p. xxx. & pp. 29-30. Translator's note: In *Re-Settlement*, as also serialized in the *Jewish Chronicle* (2/12/1887, p. 8), Wolf states that Carvajal's 'importation of bullion averaged £100,000 a year'. Elsewhere, the 5/2/1666 entry (p. 161) of the *Calendar of State Papers*, Vol. 1655-1666, reveals that, according to Carvajal's petition to Cromwell, he had imported £200,000 of Spanish money and silver bars in the last 2 years.

[71] Wolf: *Crypto-Jews*, p. 73.

work of Jewish commerce, which already covered North-Western Europe, both littorals of the Mediterranean, and the whole of the Levant, became spread over South America, the East and West Indies, Western Africa, and South-Eastern Africa as far as Hindustan and the Far East. All these colonies were in communication with each other and the early English Jews were in business relations with nearly every one of them.[72]

This overview of the situation, from a renowned Jewish historian, should be sufficient to validate what we have already stated.

Jewish Spies on His Highness's Secret Service

Cromwell wanted to use these Jewish connections not only to boost English trade but also for his foreign policy. Whether this was his own idea or it came from the Hebrews can no longer be determined. Whatever the case, there can be no doubt that Jews the world over placed themselves at Cromwell's service for espionage and rendered him great assistance.

For a long time, nothing was known about this activity of Judah, until Lucien Wolf in particular first brought it to light. A review of the relevant literature shows that the Jews' espionage successes contributed significantly to thwarting the actions of Cromwell's numerous enemies on the Continent. The future King Charles II assembled his supporters and allies (who came from all over Europe) into the region of Flanders, with the view to raising an army of men who would cross over to England and fight Cromwell in his own country. Cromwell faced almost insurmountable difficulties, especially since the Spanish support of Charles Stuart was quite strong. However, the precise information provided by Jewish espionage enabled Cromwell to nip the entire Royalist expedition plan in the bud by unexpectedly seizing his opponents' fleet at Ostend.[73]

Unsurprisingly, the head of this Jewish spy ring was in London: it was Carvajal, whom we have already discussed. In the collection of contemporary letters known as the Thurloe Papers, there is a letter written in the time and place of 'Vlyssingen, December 20/30, 1656', and addressed to 'Mr. Ferdinando Carnevall, Merchant at London', which only briefly acknowledges the late receipt of the addressee's letter 'with the inclosed' and is signed with the name 'Jacub Goltburgh'. From the title of the collection, which dates from 1752, it is clear that the name was only a pseudonym and the actual letter writer was a certain J. Butler [seen elsewhere in the letter

---

[72] Wolf: *Cromwell's Jewish Intelligencers*, p. 13. Translator's note: QVOS [Wolf: *Essays in Jewish History*, p. 111, see Translator's Bibliography].
[73] Wolf: *Cromwell's Jewish Intelligencers*, p. 13.

collection as John Butler or Jack Butler]. Further research of this name reveals a number of spy letters from this individual, which, however, were not expressly addressed to 'Carnevall'.[74]

The question then arises as to who Carnevall was and whether the letters went to him or to Thurloe. Although a distinguished historian, William Dunn Macray, argues that the name 'Carnevall' is a pseudonym, we have no hesitation in agreeing with Wolf that the name Carnevall can only refer to the Jew Antonio Fernandez Carvajal. It is true that a man like Thurloe would not be able to use the name of this well-known Jew as a pseudonym. Because if the letters, the contents of which were so important for the English government that access by unauthorized persons had to be avoided at all costs, were addressed in the manner indicated, then despite the slight difference in the name they had to have reached Carvajal, who incidentally was, as can be seen from official documents etc., often referred to as Caravajal.[75]

In another letter collection, there are further intelligence communications from Flanders, which date from February to May 1657 and are also likely to have come from Butler. However, this time they are signed neither 'Jacub Goltburgh' nor 'J. Butler', but instead 'Jean Somer'. Wolf saw the first two letters in the original, compared the handwritings of J. Butler and Jean Somer, and found them to be completely consistent, which is good evidence for the identity of the writer.[76]

It is also recorded in the documents that on 30 March 1655, a passport to Flanders was issued for one of Carvajal's employees named Alfonso de Fonseca. It cannot be determined whether this trip is connected to Carvajal's espionage activity, but based on what has been stated above, it should not be ruled out.[77]

The contents of the letters in question show that the facts reported by the spy were extremely important to Cromwell. Butler—as we shall henceforth call the spy—was, judging by the volume of communications, unable to do all of the required work on his own. Rather, he must have had various accomplices, while he himself was probably the head of Cromwell's spy ring in Holland and Flanders. In one of his letters, he explicitly refers to other

---

[74] *State Papers of John Thurloe*, Vol. V, p. 722. Translator's note: All QVOS. It should be noted, however, that although the name of 'J. Butler' appears to be later metadata, the name of 'Carnevall' is not, as it appears on the envelope in French as 'Monsieur FERDINANDO CARNEVALL, Marchand, auprès de la bourse. A Londres.' The address given ('next to the stock exchange. London.') would surely strengthen supposition that this is Carvajal. From *Cromwell's Jewish Intelligencers*, p. 97.

[75] Macray, Vol. III, pp. 242, 256 ff. & Wolf: *Cromwell's Jewish Intelligencers*, p. 6. & See, for example, *Calendar of State Papers, Domestic Series*, Vol. [Year] 1654 p. 28; Vol. 1655/6, pp. 60, 161.

[76] Macray, Vol. III, pp. 242, 256, 262 ff., 276, 283, 287.

[77] *Domestic State Papers*, Vol. [Year] 1655, p. 580.

people who are in his service. We also find that he gives very precise information about Charles Stuart's current troop strength.

However, information about the port which was to be the assembly point for the ships which would transport the invading troops to England was of particular importance, and Butler assured the unnamed addressee that he would give news of the final assembly point and number of ships well in advance. It is therefore quite certain that it was Butler's communications that enabled Cromwell to successfully attack the fleet and transport ships anchored in Ostend in good time, thereby preventing the Royalists from landing in England. In addition, Butler continuously provided precise information about the equipment and armament of the troops. He even knew and communicated the number of newly purchased weapons. With astonishing expertise, he reported on even the most intimate affairs taking place at the court of Charles Stuart. Every person of importance was apparently monitored by his secret service. One learns about the comings and goings of these people from his letters. His spies even managed to identify the individual donations that went to Charles Stuart, including the names of the donors in question. [78]

The secret service's connections went so far that it was even possible to give a precise description of the spies sent to England by Charles Stuart. It would certainly not have been difficult to have the people in question monitored or rendered harmless. [79]

However, John Butler would have earned a particularly special merit if he did indeed manage to provide Cromwell with the anticipated concrete information about the alliance treaty between Spain and Charles Stuart. The written treaty had been kept extremely secret and only two of Charles Stuart's most loyal advisors, Ormond and Sir Edward Hyde, knew the details of it, the rest of his followers being kept in the dark. Butler nevertheless undertook to procure a copy of the contract from a courtier, who had promised to get it for twenty pounds. Unfortunately, it is not possible to determine from the letters whether the intelligencer was successful.

But we can see from subsequent letters that Butler was apparently always very well informed in advance about the Spaniards' individual plans of support. For example, regarding Charles Stuart's ability to finance the expedition, Butler was able to report that the Spanish king was relying on the imminent arrival of twelve treasure galleons from the Indies which were to be met by 'twelve good ships' from Spain. Holland would also provide Charles

---

[78] *State Papers of John Thurloe*, Vol. V, p. 588. & pp. 645, 709; Macray, Vol. III, pp. 265, 276, 283. & Macray, Vol. III, p. 256. & *State Papers of John Thurloe*, Vol. V, pp. 645, 665, 709.

[79] *State Papers of John Thurloe*, Vol. V, p. 645.

with two 'men of war' from its fleet to patrol the Spanish coast, in order to
warn Spain's returning 'plate fleet' of any English navy ships in the area.[80]

Cromwell the man may also have been personally indebted to his secret
service. In one of Butler's letters, we find a warning of an assassination plot
against the Lord Protector:

> A Dutchman passed lately into England who is suspected of
> intending some attempt against the Protector; he served the
> King of Spain for a long time, and is now a great favorite with
> Charles Stuart, and resides at Sluya; he is called Colonel Pin-
> leter, a very bold fellow, of a most dissolute and vicious life; if
> any stranger frequent Whitehall, take heed to him.[81]

Unfortunately, no further details are known of this matter. We must assume
that they were able to render Pinleter harmless because of the warning.

There can be no doubt that Cromwell's successes were in no small part
thanks to the services of his Jewish spies. At the same time, Carvajal's links
to this intelligence network also give us an explanation as to why he could
always count on the government's support, regardless of his crimes.

In addition to Carvajal, another rich Jew named Manuel Martinez
Dormido (*né* David Abarbanel Dormido) may have made his connections
available for espionage purposes. When we later come to discuss Dormido in
another context, readers will fully understand why he was chosen for this
purpose. Part of his correspondence with his agents in Holland is also preserved in the Thurloe collection, and Wolf rightly argues that these communications represent only a meagre remnant of all those that must have been sent.

There are two other people involved, undoubtedly Jews: David Nasy
[Nasi] and Manoel Grasian. The former wrote to Dormido on September
10th, 1655, to inform him that 28 Spanish ships with 1010 pieces of artillery
had set sail. The crew consisted of some 11,000 men. Another 32 ships of
the Spanish fleet would soon join the first-mentioned force. The intention
was to join forces in pursuit of the English fleet. 'God grant,' Nasy concludes,
'that they never enjoy their expectations, those wicked papists; and that his
highness may remain in his arms victorious, and enjoy great success for the
good of his people.' Grasian's letter contains similar messages about the
strength and movements of the Spanish fleet and concludes: 'God prosper his
highness's forces, and of that commonwealth, which doth favor our nation.'[82]

---

[80] *State Papers of John Thurloe*, Vol. V, p. 665. & p. 709; Macray, Vol. III, p. 242. Translator's note: QVOS [Thurloe].

[81] Macray, Vol. III, p. 262. Translator's note: QVOS.

[82] Wolf: *Cromwell's Jewish Intelligencers*, p. 10. & *State Papers of John Thurloe*, Vol.
III, p. 750. Translator's note: QVOS. & *State Papers of John Thurloe*, Vol III, pp. 750-1.
Translator's note: QVOS.

The closing words of both letters are interesting in that they clearly show the attitude of the Jews towards Spain and England: the former is treated with total contempt, the latter with Jewish unctuousness.

Just as, even back then, this secret Jewish network was of great service to Cromwell, so international Jewry is still working for England in the same way today. Hilaire Belloc, the unflinchingly observant writer, writes of the present time as follows:

> The Jewish news agencies of the nineteenth century favored England in all her policy, political as well as commercial; they opposed those of her rivals and especially those of her enemies. The Jewish knowledge of the East was at the service of England. His international penetration of the European governments was also at her service—so was his secret information. With the consolidation of the Indian Empire after the Mutiny the Jews were again an ally from their traditional hatred of the Russian people, which hatred has led them in our time to wreak so awful a vengeance upon their former oppressors. The Jew might also be called a British agent upon the Continent of Europe, and still more in the Near and Far East, where the economic power of England extended even more rapidly than her political power.[83]

Carvajal's aforementioned employee, de Fonseca, is Dormido's brother. This further connection with Dormido, one of Cromwell's main spies, strengthens the previously expressed view that Carvajal was also a part of the espionage network.[84]

Dormido's services to Cromwell must have been important, considering the favor shown to him by the latter. When the Portuguese recaptured Pernambuco from the Dutch, they confiscated sizeable assets from Dormido, who asked Cromwell to appeal to the king of Portugal on his behalf. Cromwell forwarded the request to the Council of State for action on 8 November 1654. However, the Council of State 'saw no cause to make any order', let alone to appeal to the king of Portugal, on the grounds that Dormido was not a British but a Dutch citizen. Cromwell then took matters into his own hands and defended Dormido in a private letter to the King of Portugal. As a special favor, he requested that the assets in Pernambuco be returned to Dormi-

---

[83] Belloc: *The Jews*, p. 222-3.
[84] Wolf: *Crypto-Jews*, p. 70.

do. This incident should conclusively demonstrate Cromwell's stance towards the Jews.[85]

The information set out so far about the Jews' spy service is clearly proven through the historical documentation, but there is also the assumption that the Jews in general worked as spies for Cromwell. The circumstances presented do not plausibly provide for a conclusion that such activity was limited to a few specific Jews. This assumption is confirmed by the historical accounts of two reliable historians. One of them is Bishop Burnet (1643-1715), who wrote the highly acclaimed *History of His Own Time*. Given that at one point the work highlights Cromwell's relations with the Jews, it would be remiss of us not to reproduce the relevant commentary:

> I go next to give an account of Cromwell's transactions with relation to foreign affairs. He laid it down for a maxim, to spare no cost or charge in order to procure him intelligence. When he understood what dealers the Jews were every where in that trade that depends on news, the advancing money upon high or low interests in proportion to the risk they run, or the gain to be made as the times might turn, and in the buying and selling of the actions of money so advanced, he, more upon that account than in compliance with the principle of toleration, brought a company of them over to England, and gave them leave to build a synagogue. All the while that he was negotiating this, they were sure and good spies for him, especially with relation to Spain and Portugal.
>
> The Earl of Orrery told me, he was once walking with him in one of the galleries of Whitehall, and a man almost in rags came in view: he presently dismissed Lord Orrery, and carried that man into his closet; who brought him an account of a great sum of money that the Spaniards were sending over to pay their army in Flanders, but in a Dutch man of war: and he told him the places of the ship in which the money was lodged.

Through this communication, as Lord Orrery reported to him, the Dutch warship was indeed captured near Dover and the great sum of money taken

---

[85] *Domestic State Papers*, Vol. 1654, p. 393. & p. 407. Translator's note: QVOS. Aldag likely got the above reason for the Committee's refusal from Wolf, who gives it in his *Cromwell's Jewish Intelligencers* [p. 106 of *Essays*], because the entry referenced here (which is also Wolf's source) makes no mention of the petitioner's Dutch citizenship, but does describe him in the following way: 'Emanuel Martyns Dorindo, *alias* David Abrabanell, a Hebrew', which suggests that the Committee, by presenting his birth name in this way, was keen to strip his identity of any crypsis lent to him by his alias, and refused to act based on the fact that Dormido was indeed a foreign national, but one of the Hebrew nation, rather than the Dutch Republic. & Wolf: *Cromwell's Jewish Intelligencers*, p. 11.

off board under pressure from the English warships. 'Next time that Cromwell saw Orrery,' Burnet concludes, 'he told him he had his intelligence from that contemptible man he saw him go to some days before.'[86]

With this story in mind, we have better insight into an entry in the Council of State minutes of 7 September 1652, which reads as follows: 'The petition of Antonio Ferdinando Carvajal, declaring that there is some silver to be brought in a Hamburg ship to Ostend, on account of Spanish merchants, was this day read, and the manifestation therein expressed there taken notice of.' This was apparently a message from Carvajal's secret service, and English warships probably ensured that the silver did not reach Flanders. Furthermore, Carvajal's knowledge of this transport is not surprising since, as the largest merchant in this branch of trade, he would be informed by his fellow 'Spanish' peers and business friends. We find further authentic confirmation of our supposition in the pages of the so-called *Diary of Thomas Burton, esq.*, when the parliamentarian conveys the essence of Cromwell's stance towards the Jews in the following comment:[87]

> The Jews, also, those able and general intelligencers, whose intercourse with the Continent, Cromwell had before turned to a profitable account, he now conciliated by a seasonable benefaction to their principal agent resident in England.[88]

The nature of the 'seasonable benefaction' that was shown to the Jews can no longer be determined. Wolf is of the opinion that this 'benefaction' consisted of Cromwell giving the Jews assurances of settlement in England in front of an assembled Parliament. We do not consider this view to be correct, but at least one can see from Burton's report that the espionage activities of the Jews were certainly one of the main reasons why Cromwell favored them. For the sake of completeness, it should be made clear that Carvajal was the 'principal agent' of the Jews; elsewhere he is called 'the great Jew' by his contemporary Thomas Violet, from whom we will hear later. The epithets may differ, but in essence they mean the same thing.[89]

---

[86] Burnet, Vol. I, p. 122. Translator's note: QVOS.

[87] *Domestic State Papers*, Vol. 1651/52, p. 395. Translator's note: QVOS.

[88] Burton, Vol. II, p. 471. Translator's note: QVOS. It would appear that this 'seasonable benefaction to their principle agent resident in England' was not, as might be supposed, Carvajal's Letters Patent of Denization, given that Carvajal was denizenised in 1655, and this benefaction was made in 1658 according to Burton's own text (February 4th, 1658, according to Wolf in *The First English Jew*, p. 22), or in 1657 (as more improbably conjectured in the *Jewish Encyclopedia*, § CROMWELL, OLIVER).

[89] Violet: *A Petition against the Jewes*, p. 7. Translator's note: We can be sure that 'the great Jew' is the original English form of the epithet for Carvajal, as it is also quoted in the opening sentence Wolf's *The First English Jew*.

Cromwell's General Support from the Jews

Aside from the aforementioned reasons for Cromwell's support of the Jews, it should also be considered that Cromwell was likely dependent on Jewish capital, although it must be admitted that research has not yet yielded conclusive proof of this. According to the Jewish historian Lucien Wolf, there is little doubt that the Jews made money available to Cromwell, or, to be more specific, the parliamentary government. He explains that around 1643, foreign Jews from Amsterdam were found in London, who were probably attracted by the financial difficulties of the government at the time.[90]

Elsewhere Wolf expresses his opinion more bluntly, citing a letter according to which the Jews offered the Republicans 'considerable sums of money to carry on their designs'.[91]

Other writers, who were opponents of Cromwell, also claim that he received donations from the Jews. There is therefore a high probability that the Jews provided Cromwell with strong financial support. It is also quite possible that they were willing to pay Cromwell and the Republican government significant sums provided they were given certain assurances about being granted permission to trade freely in England. Since the Jews did not receive this legal assurance from Parliament under Cromwell, the offer of money may have remained.[92]

The fact that Cromwell always attached considerable importance to financial support from the Jews is evident from the fact that after the collapse of the so-called Whitehall Conference, which shall be discussed in a later chapter, he made further action on the matter dependent on the Jews paying the enormous sum of money he demanded. Whatever was the case, based on the sparse extant documentary evidence we have no doubt that large payments were made.[93]

A lot of money must have flowed indirectly into England through the immigration of Jews. We have already described the vast scale of Jewish business. One example is that of the immigrant Jew Diego Rodrigues Marques, who, with the help of relatives, brought £15,000 capital plus merchandise to London when he emigrated from Lisbon, as can be seen from his public will. One can only speculate from this fact how he must have increased his wealth, given that, in 1678, his will mentioned that gold and silver worth 1,000,545 milréis was on its way from Portugal to England.[94]

---

[90] Wolf: *Re-Settlement*, p. 4.

[91] Wolf: *Menasseh ben Israel*, p. xix. Translator's note: QVOS.

[92] Romaine, p. 5; Prynne: *Narrative*, p. 49. & Fletcher, p. 231; Henriques: *Return*, p. 67.

[93] *Nicholas Papers*, Vol. III, p. 255.

[94] Probate Office Records 1678 (Reeve Fol. 113). Translator's note: Aldag undoubtedly got his information indirectly from *Cromwell's Jewish Intelligences* (pp. 112-3), rather

But the Jews also served Cromwell in another way. Encouraged and assisted by their relatives and business contacts all over the world, they were already a people who were uniquely familiar with many countries through their wanderings and travels. At the same time, during their sojourns they were not only informed about the general character of the country in question, but also discussed the business opportunities and advantages to be gained. The aforementioned Jew Simon de Caceres, for example, had lived in South America for a long time and therefore knew the conditions there. We know that he gave Cromwell information about foreign countries and even gave him precisely formulated suggestions, which the Lord Protector mostly followed.[95]

In 1655, Jamaica was conquered by England. Caceres presented Cromwell with a memorandum titled: 'A note of what things are wanting in Jamaica.' From the contents it appears that he developed these proposals immediately after his return from Jamaica. More than anything else, he believed that an expansion of the port was absolutely necessary, which would require stones and other building materials. He gave meticulous details for the fortification of the island, down to listing and quantifying the required staff, equipment, and tools, as well as suggesting the special supplies for the troops that should be sent there as quickly as possible.[96] Cromwell appears to have been persuaded by these statements, for in one of his letters written to Major General Richard Fortescue in Jamaica in 1655, we find instructions along the lines of Caceres' suggestions.[97]

Along with this memorandum, Caceres made further proposals for the conquest of Chile. He furnishes Cromwell with a detailed description of this country and the place where the expeditionary force would land. In his opinion, four frigates and four transport ships with a thousand soldiers would be enough to conquer Chile. He thinks an island he calls Mocha is particularly suitable as a base, especially since the English could buy food there 'at easy rates' from the Indians. In addition, the latter, as mortal enemies of the Spanish, would be friendly to the English. Caceres does not forget to point out to Cromwell the six main advantages that would come from conquering Chile. More gold would be found there than in Peru, and the country was rich in fruit, livestock, and fish. In addition, the most warlike Indians lived there, who were inspired by an implacable hatred against the Spanish. Furthermore, Chile was a good base of operations for English frigates to 'scowre the

---

than the one cited, which is cited by Wolf. Wolf (ibid) also states that 'the first few Jewish settlers brought with them no less a sum than £1,500,000 in ready money'.

[95] Wolf: *Re-Settlement*, p. 5.

[96] Green, Vol. III, p. 294. & *State Papers of John Thurloe*, Vol. IV, pp. 61-2. Translator's note: This is the title of the document as it appears in the original source. Note that the petitioner's name is rendered 'Simon de Casseres' in the original document.

[97] Carlyle: *Letters*, Vol. II, p. 389-90.

whole south sea' in search of Spanish treasure ships making their way back from the Philippines and South America to the metropole. Finally, this move would also gradually push back the Spanish, as they would find themselves attacked on both sides of the Americas.

Caceres' subsequent comments were evidently made in a bid to secure the best possible positions in the expedition for himself and his ethnic kin. First of all, sailors in Holland (clearly Jews) who had already accompanied another expedition to Chile and were therefore familiar with the area should be recruited for this company. Caceres does not state them to be Jews, but the implication is clear. In addition, he also suggests that he 'shall engage some young men of my owne nation, and promise to conduct them in my owne person, by the Lord's permission; and if it seeme good unto his high-nes, negotiating all this with the greatest secrecy'. Were Cromwell to worry about this proportion of non-English on the expedition, Caceres reassures him with the final suggestion: 'That the bulk and body of the officers and company bee English; and that those of my nation, or others that shall be admitted, shall goe all upon an English account, and as Englishmen, and for his highnes service only.' Not shy to put himself forward, Caceres also con-fidently volunteered himself to 'goe in person eyther as chief in the action, or next unto him, that is chiefe therein, and upon equitable and honourable termes, as his highnes shall judge meet.'[98]

One can see that Caceres did not forget himself in his suggestions and was concerned about his own advantage. Apparently Cromwell did not un-dertake this expedition.

Wolf discovered another plan by Caceres in the Rawlinson Collection, which relates to the Navigation Act. As is well known, this plan intended to take trade away from the Dutch and increase the volume of English shipping. Caceres showed Cromwell in detail that when it came to the shipping of commodities, especially sugar in the West Indies, there was still a lot wrong with the English share in the trade. The Dutch, the Hamburgers, and the French still had far too large a share in the trade of this English colony. He then went on to show how this situation, which was unfavorable for Eng-land, could be remedied. It was particularly important to be wary of the tricks of the Dutch, Hamburgers, and other foreigners, otherwise all efforts made in this regard would prove to be useless from the start. He, Caceres, would be the right man as commissioner to carry out the measures he had designed, since he knew all the foreigners' tricks, and would only take for himself a modest 20% of all revenue resulting from the scheme. These statements by Caceres are all the more significant because it shows that the basic idea behind the Navigation Act apparently came from a Jew. The evi-dence abounds to show the extent to which Cromwell was supported by the

---

[98] *State Papers of John Thurloe,* Vol. IV, pp. 62-3. Translator's note: All QVOS.

Hebrews. He was on the lips of all the world's Jews, who expected great deeds from him for their salvation.[99]

Around 1654 or 1655—the exact year is not certain—a delegation of Jews from Asia Minor came to England under the leadership of one of their rabbis. Cromwell granted them an interview, during which they explained to him that they wanted to purchase some Hebrew books and manuscripts belonging to the University of Cambridge. Cromwell was not opposed to this plan. But they first asked for permission to take a look at the library, which Cromwell granted them. The Jews went to Cambridge, but after some time they were found in Huntingdon, Cromwell's birthplace, where, to the astonishment of the residents, they were researching his family tree. It soon became clear that they had a specific purpose in mind: they wanted to find out whether his lineage confirmed their view that *Cromwell was a Jew* and the Messiah they had long been promised. The English public received this news with a mixture of anger and derision. Finally, Cromwell himself came to hear of it, and in order to avoid the indignation or ridicule of the crowd, he was forced to expel the Jewish delegation from the country.[100]

According to Picciotto, some writers are in doubt as to whether this incident actually happened. In our opinion, it is very possible, both in general and for a special reason that has so far been overlooked by other researchers.

Through the writing of an Englishman of the time we have been informed that a large gathering of the world's Jews took place on 12 December 1650 near Budapest, a gathering which was attended by some 300 representatives of the various Jewish colonies. The Englishman, Samuel Brett, a ship's captain and surgeon, somehow had access to the event and attended all the meetings. Mainly there was heated discussion about whether or not the Messiah had yet appeared. The Jews argued for days without achieving a consensus of opinion, with the vast majority believing that he had not yet come. In any case, it is certain that the expected Messiah would have great earthly power. The decision was made to convene a similar assembly in Syria in 1653 to settle the issue, as well as other matters.[101]

We do not know whether this Syrian assembly took place, but there is nothing to say against it, and it is quite likely that once again no agreement was reached on this issue. Given the favor shown to the Jews by Cromwell as well as his great earthly power, it is understandable why some might have been inclined to consider him the Messiah. The only obstacle appears to

[99] Wolf: *American Elements*, p. 99.

[100] Tovey: p. 275. & As is well-known, the Jews do not recognize Jesus Christ as the Messiah. & Picciotto, p. 29; Romaine: *Answer to a Pamphlet*, p. 46-47; Blunt, p. 71; Wolf: *Menasseh ben Israel*, p. xli; Jesse, Vol. III, p. 88.

[101] Brett: In *Harleian Miscellany*, Vol. I (1808 edition), 379 ff. & p. 385. Translator's note: Scholarly silence over this tract may come from the fact that Brett's testimony is generally disbelieved, and, certainly, the facticity of the event was denied by Menasseh ben Israel.

have been the uncertainty of his parentage, and it is reasonable to assume that in 1653 a delegation was appointed to investigate in England. In 1654 or 1655 a delegation from Asia Minor did actually appear, as is unanimously reported, so that there can be no doubt about that aforementioned event.

Apart from these considerations, however, what is of general interest here is the fact that, even back then, the world's Jews came together to discuss common matters. This is yet more solid proof for the thesis, which the Jews categorically reject, that there is a common front among them.

Menasseh ben Israel

Now that we have received a general overview of Cromwell's stance towards the Jews and vice versa, it should not be so difficult to understand the events that followed in 1654 and 1655.

If, on the English side, Cromwell was the zealous promoter of the Jewish cause, the Jewish leader of the cause was a rabbi in Amsterdam, Menasseh ben Israel. We will have to spend some time with him, not only because of his collaboration with Cromwell, but because he was one of the first Jews to act not for a specific group of Jews, but as a leader for international Jewry. A recurring objection to one of our reasons for fighting organized Jewry is the argument that the Jewish conscious, unified will for world domination (which we believe is an objective reality), does not exist or at least cannot be convincingly established.

It must be admitted that not all attempts to provide evidence on this point have been successful. However, this is usually less due to the material itself than the way it is presented. We must get used to providing the world with unassailable evidence on this matter, which we can and must achieve by citing sources and, wherever possible, by reference to Jewish literature and historical research. Nothing helps the Jews and their supporters around the world more than departing from these principles.

It is particularly difficult to make well-founded statements about the conscious striving of the Jews towards world domination. Jewish archives like those of the House of Rothschild are, and will probably always remain, closed to the public. Furthermore, the driving forces in Judaism will naturally avoid putting their goals on paper as much as possible. Most of the time there is only circumstantial evidence to rely on, which cannot convince those who are particularly skeptical. As a result, we must be grateful for whatever documentation or other impeccable evidence that is found to justify our claim and, most importantly, to convince doubters. Menasseh ben Israel and his mission to Oliver Cromwell may be one of those cases in which there is enough compelling material to prove that the Jews of the world had a common purpose and a unified leadership.

First, let us briefly familiarize ourselves with the life of Menasseh ben Israel in order to understand why he was destined and suited for this great task. Ben Israel was born in 1604, and there is some doubt as to where he was born. However, Lisbon can almost certainly be considered his birthplace. His father was one of the aforementioned Marranos who lived in Portugal. One day he was discovered to be a secret Jew and was unable to escape the torture of the Inquisition. His assets were confiscated, and the family was only too happy to flee Portugal at the first opportunity. Like many other Marranos, they took refuge in Amsterdam, the burgeoning new center for Jewry worldwide. When Menasseh arrived in Amsterdam, his father was a broken man who found it difficult to bear his poverty. There can be no doubt that Menasseh ben Israel was already old enough to have experienced some of the Inquisition's actions against the Jews and to have absorbed them into his young mind. He would certainly have had a lasting memory of the trauma, not least because his parents would have constantly refreshed his memory with their stories. In addition, there was a continuous flow of new Marrano arrivals in Amsterdam, who reported on the harsh measures taken by the Catholics of the Iberian Peninsula against the Jews.

The Jewish character is already typically inclined towards vengeance for any perceived injustice done to him. The fact that Menasseh was no exception to this general type can be seen, for example, from a fragment of one of his letters dated 1647, in which one can sense the intensity of his rancor towards the English for their actions against his ethnic kinsmen 350 years before:[102]

> *Senhor -- No puedo enar*: that is, Sir, I cannot express the joy that I have, when I read your letters, full of desires to see your country prosperous, which is heavily afflicted with civil wars, without doubt, by the just judgment of God. And it should not be in vain to attribute it to the punishment of your predecessors' faults, committed against ours; when ours, being deprived of their liberty under deceitfulness, so many men were slain, only because they kept close unto the tents of Moses, their legislator, &c.[103]

How much more must he have sworn revenge on the Spaniards and Portuguese who, during his own lifetime, had persecuted not only his fellow Jews but his own family. Since Cromwell was Spain's greatest adversary, one can

---

[102] E. Adler: *Letter*, p. 174; Dr. Adler: *Homage*, p. 27; Picciotto, p. 25.

[103] *Harleian Miscellany*, Vol. VII (1811 ed.). p. 623. Translator's note: QVOS. As there is no verb 'enar' in Spanish, one can only imagine that it is a word specific to the Judeo-Spanish dialect [Ladino] that Menasseh undoubtedly spoke, and that the subsequent English written is indeed a translation of the Ladino, which would appear to mean that he couldn't contain his joy (perhaps better, *schadenfreude*).

imagine that Menasseh took particular pleasure in cooperating with him, as he could hope, on getting permission for mass Jewish immigration to England, to be able to build up the same dominant position in the new land that his people had once enjoyed in Spain. This would then put them in a position to be able to strike at their mortal enemies on the Iberian Peninsula.

When still a child, Menasseh ben Israel was entrusted to the renowned Rabbi Issac Uziel for his education. Under Uziel's tutelage, Menasseh was able to give his first synagogue sermon at the age of 15. When his master died in 1622, Menasseh was appointed his successor, despite being very young for the position. He was soon known in every Jewish colony in the world as one of the best rabbis. The Jews came from every country on earth to debate with him on all matters Jewish and to hear his opinions. This explains why he soon became a famous name in international Jewish circles and was acquainted with all of the world's leading Jews. The fact that he wrote extensively also contributed to the spread of his name, with works that were mainly of a philosophical and historical nature. Ultimately, however, his activity was not limited to Jewish circles; thanks to his knowledge of ten languages, he also came into contact with representatives of other nations.[104]

He married shortly after his appointment as rabbi, and the marriage resulted in two sons. To supplement his meagre rabbinical earnings, he opened a printing shop. Apparently this venture was not accompanied by great material success, as we soon hear of renewed financial difficulties. He decided to emigrate to Pernambuco, where the Jews had acquired enormous wealth after the Dutch conquest of Brazil. He had already finalized his affairs in Holland and was about to leave when two very rich Jews who had emigrated from Spain, the brothers Abraham and Isaac Pereira, persuaded him to stay. They wanted to found a Jewish school in Amsterdam and employ him as a teacher. Since the salary was sufficient for Menasseh's needs, he accepted the offer.[105]

It is no longer possible to know for certain why and through whom Menasseh ben Israel was chosen for his task in England. Some Jewish writers believe that the hospitable attitude of the Puritans as already described, combined with the literature of the time, encouraged Menasseh to begin negotiations with England. Dr. Adler and Heinrich Graetz even claim that the final impetus for him to take action was the aforementioned pro-Jewish pamphlet written by Edward Nicholas in 1648. Given that, as per previous arguments, this pamphlet may have been produced by Menasseh himself, writing under a pseudonym, Adler and Graetz's supposition may not be correct.[106]

---

[104] Dr. Adler: *Homage*, p. 27. Translator's note: Wolf (Menasseh, p. xxii) states that he was ordained a rabbi at eighteen. & Dr. Adler: *Homage*, p. 28 ff.; Hyamson: *History*, p. 145.
[105] Dr. Adler: *Homage*, pp. 32-3; Hyamson: *History*, pp. 147-8.
[106] Graetz, Vol. V, p. 104 ff.; Dr. Adler: *Homage*, p. 33; Hyamson: *History*, p. 142 ff.

Whatever the case, in our opinion, Menasseh ben Israel must have been prompted to take his fated path due to the concerns of the Jews at that time as well as the prevailing millenarian ideas that had infused the Puritan zeitgeist. Then as now, the Jewish Question had become a burning issue in many countries.

Forced by the unwelcome developments on the Iberian Peninsula which are well documented in history, thousands of Jews flooded the world. A very significant number of these refugees amassed fabulous wealth in Brazil under the protection of the Dutch. This changed when the Portuguese drove out the Dutch in the middle of the 17th century and re-took possession of their former colony. The Jews had to flee alongside the Dutch. Some of them turned to the English and Dutch colonies of the Americas, but most of them flowed back to the Jewish global headquarters of Amsterdam. Five thousand Jews emigrated from a single city in Brazil alone. One can glean from this example that numbers on the move generally must have been considerable. Most of the time they could only save their lives.

Quite apart from the fact that the all-important trade with South America had ended, which of course had negative repercussions on the prosperity of the Jewish merchants in Amsterdam, considerable funds were also needed to be raised for the maintenance of these newly arrived hungry brethren. A remedy had to be found as quickly as possible, which could best be achieved by finding new countries for the homeless Jews: a particularly difficult task. Germany had just come out of the Thirty Years' War, which meant that trade there was completely destroyed. This led to hordes of Jews streaming out of Germany into Amsterdam, intensifying the difficulties of the colony there. Whole swarms also arrived there from Poland, where one of the greatest persecutions of Jews had broken out [known today as the Chmielnicki Massacres]. Hundreds, even thousands, had migrated westwards.

An interesting document has been preserved from which it is clear that Menasseh ben Israel was also consciously pushed towards his mission by the critical situation described. In a letter dated 31 December 1655, the Dutch ambassador to the Commonwealth of England, Willem Nieupoort, informed an unnamed lord that Menasseh ben Israel would work primarily for the persecuted Spanish and Portuguese Jews: 'Manasseh Ben Israel hath been to see me; and he did assure me, that he doth not desire any thing for the Jews in Holland, but only for such as sit in the inquisition in Spain and Portugal.' The same thing is seen in a letter from the aforementioned Dormido to Cromwell dated 3 November 1654, in which he first complains about the general situation of the Jews in Spain and Portugal, and then gives a detailed description of the conditions that are so unpleasant for them. Finally, he asks Cromwell to take the beleaguered Hebrews into England. This latter source is particularly valuable to our thesis in that it represents a formal petition from Dormido, and shows that he himself was a precursor to Menasseh ben Israel's efforts in England.[107]

Another general pressing reason that concerned the world's Jews was given for their admission into England: After their expulsion from Brazil, the Jews lost all trade connections with the then-more-important southern half of the continent. Some of them made their way from Brazil to neighboring Surinam, at that time an English colony, while others went to New York, Jamaica, Barbados, or other English colonies. There they were tolerated in tacit silence, and the Jews in Europe soon established new relationships with their fellow Jews. Everything seemed to be going well. History has shown that the Jews have a special ability to quickly settle in other countries and start new business ventures with their ethnic brethren and old business friends. So it was hoped in Jewish circles that they would soon be able to get over the loss of South America, as there was the promise of new business with the West Indies and North America on the horizon.[108]

The announcement of the English Navigation Act of 9 October 1651 had a huge impact on events. This law stipulated that non-European imports into England or her colonies could only take place on English ships, and that imports from Europe of the most important goods, as well as all goods from Turkey and Russia, could only take place on English ships or on ships from the country of origin. The main purpose was to destroy Dutch trade for the next few years and thus increase English shipping. History has shown what a resounding success these regulations were for England: Dutch trade and shipping were mainly in the hands of the Jews, and they were therefore severely affected. In such cases, however, the Jews usually inveigle a war on their own behalf from their host country, which they financially support to the utmost for this purpose.

Just such an event happened during this period of history. Holland became embroiled in a war with England. Its weapons were unsuccessful and, among other things, it was forced to recognize the Navigation Act in the peace treaty. This meant that Holland's power and especially its supremacy on the seas was shattered. Judah recognized that England had the future to itself and would soon dominate the world's trade and shipping, and that the Dutch nation was too small to assert itself in the long term as a serious compet-

---

[107] Wolf: *American Elements*, p. 80. Translator's note: The controversial word choice of 'colonies', 'hordes', 'swarms' (etc.) have been translated literally from the original in order to be true to the writer's intentions, words perhaps used to reflect the attitudes of those on the ground suffering the effects of uncontrolled mass immigration, which included those Jews themselves who were long-established, and forced to donate alms for the new arrivals. & *State Papers of John Thurloe*, Vol. IV, p. 333. Translator's note: QVOS. & See Wolf: *American Elements*, Appendix, Document II (pp. 88-9) for a reproduction of this petition.

[108] Wolf: *American Elements*, p. 80 ff.

itor to the emerging England. As a result, everything had to be done to gain a foothold in England and not lose their lines of communication. With the rise of England, the Jews had to grab the chance to regain their old dominant position in the world, as they had so recently enjoyed in Spain and Holland.[109]

But it was not just the decline in Holland's geopolitical position that caused the Hebrews to change sides. Rather, their entire global trade strategy was once again up in the air, because the Jews in England's West Indian and North American colonies could no longer trade with their ethnic brothers in Amsterdam. So they faced the loss of this trading zone again. As a result, it became clear to the Jews that global traffic had to be diverted from Amsterdam to London in order not to run the risk of losing the entire trade of the new world, which they had come to view as almost their own ethnic monopoly. The only way to counteract this was to transfer their main interests to London.

And there was another reason for world Jewry to gain access to England. In all of his writings, Menasseh ben Israel was profoundly affected by the prophecy given in the book of Daniel, according to which the deliverance of the Jews would come when they were scattered throughout the world. This prophecy had become a motivating factor for Menasseh's efforts. However, according to other prophecies, the redemption of the Jews was contingent on the dawn of the thousand-year kingdom, the coming of the Messiah and the return of the Jews to the Promised Land, and Menasseh ben Israel and his followers believed in this prophecy unshakably. However, the explicit prerequisite for the prophecy to unfold was that the Jews would first have to be scattered all over the world. So what form did this have to take?[110]

It would go too far within the scope of this work to cover this topic exhaustively, which is why we shall only deal with it to the extent needed to understand the motivations and actions of Menasseh ben Israel.

Scholars have been concerned with the problem of the so-called *Ten Lost Tribes of Israel* since at least the Middle Ages, with writings on this question having been published as early as the 13th, 14th, and 16th centuries. In Asia Minor and the Caspian Sea, the Tartars were also said to be the descendants of Israel's Lost Tribes.[111]

Towards the end of the 16th and the beginning of the 17th century, it became fashionable to discuss this issue. At first it was mainly Spanish clergy who put forward the completely new theory that the American Indians were connected to the *Ten Lost Tribes*. Some claimed that they were direct de-

---

[109] Lingard, Vol. VIII, p. 374.

[110] Menasseh ben Israel: *Vindiciae Judaeorum*, p. 37. & Wolf: *American Elements*, pp. 78-9. Translator's note: This strand of eschatological or Messianic thinking is known as Millenarianism, and was particularly strong during this period in both Christian and Jewish communities.

[111] Hyamson: *Lost Tribes*, p. 116 ff.

scendants of the Israelites, while others saw the devil as their real forefather, who had endowed the Indians with Jewish customs and behavior.

One of the most illustrative books of the first theory is Gregorio Garcia's *Origen de los Indios*. In his view, the *Ten Lost Tribes* migrated throughout Asia to the shores of the Bering Strait and from there to America. Using a long list, he attempted to demonstrate the similarities between Indians and Hebrews. Writings for and against this theory appeared throughout the civilized world at that time. In England, it was not until 1650 that this theory was mentioned in a book, where it was referred to positively. Here too we find a list of customs and character traits that, in the author's opinion, could only be Jewish. The author sent a copy of the book to the aforementioned philo-Semitic pamphleteer, John Dury, who had recently visited Menasseh ben Israel in Amsterdam. On this occasion, he learned from the rabbi that a Jew named Aaron Levy, alias Antonio Montezinos, had discovered a tribe of Indians during his travels in South America that could only be descended from Hebrews. Levy had sworn a solemn affidavit to the Jewish community in Amsterdam that his statements were the complete truth. It appears that it was only from this point onwards that the Jews accepted the theory that their tribal kin were also resident in the New World.[112]

At this point, it seems that Menasseh ben Israel and his followers believed that the prerequisite for the above prophecy had almost been fulfilled. Travelers in previous years and centuries had confirmed that they had found Jews in China, Asia Minor, Ethiopia, and Russia. In general, based on the geographical knowledge of the world at the time, it was therefore assumed that Jews were settled everywhere, with one exception: England. This country therefore had to be convinced as quickly as possible of the necessity of admitting Jews.[113]

International Jewry at Work

After all this, it is clear that the Jews of the world were turning their eyes to the emerging England. Picciotto, the Jewish historian, does not doubt in the least that some of the Jews in France, Spain, Portugal, and in the Spanish Indies had 'entreated Rabbi Menasseh to be their agent to entreat this favor for their coming to England, to live and to trade here'.[114]

Apparently Hyamson was of the same opinion, though he was not as explicit. Wolf also does not seem to want to deny the cooperation of international Jewry. He reports that Menasseh ben Israel came to London accompanied by

---

[112] Hyamson: *Lost Tribes*, p. 129 ff. & p. 133 ff. & Wolf: *Menasseh ben Israel*, p. 24; Hyamson: *Lost Tribes*, p. 140 ff.

[113] Wolf: *Menasseh ben Israel*, p. 24 ff.; Dr. Adler: *Homage*, pp. 33-4.

[114] Picciotto, p. 27. Translator's note: QVOS.

three other rabbis, one from Amsterdam, another from Prague, while the third Wolf speculates as being from Lublin, who journeyed to London to tell Cromwell about the persecution of Polish Jews from his own experience.[115]

A document survives, probably prepared by Cromwell or one of his advisors, which states that on the occasion of Menasseh ben Israel's negotiations in London:

> Many Jewish merchants had come from beyond seas to London, and hoped they might have enjoyed as much privilege here, in respect of trading, and of their worshipping the God of Abraham, Isaac, and Jacob here in synagogues publicly, as they enjoy in Holland, and did enjoy in Poland, Prussia, and other places. But, after the conference and debate at Whitehall was ended, they heard by some, that the greater part of the ministers were against this; therefore they removed hence again to beyond the seas, with much grief of heart, that they were thus disappointed of their hopes.[116]

But since so many Jews from distant countries came to the conference in London, there must have been a connection between Menasseh ben Israel and international Jewry. Otherwise it is inexplicable as to why they were all in London at the time of the conference. They would certainly not want to miss a minute of the conference where it concerned getting the best deal for the Jews, as they wished to secure every advantage that might come with admission to England, while their brethren overseas avidly waited for news of the outcome of events. This is also mentioned in one of Menasseh ben Israel's tracts:

> Where, after my arrivall, being very courteously received, and treated with much respect, I presented to his most Serene Highnesse, a petition, and some desires, which for the most part, were written to me by my brethren the *Jewes*, from severall parts of *Europe*, as your worship may better understand by former relations. Whereupon it pleased his Highnesse to convene an Assembly at *Whitehall*, of Divines, Lawyers, and Merchants, of different perswasions and opinions. Whereby mens judgements, and sentences were different. Insomuch, that as yet, we have had no finall determination from his most Serene Highnesse. Wherefore those few *Jewes* that were here,

---

[115] Hyamson: *History*, p. 142 ff. & Wolf: *Menasseh ben Israel*, p. xxxvii.
[116] 'Narrative...' in *Harleian Miscellany*, Vol. VII (1811 edition), pp. 621-2. Translator's note: QVOS.

despairing of our expected successe, departed hence. And others who desired to come hither, have quitted their hopes, and betaken themselves some to *Italy*, some to *Geneva*, where that Commonwealth hath at this time, most freely granted them many, and great privileges.[117]

This is further evidence that Jews from all over Europe, if not the world, were gathered in London with knowledge of the negotiations.

However, these individuals were probably not those who only wanted to look after their own interests, but rather those who at the same time represented certain Jewish communities in other parts of the world, as one can conclude from the following:

The modern Jewish historian Cecil Roth, apparently without realizing it, succeeded in discovering extremely important documents in the Italian archives connected to this matter, thereby providing the best evidence of the Jews cooperating internationally. This shows, among other things, that a Jew from Livorno [also known as Leghorn] named Raphael Supino played a crucial role in the negotiations with Cromwell on behalf of the Jews of Italy. As a Jewish colony, after the Marranos emigrated from the Iberian Peninsula, Livorno was not only numerically very large, but was also seen as a leading city in the Mediterranean. The Jews there had been granted great privileges, and we find not only Marranos, but Hebrews from all parts of Europe who were attracted by the freedoms afforded them.

Supino belonged to one of the very oldest Jewish families in Italy. He was a wealthy merchant with connections all over the world. One of his main lines of business was to redeem the Christians and Mohammedans who had been captured by pirates in the Mediterranean. As a middleman between the pirates and the relatives of the prisoners, he certainly did not make a bad living.[118]

In an old document, there is a report from English visitors to Livorno that in 1652 they met a courteous Jew who spoke a little English, 'a very grave, proper man' who may have been Supino. What is interesting is that he told them how he 'longed to hear that England would tolerate the Jews'.[119]

In any case, it is certain that Supino appeared in London in 1655 for Menasseh ben Israel's negotiations with Cromwell, as Roth found out from embassy letters of the then Duke of Tuscany. Supino was a subject of this prince, who also had an interest in the negotiations in London and probably

---

[117] Menasseh ben Israel: *Vindiciae Judaeorum*, pp. 38-9. Translator's note: QVOS. Note that Carvajal's existing Marrano community was unaffected by the negotiations, and continued to reside in London, as before.

[118] Roth: *New Light*, p. 121. Translator's note: QVOS.

[119] Roth: *New Light*, p. 122.

feared that, in the event of an agreement, rich Jews would forsake his country for England.

This correspondence from the Tuscan embassy in London shows that Supino conducted negotiations in a prominent position alongside Menasseh ben Israel. We learn from his letters that Supino became acquainted with 'the most considerable persons of London and the Universities', either during the course of the Whitehall Conference, or while on a special visit to Oxford and Cambridge. We therefore agree with Roth that Supino was a representative of world Jewry in London.

The interest that existed throughout the then-known world in this enterprise of world Jewry can also be seen from the further correspondence on this subject that Roth discovered from the Venetian embassy in London to the Venetian government.[120] In one of the letters, the Venetian envoy Sagredo mentions that a Jew from Antwerp commenced to feel Cromwell's body all over, to make sure that he was indeed of flesh and blood.[121]

The finding that Supino worked with Menasseh ben Israel is interesting in that it shows that it was not only the Marranos, some of whom were in dire straits, who wanted to go to England, but also the Jews living unmolested and with complete freedom in Italy at this time.

But Roth made an even greater discovery for us. While he was conducting research into other matters in the former state archives of Venice, he happened upon a very old printed document, signed by Menasseh ben Israel himself, which was sent to the Jewish communities around the world on the day of his departure for London and which was written in Portuguese. Roth is surprised that Menasseh ben Israel chose this language and not Hebrew. But we do not see anything unusual about this, because at that time Portuguese was the main business language among the Jews. In addition, as Roth himself points out, there were probably further copies published in other languages. Since Menasseh ben Israel himself spoke ten languages and ran his own printing press, this assumption seems entirely justified. Finally, the content leaves no doubt that the letter was addressed to world Jewry. A translation reads as follows:

THE HAHAM MENASSEH BEN ISRAEL
to all persons of the Hebrew nation living in Asia and in Europe, especially to the Holy Synagogues of Italy and Holstein,
S. P. D. [*Salutem plurinam dicit*—bids abundant peace]

---

[120] Roth: *New Light*, pp. 123, 126 ff.
[121] Roth: *New Light*, p. 127. Translator's note: Roth's view of this tale was that it was 'no doubt an exaggeration of a little Oriental hyperbole in which one of the petitioners indulged on being admitted to audience'.

It is notorious to all those of our nation how I have labored for a long time past in order that there should be conceded to us in the most flourishing Commonwealth of England the right to public exercise of our religion, moved not only by the merit of the case, but also by certain letters from virtuous and prudent individuals: as also how, after having set out on the road on two occasions, I was persuaded by my relatives, for certain political reasons, to postpone the journey for the time being.

Now therefore do I again make known to all how, although not yet fully recovered from a long illness, moved only by zeal and love of my people, and (as I have signified) neglecting all of my private interests, I am setting out to-day on this enterprise: which I pray may be to the service of God and to our common good. It is true that certain persons who are in the employment, and above all under the protection, of most clement Princes and Magistrates, have little esteem of this perpetual care of mine. Nevertheless, considering the common applause, the general good, the affliction of those of our people who are to-day so oppressed, who could find refuge and remedy in that most mighty commonwealth, without prejudice to any other: having regard, too, for the many souls who, dissimulating their religion, dwell scattered in so many parts of Spain and France: it was impossible for me to neglect an affair of such merit, even though it be at the cost of my faculties. I have been informed by letters, and by faithful correspondents, that to-day this English nation is no longer our ancient enemy, but has changed the Papistical religion and become excellently affected to our nation, as an oppressed people whereof it has good hope.

Nevertheless, since there is nothing sure or certain in this world, I supplicate all of the Holy Congregations that in their orisons they pray affectionately to God to give me grace in the eyes of the most benign and valorous Prince, his Highness, the Lord PROTECTOR, and in those of his most prudent council, that he may give us liberty in his land, where we may similarly pray to the most high God for his prosperity. Farewell!

Amsterdam, 2 September 5415 [1655 A. D.].

(signed) o. H. Menasseh ben Israel.[122]

---

[122] Roth: *New Light*, p. 114. Translator's note: Roth's English translation of the letter is reproduced verbatim from the article cited, and a reproduction of Menasseh's original document is the cover illustration for this volume.

On the back of the document there is the following endorsement in Italian and Hebrew: 'Letter in which R. Menasseh of Amsterdam informs the Holy Congregations of his journey to England to obtain permission to found a *Beth Keneseth* or "scolla" whereat to pray.'[123]

The address and content leave not the slightest doubt that Menasseh's communication was aimed at world Jewry. The fact that he particularly addresses the Jewish communities in Holstein (probably in Hamburg, Altona, and Glückstadt) and Italy indicates that his support came mainly from these places. The former were mainly branches from Amsterdam, so had more of a Marrano character, while the latter were of a mixed nature. That the cooperation of the Jews in Italy was particularly strong is also evident from the presence of leading Jew Supino in London.

From the content we see that the previous unsuccessful efforts of Menasseh ben Israel were known to world Jewry, as it is also evident that apparently some Jews who were doing well in certain places of the world did not care about his mission.

Finally, one can safely conclude from the circular that it was not the first of its kind, but was preceded by at least one which was similar, as can be seen from his statement: 'Now therefore do I again make known to all...'

Roth admits that Menasseh ben Israel was acting 'not as a private individual, but as emissary of all the house of Israel'. But he believes that this letter from Menasseh only arose out of the rabbi's conviction of the importance of his mission and his desire for his people's prayers. We cannot concur with him on this. International Jewry was at work, Menasseh ben Israel its spokesman. Long and detailed negotiations probably preceded his journey, and, in the words of Roth himself, Menasseh 'seems to have been at the outset well enough supplied with money.' International Jewry chose him as its representative and demanded to be kept informed, hence Menasseh's circulars. How perfect the cooperation was is also shown by the fact that numerous Jews were in London with Menasseh ben Israel. International Jewry at work! It would be difficult for the Hebrews to refute the facts of this episode of their history, as presented in this chapter.[124]

Menasseh ben Israel as Spokesman for International Jewry

In a previous chapter, we saw how the ground in England was largely prepared for Menasseh ben Israel by pro-Jewish writings. The Jewish side was active primarily through its spokesman, who in 1650 published a book in Spanish, Latin, and Hebrew titled *The Hope of Israel*. In this book, Menas-

---

[123] Roth: *New Light*, pp. 115-6. Translator's note: QVOS.

[124] Roth, *New Light*, pp. 114, 115, 118. Translator's note: Both quoted elements are reproduced verbatim from page 115 of the original source.

seh ben Israel came to the conclusion that, according to the prophecies, the Jews would have to endure many sufferings, but that the bloody Spanish and Portuguese persecutions were among the worst in all of Jewish history. However, it looked to him as if the return of the Jews to the Promised Land was not far off. He dealt in great detail with the problem of the *Ten Lost Tribes* and took the view that the prophesied dispersion of the Jews around the world was complete after the discovery of America, with the exception of England.[125]

He then listed the names of famous Jewish martyrs, and attempted to demonstrate the noble character traits of the Jews. Finally, he mentioned their great achievements in politics, which they achieved through their work for the princes. He explained the Jews' 'Constancy under so many evills' as proof that 'God doth reserve us for better things.'[126]

His comments were written with England in mind, to highlight the advantages that could be obtained from the Jews. It is therefore not in the least surprising that Menasseh ben Israel published this book in English translation, probably with the help of influential Englishmen of the period—Thomas Fuller and Nathaniel Holmes likely among them. The book quickly sold out of two editions.[127]

Menasseh had written a special introduction to his translation for England, which was dedicated to 'the High Court, the Parliament of *England*, and to the Councell of State.' He highly praised the successes of the English government of the time, and was pleased to be able to dedicate his book to the English government, hoping thereby to 'gain your favor and good will to our Nation, now scattered almost all over the earth.'

The book was particularly well received in Puritan circles. The Earl of Middlesex sent a public letter of thanks to Menasseh ben Israel entitled: 'To my dear Brother, Menasseh ben Israel, the Hebrew philosopher.' On 10 October 1651, shortly after the book was published in England, we find minutes from a Council of State meeting in which it is requested that the Lord General, Lord Commissioner Whitelock, Mr. Strickland and Sir Gilbert Pickering form a committee to peruse and respond to Menasseh ben Israel's letter. It is not certain if this is a reference to Menasseh ben Israel's aforementioned dedication, but it seems doubtful as the text in question did not necessarily require an answer. Whatever the case, it appears from this record that the English government was already in contact with Menasseh at this point. A few months previously, detailed negotiations had also been underway between the Dutch and English governments. An English delegation led by one of Cromwell's relatives, Oliver Saint John, made great efforts in Amsterdam

---

[125] Roth: *History of the Marranos*, p. 262 ff.
[126] Menasseh ben Israel: *The Hope of Israel*, Section 32. p. 38. Translator's note: QVOS.
[127] Hyamson: *History*, p. 151; Dr. Adler: *Homage*, p. 33.

to link the two states as closely as possible through a solemn treaty. Menasseh emphasizes that on the occasion of the English delegation's visit to Amsterdam, a solemn invitation was extended to them by the Jews, which the English also accepted. They were welcomed into the Amsterdam synagogue 'with as great pomp and applause, Hymns and cheerfulness of mind, as ever any Soveraigne Prince was'.

It can no longer be determined what response, if any, was given to Menasseh's aforementioned letter. But it was certainly not of great importance because, as is well known, on the previous day, 9 October 1652, the Navigation Act had come into force. Apparently the Jews' negotiations with the English government did not make much progress due to the political tension between England and the Dutch Republic. One would assume that these negotiations might even have stopped after the outbreak of war in June 1652, since Menasseh was, after all, a citizen of the Netherlands and as such could not legitimately negotiate with a government with which his country was at war. Not even close. For the Jew Menasseh, the war between England and Holland was not the slightest obstacle; in fact, he was in principle prepared to come to London for the negotiation. In the English state archives we find an entry for 22 November 1652 that a passport had been issued to Menasseh ben Israel for travel to England. Almost a month later we find another entry for a Council of State meeting, referring to the passport issued to Menasseh:[128]

> Dec. 17. Whitehall.
> Pass for Menasseh Ben Israel, a Rabbi of the Jewish nation, well reported of for his learning and good affection to the State, to come from Amsterdam to these parts. All officers to give him the favorable entertainment due to well-affected strangers, they behaving themselves without offence.[129]

It is difficult to understand why a citizen of one state would negotiate with the government of another hostile to his country, and in times of war such action must rightly be regarded as treason. However, for some reason, nothing came of Menasseh's planned journey.

In the spring of 1653, Cromwell had dissolved Parliament and convened a new one on his own initiative, known to history as the Barebones

---

[128] Dr. Adler: *Homage*, p. 34. Translator's note: QVOS. & *Domestic State Papers*, Vol. 1651, p. 472. Translator's note: In 1656, Menasseh mentioned writing to the Council of State to request another passport (the first one they issued after the publication of *The Hope of Israel* being no longer valid), so this 1651 letter may have been the first passport request. See Wolf: *Menasseh ben Israel*, p. xvii. & Gardiner, Vol. II, p. 80 ff. & Wolf: p. 77. Translator's note: QVOS. & Gardiner, Vol. II, p. 82. & p. 124 ff. & *Domestic State Papers*, Vol. 1651/52, p. 577.

[129] *Domestic State Papers*, Vol. 1652/53, p. 38. Translator's note: QVOS.

Parliament, made up of Puritan clergy, officers, and religious zealots. In all seriousness, the representatives of this Parliament proposed that the Council of State should consist of 70 members, based on the Jewish Sanhedrin.

The first meeting took place on 5 July 1653. Menasseh must have immediately brought the Jewish Question before this new Parliament, which was heavily constituted in his favor, because as early as 29 July we find a letter from an Englishman according to which there had been several motions in Parliament to grant the Jews permission to trade in the same way as in Holland. Apparently they wanted Menasseh ben Israel to represent his cause in England himself. There is another official entry on 16 September which records the Council of State issuing a passport for him. However, the war between England and Holland was still not over, and Menasseh apparently did not make his trip to England, perhaps because of poor health, or perhaps because of personal considerations for his position as a rabbi in Amsterdam at a time of heightened political tensions.[130]

On 5 April 1654, England and Holland made peace, and on September 5th of the same year, the first Parliament to follow the Barebones Parliament met for the first time. This too was short-lived and fell apart in January 1655.[131]

Nevertheless, Menasseh must also have addressed this Parliament. There are no records of this in the state archives, but in the 1655 two-part treatise which has come to be known as *The Humble Addresses*, in the second part, titled *A Declaration to the Common-wealth of England,* he speaks of 'humble addresses to the late Honorable Parliament'.[132]

It is certain that the aforementioned Jew Dormido, a brother-in-law of Menasseh, went to England at the end of 1654. Dormido sent a request to the government for the admission of Jews to England, which is still preserved today. There is no need to enter into further detail on this matter as it does not contain much of interest.[133]

---

[130] Gardiner, Vol. II, p. 216 ff.; Lingard, Vol. VIII, p. 398 ff. & *State Papers of John Thurloe*, Vol. I, p. 387. Translator's note: This is the same reference as that of footnote 101 (see corresponding page for the reproduction of the original source quotation). & *Domestic State Papers*, Vol. 1653-54, p. 436.

[131] Lingard, Vol. VIII, p. 436 ff.

[132] Wolf: *Menasseh ben Israel*, p. 78. Translator's note: QVOS. Aldag appears to be mistaken in his assertion that Menasseh addressed the Parliament in person. The rest of the quotation is: '...if by humble addresses to the late Honorable Parliament, I might obtaine a safe-Conduct once to transport my self thither.' This is clearly a reference to Menasseh previously addressing the Council of State by letter, to request a passport, as is evidenced by the historical record (see footnotes 192, 201). Note also that the word 'once' in his statement indicates that he had never previously been in England prior to the October 1655 visit.

[133] See Wolf: *American Elements*, Appendix, Document II (pp. 88-9) for a reproduction of this petition.

Dormido was apparently received by Cromwell with the greatest alacrity. He immediately forwarded the request to the Council of State and recommended that it be approved and processed expeditiously. However, the Council did not follow Cromwell's instructions and rejected the application after a month with the laconic response: 'Council saw no cause to make any order.'[134]

The Jews' cause was making no progress in Dormido's hands. The Jews and their supporters recognized that only one person was able to prevail, namely Menasseh ben Israel. In October 1655, Menasseh arrived in London accompanied by three rabbis. They were received with great ceremony and accommodated in a magnificent house opposite the new Stock Exchange on the Strand, a street where mostly only Englishmen of importance and foreigners of rank lived.[135]

How were the political forces in England arrayed when Menasseh arrived? Cromwell strongly favored the Jews. The Council of State, on the other hand, was, contrary to expectation, not as favorable as had been initially assumed. Despite Cromwell's dictatorial power, public opinion could not be overlooked in all of the discussions, some of which were led by influential English people who were clearly against the admission of Jews. Popular rejection of Jewish readmission was expressed in speech and writing. Letters have survived which confirm this attitude. As one of Ambassador Francesco Salvetti's reports to the Grand Ducal Government of Tuscany stated: 'Very few of this nation are agreed to let them [the Jews] make their nest in these lands.' Ten days later, on the last day of 1655, he wrote in another letter: 'It is a matter which generally encounters great opposition, especially from the preachers, merchants, and populace.'

The same year saw the publication of a small work by the baptized Jew Paul Isaiah, that dealt with a conversation about religious matters between a Christian and a Hebrew, the latter insulting Christianity and especially the person of Jesus Christ, while the Christian defended both. Isaiah's book is of no great literary merit, but at that time it was probably suitable for influencing the masses who were all too ready to oppose Jewish entry from the outset. However, the best writing to come out over the course of the negotiations was by William Prynne, who we shall discuss in a later chapter. The accuracy of the assertion that Oliver Cromwell intended to lease the customs

---

[134] *Domestic State Papers*, Vol. 1654, p. 393; Wolf: *Menasseh ben Israel*, p. xxxiv. Translator's note: There were two petitions from Dormido involved, both of which Cromwell recommended, and both of which were rejected by the Council, but it is only the request for Jewish readmission that is of interest here. [The second petition was about the restoration of Dormido's personal property in Brazil, which has already been touched on earlier.] & *Domestic State Papers*, Vol. 1654, p. 407. Translator's note: QVOS. See also footnote 135 for more on this matter.

[135] Hyamson: *History*, p. 154; Wolf: *Menasseh ben Israel*, p. 36 ff.

revenue to the Jews cannot be verified by the extant documentation, but Thomas Violet, a contemporary of Cromwell, believed that he was willing to go this far. The people also had this fear and were extremely upset by the idea. Wolf simply describes this as an unfounded rumor that was spread to the detriment of the Jews. Exactly the same applies to the announcement that the Jews had come to London for another attempt to purchase St. Paul's Cathedral and the Bodleian Library. However, since it has already been proven in this volume that such negotiations had indeed previously taken place, it is hard to see why they could not also have been seriously discussed at this point in time, especially since these earlier proposals had likewise been put forward alongside a request for readmission.[136]

The still-strong Royalist party also did everything to disrupt the negotiations between Cromwell and the Jews. As we will see below, the Royalists had themselves established connections with the Jews, in particular to obtain Jewish financial support for the restoration of the monarchy.[137]

For the Royalists to achieve this goal, however, it was necessary that the Jews not be granted the right to settle under Cromwell's rule, because the Royalists' reward for the financial help sought from the Jews was to consist of this privilege, especially in the event of the royal family's return. If the Jews were to achieve this goal under Cromwell, they would not have the slightest incentive to offer financial backing to the Royalists. Although a reprehensible political game, in 1655 it came to the aid of the general anti-Jewish movement.

English public opinion was also supported in its anti-Jewish attitude by a foreign power—Holland—which feared that if the negotiations were to take place, rich Jews would emigrate, which displeased the government of the time, not least because the Dutch economy was largely in Jewish hands. In view of this fact, Dutch ambassador Willem Nieupoort invited Menasseh for an audience with him in London and questioned him about his intentions. He reports in a letter dated 31 December 1655, that 'Manasseh Ben Israel hath been to see me; and he did assure me, that he doth not desire any thing for the Jews in Holland, but only for such as sit in the inquisition in Spain and Portugal.'[138]

In the face of the hostile attitude of the English people, Menasseh practically only had the support of Cromwell. The men who had appeared on behalf of the Jews in earlier years were, for the most part, unable to help the

---

[136] *Domestic State Papers*, Vol. 1655/56, pp. 51, 58. & Roth: *New Light*, pp. 128-9. Translator's note: Roth's English translations reproduced verbatim from original text. & Isaiah, especially p. 36 ff. Translator's note: For more on this colourful character, see footnote 262. & Violet: *Petition against the Jewes*, pp. 2, 7.

[137] Hyamson: *History*, p. 155; Wolf: *Menasseh ben Israel*, p. 40.

[138] *State Papers of John Thurloe*, Vol. IV, p. 333. Translator's note: QVOS (sharp-eyed readers will notice that this is a previously cited quotation).

Jewish cause. Roger Williams was in America, John Sadler, given his official position, could no longer intervene in the matter as actively as before, and Hugh Peters no longer had any real influence. In addition, Thurloe, Blake, and General Monk did not want to risk alienating the city's merchants, who were the fiercest opponents of resettlement given the expected competition from the Jews.

Therefore public opinion had to be changed because Cromwell, as developments confirmed, could not force the government to approve Jewish resettlement against the will of the people.

Menasseh and his advisors believed that they could bring about this change in public opinion through a widely distributed pamphlet, which they published in two parts. The first part was titled: *To His Highnesse the Lord Protector of the Common-wealth of England, Scotland and Ireland. The Humble Addresses of Menasseh Ben Israel, a Divine and Doctor of Physick, in behalf of the Jewish Nation.* The second part had the title: *A Declaration to the Common-wealth of England, by Rabbi Menasseh Ben Israel, shewing the Motives of his coming into England.*

Hyamson and Wolf both argue that Menasseh had already completed this pamphlet before his arrival in England. The latter is even of the opinion that it was drawn up as early as 1651 with the collaboration of John Thurloe, Cromwell's secretary.[139]

As its title suggests, the first part, which is only three pages long, is addressed to Cromwell. Menasseh explained that God most favored the Jews and continued to ensure that no harm came to them. Kings such as Pharaoh, Nebuchadnezzar, Antiochus Epiphanes, and Pompey, who treated the Jews badly, had been punished by God. God's promise to Abraham—'*I will blesse them that blesse thee, and curse them that curse thee*'—appeared always to be fulfilled. In view of the recent benevolence shown by powerful people, Menasseh, as one of the least of the Hebrews, had to ask Cromwell for the grace to allow the Jews a place in England, to worship the great and glorious name of God in their own synagogues. He did not doubt that 'this most equitable Petition' would be easily granted, as even the pagans of old did grant this right, out of reverence for the God of Israel, just as the Egyptians allowed the high priest Onias to build another temple in their country. The English ambassadors had been received in the synagogues of Amsterdam with pomp and hymns, and the Jews therefore hoped that the old hatred from the time of the monarchy had been transformed into goodwill and that the rigorous laws against 'so innocent a people' would 'happily be repealed'. Undoubtedly the influence of Cromwell, who had shown them so much respect and favor from the beginning, would ensure this. In the name of the Jews, Menasseh therefore entreated Cromwell to permit the free exercise of

---

[139] Hyamson: *History*, p. 154; Wolf: *Menasseh ben Israel*, p. 38.

religion in England, and in return the Jews 'shall pray for the happiness and Peace of this your much renowned and puissant Common-wealth'.

The structure and content of these statements is typically Jewish. First there is the implied threat, because otherwise the references to Pharaoh etc. cannot be understood, and then one moves on to the sweetest flattery.

The *Declaration to the Common-wealth* is considerably longer and consists of 29 pages including the preface. In the preface, Menasseh explained the motives for his mission. In addition to the free exercise of religion for his people, he wanted a general settlement of Jews in England so that they would be scattered all over the world, a fact that was necessary for the appearance of the Messiah. He then touched on the benefits that would accrue to England through the increased importation and exportation of goods. Finally, he would welcome the arrival of Jews into England because he was so warmly attached to the English nation and has always extolled the English Commonwealth in his writing and deeds. He ends his preface with the following words, which will give the reader an idea of the techniques used to persuade the audience:

> ...*I persuade my selfe that they* [the English] *will be mindfull of that Command of the Lord our God, who so highly recommends unto all men the* love *of strangers; much more to those that professe their good affection to them. For this I desire all may be confident of, that I am not come to make any disturbance, or to move any disputes about matters of Religion; but onely to live with my Nation in the feare of the Lord, under the shadow of your protection, whiles we expect with you* the hope of Israel *to be revealed.*

He introduces the first chapter of the *Declaration*, titled 'How Profitable The Nation of the Iewes are,' with the following words:

> *Three* things, if it please your Highnesse, there are that make a strange *Nation* wel-beloved amongst the Natives of a land where they dwell, as the defect of those *three* things make them hatefull: viz. *Profit*, they may receive from them; *Fidelity* they hold towards their Princes; and the *Noblenes* and purity of their blood.

In Menasseh's opinion, profit was 'a most powerfull motive, and which all the World preferres before all other things: and therefore we shall handle that point first'. Through 'having banished them from their own Country, yet not from his Protection', God gave the Jews the natural instinct to make money and 'thrive in Riches and possessions'. Since then, the trade in currencies, diamonds, dyes, wine, oil, and other valuable commodities has been largely in their hands, and on their readmission to England they would bring with them their capital and business connections, which would cause an increase in trade, which in turn would bring in tax, and customs revenue would be increased. It was true that the Jews acquired great wealth, but this was only made possible for them by the providence of God, so that through accumulated treasure they would find favor in the eyes of the rulers and peoples.

Menasseh then explained in detail that the Jews have a trade presence in almost every country on earth. Some of them even enjoyed high honors and were privileged by their princes.

Moreover, the Hebrews had a huge advantage over all other foreigners because they never left their host nation, whereas other foreign peoples only stayed long enough to make their fortune and then return with that fortune to their native soil, 'peaceably to enjoy their estate.' The Jews, on the other hand, having no native country to which to return, stayed where they were with their wealth.

This is not the place to castigate the perniciousness of the Jews' profit-seeking to the detriment of their country, but it should be noted that this reason given by Menasseh in favor of Jewish settlement can at least be used as a counter-argument to the same extent.

He called the second chapter of the *Declaration*: 'How Faithfull The Nation of the Jewes are.' Among other things, he asserted that Jews were loyal citizens in ancient Egypt and Rome.[140]

Especially with regard to the latter example, this statement reads like a mockery of the known facts, because 'the Roman imperial period is filled with a chain of Jewish riots and unrest instigated by Jews at all ends of the empire.' The revolts they caused in Alexandria and Palestine have long been known. In 1137 they sparked a revolt in France that resulted in terrible bloodshed. The same thing happened in Persia in 1138 and 1174. A Jewish revolt against the government in Spain broke out in 1157. Many other uprisings instigated by Jews can be cited from history, but the above examples will suffice for our purpose.[141]

Near the end [p. 20], he addressed three accusations that are repeatedly made against the Jews. These '*three most false reports*' are the allegations of usury, child ritual murder, and Jewish attempts to convert Christians to Judaism. That Jews are usurers was only partially true, he asserted, and 'though in Germany there be some indeed that practice usury,' the Sephardic diaspora living in Turkey, Italy, Holland, and Hamburg rejected all usury.

---

[140] Menasseh ben Israel: *The Humble Addresses*, p. 1 ff. Translator's note: All quotations and quoted elements relating to Menasseh's two-part pamphlet are reproduced verbatim from the original source.

[141] Fried, p. 111. & Leslie, p. 29.

It was likely that Menasseh had no need to spread the word about the unassailably noble character of his ethnic kin. This task had already been done for him by Christian writers, in particular by the Englishman Henry Jessey in his book *The Glory and Salvation of Jehudah and Israel* [the only extant copy is a 1653 Dutch translation] and by Edward Nicholas.

On 31 October 1655, Menasseh waited in front of the entrance to the Council Chamber of the Council of State and asked to be allowed to present certain books, undoubtedly his own works, given that *The Humble Addresses* would have recently been published at that time.[142]

The Jews and their supporters experienced bitter disappointment with the tracts. In no way were they able to change public opinion; they only brought additional opponents onto the scene. Various tracts, such as *Case of the Jews Stated*, were published immediately afterwards by the opposing side. Prynne gives us a vivid description of the popular sentiment in the preface to his book, which he has titled 'To the Christian Reader':

> As I kept on my way, in *Lincolnes Inne* Fields, passing by seven or eight maimed Soldiers on Stilts, who begged of me; I heard them say aloud one to another, *We must now all turn Jews, and there will be nothing left for the poor*. And not far from them another company of poor people, just at *Lincolns-Inne* back Gate, cried aloud to each other: *They are all turned Devils already, and now we must all turn Jews*. Which unexpected concurrent Providences and Speeches, made such an impression on my Spirit, that before I could take my rest that night, I perused most of the passages in our English *Histories* concerning the Jews *carriage* in *England*, with some of their misdemeanors in other parts, to refresh my *memory*, and satisfie my *judgement*; making some Collections out of them, which after I enlarged and digested into this ensuing *Demurrer*...[143]

The negotiations continued, and the Council of State apparently soon dealt with the writings presented by Menasseh. In the state papers we find a list of Menasseh's various requests to Cromwell as early as November 13. Apparently, in addition to the tracts, Menasseh had submitted a special list of requests to the Council of State, the entry for which is reproduced below:

---

[142] *Domestic State Papers*, Vol. 1655, p. 402. Translator's note: (from the source) 'Order – on hearing that Manasseh Ben-Israel, a Jew, is attending at the door with some books which he wishes to present to Council – that Mr. Jessop go out to receive them, and bring them in.'

[143] Prynne, preface of his work *Short Demurrer*. Translator's note: QVOS. The preface is unnumbered, but it corresponds to pp. iv-v in both the first and second editions.

Requests to the Protector by Manasseh Ben Israel, on behalf of the Hebrew nation:

(1) To take us as citizens under your protection; and for our greater security, to order your chiefs and general-at-arms to defend us on all occasions.

(2) To allow us public synagogues in England and other places under your power, and the exercise of our religion.

(3) To give us a cemetery out of town, for quiet interment of our dead.

(4) To allow us to trade freely as others in all sorts of merchandise.

(5) To elect a person of quality to receive our passports, and oblige us to swear fidelity, in order that those who come in may live without prejudice or scandal.

(6) That we may not trouble the justices of peace with our contests, to license the chief of the synagogue, with 2 almoners, to reconcile differences according to the Mosaic law, with the right of appeal to the civil law, first depositing the sum in which the party has been condemned.

(7) To revoke all laws against the Jewish nation, that we may live in greater security.

These granted, we shall always be well affected, and pray for the success of all your enterprises. [*French, 2 pages.*].[144]

The state papers then continue with an entry stating that the request list was to be translated into English, followed by an entry listing the individuals (Lambert, Rous, Lisle, Wolseley, Pickering, and Sydenham) who had been selected to form a Committee of Council under the Lord President, so that a report could be produced on the matter. The next entry in the record to appear for that date [Nov. 13, although there is a question mark printed beside the date, and indeed the date must be erroneous—see footnote] is the following:

Report on a request for admission of Jews into England to traffic, that it is lawful in point of conscience, if certain considerations be provided for:

(1) The grounds urged by Manasseh Ben Israel, in his book lately printed in English, we conceive to be sinful in any Christian nation.

(2) The danger is great of seducing the people of this nation in matters of religion.

---

[144] *Domestic State Papers*, Vol. 1655/56, p. 15. Translator's note: QVOS.

(3) Their having synagogues and places of worship is evil in itself, and scandalous to Christian churches.

(4) Their practices about marriage and divorce are unlawful, and will be of ill example.

(5) They are proved not to make conscience of oaths made or injuries done to Christians.

(6) The inhabitants of London suggest that it will be very injurious to trade.

We therefore consider:

i. That they should not be admitted to public judicatories, civil or ecclesiastic, which would grant them terms beyond the condition of strangers.

ii. They should not speak or act to the dishonor of Christ or His religion.

iii. They should not profane the Christian Sabbath.

iv. They should not have Christian servants.

v. They should bear no public office or trust.

vi. They should print nothing in our language opposing Christianity.

vii. They should not discourage any who try to convert them, but there should be a severe penalty on any apostatizing to Judaism. [*3 pages*][145]

The Whitehall Conference

On November 14, four members of the Council of State (Lisle, Wolseley, Pickering and Rous) met under the chairmanship of Lord President Henry Lawrence to set up a Committee of Council which would examine Menasseh's proposals, and to name those eligible to speak at the Committee discussions on the matter. The very next day, the names of the 28 men selected were published, which included almost all of the important people of the time. Since legal questions also had to be resolved, the most eminent jurists Lord Chief Justice Sir John Glynne and Chief Baron of the Exchequer Wil-

---

[145] *Domestic State Papers*, Vol. 1655/56, pp. 15-6. Translator's note: QVOS. It is highly unlikely that November 13th is the date for this entry, as not only was the original document from which this entry was inserted undated and unendorsed (see text corresponding to footnotes 285 and 286 for further discussion), but common sense dictates that it is virtually impossible for a government to both form a committee and produce an official committee report in a matter of hours after the issue to be reported upon has first been introduced for consideration. However, Henriques' thesis (footnote 285), that this was an informal 'pros and cons' list that somehow found its way into official papers, where it ended up wrongly classified, may be correct.

liam Steele were appointed to the Committee, as well as distinguished dip-
lomats such as Walter Strickland, and veterans of Cromwell's old guard such
as John Lambert and William Sydenham. The City of London merchants
had sent their Lord Mayor and several aldermen, accompanied by the richest
and most powerful merchants in the form of Sir Christopher Pack, William
Kiffen, and Owen Rowe. The clergy were most strongly represented with
sixteen theologians and divines, in Wolf's words 'the flower of Puritan piety
and learning.' Among them were Dr Cudworth, Regius Professor of Hebrew, Dr. Owen, known for his advocacy of religious freedom, John Caryll,
expositor of the Puritan Bible, and Dr. Whitchcote, representing Cambridge
University. We also find Daniel Dyke, one of Cromwell's chaplains, Philip
Nye, the champion of equal rights and Henry Jessey, the Baptist Judeophile
and friend of Menasseh ben Israel.[146]

The first meeting was scheduled for 4 December 1656. Apparently the
government had held non-binding discussions with Menasseh in November.
During this period the public was only concerned with what was going on in
Whitehall, the English government district which was the venue for the conference. With the attention of the entire population, Cromwell opened the
first meeting, at which Menasseh's aforementioned proposals were read out.
It can no longer be determined whether the Jews' willingness to pay
£200,000 for the approval of the proposals was discussed on this occasion. In
any case, in a work published at the end of the 18th century, the following
text is found:[147]

> In the year 1665 [sic], Oliver Cromwell being then Protector
> of the three nations, Mannasseh Ben Israel, a famous Jewish
> Rabbi afore-mentioned, came as an Agent from Holland to
> endeavor to procure the re-admission of the Jews into Eng-
> land, and made the following proposals to the Protector, for
> which they offered no less than £200,000.[148]

---

[146] *Domestic State Papers*, Vol. 1655/56, p. 20. Translator's note: The referenced state
papers only mention three members as having been present (omitting Rous), but given that
Aldag mentions four in his text it is likely that he had referenced Wolf (*Menasseh ben
Israel*, p. 47), who lists the four members as presented above. & *Domestic State Papers*,
Vol. 1655/56, p. 23. & Wolf: *Menasseh ben Israel*, pp. xlvii-xlviii; Hyamson: *History*, pp.
157-8. Translator's note: Wolf goes into greater detail on the invitees and their respective
backgrounds, himself admitting: 'It is not difficult to see that the Conference had been
carefully organized with a view to a decision favorable to the Jews.'
[147] *Harleian Miscellany*, Vol. VII (1811 edition), p. 623.
[148] Robert Burton, p. 203. Translator's note: Quotation (and that following) reproduced
verbatim from original source. 'Robert Burton' was a pseudonym for Nathaniel Crouch.

This is followed by Menasseh's seven proposals. The writer then continues in the next paragraph: 'When these proposals were read, the Protector said: ...'

From this presentation of events, one might conclude that the offer of money was also one of the proposals and was therefore read out. Whatever the case, it is at least interesting that the writer conveyed the Jews' offer of a financial incentive. It is therefore to be expected that the Jews will characterize this published information as false or improbable, which is why it should be stated from the outset that Wolf himself used this work as an authentic source for the description of the Whitehall Conference. If he had considered this author's historical account to be untrue, he would certainly have expressed his disagreement, given that he had done so with other authors. The presumed accuracy of this information can also be concluded from the fact that a comparison of Burton's information on the proceedings of the Whitehall Conference with the official government report shows complete concordance—further proof of the reliability of this source.[149]

Furthermore, Burton [Nathaniel Crouch] was a contemporary of Cromwell, and it is therefore quite possible that he had first- or second-hand knowledge of the events in the conference room.

But there are other historical sources from which one can conclude the accuracy of Robert Burton's assertion. A namesake of his, Thomas Burton, who emerged politically around 1650 and was elected Member of Parliament in 1656, has given us the same account. In his four-volume *Parliamentary Diary* we find that Menasseh offered £200,000 for his proposals to be accepted. There is also the following snippet to be found in Henry Fletcher's *The Perfect Politician* (1660):[150]

> [H]e [Cromwell] had a promise of 200,000 from the Jews, in case he procured their Toleration here, as saith Mr. *Prynne* in his Narrative, p. 56, which sweet morsel he had swallowed by thus gratifying them, had not the design been opposed by Arguments as sharp as weapons of STEEL.[151]

Finally, a letter from 1656 has been preserved in which the writer, Colonel Richard Whitley, comments on the negotiations as follows:

---

[149] Wolf: *Menasseh ben Israel*, pp. xlix-li. & *Harleian Miscellany*, Vol. VII (1811 edition), p. 617 ff.

[150] *Dictionary of National Biography* (1886 edition), Vol. VIII, p. 17. & Thomas Burton, Vol. I, p. 309. Translator's note: Burton references his source for this assertion as 'Whitlock'. It would appear that this was either Sir Bulstrode Whitlock (1605-1675), one of Cromwell's Commissioners of the Great Seal of England, or his son William Whitlock (1636-1717), also a parliamentarian.

[151] Fletcher, p. 291-2. Translator's note: QVOS. Aldag's rendering of the quotation did not include the author's attribution to Prynne, which may have been an oversight.

> I had almost forgot that Cromwell sayes it is an ungodly thing
> to introduce the Jews; but, if he refuse them, it is because they
> refuse to purchase it at the summe desired unlesse they may
> have the authority of a parlement for theire being there with
> safety.[152]

After the Jews' proposals had been read out, Cromwell himself took the floor and laid down the program of the proceedings in two questions:

(1) Whether it be lawful to receive the Jews?
(2) If it be lawful, then upon what terms is it meet to receive them?[153]

Wolf claims that the first question was 'purely technical' and was decided positively on the first day of the meeting. To justify his claim, he cites a source [Prynne, *Demurrer* Vol. I, Preface, pp. iii-iv]. However, this source does not state what Wolf claims, given that, as it is nothing but Prynne's relation of a casual exchange with independent theologian Philip Nye, it is far from conclusive. As his conclusion cannot otherwise be drawn from the context, we believe that his position is wrong. Apart from the traditional history accounts, it hardly seems possible that even the most capable lawyers would be able to make a decision without further ado, especially since their later statements testify to detailed study and are supported by precise sources.

Finally, we found confirmation for our view in a newspaper report which states that 'nothing has been done at the moment, but the whole matter will be dealt with in detail next Friday.' Wolf's reference to Prynne cannot convince us otherwise. In his preface, Prynne does mention Nye's statement which Nye appears to believe nullifies the legal validity of the 1290 Edict of Expulsion, [i.e. 'this business had been formerly moved in the Bishops time, rather than now'], however it is a stretch to take from this one phrase that the lawyers would therefore be of the opinion that there is no law standing in the way. Indeed, we believe that if it was the case that Nye had

---

[152] *Nicholas Papers*, Vol. III, p. 255. Translator's note: QVOS [breviographs nothwithstanding].

[153] Wolf: *Menasseh ben Israel*, p. xlv ff. Translator's note: Questions reproduced verbatim from Wolf. Regarding Wolf's claim that the first question was decided positively on the first day of the conference (p. xlix), I believe that Wolf was being deliberately disingenuous here, because he does not outline what the referenced source contains to prove his thesis, and at Wolf's time of writing, Prynne was an obscure author whose text would be difficult for readers to obtain and check for themselves. In fact, the totality of Wolf's evidence is that Nye is reported as asking Prynne: '*Whether there were any Law of* England *against bringing in the Jews amongst us? for the Lawyers had newly delivered their Opinions, there was no Law against it.*' However, there is no context to say if these lawyerly opinions (assuming Nye to be a reliable witness) had been accepted or ratified by the majority of the conference.

got this opinion from a lawyer (and there is no indication in the text that he had done so) then it is likely to have been told to him in a non-binding way in his capacity as minister during preparations for the next meeting.[154]

From what can be determined, it would appear that discussions on this issue were only taken up in the negotiations following the December 4th meeting, which apparently took place on December 7, 12, 14, and 18. It is not possible to glean from the various accounts the order of appearance of the speakers from the individual estates represented. The reports in question give only a general picture, while the newspaper notices mostly only report the fact of the conference. Based on Cromwell's questions, it can be assumed that on 7 December 1655, the second date of the conference, the question was actually discussed as to whether any laws conflicted with the admission of Jews. William Steele, Chief Baron of the Exchequer, gave a very detailed report on the history of the Jews in England up until that date. He began with the period before the Norman Conquest and argued that they had already experienced harsh treatment in the time of Constantine the Great. He then provided an overview of Jewish history up until 1290 and in particular spoke about the 1275 *Statutum de Judaismo* and the 1290 Edict of Expulsion. His historical remarks were then followed by his legal opinion, which agreed with that of Sir John Glynne, Lord Chief Justice of the Upper Bench: 'There was no law which forbid the Jews returning into England; and it was therefore insisted on, that they might come upon terms and agreements, and might at first be only permitted and connived at, which might be restrained if any inconveniency happened, and that all due care might be taken to prevent their blaspheming the Lord Jesus Christ, adoring the law, and seducing others.'[155]

The reasoning for their opinion has not come down to us. However, we can assume from Prynne's evidence to the contrary that they viewed the anti-Jewish law in question as having been given only by Edward I and not at the same time by Parliament. Had that indeed been the case, the law's validity would have expired on the death of Edward I. Prynne endeavors to show that it was not simply a royal decree of King Edward I, but a law that was passed by an act of Parliament and therefore, according to the English constitution, could only be repealed by the same process. After the conference considered the first question settled, the members of the clergy were probably asked to give their opinion on the terms of Jewish readmission, since they were the

---

[154] *Mercurius Politicus*, Issue 286, 4 December 1655.

[155] *Mercurius Politicus*, Issue 187 (7 December 1655); *Public Intelligencer*, Issue 10 (7 December 1655); *idem*. Issue 11 (12 December 1655). & *Harleian Miscellany*, Vol. VII (1811 edition), pp. 618-9; Robert Burton p. 205 ff.; Wolf: *Menasseh ben Israel*, p. xlix. Translator's note: Quotation reproduced verbatim from Burton, p. 208.

most numerous and would be expected to adopt a favorable attitude due to their prior pro-Jewish attitude.[156]

But those expecting a warm clerical welcome for the Jews were to be bitterly disappointed, because just like the lawyers, the clergy also demanded numerous conditions that restricted the Jews' freedom if they were admitted. The Jewish historians Hyamson and Wolf, while discussing the clergy's 'intolerance' at length, both fail to mention that the lawyers did not approve of unrestricted admission either.[157]

The attitude of the clergy was probably determined to a considerable extent by the opinion of a very learned man, Thomas Barlow, then librarian of the Bodleian Library. He was considered extremely skilled in logic and philosophy, which is probably why he was considered particularly suitable to write the report. He later served as Bishop of Lincoln.[158]

The work in question only appeared in print in 1692. But there can be no doubt that it was already written by the end of 1655. This is known from the foreword by the publisher/bookseller, which states that the printing of Barlow's work, 'The Case of the Lawfulness of Toleration of the *Jews'*, was based on manuscripts '*written with his own Hand*' and that it 'was writ at the Request of a Person of Quality, in the late troublesome Times; when the *Jews* made Application to *Cromwell*, for their Re-admission into *England*'.[159]

In view of the care that Thomas Barlow took in drafting the report, and the position of the clergy at the time on the Jewish Question, it is worthy of a brief overview. First, the author examines the admission of the Jews from the standpoint of the state and the church.

With regard to the former, in his opinion it was first necessary to determine whether any laws against their settlement were currently in force. In contrast to the lawyers, he affirms this to be the case, but advises that this law should be repealed if it were found that the state were to be advantaged by their admission. He does not want to investigate whether or not this is the case, as this decision is a matter for the government. However, he pointed out that in the Middle Ages the Jews brought in enormous amounts of money for the Crown through taxes and compulsory contributions. In addition, the Jews were treated 'not only Unchristianly, but Inhumanely and Barba-

---

[156] *Prynne*, Vol. I, Preface (p. 'iv'); *idem*. Vol. II, p. 135.

[157] Wolf: *Menasseh ben Israel*, p. xlix; Hyamson: *History*, p. 159. Translator's note: Note that Hyamson is virtually a *calque* of Wolf. Interestingly, both authors, following Burton's *Judaeorum* (p. 204) mention the fact that Nonconformist delegate Matthew Newcomen raised the issue that 'the offering of children to Moloch, and other idolatry' might begin to take place on British shores, a suggestion which clearly sounded ridiculous enough to Wolf and Hyamson for them to repeat it in a bid to show the folly of England's Christian prejudice, but a suggestion which may give pause to the 21st-century reader.

[158] Levy: *Barlow*, p. 152.

[159] Barlow: *Case*, 'The Bookseller's Preface to the Reader' (p. 1). Translator's note: QVOS.

rously' before 1290, so 'it may be a Query whether the Common-wealth of *England* now are not bound in Conscience and Equity' to show 'real Kindness and Civility to the present *Jews*' by granting them admission to England.[160]

For him as a Christian, it was essential to determine whether it was dishonorable, disadvantageous, or scandalous to accept Jews into a Christian state. He denies this with six arguments. Jesus Christ and Christian merchants lived among Jews, and the laws of Christian countries always provided provisions for living together with them.[161]

In addition, the immigration of Jews does not appear to him to be detrimental to Christianity. In his opinion, conversion to the Jewish faith would only entail worldly disadvantages for Christians, since the Jews were 'a dispersed and vagabond People, Slaves where-ever they come, obnoxious to the Will of those Princes and States in whose Territories they live'.[162]

Finally, Barlow believes that no scandals of any kind would arise from the admission of the Jews, and therefore dedicates the rest of his work to discussing the terms of readmission itself. He goes on to state that, when readmitting the Jews, care must be taken to ensure that:[163]

> ... this Law of Moses, and the Old Testament, is (or at least should be) the adequate rule of the Jews Religion; and therefore so long as they keep to this, there is no thing in their Religion which is intollerable on this Account, as being against the Law of Nature. But if there be any thing in their Religion (as now they profess it) superinduced by Error or Custom, which is indeed against *Jus naturale*, that should not be tolerated in this, or any Christian Common-wealth.[164]

In Barlow's view, in order to convert the Jews, it was necessary to have 'Conversation and civil Communion' with them, as was done in the days of 'our Savior and his Apostles'. There was therefore nothing unlawful in their 'Readmission into our Christian Common-wealth (with those bounds and limitations which we believe and hope the Piety and Prudence of the State will put upon them)'.[165]

Barlow emphasized that the Jews should not be given too much freedom, just as their rights had to be restricted by the state. The restrictions 'anciently laid upon them' can be found in 'our Histories, in the Imperial and Canon Laws, and in the old Capitulars and Canons of Councils', and with

---

[160] Barlow, pp. 4-7. & Barlow, pp. 7-9. Translator's note: QVOS (p. 8).
[161] Barlow, pp. 9-13.
[162] Barlow, pp. 13-21. Translator's note: QVOS (p. 18).
[163] Barlow, pp. 21-34.
[164] Barlow, pp. 34-45. Translator's note: QVOS (p. 42).
[165] Barlow: pp. 45-65. Translator's note: QVOS (pp. 48, 51-2).

the prescriptions of these antique tomes in mind, the esteemed librarian recommended the following conditions:

1. No Toleration ever was, or *de jure* can be given them to profess or practice any thing against the Law of Nature.
2. No Toleration should be given them to speak any thing blasphemously or impiously against *Jesus Christ* and the *Gospel*: For though we may tolerate them in the Profession of a bad, yet not in that Blasphemy of a good Religion.
3. They never were nor should be permitted to circumcise Children of Christians, or seduce any Christians, to their Religion: Let them profess, but not propagate their Religion.
4. They were not permitted to carry any Office or Dignity in the Christian Common-weal, though it seems that sometimes even that was permitted them.
5. They were not permitted in any Suit or Difference between a *Jew* and a *Christian*, to draw the *Christian*, or his Cause before a *Jewish* Magistrate: For 'tis a ruled Case in the Imperial Law, *Judaeus Actor vel reus, Forum sequitur Christianum.*
6. They were never permitted to make Marriages with Christians, and the Glossator gives the Reason of it in Law, *Quia matrimonium debet esse communicatio divini & humani juris.* Whereas a *Jew* and *Christian* being of different Religions cannot *communicare in Sacris.* And this is consonant to the Law of the Gospel, which forbids us to be *unequally yoked,* upon which grounds, I believe all Marriages with Papists to be unlawful, that is, *Fieri non debuit,* 'tis unlawful to make such Matches, though that *factum valet,* when such a Match is made the Contract is valid.
7. Their frequent divorcing their Wives was tolerated. For though *Moses* seem to suffer it, yet the Emperors by express Edict forbid it.
8. By the Imperial Laws Polygamy, and plurality of Wives was not tolerated in them.
9. If any of the *Jews* turn *Christian* (by Civil Law) in case the *Jews* endeavored to reduce him, and maliciously injured him, they were to be burned for it.
10. They might repair their old Synagogues, but were not tolerated (by the *Roman* Laws) to build new.

11. They were not tolerated to have any Christian Servants, Nurses or Midwives. *Can Praesenti.* 1. *Extra de Judaeis. Ex concilio malis conenti.*

12. By the Canon Law they might not come abroad [i.e. leave their homes] on *Good Friday.*

13. They were not permitted to wear Garments exactly of the Christian Fashion, but were to have distinct Habits, that all might know them to be *Jews.*

14. They might not be Physicians, or give Physick to any Christian.

15. They were not permitted to be of the *Roman* militia (though they were permitted to be Advocates) by the Rescript of *Honorius*, and *Arcadius* to *Romulianus P. P.*

16. The *Jews* being the greatest Usurers in the World, and believing they may justly take the highest Use they can get, (even *Vsurae centessimae*, if they could have it) of us Gentiles, it is all the Reason in the World, they should be limited in this particular, and not permitted to take more of us, than the Law permits us to take one of another.

17. They should be enjoyned to admit of friendly Collations and Disputations sometimes about Gospel Truths, and not obstinately to reject all means of Conversion, and Conviction, and Satisfaction of those seeming Reasons which keep them off from embracing the Truth: For there will be little hopes (or possibility) of their Conversion, if they be permitted obstinately to refuse all means of doing it.[166]

After citing another old English law from the pre-Norman period, in which Edward the Confessor deemed the Jews to be under the protection and ultimately the control of the king, Thomas Barlow concludes with the following remark:

> I wish the chief Magistrate [i.e. Cromwell] could admit them on these Terms, for so they, and all theirs (*omnia sua*) should be *suum propium* [i.e. his own property], which possibly might supply him with Money and so save Taxes.
> And upon these Terms I, (and I believe every body else) will willingly consent to their Readmission.[167]

---

[166] Barlow, pp. 66-73. Translator's note: Quoted list of conditions (and other quoted elements) reproduced verbatim from original source. The list in the original source also comes annotated with references, which refer to the 26 Latin legal and historical sources which Barlow appends to the end of text for the satisfaction of the curious reader.

[167] Barlow: pp. 74-5. Translator's note: QVOS.

It is interesting that Barlow, after very detailed study, came to restrictions on the rights of Jews that are partly consistent with our current views. Here in Germany too, there is a demand for a ban on mixed marriages and the employment of Christian servants in Jewish households.

One can imagine that this carefully prepared report by a recognized scholar made a great impression on the clergy, and so it is not surprising that the majority of the conference delegates agreed with these statements.

However, when clergymen were asked to give their opinion on an individual basis, there were still some who completely rejected the admission of Jews. Their main reason for this was that they feared contact with Jews would lead to Christians being 'seduced and cheated', and that 'it would prove the subversion of many here, because people at this time were so soon drawn aside to new opinions'. Lord President Lawrence and Major General Lambert, weak-willed tools of Cromwell, argued vehemently against this view.[168]

Some wanted to see the Jews readmitted because the Hebrews only worked in trade, and not agriculture or manufacture. As a result, their entry could increase imports and thus lead to a reduction in the prices of imported goods due to a larger supply. It may be that the expected Jewish trade would cause the sales and earnings of one's own merchants to decline, but that would have to be accepted for the overall greater good, and especially since there was still the hope of converting the Jews, as the time, it was hoped, 'is now at hand, even at the door'.[169]

Prynne's erstwhile acquaintance Philip Nye and Dr. Thomas Goodwin expressed themselves in the same spirit. They argued that the Jews, 'as natural branches of the olive-tree' who were currently being persecuted everywhere, had to be supported in some way. The Marranos were being treated particularly badly and as a result should be allowed to come to England to live and trade. 'And it seems to some, that it would be very acceptable to the Lord, if favor be shewed them, so far as is lawful herein.'[170]

Joseph Caryll was of the opinion that the Jews were unjustly treated badly in the past. This crime still had to weigh on England as a sin. With consideration for their descendants, he argued, it would therefore be advisable to amend for past wrongs by accepting the Jews.

It can be seen that most conference delegates were not in favor of unconditional admission. Cromwell and his friends therefore had to try to bring about a change in sentiment by bringing in well-known people who were friendly to Jews. There was still a distinct possibility that the City's mer-

---

[168] *Harleian Miscellany*, Vol. VII (1811 edition), p. 620; Robert Burton, p. 204. Translator's note: QVOS [Burton].

[169] *Harleian Miscellany*, Vol. VII (1811 edition), p. 621; Robert Burton, p. 205. Translator's note: QVOS [*Harleian Miscellany*].

[170] *Harleian Miscellany*, Vol. VII (1811 edition), p. 617-8; Robert Burton, pp. 208-9. Translator's note: QVOS [*Harleian Miscellany*].

chants, who had not yet been heard, would form a majority with those clergy who had advocated a complete rejection of readmission.

Before the third conference session, Cromwell therefore appointed three new delegates, men who were loyal to his Jewish cause, including Hugh Peters, who, as the oldest advocate for unrestricted readmission, was known for his significant support of the Jews. To everyone's astonishment, Peters had now also changed his mind. An epistolary discussion of his speech implies that he made comments about the Jews similar to 'a people to whom many glorious promises are made, but they are as full of blasphemy as any under the sun' and 'a self-seeking generation' who 'made but little conscience of their own principles'. He also appeared to question, if only implicitly through his criticisms, whether they were Jews at all. Apparently Cromwell and the Jews had little hope of success after this last session. Thurloe, the great friend of the Jews, wrote a very interesting letter to Henry Cromwell, the commanding general in Ireland, on December 17th, 1655, in which he confirmed the above statements:[171]

> The divines doe very much differ in their judgments about it, some beinge for their admittance upon fittinge cautions, others are in expresse termes against it upon any termes whatsoever. The like difference I finde in the counsell, and soe amongst all Christians abroad. The matter is debated with great candor and ingenuitye, and without any heat. What the issue thereof will be, I am not able to tell you; but am apt to thinke, that nothinge will be done therein.[172]

Cromwell ordered another meeting to be held.

Opposition: The Anti-Jewish Prynne and His Work

Meanwhile, public opinion had become even more hostile to the Jewish cause. Prynne had worked day and night to complete the first part of his his-

---

[171] Wolf: *Menasseh ben Israel*, p. 1 (i.e. p. 50). Translator's note: I have gone back to the original source of Wolf's supposed quotation, the *Calendar of State Papers* 1655/56 pp. 57-8, and it appears, *pace* Wolf, that these are not in fact direct quotations from Peters, but an army captain talking about a report of the speech Peters made that was given to him by his correspondent, the speech itself apparently lost to history. What has been quoted from the letter, however, appears to be the gist of what Peters said about the Jews, and it indeed appears from both letters that if Rev. Peters did not go as far as to question whether the intended arrivals really were Jews, the criticisms contained in his speech certainly made the listening audience question the identity of those who said that they were Jews.

[172] *State Papers of John Thurloe*, Vol. IV, p. 321. Translator's note: Quoted verbatim from original source.

torical work on the Jews in England. Looking at this scholarly book, one has to wonder how he managed to compile, edit, and publish the material within a maximum of 8-10 days. A longer timeframe was certainly not available to him, because he began the book on December 6, and it was published immediately before the Whitehall Conference session of 18 December 1655. It is still used today as a standard work for the history of the Jews in England up to this point in time, and we too have regularly referenced it as a source. Furthermore, none of the Jewish historians have been able to accuse Prynne of inaccuracy.[173]

Given the importance of his book and the unusual circumstances surrounding its completion, we should go into some detail about the man and his work. William Prynne was born in 1600. He studied at Oxford and later became a barrister at Lincoln's Inn. However, he was not only interested in law, but also showed a special interest in spiritual and historical matters from an early age. He harshly castigated what he considered to be unhealthy mores of his age and in this way came into conflict with the royal family. After a year in prison, he was sentenced to a heavy fine and life imprisonment in 1634.

His academic titles were stripped and his name expunged from the list of barristers. Despite everything, Prynne did not lose heart. He was allowed to continue writing in prison and still managed to publish his anti-Establishment tracts. He was made to pay a hard price for his dissent, however. One by one, his ears were cut off at the pillory and the letters S. L. were branded on his cheeks, S. L. being the initials of the words 'Seditious Libel'. All of his assets were confiscated.

The English revolution of 1641 brought Prynne freedom. On 20 April 1641, the so-called Long Parliament declared his conviction illegal and restored all of his former rights to him with the promise of compensating him for all his sufferings.

He continued to act as a champion of parliamentary rights. During the disputes between the army and Parliament around 1657, he remained loyal to

---

[173] Prynne, preface, p. 1 ff. Translator's note: I have added 'the first part of' (his historical work) to Aldag's original text, because Prynne later published a second volume of the book, which was given the title *The Second Part of a Short Demurrer*. Confusingly, while it could be read as a sequel, a lot of the information in the second edition being new, much of the first volume was also reproduced verbatim in the second volume. Prynne himself saw it as a work of two volumes rather than two editions, not least to ensure the purchasers of the first book would not feel cheated, and because the second book gave him a platform to reply to the critics of his first book. (To add to the confusion, there were also two separate editions printed of Volume I, with the second edition being slightly longer than the first and with some typographical differences in otherwise identical portions of text.) Although Aldag knew of the second book, given that he references it throughout his own work, for some reason in this chapter he tends to treat the first book (and first edition of this book) as the solitary, unmarked form, which is reflected in his referencing. & Prynne, preface, p. 1 ff. Translator's note: See also Vol II preface.

the latter and was arrested by the army for his activities. After three years of incarceration, he was released, whereupon he immediately resumed the fight for his religio-political views. He was called the Cato of his age.[174]

We have already seen how Prynne was induced to write his work by his conversations with Nye and by the anti-Jewish sentiment of the people. His main purpose was to educate the English population on the real history of the Jews, which he must have succeeded extremely well in doing. His success was due to the fact that, as a lawyer, he understood that the best method of persuasion was to let the facts speak for themselves, with his references to learned and ancient sources, not least of them the Bible, being found within the main text itself or annotated in the margins.[175]

In his book, Prynne first of all points out that, as well as the anti-Jewish laws of Edward I's reign, there were also regulations in the reign of Queen Elizabeth that made it impossible for Jews to settle. The provisions of the laws passed against the Jesuits during Elizabeth's reign were also directed against the Jews. Although the Jews are not explicitly mentioned in these laws, this is only because there were hardly any Jews in the country at that time.

Numerous laws made it the duty of every branch of government, whether king or Parliament, to uphold the fundamental principle: 'SALUS POPULI SUPREMA LEX' [the welfare of the people is the highest commandment]. However, the admission of the Jews contradicted this principle, because the history of the Jews as explained by Prynne indicated that Jewish immigration into England would endanger both the wellbeing of the people and the security of the state.[176]

But the Hebrews everywhere were still exhibiting the same behavior as in ancient England, Prynne told his readers. They were 'most grievous *Clippers, Coyners, Forgers of money, Usurers, Extortioners, and the greatest Cheators, Cozeners, Imposters in the world, in all their Merchandizes and Manufactures* whatsoever...'.[177]

Throughout history they were chronicled, from the Old Testament onwards, as notorious revolutionaries who would pose a threat to any polity, even their own kingdom.

> The Jews were always heretofore a *very murmuring, mutinous, discontented, rebellious, seditious people for the most*

---

[174] *Dictionary of National Biography* (1896), Vol. XLVI, pp. 432-436.

[175] Prynne, preface, p. 5.

[176] Prynne, pp. 54-6. Translator's note: Quoted element reproduced verbatim from original source (p. 56; second edition p. 71). Note that the original quotation was also in all caps, for emphasis within the rest of the text.

[177] Prynne, p. 57. Translator's note: QVOS. Corresponding to p. 71 of the second edition, although note that some typographical elements, such as font, format, spelling and capitalization, may vary between the first and second editions.

part, not only against God, but their lawfull Governors, Kings,
Priests, Prophets, oft tumultuously rebelling against, disobey-
ing, revolting from, deposing, murdering their Kings, and
Sovereigns; and contemning, disobeying, slaying, killing the
Prophets, Messengers whom God sent unto them... And can
we then in point of piety or policy; even in these distracted,
rebellious, mutinous times, entertain, or bring in such a Nation, People as this amongst us? Or can our despised Ministry
in this age, have any hopes of reclaiming or converting such a
people, who have thus abused, murdered, stoned their own
Prophets in former times, though immediatly sent unto them
by God himself?[178]

The conversion of the Jews to Christianity would not an advantage to England, rather a danger, as it would then make it easier for them to 'seduce the
unstable people to their Judaism and Infidelity.' There already were many of
those foreigners who, in the guise of converted Jews, were abusing and
cheating the English. How much bigger would this problem be once the
Jews were permitted entry?[179]

Prynne then gave a very detailed account [pp. 73-76] of the historical
Jewish expulsions around the world. If the contemporary reader were to consider these expulsions as justified by the Jews' crimes, then he would not
understand why the Jews were being allowed back into England.

Having therefore been thus frequently banished by Christian
Kings, Princes, from time to time, at the earnest sollicitation of
their godly Christian Ministers, Bishops, People; and by our
King and Parliament too out of *England,* so long since, never
to return again, what shadow, color of Piety, Policy, Prudence,
Justice, Law, Reason, there can be for any person or persons
whatsoever to re-admit them (except the Argument of dishonest, private, filthy under-hand Bribes or Lucre, by which they
usually scrue themselves into those places, whence they have

---

[178] Prynne, pp. 64-5. Translator's note: QVOS. Corresponding to pp. 79-80 of second edition.
[179] Prynne, pp. 72-3. Translator's note: Quoted element reproduced verbatim from original
source [corresponding to page 89 of second edition]. The reality of converted Jews using
their newly found Christian status to seduce and scam well-meaning Christians of their
money is discussed in Samuel [Translator's Bibliography], which not only gives the pica-
resque life of the vagabond Russian Jew 'Paul Isaiah' (previously mentioned in this study)
and his equally roguish foreign associate 'Peter', but also discusses the phenomenon of
Catholics masquerading as converted Jews for the purposes of Catholic subversion (giving
the case of the ex-monk Alexander Ramsey the Scot, who was circumcised to become the
baptised Jew Joseph ben Israel before his true identity was discovered).

been exiled) transcends my shallow capacity to comprehend, especially at this season, when we are so over-stored with English, that some think of sending and planting Colonies in another world; whither these Gold-thirsty Jews may do well to transplant themselves, if they be weary of their former habitations.[180]

Prynne then invoked classical antiquity, in which men like Lycurgus, Plato, and Aristotle warned states not to accept strangers into their communities. It was therefore also dangerous for the English nation to allow Jews into the country, because, as he quoted from a learned scholar, himself drawing on Aristotle's *Politics*:

> *It is perillous to take Snakes into the Bosom, and Forraigners into the Commonwealth; for as they being refreshed with heat doe bite and sting; So these being enfranchised destroy the Republike. To prove this by arguments, we may consider that every Nation hath its proper manners and ceremonies which they bring along with them, & do not change with the climat when they come into another Country; Wherefore there is great danger, left by receiving strangers the ancient manners & Laws should be changed into new and forain. Now what sooner begets sedition than alteration of Laws and Customs?...*
>
> *What therefore is more perillous than the admission of Foraigners into our Commonwealth? Moreover, wherefore hath Nature instructed like to associate together with like, if it should draw men of strange and different manners into a Republike. Nature will not that sheep should be associated with wolves, neither wills Prudence that Natives should be coupled with foraigners; For* Philosophy *perswades this, that contraries cannot dwell in the same place; but strangers for the most part are enemies to the Citizens with whom they converse. Adde to this, that as Locusts are to the corn, so are foraigners to the Republike; for as they do wast and consume the grain of corn, so these devour the fruit of the Commonwealth; for although they are branches of the same plant, yet they suck not wholesom juyce but poyson from the root, wherewith at length the whole plant being infected perisheth.*

This policy of erecting barriers to the stranger, was, Prynne told his readers:

---

[180] Prynne, p. 76. Translator's note: QVOS [pp. 93-4 of second edition].

*warranted by the Jews own practise, who had no dealings
with the Samaritans, John 4:9*, and the *Samaritans* reciprocal
carriage *towards the Jews, whom they would neither lodge nor
entertain*, Luke 9, 51, 52, 53. Why we should not upon this
account seclude those alien Jews, so different from us both in
manners, customs, Laws, Religion, and obeying not the Laws
of our Saviour Christ Jesus, *it being not for the* Kings or the
Kingdoms *profit to suffer them...*

Interestingly, although he did not reference him directly, Prynne also rebut-
ted Menasseh ben Israel's aforementioned argument for Jewish readmission,
used *ad nauseam* since the 17th century: that it is the Christian duty to welcome the stranger. Prynne argued, citing many verses of Scripture, that this
Christian hospitality extends only towards:

exiles, travellers, and other private distressed strangers, coming in to lodge, or sojourn with us for a short season in our
houses, or Country, and standing in need of our relief... but especially to such who are of the houshold of faith, not Jews or
Infidels... Not to the reception of any whole foraign Nation or
Colony into our Island to cohabit perpetually with us (the only
point in question)...

Prynne also liberally referenced Scripture to show the 'illegality, folly and
sad consequences of our receiving Jews and other strangers in such a nature,
of which our Ancestors had sufficient experience in the Jewes themselves'.[181]

It is admirable with what clarity Prynne predicted the evolution of Jewish behavior in various countries and with what reasoning he spoke out
against settlement in his own country. In his view, Jews are strangers, completely opposed to the people of the host nation, whose customs and laws
they have filled with their Asian ideas and therefore completely distorted.
What profound and prophetic words of truth!

According to Prynne's citing of the Declaration promulgated by
Cromwell on 24 November 1655, it had been stated that it was *'necessary to
use all good means to secure the Peace of the Nation, and prevent further
troubles within the same'*. Prynne therefore saw the readmission of the Jews
as a violation of this declaration:

---

[181] Prynne, pp. 77-82. Translator's note: All quotations reproduced verbatim from original
source. Corresponding to pp. 96-101 of second edition.

The bringing in of the Jews at this season, when the people are so generally divided, discontented, and declare (for ought I can learn) their highest, unanimous dislike, and detestation of it, is the most probable means *to disturb the peace of the Nation*, and to engender future new troubles, Tumults within it; the generality of the people in *England*, and in other Countries, having in former ages frequently risen up in armes against them; massacred, burnt and destroyed them, notwithstanding their Kings and Magistrates Proclamations and Edicts to the contrary. And the Jews themselves in all ages having *been principle firebrands of sedition both in their own Land, and all places where they have been dispersed...* Therefore their re-admission into *England*, (especially in this unique season) must needs be diametrically contrary to the scope of this *Declaration*; and neither in policy nor prudence to be resolved on, but utterly rejected.[182]

He also pointed out that a recent law banned the former king's supporters from engaging in any kind of public activity. The government wanted to grant all of these rights to foreigners, Jews, precisely because they were Jews, but not to the other native freeborn Englishmen, 'only for their old *delinquency* in adhering to the late King and Prince (though according to their Oaths, duties and dictate of their consciences)'.[183]

A law had also been promulgated that authorized the government to expel former supporters of the king if they endangered the security of the state, and similarly allowed for the entry of Jews:

The Orders for securing the peace of the Nation, which the *Declaration* relates to; *contrary to all the Statutes, Acts, Resolutions of our Parliaments and Law-books forecited*, upon another occasion authorize *the Major Generals and Commissioners named in them. To banish and send into Foraign parts and Plantations, all persons of the royal party formerly in arms, of no estate, and living loosly, and all persons whatsoever that shall appear by their words or actions to adhere to the party of the late King or his Son, & to be dangerous Enemies to the peace of the Commonwealth*, even without and before any Legal indictment, tryal, conviction of any particular crime, for which a Sentence of *Banishment is prescribed by our Laws:* or any Judgement or Act of Parliament inflicting

---

[182] Prynne, pp. 84-5. Translator's note: QVOS [pp. 103-4 of 2nd edition].
[183] Prynne, pp. 85-8. Translator's note: QVOS [p. 85; p. 104 2nd edition].

this heavy Punishment upon them, far worse to many than death it self.

Now I shall earnestly intreat in the name and fear of God, all those whom it most concernes, to consider in their own re-tired thoughts, how unjust, unrighteous, unreasonable, un-christian and more than brutish it will seem to all Free-born English men, and conscientious Christians, both at home and abroad, and what great scandals it may bring, both upon our Nation, Government, and Religion it self, in this manner (and on this old account alone) to banish these Christian English Freemen out of their Native Country, both from their Wives, Children, Kinred, and Gods own publike Ordinances; and at the self-same time to call in foraign, Infidel Jews, (greatest Enemies to Christ himself and Christians, and in that respect more dangerous to the peace and welfare of the Nation than those thus to be banished) to supply their places, even against an express old Judgement and Edict of the whole Kingdom in Parliament, for their perpetual exile. What a sad pernicious president [precedent] it may prove in future ages, upon every new revolution to banish all English freemen of a contrary party, and call in Forraigners in their rooms...[184]

At the end of his first volume, Prynne dealt with the arguments that the Jews' allies gave in favor of Jewish admission. They claimed that the Jews would probably be converted very easily if they settled in England. This was non-sense for various reasons, as Prynne carefully explained. There were also a great many heathen who needed salvation in the blood of Christ, and he ar-gued that by this logic:

... then we ought by this allegation in the first place to call the *Turks, Tartars, Persians, Chinoys, and all other unconverted Gentile Nations into England,* and first convert them to the Christian faith, before we bring in the Jews, whose conversion is to succeed theirs, and the Gentiles fullnesse, And then we shall have Religions enough in *England* to please all *Novelists*, and a thousand aliens to each English Native.

But even if one were to disagree, it would not be necessary to bring about the general conversion of the Jews by requiring them to settle in England; this could also be achieved 'with more ease, lesse danger and prejudice to our Nation and Religion' by sending English missionaries to the 'forraign parts

---

[184] Prynne, pp. 88-9. Translator's note: QVOS. Corresponds to pages 107-8 of second edition.

where they now reside'. In addition, as Prynne argued, the Jew never converted to Christianity out of conviction, but usually only took this step out of coercion or convenience. Furthermore, as had been shown by recent events in Spain and Portugal, even a baptized Jew would still remain a Hebrew in all of his behavior.[185]

Another reason put forward by the Jews and their allies for readmission was, in Prynne's words: '*That it will bring in much present and future gain and mony to the State, and advance trading.*' In Prynne's view, this was the real reason for the English support of the Jewish cause:

> That if this argument overpoysed not the scales, that of conscience, (the hopes of their conversion) would be lighter than the dust of the balance and sticke with no man, their mony being the only engin, which hath opened the gate and passage for them into any Christian Kingdoms at first, and made new entrance for them when they have been expelled.

Money, as Prynne affirmed, was what opened their first passage into England, and was what 'kept them so long in England heretofore, till their very banishment; A sign we love their money better than their souls or our own.' Under no circumstances should Jews be allowed to pay their way back into the country:

> For the Love of mony is the root of all evill, which whiles some coveted after, *they have been seduced (or erred) from the faith,* (as thousands of late years have been), *and pierced themselvs through with many sorrows...*
>
> And therefore let us give that resolute answer to the Jewish Agents, if they proffer to purchase an indenization amongst us by their gold, as St Peter once did to *Simon Magus* in another case: THY MONEY PERISH WITH THEE...

Prynne continued his economic argument for non-admission, and the following two paragraphs serve to introduce the many complex points he makes on various aspects of the English Interregnum economy and society at large:

> The introduction of the Jews into *England* and other Nations, never advanced the publike wealthe of the Natives and Republike, but much impaired it by their Usuries and Deceits, clipping and falsifying monies, ingrossing all sorts of commodities into their hands, usurping the Natives trades, and becom-

---

[185] Prynne, pp. 90-1. Translator's note: QVOS. Corresponds to pages 109-10 of second edition.

ming such intolerrable grievances to them, that they were never quiet till they were banished, as their greatest Annoyance,
and purchased their Exiles even with publick Subsidies granted to their Kings to be quit of them, as the premises [sources]
abundantly evidence.

The Trade of this Nation flourished more after their banishment hence, then ever it did before; and their introduction
now, will but supplant, undoe our English Merchants and other
Natives, to enrich them, and some few other Grandees, who
shall share with them in their spoils and unrighteous gains... [186]

Prynne concluded his exposition, all of which is precisely referenced, with
the following observation [quoted verbatim from original source]:

I *John* 4.3. Every Spirit that* confesseth not that Jesus Christ
is come in the flesh, is not of God, and THIS IS THE SPIRIT
OF ANTICHRIST, wherof ye have heard that it should come,
and even now already is in the world.
The case of every Jewish Spirit.

All in all, this is a book that deserves to be rescued from obscurity as one of
the first scientifically based works in the fight against the Jewish spirit. It is
nothing short of astonishing how Prynne's predictions on the progression of
the Jewish system have come to pass. History has proven how the Jews and
a small gentile elite have become vastly rich at the expense of the masses.

Continuation of the Whitehall Conference

Prynne's work was a resounding success when it was published. The people
were shaken up by the facts he presented—especially since they were already strongly opposed to the Jews—as the last meeting of the conference on
18 December 1655 demonstrates. However, that 'the chamber was thronged
by a somewhat unruly crowd of violent opponents of the Jews armed with
Prynne's newly published, virulently anti-Jewish tract' could neither be established from official accounts, nor does it likely correspond to the facts. [187]

---

[186] Prynne, pp. 99-101. All QVOS. Corresponding to pp. 119-22 of second edition.

[187] Hyamson: *History*, p. 160. Translator's note: QVOS. Wolf [*Menasseh*, p. li] also paints
this scene (likely copied by Hyamson), in less thrilling terms as 'an excited crowd, armed
with copies of Prynne's newly published tract on the Jewish question, collected to hear the
debate' although he does, unlike Hyamson, add a conspiratorial note to the novelty of the
last session being made public when he says 'On this occasion the doors of the Council
Chamber were, *for some sinister reason*, thrown open to the public' (my italics). Hyamson
alleges that the events above took place on the first meeting, when in fact most sources,

There is much to suggest that the meeting was particularly bitter, but, on the other hand, Wolf's reconstruction of events from the various accounts is particularly implausible. He apparently wanted to show that, despite the fiercest opposition, Cromwell had the last word and not only intimidated his opponents into submission, but also logically refuted them. In any case, there is no detailed description of the proceedings and we can therefore only reproduce individual moments which have been reported.[188]

Perhaps—we cannot be sure—Menasseh's friend, Mr. Henry Jessey, also spoke that day. It must have been a great surprise to everyone that he took the floor. It must have come as an even greater surprise that even he did not advocate for an unconditional Jewish resettlement. Rather, he only wanted to allow the Jews to be able to settle in certain decayed ports and towns and be obligated to pay double Customs duties on imports and exports.[189]

Apparently, the city's merchants also had their say that day, arguing that immigration would only enrich the Jewish foreigners while impoverishing the native masses. In particular, Sir Christopher Pack, one of the most influential merchants in the City and considered the most eminent citizen of his day, ranged himself with Menasseh's opponents to deliver what was said to have been the most impressive speech in the entire course of the conference.[190]

Undoubtedly Cromwell also took the lead during the course of negotiations and initially emphasized that he would not make admission dependent on any conditions. The Reverend Joseph Spence reports the following anecdote which originates from the diplomat and historian Sir Paul Rycaut, who had been present at the conference as an audience member:

> The Jews had better success with Oliver Cromwell, when they desired leave to have a synagogue in London. They offered him, when Protector, sixty thousand pounds for that privilege. Cromwell appointed them a day, for his giving them an answer. He then sent to some of the most powerful among the

---

including Wolf, point to the public being allowed entry only to what was to be the final meeting.

[188] Wolf: *Menasseh ben Israel*, p. li ff.

[189] Hyamson: *History*. p. 160. & W.: *Life and Death of Jessey*, pp. 67-68. Translator's note: An interesting phenomena to note, and what has already been hinted at in this text [Peters, Jessey], is that the Englishmen who were most noted in the 1640s for their support of an unconditional Jewish readmission as part of a doctrine of religious tolerance, had all changed their positions significantly by the time of the Whitehall Conference in 1655. One Christian student of Judaism, Alexander Ross, had even come to decry Judaism and wrote the book 'A View of the Jewish Religion' (1656) to warn the English people against readmission. See Wolf: *Menasseh ben Israel*, xliii.

[190] Robert Burton, pp. 209-10; Harleian Miscellany, Vol. VII (1811 edition), pp. 620. & *Burton's Parliamentary Diary*, Vol. II, pp. 308-9. Wolf, *Menasseh*, p. li.

clergy, and some of the chief merchants in the city, to be present at their meeting. It was in the long gallery at Whitehall. Sir Paul Rycaut, who was then a young man, pressed in among the crowd, and said he never heard a man speak so well in his life, as Cromwell did on this occasion. When they were all met, he ordered the Jews to speak for themselves.

After that he turned to the clergy, who inveighed much against the Jews, as a cruel and cursed people. Cromwell in his answer to the clergy called them 'Men of God', and desired to be informed by them whether it not their opinion, that the Jews were one day to be called into the church? He then desired to know, whether it was not every Christian man's duty to forward that good end all he could? Then he flourished a good deal on the religion prevailing in this nation, the only place in the world where religion was taught in its full purity: was it not then our duty, in particular, to encourage them to settle here, where alone they could be taught the truth; and not to exclude them from the sight, and leave them among idolaters? This silenced the clergy.

He then turned to the merchants, who spoke much of their falseness and meanness, and that they would get their trade from them. "Tis true,' says Cromwell, 'they are the meanest and most despised of all people.' He then fell into abusing the Jews most heartily, and after he had said every thing that was contemptible and low of them: 'Can you really be afraid,' said he, 'that this mean despised people, should be able to prevail in trade and credit over the merchants of England, the noblest and most esteemed merchants of the whole world!' Thus he went on, till he had silenced them too; and so was at liberty to grant what he desired to the Jews. —*L. (Who had this from Sir. P. Ricaut himself...)*[191]

---

[191] Spence, pp. 78-9. Translator's note: QVOS. Note also the introduction into the story of the offer of money for a synagogue, a novel element which may indeed be correct, or may be the distortional effect of a misremembered anecdote, or legend repeated over time (Spence wrote it down c. 1730). The '*better success with Oliver Cromwell*' refers back to a previous anecdote in Spence's book, found also in Volume 3 of this study, in which it was stated that the Jewish agents on behalf of Jewish chiefs abroad had offered Lord Godolphin £500,000 (with the potential to raise it to £1,000,000) if the government would allow the Jews the town of Brentwood, along with full trading and residence rights in the town, for which they would also bring over their richest merchants, and would additionally bring 20 million pounds in cash for circulation. Lord Molesworth reported that Lord Godolphin refused, fearing, among other things, backlash from the clergy and the merchants.

Wolf rendered this part of the speech as follows:

> Then, turning to the merchants, he harped sarcastically on the
> accusations they had brought against the Jews. 'You say they
> are the meanest and most despised of all people. So be it. But
> in that case what becomes of your fears? Can you really be
> afraid that this contemptible and despised people should be
> able to prevail in trade and credit over the merchants of Eng-
> land, the noblest and most esteemed merchants of the whole
> world?' It was clear, he added sharply, that no help was to be
> expected from the Conference, and that he and the Council
> would have to take their own course.[192]

Thus the story ends very similarly to the version found in Robert Burton's
Judaeorum Memorabilia. Wolf cites the official report in *Harleian Miscellany*, *Judaeorum Memorabilia* and Spence's *Anecdotes* for his version. The
first two passages, however, are completely silent about this part of Cromwell's speech, so that Wolf could only have got his text from Spence. But
there is a big difference between the source text and Wolf's rendition: while
according to the former Cromwell himself actually described the Jews as a
very evil and despicable people, according to Wolf's version he did not insult them on his own initiative, but simply took the merchant's view of the
Jews for his argument.[193]

Why did Wolf make this change, which Hyamson, presumably in good
faith, then adopted for his own work? Was it unpleasant to him that Cromwell, whom he described as the greatest friend of the Jews, had said such
bitter words about the Hebrews?[194]

According to Spence's account, Cromwell also silenced the merchants
completely, 'and so was at liberty to grant what he desired to the Jews'.

According to the most comprehensive account, Henry Jessey's *A Narrative of the late Proceedings at White-hall, concerning the Jews* (1656), a
16-page quarto-sized chapbook which is also reproduced in the *Harleian
Miscellany,* the final meeting ended in the following way:

> All having been heard, the Lord Protector on the 18 of De-
> cember and before, professed, that he had no engagement to
> Jews, but only what the Scripture holds forth, and that He had
> hoped by these Preachers to have had some clearing of the

---

[192] Wolf: *Menasseh ben Israel*, p. liii. Translator's note: QVOS. Note also the use of the
word 'sharply', which implies a rebuke, absent from the other accounts.
[193] *Harleian Miscellany*, Vol. VII (1811 edition), p. 621; Robert Burton, p. 210.
[194] Hyamson: *History*, p. 161.

case, as to conscience. But seeing these agreed not, but were of two or three opinions, it was left the more doubt full to him and the Councel. And he hoped to do nothing herein hastily or rashly: and had much need of all their prayers, that the Lord would direct them, so as may be to his glory, and to the good of the Nation. And thus was the dismission of that Assembly.

Burton clearly used the Jessey pamphlet as his primary source, as the excerpt below shows:

> Now the Protector having heard all their sentiments upon the affair, declared, 'That he had no engagement to the Jews but what the Scripture held forth, and that since there was a promise of their conversion, means must be used to that end, which was the preaching of the gospel, and that could not be had unless they were permitted to reside where the gospel was preached. That he had hoped, by these preachers, to have had some clearing of the case, as to matters of conscience, but seeing these agreed not, but were of different opinions, it was left more doubtful to him, and the council, than before; and he hoped he should do nothing herein hastily or rashly, and had much need of all their prayers, that the Lord would direct them so as might be to his glory, and the good of the nation.'[195]

This differs considerably from the version given by Spence and shows that the greatest caution should be exercised when assessing the reliability of Wolf's presentation of events. While Wolf broadly repeats the ending of the official version, his final addition of the sentence: 'So saying, he vacated the chair in token that the proceedings were at an end', which, when read along with his addition of the word 'sharply' to describe Cromwell's tone, gives the reader the impression that he left the chamber abruptly in a fit of pique, which is not at all found in the other sources.

Today it is difficult to fathom what exactly happened after 18 December 1655. What is certain is that 'the Conference ended without further adjournment'. Diplomatic correspondence reveals that that Cromwell later heard the opinions of his ministers. We are not told anything about the outcome of this new meeting, but it is likely that no result was achieved there either. Wolf and Hyamson both state that a committee report was submitted

---

[195] *Harleian Miscellany*, Vol. VII (1811 edition), p. 621; Robert Burton. p. 210. Translator's note: Both QVOS, although in the first case I also took the spellings and other historical elements from the original pamphlet, available online at the University of Michigan Library digital collections.

to the Council of State according to which it would agree to Jewish readmission under certain conditions listed in the document, but it appears that the report was not formerly accepted by the Council. Wolf cites a report contained in surviving state papers to support this claim. It is true that this copy is undated and unendorsed, which means that there is no guarantee for the accuracy of the date of 13 November 1655 as suggested by Mrs. Everett Green in the *Calendar of State Papers*. On the other hand, while Wolf is forced to admit that there is not the slightest mention of it in the Order Book of the Council of State, elsewhere he gives the date of this document as 13 November 1655. If this date for the document is correct, then it cannot be the committee report submitted to the Council of State after the Whitehall Conference, as it would pre-date the first meeting (which took place on December 4 of that year).[196]

Cromwell had recognized from the outcome of the conference that there was still great resistance to Jewish readmission. Public opinion, which even Cromwell could not completely ignore when making his decisions, was bitterly opposed to the Jews entering England. The people could foresee the long-term consequences of approving Cromwell's request, even if Cromwell himself was incapable of doing so. As a consequence, there can be no doubt that the so-called Whitehall Conference was a complete failure for the Jews.

Nevertheless, in apparent obliviousness to the reality of what actually took place in December 1655, in 1906 the occasion of the Whitehall Conference was celebrated with a pompous banquet in London to mark its 250th anniversary. A large number of leading men attended this celebration, and the speeches delivered culminated in the highest praise of the Jews ever heard. A member of Parliament did not shy away from making Brahms fully Jewish and Goethe part Jewish, for the glory of the Jewish nation. No one, especially an Englishman, should fail to read the speeches that were given at the event. Unfortunately it would take us far too long to discuss them in detail here, but we would like to include a small excerpt from the speech of the then Earl of Crewe. After explaining that he was related by marriage to the House of Rothschild and that he himself had Jewish blood in his veins through the marriage of one of his ancestors to a Jew, he continued:[197]

---

[196] *Mercurius Politicus*, Issue 288, December 18th, 1655. & Letter sent by Salvetti dated December 31st 1655 in Roth: *New Light*, p. 130. & Wolf: *Menasseh ben Israel*, p. 56 ff. & Hyamson: *History*, p. 162. & Henriques: *Return*, p. 54. Translator's note: For the *State Papers* entry in question, see the text corresponding to footnote 221. Henriques reproduces this report in full [*Return*, pp. 52-54], and argues convincingly that it appears less like a document proposing the conditional re-entry of Jews, and more of a 'pros and cons' list made during a debate to decide whether the Jews should be allowed entry at all. & Wolf: *Re-Settlement*, p. 11.

[197] Wolf: *Whitehall Conference*, p. 276. ff. Translator's note: That the details of what actually happened in 1655 were irrelevant to the 1906 gathering is indicated by the fact that

Many of you are, no doubt, aware that books are published indicating the descent of various people in this country from the
royal family. Honest citizens study these volumes, and find
they are descended from a Plantagenet or even from a Tudor
monarch, and their satisfaction at the discovery is only tempered
by the fact that hundreds of thousands can boast the same distinction. But my suggestion is this: Some person of leisure with
a taste for genealogy should attempt to trace the Jewish descent
of what I may call the titled and untitled nobility in this country.
Without going quite so far as Mr. Lowell—for it must be admitted that there are men of tolerable intellect and good character
with no Jewish blood in their veins—yet that inquiry would
come as a revelation to some people of the extent to which
English families have been allied with those of the Jewish
race. And who shall say—I certainly shall not—that these alli-
ances have been anything but an intellectual gain, and, I have
no doubt, of moral benefit, to the people of this country?[198]

Words from a British nobleman! No further comment is needed.

As has already been well demonstrated, the majority of the Jews who
came from all over the world left London in bitter disappointment after the
Whitehall Conference. However, Menasseh ben Israel held out—and probably some other Jews with him.

The Struggle Goes On

The legal path to entry, that is, the one approval by Parliament, had failed.
The Jews therefore took the path that was not unfamiliar to them, namely,
through the back door. In the scrap remains of a letter dated 31 December
1655 that had been preserved among state papers, we find the following confirmation: "The Jews, we hear, will be admitted by way of connivency,
though the generality oppose."[199]

Even back then, the means used by the Jews were the same as they are
today: they tried to get ahead through bribery. On the same day, Salvetti, the

---

not a thing is said about the Whitehall Conference itself in the article, except for the fact
that the anniversary for the event fell on Dec 4th, 1905 [which implies that there had been
only one Whitehall meeting]. & Wolf: *Whitehall Conference*, p. 284. & Wolf: *Whitehall
Conference*, p. 285.

[198] Wolf: *Whitehall Conference*, p. 293. Translator's note: QVOS. '*Without going quite so
far as Mr. Lowell*': In one of the preceding speeches at the banquet, James Bryce MP said
that 'the late Mr. James Russell Lowell asserted that nearly all the eminent literary and
artistic men of the last two centuries had been of Jewish stock' (*ibid*, pp. 284-5).
[199] *Domestic State Papers*, Vol. 1655/56, p. 82. Translator's note: QVOS.

Tuscan envoy, wrote to his government that the Jews were doing their best to win over their opponents through bribery and thus gain their purpose '*a colpi d'oro*' [i.e. by force of gold].[200]

But the other means, so often used on such occasions, of convincing the public of the just Jewish cause through so-called 'enlightening' or 'progressive' propaganda, was also used. In particular, it was deemed essential to try to have counter-propaganda to Prynne's brilliant work. At the beginning of January 1656, a small pamphlet by John Dury [or Durie] appeared, who saw his life's goal as the unification of all Protestant states. For this purpose, he travelled everywhere and was known throughout Europe, not only because of this but also because of his writings. His pamphlet was addressed to Samuel Hartlib, a friend of John Milton's, who had made a name for himself in England as an educational reformer.

In this short tract he took the position that admitting Jews did not violate the laws of England, despite providing no evidence for this. Nevertheless, he recommends that the state put the necessary restrictions in place to 'avoid the temporal inconveniencies which may arise from their [the Jews'] covetous practices and biting usury, and other subtilities in trade, by which we of the Nation may be prejudged in our Liberty, and brought in some respect or other under their power.' However, if the state took measures against these issues from the outset, he had no concern about the settlement of Jews—on the contrary, he welcomed it, for in such an event there would be the prospect of their conversion to Christianity, which he saw as a Christian duty. But Dury then added a postscript according to which he apparently wanted to apply so many restrictions that he came very close to the aforementioned conditions laid down by the clergy. In this postscript, he offered to send a copy of the Jewish statute for the German state of Hesse, where he was residing, a statute which was well known for its restrictiveness, but which he approved of: 'Our State doth wisely to goe warily, and by degrees, in the busines of receiving them.' He once more implored the need for care when receiving the Jews:[201]

> Menasseh Ben Israels Demands are great, and the use which
> they make of great Priviledges, is not much to their commen-

---

[200] Roth: *New Light*, p. 130. Translator's note: QVOS.

[201] *Dictionary of National Biography* (1888 edition), Vol. XVI, p. 261-263. & *Dictionary of National Biography* (1891 edition), Vol. XXV, p. 72-3. & Dury: *Case*, p. 2. Translator's note: Note that the *Harleian Miscellany* reproduction is completely reliable, but those wishing to see the original pamphlet can find it on Internet Archive, its authorship misattributed to Samuel Hartlib. & Dury: *Case*, p. 8. Translator's note: QVOS. It really is quite astonishing to see how blithely some ancient commentators could countenance the irreparable destruction of the wellbeing, freedom, and security of future generations. & Dury: *Case*, p. 5.

dation here, and elswhere. They have wayes beyond all other men, to undermine a State, and to insinuate into those that are in Offices, and prejudicate the Trade of others; and therefore if they be not wisely restrained they will in short time be oppressive, if they be such as are here in Germany...[202]

One sees that in this postscript John Dury has retracted much of what he said in the main text itself on behalf of the Jews.

Another pro-Jewish treatise appeared, this time by Thomas Collier, which was probably published at the instigation of Cromwell. In the preface, the author stated that Cromwell alone had the power to help the Jews, which was why he had dedicated his work to the Lord Protector.[203]

In his introduction, Collier made clear that his treatise was intended as a refutation of the anti-Jewish publications.[204] Nevertheless, Collier could not deny that the Jews had always been an insubordinate people. He also admitted that they practiced usury, but to him this was not a big deal, given that other individuals in the country were already working in the same business. Despite this disadvantage, they were needed in England to increase trade. From the outset, deterrent laws would have to be made against usury, defaming Christ's name, and the risk of ritual infanticide[!]. The people were considerably upset at the Hebrews, which was a result of the spread of false teachings. The Jews had been given their freedom in other Protestant countries, such as Holland, so why not England as well? And when it came to trade, arguably the most important issue for the dedicatee, if not the writer himself: '... even if their trade means a loss for some rich merchants, it is generally to the overall benefit of the people: the more goods come into the country, the more plentiful and cheaper the supply.'[205]

Although the Jews had their faults, they were still the chosen of God, who would one day make them leaders of all nations and punish those who treated them badly. It would therefore, Collier argued, be better to let them come into England.[206]

Apparently this book did not succeed to swaying popular opinion to the Jewish cause, especially since Prynne published the second part of his scientific work in February 1656. In his preface to the second book, Prynne remarked that the extraordinary short deadline for his first book, which needed

---

[202] Dury: *Case*, p. 9. Translator's note: QVOS.

[203] Graetz: *Geschichte der Juden*, Vol. X, p. 109. & Collier, Preface.

[204] Collier, p. 3.

[205] Collier, pp. 7-8. Translator's note: Sadly, I do not have access to the original source, so cannot verify the wording of this otherwise incredible statement, all the more so given that it appears in an apology for Jewish readmission. & Collier, p. 9. & Collier, p. 12. & Collier, p. 13.

[206] Collier, pp. 16-7. & Collier, p. 21 ff.

to be written and in print before the end of the Whitehall Conference in order to be of any use, necessarily meant that he had had to omit a lot of relevant historical research. This research was now being published as a second volume, which those who had bought the first volume could then append to the original text. This sequel deals mainly with the period of Jewish history before the year 1230. Prynne emphasized that the Jews' ongoing state of banishment was affected by a public law of Parliament, and used the opportunity provided by a second book to refute the counter-arguments generated by the first. He also called on the public to go and look at the antique documents he had cited, which were archived in the Tower of London and which proved the facts of his thesis, thus justifying his stance against the Jews in general. This last comment is interesting for the fact that it coincides with our view that only scientifically-based educational writings will be of any use in solving the Jewish Question.[207]

Another book was written at the end of 1655, but was not published until the following year. The author only uses the initials 'W. H.' to identify himself, although it is now known that this was William Hughes, a lawyer of Gray's Inn. Judging from the scientific basis of the book, it must have been a learned personality. Here, too, there are references to old documents and manuscripts. The second part deals mainly with the Menasseh's book *The Humble Addresses*, with Hughes accusing Menasseh of not having adhered strictly to the truth. Menasseh is also accused of not answering the question of whether the Jews would really make up for the damage that they would inflict on the native merchants with the predicted increase in Customs and Excise revenue from their own trading activities [Hughes believed that they would not]. In contrast to Menasseh, Hughes did not consider it an advantage that the Jews did not have a homeland, because they—or their capital—could leave England again just as quickly as their persons and capital (as Menasseh himself admitted) were currently leaving Spain. Nor was it to be forgotten that their loyalty to the traditional royal houses and state institutions was never very strong; on the contrary, they were inclined to revolt in every place that they settled.[208] History also taught that:

> [T]he Jews at all times have so, for the most part, behaved themselves, as that they have ministered to the Christians occasion of dislike and prejudice; and that all the slaughters and massacres of them may be laid at their own doors. Here in *England*, they first begun to crucifie children and oppress the

---

[207] Prynne, Vol. II, p. 135 ff. & Prynne, Vol. II, p. 144.

[208] *Anglo-Judaeus*, pp. 51-2. & *Anglo-Judaeus*, 'The Epistle Dedicatory', p. 32. & *Anglo-Judaeus*, p 35. & *Anglo-Judaeus*, pp. 36-9. & *Anglo-Judaeus*, pp. 39-44. Translator's note: The author helpfully provides the reader with a history of Jewish revolts from antiquity onwards.

people, before they were injured, to speak on, or molested, they spoiled the coyn [coin] in *Henry* the Second his days, and yet had the priviledge of burying in all places of their abode granted. The first tumult we read of raised against them was at the Coronation of *Richard* the first, and that was occasioned by themselves, offering to come into the Kings house, notwithstanding a proclamation to the contrary.

And the occasion of the tumult at *Lin* [King's Lynn] was, their endeavour to kill a Convert: their grievous extortion at *Stamford*, *York*, and other places, drew upon them the inconveniences that followed. After this the people inraged, prosecute them as National enemies, yet they leave not off their extortions, make it their annual practice to crucifie children, conspire against City and people, still clip and spoil the coyn, as very earnest to undo themselves.

In addition, there was also the question of their national loyalty:

> *Their faithfulness* is sufficiently known, say what they will (however always to the true interest of this Nation) and if they should for better terms, play false with the State, hold intelligence with the enemies thereof, counterfeit the Coyn, clip the Money, set the Cities on fire, would not a safe prevention have proved better, than a too late remedy?[209]

After these statements, one would expect that the author would come to an outright rejection of the Jews. Not quite. Perhaps for the same reason that the book is anonymous, the author ends the book with clever diplomacy, saying that he desires the Jews 'no evil will' and hopes that they continue to flourish in the foreign lands in which they currently reside, but given their memorial they have left behind in England (as thoroughly documented in his book), the nation of Judah would perhaps be better remaining abroad, for the good of both nations.[210]

What was the situation in general, and how did Cromwell in particular behave in the months following the Whitehall Conference? Our only authoritative information about this comes from the reports of the aforementioned Tuscan envoy Salvetti to his government. On January 7 he wrote that the Jews were still hoping for a favorable decision from Cromwell. In a letter dated January 28 he wrote that Cromwell's final decision was still not

---

[209] *Anglo-Judaeus*, pp. 45-6, 48. Translator's note: QVOS. On the question of national loyalty, the author also brings up the 'Treason of *Lopez*' (p. 46).

[210] *Anglo-Judaeus*, p. 52. Translator's note: Quoted element from original source.

known. Meanwhile, Jews held their religious services in their homes. This latter remark has, moreover, led some historians to the wrong conclusion that the Jews were already allowed to freely practice their religion at this time. Salvetti then mentioned in his messages of February 4th and 11th that talk about the Jewish Question had died down and that for the time being the Jews were content to be able to go about their prayers secretly. Apparently Cromwell was happy to let them continue as long as it didn't cause a public scandal. On February 25 we learn from Salvetti that talk about the Jews was virtually at an end. That was his last word on the matter.[211]

What went on behind the scenes after the collapse of the Whitehall Conference continues to remain a mystery. It will probably never be determined why Cromwell refrained from making a decision that was favorable to the Jews. Perhaps it was the opposition from the clergy and the City of London merchants, or even the resentment of the people, that stayed the hand of the all-powerful Lord Protector. Or perhaps it had proven impossible to reach a decision on the price that Jews should pay for their privileges. As has already been mentioned, on 24 January 1656, Colonel Whitley commented in a letter to Sir Edward Nicholas that Cromwell thought it an 'ungodly thing' to admit the Jews, but that if he refused them, it would only be because 'they refuse to purchase it at the summe desired'.[212]

This anecdote about Cromwell indicates that he had little to no interest in the Jews as people, his desire to 'help' them instead motivated by how he could exploit them for political-economic gain. However, the Jewish Question was soon to return to the spotlight of domestic political events in England when, as early as March 1656, a flare-up of tensions was sparked by the so-called 'Robles case'. In the spring of 1656 war broke out between England and Spain. The Privy Council had announced its decision to confiscate the private property of all Spaniards in England for the benefit of the government.[213]

A certain Francis Knevett, an Englishman with a knowledge of Spanish, had been close to the Marrano community for a long time. By an unexplained coincidence, but likely through civil service connections, Knevett was informed of the Privy Council's decision a few days before the official announcement. He met with John Baptista Dunnington, factor to the rich Marrano *don* Antonio Rodrigues de Robles and revealed the secret to him, and in his shock at the news Dunnington blurted out that Robles and other Marranos were Spaniards [i.e. not Portuguese nationals, as had been generally presumed]. Dunnington also explained that the two ships which had just arrived in London with a rich cargo, although registered in his name, actually

[211] Roth: *New Light*, pp. 131-2.
[212] Nicholas Papers, Vol. III, p. 255. Translator's note: QVOS. The full quotation from this letter can be found earlier in this volume (see text corresponding to footnote 232).
[213] Wolf: *Menasseh ben Israel*, p. lx ff.

belonged to Robles. Of course, this could easily come out, especially if the papers were confiscated. The damage would be very great, as Robles not only had considerable stocks of goods in storage, but also had forty thousand gold ducats kept in strongboxes in his house. Dunnington admitted that similar agreements existed with other Marranos, which meant that such a decree being enforced would necessarily ruin not only the Marrano community, but also himself. In his panic-stricken state, Dunnington revealed all of his secrets. The conversation was overheard by a third person, Philip del Hoyo, who was simultaneously taking notes of Dunnington's statements. Immediately after the announcement of the aforementioned decision, all of Robles' assets, including the two cargo-laden ships, the 'Two Brothers' and the 'Tobias', were confiscated by the government.[214]

Robles sent a petition to Cromwell asking for his assets to be released. He justified it by saying that he was not a Spaniard, but 'a Portuguez borne and of the Hebrew nation'. He pointed out that he had 'resided heere many yeares and payd many thousand pounds for Customes' to the English government through his trading. He relied on the testimony of one of his young employees to claim that he had Portuguese nationality.

The Robles trial opened. During the course of witness questioning, Robles' employee declared that he could not lie—he knew for a fact that Robles was Spanish. In response to Robles' objection that he had married a woman with Portuguese nationality, the employee replied that he would not thereby acquire Portuguese nationality. Thus Robles was unable to provide evidence for his claim and at the same time was unable to refute either Knevett's testimony or the statement of Philip del Hoyo, the man who had overheard Dunnington's confession.[215]

The remaining Jews began to recognize the danger Robles was in. If it were found that he had Spanish nationality and the confiscation of his assets was therefore legal, they would have to fear the same fate. Apparently they were ready to support their fellow Jew by any means necessary. They therefore came forward as witnesses and were admitted to testify. Probably—to the chagrin of Robles and his friends—only a few said that he was Portuguese. Dunnington was also questioned and had to admit that he had previously heard everyone say that Robles was Spanish. As a result, Dunnington had never considered him to be Portuguese, although he had recently heard opposing views. It was also not true that Robles kept a lot of money in the house, according to the report of Dunnington's witness testimony:

---

[214] Wolf: *Crypto-Jews*, pp. 60-3; Henriques: Return, p. 54-55; *Domestic State Papers*, Vol. 1655/56, p. 227. Dunnington's panicked response may be due to the fact that not only would the seizure of the Marranos' goods see him irreparably ruined, but he was only 21 or 22 years old at the time of the event [based on *Crypto-Jews*, p. 81].

[215] Wolf: *Crypto-Jews*, pp. 62-3. Quotations reproduced verbatim from Wolf's appendix of the trial documents [p.77].

> [T]o the second question whether he conveyed mony out of
> his house upon Notice given him of the Seasur [seizure] that
> would be upon Spanyards I answer that I never did ether see
> him nor hear say that he ever did convey any mony out of his
> house. Besides I know sertainly that he never kept any more
> money in his house thin what he spent in the house for he not
> having a Cashkeeper did always keepe his moneys att a gold-
> smithes whose name is Mr. Backwell who reseived it and
> payd it out according to his order.

From this last part of this statement, it can be deduced that the 40,000 gold
ducats initially mentioned by Dunnington were not found during the confiscation, so he must have retracted his earlier confession to Knevett. Robles
was also questioned himself and of course claimed that he was not Spanish.
When confronted, however, he had to admit that he had lived for a long time
in Spain and in the Canary Islands, which are known to be Spanish colonial
possessions. Furthermore, he could not deny that he had been in the service
of the Spanish government for several years. Finally, witnesses said that he
had attended masses in the Spanish embassy, since he had previously
claimed to be a Catholic.[216]

An impartial judge should have found, after the evidence, that Robles
had Spanish nationality and that the seizure of the assets was legitimate. Although some Jews had stated the opposite, when weighing the value of their
statements, their own interest could not be ignored, which cast doubt on the
truth of their statements. But apart from that fact, Robles had generally been
considered a Spanish national before the trial, which Dunnington confirmed
in his initial agitation. Furthermore, if there were no concerns about Robles'
nationality, there would have been no need to register the ships that had just
arrived in Dunnington's name. Then there was the fact that Robles himself
had to admit that he had lived on Spanish territory for many years and that he

---

[216] Wolf: *Crypto-Jews*, pp. 60-6; Wolf: *Menasseh ben Israel*, pp. lx-lxv; *Domestic State
Papers*, Vol. 1655/56, pp. 227, 247, 274, 294, 316; Henriques: *Return*, pp. 54-59. Translator's note: Quotation reproduced verbatim from *Crypto-Jews*, p. 82. Wolf (ibid, p. 63),
explains this evidence for Robles' Spanish nationality in the following way: 'Seeing that,
according to his own account, he had flown from Portugal to Spain, it is probable that he
was one of the New Christians who so strangely conspired in 1641 to re-establish the
Spanish domination in Portugal, and hence his claim to Portuguese nationality would
scarcely bear a close scrutiny. Indeed, his uncle, Duarte Henriques Alvares, when asked
how it was that his nephew could venture on Spanish territory, answered significantly that
"the Portugalls who took part with the King of Spain were free to live in his territories".
One at least of the London Marranos [Simon de Souza] seems to have figured in the conspiracy of 1641.' While this provides a theoretical underpinning to Robles' Portuguese claim, it
does inadvertently lend itself to the unfortunate *tropes* that Jews have no natural loyalty to
their host nation and feature disproportionately in national ferments and revolutions.

had even been in the service of the Spanish government. Finally, there were positive statements from some witnesses that he was a Spanish citizen, so that there could not be the slightest doubt that Robles belonged to the Spanish polity, which Wolf apparently did not dispute.[217]

With all of these facts available, a corresponding verdict would probably have been expected. However, the Admiralty Commissioners, who were entrusted with this task, announced that 'they cannot ascertain whether Robles was a Spaniard or Portuguese.' The Privy Council therefore had to decide whether or not the seized assets were to remain in state custody. Its decision of 16 May 1646 was to lift the confiscation order. No reason was given for this. There should be no doubt, the Jewish writer Graetz asserts, that Cromwell brought about the decision.[218]

We ask ourselves whether once again, as with his general treatment of the Jewish Question, Cromwell's attitude was contingent on the Jews' sup-

---

[217] Wolf: *Status*, p. 178. Translator's note: Note that the statement Aldag is refers to ('as Jews, the Marranos were none the less Spaniards') can only be seen as incorrect, given that it implies that all Marranos whose Spanish ancestors fled to Portugal after 1492, over 150 years before the events in England, would still be considered Spanish nationals. Given that Wolf's wider point was about Catholicism rather than Spanish nationality, and he knows that the term *Marranos* refers both to Spanish and Portuguese crypto-Jews (*ibid*), a more accurate term for him to use would have been 'Iberians' rather than 'Spaniards'. For Wolf's view on Robles' himself, see footnote above.

[218] *Domestic State Papers*, Vol. 1655/56, p. 325. Translator's note: QVOS. For a man whose thesis is that the Jews are a separate race, and therefore cannot be a part of their host nation, Aldag, in my opinion, is being somewhat disingenuous here, for the historical record shows that this incident forced the Marranos of London to 'come out' publicly as 'of the Jewish nation and of the tribe of Judah' as a defense strategy for Robles (*Crypto-Jews*, p. 65). This fact naturally made it difficult for the Privy Council to determine Robles' nationality as Spanish or Portuguese, given that both Iberian nations had violently repudiated the Jews *qua* Jews, which included Jews living in crypsis, leaving the individuals affected with a liminal and often transnational official identity (as Robles) due to the need to escape ongoing persecution. Robles' obviously Castilian name was not the Portuguese one (Fererino) he had been reputedly given when reputedly born in Fundão, Portugal. Nor could the Council even be assured of Robles' Jewishness, given that he was uncircumcised. Indeed, the historical significance of this case is less the 'unjust' verdict meted out by Cromwell, and more the fact that, for the first time since 1290, Jews had openly admitted to having formed a Jewish community on English soil. & Wolf: *Crypto-Jews*, pp. 66, 86; Wolf: *Menasseh ben Israel*, p. lxvi. & Graetz, Vol. V, p. 117. Translator's note: It should be noted that Graetz is an unreliable source for this case, given that he gets proven facts wrong in his account (e.g. Robles was arraigned 'on the charge of being a Portuguese Papist', and his property seized 'because England was then at war with Portugal and did not tolerate Papists in general'). Therefore, Graetz's assertion, that the Privy Council set aside the confiscation 'at Cromwell's suggestion assuredly' because 'the accused was not a Catholic but a Jew', should be treated with caution. However, it is fitting to mention here that 'the great Jew' Carvajal, protected from the seizure order by his denization seven months earlier, was doubly protected from his asset seizure by a special order of the Privy Council (*Crypto-Jews*, p. 63).

ply of money. If we answer this in the affirmative, then in this case the sum must have been large enough to prompt him to make the decision that favored the Jews. Whatever the case, the reason for the outcome has certainly proved resistant to the light of day. Otherwise it would have been stated, especially since the entire factual and legal situation pointed to the opposite verdict being the correct one.

We shall now turn to the part that Menasseh ben Israel played in this affair and the activities he was undertaking in the interim. March 23rd, 1656 must have been a lucky day for him after all his many failures, because we find an entry in the public records according to which he received from Cromwell 'a pension of 100*l* per annum, payable quarterly, and commencing from the 20th day of February, 1656[-7]'.[219]

We can deduce from this that Cromwell was not ungenerous. Yet it is, in our opinion, somewhat strange that a head of state would grant a foreigner a pension in such a situation. This is all the more surprising given that Menasseh ben Israel did not even achieve success in his mission, nor was his activism approved of by the English people, the people whose money it was.

During the course of the Robles case hearing, Menasseh also took an active role. In 'The Humble Petition of The Hebrews at Present Reziding in this citty of London whose names ar vnderwritten', addressed to Cromwell and dated 24 March 1656, Menasseh's was the first of the seven Marrano names listed as signatories. In contrast to the petitions of previous years, he had scaled back his aspirations considerably. He asked only for written permission for the Jews to gather in their private houses for devotion and to have their own burial place outside of the city. Cromwell passed the request on to the Privy Council for further action, but it did not even give a response, let alone comply with the Jews' wishes.[220]

From the petition's wording it can be deduced that Cromwell had, on his own initiative, verbally granted the Jews the right to privately practice their religion, because the petition begins with the Jews thanking him for this permission, but asking for explicit written confirmation of the same. This apparently never happened. Apart from the issue of whether Cromwell's oral

---

[219] *Fifth Report of the Deputy Keeper*, Appendix II, p. 263. Translator's note: QVOS. According to letters written by Menasseh to Oliver Cromwell, and a letter written by John Sadler on behalf of Menasseh's widow to Richard Cromwell [Wolf: *Menasseh*, lxxxvi ff.], as well as in Wolf's opinion, it would appear that this pension was never paid, although Henriques [*Return*, p. 64] disagrees. In addition, John Sadler's letter indicates that Menasseh's mission to England had been the result of encouraging letters from Oliver Cromwell (and other notable Englishmen) sent out to various synagogues. Henriques [*Return*, p. 60] indicates that Cromwell gave Menasseh a pension to allay the embarrassment of the rabbi's penurious situation in England.

[220] Wolf: *Crypto-Jews*, p. 76. Translator's note: QVOS. & Wolf: *Crypto-Jews*, p. 76. *Domestic State Papers*, Vol. 1655/56, p. 237. & Henriques: *Return*, pp. 44, 61.

promise was legally valid under the English constitution, it is doubtful whether, even if this were the case, the oral promise would not be viewed as revoked by the refusal to confirm it in writing.

To support his petition and in a bid to change popular opinion on the Jews, Menasseh published another work on 10 April 1656, titled *Vindiciae Judaeorum*. The short book takes an epistolary form and is addressed to 'a Noble and Learned Gentleman' whose name Menasseh does not mention. The preface reveals that this individual had previously written to Menasseh and asked him to write this *vindication*. It is probably not wrong to assume that Prynne's educational tract must have made a deep impression on the English people, which was why the Jews and their supporters felt compelled to formulate a public response to *the Reproaches Cast on the Nation of the Jewes*.[221]

In the first section of his book, Menasseh wrote with passion about the allegation that Jews killed Christian children on their holy days: 'I cannot but weep bitterly, and with much anguish of foul lament that strange and horrid accusation of some Christians against the dispersed and afflicted Jewes that dwell among them...' In fact, according to Menasseh, Jews were not only forbidden from killing by religious law, but they abhorred such acts, given that: 'The children of Israel are naturally merciful, and full of compassion.' The incidents stated in the past by various writers and sources were either fabricated or false accusations made by Christians in order to shift their murders onto the poor Jews.[222]

The next three sections were devoted to explanations of synagogue ceremonies and the Jewish religion in general. It was also not true, as Menasseh made clear in the fifth section, that the Jews tried to convert Christians to their religion. Menasseh also saw no disadvantage in the fact that Jewish merchants had established themselves in England. If anything, the state would have an increased revenue from Customs and Excise duties and the prices of goods would naturally fall, benefitting more people. The Jews would also bring to England all of kinds of life-enhancing, hitherto unknown commodities and knowledge from far-flung places, thank to their global connections. These same global connections would ensure that the nation which treated Jews well would be extolled all over the world.[223]

---

[221] Wolf: *Menasseh ben Israel*, pp. lxiii-lxiv. Translator's note: The date is also given at the end of the main text (p. 39) of the tract itself (p. 145 if being consulted in Wolf). The full title of the tract is: *Vindiciae Judaeorum, or a Letter In Answer to certain Questions propounded by a Noble and Learned Gentleman, touching the reproaches cast on the Nation of the Jewes; wherein all objections are candidly, and yet fully cleared.*

[222] Menasseh ben Israel: *Vindiciae Judaeorum*, pp. 2-16. Translator's note: QVOS (pp. 2, 5).

[223] Menasseh ben Israel: *Vindiciae Judaeorum*, pp. 16-31. & Menasseh ben Israel: *Vindiciae Judaeorum*, pp. 31-2. & Menasseh ben Israel: *Vindiciae Judaeorum*, p. 33-4. Translator's note: Examples of the 'things so necessary for the *life of man*' that the Jews would import into England are 'wine, oyl, almonds, raisins, and all the drougs of India'

In no way were there more fraudsters among the Jews than among other nations. Rather, the Old Testament and the Talmud prohibited Jews from cheating, stealing, or robbery, whether from other Jews or from Gentiles. Prynne's statements about the punishment of the Jews under Edward I were made purely out of hatred and were completely unfounded.[224]

Menasseh concluded his remarks by saying that he still had hope for the general scattering of the Jews—'the holy people'—from one end of the earth to the other, which would necessarily include their admission to England, with all of the expected favorable consequences that this would bring. He also described what had inspired him to go on his mission to England:

> [T]he communication and correspondence I have held, for some years since, with some eminent persons of *England*, was the first originall of my undertaking this design. For I alwayes found by them, a great probability of obtaining what I now request; whilst they affirmed, that at this time the minds of men stood very well affected towards us; and that our entrance into this Island, would be very acceptable, and well-pleasing unto them. And from this beginning sprang up in me a semblable affection, and desire of obtaining this purpose.[225]

Even if Graetz thinks that the book produced 'the desired favorable effect' in England—which we believe would be the case with the Jews and their allies—Menasseh was still unable to bring about a change in public opinion in favor of the Jews. As a result, Cromwell did not dare do anything for him openly. Menasseh was devastated by the failure of his mission, but held out in London until 1657. It was only when the son who accompanied him died in September that same year that Menasseh's spirit broke and he returned to Holland, taking his son's body with him, where he followed him to the grave a few months later at the age of 53.[226]

Much has been written about the fact that the Jews were granted a burial place in February 1657, probably through Cromwell's personal intervention. Here too, it is primarily Wolf who makes this claim, which is based on

---

[224] Menasseh ben Israel: *Vindiciae Judaeorum*, pp. 34-7.

[225] Menasseh ben Israel: *Vindiciae Judaeorum*, p. 37 ff. Translator's note: Quoted element and QVOS. While he diplomatically does not name names, he implies that he knew Cromwell would be pleased at his arrival: 'And finding that my coming over would not be altogether unwelcome to him...'

[226] Graetz: *Geschichte*, Vol. X, p. 112. Translator's note: Quoted from original source. & Wolf: *Menasseh ben Israel*, p. lxviii ff. Hyamson: *History*, p. 166. Translator's note: It is worth consulting the letters referenced in footnote 327 to see the tragedy of Menasseh's last few years in England, dealing with the stresses of mounting debt and ill health, begging for pension money that had been agreed but which never came.

two documents from the years 1656/7 and 1670. The former has been lost, and its existence is only known because the document from 1670 refers to it. The 1670 document states that the lease for a plot of land in Mile End (Stepney) had been signed by 'Anthony Fernandez Carvayall' and Simon de Caceres in February 1656/7. Henriques rightly argues that it was probably just a matter of leasing a private garden (where the Jews may have secretly buried their dead), as there is nothing documented to support Wolf's theory. Indeed, the fact that the rabbi Menasseh transferred his son's body to Holland in September 1657 supports Henriques' carefully argued thesis that it must still have been illegal to burial a body with non-Christian religious ceremonies, and that Wolf's 'Jewish cemetery' was unknown to authorities. Since this issue is of minor importance to us, we can leave it at the above statements, because even if the Jews had been granted a burial place, this would not change their overall legal situation. Rather, it would only support our assertion that Cromwell generally tolerated the Jews.[227]

Another theory advanced by Wolf is that Cromwell promised general protection to the Jews in 1658, which can be deduced from his granting of John Sadler's request to allow the Jews to build a synagogue. This theory is based on a comment found in the biography written by Sadler's grandson Thomas Sadler in 1738. Henriques has also commented on this and demonstrated, by an analysis of the original manuscripts on which the 1738 comment was based, that it cannot be correct. A detailed analysis of the passages cited by Wolf also do not stand up to careful scrutiny. But this controversial issue is not of particular importance either. Even if this assurance were given by Cromwell, it should not be seen as a legally binding declaration for the future, but only as a further expression of his personal policy of toleration. We shall return to this topic shortly.[228]

We have seen above how Cromwell favored the Jews as much as possible, but how even he could only grant privileges to the extent that Parliament and the Privy Council would approve them. When Menasseh was called to England in 1655, Cromwell was certainly willing to provide the Jews with the permission necessary to legalize their residence, but even the all-powerful Lord Protector had to bow to the will of the people. After the Whitehall Conference he realized that his plans could not be achieved. He was only able to assert his influence, and only to the extent that the Jews he

---

[227] Wolf: *Re-Settlement*, p. 12 [*Jewish Chronicle*, 28/12/1887, p. 8]; Wolf: *Menasseh ben Israel*, p. lxvii; Hyamson: *History*, p. 166; Adler: *Homage*, p. 38. Translator's note: Israel Davis also gives an abstract of the lease in the *Jewish Chronicle* of 26/11/1880. & Henriques: *Return*, p. 62. & Henriques: *Return*, p. 65-6. Translator's note: Henriques is by far the most informed source on this matter.

[228] Wolf: *Menasseh ben Israel*, p. lvii; Wolf: *Status*, p. 180; Wolf: *Re-Settlement*, p. 12; Hyamson: *History*, p. 163 ff. & Henriques: *Return*, pp. 59-60. Translator's note: Again, Henriques is the better authority in this matter. & Henriques: *Return*, pp. 59-61.

wanted for special purposes were tolerated in the country. Undoubtedly, under the laws of England at the time, the Jews were not allowed to worship publicly: they were therefore tolerated in England without having any rights. They always had to be prepared to be expelled from the country if the political situation took a turn for the worse, particularly if Cromwell ceased to have influence.

It is undisputed among historians that from the middle of the 17th century onwards, England decidedly steered its social structure and mental attitude towards commercialism. In 1915, the well-known writer A. M. Ludovici had the following to say about the fruits of this revolution:[229]

> The revolting cruelties of our early factory and mining life, the appalling brutality of our treatment of children in industry, the callous barbarity of the apprentice traffic (once so scandalous in England), the hideous ill-treatment of the little chimney-sweeps, and the hard unconcern with which even the modern world allows thousands and thousands of the proletariat to be dehumanized and sickened by besotting and hopeless labors—all these things, with which no monarch, however benign, however patriarchal, can now interfere, I regard as merely part and parcel with the original brutality of the true ancestors of the modern world, the Puritan and Free Parliamentary party, whose power, whose principles and whose life-despising morality have been paramount in England ever since the last upholder of good taste and popular liberty was overthrown and murdered by them in the fatal fifth decade of the seventeenth century.
>
> And when I look around me to-day, and perceive the harsh, ugly, unhealthy, vulgar, nervous and spiritless life of modern times; when I see the seething discontent in all grades of society, and especially in the women of north-western Europe, it seems to me by no means extravagant or even fantastic to suppose that at this present moment we are witnessing the final unfolding of the bloom, the finest flower and the most perfect product of that religion of gain and greed, of trade and so-called liberty, of *uncontrolled* capitalism and unscrupulous exploitation; of the contempt of beauty, health, vigor, sexuality and high spirits, whereof the hygiene, the diet, the moral principles and the whole outlook on the world are to be sought and found in the general attitude of Prynne, Vane, Cromwell, Essex, Pym, Fairfax, Harrison, Hewson, Waller and the rest of

---

[229] To name just one: Clark: *Later Stuarts, 1660-1714*, p. 35.

odd names and natures which constituted seventeenth-century Puritanism.[230]

He convincingly argues that the struggle between King Charles I and the Republicans under Cromwell was not so much about differences in religion as about differences in economic theory. Charles I opposed with all his might the emerging financial power in the country, represented by the Puritans, who wanted to ruthlessly exploit the population for enormous profits. Indeed, he even sealed his commitment to the welfare of his subjects with his own death.[231] There can also be no question that the entire transformation in the views and mindset of the English people was caused to a large extent by Puritanism.

Another factor, for those able to perceive it, is also undisputed: the influence of the Jews in England. The most striking feature of the difference between the history of Jews on the European mainland and their history in England is that, in the latter case, the Jews never lived in ghettos when they resettled. Rather, they lived unhindered among the population and used their influence in the ways that are generally known. The Jews in England around the middle of the 17th century had already progressed to the point that their continental brethren only managed to reach at the beginning or even in the middle of the 19th century: an incredibly important factor that is either ignored or deliberately neglected by historians who are not used to thinking and researching with our historical lens.

Without going into detail as to why the Jews in England played a significant part in this transformation of English life and character, the fact itself is at least sometimes mentioned by some historians. Sir George Clark points out that the Jews played a role in the aforesaid 17th-century cultural shift in that they had considerable influence in trade, banking, and insurance. The extent to which the Jews were already influential in the commercial life of England in the first half of the 18th century is shown in a pamphlet from 1753.[232]

The change in England in the 17th century can therefore mainly be traced back to Puritanism. Both Judaism and Puritanism have a lot in common and therefore complement each other. In his book, Ludovici explained how Puritanism led to the rise of trade, but at the same time led to the ruth-

---

[230] Ludovici: *Defense of Aristocracy*, pp. 235-6. Translator's note: Other recommended books on this topic are William Cobbett's *A History of the Protestant Reformation in England and Ireland* and R. H. Tawney's *Religion & The Rise of Capitalism*. Both authors argue convincingly that this problem of self-serving English religious doctrine predates Puritanism [see Translator's Bibliography].

[231] Ludovici: *Defense of Aristocracy*, p. 31 ff.

[232] Clark, p. 35. & 'Philo-Patriae': *Further Considerations on the Bill*, p. 31 ff.

less exploitation of the people, as is always the case with the system used by the Jews.

There are significant differences of opinion on how things have developed from the 17th century to the present day. Most historians, business leaders and politicians in England see this development as a blessing. They argue that the English Empire [latterly known as the British Empire], the largest empire of all time, was built through this capitalist system. Even if we agreed with their point of view, this vision of history seems to focus too much on the last 200 years—a short period of time in the life of a people! Rather, the question should be: How will this system affect the nature and culture of the English people in the future? But such ponderings would take us into the realm of theoretical ideas, which we would like to stay away from as far as possible—our approach is one of discovering, analyzing, and synthesizing provable facts. We would rather pose the question in the following way: Has this system been a blessing for England to date, or has it already produced disadvantages that may one day in the future outweigh its advantages? Because while the question is about England's future, we can only answer it correctly if we deal with the facts of the present.

CHAPTER 3
ROYAL PROTECTORS OF THE JEWS
(1658-1714)

Jews Allied with the Royalists

Oliver Cromwell died on 3 September 1658, and his son Richard was installed as his successor that same month. Anti-Jewish forces immediately returned to the fore among the people, and after just a few weeks a certain Richard Baker presented a detailed petition to Richard Cromwell.

The City of London was probably behind this petition, as its main complaint was the decline of English trade due to Jewish competition. Admittedly, the war with Spain was taking its toll, and it was primarily 'the blood-sucking *Jews*, and other Strangers' who 'export not our Native Commodities', instead importing foreign goods of all kinds and then sending abroad England's specie [precious-metal money] 'and so they eat us out, and extract and get away the wealth of these Nations'. Baker also pointed out that '2/3 of the monies that this day is turned by exchange, is their monies, and hereby they also make great benefit on us'. In addition, the Jews in 'Italy, Portugal, Spain, Turkey, Holland &c.' had conspired to dictate their terms to English shipowners, effectively running an international cartel which has effectively turned them into the 'chiefe Traders' who 'devour this Commonwealth; and it is to be feared that in a short time they will carry away the whole wealth and treasure of these Nations'. If the English shipowners refused to accept the disproportionately low freight rates offered to them, the ships would often have to return in ballast. There was no doubt to Richard Baker that, unless something was done, English shipping, and English merchants generally, would soon be doomed to ruin.[1]

Baker made several suggestions for increasing English trade, the ninth of which is as follows:

> *To Expell or Banish the Jews*, and presently to have an exact account made up of the value of the Native Commodities they have exported, and what those they have imported amount unto; and if it be not thought fit that all the over value shall be paid unto the State, yet that they be fined, for extracting the

---

[1] Wolf: *Menasseh ben Israel*, p. 71; Hyamson: *History*, p. 167. & Baker, pp. 15-6. Translator's note: All QVOS.

wealth of their Nations: and that the like Inquisition be made
in some measure with other Strangers.[2]

The petition did not meet with any success and, as far as can be determined,
Baker did not even receive an answer, which was probably in the most part
due to the generally precarious political situation after the death of Oliver
Cromwell. The instability did not end with Richard Cromwell's abdication at
the end of April 1659, which cleared the path for the return of Charles II.

We shall now briefly examine the stance that the Jews adopted after the
Whitehall Conference towards the rising level of Royalist sentiment in England. As early as 1655 we can see that leading circles of the Royalist party
were interested in the Jews. In the previously discussed letter of 20 September 1655 from Sir Marmaduke Langdale to Sir Edward Nicholas, secretary
of the exiled King Charles II, Langdale wrote the following:

> For that clause of Mr. Overton's letter which mentions the
> Jewes, it proceded from some discourses I had with Mr.
> Brokes [Sexby] about them, who seamed much to favour them as
> necessary for a kingdome, and I believe their tenents do not much
> differ. I desired Mr. Overton to sound their intentions by some of
> his party in Holland. I am very sorry they agree with Cromwell.
> The Jewes are considerable all the world over, and the great
> masters of money. If his Majesty could either have them or di-
> vert them from Cromwell, it were a very good service...[3]

It is clear from this excerpt that the Royalists in Holland had put out feelers
for a rapprochement with the Jews living there. However, the Royalists
could not succeed, for at that very moment the leaders of world Jewry were
planning to send Menasseh ben Israel to London, as they had pinned all of
their hopes on an agreement with Cromwell.

However, the situation looked completely different a few months later,
when by February 1656 the Jews' negotiations in London had been deemed
a failure. It had become clear to them that even the all-powerful Cromwell
could not get them the necessary parliamentary approval to settle in England.
They therefore changed sides within a short time and made themselves
available to the Royalists. As can be seen from a mandate from Charles II to
General Middleton on 24 September 1656, the Royalists were already in-

---

[2] Baker, p. 17. Translator's note: QVOS.
[3] *Nicholas Papers*, Vol. III, p. 51. Translator's note: QVOS (with a few spelling conventions updated to ensure reader comprehension). As is alluded to in the main text, this letter
was also discussed in Volume 2, where the subsequent part of this quotation about the
Jews can be found.

clined at this time to make binding cooperation agreements with the Jews. This document is so interesting in every respect that we have reproduced it below:

CHARLES, by the grace, etc. To our trusty and well-beloved servant, Lt. Gen. John Middleton...:

Whereas you have represented to us the good affection which some principle persons of the Hebrew Nacion resyding in Amsterdam have expressed to you towards our service, and that they have assured you that the application which hath bene lately made to Crumwell on ther behalfe by some persons of that nacion hath been without ther consent, and is utterly disavowed by them, and they are desirous by all offices to express ther good will to us and desyre our reestablishment. Wee do heareby appointe you to lett them know how gratiously wee accepte these ther professyons, and that wee are very farr from that prejudice to them as to look on them as enimyes, and that wee shall be gladd to receave any such evidence of ther affection to us as may be an argument in better times to us to avow and declare our resolutions in ther favour.

And wee do heareby give you full power and authority to treate with such of the principle persons of that nacion who for ther interest and discretion are most fitt to be trusted in an affayre of such importance, and to assure them that if they shall in this conjuncture be ready by any contributions of mony, Armes, or Ammunicion to advance that service with which wee have intrusted you, that shall finde that when God shall restore us to the possission of our rights and to that power which of right doth belonge to us, wee shall extende that protection to them which they can reasonably expecte, and abate that rigour of the Lawes which is against them in our severall dominions, and you shall tell them that if in these our streights, when by our conjuncture with Spayne they cannot but looke upon our affayres as in a hopefull condicion, they shall lay a signal obligacion upon us, it will not only dispose us to be gratious to them, and to be willinge to protecte them, but be a morall assurance to them that wee shall be able to do whatsoever wee shall be willinge when we can justly publish and declare to all men how much wee have bene beholdinge to them, and how farr they have contributed towards our restoration, which no doubt will by all who are well affected to us be valued as it ought to be.

And wee do likewise give you full power and authority to receave all summes of mony, Armes or Ammunition as

they shall be willinge to furnish you, and acknowledgement
under your hande shall oblige us to the repayment of the same
as soone as wee shall be able in the same manner as if the
same were delivered to ourselfe, and for what you shall do in
pursuance of this our Commissyon this shall be your warrant.
    Given at Bruges [Belgium], 24 September 1656.[4]

The Jews promised money, weapons, and ammunition, resources that play a
major role in waging war. They gave all of this for a bill of exchange, based
on the uncertain future of Charles II. Because only in the event of his ascension to the English throne would he be able to pay back the money and protect the Jews in return. A good deal for both parties, but a big financial risk
for the Jews, as the success of Charles was far from assured. The fact that
they accepted the deal in spite of this uncertainty shows their enormous interest in moving the center of their world politics to London.
    Wolf has challenged the commonly held view that the Hebrews collud-
ed with both Cromwell and his adversary Charles II. To justify this, he cites
the fact that the Jews in Holland, with whom Charles negotiated, were always on the side of the Royalists, and never wanted anything to do with the
Puritans. Meanwhile, their ethnic brethren in England, such as Carvajal and
de Caceres, remained loyal to Cromwell (although there were the exceptions
of da Costa and Coronel, who always supported Charles II). There is no way
that one can follow Wolf's line of reasoning. It is beyond doubt that Charles
II or General Middleton negotiated with the Jews in Amsterdam. But we saw
previously how world Jewry, under the leadership of the Jewish colony in
Amsterdam, sent Menasseh to London to negotiate with Cromwell. There is
no evidence to prove that there were different opinions among the Jews in
Amsterdam about his departure. On the contrary, we have already seen how
Menasseh himself wrote that the Jewish community of Holland received the
English envoys with 'great pomp and applause' in their synagogue [see Volume 2]. Even if some Jews pretended to disagree with Menasseh's mission,
this was probably only a bet-hedging strategy, to save face on both sides. In
fact, it may be the exact same group of Jews that turned to Cromwell in the
autumn of 1655 as came to an agreement with Charles II the next year.[5]
    Although from the outside, the leading Hebrews who sided either with
Cromwell or Charles II were different people, given the well-known cohesion of the Jews globally, concerns arose from the outset as to whether da
Costa and Coronel were not collaborating with Carvajal and de Caceres.

---

[4] Firth: Scotland pp. 342-3. Translator's note: Translation reproduced verbatim and with
original spellings as per original source, although the i/j and u/v spelling conventions have
been updated for reader comprehension.
[5] Wolf: *Menasseh ben Israel,* pp. 73/74.

This assumption becomes a certainty when one considers that the da Costa and Mendes families are so closely related that they are effectively seen as one entity. The Mendes family, the Rothschilds of 17th century Holland, were, as has previously been stated, in close collaboration with Carvajal and Caceres in favor of Cromwell. There is too much involved in this situation to make us believe that Jews who were related and had business connections with one another took completely different political paths, especially since the goals of both strategies were ultimately the same: admission to England.[6]

The same findings and conclusions apply to Coronel, or to call him by his full name, Augustine Coronel-Chacon, who was formerly an agent of Carvajal's in Lisbon and a relative of the Mendes family. All these facts, verified by documentary evidence, should clearly prove that the Hebrews had two irons in the fire in order to secure themselves with each side.[7]

In accordance with their agreement with Charles II, the Jews distributed funds to promote the Royalist party and did everything else possible to further its cause. Coronel was a close friend of General Monk, who played a crucial role in the restoration of Charles II. So was it also Jewish money that in this case caused Monk to take this stance? We can no longer prove it, but can only conjecture due to his connection with the Jews and their known behavior in this regard.[8]

In this period of English history, we also find the oft-criticized behavior of the Jews switching sides in matters in which they want to achieve something for themselves. But what we have detailed is nothing new, even for that time. When they were expelled from the country by a decree of King James I, we find them on the side of the Republicans in England as early as 1643. Their support for Cromwell was therefore only an expression of this behavior. But how quickly they changed sides again when Oliver Cromwell's star started to fade and they came to realize that they could not expect any help from his weak son in achieving their English, and therefore global, ambitions.[9]

Richard Cromwell abdicated at the end of April 1659, and about a year later Charles II entered London as King of England. In the meantime, however, numerous political events had taken place; neither the Jews nor their opponents had been idle. Apparently the former had made a renewed attempt to secure a well-known building for conversion into a synagogue. Hence we find, in the surviving state papers, the following entry for 16 June 1659: 'The

---

[6] *Jewish Encyclopedia*, Vol. IV p. 288 (s.v. COSTA, DA, PEDIGREE); Wolf: *Crypto-Jews*, p. 72. & Wolf: *Crypto-Jews*, p. 72. Translator's note: See also Volume 2 for further evidence of this collaboration.

[7] Hyamson: *History*, p. 137. & Wolf: *Jewry*, p. 17.

[8] Wolf: *Jewry*, p. 15 ff.; *Crypto-Jews*, pp. 71, 74-5; *Status*, p. 182 ff.; *Menasseh ben Israel*, p. 73. Translator's note: Today the general's surname is more commonly rendered 'Monck'.

[9] Cunningham: *Growth*, Vol. I (The Mercantile System), p. 325.

Jews offer to buy the beautiful room in Whitehall for their synagogue, and promise not to demolish it.'[10]

This time it was not St. Paul's Cathedral that was to be used for Jewish religious services, but rather a no less well-known gala room in the government district of Whitehall. Obviously nothing came of the offer. The political conditions at the time were probably the main reason for this failure, and were why the efforts of those opposed to the Jews similarly came to naught.

This time the anti-Jewish forces were led by a man named Thomas Violet. He was a goldsmith and alderman of London. As a supporter of Charles I, he was punished by the Republicans with many years in prison. After his release, he did everything he could to uncover banned gold and silver exports. Perhaps in his extensive investigations, Violet came across export crimes committed by the Jews—who, as is well known, controlled a large part of this trade—and thus became their bitter enemy. No further details can be found in this regard. In any case, in December 1659 he appeared before Mr. Justice Tyril, to whom he verbally presented his intention to take action against the Jews using documentary evidence. Tyril seems to have agreed with Violet on the matter. However, the judge advised the goldsmith to wait until Charles II had returned to England, advice which left Violet very dissatisfied.

How much the political order was in a state of great upheaval can be seen from many other events and writings. In the latter category, a short pamphlet from 1660 with the title: *Awake O England* is of interest. The anonymous author complains bitterly about the ruinous conditions brought about by Cromwell and calls on the populace to recall King Charles II as quickly as possible. He particularly objects to the established bad practice of revealing English manufacturing methods to foreigners, given that he mentions it twice in the pamphlet:[11]

> The Mysteries of our crafts, and the Materials of our Manefac-
> toures, do find such acceptable receit in forraign parts, as un-
> conscionable men have brought the Ruines of their own Coun-
> trey into a trade...
>
> [W]e presently encounter another *Object* of our sorrows,
> the Body of our Trades is anatomized, desected, and from the
> most intrinsique secrets thereof, is discovered to Forreigners,
> all workings in wool, which together with that material have,
> by the providence of our Ancestors been, with all their Wis-
> dome, restrained from other Nations, are now so much at lib-

---

[10] *Calendar of State Papers*, Vol. 1658/59 p. 367. Translator's note: QVOS. Thomas Violet, in his 1660 *Petition*, stated that the Jews had attempted to buy the Court of Whitehall.

[11] *Dictionary of National Biography*, Vol. 20, p. 374. & Hyamson: *History*, p. 170; Wolf: *Jewry*, p. 13. & Violet: *Petition*. pp. 7-8.

erty, and by false-hearted *English* men, made so familiar to strangers, as not onely our Mysteries are laid open, but our materials are made theirs, and that trade of cloathing, which in one valuable kind of another, maintained eleven or twelve parts of our Kingdoms, is almost totally lost to *England...*[12]

Given that Jews were also among the foreigners, so we are interested by the slogan *Awake O England,* because centuries later this same call has been made once again by the English Fascists and the National Socialists.

Repelling a City Attack

On 20 May 1660, Charles II landed in Dover and on May 29 he entered London. Many issues were awaiting legislation. The Jewish Question also immediately appeared as an issue to be dealt with.[13]

All laws and regulations, in particular all of Oliver Cromwell's actions, were declared null and void unless the express consent of Parliament had been given. This meant the Jews had fought in vain for their residence permit in England, as they had only enjoyed Cromwell's personal protection. With Cromwell's death, they had no state sanction for their presence in England. We now see all the more clearly the importance of the Jewish agreements with Charles II, according to which he promised them, in the event of his return, the same personal protection that Cromwell had given them. The Jews' switching of sides had therefore been worth the financial risk, as even under Charles II they had no hope of receiving legal approval from Parliament for their presence in England. As before, the overwhelming majority of the English people were against their admission, as can be seen from the sequence of events in 1660. What is certain is that the anti-Jewish forces among the populace effectively knew nothing about the king's agreement with the Jews, and took the legal position that the Jews' residence in England was without state approval.[14]

Consequently, it is understandable that immediately after Charles II's arrival in June 1659, Violet appeared again before Mr. Justice Tyril and

---

[12] *Harleian Miscellany*, Vol. I, p. 275 ff. Translator's note: Quotations and title reproduced verbatim and with original punctuation from the original 1660 pamphlet, available online at Internet Archive. The quotations from the pamphlet (which correspond to pages 6 and 7), correspond to page 277 of *Harleian Miscellany*, which reproduces the pamphlet with the more modern typesetting, spelling and punctuation conventions of the early 19th century, making it the more readable option for the modern researcher. The pamphleteer disguises his anonymity with a pseudonym which becomes a clever pun when inserted into the rest of sentence: 'Printed for *Charles Prince,* and are to be sold at the East end of St. *Pauls,* 1660.'

[13] *Dictionary of National Biography*, Vol. IV, p. 91.

[14] Henriques: *Return*, p. 77.

asked for instructions on how to proceed with his complaint. Tyril referred him to some members of the Privy Council, whom he himself informed in detail about the laws and existing documents on the Jewish Question and with whom Violet and Tyril apparently initially discussed and prepared the case. Only on 30 November 1660, did the Privy Council eventually deal with the case, as far as can be determined from the following entry in the *Calendar of State Papers* for that year:[15]

> [Nov. 30] 140. Remonstrance, addressed to the King, concerning the English Jews, showing the mischiefs accomplished by them since their coming in at the time of William the Conqueror; the privileges which they purchased by money; their prosperity notwithstanding their oppressions and taxations, their ill-dealings and banishment by Edw. I. at the desire of the whole kingdom; yet they have since returned, renewed their usurious and fraudulent practices, and flourish so much that they endeavoured to buy St. Paul's for a synagogue in the late usurper's time; suggesting the issue of a commission to enquire into their state, and the imposition of heavy taxes, seizure of their personal property, and banishment for residence without licence, &c.[16]

It is not entirely clear whether the Privy Council only dealt with Violet's petition that day or also other people's petitions on the same matter, but it is also irrelevant. In his petition, Violet first pointed out the previous history of the Jews in England. He certainly based this on Prynne's research, which we are familiar with. What interest us, however, are his observations about the Jews present in London and their businesses. We hear that they became extraordinarily rich in a short time and caused considerable damage to the English merchants, using their wealth to take over trade everywhere. The populace's aversion to them is also very strong. Violet suggested that the king treat the Jews exactly as his predecessors had before 1290. Accordingly, it was advisable to impose special taxes on them and to consider their assets as belonging to the king. In any case, the latter should not tolerate them trading in England without a special license.

Of course, in order to monitor them, it would be necessary to appoint loyal subjects to investigate all of their transactions. Alternatively, there was nothing standing in the way of the king banishing the Jews from England once more. If the king could not bring himself to do this, he would definitely

---

[15] Violet: *Petition*, pp. 7-8.
[16] *Calendar of State Papers*, Vol. 1660/61, p. 366. Translator's note: Quotation reproduced verbatim and in full from original source.

have to place special taxes on the Jews and ensure that the English merchants were given opportunities to regain their trade.[17]

Moreover, Violet found a powerful ally in the City of London's notables, who had acted even sooner than he had to get their petition in front of the king. In the words of Lucien Wolf:

> Scarcely had Charles arrived in the Metropolis when the Lord Mayor and Aldermen of the City of London presented to him a humble petition, bitterly complaining of the action of Cromwell in permitting the Jews to re-enter the land, and asking the King 'to cause the former laws made against the Jews to be put in execution, and to recommend to your two Houses of Parliament to enact such new ones for the expulsion of all professed Jews out of your Majesty's dominions, and to bar the door after them with such provisions and penalties as in your Majesty's wisdom should be found most agreeable to the benefits of religion, the honour of your Majesty, and the good and welfare of your subjects.' The long pent-up wrath of the city found full expression in this petition, which must be read in its entirety to be appreciated.[18]

Fortunately, the contents of this petition have been preserved in their entirety for us to read, so that in this instance we have the view of a corporation and not just of an individual (the latter usually tending towards anonymous diatribes), because Jewish historians have a marked tendency to defame the character of anti-Jewish individuals, who are usually cast as scoundrels and notorious liars.[19]

The petition from the City of London is a detailed document. Here we only find sober statements from merchants about their economic situation. The trade of English companies had declined horribly solely due to the fact that the exportation of woolen and other native commodities had fallen into the hands of:

> ... such strangers both Christians and Jews who live here obscurely, free from family expenses and charge of Public offices and, by the assistance of drawers of Cloth, Packers, Clothwork-

---

[17] Wolf: *Jewry*, p. 13; Henriques: *Return*, p. 76, n. 1. & Thomas Violet's petition is reproduced verbatim in Wolf: *Status*, pp. 188-192.

[18] Wolf: *Status*, p. 182. Translator's note: QVOS. We can be sure of the order in which the king received the petitions, because the text continues: 'Mr. Thomas Violet followed with another petition, which was equally violent.'

[19] For a contemporaneous example of such defamation, see *The Great Trappaner of England* (1660).

ers & others, pretended English merchants defraud your Majesty and your Kingdom of that foreign Trade which can more than sufficiently be supplied by your Majesty's native subjects.

This 'grand complication of mischief' was all thanks to 'late usurper' Cromwell, who, prompted by his own 'corrupt interest':

> ... resolved as subtly as wickedly to let in that swarme of Locusts for a plague upon us who are now daily multiplied by the accession of whole families of them from all parts (as if your Majesty's dominions were condemned to be the Sink into which the scum of Mankind should be emptied for a plague to your subjects) from which most if not all hereditary Monarchies of Christendom are secured & against which your petitioners do humbly hope that your Majesty will provide an antidote when your Majesty shall have considered how prejudicial most Jews are ...

The king was warned not to tolerate them in the country. In other states that were by no means friendly to England, they had already managed to gain a foothold in the governments themselves. Given their ties to one another, it is entirely possible that the Jews living in England would pass on important information to their ethnic brethren living abroad:

> That those Jews having no other relation to these Kingdoms but their present liberty in order to the gaining of money and having their kindred & friends dispersed in all the Kingdoms & States of Christendom under a disguise of Christians and many of them crept into public employment under the neighbour Princes & States, those Jews doubtless here will by their correspondency with their said brethren discover the ocurrences of your Majesties affairs, as far as they can do to the prejudice of your Majesty's just & Honourable designs especially if it may serve those foreign States into whose dominions they have a free & sure retreat when they can do no further mischief here.

To make matters worse, there was also the issue of the Jews sexually exploiting the native English women and 'tainting the blood' of the nation:

> ... as to the Honour of the nations of your Majesty's dominions, they have already debauched some necessitous [destitute] ones of the weaker sex to the abominable taint of the English blood & bringing on us the infamy of a mixt nation...

Then there was the problem of fraudulent trade, and Jewish behavior generally, leading to an impoverishment and bankruptcy of the native people:

> ... your Petitioners already groaned under the wheel of their oppression; who are People that make it a practise to deceive Christians & are never just but when they cannot be otherwise; who never employ a Christian to gain a penny under them when none of their own tribes can serve them; who have found the way to buy our native manufactures on the best terms to ship them under English disguise and prostituted their price of them in foreign ports and raised the price of foreign Commodities to the great damage of your Majesty's subjects in all the ports of the Spanish and Portugal dominions so as if they be continued here that whole trade will be drained from the English to the irreparable loss of their Majesty's native People & that not only by these subtle underminings but by pure frauds also as appears by every fresh & sad experiences of several of them who having cheated other Christians in foreign parts under one name have assumed another & betaken hither and here by the confederacy of their own sort raised themselves a Reputation so as to obtain credit from your Majesty's subjects and then retired themselves with the English estates to the ruin of many good families.

The City of London therefore humbly requested that the king take action against this unregulated trade, and in particular:

> ... that your Majesty will be pleased to cause the former Laws made against Jews to be put in execution & to recommend to your two houses of Parliament to enact such new ones for the expulsion of all professed Jews out of your Majesty's dominions & to bar the door after them with such provisions and penalties as in your Majesty's wisdom shall be found most agreeable to the safety of Religion the honour of your Majesty and the good & welfare of your subjects.[20]

---

[20] Guildhall Archives, Remembrancer, Vol. IX, Nr. 44, fols. 1-18. [Reproduced in Wolf: *Status*, pp. 186-188.] Translator's note: All quotations reproduced verbatim from Wolf. Given the vast amount of breviographs and arcane spelling conventions which made the text difficult to decipher, I have found it necessary to modernise the spelling to ensure reader comprehension.

So in order to keep the race pure and to prevent the nation from being bled dry, the English people demanded the expulsion of the Jews: demands of the Third Reich!

Thus, individual Englishmen and, above all, the most powerful body of men in England, had requested the resolution of an important question. What could have been more natural than for the constitutional monarch to at least have the proposal discussed by the House of Lords and Parliament, especially since Charles II would have had to be very keen to maintain popular support after his return. But what actually happened to that properly submitted petition?

On December 7th we find in the minutes of the Privy Council the remark that the City's petition for the expulsion of the Jews was being discussed. There was also a petition from Fernandez Carvajal's widow and other Jews to be protected. That Carvajal's widow is named as one of the most important petitioners is interesting in that her husband, who died in 1659, was the main supporter of Cromwell's cause, to the great detriment of Charles II—further proof of our previously stated view that the switch of sides was not just done by a few, but by most of the Jews. How else could the widow of the alleged arch-enemy of Charles II have dared to be at the forefront of the Jewish supplicants?

The king personally saw to the settlement of both petitions and ordered that a member of the Privy Council refer the matter to Parliament. Despite the influence of the Jew-friendly General Monk, the Privy Council apparently did not dare recommend that Parliament make a special ruling, out of consideration for popular sentiment. On 17 December 1660, Mr. Hollis presented the issue to Parliament. In the Journal of Parliament for the day in question we find the following entry:[21]

> Mr. *Hollis* represents, to this House, an Order made by the Lords of his Majesty's Privy-Council, and specially recommended to this House for their Advice therein, touching Protection for the *Jews*: Which was read.
> *Ordered*, That this Business be taken into Consideration Tomorrow Morning.[22]

We agree with Henriques that unfortunately there is no entry relating to the matter in the journal the next day. On the other hand, Henriques and Wolf seem to have overlooked the following entry for December 20:[23]

---

[21] Privy Council Register of 7th December 1660.

[22] *Journals of the House of Commons*, Vol. VIII, p. 209. Translator's note: QVOS.

[23] Henriques: *Return*, 96. Translator's note: While Henriques states that as well as checking the journal for an entry the following day, he also checked the journal up until December 24th and found nothing, he nevertheless appears to be correct when he states: 'Parlia-

The humble Petition of many Merchants, Tradesmen, and Artif-
icers, in and about the City of *London*, and other Places within
his Majesty's Realm of *England*, was read; and laid aside.[24]

Admittedly, in this entry there is no mention of Jews and their previous
treatment by the Privy Council. However, there is a high probability that this
was the City of London petition discussed above. Be that as it may, in both
cases, despite the King's original recommendation that the matter be decided
by Parliament, no action—whether positive or negative—was taken.

It must really be asked why no decision was made despite the great effort on both sides. The Jewish historians Wolf and Henriques have also dealt
with this question. Wolf believes that Parliament could not have done anything because, according to him, the opinion of the judges at the Whitehall
Conference had been that 'there was no law which forbad the Jews' return
into England', which meant that the Jews had a 'fundamental legal right of
settlement'. As a result, the king would have felt no need to interfere, as the
Jews were already residing legally in England. Henriques is of the opinion that
issues concerning the Jewish Question were probably avoided in Parliament
because of 'the general temper of the House of Commons on religious questions during this reign'. However, neither historian's argument is plausible.[25]

Wolf misrepresents the fact that the judiciary's opinion under Cromwell was far from decided, especially since there were at least an equal number of jurists who took the opposite view. In addition to this, it is very likely
that Mr. Justice Tyril, who was responsible for this matter under Charles II,
agreed with the latter's position, which alone appears to have been objectively
correct, otherwise the aforementioned laws from the times of Henry III and
Edward I would not have had to be repealed by a formal act of Parliament in
1846. Finally, Wolf overlooks the fact that the City expressly requested that
new laws be passed for this purpose if necessary.[26]

Henriques is a little closer to the truth. Parliament was not inclined to
give its consent to Jewish re-admission, and so in this respect it was really
not particularly 'accessible' for any matters which concerned Jews (such as

---

ment was dissolved without ever having given their advice on the Jewish problem as they
had been requested by the Council'.

[24] *Journals of the House of Commons*, Vol. VIII, p. 217. Translator's note: QVOS.

[25] Wolf: *Jewry*, pp. 16-17. Translator's note: QVOS. & Henriques: *Return*: p. 96. Translator's note: QVOS.

[26] 9 & 10 Victoriæ, cap. 59. Translator's note: It was not until this Religious Opinion Relief Act ['An Act to relieve Her Majesty's Subjects from certain Penalties and Disabilities
in regard to Religious Opinions'] was passed on August 18th, 1846, that the Statutes of
Henry III (54 & 55 Henriciæ III) and Edward I's *Statutum de Judæismo* were formally
repealed. See: *The Statutes of the United Kingdom of Great Britain and Ireland, 9 & 10
Victoria. 1846*, p. 413.

the City's petition, or the widow Carvajal's petition), as these could necessarily lead to an unwelcome discussion of the legality of the Jewish presence
in the country. As a result, the king probably decided not to press the issue of
Jewish re-admission, but rather to leave it on a purely personal level of toleration for the time being. So the legal situation remained unchanged, and thus
remained the same as it had been under Cromwell.

Charles II, Patron of the Jews

Despite the City of London's powerful influence, the assault by anti-Jewish
forces was repelled. A result that is not surprising once one examines the
reasons for Charles II's friendliness towards the Jews.

We have already seen how the Hebrews had substantially supported the
king by supplying him money, weapons, and ammunition. It is no longer
possible to determine today how big the total financial donations were.
James Picciotto believes that these amounted to a million guilders, which
was an enormous sum for those times. He considers it possible that there are
still documents in Jewish archives in Holland which contain details of the
Jews' agreement with Charles II, including a copy of an alleged charter
which permitted the Jews to settle in England.[27]

Wolf describes Charles II's debt of gratitude to the Jews in no uncertain
terms: 'The King himself was already pledged to the Jews.' We consider this
view to be entirely correct and consider it the sole reason for the way he
dealt with the aforementioned matter. Charles II probably enlisted the help of
the Jews even after his return because, as Tovey points out, 'the Monarch...
was for ever wanting Money, and wou'd do any Thing to obtain it'.[28]

It is therefore not surprising that Charles II showed himself to be even
more gracious than Cromwell, who, as an exceptional act for one Jew, had
only ordered for Carvajal (and his two sons) to be granted denizenship. In
the case of Charles II, however, we can already see 19 such naturalizations
by the end of 1661, among which featured Manuel Martinez Dormido [Da-
vid Abarbanel], who had been such a loyal servant to Cromwell. Further
awards of this kind took place in larger numbers over the next few years.

What distinguished Charles II the most, however, was the Jew Coronel,
who worked for him in a leading position. After he officially converted to
Christianity at the end of 1660, he was knighted on 3 October 1661 under the
name of Sir Augustine Coronel (or Colonel, as his surname is spelled in *Le
Neve's Pedigrees*). However, Sir Augustine had little luck in his new dignity,
as his ethnic brethren, outraged by his conversion to Christianity, seem to

---

[27] Picciotto, p. 43. Translator's note: Picciotto states that a million guilders was equivalent
to approx. £84,000 at his time of writing (1875).

[28] Wolf: *Jewry*, p. 15. Translator's note: QVOS. & Tovey, p. 279. Translator's note: QVOS.

have persecuted him for it. We see from state documents that on 26 December 1665, he 'begs protection' against the Jews as 'their hatred will drive him to ruin', but Charles II was probably unable or unwilling to help him, because a little later in the same collection of documents we find that Sir Augustine had gone bankrupt.[29]

Charles II's public favoritism of Jews also had the effect that more and more members of this race immigrated to England. We must therefore cast doubt on Tovey's report from the 'Learned Rabbi *Netto*' who assured him that 'even so late as the Year 1663, the whole Number of *Jews* in *London* [i.e. heads of families] did not exceed twelve'. The assertions of Wolf and Hyamson, that only 35 Jewish families were settled in London at the beginning of 1661, also does not seem to do justice to the facts. Rather, Henriques' estimate is closer to the truth, which is that there were 'between Three and Fourscore Families' in London at this time. Whatever the case was, even with the latter estimate it would have been a numerically small Jewish colony when compared to the City of London's large merchant community, whose petition the king apparently supported in 1660. This is yet another example in history where it is not so much the overall number of Jews that matters in a polity, as much as the money they possess, the influence they have bought with it, and their international relationships.[30]

In the subsequent years of Charles II's reign, there continued to be an uninterrupted immigration of Jews into England, so it is therefore not unfounded for Tovey to insist that Charles II was 'their *Introducer*'. Nevertheless, the forces of self-preservation emerged once again. Thomas Violet wrote a new pamphlet against the Jews on 18 December 1660, which was published at the beginning of the following year. This little book was in the form of a petition to the king and sought above all to explain the harm that the Jews always caused, especially as it pertained to England at that time.

---

[29] Hyamson: *History*, p. 172; Wolf: *Jewry*, p. 18; Mesquita, p. 242; *Calendar of State Papers*, Vol. 1661/62, p. 214. & Wolf: *Jewry*, pp. 8, 17; *Le Neve's Pedigrees*, Vol. 8, p. 145. & *Calendar of State Papers*, Vol. 1665/66, p. 118. Translator's note: QVOS. & *Calendar of State Papers*, Vol. 1665/66, p. 137.

[30] Tovey. p. 279. Translator's note: QVOS. & Wolf: *Jewry*, p. 19. & Hyamson: *History*, p. 168. & Henriques: *Special Taxation* (II), pp. 54-55. Translator's note: QVOS. Given that this estimate is from a Jewish petition of 1689, I do not feel that Aldag is comparing like with like here, especially as, in the same sentence, Wolf goes on to say that, by the end of 1663, 'fifty-seven fresh names were added to the list of well-to-do Jews in London', which would indicate that, according to Wolf himself, by the end of 1663 there were already 92 Jewish families in London, which is more than that which Henriques reproduces from in the Jews' own petition 26 years later. Nevertheless, this does not negate Aldag's overall thesis, which is that the Jewish community, while more than doubling under Charles II, was still small in comparison to the City merchant community. That said, Wolf admits that there is no means of measuring the number of poorer Jews who had settled.

Their residence was unlawful in view of the fact that the decrees issued up until 1290 had not been repealed:[31]

> Their Banishment was so acceptable to the people who oft-
> times pressed it in parliament that they gave the King a fif-
> teenth part of their moveables to speed and execute it, and it
> was done by the unanimous desire, Judgement, Edict & decree
> both of the King and his parliament and it was total and final
> to them all never to return into England again, which Edict &
> decree though the same may not now be found extant & in the
> parliament Rolls, nor in our printed Statutes, yet it is men-
> tioned by divers Authors & in several Records...[32]

All over the world, Jews became rich by working as a closed group. They were indifferent to the country they lived in, and have no compunction about leaving one country for another. Their fraud in England was already immense. Violet suggested their banishment, but failing that, setting up an English-style Inquisition:[33]

> [Y]our Majesty (under pardon) may be advised to issue out
> Comissions in the nature of Inquisitions, and thereby empower
> some few of your discreet loyal Subjects to inquire about the
> number of the Jews in general, and of their deportments, es-
> tates, misdemeanours, Conditions, lives and Conversations,
> oppressions, affairs & Transactions, and under what privileges
> & by what authority, power or licence they do here within
> your dominion inhabit Commerce, Trade & Traffic & the like,
> by which means or by some such overtures and ways your
> Majesty may be ascertaind & satisfied of all their Transactions
> and hereby your Majesty may doubtless most legally fine,
> Tax, impose & compel them to pay what sums of money to
> your majesty as you please...[34]

Violet reserves special scorn for 'the late Usurper' Cromwell, who had received large sums from them and was not averse to bringing them into Eng-

---

[31] Tovey, p. 279. Translator's note: QVOS.

[32] Violet: *Petition*, pp. 2-3. Translator's note: Quotation reproduced verbatim (although with updated spelling for reader comprehension) from Wolf: *Status*, p. 190.

[33] Violet: *Petition*, p. 4. Translator's note: Alternatively, Wolf: *Status*, p. 191 may be consulted, although given that I do not find the referenced charges in the Wolf source, Aldag may be referring here to another of Violet's petitions.

[34] Violet: *Petition*, p. 5. Translator's note: Quotation (verbatim but with updated spelling) from Wolf: *Status* p. 192.

land in return for the revenue from customs duties. Violet also states that he had previously heard from Carvajal that Oliver Cromwell wanted to allow the settlement of 2,000 Jewish merchants in return for a payment of one million.[35]

Even this detailed pamphlet could not persuade Charles II to change his stance; on the contrary, we shall see how Judah's influence continued to grow in Restoration England.

Even before his return to England, Charles II had marriage plans. At first he had thought of marrying one of Cardinal Mazarin's nieces. After his ascension to the throne, the Spanish court recommended a Princess of Parma on his behalf. However, the French king wanted a marriage alliance with Catherine of Braganza, the daughter of John IV of Portugal, in order to bring Charles into the anti-Spanish front led by France. After long intrigues, the king was persuaded to marry Catherine.

Most historical research sees her rich dowry as the main reason for his decision. This consisted of, among other things, the transfer of Tangier and the Seven Islands of Bombay, both of which were then Portuguese possessions, and a cash sum of 2 million crusados, which was probably equivalent to around £800,000 at the time. Furthermore, free trade was guaranteed in Portugal and its colonies [Brazil and the Portuguese East Indies], an aspect in which the Jews in London were particularly interested, given that the business opportunities for their ethnic kin in Portugal were becoming increasingly limited due to the anti-Jewish movements there.

As a result, these Jews emigrated more and more to London and then set sail as merchants under English names. We have no doubt that the Hebrews worked hard to establish this Portuguese alliance. This is confirmed by the fact that on the English side it was primarily General Monk and his Jewish friend Coronel who led the marriage negotiations. Despite the persecution of the Marranos, the Portuguese court is also likely to have been significantly influenced by Jews because, despite all that had happened, the nobility and court there were still completely Jewish, as the following anecdote from the famed Marquis de Pombal (1699-1782) best illustrates:[36]

> Joseph I ordered that all Portuguese, who were in any way allied or descended from the Hebrew race, should wear a yellow hat. The old marquis shortly after appeared at court with three hats under his arm. The king, smiling, asked him, 'What he

---

[35] Violet: *Petition*, p. 7. Translator's note: QVOS. I was unable to find any reference to this 'cash-for-Jews' deal in the petition reproduced in Wolf's *Status* appendix. A researcher with access to all of Violet's petitions, ideally in the original, should be able to clarify the matter.
[36] Ranke: *History*, Vol. III, 345; Lingard, Vol IX, p. 68 ff.; Clark: *Later Stuarts*, p. 58; Chamberlayne: *Anglise Notitia*, p. 133 ff. & Wolf: *The Jew in Diplomacy*, p. 400; Margoliouth: *History*, Vol. II, p. 24. Translator's note: It should be stated that Coronel had already been baptised, and was now technically Christian at this point.

had to do with them?' He replied, 'That he had them in obedience to his majesty's command, for he did not know a single
Portuguese of note who had not Jewish blood in his veins.'
But said the king, 'Why have you three?' He answered, 'One
for myself, one for the inquisitor-general, and one in case your
majesty should wish to be covered.'[37]

The number of Hebrews in the bride's entourage also shows that this anecdote does not unjustly highlight the Judaization of the Portuguese court and
nobility. This is explicitly emphasized by all Jewish writers who have dealt
with this topic. Although there is no agreement about the individual names,
there is no dispute over their large number or their influence on the queen
and Charles II. One was the queen's personal physician, while another
served as chamberlain. A no lesser, and perhaps the most important role was
played by several very rich Jews, principal among them two brothers, Duarte
and Francisco da Silva, who were probably related to Dormido and, through
him, to Menasseh ben Israel. Duarte da Silva had been a banker in Amsterdam for a long time and had been assigned to Catherine of Braganza's entourage by order of the King of Portugal. When the marriage contract was final-
ised, he was appointed Procurator of the Treasury to the King of Portugal.
As such, his powers were very extensive.

Apparently the cash for the dowry had also been brought together by
the Jews, a group of whom formed a veritable syndicate through which they
were entirely responsible for the management of the enormous wealth fund,
from which they must also have made large profits. This, and some of their
other activities, can be glimpsed from the entries that still exist in the state
papers. From May to December 1662, we find numerous such references.
On May 23rd, a warrant was issued to Duarte da Silva 'to pay to the Duke of
York [the king's brother] 20,000*l.* out of the Queen's marriage portion.' On
June 6th and 10th, Duarte da Silva was ordered to transfer £16,000 from the
account of 'the Queen's portion' to John Loving, a teller of the Exchequer.
On June 15th, da Silva was paid £1,000 from 'the Queen's dowry', a large
sum for the time, which was probably counted as remuneration for his work.
Two further orders for withdrawals were made on June 22nd for a total
amount of £24,000. An indication that the Jews not only managed the
queen's dowry, but probably also supplied the liquidity when required,
comes an entry dated June 24:[38]

---

[37] Lindo, p. 375. Translator's note: QVOS.

[38] See especially: Wolf: *Jewry*, p. 18 ff.; Gaster, p. 97; Hyamson: *History*, p. 172; Picciotto, p. 44. & *Calendar of State Papers*, Vol. 1661/62, p. 380. Translator's note: This is the
role title as it appears in the *Calendar*. & Wolf: *Jewry*, p. 20. Translator's note: The word
'syndicate' is that used in the original source. & *Calendar of State Papers*, Vol. 1661/62,
p. 380. Translator's note: QVOS. & *Calendar of State Papers*, Vol. 1661/62, pp. 400, 403.

Warrant to Don Duarte Da Sylva to pay to Alderman Backwell 53,700*l*. out of the Queen's dowry, for moneys advanced
by him on security of the said portion.[39]

Alderman Backwell was one of the most important English bankers of the
period. While surprisingly not a Jew himself, he mostly worked with Jews,
as can be seen from his extant ledgers. Payment instructions to da Silva can
also be found on July 4 and August 13. Finally, we see more entries with
similar content on December 4 and 10. These entries are interesting because,
among the other recipients listed [the queen and John Harvey, her treasurer
and receiver-general], on both occasions £500 was ordered to be paid to Duarte's brother, Francisco da Silva.[40]

It is therefore not difficult to determine how much the position of the
Jews was strengthened by the Portuguese marriage. As the Jews acted as the
queen's fund managers, Charles II, with his eternal need for money, was
obliged to court their favor. In addition, other Hebrews in the queen's entourage ensured that the interests of their fellow kinsmen were not neglected.
Meanwhile, the Jews who had fled Portugal for London were now, in their
new guise as English merchants, able to trade with Portugal and its colonial
empire unmolested, as Jewish historians triumphantly note.[41] Indeed, Judah
could be content with its position in England. Historiography has usually
paid little attention to such events. Hopefully the world will soon see a new
historiography which takes Jewish influence into account.

Charles II's loyalty to the Jews is also evident from the fact that, to a
certain extent from 1663, and most certainly from 1664 onwards, Jews were
able to practice their religion openly. This fact has given rise to a wide variety of theories.

As has already been stated, Wolf believes that a synagogue was already
present in the earliest beginnings of Jewish settlement around 1660. Picciotto
gives the earliest proven year for this, based on the 'earliest authentic record,' as 1662, while Wilfred Samuel, in his carefully researched, 161-page
academic paper on the topic, puts it at 1657. Yet others, such as Hyamson
(before 1660) Dr. Gaster (1664), and Henriques (1662), are more conservative in their estimates. We do not wish to comment in detail on this topic as it
appears unimportant in the overall scheme of things, but for those interested,

---

& *Calendar of State Papers*, Vol. 1661/62, p. 407. & *Calendar of State Papers*, Vol.
1661/62, pp. 415-6.
[39] *Calendar of State Papers*, Vol. 1661/62, p. 418. Translator's note: QVOS.
[40] Wolf: *Jewry*, p. 19. & *Calendar of State Papers*, Vol. 1661/62, pp. 429, 459. & *Calendar of State Papers*, Vol. 1661/62, pp. 581, 587.
[41] Wolf: *Jewry*, p. 20. Translator's note: It should be noted that particular source does not
reference the trading under English names, nor, in my opinion, does it have an air of tri-
umphalism.

the cited historians have much to offer because their work is based on impeccable evidence from contemporary witnesses, documents, and archeology. However, the key takeaway is that the emergence of a public synagogue is evidence of Charles II's general friendliness towards the Jews having progressed to such an extent that by 1663 the Jews no longer saw any danger in public worship.[42]

After the City of London's petition was ignored in 1660, one would have thought that no further complaints against Jews would have been made, especially as Jewish influence continued to grow at court and elsewhere, but as early as 1664 the king had to intervene again on behalf of the Jews in his realm. As far as we can tell from the Jews' first petition to King Charles II, which was a request for him to guarantee their safety in the kingdom, they must have feared measures from anti-Jewish circles. We learn that:

> ... they are dayly threatned by some with the seizure of all their estates & are told that both their lives & Estates are forfeited to your Majestie by the Lawes of your Kingdome and particularly they are molested and disquieted by one Mr. Richaut. And att the same time they were called by the Right Honourable the Earle of Berkshire who told them he had received a verball Order from your Majestie to Protect them and in case they doe not come to a speedy agreement with him he will endeavour and prosecute the seizure of their estates.
>
> Now for as much as your Petitioners are Ignorant of any Lawes now in force which should hinder their residence in this Kingdome. They most humbly beseech your Majestie that until they shall receive from your Majestie some significacion of your Royall pleasure that they should depart the Kingdome they may remaine heere under the like proteccion with the rest of your Majesties subjects And your Petitioners shall ever bee ready to serve your Majestie with their lives and fortunes.[43]

[42] Picciotto, p. 30. Translator's note: Quoted element from original source. & Samuel, p. 3 ff. & Hyamson: *History*, pp. 168, 172, 176. Hyamson does not give the first year for what could be considered a secret synagogue, only indicating that it must have been in operation prior to 1660, as in that year, in year of the Restoration, all pretence at concealment was abandoned. He does however state that the first officially constituted synagogue, in Creechurch Lane, with a list of contributions by members, was not started until 1663, with the constitution (*ascamoth*), not formally published until April 5th, 1664. & Gaster, p. 7. & Henriques: *Return*, pp. 97-98.

[43] Gaster (p. 4) reproduces the document in full [a photograph of which is this volume's cover illustration]. Translator's note: Quotation reproduced verbatim as per original source (although with breviographs spelled out in full). I have also reproduced the second paragraph for readers to see the Jews' most certainly mendacious assertion that they 'are Ignorant of any Lawes now in force which should hinder their residence in this Kingdome'. As

As the source material for this matter solely originates from the Jews, we are unable to get the other side of the story. In their comments on this matter, Wolf and Hyamson assume that it was individual actions by the Earl of Berkshire and Mr. Richaut, but this is refuted by the text of the Jewish petition itself. Firstly, the applicants say that 'they are dayly threatned by some' and then 'particularly' Mr. Richaut and the Earl of Berkshire. From this it follows that a number of people were involved, in which the two named were probably the leaders. Wolf describes the Earl of Berkshire's actions as 'a bold piece of chantage'. He has no evidence for this, but simply relies on Dormido's knowledge of legal matters. It cannot be believed that a man of the rank of the Earl of Berkshire would dare to give himself royal authority, by pretending that he had received a verbal instruction from the king to act on his behalf. Not only did he belong to the high nobility, but he was also a royal chamberlain and a member of the Privy Council.

On the other hand, if the Earl's supposed claim of having received a royal order was actually true, it is difficult to understand what the Earl's assigned role regarding the Jews was supposed to be. One explanation is that Charles II, for some reason, wanted to once more oblige the Jews to be feel grateful for their alleged protection, and therefore perhaps only gave the Earl of Berkshire the order as a symbolic gesture in this regard. If this is indeed the case, Berkshire may have been chosen for this role given that he was the second son of the Earl of Suffolk, who, as described in the previous volume, had caused the Jews to be expelled under James I. Another interpretation of this order would be that Charles II wanted to at least outwardly appease the anti-Jewish forces for a while. Our thesis is not necessarily refuted by the king's response of 22 August 1664 to the Jews' petition. It is true that in his response he did make the following statement:[44]

> His Majesty having considered this Peticion hath been graciously pleased to declare that hee hath not given any particular Order for the molesting or disquieting the Peticioners either in their Persons or Estates, but that they may promise themselves the effects of the same favour as formerly they have had, soe long as they demeane themeselves peaceably & quietly with the due obedience to his Majesties Lawes, & without scandall to his Government.

Gaster (p. 5) points out, the King's administrative silence on this 'bold assertion' is taken by the Jews as a tacit and unassailable confirmation that they are correct. As Gaster concludes from this exchange: 'Legally they felt themselves now absolutely safe, and they enjoyed, moreover, the open favour of the King.'

[44] Wolf: *Jewry*, pp. 24-5. & Hyamson: *History*, pp. 172-3.

But what other response could reasonably have been expected from him?[45]

The Jew Dr. Moses Gaster has described Charles II's response as 'the fundamental Charter' which was 'the only instrument of royal protection and as the guarantee for the safety of the Jews in this land'. Wolf, on the other hand, explains in detail how such a label was misleading and did not correspond to the facts. Rather, it was simply a written declaration of tolerance, a 'bald and colorless assurance' that was 'a personal continuation of Cromwell's personal "connivance," and nothing more'. For the same reason, the descriptor 'The Act of Toleration', written on the cover of the document by an unknown synagogue member, was a misnomer.[46]

Another attack against the Jews had been repelled, but the next one was not long in coming. Just as news of Oliver Cromwell's friendliness towards the Jews had spread beyond England's borders, Charles II's reputation in this regard also appears to have been transnational. For example, for 5 February 1666, we find the following entry in the *Calendar of State Papers*:

> Petition of Jean d'Illan, Jew of Amsterdam, to the King, for a pass for a Holland ship to transport himself and 50 families of Jews from Amsterdam to Palestine. God has at length begun to gather in his scattered people, having raised up a prophet for them; they will pray for His Majesty when they arrive at Jerusalem. [*French.*][47]

Unfortunately, it was not possible to determine how this French-language petition from a Dutch Jew came to be presented to the king of England. But there is no reason to assume that Charles II did not comply with the request.

The anti-Jewish forces did their utmost to combat rising Jewish power. On 6 February 1671, they thought that they had might have found a new angle of attack when Parliament decided to appoint a committee 'to inquire into the Causes of the Growth of Popery; to prepare and bring in a Bill to prevent it; and also to inquire touching the Number of the *Jews*, and their Synagogues, and upon what Terms they are permitted to have their Residences here; and report it, with their Opinions, to the House...'. But this initiative also came to nothing. The Committee's report of February 17th to Parliament dealt only with the causes of the growth of Catholicism and the measures deemed necessary to combat the problem. We no longer hear a single word about the Jewish Question, which can only be explained by the fact that the king and the Jews took care not to let this matter, which was

---

[45] Gaster, pp. 4-5. Translator's note: QVOS.

[46] Gaster, p. 3. Translator's note: QVOS. & Wolf: *Jewry*, pp. 26-28. Translator's note: QVOS.

[47] *Calendar of State Papers*, Vol. 1665/66, p. 232.

sensitive for both parties, be dealt with by an official body. Once again they had managed to divert Parliament's attention away from Jewish issues by means unknown to us. But we will soon see how it took all of the king's power to avoid dealing with the Jewish Question on a legal basis. The need for this would arise more quickly than expected.[48]

In the winter of 1673, the leaders of the Jewish community were 'indicted of a riot at Guildhall, for meeting together for the exercise of their religion in Dukes Place'. The grand jury convened found the Jews guilty of the charges based on existing laws and sentenced them accordingly. An English court had thus placed itself in opposition to the king's previous unlawful orders. The Jews realized that this time their situation was serious. It was no longer Parliament whose activities could be diverted from its duties through intrigues and secret influences with the help of the king, but an English court that had clearly spoken out against them. Their salvation could only come from the king.[49]

The leaders of the Jewish community therefore immediately turned to Charles II with a petition. As justification, they referred to the king's aforementioned declaration of 1664, and pointed out that they had met the required requirements of his continued favor, namely, that they had continued to 'demean themselves peaceably and quietly, and without Scandal to the Government'. The Jews then gave the king what was effectively an ultimatum. He could either protect them, by having them 'reap the Fruits of his accustomed Clemency', or else 'give them a convenient time to withdraw their Persons and Estates into Parts beyond the Seas'. It is once again noticeable how the Jews combined humility with threats, since their leaving England would have meant great financial damage to Charles II. We already seen the same tactics from Menasseh ben Israel in the previous chapter.

Was it the ultimatum presented in the petition, or were there other considerations and forces that influenced Charles II? It is impossible for us to know from our point in history. In any case, he chose the Jews against the

---

[48] *Journals of the House of Commons*, Vol. IX, p. 198. Translator's note: QVOS.

[49] Webb, p. 39; Haggard, Vol. I, Appendix p. 2. Translator's note: QVOS [Haggard is a later reproduction of Webb]. Interestingly, similar Jewish riotous behaviour in Duke's Place, which took place just over a century later (1784) in celebration of Simchat Torah, led to a local Christian man, Porter Ridout, being set upon by a Jewish mob and robbed of a huge sum of money, which led to the death of a Jewish youth when the irate robbery victim fired his blunderbuss out of an upstairs window into the mob outside. Note that, while the jury found him innocent, the incident caused Ridout to have to sell up his coffee house and leave the area with his family. See Endelman, p. 218 for a fair overview. The Old Bailey proceedings can also be found online at: https://www.londonlives. org/browse.jsp?div=t17841020-1 and a genealogist also gives a description of the aftermath of the incident: https://the-ridouts.com/2013/04/16/jeremiah-porter-ridout-yellow-silk-shoes-and-blue-murder/. Contemporaneous press reports can also be found in online newspaper archives.

law and the grand jury's decision. The following is a report of the king's response from his court at Whitehall on 11 February 1674, when he himself was present in council:

> His Majesty in Council, taking this Matter into Consideration, was this Day pleased to order, and it is hereby ordered, That Mr. Attorney-General do stop all Proceedings at Law against the Petitioners, who have been indicted, as aforesaid; and to provide, that they may receive no further Trouble in this behalf.[50]

What a decision by a king! Bear in mind that Charles II took a step against public opinion and the law of the land in favor of a small number of people of foreign origin, when it was even questionable if this did not violate the constitution—as even the Jew Henriques rightly noted. Henriques also deals with the 'somewhat remarkable' fact that no protest about the king's action was raised in either House, which he attributes, not without reason, to the fact that 'Parliament was prorogued within a fortnight of the issue of the Order in Council, which may not have been generally known till some time afterwards.' It would appear that the Jews' allies in Parliament made sure to take care of the problem.[51]

According to the English constitution, this order from the king had no legal force. But it was, however, fresh proof to the Jews that the king would protect them even in the face of the strongest attacks. So it is also understandable that immediately afterwards they felt confident enough to end the short lease they had on a small house which had served as a synagogue, and sign a new 25-year lease for a larger premises, with the lease set to expire in the year 1700. Another consequence appears to have been the new wave of denization, with no fewer than 19 Jews becoming English denizens during this time. From the documentation that has survived, we can see that a total of 70 Jews were granted letters patent of denization during the reign of Charles II.[52]

---

[50] Webb, pp. 38-39; Haggard, Vol. I, Appendix pp. 2-3. Translator's note: Quotation and all previous QVOS. It is clear from king's response that the king must have ordered a *nolle prosequi* [an order for the prosecutor to drop proceedings] which, as we shall see, is a recurring theme with Jewish petitions to the king.

[51] Henriques: *Return*, p. 102. All quoted elements from original source.

[52] Gaster, p. 7. & Webb, Appendix pp. 17-8. Translator's note: Aldag's text gave the number as 53 persons, however going back to the original source and counting the names, there are undoubtedly 70 in the list. Readers should also be aware that, although 'letters patent of denization' is the more common form, the term 'letters of denization' is also commonly used, as seen in the historical multi-volume work *Letters of Denization and Acts of Naturalization for Aliens in England and Ireland*, which documents all of the foreigners who, from 1603 onwards, underwent this process.

In 1675 an incident occurred which was small but nevertheless significant. The king received a visit from a Jew from Holland, H. H. Jahacob Jeuda Leað, a Talmudic scholar who was given the surname Templo for his life-long interest in King Solomon's Temple. His detailed studies of the structure had led him to create models of the temple, the first of which he sold Queen Henrietta Maria, the wife of Charles I, probably on her visit to the Amsterdam synagogue in 1642. His 1675 trip to London was to show Charles II a second model of the temple, along with a printed plan. Templo was also skilled draftsman, with a particular interest in heraldry, and as such designed the Masonic coat of arms of the English Grand Lodge of Freemasons, which is still in use today.[53]

Charles II's favorable stance meant that mass immigration of Jews from Eastern Europe began as early as 1677. Apparently there were many poor people among them, as can be seen from the documents of the Jewish community that have survived to this day. For the first time, Jews from Poland and Russia poured into England. This refutes the widespread view that the only real Jewish presence in England at that time was the supposedly more civilized Sephardim. Apparently the presence of these down-and-out Hebrews in London had already made an unpleasant impression on native Londoners, because the Court of Aldermen took measures to monitor and restrict Jewish immigration, with the decree that 'no Jews without good estate be admitted to reside or lodge in London or the liberties thereof.' Nevertheless, the influence of the Jews in the city continued to grow. For 26 September 1679, we find the following entry in state documents:[54]

> The East India Company, having several ships come home, began their sale as usual last week, but, because the Jews were engaged in their Feast of Tabernacles, it was adjourned, but is now begun again.[55]

It is something of a trope in Jewish history that, whenever the Jews enjoy the all of the protection and privileges of their host nation, they always turn popular sentiment against them through some despicable act. This is what happened in London in 1680. A certain Eve Cohen from a wealthy Jewish family in Holland had converted to Christianity and eloped to London with her brother's Christian servant. Her family stopped at nothing to bring her home. We have received a detailed account of this case from the noted Scottish philosopher and historian Gilbert Burnet. He tells us how the

---

[53] De Mesquita: *Ancient Burial Ground*, p. 239.
[54] Hyamson: *History*, p. 183. Wolf: *First Stage*, p. 123. Translator's note: QVOS (Wolf), and is likewise repeated in the same author's *A History of the Jews in England* (e.g. Oxford: Clarendon Press, 1941, p. 190).
[55] *Calendar of State Papers*, Vol. 1679/80, p. 253. Translator's note: QVOS.

Jewish woman was 'daily in fear of her Life' during her flight from Holland to England because she was being followed by Jews, who pursued her all the way to London. After first unsuccessfully trying to bribe the Lavignes, the couple with whom Eve was lodging, in an attempt to see Eve persuaded to return to Holland, the Jews hounding Eve then tried and failed to have her lover Michael Verboon arrested, in a bid to get him out of the way. However, they did achieve success in bribing a sergeant and a bailiff who, together with a certain Michael Levi, put Eve in the most unpleasant situation. Her mother having made a trumped-up claim of £2,000 against her, Eve was arrested and imprisoned under the laws of the time. Her family then added three further spurious claims in a bid to strengthen their legal case, and to draw out the proceedings. However, when the Jews and their minions realized that they could not pursue their suit with the court in question, they had it referred to another court that seemed more favorable to them and which would also cause another delay, methods that are also known to us from the years prior to 1933. The Jews 'hoped now to have wearied the poor Prisoner out with Vexatious Suits and Delays'. However, the jury saw the injustice, and Eve was released.[56]

In the meantime, Eve's new husband tried to get justice for himself and his wife, but was no match for Jewish cunning and money-power, as Burnet himself notes:

> Mr. *Verboon* was advised to Arrest *Vandersee* [Eve's Jewish spurned suitor] for the false Imprisonment of his Wife; and on the 4th of *September* he Arrested him in an Action of 200*l.* which was not out of reason; but very modest for one that had suffered so many Arrests for great Sums, and all for nothing: but *Levi* soon bailed him: and so prevalent were the Arts and Presents of the Jews, that it was entered in the Books but 20*l.* So that whether they are Plaintiffs or Complainants, they are resolved to shew their skill; and perhaps have a secret Pleasure to let the World see how much their Practices can work on those who are called Christians; even in a Matter wherein the honour of Jesus Christ is so much concerned.

Despite knowing from the previous trial that they would be shown that they had no case, Eve's family launched another lawsuit, so that, during the course of the English bailiffs' attempt to arrest her husband, Eve could be

---

[56] Burnet, p. 5. Translator's note: QVOS. & Burnet, p. 13. & Burnet, p. 14-15. Translator's note: QVOS. These methods have become so common in our own recent years, to the point of prominent Jews now publicly boasting of using these methods to destroy their opponents, that the term 'lawfare' has entered common parlance.

intimidated, perhaps even injured. As a result, Eve, who was now Eve Verboon, suffered a miscarriage. The author Burnet clearly believes that the overall plan was to make sure that she miscarried:

> But the Malice of the Jews stopt not here, for perceiving that Mistris *Verboon* was by her Marriage covered from all their Suits, they resolved on another way, which looks like a Design to destroy her. *Levi* had said before my Lord Mayor, that she was within two months of her time, and therefore he could not but believe she was with Child, and very capable of being frighted into Miscarriage.
>
> But it was a sure effect of their Revenge on her Husband, against whom *Vandersee* had expressed so much malice, that he hath often said he was resolved to kill him, though he should be hanged for it. So on the second of *October*, Mr. *Verboon* was Arrested in an Action of 200l. and it appears that the Bailiffs were again instructed to behave themselves with more than ordinary rudeness: one of them was *Benedict Helm*; there were others whose Names are not known.
>
> They came at Dinner time, when they might expect to find them at Dinner together: they seized upon him at Table, and dragged him forth with their utmost violence; which when Mistris *Lavigne* saw, and withal took notice of a Coach at the Door, she immediately reflected on the Trick that they had put on them before: and therefore ran to him, and clasped her Arms about his Waste, to keep him from being thrust into the Coach. The Bailiffs, to be revenged on her, beat and bruised her Head, Brest and Body, with the greatest fury; of which the marks appear yet on her: Her Head was broke in three places, and she was thereby, as the Chyrurgeon [surgeon] has certified under his hand, in great hazard of her Life; yet she clogged them so, that they could not get their Prisoner into the Coach...

At this point, a crowd began to gather who, realizing what was happening, bundled both Michael and Eve into a nearby alehouse, from whence Eve had them send for William, Lord Bishop of St. Asaph, the cleric who had baptized her, knowing that he would have the power to stop the abduction attempt.

However, despite Mrs. Lavigne's injuries, it is Mrs. Verboon who suffered most from the ordeal:

> But though Mrs. *Lavigne* was forced to keep her Bed some time, by the Wounds and Bruises she received, yet this had a more fatal effect on poor Mistris *Verboon*; who when she saw

the Bailiffs dragging her Husband, fell presently in a swoon; and being then young with Child, was so disordered by the fright, that she has not yet recovered it; but on the 9th day after she miscarried.[57]

The Lord Bishop told the Lord Mayor of the City of London about the matter. The Lord Mayor then summoned Levi, who in this 'Conspiracy of the Jews' was Eve's mother's 'chief Contriver'. When he was interrogated, Levi admitted that it was all a ploy to force Mrs. Verboon to go back to her mother. The mayor, supported by the public, threatened to punish the Jews if they did not fully compensate Eve for 'the Costs and Trouble to which they had put her'. And if this was not carried out, the Lord Mayor assured him:[58]

> ... he would carry the Matter as far as the Law would allow him against their whole Sect: and though his time was near an end, yet he knew his Successour would pursue it with the same vigour, with which he was resolved to begin. He gave also order to some to bring him an Extract of the Laws against the Jews.[59]

Unfortunately, today it is no longer possible to determine what action, if any, was taken. Moreover, it is likely that any action would not have progressed beyond the initial stages due to certain influences at court, a thesis which is supported by the fact that nothing more is known about the case.

From Lord Anglesey's letter to the king's secretary dated 6 August 1680, which is still extant, we can see that there were indeed members of the English establishment who wanted to significantly restrict Jewish rights. Apparently there were two audiences with the king on this matter, with Sir Peter Pett also going to the trouble of examining old documents which dated prior to 1290 and lecturing on them to the king, which shows that with anti-Jewish appeals there was a tendency to recall certain pre-Expulsion legal restrictions. Lord Anglesey proposed that Sir Peter Pett should be the first Justiciary of the Jews, and also suggested that Jewish leaders should be invited to discuss, among other things, what special taxes the Jews would be willing to pay for permission to trade, residence rights and other privileges in general. Apparently, all things considered, it would appear that the plan was for the introduction of a type of Ghetto system, which was the prevailing system on the European continent at the time. The clergy were also interest-

---

[57] Burnet, p. 19-21. Translator's note: All QVOS.

[58] Burnet, pp. 19-22. Translator's note: All QVOS.

[59] Burnet, p. 23. Translator's note: Quotation and QVOS.

ed in this new scheme and were represented in this matter by the Bishop of Lincoln.[60]

It is clear then that important figures of the time had taken up the anti-Jewish cause, but the secret pro-Jewish forces still proved to be stronger. Anglesey's proposals were submitted to the Privy Council for consideration, but nothing more was heard about the matter. We can only agree with the Jew Wolf in his conclusion when he triumphantly remarks that 'powerful influences seem to have been brought against it, and it was happily dropped.' He most likely means that the Jews subsidized the king, who was always in financial difficulties.[61]

We also agree with various Jewish scholars that the entire historical evolution of Jewry in England would have taken a completely different path if this plan had succeeded. The Jews in England were ahead of their racial brethren on the European continent by almost two hundred years. Although their rights were sometimes limited, in general all options were open to them, including intermarriage.[62]

The reign of King Charles II came to an end without any notable cases arising as a result of the Jewish Question. He died on 6 February 1685; even his Jewish personal physician was unable to cure him of his illness.[63] Charles was succeeded to the throne by his brother James II, whose reign lasted only eight years. As was the case after Oliver Cromwell's death, as soon as James II took office, anti-Jewish forces clamored to find out the new king's position on the Jewish Question.

In the interest of providing a complete narrative of events, we must also discuss an event from 1672, when the 'alien duty', which was such an important issue for the Jews, was abolished under Charles II. This tax became a huge bone of contention under James II and also in the first years of the reign of his successor, William III. The 'alien duty', or 'aliens duty' as it is sometimes rendered, can be explained as follows: From the earliest times, foreigners [also known historically as 'strangers' or 'aliens'] had to pay surcharges on all of the king's taxes. For example, the goods of foreign merchants, regardless of whether they were exported or imported, were subject to special public taxes, which the foreigners could not escape by being granted patents of naturalization by the king—even though this had often been allowed to happen with the Jews under Charles II.[64]

When Charles II was crowned King of England in 1660, a law was passed to regulate his income from taxes. This law, known as the Great Statute [12 Car. II. c. 4], was only effectively repealed in 1785. According to this

---

[60] Wolf: *Status*, pp. 192-3.

[61] Wolf: *Status*, p. 185. Translator's note: QVOS.

[62] Wolf: *Status*, p. 185; also Wolf: *Whitehall Conference*, p. 280; Roth: *New Light*, pp. 134-5.

[63] De Mesquita: *Ancient Burial Ground*, pp. 241-2.

[64] Henriques: *Special Taxation* (II), p. 58.

legislation, the king was given, among other things, the income from the so-called alien duty to freely dispose of. If the 'merchant alien' (or 'merchant stranger' as he was also known in the literature) did not pay this duty proper-ly, the goods in question were liable to forfeiture. One half of the value of these goods was paid over to the Crown, the other half to the informer.[65]

It should also be said that this alien duty represented a good source of income for those entitled to it. In addition, the English merchants made sure that it was raised, as this was one of the main ways in which the competition from foreigners was made more tolerable. So it is not surprising that this tax existed as far back as the reign of King Henry VII.

It is all the more strange then that in the official statute book we find a law from 1673 [25 Car. II. c. 6] that fundamentally abolishes these tax regu-lations and stipulates that both denizens and aliens would pay the same taxes on the exportation of native commodities and manufactures as 'the naturall-borne Subjects' [i.e. native Englishmen]. An exception remained only for the export of coal. Of course, this statute was also sanctioned by Parliament, for unknown reasons.

This change of policy appears all the more incomprehensible when one considers that English trade, whose representatives were also present in the House of Commons, was significantly affected by the repeal of this tax. We tried hard to find out the reasons behind this Parliamentary approval, but all research was in vain. The press of the time provided no information, and the official reference works of the period were also silent. Unfortunately, all we are left with is guesswork. Henriques believes that the law was passed 'for the public good', in order to encourage the export trade. This view cannot be correct, since the English public in particular was never in agreement, as shall be seen from the incidents that took place during the reigns of James II and William III.[66]

We are of the opinion that the law was changed for other reasons, which are the following: Through the aforementioned Great Statute, Charles II was declared to be the recipient of this alien duty. So the decision to abol-ish the alien duty, the profits from which were seen as his personal privilege, may have been seen as largely his prerogative. It would make sense then that, if it were deemed a matter for Court rather than Parliament, that the king might have been persuaded to advocate for a tax regime that was favor-able to the Jews. For is it not reasonable to assume that Charles II in particu-

---

[65] Henriques: *Special Taxation* (II), pp. 59-60.

[66] *Statutes of the Realm*, Vol. V. p. 791-2. Translator's note: Quoted element from original source. Readers may be interested to know that an extra clause was made for English-caught fish, which was also open to global free trade. Note also that Aldag's text gives the year as 1672, as per Henriques, but the regnal year of the statute itself shows that the law dates to 1673. The text has been updated accordingly. & Henriques: *Special Taxation* (II), p. 60. Translator's note: Quoted element from Henriques.

lar could have been persuaded to abolish all alien duties in return for financial compensation from the Jews? One objection to this might be that not
only the Jews, but also other foreigners benefitted from this abolition, which
is basically true. But perhaps Charles II was willing to accept this in order to
favor Jewish interests. The law of 1673 expressly stated that denizens and
aliens would have to continue to pay export tax on coal. However, this special regulation was of no particular interest to the Jews, as the coal trade was
not in their hands.[67]

There may also be an explanation for Parliament's stance on this issue.
In period leading up to 1858 we will see how that the English populace and
the English Parliament very often have completely opposite views on the
Jewish Question. The people's representatives are for the most part apparently under some kind of influence to pursue pro-Jewish policies without regard
to the will of their voters.

This influence would appear to involve bribery. Even at this time, the
members of the English Parliament were by no means free from this type of
corruption. As is well known to historians, the process for even getting into
Parliament itself was fraught with corruption, hence the records of House of
Commons debates about the problem of members only getting into Parliament by means of buying voters. And, as it may well be argued, anyone who
can stoop to bribery is also likely to allow himself to be bribed. Just a few
years earlier, in 1662, large amounts of money had been used to persuade
Parliament to take a certain position. Louis XIV of France 'offered Charles a
considerable sum of money to purchase votes in the parliament' in favor of a
Portuguese match, while the Spanish ambassador did not shy away from
distributing money to parliamentarians in a bid to persuade them to side with
Spain's choice of a Protestant bride. When this was standard practice, why
would the Jews not also opt for this means of influence?[68]

When James II took office, various tax revenues were expressly transferred to him by an act of Parliament. Among other things, the act in question [1 Jac. II. c. 1] referred to income under the Great Statute [12 Car. II. c.
4], but the amendatory act of 1673 [25 Car. II. c. 6] was not mentioned. Giv-
en the omission of the 1673 act, the common interpretation was that it had
been tacitly repealed, in other words, that the alien duty was once again in
full vigor. The Jews must have immediately made representations about this
issue to James II, because as soon as the law came into force, the king declared through a letters patent that the alien duty would remain repealed, and

---

[67] Tovey p. 287. Translator's note: This reference appears to be incorrect, given that it
refers to James II's time. & Cunningham: *Growth*, Vol. I (The Mercantile System), p. 247.
[68] Cobbett: Vol. V, p. 434 ff. Translator's note: For those unfamiliar with the topic, historical electoral corruption was so notorious in England that the terms 'pocket borough' and
'rotten borough' have entered the popular lexicon. & Lingard, Vol. IX, pp. 71-72. Translator's note: QVOS.

a *nolle prosequi* declared by the Attorney General regarding the back taxes that were due.[69]

Now the City of London tried to persuade the James II to change his mind. However, their efforts and general displeasure made no impression on the king, and his original order remained in place. This is all the more surprising given that the City had warned him of how even a partial remission of the alien duty:[70]

> ... is a Publick Damage to the Interest of Your Majesty's Kingdoms, and a Diminution of Your Revenue, and the Trade of Your *English* Merchants, and a Means to transplant that, and the Mysteries of our Artificers into the Hands of Foreigners, to the Ruin, not only of the Trading and Working People at Home, but also of the several *English* Factories Abroad.

Even the fact that the petition bore the signatures of 65 of the most respected English merchants, at least eight of whom were Knights of the Realm, did not change the king's position. Other separate petitions from the famous trading companies the Hamburg Company and the Eastland Company, as well as additional petitions from the merchants of the west of England and the merchants of the north suffered the same fate. The number and economic power of the petitioners was certainly superior to the Jews, as they included almost all of the important English merchants. Notwithstanding, the king decided in favor of the Jews.[71]

The dispute over the alien duty was to flare up again with a vengeance in the first years of William III's reign. Before we get into that, however, let us conclude the reign of James II with the following conflict related to the Jewish Question.

As mentioned in the previous volume, there was a statute from the time of Queen Elizabeth, the 1581 Act of Persuasions, that threatened significant financial penalties for failure to attend Christian services. This regulation was by no means repealed, but had largely fallen into disuse in later decades. In the autumn of 1685, a certain Thomas Beaumont resorted to this law and brought charges against 48 Jews for violating the aforementioned statute. He

---

[69] *Statute of the Realm*, Vol. VI, p. 1 & See also Henriques: *Special Taxation* (II), p. 61. & Tovey, pp. 287, 291, 294. Translator's note: According to Tovey [p. 294], the Order of Council reversing the alien duty was dated 22nd January, 1685, [?] and came 'upon the Petition of divers Merchants of the City of London'.

[70] Margoliouth: *Anglo-Hebrews*, p. 46. Translator's note: Margoliouth also reveals that, in their efforts to get the alien duty remitted, the Jews had enlisted the help of several 'influential and liberal Englishmen, Baronets' to petition the king on their behalf. Tovey (p. 287) reveals that one of these was Sir Peter Vandeput.

[71] Tovey, pp. 287-288. Translator's note: QVOS.

even had 37 of them arrested as they were plying their trade at the Royal Exchange. The Jews saw that they could achieve nothing by resorting to the courts because the measures were based on existing laws. They therefore chose the well-trodden path of appealing personally to the king. In a petition to him, they again referred to Charles II's 1673 decision and pointed out that the prerequisite required for his royal pleasure—the Jews remaining quiet, true and faithful to the government—had been adhered to by them. The arrest had caused great damage to their reputation both domestically and abroad. At the end of their petition, they asked for 'the benefit of the free exercise of their religion', a request which would logically mean that the charges would be dropped. [72]

Just like his brother Charles II, James II issued a former Order in Council, this time on 13 November 1685:

> [H]is Majesty having taken this Matter into his Royal Consideration, was pleased to order, and it is hereby accordingly ordered, That his Majesty's Attorney-General do stop all the said Proceedings at Law against the Petitioners; his Majesty's Intention being, that they should not be troubled upon this Account, but quietly enjoy the free Exercise of their Religion, whilst they behave themselves dutifully and obediently to his Government. [73]

Was it again the 'powerful influences', to use Wolf's words, that induced Charles II to scupper the anti-Jewish initiatives of 1680? We have no reason to believe otherwise.

The fact that James II also favored the Hebrews is clear from the fact that in the first four years of his reign, no fewer than 34 Jews were naturalized—a relatively high number even compared to the awards made under Charles II. [74]

Thus we have seen that Charles II and James II were more concerned with the interests of the Jews than with those of their own subjects. It should be obvious to any clear-eyed person that this servitude did not go without services in return. The Jews' services most likely consisted of payments, since both rulers were constantly in need of money. It is worth mentioning in passing that these monarchs did not hesitate to accept annual payments of up to £100,000 from King Louis XIV of France in order to prevent any anti-French policy from Parliament. So if these kings accepted money from for-

---

[72] Henriques: *Return*, pp. 105-6. Translator's note: The fine was a ruinous £20 per month.

[73] Haggard, Vol. I, Appendix, p. 3; Webb, pp. 39-40. Translator's note: Quotation and previous QVOS (Webb, but Haggard is faithful later reproduction of Webb).

[74] Webb, Appendix, pp. 18-9.

eign rulers to suppress the will of the English people, why would they not also demand and pocket money from the Jews for the same purpose?[75]

Other Allies of the Jews: James II and William III

At the end of 1688, James II hastily departed from England. William III stood at the gates of London and entered the capital immediately after James II had fled. We know that William had had to equip a large expeditionary force for his operations. According to Jewish historians, the money for this was mainly provided by Jews. The financing was then in the hands of the Jewish banker Francisco Lopez Suasso, who later settled in England. The money was probably not paid directly to William III, but to the Dutch state. If this is true, then the amount given by the Jews may be related to the £600,000 that the English government later paid to Holland for the expedition. The Jewish historian Moses Margoliouth provides precise information about this, but without naming his sources.[76]

According to Margoliouth's account, William III's preparations for the expedition to England were at a standstill for want of funds. While he was desperately looking for a way out of his predicament, an Amsterdam Jew was brought into his presence, who bore the Prince of Orange some very welcome news:

> My Lord, you are in want in money to accomplish a great national project; I have brought you, from our people, two millions [probably guilders]. If you succeed, you will refund them to me; if you fail, we are quits.[77]

Margoliouth proudly remarks: 'It was naturally to be expected that many Hebrew merchant-princes should have settled in this country, where a sovereign reigned who was indebted to Hebrew gold for his royal diadem.'[78]

After James II's flight to Ireland, a transitional law regarding tax collection was passed by Parliament. This stipulated that the tax regulations as under Charles II and James II should be maintained until they could be formally reassessed. In the absence of any explicit mention of the 1673 law of Charles II, this would have meant the revival of the alien duty, which had only been repealed by the royal decree of James II in 1685. With the latter's

---

[75] Clark, pp. 82 ff.; 125.

[76] Picciotto, pp. 52-3; Hyamson: *History*, p. 188; Margoliouth: *History*, Vol. II, pp. 40-3; *Anglo-Hebrews*, p. 47 ff.

[77] Margoliouth: *History*, Vol. II, p. 41. Translator's note: QVOS. The same quotation is also found in the same author's *Anglo-Hebrews*, p. 48 and *Pilgrimage*, Vol. II, p. 229.

[78] Margoliouth: *Anglo-Hebrews*, p. 47. Translator's note: QVOS. A paraphrased quotation is also found in the same author's *History*. Vol. II, p. 43.

flight, however, this decree ceased to be valid and the pre-1673 situation was thus restored.[79]

A customs officer named Thomas Pennington took this legal stance when he arrested a number of Jews on 30 January 1689 on the grounds that they had not paid the alien duty that had become due again after the abdication of James II. This was not a high-handed action by an individual official, as the accounts of Jewish historians would have us believe, but rather an action that was initially approved by King William III. Pennington, with the support of a Treasury official (or 'Lord of the Treasury', to use Tovey's phrase), had informed the king of the legal situation. He had further pointed out that the express privilege of exemption from alien duty, as was stated in various Jews' letters patent of denization, did not change the general legal situation. The personal exemptions in question would have lost their legal validity after the death of Charles II or the abdication of James II. Pennington was able to convince the king that the Jews had violated the law and that as a result the goods in question would have to be forfeited and they would have to pay further fines. They would also have to pay an amount of £58,000 in back taxes which had arisen and become due since 11 December 1688. The king gave Pennington a free hand within the limits of the law, and so the arrested Jews awaited trial before the appropriate court. But once again the case would not get far.[80]

The Jews and their friends had of course not remained inactive as the crisis unfolded. Firstly, the prisoners sent a petition to the king asking for their release from prison and for a discontinuation of proceedings. They justified their petition by saying that their letters of denization and thus also their exemption from paying alien duty were in force. At the same time, they invoked the law of 1673 and the Order in Council of 1685. It is striking that they too found the latter justifications to be quite weak and therefore relied more on the former argument. Along with this petition, the Jews made every possible effort to influence the courtiers and the customs officials in their bid to get a *nolle prosequi* [an order to drop the case].

The means of this influence was probably the usual one: money. On such occasions there are usually no witnesses and so the details do not come to light. Both parties have the same interest in remaining silent, and on such occasions the historical researcher is dependent on evidence or conclusions that are described as absurd or biased by those interested in pushing a particular narrative. In order not to leave ourselves open to such points of attack, we are therefore careful to refrain from such speculation; rather, when dealing with such incidents, we rely, as far as possible, on the views of Jewish

---

[79] *Statutes of the Realm*, Vol. VI, p. 71.
[80] *Historical Manuscripts Commission*, Vol. 22, p. 35; Tovey, p. 288 ff. & Henriques: *Special Taxation* (II), p. 62; Hyamson, *History*, pp. 185-6.

historians, who can hardly be accused of an anti-Jewish bias. But here the events are such that the outcome of the matter can only be explained by bribery on the part of the Jews.[81]

In any event, the case against the Jews was not progressing very well. Pennington—relying on his king's instructions and the laws of the land—grew impatient. He made a submission to the Privy Council, which had to decide on the Jews' petition, and asked that the inquiry continue. In particular, he repeatedly sought the right not only for his own petition against the Jews to be heard before any decision was made, but also that he be given the floor as a representative of the state. His efforts were in vain however. The matter was dealt with over nine days, but Pennington, as the authority's main representative, was not heard from once, nor was any debate admitted. And as under Charles II and James II, the Privy Council, now chaired by William III, came to a decision that was incompatible with both the law and the wishes of the people: a *nolle prosequi* was issued. In the relevant Order of Council of 26 February 1689, no justification is given for this decision, despite the extensive length of the text. Rather, the decision can be summed up in the Order's final few lines:

> His Majesty taking the whole Matter into Consideration, was graciously pleased this Day in Council, to order, That Sir *George Treby*, His Majesty's Attorney General, do cause *Noli Prosequis* to be forthwith entred upon the said Informations, or any others that shall be brought against the Petitioners upon the like Account, it being His Majesty's Pleasure, that they enjoy the full Benefit of their respective Letters Patents.[82]

It should be borne in mind that, with this decision, King William III was giving up thousands of pounds of annual income. Most importantly, this decision cannot be reconciled with his initial stance, especially since at the time he had 'vowed that he would not abate the Jews of threepence of what was due to himself'. The whole nature of the proceedings, particularly the treatment of Pennington, is also very strange. Is it not it therefore reasonable to assume that William III was compensated accordingly in the form of a severance payment when he gave up this high annual income? Once again we see how the resources of the Jews are strong enough to persuade even a king of England to make such decisions.[83]

---

[81] Tovey (pp. 290-2) reproduces this petition in full. See also Picciotto, pp. 48-9.

[82] Tovey, p. 292. Translator's note: QVOS, which reproduces the full Order in Council.

[83] Tovey, p. 289; Picciotto, p. 48. Translator's note: Quoted element reproduced verbatim from Picciotto.

Another Battle

The English merchants were angry at this order from their king and openly admitted that only bribery could have brought about such a result. This is conveyed to us in particular by the philo-Semitic D'Blossiers Tovey, who would certainly have known fellow Englishmen from that time and who thus passed on an impeccable report to posterity less than forty years after the event (1738):

> [T]he Merchants complain'd that nothing but Bribery from the Jews, cou'd have obtain'd such an Order, so contrary to the publick Interest of the English Natives...[84]

Even Jewish historians seem to want to admit that bribery took place. James Picciotto, writing in 1875, cannot seem to be able to resist boasting of his nation's power in England at that time:

> Nevertheless, the Jews had so much influence at Court and among the Commissioners of Customs, that for a long time they baffled all the efforts of their enemies. They succeeded in procuring an order of Council, not only against the information brought by Mr. Pennington, but against all others that should be brought against their nation on the same grounds.[85]

However, the anti-Jewish faction did not immediately give up, but continued to fight for their rights and what they believed to be their vital economic interests. In a detailed petition, they made the customs authorities aware that the king would forfeit over £40,000 by not prosecuting the Jews' previous customs offences. In addition, by abolishing the alien duty, at least another £10,000 would be lost every year, which English taxpayers would later have to pay in the form of property taxes. The Jews were not burdened with this, due to a lack of property, and would therefore greatly benefit from this change of tax regime. The balance of trade would also be affected, and the Jews, 'by Virtue of such illegal Clauses', would be 'let loose to over-run the Trade of the English merchants, both at Home and Abroad'. Furthermore, given his current constitutional position, the king had no right to intervene in prosecutions with orders of *Nolle Prosequi,* which, the merchants argued:

> ... were a mere Snare for the Legal Prosecutors whether publick Officers or Others; for instead of reaping that Benefit

---

[84] Tovey, p. 290. Translator's note: QVOS.
[85] Henriques: *Special Taxation* (II), p. 63. Picciotto, p. 48. Translator's note: QVOS.

which the Law design'd them, they were almost ruin'd by the Charge of preparing the Suits, which were discontinu'd without any Fault of theirs.[86]

Again the Jews did everything they could to prevent the petition from being approved. But this time, all of their efforts appear to have been in vain. The pressure from the people must have been very strong, because William III repealed his previous order on 14 October 1690. The content of it clearly shows that, in the opinion of the Crown's lawyers, when both he and James II took office, the alien duty had been revived, and William III's previous decree was not valid. The authorities in question were therefore instructed to collect the alien duty exactly as they had at the demise of King Charles I.[87]

The English merchants were naturally very satisfied and thanked the king for his decision. We can only guess at the reasons for the king's change of heart, even though it was a perfectly legal decision. Was it the customs officials demanding that the law be properly applied? This seems hardly likely—as we saw with Thomas Pennington, the customs men had been unable to assert their will with the authorities. Had the king initially accepted the compensation or bribe from the Jews, and now, after receiving it, unscrupulously retreated back to the letter of the law? Perhaps. However, there is more evidence to suggest that he took the entire situation into account, particularly his desire to collect more revenue in order to continue waging his wars against Ireland and France.

Above all, he hoped to be able to raise a larger loan from the City of London for this purpose. The Jews had shown themselves very disinclined to lend the money required, as can be seen in the report of a letter from the Earl of Shrewsbury to the Lord Mayor of London dated 10 February 1690. In it, the Earl of Shrewsbury expresses his displeasure at the fact that the Jews, despite their flourishing trade in England, which they only carried on 'under favor of the Government', did not feel great desire to 'support that Government' by subscribing to the government loan. Negotiations had already been held with Jewish leaders and they had been asked whether they did not want to make some money available to pay for the army bread deliveries made by

---

[86] Tovey, pp. 290-2. Translator's note: All QVOS.

[87] Tovey, pp. 294-5. Translator's note: Bear in mind that under the common perception of the law at the time, the alien duty was only to apply to foreign-born Jewish merchants. Their sons, if born in Britain, would (under this opinion) fall under the feudal principle that all persons born in any of the King's dominions owe allegiance to the king, and would therefore be natural-born British subjects. However, this idea of *jus soli* was strongly contested by the anti-Jewish forces, who correctly saw the medieval status of Jews as still technically in force, as the civil status of Jews *qua* Jews had never been legally updated since then. See Henriques: *The Jews and the English Law*, p. 233; the appendix of the next volume, and Romaine: *An Answer*, p. 2 ff., for both sides of the controversy.

'one of their brethren' Mons. Pereyra. They only offered the amount of £12,000, 'below what his Majesty expected from them'. As a consequence, the earl, on behalf of the king, now asked him—the mayor—to send for the Jewish elders and principal merchants:[88]

> ... to let them understand the obligations they are under to his Majesty for the liberty and privileges they enjoy, and how much it is to their advantage to make suitable returns of affection and gratitude for the kindness they have received and may expect. And since the money demanded carries with it more than the ordinary interest allowed, it was supposed they would, without difficulty, raise among them 30,000*l*., or if not that amount, that they could not propose less than 20.000*l*...[89]

We do not know whether and what amount the Jews handed over in the end. It is also not known why they had been hesitant to lend money to the king. Perhaps the 7% interest rate was too low for them. In any case, their attitude shows that there had been a deterioration in the good relations between the king and the Jews, although it was probably only temporary. It may also have been a factor in the King's decision nine months later to reinstate alien duty, especially since he had to rely on the City's funds for raising his loans and it was therefore better for him to be on good terms with the English merchants. Incidentally, it is worthy of note that once again—as under Cromwell—we find a Jew in an apparently prominent position among the army contractors.[90]

Along with these battles over the alien duty, further disputes took place over the Jewish Question.

As has already been touched on, William III's first priority was to find the necessary funds for the reconquest of Ireland—which was still defended by James II—and for the war against France. Bonds had little chance of success, and so new taxes had to be levied. A committee was appointed by Parliament to find the means to add £2 million to the public revenue. It was believed that this sum, which was considerable at the time, could partly be collected by introducing a poll tax and a one-off special tax on the Jews amounting to £100,000. Under this new system, the Hebrews would have had to pay twice, as they too were to be included in the poll tax. It was expressly mandated that they should contribute the amount of £10 per head, while other taxpayers in general were to be divided into different classes

---

[88] Clark, pp. 174-5.
[89] *Calendar of State Papers*, Vol. 1689/90, p. 453. Translator's note: QVOS. Readers may be forgiven for feeling some of the medieval echoes of chapter 1 in this passage.
[90] Henriques: *Special Taxation* (I) p. 49. & Acres, Vol. I. p. 7.

according to their rank and wealth. A comparison between both groups shows that the Jews were valued quite highly. The poll tax raised £288,000.

The following year, Parliament approved another poll tax. The Jews were divided into merchants and brokers. The former were liable for £20 and the latter £5, which meant that Jewish merchants were assessed on the same level as barons and bishops, while Jewish brokers were assessed as equal to doctors, priests and lawyers. Furthermore, the rest of the Jews had to pay the amount of 10 shillings when they reached the age of 16.[91]

However, the passing of the special tax on the Jews encountered considerable difficulties, mainly due to the fact that the Hebrews tried to prevent the introduction of the tax using all means at their disposal. On November 19, a petition from the Jews was formally presented to the House by Mr. Paul Foley, MP, before the first reading of the bill had taken place, a highly irregular if not unprecedented action which immediately resulted in a protest being raised by other members. When the Speaker of the House joined in this protest, the petition was refused. The petition is not included in the *Commons Journals*; we only find an indication from *Cobbett's Parliamentary History* that some members raised their objections to the petition being submitted to the House. As this opinion prevailed [as per the rules of the House], there was no inclusion of the petition, nor the debate around admitting it, in the *Commons Journals* at all. At the same time, the Jews had spread a rumor that when the tax was imposed, they would leave the country and go to Holland. We see this in the *Calendar of State Papers*, in the entry for the 12th of November:[92]

> News letter. The Jews will rather remove their effects into Holland than pay the imposition which Parliament has designed to lay upon them, which is 100,000*l*. sterling to carry on the war; that next year the rest of the 1,400,000*l*. to be raised by a subsidy of the 2*s*. in the pound of all lands, and double of those that refuse the new oath of allegiance and supremacy.

---

[91] *Journals of the House of Commons*, Vol. X, p. 279. & *Journals of the House of Commons*, Vol. X, p. 281. & *Statutes of the Realm*, Vol. VI, p. 65. & *Parl. History*, Vol. V, Appendix 19, p. 241. & *Statutes of the Realm*, Vol. VI, p. 158.

[92] *Parl. History*, Vol. V, p. 444. & *Parl. History*, Vol. V, pp. 444-5. Translator's note: Protests came from the fact that not only was it unheard of to present a petition before a debate, but because it was against the then rules of Parliament to allow petitions against taxes, a rule which remained unchanged until 1842. Readers may like to weigh these complaints against Mr. Foley's statement made in the Jews' defence: 'I think that, for the honour of the house, you are to hear what they will say. Where you lay a general tax on the whole kingdom, you can receive no Petition against it, because all are represented here, but when there is a particular tax on men, they may petition.'

This is how the rumor was reported by Narcissus Luttrell (1657-1732):

> The 11th, the Jews petitioned the house of commons to be eased in the new tax, setting forth they cannot pay the 4th part of the 100,000*l.* imposed on them, and that if they have no redresse they must be forced to leave the kingdome.[93]

One can imagine that this threat would have had a great impact in political and commercial spheres.

However, despite the petition's absence in official sources, Henriques believes he has discovered a copy, which, judging from the document's contents, points to him being correct.[94] The content of the petition is very interesting. First we find a brief summary of the history of the Jews since Cromwell. It then points out the great importance that they have for the English economy despite their relatively small number. They:

> ... do drive a considerable Trade, exporting great Quantities of the Woollen manufactures of this Nation, and importing vast Quantities of Gold, and Silver, and other Foreign Staple Merchandizes, which do greatly Enrich the Nation, and encrease the Revenue of the Customs, insomuch that one of the said Families alone hath since the Restauration paid about Two Hundred Thousand Pounds for Customs...

Furthermore:

> [T]he Market for Diamonds in the *East Indies* was formerly at *Goa* (belonging to the *Portuguese*) and by the means and industry of the Jews the Market hath been brought to the English Factories, and by that means *England* has in a manner the sole management of that precious Commodity, and all Foreigners bring their Monies into this Kingdom to purchase the said Diamonds.

The next point was the fifth of the nine points raised in the petition:

---

[93] *Calendar of State Papers*, Vol. 1689/90, p. 318; Luttrell, Vol. I, p. 603. All quotations reproduced verbatim from original sources. Note also the double tax on those who will not swear the new oath of allegiance and supremacy, which would include the Jews. It should also be noted that the threat of the Jews removing their assets or persons to Holland did not feature in the petition itself. In addition, Luttrell states that the petition was introduced to Parliament even earlier than the 19th, but gives no other evidence to substantiate this claim.

[94] Henriques: *Special Taxation* (I), p. 41 ff. Translator's note: Henriques' paper contains all of the information from the sources mentioned, plus a reproduction of the petition in full.

5. That all the Jews together are not by much worth the Hundred Thousand Pounds designed to be raised upon them; even if all they have abroad should come safe to their Hands, without suffering Equal Losses at Sea with those of this year, and consequently it cannot be supposed that the Honourable House of Commons will go about utterly to destroy a People that have always lived Peaceably, Quietly, and Dutifully, under the Established Government; which will certainly be their Case if this Tax proceed.

The opportunity is taken, in points seven and eight, to dispel certain ideas held by some of the English populace regarding the Jews residing in England:

7. And forasmuch as it is believed by some Persons, that the *Jews* did offer a very great Sum of Money to *Oliver Cromwell* for their Establishment in this Kingdom, They do solemnly declare, they are altogether Strangers to it, and utterly deny it; And that they never gave, or offered either of the two last Kings, any Sums of Money for their Liberties, or upon any such like account whatsoever.

8. And Whereas the *Jews* are informed, that there is a rumour goes about, That what these are not able to pay, the *Jews* in other Parts will make up, looking upon them all to make but one Body, though at never so great a distance from each other: They humbly take leave to represent, that in Truth every one particular Man among them subsists of himself, without dependance on any other; And that they cannot expect any Assistance, or Relief from any other place whatsoever: But instead thereof, those abroad will certainly withdraw their Effects, and Correspondencies, and never be concerned any more with them; which will be their utter ruine, and Destruction of them.[95]

The first thing one notices about the petition's content is the Jews' objection to the apparently widespread assumption that world Jewry would give them assistance to pay the £100,000. Apparently the solidarity of Jews from all countries was already recognized in certain places, which the Jews themselves indirectly confirm by saying at one point in the petition [start of point six]: '...the *Jews* being a Nation that cannot lay claim to any Country...'. Henriques, who seems embarrassed by this remark, tries to deflect from the

---

[95] Henriques: *Special Taxation* (I), pp. 44-6. Translator's note: All quotations reproduced verbatim from original source.

truth of this phrase with the somewhat disingenuous argument that the word 'nation' had a different meaning at that time than it does today:

> It is further to be remarked that though they call themselves a nation—a word which at that time had not the definite meaning it has since assumed—they expressly declare that they lay claim to no country of their own, and that so long as they receive toleration and protection they intend to remain in the country which accords them these boons and accept it as their own. [96]

After admittance of the petition was summarily rejected at the parliamentary session on November 19th, the next debate was postponed to December 30th. No record could be found of any specific debate having taken place, although the following short entry for December 30 was found in the *Commons Journal*:

> A Bill for laying a Tax upon the *Jews* of One hundred thousand Pounds, was read the First time.
> *Resolved*, That the Bill be read a Second time. [97]

As is often the case, the official record then goes silent. This time, unlike previous occasions, the first reading had taken place on the bill, but this did not change the fact that everything that could be dangerous to the Hebrews eventually disappears without trace into obscurity. Of course, the Jews and their allies also consider how best to explain the abandonment of the bill, without, however, arriving at a particular view. There had been enough time to pass the bill into law as Parliament sat in almost uninterrupted session until January 27. The need to have funds to continue the war was more than urgent. In addition, the Jews had clearly expressed in their petition how rich they were. If the king hadn't wished to collect the entire amount, he could have at least started with a partial amount. Macaulay, who campaigned heavily for Jewish emancipation at the beginning of the 19th century, argued without substantiation: 'Enlightened politicians could not but perceive that special taxation, laid on small class which happens to be rich, unpopular, and defenseless, is really confiscation, and must ultimately impoverish rather than enrich the State. After some discussion, the Jew tax was abandoned.'[98]

Even the Jewish lawyer and historian Henriques does not agree with him. According to Henriques, people were less convinced of the injustice

---

[96] Henriques: *Special Taxation* (II), p. 58. Translator's note: QVOS.

[97] *Journals of the House of Commons*, Vol. X. p. 319.

[98] Macaulay: *History*, Vol. III, pp. 497-8. Translator's note: QVOS [p. 91 of Vol. III of 1906 edition].

than of the impossibility of the Jews raising the sum, although there was apparently no discussion of reducing the tax demand in response. But the entire tax proposal was dropped, which leads us to speculate that there were other 'unknown but powerful influences' at work which prevented the law from being passed.

The year 1694 sees the founding of the Bank of England Company. The first directors were exclusively English, and it was not until the 18th century that we find Jews in this position. At first the Hebrews were against the establishment of the bank and, together with the goldsmiths of the City of London, tried to bring it down. Among other things, the Bank of England Company was granted a royal charter to practice banking, and it also traded in gold and silver bullion. The former was previously a monopoly run by the goldsmiths, the latter was exclusively in the hands of the Jews. Both therefore saw the bank as an inconvenient competitor supported by the state. The Hebrews also apparently did not like the fact that the bank had been set up by their old enemies—prominent freemen of the City of London—without their involvement.[99]

In 1696 the young company had to go through a difficult crisis that it was only able to overcome with great effort. The reason for this was that the government encouraged the creation of a rival company, the Land Bank United, and the Bank of England was unable to meet the public demand for undamaged coins as a result of illegal coin clipping. The scale of the crime was so great that silver coins were only traded at a fraction of the official rate. It appears that the Jews were not uninvolved in this general financial crisis, as evidenced by extant state documents.[100]

According to an entry dated 14 May 1696, in a discussion about the Bank of England, it is clear that the wavering of confidence in the bank's credit was caused by the goldsmiths, aided by the unsavory business methods of the Jews:

> Some considerations had about the blow given to credit. It was considered that it rose from the malice of goldsmiths against the bank, which had lessened their profit; and the Jews combined with them; the latter had found out a new way for remittances in gold at 31*s.* 9*d.*, silver 31*s.*, and bank bills 30*s.*,

---

[99] Acres, Vol. I, p. 8. & Acres, Vol. I, p. 5 ff. Translator's note: Subsequent research has shown that certain Jewish investors did indeed take a great interest in the Bank of England from its earliest days, an interest (and involvement) which only grew as time passed. See Giuseppi [Translator's Bibliography] for further details.

[100] Acres, Vol. I, p. 66 ff. & *Parl. Papers*, Vol. V, p. 955. Translator's note: (from original source) 'The current silver coin had for many years began to be clipped and adulterated... that five pounds in silver specie was scarce worth 40 shillings, according to the standard: beside an infinite deal of iron, brass, or copper, washed over, or plated.'

which was to ruin the credit of the bank; that the goldsmiths kept up their gold, and new and broad money, and issued only clipped sixpences.[101]

The day after this discussion, the miscreants concerned were summoned to Whitehall and given a dressing-down:

> The merchant Jews called in and advised not to augment the difficulties that are now upon credit. Sir Francis Child and Sir Stephen Evance spoken with to the same purpose.[102]

Another communication dated August 6th seems to indicate that Judah was inclined to provide funds for the establishment of the land bank:

> R. Yard to Sir John [Joseph] Williamson. Little of moment has passed here since you went out of town, except what relates to the money business. This brought Lord Portland from Flanders. The gentlemen of the Land bank subscribed only 36,000*l.*, and the Jews have remitted 20,000*l.*[103]

Meanwhile, the Jews returned to the royal favor, to the detriment of the City of London, and the merchants complained about the king's poor treatment of them. They also complained that the Jews received better conditions for loans than the City, and were therefore prepared to subscribe more money on the same conditions, if they could be promised of an equally speedy repayment. The following events would indicate that the Jews had continued to gain influence:[104]

Near the beginning of 1696 a petition was submitted to Parliament regarding issues with a bill to prevent fraud and abuse in the plantation trade, which would be applied principally to the American colonies. Certainly the conditions there required urgent remedy, otherwise the law would not have needed to be passed. Unfortunately, as far as can be ascertained, the debates on the bill in Parliament and in committee have not been preserved, however, we can at least see from the *Commons Journal* entry of 5th March who among the colonists were considered responsible for these abuses:

> That, in the Bill, now before the House, for preventing Frauds, and regulating Abuses, in the Plantation-Trade, there is a

---

[101] *Calendar of State Papers*, Vol. 1696, p. 178. Translator's note: QVOS.
[102] *Calendar of State Papers*, Vol. 1696, p. 179. Translator's note: QVOS.
[103] *Calendar of State Papers*, Vol. 1696, p. 325. Translator's note: QVOS.
[104] *Calendar of State Papers*, Vol. 1696, p. 310. & *Calendar of State Papers*, Vol. 1696, pp. 310, 317.

Clause, That no Person, other than such as are Natives of *England* or *Ireland*, or born in his Majesty's Plantations, shall trade, as a Merchant or Factor, in the Plantations, under a Penalty...[105]

Accordingly, the view must have initially prevailed that the removal of aliens [foreigners] was absolutely necessary to remedy the grievances. Of course, among those who had to leave the colonies if the law came into force were, in addition to other aliens, numerous Jews. So it is not surprising that the Jews themselves submitted a petition on 12 February 1696, requesting that the above-mentioned regulation be waived, because:

> ... such a Clause will be the Ruin of many Families, who, by the Rigour of the *Spanish* and *Portuguize* Inquisitions, were forced to renounce their native Countries, and shelter themselves under the Protection of the *English* Government; to which they have ever dutifully submitted: And praying, That they may be heard, by their Counsel, at the Bar of the House, before the Passing of the Said Bill, touching the Premises.[106]

We do not know whether it was the Jews' petition or some other influence, which is so often suspected, but in any case, the clause which was so dangerous for them was omitted. As a result, the aforementioned law was passed on 10 April 1696, but without the all-important aliens clause. A compromise had been reached in which the governors and commanders-in-chief of the English colonies had to take a solemn oath that they promised to do their utmost to enforce all of the alien-restrictive clauses relating to trade which already existed in the Navigation and other kindred Acts.[107]

The Jews had won their battle to stay in the colonies. The interpretation of the law was left to the individual discretion of the powerful, and the Hebrews, as only they knew how, most certainly knew how to get the powerful onside.

---

[105] *Journals of the House of Commons*, Vol. XI, p. 491. Translator's note: QVOS.

[106] *Journals of the House of Commons*, Vol. XI, p. 440. Translator's note: QVOS. Note the historical importance of the final sentence – even as early as the 17th century, Jews evidently thought nothing of sending their lobbyists into the House of Commons Chamber in a bid to persuade MPs to side with their cause, to make eye contact with the speakers, and likely to even waylay lawmakers as they entered and left the Chamber.

[107] *Journals of the House of Commons*, Vol. XI, p. 555. & Henriques: *Special Taxation* (II), pp. 65-6. Translator's note: Obviously, if this pre-existing legislation had been in any way effective, new legislation would not have been required. A parallel case of egregious Jewish interference in the crafting of an English law originally conceived to restrict undesirable immigration, thereby rendering it completely ineffective, is the 1905 Aliens Act (see Volume 7).

Jewish Successes

Before the 17th century ended, the Jews celebrated a great victory over the City of London.

In those days, more than today, a merchant's advancement depended on being admitted to the Royal Exchange as a broker, where all of the wholesale trade took place. But the City had for a long time ensured that hardly any foreigners, and certainly no Jews, were allowed entry. The Jews were of course aware of the importance of gaining entry, and so even under Cromwell they did everything they could to ensure that at least one of their ethnic brethren became a member of the stock exchange. Despite fierce resistance, they achieved their goal, because under pressure from Cromwell, the City was forced to give a broker's medal to Solomon Dormido, eldest son of the aforementioned Manuel Martinez Dormido. This completely violated the prevailing laws, because at that time a Jew could neither become a freeman of the City nor become a broker without taking the Christian oath. However, these two legal requirements were waived for Dormido. We completely agree with Wolf that Dormido's admission, which flouted the existing laws, could only have come about through manipulation, although how this was done can no longer be ascertained from the historical record.

In the years 1671-1681, another six Jews were admitted to the Royal Exchange under the same conditions, and so we must assume that this was due to the influence of King Charles II, who was loyal to the Jews. However, disregarding laws in such cases always leads to the same result: the infiltration of extraneous undesirable elements. This is what happened to the brokers on the Royal Exchange, when, to quote Wolf, 'all sorts of disreputable aliens and bad characters forced their way through the portals of the Exchange' [*ibid.* n. 157]. In 1696 the abuses had become so serious that it became urgently necessary to exclude some of the members and reorganize the entire regulatory system, and parliamentary powers were therefore obtained 'for restraining the number and ill-practices of brokers and stock-jobbers'.

At the City's request, Parliament passed a law at the beginning of 1697 which, among other things, limited the number of licensed native brokers to 100. According to the implementing regulations that were later issued, there were an additional 12 foreigners and 12 Jews permitted. The previous requirement for freeman status [or 'Freedom of the City'] was then dropped for the Jews and the oath was modified to a form that allowed them to take it, while the foreign merchants (or 'merchant strangers')—among whom there were many Germans, Dutch, Spaniards, and French—still had to fulfil the condition of being a City freeman.

Acquiring this status was fraught with many difficulties for foreigners, and one must therefore be surprised that the Jews were able to make such considerable progress even in a city that was so hostile to them. Wolf rightly points out that the lack of native resistance to Jewish admission was 'due no doubt to fear lest a conflict with the Jews, in the then undefined, but still very real, protection extended to them by the Government, might lead to some irreparable invasion of the rights of the City'. The reader is invited to ponder why an English government was so keen to impose its will on the kingdom's most respected citizenry on behalf of a small number of Jews.[108]

In the spring of 1698, an 'Act for the more effectual suppressing of Blasphemy and Profaneness' was put before Parliament, and an amendment was inserted after its return to the House of Lords, by which all persons openly professing Judaism would have been made liable to severe penalties. We can also see what happened when this amended bill was put to the vote in the House of Commons, as reported by Luttrell in his *Diary*, dated 22 March 1698:[109]

> The commons yesterday divided [voted] about a clause in the bill against prophanesse, relating to the Jews, who deny Jesus Christ; 144 were for it, and 78 against it: so the clause was added that the Jews shal not be molested.[110]

We can see then how the Jews had made considerable progress by the end of the 17th century. They not only enjoyed the favor of the king, but also increasingly the favor of Parliament.

Moral Corruption

Over the course of 18th century and onwards, we will see that the general populace still wanted to have nothing to do with the Jews or their allies. It is therefore strange that despite this fact, most of the members of Parliament that the populace supposedly elected were almost exclusively pro-Jewish.

---

[108] Wolf: *Re-Settlement*, pp. 9. 10, 14; Wolf: *Menasseh ben Israel*, pp. 106-7. & Wolf: 'Jew Brokers' in the *Jewish Chronicle*, 16/4/1897, p. 8. Translator's note: (*ibid.*) 'How it was managed is a mystery… There was probably some bargain which is not recorded in the Guildhall archives and no doubt public opinion connived at the infraction of the law for fear of driving the Jewish trade out of the country.' & Wolf: *First Stage* pp. 132-3. Translator's note: QVOS. & Wolf in the *Jewish Chronicle*, 16/4/1897, 14/8/1903; Wolf: *First Stage*, p. 134. Translator's note: Quoted element reproduced verbatim from *First Stage*, where Wolf's source for the quotation is given as a reference to a page in Wolf's own archive. No source at all is given for the quotation in the *Jewish Chronicle* versions. & *Statutes of the Realm*, Vol. VII, pp. 285-7. Translator's note: Before the new regulation, the number of Jews working at the stock exchange must have grown to quite an extent (cf. the earlier report of Thomas Beaumont having 37 Jews arrested as they did business at the Royal Exchange in 1685). & Wolf: *First Stage* p. 134. Hyamson: *History*, pp. 208-9. & Wolf: *First Stage* pp. 135. & Wolf: *First Stage*, p. 132. Translator's note: QVOS.

[109] Henriques: *Jews and the English Law*, p. 167.

[110] Luttrell: *Brief Historical Relation*, Vol. IV, p. 358. Translator's note: QVOS.

Jewish historians attribute this stance of the decisive estates of the realm—the king and the legislative houses—to the fact that they recognized the value of the Jewish race and therefore always defended it. There is considerable debate about such an argument. Was it not rather the 'powerful influences' that Wolf spoke of, those that were invisible to outsiders and which worked for Jewish interests? In other words: Was it not money that caused the king and government to protect the Jews? Before we go into this matter further, a preliminary question must first be asked: Is it conceivable that the monarchy, the House of Commons, and the House of Lords, all so highly praised throughout history, could behave so despicably? Incidents in history point to this being the case.

We can only deal briefly here with this chapter of English history and so can only convey a few of the many salient events of that time.

In 1694, the House of Commons Speaker, Sir John Trevor, was expelled from the House for 'Corrupt Practices'. In exchange for a thousand guineas (£1,050) from the City of London, he had, in an illegal and unconstitutional manner, facilitated the passage of a bill (the Orphans Bill), which aimed to protect the City of London after it had repeatedly raided a fund for orphans to cover its own financial deficits. A smaller bribe (20 guineas) had been taken by MP John Hungerford, who had chaired the Orphans Bill committee. He too was expelled from Parliament.[111]

One of the state's highest officials, Secretary of the Treasury Mr. Henry Guy, was imprisoned in the Tower of London because he was found to have taken a bribe of 200 guineas. The public reaction with Guy, as with the case of Sir John Trevor, was one of great anger. For a long time both men were considered people who not only allowed themselves to be corrupted, but who also corrupted other House members through their high position, and with the help of their financial backers.[112]

At the same time, other notable figures were convicted of similar crimes. The biggest scandal, however, arose from the discovery of bribery on the part of the East India Company, which sought to obtain favorable decisions from the king and both legislative houses on the renewal of its charter, which gave it a monopoly on trade with the East. The governor of this company, the goldsmith and MP Sir Thomas Cooke, was immediately arrested, imprisoned in the Tower, and forced to explain the use of what otherwise appeared to be a secret slush fund of £90,000 marked for 'private service'.[113]

---

[111] *Parl. History*, Vol. V, pp. 901-907.

[112] *Parl. History*, Vol. V, pp. 885-887.

[113] *Parl. History*, Vol. V, p. 890 ff. & *Parl. History*, Vol. V, p. 913. Translator's note: Quoted element reproduced verbatim from p. 899.

Cooke's interrogation in front of Parliament was carried out in an atmosphere of great tension. Many Englishmen in high places feared for their honor because of their involvement in the affair.

The first interrogation took place on 23 April 1695. One would have assumed that the governor would have been cautious about his initial statement, for he could only expect support from his high-status accomplices if he spared them. To their horror, however, he did not make use of this opportunity, but rather revealed the truth, albeit in a tortuous form. In particular the Court of Committee wanted to know about two large items of £10,000 and £33,000. The Governor's subsequent statement, as reported by Cobbett, must therefore have caused a sensation:[114]

> To the first sum, of 10,000*l.* mentioned in the said writing, he saith, The same was paid to Mr. Tyssen in Nov. 1692: That he gave him no direction how it should be disposed; but it was in expectation to have the Charter of the East-India Company confirmed, and new regulations thereto made; and they concluded it for the service of the Company: It was intended for the king; but he could not say the king had it.
>
> He believes the East-India Company never had any Account how this 10,000*l.* was disposed of: he told the Court as he remembers, That he had disposed of the Money; and they required no Account thereof: he believes Mr. Tyssen told him, That he delivered it to sir Josiah Child, who delivered it to the king: He saith, It is a customary present: and that, in king Charles, and other former reigns, the like had been done for several years, which by the Books of the Company may appear.

Cooke could not deny that the Company was in an 'ill condition' at the time this present was made, and that he himself had advanced the sum, but repayment was not made within the intended four or five months. The £10,000 and £2,000 next mentioned in the account were paid at about the same time to Mr. Rd. Acton, who declared that 'he had several friends capable of doing great service to the Company's affairs, and several of them would speak with parliament-men'. He could not give details as to who they were, but the aim was to get an act passed by Parliament.[115]

Cooke then went on to say that the desired act was a prohibition on the establishment of a rival trading company for the East Indies, which had been planned to do business there in accordance with the king's wishes. Apart from the members of Parliament, no one else had been influenced. Various

---

[114] *Parl. History*, Vol. V, p. 915.
[115] *Parl. History*, Vol. V, p. 915. Translator's note: Translator's note: Quotations and QVOS.

lords had received large sums for the passage of the law sought by the Company, with the Duke of Leeds [also known as the Earl of Danby] having been given almost £6,000. Meanwhile, Sir Basil Firebrace received £10,000 for himself, and distributed a further £30,000 to various people unknown to the governor to secure favorable laws for the company.[116]

During his interrogation, Sir Basil denied distributing the money to influential people. Rather, he stated that it was for share losses he had incurred, and had thus kept it for himself except for an amount of £500.[117]

Firebrace's banker Mr. Fowles then gave his testimony, which was recorded for posterity with the following words:

> That he cannot remember the Names of any Members of Parliament, to whom any money was paid by sir Basil's order: That he never keeps any private Notes or Memorandums of persons names to whom he pays Money; and hath no other Accounts, to as to that matter, but what are in his Books.[118]

Further evidence revealed that consideration had even been given to bribing the queen and to providing the king with a special sum of £50,000 if he would support the Company. But the king had his agent Mr. Tyssen tell Cooke's agent Mr. Acton: 'The king would not meddle in that matter'. The king might not have accepted the money this time because he considered the sum too paltry, but the fact that anyone could even dare to make him the offer in the first place without him immediately initiating proceedings against the Company tells us all we need to know about the monarch's moral rectitude. Sir Thomas Cooke and Sir Basil Firebrace were sentenced to prison along with other participants. The case against the Duke of Leeds, then Lord President, did not progress very well and later went completely dormant. Everyone was convinced that he had received 5,500 guineas for supporting the passage of the bill favorable to the East India Company. However, it was feared in the highest circles that his conviction would implicate numerous other leading personages, so while the House of Commons initially impeached the duke for high crimes and misdemeanors on April 27th, 1695, and two days later exhibited charges against him, nothing else happened until June 24th, 1701, over six years later, when the House of Lords dismissed both the impeachment and the charges.[119]

---

[116] *Parl. History*, Vol. V, p. 916. & *Parl. History*, Vol. V, pp. 917-9.

[117] *Parl. History*, Vol. V, p. 922-3.

[118] *Parl. History*, Vol. V, p. 923. Translator's note: QVOS.

[119] *Parl. History*, Vol. V, p. 925, 929 & *Parl. History*, Vol. V, p. 929. Translator's note: QVOS, although note that this is reported speech. Note also that on this page the surname Tyssen is spelt 'Tysson'; elsewhere in the text we see 'Tyson'. Similarly, Thomas Cooke's surname is sometimes seen as 'Cook'. & *Parl. History*, Vol. V, pp. 933-942 [particularly p. 941]

There must have been considerable public dismay at the general rotten-
ness of the House of Commons, the House of Lords and the Crown. It is best
expressed in the words of the Speaker of the House of Commons when his
speech at the conclusion of the various bribery cases culminated in the
words: 'What security can the nation have, when we are bought and sold to
one another?'[120]

The following contemporary account of endemic bribery does not
therefore seem to be an exaggeration. According to this account, again taken
from *Cobbett's Parliamentary History*:

> Then was the time when a hungry member was sure of a Din-
> ner* at one or other of the public tables kept about Westmin-
> ster, and which had very lately began to be set up again, to
> feed the betrayers of their country...
>   *The practice was, that besides a dinner, when they had
> done any eminent piece of service, every one found under his
> plate such a parcel of guineas, as it was thought his day's work
> had merited.[121]

The extent of public corruption can also be seen from the fact that, of the 5
million pounds granted by Parliament to continue the War of the Spanish
Succession, only 2.5 million ended up in the Exchequer's coffers. The other
half ended up in the pockets of individuals. The events on the stock exchange probably contributed significantly to this rot, because bribery was
openly discussed there, and in 1720 it was said that 'elections for members of
parliament came to market in 'Change Alley as currently as lottery tickets'.[122]

Exchange Alley, or 'Change Alley' as it was known, although it was
shortened still further to 'The Alley' by those who frequented it most, was
for a century the centre of all dealings in stocks, shares, funds, exchequer bills
and bank-notes. An excerpt of John Francis' description of The Alley [p. 27-8]
is worth reproducing to give the modern reader a sense of the wheeling-and-
dealing, wild-west atmosphere of financial London at that time:

> Here assembled the sharper and the saint; here jostled one an-
> other the Jew and the Gentile; here met the courtier and the
> citizen; here the calmness of the gainer contrasted with the
> despair of the loser; and here might be seen the carriage of
> some minister, into which the head of his broker was anxiously

---

[120] *Parl. History*, Vol. V, p. 932. Translator's note: QVOS.
[121] *Parl. History*, Vol. V, p. 931 (footnote). Translator's note: QVOS.
[122] Francis, p. 34. & Francis, pp. 48-9. Translator's note: QVOS.

stretched to gain the intelligence which was to raise or depress the market. In one corner might be witnessed the anxious, eager countenance of the occasional gambler, in strong contrast with the calm, cool demeanour of the man whose trade it was to deceive. In another, the Hebrew measured his craft with that of the Quaker, and scarcely came off victorious in the contest; while in one place, appropriated to him, stood the founder of hospitals, impressing with eagerness upon his companion the bargain he was about to make in seamen's tickets.

Given all of this, we believe that in general circumstances it was not unusual, if not the rule, to bribe the king, the government, and the legislature. We therefore see no reason to doubt that the Jews, who were always present wherever there were trades and intrigues, also played their part.

Even back then, Jews played a significant role on the stock exchange:

> Many Jewish capitalists came over from Holland with William III. From Menasseh Lopez to Abraham Goldsmid and Nathan Meyer Rothschild, a series of Hebrew speculators held commanding positions in Change Alley or the Stock Exchange. They followed their avocation with eager zest; and their expresses from every court in Europe outstripped Government messengers with the latest news. Stock-jobbing flourished greatly, and increased in extent in the middle of the last century, notwithstanding various attempts made by the legislature to check this form of gambling.[123]

It is interesting to note that the Jews committed a fraud similar to that alleged by Rothschild after the Battle of Waterloo. One day during the reign of Queen Anne [ca. 1705], a well-dressed man, riding his horse at a furious rate, ordering turnpikes to be thrown open and sparing neither spur nor steed, rode down the Queen's Road, loudly proclaiming the death of the queen to all those who could hear. It did not take long for the news to spread everywhere. Given the uncertainty of the successor, government securities on the stock exchange fell dramatically. The Christian speculators, spooked, threw their securities onto the market and the oversupply pushed the price down even further. In the general confusion, it was hardly noticed that the Jews under Menasseh Lopez were buying up all the government securities that they could get their hands on. After a while, it was discovered that the news of the queen's death was untrue. The result of this was a rebound in stock prices and a consequent huge profit for the Jews. In what he calls 'first polit-

---

[123] Picciotto, p. 219. Translator's note: QVOS.

ical hoax on record', John Francis rightly points out: 'There is no positive information to fix the deception upon any one in particular, but suspicion was pointed at those who gained by the fraud so publicly perpetrated.'[124]

It was agreed in the decent circles of England that 'the brokers of Change Alley were the bane of the nation', with someone at the time describing Exchange Alley as:

> ... a complete system of knavery, founded in fraud, born of deceit, and nourished by trick, cheat, wheedle, forgeries, falsehoods, and all sorts of delusions; coining false news, whispering imaginary terrors, and preying upon those they have elevated or depressed.[125]

However, such a state of lawlessness was optimal for the Jews, and so it is not surprising that 'the Hebrews flocked to 'Change Alley from every quarter under heaven'. A single synagogue in London was no longer sufficient, and so, in addition to the recently enlarged Sephardic synagogue, a synagogue for the Ashkenazim was built. The continuous influx—mostly of Eastern European Jews—can still be determined from state documents, as there the entries for passport requests and other such matters for the Children of Israel are found at an unprecedented level.[126]

With such favoritism, it is only too understandable that the Jews accumulated riches upon riches, and during this period it was Menasseh Lopez, Solomon Medina and Sampson Gideon who were known for their enormous fortunes. The first name we have already mentioned. He was the man who owed his fortune mainly to the aforementioned 'queen's death' fraud.[127]

It is worthwhile spending some time on the lives of the latter two. An in-depth discussion of Sampson Gideon will be undertaken in the context of the political struggles of 1753, while Solomon Medina was at his greatest under King William III and Queen Anne.

According to one account, Medina came with the stream of Jews from Holland to England after William III's accession to the throne. However, there are doubts about the accuracy of this narrative, because according to another source, Medina paid fixed contributions to the Jewish community's coffers as early as 1677, over a decade before William III's expedition to

---

[124] Francis, p. 49. Picciotto, p. 59. Translator's note: Readers may find certain parallels between this event and the method by which Samson Gideon almost doubled his fortune in 1745-6 (see Volume 4). & Francis, p. 49. Translator's note: Quotation and QVOS.

[125] Francis, p. 61. Translator's note: Quotation and QVOS.

[126] Francis, p. 81. Translator's note: QVOS. & Margoliouth: *History*, Vol. II, p. 41 ff.; Picciotto, p. 54 ff. & See, for example, *Domestic State Papers*, Vol. 1696, pp. 211, 420, 462; Vol. 1697, p. 49, 55, 90, 115, 139, 141, 159.

[127] Picciotto, p. 59.

England. These contributions were calculated as a percentage of income. Picciotto has found that, based on the payments made, Medina must have had an income of £32,000 in 1677 and even £80,000 the following year, a considerable sum for those times.[128]

His money certainly won him the favor of King William III in one way or another, because on June 23rd, 1700 he was honored with a knighthood. This is all the more remarkable because, unlike Coronel, who converted to Christianity in 1660, there are no references to any conversion of Medina in the historical record. The conversion to the Christian faith was apparently left to his descendants.[129]

Medina was known as a merchant, but his main field of activity was as an army contractor, supplying the army with bread. He may have played the same role in England during the War of the Spanish Succession as the Jew Oppenheimer did in Austria on the same occasion. He was the reason that the Duke of Marlborough, Winston Churchill's ancestor, was dismissed from public office in 1712, and he has provided us with evidence of active bribery.[130]

Marlborough, the Ancestor of Winston Churchill

John Churchill, 1st Duke of Marlborough, was accompanied by Medina on all of his military campaigns. The latter supported him—as his fellow Englishman Cromwell had been served—by providing intelligence. Meanwhile, the battles of 'Ramilies, Oudenarde, and Blenheim administered as much to the purse of the Hebrew as they did to the glory of England'.[131]

But this close association of the Jews with one of the most famous generals of the 18th century had its downside: from a soldier's point of view, it must have been shameful to see how Jewish money had somewhat tarnished Marlborough's glory. If we dwell on this matter, it is not in the least as an attempt to belittle his deeds, which were so great for England, or to burden him with shame; rather it is to provide yet another example of how the Jewish character and Jewish behaviors are very often the cause of such irregularities or blemishes in the lives of great men as is seen with Marlborough. Although he may have been greedy for money and thus became an easy victim

---

[128] *Jewish Encyclopedia*, Vol. VIII, p. 425. & Picciotto, p. 50. Translator's note: Picciotto also details the methodology used by the synagogue to calculate each member's income tax (*finta*), and reveals that Medina was the synagogue's biggest contributor at the time.

[129] Le Neve, p. 473. Translator's note: Note that in this volume his name is rendered 'Solomon de Medena', while in the *Jewish Encyclopedia* it is 'Solomon de Medina'. & *Jewish Encyclopedia*, Vol. VIII, p. 425.

[130] Frischauer, p. 289. Translator's note: Source not found in any of Aldag's bibliographies.

[131] Picciotto, pp. 58-9; *Jewish Encyclopedia*, Vol. VIII, p. 425; Margoliouth, Vol. II, pp. 58-9. & Francis, pp. 31-2. Translator's note: QVOS.

of the Jews, one cannot imagine Medina's assistance or even instigation in this incident.

In general, the events speak eloquently to the fact that, at the same time as the Jews' greater influence in public life after 1660, bribery in connection with the perversion of justice and the commission of crimes took place in disproportionately greater frequency than earlier in English history—especially under Elizabeth and Charles I. The reader may remember Ludovici's statement [chapter 2] that the exploitation of the people began with the death of Charles I. This was also the point at which the Jews had begun to gain their foothold in England. The beginning of the general grievances from the populace along with the simultaneous appearance of the Jews must at least give us pause for thought. It is left to the reader to decide whether the presence of the Hebrews was not a *sine qua non* for the development of adverse conditions in England. Perhaps this thesis is not so implausible when one considers that it is always the Jew whose name is associated with the corruption of morals. The case of Marlborough and Medina may rightfully be consulted for proof of this.

In the autumn of 1711, there were signs that Marlborough was using large sums of money from bribes and other public funds for himself. A commission was appointed that, over the course of long sessions, tried to get to the bottom of the matter. At the beginning of October 1711, as we learn from a letter to Lord Oxford, the public was already fully aware of the facts. The Jew Medina was called as the main witness and examined under oath. The substance of his deposition best summarizes the whole situation and is reproduced in full below:[132]

> Sir *Solomon de Medina*, Knight, being sworn on the *Pentateuch*, deposeth, That from the Year 1707, to this present Year 1711, both inclusive, he has been solely, or in Partnership, concerned in the Contracts for Bread, and Bread-Wagons, for supplying the Forces in the *Low-Countries*, in the Queen of *Great Britain*'s Pay; and that he gave his Grace the Duke of *Marlborough*, for his own Use, the several Sums following, viz:

> | For the year | 1707 | --------- | 65.000 Dutch Guilders |
> |---|---|---|---|
> | | 1708 | --------- | 62.000 Dutch Guilders |
> | | 1709 | --------- | 69.587 Dutch Guilders |
> | | 1710 | --------- | 66.810 Dutch Guilders |
> | | Total | ------- | 265.614 Dutch Guilders |

---

[132] Coxe, Vol. III, p. 458.

Also Twenty One Thousand Gilders for this present Year, in Part of a like Sum with those abovementioned; all which Sums he gave his Grace, because the former Contractors had given the like Annual Sums.

He further deposeth, That he allowed Yearly, Twenty Two Wagons *gratis*, to the General Officers, Twelve or Fourteen of which were for the Duke of *Marlborough*'s own Use, and that the former Contractors did the same.

This Deponent further saith, That from the said Year 1707, to this Year 1711, both inclusive, he gave Yearly, on sealing the said Contracts, a Gratuity of Five Hundred Gold Ducats to Mr. *Cardonnel*, Secretary to the Duke of *Marlborough*, for his Trouble and Pains in translating the *Dutch* Contracts, and putting the *English* Contracts into Form. And he further saith, That for all the Money he received in *Holland* from Mr. *Sweet*, Deputy Pay-Master at *Amsterdam*, on Account of the said Contracts, he was obliged to pay him One *per Cent.* for Prompt Payment, and that the former Contractors did the same; but he found him notwithstanding so backwards in his Payments, that he complained to the Duke of *Marlborough*, and, at the same Time, acquainted him with the Allowance he made to Mr. *Sweet* of One *per Cent.* as aforesaid, and that his Grace reproved him for not paying this Deponent more punctually.

And this Deponent further saith, That it appeared by the Accounts of *Antonio Alvarez Machado*, who had supplied the Bread, and Bread-Waggons, for the Forces in the English Pay, as aforesaid, for the Year 1702, 1703, 1704, 1705, and 1706, That he gave as large Yearly Sums to the Duke of *Marlborough*, as this Deponent hath done since.

Jurat [sworn], 6 December 1711. *S. de Medina.* [133]

Medina's deposition and the entire proceedings, which was initially kept as secret as possible, quickly reached the ears of the absent Marlborough. Immediately the 'insulted general', to use Coxe's words, sent a letter of defense to the commission. The following is an excerpt from this letter:[134]

---

[133] *Report of the Commissioners*, p. 8. Translator's note: QVOS. I have, however, followed Aldag in only stating the Guilders in the accounts, omitting the *Schillinge* and the *Pfennige*, but wish to assure the reader that Medina was able to provide an account of the transactions down to the last *Pfennig*.

[134] Coxe, Vol. III, p. 459. Translator's note: QVOS.

Hague, 10 November 1711.

Gentlemen,

Having been informed, on my Arrival here, That Sir *Solomon de Medina* has acquainted you with my having received several Sums of Money from him; that it might make the less Impression on you, I would lose no Time in letting you know, That this is no more than what has always been allow'd, as a Perquisite, to the General or Commander in Chief, of the Army in the *Low Countries*, even before the Revolution, and since: And I do assure you, at the same Time, That whatever Sums I have received on that Account, have been constantly employ'd for the Service of the Publick, in keeping secret Correspondence, and in getting Intelligence of the Enemies Motions and Designs...

Marlborough then goes on to comment about the allegations regarding the use of other public funds, which are not of great interest here. However, it should be pointed out that Marlborough does not deny that he received the money from Medina, but says that he did not use it for himself, instead using it for state ends, to aid the war effort. In addition, he defends himself with the argument that the receipt of the money itself was legal because it was a legitimate additional income that had been permitted for a long time. He ends his letter with a personal address to the commissioners:

And now, Gentlemen, as I have laid the whole Matter fairly before you, and that, I hope you will allow, I have served my Queen and Country with that Faithfulness and Zeal which becomes an honest Man, the Favour that I intreat of you, is, That when you make your Report to the Parliament, you will lay this Part before them in its true Light, so that they may see this necessary and important Part of the War has been provided for, and carried on, without any other Expence to the Publick, than the Ten thousand Pounds a Year; and I flatter myself, that when the Accounts of the Army in *Flanders* come under your Consideration, you will be sensible, the Service on this Side has been carried on with all the Œcomony and good Husbandry to the Publick, that was possible. I am, Gentlemen, *Your most Obedient Humble Servant,* Marlborough.[135]

---

[135] *Report of the Commissioners*, p. 4-5; *Parl. History*, Vol. VI, p. 1057. Translator's note: QVOS (*Report*).

Marlborough's secretary, Mr. Adam Cardonnel, who was responsible for administering the bread contracts, was also interviewed:

> Mr. Cardonnel being sworn, was ask'd, Whether there are any Allowances or Presents made to the *English* General in the *Low Countries*, by the Contractors for Bread, and Bread-Wagons, he answer'd, No, not that he ever heard of, till the late Noise of Sir *Solomon de Medina*'s Evidence before this Commission.
> The Question above was asked twice, and he repeated the same answer...[136]

The Duke's secretary also stated that he had given no receipt for the skimming of the other public funds that were also in question:

> But Mr *Cardonnel*, as he declares on Oath, never gave any Receipt for any Part of this Two and a Half per cent...[137]

Marlborough thought it advisable to leave the Hague as quickly as possible and return to England. On November 17 he landed at Greenwich, 'to encounter new disgusts and aggravated indignities'. Meanwhile, the public had also become aware of the events taking place. Pamphlets appeared against the Duke, some of which were obviously motivated more by the desire to tear him down than by any real wish to report on the facts. Others—and we will only deal with these—could not understand how a man in his position could have used so much money. According to one such publication, Marlborough had an annual income from his various public offices of £62,325. Since 1701, he had received a total of £623,381 from Jews and public sources. Furthermore, he received various special payments, such as £50,000 from Holland after the Battle of Blenheim. However, the total stated in this pamphlet appears to be somewhat exaggerated and the figure of approximately £523,000 found by the commission of inquiry is more likely.[138]

The two legislative houses met in early December, which also opened up party-political battles over this issue. Marlborough's opponents did everything they could to get the investigation done as quickly as possible. They were successful, and on December 15, a motion passed in the Commons for the commissioners of public accounts to report their findings. The report was presented on December 21. First, Medina's statement and Marlborough's

---

[136] *Report of the Commissioners*, p. 12. Translator's note: QVOS.

[137] *Report of the Commissioners*, p. 6. Translator's note: QVOS.

[138] Coxe, Vol. III, p. 462 ff. Translator's note: QVOS. & For example: *No Queen; or, No General* pp. 10-11. & *Yearly Income of the Duke...* p. 1 ff. & *Report of the Commissioners*, pp. 6, 22, 23.

letter, as previously discussed here, were reproduced. The commission then took the position that such payments from military supply contracts 'can never be esteemed Legal or Warrantable Perquisites'. In addition:[139]

> ... they do not find, by the strictest Enquiry they can make, that any other *English* General in the *Low-Countries*, or elsewhere, ever claimed or received such Perquisites; but if any Instance should be produced, they humbly apprehend it will be no Justification of it, because the Publick, or the Troops, must necessarily suffer in Proportion to every such Perquisite; and how agreeable this Practice is to that Œconomy and good Husbandry, with which that Service in *Flanders* is said to be carried on, remains yet to be explained. By the Assurance his Grace is pleased to give, that this Money has been constantly employ'd for the Service of the Publick, it must be either allowed, that he relinquishes his Right to this pretended Perquisite, or that he has been wanting to himself in concealing so great an Instance of his own Generosity to the Publick.[140]

Furthermore, the statement from the Duke's secretary indicated that the matter was handled with great secrecy—evidence of Marlborough's own guilty conscience. In addition, in their opinion, Marlborough's behavior represented a major breach of trust:

> The great Caution and Secrecy with which this Money was constantly received, gives Reason to suspect, that it was not thought a justifiable Perquisite; for Mr. *Cardonnel*, the Duke's Secretary, and Auditor of the Bread Account, has declared on Oath, That he never knew or heard of any such Perquisite, till the late Rumour of Sir *Solomon de Medina*'s Evidence before Your Commissioners. By the Contracts for Bread, and Bread-Wagons, the General appears to be the sole Cheque on the Contractors; he is to take Care that the Terms of the Contracts are duly performed; he is to judge of all Deductions to be made from, and Allowance to, the Contractors; and whether in such Circumstances he can receive any Gratuity, or Perquisite, from the Contractors, without a Breach of his Trust, Your Commissioners presume not to determine. The General may with equal Reason claim a Perquisite for every other Contract

---

[139] Coxe, Vol. III. p. 469ff. & Coxe, Vol. III. p. 478. & Coxe, Vol. III. p. 478; *Parl. History*, Vol. VI, p. 1049; *Journals of the House of Commons*, Vol. XVII, p. 15 ff.
[140] *Report of the Commissioners*, p. 5. Translator's note: QVOS.

> relating to the Army, as for these of the Bread, and Bread-
> Wagon; but his Grace being silent as to this, your Commis-
> sioners ought to suppose he has not received any such Allow-
> ance, unless they shall understand otherwise when they come
> to examine into those Contracts, which hitherto they have not
> been able to do, by reason the Contractors are Foreigners, and
> constantly resident in Holland.[141]

With regard to the other amounts received, which had no connection with
Medina, it was then concluded that these were public funds and that Marlborough had also committed a criminal offence in disposing of them. The
Duke's argument of using the money to pay for espionage was refuted with
the following counter-argument:

> By the Warrant, this Deduction is reserved for the defraying
> extraordinary Contingent Expences of the Troops, from whom
> it is stopp'd: And if the Whole has been employed in secret
> Correspondence and Intelligence, there must have been some
> Neglect of the other Services for which it was originally de-
> sign'd; and such a Disposition being in no sort authoriz'd by
> the Warrant, is a Misapplication of it.[142]

Under the force of this accusation, the Queen removed Marlborough from all
of his positions on December 30, in order, as she emphasized, to ensure an
impartial investigation.

On 24 January 1712, the debate on the commission's report took place.
The best speakers were on both sides. They refrained from any harsh words
about Marlborough's service to his country and took a purely factual stance
on the report. His defense lawyers also submitted the affidavit of Jacob de
Mercado, book-keeper and cashier for the late owners of the bread company,
from which Marlborough had also received money from the bread contracts.
This employee had special insight into the business and made the following
statement (translated from French):[143]

> I the underwritten, Book-keeper and Cashier of the late Mes-
> sieurs *Machado* and *Pereira*, deceased, Contractors General of
> Bread, for the *English* and *Dutch*, during all the last War; and
> interested myself, with the late Monsieur *Machado*, in the

---

[141] *Report of the Commissioners*, p. 5. Translator's note: QVOS.
[142] *Report of the Commissioners*, p. 6. Translator's note: QVOS.
[143] Coxe, Vol. III. p. 484 ff.; *Parl. History*, Vol. VI, p. 1077; *Journals of the House of Commons*, Vol. XVII, p. 38.

Bread Contracts of this War, till the Year One thousand Seven
hundred and Six, inclusive; do hereby declare and attest, That,
during the whole Course of the last War, and of this present
War, till the aforesaid Year 1706; I say, I do declare and affirm, That the Usage and Custom was, That the Contractors
for Bread did annually give a very Considerable Present to the
Generals commanding in Chief the Armies during the aforesaid time; and also to several General Officers of lesser Rank;
which said Present, or Gratifications, were proportionable to
the Strength and Number of the Troops that composed the
Army to whom the Deliveries of Bread were made: And I do
further attest and certify, That I have always heard, from the
Persons that contracted for Bread in the First Campaigns made
by King *William*, of glorious Memory, That the said Usage of
making such Present, or Gratification, to the Generals commanding in Chief, was generally practised, and became, by
long practice, a Right established in such a Manner, that the
Contractors thought, that the Generals commanding in Chief
might legally claim the same...[144]

This statement was intended to confirm Marlborough's earlier statements, as
found in his letter of 10 November 1711. The defense more or less only put
forward the arguments used by Marlborough in his letter. His opponents, on
the other hand, took the stance of the investigative commission. By a majority of 265 votes to 155 the House determined: 'That the taking several Sums
of Money annually, by the Duke of *Marlborough*, from the Contractors for
furnishing the Bread, and Bread Waggons, for the Army in the *Low Countries*, was unwarrantable and illegal.'[145] A similar decision was made regarding the further public funds that were received by Marlborough.

The annual receipt of the 500-ducat gratuity by Marlborough's secretary, Mr. Adam Cardonnel, was also found to be 'unwarrantable and illegal'
and he was expelled from Parliament. It was also decreed that the aforementioned Mr. Sweet was to be prosecuted, because:

... the One *per Cent.*, received by Mr. *Sweet*, Deputy Pay-Master
at *Amsterdam*, upon the Payments made by him to the Contrac-

---

[144] *Journals of the House of Commons*, Vol. XVII, p. 36-37. Translator's note: QVOS.
[145] *Journals of the House of Commons*, Vol. XVII, p. 38; *Parl. History*, Vol. VI, p. 1077.
Translator's note: QVOS (*Journals*).

tors for furnishing Bread, and Bread-Wagons in the *Low-Countries*, is Publick Money, and ought to be accounted for...[146]

Queen Anne was asked to instruct the Attorney General to initiate formal criminal proceedings against Marlborough. She complied with this request, but the process was 'very moderately pursued.' The reason, we hear, was 'either by the queen's indulgence to one whom she had formerly so much trusted, or perhaps to be revived or slackened, according to the future demeanor of the defendant.' The trial that was supposed to take place eventually went nowhere.[147]

Marlborough published a defense soon after Parliament's decision, in which he gave the same apologia as found in his letter of 10 November 1711. He added that Prince Waldeck, whilst he was General of the Dutch Army in Flanders, had received the same funds. Receiving free deliveries of bread also corresponded to an 'ancient Usage', which Count Tilly reportedly partook in. Furthermore, the public did not appear to have been disadvantaged by the donations from the bread contractors, and he had not committed a breach of trust because the contracts had been signed by the Treasury. The army had never suffered from a lack of bread, and he had always followed up on the few complaints that he had received from the soldiers, regarding which he appealed to his officers to confirm the truth of his assertion.[148]

His secretary had had nothing to do with the bread deliveries and therefore knew nothing about his master's perquisite, while the Duke had had no idea about the money paid to Mr. Sweet.[149]

We shall refrain from going into the many pamphlets for and against Marlborough that were published during this period. The statement of the facts from his defense should suffice.

Marlborough tried to clear his name by claiming that the benefits from the bread contracts were legitimate additional income—in other words, that he was asserting a right. However, such a right only arises if it does not violate the written laws and—what is actually much more important—if it does not violate the sense of decency of all those who think fairly and equitably. What matters here is not the opinion of a specific circle, but rather the general public. Therefore, while the Jews and their allies may have believed that the general had a claim to righteousness, people with the generally accepted moral viewpoint could not approve of his actions. Such behavior has always

---

[146] Coxe, Vol. III. p. 486. *Report of the Commissioners*, p. 16. Translator's note: Quotations reproduced verbatim from respective original sources. Note that Coxe, as some other sources, spells the secretary's surname 'Cardonel'.

[147] *Parl. History*, Vol. VI, pp. 1077. Translator's note: Quotations reproduced verbatim from original source.

[148] *Case of His Grace*, pp. 5-6. Translator's note: QVOS. & *Case of His Grace*, pp. 10-11.

[149] *Case of His Grace*, p. 12.

been described by law and custom as bribery. Apart from the fact that an official is not free in his decisions when receiving such money, there is also the fact that public funds suffer as a result, because no one will believe that the Jews paid the amounts out of their own pockets or to the detriment of their own earnings. The bribes were immediately factored into their calculations as expenses, in other words, the state had—and still has to pay in such cases—the surcharges imposed for the crimes of its officials.

Aside from the question of additional income, the great general claimed that he did not use the money for himself, but for state purposes—espionage—a justification that has the advantage of it being impossible to provide an orderly proof of expenditure due to the nature of the activity. Did he use the 21 wagons of bread given to him by Medina for the same purpose? As things stand, there can be no doubt that Marlborough and his associates, on the one hand, and the Jews Machado and Medina, on the other, were guilty of passive or active bribery, which is also admitted by some historians.[150]

This incident joins many similar scandals in history, such as the Barmat and the Stavisky scandals—to name just a couple of worthy, or rather unworthy, examples. It is unfortunate, however, that the events just described are associated with the name Marlborough. The well-known English parliamentarian and German hater Winston Churchill is his direct descendant and one of the best-known and most zealous friends of the Jews in England.

It is not surprising then that the general public did not think much of the integrity of the Jews in such events and therefore continued to be hostile towards them. This is illustrated quite nicely by a traditional anecdote. An Englishman was in debt to a Jew who sued for repayment. There was an old law according to which a Jew could not sue in his own name, but only in the name of the king.

The hearing took place before one of England's highest judges, the notorious Lord Chief Justice George Jeffreys, known to history as 'the Hanging Judge.' The English defendant raised the aforesaid formal objection and considered the action to be dismissed. The judge asked if he had anything else to plead in his defense. The defendant replied in the negative. 'Then,' shrieked the judge, 'I tell you that even according to your defense, you must pay his demand, for he did not bring an action against a Christian, but against a Jew, and one greater than himself.'[151]

The literature also provides ample evidence that the people continued to reject the Jews. We shall limit ourselves to dealing with one book, *A Historical and Law Treatise against the Jews and Judaism*, which was first published in 1703. As the author explained in his introductory 'Epistle Dedicatory',

---

[150] Graetz: *History*, Vol. V, p. 217; Jesse: *Memoirs*, Vol. I, p. 400-5.

[151] Picciotto, p. 52. Translator's note: The judge's ruling is quoted verbatim from Picciotto.

his statements were not intended as a hateful screed, but rather as a fair debate, to which intention he has arguably remained true:

> *Gentlemen, I hope you won't mistake me, I am not for whetting the* Edge *of* Severity, *or* Insulting the Agonies *of a* Distress'd People; *but if upon a fair and impartial* Survey, *the* Jews *shall appear to be as* Impious, Dangerous, *and* Subtle *as they are here* Represented, *I hope you will Excuse me if I put you in mind that 'tis your* Duty, *nay your* Interest *to get the Matter candidly Represented, in order to their speedy* Suppression, *and to make a strict Enquiry what* English Christians *are lately Perverted to* Judaism *in* England.[152]

The Jews and their allies, however, as far as they have discussed this book at all, take a different view. But this view is probably due in the most part to the author's highlighting of facts that are inconvenient to the Hebrews. That these reports are not exaggerated can be seen from the aforementioned statements made by John Francis. Furthermore, they are only a generalization of the particulars arising from the Medina case, while the conditions described bear so much resemblance to modern conditions in all Western countries, including the erstwhile Weimar Republic, that we have no reason to mistrust the information.

In the author's opinion, which he backs up with legal sources, the pre-Expulsion laws were still in force, according to which Jews were forbidden to settle in England. However, he goes on to say the following:

> As for the great Liberty which the *Jews* now take (in this Realm) it is evident, That by our Antient Laws and Decrees, they have no Pretence, or the least Colour of Law or Right to Claim any such Privileges here; and that the Impious and Immoral Freedom which the *Jews* take amongst us, is depending upon the Force and Power of their Money; which (as we have just Reason to believe) runs through many secret Channels (in this Kingdom) Corruptly, to Support the Impious and Blasphemous Doctrine of the *Jews* against the Gospel of Jesus Christ...[153]

---

[152] *Law Treatise.* Translator's note: QVOS (page unnumbered). The *treatise* must have proved popular enough (or was considered sufficiently important) for a second edition to be published with new typesetting in 1720, although note that the 1720 edition appears to lack the Epistle Dedicatory.

[153] *Law Treatise*, p. 3. Translator's note: QVOS. One example of a Jewish mention of this book is found in Margoliouth's *History*, Vol. II, pp. 57-58, which describes the author as a 'zealot'.

Elsewhere in the text, the Jews are compared to wolves, locusts, and thorns:

> And that as Nature will not allow Sheep to Associate with
> Wolves, no more will the Law of the Gospel allow Christians
> to Associate or Intermix with *Jews*; Christians are Promised
> the State of Grace, and the *Jews*, without their Conversion and
> Repentance, totally Excluded. And as Locusts are to Corn, so
> are the *Jews* to Christians; the former Consumes the Grain,
> and the latter Undermines the Common-Wealth; The Foreign-
> ers that were Admitted amongst God's own People, Did they
> not prove Thorns and Briers to them?[154]

Above all, the rabbis had to be expelled from the country. The author then
goes on to steadfastly refute the claim that the Jews 'bring in Money, and
promote Trade' to the benefit of the nation:[155]

> It is most certain, that none but Kings and Princes, and their
> Favourites ever gained by the *Jews*; and that all Common-
> wealths have suffer'd by them to Excess. The Jews, by their
> Corrupted Charms, and Secret Intrigues, though they have no
> manner of Right to Live here, do boldly presume, not only to
> Engross the Principal Part of our Trade, now they are admitted
> Sharers in Publick Stocks...[156]

The author also details how the Jews have taken over most of international
trade, in doing so describing the mechanisms of international Jewry. He also
details their mockery of naive English largesse, and his argument against the
claim that the Jews improved English trade ends on a bitterly sarcastic note:

> The *Jews* have Engross'd the *Portugal* and *Barbary* Trade to
> themselves, and have bid very fair for the *Spanish*, they have
> out-done our *English* Merchants, and have got into their
> Hands the Trade of *Barbadoes* and *Jamaica*, whereby they by
> their Remote Correspondence, drive all the Course of our *Ex-
> change* and Merchandize before them. And by their pretend-
> ing Friendship to all Religions, they got into favour with Cler-
> gy and Laity, which gives them many Opportunities to drain
> all Christian Countries of their Coin; the *Hollanders* are so
> well acquainted with the Jews, and with their Practices, that

---

[154] *Law Treatise*, p. 13. Translator's note: QVOS.
[155] *Law Treatise*, p. 15.
[156] *Law Treatise*, p. 17. Translator's note: QVOS.

they keep them out of all Publick Stocks at Home, and Hang them up if they catch any of them in their Plantations Abroad; But here in *England* they do what they please, their greatest Sharpers they send hither, and here they are supplied by their Brethren with Money, Jewels and Goods of great Value, to make fine Shews, and gain Credit, and when they have so far got into our Debts as they can, then they march off by new Names, and leave us in the Lurch, and the Jews here helps them off with our Effects; and thus they encrease in Cheat, and multiply in Wickedness, and after this manner of Fraud they Improve the *English* Trade...[157]

So nothing has changed there then.

At the beginning of the 18th century, the Jews apparently felt that the time had come to purchase privileges and a location to form a closed settlement. They offered government minister (and close friend of Marlborough) the Earl of Godolphin £500,000 to sell the town of Brentford near London and grant numerous privileges. The Jews' agent reported 'that the affair was already concerted with the chiefs of their brethren abroad; that it would bring the richest of their merchants hither, and of course an addition of above twenty millions of money to circulate in the nation.' Lord Molesworth urged Lord Godolphin to comply with the demand. However, the latter refrained from doing so in view of the expected strong opposition from the clergy and the merchant class, although the Jews were prepared to pay up to £1,000,000 for the fulfilment of their wishes.[158]

As far as is known, during the years of Queen Anne's reign there was in fact only one important piece of legislation concerning the Jews. Around 1701, Parliament deemed it necessary to enact the following law in the event of a young Jew converting to Christianity:

---

[157] *Law Treatise*, p. 18. Translator's note: QVOS. This excerpt is particularly interesting because it reveals that a 'reactive anti-Semitism' had begun to set in with the Dutch, a natural and ineluctable process which Professor Kevin MacDonald explains at length, citing historical examples, in his landmark *Separation and Its Discontents* (1998). For a documented example of a foreign Jew gaining credit from English merchants to then skip the country without paying, see Chapter 3 of *The Sultan's Jew* for the incident involving Moroccan Jew Meir Macnin, in which he defrauded fifty English creditors when he left England for Morocco with a ship full of English cargo on credit; the cheated merchants petitioned the British government to take action on their behalf, but to no avail. [See Translator's Bibliography for both sources.]

[158] *Dictionary of National Biography*: Vol. XXII, p. 42. Translator's note: Refers to Sidney Goldolphin (1645-1712). & Spence, p. 77. Translator's note: QVOS. This story can also be found (reproduced in full from the original source) in Volume 2.

> If the child of any Jewish Parent is converted to the Christian
> Religion, or is desirous of Embraceing it; upon Application to
> the Lord Chancellor he may compell any such Parent to give
> his Child a sufficient Maintenance, in Proportion to his Cir-
> cumstances.
>   Stat. I°. *Anne* Cap. 30.[159]

There is an amusing anecdote related to this law, and we shall reproduce it
from Margoliouth's *History of the Jews in Great Britain*:

> A young Jew having embraced the Christian religion, and, be-
> coming consequently disinherited, bethought himself to take
> advantage of Queen Anne's Act. He accordingly sued his fa-
> ther for 'a sufficient maintenance in proportion to his circum-
> stances.' The parent was not disposed to submit to the act
> without a struggle; he determined therefore, to take legal ac-
> tion. Having laid the case before the most learned counsel of
> the day, and having offered a lucrative reward, if the lawyer
> could devise any plan whatever, so as to outwit his apostate
> son, the jurist promised to set his wits to work, and he thought
> a way of escape might yet be found. He said, moreover, that if
> the Hebrew client would call upon him the following day, ac-
> companied with the promised fee, he would tell him of the
> best mode of defence to be adopted against his son. The He-
> brew departed from him in better spirits than he entered into
> the barrister's house, and with characteristic punctuality he
> presented himself once more at the appointed hour before his
> legal champion.
>   'Well, Sir,' said the Hebrew, 'I hope it is all right, and
> that that rascal of a son of mine will not be allowed to eat pork
> at my expense.'
>   'I have hit upon a plan, after a sleepless night of cogitation,'
> rejoined the counsel, 'and it is the only plan that will effectually
> prevent him eating pork or anything else at your expense.'
>   The barrister paused, the client knew its meaning.
>   'There, Sir, your eyes shall not have been deprived of
> sleep, nor your eyelids from slumber for nothing. I hope you
> will consider this fee ample, and let your mouth utter the plan.'
>   The lawyer secured the liberal reward, and then with ju-
> dicial gravity propounded his matured plan.

---

[159] Tovey, pp. 295-6; Hyamson: *History*, p. 210. Translator's note: Quotation reproduced
verbatim from Tovey.

'The only way, dear Sir, to neutralise that obnoxious Act of Her Majesty, is, for you to be publicly baptised into the Christian Church. You see the law does not provide for Christian children, but it does for Jewish.'

'And is this the only plan?' exclaimed the irritated client.

'The only plan, I assure you; and its formation deprived me of last night's sleep.'

'I wish then you slept and never awoke,' muttered the disappointed Hebrew, and departed.[160]

---

[160] Margoliouth: *History*, Vol. II, pp. 55-7. Translator's note: QVOS.

CHAPTER 4

EARLY EMANCIPATION STRUGGLES AND JEWISH DEFEAT (1714-1753)

The South Sea Bubble

The Guelphs ascended the English throne after the death of Queen Anne in 1714, and the new royal family were initially faced with significant difficulties. However, things looked particularly bleak for them after the collapse of the South Sea Company:

This company had gradually taken over the entire public debt of about £30 million. In return, the government agreed to pay the annual interest on these debts for a limited period of time and, above all—and most importantly—to grant the company extensive trading privileges. Initially the company did great business and its share price rose. Later, however, the public was misled by false rumors and promises of profits, causing the shares to rise from £100 par to £1,000. A fever had gripped England. Nobles and commoners alike threw themselves into this speculative madness. Suddenly, the directors of the company sold their shares off, which was followed by a crash in the share price. Hundreds, even thousands of lives were destroyed. A major crisis hit the government.

The only way the government could save itself somewhat was by the resignation of its leading man—Charles Spencer, the 3rd Earl of Sunderland—and by punishing the main offenders—the company directors and the Chancellor of the Exchequer, John Aislabie. It is surprising that the Jews took part in the speculation but not in the actual fraud; they apparently sold their shares in a timely manner and thus suffered no damage. The Jewish historian Albert Hyamson says of Jewish participation in the affair:

> The Jews, as a whole, stood aside from the wild speculation of the time, and were among the few whose fortunes passed through the ordeal unimpaired.[1]

However, although some readers might be inclined to infer from Hyamson's careful syntax that no Jewish speculation took place, it is clear that the Jews did speculate, if not wildly. According to the records of the official enquiry set up to investigate the government's role in facilitating the disaster and to

---

[1] Hyamson: *History*, p. 217. Translator's note: QVOS.

discover criminal behavior that had taken place, Jews were buyers of the shares at prices between £150 to £300.[2]

In his recently published book, Heinz Krieger concludes from the fact that the Jews emerged financially unscathed from the affair as proof that they, together with Robert Walpole, had been behind the market manipulation. However, he has provided absolutely no evidence for his assertion. We ourselves had initially also suspected a Jewish hand in this fraud. However, very detailed investigations have not uncovered any incriminating evidence to indicate this. Neither the records of the official investigation against the guilty nor the almost endless writings of outraged and ruined Englishmen gave us any indication of complicity on the part of the Jews. And this at a particular point in history, when Englishmen would certainly not have held back with their views had they believed the Jews to be involved, there would definitely be some trace of this in the historical record were it to be true. Based on the evidence, it is therefore not possible to affirm that there was Jewish involvement, and it is left to the reader to form his or her own opinion in this regard.[3]

Krieger has also expressed the view that Walpole was friends with numerous Jews and should be held responsible for the catastrophe. The first point is true, because there is no doubt that Walpole had very close relations with the Rothschild of the period, Sampson Gideon. However, since it cannot be established that Jews were involved in the South Seas trade, their connection with Walpole is irrelevant here. Furthermore, it is clear that Walpole was not a member of the government in the years 1717 to May 1720, as stated by Krieger. Rather, he was the Leader of the Opposition and vigorously fought, through parliamentary speeches and published writing, the government's support of this company.[4]

Jews in the Colonies

Before we make any further statements about the evolution of the Jewish Question in England, we would like to take a look at the English colonies. There is substantial material available about the spread of Jews to the colonies of New World and given that most of it has already been published, we shall only go into the topic very briefly, using Hyamson's work as our source.

---

[2] *Several Reports of the Committee of Secrecy* p. 52 ff.; *Supplement to the Reports*, p. 16 ff.

[3] Krieger: p. 49 ff.

[4] Hyamson: *History*, pp. 216-7. & Haydn: pp. 156, 165, 244; G. E. C.: *Complete Peerage of England*, Volume VI, p. 129. & Oliver: pp. 238-240. Lecky: Volume I, p. 374. Translator's note: Despite his initial opposition to the scheme, this is not to say that Walpole did not personally do well out of the South Sea Bubble: according to Oliver [p. 250], Walpole bought early and sold at the top of the market, which allowed him to rebuild Houghton Hall and start a fine art collection.

Barbados is probably the English possession where the Jews first appeared openly, as early as 1628. Many of their ethnic brethren soon joined them, and trade was largely in their hands. Attempts by the English colonists to restrict the rights of Jews and to set high taxes in accordance with their large incomes, when successful, did not last long.[5]

We have already touched on Jewish involvement in the development of Jamaica. On that island too there was a steady increase in Jewish influence on the resource-rich economy. In order to protect their interests, in 1671 the English settlers submitted a petition to the Council of the Colony for the expulsion of the Jews.

They achieved the opposite. The governor of the island, Governor Lynch, forwarded the petition to England with his own personal recommendation against it, and his views were adopted by the Jew-friendly Charles II, who not only rejected their request, but recommended steps to encourage further Jewish immigration to the island. Over time, Jews came to dominate almost all aspects of trade and exchange on this island. As always on such occasions, a healthy population of a country seeks to defend itself, and so, ten years later (1681), the Council of the Island attempted to have the Jews expelled from the country. Of course, once again it was to no avail.[6]

The beginning of the 18th century even shows the Jews making efforts to gain the right to vote in the local Assembly, although all of these efforts, in 1702, 1711, and 1740, ultimately met with failure. Furthermore, the Jews themselves admit that at this time the economic position of the Jews in Jamaica 'was by then so strong that they practically monopolized the trade in sugar, rum, and molasses'.[7] Numerous Jews were also found everywhere on the other West Indian islands.

The first Hebrews on the American mainland are said to have landed in New Amsterdam—now New York—in 1654. They then spread to other parts of North America. After New York was occupied by the English in 1664, the Jews made good progress. As early as 1672 they were no longer legally considered foreigners. Although they still had some setbacks in their advancement—e.g. around 1685, retail trade was prohibited to them, if only temporarily—the last years of the 17th century saw them in possession of every freedom of trade and other privileges.

As early as 1727, there were hardly any barriers to the naturalization of the Jews in the colonies, as the oath laid down for this purpose with the final words: 'upon the true faith of a Christian' had been declared unnecessary for Jews. So a legal phrase that was considered so insignificant that it was ig-

---

[5] Hyamson: *History*. pp. 198-200. Translator's note: Note that this is prior to their resettlement under Cromwell in England itself.

[6] Hyamson: *History*, pp. 200-1.

[7] Hyamson: *History*, pp. 202-4. Translator's note: QVOS.

nored in New World from the earliest days, remained so important in the Old World that it was able to hold back the complete emancipation of the Jews in England until 1858 [see chapter 6]. In North America, of course, the omission of this oath norm had the contrary effect on satisfying Jewish desires, and so it is not surprising, given the Jewish mentality, that the Jews then went on to illegally take part in the elections of 1737. After lengthy debates in the Assembly, their votes were declared null and void.[8]

In Canada, the first reliable traces of a Jewish presence only become apparent after the French were ousted by the English in 1760. It is certainly no coincidence that the Jew of modern times followed the Union Jack.[9]

Further settlements of Jews also took place in other parts of the English colonies in America, such as Rhode Island, Maryland, Georgia, and South Carolina, although initially none of these were of great importance.[10]

All told, there is no doubt that the Jews had at least the same influence in the colonies as in the mother country, and it is therefore not surprising that it was from the New World, where the colonial societies were not as old and deep-rooted, that the first successful steps towards Jewish emancipation were taken.

Jewish Preparations for the First Emancipation Attempt

The same Jewish tactic can be proven again and again in history: they work to achieve their goals through subtle and careful changes in legislation. First, they seek from the legislature the enactment of a law on (what appears to be) a matter of minor importance: the first stage for later efforts and at the same time a test of the popular response to such a measure. If the response is not favorable then the tactic is to wait a while and in the meantime use propaganda to prepare a better public mood for the next attempt at change.

This was also the case in 1740, which will go down as an important milestone in the history of the Jews in England, despite it appearing insignificant at first glance. This is the year of the enactment of 'An Act for Naturalizing such foreign Protestants and others therein mentioned, as are settled or shall settle in any of His Majesty's Colonies in America', more commonly known as the Plantation Act.[11]

An unbiased reader would not initially realize that the law also contained drastic provisions for Jews in America. No one will think of Jews when they hear the words: 'foreign Protestants and Others'. Most people will never bother to read through long laws—the English ones are hard to beat— and if someone actually thinks of laboriously working their way through the

---

[8] Hyamson: *History*, pp. 204-5.

[9] Hyamson: *History*, pp. 206-7.

[10] Hyamson: *History*. pp. 214-5.

[11] *Statutes at large*, Vol. XVII, p. 370. Translator's note: QVOS. This statute [13 Geo. 2. c. 7] is also known to historians as the 1740 Naturalization Act.

weeds of English legalese, he is unlikely to do a minute analysis of the entire contents. He might skim through the first section of around 700 words and, depending on his temperament and interest, decide that everything in the remainder of the text is fine—or that he has really had enough of the dense, jargon-laden writing. The next two sections contain the important provisions for the Jews—although again they are only mentioned in a subordinate clause. The Jews were mentioned in the second section in such a way that they were granted an exemption from Sacramental Test, a drastic decision for the time, because previously it had had to take place before the official act of naturalization. Finally, they were accommodated in the third section by the fact that they were allowed to take the Oath of Abjuration, which they had to take upon admission to the state, without the final sentence 'upon the true faith of a Christian'.[12]

Was it the aforementioned 'powerful influences' on members of Parliament [see chapter 3], was it the clever way the law was drafted, or was it even Robert Walpole's relationship with the Jews that resulted in this law being passed without it arousing public curiosity, despite its public interest? In any case, it is clear that the clause regarding the Jews was actually obtained by deception of the people. When the Duke of Bedford, on the occasion of the Jewish debates in the House of Lords in 1753, took the floor to discuss the still-unresolved issues, he stated the following regarding the creation of the 1740 law:

> I think the American act, so far as relates to the naturalization of Jews, ought to be repealed. We know how artfully that part of the act was introduced: we know that it was passed by surprise, or rather, I may say, by stealth; for nothing relating to the Jews ever appeared in the votes, nor does now appear in the title of the act.[13]

Thus the legal clause relating to the Jews was an irregularity, or, as Coxe [Vol. II, p. 292] summed up the Duke of Bedford's view, 'introduced either by surprise or inadvertence'. This is not only the opinion of a member of the House of Lords, but also that of a member of the House of Commons, namely the Earl of Egmont. He also commented on the events of 1740:

> [I]f they [the people] have never yet shewn any discontent with the act for naturalizing such Jews as shall reside seven

---

[12] This oath, imposed in 1702, was an abjuration of the Stuart dynasty and the temporal power of the Pope.

[13] *Parl. History*, Vol. XV, p. 107. Translator's note: QVOS, see also Translator's Appendix II. Incidentally, Coxe reveals that it was the Whig politician Henry Pelham who was the promoter of this bill in Parliament.

years in our plantations, it is because that part of the act which relates to Jews was passed as it were by stealth, without ever making its appearance either in the votes of this House, or in the title of the act, so that very few of the people know that there is such an act...[14]

If we were to ask ourselves which of the previously-mentioned factors must have been relevant to the law being passed, we can now be certain that the wording of the law and the ignorance of the people contributed significantly.

It is difficult to determine how many Jews became naturalized in the colonies. During the 1753 controversy, some commentators claimed that 185 Jews had acquired British citizenship by that time, while another talked of several hundred. In Jamaica, the Jews even demanded, citing the law, that they be given the right to vote. This was refused, but it is another example of the extent to which the Jews will immediately abuse whatever privilege is granted to them.[15]

In England itself, the Jews were also eager to achieve further small successes. Under Elizabeth I, a number of distinguished merchants from the City of London had been granted privileges to trade with the Levant and a company was then founded under the name of the Levant Company, although it came to be known colloquially as the Turkey Company. The possibility of joining was subject to certain conditions and was only limited to a small number of people. In any case, the Jews were unable to penetrate society primarily because certain conditions stood against them. Almost all trade in Turkey, on the other hand, was in the hands of the Jews, and their racial brethren in England certainly expected, not without reason, a preferential position in economic relations with this country.[16]

In 1744, conditions in the Levant Company were very favorable to Jewish infiltration. For several years the Company's trade had been going downhill because the French were able to supply more suitable goods to the Turks and, due to the shorter route from southern France, at cheaper prices. In addition, there had been power shifts in the Middle East, which meant that the Company had lost purchasing and sales opportunities, but the Jews and their allies tried to publicly explain this loss of revenue as being caused by the closed nature of Arab society.[17]

In the same year, a bill was introduced into the House of Commons, according to which all British subjects could participate in the Company by paying £20 and fulfilling certain other small obligations. In the event of the

---

[14] *Parl. History*, Vol. XV, p. 158. Translator's note: QVOS.

[15] Hyamson: *History*, p. 218; Hertz, p. 62. & Hargrave, p. 78. & Hyamson: *History*, pp. 203-4.

[16] *Parl. History*, Vol. XIII, p. 895 ff.

[17] *Parl. History*, Vol. XIII, pp. 895-898; Macpherson, Vol. III, p. 240.

bill passing, nothing stood in the way of Jewish entry. The honorable Old English merchant families did not agree to this under any circumstances and therefore put up bitter resistance to the bill. The Jews naturally made every effort to oppose this resistance.[18]

Fierce debates took place in the House of Commons. The most stubborn opponent of the Jews was Sir John Barnard, the man who became London's leading merchant in the battle of 1753, and the man worked hard to defend the Levant Company in 1744. Nevertheless, the bill passed by 87 to 43 in a thin House of Commons, after which it was sent up to the Lords, which also had to give its consent for the bill to be made law.[19]

On 7 May 1744, the bill was discussed in the House of Lords. Judging from the debates recorded, it must have been a long and heated session, as we find around 40 pages in *Cobbett's Parliamentary History*. The proponents of the bill tried to show that the exclusive character of the Levant Company was the main cause of its decline, while the company's political and other difficulties were only of secondary importance. An injection of fresh blood into the Levant Company was therefore needed, and who could be more suitable for this than the Hebrews?[20]

The bill's opponents explained at great length the reasons for the current poor state of trade relations, and warned strongly against the admission of Jews. As a result, 'a multitude of low people' would accompany them to Turkey, who would represent a constant threat to England's reputation and trading rights there. But even apart from such an objection, the Duke of Bedford explained, one should remember that even if trade were to increase, the English merchants would gain nothing from this, and in fact, only lose in the long term. Since the Turkish side of the trade was controlled almost exclusively by Jews, with their well-known global solidarity that was not disputed by the other side, the Jews would direct the trade into the hands of their ethnic kin, with the end result that they would 'engross the whole trade to themselves', and the English merchants would be left completely dispossessed.[21]

Lord Delaware supported the Duke in his remarks and once again pointed out the difference between Englishmen and Jews:

> The Jews, my lords, let them be born in what country they will, look upon themselves as all of the same nation: those born in China are as much of the Hebrew nation as those born in England, or any other country; and wherever they meet, they consider themselves as countrymen: they associate to-

---

[18] Cunningham: *Immigrants*, p. 203. & Macpherson: Vol. III, p. 241.

[19] *Parl. History*, Vol. XIII, pp. 895-898.

[20] *Parl. History*, Vol. XIII, pp. 910 ff.; 933 ff.; 954 ff.

[21] *Parl. History*, Vol. XIII, pp. 908-910. Translator's note: QVOS.

gether, go to the same synagogue, speak the same language, and have the same customs.[22]

The friends of the Jews naturally had a different opinion on all of the objections raised and did not see the slightest danger of the Levant trade becoming Jewish, since the English merchants were just as capable as the Jewish ones.[23]

The opponents of the bill submitted a motion to adjourn the debates, for which they received a majority. This represented a defeat for the Jews' allies, who made no further attempt to pass the bill over the next few years. The historian David Macpherson (1746-1816) quite rightly cites the Upper House's fears of the Levant trade becoming completely Judaized as the main reason that the bill was dropped.[24]

It is strange that in 1753, when the Jews were compelled to shelve their emancipation efforts for almost a hundred years, they were able at least to achieve some success in their long-cherished ambition of forcing themselves into the Levant Company. Business was once again very bad with the company's trade, which led to the change in the admissions policy, mainly due to the argument that the economic position of the Levant Company would improve if general admission (which would include Jews) were allowed. Was the state of the Company really so perilous due to the political developments of Asia Minor, or had the Jews *fomented* this situation by working hand in hand with their ethnic brethren in Turkey to establish a silent boycott of the English merchants, thereby destroying the latter's last possibilities of prosperous trade? It is impossible for us to know, but it would not have been the first or the last time that the Jews had achieved their goals using such means.[25]

The year 1748 brought another move from the anti-Jewish faction. Even back then, Jews were heavily involved in hawking and peddling in England, both of which were banned by a special law under Queen Elizabeth, but allowed again under William III.[26] In the meantime, the abuses of this trade had become so unbearable—the peddlers cheated wherever possible, sold unfit and unusable goods, and acted as the main fences for smuggled goods in an era where a lack of orderly warehouses meant that there was no effective state control—that on 19 March 1748, a petition was sub-

---

[22] *Parl. History*, Vol. XIII, p. 924 ff. Translator's note: QVOS [p. 932].

[23] *Parl. History*, Vol. XIII, pp. 919-922 (Lord Sandys' speech).

[24] *Parl. History*, Vol. XIII, p. 963. & Macpherson, Vol. III, p. 241.

[25] *Statutes at Large*, Vol. XXI, pp. 49-53. & Cunningham: *Immigrants*, pp. 203-4; Macpherson, Vol. III, pp. 293-4.

[26] Hanway, p. 143; *Parl. History*, Vol. XIV, pp. 1391-2; 'The Adventurer' (newspaper), p. 255 (3rd April 1753). & *Parl. History*, Vol. XIV, p. 266. & *Parl. History*, Vol. XIV, p. 246.

mitted to Parliament for an abolition of the William III law. A lengthy debate on the issue took place, but it is not clear what became of the motion.[27]

Apparently, however, hawking and peddling had not been banned, because in 1753 we find the continued existence of the Hawkers' and Pedlars' Office in London, at which, among other things, licenses had to be renewed annually. It can therefore be safely assumed that this attack by the anti-Jewish faction had been defeated.

There are certain events in history whose causes can only be guessed at. However, such assumptions can become almost a certainty if they coincide with the goals of a particular interest group.

The Jewish drive to achieve supremacy within a people usually begins with the Jews first striving for naturalization, because only as formal citizens can they gradually acquire the associated privileges. In order not to arouse the hatred of Jews that usually initially prevails in a country, special tactics are required. Laws must be made to aid them in their endeavor; but they must not reveal their goal too openly lest they run the risk of rejection. So, with Jewish cunning, a bill is introduced which speaks not of the Jews, but of 'foreigners,' of whom there were many in England. For example, the Huguenots who had left France because of their Protestant faith were mostly welcome in England because of their skills from the then flourishing French industries and because they were generally few in number. Who would therefore object to their naturalization? With these and other foreigners, the Jews then slipped into a newly created government category more or less unnoticed. The aforementioned 1740 law for the colonies [the Plantation Act] is an early example of this, and without a doubt the Jews were significantly involved in the fight to pass a general naturalization bill between 1745 and 1751, which was of course introduced to the House under the title 'Bill for Naturalizing Foreign Protestants.'

Furthermore, the Jews and their allies do not deny their lively interest in such legislation. Shortly before the bill was introduced to Parliament, the Jews had been busy drafting a special immigration bill for themselves. They immediately contacted the proponents of the 'foreign Protestants' bill and asked for naturalization to extend not only to foreign Protestants but also to themselves. As the pro-Jewish Philo-Patriae further tells us, the Jews found the men concerned sympathetic to their aspirations, and they even encouraged the Hebrews to publicly announce their desire despite the great opposition in Parliament and in the nation. But fearing 'that they might prevent a measure which they believed to be for the good of the people, the Jews re-

---

[27] *Parl. History*, Vol. XIV, pp. 246-7, 250. & *Parl. History*, Vol. XIV, p. 249. & *Parl. History*, Vol. XIV, pp. 246-266.

jected this pursuit of their private interests and endeavored to advance the bill as it was'.[28]

This pharisaic and frankly mendacious statement, which comes as no surprise to those who study Jewish behavior, was refuted in 1753 by a leading Jewish ally, the MP Robert Nugent, in the course of a speech he made in defense of the Jews Naturalization Bill:

> And with respect to our liberties, everyone knows, that the liberties we enjoy is what makes the Jews so fond of coming to settle in this country. Can we, then, suppose, that they would ever contribute to the destruction of that which is their chief temptation for coming hither? Surely, Sir, the opinion of some gentlemen with regard to the Jews must be very much changed from what it was some years ago; for I remember when I had the honour to receive the commands of this House to prepare and bring in a Bill for a general naturalization of foreign Protestants (and I shall always look upon it as an honour) the Jews applied to me for a clause in their favour, and I was inclined to have added some clause for that purpose; but I was afraid lest it might obstruct the Bill, and therefore I refused to comply with their request.[29]

We have no hesitation in believing these words, because the modesty of the Jews and their consideration for the common good (as described by Philo-Patriae) is not exactly typical of them. Whatever the case, Nugent's statement confirms our assumption that the Jews were involved with the bill in question from the outset.

The legislative proposal for the foreign Protestants, which was introduced by the aforementioned Robert Nugent, was ultimately unsuccessful. Of the man himself, the following is reported:[30]

> His speeches in parliament, delivered as they were in a rich Irish brogue, often hovered on the borders of farce, but his unflagging wit usually carried him happily through his difficulties. As for convictions in politics he had none; from the first he laid himself out for the highest bidder, and as his knowledge was inconsiderable and his opinions changed with expediency, he was open to the censure of Lord George Sackville, who

---

[28] Philo-Patriae, *Considerations*, p. 22. Translator's note: For a discussion of Philo-Patriae's identity, see footnote 46. & Philo-Patriae, *Considerations*, p. 23.

[29] *Parl. History*, Vol. XV, p. 136. Translator's note: QVOS.

[30] Hyamson: *Jew Bill*, p. 158.

dubbed him 'the most uninformed man of his rank in England,' adding that nobody could depend upon his attachment.[31]

It therefore does not seem unreasonable to assume that the money of interested parties played a role with such a character, especially since bribes were the order of the day at that time. In any case, Mr. Nugent showed great interest in these questions of naturalization, because early in 1751 he introduced another similar bill to Parliament, which this time, after much heated debate, found a majority at the second reading. The Opposition had only been able to put forward a few amendments, which meant that a new second reading had had to take place. However, the third reading was unduly delayed by the death of the then Prince of Wales, giving the Opposition time to call on voters to help in the fight against the government's proposed legislation, which enjoyed warm support within the House of Commons itself. The people made their voices heard, and a storm of protest broke out. Petitions were submitted to Parliament from the City of London, Thetford, Bristol, Rochester, Oxford, Southampton, Salisbury, Gloucester, and Reading. The government bowed to public indignation and the bill was taken off the parliamentary agenda.[32]

The people's great concern for the issue is reflected in their joy at the bill being dropped. When the news of this victory reached Bristol, the jubilation knew no bounds, as a contemporary magazine's report makes clear:

> *Bristol.* On the 18th arrived an express with news that the naturalization bill, after a third reading in the house of commons, and much debate, on a majority of 13 against it, was put off

---

[31] *Dictionary of National Biography*, Vol. 41, p. 270. Translator's note: QVOS. From the following passage (*ibid*.) one may also speculate that Nugent was a Catholic 'sleeper cell' in Parliament, keen to promote non-Anglican interests for his own outsider religion, or else it could simply be that he had no firm religious conviction, and that, as the main text implies, he would adopt any religious cause for political expediency: 'Nugent was brought up as a Roman catholic, turned protestant, and, last of all, died in the bosom of the church which he had abandoned and ridiculed. Popular doubt as to the religion which he professed gave the sting to Oswald's retort to him, "What species of Christianity do you claim to belong to?"'

[32] *Parl. History*, Vol. XIV, p. 970-2. Translator's note: The source also gives the myriad reasons for the petitioners reasons for the anti-immigration stance, as well as discussing the one petition that arrived in *favour* of immigration, with the following amusing anecdote: '...and on the 28th [February] there was presented, a Petition of the merchants, traders, and others residing in or near the city of London, setting forth the advantages of a general Naturalization, and praying that the Bill might pass into a law; and it being ordered that the names of the subscribers might be read, Mr. Sydenham moved, that the clerk might read each man's name, as near as he could, as it was pronounced in the language of the country the subscriber came from or belonged to; whereupon it appeared that many, if not most of the subscribers were foreigners, or of late foreign extraction...'.

for two months; on this, the bells began to ring, and the populace assembled in great numbers, patrolling the streets with
several effigies, one of which was habited like a clergyman
(designed for the Rev. Mr. *Tucker*, rector of *St. Stephen*, who
had wrote an excellent *essay on trade*, and a pamphlet on the
pernicious use of spirituous liquors); the evening concluded
with bonfires, when the effigies were committed to the flames
with all the marks of detestation and contempt.[33]

1753: The Year of Battle

The people had successfully defended themselves against foreign infiltration
with the right instincts. It had become clear that the people's representatives,
who were generally corrupt at that time, would do nothing to obstruct the
will of foreign elements, but the populace was still healthy and strong
enough to enforce its will.

As a result, what we see around this time is a continual attack and
counterattack, with victory and defeat alternating between both sides. The
year 1753, however, was to be the culmination of the Jews' efforts and the
people's defense. The former apparently believed that their time had come.
They did not consider the failure of 1751 to be greatly significant and had
only the success of 1740 in mind. Furthermore, they were probably deceived
by their partial success with the Levant Company, the new law for which, as
evidenced by its straightforward arrangement in *The Statutes at Large* [Vol.
21, pp. 49-53], had also been passed without much difficulty. [Translator's
note: The Jews' morale may also have been boosted by the passing of the
British Subjects Act of 1751, 25 Geo 2. c. 39, which ensured 'natural-born
subjects' could inherit property from an alien parent or parents.] It is always
the same with the Jews: they always fail where instinct has to take the place
of intelligence, a consequence of the fact that they are no longer rooted to the
soil and do not understand the feelings of the national body that is alien to
them. As a result, they cannot appreciate the powers that arise from these
forces, and they were defeated in England in 1753—just as they were defeated in Germany in 1933.

Immediately after the failure of the 1751 bill, Jews continued their efforts for a general Jewish naturalization law. Slowly, very slowly, they started their propaganda machine, as can best be seen from Philo-Patriae's remarks, which should not be missed:

> [T]herefore they considered it their duty not to pursue their
> plan at first and to suppress any little selfish inclination that

---

[33] *Gentlemen's Magazine*, Vol. XXI, p. 186. Translator's note: QVOS.

each of them might have to bring up the matter, so as not to appear to beg. But later they almost unanimously agreed to go for it, making it clear that of course they did not want any new privilege. In general, the petitions were made publicly and with this justification, after which they then disseminated them among their acquaintances. So they became a common topic of conversation, especially at the end of the session of 1752. There was general (not to say unanimous) approval, but it was also considered appropriate to leave the issue until the next session, so that people had time to consider the matter.

At the beginning of last winter the conversation was renewed, the matter was considered, a formal petition was made, and no objection was found... How could such an extremely sensible matter ever be an obstacle!... The few who seemed not to understand the proposal when they first heard it being discussed, were made to see that no adverse consequences could arise from it. No effort was spared in considering every possible objection, nor was any action taken until all to whom the proposal was made were fully persuaded of the utility of such a law and of the general approval that it would receive...[34]

So they tried to convince their friends of 'the utility of the law' for two years before the bill was formally introduced. We know how 'persuasive' the Jews would have been on such occasions, and how accommodating they must have been at a time when corruption was the order of the day.

The battle began in the spring of 1753, when the Whig [i.e. liberal] Pelham government introduced a bill in the House of Lords under which foreign Jews could, under certain conditions, acquire British citizenship. At that time, there were laws in place that basically deprived them of this opportunity. Under King James I, 'in order to keep out unwanted foreign Catholics', naturalization was made more difficult by requiring, as an indispensable prerequisite, that the applicant take the Sacrament Test, followed by the Oath of Allegiance and the Oath of Supremacy shortly before the relevant state act was finalized. The former was based on the New Testament, the latter ended with the words that were so fatal for the Jews: 'upon the true

---

[34] Philo-Patriae: *Considerations*, pp. 24-5. Translator's note: Based on the circumstantial evidence around his two texts, a strand of modern scholarship has identified 'Philo-Patriae' (a pseudonym deliberately chosen to sound English/Christian) as Joseph Salvador (1716-1786), a leading member of England's Sephardic community. Certainly, contemporary Christians were not fooled by this guise, as we see from the *London Evening Post* of 22/9/1753, which described *Considerations* as being a 'doughty Piece... published certainly by a Jew under the Mark of a Christian'.

faith of a Christian'. The Jewish aspirant to naturalization could not fulfil all three requirements.[35]

In 1663, King Charles II eased the conditions of naturalization by abolishing the obligation to take the Lord's Supper in order to encourage the immigration of foreigners who could help boost underdeveloped industries such as (linen, hemp, and flax) cloth-making, twine and rope-making, and tapestry-making. If the immigrants could not prove that they possessed any of the key craft skills involved in these industries, the old regulation remained. This change in the law was of little help to the Jews. Apart from the fact that the Oaths were still in place, the Jews have almost never practiced such labor-intensive professions. As a result, they hoped to obtain the same facilities for naturalization as had been granted to their ethnic brethren in the American colonies in 1740.[36]

The long-term preparatory work was to prove to have been worth it. The Jews and their friends were initially successful across the board. The bill was brought to the House of Lords, where it was passed quietly and with great speed, although this fact has been wrongly disputed by the Jews.[37]

On 6 April 1753, the bill was submitted to a committee for consideration. The two archbishops of England and twelve bishops were present at the meeting. As far as can be ascertained, no voice was raised in objection. As early as April 10 it was announced that the final hearing would take place at the next meeting. Again the two archbishops and this time only eight bishops were present. There was a short delay, but the bill was passed unanimously by the Upper House on April 16.[38] Somewhat incredibly, it was presented to House of Commons on the same day, where it was read for the first time at the next day's session of April 17. It really could not have been fast-tracked any quicker.[39]

As we shall later be discussing this bill in some depth, it is helpful to give a brief summary of its contents.

---

[35] Oath taken by subjects to pledge their allegiance to the British king as their temporal leader. & Oath taken by subjects to pledge their allegiance to the British king as their spiritual leader, i.e. as head of the Church of England. & Parl. History, Vol. XIV, pp. 1373-4; 7. Jac. I. c. 2. Translator's note: According to Lord Dupplin [*Parl. History*], the Sacrament Test was the Anglican sacrament of the Lord's Supper, which was usually done within a month prior to naturalisation, and the oaths were usually taken at the same time that naturalisation was to be granted.

[36] *Statutes of the Realm*, Vol. 5, p. 498.

[37] Philo-Patriae: *Considerations*, p. 25.

[38] *Journals of the House of Lords*, Vol. XXVIII, p. 80. & *Journals of the House of Lords*, Vol. XXVIII, pp. 82, 84, 85. & *Journals of the House of Lords*, Vol. XXVIII, pp. 88-91.

[39] *Parl. History*, Vol. XIV, p. 1365. Philo-Patriae: *Considerations*, p. 25-26. Translator's note: Or as 'J. E.' poetically described it, 'the Bill stole in at the back Door like a Thief in the Night, on the Wings of Gold' [p. 15].

Firstly, there is a long preamble in which, among other things, reference is made to the previous naturalization laws. Then the actual bill follows with the words: 'Be it therefore enacted... that persons professing the Jewish religion may, upon application for that purpose, be naturalized by parliament without receiving the sacrament of the Lord's Supper...'. The Jews also only had to prove that they had resided in England for the previous three years without being absent from the country for more than three months at a time, and that they had been followers of the Jewish religion during these three years.

There then follows a restriction on the Jews being able to purchase or inherit an advowson [the right to recommend or appoint an Anglican clergyman to a benefice], which clearly shows the extent to which the Church of England had been compromised—its only protection against the predominance of Jewish influence in its territory being the fact that no Jew would be authorized to become a patron of a church or to purchase or otherwise acquire other rights or interests associated with any church, school or hospital. Finally, it was determined that all existing agreements regarding the disposal of church assets would be voided.[40]

After the first reading, the text of the bill was put into print and the intention was to get it through Parliament quickly. However, this plan was mainly scuppered by the fact of the Easter holidays, which meant that the second reading could not take place until May 7. This interim period gave sufficient time for the situation to be made clear to the people and to some of the MPs. The first signs of the coming storm were on the horizon, leaving the Jewish side to look forward to the second reading with some apprehension.

The debate on this issue was long, with a number of MPs from both sides giving speeches. The bill's proponents argued that the proposed law would only give Jews who were rich the opportunity to come to England and be naturalized, which would not be to anyone's disadvantage but to everyone's advantage. Furthermore, it was not to be forgotten that the Jews in England behaved well and contributed significantly to the payment of taxes. Additionally, it had been shown that the Hebrews posed no threat to retail trade. While it was true that they sold cheaper than the English merchants, this was because they were satisfied with less profit. Overall, however, this was only to the benefit of the buying public.[41]

But the Jews had an overwhelming influence in the export trade. Lord Dupplin argued that 'as the Jews by their great command of money, and by their extensive correspondence in all parts of the known world, do increase the commerce of every country they repair to, it is certainly the interest of

---

[40] *Statutes at Large*, Vol. XXI, p. 97; Hyamson: *Jew Bill*, pp. 159-160. Translator's note: Quotation from the bill reproduced verbatim from original source (Hyamson).
[41] *Parl. History.* Vol. XIV, pp. 1375, 1387. & *Parl. History.* Vol. XIV, pp. 1378-9. & *Parl. History.* Vol. XIV, pp. 1398.

every trading and manufacturing people to invite, or at least to render it possible for the rich Jews to come and live amongst them'. It is unsurprising that this argument was also wielded by other MPs, including Robert Nugent, whom we have already encountered.[42]

Reference was also made to the support that the government received from the Jews in times of extreme crisis, and that the opposition to this honorable race could only be explained in terms of base commercial jealousy. Finally, the Jews would be persuaded to be baptized.[43]

The anti-Jewish side was no less active. One of their representatives, William Northey, opened the debate and described it as almost inexplicable why Parliament found itself having to deal with naturalization bills so often. Even during the times of Cromwell and King William III, the Jews offered large sums of money for such purposes. It could hardly be assumed that this would not also be the case now, since they would have to be even more interested in becoming naturalized in England given their greater expansion in Europe, and with the increase in their wealth, paying for it would be even easier for them than before. But Northey feared that this money would not be used to the benefit of the general public.[44]

Northey also objected to any opposition to Jewish ambitions being described as 'persecution,' and presciently saw what lay ahead for a country with such a naive understanding of reality:

> [F]or what in this country we call liberty of conscience, that is to say, a liberty not only to profess openly, but even to propagate whatever sort of religion a man pleases, has too often been made a pretence for forming a party against the government. When I say this, I hope I shall not be supposed to mean, that people ought to be persecuted for the sake of religion; but there is a very great difference between this and allowing enthusiasts and sectaries of all sorts, and now at last Jews, to have a share in our government: I say, a share in our government, for by this Bill, and by the doctrine lately established by our lawyers, a multitude of Jews, may have votes for members of parliament, and we may soon have some of them in this House.[45]

He and Sir Edmund Isham further emphasized that if the bill were made law, it would be the clarion call for Hebrews 'from the remotest corners of the

---

[42] *Parl. History*. Vol. XIV, p. 1376. Translator's note: QVOS. & *Parl. History*, Vol. XIV, p. 1386.

[43] *Parl. History*, Vol. XIV, p. 1395. & *Parl. History*, Vol. XIV, p. 1385.

[44] *Parl. History*, Vol. XIV, pp. 1367-9. Translator's note: For reader edification, Northey's deeply interesting and historically resonant speech has been fully reproduced in the Appendix.

[45] *Parl. History*, Vol. XIV, p. 1371. Translator's note: QVOS.

earth' to decamp to England and buy up the country. Sir Edmund also presciently warned of the following danger, namely, the lessening power of the English to legislate for their own interests in their own land, if alien immigration were allowed to continue:

> But if those of true English blood have not now the power to prevent opening the sluice for letting the torrent in upon us, can we hope, that they will have power enough to shut it up, after the torrent is broke in, and the Jews are become possessed, not only of all the wealth, but of many, perhaps most of the land-estates of the kingdom? This hope, I am sure, is much more chimerical than the danger of our being overwhelmed by the torrent before we begin to think of putting a stop to it.[46]

But the most impressive speech must have been that of the leader of the anti-Jewish movement, Sir John Barnard, who expressed similar ideas to ours. During his lifetime, he earned the title 'Father of the City', and the epithet from Lord Chatham of 'The Great Commoner'. He had previously opposed the threat of foreign infiltration with similar interventions.[47] After the standard exculpatory preamble, Barnard's speech began on a strong note:

> The Jews, Sir, are, and always have been, the most professed enemies of Christianity, and the greatest revilers of Christ himself: they are the offspring of those that crucified our Saviour, and to this day labour under the curse pronounced against them upon that account. I know, Sir, that, as a Christian, I am obliged to love my enemy; but whilst he continues to be so, no precept of Christianity enjoins me to take him under my roof, much less to put him in a way of making himself master both of me and my roof...

He also stated that he could not comprehend the argument put forward by the bill's proponents, namely that that the new law would indirectly encourage the Jews to convert to Christianity, as conversion would bring the Jews no practical benefit.

He also felt it necessary to deal with the oft-repeated argument that Jews had founded the economy in various countries:

---

[46] *Parl. History*, Vol. XIV, pp. 1372, 1379, 1381. All QVOS. Sir Edmund Isham's full speech can also be found in the Appendix.

[47] *Dictionary of National Biography*, Vol. 3, pp. 240-1. Translator's note: Epithets reproduced verbatim from original source.

[I]t is a very great mistake to suppose, that the Jews ever did, or ever can set up trade in any country; for the origin of trade in all countries is manufacture; but none of the Jews, even of the poorest sort, are ever bred to be manufacturers or mechanics, or indeed to any laborious employment; therefore they can never be the beginners of trade in any country... In Poland there have been multitudes of Jews for many ages, yet no man will say that Poland is a trading country.

Some rich Jews helped to increase the existing trade with their liquid assets; but the majority were employed in usury, brokerage and financial speculation. However, it was correct that the Hebrews, by virtue of their worldwide connections, could initially increase exports:

For this reason, in the infancy of the trade of any country, it is right to encourage the Jews to come and settle amongst them: as the manufacturers have not then money of their own sufficient for carrying their manufacture to any great extent, and as the native merchants have not a foreign correspondence settled, perhaps, in those countries where some of their manufactures may be sold to the best advantage.

But in a country where trade and commerce have been fully and long established, where the manufacturers have money sufficient of their own, or of their friends, to carry their manufactures to the utmost extent, and where the native merchants have a correspondence settled in every foreign country where it is possible to carry on any commerce, and consequently must know where every sort of manufacture may be sold to the best advantage: in such a country, I say, it is madness, if not worse, to put Jews or any other foreigners upon an equal footing with natives, because it only enables the former to take the bread, or a part of the bread, out of the mouths of the latter, without increasing in the least the national trade or commerce; for no Jew, any more than a native, will export more of your manufacture than he can sell to advantage, and so much your own native merchants will always export, if there were not a Jew in the kingdom...

This was all the more the case, said Sir John, since there was already an oversupply of English merchants in all parts of the world, meaning that profit margins would get even thinner if Jews were admitted.

The Jews would not be of any advantage in retail trade either. The consumption of a people does not increase by admitting Jews, but an influx of

Jewish shop-keepers would inevitably cause a displacement of the Christians because 'we cannot suppose that Jew shop-keepers would sell cheaper than our English now do, but they might perhaps cheat oftener.'

At the end, Barnard warns the English people that, with such a law, England would over time be overrun by Jews, because where the rich Jew appears, the poor one also follows. The influence of the Hebrews would become ever greater; trade and exchange would be ever more controlled by them. And in the end 'they will probably leave the laborious part of all manufactures and mechanical trade to the poor Christians, but they will be the paramount masters'. [48]

What would Sir John say today if he were able to open his eyes again! All the efforts of the anti-Jewish faction and their leader—who was a 'personal enemy of Sampson Gideon'—were in vain. After a brief final statement by Prime Minister Pelham in support of the bill, the vote was taken. An overwhelming majority of 95 members to 16 voted in favor of the bill.[49]

Normally the second reading was (and continues to be) the decisive one and the third reading is hardly given any importance, especially since the defeated opposition rarely makes any effort in such cases. However, things were different this time.

The City, already well represented in Parliament by Sir John Barnard, had not yet given in. Even under the Stuart kings, it was the City who repeatedly made attacks and, if necessary, resistance against the Jews. In the earlier battles, the Jews had found little or no support there at all and therefore realized that they would have to win support in the City if they were to overcome this bulwark of Englishness.

Throughout history it becomes clear that the Jews stay true to the same well-thought-out tactics. First they try to gain influence over a country's capital city; from there they then manage to defeat the healthy countercurrents coming from the provinces. This process is completed all the faster the larger the capital city's population is in relation to the rest of the nation, and the longer—and therefore the more effective—the process of power centralization has been going on in the country. London, which had been by far the most dominant city of a long-unified England for centuries, offered the ideal conditions for this plan. We will see to what extent the Jews' attempts to 'conquer' the City of London in 1753 were successful.

---

[48] *Parl. History*, Vol. XIV, pp. 1388-1395. All QVOS. The full speech is reproduced in the Appendix and is recommended to readers for its perspicacity and prescience.

[49] Hyamson: *Jew Bill.* p. 162. Translator's note: QVOS. & *Parl. History*, Vol. XIV, p. 1417. Translator's note: Given such an overwhelming majority, I felt it instructive to add an appendix of some of the speeches given in Parliament in opposition to the 'Jew Bill' so that readers could see the overall quality of the arguments that were made against the bill, and judge for themselves the probability of bribery having played a part in this voting result.

The Jews' secret preparations for the passage of the bill were not unknown to the City's merchants. They therefore already had the intention of submitting a petition against the bill to Parliament before the bill itself was introduced. Apparently, however, they received convincing assurances that the bill would be abandoned, and the false sense of security this gave them left them on the back foot:

> The Merchants had observed with great Uneasiness, that a Bill was brought into Parliament to enable the *Jews* to be naturalized, and were very apprehensive of the pernicious Effects, which it might have upon our Trade. And they would have presented a Petition to the House very early, if they had not been well assured, that the Members who opposed the Bill understood so perfectly the bad Influence it would have upon our foreign Trade, particularly to *Spain* and *Portugal*, and were able to demonstrate it so clearly, as to have no Doubt but they should satisfy the Patrons of the Bill, and induce them to drop it. But herein they failed. The Time of passing the Bill drew nigh. And the Merchants at last found themselves under a Necessity of humbly representing to the House their Reasons against passing the Bill.[50]

Immediately after the second reading, on May 9, the City of London Corporation was convened to take action. Philo-Patriae reports that the meeting had no positive result for the opponents of the bill. We are hesitant to believe him in this since it is difficult to reconcile his statement with subsequent events.[51]

He himself had to admit that at the same time 'a few restless elements' had come together to take steps against the bill. However, later developments clearly show that it was not 'a few restless elements' but the overwhelming majority of the city's inhabitants. So we are inclined less to the narrative of his reports, and more to that of his opponents.

Afterwards, a significant number of citizens gathered to form a party to fight the so-called 'Jew Bill.' A petition was drafted and publicly displayed near the Royal Exchange. In a very short time, it was found that out of every ten Londoners, nine declared themselves to be against the bill. No coercion was exerted on them, as the Jews and their friends claimed.[52]

---

[50] Romaine: *An Answer*, pp. 66-7. Translator's note: QVOS.

[51] Philo-Patriae: *Considerations*, p. 26.

[52] Romaine: *An Answer*, pp. 66-9. & Philo-Patriae: *Considerations*, pp. 26-8. Translator's note: Also see Romaine: *An Answer*, 67-9, in which he refutes the 'aspersions' of the '*Jew* Apologist' Philo-Patriae point by point, quoting each aspersion in turn.

Because of this popular indignation, all evidence points to London's merchants having 'assembled together in Common-Council' in the Guildhall on May 21. Even the opposing side does not claim that any of the City's freemen gathered there were in favor of the bill. Rather, they unanimously decided to petition Parliament to vote against the bill, as it was against all Christian honor and would have catastrophic consequences for the trade of English merchants. The petition was presented to Parliament on the same day. Almost at the same time, many ordinary citizens petitioned against the bill, making particular reference to the disadvantage that it would have on trade.[53]

The Jews and their friends had—as usual—worked to counter this resistance: another group of City merchants and traders also submitted a petition, but this side only saw the great advantages of increased Hebrew immigration, which made the passage of the bill desirable.[54]

Half a century ago, the City stood together as one. But now the Jews had already caused a schism and, even if this was only a tiny fraction, had won over people to their cause. We know how the Hebrews gradually find friends among the population of a country, which in this case is best illustrated by the following contemporary comment:

> The Sense of the City is Nineteen out of Twenty against the *Jews*. Indeed they got some Men of Fortune to sign for them, but they were under Ministerial Influence; others were guided by their Interest, and I know some whom these charitable, merciful *Jews*, threaten'd to trade with no more, if they did not sign. And though they used every possible Art and Method to get Names to their Petition, yet, after all, the Number was not the greatest ever known.[55]

Given that Jews still use the same methods today in similar cases, we have no reason to doubt any part of this statement. The only difference between this 1753 case and today is that today, not only private individuals but entire

---

[53] Romaine: *An Answer*, p. 74; Romaine: *Modest Apology*, Preface, iii-vi; Gentleman's Magazine, Vol. XXIII, p. 246; Newspapers: *London Evening Post*, 28/7/1753, 30/7/1753; *Public Advertiser*, 22/5/1753. Translator's note: Quoted element taken verbatim from *Modest Apology*. & *Journals of the House of Commons*, 21st May 1723, p. 827. & *Parl. History*, Vol. XIV, pp. 1417-8.

[54] Philo-Patriae: *Considerations*, p. 30 ff.; *Parl. History*, Vol. XIV, pp. 1417-8.

[55] 'J. E.', p. 21. Translator's note: QVOS. One also has to wonder how many of these signatories were the same foreign-origin merchants and traders who signed the 1751 naturalization petition (see footnote 44). In the same vein, Romaine (*An Answer*, pp. 91-4) reveals that the Jews slandered anyone who opposed their naturalization as a 'Jacobite', which, along with the fact that copies of their petition had been placed all over the city, and there were agents at work 'soliciting and teasing people to sign' (p.71), may have been what intimidated some into signing their petition.

states are being subjugated (or attempted to be subjugated) through boycotts and similar means. The examples of post-1933 Germany, and Romania during Octavian Goga's reign, show that the Jews achieve these aims with varying degrees of success.

In the meantime, the Jews had even managed to convert a well-known City MP, Sir William Calvert, into one of their supporters. Until 1753 he held an influential position in the City. The people continued to accuse him of taking Jewish bribes and did not forget that he had voted for the Jews in Parliament. His constituents were soon able to give him their response to his stance: when new elections were called in 1754, his re-election bid failed miserably. [Translator's note: Readers will be reassured to know that this fine gentleman's parliamentary career was revived in 1755, when he 'won' a seat for Old Sarum, the most notorious of the rotten boroughs, which had no resident voters.]

It also came as a great surprise to the public that the Jews actually had a number of friends in the City. But the bitterness was all the greater when it was discovered that these friends were racially Jews or otherwise those who were somehow dependent on them.[56]

The third reading took place at the end of May against the united resistance of the Opposition. The various Englishmen who had signed the petition against the bill were heard. The Earl of Egmont, MP for Weobly, spoke most extensively on behalf of the Opposition, and also made a last-minute bid to save his cause when, after the third reading was finished, he put forward a motion for the bill to be adjourned. He began his speech with a warning to Parliament not to ignore the popular will. The people were overwhelmingly against the law and, unable to comprehend how it was favored by the majority of Parliament, the people's faith in the competence of their lawmakers was at great risk.[57]

He also cautioned against talk of the great advantages that arose from admitting Jews to trade. He reminded Parliament of how, in the past, the Jews destroyed the existence of individuals through their usury and other unethical methods and thus gradually incurred the hatred of the people. Today they have gone so far with their system that they have even ruined whole kingdoms, 'by aiding ministers to beggar the states they serve, by which traffic also they have greatly aided to plunge this nation into a debt of near eighty millions.' The immense fortunes of the Jews in England were not the result of honest and decent business, but were rather due to their profiteering with contracts and commissions, and speculating over the vital necessities required by the public during the last war.

---

[56] Stephenson, Vol. III, Part 2, p. 860. Translator's note: Not being in any of Aldag's bibliographies, I was unable to identify this source.

[57] *Parl. History*, Vol. XIV, p. 1418.

The Earl of Egmont also raised the specter of an eventual tyranny against the native Christian population:

> [T]he abomination in which they [the Jews] are held by the people of this kingdom, should they grow insolent, or obnoxious by their numbers, may provoke excesses against them, which, when all other arguments fail for a standing army, may furnish new ones for its support. For it is no extravagant supposition, should this Bill pass, that the consequence may hereafter be not only the establishment, but the employment of an army to knock our own Christian fellow-subjects on the head, in protection of our foreign Jews.

Then there was the risk to foreign trade. Given the aversion of the Portuguese and Spaniards towards dealing with Jews, England would come to be seen as 'the most impious nation on Earth,' with the risk of the English consequently losing all of their trade in these two countries to the benefit of France. Finally, there were fears that increased Jewish immigration and the associated foreign infiltration would have negative consequences for England's religion, politics and culture, and would risk the overall peace and tranquility of the kingdom, given that, as English land would pass into Jewish hands, the bill would work 'to turn the tables upon the Christians in favor of the Jews—to put the Jews upon the ground of the English, and the English upon the present footing of the Jews'.[58]

Neither the Earl of Egmont's long speech nor public opinion could prevent the victory of the Jews and their allies. With a vote of 96 to 55, the Opposition's motion for an adjournment was rejected and the bill was finally passed. On June 7 of the same year, the king gave his royal assent, at which point the bill officially became law.[59]

The Jews and their allies had triumphed. All of the efforts of the Opposition in Parliament and outside among the people had been in vain. The government's support for the bill was probably the deciding factor, although the king too had no reservation about giving the legislation his approval. The king, government, House of Lords, and House of Commons, the latter two with an overwhelming majority, had spoken out in favor of the Jews. The idea was now to go about calmly building on this success, until total Jewish emancipation was finally achieved. And yet nothing was to come of it. One power proved stronger than all external powers of government: the people!

Immediately after the law came into force, anti-Jewish forces took the fight from Parliament to the public square. One might have thought that they

---

[58] *Parl. History*, Vol. XIV, pp. 1418-1430. All QVOS.
[59] *Parl. History*, Vol. XIV, p. 1431. & *London Evening Post*, 8/6/1753.

would have been demoralized by such huge wasted efforts before the law was passed, combined with the final devastating failure. Nothing could be further from the truth. Whether it was the oft-lauded tenacity of the English, or the Englishman's attitude, just as often cited, of never knowing whether or not he is defeated, in short, the opponents did not give up the fight, but continued on with redoubled strength. As the Jew James Picciotto notes:

> Not many measures caused greater commotion in London, or gave rise to warmer discussion, than an Act of Parliament which merely proposed to grant a few, only a few, of the privileges of Englishmen to a very limited number of foreigners. Neither the Repeal of the Corn Laws, nor the introduction of Free Trade, nor the passing of the Reform Bill caused more excitement in their day than the question as to whether or not some scores of Dutch or German Jews were to be allowed to go through the costly proceedings to acquire the right of holding property in England.[60]

All of London spoke of nothing else but the Jews' victory. One contemporary said the law was without precedent in the history of Christendom, while another expressed the same sentiment in the following way: 'It seems as if we were arriv'd at such a critical Juncture of Time as this Nation never saw before, and I hope, never will again.' Books, pamphlets, cartoons, and newspaper articles were published by both sides. England lived as if in a fever. The talk of the day was the Jewish Question. Until 1933, no other people had defended themselves against Jewish foreign infiltration as unitedly as the English people did back then. But the Jews and their friends were not idle either, and an unprecedented flood of pro-Jewish propaganda poured over the country.[61]

A popular argument for admitting Jews was the possibility of their conversion that the law would supposedly create. The English had not neglected to send missionaries into the world to convert other peoples. Why shouldn't the achievement of this noble mission be made easier by letting the

---

[60] Picciotto, p. 80. Translator's note: QVOS.

[61] 'J. E.', p. 5. & *Reflections of the Past*, p. 3. Translator's note: As the original source puts it: 'The Act lately passed by the *British* Parliament, which paves the Way for the Incorporation of the *Jewish* Nation with so considerable a Body of *Christian* People, hath very much drawn the Attention of *Britons* in general, and very probably of learned *Foreigners* also, as it is a Thing of such a Nature, as the *Jews* never attempted before any where, or any *Christian* Government granted: For, though some have upon this Occasion asserted that *France* hath done the like, yet it is without Foundation; that Nation having only suffered them to reside among them, without taking them into their Body.' & *Jews' Advocate*, first sentence of Preface. Translator's note: QVOS.

Jews into the country and then endeavoring to convert them on the spot? As soon as the Jews were naturalized, a clergyman argued in a sermon, they would become a more civilized people, and would learn common civility and good manners towards the English.

It should not be forgotten, wrote another, that the whole world owed the Jews a great debt of gratitude for their system of morality. In particular, it was the aforementioned clergyman Josiah Tucker in Bristol who demanded the admission of Jews for religious reasons. It would be an almost inconceivable blessing if the English Church were to facilitate God's will to 'fetch home his ancient people.' Some were so certain of the Jews' conversion to Christianity that, in their opinion, naturalization could be equated with conversion. The hope was even expressed that Jewish naturalization would facilitate the Jews' return to the Holy Land, with the Jews setting off from England, and the Jewish nation of Israel restored by 1666:[62]

> Which clearly implies, that the *first Return* of these *Jews* shall be by Ships passing along the *Mediterranean*, from remote Islands: Which agrees to no nation so expressly, as to the *British* Nation, joined probably by the States of *Holland*, their near Ally and neighbouring Maritime Power. And does it not still appear the more probable, that the first setting out of the *Jews* to their own Land will be from *England*, not only by the Assistance of an *English* Fleet, but that, by the late Naturalization of the *Jews* here, they may be enabled not only to extend their Trade, enrich themselves, but purchase Ships of their own; by which Means they may not only facilitate their own Return, but likewise be aiding and assisting to bring their Brethren from other Countries...
>
> When this happy State of the *Jews* will come, we cannot exactly tell, but believe it will be very soon, altho' not so soon as Mr. *Whiston* expected; for he says, that when he was at *Tunbridge*, in the Year 1746, about his Lectures there, which he finished with the following *Memento*: 'That tho' I have been here a Fortnight, and have seen several of this Company, both Ladies and Gentlemen, at Prayers on the Week-Days, and a great Number of them at public Worship on the Lord's Day, yet have I not myself seen any of them at a Gaming-Table. And I cannot but wish, heartily wish, that nobody else had seen them any one of them at such a Place neither.

---

[62] Philo-Patriae, *Considerations*, pp. 7-13. & Winstanley, p.11. & Leslie, p. 15 ff. & Tucker: *Letter to a Friend*, pp. 13-14. Translator's note: QVOS. & Bowyer, pp. 452-458.

However, I venture to add this, which I desire you all to take special notice of, that if I be right in my Calculation, as to our Blessed Saviour's coming to restore the *Jews*, and begin the *Millennium* 20 Years hence, I cannot but conclude, that after these 20 Years are over, there will be no more an Infidel in *Christendom*; and there will be no more a Gaming-Table at *Tunbridge*.[63]

It is interesting that such public statements come predominantly from clergymen who, with few exceptions, were on the side of the Jews.

Philo-Patriae also believes that Jews can be easily converted since 'many Jewish families have already been baptized in England.' If this statement is to be believed, a mixing of Jewish and English blood must have taken place at this time if not before, since the barriers between the two peoples fell very quickly with Jewish converts to Christianity. On the other side of the issue, there was no lack of doubt about the chances of conversion, and some, including Jonas Hanway, expected the law to have the opposite effect. The Jews had already been treated with such leniency in England that—if they were to convert at all—they would have done so earlier, when more benefit could have been derived from it. The rights granted in the new law would encourage them to hold on to their faith even more, as it would encourage other Jews to immigrate into the country, meaning that the power and status of Judaism would only grow and conversion become even less likely. Similar concerns were raised in an open letter to a newspaper, in response to comments made by a clergyman on the matter.[64]

England was also associated with Jewish prophecies on the restoration of a kingdom in Palestine. As has already been touched on, one anonymous author believed he could foresee England helping the Jews in this matter. Another anonymous writer, potentially also a theologian, devotes his book more or less entirely to this idea. In his opinion there was no doubt that England would lead the Jews back to their country of origin and was destined to put the Jews on the right path of faith. With England's help, the Jews would return to Palestine. A canal would be built from the Mediterranean to the Red Sea, and the Jews would then play a decisive role in controlling this sea route due to the location of their land. The author also goes on to say:[65]

---

[63] *The Full and Final Restoration of the Jews*, pp. 14-16. Translator's note: QVOS.
[64] Philo-Patriae, *Considerations*, p. 8. & Hanway, p. 70. & *London Evening Post*, 18/8/1753. Translator's note: Note that the *London Evening Post* was published every three to four days, and so was dated for the three to four days in question (e.g. 'From Tuesday August 18, to Thursday August 21, 1753.'). For the sake of clarity, I will reference this title by the first date it was issued (e.g. 18/8/1753).
[65] *The Full and Final Restoration of the Jews*, p. 14. & *Reflections on the Past and Present State of the Jews*, p. 19. & p. 31 ff. & p. 58.

But there are other Circumstances which I have not mentioned as yet, that will induce them to heighten, as well as to perpetuate it; namely, *first*, that they will not have any *Products* of their own to trade with; and *secondly*, that they will have no *Ports* in their Neighbourhood on either on the Seas aforementioned, fit to receive *Ships of War*, and therefore, they will stand in Need of *Great Britain*, as well on Account of the *rich Products* wherewith she can furnish them, both *native* and *foreign*, as of the *Protection* which she will be able to give them by her *Fleets*, which may receive all the Stores that they may want from Time to Time for that Purpose, from *Gibraltar* and *Port-Mahon*, as to their Commerce in the *West*.

So that if *Great Britain* should think fit, at the same Time, to make a Settlement once more upon the *Isthmus* of *Darien*, which parts the *Western Ocean*, that has a Communication with the *Mediterranean Sea*, by the Streights of *Gibraltar*; and the *Pacific Ocean* that hath a Communication with the *Red Sea*, by the Streights of *Babelmandel* [Bab-el-Mandeb], an Isthmus about the same Breadth as that before spoken of, all the whole Commerce of the *Universe* in its utmost Extent, will center in her *ultimately*; though at the same Time a great Part of it must go through the Hands of the *Jews*: And in consequence thereof, all that *Peace*, *Plenty* and *Happiness* might be introduced into the World, which are the great Characteristics of the *Messiah's* Reign.[66]

Such global visions for the future will be seen again later in this study. When we now see the stubborn efforts of the English to establish a Jewish territory in Palestine, we must be surprised at how far these efforts go back. Even today, while strategic necessities and allegiance to international Jewry will no doubt exert their due influence, the history of this grand plan nevertheless remains very intriguing.

Attempts were also made to explain to the English people that a hostile attitude towards the Hebrews was against the Christian religion. A Christian was not allowed to repay like for like, and on top of that, the English still had to make amends for the harsh anti-Jewish laws before 1290. One should nei-

---

[66] *Reflections on the Past and Present State of the Jews*, p. 67-68. Translator's note: QVOS. Although the original German version only quoted the final sentence of this passage, I have chosen the larger extract because of its uncanny similarity to what has taken place since the author's time of writing. It should be noted however, that in this prophesy, the Jews would already be converted to Christianity before their return to Israel, 'and consequently they will be a quite different Set of People to what they are at present, both as to Principle and Practice'.

ther persecute them with hatred, for they were once the Almighty's favorites, nor ignore the fact that Englishmen and Jews were both of the same father.[67] Finally, the Jews were warned to end their obsession with amassing vast wealth, since one day they too would die, and be judged and sentenced.[68]

In a London newspaper, we find one Englishman countering the reference to unfair persecution of the Jews with the observation: 'there is a great Difference betwixt persecuting them, and not shewing them particular Favours', this short sentence aptly summing up the response to the complaints of persecution. It was further pointed out that the Hebrews always fought with the Protestants against the Catholics—since their religion was much closer to the former than to the latter—just as efforts were made to convince the English people of the Jews' usefulness to the economy.[69]

The Jews were in possession of unexpected financial resources, so that a large stream of wealth would enter the country along with their immigration, a circumstance all the more significant since they maintained extensive connections with their equally wealthy fellow Jews in mainland Europe. The state could also expect greater tax revenue if wealth increased, since the Jews would not leave their money idle but would invest it in trade.[70]

They already had a significant share in England's economy. However, an even greater share was still to be desired for the good of the country. Jews had now proven themselves 'not only convenient, but necessary' for English trade, the future of which could best be secured through further Hebrew immigration. In general, it is a basic rule that the more merchants a country has, the richer and more powerful it becomes. That is why the 'Turks, Infidels and Papists caress them,' despite the Jews' opinions and religious sentiments being 'diametrically opposite to those of their Protectors'.[71]

Finally, new blood and great energy would be injected into the country. Would the Jews have been able to survive all of the persecutions if God himself did not want to see their continued preservation? The centuries-long struggle had ruthlessly eradicated the weaker members of the race, making the survivors ever stronger, and more determined to achieve their goals by whatever means necessary.[72]

---

[67] Peckard, p. 11 ff. & 'True Believer', p. 2. & Tucker: *Letter to a Friend*, p. 11.
[68] *An Earnest Persuasive and Exhortation to the Jews*, p. 17.
[69] *London Evening Post*, 18/8/1753. Translator's note: QVOS. & Philo-Patriae: *Considerations*, p. 52.
[70] Philo-Patriae: *Further Considerations*, pp. 8-9. & *True State of the Case*, p. 1. & *Appeal with Due Submission Addressed to Caesar*, p. 4. & *Jews' Advocate*, p. 11; *Letter to the Public*, p. 19.
[71] Philo-Patriae: *Considerations*, p. 36 ff. & Philo-Patriae: *Further Considerations*, p. 51. Translator's note: QVOS. & Webb: *The Bill Permitting the Jews*, p. 1 ff.; *Address to the Friends*, p. 10. & 'True Believer', p. 22. Translator's note: QVOS.
[72] 'True Believer', p. 3 ff. & 'True Believer', p. 12 ff.

There were also warnings from English people among these anonymous voices. They did not consider Jewish capital necessary, as during the reign of Queen Elizabeth there had been great economic prosperity without Jews. Rather, the Jews would only create unwanted competition for the English merchants, which would ruin some of them. We find similar concerns in a major public speech warning that the rich Jews would of course do everything in their power to buy up land with their money and thus gain further influence based on the privileges associated with land ownership.[73]

However, the Jews and their allies did not limit themselves to demanding Jewish naturalization for the future development of England, but rather attempted to show that the Jews were worthy of this right simply because of the services they had rendered. They claimed that the Jews contributed significantly to the salvation of the state in the critical days and months of 1745 and 1746. During this time, the so-called Young Pretender, i.e. the last Stuart with a direct claim to the English throne, had landed in Scotland and marched with his Scottish Highlanders on London. A mood of panic arose. The Jews claimed that they overcome this panic to help the English defeat the Jacobite Rising. So it was only out of love for the king and country that they voluntarily joined the defense militia which had formed in order to defend London if necessary.[74]

It is true that a number of Jews were found in the ranks of the militia. This is surprising at first, since even the Hebrews do not deny that they abhor wielding weapons. But as soon as we learn more about the circumstances in which this took place, this exceptional phenomenon becomes explicable.

In fact, as a contemporary tells us in detail, not a single Jew volunteered. Rather, they were enrolled into military service 'by Force and Necessity.' Under the conditions that prevailed at the time, every homeowner was legally obliged to report to the militia. However, he had the option of hiring a soldier to be his replacement, but for this he had to pay a salary of 5 shillings per day. As a result, there were various Jews who were unwilling or unable to raise this amount. So it happened that some of them had to take on the duties of soldiering that they so hated—certainly to their greatest chagrin. Evangelical divine William Romaine asked if such people could be called volunteers:[75]

> Was this all their Merit, that they did what they could not
> help? They had absolutely no other Merit: They can claim noth-

---

[73] *Daily Advertiser*, 19/9/1753. & *Gentleman's Magazine*, Vol. XXIII, p. 479 ff. Translator's note: This is actually a reproduction in full of the Earl of Egmont's speech to the House of Commons against the Jewish Naturalization Bill, which has already been discussed in this chapter.

[74] Philo-Patriae: *Considerations*, p. 41.

[75] Romaine: *An Answer*, p. 83. Translator's note: QVOS.

ing but the Merit of Necessity. And I fear the *Jews* will always act in this Character, they will always be Volunteers by Compulsion, whenever they do any real Service to this Kingdom.[76]

We need not add anything to this statement by Romaine, who was one of the few clergymen to be on the anti-Jewish side of the argument.

The Jews claim as a further service to the general public that they introduced coined money in the aforementioned years of crisis and thus saved the state's credit, because some of the public withdrew considerable quantities of coined gold and silver from the bank in times of danger, and a bank run was imminent. But when supplies were almost exhausted due to this strong demand, the Jews imported gold and silver in larger quantities and made them available to the bank.[77]

It is no secret that the Hebrews do nothing without benefit to themselves, and so the Reverend Romaine's comments on this matter appear to quite accurate, according to which the Jews enriched themselves considerably from this transaction.

The Bank of England had closed its discount office to the merchants, which resulted in a general rise in prices on the stock exchange and a shortage of minted gold. The Jews then bought and imported specie [precious metal money] from Holland and Hamburg instead of accepting bills of exchange to settle their claims against foreign business associates. In this way, they made a profit of at least 7%, the difference in value between the coins and the bills; the only reason for raising the money that they had previously carried out of the country was that it was in their interest. Or as Romain put it: 'it was not their Love for the Government, but their Love for *7 per Cent'*.

Romain affirms that the City's merchants and the directors of the Bank of England soon realized that there was not the slightest merit in this act on the part of the Jews:

I believe all the Merchants in *London* have ever considered their importing the Specie in this Light: I am sure however, that the Directors of the Bank have. They saw no Merit in what the *Jews* did, no not the least. This great Piece of Service, as the Apologist relates it, could make no Amends to the Bank for their smuggling the Specie out of the Kingdom, and therefore it denied them those very Privileges, with which all the trading Part of the Kingdom were indulged: For when the Bank opened her Discount-Office to the Merchants, it re-

---

[76] Romaine: *An Answer*, p. 84. Translator's note: Quotation (and subsequent Romaine quotation) reproduced verbatim from original source.

[77] Philo-Patriae: *Considerations*, p. 42.

mained shut to the Jews, and continued shut, until very lately [i.e. about 7 years]: Insomuch that if a Christian Merchant brought a Bill with a Jew's Indorsement upon it to be dis- counted, it used to be returned undone, and this Reason was given, that probably the Christian might bring the same for the Service of the *Jew*.

The Reverend Romaine also asked the question of how was it that this English coin had found itself abroad in the first place, in order for to be so help- fully re-imported into the country. He furnishes the reader with his thoughts on the matter:

When we hear of their [the Jews'] great Merit in importing Specie, it naturally makes one enquire, how this Specie came to be exported? Who are they that carry on this illicit Trade? By whose Traffick was the Nation drained of its Specie? I do not mean, of foreign Gold and Silver, but of our own Coin. And who will point out any Persons deep in this Inquiry, but the *Jews*? And how deep they are in the Mystery of smuggling the Currency out of the Nation, every Person, who has been Abroad, must be perfectly convinced: For in what Part of *Eu- rope* do we not find *English* Gold, and in Abundance? It is not suffered to be exported by the Laws. It must be smuggled Abroad. And if the Casks in which it is exported were now and then to be opened at the *Custom-House*, and all the Coin turned out, I fancy some Quantity of little *English* Guineas would be found lying might snug in the Middle of the Cask, to the great Disappointment of *Duke's-Place*, and to the no small Joy of the fortunate Officer.

Finally, Romaine questions the supposed good deeds that the Jews put for- ward for their cause:

And now where is all this boasted Merit of the *Jews*? for which they claim their Naturalization. They first drain us of our Specie, and bring us into Distress, and then they take an Advantage of this Distress, and make a mighty Merit of bring- ing the same Specie back again, although they get 7 per Cent by it. Their fighting Merit was very insignificant, but this trad- ing Merit is very iniquitous.[78]

---

[78] Romaine: *An Answer*, pp. 84-87. Translator's note: All QVOS. Readers who wish to know more about this dual paper-gold currency economy, with a description of the various

In the critical years of 1745 and 1746 it also happened that the Bank of England's notes were offered below par: the first signs of a lack of confidence in the state's credit, with the resulting threat of a decline in the currency. All the leading merchants of the City united in these hours of crisis and published a declaration that they would redeem all banknotes at full rate: a measure which contributed greatly to the saving of the currency.

Philo-Patriae treats the affair as if the Jews could claim to have played a decisive role in this support campaign. However, he himself had to admit that out of the twelve leading merchants involved, only two were Jews. We do not know whether this is true, but assuming it is based on truth, doesn't this number of Jews speak against their predominant participation in saving the day? In reality, their help in this regard was of quite minor importance, since the aforementioned Sir John Barnard played the instrumental role in procuring the signatures of the leading city merchants as an agreement to receive the banknotes, with the full support of Mr. Lee, an English banker of Lombard Street. For his swift action in this time of panic, as well as for other eminent public services (he was also an MP and City alderman), in May 1747 the city erected a statue of Barnard on the Royal Exchange, despite his protestations.[79]

As a further service to the state, Philo-Patriae cites the fact that in the years of crisis the Jews lent considerable money upon the Land Tax: 'A quarter of the money immediately raised on this occasion came from them'.[80]

Romaine replies that the Jews had indeed made funds available to the government, but there was nothing unusual about this loan, since it offered the best security that the state could give them, and security was of particular importance during times of instability. The interest rates were also good, and so, with the best will in the world, one could not say that the Jews had in any way made a sacrifice for the benefit of the nation.[81]

But Romaine also seems to have missed the most important way of refuting Philo-Patriae's claim. We found an official list of the subscribers' names and the amounts they subscribed, drawn up at the request of some of the citizens involved in this rescue operation for the state. This list was printed together with the Guildhall Committee report in 1747. It is now clear that, of the initial subscriptions totaling £18,910, the Jews only raised the sum of £514 (and 12 shillings). It cannot therefore be said in the slightest that the

---

scams and manipulations taking place as a result, may wish to consult William Cobbett's *Paper Against Gold* (1815). Cobbett is also discussed in chapter 5, vis-à-vis his outspoken views on the Jewish Question.

[79] Philo-Patriae: *Considerations*, pp. 43-4. & *Dictionary of National Biography*, Vol. I, p. 1160. & Romaine: *An Answer*, pp. 87-8. & Orridge: p. 179.

[80] Philo-Patriae: *Considerations*, p. 45.

[81] Romaine: *An Answer*, p. 89.

Jews raised a quarter of the initial funds, on the basis of which the public felt sufficiently confident to make further subscriptions.[82]

When the list was published in the *London Evening Post*, the Jews were simultaneously asked to provide corrections if the list did not correspond to the facts. However, further detailed research in this and other newspapers found no evidence of any amendment to the published list.

This strongly suggests, alongside Romaine's points, that the Jews could not demonstrate any past services to the state that would have justified passing the naturalization law, just as Hyamson's modern perspective on the situation, which is essentially just a reformulation of the arguments made by Philo-Patriae, is likewise refuted.[83]

In contrast to the Jews and their allies, the opponents of the bill see Christianity as an insurmountable obstacle to the law, a position which they justify by saying, among other things, that the Jews are solely responsible for the crucifixion of Jesus Christ and that the principles of the Christian religion are incompatible with those of the Jewish.[84]

Frequent reference is also made to the economic disadvantages that the law would bring to English merchants. A key quotation in many arguments was a statement from the great English Lord Chief Justice Sir Edward Coke:[85]

> The *Jews* and all other Infidels are in the Eye of the Law *Aliens* in the highest Degree, *perpetui inimici, perpetual Enemies: For the Law presumes not they will ever be converted; for between them, as with the Devil, whose Subjects they be, and the Christian, there is perpetual Hostility, and can be no Peace.*[86]

In addition, the Jewish character was examined in detail. This led to conclusions about the Jewish people that are completely consistent with ours, and an Englishman today would be surprised to know that these views were once

---

[82] *London Evening Post*, 16/8/1753. Translator's note: Having looked at the original source, and found that there is no indication to show how soon these Jews subscribed after the subscription opened, it still may be the case that these Jews gave their money at a very early stage when the overall pot of funds was still quite small, and their contribution therefore relatively large, and a way of encouraging the wider public to invest. I therefore do not see this list as the conclusive proof that Aldag seems to think it is.

[83] Hyamson: *History*, p. 217.

[84] See, for example, Romaine: *An Answer*, p. 21 ff.; *Candid & Impartial Examination*, p. 10 ff.

[85] See, for example, *Appeal to the Throne*, p. 22; Hanway, p. 175 ff.

[86] Romaine: *An Answer*, p. 10; *Daily Advertiser*, 3/11/1753, 10/11/1753. Translator's note: QVOS (Romaine). The original iteration of this statement, found in *Calvin's Case (7 Coke Report, 1a, 77 ER 377)*, varies very slightly from the above version in style but not in meaning (and to no-one's surprise, Romaine's version has the word 'Jews' inserted for additional emphasis, whereas Coke solely spoke of 'All infidels').

held by the majority of the English people. As Romaine [*An Answer...*, p. 62] poetically summed up the general view among the English populace:

> We know, that Grapes do not grow upon Briars, and yet we may as reasonably expect to gather a plentiful Vintage upon our Hedges, as to find a Race of moral *Jews* growing in our Cities.

The philanthropist Jonas Hanway predicted that the Jews would bring no advantage to England's labor market:

> Among the lower classes of the people, however great their poverty, they are naturally, or by custom, averse to labor. Their religion cuts them off from commerce with the rest of mankind, and I cannot discover that they learn any art, or practice any manual labor. They are of no use in agriculture, or manufactory; neither will they serve us in our army, or navy.[87]

Hanway had the following to say about Jewish hawkers and peddlers. Note his dismissive tone regarding the complaints of the English customers, as if implying that it was all that they deserved for trusting Jewish salesmen:

> Next to these come a train of *hawkers*, and *pedlars*, and *traffickers* in every *imaginable* commodity, in every *imaginable* way, but very few in *that* which is deemed *regular, honorable*, and according to the ordinary rules of civil polity. In this general list, we must include those who buy, and sell, stolen goods. Gentlemen who have been curious in their remarks, observe that many second-hand things, exposed to sale by the *Jews* in *Flanders*, are of *English* manufacture. It ought not to be imagined that these are *all stolen*, since they *buy* great quantities, in what is generally called a *fair way*.
>
> In the light of *itinerant pawnbrokers*, and purchasers of that which the seller ought not to dispose of, a late complaint of the university of Cambridge may be urged in proof, that such kind of wanderers are oftentimes detrimental. As to the *qualities* of the goods which they *vend* up and down the coun-

---

[87] Hanway, p. 69; *Westminster Journal*, 9/6/1753. Translator's note: QVOS. As has been said previously in this study (see chapter 1), this Jewish aversion to manual labor dates from 800 A.D. onwards, in which the Babylonian Talmud became the acknowledged authority in all Jewish communities. Under this classical Judaism, the Jews 'developed a hatred and contempt for agriculture as an occupation and for peasants as a class, even more than for other Gentiles' and wherever Jewish society is to be found, in whatever form, 'it does not include peasants'. See Shahak, pp. 42, 53 [Translator's Bibliography].

try; the complaint made against them, seems to carry with it a reflexion on the understanding of the *buyers*; we will therefore pass it over, as not essential to the present argument.

It is because the Jews have an aversion to productive labor that they can only end up causing a rise the prices of essential goods, the supply of which will not change with their presence, but the demand for which can only increase with their presence as additional consumers:

> It is rather a diminution of the merit of the Jews, that their poor are really a burden to the nation. They serve for little more than to raise the price of provision to the industrious laborer, from whose shoulders they take no part of the burthen.[88]

From a criminal perspective, it would also be disadvantageous to allow more Jews into the country. As one letter-writer to the *London Evening Post* stated:

> For several Years past, most of the rich Jewels, Plate, Watches, &c. that have been stolen from the Nobility and Gentry, either from their Houses, or on the Highway, have been sold to the *Jews*; who carry them to Holland, and other Places, where they dispose of them, so that their Owners never hear more of them. Numbers of *Jews* are employ'd in this vile Traffick. Pretty Fellows indeed, and very proper for Naturalization![89]

The Jews are accused of generally being of inferior character, and are even described as 'the subtilest People upon the Earth' and 'the most contemptible People.' Romaine strongly opposes the view that Jewish wealth is of benefit to the country, because of the immoral way in which it was acquired. Their fraudulent activities would, over time, erode the all-important trust between men, blacken England's reputation in the world and be highly prejudicial to English trade. Other sources tell us that, even back then, people all over the world were being harmed by English speculators:[90]

---

[88] Hanway, pp. 67-8; also see *London Evening Post* 18/9/1753. Translator's note: All QVOS (Hanway).

[89] *Westminster Journal*, 9/6/1753; *London Evening Post* 7/7/1753, 22/9/1753; 'J. E.', p. 12. Translator's note: Quotation from original source (*LEP*, 7/7). For a thorough investigation into Jewish criminality in England during this period, see Todd Endelmen's excellent *Jews of Georgian England*, particularly the chapters 'Peddlers and Hawkers' and 'Pickpockets and Pugilists'. Chapter 4 of Felsenstein also has lively vignettes and contemporary illustrations of these Jewish ambulant salesmen [both books in Translator's Bibliography].

[90] See, for example, the *Public Advertiser*, 22/8/1753; *Admonitions from Scripture and History*, p. 7 ff. & See, for example, the *London Evening Post*, 16/8/1753. Translator's

On the banks of the Danube, the Vistula, the Rhine, and the Tagus; on the shores of the Baltic and the Mediterranean; on the plains of Poland—I have met with men who have asked me for charity, because they had been ruined by connexion with some of the first English houses.[91]

Finally, there was the charge that Jews 'are Broachers of false News; (holding Correspondence in all Parts) in order to rise or fall Stocks at their Pleasure'.[92]

The sources unfailingly tell us how the Hebrews continued to be a source of trouble. It is their general depravity that after a certain time turns the population against them, with all of the domestic political disruption that this brings, along with their eventual persecution. They also rightly aroused resentment because they rose to prominence and became rich 'wheresoever they *nest Themselves*', mainly through 'Villanies and Cheating'. In addition, they would bring unrest into the nation through their innate revolutionary spirit, as amply proven by their own history. As Romaine wrote, it made no sense at all as to why anyone would want to grant these '*Vagabond Jews*'— already described as such in the New Testament—every possible right and privilege of the free-born Englishman.[93]

The Jews and their allies did not of course remain silent about such accusations. Philo-Patriae, citing passages from the Bible, denied the Jews' immorality and concluded that some English people were worse than Jews. In England, an author going by the name of Andrew Henderson and declaring himself to be a Christian, had this to say about England's leading Jews:[94]

[N]or have the *Jews* any Power to purchase Estates without a parliamentary Authority, tho' these could not be vested in the Hands of better Men than some of the *Jews* are, such as the harmless *Sampson Gideon*, that Father of the Poor; the generous and open hearted *Mendezes*, *Franks*, *Salvador*, and others, who supplied the Nation in the midst of Distress, and so fre-

---

note: QVOS, which is itself an excerpt of a 1733 letter written by Charles II's royal historiographer to Lord Clifford, solely on the subject of Jews. See Howell, pp. 312-7 [Translator's Bibliography] for the original 1733 letter. & Romaine: *An Answer*, pp. 78-9.

[91] Francis, p. 83. Translator's note: QVOS.

[92] 'J. E.', p. 12. Translator's note: QVOS. The charge of being 'broachers of false news', as demonstrated in Volume 3 with the 'death of Queen Anne' event, will particularly resonate with readers today.

[93] Hanway, p. 166 ff.; *Gentleman's Magazine*, Vol. XXVIII, p. 479. & *London Evening News*, 16/8/1753. Translator's note: QVOS. & *An Appeal to the Throne*, p. 14. & Romaine: *Modest Apology*, p. 7. Translator's note: QVOS. The New Testament reference to *vagabond Jews* can be found in Acts 19:13 (King James Version).

[94] Philo-Patriae: *Considerations*, p. 11 ff. & Philo-Patriae: *Further Considerations*, p. 4.

quently furnished the State with Money, the Sinews of War on every Emergency...[95]

Indeed, one pro-Jewish author even goes so far as to summaries his reflections with the words: 'And I will not scruple to say, that any *Jew* is equal to a nominal Christian.' The Hebrews themselves consider it quite possible that some of these writings, most of which were published anonymously, were written by their fellow Jews. Certainly, one could assume that this latter opinion could only have come from the pen of a Jew. We can safely assume the same for the author Philo-Patriae, not least since the Jews often work under the cover of patriotic-sounding monikers such as his, which literally means 'Lover of the Fatherland.'

But in addition to the Jews, the clergy played no small part in writing these tracts, as can be seen indirectly from an open letter to a newspaper. The main content of this letter is as follows:[96]

> The Christian pastor-rabbi who recently wrote in favour of the Jew Bill had the impudence and arrogance to assert that the Jews were not only more decent and honest merchants, but people of better morals than the Christians of this country, and that the Jews were much more liable to be corrupted by their association with us than vice versa. He has...heaped great shame upon himself and his spiritual brothers with such assertions. For if we are generally worse than the Jews, it must undoubtedly be due in large measure to our clergy, who do not care for their flock as they should, who do not set them a good example, but who are so eager for their worldly riches that— instead of fulfilling their sacred duties and raising the morale of the people—they would prefer to write such pamphlets...[97]

Another commentator also does not fail to point out the undesirable situation of Jews marrying English girls.[98] Under the heading: 'History of the Future,' another article made an attempt to give an ironic depiction of future conditions that, despite certain exaggerations, reflected the populace's deep concern. The future that was predicted was one in which the sons of Gideon and others of his race would violate the daughters of Britons. The British, incensed about this outrage, would be unable to do anything about it because the authorities would protect the Jews. The Jews would even go as far as to

---

[95] Henderson, p. 30. Translator's note: QVOS.

[96] *Address to the Friends*, p. 19. Translator's note: QVOS. & Solomons, p. 211.

[97] *London Evening Post*, 30/10/1753. Translator's note: There appears to be an error in this reference.

[98] *Daily Advertiser*, 8/9/1753.

ask the government to provide them with English women, in return for which they were prepared to pay any sum. If their request was rejected, they would withdraw all of their money from government securities.[99]

Already by that time, entire neighborhoods in London must have been inhabited by Jews, because one author warns against this development and emphasizes that Leadenhall Street, Duke's Court, Broad Court, Duke's Place, Bever's Marks, Henage Lane, London Walt, Houndsditch, and Cribby Islands is full of them. There was also no shortage of voices warning of the threat of increasing Jewish influence. If the law were to be enacted, in time England would be entirely controlled by Jews. Their cunning and resources would soon undoubtedly carry them into Parliament. Even then, according to one letter-writer, the Jews were not afraid to say that the land of England would soon belong to them, which is very similar to the Jewish slogan of today: 'It is your king, but our country'.[100]

The same letter-writer, 'Civis Westmonasteriensis', also made the following startling prediction:

> The Predictions in the *Hebrew Journal*, calculated for One Hundred Years hence, may, in a Century or two, be fulfilled, and our Children, that are yet unborn, feel the direful Effects of the Pusillanimity and avaricious Passion of their Ancestors: They may see the *Jews* possess'd of their principal Offices under the Government; or at least, the principal Officers of the State... And whenever that shall be the Case, nothing but a Miracle can save the Christian Religion from utter Destruction.[101]

One would also eventually come to find Hebrews in the magistracy and the legislature. The ancient rights of the English should not be compromised for the sake of Jews, and if Jewish rights triumphed, English customs and cus-

---

[99] *London Evening Post*, 16/10/1753. Translator's note: There appears to be an error in the reference.

[100] 'J. E.', p. 13. & Romaine: *An Answer*, p. 41; Hanway, p. 160; *Full Answer to a Fallacious Apology*, p. 17. & *London Evening Post*, 17/5/1753 & 12/5/1753.

[101] *London Evening Post*, 12/7/1753 (also found in *A Collection of the Best Pieces...* pp. 66-71). Translator's note: QVOS. The reference to the *Hebrew Journal* is to remind readers of an earlier satirical article printed in the *London Evening Post* entitled 'News for One Hundred Years Hence in the *Hebrew Journal*, by Authority' (7/7/1953). The article imagines what the England of the future would look like under Jewish control. Outlandish predictions include Jews being land-owning nobility and government ministers, statues of great Englishmen being pulled down, babies being routinely circumcised in hospital, and Christians, who were no longer British subjects, being shot by government soldiers. The temple was also being rebuilt in Jerusalem, with further funds for the building being raised by a lottery in Britain.

toms would be endangered. Even the external appearance of the Jews leaves no doubt about their inner characteristics:[102]

> Their Crimes deserve these severe Lashes of Conscience, and how severe they are you may read in their very Faces. You know a *Jew* at first Sight. And what then are his distinguishing Features? Examine what it is peculiar that strikes you. It is not his dirty Skin, for there are other People as nasty; neither is it the Make of his Body, for the *Dutch* are every whit as odd, aukward Figures as the *Jews*. But look at his Eyes. Dont you see a malignant Blackness underneath them, which gives them such a Cast, as bespeaks Guilt and Murder? You can never mistake a *Jew* by this Mark, it throws such a dead, livid Aspect over all his Features, that he carries Evidence enough in his Face to convict him of being a Crucifier.[103]

Harsh words, but the truth is always bitter.

Near the end of the same tract, however, the author is resigned to summing up the situation using the following Latin phrase, which has resonated through history:

> It is an old Observation, which has been justified by long Experience, that Blindness always precedes a Judgment. The very Heathen could observe it—*Quos Jupiter vult perdere, prius dementet.* [Those whom the gods wish to destroy, they first make mad.] Our present Conduct argues some such Infatuation, and foretells the Approach of some great Calamity...[104]

The Jews and their allies believed that this fear was misplaced. Even if large numbers were to come into the country, they could not pose a threat given their numerical inferiority. According to the pro-Jewish side, the Jews were peaceful, trading people who would neither use their influence to the detriment of the country nor disperse their residences throughout the population because they knew their unpopularity with the people and therefore behaved prudently, keeping together in the same part of town. Of course, Philo-Patriae could not see any danger in the increasing influence of the Jews; indeed, he even preferred that they become landowners rather than the '*Jaco-*

---

[102] *Candid and Impartial Examination*, p. 24. Translator's note: This text is also useful for its reproduction of the original wording of the fateful 'Jew Bill'. & *A Letter to the Worshipful Sir John Barnard*, p. 5; *Court and Country*, p. 5.

[103] Romaine: *Modest Apology*, p. 8-9. Translator's note: QVOS.

[104] Romaine: *Modest Apology*, p. 15. Translator's note: QVOS. The square brackets indicate my insertion into the text, which is Enoch Powell's famous use of the phrase.

bites', who were much more dangerous for England. There was also no reason to fear the Jews entering Parliament in the future; there, as elsewhere in
general, they would only have England's best interests at heart.[105]

The internationality of the Jews and the associated dangers for a nation
are illuminated by the following comment:

> [W]e shall find, that no People on Earth are more apt to betray
> Secrets and communicate private Intelligence, from one Coun-
> try to another than the *Jews*, on Condition that they are well
> paid for it. They are a People who by their Religion are ren-
> dered indifferent, if not directly opposite to all Christians of
> what Denomination soever; and their natural Thirst of *Lucre*
> makes them careless which Party they betray, so that they can
> avail themselves thereby. Though to do them Justice, they
> generally take Care to advantage the highest Bidder by their
> Information.

The anonymous author then urgently warns of the danger of this naturalization law, which could allow the entry of the Jew into the nation's 'Councils,
or any Branch of the Government', where the secret knowledge he gained of
state affairs could, 'by his extensive Communication with his Brethren
abroad', be betrayed to 'every Court in *Europe*'.[106]

There were even voices who feared that by naturalizing the Jews, England would effectively become Jewish, which would lead to its doom. From
the *London Evening Post* of 12 July 1753:

> [T]hen as the Christians and Antichrist Jews will be natural-
> ised into one Body, so will they be into one and the same
> Guilt, one and the same Punishment; for this unnatural Naturali-
> zation will then become not only the Crime of an infidel iniqui-
> tous M[iniste]r, and his Adherents, but by passing into an na-

---

[105] *Appeal to Caesar*, p. 16ff.; *Letter to the Public*, p. 18ff.; *True State of the Case*, pp. 2-9;
Freeholder, p. 30. & Philo-Patriae: *Further Considerations*, p. 57. Translator's note:
Quoted element from original source, reproduced to remind the reader that the word 'Jacobite' was an emotive word used to trigger fear and hatred of fellow countrymen, and a
word which the Jews were not afraid to brandish for their own divisive or libellous political purposes. In this regard, see Romaine: *An Answer*, pp. 90-93 (**93**), in which he talks of
how Jews have set up the internal bogeyman of the Jacobite, in order to call anyone who
opposed their agenda this name, with the aim of discrediting and isolating him from his
fellows. & 'True Believer', p. 19. Translator's note: (from the original source) 'Is it not
reasonable to believe, that he will give his Vote on that Side of the Question which shall
appear to him to be the true Interest of the Society of which he is now become a Member?'
[106] *A Candid and Impartial Examination*, pp. 16-7. Translator's note: All QVOS.

tional Act, will pass into a national Crime; and national Crimes always did, and always will call down national Judgments.

From the 1753 tract *Admonitions from Scripture and History*:

> They blaspheme that Holy Name by which we are called, and curse us, and would at any Time destroy us Root and Branch, if they could. And their Naturalization would give them Means and Opportunities, beyond all that I have yet said; and indeed, beyond all that any Man can think or imagine, to effect this. So that we can have no Communion or Fellowship at all with Them, any farther than to allow them a quiet Being, for common Trade and Merchandize, among us. Beyond which, all Friendship with, and Charity to Them, is to join with them in Enmity against our own Redeemer; and so make ourselves Foes to our own Religion, Peace and Salvation.
>
> And, therefore, if the Attempt now said to be on Foot, to incorporate them in Rights and Privileges with our natural-born *Englishmen*, should take Place, I must look upon our own Destruction, as a People, to be the next Thing we have to expect; and that, after That, we shall never see happy Day more; but Their Sin and Guilt shall become ours; and their Judgement and Plague follow us; till God cast us out of this good Land which He hath given us; as He hath, so long since, cast Them out of Theirs.[107]

Elsewhere the same warning was expressed in verse:

> Till her [Britannia's] Sons prove honest, just, and true,
> And learn to hate, that hateful Thing, a JEW.[108]

The old wake-up call from the pre-Restoration period is heard again in various places:

> Awake, therefore, my Fellow Britons, Christians, and Protestants! It is not *Hannibal* at your Gates, but the *Jews*, that are coming for the Keys of your Church Doors.[109]

---

[107] *London Evening Post*, 12/7/1753; *Admonitions from Scripture*, pp. 7 ff., 28. Translator's note: Quotations reproduced verbatim from respective original sources.

[108] *London Evening Post*, 8/9/1753. Translator's note: QVOS.

[109] *London Evening Post*, 22/5/1753. Translator's note: QVOS.

Britons awake! let the noble spirit of *truth* and *liberty* fire all
the soul.[110]

Meanwhile, the author of *Some Considerations on the Naturalization of the
Jews* felt the following poem was important enough to put on his title page:

> *Thus Step by Step, a Nation is undone,*
> *And Prodigals lose what their Fathers won;*
> *A Jew, a Turk, or Devil may come here,*
> *And Naturalize; it will not cost them dear.*

We have seen from these brief references—taken from the flood of tracts
that were published both for and against the Jewish naturalization law—the
vehemence with which the issue was treated. Hopefully, this overview has
further conveyed to the reader that the Jews' opponents did not give in, even
when the bill was passed into law. But it must be all the more astonishing
that the bill was presented in the first place given that, based on the opinions
expressed publicly, an overwhelming majority of the populace was against it.

We can also see from many contemporary accounts that hardly anyone
in the country was happy about the law being passed. The reason had to be
that the English nation has had a deep antipathy towards the Jews since ancient times, which was particularly evident in the tumultuous year of 1753.
So it came to pass that 'the People are not pleas'd at it in the City, Town, or
Country, all murmuring; none having any other Reason, except those that
had the golden Apples.' It is therefore not going too far to say that the English people stood up as one against the law and strove to enforce their will
with every means at their disposal.[111]

How exactly did this public resentment manifest itself?

We learn from the *London Evening Post* that: 'It is rumoured that a Petition from a certain great Body is intended to be delivered to the King, praying his Majesty not to sign the Bill for naturalizing the Jews.' Apparently this
plan either did not take place or was unsuccessful, since we find out that on 7
June 1753, the king did the very thing the people wanted to prevent.[112]

Apparently the universities had not done enough to support the people
in their cause, as on October 16 a Rev. Dr. Free was reported to have given a

---

[110]   *The Court and Country Interest*, p. 6. Translator's note: QVOS.

[111]   Hanway, pp. 55, 172. Translator's note: There appears to be an error with the page
numbers of this reference. & *Appendix to Review and Letters*, p. 6. & 'J. E.', p. 16. Translator's note: QVOS. & *Parl. History*, Vol. XV, pp. 110, 128, 133; *Daily Advertiser*,
1/9/1753; *London Evening Post*, 19/7/1753, 21/8/1753.

[112]   *London Evening Post*, 22/5/1753. Translator's note: QVOS. If there was truth to the
rumour, given what we know, it is likely that the 'great Body' was the City of London
Corporation.

sermon at Oxford calling for his scholarly peers to take a greater role in the struggle, and:

> [F]or this Reason several prudent People in the *New* Interest [i.e. Whigs, who were supporters and beneficiaries of the new financial system], who were his *Well-wishers*, are now disgusted at the Forwardness of this Author, a Man of a low Station, who has lately been troubling this Place, more than once, with his *Speeches* to the Citizens, and *Sermons* to the Scholars...[113]

Further public calls for resistance were issued, and subsequent protest meetings held. In every corner of the kingdom, large crowds of people gathered to express their will. While these demonstrations are acknowledged by Philo-Patriae, he considers them to be irrelevant, as in his view they are by people in pursuit of their own selfish ends. The facts by no means support his thesis.[114]

Demonstrations took place in Warwick, Blithfield, Essex, Staffordshire, and Montgomeryshire, to name but a few locations, while in almost all constituencies, voters came together to either thank their MPs for their opposition to the bill during its passage through Parliament, or to vigorously demand such opposition from them in the future.[115]

However, a much larger number of constituency meetings have been recorded in which the members of Parliament were asked to do everything they could to repeal the law, otherwise they could expect not to be re-elected in the spring of 1754. We see such assemblies in Taunton, Reading, Cirencester, York, Bristol, Yarmouth, Haslemere, Lancaster, Gloucester, and Westminster, as well as in the counties of Kent, Somersetshire, and Middlesex, among others. This should give an accurate picture of the popular mood. In addition, attention should be drawn to the fact that as the winter session of Parliament approached, i.e. November and December 1753, such meetings became particularly frequent.[116]

This outburst of public indignation must have come as a shock to some of the MPs who had voted in favor of the bill, as can be seen in the following extract from a letter written by a Dr. Birch of London to the Hon. Philip York, dated 29 September 1753:

---

[113] *London Evening Post*, 23/10/1753. Translator's note: QVOS. This excerpt is important for showing the personal material motives behind some of the elite support for Jewry.

[114] *Gentleman's Magazine*, Vol. XXIII, p. 468; *Public Advertiser*, 10/10/1753, 11/10/1753, 12/10/1753, 17/10/1753, 19/10/1753. & Philo-Patriae, *Considerations*, p. 26 ff.

[115] *Daily Advertiser*, 20/10/1753; *Public Advertiser*, 22/8/1753; *London Evening Post*, 17/7/1753, 18/8/1753, 8/9/1753.

[116] *Public Advertiser*, 10/10/1753, 12/10/1753, 7/11/1753, 19/11/1753; *London Evening Post* 17-19/7/1753, 21-23/8/1753, 6-11/10/1753, 6-10/11/1753, 24-27/11/1753, 4-8/12/1753.

The Jews Bill is likely, among many ill consequences, to have one good effect, in relieving the next parliament from the oratory of Mr. Sydenham whose declaring for that Bill has rendered the city of Exeter implacable to him; though to acquit himself of Judaism, he dispersed printed papers, justifying his attachment to Christianity, and urging as a proof of it, his travelling on Saturdays, when the business required it, and his strict observance of Sundays. This, with some other reasonings of the same force, induced his friends to persuade him to suppress those papers, which he had not yet delivered.[117]

This following vignette should give some idea of the mood in England. However, there are a number of such reports which together provide a well-rounded picture of the situation, and which delight with the humor they contain:

A Kent MP had the misfortune of voting for the bill, the news which spread like wildfire throughout his constituency and especially his hometown. Great excitement gripped the population, and they were quite angry with their honourable representative.

He had no idea of the storm that was brewing when he returned to his constituency a short time later, happy to have escaped the sweltering heat of London in the summer. His path took him past his local public house, where he knew his best friends were having lunch at the time. He quickly decided to enter the bar to proudly introduce himself to his electorate.

When he entered, his expectations were not disappointed: upright and sedate citizens of the small town were gathered and were discussing the latest events with each other. He greeted them with a hello and asked to sit with them, as was his old habit. In his joy at seeing them again, he had not noticed that everything had fallen silent when he entered, and so was shocked when his friends expressed great regret that he would not be able to eat with them because they had unfortunately ordered pork to be served. Only then did the poor sinner realise the situation and was left in a state of bewilderment. It took him a moment to recover, and only the booming laughter of those present broke him out of his dismay.

Grabbing his hat and rushing away was one thing. On his way he passed the market square and, to his joy, spied a longtime friend and loyal voter. Glad to have found someone—and

---

[117] *Parl. History*, Vol. XIV, p. 1431. Translator's note: QVOS.

this person in particular—to talk to, he rushed to greet him. He immediately bombarded him with a barrage of questions and, in his lingering state of confusion, wanted to get more detailed information from his friend about the attitude of the others. When he paused for a moment after a question, in the hope of getting a response, he saw that his friend was looking at him interestedly but in silence. The honourable member paused and impatiently pressed him with questions about why the hell he wasn't answering. His friend surely had to hear and understand him. Without batting an eye, the brave man replied: 'Eh..., I can hear you—but unfortunately I can't speak Hebrew.' No sooner had he said these words, he left the astonished parliamentarian standing there in the middle of the square.

The *London Evening Post* of 14 July 1753, also tells the following anecdote:

> We learn, by a Gentleman just come from Cambridge, that a certain *Great Man*, who had lately made a Visit there, was, on his Departure, saluted by the People, who followed him in Crowds quite through the Town, with *Hail, King of the Jews!* [Translator's note: QVOS.]

Times of violent political conflict are always more or less the same. The people strive to use battle cries to rile up their own ranks or to inspire others with their ideas. And so it was in England in 1753. The masses of Lancashire voters wore blue ribbons at their meetings with the inscription: 'No Jews! Christianity and the Constitution!' In Somersetshire the motto was: 'No Judaism! Christianity forever!'[118]

There was a report in early June that 'a worthy Member of Parliament went out of Town to his Country Seat in Wiltshire, whose Attendants consisted of six Persons on Horseback, with Labels in their Hats, *no Jews, no Naturalization Bill, old England and Christianity for ever*'.[119]

The slogan: 'No Jews!' was one of the most common in the election campaigns, but the other battle cries mentioned above were also commonly used. Cries were often heard of 'No long beards nor whiskers! Christians

---

[118] *London Evening Post*, 17/7/1753. Translator's note: The incident of the people shouting at a politician is also reported in *A Collection of the best pieces* [p. 76], with the insult being shouted in Latin – '*Ecce Rex Judæorum*' [Behold, the king of the Jews] – and the *great man* being a government minister (assuming that both accounts are varying descriptions of the same incident). If it is indeed true that the public were shouting insults in Latin, this goes some way to discredit Hertz's characterization of 'the people at large' (i.e. the Jew Bill's opponents) as 'gin-sodden and wholly uneducated' [Hertz, p. 93].

[119] *London Evening Post*, 7/6/1753. Translator's note: QVOS.

forever!' and 'No Jews, no wooden Shoes!'. These words reverberated through the streets whenever the masses assembled for protest gatherings, and were loudly shouted from the excited processions as they moved through the Jewish-inhabited streets of London. How much it was the general battle cry is shown by the fact that the Jew Gerald Hertz (who changed his name to Hurst in 1916) chose it as the chapter title for this period of his book.[120]

The meaning of the connection between 'Jews' and 'wooden shoes' has so far remained unclear. Hyamson and Hertz are not entirely sure either, but they believe that the wooden shoes were an expression of rejection of the Huguenots. This interpretation seems to be wrong, since this year the crowd only had to deal with the Jews regarding naturalization. None of the writings discussed so far confirm Hyamson and Hertz's thesis. We believe that another explanation may come closer to the truth and therefore refer to the following extract from a poem:[121]

> (Christ save us from His enemies, the *Jews!*)
> What's this? Made free and true-born *English, Jews!*
> The Devil, Infidels! Hereticks! and Turks!
> These can't be *English*, these are Romish Works:
> Some Popish Plot, to bring in the Pretender;
> Pray Heaven guard our glorious Faith's Defender!
> Were this News true, all Hell would be let loose,
> To *Englishmen* be worse than Wooden Shoes...[122]

Accordingly, the wooden shoe seems to have been the epitome of inferiority for the Englishman of that time. The battle cry may therefore have

---

[120] Tucker: *Second Letter*, p. 3. & *Election Magazine*, p. 63. & Hertz, p. 77. Solomons, p. 207. & Hyamson: *Jew Bill*, p. 168; Solomons, p. 206. & Hertz, p. 60 ff. Translator's note: This Anglicising surname change may have been prompted as much by the desire to avoid the anti-German prejudice rampant during WW1, as much as the desire to avoid being perceived as Jewish. This would be particularly pertinent given the fact that Hertz/Hurst served as a British Army lieutenant during WW1. Given his life story of rapid social ascension to become Sir Gerald Berkeley Hurst QC, however, I suspect that both factors were at play.

[121] Hyamson: *History*, p. 222. & Hertz, p. 67.

[122] *London Evening Post*, 21/7/1753. Translator's note: QVOS. Contrary to the author's opinion, I believe that Hyamson and Hertz are correct in associating the 'wooden shoes' with the Huguenots, and that the English people had formed this synecdoche is evident from two lines in the poem 'Wherever God erects a house of prayer' by the almost contemporaneous poet Daniel Defoe (1660-1731). The poet describes the 'banished Protestants of France' (i.e. the Huguenots) as 'Two hundred thousand pair of wooden shoes, / Who, God be thanked, had nothing left to lose'. In addition, some waves of Huguenot immigration would have been relatively recent, i.e. within the last 50 years, and it was likely these immigrants were still a separate ethnic group, so it would make sense that the associated grievances around these relatively recent immigrants would be revived by the Jew Bill controversy in the minds of some of the protesters.

been chosen not just because of the rhyme, but because Jews and wooden shoes were rejected with the deepest aversion.

Although these statements already give us an insight into the tremendous agitation of the populace, we can only get a true picture when we see how the people's anger was directed at the immediate supporters of the law. They stopped at nothing, and neither the government ministers responsible nor the bishops and the clergy of lesser rank were spared.

The people could not forget that the bishops in particular had supported the Jew Bill in the House of Lords without exception—at least whenever they were present. In addition to them, the bishops of Oxford, Norwich and St. Asaph had publicly supported the Jew Bill. But the others had not taken any steps to support the people in their defensive struggle, as can be seen from the public appeals in the newspapers. Likewise, in the *London Evening Post* we find an appeal to unite those clergymen who did not side with the Jews. It was bitterly emphasized that it truly was time for some pastors to take a stand with the people, since nothing could be expected from the bishops. We find this view repeatedly expressed in the same newspaper.[123]

Given the bishops' position, it is not surprising that serious allegations were made against them. In one poem ('Judas') they are compared to Judas Iscariot, because they treacherously sold themselves for gold, and the final section of the poem deals with what should happen to these corrupt bishops:[124]

> As ancient *Judas by Trangression fell,*
> And *burst asunder* e'er he went to Hell;
> So could we see a Set of new *Iscariots,*
> Come headlong tumbling from their mitred Chariots,
> Each modern *Judas* perish like the first;
> Drop from the Tree, with all his Bowels burst:
> Who could forbear, that view'd each guilty Face,
> To cry, Lo! *Judas gone to his own Place!*
> *His Habitation let all Men forsake;*
> *And, let his Bishoprick another take.*[125]

An anonymous satirist also made suggestions for future laws, and suggested that there were already plans afoot to authorize bishops and clergy to give Jew-friendly sermons from the pulpit.[126] In one poem, we find attacks against the bishops. The fourth verse of it reads:

---

[123] Solomons, p. 207. & *London Evening Post,* 16/10/1753. & 16/6/1753.

[124] Hyamson: *Jew Bill,* p. 168.

[125] *London Evening Post* 18/9/1753; similar is the ballad *The Jews' Triumph,* p. 3 ff, in which Judas is not named, but suggests that the bishops had taken bribes. Translator's note: QVOS.

[126] Telltruth, p. 10 ff.

Let there not be a JEW at your Bottle or Board,
Leave them for the B[isho]ps, his G[race], or my L[or]d;
They will feast them with Place, and with Salary too –
But turn out all Men that will favour a JEW.[127]

There is no doubt that there were also other direct attacks on the bishops, as can be seen in the cases of the Bishops of Norwich and Oxford. Firstly, the case of the Bishop of Norwich, as described by Coxe:

> Violent expressions of public indignation occurred, in many parts of the country. The bishops, in particular, were exposed to contumely, for suffering the bill to pass, without opposition, in the House of Peers. The degree of irritation which prevailed against their order, was shewn in the insults offered to the bishop of Norwich, in every part of his diocese. At Ipswich, the very youths whom he was about to confirm, called out for circumcision; and a paper was affixed on the door of one of the churches, stating that his lordship would confirm the Jews the next day, which was their sabbath, and on the Sunday would perform the same function for the Christians.[128]

Secondly, there is the case of the Bishop of Oxford, who stood on the side of the Jews until the last minute, for which the people poured scorn on him accordingly. Evidence of this scorn can be found in the British Museum's catalogue of political and personal satires, from which we take the following cartoon descriptions.

One cartoon, titled 'The American Moose-Deer, or away to the River Ohio', is a cartoon concerned mainly with various European rivalries for the American colonies, as it depicts an American moose-deer surrounded by kings, but the cartoonist obviously could not resist poking some unrelated fun at the Bishop of Oxford, Thomas Secker, whom he depicts resting a book on the animal's rump. The book is inscribed with the number 20,000, and the words 'I'll pray for the Jews & the Marriage Act, & my King'. Both inscriptions allude to the fact that, according to the engraver, he must have been bribed with £20,000 for his support. [Note that neither the public mockery nor the allegation of bribery had any negative bearing on Secker's career; he became Archbishop of Canterbury in 1758.][129]

---

[127] *Election Magazine*, p. 74. Translator's note: QVOS.
[128] Coxe, Vol. II, p. 290; *Parl. History*, Vol. XIV, p. 1431. Translator's note: QVOS (Coxe). Note that Aldag's second cited source provides the same report of events but with different wording, citing a letter from a Dr. Birch to the Hon. Philip York as their primary source.
[129] Stephens, Vol. III, Part II, pp. 927-8 [§ 3280]. Translator's note: QVOS. The cartoon has been reproduced at the end of this chapter.

Another cartoon, titled 'The Circumcised Gentiles, or A Journey to Jerusalem' might best depict the people's attitude towards the bishops in general. The engraving depicts a Jew mounted on an ass, with a bishop seated behind him. The Jew has before him a box, labelled 'Israel's Court Plaister for Green Wounds', and he is pointing derisively to the bishop, while he cries: 'Me am Naturalize and have Converted mine Broder dat is behind.' The bishop has the Talmud under his arm, and remarks: 'We have erred and stray'd from thy ways like lost Sheep.' The New Testament is lying on the ground. The ass announces: 'I have the honour to represent my Country Gratis, which is more than my Leader can say.' This leader, who is guiding the ass by the halter, remarks: 'I don't know how it fares with your Brother behind but this I am sure of, that if Circumcision agrees as ill with him as it does with me he wont keep his SEAT long.' He holds a purse marked '100,000' and a paper pouch of 'Circumscision Salve' [sic]. On the ground lie two papers, one marked 'General Election', referring to the upcoming election, and the other 'JEWS... 96, CHRISTIANS 55', referring to the parliamentary voting result. In the distance is seen the dome of St Paul's. Underneath the cartoon the following legend is engraved:

And in every Province, and in every City withersoever the King's Commandment and his decree came, the Jews had Joy and gladness, a feast and a good day; and many of the People of the Land became Jews, for the fear of the Jews fell upon them. —Esther, Chap. VIII. Verse 17.[130]

You can see that none of the bishops stood up for the concerns of the people. William Lecky's view, which is also the view held by Krieger, i.e. that a large number of the bishops were on the side of the Jews, therefore does not correspond to the facts, just as we do not agree that the lowered-rank clergy took part in the people's fight against the law. Rather, there were only a few in this latter category, including the Reverend Romaine, who championed the people's cause through preaching and writing.[131]

We have found irrefutable evidence that the clergy even stood up for the Jews. Not only did they do this from the pulpit, but they even published their sermons on the subject. It would take too long to detail these here, but

---

[130] Stephens, Vol. III, Part II, pp. 860-1. [§ 3205]. Translator's note: QVOS. Those who would like to see a visual reproduction of this cartoon can find it on page 199 of Felsenstein [Translator's Bibliography].

[131] Lecky, Vol. I, p. 330 ff. & Krieger, p. 43 ff. [Translator's note: Reference unclear, source not in Bibliography]. & See, for example, the opinions of Walpole, Vol. I, p. 357; Abbey, Vol. I, p. 214; Hyamson: *Jew Bill*, 168; Hyamson: *History*, 221; *Parl. History*, Vol. XV, p. 119; *London Evening Post*, 21/8/1753. & For a different view, see Lecky, Vol. I, p. 330 ff. & *Public Advertiser*, 22/5/1753.

rarely has there been warmer sympathy for the Jewish cause than that which was proffered by the English clergy in this particular year.[132]

They do not appear to have tempered their stance in the face of rising public anger, as there is evidence of pro-Jewish sermons being preached at the end of October 1753 which were published thereafter for wider public consumption, while the *London Evening Post* reports of pro-Jewish preaching even taking place in early December.[133] We also hear of how, on one Sunday in late October, a Monmouthshire clergyman preached a sermon in favor of Jewish naturalization, which 'so exasperated the Congregation, that many of them went out of the Church, and those that staid behind to hear his *doughty Performance*, testified their Disapprobation by their Countenances.'[134]

Incomprehensibly, the clergy thought it wise to repeatedly speak out in favor of the law through the format of printed open letters, which was only successful in turning public opinion against them. This led people to ask indignantly where the clergy had been when the law was passed:[135]

> *Hear, O Heavens! And be astonish'd, O Earth!* The Murderers of Christ are to be incorporated into the Body of Christians! Christ and Antichrist as to be united and made one in a Christian Country! *Heu Pietas! Heu Prisca Fides!* [Alas Piety! Alas Ancient Faith!] Where are the Guardians of the Christian Religion; the Trustees of the Religion of the Nation? Where are the Embassadors of Christ? The Shepherds appointed over his Flock?... Have they, like good Shepherds, carefully watch'd over the Flocks committed to their Charge? To fence and defend, protect and preserve them? Have they not rather, like Hirelings, *seeing the Wolf coming, left the Sheep, and fled? The Hireling fleeth, because he is an Hireling, and careth not for the sheep...*[136]

---

[132] Winstanley, p. 9 ff.; Peckard, p. 3 ff.

[133] *London Evening Post*, 4/12/1753. Translator's note: The rector in question is described in the report as 'always absent half, and sometimes the whole year', with the implication that his sudden appearance in the parish, to make 'strong and judicious' objections against the 'popular Clamour' was somewhat suspicious.

[134] *London Evening Post*, 30/10/1753. Translator's note: QVOS.

[135] *London Evening Post*, 14/8/1753, 18/8/1753, 4/9/1753, 11/9/1753, 25/9/1753, 16/10/1753, 23/10/1753, 30/10/1753.

[136] *London Evening Post*, 12/7/1753. Translator's note: QVOS, with words in square brackets added for reader comprehension. This long letter comes from a particularly informed contributor, who goes on at length about the 'sacred' Talmud and Talmudic practices, including the injunction to lie on oath to Christian juries, even to commit perjury in a capital case if the accused is Christian.

It is also occasionally noted with particular astonishment when an anti-Jewish clergyman (of inferior rank, of course) is found somewhere in England.[137]

Given the odds against the anti-Jewish faction, it is understandable to see why ridicule is not neglected as a weapon of war. Thus we find poems and ballads against the clergy and a call to establish a fund to reward honorable clergymen who would 'rather starve than become apostles for circumcision'. Another clergyman, who had particularly distinguished himself in the Jewish cause, must have allowed himself to be publicly ridiculed inasmuch as we see the following report in the *London Evening Post*:[138]

> We hear from Upton in Hants, that the Rev. Mr. T—— F——, alias F—— T——, or the Disturber of Miracles, will soon be appointed Chaplain to a very eminent Jew of the City of London, for his late glorious Defense of the Jews against our Savior Jesus Christ, in the General Evening Post of Saturday the 28th of July last.[139]

The joke about a Northumberland clergyman is even less subtle. He was then called to baptize a child, but to the horror of those present, he did not baptize him but instead circumcised him. Since the priest was still inexperienced at the practice, the poor mite died from the intervention.[140]

Given all of this invective, the following account of various Jews going to a clergyman's house to play cards seems to best reflect the people's opinion of their clergymen:

> LONDON EVENING POST, July 10.
> *Extract of a letter from a gentleman at Isleworth.*
> The country since the late rain is very pleasant, and would be more so, had I not the mortification of seeing the finest seats in possession of the Jews. Since the late act, they are grown very familiar; M[ose]s H[ar]t and A[aro]n F[ran]ks particularly, who, at the last vestry held here, mingled with the rest without opposition, although two clergymen and Justice B[an]kh[ea]d were present. No less than a coach load of them

---

[137] *London Evening Post*, 14/7/1753.
[138] *Election Magazine*, p. 58; *Jews' Triumph*, p. 5. & *London Evening Post*, 16/10/1753. Translator's note: There appears to be an error with this reference.
[139] *London Evening Post*, 11/12/1753. Translator's note: QVOS.
[140] *London Evening Post*, 8/9/1753. Translator's note: There appears to be an error in this reference.

> last thursday assembled at a clergyman's house very near us to
> play at cards.[141]

At that time, it was often claimed that the bishops—and the clergy in general—were bribed. No substantiated evidence has yet been found for this allegation, but if they were not bribed, it is difficult to understand the motivation for their behavior. Perhaps it was the case that, even back then, the church's natural stance (which is still evident today) was to support the Jews. Perhaps the clergy also believed that they could convert more Jews if the naturalization law was passed. Perhaps the church was also reassured by the fact that it was itself protected against Jewish influence by special provisions in the law. Regardless of the reasoning behind this ecclesiastical support, the general public pointed out the church's favoritism towards the Jews and openly criticized it.[142]

But the people were not only deeply dissatisfied with the church and the clergy: they also denounced the pro-Jewish government with at least as much bitterness, and their anger was particularly directed against the two Pelham brothers who were the leaders of the Whig government. The older brother Thomas, the Duke of Newcastle, was the leader of the ruling Whigs in the House of Lords, while the younger brother, Henry, was Prime Minister and First Lord of the Treasury in the House of Commons. The populace saw these two men as the driving force behind the Jew Bill, and the attacks against them knew no bounds.[143]

The intensity of popular anger is shown in a cartoon with the headline: 'The Jews shaving the Parliament, or, the knowing ones taken in.' It is an engraving of a barber's shop, depicting a group of Englishmen standing around a man who is about to be shaved by the barber, a Jew, who comforts his customer with the words: 'Have Patience Gentlemen, & we will have you all out of the Realm.' A second Jew in the background shouts 'Long live Solomon the Second' (meaning the then English King George II), while a third says 'Now Crucify Christ again'. Another man says 'Money Wise King of the Jews', referring to Sampson Gideon, who is probably supposed to be represented by the barber, since the Jew in question directs his gaze towards him. On the far right of the picture stands the Duke of Newcastle. A senior rabbi addresses him with the words: 'I hope your Grace will petition the King for a Temple', to which another Jew powdering a wig replies, 'And

---

[141] *Collection of the Best Pieces*, p. 62. Translator's note: QVOS, with square bracketed content added to facilitate comprehension. The context from which this excerpt was taken (i.e. the primary source) can be found at *London Evening News* 7/7/1753 (p. 1), and may have been labelled July 10 due to the newspaper being issued over three days (i.e. between the 7th and the 10th July).

[142] *Candid & Impartial Examination*, pp. 21-22; *Public Advertiser*, 22/5/1753.

[143] Coxe, Vol. II, p. 290; Solomons, pp. 206-7.

make a new Jerusalem.' The Duke replies: 'What Might Ills have not been done by M—?' [likely Mammon]. On the left we see the Duke of Cumberland, standing near two Englishmen seated on a sofa, one of whom observes, 'They will Circumcise us next'. The Duke of Cumberland declares, 'Ha! that's true, and I'm sure I have none to spare'. The other observes, 'It is too late to repent; we may thank the D— of N————stle', thus squarely placing the blame on the Duke of Newcastle for his predicament.[144]

One would have thought that after the success of the popular movement in 1753, the antipathy towards the Duke of Newcastle would have subsided, especially given that it was he who later introduced the bill of repeal in the House of Lords, albeit only under circumstantial pressure. Not at all, as can be seen from a cartoon published after the general election of 1754:[145]

The Duke of Newcastle is seated on a chair by the side of St Stephen's Chapel, Westminster, and is fishing for partisans among the members of Parliament, or candidates for the 1754 general election. His line is dropped through the chimney of the chapel, and baited with 'Titles', 'Bribes', 'Places', 'Pensions', 'Secret Commissions', 'Army', 'Navy' and 'Excise'. In doing so, he wants to win them back to the cause of the government, whose reputation had suffered considerably as a result of the difficult year of 1753. He says to himself: 'All Vermin may be caught, tho' differently, suite but the Baite to their various Appetites: But there's a Species will take no Baite; Wou'd I cou'd Scare them away; as they're not Vermin, they will not answer my Purpose.'

The 'vermin' can be seen approaching the bait. One says 'I will get repaid', while a parson declares 'I have Got a Large Swallow, & Can digest any Thing', another shouts 'Now for a Place for 1000 Per Annum' and a variety of other people approach making similar remarks that reveal their enthusiasm for the bait on offer.[146]

Apparently the hatred against the younger Pelham was even stronger, because he was mocked in a caricature even after his death. Henry Pelham died on 6 March 1754, and the cartoon that appeared shortly afterwards shows his entry into hell, led by a demon. It is captioned: 'His Arrival at his Country Retirement & Reception.' Other evil spirits make remarks, and departed statesmen greet his arrival, including Sir Robert Walpole, who says: 'O This is a Child of my own bringing up I found him a promising Genius for dirtty Work Therefore did all I could to gain him the Succession at my

---

[144] Stephens Vol. III, Part II, p. 862 (§ 3208). Translator's note: QVOS. This cartoon has been reproduced in Solomons (illustration plate after page 224), with a small reproduction at the end of this chapter.

[145] Coxe, Vol. II, p. 291.

[146] Stephens Vol. III, Part II, p. 916 (§ 3269). Translator's note: All QVOS. The cartoon is titled 'The compleat Vermin-catcher of G— B—n, or the old Trap new baited', and is reproduced at the end of this chapter.

Retirement hither Knowing that Some of his Black Stroaks wou'd make me appear as fair as Alabaster. He has done it in several Respects but Chiefly in getting the N—t—l—n of the J—ws passed—have any of you great Genius's done any thing Equal?' Cardinal Wolsey, another condemned man, admits that he imposed many things on the people, but that Pelham far exceeded him and Judge Jeffries, the notorious 'hanging judge', admits that his own actions during life were nothing compared 'to that great Achievement'.[147]

All of the cartoons allude to the dishonorable methods of government, particularly those of the 'Two Brothers', as they were referred to by the satirists of the day. This accusation was made to them repeatedly in public.[148]

One of the many who held this view was the Rev. William Romaine. According to him, the Jews under William the Conqueror and Oliver Cromwell were introduced into England by means of bribery, and he has no doubt that 'the self-same Money-Engine' was still being used by the Jews in his day. Telltruth and 'J. E.' also express something similar. Others long for the day when these practices will come to an end, while others would like to know how much 'the baneful Influence of cursed Gold' had played its tempting part in the naturalization law.[149]

The vernacular soon found new names for England and London. The former was dubbed *Judaea Nova*, the latter New Jerusalem. So it is not surprising that we find a cartoon with the title 'A Prospect of the new Jerusalem'. In the background we see the distant outline, or the 'Pisgah sight' of St. Paul's Cathedral in the middle of numerous rooftops, indicating London, and in the foreground the Pelham brothers are standing on a hill, with the older brother, Duke of Newcastle leaning against a tree, a scroll inscribed 'Naturalization Bill' in his hand. Below him on the slope, in the foreground, lies a hideous devil with a £500,000 money bag. A group of Jews look delightedly towards London, but the most foregrounded Jew looks instead towards at the devil holding the bag, ensuring that the viewer does not miss the cartoon's principle message.[150]

---

[147] Stephens Vol. III, Part II, p. 908 (§ 3264). Translator's note: QVOS (including the idiosyncratic spelling).

[148] Solomons, p. 207. All of the cartoons were to be photographed in the British Museum and included in this book. Unfortunately, the author's sudden expulsion from Great Britain, and the war that followed, has prevented this from happening. Translator's note: To honor Aldag's intentions, the listed cartoons have been reproduced at the end of this chapter, with another featuring as the cover illustration.

[149] Romaine: *An Answer*, p. 5. Translator's note: QVOS.

[149] Telltruth, p. 4. & 'J. E.', p. 16. & *London Evening Post*, 22/9/1753. & *London Evening Post*, 30/10/1753. Translator's note: QVOS.

[150] *Collection of the Best Pieces*, p. 56; *London Evening Post*, 7/7/1953. & 2/6/1753, 18/9/1753. & Stephens Vol. III, Part II, pp. 859-60 (§ 3204). Translator's note: This cartoon is reproduced in Solomons (illustration plate after page 218), Felsenstein, p. 195, and at the end of this chapter.

We hope that the concise descriptions of the numerous writings, public letters, poems, caricatures, and demonstrations have given the reader an idea of the force with which the popular storm raged against the king, government, parliamentary representatives, lords, and clergy.

These events could not have remained hidden from the members of the government; in particular, the two Pelham brothers seem to have been very disturbed by the unrest, as can be deduced from one or two of their letters. As early as July 13, the Duke of Newcastle wrote to his brother Henry that, in view of the unrest prevailing in many places, he had asked Lord Parker to consider repealing the law, even though 'bargaining with clamor, was a dangerous expedient'. He had sent word that he would make an immediate declaration, as per his brother's suggestion, in a bid to prevent any future rioting. Just four days later, in a letter to his brother, he once again expressed his serious concerns about the spread of the popular movement. The younger Pelham replied on July 20 that he held the same opinion. He ends his letter with the following advice: 'let them take their course, and if you find it gives a real uneasiness, repeal next year, as a matter of no consequence in itself; but if it gives disturbance to weak minds, it is right to indulge them.'[151]

From the available material, it can be seen that the public storm grew ever more turbulent after the month of July. Protest meetings were held across the country and the government had no influence over the masses. If the Pelham brothers were already dismayed by the way things were going in July, the months that followed were to give them an even greater cause for concern.

England's two legislative bodies were scheduled to convene in mid-November. Under the pressure of the circumstances, the government decided to recommend the repeal of the law as the first item of business and submitted a bill to this very effect. The people had won!

Jewish historians have looked for the reasons behind the government's embarrassing U-turn and have come to the conclusion that it was forced to do so by the upcoming elections. Under the circumstances it could not have counted on a majority in the future parliament, which is why, in order to save itself, it undertook, under the Pelham brothers' leadership, the shameful task of placating the people and bringing them back onside by repealing the law. This was made all the easier for the Pelham ministry because it always put its own interests ahead of principles.[152]

We too believe that both sets of circumstances contributed to the government's behavior, although we are surprised, to say the least, that a Jew would condemn the latter decision of the Pelham ministry. But perhaps the reason for his view lies in the fact that this time a tactic of cynical expediency

---

[151] Coxe, Vol. II, pp. 467-8. Translator's note: QVOS. & Coxe, Vol. II, pp. 484. & Coxe, Vol. II, pp. 485. Translator's note: QVOS.

[152] Hyamson: *Jew Bill*, p. 174. & Hertz, p. 89.

was applied to the detriment of the race that itself makes almost exclusive use of such tactics.

In fact, the main reason was probably the threat to England's domestic political stability. There were fears that the government would be defeated in the upcoming elections of 1754, but that was not the most dangerous thing at that point in time. Given the mood of the people, the government had to reckon with the fact that violent riots would occur, with all the resulting disadvantages for the ruling class. The aforementioned correspondence between the Pelham brothers leaves no doubt about this. Even back then, people were afraid of such events. And the threat must have been much greater four months after these letters were exchanged, when the mood of the nation had grown even darker. There can be no doubt that the government bowed to the will of the people.

If one surveys history, it is rare to find a similar incident. All of the powers of the state had, in some cases unanimously, supported the law, and now they all—king, ministers, lords, bishops, members of Parliament—had to submit to the people. The Earl of Chesterfield thought differently to our view of the people's opposition. He saw it as nothing more than 'groundless and senseless clamors' instigated by politically motivated rabble-rousers, and condemned the Duke of Newcastle for allowing himself to be intimidated by it. Another contemporary figure, Horace Walpole, the youngest son of Sir Robert Walpole, took a similar view and saw it all as mainly a problem of 'little curates' and drunken aldermen. We cannot agree with these lawmakers in any way, but see in the events of 1753 the defensive struggle of a strong and healthy people against Jewish infiltration.[153]

November 15th, 1753 saw the State Opening of Parliament. The king had barely finished his speech to the assembled members of the House of Lords when the Duke of Newcastle rose and made the formal request that the Jewish Naturalization Act be repealed. To the astonishment of the House, he asked that the last part of the act be left in place, according to which the Jews were forbidden any power to dispose of ecclesiastical benefices. He justified his stance of wishing to repeal the act with the need to prevent further public reaction, the continuance of which could well end up dissuading rich Jews from living in England, which would not be beneficial to the country. Nevertheless, he considered that the latter provision regarding church rights should still be retained, especially since a lack of restriction on Jewish property rights, as regarded Christianity, would cause offence among the masses. Furthermore, he left no doubt that he personally still believed this part of the act to be correct.[154]

---

[153] Stanhope, Vol. IV, pp. 38-9. Translator's note: QVOS (p. 147). & H. Walpole, Vol. I, pp. 357-8. Translator's note: Quoted element as per original source.

[154] H. Walpole, Vol. I, p. 359; *Parl. History*, Vol. XV, pp. 91-4; Coxe, Vol. II, p. 291.

It strikes us as interesting that the act's provision for the protection of the Church was intended to be maintained, and it strengthens our suspicion that this provision represented part of the bishops' price for their support of the Jew Bill. It becomes almost a certainty when, in the subsequent debate, we find complete agreement on this point between the Bishop of Oxford—speaking for his colleagues—and the Duke of Newcastle. He stated that he was not prepared to consent to a repeal of the clause that stopped a Jew from ever being able to 'purchase advowsons, or anything that may give him a right to intermeddle in affairs relating to the Church'.[155]

Various speakers commented in detail on the act in question. Only one of the Lords, Earl Temple, spoke against the act being repealed. In his opinion, the anti-Jewish faction would also demand the repeal of the 1740 law for the colonies, and the time would not be far off when pyres would be built for the burning of Jews. Such fears could only be dispelled by not heeding the people's cries against the law and thus depriving them of any desire for further riots. From Coxe:

> He treated the movers of the opposition with contempt, and pronounced the clamour to be disaffection, clothed with superstition. He trembled lest the Plantation act, which granted Naturalisation to the Jews who resided seven years in the colonies, should be repealed. He trembled also, lest fires should be rekindled in Smithfield, to burn Jews; and declared, that the persecution of the Jews would infallibly lead to the persecution of the dissenters. Finally, he conjured the peers, as a permanent and independent body, not to be swayed in their deliberations, by that popular clamour, which had alarmed the members of the lower House, on the eve of a general election. But these and idle declamations were heard with indifference, amidst the general feeling of the legislature and the country.[156]

Lord Chancellor Hardwicke supported the government's proposal because, given the mood of the people, the Jews who were already settled in England

---

[155] *Parl. History*, Vol. XV, p. 115. Translator's note: QVOS.

[156] *Parl. History*, Vol. XV, pp. 94-99; Coxe, Vol. II, pp. 292-3; Walpole, Vol. I, p. 361. Translator's note: QVOS. Readers will doubtless be familiar with this guilt-based strategy among modern Jews, who will imply that their latest demand not being met is an indication that another 'Holocaust' is imminent, so they therefore should be given whatever they want to prove that their fears are not justified. Note also how Temple suggests that persecution of Jews will naturally end up with persecution of Christians, which looks like an early precursor of today's 'anti-Semitism is everybody's problem', or 'First they came for the Jews' rhetoric. It would be interesting to know if Lord Temple had been given help with his talking points.

would have to fear for their safety on a daily basis. He then continued, 'I am convinced the ill humor of the people would before now have broke out into violence, if it had not been for the hopes they had, that as soon as the parliament met the law would be repealed'. But he objected to the possible repeal of the 1740 Plantation Act because it has been in force for too long, and he worried that this would be a 'breach of public faith', which would threaten future immigration to these places, not just from Jews, but 'from almost every Protestant country in Europe'. Then he got to the really important point regarding the need to maintain the 1740 Plantation Act:

> Even with respect to the Jews, the discouraging of them to go and settle in our American colonies, would be a great loss to, if not the ruin of, the trade of every one of them; for we know that the trade which gives life to the whole, a trade which I do not for very good reasons chuse to name, is chiefly carried on by the Jews, by means of the correspondence they have with their brethren in other parts of America, and without which no such trade could be carried on.[157]

A typical example of English hypocrisy! The noble Lord is reluctant to mention the name of this trade, but is nevertheless concerned that this trade should not suffer because of restrictions imposed on the Jews, lest English interests in the colonies be adversely affected or the English have to dirty their otherwise clean hands. In any case, it should not be too difficult to guess this 'unspeakable' trade: it could only be *the slave trade*, which was carried out mainly by Jews.

The Earl of Granville also spoke out in favor of the Duke of Newcastle's bill. He had to admit that the clamor raised against the act had been 'pretty universal'. In his opinion, the main reason for the clamor was, however, simply because the bill had been given the wrong title.[158] He does not seem to be wrong about this, because in 1740 people had cleverly managed to use such a tactic to divert the people's attention away from what was essentially a Jewish issue.

The aforementioned speech by the Bishop of Oxford is very interesting. Richard Rigby, who had been present when the speech was delivered, described it in a letter to the Duke of Bedford as 'a miserable sermon of three quarters of an hour'. He was probably right, because the content that has come down to us confirms this judgement. It is impossible to go into all of it

---

[157] *Parl. History*, Vol. XV, pp. 99-103; Coxe, Vol. II, p. 292. Translator's note: QVOS [pp. 99-100, 102-3].
[158] *Parl. History*, Vol. XV, pp. 110-4. Translator's note: QVOS. The Earl of Granville (somewhat cynically) suggested that if the law had been titled 'an act to prevent the profanation of the holy sacrament of the Lord's Supper', no public objection would have been made.

here, but we shall reproduce a typical extract from the speech, which we believe was intended to show the public that the bishops had had a change of heart.[159]

As is already known, the Bishop had been one of the earlier advocates of the Jew Bill, and in his speech, he gives his reasons for supporting the bill. He then goes on to say:

> This, my lords, was then my opinion, and I have not yet met with any good reason for altering it; but as the act has given offence to so many of our Christian brethren, and as I do not think it a matter of a very great importance either to religion or the state, I shall in this case be ready, as I shall always be in cases which I do not think of the utmost importance, to sacrifice my opinion to the satisfaction of my Christian brethren. For this reason, I shall be ready to consent to the repeal of that part of the late act which permits Jews to be naturalized...[160]

How often do we hear such words from the clergy during similar events throughout history! On such occasions, surely it would be better for them to ensure that they have the correct position beforehand, so that if the matter is later decided to be important and the people reject their decision, there is not the need for an embarrassing climbdown.

So we see that everyone, with the exception of Lord Temple, was prepared to support the repeal bill because otherwise the 'rabble of the kingdom' might commit further and even worse stupidities. Only one person differs from this attitude in his speech: the Duke of Bedford. He pointed out that he had been against the Jewish Naturalization Bill from the beginning and therefore welcomed the repeal of the Act. But the entire act must be abolished, he told the House of Lords, because the remaining legal provision would contradict common law, according to which the Jews were still the property of the king. Furthermore, one should in no way imagine that the threat from the Jews could be averted solely by forbidding them from acquiring rights connected with the church. Instead, he explained how the opposite would be the case:

> Their power will increase with their property, and as their power increases their privileges will increase. Even at this time they have indulged with the privilege of having public synagogues, though expressly contrary to law...

---

[159] Bedford, Vol. II, p. 139. Translator's note: QVOS
[160] *Parl. History*, Vol. XV, pp. 114-7; Coxe, Vol. II, p. 292; Walpole, Vol. I, p. 359. Translator's note: QVOS (p.115).

> As dominion always will follow property, could we in this case expect they would submit to continue under the disability now proposed to be laid upon them with regard to estates relating to the church? No, my lords, they would not only repeal this law, but every law for establishing Christianity, and establish Judaism in its stead. They might then call this island their own land...

It is unlikely that they would outnumber the English, but that would not be necessary, because 'if they have the sole or the greatest command of money, they may prevail with one half of the natives to assist them in subduing the other, for we know the power of money in politics as well as in war'.

In his further remarks, the Duke of Bedford pointed out that the Jews, while remaining Jews, would always remain 'a people quite distinct and separate from the ancient people of this island', whose influence would be detrimental to the native population. The people were afraid of this foreign infiltration and therefore unanimously defended themselves against it with all the means at their disposal.

He also advocated for the repeal of the 1740 Plantation Act because this left a back door open for Jews to acquire British citizenship. The danger of England becoming Jewish, he starkly warned his peers, had not been averted, because the Jews could still of course become naturalized in the colonies and then settle unhindered in the mother country afterwards, and because of the creeping acceptance of the modern doctrine that Jews born on British territory were 'natural-born subjects':

> [T]hat modern doctrine, that every Jew born in the British dominions is, to all intents and purposes, a natural-born subject, and entitled to all the rights and privileges of an Englishman, which doctrine is, in my opinion, of much more dangerous consequence that the act which is by this Bill to be repealed, and I am fully convinced, that every sensible man in the kingdom will join with me in opinion.[161]

---

[161] *Parl. History*, Vol. XV, pp. 103-10, Coxe, Vol. II, pp. 291-2. Translator's note: All QVOS, and the full speech is available in the Appendix. The Duke of Bedford's defense of the popular opposition is historically important, because Establishment/Jewish historiography has framed the Jew Bill's opponents not as individuals motivated by legitimate concerns for their country's future, but an ignorant mob being artfully manipulated by high-level political rivals of the government who wished to swing the next election in their favor. Even at the time this framing of reality was being used by the bill's proponents to discredit the popular protests, as we see in the parliamentary speeches and *A Collection of the Best Pieces* (1753). The latter source talks of 'Hebrew sophisters' (p. 38) mendaciously using this frame of events, and responds to the charge by saying that if anything will

It can be seen that the Duke of Bedford had done the most to promote the nation's sentiment, and as such wanted the law to be repealed. How Horace Walpole could come to the opposite conclusion is not clear.[162]

The House of Lords voted to annul the entire Jewish Naturalization Act. The Duke of Newcastle's original request to leave the final clause in place was rejected.

The first and second readings took place on November 15 and 20 respectively. The third reading took place on November 23 without a division [vote], then the repeal bill was sent down to the Commons for further consideration. On November 27, the Lords were 'mysteriously summoned' by Lord Temple 'to an affair, as he told them, of great importance'. This affair was his raising of a motion to appoint a committee of judges who would determine whether the Jews could buy land and whether it would legally descend to their children. The Chancellor, Lord Cholmondeley, Lord Granville, and the Duke of Argyle opposed the motion, and nobody supported it, which led to Lord Temple abandoning the idea.[163]

Immediately after the House of Commons reconvened, member of Parliament Sir James Dashwood moved for a special session to be called to repeal the Jewish Naturalization Act. Lord Parker, a government supporter, seconded his motion that the House be summoned on December 4. However, as a result of the bill being sent down from the House of Lords on November 23, they were able to hold the second reading on November 26.[164]

Only one MP, Mr. Potter, was against the majority position, citing the high qualities of the Jews and their services to England, while Sir George Lyttelton in particular was in favor of the repeal bill as it reflected the will of the people.[165]

The second reading took place without any difficulties, but everything did not go as smoothly as might have been expected after the first debate. It was not the content of the repeal bill itself, but rather the preamble to the bill that gave rise to a heated dispute. This is how the contention is described in *Cobbett's Parliamentary History*:

> Nov. 27. In the committee, the preamble to the Bill met with some opposition. It was as follows: 'Whereas an act of par-

---

swing the next election, it will be Jews' money, which may already have been advanced for that purpose.

[162] Walpole, Vol I, p. 360.

[163] *Parl. History*, Vol. XV, pp. 117-8; Coxe, Vol. II, p. 293. & Walpole, Vol. I, p. 363. Translator's note: All QVOS.

[164] *Parl. History*, Vol. XV, p. 118; Coxe, Vol. II, p. 293.

[165] *Parl. History*, Vol. XV, pp. 119-28. Translator's note: I was unable to find direct mentions of the cited elements in this speech, although one could argue that such things are alluded to with deliberate subtlety. & *Parl. History*, Vol. XV, pp. 128-131.

liament was made, and passed in the 25th year of his majesty's reign, entitled, "An Act to permit," &c. and whereas occasion has been taken from the said act, to raise discontents and disquiets in the minds of many of his majesty's subjects; be it enacted.' Some gentlemen, who had all along opposed the Bill, thought that those words in the preamble contained an indecent reflection upon the almost universal sense of the people of England. Sir Roger Newdigate, therefore, moved to leave out the words, 'Occasion has been taken to raise discontents and disquietudes,' and to insert in their stead, 'Great discontents and disquietudes had, from the said act, arisen in.'[166]

Sir Roger Newdigate was a wealthy coal-mine owner and a man with old English ideals, an ancestor—although not a mentor—of the man who would famously fight against Jewish emancipation in the second half of the 19th century, Charles Newdegate, who shall be discussed in more detail in chapter 6.[167] Sir Roger considered the words of the preamble to be inconsistent with the facts:

> [T]he preamble which has been now read to us, gives me the utmost surprize: I cannot but look upon it as a more extraordinary instance of ministerial haughtiness and obstinacy than is to be met with in the British annals.

The preamble would give the impression that the proponents were deigning to declare the law invalid simply to satisfy the misled masses:

> If we agree to this preamble, Sir, we must agree, and every reader must suppose it to have been the opinion of this House, that the law was in itself an innocent and an useful law, but that occasion had from thence been taken by some wicked people, to raise discontents, and to disquiet the minds of many of his majesty's subjects. Now this I say, Sir, is absolutely false in fact. The occasion for those discontents and disquietudes was not taken, but given: it was the law itself that gave the occasion: the more it was considered, the more its evil and dangerous tendency appeared; so that at last a great majority, I may say almost the whole people of this kingdom, came to

---

[166] *Parl. History*, Vol. XV, p. 131. Translator's note: QVOS. This was clearly an attempt by the pro-Jewish faction to get the frame of reality they had propagated into the statute books, in a bid to make it part of the historical record for posterity, thus obliterating the historicity of a populace who had genuinely opposed the Jewish agenda.

[167] *Dictionary of National Biography*, Vol. XIV, pp. 329-332.

look upon it as an affront upon the religion we profess, and a design to introduce amongst us a large body of people, who from interest as well as inclination, nay, who for their own safety, would at all times be ready to support any scheme for the establishment of arbitrary power; and this came at least to be the opinion not only of those of the Established Church, but of almost every man in the kingdom who professes himself, or has any sort of pretence, to be a Christian.

[H]ow different those of this age who pretend to be Whigs, are from their ancestors, may appear from this preamble. Among their ancestors the established maxim was, 'Vox Populi est vox Dei' [the voice of the people is the voice of God]; but their posterity of this age in this preamble told us, that 'Vox Populi est vox Diaboli' [the voice of the people is the voice of the Devil], as it must be, if it be directed by artful and wicked men. But whatever the late patrons of this law may now think, I believe the people of this kingdom, to take them in general, are, upon mature consideration, as good judges of their own interest or honour as the majority of either House of Parliament can pretend to be...[168]

The aforementioned ally of the Jews, Robert Nugent, confronted Sir Roger. He considered Sir Roger's reasons for changing the preamble to be incorrect and therefore opposed the motion. He also tried to portray the whole matter as unimportant and ridiculous:

By these papers and pamphlets a spirit has been raised among the lower sort of people for the repeal of this act, and as it is of so little importance, I think they ought to be humoured; for this sort of people in every country, like children, take now and then a fancy to a hobby-horse, without which there is no keeping them quiet.[169]

Nugent found a wide base of support all too easily, which included Henry Pelham, Horace Walpole and William Pitt. Pelham took the view that 'the clamour was...chiefly among the vulgar and ignorant'. This point found particular agreement with another MP, Sir William Yonge, who stated that:[170]

---

[168] *Parl. History*, Vol. XV, pp. 131-4. Translator's note: All QVOS; square bracketed elements added for reader comprehension. Newdigate's speech is particularly important for its rescue of the English opposition's reputation for the historical record, which is otherwise defamed by Establishment/Jewish historiography.

[169] *Parl. History*, Vol. XV, pp. 134-8. Translator's note: QVOS [p. 135].

[170] *Parl. History*, Vol. XV, pp. 142-5, 150-3, 154-5.

... in all my travels I never met with one man of any consideration, who so much as mentioned this act for permitting the
Jews to be naturalized; therefore I must conclude, that the clamour against it has been entirely confined to the lowest sort of people, who never form any opinion from their own judgment.[171]

To this assertion, Admiral Vernon got up and replied that if the honorable
gentleman had never heard the opinion of the English gentry about the 'Jews
Bill', it was because English gentlemen were too polite to bring up the topic
in his company:

They knew that he had voted for the Jews Bill in every step it
made last session through this House, and that his friends were
the chief promoters of it in both Houses; therefore they were
too polite to condemn or find fault with it in his presence; but
their having made no mention of it is a proof, that they had so
much of the old English sincerity left, as not to applaud with
their tongues what they condemned in their hearts...

Vernon then went on to theorize what these English gentlemen truly thought
of the bill, while defending the people's right to form their own opinions, the
soundness of which were only contingent upon the adequate dissemination
of information:

[A]s the lowest sort of people so generally, and so openly exclaimed against it, I must conclude, that the honest unaspiring
country curates took care to give the people notice of a law
which they thought inconsistent with, and of the most pernicious consequence to the religion they profess, and are sworn
to propagate and maintain; for a due notice was all that the
very lowest of our people wanted for forming from their own
judgment a right opinion of this law. Such sort of people I
know, Sir, may for a long time remain ignorant of what has
been done by the legislature of their country, if no one takes
care to give them due notice of it; but when they have proper
information, whatever the hon. gentleman may think, they are
generally as capable to form from their own judgement a right
opinion, perhaps more capable than those who think themselves much more above the vulgar than they really are.[172]

---

[171] *Parl. History*, Vol. XV, p. 159. Translator's note: QVOS
[172] *Parl. History*, Vol. XV, pp. 159-60. Translator's note: QVOS. The comment about
how the people 'may for a long time remain ignorant of what has been done by the legisla-

Among the various speakers who supported Sir Roger's motion was the Earl of Egmont. Of all of them, he best understood the situation. He made clear that he understood that the preamble was purposefully inserted to ensure that a new Jewish naturalization bill could be reintroduced to the House at the first available opportunity, as the preamble ensured that blame for the repeal was placed on outside forces, rather than it being a fault within the law itself. His suspicions regarding the preamble were made all the stronger not only because of the strenuous opposition that arose to counter the motion that would slightly alter it, but also because of a maxim that had evidently been adopted of late by a great number of people within the House:

> [T]he maxim I mean is, that money does all things, and that therefore the bringing of money into the nation is to be preferred to every other consideration. But I wish that those gentlemen would reflect upon another maxim, I believe much less exceptionable, that money is the root of all evil; for whoever does reflect upon this, will be against bringing any money into the nation that may probably be hereafter employed against us. [173]

The debate indicated that the government would oppose Sir Roger's motion. Consequently, it was not surprising that his amended version of the preamble was rejected by a majority of 113 votes to 47. This is yet another indictment of the so-called democratic system, in which, according to its supporters, the will of the people will always prevail. Because in this particularly egregious case, that is unlikely to be what happened as, all things considered, only the content of Sir Roger's proposed preamble expressed the view of the nation. [174]

On the same day, November 26, the bill to repeal the act was read for the second time, and the third reading took place on November 28. However, the king only gave the royal assent on December 20. [175]

Once again, the anti-Jewish faction did not rest on their laurels. As early as December 4, Lord Harley and Sir James Dashwood tabled a motion to abolish the 1740 Plantation Act. Unfortunately, the debates on this matter have not passed down to us, which is a great pity as they would most certainly have provided some insight on the subsequent trajectory of British history.

---

ture of their country, if no one takes care to give them due notice of it' is likely to be an indirect response to Pelham's earlier argument that the 1740 Plantation Act had been in place for several years 'without causing the least murmur of among the people'.

[173] *Parl. History*, Vol. XV, pp. 155-9. Translator's note: QVOS. Readers may wish to ponder the irony that much of the money which was used to bribe Parliament, money which, as Egmont suggests, could one day be used to enslave the British, was money which itself had come from the trade and labor of slaves in the colonies.

[174] Coxe, Vol. II, pp. 293-7.

[175] *Parl. History*, Vol. XV, p. 162; *Statutes at Large*, Vol. XXI, pp. 158-9.

We can be sure that the risk of Judaization of the American colonies and possibly of the mother land itself, as a result of this law, were discussed in these debates. On the other hand, the contemporary figures who were friendly to Jews have made us thoroughly acquainted with the speeches of their partisans, who of course considered the Jews necessary for the building of the empire and especially for the American colonies. Pelham, who counted among these partisans, emphasized that: 'To part with those who hold our wealth, will be to divest ourselves of our strength.' The Earl of Egmont was right when he said that the question of money played the decisive role in everything.

Given that the government again put up opposition, the anti-Jewish faction were unable to get anywhere with this latter bill, and were defeated by 208 votes to 88.[176]

There was certainly disappointment in popular circles over the latest defeat, but this was eclipsed by the joy over the previous great success, which found expression in corresponding announcements of triumph. So we read that a few days before December 20—the day of royal assent, when the Jewish Naturalization Act was to be officially repealed—great celebrations were prepared in London and Westminster. What happened there certainly also happened in the provinces where the battle had been at least as fierce.[177]

The people had prevailed against the government, the nobility, the clergy and, last but far from least, the Jews' financial resources. There is also some evidence that the royal court may also have been on the Jews' side, which would mean that all of the state's powers had been arrayed against the populace.[178]

Background on the Original Inspiration for the 'Jew Bill'

This section will be dedicated to the question of why and through what influences the original 'Jew Bill' came into being.

As has already been mentioned, contemporary figures also considered this question, and of course we shall take their conclusions into account. They were witness to events, but their clarity of vision may have been somewhat clouded by partiality. In order to reach a reliable conclusion of our own, we must first examine whether the Jew Bill was really so important to have triggered all of these events. Views on this vary widely depending on party position.

The Jews' allies believed that the legislation would only make it possible for a few rich foreign Jews to be granted British citizenship. However,

---

[176] *Parl. History*, Vol. XV, pp. 162-3; Coxe, Vol. II, pp. 297-8; Walpole, Vol. I, pp. 364-7; Hertz, p. 92. Translator's note: QVOS [Coxe, p. 297].

[177] *London Evening Post*, 15/12/1753.

[178] *Parl. History*, Vol. XIV, p. 1365; *The Christian's New Warning Piece*, p. 6.

Philo-Patriae goes further and argues that some Jews also hoped to become landowners sooner or later with the help of the act. Upon superficial inspection, it looks as if these purposes were at least intended. But we have learned from history that the Jews' tactics have always been to legally secure rights that initially seemed unimportant to their host nation, and then gradually, step by step, achieve complete emancipation in the same way.[179]

The ever philo-Semitic Philo-Patriae may well have been correct when he stated that the Jews may have had 'some secret reasons' for pursuing the bill. Unfortunately, the otherwise well-informed author did not speculate on what these reasons might have been. So let us turn to the Jews' opponents to hear what they had to say about the matter.[180]

We do not wish to dwell on judgements that would have been regarded at the time as quite outlandish, such as that London would be sold to foreign Jews. Rather, we only want to deal with those that could have been taken seriously. The opponents saw a threat to the inheritance rights of the English in the fact that the Jews would be allowed to acquire real estate, along with the numerous privileges that this entailed. According to the naturalization bill, they would only be barred from the Privy Council, from both legislative houses and from senior positions in the military and civil service, which meant that the majority of all other positions were open to them. As one anonymous stockholder wrote to the editor of the *Gentleman's Magazine*, these new regulations would undoubtedly lead to the Judaization of the largest English banking and trading companies, such as the East India Company and the Bank of England, as the newly naturalized Jews would be able to become officers, directors, and governors in these companies.[181]

The conditions in many countries that had fallen prey to Judaization would have confirmed the accuracy of these fears.

The government's support of the bill is all the more surprising given that it must have expected a violent public backlash from the outset. Apart from the anti-Jewish element within the populace, they would have known that there would undoubtedly also be resistance from other sections of the population, such as the Catholics and certain Protestant sects, whose rights at that time were more curtailed than those of the Hebrews. William Coxe also

---

[179] *London Evening Post*, 15/12/1753.

[180] Philo-Patriae: *Considerations*, p. 40.

[181] *Motives to the Senseless Clamour*, p. 11. Translator's note: Those reading this text in the 21st century may wish to ponder the irony of this sentence. & *Gentleman's Magazine*, Vol. XXIII, pp. 479-80; *Appeal to the Throne*, pp. 21-2. & *Gentleman's Magazine*, Vol. XXIII, p. 317. & Vol. XXIII, p. 318. Translator's note: This stockholder must have been quite naive to assume that these companies were not already under substantial Jewish influence via the ability of Jews to both hold stock and vote (with votes weighted according to amount of stock held), in the elections of the directors and the governor. For evidence of this with the Bank of England, see Giuseppi [Translator's Bibliography].

opines that 'there was a culpable degree of imprudence' on the part of the government, 'in thus attempting to extend important privileges to a class of men, who by their tenets and habits, must be considered as natural adversaries to the Christian religion.'

We would like to go a little further than Coxe and take the view that, all things considered, the introduction of the Jew Bill first appears to be completely incomprehensible, which is all the more evident when one considers that only a few years before, the government had been struggling to suppress an uprising from a part of the population which wanted to reinstate the Stuarts, and that there was the added complication of an imminent general election. Finally, in many public circles, rising resentment about the increasing government debt burden was an important issue for the government. So why then did the government add to all its woes the danger of a widespread public rejection of the Jewish law, especially when the number of Jews in England at that time was 8,000 to 10,000 at most?[182]

We shall now try to answer this question in the best way we can. In purely numerical terms, the Jewish colony was too small to be a valid explanation for the government's decision. But could it perhaps not have been the same then as in modern times that this small number made the government subservient with the money at its disposal? We know that by asking this question we will immediately provoke objections from our opponents, since in their view such possibilities can only exist in the minds of deluded Jew-haters. Let us therefore first examine the participation of these few Jews in the economic life of England at that time. It will never be possible to provide precise information on this topic, as there was undoubtedly a lot of Jewish capital invested in Christian companies, which would therefore not have been externally visible as such.

Philo-Patriae has dealt with this problem in great detail. We feel able to rely on his research findings, as he certainly cannot be accused of being anti-Jewish. According to this author, 'several Jews alone have brought £1.5 million into the country.' In other words, a tiny fraction of the 8,000 to 10,000 Jews already represented considerable capital. According to Philo-Patriae's calculations, in 1753 the Jews possessed a twelfth of England's total income and controlled at least a fifth of her exports. Philo-Patriae also considered five million pounds to be a reasonable estimate of the total Jewish capital in Britain at the time, an estimate which is also shared by Josiah Tucker. It is therefore not surprising that on Jewish holidays, 'the *Royal-Exchange*, the Center of Business, is always remarkably thin.' One could even speak of an overall Jewish supremacy on the Royal Exchange, with a particular Jewish predom-

---

[182] Coxe, Vol. II, pp. 290-1. Translator's note: QVOS. & Hanway, pp. 66-67. Translator's note: Hanway gives his own estimate as 7,000, though states that the Jews themselves gave a figure of 10,000, while Philo-Patriae [see Endelman, p. 172] puts the figures at 8,000.

inance in the trading based on speculation. The Royal Exchange was already the most important stock exchange in the world around 1750, and since a substantial number of Jews were represented there, as the turnover increased, their number would have also increased steadily, making their influence on stock exchange transactions in London (and through these transactions, on a large part of the world) quite significant.[183]

Finally, the pro-Jewish side goes on to demonstrate that there were sectors of trade which the Jews not only dominated but held the monopoly position. The coral trade with India, which was flourishing at the time, was almost entirely controlled by them. This was also the case with the diamond trade and its related industries (e.g. diamond polishing, jewelry, the trinket trade).[184]

Even this brief overview of the Jews' share in the economic life of England at that time shows that their influence was vastly disproportionate to their population size.

Did this Jewish dominance remain limited to the economic sphere, or did it—as always inevitably happens—also come to have an impact in other spheres of national life, such as politics?

After considering all of the facts, we believe we can be certain that this Jewish influence in England became more than simply economic, for various reasons. The question of whether the Jews had already had a significant influence on the Masonic lodges at this time is a matter of much debate. The lodges had resumed their activity in England around 1720, but were initially not very important. However, once the leading Whigs joined, the lodges began a very rapid ascent of power.[185]

There is no doubt that the Duke of Newcastle was a Freemason, for we learn that in 1731 he was made Master of the Lodge in the house of Sir Robert Walpole. Therefore we can also be certain that the latter was likewise a Freemason. Given what we know about his stance towards the Jews from the previous chapter, is it a valid hypothesis that these two politicians may even have supported each other as lodge brothers? Although we have no evidence that the law came about because of the connection between Jews and Freemasonry, we do know that around 1740 there were already 181 Freemasonic lodges, of which many Jews were members.[186] We do not wish to deny the influence of the Freemasons, but in the absence of positive evidence in this

[183] Philo-Patriae: *Further Considerations*, p. 34. & Philo-Patriae: *Further Considerations*, p. 35. & Tucker: *Second Letter*, p. 21. & Philo-Patriae: *Further Considerations*, p. 16. Translator's note: QVOS. & Postlethwayt, Vol. I, p. 94 ff.; Jacobs, pp. 233-4. Translator's note: It is unclear what the Postlethwayt reference refers to, given that the pages are unnumbered and the book is structured as alphabetized encyclopedia entries.
[184] Philo-Patriae: *Further Considerations*, p. 44.
[185] Wolfstieg, Vol. II, p. 197. & Begemann, p. 32 ff.
[186] Begemann, p. 324.

regard, we would prefer that any conclusion we reach is based on solid, impeccable facts.

In some pamphlets, there are references to the fact that the Jews would be prepared to subscribe to a loan if the Jew Bill were passed, and a newspaper article published in Amsterdam also seems to refer to this. The Jews then declared their willingness to issue a loan with an interest rate of only 2.5%. The news about this ends with the words: 'This non-public loan may have been one of the motives that led the minister to favour the naturalisation law for Jews in England.'[187] Although a larger number of Jews were probably involved in the raising of this loan, the principal Jewish merchants of the day, listed by Picciotto, are likely to have been the main players in the task. We shall proceed to discuss some of these individuals in more detail.[188]

First, let us take a look at Joseph Salvador [Joseph Jessurun Rodriguez]. He was the president of the congregation and a partner in the well-known house of Francis and Joseph Salvador. It almost goes without saying that he had great wealth. He was the first Jew to be appointed as a director of the Dutch East India Company, and he had an international reputation as an economist. His usefulness to the state was proven by his repeated negotiation of loans for the British government. As a result, he was very well acquainted with the country's political leaders. We learn that shortly after the law was passed in the summer of 1753, 'Mr. Salvadore, the rich Jew, who married the Daughter of Baron Suasso, gave a grand Entertainment at his Seat at Tooting in Surrey, to a great Number of Noblemen and Gentlemen, Members of both Houses of Parliament.' It is not unlikely that the success achieved in the legislative houses was celebrated on this occasion. Furthermore, it has been asserted that Salvador played a significant role in the law's creation, as we learn in this news item dripping with cynical irony:[189]

> We can assure the Publick, that J[osep]h S[alvado]re, Esq; who was so extremely instrumental in procuring the late famous Naturalization Act for the Children of Israel, threaten'd, that if it did not take Place, he would leave the Kingdom of England, with all his Effects—A Menace of such Importance, that we cannot wonder at the Influence it had upon our Patriot Rulers; who, in every Instance, are surprizingly attentive to the Good of the Nation.[190]

---

[187] *London Evening Post*, 7/6/1753. Translator's note: There may be an error in this reference.
[188] Picciotto, pp. 93-4.
[189] Picciotto, p. 162-3. Hyamson: *History*, p. 212; *Jewish Encyclopedia*, Vol. X, p. 663. & *London Evening Post*, 10/7/1753. Translator's note: QVOS.
[190] *London Evening Post*, 26/7/1753. Translator's note: QVOS.

Another Jew, Solomon da Costa, may provide even better evidence of illicit influence on the country's lawmakers. He was also very rich and had mainly earned his money as a broker. He was praised for his generosity towards the poor. Apparently, however, he did not limit his generosity only to the poor, as the Whig philosopher Thomas Hollis, a personal friend of da Costa, informs us that:[191]

> To this same gentleman [da Costa] several of our leaders in the House of Commons have been in no small degree indebted for their fame there in funds and money-matters, which no one understands more clearly, deeply, than himself, nor probably so well; and by his credit with them he has been enabled to effect, at times, even national good offices.[192]

Solomon da Costa's biographer also knew of this passage and, with reference to it, established corrupt relationships between the financier and various leading personalities. Hyamson objects to such an interpretation, but fails to explain why he disagrees. Regarding another wealthy Jew, Franco, it became publicly known that on the day the Jewish law was passed he had withdrawn 27 banknotes of £1,000 each from the bank, which were undoubtedly amounts that he paid to those involved as their reward for passing the law:[193]

> The Day the *Jew Bill* pass'd, Mr. Fr*nc* took out of the Bank *Twenty-seven* Bank-Notes for *One Thousand Pounds* each.[194]

Sampson Gideon, 'The Pillar of State Credit'

To gain a proper understanding of the direct influence that the Jews had on the law being passed, we must look closely at their uncrowned king, or, in the words of the Jew James Picciotto, 'the Rothschild of the day, the friend of Walpole, the pillar of state credit'. Abudiente was his original patronymic, which he later changed to Gideon to better conform to English sensibilities.[195]

---

[191] *Jewish Encyclopedia*, Vol. IV, p. 292; Hollis, p. 614. Translator's note: It should be noted that according to the sources, much of his charity money went to non-Jews as well as to his coreligionists (i.e. it would appear to be true charity, as opposed to ethnic activism disguised as philanthropy).

[192] Hollis, Vol. II, pp. 614. Translator's note: QVOS.

[193] Hyamson: *Solomon da Costa*, p. 261. Translator's note: It is a pity that Aldag did not give the biographer's name.

[194] *London Evening Post*, 16/10/1753. Translator's note: QVOS.

[195] Picciotto, p. 60. Translator's note: QVOS. & Picciotto, p. 62. Mesquita, pp. 240-1. Translator's note: As Mesquita makes clear, the name Gideon was an existing family patronymic from his Portuguese Marrano ancestry, but Gideon's official name with the synagogue remained Sampson de Rehuel Abudiente [Picciotto, p. 64].

Gideon was born in 1699. His father, who died in 1720, left him an estate of £7,900, with which he began his career as a merchant. By 1729 he had already earned enough to start working as a broker with a capital of £25,000. Now his great rise took place. We find him in active trade relations with the East India Company and the South Sea Company, while at the same time working to gain major interests in Dutch and French government securities. There was hardly any part of the world in which Gideon did not have connections. When war with Spain broke out in 1742, his correspondence shows that he was consulted by government ministers to make the necessary arrangements to raise money for the war. To this end, he devised a scheme to raise £3,000,000, making himself answerable for a considerable portion of it. From his letters to Pelham, we can see that the very next year Gideon presented the then Prime Minister with a scheme for raising 'supplies' [funds], and another scheme in 1744, when the French fleet was in the Channel and the government securities falling daily.

By 1745 he had already accumulated a fortune of around £80,000. However, he was to experience the typical Jewish financier's career trajectory in the turmoil of 1745-1746, which allowed him to nearly double his fortune in one year. At this time, as is well known, the Young Pretender was marching inexorably on London, and the government's defeat seemed certain. Everyone was therefore trying to get rid of their government securities as quickly as possible, which ultimately had little commercial value due to a lack of buyers. Then, to everyone's astonishment, Gideon began buying up all of the government securities available. All of his cash and all of his credit was exploited to this end, and he came to hold as much paper as all the remaining speculators put together. After a short time, once it was clear that there was no longer a danger of the government being ousted, the stocks and bonds recovered, which meant that, in one fell swoop, Gideon nearly doubled his fortune.[196]

As early as 1749, Pelham called upon Gideon's services again and, at the Prime Minister's request, the Jewish financier drew up a plan to reduce interest on government securities. Of course, the holders of these bonds were not pleased and declared that they were ready to put up resistance to the change. But Gideon exerted all of his influence in financial circles and managed to convince the bondholders of the necessity for a rate reduction and the possible benefits that might accrue to them if they accepted it.

Immediately afterwards, Pelham tried to raise government funds with another individual, but this proving to be a failure, Pelham summoned Gideon again, who promised to raise the desired £3,000,000 by means of a three

---

[196] Nichols: *Illustrations*, Vol. VI, pp. 277-8. & Francis, pp. 97-8; Picciotto, pp. 60-1.

percent loan. He himself immediately subscribed the sum of £100,000, and within three days the whole amount had been raised.[197]

It can be assumed, particularly in these last two cases, that Gideon was richly compensated by appropriate payment or other concessions from the government. What this would mean in real terms can no longer be determined, but it is interesting that, as has been previously discussed, a general naturalization bill was introduced in 1750. This coincidence does not lose its significance just because Gideon publicly announced that he had nothing to do with it, as one can consider as a reliable rule of thumb that the stronger the denial, the greater the probability that the denied fact is true. Such an understanding of events may be particularly appropriate here, since there is no doubt that the Jews made serious efforts to be included in the 1750 bill and to get it passed.[198]

At the outbreak of the Seven Years' War in 1756, Gideon subscribed around £107,000 from his fortune, which had now increased to around £300,000, to what became known as the Hanover loan. Two years later, in 1758, he was very instrumental in completing the first and second payment of that loan. More than ever, he enjoyed the unlimited confidence of government ministers, notably the Duke of Newcastle. During those years the government 'almost wholly relied on' Sampson Gideon for raising the funds needed to prosecute the war.[199]

---

[197] Nichols: *Illustrations*, Vol. VI, p. 278.

[198] Nichols: *Illustrations*, Vol. VI, p. 283. Translator's note: 'He took no part in the year 1750, in the Bill for naturalizing the Jews. He was much offended with that body for making use of his name and influence in soliciting and procuring that measure, and wrote a letter addressed to the Wardens or Elders of the Portuguese Jews, dated in 1750, to withdraw himself from that communion assuring them at the same time, "that he did not by this step intend to discontinue his charity, and that he should in his life-time, and at his death, convince them of the great regard he had for the necessities of his fellow creatures." In another letter he says "the affair you mention does not in the least concern me, having always declared my sentiments against any innovation; but contrary to my wishes and opinions, it was solicited in folly, and want of knowledge, granted in lenity and good nature as a matter of no consequence, and now prosecuted with malice to serve a political purpose. It would give me concern as an Englishman, if I apprehended any danger to my country; but, as I look upon it in a trifling light, I am perfectly easy, and shall not choose to meddle either way."' *Ibid.* Given these letters, and the fact that he married a Christian, raised Christian children and gave to Christian charities, it is in fact plausible that Gideon was not very interested in the Jewish emancipation battle, perhaps (with justification, as seen three years later) fearing that being linked to Jewish activism could prove to be bad for future business and personal ventures. If therefore he was indeed influential in the later 1753 bill, it would be only at the highest levels of government, on a wink-and-nod basis, known to very few and impossible to prove. But regardless of the facticity of this non-falsifiable claim, the cartoons of the day show that the satirists believed Gideon to be the prime mover behind the issue.

[199] Nichols: *Illustrations*, Vol. VI, pp. 279-80. Translator's note: QVOS.

We have relied primarily on Nichols' account of Gideon's business career and will continue to do so as far as possible, because it is compiled from documents in the Eardley family archives and can therefore, in case of doubt, make a strong claim to accuracy.[200]

Gideon also made history in another way, as he was one of the first leading Jews to marry an English woman. His wife Jane (or Elizabeth—her first name is disputed), daughter of Charles Ermell Esq., came from a respectable family. From this point onwards, the Judaization of the English nobility was to progress slowly at first, but later more quickly and inexorably. Gideon's eldest son Sampson was born in 1745, and in 1759 the boy entered the famous English public school of Eton, which only accepted the sons from the most exclusive circles. Sampson's father had brought him up in the faith of his Protestant mother, and Gideon himself had gradually become outwardly apostate from the Jewish religion, as can be seen from his announcement to the elders of the Portuguese Jewish community in 1754 that he was leaving the synagogue.

As we shall see, Gideon had a strong sense of personal ambition, to which his religion very often proved an obstacle. The events of 1753 had probably shown him that the time for emancipation had not yet come and that it was better for him to abandon the Jewish faith. [Translator's note: It should be noted that he was never baptized, nor formally abjured Judaism.] But how much he remained a Jew at heart, even in terms of religion, is evident from the fact that when he died in 1762 he asked to be buried in the Jewish cemetery. This wish would be granted to him all the more readily by his co-religionists given that he had bequeathed £1,000 to the synagogue in his last will and testament. [Translator's note: He also never stopped paying his synagogue *finta*, which he did under the obvious anonym of Peloni Almoni.] He left his children a huge fortune, the exact amount of which differs according to different sources; e.g. one source talks of £400,000, while others of £580,000. Based on the then-much-greater purchasing power of the pound, it would have been a vast estate in either case.[201]

---

[200] Nichols: *Illustrations*, Vol. VI, p. 284. Translator's note: Gideon's son followed in his father's footsteps and changed his surname, this time to Eardley, no doubt to recall his illustrious maternal grandfather (see next footnote).

[201] Nichols: *Illustrations*, Vol. VI, p. 283; Solomons, p. 209; Landa, p. 288. Translator's note: Gideon did most definitely marry into a respectable Christian family – his father-in-law was educated at Tonbridge, Eton, Oxford, and Lincoln's Inn. See Namier & Brooke [Translator's Bibliography]. & Picciotto, pp. 61-2. Translator's note: Although most sources give 1754 as the date of Gideon's leaving the synagogue (the *DNB* giving 1753), Nichols gives the year as 1750 [see footnote 301], which would make sense, as Gideon would likely have wished to prevent future instances of the Jews using his name for Jewish activism without his consent. & Nichols: *Illustrations*, Vol. VI, p. 280. Translator's note: I did not find the cited figure at this source (it mentions a total fortune of £350,000 in

In 1757, Gideon made serious efforts to obtain a peerage, as can be seen from a letter addressed to him from the Duke of Newcastle, dated June 13 of that year. It reads as follows:

> I this morning mentioned to his Majesty what you desired about the Baronetage, and acquainted him with the service you had been of in relation to raising the supplies, and particularly how much obliged I thought myself to you, and urged the zeal you had shewn on all occasions to serve the public. The King seemed extremely well disposed, spoke very handsomely of you, and said he should have no objection himself to oblige you, but as you was not bred up in the religion of the country he was afraid it would make a noise and that in a time of Confusion and Public Distress as the present is, he was afeared they would make an Ill-use of it, and therefore desired that I would inform you in the civilest manner that it was not convenient with him to comply with your request.[202]

From this statement, we can conclude that the king and ministers were happy to raise the Jew to the nobility, but they feared the people's reaction. We can also see that the tumultuous year of 1753 was not forgotten by either the king or the government.

The correspondence between the Duke of Newcastle and Gideon that has come down to us indicate that the latter made further attempts in this regard—and that these too resulted in failure. Apparently a compromise was reached when, by a patent of nobility dated 21 May 1759, Gideon's 13-year-old son, styled in the document as 'Sampson Gideon the younger, Esq., Son of Sampson Gideon, of Spalding in co. Lincoln, and of Belvedere in co. Kent, Esq.', was raised to the rank of baronet. This rank appears not to have been to Gideon's complete satisfaction, because when he sent his son the patent, he also wrote an accompanying letter, in which the boy was exhorted to 'remember his dignity,' to 'maintain a conduct worthy of his rank,' and 'though it were the lowest hereditary honor in the country, it was frequently a step to higher.' These last words in particular seem to betray an undertone of disappointment.[203]

1759, three years before his death). & Mesquita: p. 241; *Dictionary of National Biography*, Vol. XXI, p. 289.

[202] Nichols, Vol. VI, pp 279-80; Landa, p. 287. Translator's note: The quotation is an amalgamation of the letter as found in both sources, each version having its own elision.

[203] Landa, p. 287-9. Translator's note: As Landa states, it must have particularly mortifying for Gideon that the halakhically Jewish Kitty Villareal's daughter had entered the peerage as Viscountess Galway. & Nichols: *Literary Anecdotes*, Vol. IX, p. 642. Translator's note: QVOS, although it is unclear how close these are to the original letter. Gideon

Samson Gideon not only longed for a peerage, but he had long nurtured a strong desire to become a landowner. Since this was not possible for the Jews, there were considerable difficulties in granting him an exception. Sir Robert Walpole therefore introduced a special bill to Parliament on behalf of his friend and financial advisor, under which Gideon was to be expressly authorized to purchase land. Having touched on Robert Walpole's political career, we cannot be too surprised by this action. The reader will then assume, correctly, that this bill was made law. Apparently the bill was waved through quietly, so that the public got to know virtually nothing about it. The traditional historical sources also remain silent on the matter. Gideon immediately exercised his right under this new dispensation, and we soon see him as a landowner in Belvedere, Kent, and also as owner of the manor of Spalding, Lincolnshire.[204]

Given all of this, it should now be quite clear that the Jewish Naturalization Act did not come into being without influence from the Hebrews. The Jewish side also openly admits that it was Gideon who, at the same time as the bill was going through Parliament, wanted to have the question clarified as to whether Jews could become property owners or not. As a result, one could presume that Gideon would see the law as a step closer to his desired goal.

Certainly, this is the belief of the Jew Israel Solomons, who puts forward his theory in no uncertain terms:

> It may be conjectured that Gideon undoubtedly exercised great influence with the Pelhams in promoting the Naturalisation Bill ...
>
> Gideon, perhaps from purely personal or selfish motives, was anxious for the success of the project. Should the Bill pass, it might be the stepping-stone to further concessions. He was an ambitious man, eager for social aggrandisement, with hopes of a seat in Parliament and a place in the baronetage.[205]

We do not have much to add to this statement, but we would like to point out that this would only be yet another case in history in which a single Jew was able to push through a law for his own ethnic benefit, with the help of the government, against the will of the host nation, using means that are not difficult to guess—albeit, as in this case, only for a short time.

Jr. appears to have inherited his father's aspirations to higher nobility, being raised to the Irish peerage in 1789.

[204] Nichols: *Illustrations*, Vol. VI, p. 282; Picciotto, p. 62; Hyamson: *History*, p. 224; Nichols: *Literary Anecdotes*, Vol. VI, p. 85. We must assume that the bill was made law at some point before 1759, given that Gideon's land ownership is reflected in his 13-year-old son's aforementioned patent of nobility.

[205] Solomons, pp. 210-1. Translator's note: QVOS.

Endemic Corruption

Before we answer the previously posed question about the ulterior motives
for the law that was alien to the people, we must take a brief look at the general conditions of parliamentary life and the leading politicians in the twenty
years prior to 1753.

It would probably be useful to write a book about the parliamentary
system of 18th-century England in order to correct the false impression that is
often still held about the English political scene of times past. Sadly, such a
book is outside of the scope of this study, but on the other hand, one cannot
understand the reasons for the law's existence without knowing more about
the deplorable circumstances in which it was passed. Furthermore, these
scandalous conditions show how much Jewish influence over politics can
poison the views of a nation's ruling class.

We have already briefly referred to the corruption of members of Parliament around the year 1700. Nothing would change with the accession of
the Guelphs to the throne. On the contrary—if major corruption were ever
possible in England, it was evident in their time. Parliamentary corruption
had become so extreme and Parliament so subservient to the influence of the
government, that the people feared Parliament 'becoming in time rather the
oppressor than the representative of the people.' The funds that a candidate
had to expend in order to be elected to Parliament were so enormous that
only members of rich families could stand as representatives. It was publicly
known that certain constituencies were awarded to the highest bidder. The
result of this was that the respective representatives of the people wanted to
somehow recoup the money that they had spent on their electoral campaigns,
and so it was not unusual for them to receive annual salaries from a certain
group for their behavior in Parliament. As William Lecky states in his *History of England in the XVIIIth Century*:[206]

> Great sums of secret-service money were usually expended in
> direct bribery, and places and pensions were multiplied to
> such an extent that it is on record that out of 550 Members
> there were in the first Parliament of George I, no less than 271,
> in the first Parliament of George II no less than 257, holding
> offices, pensions, or sinecures.[207]

Nothing about these deplorable conditions had changed by the time the 'battle year' of 1753 arrived. Complaints about general corruption and degeneration were repeatedly encountered. The intensity of the anger over this scan-

---

[206] Lecky, Vol. II, p. 45. Translator's note: QVOS.
[207] Lecky, Vol. II, p. 46 ff. Translator's note: QVOS (p. 47).

dalous corruption is best expressed in a newspaper article from the *London Evening Post*, an extract of which is reproduced below:[208]

> It has been often said, that Money does all Things here, and not without Reason; for are not Honours, Titles, and all the Privileges and Birthright of Britons to be bought? It matters not from whence the Person comes, or how the Gold was got; was Beelzebub himself to come in *Propria Persona*, and stand a Candidate for a Place, he certainly would carry it, if he brought Cash enough.[209]

As a consequence, in 1753 corporations of honorable men were formed to combat all of these evils. It is doubtful whether they had much success, but in any case, nothing further is known. At the time it looked as if the upcoming elections of 1754 were threatening to eclipse all other concerns. On 7 February 1754, Sir John Barnard, whom we have already encountered, moved to have the 'Bribery Oath' repealed in Parliament. He justified his request by saying that if this oath remained valid, the newly-elected members of Parliament would almost without exception commit perjury when taking their seats, since generalized bribery was already evident to everyone. His motion was rejected by the majority. Another reformative attempt by the Bishop of Worcester in the House of Lords was also doomed to failure. In the same year, Fox declined to accept leadership of the House of Commons from Newcastle, unless he received information about the disposition of the secret-service money, because, as he said, 'if he was kept in ignorance of that, he should not know how to talk to Members of Parliament, when some might have received gratifications, others not'.[210]

This general corruption of the first half of the 18th century is inextricably linked to the name of Sir Robert Walpole. As early as 1712, this arch-Whig was removed from Parliament on corruption charges and was even imprisoned in the Tower for a few months. It is sometimes claimed that the latter incident is only due to his Tory political opponents. Under Sir Robert's later era of government, there was no state institution that was not bribed. He bribed George II by getting him a civil list which exceeded his father's by more than £100,000 a year. He bribed the Queen by securing for her a jointure of £100,000 a year. He bribed the Dissenting ministers to silence by the Regium Donum for the benefit of their widows.[211]

---

[208] *London Evening Post*, 15/5/1753, 26/6/1753, 4/9/1753.

[209] *London Evening Post*, 9/6/1753. QVOS.

[210] *London Evening Post*, 24/7/1753, 7/8/1753. & Walpole, Vol. I, p. 369. & Lecky, Vol. I, p. 431. Translator's note: QVOS.

[211] Lecky, Vol. I, pp. 376, 427.

There should be no doubt that the money made available to him in the budget for secret purposes was used to bribe a majority of MPs. Although such incidents were already commonplace in the times of King Charles II, the times of Sir Robert Walpole can hardly be surpassed. As Lord Chesterfield says of him:

> Money, not prerogative, was the chief engine of his administration; and he employed it with a success which in a manner disgraced humanity. He was not, it is true, the inventor of that shameful method of governing which had been gaining ground insensibly ever since Charles II, but with uncommon skill and unbounded profusion he brought it to that perfection, which at this time dishonours and distresses this country, and which (if not checked, and God knows how it can be now checked) must ruin it.
>
> Besides this powerful engine of government, he had a most extraordinary talent or persuading and working men up to his purpose... When he found anybody proof against pecuniary temptations, which, alas! was but seldom, he had recourse to a still worse art; for he laughed at and ridiculed all notions of public virtue, and the love of one's country, calling them 'The chimerical school-boy flights of classical learning'; declaring himself at the same time, 'No saint, no Spartan, no reformer.' He would frequently ask young fellows, at their first appearance in the world, while their honest hearts were yet untainted, 'Well, are you to be an old Roman? A patriot? You will soon come off of that, and grow wiser.'

Among other things, Tobias Smollett has this to say about Sir Robert Walpole:

> He was well acquainted with the nature of the public funds, and understood the whole mystery of stock-jobbing [financial trading]. This knowledge produced a connection between him and the money corporations, which served to enhance his importance. He perceived the bulk of mankind were actuated by a sordid thirst of lucre; had sagacity enough to convert the degeneracy of the times to his own advantage; and on this, and this alone, he founded the whole superstructure of his subsequent administration.[212]

---

[212] Lecky, Vol. I, p. 427-431; Stanhope, Vol. IV, Appendix p. 35 ff. Translator's note: All QVOS [Stanhope, pp. 36-7]. Readers may also not be surprised to learn that he was noto-

Sir Robert himself evidently considered the materialist desire for greater wealth, power, and pleasure to be the only meaningful motivator in life and ridiculed the purity and patriotism of young people, while resisting every attempt to improve the system. As Lecky writes:

> Other ministers may have bribed on a larger scale to gain some special object, or in moments of transition, crisis, or difficulty. It was left to Walpole to organise corruption as a system, and to make it the normal process of parliamentary government.[213]

Just as detrimentally to the country's future, Lecky also describes how Walpole 'drove from power every man of real talent who might possibly become his rival, and especially repelled young men of promise, character, and ambition, whom a provident statesman, desirous of perpetuating his policy beyond his lifetime, would especially seek to attract'. We must surely ask ourselves, is this materialism and corruption not also the basic belief system and modus operandi of the Jews?[214]

Henry Pelham, who was responsible for the 'Jew Bill' alongside his brother, the Duke of Newcastle, also proved to be an able protégé of his friend and in-law Sir Robert Walpole. Even if they were completely opposite in character, they still had in common the general ruthless bribery of those who could be used to achieve their goals. For us it is irrelevant why Pelham did this. All that matters here is the determination of the fact. He too was convinced of the correctness of such a system, and as a result he was in no way inferior to his mentor Walpole. 'The difference was,' a contemporary reports, 'that Mr. Pelham always bribed more largely as he had more power'.[215]

Pelham's brother, the Duke of Newcastle, was no different to his brother or to Walpole, his close ally and distant in-law, when it came to corruption. In Lecky's words:

---

rious for his philandering, being an open adulterer, for his over-indulgence in fine food and drink, and for his love of obscene conversation.

[213] Lecky, Vol. I, p. 432 ff.; Francis p. 107. Translator's note: QVOS. [There would appear to be an error with the Francis reference.]

[214] Lecky, Vol. I, p. 426. Translator's note: QVOS.

[215] Coxe, Vol. I, p. 8. & *Dictionary of National Biography*, Vol. XLIV [44], p. 246; Stanhope, Vol. IV, Appendix p. 46. Translator's note: From the DNB's entry on Pelham: 'It is true that he chiefly maintained his influence in parliament by an elaborate system of corruption; but Horace Walpole, who hated him, believed that he "would never have wet his finger [in corruption] if Sir Robert Walpole had not dipped up to the elbow; but as he did dip, and as Mr. Pelham was persuaded that it was as necessary for him to be minister as it was for Sir Robert Walpole, he plunged as deep."' & Walpole, Vol. I, p. 235. Translator's note: QVOS. This is also the source for the quoted portion in the previous footnote quotation.

Newcastle is certainly the most remarkable instance on record of the manner in which, under the old system, great possessions and family or parliamentary influence could place and maintain an incapable man in the first position in the State. In private life or in a subordinate office the glaring weaknesses of his character would have been comparatively unnoticed, and he would have been justly respected as a man of pure morals, warm affections, and sincere and unaffected piety. Unfortunately, however, he inherited a greater parliamentary influence than any other English noble, and he was devoured by the most feverish and insatiable ambition. Without any of the aims or capacities of a legislator, or any sordid desire for the emoluments of office, he delighted beyond all earthly things in its occupations, interests, and dignity, in the secret and corrupt management of Parliament, in the dispensation of bribes, places, and pensions.[216]

Having been shown the corrupt political system of that period, the reader may like to guess why the Bevis Marks Synagogue received such large sums from its members and made every effort to get the 'Jew Bill' of 1753 passed into law. It is most interesting that a Jew, the aforementioned Israel Solomons, has given us information on the matter, which reads as follows:

The Bevis Marks Synagogue, the richest and most influential at that time, no doubt made great efforts to insure the success of the [Jewish naturalisation] movement, which meant so much to the majority of its congregants. Funds were subscribed in furthering the propaganda, and combating the anti-Jewish literature that flooded the country... In a conversation I had with my friend, the learned Haham Dr. M. Gaster, I gathered from him that in the archives of his synagogue the whole history of the movement from the Jewish standpoint is to be found. From it, one can gather what efforts the Jews themselves made to gain their first political victory, what was the plan of campaign, the amounts of the funds, and in which manner they were expended.[217]

Rivers of ink have flowed from Jewish pens about the 'storm year' of 1753, but no Jew has ever publicly referred to these sources, let alone published the

---

[216] Lecky, Vol. II, p. 345-6. See also Coxe, Vol. I, pp. 4-6; Walpole, Vol. I, p. 162 ff.; *Dictionary of National Biography*, Vol. XLIV [44], p. 257. Translator's note: QVOS.
[217] Solomons, p. 211. Translator's note: QVOS.

material. Why is this such a secret? The events happened almost two hundred years ago, and historians always claim that they are trying hard to discover the truth. Here, however, historians seem particularly anxious to avoid
making this material accessible to researchers. There will be a reason for
this, because the factual information that still exists in certain documents has
evidently yet to see the light of day. Perhaps this book will one day become
known in England, and material will be published to refute the accusation.
The one thing we do know is that what has been withheld from the British
public will continue to slumber in the vaults of this synagogue.

*****

At this point in the study, we can say that we have collected enough information to be able to answer the aforementioned question with confidence.
The following is therefore our final statement on the matter:

It is beyond doubt that the Jewish Naturalization Act—even if, according to the Hebrews, it was of little practical importance—was an unjustified
preference for foreigners over the native people. A large part of the English
population had fewer rights than the Jews, even though with their far greater
number and not least because of their blood connection to the English nation,
they had an incomparably greater right to at least the same treatment. If the
government still went ahead, ignoring these circumstances and despite its
own difficult domestic political situation, knowing that the vast majority of
the population would be against it (undeniable after the events of 1751, when
the previous naturalization bill failed and the people's antipathy towards the
idea was revealed), then there must have been a special reason for it to make
such a risky, unpopular move.

As is well known, in the first half of the 18th century, kings, queens,
ministers, members of the nobility, bishops (etc.) could be bought off for
certain purposes. In addition, it is also undeniable that the Jews, under the
leadership of Samson Gideon, had an overwhelming, almost exclusive influence on the shaping of the economy, on politics, and on state finances. Furthermore, they had already gained a firm footing in society, specifically, in
those circles of English society which were directly or indirectly responsible
for the fate of the country. The claims of the anti-Jewish faction that all of
these circles were bribed or otherwise unlawfully influenced by the Hebrews
are confirmed in that the Jewish side admits that Jewish money was used to
get the law made.

Therefore, given the totality of the facts, *prima facie* evidence suggests
that the law was brought into being through improper means. In other words,
all of the circumstances point to the law being passed through bribery or
other illicit influences in accordance with the then prevailing methods of the
government and the legislature. What makes things more difficult for the

Jews is that, according to known historical facts, such behavior is prevalent among them and as a result they would have to prove that this case is an exception rather than the rule.

We have described the events of 1753 in detail because they represent a rare example of the victorious defensive struggle of a healthy people. It was not 'purely religious enthusiasm,' let alone 'the shallowness of English civilization,' as Hertz would have us believe, but natural instincts to ward off foreign infiltration. Already at this time, the Reverend Romaine was shrewdly warning the English people of the '*Absurdity of introducing Party into this Debate*', as Christians were being set against Christians, when the issue was '*entirely between Christians and Jews*':[218]

> When all the other Arts of Calumny and Falsehood fail, then the *Jews* betake themselves to Party Distinctions, trying to raise a *new Jew Interest* in this Kingdom, in Opposition to the *old Christian Interest*: To which End they endeavour to divide the Nation about *their* Affairs, and to support their Cause by Party, since they find they can no longer support it by Argument. And they have already made such a Proficiency in the Science of Faction, that they venture Publicly and in Print to call all *their* Enemies, Enemies to the Government. [...]
>
> We are not surprized at the *Jews* taking these dishonest Methods of dividing us among ourselves; because they are sensible, that if these should fail them, their Cause is desperate. Unless they can attach themselves to some Party, their Interest is lost. They therefore labour this Point. It is their last Resource, and it is a most iniquitous one; because it tends to introduce some new Divisions among His Majesty's good Subjects, whose great Misfortunes it is, that they are already too much divided.[219]

These are truly prophetic words from an Englishman in the year 1753. His prophecy has now become a bitter truth not only in England, but in many countries all around the world.

---

[218] Hertz, pp. 97, 92. Translator's note: QVOS.

[219] Romaine, pp. 91-92. Translator's note: All QVOS (and with original italicization).

CHAPTER 5

INCREASING INFLUENCE OF THE JEWS (1754-1830)

The Judaization of Leading Circles

The Jews' frontal attack of 1753 had failed. It was recognized that the moral strength of the people was still too great to win the battle in this way. The enemy camp first had to be undermined in order to make it sufficiently vulnerable for a new general offensive. Thus, in the 80 years following the 1753 setback, it is possible to detect the almost imperceptible excavation taking place under the surface of England's institutions. This endeavor, to hollow out ideological foundations, was particularly focused on the stronghold of the Jews' opponents, the City of London, which had already taken the lead against the Jews under Cromwell. It was the City's representatives who most actively ignited resistance in Parliament and elsewhere, therefore change had to be brought about in the City if there were to be any chance of success.

The Jews' tactics of attrition undoubtedly include the mixing of Aryan and Jewish blood. It is probably irrelevant to discuss whether these intermarriages took place consciously with this aim in mind. In general, when it comes to the Jewish Question, it is not necessary to discuss whether some process or other to advance Judaism in a country has taken place intentionally according to a well-thought-out plan. We believe that this does happen, but the only thing that matters when deciding on countermeasures is to assess the consequences of the various Jewish behaviors and the Jewish system as a whole on the future of a people. If these prove to be detrimental, then they should be combatted purely out of the instinct for self-preservation, with no need to consider the question of whether this damage is intentional or not.

In our opinion, we do not need to decide whether intermarriage was part of a well-thought-out system for weakening the host nation, beginning mainly through strategic unions with the ruling class. One could respond that the Jew himself—as we will see later—believes in keeping his race pure and even considers it necessary for his people's future. However, a supporter of the theory that the Jews have a premeditated plan for world domination could counter this by saying that in every struggle, individual members of a group must sacrifice themselves for the greater good and so bloodlines of Jewish families must perish together with families of the host nation they have contaminated, unless the inferior race gains the upper hand in such mixing. We see that this mixing would also have an internal logic, or particular benefit, of its own, but there is no space here to go into this in more detail.

We are merely stating that, regardless of whatever view is held, throughout recorded history intermarriage has always been one of the ways in which Judah gradually attains supremacy in a polity. Given all of this, the most practical method (and the only method that works) is to decide to combat the Jews based solely on the result of their general behavior, because in the fight for the existence of a people, a defensive act cannot depend on the moral intention of the people harmed by the influence of an alien body: here the sole and exclusive decision to be made is for the preservation of the people, for which every means must necessarily be justified.

But let us return to the question of intermarriage. Before we return to English history, we must point out a general circumstance that repeatedly emerges with these unions in the history of peoples.

The first intermarriages mostly took place in aristocratic circles or at least in those closely associated with it. The nobility of the 18th and 19th centuries felt their position threatened by the capitalist, who was increasingly making advances in society, and therefore decided to join forces with him. This was particularly the case in circles that were detached from the masses. As a result, a large percentage of the nobility is no longer suitable to lead the fight against this alien influence, preferring instead to accept it into their ranks as equals. As long as the so-called monied nobility is made up of members of the same (Aryan) blood, there is no threat of a blood-based decomposition of a people. But it then becomes a crime against one's own nation if some of this blood is Jewish. Then the general adverse consequences for a national body occur, as the Jews and their descendants gradually wrest leadership out of the hands of those who had previously been responsible for the nation's fate. Imperceptibly at first, the Jew then takes over the reins of the government and the economy and, with the ruthlessness that is unique to him, suppresses the forces that are pushing upward from the people. The leading men will slowly become completely alienated, and a large part of the people will join the Jewish system for better advancement, thus strengthening the Jewish front. As a result, their power becomes ever greater and the fight of the upright people, who put their own ego aside and sacrifice their social position for the good of the whole, becomes increasingly hopeless.

Once the Jew has created this situation, he no longer remains on the defensive, but uses every possible means to silence the fighters who stand up for the people and works to ruin them in every way. This too is seen from history and is apparent to the writer of these lines from the example of many contemporary Englishmen. Therefore, once the hour of decision has arrived for the Jewish Question globally, a position will have to be taken on the extent to which some of the nobility is to be held responsible for the Judaization of a nation.[1]

---

[1] The Jew Jacob Wasserman, in his book *My Life as German and Jew* (p. 144 ff.) also attributes responsibility to the nobility.

In the final chapter of this study, we will attempt to determine the extent to which intermarriage has taken place among the English nobility. Here it is only necessary to show the beginnings of this process.

We have already seen that Gideon married into a respectable Christian family. His son, who as we know was made a baronet in 1759, in 1766 married the daughter of Sir John Eardley Wilmot, Chief Justice of the Common Pleas. He first entered Parliament in 1770 as a member for Cambridgeshire, then represented Midhurst, Coventry, and finally Wallingford. In 1789 he was raised to the Irish peerage as Lord Eardley. He was called 'Mr. Pitt's Jew' because he enjoyed the special confidence of the great English statesman. His two sons predeceased him without leaving any descendants. His three daughters married Baron Say and Sele, Sir Culling Smith, M.P., and Colonel Childers, whose best-known descendants were Hugh Culling Eardley Childers (Chancellor of the Exchequer in one of Gladstone's governments), William Eden (5th Baron Auckland), and his cousin, Miss Rolanda F. Childers.[2]

Sampson Gideon's sister, Rachel de Paiba, also married into the English nobility. Her blood can be found today in the family of the Duke of Norfolk, the Earl Marshal, i.e. the highest representative of the English nobility.[3] In 1757 Gideon married his daughter to William Hall Gage, 2nd Viscount Gage, with a dowry of £40,000, a massive amount for the time.[4]

Hertz also reports on the intermarriage of the stockbroker and dramatist Moses Mendes (d. 1758) with an English woman, whose sons adopted their mother's maiden name of 'Head' by royal warrant after his death, and whose grandson Francis Bond Head was made a baronet in 1838. We also see that in the 18th century, a certain Benjamin da Costa entered into a mixed marriage. He joined the postal service, the first civil servant of Jewish birth in England, while his son was in the excise.[5]

The Jewess Kitty Villareal [née Catherine Rachel da Costa] was an ancestor of a number of English noble families. In her first marriage, which produced two children, she was married to a wealthy fellow Jew. He left her a fortune of around £200,000 and so soon enough new suitors appeared: she married the Englishman William Mellish, who came from a distinguished

---

[2] Landa, p. 286. Translator's note: I did not find this information at the source given, however the information can be found in Namier & Brooke, § GIDEON [afterwards EARDLEY], Sir Sampson [see Translator's Bibliography]. The same source also reproduces Thomas Orde's scathing comment about Sampson Gideon's name change, which is described as 'but a half measure, for the cloven foot is sadly exposed by the preservation of Sampson.' & Hertz, p. 101. & Alger, p. 61. & Solomons: Satirical and Political Prints, p. 210; Hertz, p. 101; Mesquita, p. 241.

[3] Solomons: Satirical and Political Prints, p. 210; Mesquita, p. 241.

[4] Nichols, Vol. VI, p. 278.

[5] Hertz, pp. 101-2. Translator's note: Additional data from the Jewish Encyclopedia (s. v. MENDES [MENDEZ], MOSES) and Dictionary of National Biography (s. v. MENDES, MOSES). & Landa, p. 290.

family and who won a seat in Parliament in 1741 with his wife's money. In 1751, Mellish left the House of Commons to become Commissioner of Excise at £1,000 a year, and nine years later he was promoted to be Receiver-General of Customs at £1,500 a year. After his wife's death, he married Anne Gore, whose family was the ancestral line of the current Earl Winterton and the current Colonial Secretary William Ormsby-Gore, now Lord Harlech: both friends of the Jews and enemies of the new Germany. The latter is described by the Jews themselves as a 'true friend of the Jews.' Kitty Villareal's daughter from her first marriage, a full Jew, married the heir of the 1st Viscount Galway, which means that all of the members of this noble family descended from her. In later years, her granddaughter married the Marquis of Crewe, so this family too can also be regarded as Jewish.[6]

Abraham [renamed William on baptism], Kitty Villareal's son from her first marriage, may have tried to get into Parliament with the help of the Duke of Newcastle, as a letter makes reference to his presence at a by-election. He was married to the Englishwoman Elizabeth Hallifax, who came from a very distinguished family: one of her brothers was Samuel Hallifax, Bishop of Gloucester and later Bishop of St. Asaph, another was Dr. Robert Hallifax, personal physician to the Prince of Wales, later King George IV. A daughter from this marriage married a man who reportedly tricked her out of her inheritance, then she fell into debt and was imprisoned, while Abraham's illegitimate daughter (who inherited nothing and was apprenticed to a dressmaker) married a man named Dutton who became Mayor of Chesterfield.[7]

Charles, a son from Kitty Villareal's second marriage (to Mellish), entered Parliament for the Newark constituency in 1774 and was therefore the second half-Jew to gain a seat, as Gideon's son already had already been elected as an MP for the borough of Cambridgeshire in 1770. Charles Mellish married and had children. His son Henry Francis Mellish became a colonel in the British army and found his way into the highest circles, losing nearly all of his estates during gambling evenings with the Prince Regent, George IV. Colonel Mellish went through the Peninsular War as aide-de-camp to Wellington, before dying childless at the age of 35 in 1817. 'Is it possible,' asks the Jew Landa, 'that Wellington, who was a friend to Jewish emancipation, was influenced by Mellish, who was everybody's favorite, and whose grandmother was a Jewess?'[8]

---

[6] Landa, pp. 271-80; Picciotto, pp. 103-4. & Landa, p. 282. Translator's note: QVOS. & Landa, pp. 271, 282.

[7] Landa, pp. 282-6.

[8] Landa, p. 286. Translator's note: QVOS. It may be something of an exaggeration to call Wellington 'a friend to Jewish emancipation'—see later in this volume (text corresponding to footnote 143), and Volume 6 (text corresponding to footnotes 19 and 74) for occasions on which Wellington thwarted Jewish political plans in the House of Lords.

This short list of mixed marriages may suffice to show very clearly the influence that the marriages of a very few Jews must have had on the leading circles of the time. Even King George IV had two people around him who were related to Jews or related by marriage, Colonel Mellish and Dr. Robert Hallifax, the brother-in-law of Kitty Villareal's fully Jewish son. There can be no doubt that all of these people played their part in promoting the Jewish cause.

The descendants of the rich Jew Jacob Bernal also entered into mixed marriages. His baptized son Mr. Ralph Bernal married a Miss Da Silva, of a Portuguese-Jewish family, and became a magistrate, a land owner and a member of Parliament. In 1844, Ralph's son, Captain Ralph Bernal, married the heiress of Sir Thomas Osborne of Newtown Anner, Tipperary, and on marriage took the surname of Osborne in addition to his own, thus becoming Mr. Bernal Osborne.[9]

We also find mixed marriages in the middle classes towards the end of the 18th century. Picciotto explains this phenomenon in the following way:

> The Jews have ever enjoyed the reputation of being admirers of the fair sex. Many a Samson became an easy prey to many a Delilah. The golden tresses, the sapphire eyes, the soft voices of the fair daughters of Albion did more to draw followers from the Synagogue to the Church than is usually imagined. Nor did lovely English girls disdain the considerable fortunes and dark complexions of the Jews, more especially of those of Sephardic origin.[10]

The London Society for Promoting Christianity Amongst the Jews even went as far as to grant a type of matrimonial loan of £500 to £600 for such mixed marriages. We will hear more about this in a later chapter when we come to discuss the activities of this organization.[11]

Quite apart from the disintegration of the blood, such inter-marriage between the English and the Jews were the reason why the sharp differences that had been identified between the two groups in the tumultuous year of

---

[9] Picciotto, p. 211. Translator's note: Mr. Bernal Osborne can be found in Volume 6, working for the cause of Jewish emancipation when he supports the Jew David Salomons in his attempt to (illegally) take up his seat in Parliament.

[10] Picciotto, p. 200. Translator's note: QVOS.

[11] Picciotto, p. 285. Translator's note: This appears to be a misreading of the source, if indeed the source reference is correct—the sum is referred to in the source, but has nothing to do with marriage grants (or any sort of grant), which are not mentioned. I would cautiously suggest that if there were grants of £500 available in 19th-century England for a Christian to marry a Jew, there would scarce be a member of the poorer classes, whether Christian or Jewish, who would not contemplate entering into such a union, if only for financial convenience.

1753 were, if initially hardly visible, at least gradually eroded. Inter-marriage brought the two peoples into contact with one another, and with the help of the ever-expanding propaganda in favor of the Jews and the lack of a counter-movement, people believed that the previously prevailing prejudices had to be dropped. The existence of these mixed marriages was also a reason for the Jews' eventually emancipation, and while it may not be a major reason, it is still one which should not be overlooked.

A New Wave of Immigration

From the second half of the 18th century onwards, ever larger masses of Jews poured into England from Holland, Germany, and Poland. It was mainly external factors that caused the Jews to abandon their previous residence in favor of England, where they already enjoyed unfettered freedom at that time. The Poet Laureate Robert Southey, who in 1808 published a description of England under the pseudonymous identity of Spanish traveler Manuel Alvarez Espriella, even stated that: 'It is not merely the open exercise of their religion which is permitted them, they are even suffered to write and publish against Christianity.' As early as 1755, numerous new arrivals of Jews from Lisbon were noted. A major earthquake had caused considerable damage there, and some of the Jews likely did not want to stay there during the years of reconstruction, as such times generally yield less profit.[12]

The partition of Poland in 1772 also brought new waves of Jews. Due to the lack of any official documents, their number can no longer be determined today. But it was evidently significant, because after some time the elders of the Jewish community announced that the synagogue's charity chest was almost empty and that it was no longer possible to support the Jewish newcomers who were roaming around in droves.

In addition, increased crime was observed, with thefts and robberies committed by Jews being commonplace. A brazen murder-robbery in Chelsea, carried out by a gang of Jewish criminals, forced the government to finally take action. They contacted the Jewish community to work with them to prevent further immigration. The synagogue elders declared their willingness to assist in this endeavor, and published their decision to cease providing relief to foreign Jews 'who had left their country without good cause.' In December 1771, the government ordered immigration authorities to only admit Jews with passports issued by British representatives abroad, and ordered that Jews were no longer allowed to free passage on the king's cross-

---

[12] Picciotto, p. 180; Hyamson: History, p. 236; Rumney, p. 331. & Espriella, Vol III, p. 145. Translator's note: QVOS. Aldag was apparently unaware that Espriella was Southey's pseudonym; in the interests of accuracy all references to this author as a Spanish traveler have been updated to reflect this fact. & Margoliouth: History, Vol. II, p. 94.

channel packet boats, although for some reason this latter edict would not put into effect until October 1774, and even then likely not properly enforced [see footnote]. It evidently remained difficult for local authorities to bring Jewish criminality under control, because the Lord Mayor of London offered to grant passes to poor Jews for a return journey to the south coast of England if they agreed to return to their country of origin, where they would be transported free of charge. Unfortunately, it is not known how many people, if any, made use of this offer.[13]

The siege of Gibraltar by the French in 1781 caused new waves of starving Jews to immigrate to England. Since they had of course effectively arrived destitute, they were not particularly welcomed by the English or by their fellow Jews.[14]

The events in France and Poland, which led to the latter's renewed partition in 1793, saw new masses of Jews on the move. Once again, swarms of Hebrews poured over England. The repercussions may have been the same as before, because the government felt compelled to pass an extensive if temporary law to prevent this unwanted immigration, which placed stringent demands on the newcomers. The act, known as Lord Grenville's Alien Act, 1793 (33 Geo. III, c. 4), which was renewed annually until 1826, made a passport compulsory, and foreigners had to fulfil various conditions, for example, hand over any weapons in their personal possession. They were also subject to a strict registration requirement, and the government also had the right to assign foreigners certain places of residence from which they were not allowed to leave. Violations would be severely punished and could even result in expulsion, a fate which many Hebrews apparently suffered. Despite fierce resistance from the Liberals—here too, this party had consciously or unconsciously become an ally of the Jews—the bill had been carried by a majority in Parliament.[15]

Given these various waves of immigration, it is unsurprising that the number of Jews in England had increased considerably from the previous

---

[13] Calendar of Home Office Papers, Vol. 1770-1772, pp. 355-358; Hyamson: History, pp. 232, 237. Translator's note: Quoted element reproduced verbatim from Hyamson, p. 237. Note that the meeting held by the Home Office to restrict Jewish immigration only came about in response to the public outcry after the Chelsea murder-robbery, and the government's proposed measures to control immigration appear to have been ineffective, as per the judgement of Jewish historian Todd M. Endelman [p. 202]: 'As there was no drop in the 1770s and thereafter in the rate of Jewish immigration to England, in the level of Jewish poverty, or in the extent of Jewish criminality, it is very probable that the regulation was never conscientiously enforced.' For more on the Chelsea case, in which an eight-man criminal gang of Dutch Jews was led by a university-trained physician, and which remained infamous in England well into the 19th century, see Pelham Vol I, pp. 227-230 [both books in Translator's Bibliography].

[14] Picciotto, p. 190.

[15] Henriques: Jews, p. 232; Hyamson: History, p. 246; Statutes at Large, Vol. 39, pp. 10-24.

estimated figure [8,000—10,000]. The exact size of the population is impossible to determine, given the lack of documentation, so we have to rely on rough estimates. Around 1791 we hear from German traveler Gebhard F. A. Wendeborn that around 12,000 Jews lived in England, of which, in his opinion, around 1,000 were in the provinces. The Frenchman Jean-Louis Ferri de Saint Constant lived in England about the same time and gave the much higher figure of over 20,000. With the beginning of emancipation efforts in Parliament in 1830, a reasonable estimate for the Jewish population would be around 25,000 to 30,000 individuals for the whole of Great Britain. It should also be noted, as per Wendeborn, that the Jews living in the provinces in the late 18th century had settled primarily in Falmouth, Plymouth, Portsmouth, Exeter, Chatham, and Liverpool (i.e. port towns and cities), and that these provincial Jews were exclusively Ashkenazim, 'for the Portuguese are not fond of leaving the metropolis'.[16]

The Jews Reorganize

The Jews realized that they needed to concentrate all of their forces in the country for the next open attack. The corresponding first moves can already be seen a few years after the defeat of 1753.

On the occasion of George III's accession to the throne in 1760, the elders of the Sephardi community gathered to choose seven delegates from among their ranks who would offer their respects to His Majesty. The king is said to have received these so-called 'Deputies of the Portuguese Nation' very graciously.[17]

The Ashkenazi Jews were not very pleased that this initiative had been taken by their fellow Jews without their being consulted, and later that same year it was agreed that from then onwards both branches of Judaism would work together 'whenever any public affair should occur that may interest the two nations.' This Jewish institution that was to grow from this co-operative pact, the London Committee of Deputies of the British Jews [better known as the Board of Deputies of British Jews, or simply the Board of Deputies], came to acquire great significance. It not only looked after the affairs of the Jews in Great Britain, but also watched over the destinies of the Children of Israel throughout the world. Jews from all over the globe contacted the London Committee for help, and as we shall see, not in vain. The Jews do not deny that they used the influence of the British Foreign Office, as well as

---

[16] Wendeborn, Vol. II, pp. 468-9. & Rumney, p. 332. & Pellatt, p. IV. & Wendeborn, Vol. II, p. 469. Translator's note: QVOS.

[17] Picciotto, pp. 115-6. Translator's note: For more on this event, as well as the founding and activities of the organization that this event engendered, see Charles Emanuel's *A Century and a Half of Jewish History. Extracted from the Minute Books of The London Committee of Deputies of the British Jews* (Routledge, 1910).

other means, to their advantage. Picciotto makes the following comment on the 1760-1874 interventions of the Deputies, made on behalf of Jews as far afield as Jamaica, Romania, and Damascus:[18]

> In truth, with reference to foreign affairs, they have confined themselves to seeking the intervention of the Foreign Office, which has been granted or declined, according to circumstances. Whether the Deputies might have found other available means of action at hand is a question we need not here discuss. The creation of that institution was for a specific purpose, and the expediency of extending its general scope was a matter for the consideration of its members.[19]

Such a pity that Picciotto does not go into more detail about the other means used—we would have loved to read about such international intriguing from the pen of a well-informed Jew. But one thing is interesting: this statement is fresh confirmation that by this time London was the center of world Jewry, and, as we shall demonstrate in subsequent volumes, remains so to this day.

Certain difficulties occasionally caused disagreements in this so-called Jewish Parliament, but by the year 1812 one can rightly declare that there was complete unity. Most of better-known Jews of the first half of the 19th century held leading positions in this body. The first Rothschild, whom we shall soon discuss in detail, is also among them. The association developed a diverse range of activities after 1830, when British Jewry was struggling to achieve full emancipation. In Picciotto's words:

> The Deputies were not idle. They appointed sub-committees, drew up petitions, presented them to various authorities—from the Archbishop of Canterbury to the Chancellor of the Exchequer.[20]

So we have a united and well-guided Jewry in England that took up the fight for emancipation. After long, often broken negotiations, an agreement was also reached in the area of cooperation between the three London synagogues in 1824. It may have been the looming decisive struggle that brought about this success.[21]

The Jewish hierarchy also ensured that their most deadly weapon, money, was not lacking, by ensuring that the traditional taxes were raised on congregants' incomes. Finally, in 1794, the Great Synagogue endeavored to

---

[18] Picciotto, pp. 117-8. Translator's note: QVOS.
[19] Picciotto, p. 120. Translator's note: QVOS.
[20] Picciotto, p. 126. Translator's note: QVOS.
[21] Hyamson: History, pp. 250-1.

maintain unity by having their members sign a pledge by which they would forfeit £100 if they decided to relinquish their membership.[22]

A Tidal Wave of Jewish Crime

The Children of Israel of the lower classes traded mainly in old clothes and roamed the streets of London shouting their wares, while others made the province unsafe as peddlers.[23] The vast majority, however, were active in criminal areas and had gathered in the darkest and filthiest districts of the capital, where the Jews had formed a city entirely unto themselves. 'I began to fancy,' wrote Robert Southey, posing as a Spanish traveler on a visit to this part of the metropolis, 'that I had discovered the ten tribes.' Others expressed themselves in similar terms and spoke with contempt of such a degenerate, uncouth mob. The professor of history and retired Prussian army officer Johann Wilhelm von Archenholz, who lived in England for ten years (1769-1779), had this to say about what he saw while living there:[24]

> [A]nd the children of Israel who are obliged to quit Germany and Holland take refuge in England, where they live by cheating and nocturnal rapine, and if they do not steal themselves, they aid the thief in concealing and vending the stolen goods. Thus, they are so much abhorred by the English that the honesty of the Portuguese cannot obliterate the unfavorable impression which this troop of banditti has made on them.[25]

Another German visitor to London tells us in 1791:

> I believe few burglaries, robberies, and false coinages are committed, in which some of them are not, in one shape or another, concerned. They steal not only themselves, but assist Christian thieves by receiving their stolen goods, and buying them at a very reasonable price. In Duke's-Place, where hardly any but Jews live, during the whole night, furnaces are ready to melt the stolen silver and gold as soon as the thieves bring it, that it may be rendered indistinguishable before day-light.[26]

---

[22] Picciotto, pp. 191-2. & p. 224.

[23] Rumney, pp. 334-5; Wendeborn, pp. 470-1; Espriella, Vol. III, pp. 150-3. & Rumney, p. 336.

[24] Goede, Vol. II, p. 116. & Espriella, Vol. III, p. 153. Translator's note: QVOS. & Silliman, Vol. I, p. 133; Wendeborn, p. 470; Rumney, pp. 334-5.

[25] Archenholtz, pp. 177-8. Translator's note: QVOS from Rumney, p. 333.

[26] Wendeborn, p. 471. Translator's note: QVOS. Interestingly, the same charge, of a melting pot always burning in the Jewish quarter, had also been made in pre-1290 England with reference to the coin-clippers. Add Israel Zangwill's 1908 play of the same name,

The best and most flawless explanation was given by the Scotsman Patrick Colquhoun, who became famous for the founding of England's first modern police force, among other things. His previous work as both a merchant and magistrate meant that he was good with figures, and in a position to compile official data from primary sources about criminal activity in London and the surrounding area. His work is in no way directed against the Jews, but merely serves to soberly and clearly explain the intolerable conditions in the capital and to set out the evils to the public. At the same time, he proposed remedial measures, which attracted the interest of the king and the government. The Jew Picciotto describes Colquhoun as 'a large-minded man, desirous of promoting the welfare of Jew as well as of Christian'.[27]

It remains for others to write about the influence of Jews on England's criminality; we shall limit ourselves to a short excerpt from Colquhoun's 1796 *Treatise on the Police of the Metropolis*. In Colquhoun's view, the main reason for crime was the widespread use of stolen goods. There were upwards of 3,000 receivers of various kinds of stolen goods in London, with an equal proportion in the rest of the country. Disguised by the beggarly appearance of their junk shops, they sold the stolen valuables from the back rooms. Due to the easy sale of stolen goods of every type, employees and servants were tempted to steal from their employers.

Unsustainable conditions also prevailed in the sphere of coinage. The country was flooded with counterfeit money. The London counterfeiters also copied foreign coins, both European and non-European, which were usually sold to Jews for circulation abroad. This brought the name of England into disrepute in foreign countries such as Turkey and India, which had to deal with this fraud. Despite the police's outdated and otherwise inadequate methods of detection, 608 criminals of this type were tried and convicted in one year, yet this was just a fraction of the overall number of such offenders. With this branch of criminality making over £200,000 per year, witnesses were usually bribed or intimidated into silence. The authorities' ability to gather evidence therefore encountered almost insurmountable difficulties.[28]

Colquhoun calculated that the cost to the government and the people of London and its vicinities for all of the petty pilfering, larger systematized theft, robberies, coin counterfeiting and other currency frauds to be some £2,000,000 annually.[29]

---

which many see as the Jewish desire to 'melt down' the different ethnic and racial groups in the West, and it becomes clear that the melting pot has become a leitmotif that recurs over the centuries of Jewish history.

[27] Dictionary of National Biography, Vol. IV, p. 859, ff. & Picciotto, p. 260. Translator's note: QVOS.

[28] Colquhoun, pp. 16-9. & Colquhoun, pp. 24-30.

[29] Colquhoun, pp. 45-7.

The Jews were particularly involved in all of these crimes and even maintained single-horse carts in order to bring the embezzled and stolen items, particularly metals and ship's articles, from the provinces to London as quickly as possible.[30]

The supplies stolen, including by fraud, from the state's warehouses and dockyards in Portsmouth and Plymouth alone would have to be valued at £500,000 in peacetime and at nearly £1,000,000 in wartime, and for this too the Jews, 'who are always to be found in abundance wherever the dockyards are situated', were the best buyers.[31] This is followed by detailed observations about the widespread network of counterfeiters and their accomplices, as well as observations about the ubiquity of robbery and murder.[32]

The center of all of this criminality was London, where the Jews played a major role in coin counterfeiting. The Jews almost had a monopoly in the trade in counterfeit English copper coins and all foreign counterfeit money. Special groups of Jewish youths worked together in the circulation of this worthless money:

> In this nefarious traffic [of base coin], the lower order of the Jews in London assist the dealers in an eminent degree, particularly the circulation of bad half-pence.
>
> It has not been an unusual thing for several of these dealers to hold a kind of market, every morning, where from forty to fifty Jew boys are regularly supplied with counterfeit half-pence, which they dispose of in the course of the day in different streets and lanes of the metropolis, for *bad shillings*, which they generally purchase, as has already been stated, at 3d. each, in exchange for base copper, always taking care that the person who cries 'bad shilling' shall have a companion near him with the half pence and the unclipt shillings (which are purchased) so as to elude the detection of the Officers of the Police, in the event of being searched.
>
> These Jew boys will generally clear from five to seven shillings a day, by this fraudulent business, which why uniformly spend, during the evening, in riot and debauchery, returning pennyless in the morning to their old trade.
>
> The bad shillings thus purchased by these Jew boys are received in payment by their employers for the bad half-pence, at the rate of four shillings a dozen, and generally re-sold by these employers to *smashers*, at a profit of two shillings a doz-

---

[30] Colquhoun, p. 52.
[31] Colquhoun, p. 70. & Colquhoun, p. 77. Translator's note: QVOS.
[32] Colquhoun, p. 85 ff.

en, who speedily re-colour them, and introduce them again into circulation, at their full nominal value.

Thus it is that the frauds upon the public multiply beyond
all possible conception, by the devices and criminal manoeu-
vres already explained, while the innocent tradesman who thus
sells his counterfeit shillings to Jew boys at three-pence each,
little suspects that it is for the purpose of being returned upon
him again at the rate of twelve pence, or 300 per cent profit to
the purchasers and utterers [issuers].[33]

Colquhoun then went on to detail the rampant spread of other types of fraud,
and to do so, created the following criminal category for the Jews who were
involved in both theft and the reception of stolen goods:

> *A Class of Cheats of the society of Jews, who are to be found*
> *in every street, lane, and alley, in and near the Metropolis,*
> *under the pretence of purchasing old clothes, and metals of*
> *different sorts*, but whose chief business is to prowl about the
> houses and stables of men and rank and fortune, for the pur-
> pose of holding out temptations to the servants to pilfer and
> steal small articles, not likely to be missed, which these Jews
> purchase at about one third of the real value. It is supposed
> that upwards of two thousand of these depraved people are
> employed in diurnal journies of this kind, by which, through
> the medium of bad money and other fraudulent dealings,
> many of them acquire property, and then become receivers of
> stolen goods; thereby (while their labour produces no benefit
> to the State) employing themselves in every mischievous de-
> vice that can render them nuisances in society.

Colquhoun then went on to observe the same Jewish *mode of living* that had
first been lamented by Edward II:

> It is estimated that there are about twenty thousand Jews in the
> city of London, besides, perhaps, about five or six thousand
> more in the great provincial and sea-port towns (where there
> are at least twenty synagogues, besides six in the metropolis),
> who exist chiefly by their wits, seeing that the superstitious
> adherence to a particular *mode of living*, and to their *sabbath*,
> prevents them from placing out their children as servants, or
> apprentices, or binding their sons to mechanical employments,

---

[33] Colquhoun, pp. 118-126. Translator's note: QVOS.

or indeed to any useful art, by which they can assist in increasing the national property—in place of which they diminish it by living upon the industry of others, and by establishing a system of mischievous intercourse all over the country, the better to carry on their fraudulent designs in the circulation of base money, the sale of stolen goods, and in the purchase of metals of various kinds, as well as other articles pilfered and stolen in the provincial towns, which they bring to the metropolis to elude detection—and vice versa.

It was unbearable for the English people to endure this wave of predation. In addition to the crimes already described, the Jews evidently had no respect for the English legal system, as they did not shy away from perjury in order to evade justice for themselves and other members of their race:

> Educated in idleness, from their earliest infancy, they acquire every debauched and vicious principle which can fit them for the most complicated arts of fraud and deception, to which they seldom fail to add perjury, whenever it can be of use, in shielding themselves or their associates from the punishment of the law.
>
> From the orange boy, and the retailer of seals, razors, glass, and other wares, in the public streets, to the shopkeeper, dealer in wearing apparel, or in silver and gold, the same principles of action universally prevail.
>
> The itinerants utter [issue] base money to enable them by selling cheap to dispose of their goods, while those that are stationary, with a very few exceptions, receive and purchase, at an under price, whatever is brought them, without asking questions.
>
> The mischiefs which must result from the increase of this depraved race, arising from the natural course of population, is so obvious, that a remedy cannot be too soon applied...[34]

We have nothing to add to these statements because, given his position and impartiality, there could not have been a better authority on this subject than Patrick Colquhoun. That said, we would like to make two comments about Jews in general, which may help to illuminate some of the particularities of Colquhoun's observations.

We have regularly proffered the view that what matters in history is never the overall number of Jews in a country, but rather the extent of their

[34] Colquhoun: pp. 166-169. Translator's note: All QVOS and italicized as per original source.

influence through money and other means. This has also been proven in this example.

Their moral depravity has led them to robbery, theft, coin fraud, and receiving stolen goods. With a number of around 2,000 people, the Jews represented a large contingent of England's fences. Colquhoun has repeatedly emphasized that fences are the root of all evil. By purchasing the stolen goods, they gave the criminals fresh incentive to commit further crimes. The result of this was a complete breakdown in the relationship of trust between employer and employee, and a complete corruption of morals in public life. This sense of uncertainty was further exacerbated by the circulation of counterfeit money, which again mainly involved Jews. And all of this was brought about, more or less, by some 10,000 to 20,000 Hebrews—a tiny fraction of England's population at the time.[35]

Lastly, another important statement can be made regarding Colquhoun's semi-official report: Throughout history, Jews have repeatedly excused their people's criminality by stating that they are driven to it by the unbearably cruel treatment from their host nation. Libertarians and overly pious Christians very often confirm this view. Now here once again we have an example that thoroughly refutes this explanation, because as we previously established, even back then the Jews enjoyed every kind of freedom and saw England as the promised land. How then can one excuse the Jews' activities in England around 1800? That they had too much freedom? There is certainly some truth to that!

However, these conditions of pervasive depredation were not limited to the lower classes of the population; the Jewish *mode of living* was also felt everywhere else, especially in financial circles.

The following 'pleasant anecdote' shows how much the Jewish stockbrokers were generally hated. In 1774, the son of a very sick Jewish broker had heard that the Lord Mayor of London had been asking most carefully after the health of his father. This was likely because with the broker's death a new brokerage place would be opened up to the Jews (their places being limited to twelve on the Royal Exchange), and the privilege of a broker's medal would have to be purchased at great expense from the Lord Mayor. However, the Lord Mayor's curiosity begat a rumor on 'Change Alley' that he had openly expressed a wish for the ailing broker's death. When the indignant son confronted the Lord Mayor to upbraid him for his unfeeling conduct, the mayor is said to have replied in a way which evidently must have echoed in the public mind over the subsequent decades (this newspaper report dates from 1822):

---

[35] Editor's note: With a population of about 8.9 million, Jews represented between 0.1 and 0.2% of the total. This is yet another confirmation of the rule of thumb that whenever a given Jewish population exceeds about 0.1% of the total, trouble ensues.

The death of the Jew Broker happens very opportunely for the present Lord Mayor, who goes out of office next Friday. The circumstance will remind some of our readers of a pleasant anecdote related of Wilkes. During his mayoralty one of these brokers was seriously ill, and Wilkes was reported to be reckoning on the advantage of the disposal of the probable vacancy. The son of the broker meeting his Lordship, reproached him with wishing his father dead. 'My dear fellow,' said Wilkes, with great promptitude, 'you are completely in error: I would rather that *all* the Jew brokers were dead, than your father.'[36]

Conditions on the stock market became increasingly dire, and bribery of important people in the government continued to progress. People stopped at nothing to gain advantage. Alarming false reports were spread through newspapers, letters from abroad containing false intelligence were touted, and prominent names were used mendaciously in order to manipulate prices on the stock market. Servants and secretaries of public men were bribed for information, while some mistresses and even wives of key figures were turned into spies for members of the stock exchange. Some prominent men even abused their position, making a short-term profit from the false information they promulgated, at the long-term expense of their own reputation, and to the ruin of the men who trusted them. Once an enemy invasion of England was invented, while great men saw rumors of their illness and death spread by those gambling on their life insurance. Truth and honesty on the stock market were outdated concepts.[37]

It was unbelievable how money was made by the army contractors. Here too, bribery and fraud were commonplace:

These evils were so manifest and manifold, that, after various attempts to pass a measure which should be some check on government, a bill was introduced, by which all contracts were made subject to a species of auction, although the minister was not compelled to accept the lowest offer. During the debates which were held upon the subject, many other facts were elicited, which confirm all the previous remarks, and prove the iniquity with which the money of the country was disposed of. One member possessed a contract producing £30,000 a year more than the legitimate profit. Mr. Alderman Harley made £37,000 too much by another. On a contract for remitting gold, £35,000 was paid more than was necessary. At an earlier

---

[36] Picciotto, p. 180; Francis, p. 125; *Times*, 6/11/1822 p. 2. Translator's note: QVOS [*Times*].
[37] Francis, p. 165 ff.

period it was discovered that, out of 16,000 tuns of beer contracted and paid for, only 7,000 tuns were delivered. The rum contract was granted at 50 per cent about a remunerating price. The transport service paid 20 per cent too much. Millions were lying for years in the hands of favourite placemen, favourite agents, and favourite contractors, while the country was borrowing at an exorbitant interest; and, after a careful perusal of the evidence, there can be no doubt that the charge of corrupting the House was true; nor was it in the nature of a member of Parliament, in the eighteenth, any more than in the nineteenth century, to possess profitable contracts, the continuation of which depended on war, and yet speak honestly and earnestly for peace.[38]

Jewish Financiers

The money market was increasingly dominated by individual rich Jews. Samson Gideon and Joseph Salvador were succeeded by the brothers Abraham and Benjamin Goldsmid. More than anyone else, it was the entire Goldsmid family, initially the father Aaron, followed by his four sons George (1741-1813), Asher (d. 1822), Benjamin (1755-1808) and Abraham (1756-1810), who were to play a decisive role on the Royal Exchange.[39]

Benjamin Goldsmid had acquired a huge fortune through inheritance and marriage. So it was no wonder that after a short time he had a business turnover that could only be calculated in millions of pounds. It was not long before he and his brother were called to place the government's bonds. In Stamford Hill he had an elegant house, while in Roehampton he had built a lavish palace, the immense splendor of which was described by contemporaries, who compared it to Windsor Castle. The largest and most lavish festivals of the time were celebrated in this manor house. The guests came from the cream of the English nobility, and it was considered a mark of status in high society to frequent Benjamin Goldsmid's house. The famous Pitt was never absent from such occasions, especially as Benjamin was his favorite.[40]

Benjamin was an active philanthropist. On the occasion of one such charity event, the Duke of Kent, father of the future Queen Victoria, presided

---

[38] Francis, p. 179 ff. Translator's note: QVOS. Readers may find uncanny resonances with documented practices of recent years.

[39] Hyamson: History, p. 247.

[40] Alexander, p. 94 ff. & Alexander, p. 100. Translator's note: For a scathing, satirical commentary on the Goldsmids' wining and dining of the English elite, and their PR offensive on the English populace, see the 1806 pseudonymous article 'Jewish Predominance' in Translator's Appendix.

over the banquet, where it would appear that Benjamin Goldsmid had been sitting to the Duke's left.[41]

In later years, Benjamin suffered from poor health. He committed suicide in 1808. His brother Abraham had at least the same prominence on the Royal Exchange and played a crucial role in the government's financial transactions. At great expense, he had a palace built in Morden, which was little inferior in munificence to that of his brother. He held lavish parties there and on one occasion even hosted King George III as his guest.[42]

He did his business together with Sir Thomas Baring, head of the well-known English banking house which carried his name. In 1810 they jointly undertook to raise a government loan of 14 million pounds all by themselves. At the end of the same year, Abraham feared personal financial ruin due to bad speculation and also took his own life. Picciotto describes the public reaction:

> The news of the calamity produced an unparalleled sensation. The loss of the great loan-contractor was regarded as an event of national importance. Expresses were dispatched to the King and to the Prince of Wales. Consols fell in a few minutes from 66½ to 61¾, and omnium from 6½ to 10¾ discount. Jobbers met with anxious faces in Capel Court, and merchants attended before their time in the Exchange. Business was suspended; the news of peace or war scarcely caused equal excitement. The public journals teemed with eulogies on a man whose name had been synonymous with charity, with beneficence, with philanthropy. His remains were followed to the grave by weeping and mourning thousands, who, having experienced his generosity and liberality in life, now crowded to honour him in death.

The *Morning Post*, in the meantime, produced a eulogy that would make anyone believe that a great humanitarian messiah had passed. The following extract from its editorial will give the reader an idea of the general tone:

> Never was the stream of human benificence in so full flow so reduced by the death of one man as by that of Mr. Abraham Goldsmid. Never was the departure of a single individual so great a deduction from the comfort of mankind. It is such a one as nothing but the bounty of Heaven can retrieve. But not

---

[41] Alexander, p. 114 ff. & Alexander, pp. 110-1.
[42] Picciotto, pp. 242-52; Jewish Encyclopedia, Vol, VI, p. 30; Francis, pp. 180-4; Margoliouth: History, Vol. II, p. 128.

in an age, and least of all, in an age like this, can we hope to see another instance of a heart so enlarged by universal philanthropy.

As a public man, and a more public spirited and patriotic one than Mr. Abraham Goldsmid never did honour to any age, or country, the loss of him must be long and severely felt. But amidst all his affairs, and much less than he had to attend to would have absorbed the very souls of the worldly, he neglected not for a moment his favourite occupation, the most delightful, the most important to him of all his pursuits, the exercise of his benificence. 'He went about doing good!' How hath he wiped away the tears of the orphan! How hath he caused the widow's heart to leap for joy! So replendent on his countenance was the benevolence of his soul, that in his presence even the sick at heart forgot their sorrows... In favour of him, from every spot of earth on which he was known, will prayers, and tears, and sighs ascend with more than human energy to the throne of the Divine Mercy, to Heaven, earth, and ocean's Lord and Father of the good.[43]

Broadly speaking, a national catastrophe could not have made a deeper impression on the nation, whose fate appeared to hinge on the life of a single rich Jew! As is alluded to by Picciotto, Abraham, like his brother, was well known for his philanthropic efforts.

On this occasion we would like to briefly address the popular argument about the charity of the Jews, which does not seem to be at all compatible with their opponents' claims that they are hard-hearted and miserly. Anyone who has read through the Hebrew playbook knows that philanthropy is a well-thought-out strategy to achieve overall goals. It is clear to the Jews that every host nation has an aversion to them from the outset, which is exacerbated by the system they have introduced—high finance with all its excesses, bribes, general immorality, etc. The populace, as the object of Jewish exploitation, might look askance at the growth of Jewish power, and at the lavish, brilliant galas and banquets. Therefore the Jews will use tried-and-tested methods to nip the growth of popular resentment in the bud, and no method could be more conciliatory than the cloak of charity: sums that seem gigantic to ordinary people being given to causes that guarantee the greatest publicity. And, of course, not everyone will realize that what the Jew gives with one hand, he takes double or triple with the other.[44]

---

[43] Picciotto, pp. 252-4; Jewish Encyclopedia, Vol. IV, p. 28; Francis, pp. 184-86; *Times*, 12-13/4/1808; *Morning Post*, 9/10/1810. Translator's note: QVOS.

[44] Translator's note: One person who most certainly saw this Jewish charity with clear eyes, and wanted to explain the strategy behind it to his fellow countrymen, was the English political commentator William Cobbett (1763-1835), the nineteenth century's fore-

The opponents of our view declare that such cynical ulterior motives would never inspire Jewish philanthropy. It is usually difficult to prove a person's motives perfectly when, as here, both sides present plausible opposing motivations. In addition to the evidence already presented, our thesis is supported by the fact that such charity donations from Jews would always be publicized as widely as possible. A person who gives just to do good generally avoids making a fuss about it. Finally it would have to be proven that they are naturally kind-hearted, generous, and altruistic. This evidence is unlikely to be found, since Judah's actions throughout history, and its principles as laid down in the Talmud and elsewhere, appear to be completely incompatible with disinterested charity towards gentiles.

Nathan Mayer Rothschild and Friends

On the subject of the establishment of Jewish power in England before 1830, we must also discuss the richest of the Children of Israel, Nathan Mayer Rothschild. For the scope of this study it will be sufficient to give just a brief overview of his life.

Born in Frankfurt am Main in 1770, Rothschild emigrated to England in 1798. He initially resided in Manchester and moved to London in 1805. At the same time he was naturalized by King George III for his services to the Crown.[45]

Nathan Mayer Rothschild owes his real rise to fame to William I, Landgrave [Prince] and later Elector of Hesse-Cassel, who, with the help of his Nathan's father Mayer Amschel Rothschild, had accumulated vast quantities of wealth by selling his country's sons as mercenary troops for Eng-

---

most radical and anti-Jewish journalist. Among his extensive commentary regarding Judah in England, he made many remarks about Jewish philanthropy, perhaps most notably in the 1806 article 'Jewish Predominance' (see Translator's Appendix), and in comments such as the following:

> The nobility and gentry and clergy seem to me to have entered into a solemn league and covenant to effect their own destruction. It is as clear as daylight, that either they must be overthrown, or that the Jews must be reduced to a moderate bulk. The infernal Jews and usurers are not seen by the people. One pension, or one sinecure, is more a subject of complaint than the whole thirty millions annually swallowed up by the Jews and other devils of *Change-alley*. It is quite amusing to see how quietly the money-dealing villains go and thrust noblemen and gentlemen out of their estates. Aye, and pass for good and generous gentlemen, too, by a liberal distribution of a small part of this money, which this stupid nobility and gentry have enabled them to take out of the pockets of the people. [*Cobbett's Weekly Political Register*, Vol. LXXXII, No. 2 (12 October, 1833): pp. 111-112.]

[45] Scherb, p. 60; Wolf, p. 271.

land, particularly in America and India. This 'merchant of human flesh' invested part of his fortune in England, and Rothschild managed it to the complete satisfaction of his employer, who was considered the richest man in Europe at the time. After his escape from Napoleon, the prince became more dependent than ever on Rothschild, which Mayer Amschel exploited to his own advantage.[46]

Rothschild ruthlessly exploited the Napoleonic turmoil in Europe. After the death of the Goldsmid brothers, he took over the role of all-powerful banker on London's Royal Exchange. Only with his help was England able to send subventions to Russia, Prussia, Austria, and other states during the Wars of Liberation [Wars of the Sixth Coalition]. His sophisticated system enabled the Duke of Wellington to continue campaigning in Spain. Previously, the entire campaign had often been jeopardized by a lack of money. There is no need for further explanation of the fact that Rothschild thereby secured an unforeseen influence over the English government, which consequently did not hesitate to support his foreign policy interests.[47]

Napoleon knew about Rothschild's efforts against him, and Rothschild was one of those who contributed to the downfall of "the moneylenders' everlasting enemy." If Napoleon were to win, the 'the great Debt System which held England and the world in its merciless claws' would be defeated, and therefore, to those who benefitted from this system, no price 'was judged too high to pay for a new European war.' Is it therefore any wonder that, after the fall of Napoleon, the Rothschilds paid for Louis XVIII's expenses from London to Paris, and again on the day of his 'triumphal entry' into the French capital?[48]

What is most interesting here is the role that Nathan Rothschild also played in the preparations for the emancipation of the world's Jews. It must be left to another study to detail his activity in this regard. All that can be said is that, without Rothschild, this development would have been held back for at least another century. He ensured that the privileges already granted to Jews in all countries remained intact and were increased. For this purpose, he ruthlessly exploited the growing dependence of the various states around the world on the disbursement of his loans, which amounted to hundreds of millions of marks.[49]

---

[46] Scherb, p. 27; Wolf, p. 262; Corti, p. 53 ff.; McNair Wilson, pp. 255, 287-8.

[47] Corti, pp. 128 ff; 139-141; Jewish Encyclopedia, Vol. X, p. 943 ff. (s.v. Rothschild). & Corti, p. 169 ff.

[48] McNair Wilson, pp. 353, 364, 379. QVOS.

[49] Corti, p. 138. & Jewish Encyclopedia, Vol. X, p. 495; Wolf, p. 276. Translator's note: The Jewish Encyclopedia provides a list of these foreign government loans, which included Brazil and Russia. Wolf relates that Rothschild urged the Austrian Ambassador in London to bring the grievances of Austria's Jews to his government's attention, and in 1819

In England, too, Nathan Rothschild was omnipotent in the field of finance, and it is only to the credit of the English people of this time that for some 28 years they managed to withstand the relentless assault for Jewish emancipation that took place under Rothschild's direction [see chapter 6 of this study].

The Jewish side does not deny Rothschild's intervention in this regard. He tirelessly reached out to leading politicians of both sides and tried to put them under his spell. We can see such efforts as early as 1820. In the diary of another well-known Jew, Sir Moses Montefiore, there is an entry dated 22 February 1829, which describes how he and Rothschild 'had a long conversation on the subject of liberty for the Jews' with Rothschild saying 'he would shortly go to the Lord Chancellor and consult him on the matter.' The Duke of Wellington was very friendly with both Nathan Rothschild and his son Lionel. When he was once asked by Robert Peel to seek the Rothschilds' support for the upcoming City of London election in favour of the Tories, Wellington regretted that he had to reject such an attempt as hopeless from the outset due to the anti-Jewish attitude of the Tory party.[50]

Rothschild's methods are probably best summarized in the following excerpt from an 1829 book by a pro-Jewish writer, who wrote that:

> M. Rothschild has done more for the emancipation of the Jews, than Mr. O'Connell for that of the Catholics. By the magic power of wealth, he has rendered their obstinate enemies their tributaries; while, by the attractive seduction of gastronomic and musical entertainment, he has completely conquered the aversion of the aristocracy to mix with merchants and Jews; and were the whole Church of England to threaten anathemas against the frequenters of the wealthy financier's mansion, they would certainly prefer corporeal to spiritual comforts, and disregard the threats. Those who are acquainted with the irresistible attractions which good dinners possess for the nobility, will bear me out in this assertion— *Fruges consumere nati.*[51]

Nathan Mayer Rothschild did not live to see the emancipation of the Jews. In 1836 he died in Frankfurt am Main, and his body was taken to London. The Austrian, Russian, Prussian, Neapolitan, and Portuguese ambassadors in London attended his funeral. His estate could not be estimated with

---

Rothschild (temporarily) refused to do any business in bills coming from German cities which 'persecuted' Jews.

[50] Wolf, p. 276. Translator's note: QVOS.

[51] Anichini, pp. 9-10 (footnote). Translator's note: QVOS. The Latin phrase, from Horace, translates as 'Born to consume the fruits [of the earth]'.

certainty. The tax authorities used the figure of £100 million. He was certainly the wealthiest man in the world, and it was said in London that he paid his employees extremely poor wages, as John Francis noted in 1849:[52]

> His mind was as capable of contracting a loan for millions as of calculating the lowest possible amount on which a clerk could exist. Like too many great merchants whose profits were counted by thousands, he paid his assistants the smallest amount for which he could procure them.[53]

His brother-in-law Moses Montefiore was also one of the rich Jews who saw emancipation as their main goal. Born in 1784, he lived to the rare age of 101. He owed his wealth more or less to his collaboration with Rothschild. He managed to gain the special favor of Princess Victoria of Saxe-Coburg-Saalfeld, the mother of the future Queen Victoria. He was also on good terms with the latter. When Victoria ascended the throne in 1837, she raised Montefiore to the knighthood [the same year that he was elected Sheriff of the City of London], and in 1846 she made him a baronet for his humanitarian services on behalf of Jews all over the world. The year prior to his baronetcy he was also named High Sheriff of Kent, the oldest secular office under the Crown, dating back to Anglo-Saxon England. It is obvious that his court and government connections served him well for his advocacy work.

In our list of Jewish financiers we cannot omit Abraham Israel Ricardo, the commissioned stockbroker for the Bevis Marks Synagogue. It is almost redundant to mention that he likewise possessed a large fortune. One of his sons arguably went on to become an even greater name in England. This son was David Ricardo, the financier who gained a reputation as a political economist after converting to Unitarianism. At his death in 1823 he was Whig [liberal] Member of Parliament for the borough of Portarlington with an estimated fortune of £700,000.[54]

Finally, we would like to mention a Jew named Menasseh Lopez, who was born in Jamaica in 1755 and made his fortune there before moving to England. Picciotto describes his conversion to Christianity in the following way:

> The change in the theological opinions of Mordecai and of Menasseh Lopez happened by a singular coincidence to manifest itself at the time of a general election, and the fact was

---

[52] Francis, p. 307. & Scherb, p. 63.
[53] Francis, p. 297. Translator's note: QVOS [1855 edition]. For more on the life and times of Nathan Rothschild, see Martin (chapter XVI) and Bermant (chapter IV).
[54] Picciotto, pp. 220-1.

immediately followed by the return of Menasseh as member for New Romney.

In 1805 he was created a baronet. In the next election, Sir Menasseh secured a seat for Barnstaple, the borough for which he was again re-elected in 1818. At this point, we shall let Picciotto resume the tale:

> Curious to say, we find that an attorney, named Dance, who had insulted Sir Menasseh Lopez, incorrectly described as 'a Jew baronet', was condemned to twelve months imprisonment, and to be struck off the rolls. On the 18th March 1819, the 'Jew baronet' was found guilty at the Exeter Assize of having bribed the electors of the borough of Grampound to secure his election, and sentence was deferred. On the 13th November he was again prosecuted for a similar offence, and convicted, and he received sentence in the Court of the Queen's Bench. He was condemned for the first offence to be imprisoned for twenty-one months in Exeter Jail, and to pay to the King a fine of £10,000, and for the second infraction of the law, which had been committed in Devonshire, he was sentenced to a further confinement of three months and another fine of £2000. Notwithstanding these untoward circumstances, Sir Menasseh Massey Lopez was once more returned to Parliament, and this time he was chosen as a fit representative for the immaculate borough of Westbury.

His criminal record evidently did not prevent him from holding other high civil service positions as, at the time of his death in 1831, he was found to be fulfilling the functions of recorder at Westbury, as well as being a magistrate for two counties.

He left no descendants, which meant that his title and property worth over £800,000 was inherited by his nephew, Ralph Franco, who then became Sir Ralph Lopes after making a slight [Anglicising] alteration to his uncle's surname. Ralph's son, Sir Massey Lopes, 3rd Baronet, became a Conservative politician and, under the prime ministership of his fellow Sephardi Benjamin Disraeli, was even promoted to the office of First Lord of the Admiralty.[55]

This description may suffice for now, for it is impossible to mention all the hundreds, perhaps thousands, of Jews who were rich and influential. We consciously make no distinction between baptized and unbaptized Jews, since in our opinion there is no such distinction. On the contrary, the former were probably even more dangerous at this time than the latter, since even

---

[55] Picciotto, pp. 304-6. Translator's note: Both QVOS.

before the general emancipation they were able to slip into all sorts of powerful positions and thus serve the Jewish cause. As Picciotto admits, Jewish emancipation was ultimately achieved 'by a few solitary individuals who bore the brunt of the battle—and conquered'.[56]

The Power of Propaganda

Already at the end of the 18th century, it was noticed that forces were emerging to transform the perceptions of the masses, which is best shown by the numerous books in favor of the Jews that appeared around this time. It is striking that no important book which contains the opposing viewpoint has been found.

We would like to mention just a few of the various authors found in the public sphere around this time. The earliest appears to be someone who wrote under the pseudonym J. D. I., who did a lot for the Jewish cause around 1795. Other individuals followed with public letters and pamphlets, all of them agreeing that the Jews had been terribly wronged throughout history, a situation which continued to that day.[57]

A few years later, a well-known playwright, Richard Cumberland (1732-1811), took their side with his comedy, *The Jew*. His sympathetic Jewish characters, not least of them a Jewish hero, perhaps contributed most out of all the general propaganda to so-called polite society coming to a favorable opinion about the Jewish race. Cumberland's *The Jew* achieved great success. It was performed for the first time on 8 May 1794 at the Drury Lane Theatre and was soon performed throughout England, according to contemporary reports. It was even staged in America, France, and Germany, where it appeared in German translation as early as 1798. The audience was moved to tears by the sentimentality of the play, which is incomprehensible to us today.

The plot is briefly as follows: A rich, respected English merchant's son marries a Jewish woman—to the displeasure of both families. The resulting conflicts are resolved by the benevolent moneylender Sheva, who, in Cumberland's view, represents the archetype of the true Jew. Above all, he was concerned with portraying a Jew of generous and honorable character, in contrast to the Shylock of Shakespeare's *Merchant of Venice*. A typical excerpt of the play proves that the message was anything but subtle:[58]

---

[56] Picciotto, p. 126. Translator's note: QVOS.
[57] Picciotto, pp. 236-7.
[58] Dictionary of National Biography, Vol. V, p. 290 ff. & For the German version, see the translation *Der Jude* by Dengel. & Williams, p. 231.

CHARLES enters with SHEVA.

Charles: This is the man. My benefactor; your's Eliza; Frederic's; your's dear mother! all mankind's: The widow's friend, the orphan's father, the poor man's protector, the universal philanthropist.

Sheva: Hush, hush! You make me hide my face. [*Covers his face with his hands.*]

Charles: Ah, Sir, 'tis now too late to cover your good deeds: You have long mask'd your charities beneath this humble seeming, and shrunk back from actions princes might have gloried in: You must now face the world, and transfer the blush from your own cheeks to their's, whom prejudice has taught to scorn you. For your single sake we must reform our hearts, and inspire them with candor towards your whole nation.

Sheva: Enough, enough! More than enough—I pray you spare me: I am not used to hear the voice of praise, and it oppresses me: I shou'd not know myself, if you were to describe me; I have a register within, in which these merits are not noted. Simply I am an honest man, no more; fair in my dealings, as my good patron here, I hope, can witness...[59]

Newspaper and magazine critics could not praise this piece enough, while printed editions of the play were continually selling out, as we can see from the fact that the printed version was already in its seventh edition by 1801.[60]

Other publications also sought to clear the Hebrews of their character flaws, with the writing of Jewish surgeon and apothecary Joshua van Oven particularly standing out in this regard. In *Letters on the Present State of the Jewish Poor in the Metropolis* (1802), he demanded that steps be taken to improve the situation, particularly on the basis of Colquhoun's official crime report. He did not deny the incredibly dire reality of Jewish criminality, but did not attribute it to the depravity of the Jews, instead blaming their unfavorable economic situation. In his view, the Jewish poor should not only be

---

[59] Cumberland, p. 47 (Act V, Scene 2). Translator's note: QVOS.

[60] Williams, pp. 232-33. Translator's note: For examples of the occasional contemporary critics who found this portrayal of a wealthy Jewish financier (who secretly provides disinterested financial assistance to two young star-crossed Christian lovers and who leaves his fortune to an indigent Christian) mawkish and implausible, see p. 234 of Williams and the article 'Jewish Predominance' [Translator's Appendix]. Note also that when Cumberland staged a similar play fourteen years later in 1808 called *The Jew of Mogadore*, it was universally panned and had to close down after three or four nights [Schroeter, p. 57, in Translator's Bibliography].

asked to undertake honorable professions, but should also be given practical help to do so.[61]

The suggestions for reform made by van Oven in the aforementioned pamphlet were deemed unacceptable by the Jewish printer Levy Alexander, in the response pamphlet that he printed shortly after van Oven's tract appeared. Furthermore, the same author also strongly objected to the way the situation of Jewish criminality had been presented by Colquhoun. While the facts Colquhoun stated may have been true, Alexander argued that they should have been presented in a way that was not as offensive.[62]

Among the pro-Jewish writers, one should not forget Thomas Witherby, who advocated for a change in popular sentiment regarding the Jews through his various treatises. In his main work, *An Attempt to Remove Prejudices Concerning the Jewish Nation* (1804), which contains over 500 pages of small print, he objects, among other things, to the common English saying: 'The fellow is a perfect Jew.' This was understood to mean a person who always sought to gain the greatest possible benefit for himself, even if it meant exploiting the difficulties of others. Shakespeare may also have shown such 'popular and vulgar prejudice', Witherby argued, but it was really time to do away with such outdated concepts. All persecutions of Jews, including of those in England, were unjustified. The crimes with which the Jews were charged 'should be imputed to that general odium under which they then had the misery to live' i.e. they were driven to commit crimes by the Christians. Furthermore, in Great Britain they would have been favorably influenced by the character of the English. Given this latter argument, we would therefore have been interested to see the author try to explain away the almost intolerable level of Jewish criminal activity at that time.[63]

A certain William Hamilton Reid was also a supporter of the Jewish cause. He too emphasized that the prejudices against them needed to be

---

[61] Van Oven, p. 4 ff., 16. Translator's note: Van Oven was also a reformer, who worked to realize the reforms he had written about, and while his great Jewish welfare scheme (planned with Colquhoun) failed due to opposition, he was instrumental in founding the Jews' Free School, the Jews' Hospital in Mile End, as well as several Jewish schools and charities in Liverpool. See Jewish Encyclopedia Vol. 12, pp. 400-1 (s.v. VAN OVEN, JOSHUA), Picciotto, pp. 259-63.

[62] Alexander: Answer, p. 30 ff. & esp. p. 34 ff. Translator's note: This typically Jewish strategy of using the tone argument, i.e. of attacking a message's style to deflect from its content, will doubtless be familiar to modern readers.

[63] Witherby, p. 1 ff. Translator's note: QVOS (pp. 1-2). & Witherby, p. 19. Translator's note: QVOS. Perceptive readers may rightly speculate whether this was an early prototype of the now-common liberal/Jewish strategy of always finding a way to blame the White (i.e. European Christian) male for the crimes and failures of every other group. & Witherby, p. 37 ff.

eliminated, especially since in England they had recently become much more assimilated with the manners and customs of the country.[64]

Immediately before the emancipation struggles began, a work was published addressed to the Duke of Wellington which advocated general Jewish emancipation. The Jews not only had a right to live and enjoy, 'in common with the rest of mankind, all the advantages which society admits of,' but they are 'moreover particularly distinguished by the favor of Heaven for an uninterrupted supremacy in wealth and power, and for the homage and submission which the highest authorities on earth zealously pay them.' According to the will of God, 'the Jews should not only live, but prosper, and be protected, like the rest of human kind.' The author asked why people spurned Jews for their cold rapacity, when the same thing could be said of the English:[65]

> But who is not equally fond of money in England, where, infinitely more than in any other part of the world, every thing can be obtained by the help of money?

In addition, there was also be no one more immoral than England's 'triumphant aristocrats,' who were known to be involved in 'adultery, gambling, and (I tremble in writing it), incest, and unnatural crime,' accusations were not made against the Jews. The author's heart bled when he thought of 'the cruelties inflicted by the followers of the doctrines of Christianity upon the Jews; persecutions which must have nearly exhausted the fountain of divine mercy'.[66]

The author then points out the injustice of granting emancipation to Catholics but not to Jews, as he asks rhetorically:

> [W]hat can refrain the Constitutional King of Protestant England, who has lately signed a family compact with the sectarians of the execrated Rome, to grant the same boon to the followers of the oldest religion on record, who, by the exclusive possession of wealth, rule the moral destinies of the world?[67]

---

[64] Reid, esp. Introduction, p. 5.

[65] Anichini, pp. 5-6. Translator's note: All QVOS.

[66] Anichini, pp. 24-27. Translator's note: All QVOS. In the original text, the author has asterisked the word 'incest', as he has added a footnote in which he tells of a still-living English nobleman who had a sexual relationship with his own sister, whom he implies killed the fruit of the union to evade discovery. For a discussion of Jews and incest, see Chapter IX of Ryssen [in Translator's Bibliography]. & Anichini, p. 44. Translator's note: QVOS.

[67] Anichini, p. 10. Translator's note: QVOS.

This situation was all the more reprehensible given that the Jews had already been emancipated in France and many parts of Germany.[68]

In the same year [1829], a book was published by the English glass-maker Apsley Pellatt which also strongly advocated emancipation. His main concern was that the Jews be granted full freedom of the City of London.[69]

Publications specifically about Jewish emancipation seldom appeared before 1829. The propaganda of this earlier period only said generally favorable things about the Hebrews, without mentioning the actual purpose of the propaganda, which was to prepare the public mind for later emancipation efforts. We therefore certainly believe Picciotto when he talked of 'the awakened interest and sympathy which were beginning to be felt by thoughtful Englishmen and English women for a long-persecuted race.' We are also not surprised that even princes insisted on attending Jewish services, as Picciotto recounts:[70]

In April 1809 the Synagogue in Duke's Place experienced the unusual honour of receiving a state visit from several princes of the blood. Abraham Goldsmid attended personally at a meeting of the Synagogue on the 3rd of April, to give notice that the Duke of Cumberland, the Duke of Sussex, and the Duke of Cambridge, intended to assist at a Friday evening service. The Duke of Sussex, it is well known, always displayed much friendship and sympathy for the Jews.

On this occasion pompous preparations were made for the reception of these distinguished guests. The Wardens of the day were Messrs. Asher Goldsmid, Joseph Cohen, and Moses Samuel. The notice was short, for the visit occurred on Friday evening, the 14th April. The path of the Royal Dukes from their carriages to the entrance of the Synagogue was strewn with flowers; and their advent was hailed with the usual Prayer for the Royal Family—'He who giveth salvation unto kings'—intoned by a well-drilled choir. Some verses, written, we believe, by the late Michael Josephs, were sung; and a few copies printed on silk were distributed to a favoured number. Altogether the celebration is said to have met in the highest degree the approbation of the princely sons of George III; and the visit of the Royal Dukes still forms a tradition of glory among the older members of the Great Synagogue.[71]

---

[68] Anichini, pp. 18, 23.
[69] Pellatt, pp. 5, 8, 23-27 and passim.
[70] Picciotto, p. 234. Translator's note: QVOS.
[71] Picciotto, pp. 267-8. Translator's note: QVOS.

We will soon see that this was not just inspired by idle curiosity, but a real interest in the Jews. Finally, the following 1808 observation of Robert Southey, posing as Spanish traveler Manuel Alvarez Espriella, appears to accurately judge the mood of the nation:

> During the last reign, an attempt was made to naturalize them, in a body; and the measure would have been effected had it not been for the indignant outcry of the people, who very properly regarded it as an act of defiance, or at least of opposition, to the express language of prophecy. But this feeling has abated, and were the attempt to be renewed it would meet with little opposition.[72]

And then from Picciotto:

> As a result, we are not surprised that some of the press had also changed significantly over the intervening decades. At the beginning of the 19th century, the press published numerous essays and articles that dealt sympathetically with all questions concerning Jews. It happened so often that one can hardly believe that the public participated spontaneously and one cannot shake the thought that there was a well-directed power behind this trend. It is impossible to list the numerous articles in the various newspapers, and so the mere statement of this fact should suffice.[73]

---

[72] Espriella, Vol III, pp. 143-4. Translator's note: QVOS. Southey also tells the story [p. 145] of how in earlier years a farce called *The Jew Boy* was shut down by Jewish protests, after the Jews 'assembled in great numbers and actually damned the piece'. This leads the author to conclude: 'This single fact is sufficient to prove that the liberty which they enjoy is unbounded.'

[73] Picciotto, p. 278. Translator's note: Aldag was doubtless correct in his assertion of a well-directed power behind the press. Below are excerpts from William Cobbett, who appears to have been the sole journalist prepared to critique the growth of Jewish power in early 19th-century England. Given that Cobbett was the 'almost unique' popular writer who had an anti-Jewish stance at this time [Felsenstein, pp. 215-6, 237], and a man who used his own newspaper as a vehicle for his views, one can see why Aldag has apparently overlooked him in his survey of the contemporary literature. *See also Translator's Appendix.*

[A]nd of course, the Jew newspapers have told a lie upon Colonel Clithero. It is curious enough, that the Jew Levi, actually took an opportunity at the meeting at Bow-street on the Thursday, to *praise* the *Old Times* and the *Morning Herald*, calling them respectable papers. I have often said, that the London press, is in great part *owned by the Jews*. There was a Jew of the name of King, who owned in part or in whole, two or three of the newspapers; and I am quite satisfied that

Freemasonry

We have tried to show the various forces that consciously or unconsciously worked towards Jewish emancipation. In this context, we must also briefly touch upon the question of the involvement of Freemasonry. We have already stated our wish to discuss this matter only with the greatest caution, in order to pre-empt any accusation of a lack of solid, verifiable evidence for our claims.

Although the Freemasons have always known how to cover their tracks, it is no longer a secret that Freemasons were in close contact with the Jews, and that it was Freemasonry that largely helped pave the way for Jews to embark on their emancipation struggle. The nobility and the other ruling classes of the English nation, in which the Hebrews had long established a strong foothold through business and private relationships, were brought together in the lodges. So what would have been more a logical step than to admit their Jewish brethren according to the Masonic principle of religious tolerance, the first step on the path to social equality which would end in their complete emancipation? We soon find numerous Jews in the lodges, among whom the Mendez, Montefiores, and Rothschilds are not absent. In this way, Jewish masons were able to work from within for the cause of their fellow Jews, being able to penetrate further and further into state life with the help of their Masonic brothers in leading English circles, and were thus able to conquer one position after another.

And then there is the following anecdote that likewise seems to confirm that the Freemasons, in line with their generally pro-Jewish outlook, stood up for the Hebrews: The London Society for Promoting Christianity Amongst

---

the far greater part of them are now *in the pay* of the Jews, at any rate. [*Cobbett's Weekly Political Register*, Vol. 48, No. 4 (25 October 1823): p. 214.]

God forbid, that I should not believe, that a vast majority of this nation is yet undebased: but as far as the press can go; as far as it has influence, this verily is, the basest nation, that ever was in the world. Nine tenths of the press, which ought to be the guardian of public morals, which ought to be the support of public spirit, which ought to prevent the nation from being cheated or deluded. Nine tenths of this press, or at least a very large part of it, is absolutely in the pay of the Jews. Not a stipend received from them, perhaps; not, perhaps, so much money down upon the counter, generally speaking; but in one way or other, the tool of the Jews for pecuniary reward. [...]

Every nation, that has fostered the Jews, has become miserable in proportion to their numbers and influence. Here, they have had an influence, and have influence, such as fills one with indignation to think of; and as the system becomes more and more embarrassed, their influence becomes greater and greater— Base press of London is their tool; no man who wishes to utter a word against them, can get that word in a newspaper in London. [*Cobbett's Weekly Political Register*, Vol. 65, No. 1 (5 January 1828): pp. 22-23.]

the Jews, which shall be discussed later in more detail, was on the verge of bankruptcy and, to deal with this crisis, what was probably the Society's most important meeting since its founding was held on 29 March 1840, 'at Free-Masons Tavern'. It is up to the reader to decide whether this choice of location should be interpreted as coincidental or as an expression of the Society's close cooperation with the Freemasons. It did not stop at this one meeting at Free-Masons Tavern, as it was decreed that 'the General Committee shall meet once a month at the Free-Masons Hall, and that His Royal Highness the Patron, and the Vice-Presidents, be requested to attend it...'.[74]

Napoleon and the Jews

In addition to internal English forces, there were also foreign political events that gave the Jewish emancipation movement a significant boost: the French Revolution and Napoleon's pro-Jewish measures.[75]

The cries of distress from the rural population in almost all the eastern provinces of what was then France [roughly corresponding to the regions of Alsace and Lorraine] became more and more urgent as the Hebrews sucked them dry. Napoleon, who could not ignore this appeal for help, intervened.[76]

In 1806 he summoned to Paris an assembly of 111 Jewish notables (which later became the Great Sanhedrin), from whom he demanded a clear explanation on certain questions put to them. Among other things, he demanded assurances from them that their fellow Jews would behave patriotically and fraternally towards the local population from that point onwards and would refrain from any kind of usury.[77]

Napoleon's plan was an attempt to reform the entire life of the Jews, who, in his view, had to assimilate themselves to the views and customs of modern Europe. He considered it essential that they renounce the Halakha [the traditional Jewish law code] and the teachings that had come down to them through the Talmud and other books, in view of the fundamental

---

[74] Norris, p. 96 (footnote). Translator's note: QVOS. The (ostensible) argument for these meeting places may have been that, as the Society's members were drawn from both the Church of England and Nonconformism, Free-Masons Tavern and the Free-Masons Hall could be deemed 'neutral' venues.

[75] Picciotto, p. 234.

[76] Reid p. 1 ff.

[77] Jewish Encyclopedia, Vol. XI, pp. 46-8 (s. v. SANHEDRIN, FRENCH), also Vol. IX, pp. 167-8 (s.v. NAPOLEON BONAPARTE). Translator's note: Additional information taken from *Esau's Tears* pp. 48-50 [see Translator's Bibliography]; note that the Great Sanhedrin is also known by the closer translation Grand Sanhedrin in English-language historiography. Napoleon also instituted a debt holiday for the peasants. From Margolis and Marx's *A History of the Jewish People*, p. 613: '...in a rescript dated May 30, 1806, Napoleon suspended for a year the payment of all debts held by Jews against agriculturists in the eastern departments.'

change in overall social conditions that had recently occurred, just as he also held their reckless accumulation of money to be significantly disadvantageous to French society. When the Great Sanhedrin accepted his proposals for reformation, he assured the Jews of a complete emancipation.

We cannot go into detail here about this valiant attempt by Napoleon, but it is obvious to anyone familiar with the Jewish character that his efforts, like those of the noble King Edward I of England before him, would naturally be doomed to failure. The result of his action was, however, that all over the world, reference was made to the outcome of the events in France—Jewish emancipation—with the Jews in different countries seeking the same right with varying levels of clamor, using Napoleon as their precedent. As is to be expected, these events also had their repercussions in England.

In connection with this, we would like to briefly touch on the question that is so often asked as to why the Jews of England, under the leadership of Rothschild, fought Napoleon with all their might. This fact is very often cited as evidence of the English Jews' patriotism, given that they saw Napoleon as an enemy of England despite his pro-Jewish policies.

People who do not sufficiently understand the Jewish Question are inclined to explain these events in England with the claim, so often made by the Jews, that they were due to the fact that the Jews do not all work in lockstep, and often have major disagreements with each other. However, there is in fact no such disunity because the Children of Israel have always been united on major issues of global politics. But even putting this argument to one side for a moment, there are better ways to explain the behavior of the Jews in England.

As is well known, Rothschild founded his banking house largely with the blood money of the infamous Prince of Hesse-Cassel. His client was the creditor of almost all the princes who fought against Napoleon. Napoleon, who knew of Rothschild's activities against him, was a constant threat to Rothschild's extensive business on the continent. As a result, Rothschild could not endure such a constant threat either to his personal interests or to the general emancipation plans closely related to them.

But even without this interpretation of events, the following explanation is hard to refute.

What did Napoleon demand from the Jews in return for emancipation? Nothing more and nothing less than an improvement in their behavior towards the host population by abolishing their so-called divine and, for the most part, completely immoral laws. What did that mean? Above all, it meant that Napoleon had undoubtedly made the decision that under no circumstance would he permit the people's wealth to be sucked dry by usury and that Jews would only be tolerated in the country if they behaved decently. This was a clear indication from a powerful ruler that only he had the right to determine the laws which governed the life and wellbeing of his people.

There was no doubt in the minds of the Hebrews that Napoleon would prevail in this regard, and this was unacceptable to them.

But Napoleon went further. He had recognized that the principles of the Jews were incompatible with those of a healthy nation and that a root-and-branch reformation of Judaism was therefore necessary. In doing so, he intervened in the Jews' own lives. No matter how corrupt their values may be from our point of view, they have been sacred to the Jews for centuries and, above all, a means to an end: world domination.

So we believe that it was the Jewish Orthodox circles that not only rejected Napoleon's efforts but, given their religious beliefs, *had* to reject them. One can easily see this from certain statements made by Jewish individuals. In 1928, a very well-known Jew named Mr. Levy from Florida gave a public speech which explained how the Sanhedrin of France had been wrong in acceding to Napoleon's demand for secularization. He detailed at length how the decision was erroneous and 'destitute of the Holy Spirit' as 'the design of the law [Halakha] was to create a field of action in every occurrence of life, for the exercise of faith in the word of God; and that to separate spiritual concerns from temporal duties, was at complete variance with the object of revelation, and tended to counteract the purposes of God'.[78]

We hear this very often today. In matters where man falls short, the Holy Spirit and the will of God must be called upon for divine assistance. But no one disputes that Rothschild was also an Orthodox Jew, and so this too could also be another explanation as to why he opposed Napoleon.

Furthermore, some of the Jews did not entirely trust Napoleon's efforts. They feared that at a later date he would use all his power to put them back in their original place. That this fear may have been justified can be seen from a remark made by Napoleon regarding the great support his troops received from the Polish Jews during his war against Prussia (1806-7). When he was told about it, he reportedly said with a laugh: 'The Sanhedrin is at least useful to me.' The Jews' mistrust is further seen in the comment made by the well-known Jew David Friedländer and his friends in Berlin, which described Napoleon's convocation of the Sanhedrin as simply 'a spectacle that Napoleon offered to the Parisians'.[79]

---

[78] Thrush, pp. 99-104. Translator's note: QVOS (p. 104).

[79] Jewish Encyclopedia, Vol. XI, pp. 46-8 (s.v. SANHEDRIN, FRENCH). Translator's note: QVOS. While there may have been genuine Jewish support for Napoleon on the continent, other Jewish support was purely profit-driven, as contemporary army complaints about Jewish profiteering indicate (*Revolution and Evolution*, p. 129; *The Jewish Economic Elite*, pp. 138-9). Even Jewish historians Margolis and Marx admit that 'Napoleon was little edified by the spectacle of small Jewish traders following his armies to buy up the soldiers' loot' (*A History of the Jewish People*, p. 612). See Translator's Bibliography for all sources.

Be that as it may, we are convinced that Napoleon's endeavors stood in the way of the power-political considerations of international Jewry under Rothschild leadership. Then it was Napoleon, today it is Hitler.

The London Society for Promoting Christianity Amongst the Jews

In 1808 the London Society for Promoting Christianity Amongst the Jews was founded. A certain Mr. Joseph Samuel Christian Frederick Frey was the driving force. He was a Jew who had been born in Germany and who had converted to Christianity a few years before. While the London Society's first report of 23 May 1809 showed modest successes, the picture had already improved considerably according to the second report of 27 December. The first thing one notices is that the board was largely made up of members of the highest nobility. We find, among others, the Earl of Crawford and Lindsay, Lord Robert Seymour, and Lord Calthorpe, but also the names of baptized Jews. In the meantime, Mr. Frey was giving sermons twice a week in a chapel and had had numerous tracts printed.[80]

The second report announced that a fund was soon to be set up that would provide money to Jews who intended to marry English women. They proudly declared that they had already raised £2,280 to this end. Among the donors was the Duke of Gloucester with £20.[81]

What is striking is that no president had yet been named. Apparently they wanted to fill this position with a particularly high-ranking personage. Efforts were made in vain to persuade the Archbishop of Canterbury.[82]

The next report listed other members of the nobility on the board and reported on the great successes throughout England. Branches were being set up in larger cities everywhere, and by the beginning of June there would be around 60 of them. The amount of the endowments was also described as encouraging. In one year around £6,000 had been raised. The donors were

---

[80] Halstead, p. 18. Translator's note: However, Gidney in his official *History of the London Society* states that it was founded in 1809. [See Translator's Bibliography]. & Norris, pp. 5, 22; Goakman, p. 5. & First Report, pp. 10-20.

[81] Second Report, p. 12. & pp. 45, 60.

[82] Norris, p. 36. Translator's note: Norris reports that the Society still turned this rejection to their advantage, as it had made sure to report their solicitation to the Archbishop in the press, thereby linking his name with the London Society in the public mind. This ambitious desire [chutzpah?] to capture the very biggest names from the outset is also seen in the fact that no less than the Prince Regent, afterward George IV., was invited to become the first Patron of the Society. This invitation not being accepted, the Society eventually had to settle for the Duke of Kent [Gidney p. 37]. As the organization grew however, they did get subsequent Archbishops of Canterbury on board, in trustee and patron roles. Indeed, as Gidney's History makes clear, the London Society became a veritable Who's Who of English high society.

mainly from aristocratic circles and apparently baptized Jews who had typical English Jewish names.[83]

The activity of this organization could be felt not only in the places where it had branches but reached into every remote corner of England. The land was inundated with a flood of tracts, distributed gratis, about the customs and traditions of the Jews with a view to a better understanding of them. The fourth report appeared on 21 May 1812. It noted with satisfaction the growth of the movement, which was already demonstrated by the establishment of a total of one hundred branches in England. The postal service was thanked for sending pamphlets free of charge. Donations had increased still further. The list concerned shows around 2,800 donors, most of whom belonged to the aforementioned circles. The number of lectures on topics related to Jews had increased.[84]

The company celebrated one of its greatest triumphs in 1813. The Duke of Kent, father of the future Queen Victoria, was chosen as president. The board included a number of well-known names from the nobility. In addition to those already mentioned, we also see the Duke of Devonshire, Viscount Northland, and the Earls of Stamford, Grosvenor, and Egmont, to name just a few. Even the highest clergy believed that they could no longer remain uninvolved. So we find the Bishop of Cloyne and the Dean of Wells on the board. There were also a handful of MPs, and even the Chancellor of the Exchequer did not want to be missing from this illustrious company.[85]

A magazine, *The Jewish Repository*, was published in January 1813, which, in addition to articles on the history of the Jews since the destruction of Jerusalem, also published articles on all other questions that served to promote understanding. As soon as the magazine came out, 800 copies were sold every month and a further large number distributed free of charge. The fifth report shows that the donor list was just as long. In addition to the people already mentioned, it contained the highest members of the clergy. The Bishop of Durham alone donated £50.[86]

At the same time, the foundation stone of 'Palestine Place,' the London Society's own chapel for Christian Jews, was laid. Princes and around 1,000 members of the upper circles of British society were present. The whole thing was turned into a first-rate event.[87]

---

[83] Third Report, p. 69 ff. & p. 102. & pp. 125-182.

[84] Norris, pp. 44-5. & Fourth Report, p. 25 ff. & p. 134. & pp. 61-132. & Norris, p. 48. Translator's note: From page 5 of the Fourth Report: 'The Westminster Committee have also arranged a Lecture to Christians, on subjects relative to the Jews, to be preached at various places of worship at the west end of the town.'

[85] Halstead, p. 21.

[86] Fifth Report, pp. 9-10. & p. 14. & pp. 23-75.

[87] Norris, pp. 67-76. Translator's note: Gidney gives an extensive description of the event, stating that 20,000 spectators were present to witness the Duke of Kent laying the founda-

However, that same year, 1813, brought disaster: the Society's 'first and principal organ', the aforementioned Mr. Frey, was convicted of very immoral acts, 'as foul a charge upon his *moral* character as could possibly be preferred', that necessitated his immediate departure to America.[88]

Nevertheless, the Society overcame this embarrassing event. Apart from a temporary financial difficulty that was quickly resolved, the organization continued to extend its operations. Procuring funds from the 'little people' was also constant, with particularly good results being seen among the well-meaning Christian women who ran the 'ladies' auxiliary societies' and 'penny societies.' Here, the author hints at there being a deliberate strategy to use emotional manipulation and false representation to convince members of the gentler sex to part with their money:

> Collections after sermons were made, both in churches and conventicles, wherever admission into the pulpit could be gained; and auxiliary and penny societies spread themselves with an accelerated rapidity. But the grand financial exploit of this period was directed at the ladies, to bring them under contribution distinctly from the male part of our population. For which purpose, a contrast between their own condition and that of the *vilest Jewish prostitutes*, was obtruded upon their notice, purporting to be an appeal to them in behalf of poor Jewesses, from one of their own sex, and framed with studious adaptation to the *weaknesses* of the female character; whilst, at the same time, the Bible Society's manoeuvre of heading their circulars with influential names, taken *without their owner's consent*, was largely resorted to. The result was, that in the three years from 1813 to 1815, included in the present period, the Society drew from the well-intentioned and spurious benevolence of the nation, a sum exceeding £31,000.[89]

---

tion stone. Interestingly, Gidney describes Palestine Place, which opened in 1814, as 'the first place of worship set apart in England for Christian Jews' (p. 41), which indicates that the London Society appears to have been diametrically opposed to the spirit of Galatians 3:28.

[88] Norris, pp. 63-66, 146 ff; Goakman, pp. 58-59. Translator's note: QVOS (Norris, pp. 64-5). It is unclear what the charge was, although Norris tell us that it was 'publicly brought against him to his face, and supported by the evidence of five witnesses, who all deposed that they had within the last half-hour detected him in the commission of the alleged delinquency'.

[89] Norris, pp. 77-8; 130 ff. Translator's note: QVOS (including italicization) from original source. The exact sum raised was £31,306 and 7 shillings.

In 1828 there even appears to have been at least one joint meeting of Christians and Jews in order to bring the two together by discussing the religious questions which concerned them.[90]

It has not been possible to clearly ascertain the success that was achieved in terms of conversion. In the first 16 years of the London Society's existence, £135,000 is said to have been spent, but the total number of converts is not stated. The result was probably very pitiful, because according to Picciotto, £14,000 of donations were received in 1828, yet only two adult conversions to Christianity were recorded, along with eighteen to twenty children. This would equate to a sum of around £700 for the conversion of a single person. In reality, the overall average cost would probably have been even higher, but even considering the figure given it is shameful to think how much good such an amount could have done for the English people, whose poor then lived in almost greater misery than they do today. There was therefore no lack of voices that recommended the money be better spent on Christian charity, including from the Jews themselves. As one Jewish man, Tobias Goodman, wrote:[91]

> I come now to consider the more particular means by which the London Society 'humbly hope to accomplish this most desirable object'; they are specified as follows, page 4 'to establish a School, that they may be able to receive children wholly from their parents, and bestow upon them education, board, and clothing.' Could this event be accomplished, I think it would be difficult to find a parallel, where benevolence (if it can be so considered) is so ill applied. Are there no Christian families for whom such an establishment would be more prudent? Are there no children among your brethren, whose unfortunate state in Society deserves commisseration, and the pitying hand of benevolence? Certainly, and as certainly (in my opinion) is it a duty you owe to your own people, to provide first for them; but this will not do, a scheme must be adventured on, as unprecedented as it is chimerical, and as artful as it is unjust.[92]

---

[90] Thrush, p. 1.

[91] Picciotto, p. 285. Translator's note: The fact that these were children is particularly important given that it was known that the Society targeted the most indigent Jews in society for proselytism, and one could particularly understand a child beggar being induced to identify as a Christian, if it meant being given hot meals, shelter, clothing, and perhaps even a chance of learning a trade.

[92] Goodman, p. 13. Translator's note: QVOS. For a profile of Tobias Goodman, author and synagogue preacher, see the Jewish Encyclopedia, Vol. 6 p. 45 (s.v. GOODMAN, TOBIAS).

This brief summary of events regarding the London Society may suffice for our purposes. What conclusions can we draw from this? First of all, it is noticeable that there were branches of the Society in at least 100 towns and cities in England. If this organization had really been solely concerned with the conversion of Jews, it would only have maintained such offices in the dozen or so places which then had a reasonable Jewish population.

More than anything, a large part of the population was taught that the old prejudice against Jews was completely wrong and that it was high time that the poor Jews received forbearance and understanding, to compensate for all the persecution they had suffered. And as we have seen, vast amounts of resources were also directed out of the Christian community to the benefit of the Jewish community, to the extent that these resources were not completely wasted. Furthermore, in the highest circles, insofar as this had not already happened, the Jew and his people were made socially acceptable. The same success was also recorded among the clergy, as the donations and participation demonstrate.

Our view is merely an inference from the given facts. We shall decline to address whether these consequences were intended by the Society's sponsors and board members. Determining the subjective side of an action is always quite difficult. For this reason, that is not our aim, which is solely to gauge the empirical results that all of this activity had, intentionally or unintentionally, on furthering Jewish advancement in British society.

Laws of Attrition

The period from 1754 to the dawn of the open emancipation struggle in 1830 could be described as a preparatory period for the coming major offensive. Through the methods mentioned, it was possible to weaken the enemy's defense lines, which is best compared in the propaganda that the Reds developed at the front and within the Fatherland in the final years of the Great War. Slowly, almost invisibly, the seeds sown by the Jews and their allies grew in the hearts of the people. While the term 'Jew' was the epitome of everything bad in mid-18th-century England, by 1839 this had fundamentally changed for part of the English nation. However, it was more a case of the ruling classes giving up their initially hostile position for purely material advantage, than the populace itself changing its stance. In addition, liberal ideas about the supposed equality of all became more prevalent in the public space. But just as a good general secures favorable starting positions for the final attack through small, successful operations, thereby simultaneously increasing the confidence and courage of the troops, so the Jews and their friends created positions for themselves that were bound to be of considerable value in the final confrontation.

These small, successful operations consisted of the laws that were passed in Parliament and other important bodies, which individually only signified a small win, but together became a valuable gain for Judah. The laws initially looked harmless and often did not even contain any reference to the Jews. We like to call these types of laws 'laws of attrition'. As a result, one piece after another was gradually broken out of the defensive wall, which initially only showed small cracks and chips, without revealing to the casual observer the systematic nature of the attacks and the danger of the entire wall collapsing.

One of the laws, or rather an administrative regulation, led to the admission of Jews as solicitors in 1770. In England there are two types of practitioners of the law: solicitors and barristers. The former do not need any academic studies or even higher education. Instead, five years of practical training with a licensed solicitor, two intermediate exams and a final exam are sufficient to qualify. However, they can usually only appear in the lower courts, while barristers have no restrictions in this regard. The latter have higher education and have completed university education; they correspond to the status of our current lawyers in Germany.

Solicitors are by no means to be equated with our litigation agents. They play a greater role in that they negotiate almost exclusively with the public and, in principle, only through them is the connection established with the barrister, who hardly has any personal contact with the litigant.

This brief summary may suffice to show that a far greater influence on the public can be exercised by the solicitor. As a result, the Jews could be quite satisfied with their success. Here, too, we must point out their recurring tactic of striving with all determination to not only get to know the law of a country, but also to be significantly involved in the development of the law, which we have seen with their political lobbying, and in their desire to be admitted as lawyers and later as judges and members of Parliament. The large percentage of Jewish lawyers in all major cities of the world speaks eloquently to this fact.

On 23 January 1770, Joseph Abrahams was the first Jew to receive the honor of being admitted as an Attorney of the King's Bench, having been articled as a solicitor's clerk in 1763. On 13 February, he was sworn in as a solicitor in Chancery, being relieved of the aforementioned Oath of Abjuration by being permitted to omit the last words, 'upon the true faith of a Christian', and was just one of the later numerous Jews who were permitted to do this.[93]

It is not surprising that the Jews managed to gain a foothold in solicitors' circles so early on, as they had already won over many followers during the events of 1753. In any case, this new position gave them a wide scope for

---

[93] Henriques: Jews, pp. 205-6; Records of the Society of Gentleman Practisers, p. 288.

increasing their power, especially given that more of their ethnic kin soon joined them in the profession.

They also received tax relief. As already explained, in principle every foreigner had to pay a special 'alien duty' to the state when exporting or importing goods. With varying degrees of success, the Jews had tried to have these fees abolished under various governments. However, their aim was not to be at the mercy of individual governments, but rather to bring about a general abolition. This goal was achieved when Parliament abolished all alien duties in 1784.[94]

We have also seen that the Hebrews had been seeking the right to be granted naturalization for some time, because this was the only way to obtain the same legal status as an Englishman. As is well known, the prerequisite was to take the Anglican sacrament [of the Last Supper] and to take the oaths, which was impossible for them as Jews. They had therefore sought a law that would enable them to obtain citizenship. The events of 1753 proved how successful this was. But 1825 was supposed to bring about change. There were no more street demonstrations, let alone serious difficulties in Parliament, and almost nothing is recorded about the negotiations. According to this new law, 6 Geo. IV, c. 67, which abolished the requirement for the sacrament of the Lord's Supper, naturalization took place when the applicant had taken the Oaths of Supremacy and Allegiance, which Jews could take without difficulty because they did not contain the fatal final words of the Oath of Abjuration. What a change from the events of 1753! For the sake of completeness, it should be mentioned that further technical simplifications were introduced through corresponding laws in 1844 and 1870.[95]

The 1826 repeal of the previously discussed Alien Act of 1793 (33 Geo. III, c. 4), which was passed to protect England against the excessive immigration of undesirable elements, aroused just as little attention. The provisions contained in the Alien Act, according to which the authorities could restrict aliens to certain districts as deemed 'necessary for publick security', may have been quite uncomfortable for the Jews. The English public took little notice of the repeal of this law, which was replaced by the Regis-

---

[94] Statutes at Large, Vol. XXXIV, pp. 460-2.

[95] Henriques: *Jews*, pp. 289-9. & Statutes of the United Kingdom, Vol. 65, p. 316. & Henriques: *Jews*, p. 245. Translator's note: Mr. Hutt's Naturalization Act of 1844 (7 and 8 Vict., c. 66), introduced the convenient system of acquiring British nationality by means of a certificate from a Secretary of State. The system was further improved and extended by the 1870 Naturalization Act (33 and 34 Vict. c. 14). In addition, readers should also be made aware of the 1796 statute (36 Geo. III, c. 48) which allowed Jews to obtain naturalization in Ireland, a naturalization would of course be valid for the British Isles.

tration of Aliens Act (7 Geo. IV, c. 54), a law which was much more favorable to foreigners.[96]

Undoubtedly, these partial successes gave the Jews and their allies the courage to make new advances. In addition, the question of Catholic emancipation had dominated the public square for years. A review of the contemporary parliamentary debates in Hansard will convince the reader of how much of a burning issue Catholic emancipation had become in domestic politics. The Jews did not yet openly promote their own cause, but supported the Catholics, citing the principle of religious freedom. It is probably thanks to this joint co-operation that the repeal process of the so-called 'Corporation and Test Act' was begun in early 1828.

According to the Corporation Act of 1661 (13 Car. II, st. 2, c. 1), among other things, no one could hold office in a public legal entity, such as a municipal corporation or hold a Crown office, if he had not attended the Anglican sacrament of the Lord's Supper in the year prior to his appointment. Due to an additional law of 1718 (5 Geo. I, c. 6), the election to such an office of a non-qualified person was no longer void from the outset, but had to be challenged within a six months of his election to the office. The so-called Test Act of 1673 (25 Car. II, c. 2) also required all Crown officials, whether civil or military, to take the sacrament in an Anglican church no later than three months after their appointment, and make a declaration against transubstantiation. With both acts, the candidate for office also had to take the Oaths of Allegiance and Supremacy.

These laws made it impossible for Jews and Catholics to hold state and municipal positions. Both communities therefore had a crucial interest in their repeal.[97]

At the beginning of 1828, a bill for the abolition of both acts was submitted to Parliament.

For the first time, we meet Lord John Russell, the third son of the Duke of Bedford, who was born in 1792. While abroad in July 1813, at his father's direction, he was elected as member of Parliament for Tavistock, his family's borough, despite being a month under the minimum age [21]. From that point onwards, Russell the Whig politician cannot be ignored as a champion of all kinds of so-called freedoms in the religious and political fields. It is no surprise that in later years, assisted by Benjamin Disraeli and Rothschild's son Nathan Mayer, he became the driving force behind the emancipation of the Jews.[98]

---

[96] Henriques: *Jews*, p. 232. Translator's note: Quoted element from Statutes at Large, Vol. 43, p. 16.

[97] Henriques: *Jews*, pp. 247-9.

[98] Dictionary of National Biography, Vol. XVII, p. 454 ff.

On 26 February 1828, Russell introduced a bill to repeal the Corporation and Test Act, supported by a petition to Parliament from the City of
London, and justified by Lord John Russell on the grounds that the laws
were outdated and incompatible with the principles of religious freedom.
The bill received widespread support, but there was also no lack of opposition who rightly feared that the passing of this bill would only be the prelude
to other measures to grant further so-called freedoms. Lord John Russell still
found a majority in Parliament. The new law provided for a simple solemn
declaration as a replacement for the Lord's Supper, which Catholics and
Jews could easily make when taking office.[99]

In order to be fully legal, the law still had to be approved by the House
of Lords, which insisted on the addition of the sworn phrase 'upon the true
faith of a Christian'. This had to have come as a bombshell for the friends of
the Jews. While people had previously made a point of avoiding any mention of the Jews as a group, they now felt they had to change this strategy.
Lord Holland considered the Lords' addition to be completely impossible
because it would disadvantage the Jews. But if the words were to be nevertheless inserted, one would have to give special permission to leave them
out. Surprisingly, the Duke of Wellington, who was generally not opposed to
Jews, turned against Lord Holland. In opposition to him, the Duke spoke in
favor of the House of Lords' proposal because he perceived what were likely
to be long-term unforeseen consequences of such changes, having seen the
precedent established with another religious group:

> It was proposed that the words 'on the true faith of a Christian'
> should be left out of the Declaration with the view of admit-
> ting the Jews to office. For his own part, he did not believe it
> to be the intention of the law that Jews should, be so admitted:
> he did not believe that it was the intention of the laws that Dis-
> senters should be admitted. But, be that as it might, they had
> for the last eighty years gone on suspending these laws, and it
> was notorious that Dissenters had been admitted into corpora-
> tions, although it was the object of the original laws to keep
> them out.
>
> Now, it appeared that the legislature was perfectly well
> aware that Dissenters were admitted into corporations... Did
> not the legislature, then, know very well that Dissenters were
> admitted into corporations? Was not this law a proof that they

---

[99] Minutes of the Proceedings of the Court of Common Council, Vol. 1827, pp. 29-62;
Vol. 1828, p. 11. & Hansard, New Series Vol. XVIII, pp. 677-694. & p. 707. & pp. 677 ff,
816-833, 1180-1208, 1329 ff., 1450 ff., 1571 ff.

were acquainted with the fact? It was not so, however, with the Jews. There was no instance in which the legislature had sanctioned the admission of such persons into office. Under these circumstances, therefore, he must oppose the proposition for expunging the words 'on the true faith of a Christian.'

But there was another reason why they ought to remain. It was quite a new principle, and disliked by this country, that Jews should be admitted into corporations and public offices. If, however, the principal was to be recognised, let that question be fairly brought forward, and not be introduced, on the third reading, into a bill which originally contemplated nothing of the kind.[100]

The victor of many battles for England refused to allow Jews back-door access to positions that should be reserved for the English, without this access being properly permitted through Parliamentary debate. Wellington's opinion prevailed, and so the bill was adopted only with the proviso that the final words fatal to the Jews were to be added to the declaration. The bill was thereby amended and sent back to the House of Commons for approval. There were further extensive debates in the lower Chamber. Almost needless to say, various MPs were not satisfied with the new version. It is almost astonishing how the word 'Jew' was studiously avoided during the debates. Any casual observer would have been forgiven for thinking that it was all just a dispute between the Anglicans and the Protestant Dissenters.[101]

Lord Russell spoke once more during that sitting. Given his later stance on the Jewish Question, we would like to reproduce what we consider to be the most important part of his speech:

> The words which had been added to the Declaration by the Lords, could not be considered objectionable as a Declaration of religious opinions, for they were not so intended. The Church of the country was Christian; and to whatever denomination of Christians a man might belong, he could not object to declare, 'on the true faith of a Christian'; for when a party so declared, he could be understood to mean only on the faith of that community of Christians to which he belonged. The intentions of the Lords were, that a man should give a solemn assent to Christianity, without pointing out any particular sect of Christians. He did not think the Declaration was at all nec-

---

[100] Hansard, Vol. XIX, pp. 167-8. Translator's note: QVOS.
[101] Hansard, Vol. XIX, pp. 290-5.

essary; for many who were not Christians would not hesitate
to take it.[102]

In his opinion, it would therefore be the case that the Jew would not mind
swearing these words, contrary to their religious principles. But Lord John
must have been misinformed by his friends, because it was precisely due to
the Hebrews rejecting these words that a decades-long battle broke out. Giv-
en Lord John Russell's insouciant attitude, it is not surprising that the House
of Commons passed the bill with the amendments requested by the Lords,
making it legally binding. All of the pent-up anger of the Jews' allies came
to the fore again when MP Henry Brougham—who later continued to campaign heavily for the Jews in the House of Commons—took the floor immediately after the final important vote. In order to avoid a long debate, he had
remained silent up until that point, but now spoke to express his 'entire disapprobation' of the Lords' amendments, and to add his voice regarding 'the
injustice done to the Quakers and Jews'.[103]

All of Judah's efforts had thus proved fruitless: although the requirement to take the Lord's Supper had been waived, the Lords' insistence on
the fatal wording of the oath had created a new, insurmountable obstacle.
The situation had gone from bad to worse. But in the following year, 1829,
there was to be a victory, if only an indirect one.

The Fall of the City of London, the Bulwark of the Anti-Jewish Movement

The Jews believed that, thanks to their partial previous successes, the preparations had progressed to such an extent that they could soon make the final
assault. Over the course of the preceding narrative it has been possible for
the reader to chart the growth of Jewish power and the slow destruction of
opposition forces. The City of London had been prominent among the Jews'
opponents since Cromwell's time, and it was mainly the City which had ral-
lied the populace against the Jewish law in 1753. This bulwark had to fall. It
was, and continues to be, the heart of the British Empire, with all of the
world-dominating banks and trading houses within its walls. Then, as now,
there was little the British government could do that had not been approved
by the men of the City. So anyone who wanted to achieve something mean-

---

[102] Hansard, Vol. XIX, p. 296. Translator's note: QVOS. This debate is particularly interesting for its revelation of the extent to which Christianity as a faith had declined among
some of the leading Englishmen of the day.

[103] Statute of the United Kingdom, Vol. 68, pp. 22-25.

[103] Hansard, Vol. XIX, p. 299. Translator's note: QVOS. Note the subordinate placing of
'Jews' in Brougham's list, the second of only two references to Jews in the entire Hansard
record of the debate.

ingful could not possibly afford to have the City against him. Judah had experienced this firsthand all too clearly and had therefore taken the appropriate precautions.

The role that individual Hebrews played in the government's financial policy has already been discussed. Rich Jewish trading houses worked hand in hand with government ministers. The Jews' influence on the economy was therefore bound to increase from year to year. It was not always the actual Jewish companies themselves that came into question, but equally or even more so the English bankers and merchants who were directly or even indirectly dependent on the Hebrews, the latter thereby able to enjoy the advantage of making themselves almost invisible to the outside world.

With the appearance of Rothschild in the City, this Jewish encroachment made significant progress and thus gradually reduced economic resistance to Judah. Rothschild's weapons and methods were extremely deadly, as even a pro-Jewish writer admits that Rothschild ruthlessly ruined opponents or forced them under his yoke if they capitulated:

> Your Grace, who I have no doubt is well read in history, knows, that at every period of society the Jews have, by their industry, frugality, and perseverance, monopolized that might lever of men's minds, money; and that, notwithstanding the cruelties, oppressions, spoliations inflicted on them by their savage persecutors the Catholics, they have still preserved that privilege, and kept their enemies in a state of bondage. That at no other period of society the case has been more proved than at the present moment, is fully demonstrated by the servile obsequiousness which all the Crowned heads in Europe spontaneously evince towards the most extraordinary Jew who has ever existed since the remotest days of Moses [Rothschild]; and who, through his influence on the finances of all countries, could strike a docket against all governments, and make them bankrupts.[104]

What extent must this servitude have reached by 1830 if a subservient group had already been identified in the City as early as 1753, a group which, apparently under pressure from the Jews, approached Parliament with a pro-Jewish petition against all public opinion. People who still refuse to believe in their indirect influence today should just take a look at England and France, or remember our times before 1933. Here in Germany, the publication of sobering statistics, all based on documentation, lays out the case only too clearly.[105]

---

[104] Anichini, p. 9. Translator's note: QVOS.
[105] See the official work: *Die Juden in Deutschland.*

We therefore have no doubt that by then the Hebrews had gained predominance in the City, mainly through the English bankers and merchants who were dependent on them. Their willing creatures sat everywhere in City offices, and so the time had to come when the oldest bulwark against Jewish power would fall. It will probably never be possible to determine when exactly this happened. Clear signs were certainly visible in the petitions that the City's Common Council sent to Parliament in favor of Catholic emancipation, which stood in contrast to the City's previous policy and which were obviously intended to help pave the way for Jewish emancipation.

But for all the actual power the Jews wielded in the City of London, it had still been impossible for them to gain the freedom of the City. To acquire this privilege, it was an indispensable requirement to swear an oath on the New Testament, which the Jews refused. As early as 1739—as part of the first wave of emancipation that was already beginning—the Jews tried to take the oath on the Old Testament, which even led to a lawsuit after the City's administration refused to accept the oath. During the court case, the chief justice asked the City aldermen to explain their reasoning for the otherwise qualified Jew Abraham Rathom not being able to swear the oath in the form he liked. The City cited the ancient custom and refused to make any changes. After long negotiations, the chief justice announced the verdict that the City's handling of the matter complied with the law, and the court had no right to interfere in the form of the City's oaths. After that event, the Jews no longer dared to address the issue directly, and it would be almost another century before they achieved their aim.

But the situation was more than unedifying for Judah. London was still their actual place of settlement, where they could not receive the rights of Englishmen despite becoming naturalized in Great Britain. This was a general inconvenience to them, but it also brought individual disadvantages. Wholesale commerce within the City of London was still permitted to those who did not have freedom of the City. However, the retail trade desired by the lower classes was forbidden to non-freemen.

After 1820, fundamental disagreements emerged between the City's two main administrative bodies, the Court of Aldermen and the Common Council. The former consisted of 26 aldermen, from whose ranks the mayor was elected. Among other privileges, the Court of Aldermen had the power to appoint certain offices and exercised judicial functions in regard to licensing. With each alderman being a judge and magistrate, the Court also had official control over the City. The aldermen were also members of the Common Council, which consisted of 232 members and was the legislative body of the City of London Corporation. The friends of the Jews, half-Jews, and baptized Jews were more likely to gain access to the Common Council, whose members were elected annually by the freemen, as the Common

Council could be seen as comparable to the assembly or citizenry of a city, with the Court of Aldermen being roughly equivalent to the Senate.[106]

It is to the Court of Aldermen's credit that, in compliance with existing laws and despite the pressure that was very likely exerted on it to do otherwise, it took action against Jews who were running small trading businesses in the City without permission and against the legal regulations. This must have been a very extensive problem because the Common Council decided on 5 March 1824 to appoint a committee to investigate the issue. It was declared illegal to engage in small-scale trade without freedom of the city. The goods of violators were to be confiscated without delay and forfeited to the state. After very careful investigation in the individual districts of the City, the committee had determined that, despite this risk, a large number of people were carrying on petty trade in open defiance of the law, without being freemen of the City. It happened under the guise of being a wholesaler, as the official report shows. According to this, 'a number of wholesalers constantly display goods for sale to the public and sell them in the retail trade to the detriment of those who keep open shops.' Thus it was deemed urgent that strict measures be taken against these miscreants.[107]

Apparently, however, there were no further special measures taken by the Common Council, which certainly fits with the later attitude of this City body. The Court of Aldermen, however, had apparently taken the necessary lawful steps. In 1829, the aforementioned pro-Jewish writer Apsley Pellatt, who was also a member of the Common Council, complained that:

> In the few instances where Jews have taken retail shops in the
> City, they have been harrassed by repeated processes from the
> Lord Mayor's Court Office, and at length obliged to quit their
> houses, perhaps at a sacrifice, on payment of legal costs.

Lawbreakers are therefore pitied when existing laws are applied to them. Pellatt goes so far as to describe the regulations in question as 'a bigoted system' which was 'absurd and illiberal' and 'the legacy of the dark ages'.[108]

Pellatt asserts that there were only a few Jews who were found to be offending. What information does the official report provide in this regard? It states that in 1825 there were 142 offenders, in 1826: 303 offenders, in 1827: 600 offenders, in 1828: 1128 offenders, and in 1829: 1561 offenders, making

---

[106] Encyclopedia Britannica, 11th Edition, Vol. I, p. 533 (s. v. Alderman). Dictionary of London (1918), pp. 6, 165.

[107] Minutes of the Proceedings of the Court of Common Council, Vol. 1827, pp. 138-140.

[108] Pellatt, pp. 24, 26-7. Translator's note: All QVOS. As the reader may imagine, Pellatt was equally horrified by the proposal put forward to solve the problem, namely, that the privileges of the City freemen should be extended to wholesale as well as retail trade.

a total of 3289 offenders (that were documented).[109] These numbers are very revealing in several respects. Based on the information already presented, it should be self-evident that the largest percentage of these offenders were Jews. It also appears that from 1825 to 1829 the number of lawbreakers increased enormously. It is unlikely to be a coincidence that this increase is particularly evident after 1824, which is when it was clear that no measures would be taken against this criminal behavior, despite the recommendations of the committee appointed by the Common Council. This created an incentive for such lawbreakers to defy the law more than ever before. Of course, as always on such occasions, it can no longer be determined whether there was even encouragement from certain quarters.

Furthermore, from these incidents, further insight can be gained into general Jewish tactics. Jews often gain their first foothold by blatantly breaking the law. At first it is ignored for some reason, probably because most people do not like trouble, and to go against certain individuals, who to the casual observer appear to be doing no real harm, can backfire badly on the person trying to raise the alarm. Not being challenged, the Jews then gradually expand their position in terms of numbers and power, although still working covertly so that it is difficult for the public to see what is happening. With their new authority they intertwine as large a number of fellow Jews as possible into their network, but especially also local people.

At some point, there is a build-up of counter-pressure from the host population, a natural reaction to the untenable situation created by the Hebrews, which inevitably leads to an open determination of the facts and corresponding measures to counter the problem. At this point, not only the Jews feel threatened in their illegally-acquired position, but also the non-Jews who have become dependent on them. The aggrieved Jews and their allies start screaming blue murder, demanding that the outdated, inhumane laws that are still on the books be abolished unquestionably because, as evidence of anti-Jewish persecution, they endanger the very existence of Jews. We will see how, in the course of further events, this method was used purposefully and assiduously by the Jews, and had the same good results for the Children of Israel in 19th-century England as it has had in all countries and epochs.

Incidentally, while such Jewish protests are going on, the public, or at least the printed press posing as public opinion, often mock the 'narrow-mindedness' and 'bigotry' of those who are determined to stick to their ancestors' traditional usages. The same forces also pity those who have gotten into trouble because of these 'ridiculous' ancient laws, although in such cases it is usually overlooked that it is the Jews themselves who have created their own predicament through their overreaching and disregard for others, which means that by rights they should be made to bear the consequences of their

---

[109] Minutes of the Proceedings of the Court of Common Council, Vol. 1830, pp. 79-80.

own illicit actions. Even today, this Jewish appeal to the compassion of the masses who are not yet enlightened about Jewish behavior [the *argumentum ad misericordiam* fallacy], always yields the best results.

The Court of Aldermen's antipathy towards the Jews is clearly shown by another incident. Never in the history of England has such a conscious attitude towards race been observed as that seen in one of the resolutions made by this public body. This resolution stated: 'That it is the opinion of this Court, that it is neither politic nor advisable in this Corporation to admit baptized Jews into the freedom of this City, and that it be observed as a standing order.' In a legal dispute, descendants of baptized Jews tried to challenge this provision, especially if they came from a mixed marriage. But here too the Court of Aldermen prevailed and determined that such descendants could be excluded from the privileges of the City, given that the City was free to grant or refuse its freedom to any applicant at its own discretion. But it was again the Court of Common Council, as the legislative power of the city, which intervened after the ordinance of the Court of Aldermen had existed for twelve or thirteen years, and had it repealed in 1829.[110]

Any remaining doubts about the pro-Jewish sympathies of the Common Council must have been dispelled on 19 June 1829. We can only describe this day as decisive in the struggle for Jewish emancipation. From that day on, it was clear that the City had opened its gates wide to the enemy through gradual subversion, mainly from within. That day it was decided to ask a committee 'to report on the municipal and legal restrictions which prevented Jews from doing business in the City of London, while they had not become freemen'.[111]

It is surprising that, even at that stage, the forces of self-preservation were apparently still resisting foreign infiltration. It was not until 1 April 1830 that the various reports on the matter were published. With the exception of the Court of Aldermen, it was considered possible and sufficient to change the law through a simple administrative City ordinance. The former, however, believed that, as a result of centuries of practice, the City was bound by its own law, which could only be repealed by a formal act of Parliament. It also considered the admission of Jews impossible, because of their incompatibility with the Christian religion, which had become an indispensable, essential part of all English law. Finally, it warned against foreign infiltration, which would lead to undesirable consequences. The four other experts who were called upon, however, held a different opinion and considered that the admission of Jews as freemen was possible, as there was nothing to prevent them making the necessary oath on the Old Testament. The

---

[110] Pellatt, pp. 26-27. Translator's note: QVOS.
[111] Minutes of the Proceedings of the Court of Common Council, Vol. 1829, [19 June 1829], p. 68.

previous rulings of the Supreme Court on this matter could no longer be considered acceptable in that day and age. People went along with these expert arguments and ignored the one dissenting voice of warning. The path to freedom of the City was clear for Judah. The full proposal for the new regulations was published on 3 September 1830; it was debated on December 6 and adopted four days later, on December 10 of the same year.[112]

It was not long before the first Jew applied to become a freeman. Judah Jacobs was the first to apply for this privilege, on 2 February 1831. A glance at the relevant document register is enough to see the large number of Hebrews who took advantage of his victory in the years that followed.[113]

Jews—Freemen of the City of London!

They finally achieved their goal.

The City, which had defied the Jews for so long, had finally opened its gates to them. Soon it would be the bulwark of the Hebrews, from which they would launch attack after attack on the last of their enemies' positions. If the Jews were finally victorious after an emancipation struggle of 28 years, this fact alone was the key to their success.

Anyone who undertakes to free England from Jewish rule must first recapture the City of London. Whoever defeats them will see in England's organizational structure the means of finally asserting his power in the country.

---

[112] Minutes of the Proceedings of the Court of Common Council, Vol. 1830, pp. 40-2. & pp. 42-5. Translator's note: A topical alternative translation of '*die heutige Zeit*' could be 'the current year', given that this argument is the 'appeal to modernity' [argumentum ad novitatem] fallacy. & Minutes of the Proceedings of the Court of Common Council, Vol. 1830, p. 103. & pp. 164, 170-1.

[113] Minutes of the Proceedings of the Court of Common Council, Vol. 1831, p. 18. & Vol. 1831-1832.

CHAPTER 6
EMANCIPATION (1830-1866)

Introduction[1]

It is a rather typical peculiarity of the Jewish race that it brings with it, without fail, the seeds of anti-Semitism. Effectively, in every place where the Jewish element manages to impose itself to a considerable extent, anti-Semitism will similarly flourish and activate in a seemingly spontaneous way. It would be an unparalleled historical phenomenon if anything else had happened in England. Already at the dawn of English history, anti-Jewish attitudes can be frequently observed, which countless times are manifested in anti-Semitic revolts and in strong national and racial measures. It is sufficient to recall the expulsion of almost all Jews by Edward I, back in the year 1290, which had such lasting consequences for England. Until then, it had been the custom, later re-established, that princes and kings surrounded themselves with Jewish advisors and, above all, were assisted by a Jewish financier. But Edward was one of the few noblemen who put the national interest before all else, even his own economic interests, who listened to the prevailing mood of his people, and who expelled the Jews from the country. The people have known perfectly well, at every stage in history, what to think of Judaism. In those days, it was evident that certain cases of ritual murder and the devaluation of the currency, as well as usury on money and lands, were reasonably due to Jewish machinations; in short, the royal decree was the logical consequence of an openly anti-Semitic attitude in the people.

But this event, despite being huge and consequential in itself, did not go beyond being an episodic act. Cromwell in particular began, and energetically consolidated, not only the close union of the Jewish element with English national life, but went as far as almost to make English and Jewish political interests indistinguishable. We do not claim, of course, that it would have been possible to classify Cromwell as a philo-Semite or attribute pro-Jewish tendencies to him, far from it: Cromwell was an Englishman and nothing but an Englishman. But diverse factors had obviously made him consider it convenient to turn to and support Judaism.

Let us start with the genuinely fundamental Puritan spirit of belonging to a chosen people who are favored by God. Who could deny here the great

---

[1] Translator's note: This short introduction is found in Krueger's book *Juden beherrschen England*, a separate publication that was made of chapters 6 and 7 of *Das Judentum in England*. It has been reproduced here for its literary interest, and for its useful recapitulation of salient points in the preceding chapters.

similarity between the appreciation for outward prosperity, economic success, and social advancement, and the Jewish ideology of the Old Testament? On comparing the Old Testament with the New, wouldn't the Puritan have to give preference to the first, given its sober and clear ideology which orients its religious aspects towards outward appearances? Wouldn't the history of the people who have been divinely chosen, and therefore, politically chosen, called thus to sovereignty, be more attractive to the English Puritan desirous of world hegemony, than the New Testament doctrine of love, compassion, and renunciation?

But dispensing with this purely spiritual aspect, what Cromwell yearned for was not only to give a religious and divine character to English pretensions to hegemony, but even further, to represent and characterize the English people as those directly mandated to carry out the Old Testament's divine will of sovereignty. But Cromwell would have been a poor Puritan indeed if, as well as using tradition as justification, he had not got out of it the concrete results and material success that he did. With the new wave of Jewish immigration, called to England by the Puritans, came a good part of the connections of world commerce, which already found themselves in Jewish hands, which resulted in what was perhaps England's best ally in the fight against Holland and Spain.

All of this can only be observed and represented here in the most haphazard and vaguely detailed way, and is only directly important for being able to comprehend what came later, because it demonstrates the inner and spiritual similarity between the English Puritan and the Judaism of the Old Testament, the Old Testament coming to play something like the role of an 'allegory of national policy.' Cromwell's death, which undoubtedly left Judaism in an unfavorable and unsatisfactory situation, did very little to change the state of things. The Jewish spirit of chosenness and divine grace continued to live on in countless Englishmen, and only because of this could the Jewish emancipation movement of the 19th century take such a fateful turn, and put into Jewish hands such important posts and offices. Immediately after Cromwell, the English king returned to being surrounded by influential Jews, to whom were entrusted the main duties of the Court and posts of high responsibility, or, at the very least, he was advised by a Jewish banker. It is true to say that anti-Semitism had still not disappeared. The last bulwark against Jewish emancipation was the House of Lords, until this position was likewise assaulted and destroyed. From that point onwards, it was very rare that true instincts and racial knowledge were made visible and evident, and only religious differences were recognized and stressed.

The following pages tell of the emancipation and show how Judaism not only came to dominate the racial and national life of England, but also, going beyond this, has been dedicating all of its efforts to the conquest of global hegemony.

The Jews' Methodology: The Period from 1830 to 1866

The year 1830 had arrived. The Jews and their friends had occupied all of the positions that they felt necessary for the general attack. With calm and sangfroid, they proceeded to eliminate the last of the restrictions on them, known to history as 'Jewish disabilities.' What type of restrictions were these? This is a difficult question to answer, since, theoretically, many things were prohibited to Jews that in practice they had enjoyed for already a long time since their resettlement.

There was, for example, the problem of immovable property. Two archaic 13th-century laws which had been completely forgotten, but which were unearthed again in 1788, denied Jews the right to possess immovable property. Although these laws remained in effect, due to never having been repealed, very little attention was paid to them, which was why, in the final decades of the 17th century, it was not unusual for the Jews to acquire immovable property. Nevertheless, a longstanding and heated debate continued to rage among jurists regarding the validity or otherwise of such acquisitions, and the final word on the matter had still not been pronounced in any sense.[2]

Theoretically, neither did the Jews have the right to vote, given that, although achieving British nationality would mean the first condition for suffrage was met, to be an elector one also had to be a freeholder of immovable property in some county, or citizen of a district, in possession of all of his rights. For that reason, in the face of a lack of clarity regarding the property question, this condition was highly uncertain for the Jews, while the quality of being citizens in possession of full rights had only been granted to them relatively recently—as for example, by the City of London. Nevertheless, omitting this condition, the electoral president could demand of an elector, regarding the support for a candidate of the electoral district, to swear the Oath of Abjuration (in this case, abjuration of loyalty to the Stuart King James II and his descendants), an oath which the Jews could not swear due to the final passage 'upon the true faith of a Christian.' But regardless of these theoretical difficulties, the Jews took part in elections, a situation which continued until the definitive clarification of the problem in the year 1867, when the Jews were granted full electoral rights.[3]

---

[2] Henriques: *Jews*, pp. 191-194. Translator's note: It is likely that this is a reference to the antiquary D'Blossiers Tovey, who, in the course of research at the Bodleian Library for his 1738 history *Anglia Judaica* [see Translator's Bibliography for a recent English translation of the same], unearthed two unrepealed ordinances prohibiting Jewish land ownership. These ordinances, made under Henry III in 1271 and 1275, arguably undermined the validity of subsequent legislation made in 1723. For further information, see Salbstein, p. 48 [Translator's Bibliography].

[3] Henriques: *Jews*, pp. 246-247. Hyamson: *History*, p. 261. Translator's note: Note that some sources use the phrase 'on the true faith of a Christian', while most others use 'upon

The spheres which were totally forbidden to them included, for example, the profession of barrister (jurisconsult), as well as municipal and other official posts. In addition, it was prohibited for them to enter universities, as it was prohibited for them to become members of Parliament.[4]

The quoted final words of the Oath of Abjuration, that were generally required for the granting of such rights, signified an insurmountable obstacle for the Jews, which is why they strove to defeat them so determinedly for almost 30 years. Countless petitions were sent to Parliament, and even admitted into it, requesting the abrogation of the oath's formula, to thus make Hebrew admission possible; but equally countless were the denials that these requests merited in the House of Lords. We often find, year after year, Parliament taken up with this question and sometimes several requests of this type took place in the same year. Surely in the history of England there can be no analogous issue that excited such passions. Even though, for example, the Catholic Question was also the subject of discussion for a long time, the arrangement agreed by both legislative Houses in the year 1829 brought a satisfactory solution to all interested parties. Infinitely greater were the amounts of energy, time, effort and money that were employed to help the Jewish Question to triumph. For many years, the different electoral assemblies went under the sign of 'for or against Judah.' The parliamentary debates went on for days and even nights, but for 28 years the House of Lords resisted every Jewish assault. In accordance with the British constitution of that time, every law, to acquire legal force, had to be approved by both Houses, the House of Commons and the House of Lords. At the beginning of 1858 the resistance of the Lords still remained unbreakable. What today is not wished to be seen in most spheres of England, threatened to happen: an unprecedented constitutional crisis. In the most irresponsible way, the Jews and their friends fanned the flames in their newspapers against the House of Lords and demanded more or less openly a violent intervention into the rights of the Lords, whose undignified fate can be partly explained by this.

It is truly strange—although it causes no amazement to those familiar with Jewish methods—that general works on the history of England barely mention these battles and these crises. One finds that famous historians skim over these events in two or three paragraphs, while much less important matters are discussed at length—things that to today's average Englishman seem much more important than the Jewish Question, which eats away at his very marrow, yet nevertheless he considers trivial and therefore unworthy of mention.

---

the true faith of a Christian', an interchangeability which is quite ironic, given the central political importance of these few words over the course of the 19th century. In the interests of consistency, I have opted for the latter formulation unless directly quoting a source which uses the alternate version.

[4] Hyamson: *History*, pp. 261-262. Picciotto: p. 386.

We do not wish to enter into a discussion regarding that attitude here, but it would be interesting to know why the Jews and their friends have struggled for emancipation for almost 30 years, with all of the means imaginable, if it had been such an irrelevant matter. The terrifying ignorance of the matters regarding these historic facts has been the main motivator for us to lay out in the following chapters, with considerable detail, important speeches of the members of Parliament of that time. All of these speeches can be found in Hansard and are therefore beyond all doubt in terms of their authenticity. In addition, we have been able to verify that the content and the form entirely correspond with modern anti-Jewish conceptions, thus conclusively refuting that theory spread around by the Jews of England, that in Great Britain there has never existed powerful anti-Jewish forces. Although these manifestations frequently rest on religious bases and do not strongly highlight the racial factor, the content of these speeches will leave no one in doubt that the Jews were considered immoral and pernicious for the people.[5]

We will also spend considerable time on the attitude of the press. Lord Thomas Babington Macaulay, whose life spanned the epoch 1800-1859 and who has become known principally for his historical works, wrote the sentence: 'The one true history of a country can only be found in its newspapers.' While there might be a good deal of truth to this, one has to avoid attributing too much importance to this theory. It is interesting to gauge how the press started dedicating more and more column-inches to the Jewish Question, to eventually pass over onto the side of the Jews and their friends.[6]

In this sixth chapter of our work, we shall carefully expound how the Jews, over a period of time, set about preparing the ground for their goals, back in the years around 1830. Their victory is due in part to the press, which was kind to them and created an atmosphere within the populace which must have been favorable to them. Liberal circles similarly intervened in support of Jewish emancipation, under the banner of general liberty. But it was the organized Jewry of London which did the most work to advance the cause, through money and relationships with powerful politicians.

Behind it all were men of great energy and inexhaustible financial means, such as Lord John Russell and the House of Rothschild, which was

---

[5] Paul: Volume I, pp. 81, 119, 132-3, 212, 287, 351, Volume II, pp. 66, 82, 131, 178. Lingard: Volume II, p. 627. Brodrick: Volume II, p. 235. Low: Volume XII, p. 169. Spencer Walpole: *History of England*, Volume III, p. 77, Volume IV, p. 343. Spencer Walpole: *The History of Twenty-five Years*, Volume I, p. 171. & See, for example, Paul: Volume 1, pp. 132-135.

[6] *Dictionary of National Biography*, Volume XII, pp. 410-418. Translator's note: I was unable to find the original English form of this quotation, the closest I could find being from Macaulay's *The History of England from the Accession of James II*, Chapter XXI: 'The history of the newspapers of England from that time to the present day is a most interesting and instructive part of the history of the country.'

headed until 1836 by Nathan Mayer Rothschild, and later mainly by his son Lionel. Lord John Russell was very active for many years in English politics, while Rothschild had the money required. Along with these two, one must include Isaac Lyon Goldsmid, who similarly disposed of enormous wealth and had many friends among the aristocracy and the other ruling classes. On seeing that the Jews' efforts had been unsuccessful in the first years of their fight, he dedicated himself almost exclusively to the emancipation movement and was lucky enough to be able to witness the final victory of his racial brethren, after having been previously elevated to the nobility. The last and by no means least in this alliance was Benjamin Disraeli, who onwards from 1837—the year of his entry into Parliament—intervened on behalf of the Jews.[7]

It is instructive to say something regarding the Jews' tactics. After having achieved partial victories in the City, the Jews aimed to achieved their emancipation in one fell swoop, with a bill which would legally abolish all Jewish disabilities. This attempt having failed, they returned to the old methods: overall efforts were divided into isolated actions, to achieve the annulment of one restriction after another, thus definitively overcoming and defeating the general principle of their adversaries. In this way, the Jews also managed to gradually occupy positions from which their contributions could support the Jewish Question. The most offensive method consisted of the Jews getting themselves elected for official posts of any type, without being legally entitled to do so. Then they appealed to the popular mood, and, in the case of being excluded, complained of the injustice to the electors and the candidates. We will soon see to what extent this popular mood could interfere in such elections.

We shall also deal at length with the number of Jews in England and their main centers of settlement, which we believe is needed to demonstrate once again, with full evidence, that in all of the great revolutions produced within a nation regarding the Jewish Question, the numerical force of the Children of Israel is never the main factor, but rather the real importance lies solely in certain cliques of rich and influential Jews.

The Number of Jews in the Year 1830

The calculations of various researchers regarding the totality of Jews in 1830 do not show uniform conclusions, but the differences are insignificant. One can safely say that in said epoch, some 20,000 Jews lived in London, and some 10,000 more in the remainder of England. In 1848 the number of Jews was estimated at 40,000 souls, which stands in contradiction to a calculation made in 1853 which put the figure at 25,000, which also does not seem to

---

[7] *Jewish Encyclopedia*, Volume VI, p. 31. Translator's note: Goldsmid was the first unbaptized Jew to be given a hereditary title, when he was made baronet in 1841.

accord with the 1830 estimate. This last figure come from the Reverend Mills, who, due to his extensive dealings with the Jews, claimed to have an exact knowledge of their life. Nevertheless, although he may have erred in his rough calculation, one has to forgive him due to the lack of statistics. On the other hand, his statements demonstrate that he was, indeed, very familiar with the Jewish colony of England.[8]

He tells us, for example, that the majority of Jews had to be considered as poor, being constituted of peoples who had immigrated relatively recently and who mainly lived in London. Based on his rough calculation of 25,000, he puts the figure of poor Jews at 12,000—that is, almost half; another 8,000 are counted to be among the so-called middle class, while the remaining 5,000 must be included, in his judgement, among the wealthy classes. Only this last category should enter into consideration as those able to impose their will on the influential men of England, and it would probably only be a certain few of them—like Rothschild and Goldsmid—who with their riches and their relationships could bend the English government to their will.

We also find out through Mills that already at that time, together with London, the principal centers for Jewish immigration were the industrial cities of Birmingham, Liverpool, and Manchester.[9]

Jewish Preparations and Initial Defeats

In the preparations for their first attempt at emancipation, the documents published by Jews offer us the rare chance to perfectly comprehend the objectives and methodology of Jewish behavior. It concerns the letters from the estate of the late Sir Isaac Lyon Goldsmid who played a leading role among the Jews. Unfortunately, only a selection of these letters have been published, while the main body of them continue in Jewish hands. But even this small sample offers us a good glimpse into the secret negotiations of the Jews with England's influential men of the time.[10]

Already in 1828, Lord Holland, in a letter to Goldsmid, is recommending that the final words of the Oath of Abjuration, fatal for Jews, be eliminated by law. He assures him that he will lend all of his weight in the House of Lords to having this position accepted.[11]

Other correspondence between the two, from February 1829, informs of the maneuvers of Rothschild, who—as Lord Holland advised—was to expound to the Duke of Wellington the value to be wrought from looking kindly upon global Jewry. In the face of growing Russian influence in the

---

[8] Hyamson: *History*, p. 260. B. Montagu: p. 21. Goldsmid: *Remarks*, p. 26, 69, 70. Salomons: *Short Statement*: p. 21. & Egan: p. 36. & Mills: p. 256. & Mills: *Prologue*, pp. 5, 256-258.
[9] Mills: pp. 259-260.
[10] L. Abrahams: p. 116.
[11] L. Abrahams: pp. 134-135.

Middle East, it was indispensable for England to be assured of secret support from the Hebrews who lived there. Lord Holland continued:

> The Jews throughout those eastern countries are an active, in-
> telligent, opulent, and above all compacted and united race—
> remarkable, as you well know they are everywhere, for a rapid
> and confidential communication of their sentiments and feel-
> ings one to the other, and in possession of many of the most
> lucrative trades and professions of the country. They must
> therefore have, and in fact they have, much moral though indi-
> rect influence on the councils of the State, and still more on
> the disposition of the people.

But Jews the world over adjust their attitude to each nation's government according on how the latter treats their racial brethren. 'If then the Jews of England were on an equal footing with all their other fellow-subjects, would not their brethren of Constantinople, Turkey, and the Levant, feel that in promoting the political objects of Great Britain they were furthering the view of a friendly power...?' In view of that, by England showing herself to be generous with the Jews, in Lord Holland's judgement, 'every Jew banker, Jew physician, Jew merchant throughout Turkey, would become an active and useful partisan of the English system of policy in the Levant, whatever that system may be'.[12]

This international cooperation of the Jews with Great Britain, evidently a betrayal of the corresponding host nation—as in this case Turkey—was as a consequence the main reason that, as Rothschild explained to the Duke of Wellington, there was a need to concede an equality of rights to the Jews of England. From our perspective as Germans, we can agree with the following observation: it is very interesting for us and for our measures taken regarding the Jews.

From other letters, it can be gleaned that the progress of the law regarding Catholics was closely followed. In an extract from the minute-book of the Board of Deputies for the Affairs of British Jews, dated 17 March 1829, one reads that Goldsmid held meetings with numerous members of both legislative Houses on the Jewish Question, having also entered into negotiations with figures as important as Lord Holland, Lord Lansdowne, and other influential men. It was hoped to gain still greater influence in this sphere through Mr. Moses Montefiore.[13]

---

[12] L. Abrahams, pp. 135-137. Translator's note: All Holland quotations QVOS.
[13] L. Abrahams: pp. 139-140. Translator's note: Note that here the Board of Deputies' official name is as it appears in the original source, bearing in mind that the organization has had different official names over the centuries.

In April 1829 it is likely that new steps were taken in favor of the Jews. We find letters from Lord Holland dated April 11 and 12 addressed to I. L. [Isaac Lyon] Goldsmid, which indicate great general activity. It is interesting to note that 'Mr. R.'—undoubtedly Rothschild—had spoken to 'powerful persons' who were found to be 'friendly to the object... in view.' In addition, it appears to have been verified that the press and the public would show the greatest inclination towards supporting the Jewish Question.[14]

From the minute-book of the Board of Deputies for the Affairs of British Jews, for the session of 16 April 1829, one gleans that the Duke of Wellington, the Lord Chancellor, and other leading government representatives had promised Rothschild all of their support during the course of an interview. We also learn that Rothschild 'strenuously advised that, for the present, not a single observation should be published in the daily papers on the subject, being convinced that any controversy would prove fatal to the object in view'.[15]

Straight afterwards, work began on the bill for the annulment of existing Jewish disabilities. This bill was finished in May of the same year. Its principal demand was equal rights with the English, because the Catholics had been already been granted the same rights. But before taking the formal steps to submit the bill, the Duke of Wellington was once again asked if he was still ready to lend his support to the cause. It must surely have been an unpleasant surprise for the Jews to have heard Wellington's negative reply, which was based on the fact that regarding the Catholic emancipation law he felt that it was bad timing to launch another analogous bill for another group in the population, because at that point, one had to consider the violent attacks that would come from public opinion. When even Lord Holland seconded the Duke of Wellington's opinion, the next step of the plan was cancelled.[16]

Nevertheless, it was deemed undesirable to delay the plan for more than a few months. Already at the end of June, we find a letter from Lord Holland to I. L. Goldsmid recommending the plausibility of future moves. It indicates the need to win over a high church dignitary in the House of Lords, to win over the support of this group known not to be very favorable to Jew-

---

[14] L. Abrahams, pp. 140-141. Translator's note: QVOS. As with this and all future mentions of I. L. Goldsmid in this volume, Aldag's Roman-script German text has rendered the name as J. L. Goldsmid, an error likely due to a fault in transcription from the original Fraktur [Gothic] script of the text (I's and J's being extremely similar to the casual glance); a careful checking of Aldag's primary sources show that only I. L. [i.e. Isaac Lyon] Goldsmid is the individual in question. The English translation has thus amended all errors accordingly. This is of particular importance to mention due to the fact that a J. L. Goldsmid also did exist around the same time, being Isaac's second cousin, and he similarly used double initials for his forenames [John Louis].

[15] L. Abrahams: p. 141. Translator's note: QVOS. See also Emanuel, p. 16 ff. for complete reports of these 1829 meetings.

[16] L. Abrahams: pp. 141-144. Emanuel: pp. 16-20.

ish emancipation. It considers the Bishop of London very suitable to this end and recommends that they begin to work on him appropriately, by way of Lord Bexley.[17]

From what it would appear, some time later Lord Holland established an exact plan for subsequent negotiations, as we find notes in his handwriting which indicate this. It can be seen that he set out the matter of whether the Jews' immediate demand should be a partial or total equality of rights, and whether they wanted to present their bill first to the House of Lords or to the Commons. In his judgement, one had to consider very carefully the political party to which the sponsor of the bill would belong, in order to maximize the chance of success. He then expresses his own opinion and ends by suggesting that the best option would be that the proposition is made by a government minister, or—in the case of not finding one prepared to do it—by a bishop. Failing that, 'some member of character who voted against the Roman Catholic Relief Bill' should be sought.[18]

Apparently, the Earl of Glengall must have been another of the 'friends of the Jews,' who made propaganda designed to promote the desired law, since in a letter addressed to I. L. Goldsmid he tells him that his efforts with Lord Hertford in this direction seem to have borne fruit.[19]

Halfway through September 1829, support was also secured from the Catholic Radical MP, Daniel O'Connell. O'Connell, who with great drive had led the Catholic Question to victory, showed himself very inclined to help the Jews, whom he saw as oppressed, as was expressed in his letter dated 11 September 1929 to I. L. Goldsmid. He particularly emphasized that the Jews should force Parliament to take a decision in the face of a *fait accompli*. In a letter to Goldsmid, O'Connell wrote:[20]

> You ought not to confide in English liberality. It is a plant not genial to the British soil. It must be *forced*. It requires a *hot-bed*. The English were always persecutors. Before the so-styled Reformation, the English tortured the Jews and strung up in scores the Lollards. After that Reformation they still roasted the Jews and hung the Papists...[21]

Shortly before the bill was presented to Parliament in 1830, the member Robert Grant, who had been chosen to present the motion, wrote that certain members harbored doubts about the definitive position that they should take regarding the Jewish Question [*idem*. pp. 155-156].

---

[17] L. Abrahams: pp. 144-145.

[18] L. Abrahams: pp. 145-151. Translator's note: QVOS.

[19] L. Abrahams: p. 151.

[20] *Dictionary of National Biography*, Volume XIV: p. 816.

[21] L. Abrahams: pp. 151-153. Translator's note: QVOS.

It is unfortunate that, of Isaac Lyon Goldsmid's abundant correspondence, only this small part has been published up until now. This is particularly inconvenient due to the fact that, according to another Jewish source, among the collection in question, there are numerous letters from Lord Lansdowne, Lord Melbourne, Sir Robert Peel, the Duke of Wellington, Earl Grey, and many other influential men of the House of Lords and the House of Commons. Letters from Lord Lyndhurst—who was then Lord Chancellor—attest to the fact that this man was wholeheartedly on the side of the Jews and that he was totally prepared to use all of his influence in the service of their cause. As a member of the government, naturally, when it came to voting, he had no other option but to vote in the same direction as the cabinet, but that did not in any way affect his stance towards the issue.[22]

Through all of the above, one can see how, in the shadows, many years of effort and work went into making the final preparations. Here also we can see the game, so often suspected and so rarely admitted by the Jews, of one or more of their ethnic brethren making use of the high dignitaries of a country in order to achieve their ends. It is difficult for the members of the legislative Houses, and much less the public, to imagine the closeness of the relationship between their leading men and the Jews, and what is more, that certain moves were made by these men only after being approved by the Jews. Unfortunately, in none of the emancipation attempts of the subsequent years did this game of intrigues come to be exposed. What is certain is that the I. L. Goldsmid collection and the Rothschild archive could shed light on this matter. In the meantime, we will have to wait for the time in which this mystery can be finally solved.

Eventually, the moment arrived at which it was considered opportune to mount the general offensive. For years, the enemy's positions had been gradually undermined, and the City, previously its more solid bulwark, not only had fallen, but had even turned into the hub of the Jews' allies. The number of those from the highest spheres of life who had become supporters of the Jewish cause was now legion. As a consequence, there had never been a more favorable time to achieve victory.

The Decisive Battle Begins

On 5 April 1930, Robert Grant introduced a bill 'to repeal the civil disabilities affecting British-born subjects professing the Jewish religion'.[23] In his speech, interesting for the history of Jews in England, Grant enumerated all of the circumstances which went in favor of his proposal for new legislation. To support his thesis, he made use of, among other things, the idea that the

---

[22] Marks: p. 32.
[23] Henriques: *Jews*, p. 265. Translator's note: QVOS.

times were now sufficiently modern to end with the injustices committed against the Jews over centuries. He asserted that the restrictions were in no way justified, that the Jews had always submitted themselves to the interest of the country, and that what had been conceded to the Catholics likewise had to be granted to the 30,000-40,000 Jews of England. In his long statement, he also touched upon the arguments that were expected from the Opposition, which asserted that, regarding the Jews, 'there was something so demoralizing in the state of some of their body that they were not fit to be invested with civil privileges.' He admitted that this accusation was justified in the case of a certain few, but untrue with regards to most, and that there was not, in the whole of the land, citizens who distinguished themselves as much as the upper echelons of Jewry in terms of integrity, unimpeachability, and elevated sentiments. He agreed that the Opposition's accusation had a basis in fact regarding the lower classes, but he had to consider that, at the moment that the restrictions were abolished through the law he demanded, such a triumphal social evolution would take place that it would put an end to, once and for all, every accusation made against the Jews as a collective.[24]

Next spoke the then-main spokesman of the Opposition, Sir Robert Inglis. With eloquent and bitter words, he attacked the bill. According to the Hansard report of Inglis' speech regarding the Jews:

> It appeared to him that there was nothing in their character, conduct, history, or present condition, which justified the appeal that had been made. He maintained that the Jews were aliens, not in the technical and legal sense, when Lord Coke called them 'aliens and perpetual enemies', but in the popular sense of the word: they were aliens because their country and their interests were not merely different, but hostile to our own. The Jews of London had more sympathy with the Jews resident in Berlin or Vienna than with Christians among whom they resided—and a reference to a few instances would show that their interests were different and hostile. In one of the wars of the last century, the Jews were expelled from Bohemia for assisting an invading army, and it was well known that they importantly facilitated the retreat of Napoleon after his campaign in Russia: they furnished the means to those who were lucky enough to escape. It was a known fact also, that while we were at war with France, the Jews of London had furnished Napoleon with a loan to enable him to carry on the most determined hostility.

---

[24] *Hansard*, Volume 23, p. 1298. Translator's note: QVOS.

Hansard reports that Sir Robert Inglis went on to give other analogous examples, before he said the following:

> [B]ut the Jews might get into the House of Commons, and use that power for their own selfish and unnational purposes. They were not a sect; but to this day they called themselves a people; and they might avail themselves of their political influence for objects connected with their own aggrandisement... The Jews might obtain admission by the same means [bribery] and for the same purposes [self-interest], and an honourable friend of his had said, that he knew of four who were ready to enter the House at once: considering that there were in the United Kingdom, at the utmost, 40,000 Jews, and that about every 40,000 Christians had only one representative, this number was considerably above their fair proportion. The command of capital would enable the Jews to obtain seats, and the introduction of a Jew ought to be considered direct evidence of bribery, for it was out of the question to suppose that they would ever obtain the unbought suffrages of the people. A Jew Member would carry on his forehead the evidence of the mode by which he obtained admission...

Sir Robert ended his speech with the declaration that in no way should the Jews be admitted to Parliament.[25]

Another member, the aforementioned Macaulay, voted for the bill out of 'moral obligation.' Mr. Harrison Batley warned the Parliament that, if the bill were passed, 'twenty-five Jews would obtain seats in the Commons House of Parliament, and a few of the leading men amongst them would soon obtain as much influence there as they already had already possessed over the 3 percent Consols.' Another member of Parliament, Sir James Macintosh, declared himself, in turn, a supporter of the bill. He agreed, of course, that the Jews were a degraded people, but that this was due to the fact that they were openly despised. The moral inferiority of their character came solely from the oppression that they had long suffered, he added; it was necessary to give them rights and allow them to educate their children well, and this would undoubtedly lead to them to become better people. The Chancellor of the Exchequer also intervened with a long speech in favor of the Jews' adversaries. He attacked the defenders of the bill, according to whom it was

---

[25] *Hansard,* Volume 23, p. 1303 ff. Translator's note: QVOS.

unjust to deny the Jews the same rights as the Catholics. As Hansard reports of his closing remarks:[26]

> There was this difference between the Jews and the Catholics—that the Catholics had shed their blood for us—they had fought our battles both by sea and land—they had swelled the force of our fleets and our armies, and there was a good reason why we should not make enemies of those who had served us, and who amounted to seven million people. But the Jews had not fought our battles—they had not served in our armies and navy, and they did not amount, it was stated by a writer of their own nation, to more than 27,000 persons. The arguments which applied to the Roman Catholics, seemed to him, therefore, to have no application to the Jews.[27]

At the first reading, there was a majority of 18 votes in favor of the bill.[28]

The discussion in Parliament showed that a latent fire had been burning for some time, which, naturally, was countered by the Jews' adversaries, using all means at their disposal. The press was also brought into the polemics. It first showed itself to be quite moderate, until the great campaigns of 1847 exposed the chasm between the two opposing ideologies surrounding the Jewish Question.

The *Public Ledger* of 6 April 1830 and the *Spectator* of April 10 of the same year, quote Grant's bill and opine that the problem of Jewish emancipation should be resolved as soon as possible. The *Standard* of April 6 is similarly quite indecisive. Only the *Times* directly attacks the Jews in an article dated May 3. Among other things, it stated the following [reproduced verbatim from the original source]:

> The Jews are not, cannot be, component parts of any nation: their civil, their religious institutions forbid any such amalgamation. They are, however scattered, however distant from each other, not only, in the language of their own sacred volume, 'a peculiar people,' but a separate nation. They cannot have, they must not have, any identity of political interest with any people but their own. [...]
>
> Everything short of political identification should be granted; but that, in the nature of things, cannot be granted,

---

[26] *Hansard,* Volume 23, p. 1308. Translator's note: QVOS. & *Hansard,* Volume 23, p. 1314. & pp. 1314-23.

[27] *Hansard,* Volume 23, pp. 1323-5. Translator's note: QVOS.

[28] *Hansard,* Volume 23, p. 1336.

because a Jew cannot be a patriotic Frenchman, or German, or
Englishman, till he has put off his character of Jew. [...]

More than a third of the seats in Parliament are notoriously purchasable, and a few years might convert a British
House of Commons into a Jewish Sanhedrin...

These are truly harsh words for the Jews and their friends, which is why the
bill's second reading was awaited with mixed feelings, even more so given
that the majority of the first reading had been very marginal.

But the Jews and their friends did not stay inactive and made full use of
all of their influence on public opinion. Alongside the presentation of the
bill, they brought a petition from part of the electorate of Liverpool in favor
of the Jews; the 2,000 signatures proceeding mainly from bankers and merchants. As is known, Liverpool was one of the centers of Judaism in the
provinces, so we can suppose that under such a circumstance, not a few of
the petitioners must have been baptized Jews, non-baptized Jews, half-Jews,
friends of Jews, and people who were dependent on Jews.[29]

But for the second reading, it was decided to give an even greater show
of public opinion to Parliament. For this, a second petition was brought, this
time from what had come to be, at least, a bulwark of Judaism—the City of
London. This petition contained some 14,000 signatures, also almost exclusively from bankers, merchants, and academics—between them eleven directors of the Bank of England, 1,100 doctors, many lawyers, and thousands
of influential men.[30]

With great participation from all of the interested parties, the moment
of the second reading arrived. Lord Belgrave believed that Jews had to be
denied an equality of rights, because they were an international people and
therefore incapable of all patriotic sentiment. Sir E. Deering didn't want
them to be excluded from official posts, but he did want them excluded,
without exception, from Parliament. Sir Robert Peel also voted against the
bill, because the bill did not include the Quaker sects nor the separatists. All
of Lord John Russell's art of oratory was not enough to convince the Jews'
adversaries, which is why the bill was defeated by 228 votes to 165.[31]

The consternation in the Jewish camp was great, but not so much that
they abandoned their sought-after objective, as was shown by an event
which took place in Parliament shortly afterwards.

Between the first and second reading of the aforementioned bill, the
Jew Levi had arranged to have a motion tabled which called for clarification
on the matter of whether or not it was legal for the Jews to acquire immova-

---

[29] Egan: p. 37.
[30] *Hansard,* Volume 95, p. 1385.
[31] *Hansard,* Volume 24, p. 786-7. & p. 791. & p. 802. & p. 797. & pp. 812 and 814.

ble property. His petition had even been supported by the Attorney-General. When, further onwards, a decision was required to be taken, the member Robert Grant declared himself against, giving the reason that 'one would have to grant the Jews all of the rights or none, which was why he would not vote in favor of any partial solution'.[32]

As can be seen, the Jews still felt strong enough to pursue a full equality of rights with an open frontal attack. Of course, everything had progressed in the shadows according to the agenda, but, as had already happened once, sufficient attention had not been paid to the public mood. The first failed attempt had clearly demonstrated that the popular mood was not yet remotely propitious to the Jews' desires. It was necessary to do something that would create a change, something which would be achieved, preferably, through the 'enlightenment of the ignorant masses.' As a consequence, possession was taken of every possible means of propaganda, and it was to this that the Jews largely owed their successes in the 19th century.[33]

They began by printing the speeches made in Parliament in favor of Jewish emancipation, then distributing them immediately in large print runs. Various famous authors were commissioned to write pamphlets and bulletins in favor of the Jews. The selection was made very carefully, with the result that their efforts began to pay off handsomely. The first author to write an article of this nature, in the *Edinburgh Review* of 1831, was the aforementioned and (at the time) famous Macaulay; in his article he stated, in accordance with philosophic principles, that Jews had to be admitted into Parliament; that they already had such power in the country that they could not rise any higher; that Jews could not be held responsible for any potential lack of patriotism, as this could be seen as the consequence of treating them badly.

Jews known to the public also wielded the pen. Of these, we will only mention the two most important: Barnard van Oven and F. H. [Francis Henry] Goldsmid, the second son of I. L. [Isaac Lyon] Goldsmid. The latter particularly was greatly distinguished for his writings. He discussed at length the reasons expounded by Jewish adversaries in Parliament and sought to demonstrate, among other things, that the last words of the Oath of Abjuration were not directed in the slightest at the Jews and for that reason could not be applied to them, nor was it just to grant an equality of rights to the Catholics and deny them to the Jews. He asserted that the English were the only ones responsible for Jewish behavior, which at times was reprehensible, due to always having treated the Jews badly; that it was ridiculous to speak of a Jewish danger, when only some 30,000 Jews lived in the country, of whom perhaps only three or four would end up as members of Parliament. In

---

[32] *Hansard,* Volume 24, 236-237. & *Hansard,* Volume 25, 429. Translator's note: This reference appears to be erroneous.

[33] Shapira: p. 50. Marks p.34.

another article, he informed readers that the twelve MPs of the City and the other London districts had voted unanimously in Parliament in favor of the Jewish law; that it was not true that the Jews of England ever wanted to return to Palestine, rather, they only rejected living like slaves among the English. Goldsmid also seems assured that total victory would soon be achieved, when at the end of his arguments he rejects all compromise and demands full equality of rights alongside the English.[34]

It was reported that this propaganda had the desired effect, which must be true in part, given that on the opposing side no measures were taken which are worthy of mention.[35]

In the following years, English political public opinion was so taken up with parliamentary reforms that it was likely the reason that the Jewish Question remained relegated to second place. But this period must have been quite agreeable to the Jews, as they could use this time to make new, detailed plans for a new bill.

At the beginning of 1832, a new law granted total emancipation to the Jews of Canada. The Jews did not delay in demanding the same right in the Empire's mother country. Perhaps this fact also helped them, in January of the following year, to win a not-insignificant success—admission to the Bar.[36] The four barrister associations—called Inns of Court—had up until that point denied the admission of Jews and still demanded in 1830 the complete Oath of Abjuration. In 1833 the aforementioned F. H. Goldsmid was the first Jew to present a petition to be admitted to Lincoln's Inn, and allowed into the courtroom, with authorization not to have to pronounce the last words of the oath. Some members of Parliament opposed the request. When it was shown to the MP Lord Campbell that this was a hardship for the young Jew, due to having allowed him to study in the Inn, Campbell exclaimed: 'Hardship? No hardship at all! Let him become a Christian, and be d—d to him!' Nevertheless, the request was passed by a majority, and on 30 January 1833 the first Jew was admitted to the Bar.[37]

The oath was sworn by F. H. Goldsmid in a form which was possible for him as a Jew, and the remaining three Inns were not long to follow suit in admitting Jews.[38]

---

[34] Shapira: p. 64.

[34] Shapira: p. 67. & F. H. Goldsmid: *Remarks*, p. 9. & pp. 14-15. & pp. 18-20. & pp. 26-29. & F. H. Goldsmid: *Arguments*, p. 4. & p. 10. & p. 27.

[35] Marks: p. 36.

[36] F. H. Goldsmid: *Reply*, p. 31.

[37] *Lives of the Chancellors*: Volume V, p. 544. Translator's note: QVOS. & Admission Register no. 19, folio 65. *Records of Lincolns Inn*, Volume II, p. 127. Hyamson: *History*, p. 262. Picciotto: p. 396.

[38] Marks: pp. 13-4. & Henriques: *Jews...*, pp. 203-4.

This success must not be considered a small feat, for the profession of barrister enjoys great prestige in England and is a condition for becoming a judge and occupying top offices of state. As a result, the Jews had managed to conquer another position, achieving thus a new base for their general attack.

The Jews must have considered this partial success as a good sign, because in the meantime they once more hammered out plans for a new bill. Indeed, the time had never felt as right.

In January 1833 the recently reformed Parliament met for the first time. The Whigs, whose help the Jews continued to count on, had no less than 511 members in the House of Commons, while the Conservatives, on the contrary, had not even 150. F. H. Goldsmid addressed an open letter to the new House of Commons, expressing the hope that the Reformed Parliament would mark the commencement of its career with 'an act of justice'.[39]

The Years 1833–1834

On the 17th of April, 1823, Robert Grant, who meanwhile had come to occupy the highest office in Lord Grey's government, proposed a motion requesting a committee be named to study the existing restrictions on Jews [Jewish disabilities]. Despite protests from Sir Robert Inglis, this motion was passed without a subsequent vote. The name of this MP is often found in the course of the ensuing battles for emancipation, for which reason we should say something about his personality.[40] Sir Robert Inglis was born in London in the year 1786. After a rigorous education, he dedicated himself almost exclusively to politics and in Parliament always represented the Conservative position. He was considered the representative of the opinions which prevailed in the countryside and—perhaps only for this reason—he was not considered to be of particularly great ability.[41]

Without difficulty, Grant introduced the Jews' Civil Disabilities Bill to Parliament and effortlessly managed to gain a majority at the first reading.[42]

On the 22nd of May, Parliament proceeded to the second reading. Once again it was Sir Robert Inglis who warned against the consequences, negative in every way, that would result from the passing of such a law. He was passionately supported by Sir Oswald Mosley—the great-grandfather of the current head of the Fascists of England. The friends of the Jews, on the other hand, considered the refusal as incompatible with England's liberal principles and with the Jews' brilliant qualities. What had been expected, happened: the second reading took place with a majority of 107 votes. It goes

---

[39] Marks: pp. 37-43. Translator's note: QVOS (p. 43).
[40] Marks: p. 38. & *Hansard,* Third Series, Volume 15, pp. 310, 559; Volume 16, p. 10 ff., 725, 775, 973.
[41] *Dictionary of National Biography,* Volume 10, pp. 443-4.
[42] *Hansard,* Volume 17, pp. 205-244.

without saying that the third reading similarly found the majority required, in itself unimportant. This victory was undoubtedly due in no small part to the contributions of the Goldsmids, father and son, for while the latter with his publications created endless propaganda for the Jewish cause, the father was continually in negotiations with influential people. It was said that he could be seen every afternoon in the corridors of Parliament, talking to the members who came and went, explaining to them the benefits that would accrue from the passing of the Jewish bill. The following small anecdote is demonstrative of his Jewish zeal:[43]

> On one occasion, when it was uncertain whether the Bill would come on in the House of Commons so late in the evening, a conversation between two members pledged to support it was overheard to the following effect.
> A: 'There is little chance of the Jews' Bill coming on at this late hour of the night: I shall go home!'
> B: 'I should like to do the same, but it is useless to attempt it: there's Goldsmid keeping watch in the lobby, and he'll be sure to press me to wait on the chance'.[44]

There was no rest after the triumph that had just been won, given that for it to have legal validity, it still needed the approval of the House of Lords. The leaders of the Jews and their loyalists approached the various Peers and tried to win their support. Lord Holland even managed to get various members of the royal family to declare their support, which they demonstrated at the division in the House of Lords. All possible efforts were made to win over the

---

[43] *Hansard,* Volume 18, p. 47 ff. Translator's note: In the course of his speech, Inglis brought up the fact that no synagogue or religious Jew had pushed for emancipation, and he quoted Rabbi Joseph Crool, who had campaigned against Jewish emancipation in Britain. Crool believed that the Jews' mission was to remain as 'strangers and sojourners' in foreign lands, and that emancipation would lead to assimilation (and thereby destruction of the Jews *qua* Jews). In this, Crool shared an analogous view to Rabbi Schneur Zalman of Liadi and others who had opposed Napoleon's Jewish emancipation. Modern historiography has painted Crool as poorly educated and eccentric (i.e. of ideas not worthy of serious consideration), and yet events in the subsequent century may argue the wisdom of his case better than the *Jewish Encyclopedia* and others would care to admit. Readers may also be bemused to know that Google has classified one of the Hebrew scholar's books on the topic, *The Fifth Empire* (1829), as 'Antisemitism.'

[43] *Hansard,* Volume 18, p. 56. Translator's note: Among the things, Moseley feared that such a law 'would open the flood-gates of ultra-toleration upon the Legislature of the land' and 'the House would be Christian only nominally, and not in reality, and would inflict an irreparable injury upon the institutions of the country.' & *Hansard,* Volume 18, p. 51 ff. & p. 56. & *Hansard,* Volume 19, p. 1075 ff.

[44] Marks: p. 45. Translator's note: QVOS.

high church dignitaries, and indeed, success was achieved with the Bishop of Dublin.[45]

August 1st, 1833 marked the moment of the decisive sitting in the House of Lords. As an obvious proof of power, it was permitted that the Duke of Sussex be the first to take the floor, and he had in his hands 7,000 signatures from Westminster requesting the ratification of the bill. Next, Lord Bexley, I. L. Goldsmid's close associate, formally tabled the motion to request a second reading. The Archbishop of Canterbury was the first to take the floor for the other side. He stated that he respected the Jews' religion and morality, but that Parliament was a Christian institution, something that was not lost on the Jews. The Bishop of Chichester, on the other hand, supported the motion, as for him the Jews were nothing else but the elder brothers of the Christian faith. But when the Duke of Wellington declared himself to be against the bill, which he said was at odds with the Christian character of the country, the bill's fate was sealed, and it was defeated by a large majority.[46]

Angst and mourning reigned in the Israel camp, the fact of which could not be hidden in the article published in the *Times* of August 2, which had been circulated in the meantime around the Jews and their allies. In the article, it was stated that the bill had been defeated, but that in the next session they would bring another and it would yield a better result. By contrast, the *Morning Post* of the same date applauded the previous day's events in the House of Lords, and continued in the same vein:

> It has never yet been shown how a Hebrew, professing to adhere to the religion of his nation, can, consistently with that profession, avail himself of the privileges which it was proposed to grant. Such a Jew must, we think, consider himself, if he be consistent and conscientious, an alien in this country, and refuse the offer of admission to participate actively in our national institutions whenever that offer shall be made... [QVOS]

---

[45] Shapira: p. 81.

[46] *Hansard,* Volume 20, p. 221; Egan: p. 39. Translator's note: See also Chapter 4 of Salbstein for details of I. L. Goldsmid's prominence and militancy in the Jewish emancipation movement, and the contrast of opinion with Moses Montefiore, who preferred a gradualist, or 'stealth' approach to achieving the same goals. In Montefiore's view: 'The Jew must, in his claims and wishes, not outstrip the age. Let him advance slowly but steadily; let him gradually accustom his Christian fellow-citizens to his gradual progress and success in public life, and what may not be obtainable even by an arduous struggle, will, after a certain time, fall into his lap like ripe fruit.' [p. 86, Salbstein, Translator's Bibliography]. & *Hansard,* Volume 20, p. 222 ff. & p.238. Translator's note: Readers may find themselves reminded of Pope John Paul II's famous 1987 description of the Jews as 'our elder brothers in the faith of Abraham.' & *Hansard,* Volume 20, p. 245. & p. 249.

In any case, it will surprise no one that the Jews, despite their failure, had already decided by 18 November 1833, under the chairmanship of I. L. Goldsmid, to make new formal moves in Parliament. But not before spring, 24 April 1834, did Grant table a motion. Once again, the usual speeches took place for and against the bill, which passed easily though the House of Commons and was sent up to the House of Lords.[47]

Again the Jews failed. During the debates the Earl of Malmesbury warned that if the law were passed then one would have to admit not only Jews, but also Mohammedans, and the Archbishop of Canterbury was very annoyed that a Jewish bill had been put back on the order paper for discussion.[48]

The results showed the Jews and their friends that the opposition, despite their many preparations, was still too strong for the Jewish Question to be resolved in one fell swoop. For the next ten years, they therefore returned to their original method of achieving emancipation in stages or, as it might be better said, using the law of attrition.

A Jewish Incident: David Salomons

Already by the following year, the correctness of this tactic was proven, and it brought the Jews to a new victory: their ethnic kinsman David Salomons—whom we will frequently encounter from now on—was elected Sheriff of London and Middlesex, which did not only have the character of a municipal district, but also of a county. From the year 1828, as was commonly known, a law existed according to which everyone who took up a such a post had to swear a solemn declaration before entering into the exercise of his functions, a declaration which was impossible for the Jews due to its final words, which were so disastrous for them.

In the election of Salomons, this general situation had not been forgotten: both the electors and the elected knew perfectly well that a Jew could not legally occupy the position. Nevertheless—perhaps precisely because of that—he was voted for in order for the law to be invoked, which would in turn obligate Parliament and the House of Lords to make a decision.

David Salomons refused, as was to be expected, to swear the oath that was demanded of him, with the consequence that he was not admitted to the office of sheriff. From what can be deduced, everything had been carefully prepared for the Jewish counter-coup; the government immediately got involved with the matter and, under the direction of Lord John Russell and

---

[47] Coles: p. 1. Translator's note: The chairmanship in question was of the Association for obtaining for British Jews Civil Rights and Privileges [Marks, p. 154]. & *Hansard,* Volume 22, pp. 1372-3. & p. 1176. Volume 24, p. 382.

[48] *Hansard,* Volume 24, p. 731 & p. 722. & p. 724 ff.

Attorney-General Lord John Campbell, introduced a special bill to make it possible for David Salomons to take up his post.

One must not suppose that this bill talked about the case in question or talked generally about Jewish disabilities regarding the swearing of the oath; nor could the word 'Jew' be found in it, and nor did it mention London. The bill's title, also completely unspecific, read:

> An Act for removing Doubts as to the Declaration to be made
> and Oaths to be taken by Persons appointed to the Office of
> Sheriff of any City or Town, being a County of itself.[49]

It really is amazing to see how this was done. There could be no room for doubt, especially when, with a law having been passed in 1828 [the Sacramental Test Act 1828 (9. Geo. IV, c. 17), which replaced the Test Act of 1673], everyone knew that the Jews could not swear the oath in its established form. With many complicated clauses that a layman is barely capable of understanding, this law was designed to allow the Jews to forego the oath on taking up municipal positions. It should have been obvious to any discerning legislator that, if this bill were passed, while it would not bring the Jews the complete emancipation they desired, it would nevertheless move them closer to their goal. But the most important thing was that, were the bill made law, the general exclusionary principle would be abandoned, and the friends of the Jews would be able to point to this exception for future cases. In other words, a principle of such transcendental significance could tolerate absolutely no exception if it wasn't to end up completely undermined, and effectively destroyed forever.

It is therefore completely incomprehensible why the opposition did not fight this with all of the means available. Were they deceived by the form given to the bill? Or did they believe that they could afford to take a liberal stance as they considered themselves strong enough to be able to withstand a future bid at general emancipation? Or was the bill considered too insignificant to be a threat to the general principle? Today, on analyzing the outcome, we know that this stance was the greatest and most irreparable of the errors committed in the fight against the Jewish agenda. In any dispute with them, one must maintain the principle of 'everything or nothing', as it is a given that the 'something' invariably leads to 'everything' and is the beginning of the end. It is interesting to see the extreme rapidity with which the law was

---

[49] *Statutes of the United Kingdom*, Volume 75, pp. 127-8. Translator's note: This is the original English title of the legislation, as found in *Journals of the House of Commons*, (Volume 90, p. 543), where it is also seen in an abbreviated form as the Sheriffs' Declaration Bill (p. 498).

passed by the various parties required to ensure that a bill could become valid legislation:

On 23 July 1835, the bill was presented to Parliament and already by the following day it had passed to the first reading.[50] On 29 July, the second reading took place, after a debate on the bill had previously taken place in a 'Committee of the whole House', and on August 3 it was given definitive approval in the House of Commons. In the almost unbelievable speed of ten days, it passed through the House of Lords, normally so hostile, and on August 21 the king gave the Royal Assent, a required formality.[51]

But the rapidity of the process is not the only remarkable thing. The press barely gave it any attention, and, despite the most careful research, Hansard, generally an extremely trustworthy source, does not give us the smallest detail either on any of the debates or on the voting, which leads to the conclusion that the Jews' opponents, for some unknown reason, did nothing to stop the law being passed.[52] As soon as the law came into effect, Salomons took possession of his new office, in which he was followed two years later by his ethnic kinsman Moses Montefiore.[53]

The tactic of separating the struggle from the general principle and limiting it solely to limited domains and people had shown itself to be effective. It could be expected, then, that new victories would be won in this way, which is why, on November 18th, 1835, the same David Salomons managed to get elected to the post of Alderman of the City of London.

As had happened previously, Salomons could not take possession of his post, access to which was still controlled by the 1828 ordinance, given that the recently passed law only covered an oath modification for the post of sheriff. On 3 December 1835, accompanied by numerous electors, Salomons presented himself at the Court of Aldermen, to be officially appointed to his post. There he was advised that he had to swear the oath provided by the law of 1828, which he rejected in the same way as when he had gone for the first time to be admitted as sheriff. The Court of Aldermen did not accede to any degree of negotiation and declared his election null and void. A new election was announced and another candidate presented. Salomons protested against this new alderman with the aim of showing that his election was not valid. But the court judgement recognized that the opinion of the Court of Aldermen was in line with the law and that the second election was legally valid.[54]

Not long after his defeat, Salomons expressed in an article that, for the Jews, it was more important to know that the people chose to elect them than

---

[50] *Journals of the House of Commons,* Volume 90, pp. 482, 484.

[51] *Journals of the House of Commons,* Volume 90, p. 498. & p. 504. & pp. 543, 578.

[52] *Hansard,* Volumes 29 and 30.

[53] Hyamson: *History,* p. 263. Henriques: *Jews,* pp. 253-4. Picciotto: pp. 391-2. Wolf: *Essays*: p. 314. Egan: p. 45.

[54] Britannicus: p. 7. & Henriques: *Jews...,* pp. 254-5. Hyamson: *History...,* p. 263.

the fact that the Court of Aldermen rejected them, which meant that the fight would continue on despite everything.

The Battle Continues

In July of 1836, the Chancellor of the Exchequer presented a new bill for the general annulment of Jewish disabilities. For this attempt, the last days of Parliament were cunningly chosen, because of it being known that at such a point the members were already pretty tired of debates, especially when summer had already begun, and the majority of members were beginning to leave Parliament prematurely to begin their holidays in the spa resorts. There is no other way to explain why the debate was held in an uninterested, almost empty House, where the law was passed by only 39 to 17 votes. The action was still fruitless, however, because in the face of the Government's contrarian attitude, it did not even get as far as a second reading in the House of Lords.[55]

The lack of interest in the Jews' previous attempt must have been crueler for them than failing due to violent opposition, as it was said that they had felt this defeat as 'a crushing blow.' Nevertheless, already by the following year, we see Judah get back to work once more. Parliamentary elections were held and what nobody would have believed possible happened: a Jew—once again David Salomons—stood in Shoreham as a candidate. But this time, the majority of the constituency's electorate rejected his candidacy. It was considered insolence on Salomons' part to aspire to an office to which he had no legal right.[56]

For this reason, it is instructive to see the warning made publicly by the opposing victorious candidate, Sir Charles Burrell, during a parliamentary debate, which reveals that Salomons had practiced intolerable electoral pressure tactics:

> Truth obliged him to add, however, that the supporters of Mr.
> Salomons were, with few exceptions, of an inferior class in the
> social scale; how their votes were obtained, he would not say.
> The conduct of Mr. Salomons' supporters during the election
> was not at all creditable to them.[57]

On the other hand, with the already-cited election of Moses Montefiore as Sheriff of London, the Jews felt re-energized. During the solemn banquet held to celebrate Montefiore's appointment, the Attorney-General, latterly

---

[55] *Hansard,* Volume 35, pp. 865 ff., 1209, 1216, 1318.

[56] Shapira: p. 92. & Shapira: p. 94; Hyamson: *History...*, p. 268.

[57] *Hansard,* Volume 39, p. 515. Translator's note: QVOS.

Lord Campbell, who was also present, gave a speech in which he expressed his joy at the election outcome and gave assurances that the government would do everything in its power to grant Jews full equality:

> I am happy to say that the ancient prejudices founded on dif-
> ference of religious belief are fast wearing away, and I hope
> the time is at hand when objections on such grounds will alto-
> gether cease to operate. It is the desire of Her Majesty's Gov-
> ernment to promote such a state of things by all the means in
> their power. For my part, my opinion is that, so far from injur-
> ing the constitution, it will tend materially to uphold and
> strengthen it.[58]

As well as the support of the government, the Jews could also count on the young, recently crowned Victoria, whose attitude ran contrary to that of her predecessor, William IV. The Queen honored Montefiore repeatedly and that same year gave him a knighthood. Just as in times gone by, when the Duchess of Kent (the Queen Mother) and the Duke of Sussex equally lent the Jews their valuable help.

Disraeli on the Jewish Race

When Lord Holland and Sir Robert Grant (the latter having been knighted in the interim), both died in 1837, their seats were taken by two men who, alongside Lord John Russell and Rothschild, dedicated their lives to defend-ing the Jewish cause with the same zeal as their predecessors, but with un-doubtedly greater skill: Lord Lyndhurst and the baptized Jew Benjamin Dis-raeli, later Lord Beaconsfield. Neither played a leading role regarding Jewish emancipation, but every year they distinguished themselves ever more con-siderably with their endeavors in this field. It is even said of Lord Lyndhurst that he hoped to gain the title of 'Emancipator of the Jews', which, as we will see, was undoubtedly fitting.[59]

It is not necessary to go into too much detail about the life of Lord Lynd-hurst. Suffice it to say that he was born in 1772, in Boston (America), and that he lived long enough to almost reach his 92nd birthday. He was a jurist and, as such, occupied high and extremely important positions. He was not too scru-pulous in his political principles, and often changed his mind on issues.[60]

Disraeli, son of Jewish parents, was born in 1804. On 31 July 1817, he converted to Christianity, which meant that he had no type of difficulty par-

---

[58] Wolf: *Essays*, pp. 315-16. Translator's note: QVOS.

[59] Wolf: *Essays*, p. 317. & Campbell: Volume VIII, p. 199. Translator's note: QVOS.

[60] *Dictionary of National Biography*, Volume IV, p. 1107 ff.; Campbell, Volume VIII, p. 1 ff.

ticipating in English public life. He dedicated his young adult life to literature, and as a writer he primarily praised the Jewish race. In 1837 he entered
Parliament for the first time as a member, to later rise to the highest offices
of England. One of his best friends was Lord Lyndhurst, who also enjoyed a
close friendship with Rothschild—indeed, we have learned that Rothschild
held large galas in his honor. We see then, a triumvirate capable of bringing
about the triumph, without a moment's hesitation, of the Jewish cause.[61]

But before returning to general Jewish history, it is instructive to describe the truly eye-opening opinion held by Disraeli on the importance of
race, as well as his attitude towards Jews in general, according to what can
be gleaned from his public speeches, and still more, in his books, now
somewhat fallen into obscurity. His attitude is particularly evident in
Coningsby, or The New Generation (1844), as well as in his political biography *Lord George Bentinck* (1852). The characters who appear in the first
work had been taken from public life and only their names had been
changed. The main characters are a young Englishman, Coningsby, and his
friend and mentor Sidonia, a Jew. The Sidonia character is Rothschild.[62]
Disraeli dedicated the book *Lord George Bentinck* to his friend, the well-
known politician. In Chapter 24 of this book, Disraeli deals exclusively with
the Jewish Question, and the racial question generally.[63]

In *Coningsby* he reveals that Sidonia had visited the Jewish colonies
scattered throughout the world, discovering that the lower-class Jews found
themselves mired in the most abject poverty and filth, while those of the upper classes devoted their lives to dirty business deals; but their intellectual
development seemed to him to be as strong as ever, which is what gave him
hope. The only human quality which interested Sidonia was the intellect,
which was why he was not concerned where it may spring from, nor where
he found it. Faith, fatherland, character, class—he was indifferent to all of it
in this sense.[64]

In *Lord George Bentinck*, Disraeli confessed that the Jews were filled
with hatred for the whole of humanity, but that in view of the persecutions
that they had suffered, it could not be surprising that they fought the laws
arrayed against them.[65] The lack of understanding for the Jews had also been
the reason that 'the most skillful accumulators of property ally themselves

---

[61] *Dictionary of National Biography*, Volume V, p. 1006 ff. & Reeves: p. 230.
[62] Cf. among other sources, *Hansard*, Volume 95, p. 1321 ff.; Volume 133, p. 872 ff.;
Volume 149, p. 752 ff. T. E. Kebbel: *Selected Speeches of the late Rt. Hon The Earl of
Beaconsfield* (2 vols., 1882). & Cf. among others, *Vivian Grey* (1826), *Tancred* (1847).
[63] Disraeli: *Lord George Bentinck*, pp. 482-507.
[64] Disraeli: *Coningsby*: p. 91.
[65] Disraeli: *Lord George Bentinck*, pp. 489-90.

with the communists: this peculiar and chosen race touch the hand of all the scum and low castes of Europe'.[66]

In the same work, he also reveals that in all of the revolutions that took place around the year 1848, the Jews had always played their part. The revolutions which happened in Germany, Italy, and even France had been planned by secret organizations that likewise formed the provisional governments, which were always headed by Jews. The goal of these revolutions was to attack religion and property, and thus it came about that the People of God allied with the atheists. This fateful turn in the Jewish movement does not, in Disraeli's judgement, stem from Jewish nature, but is exclusively a consequence of the ill-treatment meted out to Jews by Christians.[67]

Despite all of the evils, humanity had much to thank the Jews for. According to Disraeli, in the arts, they had produced more than the Athenians. Their creative genius had never shone as much as at the time that Disraeli was writing, and when the Russians, French, and Anglo-Saxons, fascinated by the charms of a Mozart (!?) or a Mendelssohn, applauded in the theatre, they rendered homage to Jewish art.[68] Jews led the charge not only in music, but also in science. They were so superior that they should have enjoyed all of the honor and favors that were bestowed on the Nordic and occidental races.[69]

In *Coningsby*, Disraeli believes that he proves that there is no 'great intellectual movement in Europe in which the Jews do not greatly participate. The first Jesuits were Jews. That mysterious Russian Diplomacy which so alarms Western Europe, is organized and principally carried on by Jews.'[70]

With pride, Sidonia declares that he is preparing great international financial transactions.[71] With the greatest sarcasm, Disraeli narrates how Sidonia is called back to London in the middle of an enjoyable sojourn in the countryside, because the ministers of the British Empire cannot meet the interest payments on the national debt. He, the all-powerful international banker, now had to grant new deadlines for the payment. He scornfully asks Coningsby:

> Can any thing be more absurd than that a nation should apply to an individual to maintain its credit, and with its credit, its existence as an empire and its comfort as a people; and that individual one to whom its laws deny the proudest rights of citizenship, the privilege of sitting in its senate and of holding land...?[72]

---

[66] Disraeli: *Lord George Bentinck*, p. 497. Translator's note: QVOS.

[67] Disraeli: *Lord George Bentinck*, pp. 489-9.

[68] Disraeli: *Lord George Bentinck*, p. 493. & p. 494.

[69] Disraeli: *Lord George Bentinck*, p. 491.

[70] Disraeli: *Coningsby*, p. 103 onwards. Translator's note: QVOS.

[71] Disraeli: *Coningsby*, p. 104.

[72] Disraeli: *Coningsby*, p. 102.

The circumstance of Jews trying to extend their influence into every country of the world is likewise interpreted by Disraeli as a special quality of the Jewish character and Jewish capabilities. Of Sidonia, he writes:

> No minister of state had such communication with secret agents and political spies as Sidonia. He held relations with all of the clever outcasts of the world... His extensive travels, his knowledge of languages, his daring and adventurous disposition, and his unlimited means, had given him opportunities of becoming acquainted with these characters, in general so difficult to trace, and of gaining their devotion. To these sources he owed that knowledge of strange and hidden things which often startled those who listened to him. Nor was it easy, scarcely possible, to deceive him. Information reached him from so many, and such contrary quarters, that with his discrimination and experience, he could almost instantly distinguish the truth.[73]

Sidonia details at length the Jews' enormous influence over all the events of Europe, and states at one point in the narrative: 'And every generation they must become more powerful and more dangerous to the society which is hostile to them.' As a consequence, none of Sidonia's interests are limited by national borders.[74]

Very interesting are the reasons he gives to explain why the Jews are capable of exerting such formidable influence in the world, despite all of the persecutions which have persistently targeted them for thousands of years. In his judgement, the only thing that matters, in this sense, is the purity of his race.

> Sidonia was well aware that in the five great varieties in which physiology has divided the human species; to wit, the Caucasian, the Mongolian, the Malayan, the American, the Ethiopian; the Arabian tribes rank in the first and superior class, together, among others, with the Saxon and the Greek. This fact alone is a source of great pride and satisfaction to the animal man. But Sidonia and his brethren could claim a distinction which the Saxon and the Greek, and the rest of the Caucasian nations, have forfeited. The Hebrew is an unmixed race. Doubtless among the tribes who inhabit the bosom of the Desert, progenitors alike of the Mosaic and the Mohammedan Arabs, blood may be found as pure as that of the descendants

---

[73] Disraeli: *Coningsby*, p. 91. Translator's note: QVOS.
[74] Disraeli: *Coningsby*, p. 103 ff. Translator's note: QVOS.

of the Scheik Abraham. But the Mosaic Arabs are the most ancient, if not the only, unmixed blood that dwells in cities.

An unmixed race of a first-rate organisation are the aristocracy of nature. Such excellence is a positive fact; not an imagination...[75]

In this vein, he continues elsewhere in the text:

The fact is you cannot destroy a pure race of the Caucasian organization. It is a physiological fact; a simple law of nature, which has baffled Egyptian and Assyrian kings, Roman emperors, and Christian inquisitors. No penal laws, no physical tortures, can effect that a superior race should be absorbed in an inferior, or be destroyed by it. The mixed persecuting races disappear; the pure persecuted race remains.[76]

The same declarations can be found elsewhere, but with the addition that it is foolish to talk of the natural equality of mankind and dress it up in the garb of universal brotherhood. Reduced to real terms, it would mean the ruin of all of the great races and the annihilation of all genius in the world:

What would be the consequence on the great Anglo-Saxon republic, for example, were its citizens to secede from their sound principle of reserve, and mingle with their negro and coloured populations? In the course of time they would become so deteriorated that their states would probably be reconquered and regained by the aborigines whom they have expelled, and who would then be their superiors.[77]

This is the point of view of a leading Jew on the Jewish and racial questions. As has been shown, in his reflections, Disraeli has made no distinction between a baptized and an unbaptized Jew, but rather for him, as for us, the principle factor is race. Today, this point of view is considered erroneous and is fought against by the vast majority of the world population, especially in England. It is not surprising to learn then that one of Disraeli's contemporaries roundly attacked him for his attitude.[78]

We have nothing to add to Disraeli's opinions regarding the reprehensible aspects of the Jewish character, or of the influence, in our judgement

---

[75] Disraeli: *Coningsby*, p. 91. Translator's note: QVOS.
[76] Disraeli: *Coningsby*, p. 103. Translator's note: QVOS.
[77] Disraeli: *Lord George Bentinck*, p. 494. Translator's note: QVOS.
[78] Padley: *An Answer...*

disastrous, of the Jews on politics, economics, art, and science. It is very interesting, nevertheless, to have it confirmed that, for around a hundred years now, destructive Jewish forces have been spreading around the world, working to come to power through criminal revolutions. We see then that nothing has changed.

Perhaps more surprising is Disraeli's opinion on the race problem. Although it is sometimes unclear to us on certain points, it coincides with ours in that is also rejects race-mixing, in order to conserve strength and vigor. We have already seen to what extent we have been attacked by global Jewry precisely for this attitude, despite the fact that one of their most prominent representatives admitted it himself barely a century ago.

All of this is enough for now to demonstrate the ideology of that 'great Englishman' as he was often called in Great Britain, in what concerns the Jewish Question. Later we will see how he also did everything possible to procure for his 'superior race' the place he believed it deserved in the world.

Ritual Murders in the Orient

The year 1840 was to be an important year in many ways. Shortly before the celebration of Jewish Passover [Pesach], a Capuchin monk disappeared in Damascus. The suspicions of the populace immediately fell on the Jews, as it was suspected that they used human blood to make their *matzo* flatbreads. A Jewish barber was arrested who, apparently after heavy torture, reinforced the suspicion in order to save himself from more mistreatment. He fingered several Jews as the culprits, and six of these were arrested while the remainder escaped. However, they denied all culpability and not even the Turks' torture methods could force them to confess [see footnote following page]. Meanwhile, the indignant multitude assaulted and destroyed various Jewish houses.

The French consul in Damascus had for some time represented the interests of all the Catholics in the Middle East and it was under his mandate that the trial was held of the accused Jews, which ended in death sentences being pronounced for all of them, their guilt having been established beyond all reproach. For the sentence to be carried out, the consul needed authorization from the viceroy of Egypt, Mehemet Ali, who had jurisdiction over Damascus.

Almost at the same time, in Rhodes, a ten-year-old boy had died in strange circumstances. In this case, too, the Jews were immediately suspected. Every single European consul in Rhodes, with the exception of the Austrian representative, went to the pasha in charge requesting that certain Jews, who had been denounced by two Greeks, be punished accordingly. The Jews were arrested and, it appears, treated harshly to force them to confess.[79]

At the beginning of April 1840, a report of these events arrived in London. Without wasting any time, Sir Moses Montefiore called an assembly of leading Jews. Undoubtedly, they had quickly realized that they needed to take action immediately, not only for the sake of their accused brother Jews, but for the future of Jewish emancipation. If the death sentences were carried out, it would effectively come to be seen as confirmation of the accusation, and the Jewish fight for equal rights would be condemned to failure in the whole world—but most particularly in England, where the events of Asia Minor could be used to great effect by the Jews' adversaries.

It was for this reason that Rothschild, Isaac Lyon Goldsmid, and David Salomons gathered, along with others, in the residence of Sir Moses Montefiore, to discuss the measures to be taken. One of France's leading Jews, [Adolphe] Crémieux, was called from Paris, to ensure international cooperation. A memorandum was drawn up in which the accusation was described as a mark of shame on civilization, and which denied any guilt on the part of the Jews in question.[80]

---

[79] Translator's note: According to available sources, it appears that the boy's body was never recovered, nor was there conclusive proof that the boy had died, but no reliably objective history of this case has ever been written.

[80] Picciotto: pp. 347-50. Wolf: *Essays...:* pp. 320-1. Hyamson: *History...,* pp. 276-7. Translator's note: For the definitive English-language account of the 1840 Damascus case, see Lt. Gen. Mustafa Tlass's *Matzo of Zion / The Matzah of Zion,* (1983, first published in English 1991), published when Tlass was Syria's Minister of Defense. The book reproduces original documents of the case, including interview transcripts of the official investigation, which was led by the French consul, Count Ulysee de Ratti-Menton. While much of the testimony is classifiable as hearsay, what is of interest is the fact that of the three men who initially confessed (two Jewish servants and the Jewish barber), who apparently did so due to promises of immunity rather than torture, all of the details in their confessions regarding the killing, dismemberment and disposal of the monk and his Muslim servant accorded perfectly, despite the immediate separation of the eight suspects who were caught (another six having evaded capture).

In addition, Saliman Al-Hallaq (the barber who stated that he was financially induced by one of the wealthy Jews to slit the monk's throat in the manner of a kosher slaughter, for the bound and gagged man to bleed out into a copper basin over the course of an hour), led the investigators to both the murder location (where investigators found spattered blood on the walls and damaged tiles on the floor where the Padre Tomaso's bones had been smashed) and the sewer opening where the monk's dismembered remains had been discarded, the knowledge of which no torture could induce. Specialists went down into the sewer and recovered pieces of flesh, bone and internal organs (liver and heart). Two committees of doctors, one Muslim, the other French, examined the remains and testified that the bones were human. The Austrian consul testified to seeing some pieces of a black headdress like the one worn by Padre Tomaso, while the priest's barber testified to recognizing it as that which had belonged to the priest himself. In addition, Dr. Michael Mashaqah wrote privately of his examination of the remains, which he believed

Only someone who has studied and truly come to understand the methods of the Jews in such cases, will be able to suspect what means were used to refute the accusations and to save the condemned Jews. As usual, most of the maneuvering did not become public knowledge, but what was expressed by the Hebrews themselves was enough to reveal that febrile activity had taken place.

Before all else, it was necessary to win over the public. A report, written by the Jews, was sent as a first step to 30 newspapers, who published it immediately. With few exceptions, we see the English press striving, by all means possible, to emphasize the innocence of the Jews and the cruelty of the authorities and the Christians of Asia Minor, who had participated in the accusations; in almost all of the press, one could read nothing but praise for the poor 'calumniated Israelites.' An almost unceasing barrage in this vein was directed at the populace. On looking over the *Times* of those days, it is startling to see how often this affair was front and center of the news agenda, before which the global interests of England seemed to be of secondary importance.[81]

In the face of so much propaganda, it cannot be surprising that the City of London was to call a solemn meeting at Mansion House, to show their full sympathy for the Damascus Jews' plight.[82] A Jewish delegation went to the Foreign Office and begged the Foreign Secretary, Lord Palmerston, to inter-

---

to be of the man whom he had known personally. These included parts of an upper jawbone still retaining a lock of hair from the beard, and the remnant of the thick woolen cloth of the monk's robe, the latter recognized by the doctor as that of Padre Tomaso because it was 'unique in Damascus.' No material evidence appears to have been recovered for the monk's Muslim servant, Ibrahim Amara, although several suspects testified that he was killed and disposed of in a similar manner. One of the accused rabbis later converted to Islam and made a formal statement admitting that both men had been ritually murdered.

Given that all Western mainstream sources have worked tirelessly to misrepresent these facts and vilify the incorruptible Count Ratti-Menton, even going as far as to publicly defame his most illustrious supporter, French Prime Minister Adolphe Thiers, it is unsurprising that Aldag's presentation of the case is as above. Ironically, if Ratti-Menton had not intervened to ensure that the case was investigated to the highest standard, it is likely that the guilty parties would have been summarily executed before the European Jews could intervene to free them, and the case would have been quickly forgotten, rather than becoming an international sensation which has echoed down the centuries. Establishment historians also neglect to mention that Ratti-Menton worked to quell the Damascus public's outrage at the murder of the kindly medical holy man who was known to treat Christians, Jews, and Muslims alike, and without the Count's intervention it is likely that the Damascus Jewry would have been completely destroyed. [NB: French speakers can also consult Volume II of Achille Laurent's *Relation historique des affaires de Syrie* (1846), which reproduces all documentation in the case as well as providing additional information to the Tlass book, and which was likely written with Ratti-Menton's direct collaboration.]

[81] Emanuel: p. 35. & Picciotto: pp. 351-2. Translator's note: QVOS. & See, for example, the *Times* of 1840: 2/5, 14/5, 18/5, 28/5, 2/6, 25/6, 29/6, 2/7, 5/7, 6/7, 7/7, 15/7, 6/10, 10/10, 3/12 and 7/12.

[82] Picciotto: p. 352. Wolf: *Essays...*, p. 322. Hyamson: *History...*, p. 277.

vene immediately, a request which was promised on the spot. As the published communiqué read:

> Without wasting a moment, he would send instructions to Lord Ponsonby, the English ambassador in Constantinople, and to Colonel Hedges, the English representative in Alexandria, to raise all possible protests, with the goal of preventing the prosecution of such shameful cruelties in the current era.[83]

Shortly afterwards, Lord Palmerston held an audience with a committee from the London Society for Promoting Christianity Among the Jews (SPCJ), constituted of the Bishop of Ripon, Lord Ashley, Sir George H. Rose MP, and Sir Thomas Baring, who wished to express their profound sympathy for the Jews of Damascus and equally, to request urgently that the British government provide them with protection. In an open letter, Lord Palmerston gave his assurances that he 'would dedicate his most serious attention to the matter and would ensure that England used her full influence with the government of Constantinople and the pasha of Egypt', to accomplish the triumph of justice and prevent the repetition of such shameful events.[84]

Towards the end of the year, a deputation from the General Assembly of the Church of Scotland addressed Lord Palmerston with the same request, and asked also that, from that point on, the British government placed all of the Jews of Asia Minor under its protection.[85]

We have to ask ourselves, quite bewildered, what would induce the London Society to intervene in favor of the Jews, given that, according to its own statutes, it only aimed for the *conversion* of Jews to Christianity. Seemingly, this public move in favor of unbaptized Jews was not very well received, despite the Society's founding principle being 'to relieve the temporal distress of the Jews, as well as to promote their spiritual welfare.'

The intervention of the English government in favor of the world's Jews will be found even more often later in this study, such as has been the case precisely in recent years, with particularly strong supporting evidence being made known and published.

---

[83] *Times*, 2/5/1840. Emanuel: p. 35. Wolf: *Essays...*, p. 321.
[84] *Times*, 2/6/1840. Translator's note: The Jews also imposed their will on the French government regarding the Damascus affair. The Jewish historian Léon Poliakov, in his book *Les Samaritains* (Paris: Seuil, 1991, p. 110), admits that James de Rothschild menaced King Louis Philippe of France with the threat that he would short-sell the country's annuity bonds if the king did not dismiss Adolphe Thiers [the then-Prime Minister who had supported the Count de Ratti-Menton in his investigation], which forced Thiers to resign: *'Quant à l'affaire de Damas, les Rothchild eurent finalement gain de cause, en menaçant de spéculer sur la baisse de la rente; Thiers dut démissioner.'*
[85] *Times*, 3/12/1840.

In accordance with the desire of the last delegation cited, it was officially declared to the Turkish government that England would represent and protect the Jews of Asia Minor from that point onwards, such as France had done with the Catholics. Lord Palmerston charged the consul assigned to Jerusalem with the duty to 'use every effort for the protection of the Eastern Jews.' This aspiration was openly recognized by the Sublime Porte, and, as a consequence, the other British consuls in Turkey received corresponding instructions.[86]

The open cooperation of world Jewry is also observable around this period. Thus we can see that, from almost all parts of the world, including Hamburg, Amsterdam, Barbados, Jamaica, Gibraltar, Altona (Canada), St. Thomas, and Philadelphia, large sums of money were sent to aid Montefiore in his Jewish activism.[87] The Jews came together in the 'Alliance Israélite Universelle', which had its headquarters in Paris. However, as Lucien Wolf reminds us:

> Although its organisation afterwards became centred in Paris, the English Jews have never ceased to hold this primacy in Jewry, thanks to their liberty-loving English instincts, and to the support their work has ever received from the Government and from their Christian fellow-subjects.[88]

It almost goes without saying that international Jewry got their desired victory only with the help of the powerful British government. Sir Moses Montefiore, who directed negotiations in Alexandria and Constantinople, was officially given assurances in both cases that the Jews' innocence had been proven, which is why the imprisoned Jews were set free. For his efforts in the affair, Montefiore received a baronetcy from Queen Victoria and was lauded by members of the royal family.[89]

The events in the Orient had stirred up the compassion of the English. In the face of this wave of sympathy, the Jews hoped to be able move their plans forward, thus it is that by February 9 of the following year, the Jews returned with a new bill that would allow a Jew to take up the post of alderman.[90] To great surprise all round, the bill won a majority at the first and second readings. but at the third, in general not as decisive, it was once again defeated by the Lords.[91]

---

[86] Hyamson: *History*..., pp. 278-9. Wolf: *Essays*..., pp. 322-3. Translator's note: QVOS [Wolf].
[87] Emanuel: p. 38.
[88] Wolf: *Essays*..., p. 322. Translator's note: QVOS.
[89] Emanuel: pp. 37-40. & Wolf: *Essays*..., p. 323.
[90] *Hansard*, Volume 56, p. 507.
[91] *Hansard*, Volume 58, p, 1048. & *Hansard*, Volume 58, p. 1458.

Yet again a partial Jewish attack had been repelled. Another unsuccessful bid by Salomons in the Maidstone parliamentary elections constituted another failure.[92] This new defeat for the Jews must certainly have contributed to their decision, from that year onwards, to put all of their energy into creating a well-organized press of their own. In 1841 *The Voice of Jacob* appeared, followed shortly afterwards by *The Jewish Chronicle*.[93]

The people of Damascus, however, were still upset with the Jews. Colonel Charles H. Churchill, stationed there by the English, proposed to the London Jewish community the idea of founding a nation-state of their own in Palestine, for which it would be necessary, naturally, for the world's Jews to themselves 'take up the matter *universally* and *unanimously*' and for 'the European Powers to aid them in their establishment.' Of course, the Jews of Palestine would then be Turkish citizens, but under the express protection of the European powers.[94] In view of how events later unfolded, it turns out to be quite ironic that the Jews who lived in England had been presented with Zionist plans for the first time by a Briton of the same name as their current champion, Winston Churchill.

When in 1843 the Jews of Tétouan and Tunisia reported mistreatment, the British consul, by order of his government, protested to the bey, who then promised his support.[95]

In the second half of 1841 and in the following two years, there is no record of any particular action by the Jews to get closer to their final goals. Perhaps this is due to a certain level of fatigue and a lack of internal cohesion. Indeed, this latter thesis is supported by the fact that, within the Jewish community, the religious Reform movement had begun, a schism which seemed to absorb most of the Jews' strength as it divided them into two mutually antagonistic factions.[96]

David Salomons: City of London Alderman

David Salomons was again elected Alderman of the City of London in 1844. He was confident that this time he would be able to convince the Court of Aldermen to let him take possession of this post without the required oath, because the authorities of other cities had already dispensed with it. When he appeared in front of the council, they demanded, however, that he take the oath, which he refused with lengthy historical and legal explanations, his speech ending with the words: 'I appeal to you for justice; I look for a just,

---

[92] Shapira: p. 94.

[93] Picciotto: p. 402 ff.; Hyamson: *History...*, p. 276.

[94] Emanuel: pp. 42-3. Translator's note: QVOS.

[95] Emanuel: p. 47.

[96] Emanuel: pp. 41-50. Wolf: *Essays...*, pp. 323-6.

merciful, and liberal interpretation of the law'.[97] The denial of his aspiration was the justice his arrogance deserved.[98]

Lord Lyndhurst based his bill on the fact that many Jews had already satisfactorily taken up high positions and even some cities—like Portsmouth, Southampton, and Birmingham—had admitted them as aldermen without such an oath. In addition, the Bishop of London let it be known that he would vote in favour of the bill because not to do so 'would only raise discussion, and excite angry feelings, and lessen the grace of the boon that they were about to confer on this respectable body of men.' Nevertheless, he remained against the Jews being admitted to Parliament, and he would vote against any law in this regard. According to findings, not a single member spoke against the bill, nor did a vote take place that was worthy of mention—a good condition for it to be admitted. The motion was presented to Parliament by Sir Robert Peel personally, who also explained in great detail why he supported it. Unmoved, Sir Robert Inglis once again resumed his arguments on why the bill should be defeated and complained bitterly of how the Jewish aldermen of Birmingham had been able to attack the regulations with such impunity, which was why the Jewish nation was now going to be rewarded with such a favorable law. With the overwhelming majority of 91 votes to 10, the bill was passed into law, and on 31 July 1845, it received the Royal Assent.[99]

A truly magnificent success! The tactic of attrition, by means of fatigue and demoralization, had shown its effectiveness yet again, and Judah now had every position in the town hall lying open before it. The danger that the passing of this law represented for the Jews' adversaries was recognized in certain places. With bitter words, the *Morning Post* complained of the law being passed in the House of Lords, and described it in an editorial of 19 July 1845 as a 'blow to the old British constitution.' It was a move that seemed inconceivable to the author, who was stunned that a Conservative government had put the British constitution on the line for a handful of Jews.[100]

Soon afterwards the Hebrews won a second victory, one that paved the way for the final battle: admission into Parliament.

The following year, not only were the last doubts finally quashed on the issue of possession of immovable property, which up until that point had still not been completely clarified, but the annulment process was also begun for the so-called Statute of Jewry and the laws passed under Henry III, according to which, among other directives, the Jews were to wear special signifiers which distinguished them from other citizens. Lord John Russell once

---

[97] Salomons: *Case...*, pp. 4-34. Translator's note: QVOS (p. 34).
[98] Salomons: *Case...*, pp. 3, 4. Henriques: *Jews*, p. 255.
[99] *Hansard*, Volume 78, p. 515 ff. & p. 524. Translator's note: QVOS. & *Hansard*, Volume 82, pp. 622-7. & pp. 627-32. & p. 633. & p. 1271.
[100] *Statutes of the United Kingdom*, Volume 85, pp. 480-1.

again distinguished himself, as always, very brilliantly, and the bill passed easily through all the relevant stages in the Upper Chamber, where it had first been presented. Parliament also approved the bill in the fastest possible time, whereupon it became the Religious Disabilities Act of 1846, and passed into the Parliamentary Archives under its official title: 'An Act to relieve Her Majesty's Subjects from certain Penalties and Disabilities in regard to Religious Opinions'.[101] In this way, practically all of the biggest Jewish disabilities had been eliminated, and now only admission to the House of Commons and the House of Lords remained forbidden to them.

The Jews and their allies then began invading the newly conquered terrain, and thus the number of Jews who occupied town hall positions began to grow steadily. David Salomons, who did not waste time in getting elected yet again as a City of London alderman, could finally take possession of his post. Other Jewish advances followed: Anthony de Rothschild (one of the brothers) and Isaac Lyon Goldsmid were elevated to the baronetcy, but it was the events of 1847 which revealed the powerful position of the Jews in society, in the most obvious way.

Salomons Loses, Rothschild Wins

During this time, a general election for Parliament was announced. To general surprise, David Salomons was presented as a candidate for Greenwich (a district of London), and Lionel Rothschild, the head of the banking house, was presented for the City of London seat. Salomons only let his intentions in this sense be known on the day before the elections.[102]

The tactic of the Jews and their allies was obvious. They hoped, as with the municipal elections, to put before Parliament a *fait accompli*, by working things so that some leading Jews were elected, so that afterwards, by appealing to popular opinion, they could once again move the struggle from the terrain of the principle to the terrain of the particular. This method had shown itself to be effective for the municipal elections, so likewise on this occasion, they counted on achieving the same result.

The 29th of July was Nomination Day, the day on which the candidates for each electoral district were to be solemnly announced. In addition, the election could take place by open acclaim, providing that there were no express protests against this. As this proceeding is always used more or less as

---

[101] *Hansard*, Volume 85, p. 1254 ff.; Volume 88, p. 360 ff. & p. 630 ff., 677. & *Statutes of the United Kingdom*, Volume 86, p. 413. Translator's note: QVOS. Proof that the 1275 Statute of Jewry of Edward I was still effectively in force up until this time is the fact that the aforementioned statute is found in the 1810 edition of the royally sanctioned *Statutes of the Realm* (Vol. I, pp. 220-221), but is absent from the 1870 edition (*The Statutes: Revised Edition*, Vol I.).

[102] *Daily News*, 30/7/1847.

proof, it comes to be practically the same thing as the pre-election poll. In Greenwich, the candidates who presented themselves, besides Salomons, were Admiral James Dundas, Mr. E. G. Barnard, and Mr. Samuel Kidd. On Nomination Day, as per usual, some 5,000 to 6,000 people had turned up to listen to the different candidates' point of view in terms of their electoral program.

The pre-election poll gave Salomons the majority. Dundas and Barnard then requested the definitive election to be held the next day, which brought them full victory and Salomons defeat in the battle for a seat in Parliament.[103] Rothschild was luckier. For the most varied reasons, he clinched a decisive victory in the most important constituency of England, despite the Conservatives trying to get the electors to understand in their electoral meetings, that under no circumstance should Rothschild be elected.[104]

The Jewish-friendly press did not only look at the election result with pleasure, but considered as totally unjust the situation which had prevailed up until that point. Given the English constitution, there was no way to prevent the Hebrews exercising an indirect influence on legislation. 'By entering into Parliament,' this press stated, 'they do not acquire a new influence, so much as a just and wise recognition of that which they already possess.'[105]

There is no doubt that a myriad of factors must have contributed to ensuring Rothschild's electoral success. One of those was most certainly the organized bribery of the electors. Of course, it is difficult to prove such crimes, given that all of the participants are obligated to remain silent; but in this case, we can make such a grave statement, being able to base our allegation on an objective historical investigation. Already by July 19, a feared agent and his two assistants had left the city of Norwich for London. The honorable citizens of Norwich warned their London friends of the agent's upcoming visit, because through their investigations they had discovered that this agent had already just spent £20,000 in bribes for the election of a Liberal [i.e. Whig] candidate, and it would appear that he was now making his way to the capital on a similar mission. These facts were published in an open letter from a top Conservative in the *Morning Herald* of 31 July 1847, and we will see further on if the actions of this agent and his accomplices would not have raised a red flag.

With great participation, Nomination Day arrived, in which the different candidates for the Liberals and the Conservatives set out their political agendas. But for now, our primary concern is the circumstances around this event and in particular the electors present, who for the most part had come from the poorest and dirtiest districts of London's East End. At least three-quarters of these people were made up of Jews, 'and those of the very worst

---

[103] *Standard*, 31/7/1847.

[104] *Morning Herald*, 27/7/1847; *Morning Post*, 27/7/1847; *Standard*, 26/7/1847.

[105] *Morning Chronicle*, 27/7/1847. Translator's note: QVOS.

type and most repulsive aspect,' who did not stop shouting down the speakers they did not like. When Rothschild began to speak, one could observe the greatest silence, and only occasionally was his speech interrupted with shouts of approval, while, by contrast, the other Liberal candidates [the City of London was a four-member seat] had trouble making themselves heard through 'the howling of the rabble,' several of whom had 'wrought themselves into... a state of demoniacal phrenzy.' In short, according to the *Daily News*, the whole hustings area had been 'usurped, to the exclusion of electors, by an unwashed mass of *claqueurs*, comprising coal porters, dustmen, venders of old clothes, and others *id genus omne.*'

The provisional election results showed the Liberal candidates—and therefore also Rothschild—had won at least nine-tenths of the votes, which shouldn't be a surprise given the composition of the electors who had turned up. The Conservatives then asked for an election proper.[106]

Election day came and it appears that there were truly frenzied scenes. The longshoremen—individuals who had been given the job of bribery—were working all day, especially in the poorest boroughs of the city: Cripplegate, Bishopsgate, Smithfield, etc. These individuals, strangers to the local people, obstructed the route to the polling place, tried to turn people away, or else tried to persuade them by every means possible, and at times were seen slipping electors amounts of money ranging from three to five pounds, naturally in exchange for a Liberal vote, that is to say, for Rothschild. Some voters, who did not hide this trade, reported these offers to the Conservatives and even showed themselves open to selling them their vote for an equal (or perhaps somewhat higher) price. As the Conservatives rejected such activities, the corresponding votes fell to the Liberals.

These events could be observed again and again. In each polling place, the same tableau. The last hour of the election must have been a very serious affair. Not only was the bribery taking place more brazenly than at the start, but even the prices of the votes went up, and up to £68 came to be paid per vote, with the result that the electors who arrived late ended up well paid. With such methods, it could easily be guessed from the start who would win the elections. Lord John Russell won the majority of the votes by 7,137; then followed two more Liberal candidates—one of them Rothschild—and only one Conservative managed to get elected.[107]

It must be stressed that the facts conveyed here were published in the newspapers, which is why without doubt they were also public knowledge. What is more, these practices were openly repeated in the years that followed.

---

[106] *Daily News*, 29/7/1847; *Morning Post*, 29/7/1847. Translator's note: Unless stated otherwise, all QVOS from the *Morning Post*.

[107] *Morning Post*, 30/7/1847, 31/7/1847, 27/5/1848, 29/7/1851; *Morning Herald*, 30/7/1847, 31/7/1847; *Standard*, 26/11/1847, 21/12/1847.

In bombastic rhetoric, the Judaizing press fêted Rothschild's victory. They assured readers that, with this election, the City of London had covered itself in imperishable glory and that the Jewish Question was now practically resolved, that Jewry's triumph was of the greatest importance, not only for England, but also for the entire world. As the *Morning Chronicle* wrote:[108]

> Here we have seen a Prime Minister of the British empire [Lord John Russell] take a Jew by the hand, and go before the first of British constituencies, and say—'Help me to emancipate this man [Lionel de Rothschild] from the last wretched remnant of a stupid and insulting tyranny, and make him one of ourselves, in all the franchises of an equal and common citizenship.'[109]

There was just one thing that all of these newspapers forgot in the euphoria of their triumph: to refute the accusation from the opposing side regarding the criminal methods used in the elections. Or was it that they were not capable of doing it? Whatever the reason may have been, we still search in vain for rebuttals of the accusation.[110]

The press of the Jews' adversaries were left horrified by the election result: What a disgrace that a Jew was elected to represent the City of London! The election outcome meant that gold had triumphed. Unimaginable amounts of money—£25,000 was talked of—had been disbursed in bribes. Truly, this was a brilliant triumph for the principle of freedom of religion—a verbatim quotation from a post-election speech given by Lord John Russell. At least in Greenwich, they had had the integrity to reject the election of a Jew.

Great concerns were also harbored about the future. Nothing good could be expected from the annulment of religion and principles, for 'it was as plain as day that Rothschild owed his election to money, money, and nothing but money'.[111]

Let us briefly analyze whether or not the reproaches made by the Jews' adversaries regarding bribery were justified—reproaches which we believe can be supported for various reasons. As all of the accusations were made publicly, in the newspapers, it would have been very easy to refute them if they were not based on facts. But none of that happened. Was this silence due to an unclean conscience, or was it a fear of further riling up the enemy press, which might induce them to make new revelations? Why was there no

---

[108] *Sunday Times*, 1/8/1847.

[109] *Morning Chronicle*, 30/7/1847. Translator's note: QVOS.

[110] *Morning Chronicle*, 31/7, 3/8; *Times*, 30/7, 31/7, 2/8, 3/8; *Sunday Times*, 1/8; *Evening Sun*, 30/7, 31/7, 2/8, 3/8.

[111] *Morning Post*, 30/7, 31/7; *Morning Herald*, 30/7, 31/7.

defamation claim raised against the owners and editors of the corresponding newspapers, or against the leading Conservatives of the City of London?

Not just the press, but also a few members in the House of Commons, Mr. Bankes, and most of all Mr. Newdegate—whom we shall return to later—formally repeated these allegations. The former expressed himself in the following way: 'As to the recent and previous elections for the City of London, if report spoke true, money had great influence in turning the scales; and if, in the City of London, money could produce such results, what might not be apprehended in other parts of the country?'[112]

It is interesting to note, according to what can be gathered from Hansard, that there was no uproar or protest from the pro-Jewish MPs. All of them stayed silent, and given that not even the Jews' adversaries showed any sign of surprise at these accusations, we can conclude that the accusations must have been facts that were already very well known.

It is also instructive to verify if, given the general conditions of the elections that were held in those days, it would really have been possible to bribe in the way that had been alleged. In 1830 it was an open secret that 'more than a third of the seats in Parliament are notoriously purchasable.' Some honorable members ceaselessly called attention to such an intolerable situation, which would naturally lead to the nation's demoralization. In 1844 there were further protests against abuses of this type. Shortly before Rothschild's election, on 12 July 1847, there was an in-depth debate in the House of Lords over the fact that most MPs, even those in the highest offices of government, were not free of such methods, and that recently in one constituency, the voters had affixed to their hats, in the style of cockades, the banknotes that they had received for their votes.[113]

But nor was there any improvement in this matter over the subsequent years. To all appearances, there was little inclination to intervene, and the members of the public who cared about ending such a shameful situation complained in vain of Parliament's intentional neglect. In articles of the *Morning Post* of the 2nd and 16th of March, 1853, we see the proportions these bribes could take:[114]

> Mr. Walpole brought up the report of this committee [the Huddersfield Election Committee], which was as follows: '... That Mr. Stansfield was, by his agents, guilty of bribery and treating at the last election for the borough of Huddersfield. That it was proved to the committee that William Radford, a

---

[112] *Hansard*, Volume 116, p. 372. & Volume 95, p. 1306. Translator's note: QVOS.

[113] *Times*, 3/5/1830. Translator's note: QVOS. & *Hansard*, Volume 26, p 516 ff., p. 874; *Times*, 5/6/1844. & *Hansard*, Volume 94, p. 169 ff.

[114] *Times*, 9/3/1853, 10/3/1853; *Morning Post*, 2/3/1853, 8/3/1853, 14/3/1853; *Standard*, 22/2/1853.

publican; David Dodson, a publican; and Jacob Senior, a publican, were each of them bribed by colourable payments... That Joseph Halliwell was bribed by obtaining for his nephew, as a condition for his vote, three 25-gallon casks of ale, a portion of which his nephew gave away among the electors on the day of the election, and the remainder of which he sold at a profit. That the treating throughout the borough during the last election was general, systematic, and extravagant in its character. That between 60 and 70 public houses at the last election were opened by the agents of the sitting member. That refreshments were provided, apparently, without limit, and paid for without inquiry.

There is...a brigade of voters, as well known in the locality as any other brigade to the general public, who regard the franchise simply as a saleable commodity, and who deal with it precisely as a broker does with a gold-mining or Australian land share. They are, for the most part, gross, drunken, deboshed, idle vagabonds, who have no recollection of the past, and no thought of the future... Their thoughts and calculations extend not beyond the present, and their soul is in a beer-pot.[115]

These unpleasant events did not change in the slightest until the emancipation battle ended in 1858.[116]

As such, the Rothschild case did not constitute any kind of exception. Nevertheless, the widespread use of such methods and Parliament's lack of interest in the matter, explains perfectly why Rothschild could indulge in such behavior. Rothschild himself confirmed the suspicion of bribery at a later date, through his own statements, as he let it be understood that his election in the City of London had cost him between £20,000 and £25,000. The true cost for an election of that kind in those days was normally between £800 and £1,000, with perhaps a City of London seat reaching a maximum of £5,000.[117] Until then, Rothschild had no chance of occupying a place on the bench in the House of Commons, due to not being able to swear the required Oath of Abjuration.

The Jews and their allies began to make every preparation to eliminate, at last, the final obstacle in their way, and a new heated battle over the issue soon began in Parliament.

---

[115] Translator's note: The first paragraph is quoted verbatim from the 16 March issue, the second paragraph from the 2 March issue.

[116] *Times*, 16/8/1854, 3/4/1857, 4/7/1857; *Morning Post*, 20/5/1854, 30/5/1854, 22/7/1854, 25/7/1857; *Daily News*, 22/3/1858, 20/4/1858.

[117] *Morning Herald*, 30/7/1847. *Hansard*: Volume 94, p. 169 ff.

A New Propaganda Campaign

A new wave of propaganda washed over the country in the form of countless pamphlets. It is instructive to take a quick look at some of them.

A new booklet by Francis Henry Goldsmid complained that the Jews who had been admitted to the highest position in the state's bureaucracy still continued to be banned from Parliament, a measure incompatible with the Christian religion, given 'the foundation of the New [Testament], "Thou shalt love thy neighbour as thyself".'[118] Another writer demanded reparation for the injustice committed against the Jews up until that point, and said that the British nation, 'as a younger and beloved sister', should contribute promptly to 'the glory and happiness of restored Israel'.[119]

Barnard van Oven, who had already distinguished himself in similar matters years before, naturally could not but get involved on this occasion. He analyzed the religious reasoning of the adversaries, which he considered erroneous on all points, because 'England has ceased to be a Christian country'.[120]

In *Chambers Miscellany of Useful Tracts*, a 'History of the Jews in England' was published which, from the start, earned a large circle of readers. Nobody would have thought that the author could be the Jewess Grace Aguilar, because it is certain that then a large part of the readership would have considered elements of the work to be extremely arrogant, and would therefore have rejected it.[121]

The first part of the book condemns the cruelties committed in earlier times against the poor Jews and then praises at length the wisdom of Menasseh ben Israel. It was a lamentable situation that parts of society still continued to look down on Jews, who were 'Jews only in their religion—Englishmen in everything else.' And on the subject of Jewish disabilities, the question is asked: 'Is it not discreditable to the common sense of the age that such anomalies should exist in reference to this well-disposed and, in every respect, naturalized portion of the community?' She stated that the Jews originating from Spain were comparable to princes, while those coming from Germany still left a lot to be desired. But the fault did not lie with the Jews themselves, but with the persecutions that they had suffered in said country. If it were not for this, one would not find Jewish criminals and beggars.

After having made some descriptions of the supposed persecutions suffered by the Jews on the Continent, that then as today aroused the compassion of the English, there followed, until the end of the book, a heartfelt ap-

---

[118] Goldsmid: *Reply...*, pp. 5-7, 56-57. Translator's note: QVOS. Readers will undoubtedly be familiar with Jews teaching Christians the tenets of Christianity.

[119] Birks: pp. 7-8, 59. Translator's note: QVOS.

[120] van Oven: *Ought Baron de Rothschild...*, pp. 20, 25. Translator's note: QVOS.

[121] Levy, pp. 11-12.

peal which called for peace with the Jews and to give them everything they wanted and belonged to them by right.[122]

In addition, the Jewish-friendly press was very active and, as usual, must also have been working hard in the shadows. By every means possible and from the beginning, the Jews strove to know intimately the attitudes of the members of both Houses regarding the Jewish Question.[123]

At the start of December 1847, it was believed that preparations were now sufficiently advanced to be able to push the issue of the Jewish Question into Parliament once again, especially in view of the fact that the Jews enjoyed the full support of the Whig government. As always, the Prime Minister Lord John Russell was a prominent player in the battle, on this occasion personally tabling a motion 'that the House will resolve itself into a Committee on the removal of the civil and political Disabilities affecting Her Majesty's Jewish subjects', with the goal of thus granting, in one fell swoop, full equality of rights for the Jews.

Lord John Russell expressed himself in an excellent dialectic way regarding his bill. To judge from the extant textual evidence, the speech must have lasted for hours. From the looks of things, he dealt at length with the history of the Jews. He stressed in particular that these were people of the highest morals, unbeaten in the fulfilment of their duties to the state and their loyalty to the Crown, which was why it was a source of shame to continue depriving persons of such qualities of their rights. The Jews born in England were English and nothing else.[124]

He was followed by the leader of the Jews' adversaries, Sir Robert Inglis, who also spoke at great length and in great detail. He expressed his surprise that the Prime Minister would personally lend such support to the bill and stated that he did not share his opinions in the slightest. He said that the Jews lauded the Prime Minister's support 'with especial joy', which they saw 'as a signal augury of their approaching triumph'.[125]

> [T]his, I think, is the first country in which, without a revolution, the change [to the Constitution] has ever been proposed. And for whom is it now proposed in England? For some thirty or forty thousand strangers! For some, whose very names and titles prove them to be un-English. For those, who, as I believe, never can be English... but in the first instance I may assert, without fear of contradiction, that two centuries ago there was not one single Jew in this realm of England; that they

---

[122] Aguilar: pp. 1-13, 16-18, 22-32. Translator's note: QVOS.

[123] Myers: pp. 240-6.

[124] *Hansard*, Volume 95, pp. 1234-1249. Translator's note: QVOS.

[125] *Hansard*, Volume 95, pp. 1249-1265. Translator's note: Speech excerpts QVOS.

came in, drop by drop... Did we invite them? Did they come in
for our convenience? Did they not come in for their own?...
Do they not enjoy every social protection? Do they not live in
all luxury? Does anyone envy them the wealth which they
gain among us? But, on the other hand, can they claim from us
the sacrifice of the Christian character of our Constitution, for
the sake of admitting them to a share of governing us? Can
they ever, as true Jews, be amalgamated with us? Are they not
always, necessarily and intrinsically, a separate people?...

Benjamin Disraeli also took part in the debate. He said that the hypothesis of
Judaism being able to modify a country's Christian character was ridiculous.
In every place, one could see, according to him, the prevailing influence of
the Jews, who were superior to all other races in the world. He claimed that
the Christian doctrine itself was an eloquent testament to that, as its authors
were Jews.[126] It was absurd, therefore, to reject Jewish emancipation for religious reasons. Every holiday announced the doctrine of Jewish heroes and poets
to the people, which was proof of why the Jews were considered of higher
morals. Below are some typically representative excerpts from his speech:

> ... [F]or every Gentleman here does profess the Jewish religion,
> and believes in Moses and the prophets. (Interjection: 'Oh!')
> ... Where is your Christianity, if you do not believe in
> their Judaism?
> ... And I cannot but believe that a man owning all the
> traditions, all the habits, all the laws of a Jew—a man who
> wishes to remain inviolate the religious institutions in every
> country in which he lives—must ever look upon the Catholic
> Church, whatever may be its form, with no other feelings than
> those of the deepest interest, and, as I think, with those of rev-
> erent affection.
> ... Yes, it is as a Christian that I will not take upon me the
> awful responsibility of excluding from the Legislature those
> who are of the religion in the bosom of which my Lord and
> Saviour was born.

His speech ended by calling for eternal gratitude to the Jews and their works,
and pleading that only for this reason—and not for the fact that as citizens
and taxpayers they had the right to a seat in Parliament—Lord John Rus-

---

[126] Editor's note: The entirety of the Old Testament was written by Jews, as was the entirety of the New Testament—including Paul of Tarsus and the four anonymous (but certainly
Jewish) authors of the four Gospels. Jesus himself was an ethnic Jew.

sell's bill had to be passed. What pride, what arrogance in front of Parliament, are to be found in these words![127]

The honorable member Mr. Wood considered it an injustice that use was made of the Jews' great influence and wealth without the Jews themselves being granted rights. Meanwhile, the honorable member Mr. Henry Ker Seymer warned of allowing a single Jew entry into Parliament. Working in different ways, with the help of their money, they would not waste time in gaining new parliamentary seats.[128]

After long debates, the bill was passed by Parliament.[129] Just as on previous occasions, the House of Commons had therefore taken Jewish wishes into account. Nevertheless, despite all of the propaganda and the support from high places, they could not, in any way, silence the opposition, as is shown by the speeches delivered in Parliament and the articles printed in the press of the Jews' adversaries.

The *Morning Post* did not consider it an injustice that the Jews were denied, once and for all, the right to enter Parliament. The pro-rights reasoning that Jews were English and as such had the right to sit in Parliament was false, because 'the Jew is not an Englishman' and Jews as a group would always continue being 'natural and undoubted enemies' who must not be allowed 'the power of perverting the institutions of a Christian state'.[130]

The *Standard* also adhered to these arguments over the course of numerous articles, and added that 'never was the usurer *caste* more odious, or more justly odious, to the country than at the present moment; and it is to facilitate the admission to *power* of the usurer *caste* that the doors of Parliament are to be thrown open to the deniers of the blessed Redeemer of mankind.' Regarding the supposed 'intolerance against the Jews', it was already quite enough just having to tolerate their presence.[131]

The editorial in the *Standard* of 18 December 1847, on the topic of the 'odious and sinful' Jew Bill, contains some particularly harsh attacks on the Jews themselves. The following are excerpts of the article [reproduced verbatim from the original source]:

> We therefore must protest against the line of argument taken
> by Lord John Russell and his supporters, and tell them that the

---

[127] *Hansard*: Volume 95: p. 1321 ff. Translator's note: All QVOS. I have also included elements of the speech where were elided in Aldag's text, for their interest to the modern reader.
[128] *Hansard*: Volume 96: pp. 228-242. & pp. 481 ff.
[129] *Hansard*: Volume 96: p. 536 ff., Volume 98, p. 667 ff.
[130] *Morning Post*, 15/12/1847, 18/12/1847. Translator's note: The first quotation comes from the 18/12/1847 issue, the second quotation the 15/12/1847 issue. The later issue also questions the propriety of allowing the Jews a share in the control of the nation's political destiny.
[131] *Standard*, 26/11, 29/11, 18/12, 20/12, 21/12, 24/12. Translator's note: The quotation in the text is reproduced verbatim from the 26/11/1847 issue.

onus of proof of necessity for abolishing the Christian character of the British constitution rests upon them, not upon us, who would maintain those principles and institutions that have existed amongst us for far more than one thousand years— indeed, ever since Britain emerged from barbarism. Nothing has occurred to change the character of the Jews or their relations to us during that long period. If, therefore, we are fools and oppressors because we exclude Jews from the government of the country, our ancestors have been fools and oppressors for more than ten centuries...

Now Jews are not *Englishmen*, though born in this country; they are and claim to be *an exclusive nation*—a nation separated from all others... But, admitting, contrary to the truth, that Jews born in this country are Englishmen, Lord John Russell's proposition does not apply, for there are millions of 'Englishmen born in this country' who are excluded from sitting in Parliament by want of a property qualification, or of ability to support the expenses of a parliamentary election. We might add the millions of 'Englishmen born in this country' who have not even a vote for representatives because they do not hold a 40-shilling freehold or a 10-pound house. We pass over officers in the public service, and the whole body of the clergy, because they embrace their disqualification; but we demand to know, why the want of a given sum of money is more inconsistent with the possession of civil privileges than the want of faith in the Saviour of mankind, whom all 'Englishmen born in this country' reverently acknowledge.

The number of Jews in this country (rated by Lord John Russell at 40,000, by Lord George Bentinck at 25,000) can bear only upon the question of policy, for right is not to be determined by numbers. If the Jews have *a right* to be among our governors, no matter whether their number be ten, or ten millions, they ought to be admitted to the enjoyment of that right; but if we are free to grant or to refuse, according to the determination of policy, the number of Jews is a consideration of some weight. We should like to see a statistical analysis of our 25,000 or 40,000 Jews, as the case may be. How many of them are usurers? How many of them of the trade of *Mr. Fagan*? How many of them sheriffs' officers, members of the ring, keepers of flash-houses, or engaged in still more loathsome occupations? How many, if any, occupied in useful industry? How many ever held a plough, or are connected with the soil of the country? [...]

But their numbers, says Lord John, are not formidable as 'a physical power.' No, but they may be formidable as a vehicle of pestilence—a bale of plague-poisoned cloth may destroy more than the most numerous army, and the introduction of unbelievers into the legislature alone is enough to poison, by the contempt of religion which it evinces, the religion and morality of the nation; *and it will destroy both*, if it ever be consummated.

In an article of 14 February 1848, the *Morning Post* said the following apropos of the general character of the Jews:

As we have plunged into the unamiable, we will venture to add, that throughout the debate the general character of the Jews seems to have been dealt with but too tenderly. That there are good and generous men among them we should be sorry to deny; but when considering the question whether or no the barrier between them and the Legislature should be removed, it is fair to take their general character into account.

Now, whatever may have been suppressed by the somewhat squeamish courtesy of Parliament in these days of weak civility, we know very well that the general impression, and we believe the just impression, of the people of this country is that the Jews are more discreditable members of society than any other sect or class of the same numerical amount. Whatever is most gross and revolting in the immoralities and secret abominations of crowded communities—

'...whatever vice /
The cruel city breeds'

—is chiefly under the management of persons of the Jewish race. We do not accuse their religion, for we believe these persons have no religion. The Jews of the lower orders, says Mr. Coleridge in his 'Table Talk', are the very lowest of mankind; they have not a principle of honesty in them; to grasp and to be getting money for ever is their single and exclusive occupation. A learned Jew once said to him upon this subject, 'Oh! Sir, make the inhabitants of Holywell Street and Duke's Place Israelites first, and then we may debate about making them Christians.'

The vileness of these people in our great cities being notorious, we should think the best preparation which their great men could make for satisfying the British public that they were worthy to approach Parliament would be in strenuous efforts to reform the character and conduct of wretches who are a disgrace not merely to the Hebrew race, but to human nature itself.

In an article of 7 February 1848, the *Times* takes an interest in the Opposition's argument, according to which the admission of Jews would strip the legal institutions of their Christian character, and ends, after long consideration, with a rejection of the idea. What is strange is that the *Times* never decided to avail itself of the other arguments used by the Jews' adversaries, such as bribery, vice, and the enmity of the Jews towards the state.

Judging from the tone of the press, the opinions around this issue were much more heated than in previous times. More and more, the knowledge of this being more than a religious issue was breaking through into the press. The question that the Jews' adversaries were worriedly asking themselves was what the House of Lords would do this time, and whether it would have the courage to resist, yet again, all of the pressure being brought to bear.

On the 25th of May, 1848, the bill came before the House of Lords. Lord Brougham made an address specifically to counter the allegation, made several times in the press, that the bill had originated in a trading house in the City of London. It was out of the question, he said, that there had been any collaboration between Lord John Russell and Baron Rothschild.[132] The heated debate ended with a vote in favor of the Jews' adversaries, with which the latest Israelite attack was roundly repulsed.

Neither did the mass of the English people show itself open to supporting the Jews' desires in any way, as is shown by the petitions which were sent to Parliament in support or opposition of the bill. A quick examination of these petitions makes clear that the vast majority were against the laws in question, just as every aspect of public life signaled an anti-Jewish attitude among the people. It is true that we found out about two assemblies, held in Edinburgh and Cambridge, in favor of the Jews, but against them we also noted that there was a corresponding anti-Jewish opposition.[133]

For those who were certain of triumph, the events of 1848 must have been a bitter disappointment. But from the new wave of propaganda being pushed by the Jews, it can be deduced that the decision had been made to keep up the fight. A book was published of the most important speeches made regarding the latest Jewish bill. The author Charles Egan, a barrister, summarized the different counter-arguments made by the opposition as if it

---

[132] *Hansard*: Volume 98, 1398.
[133] *Morning Post*, 17/12/1847; *Standard*, 17/12/1847; *Times*, 17/12/1847; *Standard*, 22/12/1847. & *Standard*, 30/12/1847; *Times*, 13/1/1848, 2/2/1848.

were a legal document, and tried to refute them.[134] Later followed, among others, Henry Hughes, the perpetual curate who stood up most vehemently to counter the assertion that the Jew was an outsider in England, and the Reverend Henry Street, who called the Jews his benefactors and tried to reward them with the desired law.[135]

A year later, a new attack was initiated in Parliament, under the direction of Lord John Russell. This time he titled his bill 'Parliamentary Oaths Bill', to avoid any first impression of this being a measure to favor the Jews. In principle, it called for a general reform of the oath taken by members of Parliament; the proposed new text would thus mean that there was no longer any further obstacle for the Jews. But it was not long before the adversaries noticed the secret intention of Lord Russell.

After a skillful speech from the Prime Minister, Sir John Robert Inglis took the floor. He started with the objection that the law would only serve to facilitate the entry of Jews into Parliament, and then went on to say: 'whenever they were admitted into that House, they would form a nucleus for their own opinions, and there were many instances of a small compact body having a great effect upon the public deliberations'.[136] The honorable member Major Beresford [1st Viscount Beresford] agreed with Sir Robert Inglis. In his judgement, the main reason for the demand to modify the oath was the fact that the City of London had elected a Jew.[137] Both were supported by Charles Newdegate, who later came to be regularly prominent in the debates. As Hansard reports:

> Mr. Newdegate said, that no one could accuse the hon. Member for Tavistock of religious bigotry, since he would admit not only Jews, but Hindoos and Mahometans to Parliament. The hon. Member might be a bigot to his opinions on political economy, but not on religion certainly: he seemed to agree with Voltaire, who urged, that because Jews and Christians made money together on the Exchange, therefore that there ought to be no restriction upon the admission of Jews into the Legislature.
>
> But was there no difference between the House of Commons and the Exchange? If the House of Commons and the Exchange were the same, there certainly would be no justice in the exclusion of Jews from Parliament; but he had been brought up in a different school of belief. He had been taught

---

[134] Egan: p. 150 ff.

[135] Hughes: pp. 6-7. & Street: pp. 30-1.

[136] *Hansard*: Volume 104, 1398. Translator's note: QVOS.

[137] *Hansard*, Volume 104, p.1398.

to consider the House of Commons as the representatives of a
great Christian country, assisting a Christian Sovereign in the
discharge of her Christian duties; and he could not therefore
look to this as the denial of a right of the Jews to sit in a Christian Parliament. The right to a seat in the Legislature was spoken of as a privilege; but he (Mr. Newdegate) considered a
seat in that House not as a right or a privilege, but simply as a
trust vested in the person elected by the public for the public
good [...] if they admitted the Jews, who denied Christianity
on principle, they could not refuse admittance to the infidel. If
they admitted the infidel to the same privileges and power as
Christian Members, then it was an insult to those Christian
Members to exact from them a profession of their faith. There
was another view of the question: the Jews were a separate
people by race and by religion.

After other speeches the House proceeded to the division, where there was a
majority of 93 votes in favor of acceptance. [138]

Unexpectedly, there were some new and interesting speeches during
the third reading. The honorable Mr. Law presented a previously unheard
and complete summary of the history of the Jews in England, of which he
had personally made an in-depth study. An excerpt of his speech:

> To employ the eloquent language of the modern and accom-
> plished author of the *History of the Jews:* 'Refusing still to
> mingle their blood with any other race of mankind, they dwell
> in their distinct families and communities; and still maintain,
> though sometimes long and utterly unconnected with each
> other, the principle of national unity. Jews in the indelible fea-
> tures of the countenance, in mental character, in customs, us-
> ages and laws, in language and literature, above all in religion,
> in recollections of the past, and in the hopes of the future.
> Denizens everywhere, rarely citizens even in the countries in
> which they have been the longest and most firmly established,
> they appear to a certain degree strangers or sojourners; they
> dwell apart, though mingling with neighbours in many of the
> affairs of life.' [...]
>
> We must look therefore to some other cause than the al-
> leged principle of this Bill for its introduction, and the urgency
> with which it is advocated. The fact is, that the Jews, by their
> connexions, can command the money market all over the

---

[138] *Hansard*, Volume 104, p. 1428. Translator's note: QVOS.

world; and the money market is the secret why it is sought to
admit them into this House. [...]

Is it from the idle notion of paying a compliment to a
millionaire, who happened to be associated with the noble
Lord at the head of the Government, or is it in consequence of
his wealth and his influence, especially in the contracting of
loans, and in the money market—that this measure was
brought forward? Was it introduced from any other accident,
than because he is the colleague of the noble Lord at the head
of Her Majesty's Government, and a rich man well-backed on
the Stock Exchange? [...]

Why, I would venture to ask, should we break through
the fundamental principles of the British constitution to pave
the way for the admission of the Jews into Parliament? ...
[T]he stability of the country depends—under the Supreme
Disposer of events—upon the maintenance of our institutions
on an exclusively Christian foundation.[139]

As well as the MPs Raphael and Keogh, Newdegate intervened once more in
the debate. His speeches are of great value and are particularly interesting,
given his profound study of the works on Jewish history and his specialist
knowledge of this subject. Newdegate highlighted above all the Jews' inferi-
or character, derived from their religious principles. He was not surprised by
the general support that the Jews received in Parliament given their predominance on the Stock Exchange, the principles of which had already been imported wholesale in Parliament.[140] The efforts made by the Opposition to
thwart the bill were unsuccessful: the division went in favor of the government, at 272 votes to 106.[141]

Once again, the House of Lords became the wall of resistance which
broke the assaults of the pro-Jewish faction. The Bishop of Oxford was passionately opposed to the bill being passed:[142]

First, then, he said that there was danger, because it was impossible to measure the number of constituencies upon whom
the power of money might be brought to bear in order to secure an object which might be of great importance to the Jews;
and at the present time he thought it was especially dangerous
to increase the representation of wealth as separate from those

---

[139] *Hansard*, Volume 105, p. 1384. Translator's note: QVOS.
[140] *Hansard*, Volume 105, p. 1385. & p. 1386. & p. 1389.
[141] *Hansard*, Volume 105, p. 1430.
[142] *Hansard*, Volume 106, pp. 871-922.

other considerations which ought to qualify and control the money influence. They had of late years seen the great increase of that money power in the British Legislature, without a proportionate increase of those considerations; and therefore he thought that to pass this measure, which would give the directest representation of the most immediate money power in the country, was a real, practical and great evil. [143]

The law was defeated by 95 votes to 70. [144]

A Repeat of the Rothschild Farce

The eight days that followed this Jewish defeat in the House of Lords were surely the most instructive of the 28 years of the struggle. The sitting of the Lords which decisively brought down the bill began on the evening of Tuesday 26 June 1849. At 12.30 a.m. the debate ended with a vote. In view of the lateness of the hour, the debate was adjourned until the following day. Very early the following morning, Lionel de Rothschild resigned his seat in Parliament, triggering the need for a by-election. Immediately afterwards, the official body responsible drew up the notice for the by-election in the City and sent it to the sheriffs, into whose hands it arrived shortly before 2 o'clock in the afternoon. A few hours later, it was made public that Nomination Day would be held on Monday 2 July and that the election would take place on Tuesday 3 July. [145]

The speed at which these formalities were carried out is truly surprising. Surely there is no similar case recorded in all of English history—because normally it would take a few weeks. The *Standard* of 2 July made sure to publish the notice required, while the *Morning Herald* of the same date expressed its disgust that Rothschild had stolen a march on his rival by putting up his campaign placards on the Christian Sabbath (something that Lord Manners had not been prepared to do) and stated in its editorial:

> It must convince any man of the most plain understanding that everything was long previously arranged, and every preparation duly made to take the City of London by surprise, and thus to pretend that Baron Rothschild had made a fair appeal to that constituency, and that the appeal was followed by a true

---

[143] *Hansard,* Volume 106, p. 912. Translator's note: QVOS.

[144] *Hansard,* Volume 106, p. 920 ff.

[145] *Standard,* 28/6/1849, 30/6/1849, 2/7/1840; *Morning Post,* 2/7/1849.

and determined approval of his claim to be the representative
of this great City.[146]

On Thursday, Rothschild's candidacy announcement was published,
according to which 'justice will be done according to the forms, and in the
true spirit, of the English Constitution.' This infuriated the *Morning Herald*
of 29 July, because, according to the newspaper, all of Rothschild's maneuvering, from a man who had no right to occupy a seat in Parliament, was in
contradiction to the constitution and the laws of Great Britain.[147]

Every nook and cranny of the City was covered with posters for Rothschild, but nowhere was seen anything similar from the Jews' adversaries,
who had been caught off-guard by events, and who didn't even have time to
convey to the public whether or not an opposing candidate was to be fielded.
Initially it was considered completely pointless to field a candidate, and only
after some long debates in an assembly formed for the purpose was it decided to present Lord John Manners for the role. This decision was conveyed to
the electors in the last hours of Saturday evening, 30 June, and for this reason
it seemed very doubtful that Lord Manners could have published his candidacy announcement on the same day. In any case, his announcement only
appeared in the newspapers on Monday, the Nomination Day itself. It explained that the election had only been staged to intimidate the House of
Lords. Lord Manners would act to protect the Lords and he would try to
bring down all attempts against them.[148]

The situation of the candidate chosen to challenge Rothschild was, as
might be expected, far from satisfactory. While Rothschild worked with
electoral propaganda which had been prepared long in advance, Lord Manners did not even have a whole day available to make his own preparations,
because on a Sunday, electoral campaigning hardly ever takes place in England. Rothschild, on the other hand, was in a much more favorable position,
all things considered. His ethnic brethren worked for him even on Sunday,
and even during church hours, invaded the City with posters and election
leaflets, which must have been printed only the night before, given that they
most outrageously attacked Lord Manners personally.

The morning of Nomination Day saw a large crowd in the streets,
formed mainly of Jews from the most disreputable districts of London. It
seemed as if, on that day, not a single Jew was working at his trade. Everywhere candidacy advertisements for Rothschild, and everywhere banners
inscribed with 'Civil and Religious Liberty' or 'Rothschild.' When Rothschild was presented to the crowd, a frenzy of zealous cheering broke out; on

---

[146] Translator's note: QVOS.
[147] *Times*, 28/6/1849. Translator's note: QVOS.
[148] *Standard*, 29/6/1849. & 2/7/1849; *Morning Post*, 2/7/1849; *Morning Herald*, 2/7/1849.

Lord John Manners being presented, the words of his friend's introduction were lost in the jeers and whistles of the crowd.

Rothschild mainly spoke of the need for the equality of rights and liberties for all. When he finished his speech, the applause never seemed to end. In vain Lord Manners tried to explain his political principles to the crowd. Not even those closest to him were able to make out his words. When the uproar got too much even for Rothschild's friends, the head of the assembly tried to restore calm. He appealed to the gentility of those present, saying that it was un-English to not let the adversary speak. But these words appeared not to make the slightest impression on the crowd, for as soon as Lord Manners tried to resume his speech, the same uproar returned. In a final effort, Lord Manners addressed the gathering with the following words: 'This is said to be a contest for religious liberty and freedom, but it seems to me that liberty of speech is not included in liberty of conscience.' The pre-election poll delivered a crushing majority to Rothschild, therefore the definitive election was requested for the following day.

In contrast to the first election, and to ensure that things went as desired, Nomination Day saw all of Rothschild's supporters be invited to eat and drink their fill in various restaurants.[149]

On the day of the election itself, the disturbances reached even greater proportions than those of previous day. Just as in the election of 1847, the longshoremen once again dominated the terrain, with the same scenes repeated, and the bribes at least as large as before.

In addition, Rothschild worked with false electoral lists. The Conservative Association had already ascertained, long before the election took place, that some 1,400 people—with no right to vote or even deceased—had been wrongfully included on the electoral roll; this figure constituted a very high percentage of the City of London electorate at that time. The Conservative Association complained to the registration court for the City, asking for these names to be removed, which the president of the court rejected. However strange this may seem, it cannot be surprising when one considers that the partisanship of such public bodies had been publicly complained about for years. It was also known that the main functionary of this authority, a barrister, worked for a morning newspaper, whose editor was completely economically dependent upon Rothschild. Thus he did nothing to change such an illegal situation. Rothschild, concerned with not losing a single vote, had bought, almost without exception, all of those wrongfully registered on the list; and moreover, even men were found who were prepared to vote in the name of the deceased.

---

[149] *Time*, 3/7; *Standard*, 3/7; *Morning Post*, 3/7; *Morning Herald*, 3/7; *Morning Chronicle*, 3/7. Translator's note: The quotation from Lord Manners is taken verbatim from the *Morning Chronicle*, but his words are paraphrased differently across different newspaper titles.

Rothschild's adversaries, who did not remain idle, were already distributing in the earliest hours of the election a leaflet which said that any votes given to Rothschild would be votes which were 'lost and thrown away', because it continued to be impossible for the Jew to take up his seat in Parliament, given his inability to swear to the last words of the oath. Besides this, as a Government contractor he could not represent the interests of the constituents. The leaflet also made an allegation of corruption:

> We, the undersigned electors of the said city of London, do hereby give you notice that Lionel Nathan Rothschild, Esq, otherwise called Baron Lionel Nathan de Rothschild, one of the candidates to represent the said city in Parliament at this present election, was guilty by himself or his agents, as well of bribery as of treating and other corrupt practices, at the election of the said city held in the 29th day of July, in the year 1847, and is thereby rendered ineligible and incapable of being elected to serve as a citizen in Parliament for the said city upon the present vacancy.

The leaflet carried the date of 2 July 1849, as well as the signatures of four citizens, made in the presence of two lawyers.

A few hours later, Rothschild and his friends arranged for a leaflet to be disseminated which contained the following professional opinion of eminent barrister and member of Parliament Matthew Davenport Hill, whose name was obviously familiar enough to electors for his statement to be signed 'M. D. Hill':

> I am of opinion, that the election of the Baron Rothschild to be member of Parliament for the city of London would be a valid election, notwithstanding his religious faith and opinions; that such election is no way affected by what has taken place in the House of Lords or elsewhere; that whether or not the Baron, if elected, shall think fit to take such oaths as will entitle him to sit and vote does not touch the question of his right to be a member, and that any notice to the electors that their votes will be thrown away in the event of their voting for the Baron Rothschild will be nugatory, and ought not to be regarded.

What is interesting to note, however, is that not the slightest effort was made to refute or at least reject the allegations of bribery and hospitality ('treating').[150]

---

[150] *Times*, 4/7; *Morning Herald*, 3/7, 4/7, 5/7. Both QVOS from the *Times* article.

Rothschild was elected. How could it have been otherwise! With 6,017 votes to Lord Manner's 2,814, Rothschild scored a comfortable victory in the election. The rhyme published in the *Morning Herald* of 6 July 1849 summarized the situation very well for the majority of the electors:

> Inscribe this on your banners
> (Deny it if you can),
> 'With us it is not *Manners*,
> But *money* makes the *man*.'

At the solemn proclamation of the election result, Rothschild's great friend, Mr. Wire, not knowing what to do to praise him, attacked the House of Lords for its stance. Analogous were the declarations of the *Sun* of 4 July, who openly threatened to sanction the House of Lords if its members had the temerity to oppose the Jew:[151]

> Let them beware, lest in the midst of their interference with the prerogatives of the House of Commons of England, the latter should retaliate upon them *by refusing to grant the Supplies!* How foolish the Bench of Bishops would look in such a predicament! What a sorry figure the whole of the Peers would cut in such an event! And such an event is always possible, for (let it not be forgotten) the purse of the nation is in the hands of the House of Commons!

On the same day, the *Daily News* expressed its delight and compared Lord Manner's electoral defeat to the defeat of the young Coningsby by Sidonia in a horse race. The press of the Jews' adversaries fervently accused Rothschild of availing himself of illicit means to win the election. With ardent words, the public was urged to take action against such shameless practices.

It is very interesting to note the attitude taken by the Jewish press towards these open accusations and towards the efforts made to see Rothschild prosecuted. While the *Times* and the *Sun* maintained absolute silence—the refrain 'silence implies consent' [*Schweigen ist Zustimmung*] also applying here—the *Morning Chronicle*, the newspaper of the Rothschild court, took a careful position on the matter. In its 7 July editorial, it wholly revealed its fear of a prosecution, although naturally, it strove to create the opposite impression, as the following excerpt indicates:

> We believe that the attempt will fail. To the best of our information, the charge of bribery or illegal treating in 1847, is as

---

[151] *Times*, 5/7/1849.

utterly gratuitous as of bribery or illegal treating on Tuesday last. But assuming it to be supported by evidence, it will simply place Lord John Manners in a most embarrassing and humiliating position. It will scarcely retard the cause of toleration and enlightenment an hour; and we can hardly believe that any influential body of citizens will be found mad enough to unite in offering such an insult to the metropolis. [...]

We go further. In our opinion, a decision which should seat Lord John Manners, in defiance of a great constituency, might bring matters to a crisis fraught with danger...

One notices the fear alongside the implicit threats that perhaps would have been capable of unsettling the petit bourgeois fearful of his voting rights.

One rightly has to wonder what end could possibly have been achieved by Rothschild's resignation and subsequent re-election, but the motives are difficult to ascertain. The philo-Semitic press gives us a clue, however: with Rothschild's expected re-election it was hoped that the House of Lords would be intimidated, by presenting it with full evidence of supposed public opinion. At the same time, a farce of this kind was intended to remind the English masses of the Jewish Question, given that they were always somewhat lethargic and apt to easily forget important matters. Lastly, it would give the press a good opportunity to present this issue in a comprehensible way to the man in the street. According to the *Times* of 28 June 1849, the battle was no longer a Jewish issue and 'the Bill was not a bill for permitting Jews to sit in the House of Commons, but a bill for permitting Christians to elect them.' In other words, the backwards House of Lords had the audacity to call into question the sacred right of the freedom of the vote, even going as far as the inconceivable extreme of annulling this right with their stance. This line of argument, naturally, had to make the English citizen's blood boil, especially when he was told by the same source that it was the voting class which 'represents the principles of religious freedom and the opinions of the English people.' The City of London therefore represented the English people, in the judgement of these heroes of journalism.[152]

The Expulsion of Rothschild

Almost a year passed before serious moves were made to capitalize on Rothschild's victory, that is to say, to get him into Parliament, which continued to be impossible due to the form of the oath, particularly the Oath of Abjuration.

---

[152] *Times*, 28/6/1849; *Morning Chronicle*, 2/7/1849. Note that the subsequent quotations are reproduced verbatim from the original *Times* article.

On 12 March 1850, Parliament decided to set up a committee to study the problem of the conditions under which the Jews could take up Parliamentary seats. During the debates, the stance of Lord John Russell, in contrast to that of previous occasions, was not exactly oppositional, but *was* very reserved. Despite the committee's work, no progress was made with the issue, and it stalled at the first reading of 31 May 1850. In answer to a question made in Parliament on 22 July, Lord John Russell answered that in the current session, new advances were very unlikely to be forthcoming. We do not know the reasons that could have caused such a hesitant stance, but the newspaper of the Rothschild court expressed its dissatisfaction with this reply and continually made its displeasure known.[153] Rothschild himself then decided to reach his goal without further delay. On 25 July he convened an assembly in the London Tavern, Bishopsgate Street, where some 500 people gathered together, among them well-known Jews, such as Montefiore, Goldsmid, and Cohen, alongside, significantly, Bank of England Deputy Governor Mr. Thomson Hankey.

The *Morning Chronicle* of 26 July 1850 described in great detail the course of events, during which Rothschild was unanimously invited to take up his seat in Parliament the following day. Lord Dudley Stuart was particularly prominent at the gathering. In his judgement, the assembly was the most important ever seen in their time, and it was necessary to finally take some drastic measures. Despite the lateness of the hour, the news of Rothschild's decision spread throughout London at lightning speed. The Jews' adversaries in Parliament were also informed of the news around midnight.[154]

On the following day, the Commons was a completely packed house, as many members had attended only because of Rothschild's announced intention. Immediately before the sitting began, Rothschild arrived with a busy entourage of electors who had wanted to accompany him on his journey.[155]

There was a great air of expectation in the Parliament. All eyes were on the doorway through which Rothschild had to enter to take up his seat in the Chamber. Up until the last minute, there were some who doubted that the Jew would really have the shamelessness to force the issue of his Parliamentary seat occupancy in such a way. There was not long to wait, for soon after the sitting opened, Rothschild arrived and slowly approached the Speaker. When he came to the table to be sworn in, he was asked by the Clerk what Oath he wished to take, the Protestant or the Roman Catholic Oath. He replied: 'I desire to be sworn upon the Old Testament.' Whereupon the Clerk

---

[153] *Hansard*, Volume 109, pp. 809-816. & p. 814. & *Hansard*, Volume 111, pp. 487-8. & *Morning Chronicle*, 26/7/1850.

[154] *Hansard*, Volume 113, p. 317. Translator's note: Although Aldag does not state it explicitly here, Thomson Hankey was rumored to be of Jewish heritage.

[155] *Morning Herald*, 27/7/1850. & 26/7/1850.

stated the matter to the Speaker, and the Speaker directed Rothschild to withdraw. Rothschild then withdrew from the Chamber.[156]

As might be expected, the debate that followed the event, which concerned the aforementioned Jewish Question, was extraordinarily heated. Sir Robert Inglis was no longer the only leading anti-Jewish figure, as he was now zealously supported by two younger men, Sir Frederic Thesiger and Charles Newdegate.

The first of these men was the grandson of John Andrew Thesiger, who had emigrated from Saxony to England in the middle of the 18th century. He was highly educated as a jurist and soon became famous as the most eminent barrister of his time. He occupied high offices of state. In Lord Derby's cabinet, he was named Lord Chancellor on 26 February 1858. Later on in his career, he was elevated to the Peerage, and given the title of Lord Chelmsford. It seems an irony of fate that precisely during his time, the House of Lords was to fall to the Jews' attacks; although he had never been able to overcome his aversion to the Jews, he believed that he had to vote in favor of the Jewish bill out of solidarity with the government.[157]

Charles Newdegate was as brilliant an orator as Sir Frederic, and of the same exalted academic education as his contemporary. His surname has already appeared in this history several times; in the political struggles of 1753, an ancestor in his family had taken the lead in combatting the Jews. The young Newde-gate had dedicated his life exclusively to politics. He died on 9 April 1887 and was buried in Harefield Church. Contrary to Sir Frederic, he fought until the very last for his anti-Jewish beliefs. When in 1866 the last restrictions against the Jews were about to be legally annulled, as it was now only a matter of form, he defended his convictions as the leader of four other upstanding men. Perhaps at some point, the day will come in England when this man is given the honor he deserves.[158] These two men were those who, in debates, continued to doggedly defend the stance that the admission of the Jews to Parliament was unacceptable for multiple reasons. The day of Rothschild's withdrawal, the debate on that question did not reach a decision, which was why it was adjourned until the following Monday.[159]

The philo-Semitic press used its best rhetoric to call for further action. The *Times* condemned Lord John Russell's position as too slow and not useful to the Jewish cause; the City voters, they said, could rightly be discontented with the parliamentary sitting of the previous day. It was 'now or never'; the moment had arrived for total emancipation, the *Morning Chronicle* of July 27 predictably opined:

---

[156] *Hansard*, Volume 113, p. 297. Translator's note: Additional details and wording reproduced verbatim from the original source.

[157] *Dictionary of National Biography*, Volume 19, pp. 608-9.

[158] *Dictionary of National Biography*, Volume 14, pp. 331-2.

[159] *Hansard*, Volume 113, pp. 297-333.

There are occasions when caution is folly, when valor is the better part of discretion, when we must throw boldly and stake all, when we must burn our ships, break down the bridges in our rear, and regard retreat or escape as an impossibility. The citizens of London are placed in an emergency of this sort. Now or never, should be their cry. They will sully all their need of former honour, won in many a hard-fought battle for civil and religious liberty, unless they force the Jew question to a prosperous issue. The game is in their own hands. They have only to screw their courage to the sticking-place. If they waver, falter, or hesitate, they are lost; and a noble cause, a great principle, is for a period lost with them.

It need hardly be said that the adversary press condemned Rothschild's move in the strongest terms.

The following Monday in Parliament, the battle became heated once more. A majority forced a resolution that the Speaker was to ask Rothschild if he would be disposed to be sworn in on the Old Testament, in which case the swearing-in ceremony could take place in the aforesaid form. But due to the lateness of the hour, the act was put off until the next day.[160] The joy of the philo-Semitic press was boundless. Finally the end of the argument was in sight and victory was no longer far-off. On the following day, Rothschild would be sworn in on the Old Testament and then he could take up his seat. 'Why hadn't it been done this way from the start?'[161] Seemingly, the government had worked closely with Rothschild and chosen the most appropriate route to exclude all possible influence from the House of Lords.[162]

With the same level of tension as the previous day, the sitting of Tuesday, 30 July began. Once again, Rothschild approached the Speaker and newly requested authorization to be sworn in on the Old Testament. This time he did not need to leave the Chamber; rather an assistant very courteously handed him a copy of the Old Testament, which he had to hold in his hand during the swearing-in ceremony. Rothschild, Lord John Russell, and many like-minded others, saw themselves finally at the end goal. With impotent obstinacy, the men surrounding Sir Frederic Thesiger and Newgate remained seated.

Sure of victory and encouraged by his friends, Rothschild swore the Oath of Allegiance and the Oath of Supremacy. All that remained was the Oath of Abjuration. As with the previous oaths, the words were said, which he repeated without hesitation. Now he was almost over the finish line... then

---

[160] *Hansard*, Volume 113, pp. 397-437.
[161] *Times*, 30/7/1850; *Sun*, 30/7/1850; *Morning Chronicle*, 30/7/1850.
[162] *Hansard*, Volume 113, p. 486.

the words 'upon the true faith of a Christian' were heard. In the midst of a sepulchral silence came Rothschild's reply: 'I omit these words as not binding on my conscience.' He then went on to conclude the oath with his own words: 'So help me God.'[163]

Friend and enemy alike were stunned into silence. In the silence of the assembly, the clear voice of the Speaker rang out, and he directed Rothschild to withdraw from the Chamber. Rothschild, although hesitant, was getting ready to leave, when one of the most actively philo-Semitic members, a Mr. Hume, rose up from his seat in protest, saying to the Speaker that Rothschild had sworn the oaths in the due form. Then the Jews' adversaries recovered their senses. It appeared that they could not believe that such a skillfully prepared attack, which looked guaranteed to work, was going to be repulsed yet again. In a deafening hullabaloo of shouting, they gave free rein to their joy and to their long pent-up anger. Once more did friend and enemy strive to express their opinions, and after a third night spent on this topic, the debate was once more adjourned.[164]

What a different tableau in the press the following morning! The inexpressible heady joy had transformed into the deepest affliction, and the bitterest disillusionment was replaced by renewed confidence. The philo-Semitic newspapers desperately asked what was going to happen. Would a new election be required in the City? Would Rothschild have to wait for a new law to be passed for the oath's wording to be modified?[165]

In the opposing camp, as might be expected, there reigned the greatest joy. The *Morning Herald* of 31 July opined that ultimately, Rothschild's repeated failures were no surprise, given that, even though a Jew may become immensely rich, he would never learn to conduct himself like a gentleman:

> Why cannot a Jew, however wealthy, however educated, learn the habits and feelings of a gentleman? Why cannot he understand that frankness, straightforwardness and a noble simplicity, are among the very first requisites of a man who desires honourably to elevate himself among his fellow creatures?
>
> We might as well ask, why the majority of our brothel-keepers, spunging-house-keepers, and keepers of 'hells', have always been Jews? It is part of their punishment—it is one among many other invincible proofs that the Sacred Books, of which they have been made the guardians and witnesses, and in very deed the Word of God; inasmuch as, more than three

---

[163] Oath of Allegiance, Oath of Supremacy. [Footnote as per original German text.]

[164] *Hansard*, Volume 113, pp. 486-533. Translator's note: Rothschild quotations as per original source.

[165] *Times*, 31/7/1850; *Morning Chronicle*, 31/7/1850; *Sun*, 31/7/1850.

thousand years ago, all these characteristics, and their attendant contempt and scorn, were minutely predicted of them. [...]

The Jew who consults his true dignity will not stoop to regard with the least attention the politics of the *Goyim*. Were a really religious Jew of Poland or Germany to be desired to take a share in the affairs of state of those countries, he would regard the proposal as an insult. Mr. Rothschild only desires to mingle in English politics because he is not a religious Jew.

And this low aim, and low standard of feeling, mark every step he takes. Never would he have been in a position to fence with the House of Commons, had he not first used means to gain his seat which no high-minded man would for a moment contemplate. And what has his conduct during the last three days been? Has it not been marked by that mixture of audacity and cunning, which is the secret of modern Jewish success; but which is so peculiarly revolting to every properly-constituted mind?

Evidently the government had to pay heed to the public uproar. On 1 August, the Attorney-General announced a motion for the August 5 sitting, in accordance with which Rothschild would be prohibited from occupying his seat before swearing the Oath of Abjuration, and that Parliament would 'at the earliest opportunity in next Session of Parliament, take into its serious consideration the form of the Oath of Abjuration, with a view to relieve Her Majesty's Subject professing the Jewish Religion.' This motion was passed by the House.[166]

A carefully-crafted plan by the Jews and their allies had failed yet again, which meant that it was necessary to win over the House of Lords to achieve the legal amendment, which would have to take still more time. It is likely that they would have wanted to work unofficially to attain the majority in the House of Lords, but perhaps there were also unknown reasons which impeded immediate action. In any case, it was not until 8 April 1851 that there was a motion from Lord John Russell to appeal the resolution of 5 August 1850, according to which His Majesty's subjects of Jewish faith had to be allowed to take the Oath of Abjuration without the fatal last words. Already by the following day, the first reading took place.[167]

Once again, the heated debates in Parliament began. The Jews' adversaries were indignant that this question kept coming up so often, and they considered it to be illegal pressure on the House of Lords, which so many

---

[166] *Hansard*, Volume 113, p. 674. Translator's note: QVOS. & *Hansard*, Volume 113, pp. 814-7.

[167] *Hansard*, Volume 115, pp. 1006-1019, 1030.

times had voted against Jewish emancipation, yet which found its views snubbed by this very inconsiderate insistence from the philo-Semitic camp. In an elegant speech, Newdegate said:[168]

> It could not be forgotten that Baron Rothschild had come to the table of that House, and had gone through the oath until he came to the words 'on the true faith of a Christian'; but he did not stop at those words, but, omitting them, he had ventured, on his own authority and in his own case, to alter the substance of the oath... [T]he Speaker, in that grave, dignified and impartial manner in which he discharged all the business of that House, told the hon. Member that he had been guilty of a grave irregularity... The election in 1848, in the city of London, had been too much under the influence of the long purse of the Baron Rothschild, and the number of Jews who resided there...
>
> The Jewish religion was not the religion of the Bible, but the religion of the Talmud. It was neither more nor less than the religion of the Pharisees, perpetuated, through the Talmud, down to the present time... He would ask the honourable and learned Member whether he had ever considered the morality inculcated in the Talmud?... It allows men to detain what they know does not belong to them, if it only belongs to a Gentile...
>
> Poland might serve as a warning example of the fact that in all Christian countries where the Jews were allowed a wide sphere of political operation, corrupting and destroying elements were introduced and propagated in society, to the ruin of the State at large. In Poland, one-tenth of the population were Jews, and he need not say that she was perhaps the most miserable nation in the world...[169]

The division ended with a very thin majority in favor of the law being passed. The philo-Semites achieved a majority of only 25 votes; this figure had never been so low, it being likely that many members had felt so indignant on seeing the tactic to force emancipation that they went over to the side of the Jews' adversaries. In any case, it had been noticed that opposition had grown in Parliament and also in the country.

---

[168] *Hansard*, Volume 116, pp. 367-412; Volume 117, pp. 1096-1102.

[169] *Hansard*, Volume 116, p. 368 ff. Translator's note: This is Aldag's extremely abridged précis of a 16-page-long speech, which was evidently seen as important enough to the public to be published contemporaneously as a booklet. Details of this booklet (available online) can be found in the Translator's Bibliography. The excerpts here are reproduced verbatim from the original source.

At the end of June, new deliberations took place regarding the form of the law, and 3 July saw the final reading in Parliament.[170] On this occasion, as always, the Jewish attack failed in the House of Lords. Nothing could alter this course, not even the argument expounded by the Bishop of Norwich, according to whom the previous stance of the majority of the Upper Chamber had to derive from 'that wicked and persecuting spirit towards their Jewish brethren, which was the reproach of Christendom in former times.' On 17 July 1851, the bill approved by the Commons was defeated at the second Lords reading.[171]

For a Second Time: David Salomons

Although in the aforementioned way, it had again been shown, as so many times before, that the admission of the Jews was not desired, the Jews did not take any lesson from that fact.[172] Shortly before the decisive reading of the bill to modify the Oath of Abjuration in favor of Jews, when fierce battles would break out in Parliament and the public would again take a lively interest in the Jewish Question, news spread that David Salomons, regardless of the fruitless attempts that he had made up until that point, was returning to stand as a Parliamentary candidate for Greenwich in the elections that were to be held on June 27.

The Jews' adversaries were beside themselves, especially in view of the fact that the Conservative Party appeared unwilling to field a candidate: it was disgrace for this locality, so famous as a geographical center, to be represented by a Jew. We cannot but reproduce part of the article published in the *Morning Herald* of 23 June, which, to mark the candidacy of Salomons, dealt with the Jewish Question in general and made the following declarations, which we fancy could have been written today:[173]

> In this country, they [the Jews] are but wayfarers, dwelling here only through accidental circumstances. They are English Jews, just as elsewhere they may be French or German Jews, but they can scarcely be called Jewish Englishmen. Is it for the welfare of this kingdom to make men legislators whose sympathies are centered in another land? Who take up their abode wherever a thriving trade can be pursued—to whom political freedom is nothing, save as it promotes their commerce or secures their gains? Wherever the Jew thrives the most surely,

---

[170] *Hansard*, Volume 116, p. 409. & pp. 1096-1102, Volume 118, pp. 142-7.

[171] *Hansard*, Volume 118, pp. 859-909. Translator's note: QVOS (p. 902).

[172] *Hansard*, Volume 118, p. 984.

[173] *Morning Post*, 23/6/1851, 27/6/1851; *Morning Herald*, 24/6/1851, 26/6/1851.

there is the land of his temporary adoption—his counting-house is his country, and his most cherished political aspirations (apart from Jerusalem) mostly confined to matters which affect the fluctuations of the Stock Exchange... Nationally, however, they have no sympathies with us; they are among us, but they are not of us, and it is far from evident how this country will be benefited by advancing them to power.

In the meantime, Nomination Day arrived. Besides Salomons, Mr. Chambers and Mr. Wire presented themselves as candidates. To general surprise, Mr. Chambers withdrew on the eve of the election for no apparent reason, and Mr. Wire undertook the fight against Salomons alone. He was the one who, in 1847, after the first election of Rothschild, could not have made himself more prominent in celebrating that great day. But, even disregarding that fact, it was widely known that he obeyed the Jews completely. London's organized Jewry deputized him for missions of every type. Once they even sent him to Jerusalem for an extended period. For such reasons, as the *Morning Herald* stated, it could surprise no one that 'he has acquired a certain Israelitish taint'.[174]

The election was awaited with the greatest tension, as it was wondered if it were possible that Salomons really would win, 'cost what it may, by dint of the beer-cask and the brandy-bottle'.[175]

The sun beat down from a crystal-clear blue sky when the electors and the curious gathered in the square of St. Alfege Church. A large number of dodgy-looking characters had been specially stationed in front of the speakers' tribunes, and they were making an atrocious racket. One could not help but get the impression that many of them were no longer in their right mind. As will be shown later, Salomons had not restrained his spending and had invited everyone to drink beer and brandy to their fill, just as he had advertised. It was natural, therefore, that the guests expressed their gratitude by silencing Salomons' adversaries with an infernal uproar. To achieve a still greater effect, Salomons had arranged for a battery of bells to be given out, which were well used by the mob to hail their benefactor and drown out with a 'deafening clang' any awkward questions put to 'Alderman Shalomonsh' as the *Morning Herald* dubbed him.

---

[174] *Morning Herald*, 17/7/1851. Translator's note: QVOS. In the same issue, Wire is also deemed to be 'little better than a Jew "once removed",' and the elector's choice to be between 'a Jew and his shadow.' Editor's note: This bears a remarkable resemblance to present-day America, where various candidates of the two main parties, who differ in so many regards, all function as "shadow Jews," i.e. they work arduously on behalf of Jewish and Israeli interests—as much or more so than actual Jews would.

[175] *Morning Herald*, 26/6/1851. Translator's note: QVOS.

As the pre-election poll came out in favor of Salomons—and nothing else could have been expected, given the composition of the crowd—the opposing party saw to it that the definitive election was set for the next day. This election barely differed from that of Nomination Day: once more the drinks flowed in rivers, paid out of Salomons' pocket, and even cold hard cash was handed out to get votes.[176]

It cannot be surprising, therefore, that Salomons came out on top this time. Among the totality of the votes, some 1,500 abstentions were registered, which the *Morning Herald* of 17 July 1851 rightly attributed to the fact that 'they [the voters] could not recognize in the two candidates any opposition sufficiently antagonistic between Jew and Christian to induce them to vote at all....'

On Saturday, 28 June, at 11 o'clock in the morning, the Greenwich election result was published. The huge crowd who had gathered found out that Salomons had won 2,165 votes; Wire, by contrast, only 1,278. Salomons presented himself to his excited electors, whose 'hurrahs' never wanted to end. He conveyed his steadfast decision to go to Parliament the following week. He only had to relax for a few days after the hard work of the election, and besides, he had to agree with the government on the most appropriate day to appear, in order not to disturb any important debates that already been organized.

Then it came to Wire's turn to speak. He expressed that, as a matter of principle, he had carried out the electoral battle only by licit means. The methods which his adversary had resorted to, he himself had rejected, which meant that he had not bought votes, nor had restaurants or taverns open, nor arranged for groups of musicians. His words were received with a deafening wall of shouting and only with the greatest effort was he able to finish his speech. Immediately afterwards, Salomons stood forward to speak, not to reject Wire's accusations, but only to give thanks to the returning officers who had been present at the election. A roar of approval rose up from the crowd, and the solemn declaration of the election results was finished.

The press of the Jews' adversaries did as much as they could to inform the public of the methods employed by the Jews. They did not go as hard on the electors of Greenwich as they could have, as they considered it understandable that the electors had little choice, and 'if they *were* to have a Jew, they might as well have "the real thing".' As the *Standard* explained it:

> The result of the Greenwich election is no otherwise unsatis-
> factory than that it proves the borough to be in a state so de-
> graded that no sincerely Christian man, otherwise eligible,

---

[176] *Daily News*, 27/6/1851; *Morning Herald*, 17/7/1851. & *Standard*, 17/7/1851, 22/2/1853; *Morning Herald*, 17/7/1851; *Morning Post*, 30/6/1851.

would offer himself to the electors. If the choice of the respectable electors has fallen upon a Jew, it was because the
contest lying between a Jew and a gentleman who has for a
long time acted as the partizan of Jews, they preferred the Jew,
we suppose upon the same principle upon which *Macbeth*
says, 'let *them* appear' when, questioned by the ladies met in
his morning walk, whether he preferred to be instructed by the
ladies themselves or '*by their masters*'.[177]

Despite his best intentions, Salomons did not present himself in Parliament as soon as he had stated. It would appear that the government, who
looked upon him kindly, made him change his mind, as on 3 July, Lord John
Russell communicated to the House of Commons that Salomons wished to
give up his plan until the House of Lords dealt, one way or another, with the
Jewish bill which was pending approval.[178]

As is known, late into the evening of 17 July, the bill was defeated by
the House of Lords. All of the newspapers published articles about this
event. *Would Salomons dare go to Parliament and renew the determined
struggle of so many years?*, asked the *Morning Herald*. The *Times* of the
same day, evidently as well informed as always, answered the question in
this way: 'There is not the least doubt that they [the Jews] will do it. Their
vitality and their tenacity will always overcome every setback...'

The sitting of 18 July in the House of Commons was about to take
place. No sooner had the Speaker opened proceedings than Salomons appeared and determinedly approached the Speaker, of whom he asked permission to take the three oaths on the Old Testament. His wish was granted. The
first two oaths were taken without difficulty, but he substituted the fateful
words of the last oath with the phrase 'so help me God.' Afterwards he took
out a piece of paper and read the declaration that the last words of the Oath of
Abjuration were not binding on his conscience, but that he had otherwise fulfilled all of the legal requirements and had a right, therefore, to take up his seat.

The clerk informed the Speaker that the final words of the oath had not
been pronounced and that the document read out by Salomons had been
handed over, at which point the Speaker declared: 'The honorable member
has not heeded the prescribed form of the oath, for which reason it is my
duty to direct him to withdraw to behind the bar [the Bar of the House].'

---

[177] *Standard*, 28/6/1851; *Morning Post*, 30/6/1851; *Morning Herald*, 17/7/1851 (from
which the first quoted element is taken). Translator's note: The quotation from the *Standard* has been inserted into the text due to its perceived interest to the reader, and as an
exemplar of English wit. As with the *Morning Herald*, the *Morning Post* strongly infers
that the electoral outcome was determined by the copious amounts of alcohol provided by
the winning candidate.

[178] *Morning Herald*, 4/7/1851.

Salomons had followed the course of events very nervously, and became yet more nervous. But, to widespread surprise, he did not pay attention to the Speaker's direction. Of course, he hesitatingly moved away from the Speaker's table, but he sat down on the bench immediately below the ministerial bench, beside the member Sir W. Molesworth. This immediately triggered a deafening racket, mixed with loud cries of 'Withdraw!' and 'Order!' The commotion continued to get worse by the second and reached a crescendo when it was noticed that Salomons was trying to talk to the Strangers' Gallery: a second violation of the rigorous rules of the House, surely never before seen in English history. The anger of the Jews' adversaries was now beyond measure.

It was only after some considerable time that the Speaker managed to restore order, and he once again directed Salomons to leave the Chamber, given that he had not taken the Oath of Abjuration in the prescribed form. Salomons stood up and went towards the bar, before which he stopped again, hesitating. Once more an indescribable tumult rose up, once more shouts were heard of 'Withdraw!' and 'Order!', and Mr. John Abel Smith approached him and led him out to behind the bar. Salomons remained there.

Meanwhile, Sir Benjamin Hall had got up and declared himself in support of Salomons, saying that he would submit to the Speaker's request. When he tried to make a new declaration, he was interrupted by Sir Frederic Thesiger, who had stood up and asked the Speaker for permission to take the floor. Once more returned the deafening commotion. When members from the opposite side called him to order, he shouted that it was precisely of order that he wished to speak. 'I apprehend,' he continued, 'that the worthy alderman has not obeyed the order of this house' (cheers from his fellows on the Opposition benches). 'He has not withdrawn, but is at present standing within the house, and it is my duty to call the attention of the house to that circumstance.'

Despite the third direction from the Speaker, Salomons continued to stand irresolutely between the bar and the door of the Chamber. Finally he went up the steps to the Lords' Gallery, on the left-hand side of the door on entering, and stayed there for the remainder of the discussion.[179]

After order had been restored, Sir Benjamin Hall asked the Chancellor of the Exchequer, standing in for the Prime Minister, whether he would instruct the Attorney-General to prosecute Salomons for his conduct. The Chancellor, in consideration of the absence of the Prime Minister Lord John Russell, stated that it would be best to defer an answer to that question.[180] After some skirmishes between the supporters and the adversaries of the Jews, it was agreed to adjourn the debate until Monday, July 21.

---

[179] *Standard*, 19/7/1851. *Hansard*, Volume 118, p. 979 ff. Translator's note: QVOS.
[180] *Hansard*, Volume 118, pp. 981-2.

Immediately before this sitting began, the Jew Salomons was once more observed, this time already seated expectantly behind the bar. A repressed tension reigned in the Chamber. The places for spectators were full, and outside there was a packed crowd of those who had not managed to gain entry. Everyone anxiously awaited what would happen.

After the opening of Parliament, the Speaker read out a letter from Salomons requesting, among other things, the rectification of Friday's protocol; he rejected all of Salomon's requests out of hand, and no member contradicted him.

Immediately afterwards, the House passed to the order of business. As first speaker, Sir Benjamin Hall asked the Prime Minister, now present, if the government would instruct the Attorney-General to prosecute Salomons for his conduct of the previous Friday. Lord John Russell answered no, 'but he reserved to himself the discretion of doing so hereafter should circumstances appear to warrant such a course of procedure'.[181]

Barely had he announced this decision when Salomons crossed onto the floor of the house and sat on the front bench, which was reserved solely for ministers. This unleashed a deafening furor, which was more intense and lasted longer than that of the previous Friday. After a certain calm had been restored, the Speaker exhorted Salomons to leave the chamber immediately. But Salomons did not give the slightest indication of moving from his seat.

During the resultant deafening uproar, the Prime Minister got up, evidently with the intention of speaking, but all of his efforts were in vain and he did not manage to say a single word.

The member Chisholm Amstey was seen passing a piece of paper to the Speaker and then talking to him. Only after considerable time was the President able to establish even a modicum of order. As a first thing, he announced that the honorable gentleman Mr. Amstey had tabled a motion which he regretted having to reject.

Then Lord Russell got up once again, but just as before, his attempt to take the floor was condemned to failure, due to the roar of shouting that started up again with all of its earlier intensity. Resigning himself to this fact, he sat down again. Salomons continued impassive in his seat, although he did shoot the odd fearful glance towards the angry faces of his adversaries, whose shouts of 'Withdraw!' continued to ring in his ears.

The Right Honorable Speaker, out of his wits, who surely had never believed that such a thing could ever be possible in the English Parliament, tried to restore order through gestures. He requested that the Chamber and the government help him to expel Salomons. Hurrahs and other signs of approval followed.

---

[181] *Hansard*, Volume 118, pp. 1143-5. Translator's note: QVOS from the *Standard*, 22/7/1851. The *Morning Post* of 22/7/1851 reproduces Salomon's letter in full.

Once more Lord Russell rose from his seat and managed, finally, to make himself heard. It would appear that he too had come to find the situation disagreeable, and to everyone's surprise personally requested 'that the honorable member withdraw.' This was met by a cacophony of shouts of approval from the Jews' adversaries. Sir Robert Inglis supported the motion. This was surely the first agreement between these two adversaries regarding the Jewish Question.

But with equal speed, a motion from Mr. Bernal Osborne came from the other side of the Chamber, asking that Salomons be admitted in due form and that he be authorized to occupy his seat. The motion was supported by Mr. Amstey. A new uproar, and between constant interruptions, the latter tried to explain his stance. Meanwhile the Speaker strove to expel some unknown individuals from the House—among them most certainly Jews—who tried to cross into the members-only part of the Chamber. The whole scene was one of indescribable confusion.

Finally Mr. Amstey finished his statement and asked for the debate to be adjourned. Salomons continued unperturbed in his place. They then moved to a vote on Amstey's motion, which was defeated by a crushing majority.

To the horror and displeasure of most of the Chamber, it was seen that Salomons had had the audacity to vote as well, which contravened the traditional rules in two ways: on the one hand because, as the Speaker had explained to him, he did not have the right to be in the Parliament, much less to vote; on the other, because members never intervened in the decisions which involved them directly.[182] The commotion continued almost uninterrupted and even the public took part in it to an extent that had never been seen, for which reason the Speaker ordered the galleries to be cleared.[183]

The Speaker wanted Bernal Osborne's motion to be voted on straight away, when he was interrupted by a member who wished to make a statement on this intention. Thunderous protests came from most of the members and speeches were aborted due to the incessant noise. As so many times before, comments were made on the pros and cons of Jewish admission, and worthy of being cited is a warning from the honorable gentleman Mr. Bright, according to whom Queen Victoria herself had a burning desire to see the question settled in favor of the Jews.[184]

Once more, the House was nearing a vote on the motion. Immediately beforehand, Salomons, who was still present, announced, through the mediation of the member John Abel Smith, that on this occasion he would leave the Chamber for the division, but that all decisions would be reserved on the

---

[182] *Hansard*, Volume 118, pp. 1145-1148. Wolf: *Essays...*, p. 332. Goldsmid, A.: *Report...*, p. iv. & *Hansard*, Volume 118, pp. 1205-6.
[183] *Hansard*, Volume 118, p. 1163.
[184] *Hansard*, Volume 118, p. 1199.

outcome of subsequent events. After this resolution was announced, Salomons got up, bowed to the Speaker, and left the Chamber. Bernal Osborne's motion was defeated by a considerable majority.[185]

No sooner was the division over than Salomons, under the shout of protest from his adversaries, came back into the Chamber and took up his previous position on the ministers' bench.

The member Amstey repeated his request for an adjournment, which was met, to general surprise, by the forceful protests of Lord Russell. Salomons then stood up to speak. This sparked an inconceivable tumult, and only after a good while did he managed to make himself heard. The shouts of 'Withdraw!' did not stop. Finally, one could make out a part of his speech. He said that his attitude was not due, in any way, to an irreverence towards the Speaker, but to the fact that by his conduct he only wanted to defend the rights which, in his judgement, were rightfully his.

There followed speeches from other members. The division resulted in a majority defeating Amstey's motion to suspend the sitting. Immediately afterwards, the Speaker called for another vote, this time on Lord Russell's earlier motion concerning Salomons' expulsion. This resulted in a crushing majority in favor of expulsion. Nor on this occasion did Salomons have the slightest qualm about casting his vote in both divisions.[186]

The Speaker then expressed his confidence that 'the hon. Member for Greenwich had heard the decision of the House, and hoped that he was prepared to obey it.' However, as is read in the Parliamentary minutes: 'Mr. Alderman Salomons continuing to sit in his seat, Mr. Speaker directed the Serjeant-at-Arms to remove him below the bar. Whereupon the Serjeant-at-Arms having placed his hand on Mr. Alderman Salomons, he was conducted below the bar.'[187]

As a result, Salomons had pushed things so far because he had every intention of forcing his removal, behavior which in reality only a Jew is capable of.

The sitting, which went on into the small hours of the morning, ended with a question from Mr. Bernal Osborne, who asked if the noble lord would direct Mr. Salomons to be prosecuted. The Prime Minister answered, to cheers and roars of laughter, that if the honorable member for Greenwich really wished to be prosecuted, he had no doubt that he would find plenty of persons willing to do it for him. Once more, then, the idea of a trial was deftly rejected. Due to the lateness of the hour, an agreement was reached to adjourn the debate, and on 22 July they returned to work extensively on the matter, likewise debating until deep into the night. Salomons, also present at

---

[185] *Hansard*, Volume 118, pp. 1205-8.
[186] Goldsmid, A.: *Report...*, p. VIII. Wolf: *Essays...*, p. 333.
[187] *Hansard*, Volume 118, p. 1216. Translator's note: Both quotations QVOS.

this new sitting, was now seated in the front row of the gallery, a row which was normally occupied by the Peers of England. After much to-ing and fro-ing, the debate was adjourned yet again.[188]

On 28 July, the debate resumed, and it began with the reading of a let-ter from Salomons dated July 25. The letter contained the message that two charges had already been made against him for his conduct in Parliament. It then went on to discuss the request made on the same date by the Greenwich electors, who asked that they be granted authorization to be represented by a lawyer, to demonstrate before Parliament their right to elect whomsoever they wished as a member of Parliament. At the same time, a petition had been presented on behalf of the electors of the City of London asking that it be permitted for Rothschild to take up his seat and that a lawyer of recog-nized standing be likewise admitted to the House in order to take part in the pertinent debates. As can be seen, the cooperation between both Jewish elec-toral districts was working perfectly.

Both requests were dealt with separately, but, after heated debates, the majority rejected every demand made in each. A motion requesting the mod-ification of the Oath of Abjuration was also defeated by a majority of 38 votes, and a request, according to which Salomons would not be authorized to occupy his seat before having taking this oath in the due form, was passed by 123 votes to 68.[189]

Every reader will concur that this was the longest and most tenacious attack from the Jews. We ourselves believe that Salomons' behavior is frankly monstrous, and the press response to it is interesting. What is surpris-ing is that the *Times* dedicated few column inches to the events, instead writ-ing merely about the theoretics of the problem in general, without going into details about the real-life case that was actually happening. In their opinion, it was now time to settle the problem through the mediation of the courts of justice.[190]

The *Daily News* attributed the tumultuous scenes in Parliament only to the House of Lords' position, a completely deplorable situation in the news-paper's opinion, because the House of Commons represented the whole na-tion, whereas the House of Lords were only representative of a small class. But in the course of the subsequent development of events, it believed that the conduct of Salomons and his ethnic brethren had gone too far, which was why it distanced itself from them.[191] The *Spectator* and the *Observer* de-

---

[188] *Hansard,* Volume 118, p. 1217. & *Standard,* 23/7/1851. & *Hansard,* Volume 118, pp. 1318-66.
[189] *Hansard,* Volume 118, pp. 1573-1629.
[190] *Times,* 21/7/1851, 22/7/1851, 28/7/1851, 30/7/1851.
[191] *Daily News,* 22/7, 23/7, 24/7.

scribed Salomons' behavior as imprudent and not at all productive to the cause of emancipation.[192]

To cut a long story short, we cannot quite shake off the impression that the vast majority of the philo-Semitic press received the events in Parliament with great displeasure. Thus one notices their efforts to avoid informing on the events to the greatest extent possible. The same tendency appears to prevail in the *Manchester Guardian*, although it could not help but admire Salomons' courage:

> But, whatever may be said of Mr. Alderman Salomons, at least it must be admitted that he has shown great courage and fearlessness of the consequences in thus pressing his pretensions to a practical conclusion—at no small risk and hazard to himself.[193]

The anti-Jewish press brutally condemned Salomons' behavior, as was expressed most notably in the *Morning Post* and the *Standard*. In their editorials of the July 19, 22, and 23, 1851, they describe the insolent behavior of this gentleman and his friends, and state that it would be near impossible to be able to find such a shameful event in the history of the House of Commons. They saw the greatest insolence in the fact that Salomons not only had had the audacity to appear in Parliament, but also to vote. The *Morning Post* of July 19 wrote:

> Mr. Salomons has the folly and impertinence to defy Lords and Commons alike, and to set up against the statutes of the realm, of which he calls himself a faithful subject—his own opinion on his own cause.

The *Standard* gave a lavishly detailed account of events. It was disgusted to the highest degree that Salomons, as an outsider, had had the temerity to conduct himself in such a manner and had not been satisfied with only one illicit appearance in Parliament:

> A renewal of Mr. Salomons' impudent attempt caused a repetition of the bear garden scene in the House of Commons last night, if possible more disorderly and disgusting than the scene of the night before. The proceedings were as riotous and irreverent as the exhibition presented by worshippers in a Jew-

---

[192] *Spectator*, 26/7; *Observer*, 20/7.
[193] *Manchester Guardian*, 23/7. Translator's note: QVOS.

ish synagogue; and every one who has witnessed that knows what such a scene means.[194]

Salomons' participation in the sittings had consequences in the law courts. There existed a law dating from the time of King George I which imposed severe penalties for such contraventions. Accordingly, anyone who broke this law would have to pay £500 in each instance. This law would also see him divested of many rights, among them the right to be a guardian of minors, which meant that in such circumstances he could not legally represent even his own children. In addition, he could not seek legal protection for attacks against his property, nor would he have the right to demand the return of assets which had been taken from him. Finally, he was deprived of the right to occupy official positions or to take part in elections, which meant that the man thus condemned found himself in worse circumstances than the man dispossessed of civil rights today. As a consequence, if he were to be found guilty, the consequences for Salomons would necessarily be extremely grave.[195]

As the government, despite this law, did not proceed against Salomons for unknown reasons, two private individuals raised separate lawsuits against him, each asking for the law to be applied. One of the lawsuits was withdrawn, probably as the result of an agreement between the litigating parties; the other, by contrast, was taken to the Court of Exchequer, under the case title *Miller vs. Salomons*.

On 9 December 1851, the pre-trial hearing was held in front of four barons [judges] and a special jury. After a brief round of arguments, it was decided to take the matter to the plenary session, given the importance of the question.[196]

On January 26 and 28, 1852, the case was formally heard. Salomons had hired for his defense no less than three barristers, among whom figured his ethnic kinsman Augustus Goldsmid. In the course of the judgement, the accuser, according to the accused, withdrew two of the accusations and the judgement was limited to a single event, allegedly to simplify proceedings.[197]

Salomons defended himself mainly by expressing that, in his judgement, he had had the right to remain in the debating chamber, and even to vote during the debate, because he had sworn the oaths in terms of their essential elements. He declared that the final words 'on the true faith of a Christian' could not be considered an essential element, which meant that it

---

[194] *Standard*, 19/7/1851, 22/7/1851, 23/7/1851, 29/7/1851. Translator's note: QVOS from the 23/7/1851 issue. A Bear Garden was a venue in which bear-baiting, bull-baiting, and other unsavory animal and human blood sports took place. There were various such arenas in existence in London between 1576 and 1835.

[195] *Hansard*, Volume 121, pp. 190-1.

[196] Goldsmid, A.: *Report*, p. XI.

[197] Goldsmid, A.: *Report*, p. 66.

did not matter whether such words had been omitted or not. Moreover, the law regarding the Oath of Abjuration was no longer in effect and by a special dispensation of 1838 it had been permitted for him to swear the oath in the form in which he had sworn it.[198]

The public took a lively interest in the arguments. To widespread surprise and against English custom, after long deliberation, the verdict was not made public at the end of the session, nor the following day. The reason given by the Chief Baron of the Exchequer [the presiding judge] was the following, according to newspaper reports: 'as it involved questions of great importance, the Court, with reference to that and to the great length of the argument, would wish to consider its judgment, in order that they might have an opportunity of looking over the acts. The judgment, without pledging themselves to any particular day, would be given shortly'.[199]

It was still a long time waiting for the verdict, which was eventually published on 19 April. It went against Salomons. According to its terms, he not only had to pay a fine of £500, but it also added the aforementioned penalties, such as the exclusion from official posts, etc.

In accordance with English procedure, in a collegial court, each judge has to make known his views on the case. Thus it was found that, of the four judges, one had found the accusation unjustified, opining that the final words of the Oath of Abjuration could not be considered a touchstone of the Christianity of whoever took the oath, as it had only been introduced with the goal of ensuring that it would bind the conscience of Catholics even tighter. For this reason, he considered it absolutely absurd that these words be demanded of a Jew, and its omission could have no bearing on the legality of the oath.[200] By contrast, the other judges, including the presiding judge Lord Chief Justice Baron Pollock, considered the final part of the oath to be important and indispensable, without which the oath could have no value at all.[201]

The public, which must surely have included influential men of the England of those days, had followed the various judgements very attentively. In the camp of the Jews and their allies, the greatest sense of consternation prevailed, while the adversaries applauded with satisfaction the verdict's reasoning, reasoning which demonstrated that the Jews were not capacitated to take up seats in Parliament:

> Baron Rothschild, in London, and Mr. Salomons in Greenwich, ought now to bow to the supremacy of the law, and to

---

[198] Goldsmid, A.: *Report*, p. 24 ff. Translator's note: QVOS.

[199] *Times*, 27/1/1852, 29/1/1852. *Morning Herald*, 27/1/1852, 29/1/1852. Translator's note: QVOS from the *Times* 29/1/1852 issue.

[200] Goldsmid, A.: *Report...*, pp. 66, 94.

[201] Goldsmid, A.: *Report...*, pp. 94-134.

withdraw their claims. A solemn decision has been given that the law permits them not to sit in Parliament. Such being the case, to persist in getting returned, simply (as both of these gentlemen *were* returned) by the weight of the purse—is to express a plain resolution that the law shall be altered, not because it ought to be altered, or because the people of England wish it altered—but because two or three wealthy Jews resolve that it shall be altered; and carry out that resolution by a pertinacious assault on the firmness of the two houses...[202]

Salomons lodged an appeal, which was debated by the Court of Exchequer Chamber in 1853. The appeal was unanimously rejected as groundless, leaving the lower court's sentence in place. The then-Chief Justice, Lord Campbell, a declared philo-Semite who occupied the presidency, could not reject the lower court's findings. In an addendum to his pronouncement, he emphasized how much he regretted the legal situation, but that he hoped that this would be modified in favor of the Jews. Lord Campbell's attitude is perfectly understandable when one takes into account that even in the House of Lords, he had declared himself proud to call Salomons his friend.[203]

In 1854, Salomons presented a 'writ of error'—a type of legal order—to the House of Lords as the final court of appeal, of which more shall be discussed later. Neither in 1855 nor in 1856 was any decision made. On 21 July 1857, Lord Campbell asked the House of Lords if the writ was going be determined or dismissed, and in the case of it being determined, when the hearing was to take place. The need for a decision was pressing, because public opinion, that up until recently had been in harmony with the anti-Jewish stance of the Lords, was starting to show certain changes, particularly in the previously anti-Jewish spheres of Conservatism. This observation from a philo-Semite is very interesting because, if it is correct, then public opinion must have been anti-Jewish at least until July 1857. Later in the same speech, Lord Campbell asked that the *Miller vs. Salomons* case be dealt with as soon as possible. The Lord Chancellor responded that it was a matter for the interested parties whether or not the cause was debated, as up until that point, both parties had applied for the cause to be stood over; a further joint application was made that the case might stand over for another two months, which was why another postponement had been granted, from June 15 to August 15, which would take the matter into the next session.[204]

Progress on the issue remained more or less stalled and was probably declared over once the Jews achieved their 1858 victory.

---

[202] *Morning Herald*, 20/4/1852. QVOS.

[203] Henriques: p. 276. & *Hansard*, Volume 147, p. 108.

[204] *Hansard*, Volume 147, pp. 108-16.

We shall remember that the sensational verdict of the lower court was published on 19 April 1852. With that verdict, until its annulment, Salomons' entire existence remained endangered, which is why the Jewish camp decided to take the appropriate rescue measures.

The use of the legal system served perfectly to change this state of affairs.

Already by the 4th of May, that is, only two weeks later, Lord Lyndhurst introduced a bill [the Disabilities Repeal Bill] to annul the law which had allowed Salomons to be convicted, by way of substituting it with a new one which would only involve financial penalties for such contraventions, without further disadvantages for the man so convicted.[205] Lord Lyndhurst was warmly supported by Lord Campbell, who branded the severity of the punishment of the old law as 'a disgrace to the age in which we lived; they were the remnants of the barbarous prejudices of former times'.[206]

At this time, a Conservative government headed by the Earl of Derby was in power. It seems like an irony of fate that it was this very man, who until then had always been anti-Jewish, who supported the bill as leader of the government. This support was not lessened in any way by the objection of having had to consult with the other members of the cabinet. After Lord Campbell had additionally requested that the law be retroactively applied to 1 January 1851 [in order to indemnify Salomons], the bill was admitted at the first reading.

On the 7th and the 17th of May, the other two required readings took place in the House of Lords.[207] The first two readings were approved without debate in the Lower House. The third reading was attempted so late at night that nobody was interested in it any longer. But a member [Mr. Mullings] protested against the bill 'being proceeded with at that late hour', a protest to which Mr. Newdegate added his support. Newdegate made clear that he would vote against the bill, and stated, among other reasons for this decision: 'With respect to any disabilities which had been incurred by Mr. Alderman Salomons, he had incurred them with his eyes open, and well knowing the consequences of his acts.' Due to the lateness of the hour, it was agreed to end the sitting, and the debate was adjourned until June 21.[208]

When the June 21st sitting began, Mr. Newdegate again protested vehemently against the law that his adversaries were striving to institute. 'He believed that the action brought against Mr. Salomons by Mr. Miller was a collusive action, and if the penalties could be evaded by a collusive action, any one might vote here night after night without punishment.' As his theory of collusion 'had been held by the Lord Chief Baron' himself, Newdegate

---

[205] *Hansard*, Volume 121, pp. 190-2.

[206] *Hansard*, Volume 121, p. 193. Translator's note: QVOS.

[207] *Hansard*, Volume 121, p. 194. & pp. 198-9. & pp. 354, 733.

[208] *Hansard*, Volume 122, pp. 1, 331. & pp. 697-8. Translator's note: QVOS.

asked that the progress on the bill be suspended for three months, practically a rejection statement, 'so that the House might have time to inquire into its effect' given the potential for 'the most dangerous consequences.' Mr. Roundell Palmer, another member, pointed out that the bill had been presented by a Conservative. Newdegate understood this as an appeal to his duty as a Conservative member and to his consequent sense of solidarity with his party, and thus consented to withdraw his amendment, but not without expressing his misgivings about the implications of Parliament being able to override the authority of the Court of Exchequer, and most certainly with great repugnance on his part. The bill was then passed into law without difficulty.[209]

As the law could be applied retroactively, the sentence pronounced against Salomons only remain valid in terms of the financial penalty element. We see that what was possible in the days of Sampson Gideon was even more the case a hundred years later. There can be no better proof of the state of servitude to the Jews that was suffered by the classes who in those days governed England.[210]

New Battles

Not only the legislative bodies, but also the completely impartial judiciary had a clear position against Jewish emancipation. And public opinion continued to be equally opposed to the Jewish agenda. It is truly surprising then that, despite everything, yet again the Jews renewed their efforts to attain their goal with the help of their powerful protectors. New attacks were soon to start. Meanwhile, Lord Derby's cabinet had been substituted by Lord Aberdeen's, in which Lord Russell acted as Foreign Secretary; it was in this capacity, in February 1853, that Russell presented a motion to Parliament which proposed: 'That this House do resolve itself into a Committee to take into consideration certain Civil Disabilities affecting the Jews'.[211]

Sir Robert Inglis pointed out once more that the Jews were and would always continue to be a separate nation. For this reason, they could not be granted, under any circumstance, admission to Parliament. Sir Robert Peel expressed surprise that so much noise was being made over thirty thousand Jews among thirty million Christians. Although the defenders of the Jews were apt to lavish all of the highest praise upon this group, it was important

---

[209] *Hansard*, Volume 122, p. 1127. Translator's note: QVOS. It is also interesting to note that Newdegate claims that the presiding judge also refused to admit the Hansard records as evidence of Salomons' behavior during the trial. & *Hansard*, Volume 122, pp. 1128-9.
[210] *Statutes of the United Kingdom*, Volume 92, p. 107.
[211] *Hansard*, Volume 124, p. 604. Translator's note: QVOS.

that the negative aspects of the Jewish presence were not forgotten. To quote at length:[212]

> It was not solely upon religious grounds that he opposed the introduction of the Jews into the House, but because he had considered that those words, 'On the true faith of a Christian,' represented a great principle; and, denying, as the Jews did, the fundamental principles of Christianity, it was incompatible and inconsistent with the dignity and character of the Christian Parliament to admit them to the exercise of the highest functions of the State. This measure was unwise and unnecessary, and, consequently, impolitic. It was idle to say we need be under no apprehension of their swamping our institutions, or filling all of the high offices of State. He did not believe any other constituency besides the City of London could be found confiding its political interests to a Hebrew legislator; but really we had seen of late such remarkable changes and contradictions, that it was almost impossible to argue what consequences might result from either men or measures, and he could not consent to run the risk of the possibility of that which might occur, and of the interests of the Church of England being submitted to the legislation of the Jews.
>
> What was the character, and respectability, and moral influence of the Jewish community in England? Their numbers were not above 30,000—30,000 among 30,000,000; but it would not matter one straw if there were 30 or 30,000, provided the principle was good, and there was a necessity for Parliament to interfere. Their charitable disposition and general good conduct he was perfectly ready to admit were worthy of our consideration; but he did not think that there was a title to all the great encomiums that some were in the habit of passing upon them in that House when such measures as the present were being considered.
>
> He would merely refer the House to what passed before the Select Committee on Juvenile Offenders. There it appeared in evidence that the chief instigators of crime in the metropolis were Jews. This was literally what appeared in evidence, and the statement was justified on the ground that the Jews almost exclusively afforded facilities for the disposal of

---

[212] *Hansard*, Volume 124, p. 604. & p. 610. Translator's note: QVOS. I have also included elements of the speech where were elided in Aldag's text, for their interest to the modern reader.

stolen goods. He maintained, that if this was the case in the
metropolis, it must be so in all the great centres of population—in Manchester, Liverpool, Glasgow, Birmingham—and
therefore the Jews were not, as a body, entitled to those high
encomiums which were generally passed upon them.

The House, however, must consider that they were now
merely considering a personal affair of the noble Lord the
Member for the City of London. That noble Lord had the honour of representing the City of London with a Jew, and he had
given a pledge that he would annually bring forward in this
House a measure upon the subject of the Jews' disabilities.
Now, Baron Rothschild was probably a very worthy man—
they all knew he was a very *wealthy* man—but he (Sir. R.
Peel) did not think he was entitled to a seat in that House on
account of his wealth, for everybody was perfectly aware how
that wealth had been amassed. It was only last night he had
read in a newspaper which was very well informed upon foreign subjects, that the House of Rothschild had consented to
grant a loan to the Government of Athens, with very considerable guarantees, at the rate of 9 per cent; and they could consequently very well understand how the Rothschild family had
amassed their wealth. He was ready to admit that Baron Rothschild might be a very worthy man; but, at the same time, as
much had been said by the President of the Board of Control
(Sir C. Wood) about gagging the French and Belgian press, no
one had done more to gag the expression of liberal opinions
throughout the world than the House of Rothschild, from the
loans contracted with despotic Governments, like, for instance, that of Naples.

But, even supposing Baron Rothschild to be a very worthy
man, he, for one, had expected, considering the qualities of the
noble Lord who represented the Government in that House,
and that the Government represented all the political factions
that had combined to oppose the late Government, that the
country would have received at his hands some measures
more practical and more important for the material interest of
the people of this country. In 1851 and 1852 they had been
distinctly told by the noble Lord of the absolute necessity that
existed for a new Reform Bill; and yet now that the noble
found himself leader in the House of Commons for a coalition
Cabinet, that measure was almost indefinitely adjourned. At
Carlisle, at Southwark, and in the City of London, we had
heard of nothing else but allusions to the gross bribery, corrup-

tion, and intimidation which had prevailed over the country at the last election... however, the noble Lord had thought proper to adjourn weightier considerations of Government for the purpose of hurriedly introducing a Jew Bill...

[H]e for one, upon conscientious convictions, believing that he was best fulfilling the wishes of those whose opinions he was to a certain extent bound to consider, believing also that in so doing he was giving a fair interpretation to the views of the people of this country, he gave to this Bill his most determined resistance...[213]

After the debate, the division took place, which resulted in a narrow majority, of 234 votes to 205, in favor of the bill.

Then a committee was named which was tasked with establishing the wording of the law. On 1 March 1853, the first reading took place, followed by the second reading on May 11. Once again, passionate arguments took places between the two camps. The anti-Jews were primarily represented by the members Sir Frederic Thesiger and Mr. Charles Newdegate [see footnote]. The first went back to pointing out that the Jews, as a separate nation, could not be granted any seat in the Parliament, while the second emphasized that even in Cromwell's time the Jews had made improper demands. The honorable member Mr. Drummond was reported as declaring that:[214]

They [the Jews] were looking forward to the time when they should trample upon the Gentiles like ashes under the soles of their feet. They cared very little about principle, but a great deal about interest. [...]

He had been struck by a passage he read not long ago, in which it was said that the time was when the nations of the earth were bound together in unity with Rome for their universal centre, while the talisman which bound them was *credo*. True we were still bound together, but our centre was the

---

[213] [Aldag's note:] There is a delicate irony in the original English which results from the wordplay of 'worthy' and 'wealthy.' Translator's note: QVOS, although I have italicized the word 'wealthy' in the text at the juncture of which Aldag remarks, as it would doubtless have been stressed by Peel as he spoke, to underscore the pun.

[214] *Hansard,* Volume 125, pp. 71-118, 166-72, 1217-1290. & p. 79. & p. 87. Translator's note: The original text gives 'Mr. Bernal Osborne' as the second anti-Jewish MP. This is clearly an error on Aldag's part, as Ralph Bernal Osborne (the Osborne surname being taken from his wife on marriage) was of Sephardic Jewish descent and argued consistently in Parliament for Jewish emancipation, including in the debate indicated here. Given that Charles Newdegate also took part in this debate, one must assume that this was the name Aldag intended.

Stock Exchange, and the talisman which governed us was not *credo*, but *credit*. It is not *credo*—no-one says *I* believe in anything; but *credit*: he believes someone else. The Bill before this House originated in these circumstances: The rabble of London, partly out of the love of mischief, partly from contempt of the House of Commons, and partly from a desire to give a slap in the face of Christianity, elected a Jew.[215]

He also declared that, if it were believed that Jews could be admitted to Parliament in such circumstances, then Parliament should do so, but that he, 'with a safe conscience, could not and would not'.[216]

The honorable member Mr. Herbert, who spoke in defense of the bill, reproached the anti-Jewish faction for their argument that the Hebrews were a separate nation with negative qualities:

You exclude him, you say, on account of his nationality, his origin, and his race; but if that be true, and if you say there is an inherent nationality about the Jew—about his race and about his origin—why do you not exclude a converted Jew? His race, his origin, and his blood are the same; and on what principle did you allow a converted Jew to sit in Parliament for several years?[217]

This last statement is very interesting because, in accordance with our current views, what is effectively exposed here is an internal contradiction within the anti-Jewish argument.

The debate lasted for two days and two nights. In the division after the second reading, the philo-Semites emerged victorious with a majority of 41 votes. As before, for the third reading the government took refuge in a typically parliamentarian maneuver to get the bill passed quickly and smoothly. Just before Easter, deliberations about a bill which was part of the order of business were suddenly interrupted and, out of the blue, the Jewish bill was unexpectedly put before Parliament. Most of the members were already enjoying the Easter holidays, but the few members who remained protested almost unanimously against such a tactic. The particularly strong protest

---

[215] Translator's note: In the original text, Aldag added an extra footnote to reproduce this wordplay in English, because 'the delicacy of the English text cannot be fully reflected in translation.'

[216] *Hansard*, Volume 125, pp. 94-96. Translator's note: The full extract from Drummond's speech has been reproduced verbatim from the Hansard, although the 'I' has been italicized here to aid comprehension, as this would have undoubtedly have been stressed during the speech.

[217] *Hansard*, Volume 125, p. 102. Translator's note: QVOS.

from the member Mr. George Henry Vansittart obliged the government to abort their plans for a third reading that day. The same thing took place on 15 April 1853. Once again there were heated debates. The member Mr. Charles Cumming-Bruce made clear that 'if the Duke of Wellington was alive, the government would not have dared to act as they had done in the matter'.[218]

During the course of the debate, a very interesting speech was made regarding events that had taken place in Palestine. It came from the member Mr. William Kirk, who spoke in favor of the Jews:

> It was now a period of 3,774 years since it pleased God to choose that people as a peculiar race, and in selecting Abraham as their great progenitor he used these remarkable words, 'I will bless them that bless thee, and curse him that curseth thee; and in thee shall all the families of the earth be blessed.' [...]
>
> The Jewish people resident in this country seemed to be most anxious to have representatives of their own race in the House of Commons. Might not that desire be an indication of the coming fulfilment of the prophecy as to their restoration? Might it not be in the designs of Providence that the leaders of the Jews in this country should obtain seats in our House of Parliament, in order that they might become thoroughly acquainted with our mode of legislation, and subsequently legislate for the Jews in their own country after the English model? This House being, as it were, a sort of normal school for their instruction, would not the admission of Jews to our Legislature induce the Jews, when restored to their own land, to become the firmest friends of Great Britain?
>
> And the friendship of such a people, when restored, and in possession not simply of Palestine, as they had in the days of David, and Solomon, but of all that was originally promised to them, of the whole of the land extending from the Euphrates to the Nile, and from the Mediterranean to the Indian Ocean, would be of no little advantage to the people of these realms. That land which would come into the possession of the Jews would be the most fertile and the most desirable in the world. It would form part of the highway from Great Britain to Indian and Australian Colonies. The Jews, in possession of their own land, would undoubtedly become one of the most important nations upon the earth. That was prophesied of them. Upon every ground, therefore, both of justice and of public policy,

---

[218] *Hansard,* Volume 125, p. 167 ff. & pp. 1217-1290. & p. 1220. Translator's note: QVOS.

he called upon the House to vote in favour of the third reading of the Bill.[219]

It is interesting, to say the least, that already in 1853 an English member of Parliament had declared himself in support Palestine being given, along with the concession of large swathes of adjacent territories, to the Jews.

At the end of the debate, Sir Robert Peel spoke once more about the problem as a whole:

> It so happened that at this moment there were two countries in Europe, one where restrictions were being enforced against the Jews, and another where complete emancipation had been effected. If he might be allowed, he would take one first, and then the other. Intelligence had just been received that the Emperor of Russia had published a ukase prohibiting Jews from representing Christian trading and commercial houses in that country; and he did not think the conduct of the Emperor Nicholas was much to be blamed. But suppose it was; let the House just look at home awhile. Here we saw the most extensive trading and commercial community in the world confiding a portion of its political rights to a wealthy citizen of the Jewish race, a kind of Goliath of Gath. He knew perfectly well that the City of London might return for its representative, constitutionally speaking, whomsoever it pleased. Hon. Members, perhaps, might recollect that in the time of George II and George III, the borough of Sudbury was commonly advertised for sale to the highest bidder. What the Marquess of Broadacres did there, was there any reason why the Wiseacres of Portsoken should not do in the City?
>
> Still, they would never be able to persuade him that the trade, commerce, and influence of the City of London were, or could be, judiciously entrusted to this Mr. de Rothschild. He doubted very much if they would be able to persuade the people of England that the influence of the representatives of the City of London, which had so long been the stronghold of freedom and liberty, ought to be entrusted to an Austrian Consul General—to the wealthy representative of a moneyed family, which had certainly done more than any other family in the world to gag and stifle liberty. He was one of those who thought that the City of London ought to be represented either

---

[219] *Hansard*, Volume 125, p. 1226 ff. Translator's note: QVOS.

by some great political character, or by some of the merchant princes of the empire.

As far as regarded great political character, he did not think the City could have made a more judicious selection than the noble Lord opposite, for he stood high in the opinion of his fellow-countrymen as an enlightened statesman; but he did not hesitate to say that the selection of Mr. de Rothschild as the representative of the commercial influence of the City of London was, to his mind, the greatest possible slur upon the character and respectability of the City. (*Cries of* 'Oh, oh!') He said, 'to his mind' and he repeated it. (*A laugh.*) Yes, to his mind it was a great slur upon the character and respectability of the trade and commerce of the City of London to have made such a selection.

He would now take the other case to which he had referred, where complete emancipation had been voted to the Jews. It had happened that in the States of the Prince of Meiningen [Germany], the representatives had voted complete emancipation to the Jews; and what had been the effect? Why, that the sovereign prince had been inundated with petitions from his subjects, those petitions begging him to resist what their representatives had passed. He did not know whether the House would care for what took place there; but what, he would ask, was the case with the petitions in this country? He found that there had been 35,000 signatures attached to the petitions against the measure presented to that House since the second reading of this Bill. Those petitions, he contended, were entitled to great respect; but how many were the petitions on the other side? Very few indeed.

But in considering the merits of the case, he would just take one petition in favour of the Jews, and one against; he would take the petition from the Corporation of the City of London for, and that from the University of Oxford against; he would take that for, which—as the *Times* newspaper, that recognised organ of public opinion, said—came from 'the scandal and the nuisance of the metropolis'; and the other against, from the most learned and enlightened community in the empire.[220]

Despite the best efforts of the anti-Jewish faction, the bill was approved with a majority of 288 votes to 230.

---

[220] *Hansard*, Volume 125, p. 1273. Translator's note: QVOS.

The bill passed by Parliament was sent, as usual, to the House of Lords, and the philo-Semites could this time harbor hopes of also gaining a majority in the Upper House. The then-Prime Minister, the Earl of Aberdeen, had voted in previous years as a member of the House of Lords against the Jewish bills that were presented at the time. As he was the one who sent the bill to the House of Lords, it was trusted that his personal supporters would follow his example and vote in favor of the bill, which would have been sufficient to achieve, finally, its approval. But yet more the people who believed this were deluding themselves: after long debates, the House of Lords again defeated the bill, on this occasion with 164 votes to 115.[221]

It is also instructive to look at the attitudes of the press from both sides regarding this attempt. The *Times* maintained the belief, almost inconceivable, that 'the religious antecedents of the Jews constitute the only real objection to the privileges now claimed for them.' Seemingly, the *Times* had not found out about Newdegate's speeches, which, as is known, did not limit themselves in any way to such reasons. Only on one occasion did the *Times* deal with the assertion from the opposing camp that the Jews were international. From what can be observed, it was considered a highly inaccurate and inappropriate argument to use when the question was being discussed.[222]

The *Morning Post* was angered that the Jewish Question was brought up relentlessly in Parliament. The only reason for it was that Rothschild wanted to enter Parliament, whatever the cost, and the government was supporting him in his ambitions.

> If a small man like Mr. Moses, the vendor of new clothes, or Mr. Isaacs, the vendor of old ones, had demanded a seat in Parliament upon his own simple right as an English citizen, would the Leader of the House of Commons have moved heaven and earth to get him in? We think not. The little Jew would have been met by a reminder of the unit's place he occupied among the millions of his Christian fellow-citizens. But because the Croesus of the day, the convenient agent of continental Governments, the negotiator of enormous State loans, the refuge of exhausted Exchequers, and the key-holder of half the coffers of Europe, is ambitious of a seat in Parliament, therefore the first principles of our legislation are to be invaded and set at nought for his special benefit...[223]

---

[221] *Hansard*, Volume 126, pp. 754-796.

[222] *Times*, 26/2/1853, 14/3/1853, 18/4/1853. Translator's note: QVOS from the 26/2/1853 issue. & *Times*, 18/4/1853.

[223] *Morning Post*, 16/3/1853. Translator's note: QVOS.

The *Standard* showed its disgust in a similar way. It accused Lord Russell of having shady dealings with Rothschild, who contributed to the Russell's election costs and had the Jewish electors give Russell their votes in exchange for Russell, as his part of the 'vile bargain', presenting one bill after another which furthered the Jewish agenda. These accusations must have had some basis in truth, as no legal action was taken against the *Standard* for libel or any similar charge.[224]

It was not only the press that considered Jewish ambitions to be completely inappropriate; by means of petitions, the vast majority of the population also showed their aversion. For example, in the debates on the latest bill, which took place in March, many petitions from individuals and whole districts were read out, against which there were none in favor of the Jews. The month of April brought even better proof: compared with the countless large petitions presented by individuals, towns, cities, and communities, only a very few were found in favor of the Jews. July showed the fullest evidence of this prevailing mood, with 1,055 petitions containing 34,525 signatures against the Jews, and only seven petitions containing 450 signatures in their favor. As can be seen, the people still wanted the Jews to remain excluded from the legislative bodies.[225]

This anti-Jewish stance of the people was certainly due to the great Germanophile Thomas Carlyle taking up the pen to attack the Jews.

Once more, the opposing camp fought for their agenda with new pro-Jewish propaganda leaflets—some of which came from the pen of well-known Nonconformist minister John Stoughton, which demonstrates yet again how, in every epoch, numerous servants of the Church were willing to actively intervene in favor of the Jews. This British shepherd of souls opined that the world owed a lot to the Jews for their qualities and their success in the sciences and the arts, all the more so for their ill treatment in the past. According to him, it was inconceivable that these 'benefactors of the human race' were persecuted and treated like dogs in England, since, according to all indications, 'the Jews were after all to be the final saviors of the world.' It will be no surprise, then, that Stoughton came to the conclusion that the Jews could not be let into Parliament too soon.[226]

*****

A year later, 6 February 1854, Lord John Russell returned to presenting another bill in Parliament. This time he changed tactic, because it was not a bill

---

[224] *Standard*, 21/2/1853, 25/2/1853. Translator's note: The phrase 'vile bargain' is found in both issues.

[225] *Times*, 9/3/1853, 10/3/1853. & 15/4/1853, 30/4/1853. & *Standard*, 26/7/1853.

[226] Stoughton: pp. 9-12, 22-25, 27-30. Translator's note: QVOS (pp. 27, 28).

for the general elimination of Jewish disabilities, but only a bill for modifying the Oath of Abjuration. The bill was titled 'Parliamentary Oaths Bill' and aimed for the three aforementioned oaths to be replaced by one integrated oath. In addition, the oath designed for Catholics would thus would be annulled by a special law, so that a common oath for all British citizens could be implemented.

It would appear that there were two reasons for pursuing this variation: Firstly, it was likely that they did not wish to openly signal to the public that the Jews could gain entry to Parliament in the case of this law being passed; secondly, it was desired to win over the Catholic members, because with their support the chance of success seemed more certain.

The first reading took place without a debate and, moreover, without a vote worthy of mention. At the second reading, Sir Frederic Thesiger returned to being very active, acting as an attack dog in the debate. He continually warned the Chamber that it was solely the Jews that were yet again behind this bill and that it must not let itself be fooled by the fact that the Catholics were also mentioned in the text. He was scathing of Russell's connivance with Rothschild, which had led to his continual failed attempts to push through the Jewish agenda, and warns those present:[227]

> [I]nflamed, rather than discouraged, by successful opposition, he [Russell] now proposes to break down some of the defences of our Protestant Constitution, in order that he may be able to march over their ruins with the Jew [Rothschild] by his side, and seat him in the Legislature.[228]

In Thesiger's judgement, the proposed new oath did not offer sufficient security to the Protestant government of England due to the modification of the Catholic oath; it had not to be forgotten that it had been not long since the Pope had shown aggressive ambition for all Catholics, which was not in consonance with the national and Protestant interests of England.

In the course of the debate, the Opposition received support from an unexpected source. Disraeli suddenly spoke against Lord John Russell to some of the previous defenders of the lifting of Jewish disabilities. He declared that in view of the cited ambitions of the Pope, he could not give his approval to the bill—as far as it concerned the Catholics. But as the bill came as a whole, and could not therefore be separated, he greatly regretted not being able to vote in its favor.

---

[227] *Hansard*, Volume 130, pp. 272-282.
[228] *Hansard*, Volume 133, p. 870 ff. Translator's note: QVOS. Note that in this speech Thesiger also reveals that the Parliament had received, as of the previous day, 481 public petitions against the bill, which in total contained no fewer than 60,171 signatures.

In addition, he did not consider it proper that nowhere in the bill did the word 'Jew' appear, as it would not be clear to the broad masses that with the passage of this bill, the Jews would finally achieve their much-deserved equal rights. The Jews had a right to a full and complete emancipation, visible to the eyes of the whole world, which was not observable in Lord John Russell's bill. Otherwise, the Jews could wait tranquilly for their eventual full and complete emancipation, as the Almighty Being, who had never deserted them, would lend them his support.[229]

It is very likely that Disraeli's behavior brought many hitherto supporters of Lord John Russell to the side of the opposition. Thus the supporters of Jewish emancipation had to watch as the bill did not even pass the House of Commons, but was defeated, albeit with the slimmest majority, by 251 votes to 247.[230]

The Jewish press, moved by the latest failure, attributed the defeat exclusively to the fact that on this occasion the enemies of the Jews and the enemies of the papists had marched together to win the battle. When the bill appeared, the *Times* did not step back from their position, not even before the proposition that, in the case of the bill being defeated by the House of Lords, it could trigger a dissolution of Parliament and the naming of a hundred new Peers, favorable to the Jews, to thus gain an absolute majority of philo-Semitic lords in the Upper House. The *Times* was recommending, therefore, a revolutionary new act of legislation, almost never before seen, which would have necessarily transformed the nation's political life at the most profound level. And all that for some thirty thousand Jews in a population of thirty million![231]

Lord John Russell had undoubtedly committed a tactical error on presenting the bill to Parliament in the way he had authored it, shortly after the publication of the Pope's aspirations. In any case, it would surely have been preferable to modify or abandon the bill after finding out Disraeli's position on it. It is also likely that the incredible events surrounding Salomons' intrusion into Parliament were still fresh in the collective memory of the English public, due to which the former lost his sympathetic aura of 'poor, unfairly persecuted Jew': this was a far from insignificant factor because it is known that, almost instinctively, the English nation always sides with the underdog, whether this be justified or not.

Progress and Resistance

Recent events in the fight for emancipation had taken a very unhappy turn for the Jews, despite the support lent by powerful sponsors. Furthermore,

---

[229] *Hansard*, Volume 133, p. 963 ff.
[230] *Hansard*, Volume 133, pp. 971-4.
[231] *Times*, 25/5/1854, 26/5/1854.

public opinion was more set against them than it had ever been. For this reason, it must have been clearly observed that the Jewish movement needed to take a break to get over the latest failures, because, in contrast to the previous standard practice in such situations, no action was undertaken in Parliament in the remainder of that year, nor in the year after that. Nevertheless, the Jews did win some partial victories to add to their tally.

The universities had been barred to Jews for a long time. Various laws promulgated during the reigns of Elizabeth, James I, and George I had prohibited their admission. Oxford University was the first to take an interest in the Jewish Question regarding admission. In 1854, the Oxford University Reform Act was passed, which decreed that: 'It shall not be necessary for any person, upon matriculating in the University of Oxford, to make or subscribe any declaration or to take any oath, any law or statute to the contrary notwithstanding.' This made the entry of Jews into Oxford possible. This example was followed in 1856 by the University of Cambridge. The remaining universities did not delay in adopting this measure.[232] But it was only in 1871, with the Universities Tests Act, that a unitary regulation was finally brought in. Of course, it was through this law that the Jews were also granted full freedom of education.[233]

The practice of the profession of educator or teacher had been just as prohibited to Jews for a long time. Here also the main obstacle was constituted by the swearing of the oath. In addition, there existed another law, the so-called Act of Uniformity, which dated back to 1662. This act, among other requirements, demanded that every professor, tutor, and schoolteacher had to sign a declaration in which he gave his conformity to the Liturgy of Church of England, as it was by law established. In accordance with this law, all teachers and tutors for private homes had to obtain a license from the bishop of their diocese to be able to practice their profession. Any contravention of this law was punishable with imprisonment for up to three months. As would be expected, only the members of the Anglican church, and not the Jews, received such a license. This situation was only modified in 1846 with the aforementioned Religious Disabilities Act, which authorized the Jews to be private tutors. The final restrictions on the ability to teach were eliminated in 1871 with the Universities Tests Act.[234]

The strength of the City of London's support for Jewish interests can be seen in the election of 30 September 1855, which elevated Salomons to the office of Lord Mayor. Only someone familiar with English society can comprehend the high honor and at the same time the power that the Jews had

---

[232] 1 Eliz. c. 1. & 7 Jac. I. c. 6. & 1 Geo s. 2. c. 13. & 17 and 18 Victoria c. 81. Translator's note: QVOS: (https://www.legislation.gov.uk/ukpga/Vict/17-18/81). & 19 and 20 Victoria c. 88.

[233] 34 and 35 Victoria c. 26.

[234] 13 and 14 Car. II c. 4. Translator's note: For details on how the 1558 Act of Uniformity affected the Jews, see Volume 2 of this study. & Henriques: p. 130. & 9 and 10 Victoria c. 59.

thus achieved. Nevertheless, their joy at this success was somewhat lost in the prevailing euphoria over the capture of Sevastopol.[235]

On 9 November 1855, David Salomons was invested into his new office with all pomp and ceremony. A huge banquet at the town hall was thrown in his honor, and it was attended by Queen Victoria's husband, Prince Albert. One of the highest dignitaries of the Church, who was also present at the banquet, became so enthused by the grandness of the occasion, that he addressed the royal guest with the following words: 'Thanks be to God, Your Royal Highness, we have found, at last, a true gentleman for the post of Lord Mayor.' 'Yes, my lord,' answered the prince, 'but we have had to seek him outside of Christian circles'.[236]

Salomons had, in the 19th-century alone, three Jewish successors to his post: Sir Benjamin Samuel Phillips (1865-1866), Sir Henry Isaac (1889-1890), and Sir George Faudel Phillips (1897-1898).[237]

This new success, as well as the collapse of Lord Aberdeen's coalition government, inspired the Jews and their allies to resume the attack.

The new government was formed by Lord Palmerston, who looked benevolently upon Jewish emancipation, but, to general surprise, neither did this government initially show the slightest inclination to make a spontaneous intervention in Parliament in favor of the Jews. It is not known if it was the government or the Jewish camp who compelled MP Milner Gibson to present a new bill of this type to Parliament on February 22. What *is* known is that this member introduced a private member's bill for the annulment of the Oath of Abjuration, in the first week of the Parliamentary session.[238] This bill, like the one before it, avoided all mention of Jewish disabilities. In addition, it was skillfully based on the assertion that the Oath of Abjuration was antiquated and in need of annulment, which was even the opinion of the anti-Jewish faction.

As has previously been stated, this oath demanded that the subjects of the English monarch abjure all loyalty to the Pretender (the last of the Stuarts) and to his descendants. But as there was no longer any Stuart descendancy, there was no longer, in reality, any need for the oath to be taken.

The close cooperation between the government and the bill's sponsor is proven by the fact that the government immediately began deliberations on the bill, to which they lent their full support. Lord Palmerston and—as always—Lord Russell, were the spokesmen for the philo-Semites. To the al-

---

[235] *Morning Chronicle*, 1/10/1855.
[236] *Morning Chronicle*, 10/11/1855. Translator's note: As a point of interest, the newspaper was keen to remind readers that 'the present Lord Mayor is the first of his race who has held the office.' I was, however, unable to locate the original form of the quotation in the text above.
[237] Wolf: *Essays...*, pp. 328-29.
[238] *Hansard*, Volume 140, p.1288.

ready cited reasons in favor of the bill, they added that in the epoch in which the oath was instituted, there were hardly any Jews in England, which meant that the legislator's intention could not have concerned Jews when the measure was taken. In any case, the general situation was such that the oath would have to be annulled, being an obstacle to the achievement of equitable rights for Jews.

Once more, the battle began in its accustomed format: debates that lasted entire days with all types of reasoning employed by both sides, and at the second reading in Parliament, the Jews triumphed, with 230 votes to 195. The spokesman of the adversaries, Sir Frederic Thesiger, tried once more to impede a second reading, but his motion was defeated, by 159 votes to 110.[239] It almost goes without saying that the House of Lords once more rejected the bill, by 110 votes to 78.[240]

The impotent rage of the Jews and their allies was aimed mainly at Lord Derby, under whose direction the House of Lords had repelled this attack. The gazette of the Rothschild court almost surpassed itself with its insults, as can be seen from the opening of one of its articles:[241]

> With a solemn gravity which rendered the hypocrisy of his proceeding only the more offensive, Lord Derby last night introduced in the House of Lords his Bill for 'the amendment' of the Oath of Abjuration... Those who regard this movement from a larger and more liberal point of view, only see in this new Bill a poor and petty attempt to offer an insult to the representative branch of the Legislature, quite unworthy of any man aspiring to the position of statesman...[242]

Note also how, on this occasion, disillusionment transforms into new threats against the Jews' adversaries.

The fact that the government found itself in great financial straits after the Crimean War and that Rothschild had taken it upon himself, as so many times before, to arrange a loan of some five million pounds to cover the

---

[239] *Hansard*, Volume 141, pp. 703-759. & Volume 142, pp. 595-605, 1165-1197.

[240] *Hansard*, Volume 142, pp. 1772-1895.

[241] *Times*, 23/6/1856, 24/6/1856.

[242] *Morning Chronicle*, 25/6/1856. Translator's note: QVOS. We can see from this excerpt that Lord Derby looked to counter the attack by seeking to amend the original bill rather than rejecting it outright. Such an amendment would no doubt ensure that the oath retained its Christian component, while removing the part about abjuring the Stuart ascendancy, the ostensible reason for the bill's introduction. This would leave the pro-Jewish faction with no official cause for complaint, which is doubtless the reason for the journalist's sophistic attempt to sway his readers emotionally, because, knowing that his faction is being outmaneuvered, his only recourse is to attempt to shame or belittle Derby for his actions.

debts, must have played no small part in the government's involvement in the bill.[243]

One could be forgiven for thinking that the Jews had become disheartened. It is particularly surprising that there were always governments ready to support Jewish emancipation bills and yet the Jews came away with one defeat after another.

In the spring of the following year—1857—new parliamentary elections were held. It seemed that finally the moment had arrived for the definitive victory after all of the Jewish efforts. Lord Palmerston not only found his old majority back in Parliament once more, but also that his party had gained many more seats. In addition, Rothschild had again been elected as an MP for the City of London. Initially, great fears had been harbored for his chances of victory, because the elections had been arranged for Saturday, 28 March, and it was feared that the Jews, a very religious people, would not go near the ballot boxes. But Rothschild could not give up on their support. During the morning hours their participation was very weak, but when the synagogues emptied out, they were seen voting in large number, because the rabbis had given the interpretation that the exercise of a public right was not incompatible with the God-given commandments. To everyone's surprise, this time Rothschild managed to win even more votes than Lord Russell, for which the joy, as well as the joy at both being re-elected, naturally overflowed in Jewish circles.[244]

Already within six weeks of the elections being held and immediately after the new Parliament was opened, the Jewish Question was yet again on the House of Commons table. This time it was the Prime Minister, Lord Palmerston himself, who felt sufficiently powerful to undertake the fight, perhaps confident in his evident success at the election and in his large majority in the House of Commons. His bill set out for the three different oaths to be replaced by one alone. He had made the issue so much his own that he even apologized to Parliament for having taken up the matter himself instead of entrusting it to Lord Russell. He observed that the passing of the bill would make it possible for Jews to occupy seats in Parliament, but that the special 1829 oath for Catholics would not undergo any change whatsoever. He had learned, then, from previous years: the Catholic Question would remain intact. The new oath proposed by Lord Palmerston planned to exclude those contentious final words that had been fought over so intensely for so many years.

Sir Frederic Thesiger first gave a thorough historical summary of the battle that had taken place up until that point. He considered a synopsis necessary, because many of the new MPs would likely be unfamiliar with the

---

[243] Paul: Volume II, p. 56; Reeves: p. 248.
[244] *Times*, 28/3/1857, 30/3/1857.

various phases of the battle. He limited himself to this exposition, having evidently decided to save his arguments against the opposition for a more opportune juncture. For this reason, the first reading took place almost without any resistance whatsoever.[245]

At the second reading, there were also no opposition speeches. Sir Frederic Thesiger only made a statement to the effect that the anti-Jewish faction would give the bill their approval if it were to be amended so that the oath included the phrase: 'And I do make this promise, renunciation, and declaration, heartily, willingly, and truly, on the true faith of a Christian.' The philo-Semites wholeheartedly opposed this amendment, because the amendment would ensure that Jewish access to Parliament remained blocked. The subsequent debate lacked nothing of the aggression and duration that had characterized the previous ideological clashes. But the situation soon turned against the Opposition when a leading Conservative, Sir John Pakington, who up until that point had always been on the anti-Jewish side, declared that he was against Thesiger's motion for an amendment:

> I must say, that I deeply regret the manner in which Her Majesty's Government have brought this subject before the House. I think it desirable to retain the words 'on the true faith of a Christian' for those who do not object to them. They give additional solemnity to an oath to which it is most desirable to impart as much solemnity as possible. I am sorry that the Government have decided to change the shape of the oath in that respect, and I think they would have adopted a far wiser course if they had allowed Christians to take the oath and to conclude it with that solemn form of words to which we have been so long accustomed, and had proceeded to effect the emancipation of the Jews by a Bill similar in principle to that by which the Roman Catholics were formerly emancipated...
>
> As, however, the Government have decided upon proceeding in this way, and as I have made up my mind that I can no longer conscientiously continue to oppose the admission of the Jews, it only remains for me—and I do it with regret—to support that form of proceeding upon which the Government have decided.[246]

As a consequence, the Conservative Party began to show uncertainty and disunity over the Jewish Question, which had to lead to victory for the Hebrews.

---

[245] *Hansard*, Volume 145, pp. 318-38.
[246] *Hansard*, Volume 145, pp. 1817-1823. Translator's note: QVOS.

Sir Frederic Thesiger's motion for an amendment was rejected by 341 votes to 201: such a crushing defeat for the anti-Jewish faction had not been seen in years. There was no doubt, therefore, that the third reading would result in a favorable outcome for Jewish emancipation, which is what effectively happened.[247]

Everything yet again came to depend on the position of the House of Lords, in which a majority was finally expected, given that the anti-Jewish faction had been so roundly defeated in the Commons. In addition, the government had given their full support to the bill being passed. Lord Derby, the leader of the Conservative opposition in the House of Lords, asked for the debate over the bill approved in Parliament to be adjourned for six months, a motion that, were it to be accepted, would amount to a refutation of the bill. In an explanation of the reasoning which obliged him to present his motion, Lord Derby said the following:

> I am not going to say a single word to disparage the Jews either in this or any other country. I admit the undoubtedly high antiquity of their nation. I admit that they have been, and may in some future time again be, the most favoured of all the nations of the world. I admit that, in point of eminent abilities, of natural qualifications, and of talents of various descriptions, they stand as high as any nation in the world; but I am not prepared to deny to them that which I am sure they themselves would be the last to abjure—namely, their nationality, and their character as a nation. Although they are scattered by Divine decree over the whole face of the earth, they retain unbroken the chain of their nationality, and they do look forward to that period when, as a nation, they shall have restored to them their national rights and their national territory...
>
> My Lords, the Jews were in Egypt, they are in England, and in every other country to which the decrees of Divine Providence have driven them, a nation within a nation. No doubt, they submit to the laws, and discharge the duties of citizens. In this country they are entrusted to the highest possible degree with the carrying out of the laws, with functions of trust, and with the administration of justice. That which alone is withheld from them is a voice in making the laws, and that is withheld because those laws are to regulate a Christian community.
>
> My Lords, I say that the Jews do look forward to a period when another and a greater exodus shall collect them from all

---

[247] *Hansard*, Volume 145, pp. 1101, 1341, 1759-1868; Volume 146, pp. 143-148, 347-365.

the countries of the World over which they are dispersed, and shall bring them back into their own country, and to the enjoyment of their own privileges. They retain their laws; they retain their peculiar customs. Though among us, they are not of us. They do not generally associate freely with their fellow-subjects; they have interests wholly apart. Between them and us there is an impassable gulf; their most important interests, their highest principles, their greatest views are altogether alien and foreign from ours. It may truly be said of them as was said by a noble and learned Friend behind me (against whom the expression excited considerable obloquy) of another people, that they are 'aliens in blood, aliens in religion, and aliens in language.' [...]

[I]t is the undoubted right of every citizen to enjoy by an indefeasible title all the rights and all the privileges—for my noble Friend [the Earl of Granville], I think, added the word 'privileges', and if he did not he ought to have done so—of citizenship. But in saying that the withholding of any of these rights, the depriving them of, or rather not conferring upon them, any of these privileges, is a remnant of persecution, my noble Friend altogether begged the question as to what are the rights and what are the privileges of citizenship. There are undoubtedly rights which are indefeasibly attached to every citizen of a free country. He has undoubtedly a perfect right to claim security for his person, security for his property, and the free enjoyment of the rites of his religion; and from none of these is the Jew in this country in the slightest degree debarred. But he cannot claim as a right—it is conferred upon him as a privilege—the power of legislating for the community at large—which you do not give to every man, but which you confide to certain individuals selected from the community as properly entitled to exercise these privileges. Certain duties, certain obligations, certain restrictions, have at all times been imposed upon the privilege of sitting and voting in Parliament. [...]

Now, I do not think, on the whole, that I should feel comfortable if a Jew were made Chancellor of the Exchequer. He may very possibly have some natural sympathies which would interfere with a due discharge of the duties of his office. The Chancellor of the Exchequer may be a Jew under this Bill, and very possibly will be ...

He then goes on to remind Lord Granville, who had argued that the clause 'upon the true faith of a Christian' had been inserted for the Jesuits and had been intended for the Jews, that the reason that the Jews had not been provided for in the original oath was not because they were perceived as permitted to exercise power, but because they had been banished from the kingdom over three centuries before and, at the time the act of the oath was passed, 'they were, and for many years afterwards remained, in that condition of absolute banishment.' He then highlights the fallacy of Granville's argumentation with the following:

> Why, to talk of introducing an Act of Parliament to prevent persons from sitting and voting in Parliament who could not even enter the kingdom, and to say that because words prohibiting them to sit and vote in Parliament were not directly pointed against the persons who could not enter the country, therefore it was not the intention of the Legislature to exclude them, is as much begging the question as if it were to be said that because in the oath of supremacy we declare that no foreign prince or potentate hath any power, ecclesiastical or spiritual, in this kingdom; therefore, because we do not introduce the word 'temporal', we admit that foreign potentates have temporal jurisdiction in this country.

The now elderly Lord Lyndhurst spoke at great length in favor of Jewish emancipation, but in the division of 10 July 1857, the bill was again defeated by 171 votes to 139.[248]

As had happened so many times before, the Jews' efforts had failed. One would be forgiven for thinking that they and their supporters must have lost hope forever, especially in view of the fact that even the most diehard supporters of the Jews had to admit that most of the population continued to support, as ever, the House of Lords' position. But that was far from the case. With a persistence specific to the Jewish race, a new bill replaced the old one. The plan being banked on was to exhaust the anti-Jewish faction so that, at some point, they would let their guard down. As we know today, this relentless attack is an intrinsic part of Jewish tactics.[249]

Thus it should not surprise us that it was only a week later that the Jewish emancipation issue, so often debated in the House of Lords, was back to being debated in the Commons. The government, led by Lord Palmerston, frankly admitted that it was not inclined to persist with the Jewish cause,

---

[248] *Hansard*, Volume 146, pp. 416, 1209-1278. Translator's note: Derby's speech extracts are reproduced QVOS. Additional text from the speech are also included for its perceived reader interest.

[249] *Hansard*, Volume 147, p. 111. Editor's note: This has strong echoes to present-day efforts to relentlessly push such vices as gambling, pornography, and legalized drug use on a generally unwilling public.

given that it had already done enough with the approval of the bill that had just been defeated by the House of Lords.[250]

Meanwhile Rothschild had resigned from his seat in Parliament, but in the by-election that was called as a result of this move, he once more presented his candidature. Once more he was elected. His resignation must therefore have been a tactical move for further measures, to demonstrate in subsequent battles that the indomitable will of the City was that a Jew be admitted to Parliament.[251]

Rothschild had been elected by proclamation in a public assembly, for there was no other candidate running in the election that the *Standard* described as a 'solemn farce.' The body of voters, as always a 'motley assemblage', was 'almost wholly composed of the members of the Jewish fraternity'.[252]

Not only did the press of the Jews' adversaries brand the election a farce, but it was disgusted that time was being wasted on such a trivial matter; with so many varied and important British interests at risk due to the Indian Mutiny, it could not understand why the populace was being inconvenienced with an issue of such little importance.[253]

Jews and Lords

Public opinion continued to be very divided with the regards to the course of events. The *Times* could not have gone any further in its thundering condemnation of the stubbornness of the Lords. It was incomprehensible, the newspaper claimed, that Rothschild, already elected so many times by the City for some ten years, had still not been able to take up his seat in Parliament. The fury of the *Times* was inexplicable, because Rothschild had stood for election in full cognizance of the legal situation and could therefore not complain of the consequences. Undoubtedly, with their old tactic, the Jews would continue to wear down the positions of their adversaries. Relentless attacks were essential and one bill had to follow another, until the haughty lords eventually gave up all resistance. The House of Commons had to find the courage to grant Rothschild his seat, in contravention of the law and the constitution. Then it would be left to the Upper House to react.[254]

But in its article of 20 July, the *Times* reflected on the fact that they still saw themselves as very far from the finishing line:

> There is no chance whatever that the Lords will give way...
> There will always be for the next 20 years a Jewish member

---

[250] *Hansard*, Volume 146, pp. 1699-1704, 1772-1780.
[251] Henriques: p. 285.
[252] *Times*, 24/7, 29/7; *Standard*, 29/7. Translator's note: All QVOS from the *Standard*.
[253] *Standard*, 29/7; *Morning Post*, 29/7.
[254] *Times*, 16/7/1857, 20/7/1857, 24/7/1857, 4/8/1857.

legally elected, but incapable of taking his seat, unless the
House of Commons proceeds to settle the question on its own
authority. Now, necessity knows no law; a grievance and an
anomaly are to be removed, and can only be removed by the
separate action of the Commons ...

This article was practically an exhortation to violate the constitution, at a
time when England was battling hard for the continued existence of her Empire and was in the midst of putting down a dangerous rebellion in India
which demanded the use of all of her strength.

In the meantime, Britain saw the founding of the *Daily Telegraph*,
whose position on the Jewish Question was no different to what can be observed today. In its editorials, it raged against the Lords' reactionary position
of so many years standing:

The Tory aristocracy, the Tory hierarchy, have now been exhibited in their real characters; they are the most dangerous
and the most seditious classes in the country. The people, the
Commons, and the Crown are willing to work together, in order to dedicate a peace-offering of conciliatory legislation to a
long-persecuted sect; but a confederacy of earls and prelates,
who, like wizards haunting a pagan ruin, forbid the progress of
a timely and beneficent measure, and thus perpetuate an exas-
perating feud among the guardians of the Constitution...[255]

The anti-Jewish press was joyous at the new victory, explaining the
House of Lords decision as the only one possible and continuing to affirm
that the Jews were "'wayfarers and sojourners, as their fathers were" ...
Would conscientious Jews permit Christians to sit in their Sanhedrim and to
take part in the framing of Jewish laws and ordinances?'[256]

The *Morning Post* warned, justifiably, that the national effort to put
down the rebellion in India was much more important than satisfying the
ambition of a millionaire Jew and pitting one House against the other:

[T]here are at the present moment other subjects more worthy
of the attention of the good citizens of London than the claims
of Baron Rothschild and those of his co-religionists of the
Jewish nation... We therefore tell the citizens of London that,
at a crisis like the present, they may, and ought to, devote
themselves to objects more worthy of regard than the re-

---

[255] *Daily Telegraph*, 11/7/1857, 13/7/1857. Translator's note: QVOS (13/7/1857 issue).
[256] *Morning Post*, 11/7/1857. Translator's note: QVOS.

election of a rich Jew, and the perpetuation of a most unseem-
ly and most unnecessary contest between the two branches of
the Legislature.[257]

New battles for that year were not expected, especially given that it was
unlikely that Parliament would sit again. But extraordinary circumstances
necessitated a new summons at the end of autumn 1857. Nevertheless, Parliament only met in December. It had been envisaged that the only topic under discussion would be the economic crisis and how to deal with it, but in
the December 10 sitting, Lord John Russell took advantage of the occasion
to introduce a new bill in favor of the Jews, which, just as before, proposed
the substitution of the three oaths for a single one. The text was analogous to
the one which had been passed by the Commons in the spring of the same
year, but which had been defeated by the House of Lords; with the result that
the fateful words still remained in the oath, the words which, according to a
passage contained in the bill [Clause 5], the Jews would be able to leave out.

Sir Frederic Thesiger and Mr. Newdegate protested, but the first reading took place without any great setbacks and ended with a victory for
emancipation.[258] The second reading took place on 10 February 1858, likewise with no great debate, because Sir Frederic Thesiger tabled a motion
which proposed the exclusion of the passage intended for the Jews [Clause
5]. But he never got to make his case, because the bill was first put in front of
a committee.[259]

The final debate before Parliament was delayed by the fall of Palmerston's cabinet. Then the Conservative Party, led by Lord Derby, came to
power. In the beginning, the philo-Semites abandoned their hopes of soon
being able to reach their objectives, because only a few months earlier, Lord
Derby had been the head of the Jews' adversaries in the House of Lords. But
confidence returned when Lord Derby admitted some of the biggest supporters of the Jewish cause into his cabinet as ministers, among them Lord Stanley (his own son), Attorney-General Sir Fitzroy Kelly, and lastly Disraeli,
who had risen to become the Chancellor of the Exchequer and whom 'the
Tories now reluctantly and shamefacedly acknowledge for their chief in the
House of Commons.' These men had a lot of influence over Lord Derby, and
it was not long before he too showed no inclination towards a committed
stance on the issue.[260]

In view of this, on 18 March 1858, the House of Commons returned to
debating on the bill introduced by Lord John Russell which had still not been

---

[257] *Morning Post*, 21/7/1857, 22/7/1857, 29/7/1857. Translator's note: Quotation inserted
for perceived reader interest, reproduced verbatim from the 29/7/1857 *Morning Post* issue.

[258] *Hansard*, Volume 148, pp. 469-99.

[259] *Hansard*, Volume 148, pp. 1084-118.

[260] Campbell: Volume 8, pp. 199-200. Translator's note: QVOS.

dealt with. The longstanding great orator against the Jewish cause, Sir Frederic Thesiger, had ascended under the new government to the rank of Lord Chancellor, whereupon he was bestowed the title of Baron Chelmsford, and as such was no longer a member of Parliament, but a member of the House of Lords. In these difficult days of the final battle, the mission thus fell to Mr. Newdegate to lead the House of Commons' adversaries on his own. He thus tabled the amendment initially announced by Sir Frederic Thesiger in the previous session, which sought to remove Clause 5, the specific passage which would permit Jews to omit the Oath of Abjuration's final words.

In the course of the debates, it was quickly observed that the number of the Jews' adversaries had considerably diminished, as was confirmed at the division. Newdegate's motion was defeated by a large majority and shortly afterwards the second reading passed. The third reading, on 12 April, did not even bring a division worthy of mention.[261]

With incredible speed, the bill was sent up to the House of Lords. Evidently it was intended to capitalize on the sound defeat of the anti-Jewish faction, since already by the day after the third reading in the Commons, the bill was debated for the first time in the Lords. As in the majority of cases, on this occasion was there no attempt at any counter-argument during the first reading.[262]

The second reading was due to take place soon afterwards because the government did everything possible to accelerate it, and only a week later the much-anticipated debate took place amid great tension. The House of Lords awaited the debate with the greatest interest, and were particularly keen to see what Lord Derby's position would be. Lord Derby, with the general consensus of those present, stated that he would welcome the alteration of the 'obsolete and quite unnecessary' parts of the oaths to meet modern needs, but in terms of the Jewish Question, he felt compelled to stand firm in his long-held point of view, despite the contrary opinion of at least three of his colleagues in the other House, and he would 'certainly support any Motion which may be made for that omission of that clause which exempts persons of the Jewish persuasion from taking the oath which, by this Bill, is imposed upon the rest of Her Majesty's subjects.' From his speech, we also get the sense that he was desirous to have it known that his inexpedient contrarian stance was borne solely of the dictates of his conscience and his reason, which as a responsible statesman he was compelled to follow:

> I confess I much wish that I could say, honestly and conscientiously, that I had changed my opinion on this subject; because great inconvenience, to say the least, has resulted from the

---

[261] *Hansard*, Volume 149, pp. 294-305, 442, 466-550, 946.
[262] *Hansard*, Volume 149, p. 946.

protraction of this discussion. But, my Lords, not having changed my opinion, not having seen any reason to change it, not being satisfied of the validity of the grounds on which the admission of the Jews to Parliament is supported, and not seeing in the circumstances of the case any reason for changing my course while my opinions remain the same, it is with some regret, but, at the same time, without hesitation, that I am compelled to tell my noble and learned Friend, that for my part, I cannot this Session take a course different from that which I have pursued on former occasions.[263]

In the April 27 sitting, the man formerly known as Sir Frederic Thesiger, now Lord Chelmsford, took the floor. He pointed out that all of the reasons enumerated (the 'claims of the Jews') could not persuade him, the Englishman who had spent so long fighting against Jewish emancipation, to reject the evidence brought by the adversaries. He said that this was not a case of judging the matter based on a few exemplary Jewish individuals, but on the Jewish people as a whole, and declared:

I need scarcely assure your Lordships that I am influenced by no personal feeling—that I am actuated by no prejudice upon this question. I feel only an earnest desire to support a principle which I believe to be necessary to maintain in order to secure the welfare and even the character of this country.

His speech went on at length about how admission of the Jews—as Jews—would necessarily de-Christianize the Parliament, given that, with no test of Christianity to be exacted from every individual, members of Parliament could no longer be held to the moral standards of the Gospel, and Jews as a group were known to possess 'the most inveterate hostility to the Christian religion.'

He reminded his fellow Lords that the maintenance of the Christian religion was 'the most essential of our legislative functions' because it was through the Christian religion that the rulers of the nation were consecrated to their duties:

[A]nd what are those duties? Not merely the control and direction of matters of lowly worldly policy, of earthly power, or commercial property; but the eternal welfare of the people is committed to our legislative guardianship.

---

[263] *Hansard*, Volume 149, 1479. Translator's note: All QVOS.

For these and other reasons, Lord Chelmsford moved to omit Clause 5, the specific passage in the bill which authorized Jews to omit the fateful last words of the oath, and exhorted his colleagues not to be pressured, 'against our judgement and our consciences' by the House of Commons, which was threatening to create a constitutional crisis over the matter. He warned that such an act of submission, in a bid to maintain political stability, would 'leave us nothing more than a registry office for the decrees of the House of Commons'.[264]

Lord Lyndhurst protested, but he could not prevent the vote ending in favor of the opposition led by Lord Chelmsford.[265]

As always, it has been shown once again that, despite all of the propaganda and the influence of powerful circles, the majority of the population wanted nothing to do with the Jews: a sign of a healthy opinion and of the strong resistance from the English nation of that time against the foreign infiltration that threatened their existence.

In the first months of 1858, the vast majority of the native population continued to be against the Jews being admitted into Parliament, as is shown by the evidence of the petitions sent to the two legislative Houses by cities, districts, and private individuals. While around the time of the March 17 and 22 debates, numerous petitions arrived to Parliament that were against the Jewish bill, not a single one arrived that was in favor of the Hebrews.[266]

The populace's reactionary attitude was made even clearer during the debates that took place in the House of Lords, when Lord Lyndhurst, during his motion for a second reading, presented a single petition in favor of the Jews, while numerous individuals and some sixty cities, towns, and districts asked that Jewish exclusion be continued. There was an analogous situation on April 27, when the Earl of Granville likewise presented a single pro-Jewish petition. But the following day, the overwhelming majority made their voices heard, when against 50 pro-Jewish petitions containing 2,793 signatures, a total of 224 anti-Jewish petitions with 11,359 signatures freshly revealed the true will of the people.[267]

As usual, the *Times* was not very happy at the course of events, but we have no wish to reproduce more of their emotional outbursts here; rather, we will only discuss their polemics inasmuch as they touch on the arguments of the anti-Jewish faction. With ever more evidence, the anti-Jewish faction was proving in Parliament and in the press that the Jewish Question was not just a religious issue, but that it mostly concerned many other factors. There was a fear of the Jewish amorality that was reflected in their doctrines and

---

[264] *Hansard*, Volume 149, pp. 1758-68. Translator's note: All QVOS, and additional elements of the speech have been included for their perceived value to the reader.

[265] *Hansard*, Volume 149, pp. 1477-1486, 1758-1797, 2009.

[266] *Times*, 18/3/1858, 23/3/1858.

[267] *Times*, 23/4/1858, 26/4/1858. & *Times*, 27/4/1858. & *Hansard*, Volume 149, p. 1785.

literature. The Hebrews continued to be rejected because they were foreign to the national body. The *Times* was incensed by such reasoning and declared that these statements could not refer to modern Jews, who had not suffered these problems for a long time. It was, therefore, monstrous that the English nation was criticizing the Jewish race:

> But it is a fine thing for a *parvenu* nation like ourselves, barely a thousand years old, at this corner of the world, to find itself following in the path of obstinate old Pharaohs, big, insolent Philistines, Assyrians, Babylonians, Græco-Asiatic dynasties, Cæsars, and a thousand other Royal and Imperial persecutors. The persecution has always been of the wanton, capricious, and almost childish character; playing fast and loose with its victims, pampering, plundering, coaxing, insulting, giving a little line, and then pulling it up with a jerk ...[268]

It is somewhat eye-opening that the *Times*, then as now the leading newspaper of England, had the audacity to judge its own nation as inferior to that of the Jews.

Once more then the Upper House had become an insurmountable bulwark. According to the English constitution, the amended bill had to return to the Lower House, where it had to be expressly ratified in its new form. Lord Russell, in irascible statements, pointed out that the Commons could not approve the amended bill, because it continued to bar Jews from access to Parliament.

On May 13, the House of Commons also authorized for certain members—among whom Rothschild was again counted—to hold a conference with representatives from the House of Lords, in a bid to deal with the issue and in the hope of arriving at an agreement. What an affront to the members of the House of Lords! It is surprising then, that they approved the Commons proposition and promised to appoint their own corresponding committee.[269]

The conference was soon held, which was of course attended by Rothschild, and at which all of the various points of contention were covered. Seemingly, the members of the House of Lords promised that the matter would again soon be put to a debate and everything possible would be done to get the House of Lords to change their position. Indeed, on May 31, the Earl of Lucan presented his fellow lords with the brief Report of the Conference which requested the striking out of Clause 5 (the final oath words which were so fateful for the Jews). He stated that it was not necessary to take as evidence of public opinion the public petitions which campaigned

---

[268] *Times*, 18/3/1858, 23/3/1858. Translator's note: QVOS from the 18/3/1858 issue.
[269] *Hansard*, Volume 150, pp. 529, 530. & pp. 763-4.

against Jewish admission, as 'the number of these petitions was extremely small', but rather in his opinion the Lords should consider important that 'it was a fact beyond all dispute, that nearly the entire press of the country supported the policy of admitting Jews to a seat in the Legislature'.[270]

Up until recently, Lord Lucan had been one of the Jews' main adversaries in the House of Lords. It therefore was a source of painful consternation to see him, for no apparent reason, suddenly declare himself to be a supporter of the Jewish cause.

The House had still not got over its shock when another of the main members of the anti-Jewish faction, the Earl of Stanhope, likewise abandoned its ranks. In 1856 he had headed the House of Lords' opposition to the bill proposed by the MP Mr. Gibson. He attributed his conversion to 'the largely increased majority in the House of Commons in favor of the admission of Jews to Parliament. That majority had more than trebled in two years.' This for him was a much stronger sign than there being 'a majority in the country against the measure', a fact which was always assured by the Jews' adversaries and perhaps existing in reality, but never at all proven. In terms of the number of people in opposition, there did not exist, in his judgement, any sure way of measuring them; while the voting in Parliament was decisive. Admitting the Jews could not be anti-Christian, given that 'a considerable number of the right rev. prelates, among others, had shown themselves favorable to the admission of the Jews.' He also pointed out that 'a Jewish gentleman had within the last two years been unanimously elected to occupy the high office of the Lord Mayor of London' and that 'the heads of all the great parties of the State by turns partook of that gentleman's hospitality, and exchanged compliments and courtesies with him.' In view of the reasons given, he saw himself obliged to recommend that the Jews be admitted.[271]

We cannot rid ourselves of the impression that the Earl of Stanhope was himself one of those men who were invited to these lavish Jewish banquets and 'exchanged compliments and courtesies.' This event shows with full proof the soundness of the principle that, when it comes to the Jewish Question, no exceptions or limited allowances must be made, lest the principle be gradually and subtly undermined.

It was to be a day of surprises. Immediately after the Earl of Stanhope's speech ended, the Earl of Clancarty got up to speak. He had suddenly gone over to the anti-Jewish camp because, as he declared, in view of the fact that the Jewish Question had come to dominate the entirety of domestic political life, he had studied this issue in great detail. In his previous opinion, he had considered it unjust to deny the Jews certain rights as English citizens. But

---

[270] *Hansard*, Volume 150, 859, 1147. & pp. 1139-42. Translator's note: All QVOS.

[271] *Hansard*, Volume 150, pp. 1142-9. Translator's note: All QVOS.

now he harbored serious misgivings that it was appropriate for him to stand for their cause, and he went on to give the reasons for his change of heart:

> Let the claims of the latter be admitted upon the principle contended for by the House of Commons in their fourth Reason against your Amendment—namely, that 'the infliction of disabilities upon any class of Her Majesty's subjects solely on account of their conscientious adherence to their faith, savours of persecution'; and you must admit, also, the Mohammedan, the Hindoo, heathens of every denomination (millions of whom at this moment are dependent upon the kind of government Parliament may impose upon the Indian empire), and the professed infidel, who is commonly quite as bigoted in his own peculiar views as the most superstitious votary of any false system of religion. Religious tests of every kind must be abolished as qualifications for access to the great Council of the Nation, for they could be of no possible value.
>
> Nor could you consistently any longer require the Sovereign to make profession of a particular form of religion: the King has as good an abstract right to hold and profess what religious opinions he pleases, as have the King's counsellors: so that, upon the principle contended for by the Commons, in time future government and the guardianship of the rights of a people at present blest with the enjoyment of freedom beyond any other nation in the world, might fall into the hands of a Sovereign of any, or of no religion, and of a godless Parliament. [...]
>
> The House of Commons appears to have fallen into the error of regarding seats in Parliament and offices in the State as the inherent rights of British subjects intended for the individual benefit of the persons holding them. A participation in the government of this great country is, indeed, a great and distinguishing privilege; but it is still more to be regarded as a trust conferred for the benefit of the community [...]
>
> Looking back to Magna Charta, the Barons of Runnymede in that, the first charter, of British liberty, notice the Jews only as money-lenders. History does not record their ever having taken arms in the country's defence, or ever having taken part in, or sought admission to the national councils, they have ever been and sought so to keep themselves in every country where they are found, a nation apart, aliens from all around them in blood, in religion, and in social interests.

I believe, that the feeling among them generally is still the same, and certainly, but for the wishes and personal popularity of Baron Rothschild, backed by his enormous wealth and the great political weight of his family, we never should to this day have heard of the Jewish claims. I have not the honour of Baron Rothschild's acquaintance, but from all I have heard of him, I do not apprehend that if he should obtain his seat in Parliament his conduct would be other than that becoming a British legislator...

A man so highly esteemed is not likely to do discredit to the choice of his constituents, or to be disposed to damage that free constitution under the protection of which he has preferred to live; but his admission, as a Jew, to the Councils of the nation would be subversive of the great and essential principle of the constitution which connects the maintenance of the Christian religion with the general government of the country.

The Earl of Clancarty cleared recognized the tactic of the Jews, which was to separate the main question from the principle, and due to his understanding of the real Jewish intention, arrived at the reactionary attitude towards emancipation. He cautioned his fellow Lords against 'seeking popularity', as the Lower House had done, and instead reminded them of their 'higher mission as hereditary legislators' which made it more especially their duty to act as 'guardians of the constitution.' Then followed another sensational event.[272]

Lord Derby showed himself willing to come to a compromise in order to solve the problem. He considered that the moment had come to listen to the majority in the House of Commons, which meant that he was required to forgo his own opinion. He could only do this if he could count on the full support of the population at large, but he had seen that the mood of the country was one of indifference towards the Jewish Question. It was likely that the proposition made by Lord Lucan was a solution, which, nevertheless, he would have to examine very carefully. It seemed to him that the best course would be for Lord Lucan's ideas to be specified in a dedicated bill, which is why his recommendation was to maintain the current position until the time came for the proposition to be dealt with in greater detail.[273]

What a skillful maneuver by the Prime Minister! To all appearances, firmly determined to cede to Jewish aspirations, he wished to gradually ac-

---

[272] *Hansard*, Volume 150, pp. 1149-56. Translator's note: All quotations and quoted elements from Clancarty's speech are QVOS, and additional quotations have been inserted for their perceived historical interest.

[273] *Hansard*, Volume 150, p. 1156 ff.

climatize public opinion to his stance that was opposed in every sense to his previous one. In reality, he had already changed his point of view when he approved Lord Lucan's 'compromise' solution in principle, although he wanted to see it delayed, if only for a short while.

As Secretary of State Lord Malmesbury also shared the Prime Minister's point of view, it seemed that the majority was against the immediate commencement of debates around Lucan's proposition, which was why the latter withdrew it for the interim.

Lord Lyndhurst, the leader of the philo-Semites, gave a long speech in which he enumerated the compelling reasons which made Jewish admission a necessity. At the end, he asked for the House not to insist upon amendments to the bill already passed by the House of Commons, that is, he asked for the direct admission of Jews to Parliament.[274]

Against this bill the Lord Chancellor Lord Chelmsford protested most vehemently. He impartially analyzed the reasons expounded by the parliamentary committee for their decision and arrived at the conclusion that none of these reasons was sufficiently convincing to qualify the House of Lords' position as erroneous. The House of Lords then agreed to maintain their current position, but that 'a Committee [be] appointed to prepare Reasons to be offered to the Commons for the Lords insisting on their Amendments to the said Bill, to which the Commons disagree'.[275]

This agreement from the House of Lords, which seemed only provisional, was a true masterstroke of parliamentarianism: to accustom one's own ranks to the change in position, one gave the appearance of leaving things as they were. The new framing of the problem meant that valuable time was bought, which could then be used to apply pressure against the anti-Jews at a personal level, with the goal of thus winning ground for the final agreement. In any case, it was apparent that there was a desire to avoid any new debates on the issue, which could lead to hindrance or interruption of the procedures relating to the agreement in Parliament.

In the week which followed this sensational debate, two bills were introduced: one from Lord Lyndhurst and the other from Lord Lucan. The first proposed that the three oaths were substituted by one single oath, and that certain necessary accommodations be created for the Jews. The second, known as 'Lord Lucan's bill', pursued the same objective, authorizing both constituent Houses to allow a Jewish member to exclude the fateful final words and to give analogous authorization in any similar case.[276] But due to the absence of the Prime Minister, the debates on these two bills were postponed for the interim.

---

[274] *Hansard*, Volume 150, pp. 1177-1185.

[275] *Hansard*, Volume 150, p. 1185. Translator's note: QVOS.

[276] *Hansard*, Volume 150, p.1600. & pp. 1619-98.

On 1 July 1858, the anxiously-awaited debate took place in the House of Lords. The Prime Minister's definitive position continued to be publicly unknown. But this uncertainty soon disappeared when he became the first person to take the floor in the debate. After a brief listing of the numerous bills that had not merited approval from the Upper House, he declared that he had not changed his opinion in the slightest. Nevertheless, it was necessary to end the prevailing conflict between both Houses, which threatened to gravely imperil the entire political system. It was only because of this threat that he felt compelled to lend his support to one of the bills, which was why he stated his preference as being that of Lord Lucan.[277]

Although the Prime Minister's position had long seemed uncertain, the Chamber was surprised by his statement. Lord Lucan, who supported his bill energetically, expressed that, in his judgement, the overarching mood in the country was one of the most perfect apathy and indifference to the admission of Jews to Parliament, for which reason the House of Lords could use their own judgement to decide what was best for the country.[278]

Of the anti-Jewish faction, it was the Earl of Clancarty who was the first to take the floor. He first of all reproached the Prime Minister for having 'changed his colors' to favor the Jews:

> My noble and gallant Friend was the first to go over—he was the last from whom I should have apprehended such an example. I had always regarded him as a man of great determination, and from the gallant profession he belongs to, the least likely to have entertained a thought of yielding or turning; but I am bound to say that in announcing his change my noble Friend did state what at once disentitled the opponents of the Jewish claims any longer to expect his co-operation; nay, he showed conclusively that his vote should always have been given on the other side.[279]

What he found most regrettable was that Lord Derby had not hesitated in declaring that his stance on the issue would remain unchanged, but that he had only surrendered out of expediency. A compromise on one of the greatest principles of the constitution! Inconceivable, for principles will tolerate no compromise and will never change!

Lord Berners equally rejected a compromise on such an important matter of principle. If the principle was shattered, the danger which he apprehended "was not a collision with the House of Commons, but with the

---

[277] *Hansard*, Volume 151, p. 693.

[278] *Hansard*, Volume 151, pp. 702-704.

[279] *Hansard*, Volume 151, pp. 704-713. Translator's note: QVOS.

Crown itself, should once a Radical Prime Minister accede to office, and create a Jew Member of their Lordships' House." And a Jew in the House of Lords would mean that, from that point on, "neither their Lordships' House nor the monarchy would be longer safe".[280]

The Duke of Cleveland and the Earl of Granville declared themselves in favor of the compromise, while the Duke of Rutland declared that, despite unproven claims to the contrary, the majority House of Commons' opinion on this matter 'was no accurate test of the real desire of the country' and that Jewish emancipation would be 'repugnant to...the best interest of the people of England.' For this reason alone, the compromise had to be rejected.[281]

The Bishop of Oxford and the Viscount of Dungannon both declared that in many respects they would prefer a Muslim to a Jew, as they saw the Muslim as closer to the Christian faith. In the words of the Bishop, which were seconded by the Viscount: 'The Jew declared that the Central Point of the Christian faith was an imposter, and the Mohammedan at least, admitted our Savior to have been the second of Prophets'.[282] But this time all of the opposition's efforts were in vain, even in the House of Lords. For the first time, the philo-Semites triumphed, with 143 votes to 97. The *volte-face* of the Prime Minister had clearly taken its toll.

It was decided to advance Lord Lucan's bill to a second reading and refer it to a Committee of the Whole House on the following Monday. The Committee added two further paragraphs; according to the first, the Jews were to continue to be excluded from, among other things, regency control, and the positions of Lord Chancellor and Lord Lieutenant of Ireland. The second prohibition, that of Lord Chancellor, is still in force and its content is that the right to represent the prebends of the Church passes to the Archbishop of Canterbury as soon as this enters the radius of any office held by a Jew in the Crown's domain.[283]

The bill, thus amended, passed to the third reading in the House of Lords on July 12. The opposition did not appear to be disheartened in the slightest. This time, it was the Earl of Harrington who distinguished himself as the most impassioned orator of the anti-Jewish faction:

> My next reason for opposing the admission of Jews into our Parliament is, that they are the great money-lenders—the great loan contractors of the world. It may be said that they do lend to all alike, that they are more free-traders in money. Yes; it matters not to them whether they lend their money to support

[280] *Hansard*, Volume 151, p. 713. Translator's note: QVOS.

[281] *Hansard*, Volume 151, p. 715. & p. 717. Translator's note: QVOS.

[282] *Hansard*, Volume 151, p. 725. & p. 721. Translator's note: QVOS.

[283] *Hansard*, Volume 151, pp. 726-30. Translator's note: Note that this vote took place Thursday, July 1, so the next stage was voted to take place only two working days later.

a good or a bad cause; to support liberty or despotism; to further the great ends of their own country, or to lend their money to a nation directly opposed to it.

Hence it follows, that the despotic nations of the world, now unfortunately in the ascendant, are enabled to keep up large standing armies in times of peace, and to make other nations, and to make England do so likewise, because they do well know, that when the occasion requires it, either to put down the rising spirit of reform in their own countries, or to act against other states, they can call on these loan contractors for the sinews of war. The consequence is, that the nations of the world are groaning under heavy systems of taxation, and of national debts [...]

It may be said, why persecute the many on account of the misdeeds of the few? Why persecute the whole Jewish race, some 30,000 in this country, on account of certain loan contractors, who have lent, or may lend, their money to despots—who make use of this Jew wealth to destroy the liberties of Poland, Germany, Hungary, Italy, or other nations? Why, for the reasons just stated, and because 'the many' are the great contributors—not only here, but in every other country to these loans, and but for their contributions, these loans would with difficulty be carried out.

Besides, these *millionaires,* these loan contractors, are the very men who would stand on your public hustings and make their impassioned, their sweet orations in favour of public liberty —whereas, they have ever been the greatest enemies to freedom. Why, I would ask, and for what have they been ennobled? Is it, or is it not, for having lent their gold to despots? My Lords, these loan contractors are the pets, the Poloniuses of arbitrary Courts.

He then went on to analyze the reason why Jews had been elected in some electoral districts, and why, with what had already been seen of events, the Hebrews could not be trusted:

Yes, but the constituencies are not Jews—they would not elect these loan contractors. My Lords, I would not trust them. I do well remember that some few years back, it was in 1853, not less than sixty constituencies were accused of corruption, and as many election committees sat for months investigating these matters, and by their investigations pointing out certain remedies for the future. Above thirty of these constituencies were found guilty. Would you then again open the flood gates of corruption?

My Lords, I contend that a loan contractor, be he Christian or be he Jew, who would lend his money to support despotism, would not deserve the proud honour of a seat in the House of Commons. My Lords, I would rather see a good Mohammedan, or Hindoo, sitting in the House of Commons, than I would a Jew loan contractor. In point of fact, would it not be far more natural, more just, that 180,000,000 of British subjects should have a representative in the House of Commons, to point out how the tax screw pauperises and tortures...than that a few Jews should have their representatives there? Why there never was a few men in any great State who possessed such a mighty influence as these Jews do here at this moment. Have they not a considerable body of this House voting for them? Have they not a majority in the House of Commons? Add to this a portion of the Press—the most powerful political engine that ever existed, all supporting them. (*Hear!*) Yes, but there is a power still stronger than all these combined, and that power is the moral and religious people of this country, who, however seemingly apathetic, are decidedly opposed to the admission of Jews into Parliament.[284]

He saw himself obliged once more to warn against the Jews, who had forced all of the nations to take on huge national debts, under the heavy yoke of which the entire world suffered greatly. For all of these reasons, the Hebrews did not deserve for their power to be increased still further with their admission to Parliament.

In a bid to counter such strong statements, Lord Derby replied that there were also Christian usurers.[285]

The Earl of Harrington responded that he had long predicted the regrettable result of all of these parliamentary battles. 'He, however, ventured to remind the noble Earl [the Earl of Derby], and the House, that during the last Crimean war, large sums of money were sent by Jews and others from this country to Holland, as contributions to a Russian loan.' This loan was then used by Russia, England's bitterest enemy, to aid in prolonging the war against England and her allies. 'An Act was subsequently passed, making it a misdemeanor for any British subject to subscribe to a loan raised by the

---

[284] *Hansard*: Volume 151, p. 1261 ff. Translator's note: QVOS.
[285] *Hansard*, Volume 151, p. 1264.

enemy. Could then, the loan contractor, the head and front of the offending party, be deemed a proper subject to sit in Parliament?'[286]

There followed an equally rousing speech from the Earl of Galloway. He 'foresaw that the time might not be far distant when a profligate Prime Minister of this country might receive a large bribe for recommending the creation of a Jewish peer.' Galloway was sufficiently astute to pre-empt the predictable argument from the other side that this would not be possible:

> It might be said upon the other hand that the House [of Lords] would have the power of rejecting such a peer; but it was by a very small majority indeed that the Jews had been excluded from the House, and when he recalled to mind how many peers might be added to that House in a few years, he could picture the creation of a number of peers, sufficient to vote for the admission of Jews, the Minister for the time being recommending it, so that the House might be inundated with admissions of that description.[287]

All efforts were once again futile. The third reading also won a majority, with which the Jews had practically won the fight.

As it is not easy to comprehend the situation in its entirety, the following brief summary may be instructive:

As is known, the House of Commons first passed a bill which provided for the exclusion of the oath words which were impossible for the Jews, but it was rejected by the House of Lords, who amended the bill to ensure that the most crucial excluded words were reinserted. According to the constitution, the bill had to be approved by the Commons in this new, amended format. A House of Commons committee rejected this supplementary text with the well-known nine points and argued their various objections with representatives from the House of Lords. The issue was left in paralysis by the bill which had meanwhile been passed by the House of Lords [Lord Lucan's bill], because the attention of both Houses was now focused on the aforementioned events taking place in the House of Lords. After it had been passed by the Lords, the Commons now had to deal with the new bill as well as deal with the previous amended bill, and then have it approved by the House of Lords. An unexpected twist: the House of Lords had not withdrawn their protest against the first bill, but continued to insist that the essential final words of the oath be included.[288]

---

[286] *Hansard*, Volume 151, p. 1264. Translator's note: QVOS.

[287] *Hansard*, Volume 151, p. 1265. Translator's note: QVOS.

[288] *Hansard*, Volume 151, pp. 1243-1257.

With astonishing speed, the House of Commons began the debates on the two bills.

On 16 July 1858, that is, four days after the approval of Lord Lucan's bill in the House of Lords, the Jewish Question was once more back on the Order Paper of the Commons Chamber. Lord John Russell was first to introduce a motion to propose that the House proceed to the second reading of Lord Lucan's bill. That day must surely have been the greatest of his parliamentary career, for he had finally achieved the goal that he had pursued with such tenacity: the admission of the Jews to Parliament. It was beyond doubt that the Commons would likewise reach the majority necessary to pass the bill that had already been passed in the House of Lords. Nevertheless, the anti-Jewish faction put up a defense until the very last.

The main burden of the struggle was borne on Mr. Newdegate's shoulders. He took the floor as soon as Lord John Russell's motion was presented:

> I desire not to speak disrespectfully to this House when I say that I am firmly convinced—more firmly convinced perhaps than I have ever been—that those who advocate the admission of the Jews to Parliament do not truly represent the feelings of the people of this country; I say this because, that since it has been felt that this change in the law is now, I fear, inevitable, I have seen no indications of satisfaction on the part of the people in whose name the change has been urged. I therefore feel entitled to assume that the measure has been forced upon the country; for, so far as I can observe, the only feeling which the probability of its passing has caused throughout the kingdom is one of disappointment, enhanced, perhaps, by the fact that the proposed change is to be effected by the powerful aid of one from whom such a measure was little to be expected. Hon. Members opposite can show me no demonstrations of satisfaction to prove that, in seeking to abrogate the Christian character of Parliament, they are acting thoroughly in accordance with public opinion. [...]
>
> I can regard this as no settlement whatever. It marks our first entrance upon a new phase of political existence for the country. It is the first step in a course which I myself view with the greatest apprehension; and I very much doubt whether many hon. gentlemen on the other side have weighed the extent of the change which they are about to effect; but of this I am confident, that wherever in a State this principle has been introduced, wherever a State that was Christian by its constitution has ceased to be so, the freedom of that State has not been

long maintained; and I challenge hon. gentlemen to produce me an instance to the contrary.[289]

The honorable member Mr. Spooner supported Mr. Newdegate and added, among other points, that up until the July of that session, there had been only two petitions before the House in favor of Jewish admission, and those petitions had contained two signatures, whereas there had been 250 petitions received that were against the measure, and these were signed by a total of 11,808 persons.[290]

But all resistance was in vain: the second reading of Lord Lucan's bill was approved by 156 votes to 65.

The third reading of the bill, which took place on 21 July 1858, could not now yield an uncertain outcome, although once more during the event the anti-Jewish camp defended their position with the fortitude of brave men making their last stand. Mr. Warren reminded the House that the 'admission of Jews into the Legislature is opposed to public opinion and the wishes of the people, which ought to be distinctly ascertained by means of a general election before taking a step so seriously affecting the constitution of the Legislature.' He also pointed out that the petitions received during that session up until the day of his speech regarding Jewish emancipation showed a total of 14,500 petitioners against the bill, with those in favor 'only between 300 and 400', obvious proof of the true opinion of the people. He did not harbor the least doubt that if the bill became law, it would be 'derogatory to the dignity of this House... [T]he usual organs will announce to the country and the world at large that the result was received with vehement cheering; but from that moment I believe will date the decline of the moral and religious influence of the House of Commons'.[291]

Newdegate again got up to speak, and used this final juncture to make a personal *j'accuse* against another member of the House, whose covert actions Newdegate had evidently been observing for some time:

> I do not defend the conduct of Lord Derby, who has agreed to a measure contrary to his principles, because I think he ought to have appealed to the country. I see, in the form of this measure, that it is the intention of its framers to give this House time to reflect, which, in reality, is a recognition of the fact that the country ought to have been appealed to. I cannot say anything in condemnation of the principle of this Bill, and

---

[289] *Hansard*, Volume 151, p. 1615 ff. Translator's note: QVOS, with the second paragraph inserted for its historical interest.

[290] *Hansard*, Volume 151, p. 1620.

[291] *Hansard*: Volume 151, 1889. Translator's note: All QVOS. Warren's speech also lets it be known that Baron Rothschild is watching proceedings from the Peers' Gallery.

of its tendency to destroy the Christian character of this House, that I have not already ventured to state; but when the conduct of Lord Derby is assailed, I cannot bear all the imputations which are heaped upon him, without calling attention to the difficulties of his position.

Now, who has been the main promoter of this infraction of the Christian character of Parliament on this side of the House? Why, the Chancellor of the Exchequer [Disraeli]. We know that the Chancellor of the Exchequer—himself of Jewish extraction—fosters towards the Jewish race feelings which one can trace in almost every work of fiction which he has written. Especially do we find that feeling honestly and frankly declared in the chapter which he has interpolated in his biography of Lord George Bentinck. He claims as the right of the Jewish race the government of the other races of mankind, and claims for them this supremacy, whilst they remain in the present state of rebellion against their own true King...

When, therefore, I see sitting on these benches, and taking a leading part among the members of this party, one holding these opinions, who has declared them, and uses his influence to carry them into effect, I will not hear Lord Derby's difficulties underrated in regard to this question. I have seen several leading Members of the Conservative Party brought over to his opinions by the Chancellor of the Exchequer. And when the noble Lord at the head of the India Board seceded from his noble father's opinions on this question, and joined the Chancellor of the Exchequer, I felt that Lord Derby's position, sooner or later, might become intolerable, and that there was great danger that by degrees he would be forced from the high position which he has held for many years, as leader of the great party whose pride it still is to be the defenders of the Christian character of Parliament and of the State.

In my anger I will have justice—I will not hear Lord Derby's difficulties undervalued; and although I lament that he has succumbed, I see in this a manifestation of a weakness, which is natural, however much it is to be deplored.[292]

But not even this new warning from Newdegate about the Jews' real intentions was enough to impede the bill being passed. With 129 votes to 55, the

---

[292] *Hansard*, Volume 151, p. 1895. Translator's note: QVOS. Interestingly, Newdegate then goes to expound at length his belief in a Jesuit plot to undermine the Revolution of 1688, using Liberalism (in his words, 'pseudo-Liberalism') as its revolutionary vanguard.

adversaries of the Jews were finally vanquished. Thus ended the last battle for Jewish emancipation.

Judah Has Triumphed

Immediately after the division, Lord John Russell stood up and reminded the House that the previous bill still had to be dealt with, according to which the Lords called for the final oath words, so injurious to Jewish interests, to remain in the oath:

> The Lords had sent down the general Reasons which moved them to exclude the Jews from Parliament in any case whatever, but had accompanied those Reasons by another Bill which provided for the admission of Jews. Of course, that being so, it was unnecessary for this House to resist the Lords' Amendments, because their Lordships had departed from their own Reasons.

Therefore, in view of such a contradiction, it was sufficient for the House to considered the matter settled and to proceed from this position.[293]

The MP Spooner similarly opined that the Lords' objections now no longer had a point to them and proposed a motion that Lord Russell's motion to the House be supplemented with the words 'that said Bill being in direct contravention to the clear and cogent reasons assigned by their Lordships against the enactments of such Bill [the admission of the Jews to Parliament]'.[294] But Mr. Spooner's motion was rejected. It was likely that there was no desire on Parliament's part to highlight the esteemed Lords' indignity at having put themselves in this self-contradictory position.

Parliament then came to the resolution that 'this house does not consider it necessary to examine the Reasons offered by the Lords for insisting upon the exclusion of Jews from Parliament, as by a Bill of the present Session, intitled "An Act to provide for the Relief of Her Majesty's Subjects professing the Jewish Religion," their Lordships have provided means for the admission of persons professing the Jewish Religion to Seats in the Legislature'.[295] The content of the resolution was practically the same as Mr. Spooner's motion, except that it did not make the contradiction in the Lords' actions so obvious.

---

[293] *Hansard*, Volume 151, p. 1902. Translator's note: QVOS.
[294] *Hansard*, Volume 151, p. 1903. Translator's note: QVOS.
[295] *Hansard*, Volume 151, pp. 1905-6. Translator's note: QVOS.

With this decision, it was possible to put an end to the 28-year battle between the Jews and their adversaries. On 23 July 1858, the Queen gave the Royal Assent to Lord Lucan's bill, which thus brought it into law.[296]

A few days later, Rothschild presented himself at Parliament and was sworn in, thus becoming, for the first time, a legal member of the House with full parliamentary rights.

As the reader will remember, July 16 saw the second reading of Lord Lucan's bill, which was the decisive reading for most bills. The Jews' adversaries realized at that point that the battle was, to all intents and purposes, lost. As a last resort there was nothing left but an appeal to Queen Victoria, who had to give the Royal Assent to the bill that would soon be passed. According to the old English constitution, every Englishman had a right to beseech the Queen to deny the Royal Assent.

For this reason, on July 19 a number of barristers addressed the following carefully-worded petition to the Queen:

> To Her Most Gracious Majesty the Queen.
> The humble Petition of the Members of the English Bar
> whose names are underwritten:
> Sheweth,
> That, because Christianity is interwoven with the laws of England, and because every Jew who has a sincere attachment to the faith of his forefathers must be averse to Christianity; we consider that a Jew cannot be a fit Legislator for the Realm of which Your Majesty, by the Grace of God, is Queen: and therefore humbly pray Your Majesty to withhold the Royal Assent from a Bill introduced into the House of Lords with a view of admitting Jews to sit in Parliament.

The petition was deposited in the Post Office so early on the morning of Tuesday, July 20, that, if duly delivered, it must have been received at the Home Office before the start of business on the same day.[297]

The English authorities were (and are still today) known as people who to least acknowledge receipt of a document on the day it is received. But in contravention of this general rule, the petitioners were only notified on the 23rd of July that 'any Petition to The Queen respectfully and properly worded, which is transmitted to this Office, will be laid before Her Majesty'.[298] As a consequence, the response, or better said the rejection letter, arrived the very day that the Royal Assent was being given to the Jewish bill.

---

[296] *Hansard*, Volume 151, p. 1967.
[297] Edison: *The Question*, pp. 14-15. Translator's note: Petition QVOS.
[298] Edison: *The Question*, p. 17. Translator's note: QVOS.

Edison rightly notes that it is extraordinary that the petitioners—barristers by profession and so experts in such matters—would not have chosen the correct form.[299] Furthermore, in any case, one would have been able to expect that the petitioners were notified by July 21 at the very latest. The petitioners could then have asked a Peer to pass the petition directly to the Queen during an audience. The necessary back-up measures would have already been taken in the eventuality of the Home Office presenting difficulties. Undoubtedly, among the highest-born aristocrats, they would have found at least one lord who was perfectly willing to make use of his right, as a hereditary counsellor of the Crown, to present the petition to the Queen by July 22 at the latest. With an immediate response, the matter of the petition's wording could have been cleared up in a timely manner by personal interview, and that the corresponding changes made.

In view of what happened, one cannot but get the impression that the intention was to stop, by whatever means necessary, the petition being presented to the Queen before she could give the Royal Assent; otherwise there is no explanation for the fact that the Home Office waited until the day that the bill was made law to give a response, especially because this response was a refusal to process the document for supposed wording issues.

The 28-year battle for Jewish emancipation was over. How dishonorably had the anti-Jewish resistance been demolished! But before giving our opinion on this event, we must first see what the press had to say. Specifically in the last months leading up to emancipation, the *Morning Post* had directed its fire most bitterly against the Jews, whom it continued to see as an existential threat to English life: 'Civil and religious liberty,' it emphasized, 'has nothing to do with this matter, but Mammon worship undoubtedly has'.[300]

Regarding the earlier stages of the political battle, we have often seen the *Morning Post*'s opinion of the House of Lord's position, which it applauded every time the House of Lords repulsed a Jewish attack. But as indicated by the following excerpt [reproduced verbatim] from the 14 June 1858 issue, the *Morning Post* had run out of sympathy:

> [T]he House of Lords, by the policy which it has pursued, has placed itself in a most extraordinary and discreditable position. Yielding to the pressure of the House of Commons, it has passed Lord Lucan's measure, and yet it has carried, by a considerable majority, reasons for disagreeing to the first Jew Bill, which, if they mean anything at all, mean that the Jew, as an

---

[299] Edison: *The Question*, p. 15 ff.
[300] *Morning Post*, 11/3, 18/3, 19/4, 23/4, 28/4, 29/4, 12/5, 2/7, 6/7, 14/7. Translator's note: QVOS from the 18/3 issue.

impugner of the Christian faith, ought to take no part in the legislation of a Christian country. [...]

If their lordships' reasons be valid, the measure which they have sanctioned must be altogether inexpedient and unnecessary. But the surrender of a high duty which the Lords have made, as well as the transparently inconsistent nature of their proceedings, fully justifies Lord John Russell in saying that the House of Commons possesses a paramount power in the State. [...]

[W]e cannot conceive anything more damaging to the independence and character of the House of Lords than a proceeding which declares on the part of their lordships a cowardly submission to expediency, not to say pressure, and at the same time seeks to gratify a foregone and determinate conclusion by reasons which, if they are worth anything, demonstrate that their conclusion is utterly and hopelessly inconsistent and indefensible. [...]

Five-and-twenty years ago the Lords gave way on the subject of the Reform Bill, at a time when the alternative was a swamping of the peerage or a revolution. In this present instance their lordships have given way to the threats of the Commons, and they have done more—they have exhibited a degree of cowardly subserviency which has only rendered more clear and more emphatic the reasons by which they have supported their conclusion that members of the Jewish nation ought not to sit in a Christian Legislature. A precedent has therefore been set, which, we regret to say, may to-morrow be effectually invoked for the purpose of ignoring the independent discretion and free action of the House of Lords.

And in an article of July 6, it once more unleashed its full fury at the course of events:

The House of Commons, when this Bill is passed, may resolve that Baron Rothschild be seated, and he will be seated accordingly. Then we shall see the spectacle of a man who loathes and derides the Christian religion, who rejects and scorns the claims of that Divine Being whose incarnation is the keystone of all Christian hope, and who, by the tradition of his fathers, is bound to regard the Gentile world as a race of dogs, and Christians as something worse, sitting in a professedly Christian assembly, making laws affecting Christianity, affecting the Church, her ministers, and her lay rights; and we shall have Lord John Russell looking complacently on and declaring it to be the legitimate and proper development of the English Constitution. Verily this is progress! And progress at the hands of a Conservative Ministry and by its aid.

Never was anything more unaccountable than the energy which the Conservatives have shown in passing Whig measures, and foregoing all that they have hitherto held and taught as essential to the safety of the country and the preservation of honest legislation.

In the course of its short existence, the youthful *Daily Telegraph* had become one of the main cheerleaders in the fight for the Jewish cause. In March 1858, when its perspective was still not too refined, it directed its ire mainly at Mr. Newdegate. According to an editorial of the March 24 issue [excerpt reproduced QVOS]: 'It is not fit that Mr. Newdegate, who is intellectually unworthy to occupy a seat in Parliament, should be beaten every year in order that an inferior section in an inferior House should gain a victory.' When the probability of victory began to lean more and more towards the side of the Jews, the *Daily Telegraph* continued pouring mockery on Newdegate, while at the same time lionizing the Jewish race. It exclaimed triumphantly:

The ten years' debate is concluded; the Peers have yielded to the Commons; Mr. Newdegate, unless his sincerity should induce him to resign, will be compelled to sit under the same roof with Baron Rothschild; and Lord Chelmsford, from the elevation of the woolsack itself, will, in powerless exasperation, witness the entrance of a Jew into the British Parliament ...

[T]here is no imaginable reason why a Jewish member of Parliament should not serve his country with quite as much distinction, and with far more sincerity, than many a leading Whig or thoroughbred Tory. It is not for the Conservatives, at any rate, to disparage the intellect that warms the blood of the Hebrew nation...

No one can pretend to be ignorant that Mr. Disraeli is Jewish to the inmost fibre of his frame, that he was born a Jew, that he was consecrated as a Jew, that he is a Jew in spite of recantation. At all events, he belongs to the people whom Mr. Newde-gate holds to be accursed; and yet Conservatism follows his lead, because its own mind has been exhausted, and because he can supply the mental and intellectual deficiencies of his party...

> [B]ut, at all times, the Jewish mind has been one of supe-
> rior business capacity—large, firm, quick-sighted, and reten-
> tive; these have been its intellectual traditions for hundreds of
> years...[301]

The *Daily News* and the *Spectator* wallowed, as they say, in praise for what had been achieved. Surely soon there would also be a Jewish Peer in the House of Lords. For the actions of the Lords, the people who had made the triumph possible, they only had words of disdain, and these were directed at the Lords' contradictory behavior.[302]

The *Times*, naturally, applauded the course of events, but felt nothing but contempt for the Lords' and the Conservative government's conduct. In its opinion, 'for the promotion of any Liberal measure, a Whig ought to be in opposition, a Conservative in office.' But no article better reflected the *Times*' scorn for the Lords than its editorial of July 21:[303]

> [T]he best-bred gentlemen in the world have, in Parliament as-
> sembled, just committed a *gaucherie* of the grossest descrip-
> tion. Twenty Jews dressed in full gabardines, and swearing by
> Moses, could not have inflicted so staggering a blow to the
> dignity of our House of Lords as that House has in its blind-
> ness dealt itself. The Lords have spoken brave words, and
> have eaten the leek. They have emancipated the Jews, and
> have favoured the House of Commons with certain 'Reasons'
> why they ever had refused and ever would refuse to emanci-
> pate them. They have not yielded with a protest; they have not
> said, with a certain lordly scorn, 'Well, well, let these clamor-
> ous Commons have their own way; it is scarcely decorous for
> us to contend longer with them,' but they have themselves ini-
> tiated the thing they abhor.
>
> The Jew Bill is a Lord's Bill—volunteered by the Lords—
> passed by the Lords. The position of Lord Derby and his Peers
> is not that of the tolerant Mussulman who allows a Christian to
> eat pig in his presence, merely holding his own nose and turn-
> ing away his eyes from the abomination. Their act is that of
> the obsequious Moslem who goes and fetches the pork, offer-
> ing it to his Christian master, but crying out all the time that
> the Prophet will terribly punish all who eat pork. 'Never,' say
> the House of Lords, 'will we pass the Oaths Bill, because the

---

[301] *Daily Telegraph*, 11/5, 15/5, 2/7, 3/7. Translator's note: QVOS from the 3/7 issue.
[302] *Daily News*, 11/5, 1/6, 2/7; *Spectator*, 1/5, 15/5, 5/6, 3/7.
[303] *Times*, 11/6, 14/6. Translator's note: QVOS from the 11/6 issue.

Jews always were excluded, because exclusion from seats in Parliament on the ground of religious opinion is a principle, because the Jewish disbelief constitutes a moral unfitness to take part in legislation, and because we have always shown a firm adherence to the principle of keeping Parliament an exclusively Christian assembly. We can't do it—it is impossible.'

'But, while we are discussing Parliamentary matters, here is a Bill which we have passed, and which we should be glad if you will consent to. It is called "A Bill for the Relief of Her Majesty's Subjects professing the Jewish Religion." It is to enable the Jews to sit in either House of Parliament.' Anybody who can read may see that this is a fair abstract of the Lords' 'Reasons' and of the Lords' Jew Bill. What can be said to such implacable talkers and to such docile actors? [...]

Had the Lords held out for five years longer they would not have done their Order so much harm as they have by the manner of this surrender. We English have a great admiration for dignity, but we have a very critical eye for the article. We have, moreover, a strong sense of the ridiculous; and surely nothing can be more ridiculous than presenting your sword hilt and at the same moment shouting out 'No surrender!' Unfortunately, they have acted under the counsels of some who seem to think that it is not inconsistent with the true dignity of English gentlemen to say one thing and to do another ...

Undoubtedly, the Jews' success in 1858 has to be attributed mainly to two men: Disraeli and Lord Derby. For this reason, we are going to take a look at what the press thought of these two figures.

When, as it seemed, the Jews had been newly defeated in the spring of 1858, the philo-Semitic press solely blamed Disraeli for the fiasco. The *Spectator* of May 1 reproached him with the following:

So little has Mr. Disraeli done for the measure which he has professed to support alike on the score of his race and of his judgement.

Similarly, the *Times* of April 28 found only the bitterest words for him:

For the conduct of Lord Derby and the Lord Chancellor [Lord Chelmsford] the country might have been prepared; but what we have reason to complain of is the weakness and political cowardice of another member of the Cabinet. Mr. Disraeli has identified himself with the cause of Jewish emancipation. He has written on the Jewish race; he has not only apologized for them, but he has glorified them above all races. If there is any point on which he might be supposed sincere, it is the deliverance of the burden which persecution formerly laid on them; and never had any man so fair an opportunity of accomplishing a great work ...

What a change of tune from the same newspaper two months later! They did not only congratulate Disraeli for the triumph, but they also applauded him as 'a politician of genius.' It is not necessary, of course, that we linger on this *volte-face*, because even for a newspaper like the *Times* it must have been somewhat unprecedented to go from branding someone a 'coward' to a few weeks later lauding him as 'a politician of genius'.[304]

On the other hand, the totality of the press—of both supporters and adversaries—showed itself to be quite of one mind, notwithstanding the notable exceptions of the *Daily News* and the *Times*, regarding the conduct of Lord Derby. We do not wish to reproduce here the judgements of the newspapers which had been anti-Jewish up until then, except to say that it is to be understood that the most serious accusations were made against him. We will discuss rather the viewpoints of the philo-Semitic camp, which had every reason to be grateful to him. But on the contrary, they only expressed scorn for this archetype of the parliamentary system, and they gave him what he deserved.[305]

The *Daily Telegraph* made every effort imaginable to expose him to public contempt; in its article of July 2 it hurled its most vitriolic abuse:

> Lord Derby did penance last night, with his neck in the Liberal halter, and with the worst grace conceivable acquiesced in a compromise on the Oath's question. Never, perhaps, did a Minister of the Crown stand so humbled in the presence of the Legislature and of public opinion. He was in truth retracting the policy of a life-time, avowedly deserting a principle he holds sacred to keep his party in office—creating a schism among his followers in order to pacify his opponents—digesting, in fact, the bitterest mortification for the sake of overcoming a political difficulty. While he was in the attitude of contrition—while he was stifling his pride—while he was doing that which made the elders of the Conservative peerage

---

[304] *Times*, 3/7/1858. Translator's note: The quoted term 'a politician of genius' is as it appears in the original article.
[305] *Daily News*, 2/7/1858; *Times*, 2/7/1858.

ashamed of their leader, he might surely have adopted a less
pitiable evasion than Lord Lucan's bill [...]

For ten years Lord Derby opposed the admission of
Jews, and was supported by his party; Mr. Newdegate was not
more vehement; and again and again Parliament was implored
not to challenge the divine wrath by forsaking the principle
that righteousness exalteth a nation. But now, the loaves and
fishes have worked a miracle, and the head of the House of
Stanley appears like a heretic in buckram who has been terrified into orthodoxy, with the penitential bill in one hand and
his reasons for accepting it in the other—with Lord John Russell's maxims sealed to his forehead, and Lord Chelmsford's
appeals lying at his feet, preparatory to being burned by the
common hangman. So passes away the glory of Conservatism ...

This brief summary of the main press opinion renders our critique of
the last battles and the defeat quite redundant. We have hardly anything to
add to the judgement on Lord Derby. What an irony of history, that it was he
of all people, after so many years of being at the front of the fight against the
Jews, who was the one that at the decisive moment helped them to victory,
after a few months before he had repelled their attacks by sticking to his
principles. Even during the days that he turned his coat, he continued to hold
fast to his principles, according to his own words. How could he then do
something that was contrary to them in every way? The explanation can only
be that, as the archetype of the parliamentary politician, he could no longer
keep track of his contradictory maneuvering.

Perhaps his reasoning can be explained from the perspective of a desire
to keep his position at all costs, or because pressure had been exerted on him
by the Jews or the Jews' supporters. Disraeli was part of his cabinet, as during that period he had risen to become the leader of the Conservatives, so he
would have been able to undermine the ancient bastion against Judaism from
the inside. It was not for nothing that some newspapers wrote that the Conservative Party had had to surrender itself to a Jew, in order to get new ideas.
In these bitter words there is a lot of truth, because it is only this way that it
has come to be possible that within the English Conservative Party today one
finds theories that can only be Jewish in origin.

We have still to discuss in depth the subject of Disraeli the man. Only
one thing needs to be said before we do this, and that is, that nobody did as
much as he did to transform English political ideology. He wrapped himself
in the cloak of aristocracy and English Conservatism, and the wider public
did not notice that, despite his writings and speeches, in his perspective and
his disdain for other races, he had continued to remain a Jew, specifically a
pureblooded Jew of very exceptional qualities.

Lastly, we cannot spare criticism for the conduct of the Lords: they had in their hands the power to continue to repel the Jewish attacks. They were not defeated by the battle itself, but instead by a law which they themselves proposed, which made it possible for the Jews to achieve their longed-for objective. Never was a battle so ignominiously lost by such an illustrious assembly as the one that was lost by those Peers of England.

These 28 years of struggle in England are proof of how the Hebrews achieved emancipation, and with this emancipation, power, by all means licit and illicit. The end point could no longer be distant, once the principle had been infringed, no matter how slightly. Judah will always exploit the most trivial opportunity to consolidate its position and strengthen its influence. It may perhaps seem hard to some people that all compromise with the Jewish Question should be dismissed out of hand. But history shows us repeatedly that there is only the choice of either tolerating Jews completely or not tolerating them at all. Any deviation from this rule is the beginning of the end, and the end is the sovereignty of the Jews.

Lastly, we have to stress once more: whoever wishes to liberate England from the Jews will have to act as they do, which is to say, the path towards victory starts in London.

Even the Jewish barrister and author Henry Henriques openly states: 'The settlement [of the Jewish emancipation question] seems to be destitute of principle and innocent of logic', but he believes that there was no other choice, given how intolerable the domestic political situation had become, especially in view of the fact that they could not dare to let the people decide the question. We also believe that this would have been a very dangerous option, because the English of 1858 would have voted against Jewish emancipation with a crushing majority. Nevertheless, England considered itself, and still considers itself, an especially great democracy and perhaps one day an Englishman will be able to explain the object and purpose of a democracy if the opinion of the populace is not only not counted, but decisions are made which expressly go against the populace's wishes and objectives.[306]

The Jewish position did not take long in consolidating itself still further. The Lucan law in principle allowed the Jews to forego the final words of the oath, but for this to happen, it was necessary in each case to obtain the House's approval. This state of affairs was very disagreeable to the Jews and their supporters, since any change in political circumstance could breathe new life into the old opposition. It was crucial, then, to eradicate this danger once and for all, which could only be achieved by a new law. In 1860 a new bill was introduced to this end, which was passed without any kind of diffi-

---

[306] Henriques: *Jews...*, pp. 297-300. Translator's note: QVOS (p. 297).

culty. Meanwhile—imagine, in only two years!—the adversaries of the Jews
had disappeared to such an extent that barely any debate took place.[307]

Already by 1866, Parliament was back to dealing with Jewish interests.
It aimed to establish for all members of Parliament and the House of
Lords—whatever their religion—a new common oath without the final
words 'upon the true faith of a Christian' which in principle still existed.[308]
Nor on this occasion was there an opposition worthy of mention. Disraeli
directed the action and made a long speech explaining why the bill should be
passed. From an impossible but not disheartened position, Mr. Newdegate
delivered a meticulous and impassioned speech against the bill. He accused
Disraeli in particular of wishing to use this law to obtain still greater advantages for his racial kin. He also warned the House of his belief that 'this
measure is intended to facilitate still greater changes, and to render these
changes, by making them step by step, insensibly less unpalatable to the
country, because not fully understood'.[309]

But the strength of the anti-Jewish faction had diminished so much in only eight years, that in the division they counted for only five votes against 298.

The bill was then sent, as usual, to the House of Lords, in which it was
also seen that the longstanding opposition against the Jews had become a
shadow of its former self. The same powerful and influential circles of interest must also have been at work in the Upper House for even the most stal-
wart of the old adversaries to be silenced. Even the political world's former
champion for the people's cause, Sir Frederic Thesiger, latterly Lord
Chelmsford, no longer maintained his resistance. He based his change of
position on the fact that in past times he had maintained his opposition 'upon
principle, and upon principle alone.' As in 1858 the law had been passed by
the aforementioned compromise, it seemed to him that the principle had
been so violated that today it was no longer worth opposing the bill. Previous
laws had already swept away all of the Jewish disabilities, which meant that
any opposition now would have to be looked upon as an insult to the Crown.
There was practically no obstacle left to impede the Jews from entering the
House of Lords, which meant that there really was 'nothing left worth con-
tending for.' The principle, which he had defended so steadfastly in another

---

[307] *Hansard*, Volume 157, pp. 960-3, 1916-9; Volume 158, pp. 205, 1507, 1745-50.

[308] *Hansard*, Volume 181, pp. 453-59, 1712-37; Volume 182, pp. 289-314, 480-3, 510-8,
1322-55, 1619-28, 1759, 2176.

[309] *Hansard*, Volume 181, p. 1712. & p. 1733. Translator's note: QVOS. Also note that I
could not find Newdegate's stated charge against Disraeli within this particular speech, but
as it was known that Newdegate had made a similar charge against Disraeli at least once
before in Parliament (as outlined in this volume), it may be that this charge appears in
another debate, and Aldag cited it here in error.

era, had been sacrificed, which was why he no longer saw any reason to vote against the bill being read.[310]

Perhaps with this speech Lord Chelmsford did not intend to justify the abandonment of his previous position, and that his actions were rather to be interpreted as a resignation to the fact there was nothing left to save. Of particular interest is his discursive pivot to any opposition being potentially seen as insult to the Crown. What a change had taken place in English life in the short space of eight years!

As can be seen, Judah had broken all resistance. How bitterly true were the words of the Earl of Clancarty when, during the one of the last debates that took place in the House of Lords in 1858 on the subject, he made the observation: 'principles do not change and they admit of no compromise.'

One would be forgiven for thinking that with such a state of affairs, no opposition speech would be made regarding this bill. But the Marquess of Bath accused Lord Chelmsford and Lord Derby of betraying their principles, and he reminded the members of the House that they could consult Hansard to find the arguments expounded by these two men in their many speeches against the Jews. In another era, Lord Derby had appealed to House to exclude the Jews from Parliament, for being outsiders in race and religion. Now the two men were unabashed in their support for the Hebrews.[311] But the Marquess of Bath found himself quite alone, and no vote was held that was worthy of mention, a sign that there was now hardly any opposition. Judah had triumphed in England, once and for all.

What a similar change had taken place in the press! The vast majority of newspapers did not make the least mention of these events in the constituent Houses.

Conclusion

With the achievement of the Jews' aims in Parliament, the Jewish fight for political emancipation had come to a close, at least formally. The road was now clear for new advances in British society, advances which would be truly decisive and transcendental.

Although the preceding account of all of the various Jewish attempts to enter Parliament and the state administration of England can appear fatiguing at first glance, due to the sameness of the arguments from both sides and the stereotypical constant repetition of the same methods, this uniformity demonstrates a Jewish political will which is consistent on every point and an extreme determination to achieve political emancipation. With these events, which ended in the submission of a House of Lords which had resist-

---

[310] *Hansard*, Volume 182, 1349, 1622. Translator's note: QVOS.
[311] *Hansard*, Volume 182, p. 1618.

ed until the last moment, what is revealed is the great importance that the Jews attributed to this tactical position. Furthermore, we recognize in these facts just how deeply England had been overwhelmed and conquered—the England that is already a thing of the past. The path had been cleared not only for the removal of the last of the Jewish disabilities, but still further, for Jewish domination over England. The key that opened all doors and portals was in the hands of Jewry: the last bastion of a pure race had fallen.

The next chapter of this study is dedicated to demonstrating with a terrifying clarity how Jewry recognized the value of this tactical position and, above all, how they took advantage of it. How the phrase 'Jews rule England' went, by means of the methods revealed in this study, from a slogan to a most dangerous reality. We will strive to document this reality, in all of its depravity, in the subsequent and final chapter.

CHAPTER 7

JEWISH DOMINATION, PART ONE
(1867-1933)

Prime Minister Benjamin Disraeli, or Politics and Character

In the preceding chapter, we have seen how the Jews in England not only knew how to gradually furnish themselves, over the course of 200 years, with full civil rights, but also how to prepare the ground for their subsequent domination of society. The successive years show clearly how, almost simultaneously with the total final victory of emancipation, the Jews began their advance upwards to the highest social positions. This was expressed most obviously in the personage of Benjamin Disraeli, later Lord Beaconsfield.

Disraeli has already been discussed over the course of the previous chapter in terms of the battles for emancipation; it is he, particularly, who by means of his politics and together with Lord Derby, ensured that Judah and the emancipation cause emerged triumphant. When in February 1868 Lord Derby resigned from the prime ministership for health reasons, Queen Victoria named the Jew Disraeli as his successor. And even though the latter's first prime ministerial term was short, he nevertheless returned to the office at the beginning of 1874, when he went on to exercise its functions without interruption until 1880. In between his terms as prime minister, Disraeli, as leader of the conservatives, intervened in every political event, thus ensuring that his influence was ubiquitous.

Disraeli is fondly remembered by the vast majority of the English people and enjoys the reputation of being one of the greatest statesmen. This is based on his domestic policies, which had positive repercussions on the British people and which have rendered their fruits up until the present time; but special praise is reserved for his foreign policy successes, as he contributed greatly to strengthening British prestige in the world.

Thus, by the purchase of a large part of the Suez Canal stock, he ensured the domination of both this crucial maritime thoroughfare and of Egypt itself. Additionally, in 1878 he was able to incorporate the island of Cyprus into the British Empire, which meant the beginning of English hegemony in the Near East. Immediately afterwards, he established, with a victory over Afghanistan, the strategic positions which were crucial to defending India's famous northeastern frontier from the Russian threat, and finally, after the war against the Zulus, he strengthened English dominance in southern Africa.

Let us begin, with both frankness and objectivity, to consider critically whether Disraeli was really such a benefit for Great Britain or whether there are not negative aspects which at least annul his foreign successes. This analysis is all the more necessary given that today there are still leading Conservative circles which assert the need to direct the Party according to the 'eternal principles of that great man.' But these principles can only be understood when one forms an idea of his works in terms of both domestic and foreign policy.

It was as early as 1832 [at age 28] that Disraeli first tried his luck in politics. He had given himself heart and soul to the Radical party, and stood as a candidate for the High Wycombe constituency during the parliamentary elections. He was not successful on that first occasion and nor did the subsequent by-election in the same ward carry him to Parliament.[1] When in 1833 it looked like a new election was to take place in Marylebone, he distributed a leaflet of radical ideas to publicize his political opinions to the electorate, with a view to his possible candidacy; but contrary to expectations there was no new election held.

Over the course of this and successive years, there emerged the first clues that the future belonged to the Tory party, under the leadership of Sir Robert Peel. In addition, it was no secret that the agrarian circles, who for the most part were to be found in the same party, needed a new leader. Whether it was these or other motives which induced Disraeli to cross over to the Tory camp, will for the moment remain a moot point. In any case, it was shortly after the publication of his leaflet full of radical ideas that Disraeli discovered his calling was with the Conservative party. Thus we find him in 1834 converted into a very active Conservative, now a member of a 'Commission for the Compilation of Rural Abuses and the Measures Necessary to Suppress Them' [N. B.: not the original English phrasing]. In any case, it is characteristic of the Jew Disraeli to consider himself competent to give an expert judgement on agrarian matters.

But nor did his passing to the Tories lead him to Parliament in the following years, and it is only in 1837 when he finally manages to enter the House of Commons.

In May 1839, at only 35 years of age, he marries a fifty-something woman, the rich widow of his colleague Lewis. General opinion was almost unanimous in that this was not a love match, but because Disraeli needed his new wife's money to settle the debts that were increasingly hanging over him.[2]

In the interim, he had been strengthening his position within the Tory Party, and during all of those years he never tired of lavishing mindless praise on the leader, Sir Robert Peel, in diaries, books, and public speeches. Everywhere he intoned the song of songs of 'the greatest statesman of his age' and he designated himself with regard to Peel as a 'humble, but fervent

---

[1] Raymond, pp. 49-51.
[2] Raymond, p. 92.

supporter.' Sir Robert, who did not return these sentiments in the slightest, openly showed Disraeli his aversion to him. He despised all those 'whom he never expected to head an assault.' Sir Robert's attitude is all the most explicable when we find out from the Duke of Wellington that Peel was 'the most sincere man that he had ever met'.[3]

In 1841, Peel was called to form a government. On the list of ministers' names being published, Disraeli was greatly disappointed to see that he had not even been considered for an undersecretary post. Nevertheless, he knew how to hide his disappointment and even went to the extreme of continuing to praise and defend his leader in public. But the fact that this disappointment was the motivation for an enmity towards Peel should not be seriously doubted, although the first clues of this were only to manifest much later.[4]

Between the Tories (conservatives) and the Whigs (liberals) there existed at that time a fundamental divergence on economic questions: the former were supporters of so-called Protectionism and the latter, of Free Trade. The controversy surrounding the Corn Laws played an important role in exacerbating these differences. By a new law of 1828, the radical prohibition on importation was lifted, being substituted by a tariff which was raised up considerably to a certain minimum price. Once the grain had gone over this price, the tariff was reduced accordingly. But this still served to protect domestic agriculture and assure farmers of a decent price for their grain. For some time, the liberals had harbored the intention of lowering the guaranteed price of grain and allowing for a more or less free importation from abroad, but they always came up against the most energetic opposition from the Tories.

It therefore caused a sensation when, in 1842, Peel presented to Parliament a plan to reform the Corn Laws, according to which there would be, incidentally, a minimum set price which was considerably lower than the previous prices. In addition, he intended to eliminate the oscillating tariff and substitute it with some customs duties which would practically lower the previous Protectionist tariff by half. Another surprise came from his declaration that he wished to see a consideration reduction of the customs duties on 750 classes of foodstuffs, with which Peel, who had always come out in defense of the Protectionist tariffs, was exhibiting a great shift away from his old principles. It was, then, only one step away from the Free Trade championed by the liberals, whose point of view could be seen in Peel's speech when he laid out his reasoning for the bill before Parliament, and declared

---

[3] O'Connor: Volume I, pp. 346, 457, 490, 692. Translator's note: QVOS. & O'Connor: Volume I, p. 482. MacColl, p. 1004. Translator's note: QVOS (O'Connor). & O'Connor: Volume II, p. 287.

[4] Francis, p. 56. O'Connor: Volume I, pp. 457, 483 ff., 693.

that the government had decided on the suppression of all Protectionist tariffs in accordance with the general Free Trade ideology.[5]

His propositions were the butt of the liberals' mockery, who accused him of copying their ideas and of betraying his own principles. Many of his supporters backed these reproaches and the result was a split in the cabinet, which led to the Duke of Buckingham's resignation. In the House of Lords, the supporters of the Protectionist tariffs pointed out that the measures would be detrimental to agricultural interests. A member of Peel's party even went as far as to stand in open opposition, due to Peel having abandoned the policy of agricultural protection. The press of both sides largely adopted a similar stance regarding the issue.[6]

Disraeli did not belong, in any way, to the group within his party who with words or deeds expressed their discontent with their leader's position, but was rather, on the contrary, one of Peel's most active defenders against the attacks from his adversaries. He even tried, when faced with the liberal accusation that Peel had stolen their principles, to demonstrate the opposite, despite knowing perfectly well that Peel's measures belonged to the liberals, who were correct in designating them part of their ideology—an ideology which had been fought by the Tories for years.

Nevertheless, Disraeli once again waited in vain for Peel to appoint him to an important post. As a consequence, the first overt attacks against Peel began over the course of 1843, although still within very moderate limits. But in subsequent years, their enmity became more and more obvious.[7]

In 1845 there was again a great famine in Ireland, and as a solution, Peel proposed to his ministers that the ports be opened to the free importation of grain. Everyone knew that this was the beginning of an open practice of Free Trade. Various government ministers rejected such a broad measure and Peel had to resign from his cabinet as a result. But as Lord John Russell was not in a position to form a new government, Peel was once more entrusted to do so.[8]

In the Conservative ranks meanwhile, a great indignation had arisen, and all over the country, protests were taking place. The Duke of Buckingham, who had already shown his opposition to Peel's domestic policy, joined forces with the Duke of Richmond to lead the irate opposition. In 1846 Peel had to request authorization from Parliament for his measures, and even when in previous years there had been increasingly heated arguments between him and Disraeli, nobody could have foreseen the events that were to come.

---

[5] *Dictionary of National Biography*, Volume 15, pp. 633-4. O'Connor: Volume 1, pp. 461-3. & Prentice: Volume 1, p. 333 ff. & *Hansard*, Volume 63, p. 351 ff.

[6] Stanhope: Part II, pp. 100-1. & *Hansard*, Volume 62, p. 608. & p. 54. & O'Connor: Volume I, pp. 467-8.

[7] O'Connor: Volume I, p. 482 ff.

[8] O'Connor: Volume I, p. 563 ff.

When the orators who supported Peel had finished their speeches, Disraeli made his position on the matter be known. Without leaving room for doubt, he made clear that he was completely on the side of Protectionist tariffs, and reproached Peel and his supporters, saying: 'Let men stand by the principle by which they rise—right or wrong. I make no exception. If they be in the wrong, they must retire to that shade of private life with which our present rulers have often threatened us.' In all of history, he could not find a similar case with parallels to Peel's conduct. In his opinion, the Tories would have lost their position as a party if their electors, instead of betraying them, had not remained faithful as always, and now he believed that he belonged 'to a party which can triumph no more; for we have nothing left on our side except the constituencies which we have not betrayed.' For a man like Peel, who was swayed by whichever wind prevailed, Disraeli made clear that he had lost all respect:

> [M]y conception of a great statesman is one who represents a great idea—an idea which may lead him to power—an idea with which he may identify himself—an idea which he may develop—an idea which he may and can impress on the mind and conscience of a nation. That, Sir, is my notion of what makes a man a great statesman.[9]

Disraeli also highlighted over the course of subsequent debates that he could not believe in the claims made of Free Trade principles, which in his opinion would necessarily lead to the country's ruin.[10]

Disraeli was supported most decisively by Lord George Bentinck, but despite this, Peel maintained his grip on power with a majority of 97 votes.

But the battle continued and, to the great surprise of the general public, Disraeli and his supporters managed to bring Peel down in June of the same year, on the occasion of a bill being passed that had nothing to do with the previous issue.[11]

The introduction of Free Trade by Peel had had the consequence of creating a split in the Tory Party. The majority remained in the original party, after having made their position clear on the Protectionist tariffs. These members were formally led at the start by Lord George Bentinck; but the latter found himself, nevertheless, entirely under the Disraeli's influence. And when Bentinck resigned from his leadership position in 1847 due to

---

[9] *Hansard,* Volume 83, pp. 111-123. Translator's note: all QVOS.

[10] *Hansard,* Volume 83, pp. 1318-1347.

[11] *Hansard,* Volume 87, p. 1027 ff.

differences on religious questions, the path was thus clear for Disraeli to take the reins of Tory leadership with no limitations.[12]

From that moment onwards, he did everything possible to impose his ideas and principles on the new party, made up of the Conservatives who had once had Peel as a leader. In the following years, they made sure to inscribe the Protectionist principle on their banners, and defined themselves by this issue.

After Peel's fall, a coalition was formed in Parliament, which successfully defended Free Trade from attacks by Disraeli and his supporters. Outside of the parliamentary precinct, the battle also continued between the Protectionists and the Free Tradeists, with the public's concern over the issue at times spilling over into bloody clashes between each side's supporters.[13]

When Parliament was opened in 1849, Disraeli once again declared himself in favor of Protectionist tariffs. In a speech, he asserted to the Commons: 'In my opinion the new commercial system...has had a trial, a fair trial, and has failed.' And as late as 1850-1851, the Conservatives led by Disraeli made clear every so often that they continued to remain just as loyal as before to Protectionist principles.[14]

In the spring of 1852, a Conservative government was formed under Prime Minister Lord Derby, in which Disraeli was assigned the chancellorship. Now it had to be decided, if the latter and his supporters were ready to convert the promises they had made to the farmers into action, and abolish the Free Trade introduced by Sir Robert Peel. Disraeli gave evasive answers in Parliament. Lord John Russell reproached this conduct in the harshest terms. It would appear that they wanted to keep Free Trade, a principle for which Russell's government had been forced to resign, in order to stay in power.

In August of the same year, a general election was called and, in November, the new Parliament met for the first time. Everyone knew that Disraeli could not shy away from adopting an official position for much longer.[15]

The debate raged for three days and nights and despite the efforts made by supporters of both sides, Disraeli could not be drawn, at the beginning at least, to give a clear answer. But gradually he started to reveal that he was not planning to apply the Protectionist principles that he had defended for so long. The attacks that this policy shift provoked were hard and even went as far as reproaching him for a lack of dignity. The accusations reached their peak when Mr. Sidney Herbert reminded Disraeli of his stance of previous years:

---

[12] *Dictionary of National Biography*, Volume 15, p. 665.

[13] O'Connor: Volume II, pp. 138, 146-7.

[14] *Hansard*, Volume 102, p. 82 ff. Translator's note: QVOS. & *Hansard*, Volume 114, p. 1021.

[15] *Hansard*, Volume 119, p. 1052 ff.

We all recollect the period that intervened between 1846 and 1852. Was the country quiet? Was there no agitation upon this question? At market tables—in theatres—at protection societies, one hundred in number, was everything said with a view to secure the stability of the policy of 1846? For my part, I acquit the right hon. gentleman the Chancellor of the Exchequer, as far as his own convictions are concerned, of the charge of having ever been a protectionist. I never for one moment thought he believed in the least degree in protection. I do not accuse him of having forgotten what he said or what he believed in those years. I only accuse him of having forgotten now what he then wished it to appear that he believed.

He continued by listing everything that Disraeli had done to further the establishment of Protectionist tariffs, and how it would be unthinkable for him to declare that he had never been a supporter of Protectionism. He then went on to accuse Disraeli of calumniating Peel the man, by questioning his motives and integrity, when Disraeli himself went on to follow Peel's course of action:

I knew Sir Robert Peel during my whole life almost—I admired him as a politician—I followed him as a leader—and I loved the man. He was a man, mind you, susceptible—proud, and justly proud, of the purity of his motives—jealous of his honour. I sat by him night by night on that bench when he was attacked by the foulest language, and accused of the meanest crimes. But Sir Robert Peel was a man of a generous nature—he was one who never rejoiced in the humiliation of an adversary; and he would have recollected this—that the humiliation, if humiliation it were, was an humiliation to be inflicted not only upon those who had assailed him, but also upon Gentlemen for whose character he had the warmest regard.

I don't confound hon. Gentlemen opposite with those who calumniated Sir Robert Peel. I recollect even at the moment when party strife was embittered to the uttermost—when men's passions rose high—when great disappointment was felt at the course Sir Robert Peel had taken—even at that moment there were hon. gentlemen opposite who continued a general support to his Government, and who never, when they opposed this very Bill, either threw a doubt upon his motives or assailed his integrity. I say, then, that the memory of Sir Robert Peel requires no vindication—his memory is embalmed in the grateful recollections of the people of this country; and I say, if ever retribution is wanted—for it is not words that humiliate, but deeds—if a man wants to see humiliation—which, God knows, is always a painful sight—he need but look there [*pointing to the Treasury bench*].[16]

During his speech on the previous day, the member Mr. Bernal Osborne showed a similarly damning view of Disraeli:

And then the right hon. gentleman [Disraeli] came to the House in a November Session in 1852, and, with a face which he never saw equalled in the theatre, he dared to tell the House that he had never attempted to reverse the policy of Free Trade! He said, too, that the Earl of Derby had never done so.[17]

Disraeli gave some perfunctory excuses for his contradictory behavior: 'The spirit of the age tends to free intercourse, and no statesman can disregard with impunity the genius of the epoch in which he lives.' 'In that case,' retorted the Marquis of Granby, 'some reparation is due to the memory of Sir Robert Peel.'[18]

Given that Disraeli maintained Free Trade, his former adversaries, whom he had once battled fiercely, had no reason to vote against him. They and some of his party declared themselves to be in agreement with his policy. Only the principled members of the Conservative Party, 53 in number, voted against it.[19]

A new incident in 1852 gave rise to widespread unfavorable criticism of Disraeli's behavior. In November 1852 the funeral of the Duke of Wellington took place and it fell to Disraeli, as Prime Minister of the House of Commons, to give him the final farewell. He fulfilled his mission with a panegyric full of flowery language despite having previously made patently obvious, on various public occasions, his aversion to grand strategy as much as to professional soldiers.[20]

On 17 November 1852, the *Globe* newspaper published an article on a news item which became known under the title 'Curiosities of Literature' (a pun on Disraeli's work of the same name) which gave a side-by-side comparison between Disraeli's eulogy and an 1848 funeral speech by Monsieur Thiers, in honor of the Marshal of France, Gouvion de St. Cyr. The article revealed how a transcript of the latter had appeared in a French magazine, which was then translated and printed in the 4 July 1848 issue of the *Morn-*

---

[16] *Hansard*, Volume 123, pp. 602-14. Translator's note: QVOS.

[17] *Hansard*, Volume 123, pp. 536-50. Translator's note: QVOS.

[18] *Hansard*, Volume 123, pp. 387 ff., 498 ff., MacColl, p. 1005. Translator's note: QVOS [MacColl]. & MacColl: p. 1005. Translator's note: QVOS.

[19] *Hansard*, Volume 123, p. 701 ff.

[20] Raymond: p. 196.

ing Chronicle. Without the slightest doubt, Disraeli had copied the speech in question, given that not only did it contain the same thoughts, but entire sentences and even half a page of the Thier's eulogy had been plagiarized verbatim. The English public was beside itself with anger, and its displeasure was shown in its fierce attacks against Disraeli; as rightfully there prevailed a great bitterness about the fact that such an affront had been committed against one of their greatest sons and that Disraeli had not even bothered to find his own words of gratitude and praise for the occasion of the Duke of Wellington's passing.[21]

There was another controversial revelation which did nothing to help strengthen confidence in Disraeli's party. It was discovered that the Secretary of State for War, who was also a member of the Privy Council, was mixed up in a serious bribery case.[22]

In 1867 we come up against another scandal, which again confirms the lack of rigor with which Disraeli held his own principles.

After the death of Lord Palmerston in 1865, Lord John Russell returned to the heights of power. In his opinion, the best way to quell the agitation prevailing at that time among the general populace was to reform the electoral system. For this reason, in 1866 the government introduced the corresponding bill into Parliament. This bill was broadly based on the 1832 reform model, which in its time had counted on strong support from Disraeli. According to the opinion which the latter then held, the reform was 'a means to a great end'.[23]

In the House of Commons debates, Disraeli proved himself to be, with his strong support for the bill, one of Gladstone's fiercest adversaries. The new reform proposals, which to the general public seemed moderate, would, in Disraeli's opinion, lead to an Americanization of the British constitution, with the result that:

> ... the great elements of our civilization would disappear, and England, from being a first-rate Kingdom, would become a third-rate Republic... I think that this House should remain a House of Commons [i.e. for the middle classes], and not become a House of the People, the House of a mere indiscriminate multitude, devoid of any definite character...[24]

---

[21] Raymond: pp. 196-7. O'Connor, Volume II, pp. 281-7.

[22] O'Connor: Volume II, p. 263.

[23] O'Connor: Volume I, p. 76. Translator's note: QVOS.

[24] *Hansard*, Volume 183, pp. 74 ff., esp. pp. 103-13. Translator's note: QVOS (pp. 103-4).

The Russell government was defeated by a vote due to the debates over this bill, which forced it out of office. It was replaced by a cabinet under the orders of Lord Derby and Disraeli.

On 18 March 1867, Disraeli introduced his Reform Bill, which envisaged reforms which were considerably more far-reaching than those which only shortly before he had fought so rabidly against until their defeat. He managed to silence his adversaries and got his reform proposals passed.[25]

Next, we wish to briefly address the aforementioned foreign policy events, as they relate to Disraeli the man. On 26 November 1875, it was made public that the British government had bought 176,602 shares in the Universal Company of the Maritime Canal of Suez, for the price of 3,976,582 pounds sterling. The news was received, on the whole, as a pleasant surprise, especially due to the fact that these shares had run the risk of suffering a big drop in price, which would have harmed, among others, many English shareholders. The idea of the purchase did not come, as it generally assumed, from Disraeli, but from a certain Mr. F. Greenwood, editor of the *Pall Mall Gazette*, who spoke of it, on the occasion of a banquet, to the Jewish Mr. Oppenheim. The latter in turn passed on the proposition to Disraeli, who immediately approved the scheme and made contact with Rothschild to organize the purchase. It seems that Rothschild had likewise already drawn Disraeli's attention to the possibility of the acquisition. It is recorded that Rothschild paid in advance, some four million pounds, to the seller, the khedive of Egypt:[26]

> His Highness the Khedive having proposed to sell his Shares in the Suez Canal Company to Her Majesty's Government for 4,000,000l., Her Majesty's Government accepted the proposal, supposing that His Highness was still in possession of the full number (177,642), formerly belonging to him; but His Highness subsequently informed them that he had parted with some Shares, and that the number in his possession actually amounted to only 176,602, a reduction corresponding to the reduced number was accordingly made in the Purchase Money, which amounts to 3,976,582l. 2s. 6d. Messrs. N. de Rothschild undertook to pay the above-mentioned sum to the Khedive in anticipation of the Vote of Parliament; and, in consideration of their trouble and Risk, it was agreed that Her Majesty's Gov-

---

[25] *Hansard*, Volume 186, p. 6 onwards, p. 472 ff.; MacColl: p. 1008 onwards.
[26] Clayden: pp. 154-158. O'Connor: Volume II, pp. 600-1. Raymond: p. 308.

ernment should pay to them a commission of 2½ per cent on
the Purchase Money, or 99,414l. 11s. 1d.[27]

Most of the public did not agree with Rothschild being used for the
transaction. Thus, among others, Gladstone pointed out that, for at least the
last sixty years, the government had customarily used the official banking
institution for such transactions, that is to say, the Bank of England. To date
it has not been possible to find out why a private bank was the recourse of
choice. In addition, Rothschild offered no guarantee that the government's
intentions relating to the purchase were to remain a secret. On the contrary,
all of the circumstances gave the impression that the plan had likewise come
to be known by other circles at the same time and that these had also acquired Canal shares; since these shares, given the projected official purchase,
would have to go up in value.

Even with that aside, there is no way that a 2½ percent commission
could be designated a proportional recompense for Rothschild's effort and
risk. His labor was insignificant, and the second factor did not even exist,
given that the British government was in any case good for a four-million-
pound credit and that it was a matter of honor for the sum total to be repaid.
This meant that Rothschild's commission represented a return on the advanced capital. And as the amount had only been advanced for a maximum
of three months, it resulted in Rothschild having lent his money at the outrageous rate of ten percent annually, and having received besides another five
percent, which it fell to the khedive of Egypt to pay. As a consequence,
Rothschild had obtained in total an interest of fifteen percent; this was, then,
the price at which the British government could obtain credit on the national
market in 1875.[28]

After Gladstone's speech, the Chancellor of the Exchequer was forced
to recognize that there truly was something extraordinary in the fact that they
had turned to Rothschild and not the Bank of England, but that it was due to
the fear of the latter not being able to work with sufficient rapidity and the
fear of burdening it with such risk. It was also true that Rothschild earned, in
addition to his commission, the aforementioned five percent, but that this was
totally irrelevant given that the British government did not have to pay it.[29]

---

[27] *Accounts and Papers of the House of Commons*, 8 Feb—15 Aug. 1876, Volume 49, p. 649. Translator's note: QVOS.

[28] *Hansard*, Volume 227, pp. 584-607. Translator's note: It may interest readers to know that the poet Ezra Pound objected to Suez Canal share purchase because of its usurious nature, which resulted in Rothschild's commission being paid by the English public. But his first objection to the transaction was that it was the result of an executive decision on Disraeli's part which was without legislative approval from, or even the consultation of, Parliament. See Henderson [Translator's Bibliography].

[29] *Hansard*, Volume 227, pp. 607-620.

The English people were to continue being taken up with problems of the Near East in the following years.

Disraeli's Foreign Policy

England, which for some time had been representing Turkish interests, especially as they related to Russia, could not and would not consent to a Russian presence in the Mediterranean. But at the same time, it was also about guarding the financial interests of the City of London.

For some twenty years, the Turkish government had been receiving easy loans from London, and the following passage explains how this gave large numbers of British people in the middle and upper ranks a strong pecuniary interest in the preservation of Turkish rule, while Turkey itself fell irremediably into ruin:

> Most of them [the loans] were issued at prices which proved irresistibly tempting to avaricious investors. Five millions of bonds were issued in 1858 at 62½ per cent, bearing 6 per cent interest; another eight millions were issued in 1862, at 68 per cent, bearing the same interest. In 1863 eight millions were issued at 72 per cent; and in 1865 six millions more at 66 per cent. In the same year the interior debt was consolidated, and nearly a hundred millions were borrowed at five per cent interest, the price of issue being about 50 per cent. In 1869, twenty-two millions of bonds, bearing 6 per cent interest, were issued at 60½ per cent; five and three quarter millions more at 73 per cent were issued in 1871; and twenty-seven and three quarter millions in 1873 at 58½ per cent. In 1872 eleven millions had been borrowed in the same way at 9 per cent interest, the amount paid for each £100 being £98 10s. In this gambling fashion a large debt had been accumulated within twenty years, and the lenders had received from ten to twelve per cent on the money they had actually advanced.[30]

At the end of 1875 or the beginning of 1876, Turkey declared that it was not in a position to meet its financial obligations in the expected form. The consternation in England was naturally great, especially for those who had placed all or part of their meagre savings in Turkish bonds.

Meanwhile, the news coming out of Turkey grew ever more alarming. The Christian population of the Balkans found themselves in more or less open rebellion and demanded their autonomy. All of the great Continental

---

[30] Clayden: pp. 158-9. Translator's note: QVOS.

powers supported this aspiration in the so-called Berlin Memorandum. Only England, under a Disraeli government, stopped this from going ahead.

In the summer of 1876, the first news arrived of the cruel massacres carried out in Bulgaria. In England, the vast majority of the populace harshly condemned Turkey's actions. One of the few who was not in the slightest moved by events was Disraeli. He dismissed it all as 'coffee-house babble', despite the existence of official reports from the relevant consuls which substantiated the claims. Gladstone, on the other hand, condemned what he called the 'Bulgarian Horrors', and demanded it be stopped. But City finance was completely on Disraeli's side, and due to this even refused to give help to a collection that was being made for Bulgaria. Rothschild showed himself to be in particular agreement with Disraeli's position, 'Mammon having declared on his side', as the historian E. T. Raymond put it.[31]

The Continental powers, particularly Russia, presented conditions to Turkey with an established deadline to put an end this general state of affairs in the Balkans; England did not in any way bring her influence to bear on the success of this request. Turkey deduced from this passivity that if it came to the crunch Turkey could count on England's assistance, and thus April 1877 saw the start of the Russo-Turkish War.

In the English cabinet, there was no idea regarding the strategy to be adopted. Disraeli was completely on the side of the Ottoman Empire, while Lord Derby, as Foreign Secretary, and the Liberal party which found itself in opposition, did everything possible to prevent help being given to the Turks. The latter, buoyed by the conduct of the governing party in the British Parliament, were able to continue harboring hopes for an alliance with England and so did nothing to come to peaceful terms with Russia. To this must be added the fact that Disraeli did not hesitate to come out in defense of the inviolability of the Ottoman Empire.[32]

Turkey was completely vanquished in the war, and peace was reestablished with the Treaty of San Stefano. Disraeli considered the peace agreement established for the Balkans and Asia as intolerable for Turkey and England, and left Russia in no doubt that England had to intervene on Turkey's behalf. In accordance with this, he initiated war preparations to great public fanfare. Lord Derby resigned from his post as Foreign Secretary, given that in the interim he had become convinced that the Prime Minister was coming out publicly to defend Turkey's inviolability, when in fact he was planning to participate in a carve-up of said country. In order to avoid playing a part in this game, Derby tendered his resignation.[33]

---

[31] Raymond: pp. 314-9. Translator's note: QVOS. & Raymond: pp. 321-2. Translator's note: QVOS. Note that E. T. Raymond was a pen-name of Edward Roffe Thompson.
[32] Clayden: p. 328 ff.; Raymond: p. 331 ff.; O'Connor: Volume II, p. 353 ff.
[33] Raymond: p. 333.

The British government formally announced its position to the Russians, and the fruit of the subsequent negotiations, among other things, was the Congress of Berlin. The secret conversations between the British government and the Russian ambassador did not become publicly known. On 30 May 1879, which is to say, two months before the Congress was due to be held, England and Russia came to terms.[34]

One of the main points of the secret agreement was that Russia would make the commitment to England not to attempt any future expansion in Asia which would be to the detriment of Turkish interests. However, that same day, Lord Salisbury had instructed the British ambassador to Constantinople to offer the Turks a defensive alliance 'against any further encroachment by Russia upon Turkish territory in Asia'; but at the same time, it was made clear to the Turks that this protection came at a price, and accordingly the demand was made that Turkey cede the Mediterranean island of Cyprus.

The Turks agreed to this reluctantly, as they knew that England had given their approval to the Russian territorial gains of the last war, 'in respect of Batoum and the fortresses north of the Araxes', and so the loss of Cyprus was indeed keenly felt. But mindful of Russian attacks, which they believed to be a credible future threat, they accepted England's offer and the Anglo-Turkish Convention was solemnly signed on June 4.[35]

In the Congress, it became clear that Disraeli broke the promise he made to Greece, even though it was thanks to this promise that Greece did not intervene in the war against the Turks. When the Greeks started to present new difficulties regarding the transfer of Cyprus, Disraeli quickly abandoned his plans to demand, as had been promised, the territories of Crete, Thessaly, and Epirus for the Greeks. In this way, Greece, who had completely trusted in England's support, came away empty-handed.[36]

The Romanians found greater favor from Disraeli on solemnly guaranteeing, in accordance with the demands of the peace treaty, the protection of the Jews against the abuses of the populace.[37]

This Jewish success was due to prior secret negotiations that had gone on for over ten years, which is revealed in a Blue Book published by the English government in 1877. From this book, it can be deduced that, for years, the representatives of international Jewry and the English government

---

[34] Clayden: p. 414 ff. Translator's note: I have translated England as it is in the original text (i.e. as a metonym for Great Britain which reflects the reality of England being the prime mover of the Union nations), but I have changed the 'English government' of Aldag's text to 'British government' in the interests of accuracy. As the interchangeability of these terms throughout this study shows, these concepts of 'England' and 'Great Britain' were very much interchangeable in the author's mind.

[35] Clayden: pp. 428-430. Translator's note: QVOS.

[36] Clayden: pp. 426-430. Raymond: pp. 338-9.

[37] Wolf: *Essays...*, p. 405.

were in constant correspondence about the treatment given to the Jews in Romania and Serbia. The Foreign Minister was overwhelmed with reports and telegrams regarding the persecutions which targeted the Jews. Representatives of international Jewry, such as Baron Rothschild, Sir F. Goldsmid, Sir M. Montefiore, the chief rabbi and other influential Jews demanded that the Foreign Office give instructions to their representatives in the countries concerned to make it very clear to the authorities of those places, and even to their sovereigns, that their treatment of Hebrews up to the present time was contrary to the norms of the civilized world and that the Romanians and Serbians could not expect to receive support for their aspirations of independence, as long as they did not treat the Jews more kindly.

But it was not only the influential Jews of England who demanded an intervention from their government in favor of their ethnic kinsmen abroad —the President of the Alliance Israélite Universelle in France also addressed the British Foreign Minister with the same desires. That this request was from an international association did not mean that the Foreign Minister thought fit to abstain from dealing with the matter personally. On the contrary, perhaps it was precisely the fact that this came from international Jewry was what induced him to take the stance he did. Every Englishman should read this collection of official correspondence, in order to begin to understand once and for all how the government of that time intervened in favor of the Jews, without this bearing the slightest relation to any English interest.

A study of the Blue Book likewise leads to a recognition of how so much time was wasted in giving the Romanian and Serbian governments rules of conduct regarding treatment of the Jews. The consuls, the consul generals, and every class of diplomatic representative had to draft long reports, while the ministers had to personally and forcefully admonish the sovereigns every so often and, in the case of these admonitions not being heeded, threaten them. All of this took place not to safeguard British interests, but to satisfy the desires of international Jewry. The sheer number of these interventions is clear from the fact that the Blue Book contains no less than some 400 printed pages, with 357 letters, reports, telegrams, etc.[38]

Due to limited scope of this work, we are not able to detail here the foreign policy decisions taken by Disraeli which led to the Second Anglo-Afghan War of 1878-1880 and the Anglo-Zulu War of 1879.

Disraeli's Conduct and Influence

A cursory glance over Disraeli's conduct shows with total clarity that he only had principles wherever these coincided with his personal interests, be

---

[38] For further details, see *Accounts and Papers of the House of Commons* (1877), Volume 99, p. 141 ff.

these in success, love, or hate. Perhaps his fundamental principle was not to have any principles. Perhaps it is possible to argue for this philosophy of conduct, in which better outcomes for the people and the state can perhaps justify—but only perhaps—a lack of principles as standard. But how little does this case apply to Disraeli, when an analysis of his character and dealings reveals the true motivations for his conduct. A few key examples will suffice to bring Disraeli's nature back to the reader's mind:

Together with Peel, he was a champion of Protectionism, and alongside Peel had a change of heart in 1842. In 1846 he was once again a passionate defender of Protectionist tariffs and he defeated Peel on that basis. But in 1852, during his stint in government, he not only declared himself once more a supporter of the Free Trade policy, but even went as far as to insist that he had never come out in defense of Protectionism.

Could there be anything more obvious than such a U-turn? The same thing happened with the electoral Reform Act of 1832, which he praised the year that it became law, then censured in Parliament in 1866 for being 'Americanizing', only to introduce a few months later, once the government had fallen and he was a member of the new one, a bill which went much further than the reform measures proposed by the cabinet which he had brought down.

And with what speed did he switch from praise to condemnation of Peel because the latter had not given him a post in his government despite all of the flattery! Then there is the fact that, while there is no doubt that the Suez Canal share purchase was a good thing for England, it was Disraeli, Rothschild, and Oppenheim who did the deal.

In foreign policy, he played the same game that has such parallels with the events of our time. Due to the conduct of Disraeli's cabinet, Turkey was encouraged to get into a war with Russia, because of the guarantees that had been given to protecting her territorial limits. And what was the result? Turkey completely defeated, and England enriching herself at Turkey's expense with the cession of Cyprus.

It might be that Disraeli's love of Turkey has its origins in the efforts made by England for so many years to sustain the country. Nevertheless, there should not be the slightest doubt about the influence that City interests had on him, likewise his hatred for Russia and the Balkan Christians, realities that also did not escape the attention of his contemporaries. O'Connor leaves no doubt in this regard, and Gladstone was convinced of it, saying one day to his friend, the Duke of Argyll: 'I have a strong suspicion that Dizzy's crypto-Judaism has had to do with his policy: the Jews of the East *bitterly* hate the Christians, who have not always used them well.' Other politicians similarly expressed their opinions on this matter. 'Dimly, and, it may be, unconsciously,' says Raymond, 'the Prime Minister was feeling the influence of his blood.' In other words, the Jew Disraeli did not let himself by guided purely by English interests when making decisions of such magnitude, but also by Jewish interests, to the same extent if not more.[39]

But let us put this to one side: England has to come to terms herself with these figures and this historical past. What interests us here—and it seems not only symbolic of his age, but also for the destiny of England—is Disraeli's type as a Jew.

Disraeli is the founder of the modern Conservative Party, which governs today. With Peel's departure from the Tories, a new structure emerged, a product of Disraeli's ideas. In a short time, he managed to drag the majority of his supporters into dishonorably changing all of their positions, despite his being a Jew and the party he led blocking Rothschild from entry to Parliament year after year. But ultimately it was the Conservative government under the orders of Lord Derby and Disraeli which assured the final Jewish triumph; with the call of the blood being undoubtedly the decisive factor for Disraeli.

It remains almost inexplicable how this political adventurer—as he was often called—managed to seize the leadership of the Conservative Party. It is possible that after Peel's withdrawal, the Conservatives did not have anyone who could be a better spokesman for them in Parliament than Disraeli. But the more his ideas spread among his supporters, the more the latter became dependent upon him, given that only from him could they get an explanation of the party program and its practical application. It might also be, as O'Connor states, that Disraeli brought to the Tories, through his novels and particularly through his biography of Lord George Bentinck, the proof that his ethnic brethren had always belonged by nature to their party and, in every age, to the best of politics, art, and religion, as we can still recall from Disraeli's speeches cited in the previous volume, given that according to the latter, the Jews are, properly speaking, the true Christians. Thus, he had worked from the earliest opportunity to convince his fellow party-members that the Jew and only the Jew was the most suitable being to lead humanity.[40]

All of this certainly contributed to the gradual imposition of his leadership on the Conservatives. But this seems to have only been possible because the Tories' previously fundamental ideals had outlived their usefulness, or because the Tories were already so far removed from these ideals that there was virtually nothing left of the true conservatism of the age of Charles I. But be this as it may, it cannot be denied that the ideals of the Conservative Party found their representation in a man who until his dying moment always proclaimed that he was, and would always be, a Jew. In other words, he was a foreigner who, as Raymond underscores, 'often made gross mis-

---

[39] O'Connor: Volume II, pp. 649-50. & Abbott: pp. 438-9. Clayden: p. 394. Brasol: p. 184. MacColl: pp. 1001-2. Translator's note: Gladstone quotation QVOS [Abbott]. & Raymond: p. 317. Translator's note: QVOS.

[40] O'Connor: Volume II, pp. 150, 463-6, 641-2.

takes' when he 'attempted to think in English terms.' Therefore we believe, alongside O'Connor, that under Disraeli's leadership, the Conservatives distanced themselves considerably from the 'national ideals of the real Englishman' and that these politicians 'were not Englishmen or Conservatives, but strictly Disraelites.'[41]

But not only had the principles of the Conservative Party been changed, but those of England. The general social situation found itself in the throes of transformation. With the abolition of customs tariffs on grain, agriculture was ruined, a situation which is still the case to this day, as we shall see further on. Before the days of Free Trade, the peasant was all-important; after it, he was nothing. The introduction of Free Trade saw the perishing of a healthy peasantry that had been the pride of England. From that point onwards, the whole life of the country has been ruled solely from the point of view of money.[42]

And all of this was in no small measure the work of the Jew Disraeli, who remained in life-long devotion to the memory of Henry St. John, 1st Viscount Bolingbroke, whom he saw as his 'beau ideal of a patriotic statesman' and 'the father of modern Toryism' and (according to one of Disraeli's many panegyrics to his hero) 'in whose writings I have ever recognized the most pure and the profoundest sources of political and constitutional wisdom.' However, MacColl then goes on to say this about the man:

> Now what manner of man was Bolingbroke? His life, political and private, is as well known as that of any character in English history. It is, therefore, unnecessary to go into details; but it is no exaggeration to say that Bolingbroke was the most brilliant orator, the most sparkling writer, and one of the most profligate noblemen of his time: in morals a rake; in politics an unprincipled schemer, who joined and betrayed all parties by turns; in religion a believer in a kind of vague and nebulous deism. Violent and bitter attacks on Christianity are scattered over his writings.

Talking of another similarly immoral hero of Disraeli's, the dissolute Count d'Orsay, MacColl says the following about Disraeli's judgement of what makes a 'great man':

> If a man makes ambition the one aim and purpose of his life, and if he shows intellectual power and determination of will

---

[41] Raymond: p. 324. Translator's note: QVOS. & O'Connor: Volume II, pp. 617-622, 642, 653-4.
[42] O'Connor: Volume II, pp 42-44.

adequate to the end in view, the moral character of the means employed is, in Mr. Disraeli's opinion, a matter of little or no moment.[43]

Disraeli may have been the one who made the slogan 'Perfidious Albion' a permanent phrase in history.

J. B. Firth, a well-known historian, expressed on one occasion in the *Daily Telegraph* that Disraeli's genius made the Disraeli tradition permanently secure, and that 'each successive Conservative Conference bears witness to the vitality of the seed which he sowed in the minds of his political supporters'.[44] He did not take to the tomb, then, his ideas and principles.

Leading Jews as Shapers of English Life

Just as Disraeli's influence on the political principles of Great Britain extended long after his own lifetime, so the Jew George Jessel's spirit continues to be alive today in English jurisprudence. Son of a rich businessman, he was born in London in 1824. After being educated in a Jewish school, he went to university, where he passed his studies in mathematics and natural sciences. Later he dedicated himself to legal studies and soon became a well-known lawyer, who at his peak earned between £20,000 and £23,000 per year.

In 1868 he was elected a member of Parliament for the Liberal Party, and in Parliament he very soon enjoyed the fame of being one of the most expert members when it came to drafting bills. In 1871 he was named Solicitor General, that is, a law officer of the Crown without a seat in Parliament, and two years later was made Master of the Rolls (i.e. the Keeper of the Rolls and Records of the Chancery of England), and at the same time, a member of Privy Council.

This period saw fundamental reorganizations in the English court system. The law of judicial constitution, the rules of judicial proceedings, and the patent law were all radically modified. These were the first steps towards the transfer of the old customary law and the existing statutory provisions into a single legal system. Jessel was very intensely involved in all of it.

In accordance with the new laws, Jessel was, as Master of the Rolls, simultaneously President of the Civil Division of the Court of Appeal of England and Wales. Even today his interpretations of statutes, regulations, and common law are considered to be the best in English jurisprudence. They are of particular importance in English law because, over time, decisions by recognized judges in practice almost take on the character of laws.

---

[43] MacColl: pp.996-7. Translator's note: All QVOS. Extended quotations added for reader interest.
[44] *Jewish Chronicle*, 23/10/1936. Translator's note: QVOS.

For this reason, Jessel is referred to as 'a legislative judge', whose authority remains undisputed to this day.

In addition to his duties as a judge, Jessel also had significant other offices. He was the working head of the patent office for over ten years, an inspector of the trademark register, a fellow of the Royal Society and a trustee of the British Museum. Finally, in his capacity of Master of the Rolls, he supervised the official historical publications compiled from minutes and manuscripts, the so-called Roll Series, which have been largely the subject of our investigations. He was an honorary vice-chancellor of the University of London and vice-president of the Anglo-Jewish Association. As can be seen, he could not complain about a lack of public duties. His bust can be found not only in the most prominent place in Lincoln's Inn, but also in the lobby of the Royal Courts of Justice.

He was knighted in 1872; he died eleven years later, in 1883. A baronetcy was conferred upon his heir, Charles James Jessel, in the same year; a rank which was similarly conferred upon his second son, Herbert Merton Jessel, in 1917. Charles James has held high positions in government and administration, and Herbert's son has been married to the daughter of the well-known Marquis of Londonderry since 1935.[45]

The year 1885 was to bring the culmination of Jewish aspirations for power. Nathaniel Meyer Rothschild was made a Peer of England and, as such, entered the House of Lords. He also became a member of the Privy Council in 1902. At Trinity College, Cambridge, he became friends with the future King Edward VII, who regularly bestowed favors upon him. His positions in the economy are so numerous they can barely be listed, the most important being undoubtedly that of Governor of the Bank of England.[46]

Farrer Herschell was one of the Jews who played a significant role in politics at the end of the 19th century. He was originally a barrister and was elected to Parliament in 1874. Under Gladstone, he was promoted to Solicitor General in 1880, and was knighted weeks later. In 1886 he was made a baron and appointed Lord Chancellor. Thus the Jews had also provided a Speaker in the House of Lords.[47]

Lord Herschell's daughter is married to Brigadier General R. M. Yorke, and they have two daughters.[48] His grandson is the current Baron Herschell, whose many honorable positions include that of Page of Honor to the King.[49]

---

[45] *Jewish Encyclopedia*, Volume 7, pp. 158-9. *Dictionary of National Biography*, Volume 10, pp. 805-807. & *Who's Who 1938*, p. 1773.

[46] *Jewish Encyclopedia*, Volume 10, p. 503.

[47] *Jewish Encyclopedia*, Volume 6, p. 363.

[48] *Who's Who 1938*, p. 3730.

[49] *Who's Who 1938*, p. 1557.

These few examples may suffice to show the extent of the influence and positions achieved by the Jews in Great Britain immediately after their emancipation. In politics, law, and economics, areas among the most powerful in a state, they wielded considerable influence.

Jewish Financial Scammers: The Honduras Loans

From the plethora of financial scandals that were commonplace around the 1870s, we shall discuss just one case in order to demonstrate how the Jews were also influential in this sphere of activity.

Around the aforementioned decade, England and France in particular were flooded with foreign bonds, most of which were practically worthless just a few years later because interest was no longer paid on them and the securities were only quoted on the stock exchanges—if at all—for a fraction of their face value.

By 1875 the situation had become untenable. Foreign bonds totaling £240 million were in default on interest payments. Many British subjects were completely ruined as a result. Public officials and civil servants had to give up their posts, because not only had they lost their entire fortune, but had also incurred debts as a result of their bad speculation. Widows and the elderly who had invested their money in these bonds found themselves without means to live and did not know how they were going to survive from that point onwards. The misery was indescribable.[50]

On 23 February 1875, Sir Henry James moved Parliament to immediately appoint a select committee, which came to be known as the Foreign Loans Committee, to investigate the circumstances which had led to this disaster. The proposal met with no opposition and it was agreed to only deal with one part of this complex issue: the bonds for Honduras, Costa Rica, Santo Domingo, and Paraguay. The total value of these bonds amounted to some ten million pounds and was therefore small in relation to the total amount of 240 million pounds. In any case, it was believed that after examining the aforementioned cases, the Committee would have sufficient knowledge of such transactions as a whole because they were all more or less set up the same way. The results of the investigation fully confirmed this assumption.[51]

Parliament appointed a Select Committee of 17 members, which held its first meeting in March. It is impossible to give a detailed description of the meetings that lasted until July. The official files which were printed and published contain no fewer than 6,680 recorded questions and answers from the witnesses and experts involved. The Committee's minutes, annexes, and

---

[50] *Hansard*, Volume 222, pp. 773-777.
[51] *Hansard*, Volume 222, pp. 772-787.

report filled 719 large pages crammed with small print. The newspapers covered the results of these investigations every day.

We want simply to get an insight into the machinations of the financial racketeers, based exclusively on the what was found with regards to the bonds raised for the state of Honduras. In 1867, the state of Honduras was little more than a wilderness, and there was no mention of an orderly financial economy. How small the state revenue was is shown by the fact that the state in question was unable to pay the interest of £1,632 on an old loan and had been in arrears for some time.[52]

However, this did not stop a clique of unscrupulous people from issuing public bonds worth over £6,000,000 between 1867 and 1871. The interest, including the repayment premium, totaled £700,000 annually.[53]

The main participants in this business were: the Honduran consul in London (Don Carlos Gutierrez), a certain Monsieur Lefevre, and the Bischofsheim & Goldschmidt company. The owners of the latter were Jews, while we similarly have little doubt about Lefevre. Before these events, Lefevre had already been sentenced in France to two years of prison for breach of trust. Afterwards he suddenly appeared in London and founded two small, insignificant companies, the purpose and aims of which were very unclear. He soon entered into a commercial relationship with the well-known Jewish company Bischofsheim & Goldschmidt; from that moment, he rose rapidly and displayed immense wealth. When the situation in England became too difficult for him due to the investigations, he returned to France and thus avoided being questioned by the committee. The consul of Honduras invoked his diplomatic immunity and likewise did not appear to give evidence. The third member of the group, Henry Louis Bischofsheim, had a representative provide a medical certificate from Sir James Paget and Dr. J. D. Chepmell—respected doctors—which stated that his health did not allow him to be questioned.[54]

So the Foreign Loans Committee had to struggle with great difficulties, and the *Times* rightly noted in long articles of September 23 and 24, 1875, that this and the withholding of important documents, which the Committee also pointed out in its final report, made it completely impossible to establish the full truth about what had gone on.[55]

The investigation brought to light the most scandalous fraudulent practices, and the public front for these practices were, among others, an employee of the Bischofsheim & Goldschmidt company, the Jew Davids, who appeared to the public as a so-called trustee.

---

[52] *Accounts and Papers... 1875*, Volume XI, pp. IV, V.

[53] *Accounts and Papers... 1875*, Volume XI, p. XXIV.

[54] *Accounts and Papers... 1875*, Volume XI, p. 117.

[55] *Accounts and Papers... 1875*, Volume XXV.

With the first bond of one million pounds, the aforementioned Jewish company undertook to place it in England and France. What commission the company had been guaranteed for this could not be determined directly from the documents, but it could be indirectly concluded that it was no less than £82,000. Apparently the loan was intended for the construction of a railway that would connect the Atlantic and Pacific Oceans. As security, the future net surpluses from the income of this company were pledged and a first mortgage was supposedly registered on the domains and the mahogany forests of the state.

Initially, the public wanted nothing to do with the bonds, and despite all efforts over several months to elicit interest, no more than £10,000 had been subscribed—which the Jewish company itself had taken over. Then Lefevre showed up and undertook to place the remainder. However, he did not purchase the bonds at the issue price of 73% of the nominal value, but at 68%. But nor could he apparently place more than around £175,000. A new contract between Lefevre and Bischofsheim & Goldschmidt was signed, with more favorable conditions for the latter, and although buyers were finally found for the rest of the loan, it was only because Lefevre persuaded various brokers to use illegal business methods. He put at their disposal, among other things, bonds below the issue price of 73%, which obligated him to not to put any further bonds onto the market within a certain period of time. As soon as the prices on the stock exchange fell, this consortium of scammers made purchases through an intermediary, thus artificially driving up demand to make the bond price rise again. In this way it was possible to drive the shares up to 94%.

In May 1869 a new loan of £2,500,000 was issued for Honduras, although at most a small portion of the first had been sold. The bonds for this new issue were also placed using the methods described above.

In the spring of 1870, the same people decided to issue a new round of government securities. The public had already become suspicious because this amount was likewise supposed to be used for the building of the railway. By means of new trickery, attempts were made to restore wavering trust.

As is already known, according to the terms of the 1867 loan, the state's mahogany forests had been pledged alongside other assets as security. In addition, it was determined that the company Bischofsheim & Goldschmidt should at the same time be conceded total distribution rights to the commodities obtained. It was in this context that the following notice was placed in the 'Money-Market & City Intelligence' section of the *Times* dated 11 June 1870:

> The A. N. Lezard and the Hope have arrived in the West India Docks from Truxillo (Honduras) with cargoes of mahogany and fustic, consigned to Messrs. Bischoffsheim and Gold-

> schmidt on account of the Honduras Railway Loan. Advices
> just received state that the Grenmar and Queen of the South were
> loading at Truxillo with similar cargoes on the same account.

In fact, these and three other later shiploads had arrived in London, but what was left out was the fact that they did not come from the state forests, but were purchased privately in Honduras and were additionally of very poor quality. The Bischofsheim & Goldschmidt company—or one of the other accomplices—had made these purchases themselves and paid for them using the funds from the previous bond-holders.

The public's trust, thus newly regained, given that the payment of interest and capital was considered assured through this transaction, was exploited to announce the conditions of the new bond. The amount was again approximately £2,500,000, and the same items that had already been pledged were once more offered as security. But this time they went so far as to declare that all assets and income of the state of Honduras were security for the loan. Honduras was obliged to sell to Bischofsheim & Goldschmidt all of the products of state assets that were destined for export and to deposit the proceeds into the fund for loan repayment. In other words, *the entire state of Honduras* was mortgaged to the Jews, and it was only allowed to do business with them.

All of the money raised from the bond was also to be directed to a fund. The trustees consisted of five people, one appointed by the state of Honduras and the remaining four by the aforementioned Jewish company. Bischofsheim & Goldschmidt was also entitled, but not obliged, as trustees for the bond-holders, to confiscate and manage all of the state of Honduras' assets at home and abroad, in the event of the non-fulfillment of its obligations.

Again it was the same group that used fraudulent methods to raise the loan funds. At times, up to 100 people were connected to each other, buying up the securities when prices threatened to fall and selling them again when the market for the bond was firm. A single speculator once bought and sold the entire bond stock. If prices could not be maintained using such methods, the consortium resorted to other deceptive tactics.

Thus, on 1 April 1871, it was declared that £50,000 would be drawn from the bonds and redeemed by the state of Honduras at par. Since the bond price was not bad at this time, but still far from par, this was a new incentive for the buying public. In addition, the draw was intended to show that the financial situation of the government in Honduras was very healthy. In fact, of the securities drawn in the 'lottery', only those worth around £17,000 were in the hands of people who were not part of the plot, so only this sum was paid out. However, it was not provided by the state of Honduras, but was taken from the proceeds of the last bond. The interest and capital repayment schedule was also only made possible in this way.

With such manipulations, an unbroken series of loans was naturally made possible and necessary, the ongoing costs of which were only covered by the issuance of new bonds.

When, at the end of 1871 in England and the summer of 1872 in France, further attempts to keep the scheme going were unsuccessful, the entire fraudulent house-of-cards collapsed because the state of Honduras was unable to pay even a penny of debt service. All of the bonds fell to rock bottom in 1872. It was quoted at around 6% of book price in July 1875 and only 3% in September of that year. The *Times* of 23 September 1875, in their report on the Foreign Loans Committee, quoted a country clergyman who had been unable to resist speculating, who thought that there must have been an earthquake 'which had swallowed the whole of the precious place up.'

The magnitude of the fraud is evident from the Committee's findings, *viz.* that the state of Honduras received approximately £60,000 and the railway contractors received approximately £700,000 for construction, while the remainder of the multi-million-pound loans had been used for things that had nothing to do with the purpose stated in the bond. Thus, no less than a million pounds ended up in Lefevre's hands to compensate him for supposed commission and publicity expenses.

The parties who suffered were the state of Honduras and the public. The former had an abandoned, half-built railway line of around 80 km and an annual interest burden of around £700,000, which could never be paid, given that, as it has already been stated, the Honduran state had not even been able to repay the sum of £1,632. The misery of the public investors left holding the bonds has already been described.

The Foreign Loans Committee found that the same fraud had taken place in other countries, with only a variance in some of the main characters. But Jews also set the tone in those places. Among the various players, we find the involvement of the well-known Jewish bank Erlanger & Co. The public of France and England therefore suffered the loss of about £240 million, that is to say, five billion marks, due to Jewish fraud.

And what happened to everyone involved in the crime? Let the reader guess: Nothing! Nothing at all![56]

The Foreign Loans Committee took a position which appears more than strange. Apparently it let itself be guided by the opinion of Nathaniel Meyer Rothschild, who, called as an expert, was of the opinion that the sole culprit for this affair was 'the people's desire to get the highest possible interest on their money.' 'Do you suggest, Sir, to remedy this situation?' the chairman then asked him. 'No, not at all,' replied Rothschild. When the chairman pressed him further whether this was not a very serious evil, Rothschild made no answer to this categorical question, but spoke of the abuse of

---

[56] Clayden: pp. 142-3. Sinclair: Appendix, pp. 129-30.

the investment funds from the Honduras bonds. During the cross-examination, he refused to make any suggestions of his own to avoid such frauds in the future, saying he had only come to criticize the suggestions that others had already made in this regard. The Committee was completely satisfied with this response.[57]

In the face of such an attitude, one cannot be remotely surprised by the report. At the end of their investigation, the members of the Committee made some suggestions for remedial action in the future. They dealt with, among other things, the question of whether one should enforce by law that those people who—as described above—artificially influence prices on the stock exchange by buying and selling depending on the market situation, should be made to work openly and with full public knowledge instead of being allowed to carry out their manipulations in secret. 'It has been communicated to the Committee,' they concluded, 'that if such a law were passed, all transactions in public bonds for foreign loans would go to foreign countries.' The Committee agreed that the profits from such transactions must be kept in England and that such legislation was therefore impossible.

However, it was believed that the main cause of this bitter experience was the gullibility and greed of certain sections of the population:

> These types of people seem to measure the value of the promises made to them not by the rules of any experience, but only by their own unrealistic expectations. This has made them easy prey for those who, relying on such gullibility, have fraudulently obtained their money from them.
>
> The Committee does not believe it is its duty to place any blame on the various parties involved in these transactions. It is generally agreed that...the cause of the collapse is equally attributable to all those who have interests, rights, claims, grievances or any other participation in the matter. It is a kind of original sin that taints even the most innocent who have anything to do with the affair.[58]

As we do not feel it is out place to render an opinion on the Committee's statements, we shall leave it to the reader to decide whether it is the small investor or the international Jewish financial racketeers who should be held responsible for fraud on such a scale. Certainly, there was at least one man in English public life, albeit a Scotsman, who was not afraid to point the finger at the heart of the problem. In 1877, the Liberal MP Sir Tollemache Sinclair wrote:

---

[57] *Accounts and Papers... 1875*, Vol. XI, pp. 266-7.
[58] *Times*, 23/9/1875, 24/9/1875. *Accounts and Papers... 1875*, Volume XI, pp. XLIV-L.

Everyone who has read the report of the Select Committee on Foreign Loans knows of what untold millions we are robbed by Jews who bring out rotten loans, and other public compa- nies, then rig the market, and wriggle out themselves, and the cement in the edifice of their fortune is moistened with the tears of the plundered widow and orphan.[59]

Apparently, however, the *Times* took the Select Committee's view that the purchasers of such securities were as much to blame for the scandal as the fraudsters. This was because, in the newspaper's view, they should have anticipated from the outset, given the very favorable returns on offer, that there was a strong possibility of losing their money. Can we be at all sur- prised that nothing happened by way of repercussion when this is the pre- vailing attitude? Even today, five million pounds are lost each year on the Stock Exchange due to fraudulent transactions.[60]

Anti-Jewish Forces

At the end of the last century, however, there was no lack of upright men in England who spoke and wrote against such behavior. The following is an excerpt from the essay 'The Jews: A Deferred Rejoinder' by Professor Goldwin Smith (1823-1910), a prominent and well-respected Oxford don:

> The age is propitious to the operations of the Hebrew: the use of force, as we have said, is by our present civilisation forbid- den, while the use of unscrupulous cunning is permitted and protected by the law. Rob a man on the street, and you will go to prison; fleece a thousand on the Stock Exchange, and you will dwell in a palace with an aristocracy at your feet. The power of wealth and of things which wealth can buy is im- mense. Stock-jobbing is rife, and financial craft, by dealing with the circulating medium, transfers to itself, on a large scale, the product of honest labour. By the decay of religious belief, the moral sinew of society has for the time been weak-

---

[59] Reproduced verbatim from Sinclair's *A Defence of Russia and the Christians of Turkey*, Vol. II, Appendix pp. 129-130.

[60] *Times*, 23/9/1875. & *Daily Telegraph*, 22/11/1938. *Daily Express*, 22/11/1938. Transla- tor's note: The *Daily Telegraph* article, 'Measures Against Share-Pushers', which reports on MPs' comments about an anti-fraud bill, includes quotes from Sir George Broadbridge ('It should not be forgotten that the moving spirits in these fraudulent firms were to a large extent undesirable persons of foreign extraction.') and Mr. Bellenger, who welcomed a bill which would 'clip the wings of those birds of passage who have long battened on the social system'.

ened, and the strength of resistance to anything which assails
us on the side of material interest has been proportionately reduced. Party divisions present fatal openings for Hebrew Op-
portunism; international quarrels lend themselves to the action
of a Cosmopolitan Ring, playing off one nation against another for the advancement of its special interests and the accomplishment of its designs...

Above all, there is the Press—at once the great benefactor and the great peril of society at the present day—the anonymous organs of which are fearfully liable to fall under the secret influence of moneyed intriguers, and to become in their
hands the means of fabricating public opinion on all questions,
political, social, and personal, as well as commercial. It is
needless to dilate on the fell ascendancy which may thus be
gained. No one who has not specially inquired can be aware to
what an extent the Newspaper Press in all countries, as well as
the agencies for the transmission of intelligence, are becoming
Jewish: not only are the relations often indirect as well as confidential, but the Jewish journalist seems to be fond of assuming a Christian name.[61]

In connection with the Eastern Question, the aforementioned MP Sir
Tollemache Sinclair, who was well-known in Disraeli's time, wrote a major
work, *A Defence of Russia and the Christians of Turkey* (1877), which explained to the public that the Jews had committed acts since time immemori-
al which could not be reconciled with our concept of honor and decency. As
Sinclair wrote:

I think I have established that the Jews are not, and never have
been, worthy of our esteem and regard, and that they are the
eternal and implacable enemies of the Christian; consequently,
it would be madness to follow their advice to go to war with
Russia, but wisdom always to take the opposite course to that
which they recommend.

He cites the Old Testament at length to demonstrate their moral corruption,
and shows how the historical record has handed down an unbroken chain of
their crimes, not least of them pitiless usury:

---

[61] Smith: pp. 707-8. Translator's note: QVOS. For an overview of the extent to which the
English press at Smith's time of writing was Judaized, see Chapters XVII, XVIII and XIX
of Joseph Banister's 1907 [1903] *England Under the Jews* [in Translator's Bibliography].

> If a man falls into the hands of a Christian money-lender, he contents himself usually with bleeding him, as it were, in a single vein, while the Jew, who is *hostis Gentili generis*, bleeds every vein and artery, and leaves you penniless, like a squeezed orange, or like the stock-meat which a cook makes into a transparent jelly by pressing out the whole of the juice, so that even the dogs will not eat the tasteless fibre which remains.

He also warns, among other things, about the danger of interbreeding with them. For centuries there had been mixed marriages between the English and the Jews, which could no more be combined than oil and vinegar.[62]

The well-known adventurer Sir Richard Burton also belongs to the list of anti-Jewish writers of this time. At his death, he had published no fewer than 48 works and left numerous others unfinished. One of these was the book used for this study, in which he deals with both the Jews in general and the Jews of England in particular. In his opinion, the broad masses in England are only ever told about the charity, thrift, and other good qualities of the Jews. Only a few people know that '[the Jew] alone eats bread, not in the sweat of his own face, but in the sweat of his neighbor's face' and earns his money through usury and fraud, becoming rich while 'the working-men starve in the midst of gold.' In every age, Jews are found to be receivers of stolen goods and owners of gambling dens. They deal in obscene literature 'calculated to pervert the mind of youth.'[63]

As stated above, Burton's book was only published after the author's death. The book's editor, William Henry Wilkins, has given us the very interesting reason for this posthumous publication. According to his account, Burton was British consul in Damascus from 1869 to 1871. He spoke the local languages and went around the city disguised as a native. His investigations into the ritual murders practiced among the Jews in Asia Minor bore splendid fruit. At the same time, he also enquired into the mysterious circumstances of the murder of Father Tomaso in Damascus in 1840. His prying into this matter did not go unnoticed by the Jews who resided there, and it aroused their extreme displeasure. This hostility was the reason that he was recalled in 1871 by Lord Granville, then Foreign Secretary. But it was not possible, nevertheless, to prevent Burton from compiling the extensive material that he had collected into a book while in his new post as consul at Trieste. His manuscript was finished in 1874.

---

[62] Sinclair. See, for example, the appendix, 'The Jews, The Implacable Foes of the Christians', pp. 112-154. Translator's note: QVOS (Vol. II, pp. 131, 135).

[63] Burton: *The Jew, the Gypsy and El Islam*, Prologue, p. V. & p. 20 ff. Translator's note: All QVOS.

A year later, while on holiday in England, Burton presented his manuscript to an 'influential friend, who was highly placed in the official world.'
This friend strongly advised him against publication, 'owing to the anti-
Semitic tendency of the book.' Other friends advised him in the same way,
pointing out that 'so long as he remained in the service of the Government of
a country where the Jews enjoy unprecedented power and position, it would
be unwise, to say the least of it, for him to make enemies of them.' These
warnings deterred Burton from publishing and he took his manuscript back
to Trieste. His friends were also endeavoring to get him the post in Tangier,
which would only have been a normal promotion given his seniority.

Year after year, Burton waited for the promotion he deserved. In vain.
Sir William Kirby-Green was appointed to the coveted post in 1886. This
apparently angered Burton to such an extent that he once again decided to
publish the book, regardless of the consequences. In the meantime, his wife
worked to ensure his right to the payment of the pension to which he was
entitled before he left the service and carried out his intention regarding the
book. But the bureaucratic process was continuously delayed for years at a
time, and Burton died before they would grant him retirement.

His widow also died before the book was published, and she had left
instructions for this to be carried out as quickly as possible. However, Burton's findings on Jewish ritual murder in connection with the 1840 murder of
Father Tomaso were not made available to the public, although, as editor
William Henry Wilkins emphasizes, these findings would have caused a
great stir. 'It may well be,' Wilkins continues, 'that the superstitions and
cruelties of the Eastern Jews have been generated in them by long centuries
of oppression and wrong. From these superstitions and cruelties, the enlightened and highly favored Jews in England naturally shrink with abhorrence
and repudiation; but it does not therefore follow they have no existence
among their less fortunate Eastern brethren.'[64]

The omission of the chapter about ritual murder was not voluntary, but
imposed by the Jews. Apparently, before the book itself was published, the
publisher had already published an index from which conclusions could be
drawn about its contents. When it was learned that the book was to be published, as well as translated into other languages for publication abroad, the
Board of Deputies of British Jews 'threatened the Publishers and Editor with
libel proceedings if the work appeared. The Rabbis of all the principal foreign centers were warned of the book, and were advised to take steps locally
to prevent publication.' It is very likely that these Jewish actions caused the
ritual murder section to be removed from Burton's book, not least because

---

[64] Burton: *The Jew...*, Preface, pp. VII-XI. Translator's note: All QVOS. Wilkins' own
books are referenced in the later chapter on mass Jewish immigration.

the Board of Deputies' own minute-book admits: 'as a result of the steps taken by the Board, the book appeared with the obnoxious chapters omitted'.[65]

Interesting conclusions can therefore be drawn from the circumstances surrounding this book. The editor's statements prove without a doubt that Burton's investigations into this subject provided evidence of Jewish ritual murder. There is relatively little reliable material from modern times about these accusations against the Jews, and it is therefore all the more regrettable that scholars have not been given access to these sources.

Furthermore, we once again find irrefutable evidence of international Jewry's collaboration. The Jews in Smyrna felt threatened by Burton's research and therefore turned to their comrades in London, who brought their influence to bear on the situation, with the result that the Foreign Minister himself acceded to their requests.

The supposed supremely English value of 'freedom of expression' is also brought under the spotlight of truth: a scientific work, even before publication, had the consequence of bringing complete disgrace down on the head of a lauded official because he had dared to make anti-Jewish statements available to the public.

To shed further light on Burton's fate, it should be noted that it was none other than Lord Rosebery who forever dashed Burton's hopes of a transfer to Tangier by appointing another official. Lord Rosebery, at that point Foreign Secretary, later Prime Minister, was married to a daughter of Rothschild, and therefore was closely connected to international Jewry.

Lord Rosebery has since died and was succeeded by his son, the current Earl of Rosebery. The current earl bears not only the first name of his maternal grandfather—Meyer—but also the facial features and bearing of his Jewish ancestors. With more than 50,000 *Morgen* [31,250 acres] of land, he is one of the largest landowners in England.[66]

His sisters, likewise half-Jewish, also married into the high nobility. One sister became the wife of Lieutenant-General Sir Charles Grant, while the other is the wife of the well-known Marquess of Crewe. As is well known, the current Lord Crewe declared with particular pride at a banquet in

---

[65] Emanuel: pp. 142-3. Translator's note: All QVOS. Interestingly, the British public could read details of Jewish ritual murder earlier in the Victorian era, and changes made to later editions of a popular reference work support the thesis that rising Jewish influence led to the curation of publicly available information. Readers may wish to consult an 1840s edition of *Haydn's Dictionary of Dates* (s.v. 'Jews') to see statements regarding three Jewish ritual murders of children in medieval England (two completed, one thwarted but with mutilation), along with a ritual murder in Paris. However, from the 1870 edition onwards, all incidents of Jewish ritual mutilation/murder are absent from the 'Jews' entry, although the incidents of persecution by the host population are of course still featured. [See Translator's Bibliography]

[66] *Who's Who 1938*, p. 2918.

1905 that he was of Jewish descent and that his wife belonged to the Roth-schild family.[67]

One of his daughters is married to Sir Edward Coates, another to the Honorable George Colville, son of Viscount Colville of Culross. The other two are the wives of Major J. H. Dodds and the Duke of Roxburghe respectively.[68]

England and World Jewry

The books mentioned in the last chapter were expressions of the anti-Jewish sentiment which had reawakened among the people. Of course, this hostile current was not lost on the Jews. They therefore considered a stronger organization necessary, especially since the Jews' institution in England was to all effects outdated and the French one, the Alliance Israélite, barely existed after the war of 1870-71. Under the principal leadership of Sir Francis Gold-smid and Dr. Benish, the then-editor of the *Jewish Chronicle*, the existing organization was completely rebuilt, headed by, among others, the afore-mentioned Sir George Jessel. Later we find Baron Henry de Worms, later Lord Pirbright, in a leadership position.

From now on, according to the Jews' own statements, it was once again fully justifiable to claim that London was their world center, to which all persecuted brothers could turn their eyes and expect to receive assistance. On the occasion of the persecution of the Hebrews in Romania, debates took place in Parliament in which members of all parties spoke out in favor of the poor victims. Delegations were sent to ministers, and the opinion everywhere was that the persecutions were 'a disgrace to modern civilization'.[69]

To what extent Jewish power had already spread in past times can be seen from a summary of the interventions carried out on their behalf by the British government between 1860 and 1910. This is the only way to truly demonstrate the extent to which the British government has been turned into a tool of world Jewry in past decades. We know that this assertion requires irrefutable proof, which we can provide, once again, with the help of the Hebrews themselves. One of their ethnic kinsmen, Charles Emanuel, has published excerpts from the minute-books of the meetings of the London Committee of Deputies of the British Jews [known today as the Board of Deputies of British Jews], which is a treasure trove of proof for our supposition, and which we will cite exclusively as there is no more impeccable source. In addition, other official documents are referenced for readers to

---

[67] *Who's Who 1938*, p. 1343. & *Transactions of the Jewish Historical Society of England*, Vol. 5, p. 293

[68] *Who's Who 1938*, p. 656. & p. 691. & p. 924. & p. 2939.

[69] Wolf: *Essays*, pp. 351-2. Translator's note: QVOS.

consult for further information, such as the Blue Book, which documents the treatment of Jews in Serbia and Romania.[70]

With all of the relevant interventions by the British government, it remains irrefutable that the entire Foreign Office apparatus and the use of English global power serve not only for the attainment of British interests, but are also fully at the disposal of world Jewry.

Furthermore, this interference in the affairs of foreign countries cannot be explained by a certain kind-hearted attitude on the part of the English, because their entire history is a chain of brutality against the peoples they have subjugated. One need only think of the extermination of the natives of North America and Tasmania and the atrocities in India, as well as the suffering of Boer women and children in the concentration camps, which is still fresh in everyone's memory. With this in mind, it could only have been a concern for Hebrew interests that guided the British government to such actions. A further logical conclusion of establishing a dependence on international Jewry should not be considered too outlandish.

But now to the individual cases. In 1860, the memory of Father Tomaso's 1840 murder in Damascus was revived when a memorial plaque was placed in a Capuchin chapel of that city, which stated that Tomaso had been murdered by the Jews. The Foreign Office in London was made aware of this inscription and decided to intervene to have the plaque removed. 'As a matter of fact,' Emanuel reports, 'a little later an accidental fire removed both tablet and chapel.' Apparently, following this 'accidental fire', unrest against the Jews began, and the Board of Deputies called on the Foreign Office to intervene: 'Lord John Russell sent instructions to the British Ambassador at Constantinople to take immediate steps for the protection of the Jews. This he did with such energy that many of the oppressors were punished, and the accused Jew was set free.' Emanuel does not reveal what caused the unrest or why the Jew was imprisoned. But there can hardly be any doubt that all of this was connected to the burning of the chapel.[71]

In the same year, news came of poor treatment of Jews in Persia, where the Jewish quarter in Hamadan had been ransacked. Warnings from the British envoy to the Shah not only went unheeded, but also led to further punishment of the Jews. The British envoy was then instructed to make another protest, the outcome of which was not reported.[72]

The Foreign Office intervened in similar matters with the governments of Wallachia, Corfu, and Tripoli over the next two years, mostly with suc-

---

[70] Emanuel: Note the title page. Translator's note: The title page shows that the entire contents of the book was taken from the London Committee's minute-books, as Emanuel was the Committee secretary and minute-book custodian. Note that all other references to this organization shall be made as the 'Board of Deputies' to prevent confusion.

[71] Emanuel: pp. 76-7. Translator's note: QVOS.

[72] Emanuel: p. 76.

cess. When the Jews who had emigrated from Russia to Jerusalem in 1863 gave up their citizenship, they were immediately placed under the protection of the British consul on instructions from London.[73]

For the year 1865, the minute-book recorded the following events relating to Serbia:

> The year opened with the news that a memorial to the Prince of Servia as to the unhappy conditions of his Jewish subjects had been duly delivered through Her Majesty's Consul-General, with a recommendation that he should give it his favourable consideration. News was further received that the Consul-General had summoned the heads of the Jewish Community, and had informed them that he had received instructions to do what he could in their behalf. In April, however, fresh outrages necessitated a further application to the Foreign Office, which made fresh representations. The Prince, in acknowledging the Board's memorial, assured the Board of his solicitude for his subjects, without distinction of creed, and that the temporary disabilities of the Jews would be removed as occasion permitted.[74]

The same promise was made by the Shah of Persia after repeated requests, but it would appear that these promises were not made seriously, as in the following years the British Foreign Office saw itself obligated to intervene once more in favor of the Jews.[75]

The next four years would see a number of different requests to Romania. Lord Stanley had replaced the Earl of Clarendon as Foreign Secretary, and declared to the Jewish leaders that 'he would always be ready to employ his good offices to save the Jews from persecution.' When in 1867, in spite of earlier promises from the government concerned, the Jews in Romania were declared vagabonds and delivered over to the soldiery for expulsion, the British representative was instructed to speak to the reigning prince personally and demand that the officials in question be punished. The following year the Romanian government guaranteed general protection for Jews. But when anti-Jewish measures became known shortly afterwards, the British Consul General, on the personal instruction of the Foreign Minister, protested vigorously against them.[76]

---

[73] Emanuel: pp. 77-8. & pp. 80-1.
[74] Emanuel: p. 82. Translator's note: QVOS.
[75] Emanuel: p. 84.
[76] Emanuel: p. 85. & p. 86. & p. 87. & p. 90.

In 1869, Serbia gave great cause for concern to international Jewry. As a result, the British government left no doubt that Serbia would only receive Britain's support against Turkey if it granted Jews complete religious equality.[77] In the years 1872, 1875, and 1876 the Foreign Office again supported the Jews in Turkey and each time succeeded in satisfying their demands.[78]

When, in 1876, conditions in Zergoon (Persia) deteriorated for the Jews and they appealed to the Board of Deputies in London for help, the Foreign Office telegraphed instructions to the British representative to demand immediate protective measures from the government. An order was at once given to the Governor of the city to take the Jews under his special protection.[79]

Over the following decades, Romania and Morocco in particular were subject to British protests of this type. In 1876, discussions took place about concluding a trade agreement, with Romania on one side, and England and France on the other. The original proposals for this would have excluded the Jews in England from the trade benefits granted therein. The Jews got wind of it and in a memorial protested against this clause in the treaty. A copy of the memorial was sent to the Alliance Israélite in Paris. In light of this, the Foreign Office assured the Board that a treaty on the lines proposed would never be signed by British government. Emanuel then adds: 'The Board was able to inform it [the Foreign Office] that the French Government was similarly minded.' [80]

In the same year, expulsion decrees for Jews were issued in individual districts of Romania. At the request of the Foreign Office in London, these regulations were not only repealed, but four officials responsible for them were fired.[81]

As the Berlin Conference approached, the Board of Deputies in London presented the British government with a request to demand measures for the freedom and equality of the Jews in Romania and other Balkan states, in the event of said states making a declaration of independence. We will remember that Disraeli intervened in this regard. However, the Hebrews were by no means satisfied with the agreements he had made, and they expressed their disappointment in a special letter to Lord Salisbury, in which they claimed that the British government had been duped by Romania. In 1884, the Jews believed that Romania had violated the treaties concluded in Berlin to their detriment and therefore requested the intervention of the British government in Bucharest.

For the first time, they received a negative response, and experienced the same outcome the following year. Lord Salisbury explained to them that

---

[77] Emanuel: p. 91.
[78] Emanuel: pp. 95, 102, 103-4.
[79] Emanuel: pp. 102-3.
[80] Emanuel: p. 104. Translator's note: QVOS.
[81] Emanuel: pp. 105-6.

this was an internal Romanian matter in which it was not possible to get involved. This rejection is probably due to Lord Salisbury's general attitude towards the Jews, which was not particularly friendly. At that time, he was Prime Minister and at the same time managed the Foreign Ministry. This period of his government as well as those subsequent are remarkable in relation to other cabinets for the almost complete absence of such interference. We shall return to Lord Salisbury later.[82]

Morocco was to become the subject of British protests in 1876, 1880, 1885, and 1887. When the British warnings in the penultimate case were not enough, Britain acted together with France, the United States and Italy.[83] In the period from 1889 to 1896, it was likewise achieved in Morocco that the Jews were widely protected in every instance and that any native Moroccans involved in anti-Jewish incidents were severely punished.[84]

In Corfu in 1880, a criminal trial was held against Jews accused of ritual murder after the body of a Greek boy was found in Alexandria, a few weeks before Passover. At the request of his ethnic brethren, the Foreign Office appointed a British Commissioner to take part in the trial. The Jews were acquitted.[85]

In Turkey in 1888, Foreign Office interventions to rescind Ottoman restrictions on 'foreign Jews of the industrial class' residing in the Holy Land were also successful.[86]

In Malta in 1892, under the imprimatur of the local Roman Catholic archbishop, a leaflet was publicly sold which accused the Jews of ritual murder, and which urged the populace to keep a close guard over their children. The Jews of Malta, according to general custom, turned to London, with the result that Lord Ripon of the Foreign Office sent instructions to the Governor for the protection of the Jews. Furthermore, at the instigation of the Jews in London, the Archbishop of Westminster asked his colleague in Malta to use his influence to have the leaflet withdrawn. This intervention also had its desired effect.[87]

In the same year, the Jews in Switzerland were disturbed by a bill that would ban the kosher slaughter of cattle [*shechita*]. If the bill were to be made law, international Jewry feared that this might incentivize other nations to follow suit. And once again it was Lord Rosebery who intervened on behalf of Jewish interests by passing this communication on to Lord Ripon at

---

[82] Emanuel: pp. 107-9. & p. 110. & pp. 120-1. & pp. 122-3.

[83] Emanuel: pp. 104, 110, 121, 125.

[84] Emanuel: pp. 128, 131, 133, 136, 137, 140.

[85] Emanuel: pp. 114-115. Translator's note: This is not to be confused with the Corfu ritual murder case of 1891, for which the British sent warships to the island to 'restore order' (*idem*, p. 132).

[86] Emanuel: p. 126. Translator's note: QVOS.

[87] Emanuel: p. 133.

the Foreign Office. An article was immediately published in the *British Medical Journal* stating that, according to scientists, the Jewish method of slaughter was the least cruel and most effective, an article which was circulated in Switzerland. Lord Rosebery kept the Board of Deputies regularly updated on this matter. The bill was rejected in Switzerland's National Council by a narrow majority, meaning that further measures from London were unnecessary.

Further Foreign Office interventions also took place in Persia that year.[88] In 1890 a Jew was killed in Shiraz (Persia), and at the instigation of England the perpetrator was punished and the Jew's family compensated. Two years later, Lord Rosebery demanded protective measures for the Jews given the riots taking place there, and troops were brought in to restore order. In the same way, similar riots were prevented in 1898 and 1907.[89]

But what most concerned the Jews and the Foreign Office from the close of the nineteenth century onwards were the events taking place in Russia. When the rights of Jews in Russia were again restricted in 1890, a meeting was held at the Guildhall, chaired by the Lord Mayor of the City of London, which 'denounced the persecutions of the Jews as a scandal to Christianity.' A memorial was drawn up and sent to the Tsar, but he refused to receive it. This time the British government felt it was unable to intervene as it was 'a matter of domestic legislation.' Nevertheless, it directed its representative in Odessa to submit reports on the impact of the legislative measures.[90] Nevertheless, in 1904, 1905, 1906, and 1910, the Foreign Office actively worked in favor of the Jews in Russia and each time ensured that nothing was done against them.[91]

This short summary, by no means exhaustive, of the interventions made by England on behalf of the Jews, clearly demonstrates the extent to which world Jewry and Great Britain have been working in collaboration for a long time. One can go even further, and say without exaggeration that it is truly difficult to determine any major difference between these two forces. The Jews themselves make no secret of their prevailing power, as can be seen from the following statement by the Hebrew Simon Wolf:

> We all know that the first bankers in the world—Rothschilds—are Jews; we know that they control not only the money market, but also the political destiny of the European world. [...] The Press of Europe is mostly controlled by Jews;

---

[88] Emanuel: p. 134.
[89] Emanuel: p. 128. & p. 134. & pp. 144, 172.
[90] Emanuel: pp. 129-30. Translator's note: QVOS.
[91] Emanuel: pp. 161, 165, 167, 185.

the leading editors are Jews. [...] The revolutionary feeling in Europe owed its life and stimulus to Jews...[92]

The Boer War, A Jewish War

The close ties between the Jews and England also emerge from the causes that led to the Boer War in 1899. The Boers had emigrated from the Cape Colony, which was under English rule, in the first half of the 19th century because the English did not allow them to develop their own cultural life.

They colonized, among other territories, the Transvaal, which since 1884 had merged with other small Boer free states to form the South African Republic. In all of the years before and after this founding, there were legal disputes with the English until the outbreak of war. And when, in 1886, rich goldfields were discovered within Boer territory, it was obvious that the English would soon try to incorporate this country into their colonial empire.[93]

The gold industry resulted in many Englishmen emigrating to the Boer republic, and they settled mainly in Johannesburg. Because of English allegations of poor treatment and the Boers' denying them full citizenship, England believed it was entitled to make harsh demands on the country's owners. The partial rejection of these demands and other circumstances ultimately led to the outbreak of war.

At least to the same extent—and many believed that it was the only reason —there was another cause of the war, namely, the desire of the Jewish-owned gold industry to come under England's rule. To understand this, we must take a brief look at the conditions in the Boer Republic at the time.

The center of the gold industry, Johannesburg, had grown to around 100,000 inhabitants in a very short time. The shops and places of entertainment were in Hebrew hands, and as early as 1900, half of the land in the Transvaal and nine-tenths of the national wealth belonged to Jews. In the opinion of J. A. Hobson, who expressly stated in his book that he in no way agreed with 'the ignominious passion of *Judenhetze* [Jew-hatred],' Johannesburg was undoubtedly 'the New Jerusalem'.[94]

Even if the number of Jews was relatively small at around 15,000, they still dominated the whole life of this city. The gold mines were almost entirely in their hands, headed at that time by the so-called Eckstein Group who, alongside the company Wernher, Beit & Co., controlled, among other assets, no fewer than 29 mines, with a market value then of some £76 million. And everywhere were similar companies with great monopolistic influence over the country's entire economy. The City of London, including Rothschild,

---

[92] Simon Wolf: pp. 36-9. Translator's note: QVOS.
[93] Reitz: p. 36.
[94] Hobson: *The War in South Africa...*, pp. 11-13. & pp. 189-90. Translator's note: QVOS.

likewise had major interests in the gold industry. Names such as Albu, Barnato, Neumann and others were and still are influential in the Transvaal. All other branches of industry were largely in the hands of the Jews, regardless of whether these were wholesale or retail trade. Under such circumstances, it was inevitable that the stock market transactions would also be controlled by the Jews. The stock exchange was closed on Jewish holidays. As usual, the Hebrews were also heavily engaged as moneylenders, and the colonists and Boers on their farms were completely indebted to them. But they had gained their greatest influence by controlling most of the press and thus public opinion. The predominance of the Jews was so great that some entertainment venues were not open on Jewish holidays.[95]

The Jews were dissatisfied with the Boer government for various reasons. Apart from what they considered to be too-high dynamite prices (there was a state dynamite monopoly in which the Jews were not involved) and the excessive cost of rail freight (the railway was also almost exclusively owned by the government), the main issue for the constant complaints from Jewish groups was the wage structure and the social question intimately linked to this.[96]

The Jews' main aim was to introduce wages that were as low as possible, which did not go above 55% of the gold mines' total expenses. They therefore lobbied the government to demand that contracts be agreed with the Kaffir chiefs to send labor as cheaply as possible, but the government did no more than it considered convenient to the public interest. A major shortage of workers arose, which resulted in an increase in wages. This development could only be remedied by bringing in black labor from the neighboring British colonies for the benefit of the companies, and the leading Jews in the gold industry strongly emphasized this necessity. As one, a Mr. Rudd, put it:

> If under the cry of civilization, we in Egypt lately mowed down 10,000 or 20,000 Dervishes with Maxims [machine guns], surely it cannot be considered a hardship to compel the natives in South Africa to give three months in the year to do a little honest work.[97]

In addition, the economic situation in the English colony of Rhodesia was very bad, where the leading gold industry companies also had major interests. It was hoped that the losses suffered there could easily be offset by

---

[95] Hobson: *The War in South Africa...*, pp. 90-5.

[96] Hobson: *The War in South Africa...*, pp. 26-7, 230. Reitz: p.62.

[97] Hobson: *The War in South Africa...*, p. 230 ff. Translator's note: QVOS [p. 235]. It may also interest readers to know that Mr. Rudd [*ibid.*] also decried popular white opposition to his plans as 'a morbid sentimentality among a large section of the community on the question of the natives'.

the large surpluses expected from the South African gold mines. However, the annexation of the Transvaal was necessary for the merger of these businesses.[98] In view of all of these factors, the goal of the Jews and their friends was to overthrow the Boer government and have the country occupied by the English.[99]

It was, of course, impossible to communicate these reasons to the British public. Others would therefore have to be invented in order to have a pretext that would justify going to war.

Nothing could be easier. There were reports of alleged attacks by the Boers against the British who lived in Johannesburg and the surrounding area. Whether and to what extent these were illegal measures is virtually impossible to determine today. In any case, the incidents were of minor importance and were only artificially turned into barbaric atrocities against British subjects by English news articles and their accompanying editorials. The main people who helped here were the press, as well as the Jews and their allies, who had already prepared the ground well. The Eckstein and Barnato group owned the majority of shares in Cape Town's leading evening newspaper, the *Cape Argus*, and then soon came to control almost all other important newspapers in that English colony. Eventually even the most influential newspaper of Cape Colony, the *Cape Times*, was bought up by the Jews and their allies, along with other newspapers published in Port Elizabeth, Durban, and other important localities. The strategy was, above all, to convince the Cape Colony populace that there was only a constant state of insecurity in South Africa because of the independent Boers.

In the Boer Republic, the press was also controlled by the same groups, which had cunningly founded various daily newspapers in recent years, all with the same goal of opposing the Boer government and provoking a crisis. The *Star* and the *Leader* ensured above all that their reporting of incidents was bound to injure the pride of the English.[100]

But it was winning the public opinion of England which most concerned the Jews and their allies. It was not too difficult, as the press of the mother country mostly reproduced verbatim the reports from the South African newspapers, so that the same exaggerations were published in Britain. The three largest newspapers of the Conservative Party even received their news directly from the editorial team of the aforementioned *Star*, while another Tory newspaper received theirs from the *Leader*. Liberal newspapers were also provided with news largely from the Jews and their friends. Even after the war broke out, it was only in this way that initially the London press was informed of what was happening in the theatre of war; reports were syn-

---

[98] Reitz: p. 60.
[99] Stead: *The Scandal...*, p. 7.
[100] Hobson: *The War in South Africa...*, pp. 206-15.

dicated of unspeakable atrocities by the Boers, and these were all too readily believed by the credulous everywhere.[101] Thus, even at the time, there was no doubt in the minds of insightful individuals that the press had worked to make the English population—first that of South Africa, followed by that of Great Britain—ready for war.[102]

The war certainly brought about one of the most valuable land acquisitions for the English Crown, but without securing any advantage for the individual Englishman in Africa. Nor can one talk of English rule in South Africa, given that the entirety of life there was ruled by the Jews.

Thus the conquest of the Boer Republic only served to strengthen the power of international Jewry and its allies, since the importance of this acquisition is evident from the fact that South Africa has long been producing 50% or more of the world's total annual gold output. We will even see in a later chapter how today one can speak credibly of a Jewish global monopoly on gold.

Edward VII, Friend of the Jews and Supporter of Coterie Politics

In 1901 Queen Victoria died. Her son, Edward VII, succeeded her to the throne. And if the Boer War was one of the most important milestones of Jewish dominance in Great Britain, it is fair to say that the reign of Edward VII brought the Jews their crowning glory.

His preference for Jews is so well known that only a few details need be given. His greatest confidants were the three Rothschild brothers, of whom Alfred is described as his dearest friend. The Sassoon family could also not complain about not enjoying great affection from the monarch. Sir Ernest Cassel is usually described as his closest friend, whom the king made, along with another Jewish friend Sir Edgar Speyer, a member of the Privy Council. Sir Ernest was perhaps, next to Rothschild, the most influential banker of his time and possessed a massive fortune. He was born in Cologne and had worked hard behind the scenes for an Anglo-German rapprochement, to this end setting up the Anglo-German Fellowship, a society to promote friendly relations between the Germans and the English, and putting £200,000 at its disposal. His daughter is the wife of the well-known Lord Mount Temple, and she has two daughters from this union. One of them married Captain A. Cunningham-Reid, a Conservative MP, and the other married Lord Louis Mountbatten, a member of the nobility who has been the King's aide-de-camp since 1937. Mountbatten is closely related to the royal family. His father, the erstwhile Prince of Battenberg, who felt it his duty to

---

[101] Hobson: *The War in South Africa...*, pp. 215-22.
[102] Hobson: *The War in South Africa...*, pp. 227-8. Stead, in the prologue of Reitz's book, p. VIII.

anglicize his name in 1917, was married to Princess Victoria, the daughter of Grand Duke Ludwig IV of Hesse and his wife Alice. The latter was the daughter of Queen Victoria.[103]

All of King Edward VII's Jewish friends belonged to the most influential financial and industrial circles. This is shown most clearly in a letter from Kaiser Wilhelm II to Prince von Bülow, in which the Kaiser writes as follows:

> Ballin told me that Wernher Beit had visited him lately. He (Beit) is the great speculator and Stock Exchange jobber of the City, one of the organisers of the Boer War and African mining swindles. He takes care of all the speculations of His Majesty, who must be almost a partner in his transactions. He must always be providing His Majesty with heaps of gold, of which he is always in need. One may say, 'he runs the king'.[104]

In view of all of this, it is not difficult to imagine the extent to which the king favored the Jews, whom he tried to make socially acceptable if this were not already the case. In England this often happens when those concerned aspire to become members of gentlemen's clubs. However, the king encountered very strong resistance to his efforts in this regard and was not always successful. It is for this reason that he founded the Marlborough Club and only invited as members those who did not oppose the admission of Jews. Today the club is still one of the most exclusive in London.

---

[103] *Jewish Year Book 1937*, p. 368. & Jackson: p. 193. Translator's note: For a lively contemporary portrait of the king's relationship with his powerful Jewish friends, including Cassel, see Chapter XXIV of Banister [Translator's Bibliography]. & *Jewish Chronicle*, 7/5/1937. & *Who's Who 1938*, p. 797. & 2496-7.

[104] 'Spectator': *Prince Bülow and the Kaiser*, p. 193. Translator's note: The Oakley Williams translation [London: Thornton Butterworth, n.d.] cited by Aldag here does not contain this quotation beyond the first sentence (found on p. 206). In *Letters of Prince Von Bülow* (trans. Frederic Whyte, London: Hutchinson & Co., 1930), the phrase 'one of the organizers of the Boer War and African mining swindles' is missing from the quotation, which is otherwise as it has been reproduced above. Yet the full quotation as Aldag gives it was known in the German-speaking world, having appeared in books published in 1925 (*Die grosse politik der europäischen kabinette, 1871-1914*) and 1930 (*Fürst Bülow und der Kaiser*, the German original of the book cited by Aldag), so it appears that the quotation was edited down for the Anglosphere to minimize controversy, and Aldag was unaware of this. For example, Arthur Leese in his *Gentile Folly: The Rothschilds* (1940), repeats the edited quotation, likely taken from Whyte, which, given Leese's agenda, supports the thesis that the full original version of the letter (as shown above) was unknown to English speakers. Given that the MP Mr. A. B. Markham, was successfully sued for libel by Messrs. Eckstein, Wernher, Beit & Co. for having repeated his House of Commons comment of 19 March 1901 outside of the House after having being dared to do so, in which he called the company 'a gang of common thieves and swindlers', one can understand why the editorial decision was made.

The fact that he ended cordial relations with a very worthy cabinet minister also testifies to the king's determination to do everything for his Jewish friends. In this case, it was the aforementioned Lord Salisbury, whose reasons for his resignation are still not entirely clear today. Although his poor health probably gave some impetus to this decision, there is, among other reasons put forward, much evidence to suggest that Lord Salisbury was unwilling, despite constant pressure from Edward VII, to include one of the latter's Jewish friends on the coronation honors list, in order to elevate his friend to the peerage. When the king insisted unconstitutionally upon his request, Lord Salisbury submitted his resignation.[105]

The Jews Flood into England

Under King Edward VII, a new law was passed to prevent unrestricted immigration to Great Britain. This was the culmination of a years-long struggle between both sides on the issue of immigration control. In the second half of the 19th century, huge masses of migrants flowed from east to west, made up mainly of Jewish elements. Since the end of the Crimean War, there had been a steady year-to-year increase in immigration from Russia which at the time, it must be remembered, also included Poland and Lithuania.[106]

Apparently the new naturalization law of 1870 had produced an incentivizing effect for foreigners, as according to this, under favorable conditions, they were able to obtain naturalization after just a few years.

After 1882, a torrent of Eastern Jews [*Ostjuden*] poured over England, when Russia passed its famous May Laws of that year. These tightened the existing regulations that Jews were only allowed to live in the countryside under very specific conditions, which included having to prove that they had already lived there for some time, otherwise they had to return to the nearest town. In addition, they were only allowed to stay within fifteen precisely designated provinces of the then Russian Empire. The result was that the cities in the affected areas were overcrowded, which meant that the Jews had to look for other places to settle.

Most of them turned to England and America for succor, and just as today, there were protest gatherings against such laws, which were continually excoriated as a disgrace to civilization. In London, at one such meeting held at Mansion House for the poor persecuted Jews, a total of £108,000 was raised and handed over to the corresponding refugee committee.[107]

The Jews arrived mainly by ship from Hamburg and Bremen, and were mostly landed in London and Hull. There were practically no difficulties

---

[105] Keith: pp. 105-6.
[106] Wilkins: *Alien Invasion*, p. 18.
[107] Landa: p. 7 ff.. Wolf: *Essays...*, p. 358.

with immigration. At that time in England there was no requirement to have a passport or to register with the authorities. There was only one immigration law, from the time of King William IV [the Alien Act], which had been passed around fifty years previously and therefore no longer fitted the changed circumstances. This law simply required the captains of incoming ships to prepare a passenger manifest of foreigners on board [known historically as a 'return'] and hand it over to the customs officer on duty. There was no provision for any kind of ban on landing, so anyone who wanted could come to England. The newcomers usually presented a deplorable sight, which is known, among other ways, from the accounts of customs officers who had worked for many years in the London port and who were called to give witness statements before a Parliamentary committee in 1889.[108]

According to these witness statements, the passengers of such immigrant ships were completely without resources. With very few exceptions, they arrived in England without luggage, and usually only had a bit of dry bread and a herring tied into a handkerchief; their clothes were filthy and often torn to rags. They were almost exclusively Polish, Russian, Lithuanian, Galician, and German Jews, and when such ships arrived, one could see their ethnic brethren standing around the dock waiting for them. The authorities had no interest in determining what became of them. They were mostly seen disappearing in the direction of the East End of London, particularly the Whitechapel area.[109]

It was not London alone that was blessed with these Jews. Many other cities, particularly Bradford, Hull, Manchester, Glasgow, and Leeds, were also populated with them. The result of this was that there was a severe housing shortage in the cities concerned. Entire city neighborhoods were evacuated by the English population, who could not stand the filth and stench in them. An idea of the situation that the natives of England found themselves having to tolerate can be seen in the following extract from newspaper article 'Sanitation and Whitechapel', taken from the *Eastern Post and City Chronicle*, 22 November 1884:[110]

> [T]he great difficulty the [Whitechapel Board of Works] officers have to cope with is in the fact that a very large number of the houses in the district are occupied by foreign Jews, who either do not know how to use the latrine, water, and other sanitary accommodation provided, or prefer their own semi-barbarous habits, and use the floors of their rooms and passages and yards to deposit their filth. Even in places where caretakers see

---

[108] *Accounts and Papers... 1889*, Volume 10, pp. 267-9.
[109] *Accounts and Papers...* 1889, Volume 10, pp. 315-333.
[110] *Accounts and Papers...* 1889, Volume 10, pp. 333-42, 348 ff.

that yards and closets are cleansed every morning, dirt and destruction follow the same day.

To what extent this immigration was overwhelming the native population can be seen in the example city of Leeds. The number of Jews there had increased so much that the English population was extremely unhappy. It was not possible to determine exactly how many of them had settled there, because neither authorities nor private individuals had bothered to adhere the aforementioned law, which had effectively fallen into disuse.

Official censuses were also inaccurate, as we shall see. How different opinions were about the number of Jews in a medium-sized city like Leeds, which had a population of around 370,000 at the time, can be seen from an official survey on the matter. The rabbi of the Jewish community called to make a statement put the number at a maximum of 6,000, while a doctor who had a large practice in the Jewish districts put it at 15,000. A Leeds councilor, however, estimated there were at least 30,000 souls.[111]

Things had also gradually worsened in certain parts of London, such as Hackney, Shoreditch, and Whitechapel. The number of Jews settled there had tripled to quadrupled in six to eight years, which meant that the English population had already been pushed out of entire streets.[112]

After all of this, it is not surprising that the English, who did not wish to tolerate this foreign invasion, complained about this state of things both in Parliament and in public, and urgently demanded a solution. The Jews and their friends, on the other hand, were hostile to these efforts. Nevertheless, in 1889 the aforementioned committee was set up in Parliament, which was initially intended to determine the extent of the immigration and, as far as possible, its disadvantages. It met over the months of May and June and, after hearing numerous statements, to which we have already partially referred above, produced an extensive report.

At the end of the report, the committee summarized its findings in seven points, and in five paragraphs gave its suggestions for improving the situation. In this report, they stated, among other things, that immigration was increasing significantly and that 'the poorest and worst class would remain in England.' However, the report did not call for restrictions on immigration, as a law to do so would cause too many difficulties. One should simply take measures to carry out an accurate official census of foreigners in the future.[113] Given this fact, it is all too understandable that the influx of Jews increased from year to year.

---

[111] *Accounts and Papers... 1889*, Volume 10, pp. 335-48.

[112] *Accounts and Papers... 1889*, Volume 10, p. 348 ff.

[113] *Accounts and Papers... 1889*, Volume 10, pp. 274-5.

In the meantime, unbearable conditions had arisen in the economy in terms of daily wages and other working conditions. In 1890, the so-called Sweating Committee met under Lord Dunraven, who, after lengthy investigations, drafted the report to be submitted. His view, that the anti-social working conditions were mainly due to immigration, was not shared by the other members of the committee; they refused to approve the draft, whereupon Lord Dunraven resigned his chairmanship.

In the same year, opponents of unrestricted immigration tried to draw public attention to the danger of foreign infiltration. They called meetings in which Lord Dunraven and Sir Howard Vincent were keen participants. Arnold White and W. H. Wilkins, Lord Dunraven's former secretary, also held leading positions. Wilkins, in an impassioned article in the *National Review* of September 1890, accused the pauper Jewish immigrants of despoiling the native English of their birthrights.[114]

The advocates for immigration, who were mostly found in liberal circles, did everything they could to downplay the threat as non-existent. They referred, among other things, to the now-published official statistics from the Board of Trade, which differentiated between migrants in transit and those who remained in England. Their opponents, however, emphasized that the publication in question did not correspond to the facts of reality for various reasons. We will see to what extent these opponents of immigration were right.

Meanwhile, Jewish immigration grew to ever greater proportions, especially given that, in 1890, Russia passed new regulations to implement the May Laws of 1882, which spurred even greater migration of Jews from east to west. Another Mansion House meeting took place to protest the Tsar's barbaric measures, and again a sum of around £100,000 was raised.

Nevertheless, there was such a widespread interest in the whole question of immigration that even the Liberal government which came to power in 1892 could not completely avoid the issue. Initially, however, actions were limited only to new investigations being carried out, and two members of the committee set up for this purpose—one of them named Schloss—were sent to America to investigate the legal restrictions to immigration that had been introduced there.[115]

On 11 February 1893, the problem was the subject of a long debate in Parliament. The opponents of the foreign infiltration of England were led by MP James Lowther, who pointed out that public corporations and trade associations found further immigration intolerable. The official statistics on immigration, he told the House, were worthless for assessing the situation. It would happen that the passenger manifests that the ship's captains had to

---

[114] Landa: pp. 12-14. Translator's note: This is the aforementioned William Henry Wilkins who edited Sir Richard Burton's book, *The Jew, The Gypsy and El Islam.*
[115] Landa: pp. 14-20.

prepare by law, a law dating from the time of King William IV which had been 'dragged from oblivion by the Select Committee' and on which the official censuses were based, were often prepared by the cabin boys of the steamers in question. In addition, one would rely entirely on the information provided by the immigrants and no steps were taken to determine if the declared transit passengers continued on their stated onward journey. And due to the new, stricter immigration regulations in America, there was even the risk that many of these declared transit passengers would be forced to remain in England in any case, being 'utterly unfit and destitute.' The inward flow of foreigners, with the intensifying factors of the immigrants being concentrated into certain areas, and in particular trades, was having the effect of displacing 'for the most part the best blood of the country', as the English themselves were driven to emigrate.[116]

Lowther's speech was constantly interrupted with disingenuous questions from the Jewish MP Sir Julian Goldsmid, who over the next few years became very vocal in his support of unrestricted immigration. As chairman of the so-called Russian-Jewish Committee, he played a very active role in promoting its interests.

Over the course of the debate, Lowther wanted to know the whereabouts of the immigration restriction bill of the previous government. Sir Charles Dilke told him that he had made inquiries about the bill, but 'could find no trace of it.' Mundella, the President of the Board of Trade, reported to the House that he had 'made inquiries if any Bill existed...but there was not a vestige or a scrap of a Bill left behind by the late Government.' But another MP, Mr. Stuart Wortley, contradicted the assertions of previous two gentlemen when he stated: 'I have seen the Bill.' Of course, given the Liberal government's reluctance to impose immigration restrictions, this stance was not surprising.

As the debate progressed, the immigration supporters argued that poor Jews could not be deprived of the opportunity to immigrate to England. They had suffered so inhumanely under the harsh laws of Russia, 'a despotic country', that that they had to be granted refuge, the supporters argued. After all, how much we owe them! Consider the great achievements of Disraeli, himself the son of 'destitute aliens.' Moreover, one should not worry about the supposedly degraded immigrants, because for every one of them who entered, ten Englishmen of the same class emigrated. In fact, Jews were, 'as a rule...fairly intelligent, exceedingly industrious, and extremely sober, and their faults were only those which they would expect to find in a persecuted and a hunted people.' And was it not that 'that great right of asylum...had always been vaunted as the boast of England'? Was not England 'the great sanctuary of the world'? These remarks were made principally by Sir

---

[116] *Hansard*: Series IV, Volume 8, p. 1154 ff. Translator's note: QVOS.

Charles Dilke and Mr. Mundella, but also by Rothschild and Goldsmid, who ably insinuated that the factual economic and social arguments made against mass immigration were simply a cover for the corresponding speaker's anti-Jewish religious bigotry, as we see from the protests recorded in the transcript that this was evidently a charge with which the opponents of immigration were fearful of being smeared. Perhaps unsurprisingly, the emotive thesis of the pro-immigration side prevailed at the vote, with the result that no legal restriction was imposed on immigration.[117]

However, in May 1894 a long report containing many tables of statistics was published by the Board of Trade, summarizing four years of investigation. But as before, the difficulties associated with accurately registering all foreigners were pointed out, especially since passports were not yet compulsory in England. After 1890, it is true that the aforementioned passenger list was required of ship's captains arriving at 26 ports in England, but in Dover, Folkestone, Harwich, Southampton, and Newhaven, only the steerage passengers were counted and identified by name.[118]

A large part of the report is devoted to the lives and activities of the Jews in London, and from it we learn that they used every free minute to take part in discussions about the Talmud. The general complaint was that they had no morals in their trading practices and did not honor contracts. It is no secret, the report stated, that the populace hates the Jews, who already dominate the clothing, footwear, hat, and cigarette industries.[119]

At the end of the report, reference is made to the cause of this Jewish mass immigration from the then-Russian Empire. Not only were the restrictions there causing Jews to come to England in ever greater numbers, but it was also widely known in Russia that, in England, the Jews found every kind of freedom and every support imaginable from their ethnic kinsmen.

No proposals were made to change the situation. However, it was believed necessary to point out the danger that lay in the population's contact with Jews, who were not always clean, and the resulting consequences. However, when deciding on the future measures to be taken, it was stated that no store should be set by the outward appearance of the newcomers, who also tended to show worthwhile qualities during their residence in the country.[120]

As a consequence, everything remained as it was before, and it was left to the Liberal government to take any measures that it felt appropriate, something that, as always, it showed itself very disinclined to do. As a result, Lord Salisbury, who was part of the Opposition, introduced a bill in the House of

---

[117] *Hansard,* Volume 8, p. 1184, & p. 1210. & p. 1209. & p. 1185 ff., p. 1209 ff. Translator's note: All QVOS.

[118] *Accounts and Papers... 1894,* Volume 68, p. 351.

[119] *Accounts and Papers... 1894,* Volume 68, p. 390-1. & p. 439 ff.

[120] *Accounts and Papers... 1894,* Volume 68, p. 482 ff.

Lords which did not provide for a general restriction on immigration, but merely sought to make it particularly difficult for criminal elements to enter England freely. The debate for this bill, known as the Aliens Bill, took place on 6 July 1894.[121] After a heated argument between Lord Salisbury and Lord Rosebery [the then-Prime Minister, who as previously stated was married to a Rothschild], as well as a closing statement by the Jewish Lord Chancellor Lord Herschell, who also spoke out against the bill, the Aliens Bill proceeded to a second reading despite opposition from the Liberal peers.[122]

A few weeks later, the then-Lord Londonderry asked Lord Salisbury about the progress on his bill, to which the latter replied:

> There is no doubt that the Government is entirely master of the time of the House of Commons, and that they have not only the power of rejecting a Bill which has been discussed, but they have the power to refuse the time to have it discussed at all. The Leader of the House of Commons stated in emphatic language—in very usually forcible language—that he would not find time for the discussion of this Bill.

Lord Salisbury continued in his reply by saying that he did not wish to push his bill further until he could be assured of it at least being discussed in the House of Commons. In fact, this bill similarly ended up disappearing without a trace.[123]

The next few years seemed to bring the legislation longed for by a large part of the population, especially since Queen Victoria's Speech from the Throne, delivered when the new government took office in 1896, contained a strong promise in this regard. But despite all of the pressure from interested parties, nothing happened, and the Queen's Speech of the next year on the activities of the government was completely silent on this question. The same thing happened in 1898. To everyone's surprise, Lord Hardwicke introduced Lord Salisbury's earlier bill in the same year, but nothing more was heard of this bill either. Then came the Boer War, which, despite an attempt by MP Sir Howard Vincent, made any legislative action impossible, as in the government's view the matter was trivial in comparison to the war. It was only when the war was over and the subsequent elections brought new men into parliament that the struggle was to flare up more fiercely than ever.[124]

---

[121] *Hansard*, Volume 26, p. 1047 ff.
[122] *Hansard*, Volume 27, p. 147 ff.
[123] *Hansard*, Volume 28, p. 889. Translator's note: QVOS. & Landa: pp. 22-23.
[124] Landa: pp. 23-26.

A new member of parliament had been elected who rose to become a leading opponent against England's foreign infiltration. He was Major William Evans-Gordon, whose constituency was at the heart of the action in Stepney, a neighborhood in the East End of London. For some time before, he had gathered together all of the English people who were resisting the ever-increasing Judaization of the East End, and he brought their efforts together into a unified system. It was thanks to his initiative that a markedly anti-Jewish organization, the so-called British Brothers' League, came into existence. Meetings were held everywhere to wake up the masses and to promote active measures of defense against foreign infiltration. Such meetings were often preceded by demonstrations which marched through the most threatened neighborhoods.

The work of these self-preservation forces found great resonance with the nation, and for the second time since emancipation, an anti-Jewish wave swept through England. Again, it was the Jews themselves who had created this mood with their pressure on English life. Their monopoly on the clothing and shoe industries was greater than ever before, and they had depressed wages in these spheres to an unbearable extent. The Judaization of the East End progressed at an incredible pace. What not long before had been workers' houses with their gardens, was now replaced by sweatshops, whose owners and the workers inside were exclusively Jewish. On the grounds which had previously been set aside for gardens, new sweatshops had been built, and in the streets, masses of Jewish old-clothes men and street vendors scurried to and fro. Selling stands had been set up everywhere, and one street after another had been abandoned by the English population, leaving the chapels and churches of these districts deserted.

In those days, just as today, people believed that they were not in an English city, but in a purely Jewish city. On some of the shop fronts, the names of the Jewish owners were written in Hebrew letters. Even the fire alarms had English and Hebrew printed on them. In a very short time around the turn of the last century, Jews had come to completely occupy around 107 streets in the East End borough of Stepney. Countless others were already predominantly Jewish and are now entirely in the hands of the Hebrews. The density of the population had the sense of being at its very limit. Most families, many of them quite large, only had one room that served all purposes.[125]

There was not the slightest sign that the Jewish immigrants belonged to a better class than the previous interlopers. They were filthy and had absolutely no resources. A 1905 article from the *Times* (below) gives an impressive description of the public health and financial implications for Londoners receiving these new arrivals:

---

[125] Russell: p. 68 ff. & Evans-Gordon: pp. 10-19.

ARRIVAL OF ALIENS IN LONDON.

At the Bermondsey Borough Council last night, the Public Health Committee reported that information was received in the early part of last week that a number of aliens were being landed by ships from Russia at Hay's Wharf. The medical officer at once wrote to the port sanitary authorities requesting them to be good enough to advise him as to the arrival of vessels carrying them. On September 29 notice was received of the arrival of the steamship Micail from Riga at Hay's Wharf at 5.20 p.m. On arriving at the wharf, the medical officer found that the ship contained 325 aliens, mostly Jews, from Russian Poland. They seemed to be very poor, ill-fed, badly clothed, and some of them were not very clean. About three-fourths were passing through to the Argentine, Canada, and the United States, the rest remaining in London.

The port medical officer and his assistants examined them all carefully at Gravesend, and took the names and addresses of those who were to remain in London. These addresses were forwarded to the respective sanitary authorities. Those who were on their way to America were conveyed across London to St. Pancras in the private omnibuses of the Midland Railway Company. It seemed to the medical officer a somewhat objectionable use of these vehicles, and he wrote to the railway company suggested that if they have not already taken precautions against the possibility of infection or vermin before these omnibuses are hired out to the public again, they ought to do so. Those aliens who were going to various parts of London were conveyed in open brakes. The wharfowners, as well as shipowners, are in the habit of cleansing and disinfecting the places occupied by these people, and the medical officer thinks the omnibuses should be subjected to similar treatment. The medical officer is also communicating with the owner of the brakes. The report was adopted.[126]

The publication of this article caused great displeasure among the Jews, and one of their representatives wrote an open letter to the *Times* objecting to the findings of the health official concerned. The Jewish immigrants who had

---

[126] *Times*, 4/10/1905. Translator's note: Article reproduced verbatim and in full from original source for reader interest.

been conveyed to the Jews Temporary Shelter in Leman Street, Whitechapel were received by the shelter's secretary:

> who also bears testimony to their excellent outward appearance. Some of them might not have been very clean, but this is no reflection on the immigrants, for we must remember that the voyage occupies six, and sometimes seven, days, and that the boats from the Baltic ports include in their cargoes hides which emit offensive smells...[127]

However, this view seems to have been held only by the Jews, for respected men repeatedly expressed in public very different views. The following selection of quotations from a *Times* report of 3 May 1905, of the previous day's Parliamentary debate over an immigration restriction bill, will give a flavor of some of the sentiment expressed in the House of Commons:

> Mr. H. Lawson [who began his speech with a reminder to the house that he is half-Jewish, which presumably allowed him to be more candid about the ethnic aspect of the issue]: ... There was no question but that a great number of the men now brought before the Courts of London were the scum of the Jewish community, and this Bill would do much to prevent such men from entering the country...for now there was a continual immigration of the unfit and degenerate... The worst of the present situation was that we were parting with the strong and fit and taking in the incapable and the helpless. (Cheers.) We were left with the derelicts of Europe. (Cheers.) ...
>
> Mr. Hayes Fisher: ... the thousands upon thousands of criminal aliens of all descriptions now infesting the country ...
>
> Mr. Buxton (Tower Hamlets, Poplar): ... He felt very strongly that the present admission of these uneconomic and socially undesirable aliens required regulation and discrimination, and that it was time some entrance standard was set up. (Ministerial cheers.) The only immigrants to which he had any strong objection were Russians and Poles, who, unfortunately, were coming into the country in greater numbers year by year. He was quite certain that very few of them added to the strength, the wealth, or the welfare of the nation. (Ministerial cheers.) The objection he had to them was that they were in a totally different state of civilisation from what we desired in this country: that neither in race, religion, feeling, language,

---

[127] *Times*, 9/10/1905. Translator's note: QVOS.

nor blood were they suitable or advantageous to us, and that they were by [far] the most destitute of all the aliens who came to these shores...

It was perfectly true that many of these aliens were in course of transit to America, but the most efficient and the most enterprising went to America, and the least efficient were left in this country to do us harm. The result was that we were getting from Eastern Europe the refuse of the refuse... What they wanted to do was, in the first place, to put up a notice, "Rubbish will not be allowed to be shot here." (Ministerial cheers.) ...

Even the American, James Davenport Whelpley, in his impartial 1905 study of the problems attendant to mass immigration in Western countries, is forced to admit the following:

> For years, England has been a sort of clearing-house for unde- sirable emigration to the United States from many countries. Many emigrants rejected for passage at Continental ports found it easier to get to England than to return to their homes. The enormous alien and British emigrant traffic from British ports has resulted in the refuse being left upon British soil. The greater number of deportations from the United States are re- turned to England, even though they may have come original- ly from other foreign countries. The effect of this upon the British population is almost indescribable. Charitable institu- tions, prisons, and hospitals are crowded with aliens, and some of the trades are so burdened with this low grade of labour that the British workman is driven out.[128]

The truth of these assertions soon became clear from the fact that crime in- creased significantly. In business, the Jew typically resorted to 'palpable ly- ing and cheating'.[129] Even a Jewish writer believed this statement to be cor- rect and had to admit to the reader:

> One is sometimes tempted to conclude in despair that the bulk of the Polish immigrants have no sense of truth whatever. No more painful spectacle can be witnessed than the hearing of a summons at an East-End police court, where the parties con- cerned are foreign Jews. Obvious perjury, on the smallest

---

[128] Whelpley: pp. 26/27. Translator's note: QVOS.
[129] *The Jew in London* [Russell's essay: p. 37]. Translator's note: QVOS.

provocation, is committed in case after case. The comments of Judge Bacon at the Whitechapel County Court on this fact have been at times severely criticised by the Jewish press. His generalisations may have been too sweeping, being based on his experience of petty litigation, where the seamy side of life is necessarily prominent. At the same time, his remarks have been based on a substantial sub-stratum of truth. It is the experience of most visitors amongst the foreign poor for charitable societies, that although absolute imposture is exceptional, falsehoods with regards to the details of cases are constantly met with.[130]

Jewish minors involved in misdemeanors and crimes were increasingly common, and other crimes of deception were likewise to be expected in a group with the aforementioned 'taint of untruthfulness.' Of the names of the offenders listed on return of convictions, which was periodically issued in the minutes of the London County Council for the use of false weights and measures (and kindred offences) 'an altogether undue proportion of them appear to be foreign Jews.'[131]

Then there were the other typical crimes that the authorities had to take action against. So we find a lot of prostitution and illegal [alcohol] distillation. Counterfeiting of banknotes and stamps was not uncommon, and fraudulent bankruptcy was one of the most common Jewish crimes at that time. East London had 'far too many cases where the Bankruptcy laws are evaded by persons who pass through the courts and reappear in business with suspicious celerity and without apparent loss.' It was determined by the relevant courts that over a period of three years, creditors had lost a total of £1,220,850 in such bankruptcies. Four fifths of public debtors had gone bankrupt more than once, putting the public at a loss of a further £354,600. And as early as 1893, an official statement was made that the cost to the taxpayer for housing convicted immigrants alone was estimated at £30,000.[132]

With the passage of time, one finds more and more intermarriage, which, according to our racial theory, must necessarily lead to disastrous consequences for a nation.[133]

These intolerable conditions created by the Jews could not be hidden from the public. Nevertheless, only some English people believed that it was

---

[130] *The Jew in London*, pp. 171-2 [Lewis]. Translator's note: QVOS.

[131] *The Jew in London*, pp. 172-3 [Lewis]. Translator's note: QVOS. Also see Evans-Gordon: p. 263 ff., p. 293 ff.

[132] *The Jew in London*, pp. 173-6 [Lewis]. Landa: pp. 158-163. White: p. 191. Evans-Gordon: p. 265. & *Accounts and Papers... 1903*, Volume 9, p. 27. Evans-Gordon: p. 267 ff. Translator's note: QVOS from Lewis p. 173. & Evans-Gordon: pp. 261-2.

[133] *The Jew in London*, p. 39 [Russell], p. 167 [Lewis].

necessary to intervene to prevent further immigration, while others never tired of claiming that the dangers were non-existent. The aforementioned Arnold White believed that 'these people are in the nature of poison to the immediate interests of the nation.' And in *The Modern Jew,* he lamented the fact that 'our rulers and statesmen generally do not appear to have given serious thought to the consequences of the coming invasion.' If this continued, the people of England would 'wake up one morning only to discover that they have parted with the realities of national life, and are dominated by cosmopolitan and materialist influences fatal to the existence of the English nation'.[134]

It must not be forgotten that Jews, unlike previous immigrants such as the Huguenots and the Hollander refugees, did not assimilate into the English people. They would always remain a foreign body. One had to fear that the Jews would soon exercise a dominant influence in England, and he, White, was unfortunately not convinced that they would then be guided solely by British interests. History has already shown that this was the case in France and that they did not even maintain solidarity with their own ethnic kinsmen. He also opined that one must expect the press in England to soon find itself completely under Jewish control, a development that had already taken place on the continent. The same thing could also be said of international finance. The Jews in England already controlled so much of the country's finances and press that any ministry that did anything against the entrenched strength of the Jews would inevitably be unseated. With immigration, this would become more and more the case.[135]

The onslaught of anti-Jewish activists became increasingly intense, and the government could no longer evade demands for an in-depth investigation. On 28 January 1902, the government announced that it would set up a Royal Commission in the near future, which convened for the first time on 24 April 1902.[136] The Commission was composed of seven members, including Lord Rothschild, 'so that the Commission might be recognized as free from all bias against the alien' and Major Evans-Gordon. The chairmanship was in the hands of Lord James of Hereford. Forty-nine meetings were held. The Commission's activities, including the preparation of the 1,100-page report, spanned a period of just under one and a half years. A total of 175 witnesses and experts were examined and 23,639 questions and answers recorded. The Report of the Commission was completed on 10 August 1903.[137]

---

[134] Landa: p. 61. Translator's note: QVOS. & White: *The Modern Jew*, pp. XI-XII. Translator's note: QVOS.

[135] White: *The Modern Jew*, pp. XII-XV. & p. 193 ff.

[136] Landa: p. 29. Evans-Gordon: p. 276. Abbott: p. 460.

[137] *Accounts and Papers... 1903*, Volume 9, p. 1 ff. *Jewish Chronicle*, 14/8/1903. Translator's note: QVOS from the *Morning Post*, 14/8/1903. For a spirited analysis of the Jewish influence over the Royal Commission, the selection of its commissioners, its line of ques-

The report initially dealt with the causes of immigration from Eastern Europe. The Commission had ensured its source of accurate information on the topic by sending Major Evans-Gordon to the area. It was found that most of the immigration that had taken place since 1880 consisted of Eastern European Jews. As soon as these Jews had saved some money in England and America, they sent it to their relatives who had stayed behind. These Jews considered London and New York as a heaven on earth, where one could become rich in a short time. As a consequence, it was not only coercion and oppression, but also the force of attraction that sparked the desire to migrate West.[138]

The main stream of migration flowed into England via Hamburg, Bremen, Rotterdam, and Libau [Liepāja, Latvia]. Four steamers arrived weekly from Hamburg alone, three each from Bremen and Rotterdam, and one from Libau. Upon their arrival, the Jews, regardless of whether they planned to remain in England or were in transit to America, would be met by members of the Jewish organization Jews' Temporary Shelter. From enquiries, it was revealed that 24.8% of those aliens who arrived in 1901 and 1902 did not have a penny. Over the previous eight years, the average percentage of penniless arrivals had been 22%, while a further 15% had less than ten shillings.[139] Very detailed investigations once again confirmed the criminality of the immigrants and the overpopulation of the East End of London, with all of the attendant horrors this caused.[140] The summary of the findings was that an extraordinarily large number of Eastern Jews had immigrated and, with this in mind, it seemed advisable to allow immigration only under certain conditions, with settlement in pre-determined localities.[141]

The proposals to remedy the situation were in no way aimed at restricting immigration; rather, they were aimed only at ensuring that provision were made for official and accurate data-collection. Only in the case of a foreigner committing a crime in the first two years of his stay should a specific court be authorized to expel him. In order to avoid overpopulation, certain city districts were to be declared restricted areas in which the settlement of new arrivals was prohibited.[142]

Lord Rothschild and Sir Kenelm Digby had only agreed to this report subject to presenting their own Minority Report. In it they stated, among other things, that the assertion that the increase in crime was the result of Russian-Jewish immigration was unjustified. But what they most objected to

---

tioning, and its limited coverage in the newspapers, see Banister, Chapter XXIII [in Translator's Bibliography].

[138] *Accounts and Papers... 1903*, Volume 9, p. 10-1. & p. 12.

[139] *Accounts and Papers... 1903*, Volume 9, p. 17. & pp. 19-20.

[140] *Accounts and Papers... 1903*, Volume 9, pp. 25-7. & pp. 30-5.

[141] *Accounts and Papers... 1903*, Volume 9, p. 48.

[142] *Accounts and Papers... 1903*, Volume 9, pp. 48-51.

was the suggestion that future immigrants should only be allowed to settle in certain districts.[143] Despite this, the report immediately met with criticism from the public. Arnold White expressed his concerns in an open letter. He did not believe that the proposed system of restricted zones would be made law in Parliament. 'It seemed that the Commission's members underestimated the enormous influence of Jews in politics and the press, and overlooked the fact that their supreme chief did not agree with their proposals. In recent years he, White, had come to the realization that no measures whatsoever could be taken without the consent of Jewish leaders.' And in any case, he believed that the Jews would simply flout any laws that were put in place.[144]

Some of the press rejoiced at the report's statement of facts, about which there had long been widespread claims to the contrary. As H. W. Wilson of the *Daily Mail* declared:

> This country has become the dumping-ground for the human waste product of other nations. The pauper, the criminal, the lunatic have been shot upon British shores, to compete with the British worker for his wages or to draw upon the British ratepayer for support ...

The same writer was also unafraid to mention that the immigrants driving down the housing and industrial conditions of the native workers were 'foreign Jews' and similarly pointed out that it was Lord Rothschild who opposed the amelioratory measures proposed by the Commission:

> Lord Rothschild wishes the municipality to undertake the task of providing house-room, and would not sanction the marking-off of prohibited areas. But the task of accommodating with good house-room the refuse of the Continent is very much like that of pumping dry the Atlantic.[145]

Another newspaper pointed out that all of the foreigners, who were mainly Eastern European Jews, had been allowed in out of false sentimentality:

> [T]he catchword of a Free Asylum has been employed to keep open the doors of England to the scum of all nations. It is time that we stopped this parrot-cry, and faced the situation like

---

[143] *Accounts and Papers... 1903*, Volume 9, pp. 51-9.
[144] *Sunday Sun*, 16/8/1903. Translator's note: Quotation translated from Aldag's German text as the original source could not be found—it would appear that the attribution of this source to the *Sunday Sun* is a referencing error on the author's part, as apparently the *Sunday Sun* did not come into existence until 1919.
[145] *Daily Mail*, 13/8/1903. Translator's note: Excerpts QVOS.

sensible people, without any undue leaning towards the senti-
mental. After all the first duty of a nation, as of a family, is to
itself. The old familiar proverb has it bluntly that charity begins at home...

[A] nation has a right to defend itself whether from the
outright assaults of a rival or from the more insidious attacks
arising from the percolation of foreign undesirables into the
country. In the phrase which has been reiterated for the last fifteen years, Great Britain has long been the dumping ground of
the refuse of Europe...[146]

Even the *Daily Telegraph* itself [i.e. a newspaper known for its philo-
Semitism], in an article of 12 August 1903, recognized that the bulk of immigration was due mainly to Jews from the East.

However, the people of London saw some signs of progress in the report and, at a mass demonstration of the Immigration Reform Association at
the People's Palace on November 10, demanded that the government introduce the corresponding legislation 'at the early possible opportunity in the
forthcoming Session of Parliament'.[147] But Home Secretary Aretas Akers-
Douglas did not present such a bill, that is to say, one that would essentially
follow the Commission's proposals, until 29 March 1904. And although it
provided for a certain level of scrutiny of the newcomers' personal circumstances, in no way could this be described as a restriction on immigration.
The minister likewise made clear, in the opening remarks of his introductory
speech, that with what came to be known as the Aliens Bill, 'we have no
intention whatever of unnecessarily interfering with the admission into this
country of foreigners, or of throwing any unnecessary difficulty in the way
of their general entry into this country.'

However, since the judiciary and the police had meanwhile been bom-
barding the government with reports about the huge increase in immigrant
convictions, which had gone up 'by no less than 55 per cent' over the previous five years, with the attendant state costs in maintaining this 'large alien
prison', it had been decided, said Akers-Douglas, 'on these grounds, and on
these grounds only', that 'some interference on the part of the State' was
urgently required and certain officials be given the opportunity to exclude
undesirable elements. Nevertheless, this putative exclusion was only to be
applied to those who had committed an extraditable crime within the previous five years, prostitutes and pimps, and those with 'infectious or loathsome

---

[146] *Morning Post* 12/8/1903, 14/8/1903. Translator's note: Excerpts QVOS from the
14/8/1903 issue.
[147] *Times*, 11/11/1903. Translator's note: QVOS. Note that the demonstrators were keen to
have known that this 'was not a question of religion' but rather that the foreigners were
objected to 'on account of the quantity and quality of them'.

diseases.' Those were virtually the only restrictions to be imposed on immigration, and even the fate of these cases was to be ultimately decided by the Home Secretary himself.[148]

After heated debates and obstruction from the Liberals, as a result of which, according to Prime Minister Arthur James Balfour, no more than two lines of the bill were worked through by the Standing Committee each day, the government announced on 11 July 1904, to everyone's astonishment, that it had withdrawn the bill and that it would introduce a new one in the next Parliamentary session.[149]

Judah Caught in the Crossfire

What had happened to the Aliens Bill? Was it really just the Standing Committee's report that had caused the government to withdraw the bill, or were there other, much more important things going on behind the scenes?

To answer this question, we must first return to what was happening outside Parliament. As early as May 1903, while the Royal Commission under Lord Heresford was still investigating the entire immigration situation, the Jews had called a protest meeting led by the Zionist Israel Zangwill, who even at that time, around four months before the report was published, was able to explain the Commission's report proposals to the audience. Today it is almost impossible to determine how he had come by this knowledge, but it is not implausible to assume that it came from a member of the Commission. It is also natural that, in this case, the first suspicion would fall on Lord Rothschild.

In his address to the Jews, Zangwill expressed his fear that in the future one would have to expect not only the exclusion of unwanted foreigners, but also far more drastic measures. The Jews had been resident in England for a

---

[148] *Times*, 1/4/1904. *Hansard*, Volume 132, pp. 987-991. Translator's note: All QVOS [Hansard]. Both sources between them also give full details of the bill, including the other few restrictions for entry, which I presume Aldag has omitted due their nature of being easily hidden, subjective/difficult to quantify, and/or impossible to implement in the real world. Readers may also wish to look at the provisions within the final legislation itself—Aliens Act, 1905—available at the legislation.gov.uk website.

[149] *Hansard*, Volume 136, pp. 1220-1. Translator's note: According to the *Times* article of 12/7/1904, during Balfour's speech, ministers clarified by means of shouts that the Standing Committee's progress on the Aliens Bill was in fact only 'half a line a day.' It would appear that 30-year-old Winston Churchill was instrumental in this situation, because, as we read in the *Jewish Chronicle* of 7/1/1904 (pp. 16-7), Nathan Laski assured his fellow Jews at a protest meeting against the bill in Manchester that Churchill 'had seen Lord Rothschild with reference to the Bill' and, as a result, 'Mr. Churchill was practically leading the attack on the Bill in Grand Committee.'

long time, but if things were to continue at the current pace, one would even have to expect anti-Jewish riots in London.[150]

A year later, Zangwill held another Zionist meeting in which he triumphantly pointed to the accuracy of his prophecies of the previous year, and again drew attention to the growing anti-Jewish sentiment in the country.

This reached the ears of Prime Minister Balfour, who explained in an open letter that 'the Aliens Bill is designed to protect the country, not against the Jew, but against the undesirable alien, quite irrespective of his nationality or his creed. I should regard the rise and growth of any anti-Semitic feeling in this country as a most serious national misfortune.'

Then as now, the clergy worked on behalf of the Jews. At a meeting of the Community of British Jews, a clergyman declared that the Jew had been a blessing to the East End of London, while the distinguished prelate Bishop Welldon, in his Good Friday sermon of 1904 which was preached in Westminster Abbey, exhorted the faithful to be an imitation of Christ's example, and to demonstrate their faith practically by contributing to the East London Jews' Fund, which would be, he said, 'the best return they could make for the crucifixion of their Lord and Master. The Jews gave him strife, and encompassed his death; we gave them sanctuary and kindness, and without one word of reproach.' Incidentally, the Bishop of Stepney followed his example the next year, in exhorting his faithful during Holy Week and Good Friday to donate to the same Jewish fund. The thoughts of the season, he said, would be incomplete unless Christians gave a place to those 'whose rejection of their own Messiah has been one of the great tragedies of history.' He went on to describe how the Diocese of London treated the East End Jews as neighbors and parishioners, and by the tact and patience of the fund's workers 'the barrier of prejudice, built up by long years of persecution at the hands of Christians, is being rapidly removed'.[151]

But the Jews and their friends did not limit themselves to protest or sympathy demonstrations. On 20 May 1904, which is to say, some four weeks after the second reading of the latterly-withdrawn bill, a delegation of leading Jews, consisting of Lord Rothschild, Leopold Rothschild, Sir Samuel Montagu, Member of Parliament Mr. Samuel and others, paid a visit to the Home Secretary. They presented him with a long complaint about the bill being debated in Parliament, as it would impose undue hardship and likely restrict immigration, and which could only be detrimental to England, which had so far greatly benefited from Jewish immigrants. They also made a commitment to ensure that no Jewish newcomer would be a burden on the

---

[150] *Daily Chronicle*, 18/5/1903.
[151] Abbott: p. 466. Translator's note: QVOS. & Abbott: p. 468; *Standard*, 2/4/1904; *Times*, 17/4/1905. Translator's note: All QVOS [Abbott/*Times*]. Note that Abbott's 1907 textual rendering of Bishop Welldon's speech did not give reverential capitalization to Christ's pronouns.

state for the first two years of his stay, and that they would also, on their own initiative, work to exclude criminals.

In a leaflet distributed to the public, they reiterated their position and emphasized that the proposed legislation would be to the detriment of those persecuted for religion and politics and might even make it impossible for them to enter England. According to Charles Emanuel:

> The pamphlet showed that the Bill as drafted would enable old-established foreign settlers to be forcibly ejected from their homes in this country without compensation, that it gave power to eject those who arrived without an official passport or certificate of character, which would include all those flee- ing from persecution in Russia or Roumania, and that it gave no right of appeal to be rejected.

What was the success of these efforts? Let Emanuel answer as an authorita- tive source:

> A deputation from the Board waited on the Home Secretary and stated its objections to various provisions in the measure, and he promised that their view should be considered. The bill was subsequently withdrawn.[152]

What was it Arnold White had been quoted as saying on 16 August 1903? 'No measures whatsoever could be taken without the consent of Jewish leaders'? Events have been shown to prove him right.

A novella by the Jewess Violet Guttenberg is in many ways character- istic of the prevailing general mood among Jews at that time. The author narrates a love story between a Jew and an Englishwoman, the daughter of the staunchly anti-Semitic Prime Minister Moore. The two young people get married without his knowledge. Shortly afterwards, at the request of the Prime Minister, a law is passed requiring all Jews to leave England. As a consequence, most of them then emigrate to Palestine, with the result that England's economy virtually comes to a standstill. There is unemployment and poverty everywhere.[153]

The Prime Minister's daughter accompanies her husband to Palestine, and when she later returns home for a visit, she finds her father made a nerv- ous wreck because he is still preoccupied almost exclusively with the Jewish Question. A member of the government tells her openly: 'England can not

---

[152] Emanuel: *A Century and a Half...*, p. 162. Translator's note: Both QVOS.
[153] Guttenberg: p. 283 ff.

get along without Jewish money and Jewish brains; and she's shipped all the best of it away—sent it to Palestine to enrich the Holy Land.'[154]

The Prime Minister eventually changes his mind, repeals the expulsion law, and because all the Jews return, England is rich and happy again:

> 'Moore—the anti-Semite—is dead.' 'And Mr. Moore the Christian statesman lives!'[155]

The bias of this book is so obvious that no comment is required.

But the fight wasn't over yet. Both parties continued to agitate for their views. For the forces of self-preservation Major Evans-Gordon was a prominent champion; for the opposite side, among others, Winston Churchill. The former did everything to ensure that efforts to restrict immigration did not come to a standstill. Fundraising was organized to continue the fight. At meetings, Evans-Gordon pointed out that the overcrowded ghettos of Russia, Poland, Romania, and Austria-Hungary would throw an inexhaustible supply of new masses onto the shores of England. The Radicals only spoke of 'the liberty of the—foreign—subject, but nothing about the liberty of the British workman to live in his own country.' He also called attention to the fact that twelve ships carrying strangers arrived every week at the Port of London alone, of whom some 40% were destitute. How was this supposed to end? Over the last five years alone, the government had already had to pay a total of some £629,000 for the prison costs of 13,114 alien criminals.[156]

Other voices also came forward to demand a definitive solution that would be satisfactory to the people. Again it is Arnold White who points out the importance of the issue:

> But it is certain that any Alien Bill, before it becomes law, will raise the Jewish question throughout the world, for the reason that the money of the world is mainly in the hands of the race chiefly affected by the proposed measure of restriction.

He suggests that England should call a conference of Europe's Jewish leaders, along with the governments of Russia, the United States, Canada, and Romania. Pressure could be brought to bear on Russia because, being currently at war with Japan she was in need of money, and:

> [T]he gold by which Russia continues to make war is gold under Hebrew control... In the whole course of European history,

---

[154] Guttenberg: p. 294. Translator's note: QVOS.
[155] Guttenberg: p. 316. Translator's note: QVOS.
[156] *Times*, 8/8. & 18/11. & 12/7. Translator's note: QVOS. & *Times*, 8/12, 15/12.

the Jewish community has never had a more favourable opportunity of compelling Russia to come to terms on the treatment of her Jewish subjects. With the diplomatic assistance of Great Britain and the United States the interchange of views at a conference on the Jewish question between the Powers interested and the heads of the Jewish community might solve, and could not complicate, a problem that otherwise threatens to be insoluble.[157]

But the other side was also at work, subverting the opposition's position while pretending to be part of that opposition. It held 'anti-immigration' meetings and infiltrated the genuine anti-immigration movement. The following newspaper article illustrates this phenomenon perfectly:

ALIEN IMMIGRATION. A meeting of the Kensington Branch of the Women's Liberal Unionist Association was held on Friday afternoon, by permission of Mrs. Richards, at 19, Wetherby-gardens, South Kensington, when the subject for discussion was alien immigration. Mr. Leo Maxse presided, and there was a large attendance. Major Hills, R. F., in opening the debate, gave an historical account of the question of alien immigration. Miss Hyams, speaking with personal knowledge of the Russians and Poles in the East-end, maintained that the standard of living was not so low as had been made out; it was only on the aliens' first arrival that the standard was low. She advocated the exclusion from England only of the morally and physically unfit, and maintained that those aliens who were now in England were a benefit to the country which had sheltered them. Mr. Maxse appealed to the meeting to urge upon the Government to carry out what they had promised to do in this matter.[158]

Winston Churchill played a leading role in this subversion. His father, Lord Randolph Churchill, had borrowed £5,000 from Rothschild and used it to buy shares in gold mines in South Africa. After a certain time, due to a lack of money, he had to sell two-fifths of them; the remainder were later sold after his death [in 1895] for £70,000 as the share-price had since risen exponentially. Incidentally, he was one of Rothschild's closest friends and was a regular guest at his country estate in Buckinghamshire.[159]

---

[157] *Times*, 24/12. Translator's note: QVOS.
[158] *Times*, 13/2/1905. Translator's notice: Article reproduced in full and QVOS.
[159] Smalley: pp. 291-2.

Winston Churchill had switched from Conservative to Liberal in Parliament shortly before the events described. He had already spoken out openly against the Aliens Bill in May 1904. In a letter to a Jew in Manchester, written that same month, he described the government's efforts as 'an attempt on the part of the Government to gratify a small but noisy section of their supporters, and to purchase a little popularity in the constituencies by dealing harshly with a number of unfortunate aliens who have no votes'.[160]

When in 1904 it became clear to the most perspicacious that the proposed legislation would not be passed in the House of Commons, the triumph of the Jewish press knew no bounds. Churchill was given the highest praise and thanks for his intervention on behalf of the Jews.[161] He also advocated for amendments to the new bill in public meetings while the Parliamentary debates of 1905 were taking place, and likewise in that year the Jews did not forget to publicly mention Churchill's services to their cause.[162]

Both parties knew that the abandonment of the 1904 bill did not in any way resolve the situation. Rather, the opponents of immigration had become even more agitated, as demonstrated by, among other things, an incident in Ireland. In Limerick, the Catholic population had protested against their exploitation by the Jews. They were led by their clergy, in particular the charismatic and eloquent Father Creagh, a holy monk of the Redemptorist Order, whose gifted preaching incited the populace to a holy crusade of collective action. As he told his flock: 'It would be madness for a man to nourish in his own breast a viper that might at any moment slay its benefactor with a poisonous bite. So it is madness for a people to allow an evil to grow in their midst that will eventually cause them ruin.'

---

[160] Abbott: p. 465. Translator's note: QVOS. The letter recipient was, in fact, Mr. Nathan Laski, President of the Manchester Great Synagogue, and the full letter, in which Churchill expresses an utter contempt for the interests of the British people, particularly the working classes, can be found in the 3/6/1904 issue of *Jewish World*.

[161] *Jewish World*, 24/6/1904, *Jewish Chronicle*, 24/6/1904. Translator's note: There may be a referencing error for these publications, as I could find nothing in these particular issues but impartial reporting on events, i.e. no evidence of Aldag's assertion. The only thing that might resemble gratitude is in the *Jewish Chronicle* issue, which had news that Churchill had been 'entertained...along with several prominent Jewish and Christians citizens at dinner' at the residence of aforementioned Mr. Nathan Laski (p.29).

[162] *Times*, 30/6/1905. Translator's note: Churchill's proposed amendments were designed to make the bill completely useless. In addition to an exception for the victims of political persecution, Churchill proposed there also be an exemption for 'victims of religious persecution' as well the right to appeal for those who were refused permission to land, or who were threatened with expulsion. He also said that there should be no distinction made between the rich and poor immigrant, but 'one law for all immigrants.' & *Jewish Chronicle*, 15/12/1905 (pp. 9-11). Translator's note: An example: "Mr. Winston Churchill's splendid fight in Grand Committee against the first Aliens' bill will long linger in the recollections of those who witnessed it."

While there had been hardly any Jews there at the end of the 19th century —in 1871 only two Jews were counted in the Limerick census—they had now settled in larger numbers, with at least thirty-five families present, and had quickly taken over trade. Soon a large part of the farmers were in debt to them, against whom the Jews acted ruthlessly as soon as payment became due. This angered the population so much that they refused to sell any food to the Jews and even began a complete boycott against them. Jews could barely be seen in public without having to fear for life and limb. Attacks were not uncommon and stones were thrown at them when they showed their faces in public. This situation lasted for a good while, and led to the ruin of the Jews, who, given the nature of the siege, would likely have starved to death in their homes if some Protestant gentlemen had not rendered assistance, which was done in utmost secrecy for fear of 'drawing down upon themselves the pious wrath of the Redemptorist monks and of the 6,000 brethren of the Confraternity of the Holy Family.' However, after a press campaign had roused public opinion in England, the government was forced to intervene and charitable associations hastened to the Jews' relief.[163]

When, at the beginning of 1905, the government had still not made any moves to resolve the situation, the public became impatient, as demonstrated by the constant questions that were raised about this matter in Parliament.[164] On 18 April 1905, the bill was finally introduced into Parliament by Home Secretary Akers-Douglas.

This showed, among other things, that circumstances would no longer tolerate any further delay. In 1903, 82,000 foreigners had landed in England, the vast majority of whom remained in the country. The associated evils were increasing on a daily basis. Crime had increased. The police and judges continually sent him complaints. Above all, the bill provided for the deployment of immigration officers to eight pre-determined ports, where 97% of foreigners currently landed and where all future immigrants would be made to land, and these officers would decide whether or not entry would be granted. In the case of a negative, the party concerned would have the right to appeal to a designated local court. In addition, there were also provisions authorizing the expulsion of undesirable elements.[165] Sir Charles Dilke objected to the contents of the bill, but the bill passed its first reading, with the vote going against the Liberal Party.[166]

On 2 May 1905, the debate on the second reading took place. And again it was Sir Charles Dilke who was the first to speak for the Opposition. The figures cited by the government were completely exaggerated, just as

---

[163] Abbott: pp. 469-72. Translator's note: QVOS, and additional elements inserted for reader interest.

[164] *Hansard,* Volume 143, pp. 212, 956, 1734/35; Volume 144, p. 1018.

[165] *Hansard,* Volume 145, pp. 464-468.

[166] *Hansard,* Volume 145, pp. 468 ff.

the case for the negative effects that resulted from current immigration was 'so miserable and trivial.' In his opinion, 'asylum in the past has been of benefit to this country, and I believe we derive benefit from it still.' He also pointed to evidence for the complete assimilation of immigrant Jewish children, who were now, apparently, more English than the English:

> Evidence was given before the Commission by the school authorities and others in the East End who are most competent witnesses. The overwhelming weight of testimony is on the side of those who say that these children are completely English. The typical evidence was that of the master of Betts Street School, who pointed out that the English history of the Jewish children was infinitely better than the English history of the average English children, and that the children were proud to become English. I think that the whole history of the United States, where you have seen the whole of the alien emigrants moulded into an essentially English race, proves that the spirit is far more important than the birth.[167]

He would, however, give his assent to the part of the bill that would keep out the sick and criminals. He was supported by Mr. Trevelyan and other Opposition members. The latter also included the Jew Herbert Samuel, who believed that the immigration level was tolerable and that the crime figures should be treated with extreme caution. In any case, the poor were fully supported by the Jewish community.[168] He was opposed by the Hon. Harry Lawson, who declared his own half-Jewishness early on in the debate, perhaps in a bid to pre-empt any accusation of anti-Semitism. In fact, he told the House, Jews made up 'a great number of those now brought before the Courts of Justice in London.' He went on to say:

> [T]here are thousands of immigrants who cannot be regarded as refugees, who are chronic paupers, and who come from Russia or Poland in the hope of getting something from the Russo-Polish fund of which they have heard such exaggerated accounts. That is one of the features most noticeable in this recent incursion of Jewish refugees. There have been more beggars in the streets, and more beggars, unfortunately, among children in the streets, and the reason is that you are getting the less fit and capable of these people. That is what we notice in the doctrinaire protests raised against this Bill. There is a want,

---

[167] *Hansard*, Volume 145, pp. 689-99. All QVOS.
[168] *Hansard*, Volume 145, p. 724 ff.

on the other side, I fear, of the sense of historic perspective. They still seem to think that we are getting the energetic, the able, and the competent aliens. That was the fact in the past. Whether they were Walloons or Huguenots or Jews, we had formerly coming into this country those who were most likely to contribute to its prosperity. But now the exact opposite is the case. Now we are getting the untransportable—those who cannot get into America, and whom the shipping companies will not take to America. [...]

Unfortunately, as we know, the greater number of those who are rejected in America come back here. I have got a case in point where there was a large number of aliens on board the liner 'Carpathia' who were refused admission at New York. An attempt was made to land them at Fiume, but the Italian authorities objected to allow this, and these people came to England. Time after time, the same thing occurs [...]

The case in regard to immigration in this country is summed up by the words used by the German official at the ports of embarkation: 'Utterly destitute and friendless who can just afford a ticket to Grimsby go to England.' I think I have said enough as to the character of the immigrants. The truth is that we get the floating scum—those who would go anywhere and do anybody and those who are a burden to their own community, if not a burden to the public at large. These are the people who bring scandal on themselves and on those with whom they are associated.

He then went on to speak of the dire housing conditions in the East End of London that needed attention. To compound this problem, in a very short time, rents had increased threefold due to overpopulation. The misery and distress there was very great, and a solution would need to be found. He concludes his speech with the following remarks:

The present situation is that we are sending out the fit and the strong and taking in the incapable and the helpless. If hon. members studied the figures of immigration into Canada, they would find that the very flower of our working class was being sent out there, and in return we are getting those whom it is impossible to induce the United States to accept. And who are left here? The derelicts of Europe ...

One feels that this unrestricted flow will be likely to weaken and vitiate the whole stream of our national life. We talk of 'man-power', but the man-power behind the Empire is not likely to be improved by the introduction of new diseases and the constant influx of people dumped down on this country because no other country will take them. This Bill is not only due, but in the view of those I speak for, is already overdue, and I think it is time that we cried 'Halt' to what is becoming a backward march to physical degeneration.[169]

Major Evans-Gordon had spoken earlier in the debate, in which he gave the facts of the immigration figures that Sir Charles Dilke had tried to deny, and reminded the House that the Census and Board of Trade Returns automatically counted the children born in England of immigrant people as 'English', thus handily reducing the official foreign population figures by some 50%. From the same speech:

The House has to face the fact that during the last few years the area occupied by aliens in the East End of London has increased rapidly; it has doubled, trebled, quadrupled. Streets and districts formerly entirely English have become almost entirely foreign in character. We have the evidence of Chief Inspector Malveney, of the H Division, that in six years, 107 whole streets in Stepney went out of English occupation into foreign occupation... Three years ago the Bishop of Stepney said that in some districts where there was formerly evidence of comparative wealth and comfort these had been absolutely wiped out, and the East End of London was being swamped by aliens who were coming in like an army of locusts, eating up the native population or turning them out. Their churches were being continually left like islands in the midst of an alien sea. And yet in the face of these statements the right hon. Baronet says that the whole thing is moonshine and a figment of the imagination. Not all the Blue-books or statistics in the world can controvert these incontrovertible facts. I have made inquiry on the spot myself.

He also called attention to the hypocrisy of the Jews themselves, who were themselves selective when deciding on the quality of Jews who should populate their own colonies, yet libeled the English trying to do the same for England as 'anti-Semitic':

---

[169] *Hansard*, Volume 145, pp. 733-740. Translator's note: All QVOS. Harry Lawson (full name: Harry Lawson Webster Levy-Lawson) inherited his father's title of Baron Burnham in 1916 as well as inheriting his father's ownership and management of the *Daily Telegraph* newspaper. He was created Viscount Burnham in 1919.

Again, it is sometimes said that we cannot do anything to help our own people without being cruelly unjust to the immigrants who come here, especially Jewish immigrants. Now what are the precepts and practice of the Jews themselves in this matter? Do they allow all their own people, irrespective of their industrial fitness or capacity, to go to their own colonies in the Argentine Republic and elsewhere? Not at all. Everybody is subjected to the closest scrutiny before he is allowed to start—scrutiny as to his antecedents, character, health, and fitness in every respect.

So much is this the fact that Mr. Zangwill, when recently discussing the proposed East African colony for Jews, made this remarkable statement—he said, 'the colony was not to be the dumping ground for refugees.' No, Sir; the privilege of being the dumping ground is reserved for this country, and when anyone dares to lift a voice in protest, or ventures to suggest that the same precautions should be taken here as are taken by the Jewish community themselves, we are denounced as Anti-Semites. We have no wish, and I say no reason can be given for saying we wish, to exclude persons from this country because they are Jews. Our desire is not to exclude undesirable aliens because they are Jews but because they are undesirable aliens.

In closing, he reminded the House about a much-neglected party in the debates, the working-class Briton:

We hold that immigrants coming here should be submitted to the same process of selection as they have to submit to in other countries, and that the people sent here from abroad should be the best and not the worst of the population. We desire to rid our gaols of foreign criminals and our streets of foreign prostitutes and souteneurs, but, above all, we desire to save our own poor and working classes from an influence which must tend to make their lives more painful and more difficult, and deprive them of what we believe to be the most elementary of all their rights, namely, the opportunity of earning a living in their own land.[170]

---

[170] *Hansard*, Volume 145, pp. 706-724. Translator's note: All quotations from Evans-Gordon are QVOS.

Joseph Chamberlain was also in favor of restricting immigration, and reminded the house that it was not correct or fair to accuse those who were critical of uncontrolled immigration due to its negative impact on both working-class Jew and Gentile alike: 'It is often said that anybody who looks at this question as I do, entirely from a British point of view, is guilty of anti-Semitism. There is no feeling of anti-Semitism in the movement against this immigration'.[171] After Prime Minister Balfour's closing speech, the debate ended with the second reading of the bill.[172]

Lengthy deliberations by the committee followed. It is impossible to detail all of the proposed amendments and speeches given. Here, too, it was primarily Churchill who stood out among the opponents of the bill. This was followed by more interminable debates in the plenary sessions of the House of Commons. The Aliens Bill finally passed its third reading on July 19. It also found the necessary majority in the three required readings in the House of Lords.[173]

The Aliens Act stayed within the framework of Akers-Douglas' aforementioned statements. It should also be added that in addition to criminals, sick people, and idiots, those who were completely destitute were also to be denied entry. However, the restriction for the latter should be lifted if they could prove that they would be assisted in England or that they had left their country of origin as refugees who were being persecuted for their religious or political views.

It is obvious that this provision would continue to allow Jews unhindered immigration. In any case, they were already seen as a poor, persecuted people by a large part of the English population, or else found the support of well-organized and well-funded Jewish welfare institutions. The regulation regarding the admission of political and religious refugees was inserted into the law at the instigation of the Board of Deputies of British Jews, who enlisted the help of legislators Lord Hugh Cecil, Sir Charles Dilke, and Mr. Robson. In his book which details the Board's activities, the aforementioned Charles Emanuel shines a light on how the Jews mounted their pressure campaign:

> A fresh Aliens Bill was introduced this year [1905], and was the subject of a detailed report which advocated various essential amendments. A copy of the report was sent to every Member of Parliament, the leading newspapers, and to the principal officers of every provincial synagogue, asking the latter to bring the Jewish view of the necessary amendments before their local Member [of Parliament]. Three thousand

---

[171] *Hansard*, Volume 145, pp. 763-7. Translator's note: QVOS.

[172] *Hansard*, Volume 145, p. 805 ff.

[173] *Hansard*, Volume 148, pp. 270, 272, 277, 280, 295-6 and others. & *Hansard*, Volume 149, p. 1257. & p. 1299; Volume 150, p. 740 ff.

copies were circulated in Manchester alone. Sir Charles Dilke consented to take charge of the amendment which provided a loophole for the admission of victims of persecution abroad. Mr. Robson took charge of an amendment providing a right of appeal for rejected aliens, and steps were taken to see that the other amendments asked for by the Board, were placed before Parliament.[174]

In each of the pre-designated immigration ports, where the ships with new arrivals were obligated to dock, a new type of immigration center was set up. Each one was staffed by three people and had, among other functions, the task of deciding on the affected party's grounds for appeal in the event of a refusal of entry. The implementation of the regulations was largely left to the authorities. However, all of these regulations only applied to ships that had more than twenty immigrants on board. Others were able to land their passengers wherever they wanted and everything stayed the same as before.[175]

So this was the result of almost twenty years of struggle, both in the public sphere and in the legislative houses. Three commissions—four if you include the Sweating Commission of 1890—had worked tirelessly for years to achieve this pathetic compromise.

The law came into force on 1 January 1906. One would have assumed that the Jews and their friends would be completely satisfied. Not even close! And so we have the rare situation where both sides complained about the law and criticized those responsible for it. One of them, Mr. Balfour, even felt the need to publicly express his sympathy for the Jews. And thus we hear that under his patronage a large charity concert was held in aid of the Russo-Jewish Fund. Other patrons of this event included the Bishop of London, Sir Albert Rollit, Sir Marcus and Lady Samuel, Israel Zangwill, and Rufus Isaacs. Mr. Balfour had since resigned with his government. In the subsequent general election, the Conservative Party he led was completely defeated, and the Liberals formed the new government with a large majority. Herbert Gladstone was made Home Secretary, and his Under-Secretary of State was the Jew Herbert Samuel, now Lord Samuel.[176]

As early as March 1906, an order from the Home Office provoked the indignation of Major Evans-Gordon's supporters. An instruction had been issued to immigration officials that if there were any doubt about arrivals' claims of political or religious persecution, the benefit of the doubt was always to be given, and they be allowed to land. The following is a reproduction of the instruction:

---

[174] Emanuel: pp. 165-6. Translator's note: QVOS.

[175] Law Reports 1905, pp. 22-7.

[176] *Times*, 2/1/1906.

INSTRUCTION TO IMMIGRATION OFFICERS.

In all cases in which immigrants, coming from the parts of the Continent which are at present in a disturbed condition, allege that they are flying from political or religious persecution, the benefit of the doubt, where any doubt exists, as to the truth of the allegation will be allowed, and leave to land will be given.

Gladstone and his friends viewed this arrangement as merely a rule of interpretation of the law, which would not in any way alter its meaning. Major Evans-Gordon expressed the greatest indignation at this situation and declared that 'the whole Act became null and void under those conditions', given that every newcomer would therefore claim to belong to this category. In a like manner, he blasted MPs who made 'capital out of charges of alleged hardship arising from the rejection of diseased persons', reminding them that their constant demand for leniency out of sympathy for certain individual cases of immigrants with contagious diseases would inevitably lead to all diseased people having a case for entry, as 'the question was one of principle.' He reminded the House of 'our bounden duty' to protect the British people from needless suffering. 'Steps had been taken to protect the cattle of this country from infection from abroad, and was it reasonable when such a disease as miners' worm was imported to raise an outcry against sending immigrants back who were suffering from that and other dangerous diseases?'[177]

It soon became apparent that the fears of those who had opposed this ministerial instruction were coming true. The *Times'* special correspondent, who had been eyewitness to events, reported that those entering the country would readily 'tell their stories' to the well-trained immigration officers concerned, some of whom were multilingual in German and Yiddish and who made sure to 'display no harshness of bearing or disposition' towards the 'fairly treated' newcomers; and in keeping with the spirit of the aforementioned ministerial order, these people were freely given permission to enter.[178] It should not be difficult to guess who was behind this measure by the Home Secretary. Most Jewish immigrants said that they were being persecuted because of their religion or politics.

---

[177] Landa: p. 222 ff. Translator's note: Instruction text and Evans-Gordon QVOS. & *Hansard*, Volume 153, p. 1312 ff.; *Times*, 15/3/1906. Translator's note: QVOS [Hansard].

[178] *Times*, 26/4/1906. Translator's note: All QVOS. The eyewitness also reported that 'the immigration boards...are summoned so seldom and so irregularly that I have not had the opportunity of observing the proceedings' which again points to the interview process being a mere formality.

One newspaper complained bitterly that England had become 'the dumping ground for the moral and physical waste of Europe.' This would necessarily lead to the degeneration of the British nation.[179]

The Jews and their friends protested against the treatment given to the newcomers. The Jew Landa, who, as a correspondent for the *Jewish Chronicle* and later the *Jewish World*, had been tasked with attending the appeal proceedings of rejected immigrants, complained about the inadequacy of the appeal process. In his view, the assessors of the Immigration Board in question were guided by a combination of prejudice and incompetence. Very often the complainants' stories were not believed and they were even accused of telling untruths.[180]

Winston Churchill continued to work for Jewish interests and promised to solve their problems as soon as he had the personal influence to do so. He did not shirk from giving these assurances to various Jewish organizations, such as the Achei Brith Society. As the *Manchester Guardian* reports in 'Mr. Churchill and the Jews':

> Mr. Churchill, in addressing a Jewish audience at the rooms of the 'Achei Brith' Society on Sunday evening, appealed for their support on account of the work he had done for Jews in connection with the Aliens Bill. With regard to the first measure on the subject, men like Sir Charles Dilke, Mr. Herbert Samuel, and himself had striven their utmost to wreck that bill, and he (Mr. Churchill) it was who got the credit, together with the odium, of defeating it.[181]

Since 1906 Churchill had been Under-Secretary of State for the Colonial Office, and so the Jews had another friend at the highest level. When he became President of the Board of Trade in 1908, his position of influence was strengthened still further. His constant support of the Jews did not escape the public's notice, as demonstrated by a report in the *Manchester Guardian* of 21 April 1908. The following is an excerpt reproduced verbatim from this report:

> He [Mr. Nathan Laski] said candidly that in spite of anything Mr. Joynson-Hicks might say, he was first and foremost a Jew; and in spite of his lifelong adhesion to Liberalism, if Mr. Churchill had not satisfied him on the questions which they had put to him as Jews he would not have been on his plat-

---

[179] *Daily Mail*, 15/3/1906.

[180] Landa: p. 199 ff.

[181] *Manchester Guardian*, 9/1/1906; *Jewish Chronicle*, 14/12/1906. Translator's note: QVOS. For more on the carefully orchestrated strategies to destroy all attempts at immigration restriction, see Chapters XXV and XXVI of Banister [in Translator's Bibliography].

form that day. It was because he was able to get more from
Mr. Churchill than from Mr. Joynson-Hicks that he supported
Mr. Churchill. –(Cheers.)

The Hebrews' joy at Churchill's appointment as Home Secretary in 1910
knew no bounds. They discovered triumphantly that from then on, he would
supervise the implementation of the Aliens Act. Based on his previous behavior, it was known that he would take care of the Jews. As the *Jewish
Chronicle* reported:[182]

> Our own community, however, will have a special interest in
> Mr. Churchill's promotion. As Home Secretary he will have
> charge of the administration of the Aliens Act; and after the
> prominent part he took in the opposition to that species of leg-
> islation, and his sympathetic replies to Jewish deputations, we
> may at least expect a more generous attitude towards Jewish
> representation on this subject than was manifested by his pre-
> decessor. Mr. Churchill, in his new post, will also have a more
> important voice in the naturalisation question than he could
> previously lay claim to.[183]

His help soon became visible to the outside world. At the suggestion of the
Jewish community, he appointed three Jews as assessors to the aforementioned Immigration Boards.[184] Shortly after taking up his new office,
Churchill also fulfilled the Jews' long-expressed wish that the appellants
would in future be allowed to have legal representation when they appeared
before the Immigration Board. The Jews immediately set up a special committee to ensure that defense lawyers would be appointed in a timely manner
if required.[185]

We see, then, that the situation with regard to immigration was practically the same as before the law was passed, that the situation had actually
only changed in a formal sense and that it had in no way led to a restriction
on immigration. Nevertheless, Jews in England remained dissatisfied with

---

[182] *Jewish World*, 10/6/1910. Translator's note: A. K. Chesterton quotes this issue as saying the following: 'A victory at last! After nearly four years' ceaseless agitation... A great
victory has been won against the Aliens Act... The Home Secretary (Churchill) deserves
our warmest thanks; he had nobly fulfilled his pledges, and at the earliest opportunity. For
ourselves, we never doubted his sincerity.' [*The Tragedy of Anti-Semitism*, pp. 87-8, see
Translator's Bibliography].

[183] *Jewish Chronicle*, 18/2/1910. Translator's note: QVOS.

[184] Emanuel: pp. 182-3.

[185] Landa: p. 208.

these legal provisions, which they considered to be a personal insult, as the following extract from a *Jewish Chronicle* editorial demonstrates:

> But the officials under the Aliens Act can never be relied upon to do the right and merciful thing. Placed all of a sudden in supreme control of perfectly innocent men and women and endowed with absolutely unrestricted powers, they lapse almost inevitably into cruelties that ought not to be known in the country which voices so righteous an indignation over oppression practised elsewhere. The Immigration Board, we notice, rejected an alien, although his sister was positively in need of his services in her business and could therefore have given him employment. In another case a girl was dismissed, although her uncle, who had two thriving businesses, had desired to put her in charge of one of them.
>
> For our part, we fail to comprehend the whims which lead to give such decisions. This arbitrary and capricious tossing of unfortunate people backward and forward across the ocean is totally inconsistent with every canon of human right; and it is time that some protest was made against its continuance. It is monstrous that the destinies of perfectly harmless people should be subjected indefinitely to some obscure little tribunal set up by a reactionary law.[186]

Jewish Demographics up to 1914

At the end of our discussion of the history of Jewish immigration to England between 1881 and 1914, we have to deal with the rather difficult matter of attempting to determine the total number of Jews in Great Britain up to 1914. This endeavor is hampered by many obstacles, with the result that only an approximate estimate can be given.

We will only use the minimum figures that we believe should be taken in account, in a bid to avoid any overestimation. There are various points of reference that are useful for this census. First of all, the statistics for Jews and the official census of foreigners residing in England are available. In addition, we still have the total number of annual immigrants compiled by the Board of Trade. None of these sources will lead us to a correct and unquestionable result, but we believe that by using the latter, with certain corrections, we can achieve our goal to some extent.

---

[186] *Jewish Chronicle*, 19/11/1909. Translator's note: QVOS. Modern readers will undoubtedly be very familiar with the textual strategies employed in this excerpt.

The Jews themselves have to admit that when they do their own censuses, they are partly dependent on guesswork and that their estimates are probably lower than the actual figures. This is probably not entirely unintentional when it comes to the Jewish population. We have seen previously how for years there had been a public battle to restrict immigration which remained ongoing and which in addition was strongly directed against the Jewish element of the problem. The Jews therefore had the greatest interest in keeping the official figures as low as possible, which was clearly evident in 1889 when Rabbi Abrahams was examined before the Parliamentary Commission and questioned about the overall Jewish population in Leeds. He set the figure at a maximum of 6,000 souls, while two other expert witnesses gave it as 15,000 and 30,000 respectively.[187]

In addition, the Jews expressly emphasize that they only included religious Jews. However, this is not enough, since our estimates take into account the number of racial Jews.

Finally, the statistics for the Jews may not be correct for another reason. According to them, we find the following Jewish population figures for the following years:

1891: 64,280 in London;   101,189 in England
1901: 97,000 in London;   144,000 in England
1903:106,550 in London;   188,000 in England

In the period from 1891 to 1901, the total number is said to have only increased by 33,000, and of this increase 10,000 was due, according to the Jews, by an increase in births, with only the remainder being due to immigration. This would amount to an annual average of only 3,300 Jewish immigrants. Can it truly be believed that such a level of immigration would have led to all of the aforementioned upheavals in English life, with the consequent political struggles in the legislative houses and in the public sphere?[188]

We also firmly believe that we cannot trust the official censuses, but due to the lack of better reference points, we will use some of the figures contained in them to assist with our estimate. The Board of Trade claims to have used the official immigrant census figures in its 1894 report, but does so in a way that we find unacceptable. It compiles the total figures for traffic to and from England for the years from 1890 to 1893. It then deducts the latter from the former and then arrives at a net surplus, from which it then deducts those people who are listed as sailors. In this way, leaving out the year 1890, it arrives to the following figures:

---

[187] *Jewish Year Book 1900/1*, p. 26 ff.
[188] *Jewish Year Book 1900/1*, p. 26 ff.; *Jewish Year Book 1903/4*, p. 218 ff.

1891:   9,797
1892:   10,349
1893:   9,760[189]

This method can only be condemned in the strongest terms, because the traffic from England includes the thousands of emigrants of English blood who are being replaced by Jewish immigrants. The difference between incoming and outgoing traffic can therefore never represent the displacement of population. The Board of Trade does not overlook this flaw in its data-gathering, but considers it to be irrelevant when taken in the context of the overall situation.

The Commission of 1903 took the position that although the official censuses could in no way claim to be accurate, they must be approximately correct because the Board of Trade's annual immigration figures were considered unacceptable as evidence. We know that Rothschild and Sir Kenelm Digby raised strong objections to the published report. Given the composition of the Commission—even aside from these two—it is clear that compromises must have been made with the other assessors in order even to get to a final report. One only has to look at the witness statement of Evans-Gordon on this point to agree with the above hypothesis, as he considered the official findings to be significantly incorrect, but nevertheless later signed off on the report as a member of the committee.[190]

Major Evans-Gordon is of the opinion, among others, that the Jew generally avoids being counted because he always believes that there are certain disadvantages associated with this, even if it is only the danger of correct tax registration. Aside from this fact, it was not lost on the Commission that there was a possibility that the officials in question were incompetent and, furthermore, that the immigrants did not yet have a sufficient command of English to complete the questionnaires, which were not always easy to understand. In addition, one would also have to reckon with the possibility that those concerned would intentionally misrepresent their nationality.[191]

However, we too have further concerns about the accuracy of the official censuses. It is a phenomenon often observed that, in those days just as today, Jews would change their name to an English one as soon as possible and then present themselves to the outside world as English. This can be done in England almost effortlessly and requires minimal involvement of the authorities. The Jew Landa agrees, but in such a case, he thinks it is right to list such a foreigner in the statistics as an Englishman; the fact that 'to avoid

---

[189] *Accounts and Papers... 1894*, Volume 6, p. 354 ff.
[190] *Accounts and Papers... 1903,* Volume 9, p. 91 ff.
[191] *Accounts and Papers... 1903,* Volume 9, p. 20.

recognition as a foreigner was the surest sign of having acquired English characteristics.' We do not agree with this reasoning.[192]

In addition, those who had since acquired British citizenship were not included in the foreigner statistics. This likewise does not meet the requirements of our estimate, since a Jew does not become a Briton through admission to the British polity.

Moreover, the children of Jews born in England were no longer registered as foreigners, regardless of whether the parents were naturalized or still retained their original nationality, as according to English law, everyone born on British soil acquires British nationality [i.e. *jus soli*]. This was, in Evan-Gordon's opinion, 'the most serious omission as regards the Census figures' given that '[t]he Hebrew race is exceptionally prolific'.[193]

With all of this said, we can only use the official foreigner censuses as a rough guide for our estimates because nothing better is available. This is the case regarding the period prior to 1881, because it was only in 1879 that immigration statistics began to be compiled, albeit initially very inadequately.[194]

For this reason, we have used the following methods of calculation:

1. Until 1881, the official foreigner censuses serve as the key reference point.
2. From 1881 until 1907, the immigration statistics are used.
3. After 1907, figures are freely estimated.

According to the official census from 1889, there were 136,000 foreigners in England. We have already seen how this figure is almost certainly inaccurate and does not remotely count all of the people in question. So it would hardly be unfair to use these figures as a basis for calculation, even without taking into account those foreigners in England who are not Jews. However, in order to forestall as far as possible the accusation of inaccuracy or partiality, we will only assume that 75% of this official figure are Jews. We will also apply this percentage to the numbers found later, and we believe we are entitled to do this based on the following considerations.

According to the evidence previously expounded, there can be hardly any doubt that the masses who had streamed into England from Europe during that time belonged overwhelmingly to the Jewish race. Since 1856, Jews had been entering Great Britain in increasing numbers. Undisputedly, the introduction of the May Laws in 1882 and the stricter implementation regulations in 1890, which aggravated the 1882 laws still further, caused the

---

[192] *Hansard*, Volume 8, p. 1157. & Landa: p. 27. Translator's note: QVOS.

[193] Evans-Gordon: p.243 ff., 270. *Accounts and Papers... 1903*, Volume 9, pp. 30, 1053. Translator's note: QVOS [Evans-Gordon, p. 244].

[194] *Accounts and Papers...1889*, Volume 10, pp. 268 ff., 325 ff.; *Hansard*, Volume 132, p. 987 ff.; *Hansard*, Volume 133, p. 1083.

greater increase from year to year. The entire literature on the immigration issue treats the question as almost exclusively Jewish and also mostly emphasizes the great predominance of the Jewish race among the immigrants from the (then) Russia Empire, Austria-Hungary, Germany, and Romania. Copies of transcripts from the debates held in both legislative houses likewise convey the same impression. And whatever doubts may still linger are quashed by the evidence gathered by three or four different commissions, as a glance over their extensive records will confirm. Furthermore, it is also indicated by the names themselves of the later naturalized people, more than 75% of which unmistakably point to their Jewishness. Finally, the proceedings of the various commissions deal almost exclusively with questions relating to Jews.[195]

We therefore have no reservations about viewing the 75% rate for the official immigration census of 1881 and for the results of later immigrant censuses as appropriate and correct. This principle, when applied to the official census of 1881, results in a Jewish community of 102,000 people out of a total of 136,000 foreigners.

The next determination is supposed to cover the years 1882 to 1888, even though it is very unlikely that the arrivals of 1881 were in any way recorded in the official census. However, in the interests of the desired accuracy, this will be assumed.

The immigration figures from 1882 to 1888 are likewise very inaccurate, because as we have already previously discussed, the Alien Act of King William IV, from which immigration figures had traditionally been compiled, had been allowed to fall into disuse. It was only reintroduced around 1880 in London, Hull, Grimsby, and Southampton. All other ports continued as usual in their refusal to implement this law. London, however, appears to have carried out reasonably detailed research and we will therefore only consider this data, which indicates that 81,896 foreigners landed in the port of London during the period mentioned. How many of these were just passing through cannot be determined with certainty. An official analysis made on one ship chosen at random showed that it was 9%. We are prepared to increase this percentage to 10% and subtract it from the total, so that we get 73,706 people. If we then calculate that of these, 75% are Jewish immigrants, we get a total number of 55,281.[196]

As a result, we have not taken into account the arrivals in all the other ports and are only considering 75% in each case in question as being Jews,

[195] Landa: p. 8 ff.. Evans-Gordon: p. 4 ff.; Wilkins: *The Alien Invasion*, p. 1 ff.. Wilkins: *The Immigration...*, p. 1 ff. Abbott: p. 461 ff. Also see Russell/Lewis. & *Accounts and Papers... 1903*, Volume 55, p. 44 ff.; ... *1904*, Volume 78, p. 341 ff.; ... *1905*, Volume 62, p. 409 ff.; ...*1906*, Volume 96, p. 781 ff.; ...*1907*, Volume 66, p. 712 ff.
[196] *Accounts and Papers... 1989*, Volume 10, p. 268-9. Wilkins: *The Alien Invasion*, p. 27 ff.

despite the fact that the official interviewed about this only spoke of Jews and their destitute state upon arrival.[197]

For the years 1889 and 1890, we will only use the same annual average as for the period from 1882 to 1888, despite the fact that increasing immigration figures were noted for these latter years. This amounts to around 8,000 people, so we get a further total of 16,000 for those two years.

The next uniform period extends from 1891 to 1904. Here we basically used the official immigrant censuses with certain modifications which shall be discussed. We have already explained how we also consider these surveys to be inaccurate. In the years after 1891, however, further deficiencies in reporting emerged that make the relevant findings appear to be too low rather than too high.

As before, the lists were drawn up by more or less capable members of the incoming ships' crew. They relied on the information provided to them by the passengers. The officials accepted this as correct and did not care whether a newcomer was actually in transit to another country or not. Confirmation of this can be found again and again in the statements of the various officials examined on this matter. So there is a strong possibility that many passengers who said that they were in transit remained in England. Others believe that many immigrants only pretended that they wished to remain in England, or they later changed their minds and went on to America, which would mean that the number of people passing through is larger than that recorded in official statistics. It may be true that the official immigration counts are incorrect in this respect too, as far as individual people are concerned. Nevertheless, we believe that the overall figure is correct. After 1893, American immigration laws changed, making entry much more difficult. Many people therefore gave up on the dream of America, and remained in England, or else were returned to England after an unsuccessful attempt to land on American shores. As a consequence, it may be that more people actually remained in England than appear in the official statistics. But here too, in the interest of the most accurate estimate possible, it is instructive to weigh both possibilities against each other.[198]

It must also be added that, according to the information already provided, the Board of Trade had not the slightest inclination to publish the real immigration figures, which would reveal much higher numbers. In fact, many disbelieved the Board's numbers, including Lord Salisbury, who, during an 1894 debate on the Aliens Bill, accused the Board of 'sweating the figures down', a deliberately evocative turn of phrase:

---

[197] *Accounts and Papers... 1989,* Volume 10, p. 325 ff.

[198] *Hansard,* Volume 8, p. 1158. & Landa: pp. 14-5. & Wilkins: *The Alien Invasion,* pp. 27-9.

My Lords, I freely admit that in bringing forward a Bill of this character from the Opposition side of the House, I am challenging the conduct which the Government have pursued, and trying to point out to them that they have not met the crisis through which we have been passing in the manner which their duty and their position demanded. But I will deal, in the first place, with the least important points to which the noble Earl [Rosebery] referred. He informs me that the Board of Trade have sweated my figures down. I readily admit that the Board of Trade are great adepts in that art, but for my part I prefer figures for use that have not been sweated.[199]

The Jews and their friends also considered the immigrant censuses to be unsuitable as a basis for policy because among those who were not in transit there were tourists or business travelers who returned to their country of origin. This might have been true in for a small number, but it is, nevertheless, an improbable supposition, given that only those arrivals who did not travel in first or second class were ever counted, i.e. only as passengers in third class or steerage, where you would hardly find any tourists or wealthy merchants. Rather, it can in fact be assumed that among the first- and second-class travelers, there were also quite a few Jews who settled permanently in England. Here, too, one could, if anything, allow for an increase in the official figures, but we shall refrain from doing so in the interests of finding a total number which cannot be refuted as exaggeration.[200]

The other side insists that those listed as seafarers be deducted from the annual total from those not in transit. In this, too, we shall to follow their wishes, although we have strong reservations about doing so.

The evidence taken by the commissions in 1889 and 1903 showed that the complete opposite was the case. According to customs officials, it was not uncommon for migrants who worked their passage to England on the ship to be listed as sailors. So they were employed, among other things, as guards on pony transports, and they too, alongside others not listed as sailors in the official censuses, often settled permanently in England.[201] Indeed, even the greatest expert of the Board of Trade expressly stated before the Commis-

---

[199] Hansard, Volume 27, p. 132 ff. Translator's note: QVOS. It may also interest readers to learn that, in this debate, the Lords who argued against Salisbury's claim of (immigration numbers being higher than official statistics) were Lord Rosebery [married to a Rothschild] and Lord Herschell.

[200] Wilkins: *The Alien Invasion...*, p. 32-3. Landa: p. 231. *Times* 1/1/1906. *Accounts and Papers... 1894*, Volume 68, p. 352.

[201] *Accounts and Papers... 1889*, Volume 10, pp. 321, 323, 328. & *Accounts and Papers... 1903*, Volume 9, p. 77, Question 207 ff.; p. 92, Question 434 ff.; p. 658, Questions 16, 572 ff.; *Hansard*, Volume 27, p. 132 ff.

sion of 1903 that 'in his opinion it was wrong to deduct them all.' Nevertheless, we will deduct them in full and not count them as immigrants.[202]

Lastly, there is one final and important circumstance which bolsters our
thesis on the inaccuracy of the Board of Trade's figures. According to Board
of Trade's system, every two children were listed as one adult in the official
statistics. How important this is for accurate reporting can be deduced from
the following example.[203]

We know that the families of Jews, especially the Eastern European
Jews, are very numerous. Five to six children in a family is not uncommon.
But here too we would like to submit to the judgment of Rabbi Abrahams
from Leeds, who was officially interviewed on this matter, and who stated
that the average was a family of five members, i.e. three children. So if a
total of 400,000 people appear in the official immigration statistics within a
certain period of time, in our opinion, around 571,000 people actually immigrated. But we shall refrain from taking this into account in order to make an
estimate that is as error-free as possible.

If we use the official immigration lists from 1891 to 1904 with reference to the aforementioned methodology, we arrive at the following results:

1891 28,270
1892 22,137
1893 21,296
1894 18,861
1895 20,634
1896 24,987
1897 28,089
1898 28,486
1899 37,522
1900 47,555
1901 40,318
1902 51,409
1903 69,162
1904 82,874

TOTAL   521,600[204]

For the years 1905 and 1906, a distinction was no longer made between
transit travelers and those coming to settle, and instead a different system
was introduced, which was again tailored towards different aspects in both

---

[202] *Accounts and Papers... 1903*, Volume 9, p. 887, Question 22367.

[203] *Accounts and Papers... 1903*, Volume 9, pp. 19-20, p. 108, Question 864; p. 124,
Question 1321. Wilkins: *The Alien Invasion...*, p. 33.

[204] *Accounts and Papers... 1894*, Vol 68, p. 357. *Accounts and Papers... 1903*, Vol 9, p. 947.

years. The details are of little interest, since the final total is almost the same as in 1904.

On the other hand, it can be assumed that the immigration figures of Eastern Jews from the former Russian Empire would at least have remained the same, given that, as a result of the Russo-Japanese war and the subsequent turmoil, more Jews left Russia than ever. One must also take into account that, after 1 January 1906, i.e. after the Aliens Act came into force, it was 'notorious' that the law was being freely evaded by having the immigrants arrive on ships carrying no more than twenty passengers. Because as has already been stated, such ships did not fall under the provisions of the law. The passengers were able to land anywhere on the coast, and no investigation by officials took place. A consequence of this, among other things, was that these immigrants were not included in the statistics. If we therefore use the 1904 figure of 82,874 for each of the years 1905 and 1906, then by applying our rate of 75% we arrive at the [very] conservative estimate of 62,154 for each of these two years.[205]

For the subsequent years, the criteria for data collection were changed yet again. Censuses were based on immigrant ships which had arrived from specific ports in Germany, the Netherlands, Finland, and the Russian Empire.

We believe that if we take solely the immigrants from the ports of the last two categories, we should come fairly close to an accurate estimate. It should be noted that this means that we are not taking into account all the arrivals from other nations, nor those who circumvented the law in the manner described above. This brings us to 66,000 and 19,000 people for the years 1907 and 1908, respectively. By then applying our schema of 75%, this gives a total of 63,750 Jews.[206]

From 1909 onwards the system was changed yet again and it was made—probably deliberately—so opaque that it is difficult to find any indications that point to the immigrants being of Jewish origin. For this reason, we believe that we can base our calculations on the low 1908 figure of 14,250, which is to say, we can estimate that every year 14,250 Jews landed. This results in 71,250 Jewish immigrants arriving to England for the period from 1909 to 1913 inclusive. Calculations for the year 1914 will be avoided due to the outbreak of war, although it must be said that most of the immigration for that year would have already taken place before work broke out, as the numbers usually fell sharply during the autumn and winter months.

---

[205] *Accounts and Papers... 1906*, Volume 96, p. 781 ff.; *Accounts and Papers... 1907*, Volume 66, p. 712 ff. & *Hansard*, Volume 153, p. 1313. Translator's note: 'Notorious' is quoted from original source, although it must be noted that the speaker Evans-Gordon errs when he refers to the maximum being twelve—the legislation itself shows the maximum to be twenty.

[206] *Accounts and Papers... 1908*, Volume 87, p. 909 ff.; *Accounts and Papers... 1909*, Volume 70, p, 499 ff.

Our calculations give then the following results:

until 1881	102,000
from 1882 until 1888	55,521
from 1889 until 1890	16,000
from 1891 until 1904	391,200
from 1905 until 1906	124,308
from 1907 until 1908	63,750
from 1909 until 1913 or 1914	71,250
TOTAL	**823,789**

As a result, we have no reservations about estimating the number of Jews in England by 1914 at 850,000, especially given that this calculation does not take into account the excess in births for the 1881-1914 period, i.e. a period of 33 years.[207]

It is completely impossible that this large-scale immigration within such a relatively short period of time could have had no detrimental consequences for the British nation. One should not overlook the fact that the British population within Europe did not exceed 40 million during these years. In addition, this immigration must have had a further undesirable effect if at least as many English people left their homeland as Jews entered during the same period. That this was indeed the case is confirmed by a glance at the official surveys for English emigration over this period. Nor was this danger unknown to the English themselves. Whelpley laments the fact that, in his opinion, around 75,000 foreigners landed in the country in 1904, while correspondingly around 80,000 Britons emigrated. The latter were replaced by inferior individuals who could only have a detrimental influence on the life of the nation.[208]

We have covered this topic extensively because we consider it indispensable for assessing current events in England, which will be covered in later chapters. Furthermore, the above estimate is in such stark contradiction to the figure provided by the Jews themselves that a detailed justification seemed necessary. The Jews stated that their population in Great Britain was 245,500 by 1914. We shall leave it to the reader's discretion to form an opinion on the two opposing figures based on the facts presented. But we also

---

[207] Editor's note: If there were 850,000 Jews in England in 1914, this represents 2.3% of the total of 36.2 million. This is the approximate percentage in the US today. We must again note that Jewish corruption of society seems to begin when they exceed about 0.1%. Also, it is striking to observe that the Jewish population in England today is listed in official sources as about 300,000, or around 1/3 of the figure from 1914—even as the English population rose to 58.6 million. Based on the above history, we may assume that present-day figures are comparably understated.

[208] *Statistical Tables 1907*, Volume 44, p. 350. & Whelpley: p. 26 ff., 41 ff.

feel it necessary to stress, once again, that our estimate represents the minimum possible number.[209]

The Marconi Scandal

Not only had the number of Jews in England increased considerably, but they had likewise gained an ever-greater influence, which was to some extent visible to the outside world. Thus, in addition to Rothschild, three other Jews had since been made Peers of England. They were Lord Michelham and Lord Wandsworth, both originally named Stern, and Lord Swaythling, formerly known as Sir Samuel Montagu. Towards 1914 we find no fewer than 22 barons and 15 knights of Jewish blood. Six Jews, namely Lord Rothschild, Lord Reading, Sir Alfred Mond, Herbert L. Samuel, Sir Edgar Speyer, and Edwin Samuel Montagu, were members of the Privy Council at this time, and there were 16 avowed Jews among the members of Parliament. How many baptized Jews, half-Jews, or quarter-Jews there were in Parliament at the time is almost impossible to determine today.[210]

We shall first concern ourselves with Herbert L. Samuel and Lord Reading, previously known as Rufus Isaacs. The former was Postmaster-General, the latter Solicitor-General in Asquith's Liberal cabinet.

Rufus Isaacs had an adventurous career. As a boy, he ran away from his parents. He later became a stockbroker, went bankrupt and, as a result, lost his license to trade on the Stock Exchange. He then turned to law and qualified as a barrister. It took him five years to pay off his previously accumulated debts. After just ten years of practice, he had an annual income of £7,000, which increased to £30,000 between 1900 and 1910. In October 1904 he was elected to Parliament as a Liberal MP, appointed Solicitor-General in March 1910, and Attorney-General in September of the same year.[211]

Herbert Samuel also belonged to the Liberal Party and was a member of Parliament since 1902. From 1905 to 1909 he was Under-Secretary of State for the Home Department, and his roles included that of Postmaster-General from 1910 to 1914.[212]

Both Jews, together with David Lloyd George and Godfrey Isaacs, Rufus Isaacs' brother, were the key figures in the Marconi scandal. To give an even approximately accurate history of this saga would, as L. Maxse, owner and editor of the *National Review*, rightly opined at the time, 'tax the pen of a Conan Doyle, assisted by the brains of a Sherlock Holmes.' It is not simply a matter of having to work through the extremely large volume of

---

[209] *Jewish Year Book 1915*, p. 167 ff.

[210] *Jewish Year Book 1911*, p. 278 ff.; *Jewish Year Book 1914*, p. 175 ff.; *Jewish Year Book 1915*, p. 177 ff.

[211] Jackson: pp. 1-3. & pp. 18, 136. & pp. 103, 135-7.

[212] *Who's Who 1938*: p. 2979.

documentary material, but also understanding the many behind-the-curtain dealings that have never been fully clarified, even after an eight-month-long investigation.[213]

The recently-deceased [in 1937] Marconi's great contributions to wireless telegraphy are well known. In England, his progress was due, not only to his genius, but to Jewish financiers. Nor could he have ever complained about his treatment by the Patent Office or about how the Court of Chancery settled the legal disputes over his patents. It is therefore not surprising that he was usually able to prevail over his competitors in business matters, even though at times their inventions were at least as valuable as his.[214]

In October 1909, the Marconi Company informed its shareholders that, for a fee of £15,000, it had sold to the English government [under the name of the Post Office] all of the coast stations in the United Kingdom, along with the right to use the Marconi patents installed therein and any future patents and improvements for the term of 14 years.[215] Shortly after this contract was concluded, patent disputes arose over competing inventions; among others, the Marconi Company had a particular interest in having the Lodge-Muirhead patent declared null and void due to expiry, given that the latter was its most formidable competitor. To everyone's astonishment, the Marconi Society found support from the Crown due to the mediation of their lawyer Sir Rufus Isaacs.[216]

Two months before the appointment of Rufus Isaacs as Solicitor-General, that is to say, in January 1910, Rufus Isaac's brother Godfrey had been appointed director of the Marconi Company. There was a general puzzlement as to why he of all people had been chosen, given that until then, Godfrey had shown neither the ability nor the merit for such a great position. On the other hand, it was common knowledge that in the past Sir Rufus Isaacs had almost always been in some way involved in his brother's often unhappy ventures.[217]

Despite Crown intervention, the Lodge-Muirhead patent remained valid, which entailed settlement negotiations between the Marconi Company and the holders of the former patent, Sir Oliver Lodge and Dr. Alexander Muirhead, who had cared less about protecting their patent rights than they had about trying to convince the government of their invention's usefulness as a public service that would benefit the nation, efforts which had gone in vain for four years. The futility of their efforts were later explained by the fact that elements of the very government they were trying to persuade were

---

[213] *National Review*, Volume 61, p. 405. Translator's note: QVOS. As if to prove the author's thesis, the article on the topic then goes on for 200 pages.

[214] *National Review*, Volume 60, pp. 200-2.

[215] *National Review*, Volume 60, p. 204.

[216] *National Review*, Volume 60, p. 205.

[217] *Accounts and Papers... 1912-3*, Volume 8, p. 12 ff.

in league with the Marconi clique, and so were deliberately stringing these good men along for years while their confederates worked to steal the duo's invention.[218]

When Rufus Isaacs became Solicitor-General, his brother Godfrey entered into negotiations with Postmaster-General Herbert Samuel to establish a network of wireless stations across the British Empire. These negotiations dragged for a long period of time, and were only accelerated after a recommendation from the Imperial Conference in 1911. Even then, no other inventions were used for comparison, and only the Marconi company was requested to put in a definitive tender.[219]

In the event of an agreement, the Marconi Company would make its major stations at Poldhu and Clifden available and promised a further expansion of its system at various points in the British Empire. Incidentally, nobody had bothered to check whether the two stations being offered were suitable for the intended purpose. The government experts at the Admiralty and the Post Office did not request any evidence of successful prior functioning. This would have been all the more necessary since it would be on the basis of such evidence that the contractual conditions and all calculations were made. It was left to various officials in seven or eight departments at the Treasury to draft the contract. As for negotiations with the other contractual party, these officials had to deal exclusively with the cunning Godfrey Isaacs, who had quite openly expressed to them that the Marconi Company was in a privileged position due to his brother Rufus.[220]

In January 1912 the negotiations had already made considerable progress. On the 17th and 24th of the month in question, the final meetings were held by the relevant committees, in which the only items of concern were, in Herbert Samuel's words, 'the purchase price, the duration of the contract and the ongoing patent fees'.[221]

Lord Murray (one of the leading Liberals), Sir Rufus Isaacs, and Chancellor of the Exchequer, [49-year-old] David Lloyd George, spent their holidays in Villa Dragonier on Cape Martin at the beginning of January. At this time, the first of these men sent the following telegram to his stockbroker Fenner: 'Write to me about how things are.' Mr. Fenner responded with the following: 'Another stock that has risen significantly over the last few months is the Marconi Company. Apart from this, the market is presenting a downward trend'.[222]

Meanwhile, the Marconi Company's negotiations with the government continued, with Samuel representing the British government's interests. In

---

[218] *National Review*, Volume 60, p. 205.
[219] *Accounts and Papers... 1912-3*, Volume 8, p. 761.
[220] *Accounts and Papers... 1912-3*, Volume 8, pp. 708-9. & pp. 904-5.
[221] *Accounts and Papers... 1912-3*, Volume 8, p. 763.
[222] *Accounts and Papers... 1912-3*, Volume 7, pp. 738-41.

the final negotiations, Godfrey Isaacs was granted even better conditions regarding patent fees. And on 7 March 1912, Samuel hurriedly accepted the Marconi Company's final offer, subject to the approval of Parliament.

The text of the contract included, among other things, the stipulation that the Marconi Company would receive £60,000 for each of its stations and 10% of the gross income from all stations to be established under the terms of the agreement. A term of 28 years was agreed, but the government had the right to withdraw from the contract after 18 years. In this case, however, the government could not make any further use of Marconi's patents in the future. The Marconi Company had the exclusive right to install whatever devices it deemed necessary, including those that had nothing to do with their patents. The company continued to act as a kind of technical consultant for the government. It even went so far that in future the government had to submit to the Marconi Society for appraisal all the details of any new invention offered to it, which it might intend to install in one of the stations built under the contract. Details of this agreement were communicated to shareholders in a circular dated March 9.[223]

On the same day, Godfrey Isaacs embarked for America to sort out the affairs of the subsidiary company there, of which he was also a director. The majority of its shares were owned by the English company. Conditions in America were not the best for the Marconi invention, as a major lawsuit was pending over the alleged infringement of a United Wireless Company patent. Godfrey Isaacs managed to acquire this competitor for the British company. The purchase price consisted of the transfer of 700,000 shares from the American Marconi company. In addition, another contract was concluded between the English and the American company, according to which the former sold the rights transferred from the agreement, and indeed all of the assets, to the American Marconi company for approximately twice the price. They also agreed that each of them would have to set up a station on both banks of the Atlantic in order to ensure wireless communication between Europe and America, as well as a future close cooperation between the two entities. It was also decided to increase the American company's share capital to ten million dollars, and if any of the shares in question did not find buyers in America, the British company was granted the right to issue these unsold shares at par within one year. Finally, the two Marconi companies reached agreements with a third company for a joint news service.

Under no circumstances were any of these contracts to be disclosed to the public before the American company had approved the new share issue.

---

[223] *Hansard*, Volume 42, pp. 667-750. Translator's note: Researchers may wish to consult this debate ('Marconi Wireless Telegraph Company, Limited', House of Commons, 11 October 1912) for the expert way in which Sir Henry Norman exposes all of the absurdity and blatant corruption in the Marconi contract. & *Hansard*, Volume 42, p. 685 ff. & p. 669.

Sir Rufus Isaacs sent the following official telegram to a Marconi Society banquet in New York on 17 March 1912, saying: 'Please congratulate Marconi and my brother on the success of the wonderful enterprise. I wish them all success in New York'.[224]

In the aforementioned agreement, Godfrey Isaacs was personally granted the right to place 500,000 shares at five dollars or one pound sterling each. He had already managed to place 400,000 of these shares in America, which meant that on his return to England he only brought the remaining 100,000 back with him. The public was also unaware of this agreement.[225]

On 8 April 1912, Godfrey Isaacs returned to England and the very next day had a meeting with his brother Rufus and a third brother Harry. He informed them in great detail of the arrangements made in America and explained to them that the stocks in his hands would rise considerably. Nevertheless, he would offer them the entire share package at par. Sir Rufus refused to accept any of the shares. Harry, on the other hand, took over 56,000.[226]

Immediately after this conversation, Godfrey Isaacs learned from various quarters that strong opposition was brewing in Parliament against the British government's contract with the Marconi company. Great difficulties had therefore to be expected in obtaining approval from the House of Commons, especially since very influential members of Parliament were among the opponents of the contract. Because of this, Godfrey Isaacs by no means believed that the final acceptance of the contract was in any way guaranteed. In the meantime, his brother Harry did not desist in his efforts to sell shares in the American company to his influential brother Rufus. On April 17 Harry's efforts paid off: Attorney-General Sir Rufus Isaacs acquired 10,000 shares from the holdings of Harry Isaacs. They were not actually handed over to him, but rather Rufus held a proportionate share in the latter's entire share package. The price had been set at £2 per share as these shares, which were still unlisted on the stock exchange, had doubled in price.[227]

In evidence later given, Sir Rufus Isaacs stated that he had had no reservations about making the deal with his brother Harry. He had felt it necessary to reject the first share offer, which came from his brother Godfrey, because Godfrey was a businessman whose company was about to contract with the government, which was not the case with Harry. As a result, Sir Rufus had no compunction about making the purchase, especially since his brothers had explained to him in detail that the American company had nothing to do with the English company.[228]

---

[224] *Accounts and Papers... 1912-3*, Vol. 8, p. 12; 1913, Vol. 7, pp. 124-7.

[225] *Hansard*, Vol. 54, pp. 394-5.

[226] *Hansard*, Vol. 54, p. 455.

[227] *Hansard*, Vol. 54, p. 456. & pp. 395, 457. *Accounts and Papers... 1913*: Vol. 7, pp. 127-9.

[228] *Hansard*, Vol. 54, pp. 398, 436; *Accounts and Papers... 1913*, Vol. 7, p. 129.

Sir Rufus Isaacs was a close friend of Lloyd George and Lord Murray. On the evening of April 17, Sir Rufus went to these two and informed them of his deal with Harry Isaacs. If they were also interested in the shares, he would be disposed to hand over a thousand to each of them, after which both of them first inquired about the payment terms. Sir Rufus replied that they did not need to worry about the payment, that he would give them notice well in advance if he needed the money. He further explained to them that, according to his brother Godfrey, there was no relationship between the English and the American companies. Lloyd George and Lord Murray then each took a thousand shares at a price of £2 each.

After the luxury ocean liner Titanic sank on 14 April 1912, the shares were listed on the Stock Exchange on April 19 and the important aforementioned American agreements were announced to the public. This timing was even more favorable by the fact that the importance of wireless telegraphy had become clear to the whole world in view of the Titanic disaster. On the same day, Lloyd George called his broker and told him that he owned shares in the American Marconi Company. The broker replied that he did not consider this investment to be a good one because, in his opinion, the company was overcapitalized and the entire circumstances surrounding it reminded him too much of the last major scam, the Barnato stock scam. Lloyd George apparently did not take too kindly to this hint as he immediately ended the conversation.[229]

The shares opened at £3¼ on the morning of April 19 and rose to £4 the same day. The Attorney-General immediately sold 7,000 of his remaining 8,000 shares at an average price of £3½. Lloyd George and Lord Murray together sold 1,714 shares at £3 $5/32$ on April 20, making £2,200 from the operation. Both ministers purchased 3,000 new shares on May 22 at a price of £2 5/32. Lord Murray had previously bought 2,500 shares at £3¼ on April 18 and a further 500 on May 14 at a lower price using Liberal Party funds.[230]

Rumors were already flying around the stock exchange in April that there were ministers who had interests in the Marconi company. On June 13, Sir Henry Norman asked the Postmaster-General, Herbert Samuel, to inform him of some of the terms of the contract, but Samuel replied that 'it would not be convenient to furnish the details asked for'.[231]

On July 19, the General Post Office published the details of the contract. Shares jumped vertiginously to £9.15, and the rumors in the City about certain ministers doing business in Marconi shares became more and more intense. In June, a daily newspaper printed a single article on this issue, while references to it increased throughout July. The periodicals leading this discussion were

---

[229] *Hansard*, Vol. 54, p. 395. *Accounts and Papers... 1913*, Vol. 7, p. 194 ff.
[230] *Hansard*, Vol. 54, p. 399. & p. 635.
[231] *Hansard*, Vol. 42, p. 669. Translator's note: QVOS.

the *Outlook*, the *Eyewitness* and the *National Review*. In the last of the three, a certain Mr. Lawson compared this stock speculation to the South Sea Bubble. Other periodicals described the ministers' participation as corruption. The Liberal government's press continued to remain silent, and did not even comment on the strong criticisms, which was all the more inexplicable given that the opponents' press was increasingly demanding an investigation.[232]

At the end of July or beginning of August—apparently those involved did not know exactly when—Lord Murray and Sir Rufus Isaacs informed Prime Minister Asquith of their involvement in the American company, but without informing him of the details, such as, for example, the number of shares they each held or the different phases of the transaction. However, they made sure to explain to him that American company had nothing to do with English one. Asquith then claimed to Parliament that the Attorney-General Rufus Isaacs had sent him a letter on the matter, repeating what had previously been said, but that he had not kept it.[233]

After July 19, Samuel did everything possible to get Parliament to approve the contract as quickly as possible. During one of the last sittings of August, he tried to persuade the Opposition to refrain from the resistance that had already been shown during the debates. It was at this time too, that Samuel, according to his statements, was informed by Lord Murray of the ministers' transactions. He also considered this involvement to be insignificant because he believed Murray's statements that there was no connection between the two Marconi companies.[234]

On 6 August 1912, the Prime Minister announced that, in view of the great opposition to the contract that was already evident, he would allow an enquiry on the matter, although there would only be time for this after the summer recess. Regardless, Samuel approached Major Archer-Shee, who led the Opposition, and tried to persuade him to abandon his concerns and refrain from protracted debates. The adjournment of the enquiry until after the recess already meant an unduly long delay, Samuel argued, which was undesirable in view of the international situation and the urgent need to install wireless telegraph transmitters. Major Archer-Shee refused this request.[235]

A technical official from the General Post Office also took part in one of the negotiations with the British Marconi Company, and on this occasion became acquainted with some of the terms of the future contract. This engineer, Mr. Taylor, bought a few shares in the British company because he

---

[232] Jackson, p. 168; *Accounts and Papers... 1912-3*, Vol. 8, pp. 12-3. & p. 13; *Hansard*, Vol. 54, pp. 459, 474.

[233] *Hansard*, Vol. 54, pp. 552-3.

[234] *Hansard*, Vol. 42, pp. 728-9; Vol. 54, pp. 506-7; *Accounts and Papers... 1913*, Vol. 7, p. 310.

[235] *Accounts and Papers... 1913*, Vol. 7, pp. 310-1.

considered them a good investment for his small fortune. After a while, however, he sold them in view of the rising prices.

The matter came to the attention of Samuel, who ordered for the facts of the case to be established. The Postmaster-General acquitted the official of corruption charges, but punished him with demotion for his insider trading.[236]

On 11 October 1912, Asquith fulfilled his August promise to set up a Select Committee. The request in question was made by Samuel because Asquith was allegedly unable to attend the meeting due to a minor illness. A heated debate took place in which the government was heavily reproached for the terms of the contract. Of course, the ministers involved also had their say, rejecting all allegations as unfounded and defending themselves against the supposedly untrue allegations in public.[237]

Sir Rufus Isaacs declared that he was in no way involved in the British Marconi Company's negotiations with the government. He did not even have any official or private information about the progress of events. He only found out about it by chance at a social event a few days before the agreement was published. The Attorney-General went on to solemnly declare that:

> Never from the beginning, when the shares were 14s., or £9, have I had one single transaction with the shares of that company. I am not only speaking for myself, but I am also speaking on behalf, I know, of both my right hon. friend, the Postmaster-General and the Chancellor of the Exchequer, who, in some way or other, in some of the articles, have been brought into this matter.[238]

His statement was then corroborated by Samuel in a lengthy speech, who also went on to emphasize once again that not a single member of the government had any interests in the British Marconi Society and that the public claims to the contrary were 'wicked and utterly baseless slanders'.[239]

The Chancellor Lloyd George pretended not to know what the rumors were and called for the situation to be clarified. He called for an open debate before a Select Committee in order to deal with 'these rumors, these sinister rumors, that have been passed from one foul lip to another behind the backs of the House'.[240]

At the end of the sitting it was decided to form this Select Committee, which was given the power to summon persons and request papers and records. Nine members of the ruling party and six members of the Opposition

---

[236] *Hansard*, Vol. 52, pp. 1864-5; Vol. 54, pp. 453-4, 510-2, 649.

[237] *Hansard*, Vol. 54, p. 553; Vol. 42, p. 667 ff.

[238] *Hansard*, Vol. 42, p. 716 ff. Translator's note: QVOS.

[239] *Hansard*, Vol. 42, p. 725 ff. Translator's note: QVOS.

[240] *Hansard*, Vol. 42, p. 714. Translator's note: QVOS.

were appointed as the Committee members. Committee decisions were to be taken by a simple majority.[241]

The Select Committee sessions began immediately afterwards. All kinds of witnesses were heard and a wide variety of documents examined. The only people who were not called to give a deposition were the ministers against whom the accusations were made, despite the fact that, given the fact that the witnesses had to make sworn statements, had these men been called the situation could have been clarified with the utmost speed. Thus the months of October, November, and December were filled with Committee sessions.

On 13 January 1913, Lord Murray left England, ostensibly to pursue his major business interests abroad, which would keep him away from home for some months. Neither he nor his accomplices had told the Committee anything about their transactions. Before his departure, he visited his brother, the MP Captain A. Murray, and gave him the Liberal Party's 3,000 Marconi shares. 'He suggested,' Captain Murray later testified, 'that they should be kept until the Marconi affair was settled, so that no one but himself would be implicated.' And to lend credit to his statements, nor did he not tell anyone about the matter. It was not until 15 June 1913 that the transactions became public, as a result of the bankruptcy of Lord Murray's broker. The Select Committee immediately telegraphed a request to Lord Murray to return to England so that he could make a statement, but he refused this request, citing his business obligations and the long distance involved. The trip would likely have taken four weeks at most.[242]

On 19 June 1913, Prime Minister Asquith stoutly defended Lord Murray, declaring that in his several years of close dealings with the man, 'I never saw anything in his language or his conduct which led me to entertain the faintest doubt, either of the soundness of his judgment or the integrity of his character.'[243]

In the first week of 1913, Lloyd George and Sir Rufus Isaacs once more visited Prime Minister Asquith and finally gave him all the details of the matter. Apparently, they informed him for the first time about the second share purchase that Lloyd George and Lord Murray had made in May. They agreed with the Prime Minister to disclose the transactions to the Committee as quickly as possible, but Lloyd George and Sir Rufus nevertheless failed to do so.

Instead of this, the latter asked Liberal MP James Falconer, a Committee member, for an interview which took place 'some time towards the end of January, or about that date', during the course of which Isaacs communicated to him the various transactions as he thought appropriate, in view of the cross-examination to which Falconer subjected him. But Falconer also

---

[241] *Hansard*, Vol. 42, p. 750. & *National Review*, Vol. 61, pp. 473 ff.

[242] *Accounts and Papers...1913*, Vol. 7, p. 736 ff.; *Hansard*, Vol. 53, pp. 1246-7.

[243] *Hansard*, Vol. 54, p. 554. Translator's note: QVOS.

kept the confession to himself. According to his own statements made in Parliament months later, on June 19, Falconer believed he was entitled to do this because 'the meeting was understood by him and by me to be private' and if he had passed it on to the Committee there was the risk that the press would find out about everything.[244]

Meanwhile, Marconi had rescinded the contract on January 27 due to an alleged delay in its implementation.[245]

Even by February 1913, the ministers in question had still not testified before the Select Committee. Earlier in the same month, a paragraph had appeared in the French newspaper *Le Matin* under the heading '*un scandale financier en Angleterre.*' Many similar articles had previously appeared in the English press, one of which, published in *The Eye-Witness*, had prompted Godfrey Isaacs to file a lawsuit for criminal libel, the hearing for which was still to take place. On February 27, *Le Matin* was served with a similar libel claim, with the hearing starting as early as March 19. During the course of the *Le Matin* trial, the transactions by Herbert Samuel and Sir Rufus Isaacs were publicly admitted for the first time. 'This disclosure', as Stanley Jackson, Rufus Isaacs' biographer put it, 'fell into the country like a lighted torch into a pile of resinous wood.' Isaacs had already been questioned by the Select Committee beginning on March 25, an interrogation which continued for three days straight. Despite many remonstrations, Isaacs stuck firm to his previous statements.[246]

The Committee continued to meet with minor interruptions from October to June. Many witnesses and experts appeared and numerous documents were examined. Approximately 30,000 questions and answers alone were recorded, with the documentary evidence compiled into two voluminous printed tomes.

Immediately after the completion of the evidence-taking, two separate drafts of the report destined for Parliament were presented to the Committee. One was from the Committee chairman, the other from Lord Robert Cecil, a member of the Opposition. According to the former, the report should pro-

---

[244] *Hansard*, Vol. 54, p. 581 ff. Translator's note: QVOS from Falconer's original testimony.

[245] *Accounts and Papers... 1913*, Vol. 7, p. 131.

[246] *Accounts and Papers... 1913*, Vol. 7, p. 165 ff.; *Hansard*, Vol. 54, p. 637 ff.; Jackson, p. 170 ff. Translator's note: Newspaper heading and Jackson QVOS. Jackson (p. 168) makes clear that the British newspaper involved in the libel lawsuit was Hilaire Belloc's *The Eye-Witness,* and the writer/editor sued was Cecil Chesterton, brother of Gilbert. Given the fact that *The Eye-Witness* had already been deemed an anti-Semitic publication for its open discussion of Jewish interests, and the fact that the lawsuit was initiated by Godfrey Isaacs, the brother of the Attorney-General Rufus Isaacs, it can be no surprise that Chesterton was found guilty of libel and fined £100, plus Isaacs' court costs (just over £1504), and sentenced to remain in prison until the monies were paid [see Donaldson, pp. 172-92—Translator's Bibliography]. The question therefore remains open as to whether this ostensible libel case also had a dimension of ethnic lawfare.

ceed to a summary of the facts, followed by a mild reprimand of the ministers involved. Lord Cecil's report solely stated the clearly proven facts, but proposed, by contrast, a sharp rebuke to the ministers' conduct. To everyone's surprise, the Committee did not accept either of the drafts, although it acted as if it had taken the Chairman's draft as the basis of the final report. In reality, however, the majority of the Committee, which, as is well known, consisted of members of the ruling Liberal party, modified the report in such a way that little of the chairman's original statements remained. With the deletion of 26 paragraphs, most of the facts were omitted.

In any case, the Select Committee report affirmed that Sir Rufus Isaacs had taken sufficient steps to ensure that the American Marconi Company had no interest in the contract to be made with the British government. This good faith was also supposed of the other ministers. Furthermore, nor did the American company have any interest in the benefits which would accrue from the contract in question. Additionally, the British company and its director Godfrey Isaacs had had nothing to do with the ministers' transactions. Rather, the ministers would have only had a slight connection, if any, with Harry Isaacs. Therefore, no type of reproach could be made to any of the parties involved regarding the acquisition of the shares.

In the final paragraph, the committee summarized its report by saying that 'all of the ministers involved in the affair had acted in the honest belief that they were doing nothing that would put them in any way at odds with their duties as ministers of the Crown'.[247]

However, the Liberal party's opponents were not satisfied with this statement and on 18 June 1913, Mr. George Cave presented the following motion to the House:

> That this House regrets the transactions of certain of His Majesty's Ministers in the shares of the Marconi Company of America, and the want of frankness displayed by Ministers in their communications on the subject of the House.[248]

The matter was again dealt with over the course of two days. Sir Rufus admitted that it would have been better to report everything to Parliament on 11 October 1912. However, since the attacks made against them only related to the British Marconi Company and their alleged connections to it, they saw no reason to make any announcements about their interests in the American company, especially since it had no relations with the British one. He made a point of emphasizing that the shares came from his brother Harry, who had

---

[247] *Accounts and Papers... 1913*, Vol. 7, pp. 100-1.
[248] *Hansard*, Vol. 54, p. 391. Translator's note: QVOS.

no relationship with the Marconi Company.[249] Lloyd George also regretted not having revealed everything to the House, and emphasized that he did not speculate with the shares, but viewed them solely as an investment. After both ministers made their statements, they left the Chamber.[250]

All of the Opposition's efforts to get their motion passed were unsuccessful, and Parliament, with its Liberal majority, determined that the ministers concerned acted solely in good faith, and reprobated 'the charges of corruption brought against Ministers which have been proved to be wholly false'.[251]

In our opinion, this decision was undoubtedly made for party political reasons and cannot stand up to any impartial judgement. The same may be seen as yet another sign of the extent to which the British government of the time was prepared to protect the Jews and their friends, even in scandals. In any case, one will not be surprised at the outcome of this affair if one considers that—quite apart from those involved—other ministers with Jewish blood or with close ties to Hebrews also threw the weight of their influence into the balance. When we say this, we are thinking particularly of the Marquess of Crewe, who held two offices, namely Lord Privy Seal and Secretary of State for India, and of Winston Churchill, then First Lord of the Admiralty. Even a layperson's understanding of justice must instinctively lead them to reject such a verdict. It is therefore instructive to add some legal considerations to the matter.

Parliament's view, that Sir Rufus Isaacs (and therefore also Lloyd George and Lord Murray) had nothing to do with Godfrey Isaacs and therefore nothing to do with the British Marconi Society, is completely absurd. Furthermore, even if Harry Isaacs acted as the seller of the shares, it is clear that the director of both companies, Godfrey Isaacs, informed his brother Rufus immediately after his return from America about the business he had done there and the resulting favorable situation of the American company, just as the transfer of the ten thousand shares can only be explained by the fact that the three brothers were closely linked to one another not only by blood but also by business.

By purchasing the American shares, however, the ministers also acquired interests in a company whose fate was closely linked to that of British Marconi Company, as the British company's entire credit was used to restructure the American company, the British company owned a controlling 56% share of the American company, and the flotation of the American company in Britain 'was absolutely dependent on the British company', as one of the American directors had averred. How closely the administration

---

[249] *Hansard*, Vol. 54, pp. 422-38.
[250] Hansard, Vol. 54, pp. 438-9, 484.
[251] *Hansard*, Vol. 54, pp. 663-70. Translator's note: QVOS.

of the two companies was linked is shown by the fact that three members served as directors of both companies.[252]

Since the motive for an individual's way of behaving always serves as a lawyer's point of reference, the question arises as to whether Godfrey and Harry Isaacs had an interest in winning over their brother Rufus and other cabinet members to the Marconi Society cause. This was undoubtedly the case, because when Godfrey Isaacs returned from America it was already clear that there would be great opposition to the contract agreed between the government and the Marconi Company. So what could be a more obvious move than to interest powerful friends who could also gain money as a result? There was no better middleman for this than Rufus, who won two other cabinet members and the ruling Liberal party over to the cause by means of share distribution.[253]

It is not difficult to see how the Marconi company was favored when we remember the support that was given in the aforementioned patent dispute case, and the very unusual contractual conditions, which not only granted the company a type of monopoly status, but also allowed practically no other invention or innovation to emerge in the sector.

The advantages that the ministers obtained through their association with the Isaacs brothers—even if only indirectly—are undisputed. Before the public announcement and the first official listing on the London Stock Exchange, they received information that was only accessible to a very small circle of initiates and which would have guaranteed large profits for anyone in the know. Furthermore, it should not be overlooked that they did not have to spend a penny of cash to purchase the shares, so the profit they realized would almost seem like a gift. The ministers' excuse that they viewed the shares as a good investment is extremely flimsy, especially since they cashed out this 'investment' in a matter of days.

This is a matter then, if not of outright corruption, then at least of unauthorized speculation [insider trading] which, in a similar case in 1854—as one MP pointed out—led to the immediate dismissal of a minister's private secretary. Apart from that, the case of the ministers is ultimately no different from that of the General Post Office official whom Samuels himself punished for his conduct. In our opinion, it is irrelevant that the official in question had bought shares in the British company rather than the American one, because, as has been explained, this has no bearing on the merit of the case. But, as always, the little players are hanged while big players go free.[254]

---

[252] *Hansard*, Vol. 54, pp. 639, 651. Translator's note: QVOS. & *Hansard*, Vol. 54, pp. 398-9, 458-9, 567-8, 614, 639-40.

[253] *Hansard*, Vol. 54, pp. 456, 481-2, 508.

[254] *Hansard*, Vol. 54, pp. 510-2.

Given the attacks in the press and the rumors circulating in the City of London, nothing could have been more appropriate than to make a statement in Parliament at the beginning of August 1912. But the opposite thing happened: one of the inner circle, Samuel, did everything in his power to have the matter rushed through in the last or penultimate sitting of the summer session, and to avoid a parliamentary Select Committee being set up. His efforts to this end almost make him an accomplice in the matter. Asquith, as Prime Minister, also had a duty to get his ministers to reveal their role in the scandal, and not only did he do nothing, but he even stayed away from the crucial sitting of 11 October 1912. Equally strange is the behavior of the Liberal press, which remained more or less silent in the face of all of the rumors and attacks.

However, the attitude of the ministers directly involved is completely indefensible. All of them should have made to at least give a statement at the October 11 session, as this information ended up being revealed five months later during the course of the *Le Matin* trial. All attempts to justify this behavior are excuses and are irrelevant to the matter. One cannot help but get the impression that this *Le Matin* lawsuit was only filed in order to make a long-needed statement and at the same time to undermine possible accusations of concealment.

In this way, the ministers believed they could save face by finding an opportunity to reveal the cards, something which up until that moment had been not been done. This supposition becomes all the more plausible when one considers that similar accusations had already appeared in the English press for months. [255]

The bad conscience of those involved is also documented in the behavior and statements of Lord Murray's brother. He justified his previous silence by saying that he believed that, in the interests of the Liberal Party, he could not appear as a witness due to the risk of reputational damage. A very strange view to hold if everything was above board and he had nothing to hide.

The composition of the Select Committee, with a majority of Liberal MPs, guaranteed from the start an outcome which would be acceptable to the government, as the entire course of proceedings came to confirm. It is otherwise inexplicable that the ministers who were the objects of the attacks in Parliament and the press were not heard immediately, but only after the Committee had already been active for five months and only after their

---

[255] *Accounts and Papers... 1913*, p. 366 ff.; *Hansard*, Vol. 54, p. 473-477. For more on the English dissident press belief that the *Le Matin* lawsuit was a 'Jewish conspiracy' to enable a controlled disclosure, see Holmes, p. 74 [Translator's Bibliography]. While Jackson [pp. 170-1] does not imply there was a conspiracy with the French newspaper to create the conditions for a 'confession', he does reveal that *Le Matin* issued a full and frank apology when the complaint was raised, and did not defend the lawsuit, which meant the need for Isaacs and Samuel to thrash the matter out in court was quite redundant.

statement in the *Le Matin* trial had been made. This partiality is further evident from the conduct of the Liberal Mr. James Falconer, who, as a member of the Committee, had more or less the capacity of a judge in the matter. As such, he should have either recused himself at the outset from accepting a confession from Sir Rufus Isaacs or, on deciding to accept it, forwarded it to the Committee. The reasons for his silence can only be described as a poor excuse, since the press had a well-founded interest in publishing the evidence.

The clear partiality of the Committee and its efforts not to shed light on the matter under any circumstances became particularly clear during the questioning of the broker Percy Heybourn, who had worked mainly for the Marconi Company. When Conservative members of the Committee demanded to know the names of those who had likewise acquired a significant number of shares, Heybourn refused to testify. Against the protests of the Conservatives, he was granted the right to refuse to testify on this point by a majority vote. The discovery of this information through the investigative process would have been extremely important, as the other people involved would probably have been identified. Given his behavior during the proceedings, it would not be an outlandish assumption to believe that Samuel must have been implicated.

Lastly, the attitude of most of the Committee was revealed when the report was produced. There was no criticism of the ministers' machinations, nor was there a summary of the facts necessary to assess the case. While the former could potentially be argued as the result of a difference of opinion, the latter is a violation of a universally practiced rule for which there is not the slightest justification.

All things considered, the Marconi scandal should be seen as one of the great examples of where Jewish influence eventually leads. Lord Robert Cecil described the ministers' behavior as an impropriety but declined to go as far as to call it corruption. We have strong doubts as to whether he is right. But let us not forget that even Lord Cecil's mild assessment was considered too harsh by the majority of Parliament, which acquitted the ministers of any wrongdoing.

It might interest the reader to know what happened to each of the main participants. David Lloyd George's upward trajectory is so well known that not another word need be said.

Meanwhile, on 20 October 1913, four months after these events, Sir Rufus Isaacs was made Lord Chief Justice, the highest judge of the common law, and at the same time elevated to the peerage as the Marquess of Reading. During the war he was an extraordinary ambassador to the United States as President of the Anglo-French Mission, and it was thanks to him that the huge joint loan of $500,000,000 was secured, which was to be spent in America on munitions. Isaacs also contributed greatly to America's entry into the Great War. Unsurprisingly, he was considered one of Lloyd

George's principal allies.[256] On 6 January 1921, he was entrusted with the office of Viceroy of India. After five years in this role, he went on to become a director in major corporations, including ICI. His work in the construction of Palestine for the Zionist cause was significant. In 1931 he became Secretary of State for Foreign Affairs. It almost goes without saying that he was hostile to the Third Reich, which is reflected in his speeches to the House of Lords. He died in December 1935.[257]

In addition to the offices already mentioned, Herbert Samuel held the highest positions in the British government, including Postmaster-General (1915-1916) and Home Secretary (1916). In 1919 he was Special Commissioner for Belgium and from 1920 to 1925 he was the first High Commissioner for Palestine, a post which fit with his fervent Zionism. He then went on to hold various high positions in Britain, including that of the Home Secretary (1931-1932). In 1937 he was raised to the peerage as Viscount Samuel.[258] Thus it can be judged that the Marconi scandal in no way harmed the ascent of any of its main participants.

Sir Stuart Samuel

While the parliamentary Select Committee was meeting to investigate the Marconi affair, a new scandal came to the attention of the public.

The India Office had to make continuous purchases of silver for the Indian currency, which had long been made through brokers appointed by the Bank of England.[259] At this time, as previously mentioned, the Marquess of Crewe was Secretary of State for India, and from the beginning of 1910 onwards, his Under-Secretary of State was the fully Jewish Edwin Samuel Montagu, who had been a Liberal MP since 1906. Montagu's brother Samuel Montagu, Lord Swaythling, was a partner in Samuel Montagu & Co., one of the largest banks in London. Another partner in this company was Sir Stuart Samuel, a brother of the aforementioned minister Herbert Samuel, who also served as MP for Whitechapel in Tower Hamlets.[260]

In contrast to previous practices, the Marquess of Crewe, as Secretary of State for India, gave the company Samuel Montagu & Co. the order on 4 March 1912 to purchase silver to the amount of £500,000. The firm was not one of the designated brokers that the Bank of England had previously employed for these operations. The attempt was made to justify this measure by saying that the prices for silver rose every time the existing brokers showed

---

[256] Jackson, pp. 181-191.

[257] Jackson, pp. 238 ff., 287-296.

[258] *Who's Who 1938*, p. 2979.

[259] *Hansard*, Vol. 44, p. 686.

[260] *Who's Who 1912*, pp. 1504, 2065. & p. 1877.

interest in buying, because the British government was rightly suspected to be behind it.

It may be that this was true, but we cannot believe that it was the main reason. It makes much more sense to attribute this move to the purely Jewish connections, because all of the people mentioned so far are Jews or have Jewish blood in their veins. Even the head civil servant of the India Office who placed the first order with Samuel Montagu & Co. bore the surname of Abraham, as can be seen from bank document dated 25 March 1912, which refers to Mr. Abraham's letter of March 4. By September 1912, i.e. after seven months, the India Office had purchased silver worth around eight million pounds sterling from the aforementioned Jewish company. Another well-known Hebrew, Sir Felix Schuster, also played a leading role in these transactions by means of his position as governor of the important Union of London & Smiths Bank. At the special request of Samuel Montagu & Co., payments for the silver purchases had to be made through this bank. As can be seen, it was almost impossible to have set up a more exclusively Jewish operation.[261]

It would not be too long before the public became aware of this situation, which was made public by Sir Frederick Banbury on 7 November 1912. At the same time, Banbury asked the Prime Minister whether the government was aware that Sir Stuart Samuel's partnership in the company Samuel Montagu & Co. was a punishable offence under a statute of King George III (22 George III, c. 45). The Prime Minister replied that he had already referred the matter to the law officers of the Crown for their opinion.[262]

This law from 1782 had become necessary at the time in order to prevent and punish the common immoral practice of the government granting public contracts to certain members of Parliament in exchange for their votes of support in the House of Commons. In other words, such an offence met the criteria of corruption.[263]

It should be quite obvious that this law applied to the events described above. Sir Stuart Samuel was an MP and his company had won a public contract. The Attorney-General Sir Rufus Isaacs gave lengthy speeches to argue that the case was one of dubious interpretation. It was not known whether this was a government contract within the definition given by the law or whether the law also applied to matters that were unrelated to the mother

---

[261] *Accounts and Papers...* 1912, Vol. 61, pp. 553, 537. & pp. 553-637. & *Who's Who, 1912*, p. 1896. & *Accounts and Papers... 1912/13*, Vol. 61, pp. 532-3.

[262] *Hansard*, Vol. 43, p. 1434. Translator's note: The statute is titled 'An Act for restraining any Person concerned in any Contract, Commission or Agreement made for the Publick Service from being elected or sitting and voting as a Member of the House of Commons' and can be found on pp. 170-2 of *The Statutes: Revised Edition. Vol. III. 11 George III to 41 George III* (London: Eyre and Spottiswoode, 1872).

[263] *Hansard*, Vol. 44, p. 688.

country. He was of the opinion that this question could best be decided by a Select Committee composed of members of Parliament.[264]

We see then, how another Jew took charge of the case and defended it, something for which he was reproached by the MP Bonar Law, who pointed out that Isaacs appeared to be more concerned with defending the government's position than providing an impartial legal opinion.[265]

The Opposition under Lord Balcarres considered Sir Rufus's view to be incorrect, since a legal precedent in 1907 meant that the law had to apply to the present case. In the matter to which he referred, coal had been purchased by the India Office, which itself had written a special paragraph in the contract about the need to observe the 1782 law. Lord Balcarres asked whether Sir Rufus Isaacs seriously believed that the law made any distinction as to whether one bought coal or silver. The respondent declined to answer.

Lord Balcarres further demanded that this legal question should not be decided by parliamentarians, but should be examined by judges, given that since 1869 there had been the justified tendency to avoid having parliamentarians make decisions in such situations, given that the matter was to determine whether or not a member of Parliament had forfeited the right to his seat due to an unlawful act. However, Balcarres' will did not prevail and the Liberal majority decided to set up a Select Committee made up of parliamentarians to examine the case.[266]

After the Committee had met for a few months, it was apparently no longer possible to evade the Opposition's demands and, in accordance with a further resolution of 31 January 1913, the House resolved that the issue should be presented to the king in the hope that he would refer the case to the Judicial Committee of the Privy Council.[267]

In the meantime, it emerged that, in addition to the silver contracts, contracts had been signed between Samuel Montagu & Co. and the Secretary of State for India under which the latter received short-term loans. They had also made agreements on the purchase of bills and treasury bonds from the Indian administrations. The judges' verdict of 11 April 1913 determined that these actions fulfilled the requirements and application of the aforementioned law because it was clearly a matter of public contracts. As a consequence, Sir Stuart Samuel lost his seat from the day that the contract was signed and was no longer authorized to serve as a member of Parliament, nor vote in the House of Commons.[268] In such a case, the 1782 law further provided that a member of Parliament who voted in spite of his disqualification was liable to pay a fine of £500 for every occasion of his voting. As a result,

---

[264] *Hansard*, Vol. 44, pp. 685-698.

[265] *Hansard*, Vol. 44, p. 702.

[266] *Hansard*, Vol. 44, pp. 698-707. & p. 743.

[267] *Hansard*, Vol. 47, pp. 1747, 1959; *Accounts and Papers... 1912-13*, Vol. 9, p. 455.

[268] *Accounts and Papers... 1913*, Vol. 51, pp. 455-8.

Sir Stuart Samuel had incurred a total penalty of between £45,000 and £50,000.[269]

The opinion of the *Times* newspaper on this verdict is very interesting:

> Sir Stuart Samuel was, of course, morally innocent, and there will be sympathy with him as to his loss of his seat and as to the action for penalties to which he is exposed. But we cannot regret that there is no relaxation of the spirit or letter of a wholesome enactment. Ours is a purer atmosphere than that of 1782.[270]

The court costs were £1,055, but these were described by the government as public costs, and therefore not recovered from Sir Stuart Samuel.[271]

According to his friends, the convicted man should in no way pay the fines that were due. As early as May 1 and May 7, the MP William Thorne asked the Prime Minister if the government intended to bring in an Indemnity Bill for Samuel, which would relieve him of the penalties incurred through voting in the House.[272] On May 8, Attorney-General Sir Rufus Isaacs presented the Sir Stuart Montagu Samuel Indemnity Bill, the description of which reads as follows:

> To indemnify and to relieve Sir Stuart Montagu Samuel, baronet, from any penal consequences which he may have incurred or suffered by sitting or voting as a Member of the House of Commons during a time when the firm in which he was a partner were executing, holding, or enjoying a contract, agreement or commission made or entered into with the Secretary of State for India in Council, and for purposes incidental thereto.

The first reading then took place immediately.[273] However, it soon became apparent that the government would find a large, determined opposition to this bill. Therefore—allegedly due to a lack of time—no further action was taken in Parliament. However, it looks as if the opposition had made demands that the company Samuel Montagu & Co. was not prepared to meet. Bonar Law had requested that all of the company's books be audited by a

---

[269] *Hansard*, Vol. 43, p. 1435; Vol. 44, pp. 713, 718.

[270] *Times*, 12/4/1913. Translator's note: QVOS.

[271] *Hansard*, Vol. 52, pp. 1191, 1849, 2206; Vol. 53, p. 314.

[272] *Hansard*, Vol. 52, pp. 1365, 2063.

[273] *Hansard*, Vol. 52, p. 2253; *Accounts and Papers... 1913*, Vol. 5, p. 737. Translator's note: QVOS [Hansard].

sworn auditor, a request which the company believed it was obliged to refuse because their clients' transactions would then become public.[274]

No further attempts were made by the government to pass the law in the meantime. On the other hand, nor was anything done in an official capacity to collect the fines. Thereupon three people exercised the right of the 'Common Informer', a right of accusation, to take legal action against Sir Stuart Samuel regarding his sentences. Two claims were dismissed on a technicality at first instance, while the third claimant won a £13,000 judgment. All of the verdicts were appealed, however there were no new proceedings. Apparently the parties had settled out of court as each withdrew their appeal. The nature of the agreement was not disclosed. The same circles that had wanted to exempt Samuel from punishment by law had certainly also helped in a similar way.[275] Sir Stuart suffered no other negative consequence as a result of his behavior.

On 21 April 1913, the Solicitor-General moved to declare vacant the seat that Samuel had previously held—albeit in consideration of the decision of the Judicial Committee of the Privy Council—which meant that a new election for Whitechapel became necessary. With the approval of the Liberal Party, Sir Stuart Samuel stood for re-election and won back his seat with a 'greatly reduced' majority on April 30. His absence from Parliament was therefore very short. The *Times'* special correspondent notes in the editorial 'The Whitechapel Election: British Jews and Russia' of April 29 that this election hinged on the Jewish vote:[276]

> Although, as I have explained before, not more than half of the voters in Whitechapel, and possibly only 40 per cent., are Jews, they are dominating the election to an extent hitherto unapproached in the constituency. Of course, the Division is an exceptional one, and the circumstances are unusual. Jewish questions would certainly not be so prominent were it not for the fact that many Jews in the East-end have been persuaded that there is some sort of anti-Semitic movement on foot. The politicians are naturally seeking to reassure them on this point, and so it comes to pass that one can hardly consider the con-

---

[274] *Times*, 23/7/1913; *Hansard*, Vol. 54, pp. 534, 541; Vol. 55, p. 1847; Vol. 56, pp. 1742, 2247, 2279. & *Times*, 8/8/1913; *Hansard*, Vol. 56, pp. 2247, 2248.

[275] *Times*, 17/1/1914, 10/2/1914, 12/2/1914, 13/2/1914, 17/2/1914, 18/3/1914, 24/3/1914.

[276] *Hansard*, Vol. 52, p. 61. & *Times*, 23/4/1913, 30/4/1913, 1/5/1913. Translator's note: Quoted element from 1/5/1913 article, which informs that Samuels won by a majority of only 166 votes, out of a total of 3278 votes cast. The narrowness of Samuels' win may be due to the fact that, while his rival Browne was not Jewish, he was happy to do a tour of the back streets of Petticoat Lane with a well-known Jewish boxer (*Times*, 30/4/1913).

test without dealing with it in terms of the Jewish vote and by the measure of Jewish interests.

Incidentally, we would not wish to neglect regaling readers with the beginning of Samuel's address to his electorate after the victory:

> I won because both Tory and Liberal thought I had been very hardly [harshly] treated, and many who did not vote for me before voted on the present occasion. I was very heavily handicapped owing to the fact that out of the nine days available for the election six were either Jewish feasts or the Sabbath. I had great influences brought to bear against me, especially the Church. Whereas I have never opposed the Church, the whole organization of the Church was against me.[277]

With the best will in the world, we cannot see how he was 'hardly treated.' In the interests of the English people, let us only hope that his reference to the supposed voter indignation at his treatment referred solely to Jews with British citizenship.

Anti-Semitic Voices

As always in history, the phenomenon of anti-Semitism emerges when the pressure of the Jews on the very life of the host nation and their harmful influence on the masses becomes apparent. The history of England since the earliest times is a particularly good example of this. One can therefore in no way agree with the opinion expressed by the Jew Louis Golding that 'anti-Semitism did not come into being because some Jews, or even because all Jews, were dislikeable. Its original grounds were religious—not personal, not social, not economic, not political.' Rather, the anti-Jewish tendency is born out of the need to defend against Judaism, alien to all European peoples, as was again evident in England from around 1910 onwards.[278]

In 1909 in London, a pamphlet was published which made violent attacks against the Jews, and it listed all of the fields of industry in which Jews were already predominant. The *Times* was called a Jewish newspaper which would not have hesitated to bring down an outstanding general, and it noted that the immigration of Jewish fraudsters, bankrupts, and perjurers was still

---

[277] *Times*, 1/5/1913. Translator's note: QVOS.
[278] Golding, pp. 12-13. Translator's note: QVOS.

increasing. The leaflet carried the title *Britons Awake!*—a battle cry which, as we have seen, has been used against the Jews since ancient times.[279]

In the *National Review* of 1911, we also find a warning about the Jewish danger, and a reproach of the Radical journalists who put themselves at the service of the Hebrews:

> Unsuspecting Radical journalists who are engaged in this disgraceful business, which discredits them and dishonours their profession, should ask themselves what they hope to gain by joining hands with the International Jew who is permanently on the war-path in the interests of the most reactionary and dangerous Power in Europe...[280]

Other articles of a similar nature appeared in the general press. The Jews themselves note with regret that at the time of the Marconi and Samuel scandals there was great bitterness among the English against the Jews. One member of the House of Commons in particular distinguished himself with anti-Jewish speeches and violently attacked what he described as the Anglo-Jewish plutocracy. 'In responsible circles,' the Children of Israel conclude in their reflections, 'no significance was attached to these incidents.' A fact which was unfortunately all too true.[281]

The Jews in the Great War

The Great War interrupted the development of growing anti-Semitism. It is not uninteresting to see the role that the Jews played as soldiers in Great Britain during this time. Here we first want to reproduce the official state-

---

[279] 'Englishman', pp. 1-7. Translator's note: The phrase 'Britons Awake!' also became the title of a 1930s BUF marching song, the lyrics of which can be found in Holmes, p. 103 [Translator's Bibliography].

[280] *National Review*, Vol. 58, p. 683. Translator's note: QVOS.

[281] *Jewish Year Book, 1937*, p. 359. Translator's note: The MP referred to is likely to be Conservative MP Rowland Hunt (1858-1943), who was a supporter of the National League for Clean Government. The speech referred to is likely to be the one given at a League meeting on 8 December, 1913, not in the chamber of the House of Commons as the text might suggest, in which Hunt is reported to have said, among other things: 'We are really in danger of being ruled by alien votes and foreign gold... The aliens and foreign plutocrats are driving out British blood' [see Holmes, p. 102]. Note that the Jews are referred to euphemistically—already by this time the social taboo of saying the word 'Jew' is in firmly in place for Englishmen of consequence. For further evidence of the Jewish control of the public space in England by the 1900s, see the 'Preface to the Third Edition' in *England Under the Jews* [in Translator's Bibliography], a book which was self-published and had to marketed by private peer-to-peer and word-of-mouth techniques.

ments made by the Jews in this regard and only then see whether they perhaps forgot or overlooked the need to convey further facts.

The Jewish War Services Committee had Rabbi Michael Adler publish a brief overview of Jewish participation in military service. This estimated the total number of Jews in the British Empire at 420,000 people. At the outbreak of war, 600 of them were in the reserves and militia, 400 in the regular army and 50 in the navy.

However, these numbers are said to have increased immediately after the declaration of war, so that by the time compulsory military service was introduced, around 10,000 Jews, including 1,140 officers, were already members of the armed forces. By the end of the war, around 50,000 Jews were said to have been called up to fight for the flag. Even a Jewish regiment was formed in England in 1917 and commanded by a non-Jew, Colonel Patterson. The orders in this regiment were said to have often been given in Yiddish. Later, two more Jewish battalions were formed, although their troops came from America and Canada. These battalions were sent to Palestine in 1918, where in September they took part in the last British offensive. The so-called Zionist Mule Corps was established in Egypt in 1915, with the aim of transporting ammunition on the Gallipoli front, and was dissolved in January 1916. As we were told by English participants in the war, Tommy soon found a motto for these units: 'No advance without security.' Unfortunately, the double meaning contained in the English is lost in the German translation. It means both 'No loan without security [i.e. collateral]' and 'No moving forward without cover'.[282]

No fewer than 20 Jewish lieutenant-colonels and numerous Jewish majors belonged to the officer corps, and there was even a Jewish brigadier-general named Herbert Spencer Seligman. In 1918, the Jew Sir John Monash was named Commander of the Australian Corps in France and promoted to lieutenant-general. Sir Philip Sassoon was private secretary to Field-Marshal Sir John French, and later held the same post under Field-Marshal Sir Douglas Haig. The Jewish Secretary of State for War, Leslie Hore-Belisha, who has since been dismissed from the post, served in the Royal Army Service Corps. In *Who's Who* his military service is stated as 'served in the army during the World War.' This vague description is in complete contrast to the current norms, which always gives the rank and the unit of the person in question. One has to wonder why such standard information was omitted from Hore-Belisha's profile.[283]

---

[282] Adler, pp. 1-4; *Jewish Chronicle*, 24/1/1936, 23/4/1937. & *Jewish Year Book*, 1937, p. 364.

[283] Adler, pp. 6-12. & *Times*, 30/5/1938; *Daily Telegraph*, 30/5/1938; *Daily Express*, 30/5/1938. Translator's note: The original German states that Hore-Belisha was '*offizier im Train*', i.e. an officer in the rear. I have added the element of Royal Army Service Corps as the *Daily Telegraph* article states that it was his unit, where he rose to the rank of major. & *Who's Who, 1938*, p. 1640.

Some Jews were also in the air force. According to the official Jewish report, the team included a large number of tailors and other tradesmen. The latter were responsible for maintaining the machines and working in the Film and Photographic Unit.[284]

According to Adler's sources, 2,324 Jews died in the Great War, and according to a report in the *Jewish Year Book*, the Jewish death toll was 2,420. But this refers to the Jews of the entire British Empire and not just the mother country. Accordingly, if the figure of 420,000 given by Adler above is assumed to be correct, they lost about 5.5 men for every thousand. If, on the other hand, we take the minimum number of 1,200,000 to 1,500,000 as the total Jewish population, which is our estimate, we arrive at a maximum of two men per thousand. If we consider that the number of casualties our brothers sustained in the Sudetenland was 44 per 1000, a figure that we have just come across by chance, then one cannot speak of a very great sacrifice by the Children of Israel. Nevertheless, the Jews in England were zealously keen to point out that the widely held view of the Jews being cowards and shirkers during the Great War was a very gross distortion of the facts.

Apparently this idea is even more widespread today, if the following letter to the *Jewish Chronicle* is at all representative of the common view in 1938:[285]

> 'It Can't Happen Here'
> Last Thursday at our local cinema when the newsreel of the Jewish ex-Servicemen's parade was thrown onto the screen and the commentator stated that some 50,000 Jews had fought for the British Empire, two people behind me remarked: 'They probably had cushy jobs behind the lines or only fought under conscription. They deserve all they are getting on the Continent.' The last incident must surely prove the fallacy of 'It can't happen here.' —Mrs. S. Sharpe, 74, Barrington Court, Muswell Hill. No. 10.[286]

In reality, the Jews were not particularly keen on the war. During the war, one of them felt compelled to publish a pamphlet in which he defended the attitude of his fellow Jews who had immigrated from Russia. According to him, the Hebrews could not be blamed for not wanting to go to war, because the nation of their former hosts—Russia, England's allies—would still do nothing for the freedom and good treatment of their brothers who re-

---

[284] Adler, pp. 14-15.
[285] Adler, p. 5. & *Jewish Year Book, 1937*, p. 343. & *Deutsche Zeitung für Großbritannien*, 29/10/1938. & *Jewish Chronicle*, 14/10/1938.
[286] *Jewish Chronicle*, 18/11/1938. Translator's note: QVOS.

mained there. Efforts were underway to deport Russian-born Jews born from England in the event of dodging enlistment. In the *Jewish World* of October 4, 11, and 18, 1916, such an intention is described as extremely cruel because those concerned had spent their entire lives in England and were complete strangers to Russia. From Leeds, one of the main Russian-Jewish settlements, it was reported with displeasure that all Russian Jews had refused to volunteer for the flag despite being asked to do so. Even Jews with British citizenship who had to enlist after the introduction of compulsory military service did not fulfil this service to the nation, and were widely reported to have escaped in large numbers to Ireland. In Belfast alone, during a single police operation, eighteen Jews were charged with this crime.[287]

Unpleasant scenes also took place in London. A court martial had been set up in Stepney, a predominantly Jewish district in the East End. Most of the time it was Jews who had to answer for shirking, and their relatives and friends, who also attended the hearing, rioted in a shameless and unpatriotic manner so that the auditorium had to be evacuated. The Hebrews themselves admitted that Jews were resorting to 'shamming, malingering, bribery, corruption and downright fraud' to escape, or obtain exemption from, military service. Even in 1917, everything was done to prevent the conscription of Russian Jews. A mass meeting against deportation and forced conscription into the army was organized by the Foreign Jews Protection Committee. The chairman was Lord Sheffield, whose daughter had married the Jew Edwin Samuel Montagu, who has already been discussed. The Russian Jews declared that the English should only go to war themselves. England was not Jewish land, and the more English men were killed, the more jobs there would be for the Children of Israel. Negative news also reached London, such as the 1918 incident in which no fewer than 54 Jews were sentenced for mutiny in Palestine. After the war ended, it was the same situation in England as in Germany. Many intermarriages had taken place, and the Jews had

---

[287] *Times*, 8/12/1924. Translator's note: It is likely that the author is referring to this excerpt from the article 'Alien London': 'The behaviour of the alien Jews in the East-end during the war was often unsatisfactory. They indulged in wholesale panic during the air-raids, and in too many cases did their best to avoid military service, not only in the Russian Army, which was explicable enough, but in the British.' & Wassilevsky, pp. 1-8. Translator's note: In 1916, there were estimated to be some 25,000-30,000 alien Russian Jews in England [Holmes, p. 126]. & *Daily Chronicle*, 30/3/1916. Translator's note: The chief constable, in a letter to the Home Office, stated that of the approximately 1,400 military-age alien Jews in Leeds, who were chiefly Russian Jews, only 26 had joined the forces. The resentment that this mass non-participation provoked in the English population, especially in those who returned injured from the front to find Russian-Jewish men 'promenading about our principal streets and the various pleasure resorts', sparked anti-Jewish pogroms in Leeds and London's East End in 1917, as English casualties mounted and the war grew more desperate [Holmes, p. 131 ff].

filled the jobs and commercial positions of the Englishmen who had been in the trenches.[288]

The Balfour Declaration

As we have seen, it could hardly have been the military service of the Empire's Jews in the trenches that led to the well-known Balfour Declaration of 2 November 1917, according to which the Jews were promised Palestine. Before we go into detail, however, we must give a brief outline of English public opinion over the previous two centuries regarding the return of the Jews to Palestine.

It is impossible to give an exhaustive account of this within the scope of this study. As the Zionist leader Sokolow's two-volume book has already shown, this would require several years of work. London has been the center of world Jewry since the 17th century. What has already been discussed over several chapters should be sufficient proof of this. We have also shown the extent to which the ruling classes in England have been dominated by Jewish influence for decades, if not centuries. But the teachings of Puritanism also have a lot in common with Jewish ideas. This has resulted in the adoption of Jewish principles, which are primarily taken from the Old Testament.

Certainly this has also happened to a certain extent in other nations, but to go by the attitude of the British clergy and numerous British writers, this tendency cannot have been surpassed in any other country. Sokolow rightly refers to the scriptural influence on the entire works of Francis Bacon (1561-1626), and points out the same Hebrew spirit in the works of John Milton (1608-1674), especially in *Paradise Lost*. Other great figures of English literature such as Abraham Cowley (1618-1667), Bishop Jeremy Taylor (1613-1667), Archbishop John Tillotson (1630-1694) and Dr. Isaac Burrow (1630-1677) manifest the same spirit. The poetry of Alexander Pope (1688-1744) also shows a close relationship with the Bible. The 18th century continues

---

[288] *East London Observer*, 1/4/1916. & *Jewish World*, 12/4/1916; *Jewish Chronicle*, 7/4/1916. Translator's note: QVOS (the *JC*, p.11). & *Who's Who, 1917*, p. 1642; *Daily Mail*, 2/6/1917. Translator's note: The FJPC was regarded by the police as 'stuffed with revolutionaries and anarchists.' One Home Office official, exasperated by the activities of leading activist Solly Abrahams alias Abraham Bezalel, gave him a third alias of 'Belzebub' [Holmes, pp. 128-9]. & *Daily Sketch*, 2/12/1915. & *Jewish Chronicle*, 23/1/1920 p. 33. Translator's note: I have specified 'Russian Jews' rather than the original 'Hebrews' regarding the militant refuseniks, because the German Jews of England were a separate demographic category in this instance [for more on the German-Jewish experience of the war, see Chapter 8 of Holmes]. Heartbreakingly, prior to 1914, prominent German Jews in Britain were attacked in the press for trying to prevent a war with Germany and for trying to establish an Anglo-German friendship, a movement which, had it been successful, would have undoubtedly prevented the catastrophic tragedy that was to befall Britain and Europe [see Holmes, pp. 82, 257-8]. & *Daily Express*, 4/12/1920.

this tendency with individuals such as James Thomson (1700-1748), Edward Young (1683-1765) and Dr. Mark Akenside (1721-1770). Even the 19th century is still full of these traces. We need only consider Lord Byron (1788-1824) and Thomas Moore (1779-1852).[289]

This centuries-long conception of the world must have left its mark on the English collective psyche. Sokolow points out that in earlier times, for this reason, people had already compared England with Israel. Given all of this, we have no hesitation in agreeing with Sokolow's judgement that England, in contrast to other peoples, was even more influenced by Israel than by Greece and Rome. The natural consequence of this fact is that England feels a duty to the Jews as its teachers and is full of admiration for this race. Thus we find very early expressions of the idea that the Jews should be helped to return to Palestine. This view was shared by, among others, the aforementioned figures of the 18th and 19th centuries, as well as by Thomas Newton (1704-1782), later Bishop of Bristol, and Samuel Horsley (1733-1806), Bishop of Rochester and later Bishop of St. Asaph. So we have likewise no reason to doubt Hyamson's assertion that 'Judaism in one or other of its senses had become almost a passion among certain classes of the people'.[290]

It is therefore not surprising that in 1804 the Palestine Association was founded in London with the aim of procuring and publishing information regarding the history, geography, people, and climate of the Holy Land. The London Society for Promoting Christianity Amongst the Jews, which has already been discussed, turned its attention to Palestine in 1822, thirteen years after the society itself was founded.[291]

Sokolow calls the Palmerston period, i.e. the years from 1837 to 1852, 'a great time in England for the idea of the Restoration of *Israel*.' Even back then, in view of the conflicts between Sultan Mahmud II and his insubordinate Governor-General of Egypt, Mehemet Ali, who was supported by England, it was hoped that England would plant its banner in Palestine or Syria in the resulting negotiations. The Jews and their allies were at work to secure Palestine. It was particularly the *Times* that tried to win over British public opinion over the course of 1839 and 1840. Thus, on 17 August 1840, an article appeared with the headline 'Syria—Restoration of the Jews.' It pointed out, among other things, that 'a nobleman of the opposition' (probably the seventh Earl of Shaftesbury Lord Ashley), was already very interested in the question. This nobleman had already carried out a survey into whether, if the situation were to arise, rich Jews would be prepared to return to Palestine

---

[289] Sokolow, Vol. I, pp. 1-12.

[290] Sokolow, Vol. I, pp. 1-2. Translator's note: A reminder to the reader that Sokolow was writing in 1919, and the 'Israel' he refers to is the Jewish people and their Old Testament literature, not the territorial polity given that name in 1948. & Sokolow, Vol. I, pp. 56, 91-3. & Hyamson: *British Projects*, p. 1. Translator's note: QVOS.

[291] Hyamson: *British Projects*, p. 3.

and invest money in agriculture there, as well as finding out when they could begin the process of migration, and whether they would consent to live under Turkish sovereignty but with their rights protected by the five European powers. This article resulted in a letter from 'An English Christian' being published in the *Times* nine days later, which urged that England should buy Palestine for the Jews.[292]

It soon became apparent that Lord Shaftesbury was using all of his connections for the Jewish cause to make the Palestine project a reality. As a relative of Palmerston, he had easy access to that statesman at any time and did not fail to make use of that advantage for his cause. His enthusiasm for the Jews went so far that he learned Hebrew and was in close co-operation with the clergyman Alexander MacCaul, who had spent many years among the Jews in Poland and who was subsequently the first to receive the offer of the Bishopric of Jerusalem. But all of his efforts to have Palestine allocated to the Jews came to nothing.[293]

Nevertheless, further efforts were made in this regard. In 1844, the Rev. T. Tully Crybbace held a meeting in London to form the 'British and Foreign Society for Promoting the Restoration of the Jewish Nation to Palestine.' He declared that England should use all its might to make this dream a reality. 'The believing people of England are especially called upon, and commanded, to use the appointed means of accomplishing this work of God.' Not only would this be a work of prophecy, benevolence, and generosity, but it would at the same time protect England's geopolitical interests in the Middle East and beyond. With this in mind, pamphlets were printed and lectures were planned for the principal towns of the country to arouse public opinion on the question.

Similar ideas were also spread in the literary field, with some of the main writers on this issue being the Rev. Samuel Alexander Bradshaw, the colonial civil servant E. L. Mitford, Colonel George Gawler, and the Rev. A. G. H. Hollingsworth. According to Gawler, only the Jewish people could save Palestine and the East, of course under the protection of England. Hollingsworth also made the same suggestions in a book of 1853, at the same time pointing out Palestine's existing mineral resources. By means of gradual colonization, the Hebrews would form a powerful state and no one would ever again dare to persecute the Jews. In an earlier book of 1849, Hollingsworth also dealt with the various prophecies concerning the coming Jewish kingdom. According to the prophesies that Hollingsworth set forth, with the elements

---

[292] Sokolow, Vol. I, p. 101. Translator's note: QVOS.
[293] Sokolow, Vol. I, p. 101 ff.; Hyamson: *British Projects*, p. 3 ff.

cited from Bible verses referenced in the margins, the Jews would have all of the power because of their vast wealth and divine favor:[294]

> The POLITICAL POWER of the new kingdom is even more surprising than its religious influence. 'Kings' by their ambassadors are represented in the rising state, 'Queens' are royally present at their new courts. Their respect for the kingdom can only arise from its power and importance, and *several states* even consider themselves honoured by being admitted into treaties of alliance, for they 'bow down', 'they lick up the dust of thy feet.' Their fleets are placed at the disposal of the Hebrew Government. Their assistance is in some cases gratuitous. Gentile gold is collected for Hebrew purposes. 'Strangers' assist in building the new towns. 'Kings minister' unto them. The land 'forces' of mighty nations defend, and are allied with the kingdom. And those who oppose or 'contend' with them are threatened with all God's severe judgments. Some are utterly extirpated, and others change their policy and send ambassadors to represent them in the Hebrew state, because 'God hath glorified the nation, and they that despised it', then come 'bowing down', 'bending' and calling Jerusalem 'the city of the Lord, the Zion of the Holy One of Israel.' They shall possess 'double' more favour than during the reign of Solomon. 'All kings shall behold its glory.' Like a flowing stream it shall pervade all nations. And they 'will be a crown of glory in the hand of the Lord, and a royal diadem in the hand of her God.'
>
> The WEALTH of this new kingdom is described in terms not less extraordinary than her power. Riches are one of the elements of Political influence. The Jews in their scattered nobles and families possess more of this element than any other people in the world. Gold, silver, iron, metallic ores in the bosoms of their awful mountains, a just taxation under the new Government; the Gentile source in their former mercantile pursuits, from whence 'the milk' of their wealth has flowed, are described in language which flashes and glows on the page of Holy writ with a supernatural splendour. Their po-

---

[294] Sokolow, Vol. I, p. 133 ff.; Hyamson: *British Projects*, pp. 12-16. & Hollingsworth: *Remarks*, p. 11 ff. & p. 39 ff.

litical institutions are permanent, and will neither want Reformation or revolution.[295]

In 1865, the Palestine Exploration Fund was formally constituted to explore Palestine, which, among other things, was to carry out detailed and systematic scientific research of all aspects of the Holy Land, including the geological structure. This company enjoyed the full support of the government and influential circles, and the War Office even granted the services of Royal Engineers for the execution of excavation work.[296]

It goes without saying that the movement for the return of the Jews was also supported by Disraeli. As early as 1833 he had unequivocally promoted this idea in his novel *Alroy*, just as he expressed hopes for the return of his race to Palestine in other works such as *Tancred* and *Coningsby*. At the end of the 19th century, it was Colonel Claude Reignier Conder who took the leading role in promoting these efforts, while Lord Shaftesbury and his friend Laurence Oliphant also continued to promote the Jewish cause. The latter proposed acquiring a concession from the Turkish government for the fertile northern half of Palestine, which would advantage both countries as England would gain further political power and Turkey would gain money. Oliphant, along with Baron Edmund de Rothschild, helped with the efforts to create Jewish colonies in Palestine.[297]

But in the judgement of the Jews themselves, the person who best dealt with this issue was George Eliot [aka Mary Ann Evans] in her book *Daniel Deronda*, as she described how the Jews would demand the rights of freedom and equality to which they were entitled. The Jews considered the work so important that during World War II it was translated into Hebrew along with Disraeli's *Tancred*.[298]

Despite all this support, no practical progress had been made on this issue. However, the effort resumed with renewed vigor when, in 1897, the First Zionist Congress was held, which also saw the movement given its own name. At the beginning of the 20th century, the then-leader of the Zionists, Theodor Herzl, established close ties with Colonial Secretary Joseph Chamberlain, Secretary of State for Foreign Affairs Lord Lansdowne, and Under-Secretary of State for Foreign Affairs Lord Percy. The British government offered the Zionists El Arish, part of so-called Egyptian Palestine, as a replacement for Palestine. A joint commission was sent out to examine settle-

[295] Hollingsworth: *Holy Land,* pp. 227-8. Translator's note: QVOS.

[296] Sokolow: Vol. I, p. 62.

[297] Disraeli: *Alroy,* Vol. I, pp. 23 ff., 147 ff., 269 ff.; Vol. II, pp. 36 ff., 119 ff. & Hyamson: *British Projects,* p. 23; Sokolow, Vol. I, p. 140 ff. & Hyamson: *British Projects,* pp. 24-6. & Sokolow, Vol. I, pp. 206-8. & Hyamson: *British Projects,* pp. 28-32.

[298] Sokolow, Vol. I, pp. 209-10. & Sokolow, Vol. 2, p. 43.

ment options. However, the report that was produced was not even published and the project was quietly dropped.[299]

This is said to have been a great disappointment for Joseph Chamberlain who, on one of his trips to the African colonies, thought that he had found a suitable place for the Jews in a part of Uganda. He immediately reported this to Lord Lansdowne and Lord Percy, who were also enthusiastic about the plan. In a 1903 letter from the Foreign Office to the Zionists, Lord Lansdowne announced that he had 'studied the question with the interest which His Majesty's Government must always take in any well-considered scheme for the amelioration of the position of the Jewish race.' He then went on to detail the government's proposals for the scheme in British East Africa, which were 'the grant of a considerable tract of land, the appointment of a Jewish official as the chief of the local administration, and permission to the colony to have a free hand in regard to municipal legislation, and as to the management of religious and purely domestic matters, such local autonomy being conditional upon the right of His Majesty's Government to exercise general control.' The Zionists withheld their decision on this offer until after their leading members all over the world had been consulted. When, after two years, no final position had been taken, Joseph Chamberlain's successor, Lord Alfred Lyttelton, made the proposal again. Due to opposition from Jews who wanted Palestine or nothing, the British government's plan was rejected some time later.[300]

The Zionists, of course, did not stop striving to implement their program. The Great War was to bring them the fulfilment of their desires.

With Turkey's entry into the war against England, the Zionists soon realized that there was the possibility of making their millenarian dreams a reality in the event of Turkey's defeat. Countless meetings took place around the world to discuss the next steps. From the outset the Hebrews were clear that all necessary measures would have to be taken from central London. It was Dr. Chaim Weizmann, a Russian *emigré* who lectured in Chemistry at Manchester University, who took the leading role. He was supported, among others, by the Jew Nahum Sokolow and Chief Rabbi Dr. Joseph Hertz. It was agreed that first the public had to be won over to the Jews' plans by means of the press. To this end, the right connections were made and support was easily found. Above all, a leading journalist at the time, C. P. Scott, editor of the *Manchester Guardian*, was particularly prominent in his support of the Jews.

It was also not difficult to find a sympathetic ear among cabinet members. Some of them, such as the Marquess of Crewe, Herbert Samuel, Edwin

---

[299] Sokolow, Vol. I, p. 268 ff. & Hyamson: *British Projects*, p. 38.
[300] Sokolow, Vol. 2, p. XLV; Hyamson: *British Projects*, pp. 39-40; Hyamson: *History*, p. 297. Translator's note: QVOS.

Samuel Montagu, David Lloyd George, and Winston Churchill, have already been discussed earlier. In a public lecture, Herbert Samuel stated that he had no share in the initiation of the negotiations which led to the Balfour Declaration. But this in direct contradiction to the assertions of two leading Zionists, the aforementioned Nahum Sokolow and Samuel Landman. The latter expressly emphasizes that it was above all Herbert Samuel who, alongside the aforementioned C. P. Scott, was able to persuade the cabinet to take up the Zionist cause. Landman should actually have precise knowledge of this, since he had been actively working in Zionism for years and was the solicitor and secretary of the Zionist Organization from 1917 to 1922. Likewise, Sokolow's statements leave no doubt as to Herbert Samuel's active collaboration. In Sokolow's own words, Samuel 'had given great and never-to-be forgotten services in the cause of the Zionist idea' which he 'championed...with the full force of his convictions.' In Sokolow's report of Samuel's own words at the Balfour Declaration celebration on 2 December 1917, which took place at the London Opera House, 'he has stood for Zionism not only in the Cabinet, but also outside it'.[301]

The House of Rothschild also helped the Zionist cause in every way, so international Jewry could certainly not complain about the quality of its support.[302]

During the course of 1916, in addition to the Jews and their allies in the cabinet, a pious Catholic raised by Jesuits, Lieutenant-Colonel Sir Mark Sykes, became enthused for the Zionists' plans. As Under-Secretary to the War Cabinet, he was a government expert on Near Eastern issues. Great help was also provided by the Englishmen Sir Ronald Graham, General Sir George Macdonagh, Mr. G. H. Fitzmaurice, and the former Colonial Secretary W. Ormsby Gore.

A certain Mr. James Malcolm in particular brought the Zionists' aspirations to Sykes' attention, and asserted to him and other members of the English and French governments that only the Zionists would be able to bring the USA into the war on the Allied side, after all previous attempts to do so had failed. He further explained to these powerful men that the Zionists were in no way pro-German, but only anti-Russian. Sir Mark Sykes on the British side and François Georges-Picot on the French side finally came to the view that securing the co-operation of Zionist Jews was 'the best and perhaps the only way' to induce President Wilson to enter the war. This was thought to be all the easier because he listened almost exclusively to the advice of the Zionist Louis Brandeis, a Supreme Court justice. Of course, as part of this '*quid pro quo* contract,' the Jews had to be assured of something in return, which according to their plans could only be Palestine.

---

[301] Sokolow, Vol. 2, pp. 22-42. & Bolitho, *Twelve Jews*, pp. 276-7. & Landman, p. 3. & p. 2. & Sokolow, Vol. 2, p. 47. Translator's note: QVOS.
[302] Sokolow, Vol. II, p. XIX.

After long deliberations, the British government commissioned Sir Mark Sykes for the role and an agreement with the Zionists was reached which, with the help of the Foreign Office, was sent out to every place where a Zionist movement could be found. Immediately afterwards, 'the change in official and public opinion as reflected in the American press in favor of joining the Allies in the War, was as gratifying as it was surprisingly rapid.' Samuel Landman, to whom we owe these previously little-known facts regarding this 'necessarily secret "gentleman's" agreement of 1916,' also points out with particular pride that it was the 'hitherto unsuspectedly powerful forces of Zionist Jews in America and elsewhere' who had brought America into the war.[303]

Thus we have finally learned the truth from one of the Jews involved in the affair. So it was not the merits of a brilliant chemical discovery by Dr. Weizmann which brought about the later Balfour Declaration, as Bolitho seems to want us to believe. Likewise, the idea of the Balfour Declaration being simply a result of Britain's leading statesmen, in an altruistic and romantic gesture, wishing to give the oppressed Jews the right to self-determination is probably of such little veracity that to all intents and purposes it does not need to be given serious consideration. Indeed, according to Harold Temperley, there was in fact significant opposition to the Zionist plan and the agreement was only signed out of dire necessity:[304]

> But when the matter came before the Cabinet for decision, delays occurred. Amongst influential English Jews, Zionism had few supporters, at all events for a Zion in Palestine. It had still fewer in France. Jewish influence both within and without the Cabinet is understood to have exerted itself strenuously and pertinaciously against the policy of the proposed Declaration.
>
> Under the pressure of Allied needs, the objections of the anti-Zionists were either over-ruled or the causes of objection removed, and the Balfour Declaration, as we have seen, was published to the world on 2nd November 1917.[305]

The Jews were extremely embarrassed by Landman's publication, as is reflected by Albert Hyamson's article in the *Jewish Chronicle* of 17 April

---

[303] Sokolow, Vol. II, p. XIX. & Landman, p. 3. & pp. 3-5. Landman in the *Jewish Chronicle* of 7/2/1936. Translator's note: All QVOS.

[304] Bolitho, *Twelve Jews*, p. 280. Translator's note: Weizmann reportedly perfected a method for obtaining alcohol from wood, which was useful in explosive production. Mr. Lloyd George was apparently so grateful for this discovery that he asked Weizmann how he could be repaid for this knowledge, and Bolitho implies that this is how the Balfour Declaration came about.

[305] Temperley, Vol. VI, p. 173. Translator's note: QVOS.

1936. Hyamson describes Landman's essay as erroneous and dangerous from the Jewish perspective, and also states: 'It is almost as dangerous to suggest that Western Jews put their own supposed interests as Jews before their allegiance to the States of which they were citizens.' Elsewhere, we find Henry Wickham Steed, the former editor of the *Times*, writing almost the same account of events as Landman had. That Steed was complete unconnected to Landman is supported by the fact that Steed published his information twelve years prior to Landman's essay and, unlike Landman, probably received his information directly from the government, i.e. the other contracting party in the agreement. This can be inferred because as Steed's memoir continually demonstrates, the journalist maintained the best of relations with the government. Finally, this version of events as presented by Landman and Steed is also supported by Temperley.[306]

Apparently all parties remained in constant contact after the conclusion of this contract, which was apparently not put down in writing. Another meeting took place on 7 February 1917, attended by Sir Mark Sykes, Lord Rothschild, Nahum Sokolow, Herbert Bentwich, Joseph Cowen, James de Rothschild, Harry Sacher, Herbert Samuel, and Chaim Weizmann. Also present was the rabbi Dr. Moses Gaster, in whose house the deliberations took place. Sokolow was given the task of contacting the other Entente Powers to discuss the Zionist question.

In March 1917 Sokolow went to Paris, where he was assured of the French government's full support on all matters. The Zionists in America and Russia were immediately informed of this by telegraph. Sokolow traveled to Rome in May, where he had the same success. He had conferences with the cardinals, especially Cardinal Gasparri, and received an audience with the Pope on May 10. According to Sokolow: 'These conferences led to a most satisfactory attitude on the part of the Vatican towards Zionism'.[307]

In the meantime, Weizmann had done all of the preparatory work necessary to influence public opinion in England. Two magazines, the *Zionist Review* and *Palestine*, had been founded. The Jewish communities in the country were slowly being prepared for the Allies' agreement with international Jewry, which had not yet been published. At the Conference of the English Zionist Federation, held in London on 20 May 1917, Weizmann, who was Chairman, explained in his opening address that the Zionist Movement was 'never built...on the sufferings of our people in Russia or elsewhere.' Rather, the cause of Zionism was the 'ineradicable national striving of Jewry to have a home of its own—a national center, a national home with a national Jewish life.' He also did not neglect to mention that the highest Catholic circles were favorable to their plans:

---

[306] Steed: *Thirty Years*, Vol. II, pp. 391-3. & Temperley, Vol. VI, p. 172-4.
[307] Sokolow, Vol. II, pp. 52-3. Translator's note: QVOS.

> We have assurances from the highest Catholic circles that they will view with favor the establishment of a Jewish national home in Palestine, and from their religious point of view they see no objection to it, and no reason why we should not be good neighbors. And good neighbors I hope we shall be.[308]

Article after article appeared in the general press in favor of the Jews, with the *Times* once more leading the way. On 23 October 1917 it published an editorial with the title: 'Palestine for the Jews: British support of the proposal.' The *Westminster Gazette, Spectator, New Statesman, Nation, Weekly Dispatch, Sunday Chronicle, Manchester Guardian, Liverpool Courier, Yorkshire Post, Daily News* and many more began a real campaign on behalf of the Jews. On October 26, the *Times* ran an editorial strongly urging the government to issue a pro-Zionist statement.[309]

Exactly the same methods were used in America. The Zionists there were in a constant communication with their ethnic kin in England, and as a result 'there was perfect unity among the Zionists of both hemispheres.' Sokolow describes the period of August to November 1917 as an exceedingly busy time, because the Zionists had not only to continue garnering support for their movement, but also to defend themselves against attacks made both in manifestos and behind the scenes. Landman states that Dr. Weizmann turned to General Macdonagh to request an exemption from military service or army discharge for himself and for other Jews, such as Leon Simon, the then president of the Postal Savings Bank, Harry Sacher, Simon Marks, Albert Hyamson, and Shmuel Tolkowsky. It almost goes without saying that this request was approved by the general who sympathized with the Zionist cause.[310]

Apparently the British government had hesitated for a long time to publish its agreement with the Zionists. The government's reticence would not least be due to the fact that in 1915 it had already made the same promise regarding Palestine to the Arabs, who had fought for the British during the war. However, the Jews finally forced the government's hand, and on 2 November 1917, Foreign Secretary Arthur James Balfour issued a statement of support in the form of a letter to Lionel Walter Rothschild, which became known the world over as the Balfour Declaration. The letter reads as follows, in full:

---

[308] Sokolow, Vol. II, pp. 52-8. Translator's note: All QVOS.

[309] Sokolow, Vol. II, pp. 72-9. Translator's note: Sokolow also lists other newspaper and magazine titles involved in this campaign, and reproduces excerpts from many of the articles in question. The *Times* editorial title in the main text is as it appears in Sokolow.

[310] Sokolow, Vol. II, p. 79 ff. Translator's note: QVOS (p. 80). & Militant Christian Patriots, p. 14. Translator's note: The general referred to may be Lt.-Gen. Sir George Macdonogh, whose name is rendered in various ways in the historical sources.

Foreign Office, November 2nd, 1917
Dear Lord Rothschild,

I have much pleasure in conveying to you, on behalf of His Majesty's Government, the following declaration of sympathy with Jewish Zionist aspirations which has been submitted to, and approved by, the Cabinet.

'His Majesty's Government view with favor the establishment in Palestine of a national home for the Jewish people, and will use their best endeavors to facilitate the achievement of this object, it being clearly understood that nothing shall be done which may prejudice the civil and religious rights of existing non-Jewish communities in Palestine, or the rights and political status enjoyed by Jews in any other country.'

I should be grateful if you would bring this declaration to the knowledge of the Zionist Federation.

Yours sincerely,
Arthur James Balfour[311]

We are not surprised, and hopefully nor is the reader, by England's alliance with international Jewry. The only new thing about the Declaration was that this was the first time that an instance of English-Jewish collaboration had been published in a formal way for everyone to see. The well-known historian Harold Temperley comments on this as follows:

Support of Zionist ambitions, indeed, promised much for the cause of the Entente. Quite naturally, Jewish sympathies were to a great extent anti-Russian, and therefore in favour of the Central Powers... [T]he German General Staff desired to attach Jewish support yet more closely to the German side. With their wide outlook on possibilities, they seem to have urged, early in 1916, the advantages of promising Jewish restoration to Palestine under an arrangement to be made between Zionists and Turkey, backed by a German guarantee... In fact in September 1917 the German Government were making the most serious efforts to capture the Zionist movement.

Another most cogent reason why the policy of the Declaration should be adopted by the Allies lay in the state of Russia herself. Russian Jews had been secretly active on behalf of the Central Powers from the first; they had become the chief agents of German pacifist propaganda; by 1917 they had done

---

[311] Sokolow, Vol. II, p. 83. Translator's note: Letter QVOS (double-checked with an online photograph of the original letter).

much in preparation for that general disintegration of Russian national life, later recognized as the revolution. It was believed that if Great Britain declared for the fulfilment of Zionist aspirations in Palestine under her own pledge, one effect would be to bring Russian Jewry to the cause of the Entente.

It was believed, also, that such a declaration would have a potent influence upon world Jewry in the same way, and secure for the Entente the aid of Jewish financial interests. It was believed, further, that it would greatly influence American opinion in favour of the Allies. Such were the chief considerations which, during the later part of 1916 and the next ten months of 1917, impelled the British Government towards making a contract with Jewry.[312]

These statements stand in sharp contrast to those of Dr. Weizmann, who can only identify idealistic reasons for the Balfour Declaration, as we can see when, in 1936, he was questioned during the proceedings of the Palestine Royal Commission:

Dr. Weizmann explained that the Balfour Declaration was not a piece of War propaganda, and its object was not to enlist the sympathies of the rich Jews. As a matter of fact, rich Jews everywhere opposed Zionism. The Balfour Declaration was the result of mature thinking and repeated consideration by the British Empire. It was given because the British people desired to make a contribution to the solution of the world Jewish problem.[313]

Once again, after the Balfour Declaration was published, the press (with very few exceptions) came out once more in defense of the Jews. It was an 'epoch-making' event, readers of the *Daily Chronicle* were assured. Years later, however, the *Morning Post* had strong words to say against this government policy. In an editorial dated 16 October 1922, it complained about the adverse consequences that had arisen for England from the 'Zionist adventure.' 'We have often complained,' it explained, 'about the atmosphere of intrigue and mystery in which the agreement took place. We do not like the coincidence of the Balfour Declaration coming at a time when Britain was in great distress, as it has the strong flavor of blackmail'.[314]

---

[312] Temperley, Vol. VI, pp. 172-3. Translator's note: QVOS.

[313] *Jewish Chronicle*, 27/11/1936. Translator's note: QVOS.

[314] Sokolow, Vol. II, pp. 84-99. Translator's note: QVOS [p. 84]. All of the pages cited contain excerpts from a wide variety of British press titles, and all of them praise the Zionist project to the skies.

Immediately after the Declaration was issued, a Jewish Department was opened in the Ministry of Information, a department in which several Zionists served, and 'of which the leaders of the Zionist movement made astute use.' Wolf is right to see this as the British government putting out a public signal that it was on the side of the Zionists. While the department's leading civil servant was a non-Jew, Sir Lancelot Oliphant, this did not matter in itself because he 'was a relative and namesake of a famous diplomatist, journalist, and man of letters who is remembered as one of the pioneers of the Zionist idea'.[315]

On 2 December 1917, a large Jewish demonstration took place in the London Opera House as a way of expressing their gratitude to the British government. The function was led by Lord Rothschild. Other speakers included Lord Robert Cecil, who today continues to be one of the strongest allies of the Jews, and Herbert Samuel. The latter said, among other things, that 'it may be that the genius of the Jewish race will again be able to give the world a brilliant and distinctive civilization.' It is not uninteresting to note who among the leading circles of England at the time professed themselves to be friends of international Jewry with warm congratulatory telegrams. We find among them Viscount Grey, Arthur Henderson M.P., the Marquess of Crewe, Viscount Bryce, the Earl of Selborne, Lord Hugh Cecil, Lord Sydenham of Combe, Lord Emmott, Lord Tennyson, and the Rev. James Cooper, Moderator of the General Assembly of the Church of Scotland.[316]

Jews in Versailles

After the war ended, the promise made to the Jews in the Balfour Declaration had to be kept by the Paris Peace Conference. No fewer than 75,000 Jews in England sent a petition to Paris requesting the establishment of a Jewish state in Palestine.[317]

As is well known, the British delegation was led by Lloyd George, a man about whom we have already heard various things regarding his relationships with the Jews. We would only like to point out that around this time he was so much under their influence that it even came to the public's attention. The Jewish members of the delegation were Sir Philip Sassoon, Lord Reading, Louis Namier, Alfred Mond, and Edwin Samuel Montagu.

The first of these men was a member of the Sassoon family, the Rothschilds of the East. Sir Philip had been a member of Parliament since 1912,

---

[315] Landman, p. 6. Translator's note: Wolf (*Essays*, p. 407) states that the Jewish Department was organised as part of the Foreign Office, so it may be that the Jewish Department (or Jewish Section) passed to the latter ministry at a later date. The quoted element also comes verbatim from Wolf. & Wolf: *Essays*, p. 407. Translator's note: QVOS.

[316] Sokolow, Vol. II, pp. 99-112. Translator's note: QVOS. & Sokolow, pp. 113-116.

[317] *Morning Post*, 6/3/1919.

and from 1924-1929 and again from 1931-1937 he served as Under-Secretary of State for Air, then in 1937 became First Commissioner of Works, a post which he held until his death two years later. He had also served as Lloyd George's private secretary. The aforementioned Jew had such an influence over the latter that it 'aroused much comment among the general public.' Regarding Montagu's participation, the *Morning Post* of 20 March 1919 rightly noted that in this position he could give his company, Samuel Montagu & Co., valuable insider advice. He was accompanied by his Jewish secretary, Arthur Samuel (later Lord Mancroft), who at the time was the Conservative member of Parliament for Farnham, and who went on to hold other high positions in the British government, including Under-Secretary of State in the Foreign Office, Secretary for Overseas Trade and Financial Secretary to the Treasury. Samuel's numerous publications on economic issues are well-known.[318]

Other full Jews were Sir Cecil Hermann Kisch and E. G. Abraham. The former belonged to the Russia department of British military intelligence. As was to be expected, as a Jew, he had considerable antipathy towards Russia, and as a result was not free from prejudice in his analysis and decision-making. This was expressly confirmed by one of his colleagues, who was otherwise full of praise for him. Today he is an Assistant Under-Secretary of State for India.[319] Abraham was British secretary in the Supreme Council of the Peace Conference and therefore took part in the most confidential and important decisions. For this reason, we can discount Wolf's claim that no Jew, with the exception of the interpreter Prof. Paul Mantoux, penetrated this Holy of Holies. We also find the part-Jew Sir Percy Radcliffe acting as the chief of the military delegation, given that his superior, the Chief of the General Staff, was often tied up in London.[320]

The Jews were represented by a special delegation that worked hand in hand with the British government's delegation. This Jewish delegation included Sir Stuart Samuel, Henry Henriques [perhaps better known as H. S. Q. Henriques], Claude Montefiore, and Lucien Wolf. They formed an exclusively Jewish conference with Jews from other countries, who together discussed all issues that affected them. Sir Stuart Samuel was also the British government's envoy on the official joint US-UK commission who went later that same year to investigate the alleged pogroms in Poland. Wolf was a leading delegate of this Jewish clique at Versailles and is described by his ethnic brethren as the father of the Minority Treaties which came out of the Peace Conference. At the London banquet thrown in his honor by the Mac-

---

[318] *Jewish Year Book, 1938*, p. 498; *Who's Who 1937*, p. 2974. & Brasol, p. 207. Translator's note: QVOS. & *Jewish Year Book*, 1937, p. 490; *Who's Who 1937*, p. 2959.

[319] Beadon: pp. 37-40. & *Jewish Year Book*, 1938, p. 461.

[320] Beadon, pp. 41-45. & Wolf: *Essays*, p. 407-8. & Beadon, p. 15; *Fascist*, June 1937.

cabeans in 1920, the following statement made by Zionist leader Israel Zangwill is interesting:[321]

> Honour to whom honour is due, and all honour to Lucien Wolf, the man who fought for Jewish rights at Versailles last year... The Minority Treaties were the touchstone of the League of Nations, *that essentially Jewish aspiration*. And the man behind the Minority Treaties was Lucien Wolf.[322]

But it was not just the English who came to Paris with such a heavy Jewish entourage. Clemenceau's private secretary at the Conference was the notorious Jew Georges Mandel, who worked as a middleman between the Stock Exchange and the Quai d'Orsay. The Romanians had chosen the Jew Salomon Rosenthal as their legal advisor. Even the Poles had sent a Hebrew, Stephen Markowski, as their financial expert, who in turn took two fellow Jews with him as his assistants. Lithuania sent the lawyer Rosenbaum (who held the rank of Assistant Minister for Foreign Affairs), and Ukraine sent the Kiev lawyer and Itoist Arnold Margolin, as well as Samuel Zarchi, whom Wolf describes as 'a London physician who had previously practiced in the Whitechapel Road.' Jewish participation can also be seen from the fact that the Treaty of Versailles was signed for France by Louis Klotz, for India by Edwin Samuel Montagu, and for Italy by the half-Jew Baron Sonnino, Italy's Minister of Foreign Affairs. Of the German delegation, Brasol states simply that it 'was so obviously dominated by Jewish banking interests that it became known as "The Warburg Delegation".'[323]

The Americans did not lag behind the British when it came to favoring the Jews. The loyalty that President Wilson and Colonel House had for the Jews is world-famous. With [Bernard] Baruch's arrival in Paris, everything was ordered and determined according to the interests of international finance. In addition to Warburg, it was the influence of Jews such as Felix Frankfurter and Jakob H. Schiff who completely dominated Wilson and his decisions. The Jews Henry Morgenthau, Oscar Straus, and Louis Marshall were also attached to the American delegation. At the same time, as always happens on such occasions, Freemasonry will doubtless have played a role.

All in all, it appears that Lucien Wolf was not exaggerating when he said, after the Versailles Treaty, that 'the Peace Treaties, so far as the Jewish

---

[321] *Jewish Year Book, 1937*, pp. 632-3; Lane, p. 124.

[322] *Jewish Guardian*, 11/6/1920. Translator's note: QVOS from Lane, p. 124, which reproduces the excerpt from the *Jewish Guardian*. It is not known if the italics were added by Lane or were part of the original *Jewish Guardian* transcription.

[323] Wolf: *Essays*, pp. 406-10; Brasol, p. 207. Translator's notes: Quotations reproduced from Wolf and Brasol respectively. Wolf (p. 409) also reports that Klotz signed the 1919 Treaty of Saint-Germain on behalf of the French nation.

aspect was concerned, gave them all they asked for, and a great deal more than they dreamt of getting when the Peace Conference opened.' Fortunately, this Jewish dream is now over.[324]

England's Palestine Policy

The post-war history of Palestine and the issues surrounding it would fill another volume. Hence why we shall only touch upon those events which have been largely forgotten or which have not become widely known.

The British Foreign Office had learned the value of supporting international Jewry and therefore saw, in Landman's words, 'the great potential value of Zionism in future as an instrument of British foreign policy.' The international events of 1938 have shown all too clearly that this is still the case today. Although the special department for Palestine was transferred from the Foreign Office to the Colonial Office after the 1921 Cairo Conference chaired by Winston Churchill, this is only one aspect of the issue and is only related to Palestine's administration. While receiving a Jewish delegation, Churchill expressed his belief that 'the establishment of a Jewish national state in Palestine would be a blessing to themselves, to Great Britain and to the whole world'.[325]

But British foreign policy was (and is) not the only domain decisively influenced by international Jewry, as its influence can also clearly be seen in Britain's domestic policy, which we shall endeavor to prove in the next chapter. Here it is sufficient to refer to a letter from the Jews that was revealed to the public.

At the end of 1922, with a general election looming, it was noted that the Jews were very active. They sent circulars to their gentile allies and fellow Jews calling on them to form a group that would 'ensure the guarantee of as many parliamentary candidates as possible that they would support the Zionist program. Specifically, it is first only required to find out their position, i.e. to what extent the candidates in question declare themselves to be neutral, or for or against Zionism.' If at all possible, the group should try to obtain solemn promises of support. Concerning this matter, the Jews then issued the following instructions:

> Extra care must be taken in questioning the candidate on this point before trying to obtain a written promise of this kind. In certain cases it is preferable to settle for a candidate's silence on the matter rather than to receive an outright rejection. From other candidates, a written assurance will probably be obtained

---

[324] *Times*, 15/12/1919. Translator's note: QVOS.
[325] Landman, p. 6. Translator's note: QVOS. & *Jewish Guardian*, 22/4/1921.

without particular difficulty. Otherwise, it shall be assumed
that the friends familiar with each individual situation shall
proceed with all necessary discretion.[326]

How international Jewry watched over the establishment of the British administration in Palestine can be seen from the fact that in 1922 many civil
servants were dismissed, allegedly for reasons of economy. What was striking about these dismissals was that, of those men who were dismissed, not
one was a Jew or an Englishmen who was known to be philo-Semitic. These
measures must be attributed in at least some measure to Herbert Samuel,
who had been High Commissioner for Palestine since 1 July 1920.[327]

Needless to say, the Jews found great public support everywhere for
their plans in Palestine. In this context, we would like to focus on just one
personality who deserves a special mention for his importance as a journalist
and for his influence in general: Herbert Sidebotham. Sidebotham published
four books on the issue. Palestine, in his opinion, 'is crucial for England's
strategic position in the Mediterranean. Furthermore, it is of crucial importance
for the future of the Jews, in order to allow their genius to be fully effective
in the interests of England.' It is very revealing about the general political
situation, which Sidebotham often deals with in the major London newspapers, to know that in his view it is 'it is a false democratic and liberal attitude
that a country which happens to be inhabited by one race or nation, must be
occupied by this people for all time in order for them to have control of it.
The possession of the land must be generally and permanently beneficial to
the whole world, otherwise it loses its moral and political justification'.[328]

We believe that it is common knowledge that some of the Jews demanded further support from England on the Palestine Question. According
to Landman's statements, there are two opposing tendencies which dominate
within Zionism. One is described by him as right-wing, while the other represents Marxist-Socialist views, which, with its model of small, collectivist
communities, allegedly contradicts the principles laid down by Theodor
Herzl, which clearly envisage an independent state in Palestine. This latter
tendency, headed by Dr. Weizmann, is the one which most strongly represented in Palestine. Meanwhile the former tendency, represented by the New
Zionist Organization founded by Vladimir Jabotinsky, is not satisfied with
the territorial aspect of the Palestine settlement, and demands the sparsely-
populated Transjordan in order to accommodate all of the Jews wishing to
immigrate. Naturally, with its 'land hunger', as Landman describes it, Jabotinsky's movement rejects any division of Palestine. Apparently, however,

---

[326] *Morning Post*, 6/11/1922.
[327] *Morning Post*, 18/3/1922. & *Evening Standard*, 6/7/1937.
[328] Sidebotham, *Future*, pp. 5-8; Sidebotham, *British Imperial*, pp. 1-2. & pp. 11-12.

it is the faction led by Weizmann which currently has the most influence within international Jewry.[329]

On 13 August 1937, the *Jewish Chronicle* published an in-depth article, according to which the division of Palestine had already been discussed and an agreement reached between Weizmann and the then-Colonial Minister and great friend of the Jews, [David] Ormsby-Gore, before the Palestine Commission set up by the British had even had the chance to make its suggestions regarding the issue. So here again one can see the Jewish conspiracy behind the curtain of public life pre-arranging outcomes before they happen and the confirmation that England dares do nothing without the prior approval of international Jewry.

In the discussions about the partition plan, the two strategies mentioned by Landman emerged. Ormsby-Gore, and therefore the government, advocated partition, which was opposed by the radical Jews and their allies. This was particularly evident during the House of Commons debate on the issue which took place on 21 July 1937. Given what we have already discussed, the reader will not be surprised to learn that David Lloyd George and Winston Churchill belonged to the second camp. Lloyd George also penned the article which was published in the *Sunday Express* of 18 July 1937, which praised the cultural work carried out by the Jews in Palestine, for which around 77 million pounds had already been spent, while he sharply criticized support for the government's partition plan.[330]

The Jews inform us on other occasions of the British government's subservience to them. In July 1937, the *Free Press* reproduced an article from the American Jewish newspaper *California Jewish Voice* of 7 May 1937. According to this article, the well-known American Jews Rabbi Stephen S. Wise and Louis Brandeis protested to Roosevelt about the fact that during the meeting of the Palestine Committee, there were attempts to stop Jewish immigration. Roosevelt agreed with them and accordingly telegraphed Anthony Eden, then Britain's Secretary of State for Foreign Affairs, who immediately acceded to the request.

We are all sufficiently informed about the situation in Palestine. Britain sends her best sons there to protect the Jews against the Arab freedom fighters with their well-founded rights. Sidebotham, writing under the pseudonym of 'Scrutator' in the *Sunday Times* of 23 August 1936, referred to the fact that Palestine represented a difficult problem for England, but reminded readers: 'The alliance between England and Zionism is not some hobbyhorse of Balfour's, but a common mission and a useful tool of British imperialism in the Near East.'

---

[329] Landman: pp. 10-20.

[330] *Daily Telegraph*, 22/7/1937. Translator's note: Readers are invited to make a comparison with the situation today.

Another important Englishman, namely Field-Marshal Sir Henry Wilson, recognized the difficulties for international politics that arose from Britain's collaboration with international Jewry and in 1922 publicly pointed this out: 'We find ourselves in Palestine because a few years ago Mr. Balfour gave a speech. And we stayed there because the politicians were told that, in the event of our evacuating, we would have organized Jewry against us in every capital in the world'.[331] He was murdered some two months later.[332]

---

[331] *Evening News*, 3/5/1922.

[332] *Dictionary of National Biography*, Vol. 1922-30, p. 916. Translator's note: Official reports say that on 22 June 1922, Wilson was assassinated on his London doorstep by two members of the revolutionary Irish Republican Army.

CHAPTER 8

JEWISH DOMINATION, PART TWO
(1933-1942)

England's Impotence

The enormous influence of the Jews in England is beyond all doubt. Before 1933, we in Germany experienced firsthand what this influence leads to. But here the Jew had not been able to establish his power as deeply as he had in England. Given this fact, can one really believe that the British nation could return to being as it was in the time of Elizabeth I and the first two Stuarts? Do we really believe that three hundred years of Jewish domination in England have gone by without leaving its mark on the national body? This is only plausible if one denies the Jewish danger and the associated disadvantages they bring to a people.

But not even the most incredulous would dare to make such a claim, because in this respect History itself is too big an accuser to ignore. Let the reader consider our previous account of the facts of English history, which is based both on Jewish sources and on official material. Counterfeiting currency, usury, receiving stolen goods, bribery, and other crimes mark the trajectory of the Jews in a country that they themselves admit has given them the greatest freedom since Cromwell's time. The excuse that is repeatedly given for their crimes, that their behavior was solely the result of circumstantial pressure, has no basis in fact, at least in England. Our historical report has already shown the level of morality that generally prevails in England whenever a financial scandal comes to light. Based on the information we have provided so far, there can hardly be any doubt that this attitude arose through the merging of Puritanism with Judaism over the centuries.

Does the British people, as a result, show signs of decline? We dare to say yes without hesitation. However, before we explain the reasoning for our judgement, let us see what prominent Englishmen have had to say about the matter.

Lord Shaftesbury, the great friend of the Jews, proclaimed as early as 1848: 'Nothing can save the British Empire from shipwreck.' The following year, even Disraeli expressed the view that 'in industry, commerce, and agriculture there is no hope.' He certainly did not blame his fellow Jews for this fact any more than Shaftesbury did. In 1852, the dying Duke of Wellington

announced: 'I thank God that I shall be spared from seeing the consumma-
tion of ruin that is gathering around us'.[1]

It would appear, according to the opinion of the *Daily Express*, that
none of these three men were correct, because England has still not sunk into
ruin. But is the complete destruction of Britain's power, visible to the outside
world, necessary to confirm the views of these three 19th-century figures?

First of all, we must not overlook the fact that 19th-century England
could not be challenged by any world power. France, defeated everywhere
by England in the 18th century, had brilliant plans for North America and
India, but these had failed because France's power was dissipated and bled
to death on the battlefields of Europe. It therefore no longer had sufficient
forces to defend and consolidate its overseas possessions and, specifically, to
be able to confront England, which was solely focused on empire-building.
Napoleon's attempts to correct the mistakes of his predecessors failed because, among other reasons, he made too many enemies at once and united
Europe against him before he was able to strike a decisive blow against England, his greatest adversary.

Due to a lack of unity, 19th-century Germany had neither the strength
nor the necessity to seek a confrontation with the British Empire. And in the
years following 1870, it first had to deal with the domestic issues arising
from unification. Russia had been kept down by the Crimean War and was
later contained with the help of various allied powers. Japan and America
were also eliminated as rivals during this period.

Hilaire Belloc, a leading historian and writer, called England's attention
to the various detrimental changes in her national body that were attributable
to what he called her Commercial Spirit. In the current epoch, abstract
wealth—money—was the only test of excellence, Belloc said, not the quality
of production. Agriculture, crafts, and peasant life in general, incompatible
with these principles, were therefore doomed:

> [I]t must be clear that the Commercial Spirit militates against
> the existence or survival of a peasantry. A peasant State is
> primarily productive: it cannot survive instability of owner-
> ship, nor does it envisage wealth as figures but as things. It
> will even regard money itself as a thing and cry out against a
> debased currency as a form of theft—an injustice. It will insist
> on a currency of real materials—such as the precious metals.
> But the Commercial State is content with an imaginary cur-

---

[1] *Daily Express*, 29/10/1938. Translator's note: All of these quotations are relatively famous and are given in their original English versions, although the Wellington quotation is
sometimes found with minor variations, with the year of attribution generally given as
1851 or 1852.

rency the unit-values of which fluctuate at the will of the authorities. To the one a king who issues false money is a criminal: to the other he is a statesman. So antagonistic are the spirits of Commerce and of Husbandry that the preponderance of the one endangers the very life of the other. Commercial habits will be clumsy and impeded in the peasant State. In the Commercial State, the peasantry will be destroyed.[2]

Even if Belloc does not explicitly mention it, we would like to assume, in view of his statements elsewhere, that he understands that the Jews are indirectly responsible for this process, despite his strong disavowals of enmity towards them in his book *The Jews* (1922).

In Belloc's opinion, expounded most extensively in *The Jews*, the Jew in England enjoys a social position that he does not find in any other country in the world. He has even penetrated the most exclusive of institutions, the British nobility, changing it forever with his blood:

And the Jew pointed to the English State as that one in which all that his nation required of the *goyim* was to be found. He here enjoyed a situation the like of which he could not hope to enjoy in any other country of the world. All antagonism to him had died down. He was admitted to every institution in the State, a prominent member of his nation became chief officer of the English Executive, and, an influence more subtle and penetrating, marriages began to take place, wholesale, between what had once been the aristocratic territorial families of this country and the Jewish commercial fortunes.

After two generations of this, with the opening of the twentieth century, those of the great territorial English families in which there was no Jewish blood were the exception. In nearly all of them was the strain more or less marked, in some of them so strong that, though the name was still an English name and the traditions those of a purely English lineage of the long past, the physique and character had become wholly Jewish and the members of the family were taken for Jews whenever they travelled in countries where the gentry had not yet suffered or enjoyed this admixture.

---

[2] Belloc, *Contemporary England* p. 59 ff. Translator's note: QVOS (p. 62), and inserted into the text for reader interest. Note that Belloc was also very aware of the Jewish role in these nefarious changes to the country, as in his early political satires, beginning with the 1903 masterpiece *Emmanuel Burden*, his regular allusions to negative Jewish influence are easily discernible to the initiated.

Belloc also leaves the reader in no doubt that he regards Freemasonry as a tool to achieve Jewish aims, just as the British state itself was a similar such tool to be used on behalf of Jews worldwide:

> Specially Jewish institutions, such as Freemasonry (which the Jews had inaugurated as a sort of bridge between themselves and their hosts in the seventeenth century), were particularly strong in Britain, and there arose a political tradition, active, and ultimately to prove of great importance, whereby the British State was tacitly accepted by foreign governments as the official protector of the Jews in other countries. It was Britain which was expected to interfere, within the measure of her power, whenever a persecution of the Jews took place in the East of Christendom: to support the Jewish financial energies throughout the world, and to receive in return the benefit of that connection.

Belloc further points out how the change in the Jews' political position in England led to a re-assessment of the Jew in literature and historiography. Within English fiction, the Jew would no longer be generally viewed as the moral inferior, but 'as an exalted character, quite specially removed to his advantage from the mass of mankind.' Within historiography, distortions began to be inserted into the tradition which have since become conventional wisdom:

> A convention arose that in the clash between the Jews and the English of the Middle Ages, the Jews were invariably right and the English invariably wrong. Where the struggle was between the Jew and the non-Jew abroad, the historian exceeded all bounds. The European hostile to the Jew was a senseless monster, and the Jew hostile to the European was a holy victim.
>
> The whole story of Europe and of this country, in so far as it was affected by this very considerable factor, was distorted through suppression, and false emphasis and quite exceptional lying.
>
> The general reader of history neither knew what part the Jewish question had played nor the claims that could be advanced for his own race in the conflict. And as historians live by copying one another, the legend was established in every school and college.

When the Jewish advance through English society was over, the Jews 'in proportion to their numbers, held a power in this country beyond anything that has been seen in any other of the world.' Not even Poland at the end of the Middle Ages came close to the situation found in modern Britain. As Belloc went on to explain:

> Every English Government had (and has) its quota of Jews. They had entered the diplomatic service and the House of Lords; they swarmed in the House of Commons, in the Universities, in all the Government offices save the Foreign Office (and even there, representatives of the Jewish nation have recently entered); they were exceedingly powerful in the Press: they were all-powerful in the City. No custom unsympathetic to their race, from the duel to popular clamour, survived.[3]

In his book *The Alien Menace*, Lieutenant-Colonel A. H. Lane no less strongly emphasized the disastrous influence of the Jews and the harm this caused to the English nation. We shall return to this book in a later chapter.

The well-known writer of the younger generation, Beverley Nichols, has also pointed out the decline of British power both domestically and abroad, in his recent book *News of England* (1938):

> The position is one of extreme danger. On the material side we have the prospect of an undisciplined nation with a declining population in possession of an utterly unreasonable proportion of the world's riches. This nation, which is led by a committee of dreamers and grandfathers (whose faltering steps are hampered by an irresponsible and ignorant opposition), finds itself confronted by new nations of immense strength, led by young and ruthless men, whose fingers are itching to pick out pockets. [...]
>
> England, it would appear, no longer cares about England. With equanimity the majority of the population has witnessed the destruction of London, and its transformation into the shoddiest capital in the world. With hardly a protest we have assisted at the desecration of the countryside, till every other village is an advertisement of the fact that we are not only a nation of shopkeepers but a nation of usurious vandals.
>
> With sang-froid we tolerate slum conditions which the authoritarian states, with their empty treasuries, would not tolerate for a month. With indifference we accept a chaotic and antiquated road-system, which is paralysing our transport and filling our cemeteries.

---

[3] Belloc: *The Jews*, p. 222 ff. Translator's note: All QVOS.

Further on in the book, Nicholas wonders how later generations will explain the decline and fall of the British Empire:

> We have had so many shocks, since the war, that we seem to think that this is a perfectly normal situation. Actually, of course, it is so fantastic that future historians, poring over yellowing documents in an effort to form a final verdict on the Decline and Fall of the British Empire, will rub their eyes and say, 'There must be some other explanation, some subtle, secret thing which caused this madness. After all, the men who had charge of the Empire's destinies were not, by the ordinary standards of education, half-wits. They were not, by the ordinary standards of morality, rogues. And yet...look at what they did!'[4]

Apparently, Nichols does not see this 'subtle, secret thing' to be the Jews. Although he has no love for the Jewish financier, he considers the Hebrew to be indispensable to the British Empire, and compares the Jew to ivy:

> Let us imagine, however, that we can forget all feelings of humanity. Let us regard anti-Semitism from a purely utilitarian point of view. Is it for a moment conceivable that the British Empire, which is of all institutions the most precarious and the most ramshackle, could possibly tear out the Jews from its midst, and continue to survive? The briefest consideration assures us that if it attempted such a drastic surgical operation, it would crash in ruins. It would crash as certainly as an ancient building on which the ivy had for centuries encroached. You may call the ivy a parasite. You may suggest that it had stretched its tendrils too deeply into the crevices, that it was eating into the very fabric of the stone. That may be true. But try to tear it away, and you will bring down, not only the ivy, but the entire structure.
>
> Would it not be better to trim the ivy?
>
> I do not think that the metaphor is either inappropriate or far-fetched. The ivy is a parasite. The Jew is a parasite. But the ivy, on an ancient structure, is not only a parasite but a support. And the Jew, in an ancient structure like the British Empire, is not only an alien but an asset.[5]

---

[4] Nichols, pp. 3, 9-10. Translator's note: Both QVOS.

[5] Nichols, p. 279. Translator's note: QVOS. On the following page Nichols laments not being able to have a mature conversation about realities concerning Jews, writing: 'a modern journalist who does not constantly scream hysterical abuse of the whole German people is at once labelled an anti-Semite... The modern intellectual does not debate. He de-

Nichols would have done better to apply the analogy to two living concepts, portraying the British Empire as a mighty, profusely branching tree. He would probably have come to the conclusion that the creeper had sucked the tree so dry of sap that it was almost dead...

The well-known Nietzsche translator and writer A. M. Ludovici, who undertook a lecture tour through Germany in 1938, should not be missing from the list of men who have relentlessly exposed the decline of the British nation. In at least three of his publications, the facts of the Jewish influence and the decline of English life have not only been established, but this decline is squarely attributed to the Jews.

His elegantly and scientifically-written book, *Jews and the Jews in England*, was published at the beginning of 1939 under the pseudonym Cobbett. Ludovici has no doubt that the Jew and only the Jew is to blame for the decline of the British nation. The general public still believes that they live in merry old England. However,

> [A]t bottom, the nation is really unrecognizable. The age-long rake-off of the transformed ruling or possessing classes— whether Jews or Englishmen—who have considered profit rather than service, quick and clean sources of income rather than production, has left the people and their soil not only disintegrated but exhausted. Everywhere in plant, animal and human being there are signs of generations of ruthless exploitation, systematic devitalization. The people no longer even care for the greatness on which their ancestors squandered their blood and treasure.

In his guise as Cobbett, Ludovici warned against the danger of seeing England's ills as being caused simply by the presence of Jews, when the problem had evidently extended beyond this one ethnic group:

> Modern English life is bristling with evidence of the victory of the Judaized Englishman and of Jewish values. What sense, then, would there be in so empty a gesture as excluding the ethnic Jew and retaining his Gentile understudy? What pur-

---

nounces.' He also repeats Mosley's point that 80% of Britain's fraudulent bankruptcies of the previous ten years were Jewish. However, given that 'I abhor anti-Semitism', Nichols says that the solution must be to make more rigorous laws, or else to agree with one of his Jewish friends who observed that 'people who were so stupid deserved to be robbed.' Nichols, who admits to have a 'sneaking sympathy' for this 'Jewish point of view', is apparently oblivious to the fact that the low-trust, amoral society which results from such apathy towards dishonest, anti-social, and predatory behavior is exactly the kind of society he had previously bemoaned that England had become.

pose would be served in excluding the Jew and in continuing to worship at the shrine of his idols?

No exclusion of the Jews from the administrative or cultural life of England, therefore, could be more than a piece of shallow, hysterical patriotism, if it did not contemplate and include the far more fundamental but infinitely more difficult task of freeing the country of its wrong values. And all bodies of Englishmen who seriously wish to recover English civilization at this stage cannot be regarded as any more than emotional and hysterical flag wavers if they do not see the compelling need of that infinitely difficult task—the task of accompanying any gesture of organized reform by a frontal attack upon the Judaized elements in their kith and kin and their own Judaized values.

However, the writer is not optimistic about the long-term prospects for such a revolution being possible in England:

But such a transformation and wholesale demonetization of established values is a stupendous undertaking, and although none other offers any hope, it may be questioned whether at this stage in our history we still possess the energy, the fire and the will which alone could be adequate to carry through such a fundamental and far-reaching change.[6]

Ludovici's writings in general advocate a regeneration of the English nation through a return to the traditional virtues, but the mere suggestion of this is so absurd to most English people that they do see the need to concern themselves with the question. He is of the opinion that the system prevailing in England is detrimental to the nation. At least two thirds of the population are dissatisfied and resentful. There is a deep divide between employer and employee as relations become 'less and less human', leading to all sorts of undesirable outcomes. With no regard to the spiritual and physical condition of the people, the only factor considered important is the accumulation of capital. The health of the population is only of secondary importance to those in power. The most important demand for a people, keeping the nation clean of alien, undesirable elements, had also been forgotten for a long time. In connection with this question, Ludovici then states that when deciding

---

[6] 'Cobbett', pp. 111-117. Translator's note: All QVOS. In the original text, Aldag appears unaware that Cobbett was a pseudonym, much less a pseudonym of Ludovici (as chapter 5 makes clear, the figure of William Cobbett appears to have missed Aldag's literature review, or he would surely have understood that this name had to be pseudonym). In the interests of clarity and truth, I have updated the text for the benefit of the reader.

whether to admit foreigners, especially Jews, into the land, the so-called morality of the decision is irrelevant, because in all decisions which affect a nation there is only one commandment: do only what benefits the long-term preservation and wellbeing of the people.[7]

Ludovici also castigates England's modern socio-economic system, in which he evidently sees Jewish ambition as being the crucial factor in its emergence:

> To own property without responsibility, to own industrial interests without performing any function in regard to industry, these are two of the developments which ever since the Commonwealth have done most to bring discredit upon Capitalistic organisation; and, in the sense that they are inseparable from the purely usurious character of the modern financial control of trade, we are justified in at least formulating the question of whether the return of the Jews in large numbers, ever since 1656, may not have had something to do with this un-English development of the country's economic organisation.
>
> There is, moreover, this serious view to be taken of the Jewish question—a view which, to the best of my knowledge, does not appear to have been stated elsewhere—namely, that since the Jew approaches the society in which he resides, more or less as a stranger, he and those he influences will naturally strive to break down as far as possible all the barriers in that society which tend to perpetuate his strangeness, or to bar his access to complete citizenship. This means that the Jew's form of power—wealth—will find itself opposed to all other kinds of power, such as Gentile aristocratic lineage, Gentile aristocratic character and prestige, hereditary honours of all kinds, and, above all, national solidarity (by this I mean loyalty between the various classes), which are all things that cannot be bought, which have no market price, and which the Jew cannot get possession of, or form part of, no matter how rich he is.
>
> Now where the Jew becomes powerful, it will be found that these things tend to fall ever more deeply into disrepute, and the tendency will be to make rank, status, citizenship, nationality and prestige depend entirely upon purchasable symbols, or outward signs—whether these happen to be titles, honours, a reputation for charitable or patriotic munificence, valuable old masters, or expensive horses and cars. Hence the

---

[7] Ludovici: *Aristocracy*, pp. 35 ff., 44 ff., 166 ff. Translator's note: Quoted element reproduced from page 44.

inevitable association of Jews in Germany, France, England and elsewhere, with a Liberal plutocratic order of society, standing opposed to a proud hereditary aristocracy struggling to uphold tradition, lineage, the national character and inter-class loyalty.

The fact that anarchy is always next door to a Liberal plutocratic order of society, lends a note of gravity to this view of the Jewish question, which it is only prudent to appreciate at its proper worth, without the exaggerations either of emotional bias or panic. And those who see in the last eighty years of English political life, a tendency to depreciate all those symbols of honour and prestige, which cannot be bought or acquired by wealth, and who find even powerful Gentiles in the land now advocating and promoting this tendency, might do well to enquire into the influence of the Jew, and the benefits ultimately reverting to him through the success of this development.[8]

Time and space impede us from reproducing other valuable excerpts from this British writer. There are several analytical works by him that are well worth reading, and it would be timely for some of his books to be made available to the German public. It is unfortunately the case that we are mostly introduced to English writers who, due to their very affiliation with the Jewish system, continue to portray the England of today and of the past in a light that does not at all correspond to the facts. In this too, Ludovici has done pioneering work without having yet achieved anywhere near the level of commercial success that his work deserves.

Last but not least, there are the two men who, in their own way, are leading the fight against the Jews and the decline of England: Arnold Leese and Sir Oswald Mosley. The former is the leader of the Imperial Fascist League (IFL), whose policy regarding the Jews is the same as ours, and which sees the Jews as the greatest danger to England. Sir Oswald is the leader of England's most important fascist and nationalist party, the British Union of Fascists (BUF), which pursues a strident anti-Jewish policy, although its justification differs from ours. According to their platform, the English National Socialists attack the Jews neither because of their religion (the BUF principle being one of complete religious toleration) nor for reasons of racial prejudice (because in their view that would be detrimental to the multi-racial British Empire). Rather, the BUF's 'quarrel with the Jewish interests' is because 'they have constituted themselves a state within the nation, and have set the interests of their co-racialists at home and abroad above the interest of the British State.'

---

[8] Ludovici: *Conservatism*, pp. 118 ff., 138 ff., 152-5. Translator's note: QVOS [pp. 154-5].

Mosley gave an outstanding example of such conduct when he wrote of 'the persistent attempt of many Jewish interests to provoke the world disaster of another war between Britain and Germany, not this time in any British quarrel, but purely in a Jewish quarrel.' The course of world events have since proven Mosley to be correct.[9]

We believe that for our purposes it will suffice simply to enumerate these men of England who describe Jewish rule as harmful to their people. In the following, we will endeavor to provide incontrovertible evidence for their assertions. For this we will have to take our investigations into the individual branches of English public life in which Jewish participation can be demonstrated.

We are well aware that, given the scope of this work, we can only skim the surface of each topic, but in our view, it is not necessary to have make an exhaustive investigation of the Judaization of each individual sector. Apart from the lengthy research which would be required, we are not at all sure that we could get to the bottom of the issue under the current English system, because, for example, the trading companies and financial trusts are so intertwined that one would have to be an insider—i.e. one of the Jews or their friends—to be able to uncover everything. Then to cite just another strategy of deliberate obfuscation, there is the fact that the banks manage blocks of shares—often the majority of certain companies—in trust, so that it is not possible to determine through the public registers the identity of the actual owner.

Furthermore, the indirect influence of the Jews, i.e. the dependence on them that is created by certain circumstances, cannot be measured at all in an economic system like the English one, despite the fact that said indirect influence is at least as great as their direct influence, if not even greater. Nevertheless, we hope that the subsequent findings of our investigations will convince even the biggest doubters that there is unlikely to have ever been a country in history that has been more subservient to the Jews than Great Britain is currently.

How Many Jews Live in the British Empire?

Before we proceed to the aforementioned investigations, we wish to deal once more with the difficult question of the size of the Jewish population in the British Empire and, where applicable, in England alone. We have con-

---

[9] Mosley, pp. 58-9. Translator's note: All QVOS. The aforementioned Leese also wrote on the topic of Britain entering WW2 for Jewish interests. However, as Leese was imprisoned without charge or trial in 1940, along with a thousand others, under Defense Regulation 18B, which suspended *habeas corpus*, he was unable to publish his book *The Jewish War of Survival* until 1945, too late for Aldag's study, but one which I am sure would have been cited had it been contemporaneous. See Macklin, p. 52 ff. [in Translator's Bibliography] for more information on Leese's internment.

stantly reiterated that when it comes to the Jewish Question, it is never a matter of the numbers of Jews in a country, but rather the level of their influence over the state and economy concerned, and on national life generally. That said, the overall number of Jews still has a certain importance, because the greater the blood ratio of the Jewish population to the indigenous, the greater the danger of racial decomposition and Judaization. The general Jewish and Judaism population also becomes the reservoir from whose lowest layers the Hebrews continually receive a refreshment of new blood. These are not infrequently the elements who push forward with their instinctive desire for money and power and ensure that the Jewish advance does not come to a standstill due to the fatigue or degeneration of the leading families.

It is extremely difficult to arrive at a demographic estimate for the period up to 1 January 1939. Here too, we will state the figures at the lowest end of the estimate range, in order to safeguard the scientific accuracy of this study.

Official immigration statistics are currently presented in such a way that it is difficult to find in them any useful points of reference from which we could base our calculations, and this is even more the case now than it was with the statistics of previous years. As a result, efforts in this regard must necessarily be limited to very scarce and often vague data. In the case of the Dominions and the Overseas Territories, this data becomes so scarce that we have had to rely exclusively on Jewish sources.

Accordingly, the number of Jews in India would therefore have to be estimated at around 25,000, a figure that is evidently too low given the size of India and the influence of Jews in the big cities. We have been told by English people living in India that the influx of Jews after 1933 was quite significant. In particular, they have recently noted a predominance of Jews in the medical profession. And of those occupying important positions in India we find, among others, Sir Sassoon David, Mayor of Bombay, and Sir David Ezra, Mayor of Calcutta.[10]

In New Zealand, the colony of Jews consists of 5,000 to 6,000 souls. Nevertheless, a Jew, Sir Julius Vogel, has already become Prime Minister and another, Sir Michael Myers KCMG, has become Chief Justice.[11]

According to the Jews' own statements, the proportion of Jews in Australia's population is also only small. The first settlers arrived in 1821, and today there are said to be 22,000 to 23,000 Jews there out of a population of around 6.5 million. As always, they can be found in the big cities: 10,000 in Sydney, 9,000 in Melbourne, 500 in Adelaide, 400 in Brisbane, and 2000 in Perth. They are mainly engaged in trade and finance, and their influence is very significant. Prominent among the leading Jews are the former Attorney-General and later Governor-General Sir Isaac Isaacs, Chief Justice Sir Julian

---

[10] *Jewish Chronicle*, 7/5/1937, p. 35.
[11] *Jewish Chronicle*, 15/5/1936, p. 13; *Jewish Year Book 1938*, p. 343.

Salomons KC, Chief Justice H. E. Cohen (the highest judge in New South Wales), and the aforementioned Sir John Monash, who commanded the Australian Expeditionary Force in France. The number of Jews who have been in Parliament and in high positions is legion. The Jews note with particular satisfaction that there is not a trace of anti-Semitism to be found in Australia and that many intermarriages take place.[12]

The strength of Jewish influence in Australia can be seen from the fact that at the end of 1938 this country was the first to declare its willingness to settle 15,000 Hebrews over the subsequent three years. The explanation for this is that in the days of the September crisis of 1938 a rumor was circulated that a large Japanese naval force was cruising off New Guinea, ready to strike Australia should war break out in Europe. Only because of this danger did people recognize the sparse population as a serious disadvantage, and as a result they wanted to call in new settlers for the defense of the country. We only fear that the Australians will experience severe disappointment in this regard, and we are surprised that no effort has been made to invite the English, who incidentally have little desire to emigrate.[13]

In Canada, there is a colony of around 200,000 Jews in relation to the total population of around 13 million. The Hebrews themselves do not provide any consistent data on this. For example, they put the number of Jews in Canada at 156,176 or 160,000, while in the same breath say that it is twice as large as the Jewish community in Australia and South Africa, which would make this number greater than 200,000. After London, Canada has the two largest population centers of Jews in the British Empire, with Montreal containing 58,000 Jews, and Toronto with 45,000. It is therefore no surprise that a recrudescence of anti-Jewish agitation is already emerging in Canada, led by H. H. Beamish, who has declared war on the Jews and their allies.[14]

In our previous discussion on the reasons for the Boer War, we have already stated to what extent South Africa was Judaism at that time and how the nation's life was dominated by the Hebrews. It need hardly be said that this did not diminish under British rule. On the contrary, as is well known, the Boer War was fought to secure the immense wealth of this country for the Jews and the British.

---

[12] *Jewish Chronicle*, 7/5/1937 p. 32. Editor's note: There are currently around 115,000 Jews in Australia, roughly 0.4% of the population. But Jewish influence is utterly dominant there today.

[13] *Jewish Chronicle*, 23/12/1938, pp. 16, 28.

[14] *Jewish Chronicle*, 7/5/1937, p. 34, 3/9/1937, p. 50; *Jewish Year Book 1938*, p. 343. Translator's note: The JC of 25/6/1937, p. 23 reported that Beamish was reportedly active in Canada and said to be attempting to resurrect the Canadian Nationalist Party in Winnipeg, but the 3/9/1937 issue suggests that his influence had not managed to extend beyond Winnipeg itself, while the other issues only talk about anti-Jewish feeling being a problem in the province of Quebec, due to its French Catholic heritage.

Should we be surprised that, even according to the Jews, out of a total White population of around two million, no fewer than 95,000 of their ethnic brethren settled there? This number would certainly have increased if immigration restrictions had not been imposed, despite the extreme resistance of the Jews already there. As early as 1930, it was ordered that annual immigration from Eastern and Southern Europe should not exceed 50 individuals. And in accordance with a new law of 1937, Jewish immigration is completely prohibited.

With this legislation, we cannot help but get the impression that the Jews in South Africa agreed to these measures behind the scenes, because they understand that with a further Judaization of the country, they would have to deal with the existing anti-Semitic forces growing stronger in response. The strong Nationalist Party is led by the extremely active Dr. D. F. Malan, a former cabinet minister who is a minister of the Dutch Church. According to one of Malan's public statements, made at a party meeting in the Transvaal in October 1936, he attacked the government for permitting Jews to immigrate into the Union and stated that South Africa had long ago reached the stage where she had absorbed the maximum number of Jews to not trigger an anti-Semitic reaction. He also made clear that, were he to seize power, he would not hesitate to take the same measures against the Jews as have been done here in Germany. It was thanks to his campaigning for a private bill, in which new immigrants would have to be tested for race and assimilability, Yiddish discounted as a European language, and certain businesses, occupations and trades to be closed to 'foreigners', which he claimed had flooded into South Africa, that the government rushed its Aliens Bill through Parliament in January 1937, made effective on February 1. However, Dr. Malan has since claimed in meetings that despite the ban, Jewish immigration has been continuing to take place. Evidence of rising anger is shown from the fact that, in late 1938, the synagogues in Johannesburg were being guarded by special police detachments.[15]

It is impossible to outline here the influence of the Jews in South Africa, for it would require a special study of its own. We would dare to say, however, that despite their power in the United States, the Jewish quest for global hegemony will collapse if they lose South Africa along with England. This is where their greatest wealth currently comes from, as the gold and diamond industries, along with other sections of the economy, are almost entirely in their hands. The most recent census, made by the Jews themselves, of the Jewish population in South Africa and Rhodesia gives a total of 102,000 individuals. According to the same, the Jewish colony in Rhode-

---

[15] *Jewish Chronicle*, 7/5/1937. Translator's note: It should be noted that the Aliens Act did not prevent against the entry of 'natural-born British subjects', who could obviously be Jewish. & *Jewish Chronicle*, 3/9/1937, p. 50; 18/11/1937, p. 38; 2/12/1938, pp. 18, 36.

sia amounts to 7,000 souls, a relatively high figure given that the total European population is just over 60,000. Their overwhelming influence in South Africa's economy stems from the fact that the Jews Sir Lionel Phillips, Sir Ernest Oppenheimer, Sir George Albu, Louis Reyersbach, and Ernest Friedlander are among the former presidents of the Chamber of Mines.[16]

Jews have held the highest positions in government, administration and politics. Thus, Sir Richard Solomon was Lieutenant-Governor of the Transvaal and later High Commissioner for South Africa in London, his main duties in the latter role corresponding to those of a plenipotentiary dealing with the Imperial Government in London. Sir Ernest Solomon was a member of the Transvaal Government, Sir William Solomon was Chief Justice of South Africa. In addition to those already mentioned, many other Jews were raised to the knighthood or even the baronetcy, with Sir Siegmund Neumann, Sir Lionel Phillips and Sir George Albu being examples of the latter. In the South African Parliament, we find Jews such as G. Hartog, C. P. Robinson, Morris Alexander, and Sir Ernest Oppenheimer in leading positions. Every town of importance in South Africa and Rhodesia has already had at least one Jewish mayor.[17]

This summary of the main centers of Jewry in the British Empire may suffice for our purposes. Jews are generally found wherever there are opportunities for rich pickings. Thus, they have long dominated the sugar industry in the West Indies, where, according to eyewitnesses, conditions that are almost medieval still prevail and have repeatedly been the cause of unrest.

Determining the total population of Jews in the Dominions and Overseas Territories of Great Britain is extremely difficult. Based on their own estimates, the Jews probably number around 330,000 to 350,000 people. We have already outlined our concerns about the accuracy of such statistics. Aside from these concerns, the Jews themselves have confirmed that only religious Jews have been included in their estimates, but as is known, we go further and include every racial Jew in our estimates. The official censuses carried out in Germany after 1933 have shown that the percentage of Jews who have been baptized is not insignificant. In addition, studies done around this topic here in Germany and recently in Italy have come to prove that previous statistics, regardless of the type, were always inaccurate because they were published by Jews (or those dependent on Jews) who had an interest in keeping the figures as low as possible. Finally, there are many Jews who are 'averse to being marked down as Jewish' in official surveys, as stated in the *Jewish Chronicle* article 'Jews and the National Register' (6 January 1939, page 11).

---

[16] *Jewish Year Book 1938*, p. 344.
[17] *Jewish Chronicle*, 7/5/1937, p. 37.

Given all of this, we have no reservations about estimating the population of Jews in the British Empire at 500,000. This figure excludes the mother country, which shall now be dealt with below.

*****

In accordance with our calculations, which have been fully expounded in a previous chapter, our estimate of the number of Jews in England by 1914 was 900,000, while the Jews themselves put this number at about 250,000. In their statistics for 1938 they put the number at 333,000, which means, in their opinion, that an increase of almost exactly a third has occurred. To be clear, we also support this proportional increase, but not from the starting figure of 250,000, but naturally from that of 900,000. As a result, we have arrived at our own estimate of there being approximately 1,200,000 Jews in England as of 1 January 1939.

As early as 6 July 1930, the newspaper *The People* reported that England had 1,500,000 foreigners resident at that time, nine-tenths of whom came from the former Russian Empire. We have seen that the newcomers from Eastern Europe were almost exclusively Jews, so that based on this estimate our figure does not seem exaggerated, especially given that after 1933, as we will show, immigration to England reached unprecedented proportions.

As early as 1926, A. M. Ludovici estimated the number of Jews in the United Kingdom at one million. Today, as he explained to us personally, he too does not hesitate to use a higher figure.[18]

What evidence is there to indicate that the proportional increase that we adopted from the Jews corresponds in any way to the facts? To find out, we must first divide the post-war period into two immigration periods: the period after 1918, when the war ended, and the period after 1933, when Adolf Hitler came to power.

The Zionist leader Jabotinsky, rightly pointed out in 1916 that after the war, 'tens of thousands of destitute Jews will rush from the ruined Pale [Russia] to this country'.[19] Immigration is said to have increased considerably as soon as the hostilities ended. Mr. William Collinson, General Secretary of the National Free Labor Association, reported in 1921 that '3,000 aliens are coming into England every week. They come in rags and covered with lice.' The wave of immigration does not seem to have abated the following year either. The chattering classes were shocked to see that the number of foreigners was increasing day by day, depriving the British, who had fought to

---

[18] Ludovici: *A Defense of Conservatism*, pp. 155-6. Translator's note: Ludovici makes clear that he has included in this figure 'the non-religious Jews, the Jews who do profess themselves as such, of which there is a vast number, and the half- and quarter-Jews, who are the outcome of miscegenation'.

[19] *Jewish Chronicle*, 30/6/1916, p.16. Translator's note: QVOS.

defend their country, of work and bread. Even the public were forced to grapple with this question. It was discovered that shocking conditions prevailed just a few minutes from the center of the cosmopolitan city of London. Entire streets were reminiscent of the Eastern European ghettos, 'resembling those to be seen in Odessa or in the towns of Galicia.' These newcomers made no attempt to shed their peculiarities and habits, and 'look[ed] upon their Gentile fellow-citizens...with suspicion and with a certain contempt.' The *Times* editorial which described the situation in 1924 was unabashed in the opinion that the alien Jews of London 'do not form a desirable element in our population, and still less a desirable element in our electorate'.[20]

'Alien London', the anonymous series of articles in the *Times* which was introduced by the aforementioned editorial, vividly described the cultural norms, labor patterns, living conditions, and political tendencies of the alien Jewish population, who were gradually displacing the existing British population [both Jew and Gentile] from the East End of London. The author of the articles ('Our Special Correspondent') revealed that on 30 September 1924, no fewer than 214,869 unnaturalized aliens had been counted in Greater London. According to the English methodology of data-gathering, this figure does not include people who had been in the UK for less than two months or who were under 16 years old at the time of the count. It should not be an exaggeration if the latter categories were to account for a quarter of the overall total. This being the case, we can surmise that there were over 250,000 unnaturalized aliens in London in 1924. Based on our previous-discussed percentage of 75% (to err on the side of caution), we come to the figure of 180,000 to 200,000 Jews who did not yet have British citizenship.[21]

---

[20] Banister, p. 81; *Daily Graphic*, 24/5/1921. Translator's note: QVOS (Banister). & *British Legion*, November 1922; Banister, p. 104. & *Times*, 27/11/1924, p. 13. Translator's note: All QVOS. The *Times* editorial of 8/12/1924 is even more strident on the unacceptability of Jewish non-assimilation and its danger to the British state, e.g.: 'No nation welcomes the settlement within its borders of an alien population, living its own separate life and preserving its own characteristics from generation to generation. No nation can desire that such a population should share in the political system of the country... Men of the same blood and the same creed, who live together and work together, naturally tend to think in the same way; and some of the thoughts, which these men have inherited in the Ghettos of Poland and of the Russian Pale and have brought with them to this country, are not wholesome for the general community or for the State.'

[21] *Times*, 27/11/1924, 28/11, 2/12, 4/12, 8/12 (see also the editorials of 27/11 and 8/12). Translator's note: After the final (fifth) instalment, the series was epilogue in the 16/12 issue by a reply letter from Lord Rothschild, in his capacity as Vice-President of the Board of Deputies, on behalf of British Jews who were unhappy at some of the statements made within the series, in particular raising the strawman of the writer treating the British-born children of alien Jews as aliens, rather than British. Rothschild also alleges that moral and hygiene standards actually 'vastly improved' in the East End after 1881 (!). Interestingly, the *Times* granted their journalist a right of reply to Rothschild's letter within the same issue, in which he masterfully acquits himself of any implication of bigotry or anti-

The government's immigration statistics are unsuitable for our purposes because the tendency is to set the figures for immigration against those for emigration (i.e. to generate a figure for net migration) in the belief that adverse consequences will only arise in the case of a surplus in the former category. This fallacious thinking, which erroneously takes a quantitative rather than a qualitative view of human beings, has already been discussed in a previous chapter and therefore need not be elaborated on further.

Nevertheless, we can use some official figures in the calculation of our estimate. On 25 November 1924, the then-Home Secretary, Sir William Joynson-Hicks, made interesting remarks at a reception for members of the National Citizens Union who had approached him on this matter. According to these remarks, 321,451 foreigners had entered the country in the first nine months of that year, while only 311,576 had left. This meant that 10,000 foreigners remained in the country. According to the documents available to him, 272,862 foreigners were registered with the police, several hundred fewer than in 1922 and 1923.[22]

Here too, with reference to our previous statements in this regard, we have no hesitation in assuming that 75% of these registered foreigners were Jews. Let us also not forget that young people under the age of 16 were not counted.

In 1927, the question of immigration appeared to have been a matter of public interest. At this time, Sir W. Joynson-Hicks was also Home Secretary, and in this capacity informed Parliament on July 14 that 367,000 foreigners had entered Britain, but that nevertheless about the same number had left. At that time, 53,000 foreigners were registered as residents of the country. In 1924, 935 foreigners were naturalized, while the following year saw 1074 naturalizations and in 1926 there were 1345. The Home Secretary viewed the previous year's increase in naturalizations as proof of the groundlessness of the accusations made against him that he was prejudiced against foreigners.[23]

In the summer of 1927, the House of Lords debated a bill which would restrict immigration. The *Annual Register* noted with satisfaction in December of that year that 'the hated immigration restriction bill...had been dropped due to lack of time...'.[24]

We believe that all of the data on the first post-war immigration period [1918-1933] are sufficient to show that our estimate of an increase of 300,000 people had likely already occurred during this time. However, any

---

Semitism, as well as debunking Rothschild's claims. This is also the letter from which Aldag takes his immigration figure above. These well-written and balanced articles are recommended to any student of British social history and inter-community relations.

[22] *Annual Register*, Vol. 166, pp. 125-6.

[23] *Annual Register*, Vol. 169, p. 69.

[24] Annual Register, Vol. 169, pp. 73-126.

remaining doubts about this figure will disappear completely as soon as we present the immigration data for the period after 1933.

As is well known, the migration of Jews from Greater Germany, including Austria and the Sudetenland, largely went to England and France. One only has to take a trip from Germany to England by train or ship to be able to appreciate how many hundreds and thousands of Jews are pouring into the British Isles. The staff of the transport companies concerned give repeated assurances that this is the permanent state of things. One is reminded of the period around 1900, which has been extensively detailed in a previous chapter. Only those who have taken the trouble to observe the traffic in the Jewish aid organizations in London can begin to appreciate just how wide Great Britain has opened its doors to Jews.

Here too it is difficult to obtain official numbers. Even where they are available, we have great reservations about regarding them as accurate. It appears to be a peculiarity of the English that they generally lack organizational talent and as a result struggle to produce impeccable statistics. That said, cases continue to come to public attention in which Jews somehow end up in England having flouted immigration laws. Then there are the marriage agencies that find Englishmen who, for a fixed fee, are willing to wed foreign Jewesses in sham marriages. After the civil wedding, the couple separate and, in most cases, never see each other again, but the Jewess is now a British citizen. It would appear that the authorities are doing everything they can to facilitate Jewish immigration, which may explain their lack of interest in keeping good statistics on the matter.[25]

As always, we need not infer this from the well-known philo-Semitism of the system currently in place in Britain, but from the Hebrews and their friends themselves, who have furnished us with the necessary details. They have an organization called the Jews' Temporary Shelter, which is closely linked to the Home Office. According to reports from the Jews in 1928 and 1929, this organization almost always receives the necessary immigration permit for Jews whose relatives are already in England. We have no reason to believe that relations between Jewish immigrants and the state have not cooled in any way since then. Just recently, a recent Jewish arrival publicly emphasized that 'everywhere...I have found courtesy and kindness and real

---

[25] See, for example, the *Times*, 7/1/1939, p. 9. Translator's note: The article concerned is titled 'Control of Refugee Relief', and after a discussion of the need for a coordinated response to the problem, the article's final paragraph reads: 'Another batch of Jewish refugee children from Germany landed at Harwich yesterday and went by motor-coach to the Dovercourt Bay holiday camp.'

human feeling. Officials at Croydon, at Bow Street, and at the Aliens Department (Stanley House), have been wonderful'.[26]

However, nothing better demonstrates the former Home Secretary Sir Samuel Hoare's willingness to help than the following incident: the chairman of the Aliens Committee, a Mr. H. S. Schildkraut (Order Achei Brith and Shield of Abraham) and Mr. Isaac Landau (United Synagogue) went to see Hoare for a meeting in April 1938 and then expressed his delight at the Home Secretary's warm welcome. Sir Samuel was not only forthcoming, but Schildkraut reported that he 'could not recall any interview with a Minister of the Government which was conducted in such a homely and friendly atmosphere as this one' while Laudau was struck by how Sir Samuel 'expressed real and genuine sorrow at the unhappy lot of these poor people.' Of Sir Samuel's own statements, only one need be mentioned, made in May 1938 during a speech at the Rotary Club conference in Blackpool: 'In accordance with democratic ethics, there is not enough that can be done for the Jews'.[27]

There is very little evidence to support the officially-admitted figures for Jewish immigration. Thus, Sir Samuel Hoare responded to a question in Parliament that from the 1st to the 29th March that year (1938), 1,317 Austrians had been given leave to land in England. There can hardly be any doubt that these were almost exclusively Jews. He did not say how many had arrived from Germany and other parts of Europe. There were certainly at least as many again. At the end of November 1938, Sir Samuel Hoare, in response to a question from a member of Parliament, gave further details about the immigration of the so-called refugees. According to this information, there were 10,974 refugees who had arrived in England since 1933. Of course, it remains unclarified what the basis was for such a classification. It looks as if a number of people whom we consider to be Jewish immigrants were not included in the estimate, because immediately afterwards the Germans were established in the statistics with a total of 21,871 and the so-called Austrians with 16,606. So the total is, as a consequence, 37,877 (not counting the refugee figure). This again does not take people under the age of 16 into account, so another quarter of this sum needs to be added to the total.

After all of this, one can count on there being around 50,000 German citizens, to which the individuals designated as refugees must also be added. In this way, we arrive at a number of around 60,000 people with German citizenship, which, if we apply our previously defined standard of 75%, would make around 45,000 Jews. Anyone who has a reasonable overview of the general situation can only smile at these official figures. Almost every

---

[26] *Jewish Chronicle*, 23/3/1928 p. 29; 12/4/1929 p. 28. & *Jewish Chronicle*, 6/1/1939. Translator's note: QVOS (p. 27). Note that the letter-writer, Hans Pasch, still complained that Woburn House could be more efficient in their processing of claims.

[27] *Jewish Chronicle*, 15/4/1938. Translator's note: QVOS (p. 13). & *Observer*, 8/5/1938.

week, even the English newspapers reported on the arrival of mass transports of Jewish immigrants. The *Daily Express* wrote on 20 October 1938 that the government had approved 150 entry permits for arrivals from Czechoslovakia. On November 1, the same newspaper announced the arrival of the first 34 of 350 'anti-Hitlerites', the remainder of which were to arrive imminently. At the same time the newspaper published a picture showing the arrival of these people, and there should be no doubt that they were exclusively Jews. At the end of November, Sir Samuel Hoare announced in Parliament that an unlimited number of Jewish children should be admitted to England. According to a report in the *Daily Express*, 300 arrived on November 29, and about a week later 1,000 arrived from Vienna, which represented the first transport of a total of 3,000 children that were expected from the city in question.[28]

Contrary to expectations, two English newspapers have provided us with some basis for our estimate. At the end of October 1938, they managed to obtain from the Home Office the latest official figure for the total number of non-naturalized foreigners up until May 1938. Curiously, the figures for all subsequent months are not available. According to this statistic, 196,852 non-naturalized foreigners were registered with the police in England and Wales by the end of that month. One of these newspapers rightly pointed out that, since then, the total must surely have gone up significantly due to the recent political events in Central Europe and that the foreigners in Scotland and Ireland were not included in that figure.[29]

The naturalization figures also speak eloquently about the ever-increasing foreign infiltration and Judaization of the British people. In six months of 1938, namely from March to September, as many foreigners were naturalized as in the entire previous year. Furthermore, in the last two months of 1938 alone, there were at least 130 name changes that took place for Jews adopting an English surname. In this way, all the Abrahams, Isaacs, Levys (etc.) become Morris, Harris, Lewis (etc.), names that 50 years ago allowed a family to be recognized for its English roots.[30]

In light of all of this, we have no doubt that the total Jewish population of Great Britain has increased by 350,000 people since 1914. And in this instance, just as with our first [1914] population estimate, we have not taken

---

[28] *Jewish Chronicle*, 8/4. & 2/12. & *Daily Express*, 22/11. & 13/12; *Daily Telegraph*, 6/12, 8/12.

[29] *Sunday Express*, 23/10/1938; *Daily Mail*, 2/1/1929.

[30] *Sunday Express*, 23/10/1938. & *London Gazette*, 1938, pp. 6856-8226. Translator's note: From the first article of 'Alien London' [*Times*, 27/11/1924]: '...many Jews of recent foreign origin have taken English surnames. Thus in Stepney and Whitechapel such names as Morris, Harris, Cross, Lewis, and Davis are regarded as Jewish unless there is proof to the contrary, and one wonders how many of those who made the change since the war have conformed to the law.'

the excess births into account, despite the fact that this percentage is unlikely to be small. According to their own statistics, the world population of Jews was 13,168,924 in 1914, the year of our first estimate, and 16,113,000 in 1938. According to these figures, an increase of about 20 to 25% took place, which, applied to England and our 1914 estimate, would produce almost the same result even without the subsequent immigration. Therefore, if immigration plus a birth surplus of 30% was used to equal 350,000, we would arrive at a total estimated minimum of 1,200,000. Thus, taking into account the data available for the Dominions and Overseas Possessions, we arrive at around 1,700,000 Jews for the British Empire.[31]

We cannot agree with the estimate made by Leese's movement, the IFL, which puts the number at 2.5 to 3 million for the mother country alone. Nor do we believe that Lord Northcliffe's view, according to which the Jewish population of London was already at 1.5 million in 1919, should be taken too seriously.[32]

The Royal Court and the Nobility

As has already been explained, the extent to which the Hebrews are numerically represented in a country is not the decisive factor, but it is rather their economic, political, and personal influence and the positions of power they create as a result.

In a country where money is everything, it is therefore only too understandable that Jewish wealth was the key that opened all doors in the United Kingdom. Jews also enjoy full social equality and are even welcome at court. Very close to the king there are people of Jewish blood and with close Jewish ties, such as Lord Herschell and Lord Mountbatten. But the court's sympathy towards Jews is also illuminated by other examples.

Thus we hear of the king and queen enjoying a luncheon with Sir Isaac Isaacs, the former Governor-General of Australia, and his wife Lady Isaacs. This attitude of the court was particularly evident during the coronation celebrations of 1937, on the occasion of which the now oft-mentioned Herbert Samuel was raised to the viscountcy and the press magnate Julius Salter Elias was raised to the baronetcy. Louis Saul Sterling, with his great economic influence, and Maurice Block, with his positions in municipal administrations, were knighted. Numerous other honors were also bestowed on other Jews.[33]

At the coronation ceremony in Westminster Abbey, to which only the most select were invited, various Jews were present, including the Chief

---

[31] *Jewish Year Book 1915*, pp. 167 ff. & *Jewish Year Book 1938*, pp. 343 ff.

[32] *The Fascist*, April 1937. Translator's note: This is also confirmed in Macklin, p. 47 [see Translator's Bibliography]. & Clarke, p. 125.

[33] *Jewish Chronicle*, 15/5/1936, p. 10.

Rabbi of England, the President of the Postal Savings Bank and ardent Zionist Leon Simon, Mr. and Mrs. Ben Zvi, and Mr. S. D. Fresco (representing H. M. Exchequer and Audit Department).[34]

At the subsequent festivities at court, Jews were represented in large numbers, some of whom were introduced by fellow Jews, and others by prominent Englishmen. According to the attendance list, the following were presented:

> Miss Ruth Ezra, by her mother Mrs. Alfred Ezra;
> Lady Franklin, by Lady Samuel;
> Mrs. Adrian Franklin, by her mother-in-law Lady Franklin;
> Mrs. Cecil Kahn, by her mother Mrs. Frank Pollitzer;
> Miss Pamela Laski, by Lady Rossmore;
> Mrs. John Makower, by her mother Lady Franklin;
> Lady Mancroft, by Mrs. Stanley Baldwin;
> Mrs. Frank Pollitzer, by Lady Simon;
> The Hon. Renetta Samuel, by her mother Lady Mancroft;
> Miss Clarice Joseph, by Lady Joseph;
> Mrs. Edward Judah, by the Marchioness of Zetland;
> Miss Mathilde Marks, by the Hon. Mrs. Partrick Johnstone;
> Miss Ann Mocatta, by her mother Mrs. Owen Mocatta;
> Miss Daphne Sebag-Montefiore, by Mrs. Vincent Massey;
> Mrs. Alfred Salmon, by Lady Salmon.[35]

The court's later events included the following introductions to the king:

> Lord Mancroft, by Sir George Penny, MP;
> Mr. Montagu Lyons, KC, MP, by the Secretary of State for Air;
> Lieutenant-Colonel Alroy Cohen, by the Colonial Secretary;
> Siegmund Samuel, by the High Commissioner for Canada;
> Mr. Max Seigler, by the High Commissioner for Canada;
> Mr. Aubrey Solomon, by the Colonial Secretary.[36]

On the occasion of a garden party at Buckingham Palace we note, among many other Jews, Sir Philip and Lady Hartog, Lord and Lady Samuel, Mr. Leon Simon and his wife, and Colonel and Mrs. H. L. [Henry Louis] Nathan. Colonel Nathan is currently serving as Chief of National Service.[37]

---

[34] *Jewish Chronicle*, 14/5/1937, p. 8.

[35] *Jewish Chronicle*, 14/5/1937, p. 8-9.

[36] *Jewish Chronicle*, 4/6/1937, p. 11.

[37] *Jewish Chronicle*, 30/7/1937, p. 9

Well-known Jews also socialized with all members of the royal family: at a small dinner hosted by the Princess Royal (the king's sister) and her husband, the Earl of Harewood, one of the highest Freemasons in the country, there were numerous Jews present: Lord and Lady Duveen, Sir Leonard and Lady Franklin, Sir Percy Harris, Alderman and Sheriff Sir Frank and Lady Pollitzer, Mr. and Mrs. Philip Guedalla, and Mr. Humbert Wolfe.[38]

Such incidents are so numerous that it is impossible to mention them all, but the examples listed will suffice for our purposes.

The awarding of medals and other awards to Jews is also not uncommon. Percy Cohen received the insignia of Commander of the British Empire from the king, while Ezekiel Cohen, the Principal Clerk of the Office of the High Commissioner for Basutoland, the Bechuanaland Protectorate and Swaziland, was made a member of the Imperial Service Order. Other Jews who featured in the Royal Birthday Honors List were Rabbi David Isaac Freedman (O.B.E.), Mrs. Zara Baar Aronson (O.B.E.) and Avinoam Yellin (M.B.E.), while the Mayor of Tel Aviv, Meir Dizengoff, saw his existing O.B.E. upgraded to an honorary C.B.E. The Jews did very well again in the New Year Honors list of 1939, with knighthoods bestowed upon Dr. Adolphe Abrahams (Dean of Westminster Hospital), musician Robert Mayer, and Honorary Colonel Benjamin Hansford (a member of the Stock Exchange), while numerous other Jews were decorated with lesser honors. The brother of the aforementioned Dr. Adolphe Abrahams, Sidney Abrahams, is Chief Justice of Ceylon and is also a knight of the realm. These brief examples, which cover a period of two to three years, also serve as examples of how much the Jews are favored by the royal court.[39]

Throughout this study, we have often referred to the ties between the nobility and the Jews in connection with other questions. We shall continue to do so, given its importance in understanding how Jewish power works, but in this section, we shall turn our attention to certain families that might otherwise go unnoticed.

We shall start with Baron William Burnham. We would like to say in advance that the English noble families retain not only their noble names but also their former family names. Thus, Lord Burnham's real name was originally Levy, which he changed to Lawson to make it more English-sounding. His ancestors bought the *Daily Telegraph* in 1855, within months of its founding, which explains why, as the struggle for Jewish emancipation neared its end, this newspaper could not do enough to champion the Jewish cause. A member of this family married Major John Spencer Coke, son of

---

[38] *Jewish Chronicle*, 4/6/1937, p. 11.
[39] *Jewish Chronicle*, 21/2/1936, p. 22. & 26/6/1936, p. 10. & 6/1/1939, p. 13. & *Observer*, 8/1/1939.

the Earl of Leicester, who has been Gentleman Usher to the King since 1937.[40]

We also find Baron Herman Michelham, whose family name is Stern, and Baron Percy de Worms, a barrister. Viscount Erleigh is the son of the current Marquess of Reading, whose family name is Isaacs. We should mention in passing that Lady Reading is active in the current war as head of the Women's Voluntary Services for Civil Defense (WVS). The first posters advertising entry into this organization showed a fresh-faced, blonde girl. Lady Reading, who found this type 'too German', asked for a brunette beauty for her propaganda material.[41]

Barons Philip Montefiore Magnus, Lionel Faudel Phillips, chairman of Faudels Ltd., and Michael Bernard Oppenheimer are also full-blooded Jews. Baron Oppenheimer's wife is a daughter of Sir Robert G. Harvey, while his other daughter is married to Captain Harold Harington Balfour, Member of Parliament and Under-Secretary of State for Air.[42]

Baroness A. Foley is the daughter of the Jew H. Greenstone of South Africa. The mother of the current Baron John Peter Fitzgerald was the Jewess Bischofsheim. His wife, who does not appear to be Jewish, recently made a name for herself when she organized a collection of gold and silver items, named 'Lady Fitzgerald's Jewel Fund.' This initiative appealed to 'every Jew and Jewess' to make 'the Golden Sacrifice', in which their precious items of any description would be turned into Palestinian land for Jewish immigrants (or as one headline read, 'Gold, Silver and Jewels into Land').[43]

The son and heir of the former Foreign Minister Viscount Halifax, who owns no less than 38,400 *Morgen* [24,000 acres], married into the Rothschild family, and the wife of the Marquess of Cholmondeley comes from the oft-cited Sassoon family. The Marquess of Castle Stewart is married to the Jewess Eleanor Guggenheim of New York; the Marquess of Tweeddale, with a 64,000 *Morgen* [40,000-acre] property, is married to a daughter of Lewis Einstein. Barons John Blunt and Thomas Colyer-Fergusson, as well as Viscount Blegisloe, also have Jewish wives, as does Baron Howard de

---

[40] *Who's Who 1939*, p. 451. See also p. 1029 (Faudel-Phillips). & p. 636.

[41] *Who's Who 1939*, p. 2192. & p. 3493. & p. 938.

[42] *Who's Who 1939*, p. 2077. & p. 1029. & p. 140.

[43] *Who's Who 1939*, p. 1069; *Jewish Chronicle*, 14/10/1938, p. 13; 21/10/1938 pp. 15, 22. Translator's note: All QVOS. As might be expected, this highly emotional appeal from the Zionists ('The Jewish people fights with its back to the wall...') resulted in a huge response, particularly from poor Jews who had felt compelled to play their part (unsurprising, with manipulative slogans such as 'Every Jew and Jewess must share in the Golden Sacrifice!' and 'No Jew will refuse in our hour of need.') and could ill afford their donation. As the full-page advertisement in the 14th October issue literally underlined, 'no gift is too humble, no sacrifice too great'.

Walden, who owns almost all of Oxford Street, one of the main shopping streets in London.[44]

This brief overview in conjunction with the earlier and subsequent elements of this study will provide some insight into the Judaization of the nobility, although by no means do we claim this list to be exhaustive. To the persons named must be added all those who descend from these marriages or who are related otherwise to them, and it must be admitted that this is a large number. In addition, we can identify many nobles who have made the Jewish cause their own, and who therefore defend the Jews at every opportunity, but we could not possibly name all of them.

Thus, we find at the banquets of the association of Jewish businessmen, the so-called Maccabeans, among others: Lord Blanesburgh, the Marquess of Hartington, Sir Herbert Samuel, Sir Samuel Gluckstein, and the Master of the Rolls Lord Wright. The dinner for the 'Friends of the Hebrew University' in 1937, hosted by Sir Robert and Lady Mond, was attended by Lord Rutherford, Lord and Lady Hailey and other members of the highest social circles. It is also interesting that Lord Peel, the late chairman of the Palestine Royal Commission, which drew up the partition plan, employed a Jewish woman as his secretary. The former Lord Chancellor Viscount Sankey particularly identifies with the Jewish cause and actively intervenes on their behalf on every possible occasion.

In his presiding role at the lecture given by Dr. Cecil Roth on 'The Jewish Contribution to Civilization' which took place in the Ernst Schiff Memorial hall of the Great Synagogue, Viscount Sankey declared of the Jews: 'We cannot get on without them.' The nephew of the well-known Arthur James Balfour, Viscount Traprain, particularly distinguished himself in his support of the Jewish cause when he offered Whittingehame House for the use of Jewish refugee children, and on the occasion of the huge pro-Jewish rally held in the Royal Albert Hall that became known all over the world, Lord Dunsany sent in a poem that he had written in December 1938, in which he expressed his confidence that Israel's foes would be defeated. The fact that at this meeting the Catholic Cardinal Archbishop of Westminster, Dr. Hinsley, sat on the same platform as the Chief Rabbi requires no further comment.[45]

---

[44] *Who's Who 1939*, pp. 1341, 3474, 2599, 2754. & p. 584. & p. 541. & p. 3237. & pp. 303, 656, 296. & p. 1563. Translator's note: More names of aristocrats with known or suspected Jewish heritage (or marital connections to Jews) can be found in Arnold Leese's *Our Jewish Aristocracy* (1936).

[45] *Jewish Chronicle*, 3/7/1936. & 28/5/1937, p. 9. & 19/11/1937 p. 11. & 17/12/1937 p. 12. Translator's note: The source reports on Sankey agreeing to preside at the upcoming Lucien Wolf Memorial Lecture. & *Jewish Chronicle*, 9/12/1938 p. 13. Translator's note: QVOS. Sankey's remark was his clever wordplay response to those who said (in his words): 'We cannot get on with the Jews.' & *Jewish Chronicle*, 9/12/1938 p. 8. & 9/12/1938 p. 33.

A glance at the list of donors to the various funds for Jewish emigrants best shows the sympathy of the nobility. The same applies to Jewish social events attended by members of the nobility. It is impossible to mention them all. In short, it can only be said that, in case of doubt, virtually every member of the aristocracy must be assumed to be sympathetic to the Jews unless proven otherwise.

Statesmen Sympathetic to Jewish Interests

Given this attitude of the nobility, it should not be difficult to guess the attitude of the House of Lords on Jewish issues. Whenever there are such debates in the Upper House, the Jews find, with no exception, the most ardent support. We have already shown that the main statesmen, even when they were not Jewish, for the most part did not stand in the way of Jewish aspirations and indeed encouraged them in every way.

One only need consider the close ties that Lloyd George always had with the Jews. When, on 19 October 1922, circumstances forced him to resign from his office of Prime Minister, the Jews were inconsolable. The following excerpt is from Lloyd George's own pen, taken from one of the *Daily Telegraph* articles he wrote in 1923 to champion the Zionist cause:[46]

> Of all the bigotries that savage the human temper there is none so stupid as the Anti-Semitic. It has no basis in reason, it is not rooted in faith, it aspires to no ideal—it is just one of those dank and unwholesome weeds that grow in the morass of racial hatred.
>
> How utterly devoid of reason it is may be gathered from the fact that it is almost confined to nations who worship Jewish prophets and apostles, revere the national literature of the Hebrews as the only inspired message delivered by the Deity to mankind, and whose only hope of salvation rests on the precepts and promises of the great teacher of Judah.[47]

---

[46] *Jewish Chronicle*, 27/10/1922, p. 13; 3/11/1922 p. 16. Translator's note: Not only was Lloyd George's political downfall 'keenly regretted' by the Jews in Britain, but even Jews abroad, 'particularly in Eastern Europe' expressed 'genuine sorrow' that their champion had gone (quotations from later issue). Lloyd George's downfall came after his position had been greatly weakened by a scandal which had erupted that summer over the revelation that he had been selling peerages (from 1917-1922 over 120 hereditary peers were created, as well as many knighthoods), with the price list being set at £10,000 for a knighthood and £40,000 for a baronetcy. Research remains to elucidate to what extent the Jews availed themselves of this fire sale of social status and institutional power.

[47] *Daily Telegraph*, 14/7/1923; Banister, p. 115. Translator's note: QVOS.

How much his sympathies lie with the Jews can also be seen from his essay in the April 1937 issue of *The Strand Magazine*, according to which he describes the Jews as the most admirable race that has ever lived on the earth.[48]

Sir Austen Chamberlain (1863-1937), older half-brother of the current Prime Minister Neville Chamberlain, is linked to many damaging measures against Germany. Perhaps unsurprisingly, he was also a great friend of the Hebrews, evidence for which is shown in many sources, including his obituary in the *Jewish Chronicle*. The following is an excerpt from said obituary:

> When the savage Nazi onset came in Germany, his was among the first voices in this country to be raised in indignant protest. Again and again, within Parliament and without, he condemned, in ringing tones, the cruelty and the meanness of the German oppression. And springing from ardent sincerity and carrying all the authority of an eminent leader of British opinion, his burning utterances struck dismay into the hearts of the oppressors as the words of few other public men could have done. Never can the service he thus rendered the Jewish cause be forgotten. His memory will be cherished as that of one of the *Chasidai Oomot Haolam*—a righteous non-Jew who hated wrong and loved the right, and a friend whose name will be written in letters of gold in the tragic pages of Jewish history. Abiding peace be unto him![49]

Former Prime Minister Ramsay MacDonald was also completely under the spell of Judah. According to his former colleague Michael Marcus, himself a Jew, MacDonald considered that 'Zionism without Socialism was unthinkable', just as he was 'genuinely devoted to the Zionist ideal.' Marcus himself was 'often impressed with the fact that MacDonald drew much of his political inspiration from Jewish sources'.[50]

When MacDonald died, the Children of Israel also dedicated an honorable obituary to him, in which they particularly emphasized his services to the Zionist movement. His private secretary was the Jew Rose Rosenberg, and in the *Forward* of 14 October 1922, MacDonald was quoted as saying:[51]

> I have been an unswerving hopeful regarding the Moscow Government... We can now take the Moscow Soviet Com-

---

[48] *Jewish Chronicle*, 26/3/1937, p. 15. Translator's note: The JC source is simply an advertisement for the article, which is titled 'What has the Jew Done?'—it does not quote directly or otherwise indicate the article's contents.
[49] *Jewish Chronicle*, 19/3/1937, p. 12. Translator's note: QVOS.
[50] *Jewish Chronicle*, 9/12/1938. Translator's note: All QVOS.
[51] *Jewish Chronicle*, 19/11/1937.

munist Revolutionary Government under our wing, and clothe it in the furs of apology to shield it from the blasts of criticism.[52]

Ramsay MacDonald's successor, Stanley Baldwin, the current Earl Baldwin of Bewdley, has proven on numerous occasions his embrace of the cause of Judah. When Baldwin resigned the Prime Ministership in 1937, the *Jewish Chronicle* of April 16 of that year dedicated an article full of praise for him, of which the following is an excerpt [QVOS]:

> They [Jews] will honour the man who shunned the ways of the Continental despotisms and in his parting words warned his countrymen solemnly against them. They will see in him the statesman who never hesitated to avow himself a disciple of the Jew, Disraeli—'remember that our party,' he adjured his constituents last week, 'has always stood, in Disraeli's words, for the maintenance of the Constitution.' And they will not forget either the support of Zionism which he offered in company with other famous men when he protested against the watering down of Jewish hopes, or the fact that it was under his Premiership that a blow was struck at pernicious anti-Jewish propaganda in the Metropolis.

This claim is confirmed in the statement made by Baldwin himself, when he made a public speech which referenced 'that great man': 'I have tried to mould my policy, my speeches, and the policy of my party on the principles of Disraeli.'[53]

However, Baldwin gave the best proof of his attitude towards the Hebrews through the establishment of the Lord Baldwin Fund for Refugees. In a radio address of 7 December 1938, which was simultaneously broadcast in the United States, Baldwin made an eloquent appeal to the English nation, an appeal in which he invoked the nation's Christian values, to support the Baldwin Fund as much as possible.[54]

---

[52] Lane, p. VI. Translator's note: Aldag bases his statement regarding Rosenberg on the attribution of Lane's *Forward* quotation to Rosenberg, an understandable error given the ambiguity of Lane's syntax, but having checked, this statement was actually made by MacDonald himself. The fuller quotation above, with attribution, was reproduced from the Hansard record of a speech made by Commander Southby in the House of Commons debate of 2 March 1931, titled 'Grey Seals Protection Bill Lords' (Vol. 249, p. 149). However, weighed in the balance of probabilities, it is highly unlikely that Rosenberg did not share her master's political sympathies.

[53] *Jewish Chronicle*, 15/5/1936 p. 13. Translator's note: QVOS.

[54] *Times*, 9/12/1938 [the radio broadcast transcript is reproduced on p. 16, the *Times* opinion on p. 17], 10/12/1938.

In view of what has been discussed above, we need hardly bring up the former Home Secretary and Lord Privy Seal Sir Samuel Hoare, whom Churchill has since removed from his post as Secretary of State for Air [as a punishment for his support of appeasement], and then effectively exiled with an ambassadorial position in Madrid. Although Sir Samuel only enjoyed his office as aviation minister for a short time, it is significant that one of his department advisors was the Freemason Lord Riverdale, who was known as Arthur Balfour until 1935. This Arthur Balfour was connected to the famous Arthur James Balfour, known for the Balfour Declaration. Hoare also had Harold Harington Balfour as his Undersecretary of State. Hoare's sister-in-law married two Jews in succession, first Sir Michael Oppenheimer and then Sir Ernest Oppenheimer, the leading man in the gold, copper, and diamond industries of Rhodesia and South Africa.

The former Secretary of State for the Colonies William Ormsby-Gore, who has already been mentioned several times, is so much in the Jews' thrall that when he acceded to the aforesaid post, the *Jewish Chronicle* of 5 June 1936 devoted an article to him with the sub-headline: 'Mr. Ormsby-Gore as Champion of Zionism.' The article begins with an epigraph from an earlier edition of the *Jewish Chronicle* (8 October 1920): 'Of the many non-Jews who have championed the Jewish National Cause, none has done so with greater knowledge, steadier purpose, or more passionate zeal than the Hon. W. Ormsby-Gore.'

However, this was not just the typical unctuous flattery from Jews looking to get a politician on side—the article contained many references to the minister's own words, which left no doubt about his personal position on Zionism, as indicated by the following extract:

> [H]e said, in an interview with *The Jewish Chronicle*, that he accepted Zionism as a solution of the Jewish problem, 'firstly, because the Bible continually points to Palestine as Israel's most permanent habitation; and secondly, because local conditions in Palestine demand it.' [...]
>
> Mr. Gore gave further advice, that time has already justified, when he said to the Central London Mizrachi Society in June, 1921: 'The Moslem Nationalist Movement is not merely anti-Jewish, it is also anti-British, and is really anti-Western.' [...]
>
> [H]e made a particularly inspiring speech at the tenth Anniversary Dinner of the Balfour Declaration in 1927. What attracted a Gentile like himself, he said, to assist wherever he could the progress of the Zionist movement, was the thought that from those wonderful hills, from that fascinating country, there had come the greatest forces in history that had made for the ideal side in human nature. The Zionist movement might

produce, not necessarily in the first generation, or even the second or the third, from the soil of Palestine and from the historical race associated with Palestine, the inspiration that would bring healing for the whole of our human family.

Mr. Ormsby-Gore repeated this idealistic note at a dinner of the Anglo-Palestinian Club in 1931. 'Zionist must have its political side,' he admitted, 'but as he saw it the Zionist movement was essentially something which transcended politics and could not be interpreted in purely political terms. It must have a body in Palestine; it must have a basis, but the essence of it was this—the belief that the Jewish people, as a people, still had it in them to contribute to the idealism and the culture and knowledge of the world as Jews, not as English Jews or German Jews or Polish Jews or Sefardim or Ashkenazim, but as Jews.'

As we lack the time and space to detail every pro-Jewish statesman who rose to eminence after the Great War, we must necessarily limit ourselves to a small selection.

Winston Churchill, Prime Minister and at the same time the nation's first Minister of Defense (a self-created position), has never hidden the extent to which his sympathies lie with the Children of Israel. We have already seen his close collaboration with the Hebrews. His zeal has not diminished, as demonstrated by his constant advocacy of their cause in Parliament and in public. With eloquent words, he demanded help and support for 'the Jewish race' in Germany, which was 'being subjected to the most horrible, cold, scientific, brutal persecution—a cold pogrom', and he also drew up his own plan for solving the problems in Palestine:

> His plan was to fix the immigration of Jews into Palestine for ten years at 30,000 to 35,000 a year, a figure which, he calculated, at the end of the ten-year period would not have decisively altered the balance of the population. If the Arabs did not agree to this plan or accept the offer, Mr. Churchill would have us look to the strong armament of the Jewish population.[55]

Today he proves more than ever to be a willing tool of Judah, his stance best shown in the following statement, made during a 1926 speech in the House

---

[55] *Jewish Chronicle*, 27/3/1936 p. 11; 3/9/1937, pp 24-25; 2/12/1938 p. 16. Translator's note: QVOS from the March and December issues.

of Commons: 'Almost continuously in my political life, I have been in friendly, pleasant relations with the Jewish community'.[56]

Neville Chamberlain, who lost his position as Prime Minister to Winston Churchill and then served as Lord President of the Council until his death, is said to have Jewish blood according to Arnold Leese's 'His Majesty's New Sub-Government.' To prove this claim, Leese cites various sources and quotations, none of which we were able to examine. In any case, it is clear that Neville's father Joseph Chamberlain and his stepbrother Sir Austen Chamberlain always supported Jewish interests. Neville, who was the first to propose the settlement of Hebrews in German East Africa, has also repeatedly demonstrated his pro-Jewish orientation.[57]

The former Secretary of State for Foreign Affairs and current Ambassador to the United States, Lord Halifax, whose son and heir, as has been stated, is married to a scion of the House of Rothschild, has demonstrated his loyalty to the Jews so often that it is unnecessary to go into further detail.

The Semitic connections of the former War Secretary, now Foreign Secretary, Anthony Eden—a student of Baldwin—are so obvious to everyone that we need hardly repeat what is known. As the *Evening Standard* of 5 August 1938 reports, Eden is said to be strongly supported in his politics by the so-called Fabian wing of the socialists under the leadership of the Jew Israel Sieff.

The Marquess of Zetland, the former Secretary of State for India whose wife introduced a Jewish woman to the court during the coronation celebrations, also maintains very close ties with the Jews. One of the highest officials in the India Office is the Jew Sir Cecil Kisch, and his advisors are the Jews Sir Henry Strakosh and T. E. Gregory Gugenheim, who is known for his economic publications.[58]

When choosing Zetland's successor, Winston Churchill decided upon the apparatchik of the Conservative Central Office, L. S. Amery, who is said to have Jewish blood. Staunchly anti-appeasement, at a mass protest meeting at the Royal Albert Hall against Germany's anti-Jewish measures, Amery made a vehement speech which went down well with the crowd:[59]

> And the passages which drew the loudest applause—including
> that in the excellent speech of Mr. Amery, who announced

---

[56] *Daily Telegraph*, 19/1/1926. Translator's note: QVOS. Joseph Banister, in Chapter XXIV of his *England Under the Jews* also provides a scathing overview of Churchill's early political career.

[57] *Daily Telegraph*, 22/11/1938.

[58] *Jewish Chronicle*, 14/5/1937, p. 9. & *Jewish Year Book 1937*, p. 457. & *Who's Who 1939*, p. 3071. & p. 1293.

[59] Banister, p. 154. Translator's note: 'Early Life' indicates, with good documentation, that his mother Elisabeth Johanna Saphir (1841-1908) was Hungarian Jewish.

that he represented Conservative Party headquarters—were those which demanded the wider opening to the refugees of the gates of Palestine.[60]

The former education minister Herwald Ramsbotham, now Viscount Soulbury, is married to the fully Jewish Doris Violet de Stein. During his previous stint as Prime Minister, his closest aide was Sir Charles Fraser Adair Hore, Hore-Belisha's stepfather.[61]

Alfred Duff Cooper, Churchill's former Minister of Information and current Chancellor of the Duchy of Lancaster, resigned from his post as First Lord of the Admiralty in protest against the 1938 Munich Agreement. His devotion to Jews is just as notorious as his hatred of Germans. Significantly, the late Jew Otto Kahn of Kuhn, Loeb & Co. was his child's godfather.[62]

Herbrand Sackville, the 9th Earl de la Warr, former President of the Board of Education, and then First Commissioner of Works until October 1940, expressed his feelings in a public speech during a National Labor demonstration in Bradford. In his 1938 speech, he described the Third Reich's treatment of the Jews as 'a defiance of every canon of civiliza-tion...that aroused anger and dismay in every quarter of the globe.' During the Great War he initially refused military service.[63]

Sir Kingsley Wood, who was Lord Privy Seal and more recently Secre-tary of State for Air, now serving as Chancellor of the Exchequer in the Churchill cabinet, publicly praised the Jews' great contributions to the Brit-ish Empire and expressed the hope that Great Britain would always continue to reject racial differences.[64]

As Parliamentary Secretary to the Ministry of Shipping, the Jew Sir Ar-thur Salter is also a member of the Allied Maritime Council to control the use of British and French shipping, which was set up in March 1940.[65]

Sir Edward Grigg, the former Financial Secretary at the War Office, now an Under-Secretary of State for War, is known for his extremely philo-Semitic stance. It was he who repeatedly advocated the incorporation of German East Africa in flagrant violation of the terms of the mandate, just as

---

[60] *Jewish Chronicle*, 9/12/1938, p. 11. Translator's note: QVOS.

[61] *Who's Who 1939*, p. 2633.

[62] Seton Hutchison, p. 3.

[63] *Jewish Chronicle*, 9/12/1938, p. 34. Translator's note: QVOS. Note that this is a sum-mary report of the speech, so the speaker's exact words/phrasing may have differed to those reported. & *Who's Who 1939*, p. 827. *Frankfurter Zeitung*, 28/10/1938.

[64] Query, p. 27.

[65] *Daily Herald*, 27/3/1940. Translator's note: This would be a reprisal of his role in WWI, when he helped establish, and chaired, the Inter-Allied Maritime Transport Council (AMTC).

he repeatedly demanded that Jewish emigrants from Germany be granted special advantages in the colonies.

The president of the Postal Savings Bank is Leon Simon, an ardent Zionist.[66]

Another former cabinet member is Earl Winterton, Chancellor of the Duchy of Lancaster until January 1939, then Lord Treasurer, whose sympathy for the Hebrews is best illustrated by the fact that in his capacity as a government representative he played a leading role in the international conference which took place Evian-Les-Baines whose aim was to resolve the difficulties of Jewish refugees.[67]

After the Great War, there was hardly a cabinet in which full Jews were not represented. In the so-called second coalition government under Lloyd George, Edwin Samuel Montagu was Secretary of State for India. Sir Alfred Mond, the later Lord Melchett, whose family we shall discuss later, was First Commissioner of Works, and then Minister of Health. Sir Rufus Isaacs, later Lord Reading, infamous for the Marconi scandal, went on special government missions abroad and was Viceroy of India from 1921 to 1926.

After the fall of Lloyd George in 1922, we find Sir Arthur Samuel as a senior official in the Treasury and from 1924 onwards the aforementioned Sir Philip Sassoon as Under-Secretary of State for Air, who later held the post of First Commissioner of Works until his death in the summer of 1939.

Under the Labor governments of 1924 and 1929-31 we find the Jewish MP Emanuel Shinwell as Secretary for Mines and the Financial Secretary to the War Office. The Lord Justice of Appeal, Sir Henry Slesser, is also said to be of Jewish heritage. He was Solicitor-General in 1924.[68]

When Sir Hebert Samuel returned from his post as High Commissioner for Palestine in 1925, he was appointed chairman of the Royal Commission on the coal-mining industry (which became known as the Samuel Commission) and played a major role in the General Strike of 1926.

When the so-called National Government was formed in 1931, important positions again fell into Jewish hands. The Marquess of Reading was made Foreign Secretary, Sir Herbert Samuel was made Home Secretary, and Sir Philip Sassoon once again became Under-Secretary of State for Air. During later cabinet reshuffles, the Jew Leslie Hore-Belisha became Minister of Transport, and later rose to the position of Secretary of State for War; he is undoubtedly still remembered for his resignation from this post at the start of 1940. Sir Herbert Samuel later became the Liberal Leader of the Opposition.[69]

---

[66] *Jewish Year Book 1937*, p. 497.

[67] See, for example, *Daily Telegraph*, 5/7/1938, 13/7/1938, 16/7/1938.

[68] *Who's Who 1939*, p. 2939.

[69] *Jewish Year Book 1937*, pp. 361, 371; *Jewish Chronicle*, 24/1/1936, p. 30.

Jews were in the highest places everywhere. We can therefore refrain here from discussing those cabinet members who were part-Jewish or simply Jewish sympathizers in order to give the reader an impression of the direct Hebrew influence over government policy-making.

Given this state of affairs, one will no longer be surprised at Britain's long-standing philo-Semitic politics, which in foreign policy has always meant standing against the measures of the Third Reich and which has ultimately led to war.

With regard to the composition of Churchill's cabinet as it appears at the time of writing (June 1942), it is noteworthy that, in contrast to the long-standing practice of British government circles, today there appears to be no Jewish minister, secretary of state, or under-secretary of state. In view of Churchill's emphatically pro-Jewish stance, one wonders what reasons there might be for this. There can be no avoiding the fact that anti-Semitism is spreading more and more throughout England, as can be seen from the speeches of leading politicians and from the statements made repeatedly in the *Jewish Chronicle*—especially since 1941. Apparently the Jews, especially in view of Britain's difficult military situation, consider it more prudent to stay out of positions of responsibility—on the one hand in order not to provide targets for attack against the Jewish race, and on the other hand also in order to be relieved of all future responsibility if Britain is to be defeated.

The Jewish MPs, especially Leslie Hore-Belisha and Emanuel Shinwell, even often indulge in particularly strong criticism of the Churchill cabinet's activities—so that, in the event of the collapse of the Empire, they can say that they had warned in good time, but no one had listened.

It is evident from the behavior of the Jews that they are already expecting the dissolution of the British Empire and are limiting their direct influence on government primarily to the Empire's prospective heir: the United States of America.

In domestic policy, this preferential treatment of Jews and their friends is clearly shown in the law passed a few years ago, which has since come to be known as the Public Order Act 1936, which in its spirit and purpose is directed exclusively against Sir Oswald Mosley's political movement. The bill was presented in Parliament in response to the alarm caused by the growth of Mosley's party, which was not wrongly attributed to the positive impression that his uniformed supporters made on public opinion. The Act imposed a ban on political uniforms in public and placed significant restrictions on meetings 'of a provocative character' and street marches. The extent to which double standards were applied is demonstrated by the fact that the renting of public halls to fascists for meeting purposes was denied outright, even for events that were supposed to be restricted to party members, while on the other hand the same halls were let out unreservedly to communists and Jews.[70]

Foreign Policy Incidents

In 1919, London heard about Jewish pogroms in Poland. One would probably not be mistaken in assuming that the rumors of large-scale massacres were circulated by the Jews. In any case, the British Foreign Office immediately announced that Britain would withdraw all of her support for Polish aspirations if the persecution did not stop immediately.

Sir Stuart Samuel, notorious for the aforementioned silver purchasing scandal, was commissioned by the British government to investigate the facts on the ground. The *Morning Post* managed to prove, based on reliable sources, that there was not the slightest suggestion of pogroms or mass murders, and that the Jews in question had met their death by misadventure in chance street fights. In an editorial, the *Morning Post* asked the Foreign Office where the false news had originated from and why they had sent such a dubious personage like Sir Stuart on an official mission to Poland. At the same time, it protested against such a biased stance from the Jews, who on this occasion had once again openly shown that they obviously did not feel like they were English.[71]

---

[70] *Jewish Chronicle*, 3/9/1937, p. 48. Translator's note: QVOS. This term 'of a provocative character', which alludes to Section 5 of the Public Order Act, was the key to Jewish groups getting BUF meetings shut down. Section 5 reads as follows: 'Any person who in any public place or at any public meeting uses threatening, abusive or insulting words or behavior with intent to provoke a breach of the peace or whereby a breach of the peace is likely to be occasioned, shall be guilty of an offence.' Given that what could constitute a provocation is subjective, and that provocative language or behavior could itself be maliciously provoked, Section 5 was exploitable by interested parties. Note also that it was the so-called Battle of Cable Street which prompted lawmakers to decide to restrict civil liberties. See Chapter 6 of Lebzelter [Translator's Bibliography].

[71] *Morning Post*, 20/3/1919, 11/4/1919, 30/4/1919. Translator's note: It should be noted that the *Morning Post* was a notorious anti-Communist newspaper around this time, not without reason fearing an imminent 'Judeo-Bolshevik' revolution in England (and the world). The editor, H. A. Gwynne, in his deep study of the *Protocols* and the Jewish involvement in the Russian Revolution, wrote the Introduction to *The Cause of World Unrest* (1920). Although opinions varied as to the cause of the violence in Poland, with anti-Bolshevism, anti-Zionism, economic competition and anti-Semitism variously being given as reasons (depending on the *ethnos* and political persuasion of the judge), there can be no doubt that there was indeed violence against Jews (if not Jews *qua* Jews), and while it was not as bad as some reports suggested, it was definitely more serious than the odd street fight. The disagreements triggered by the conclusions reached in the Morgenthau Report (1919) show just how contentious the interpretation of events in Poland was, and the impossibility of getting all sides to come a semblance of consensus.

However, the most striking example of biased foreign policy took place in February 1938. In Romania, the Goga government had come to power, and its policies, particularly on the Jewish Question, were soon clear to anyone with insight, especially when it prepared legal measures against the Hebrews. Not only the Jews in Romania, but all of international Jewry were alarmed. Thanks to the publication of the Jew Charles Emanuel, we know what usually happens in such cases: an appeal immediately goes out to London. Nor was this case any different. The British and French governments made official protests to the Romanian government, citing the Versailles Minority Treaties of 1919, constituted, as is known, by the Jews. We will never forget how, for example, the *Evening Standard* had posters which announced in huge letters: 'Jews—Britain tells Roumania.' From the reports in English newspapers, the interference of international Jewry was clearly visible: Romanian securities had been allowed to fall on stock exchanges around the world and a silent boycott had already been imposed on the country's economy. The following report from a newspaper's diplomatic correspondent shows that everything was directed from London: 'A person close to the court in Bucharest reported to me that Goga's dismissal was of a most summary nature'.[72]

When Goga was summoned for an audience with the king, he had no idea of his dismissal. The day before, the King [Carol] had received a detailed report from the Governor of the Bank of Romania on the country's financial situation, which had been provoked by the government having the wrong policies. The governor made it clear that the continued oppression of the Jews, who controlled the economic life of the country, would bring about a sudden collapse. Transactions of all kinds and the payment of taxes had come to a halt. King Carol was horrified by these facts, which had previously been withheld from him. His decision to dismiss Goga was accelerated by the fact that the king was influenced by an urgent warning from a place that under no circumstances could he afford to ignore. The warning culminated in the fact that the King's planned visit to London had to be postponed until the situation in Romania had been rectified.

---

[72] See, for example, *Berliner Tageblatt*, 5/1/1938. & *Evening Standard*, 5/1/1938. Translator's note: The article to which the poster so tersely referred carried the headline and sub-headline: 'Britain Tells King Carol of Pledges. Jews' Rights Guaranteed in Post-war Treaty.' & *Evening Standard*, 10/2/1938; *Times*, 12/2/1938. Translator's note: The *Evening Standard* article reports on the Governor of the Bank of Romania's audience with the king, in which he details Romania's dire financial situation. & *Jewish Chronicle*, 24/11/1922. Translator's note: The *Times* of 12/2/1938 (p.12) reports that, on the morning after Goga's dismissal: 'Rumanian Government bonds appreciated by 8 per cent, and industrials reached pre-Goga levels on the exchanges to-day. Buying and selling were brisker than they were six weeks ago.'

As can be seen, nothing has changed since Emanuel's books: international Jewry is at work with the help of their London headquarters.

Jews in the Political Parties and in Parliament

It is necessary to know to what extent the British Parliament is under Jewish influence. A reader who is enlightened about the Jewish Question would probably agree with us from the outset that the number of Hebrews in Parliament is not the decisive factor. Nevertheless, it would be instructive for the reader to have a brief overview of the situation.

After the elections of 1906 and 1910, 16 Jews entered the House of Commons on each occasion. The last general election [1935] brought 18 Jewish representatives into Parliament, namely:[73]

H. Day (Labor),	Sir Isidore Salmon (Conservative, deceased 1941),
D. Frankel (Labor),	Sir A. M. Samuel (Conservative),
L. H. Gluckstein (Conservative),	Marcus Samuel (Conservative),
Sir Percy Harris (Liberal),	Sir Philip Sassoon (Conservative, deceased 1939),
L. Hore-Belisha (National Liberal),	E. Shinwell (Labor),
Dudley Joel (Conservative),	S. Silverman (Labor),
T. Levy (Conservative),	E. A. Straus (National Liberal),
A. M. Lyons, KC (Conservative),	Louis Silkin (Labor)
James de Rothschild (Liberal),	Sir Alfred Lane Beit (Conservative).

This number has now increased by at least two due to by-elections that were made necessary by the resignation of MPs. The Jew Colonel Harry Louis Nathan (Labor) was elected in Wandsworth in 1937 and Daniel L. Lipson (Independent Conservative) in Cheltenham the same year. To these we can probably add Mrs. Jennie Adamson, who entered Parliament in 1938, and of whom, unlike the previous cases, we are not totally sure whether she is Jewish. But in any case, she is very active in supporting Jewish interests and speaks at Zionist meetings.[74]

There is no doubt that there are more full- and half-Jews in Parliament, but their total number cannot be determined with sufficient certainty, given that our best sources of authority, the *Jewish Chronicle* and the *Jewish Year Book*, list only denominational Jews. However, in the interest of ensuring a

---

[73] *Jewish Chronicle*, 24/11/1922 p. 10.

[74] *Jewish Chronicle*, 7/5/1936. Translator's note: He was later made a hereditary peer, becoming Baron Nathan in 1940. & *Jewish Chronicle*, 3/9/1936. & 25/11/1938, pp. 31, 44. Translator's note: I was unable to find information from the reference provided. In any case, there is no extant evidence to indicate that Jennie Adamson was Jewish. However, she was Scottish, and given that Scots and Jews have practically identical political tendencies within the Westminster system (as anyone who remembers the New Labor years will attest), the suspicion on Aldag's part is understandable.

scientific study, we must refuse to base our assertions on assumptions, even though these are usually well-founded when it comes to the Jewish Question.

What is certain is that the number of Jews in Parliament is completely out of proportion to the Jewish population, but is, nevertheless, smaller than could be expected. Even so, these Hebrews exert a disproportionately large, direct influence. We need not speak of Hore-Belisha, who has since resigned from his post of Secretary of State for War. Thomas Levy was chairman of the Textiles Committee in the House of Commons. Although Lewis Silkin does not serve as a chairman on a parliamentary committee, he does chair the Housing and Public Health Committee of London County Council. Perhaps the most important committee in Parliament is the Select Committee on Estimates, which deals with the most secret matters of state and has to prepare not only budget estimates, but also proposals for the use of funds to be spent in the public interest. Until his death in 1941, the chairman of this committee was the Jew Sir Isidore Salmon. Salmon was closely linked with J. Lyons & Co. Ltd., the British restaurant chain, food manufacturing and hotel conglomerate, over the years holding various positions within the company as director, managing director, and chairman. Because of this corporate catering background, he also held the office of honorary catering advisor to the British Army, to advise on troop provisions, which, as a military supplier himself, he had an all too understandable interest.[75]

In any case, it appears that the Jewish cause in the British Parliament is in excellent hands with the non-Jewish MPs who are allies. Here, too, it would be impossible to name all of the representatives in question and all of the pertinent facts. A study of the debates on Jewish issues in Parliament, particularly in recent years, shows that almost all MPs, regardless of party, are united in protecting Jewish interests. How far this goes can be seen in a news article from the *Jewish Chronicle* of 18 November 1938, according to which Colonel Josiah Wedgwood tabled the following amendment to the Address in reply to the Speech from the Throne: 'But humbly regrets that in view of what has happened in Germany during the last week, H. M. Government has not yet seen fit to allow the Jewish refugees from Germany increased facilities to go to Palestine during the next six months.' In half an hour, signatures were collected from about 35 MPs on the move, and those members of Parliament who refused to sign 'refused generally because they thought "Palestine" should be replaced by "British Empire".' So this latter category are those members who are even more pro-Jewish and for whom immigration to Palestine alone is not enough.

---

[75] *Jewish Year Book 1937*, p. 466; *Who's Who 1939*, p. 1883. & p. 2913. Translator's note: Wikipedia informs us that as a backbencher, he introduced a bill to reform the firearms laws, which eventually became the Firearms Act 1934. He became Baron Silkin in 1950. & *Daily Express*, 1/11/1938.

We wish only to highlight a few of the non-Jewish MPs from the rest because of their special, constant championing of the Hebrew cause, and Colonel Wedgwood is at the forefront of all pro-Jewish actions inside and outside of Parliament. According to the magazine *Jewry Über Alles* of March 1923, he was even made an honorary member of the Zionists, which may well be true, especially given that in 1922 he went to America to collect money for the Zionist cause, and was greatly fêted by the Jews on his return. Another MP, Commander Locker-Lampson, is also known for his active advocacy for the Children of Israel. In April 1938 he made a name for himself because of his proposed law, titled the 'Jewish Citizenship Bill', which proposed to offer every Jew in the world citizenship in Palestine. Since Palestine is a mandated territory of Great Britain, anyone with such citizenship would automatically enjoy the protection of England.[76]

The general attitude of parliamentarians can also be seen from the fact that leading MP Hugh Dalton, who under Churchill became Minister of Economic Warfare, publicly declared: 'In quality of citizenship, the British Jew is worthier and finer than the British Fascist.' The member of Parliament Beverley Baxter recalled how, while he was still a parliamentary candidate and brought before the Conservative Executive Committee, he was asked whether he was Jewish. He replied: 'I have not the honor to belong to that great race.' These words drew warm applause from those present. The *Jewish Chronicle* then went on to report on the rest of his answer:[77]

> There was one institution in this country which stood solidly as the friend of the Jewish race and that was His Majesty's House of Commons. He prophesied that the time would never come in this country when the Jewish people, who had enriched the life of the country to such an extent, would be challenged. But if there should come a suggestion of a challenge, he promised them that in the very seat of power in this country it would be suppressed like the festering evil thing it was.[78]

We do not think that we have been too harsh in our judgment of Parliament. Given these circumstances, one can also see why all of the political parties would be loyal to the Jews.

The Liberal Party, as we have already shown, has been in thrall to the Jews for a long time. As of the time of writing, it has only a few representa-

---

[76] *Morning Post*, 7/10/1922. & *Jewish Chronicle*, 19/3/1937, 28/10/1938, 2/12/1938. & 15/4/1938 p. 16. Translator's note: As we have seen, the enactment of this law has since come to pass for the land of Palestine, if under Israeli rule rather than British, with the Law of Return (1950).

[77] *Jewish Chronicle*, 25/12/1936, p. 13. Translator's note: QVOS.

[78] *Jewish Chronicle*, 15/5/1936. Translator's note: QVOS.

tives in the Commons. Nevertheless, as has already been stated, we can identify four Jews among them. For this reason, during a by-election in 1923, the Jews of East Willesden are called on to vote for the Liberal candidate Johnstone 'who will look after the Jewish Interests' with the same advertisement reproducing an extract from Johnstone's election address: 'Our duty no less than our vital interests, demands the fulfilment of our Mandate in regard to Palestine.'[79]

We have also already learned how the main founder of the Labor Party, Ramsay MacDonald, felt about the Jews. His former colleagues were just as zealous on Jewish issues, for which the Jews repeatedly showed their gratitude, and who at times signaled their close solidarity with the Marxist workers' party. The aforementioned MP Henry Slesser is said to have made a point of emphasizing that the Labor party was not socialist, but Jewish. Meanwhile, the party itself was keen to show the Jews that it was the party best suited to defending Jewish interests, something which it demonstrated repeatedly. At the end of 1938, for example, the Labor Party tabled the following motion:[80]

> That this House notes with profound concern the deplorable treatment suffered by certain racial, religious, and political minorities in Europe and, in view of the growing gravity of the refugee problem, would welcome an immediate concerted effort amongst the nations, including the United States of America, to secure a common policy.[81]

---

[79] *Jewish Year Book 1937*, pp. 443, 478, 488, 504. & *Jewish Chronicle*, 2/3/1923; Banister, p. 87. Translator's note: QVOS (JC). Amusingly, right next to the advertisement in which these elements appear, there is an election advertisement for the Conservative candidate, whose pitch to Jewish voters states bluntly (and mostly in all caps, unlike his rival's advert): 'THE LIBERAL CANDIDATE STATES THAT HE WILL FURTHER JEWISH INTERESTS!!! HOW CAN HE? HIS DIMINUTIVE PARTY ARE NOT EVEN IN POWER. THE BEST THING THE JEWISH ELECTORS CAN DO IS VOTE FOR STANLEY. Conservatives have always furthered Jewish interests.' Amusement aside, both advertisements highlight the fact that Jewish voters appear(ed) to vote based on their own ethnic group's particular interests, rather than on the best interests of Britain as a whole.

[80] *Jewish Chronicle*, 29/9/1922, 16; 14/12/1923 p. 5. & *Morning Post*, 28/7/1923; Banister, p. 13. & *Jewish Chronicle*, 30/11/1923. Bannister, p. 125. Translator's note: The JC reference must refer to the open letter on page eight of this issue, written by Labor officials, which lists how the Labor Party supports various Jewish interests, e.g. recognizing the Jewish National Home in Palestine, working to combat anti-Semitism, condemnation of cordial foreign relations with Russia, championing of rights of oppressed minorities globally, fighting in Parliament to ensure aliens get the same unemployment and pension benefits as 'Britishers', etc.

[81] *Jewish Chronicle*, 18/11/1938. Translator's note: QVOS. Note that Aldag did not detail this motion, which has been included here in the interests of historical accuracy.

A little later, the leader of this party, Major Attlee, insisted on speaking at a protest meeting in the same spirit—the same Mr. Attlee whom Churchill brought into his war cabinet and under whose leadership the Labour faction of Parliament became one of the Great Britain's most rabid warmongering groups.[82]

But the Conservative Party, which currently has the majority in the House of Commons, is also completely loyal to the Jews. The Jewish domination of the party is most clearly seen by the fact that there are a disproportionate number of Jews in Central Office, the party's executive headquarters. A nice little anecdote in this regard tells of a general who visited the office in question and was met by a Jew, to whom he explained that 'he would never bring his matter to a Jew.' On saying these words, he handed the Jew his card and asked to speak to an Englishman. It is not known whether he was successful. However, it is clear that the Jews, today just as in the past, hold leading positions in the Tory Party's central administration, which has great influence in the nomination of candidates and other important matters. Lord Jessel used to be the party's treasurer. Today the most powerful man is Sir Albert Clavering, son of Isaac Abraham Clozenburg, an Eastern European Jew who in 1920 changed his original name to that of Clavering.[83]

Another Jew, Percy Cohen, is Head of the Library and Information Department, and was honored by the king the 1936 New Year Honors List. Recent publications show the extent to which the Conservative Party has succumbed to the main principle of Judaism, namely the pure principle of money. According to these sources, each individual electoral seat is put up for bid and literally sold during elections. For constituencies in which one can count on a Conservative victory and thus the election of the candidate in question, the candidate must make large amounts of money available. He must also pay the election costs, which range anywhere from £400 to £1,200, and at the same time pay between £500-£1,000 annually to the local Conservative Association. Candidates who are only able to raise at least half of the electoral expenses required and who can only contribute £250-£400 annually to the Association are put forward where the electoral prospects promise much less success, and those who can contribute nothing to the election costs and only £100 to the party coffers are unlikely ever to get into Parliament.[84]

Furthermore, as an election advertisement for the well-known MP Colonel Stanley shows, the Conservatives proudly state that they have always supported the Hebrews. This election advertisement is addressed to the

---

[82] *Jewish Chronicle*, 13/1/1939 p. 25.

[83] *British Guardian*, September 1924. & *National Citizen*, February 1937.

[84] *Jewish Year Book 1937*, pp. 388, 417; *Who's Who 1939*, p. 635. & *Evening Standard*, 4/1/1939. Translator's note: All of the figures given and allegations made are verified in the top story of this issue, which came from a prospective Tory candidate-turned-whistleblower.

Jews and points out that only Colonel Stanley from the well-known Derby family is a suitable candidate for them, since 'Conservatives have always furthered Jewish interests.' Truly a worthy successor to Hore-Belisha, even if the latter soon lost his War Minister post under Winston Churchill to Anthony Eden![85]

Now we shall give a brief outline of how much the upper class in England are subordinate to the money principle.

It had long been known that honors and titles were being bestowed according to the amount of money that was being paid in certain places. On 6 March 1919, an article appeared in the *Morning Post* with the headline: 'Democracy and Corruption.' The article made reference to debates in the House of Lords, through which the public finally learned how a noble title could be bought through donations to party coffers. The *Morning Post* expressed its deepest disgust at such behavior. All respect for England's highest honors had disappeared, and it could not be described as anything other than corruption and secret bribery.

Even today, it is said that nothing has changed, and one can judge to what extent the Jew has taken advantage of such circumstances. In a recently published book, Ramsey MacDonald is accused of having a certain individual raised to the baronetcy on the basis of certain donations, and Belloc also speaks out against such evil in one of his latest books.[86]

In this book, Belloc highlights the corruption of Parliament. Of course, he is not surprised that the public tacitly tolerates this, since the traditional British mentality sees nothing criminal in it. Unfortunately, Belloc did not provide us with any precise information about the nature of the corruption.

In addition, the fact that many members of Parliament are also directors of companies is likely to constitute corruption in a broader sense. In 1912 we are told that 25 MPs were already acting as directors for 41 public companies and 10 were acting in the same capacity for railway companies. Apparently this has become the norm today. As Lt. Col. Lane outlines in his book, *The Alien Menace* (1934), in the Parliament of 1924-1925 no fewer than 694 companies were represented by 766 directors. The Parliament of 1932 had 691 members and the 1934 Parliament had 581 members, representing 646 and 546 companies respectively. Lane rightly denounced this situation and

---

[85] *Jewish Chronicle*, 2/3/1923. Translator's note: QVOS. See Footnote 574 for more details on this advertisement.

[86] *Jewish Chronicle*, 9/12/1938, p. 32; MacNeill Weir, p. 160. Translator's note: According to the JC, the individual concerned, who had been raised to the baronetcy, was biscuit-tycoon Sir Alexander Grant, a Scotsman like MacDonald. MacNeill Weir's accusation was based on the 30,000 biscuit shares and Daimler motor car that Grant had gifted MacDonald prior to the baronetcy, although in MacDonald's defense it was revealed by Sir Laming Worthington-Evans that Grant had been recommended for the baronetcy by the previous Conservative government. & Belloc: *Contemporary England*, p. 70 ff.

argued that Parliament had come to represent only the special interests of commerce and finance, which were in turn controlled by Jews (as we shall endeavor to prove below):[87]

> Ex-Cabinet Ministers and ex-Civil Servants have obtained very lucrative appointments in the City, especially in firms dominated by Aliens. The business relations of these Alien-controlled concerns with Governments are now so constant and important that it is obviously a distinct advantage for these concerns to have leading politicians and ex-Civil Servants on their Boards of Directors, or as advisors.
>
> In this way, much valuable information may be gained and many useful concessions obtained. This is no doubt the explanation of how Aliens, who control large companies and combines, have, especially during the last decade, exercised a sinister power on the governments of this country. These Aliens move in all circles —social, political, and diplomatic. They find out which of our leading men or rising politicians are pressed for money, and, gradually approaching them, offer them jobs or directorships. [...]
>
> It is no secret that some of our leading men who have been in Parliament for years have been subsidized directly or indirectly by Aliens, from the time they entered the House of Commons and in some cases before that time, for no ostensible reason. This, to a great extent, explains the extraordinary happenings so markedly evident, especially during the past decade, which have so puzzled those who take an intelligent interest in the affairs of our unfortunate country.[88]

One can imagine how such commitments determine the attitudes and positions of these members of Parliament. A member of Parliament who is also a company director is at least indirectly influenced in his decisions because, in his own interest, he cannot go against the interests of his company. Lane later calls attention to the inherent danger in trying to serve two masters, and particularly to the fact that the MP who has tailored his lifestyle to the increased income from his directorships will later be unable to turn back, leading him to become ever more dependent on the real directors of these companies. Lane also describes it as dangerous for healthy government that

---

[87] *Hansard*, Vol. 43, p. 1721.
[88] Lane, pp. 137-9. Translator's note: QVOS. Note that 'alien' was the euphemism of the time for 'Jew.'

ministers and other high-ranking officials accept City directorships after their term in office.

Consider, for example, the recent case of Maurice Hankey, who for almost twenty years held the post of Cabinet Secretary, one of the most important positions in the British state structure; on his resignation in 1938, he became a director of the Suez Canal Company. Furthermore, the rumors persist that he too is a Jew or of Jewish blood, and it is therefore unsurprising that Churchill chose him for his new cabinet.[89]

Jews in State Bureaucracy and Law

In this section, we will endeavor to give the reader a brief impression of the Judaization of public administration and the judicial system.

The Judaization is most evident in the municipal administration of Greater London, known as London County Council. Sir Percy Simmons has held high positions within the LCC for years. He was a councilor from 1910-1919, then chairman of the London County Council in 1921-22, chairman of the Fire Brigade for five years, chairman of the Public Control Company for three years, chairman of the General Purposes Committee for two years, chairman of the Theatre and Music Hall Committee for four years, and chairman of the Improvement Committee for seven years. As we have said, in 1922 Sir Percy held the extremely important post of chairman of the London County Council. For the following two years, this position was not occupied by a Jew, but the deputies were Jews, namely Nettie Adler and Sir Isidore Salmon, the latter being, until his death, chairman of other committees and institutions in addition to his aforementioned position in Parliament.

As early as 1925, however, there was once again a Jewish LCC chairman in the person of Sir Oscar Warburg. He also held many other important positions in the administration, as did Sir Max Bonn. Sir Samuel Joseph was a councilor and sheriff of London. At the same time, he was twice elected mayor of the London borough of Marylebone. Sir Philip Henriques held high positions in the City of London, and during the Great War he was in the Ministry of Munitions. Sir Frank Pollitzer was a councilor and sheriff of London, while George Heilbuth was mayor and deputy mayor of Westminster, as well as chairman of countless committees and other bodies. A. Instone was formerly active in the intelligence service of the General Staff and was later mayor of the London borough of Paddington and a city councilor. Isidore Jacobs previously held the offices of sheriff and alderman in the City of London. Santo Jeger served as Justice of the Peace and later as mayor of Shoreditch, with Councilor J. Abrahams as his deputy, who succeeded him

---

[89] *Who's Who 1939*, p. 1369. & *Jewry Über Alles*, August 1922, September 1923; *Sunday Express*, 25/6/1922.

the following year. The barrister Frederick Levy held high positions in the LCC administration, and Louis Lewis was mayor of the suburb of Islington. Marcus Lipton and J. Somper were also in the London administration, the latter as mayor of Stepney, a borough of the capital. Mrs. H. L. Nathan held important positions in Greater London, the solicitor A. Samuels was (among others things) chairman of the Public Control Committee of London County Council, M. Streimer (among other things) was mayor of West Ham, Mrs. Helena Roberts, mayor of Stepney and John Genese, mayor of Hackney. Finally, there is the barrister Jacques Abady, who, among other things, was mayor of Westminster. In the London County Council elections of 1937, 12 of the 16 Jewish candidates were successful.[90]

The individuals mentioned represent only a small selection of Jews who held high positions in Greater London after the Great War. By no means can we claim that the list is exhaustive, especially since, in view of our aim to use only completely impeccable sources, only religious Jews are included in the above compilation.

Judaism can also be seen everywhere else in the British administrative structure. Thus, for example, Sir Ewart Levy was High Sheriff of Leicestershire. In addition to being the mayor of Richmond, Norton Courlander held other high administrative positions. J. Goldston was twice mayor of Stockton and H. Howitt was twice mayor of Richmond. Julius Jacobs held high positions in Liverpool, likewise R. Levy in Glasgow. D. Lipson and B. Marks were the mayors of Cheltenham and Hove respectively and also held other important offices. Montagu Lyons is Recorder of Grimsby, and Samuel Morris is the mayor of Doncaster.[91]

We also found and still find Jews in high positions in the government ministries, such as Colonel Charles Cohen in the Colonial Office, Sir A. Green in the India Office, Albert Hyamson in the Colonial Office, and H. Infield in the erstwhile Commission for the Upper Silesia Plebiscite. Louis Infield was Assistant Secretary in the Ministry of Health and vice-chairman of the International Committee of Enquiry under the Spa Protocol in the

---

[90] *JWB37*, p. 497; *WW39*, p. 1915. & *JWB37*, p. 400; *WW39*, p. 23. & *JWB37*, p. 490; *WW39*, p. 2806. & *JWB37*, p. 509; *WW39*, p. 3489. & *JWB37*, p. 409; *WW39*, p. 316. & *JWB37*, p. 455; *WW39*, pp. 1710-1. & *JWB37*, p. 444; *WW39*, p. 1463. & *JWB37*, p. 482; *WW39*, p. 2556. & *JWB37*, p. 443; *WW39*, p. 1448. & *JWB37*, p. 449. & *JWB37*, p. 451. & *JWB37*, p. 453. & *Jewish Chronicle*, 12/11/1937, 11/11/1938. & *JWB37*, p. 464. & *JWB37*, p. 466. & *JWB37*, pp. 467, 501. & *JWB37*, p. 478. & *JWB37*, p. 492. & *JWB37*, p. 505. & *JWB37*, p. 387. & *JWB37*, p. 434. & *JWB37*, p. 398; *WW39*, p. 1. & *Jewish Chronicle*, 3/9/1937 p. 49. Translator's note: Incidentally, three out of the twelve new councilors were already serving MPs, which speaks to the consolidation of power within certain individuals.
[91] *JWB37*, p. 465; *WW39*, p. 1882. & *JWB37*, p. 419. & *JWB37*, p. 437. & *JWB37*, p. 447. & *JWB37*, p. 452. & *JWB37*, p. 465. & *JWB37*, pp. 467, 470. & *Jewish Chronicle*, 4/6/1937. & 3/9/1937.

Ruhr. Meanwhile, Reuben Kelf-Cohen is in the Board of Trade, B. Kisch and H. M. Kisch in the India Office, and Sir Matthew Nathan in the Colonial Office. This list too could be expanded considerably.[92]

The influence of Jews in semi-official institutions is also notable. Sir Eliot de Pas was chairman of the West India Committee from 1928 to 1936, and Baron Mancroft of Mancroft was a member or chairman of so many similar bodies that it is impossible to name them. A glance at the corresponding entry in *Who's Who* is sufficient to confirm this. The same can be said about Baron Hugo Hirst, who, among his other influential committee roles, until recently served as President of the Federation of British Industries. Last year he received the special distinction of being appointed alongside four other major industrialists to a committee that advises the government on rearmament. Baron George May, a non-Jew but married to a Jew, has been the chairman of the Import Duties Advisory Committee since 1932. Until 1931 he was director of the British Overseas Bank. Finally, we must not forget Saul Doffmann, the former president of the Northampton Chamber of Commerce, nor Sir Benjamin Drage, who did much work for the Imperial Institute.[93]

With our experience of how they were in Germany, Austria, etc., it should not be surprising that the Jews also exert a considerable influence in the English judicial sphere. We are already familiar with the level of power they generally gain as a result, and this is increasingly the case in England. There has probably never been a country in all of history in which lawyers play as big a role as they do in England. The very wording of the laws and the arcane procedural language is so completely different to ordinary language that many English people, perhaps most of them, find themselves helpless when it comes to drafting even the smallest contracts. Lawyers have to be present everywhere, and one cannot help but get the sense that they themselves were the ones who deliberately brought about this state of affairs over the centuries. As Belloc describes the situation:

> Be it remarked that one factor in the particular case of the English Aristocratic State is the exceedingly powerful lawyers' corporation.
>
> In all ancient European States the legal profession plays a great part: we know the part it played for instance in the old

---

[92] *JWB37*, p. 412; *WW39*, p. 633. & *JWB37*, p. 440; *WW39*, p. 1278. & *JWB37*, p. 448; *WW39*, p. 1614. & *JWB37*, p. 449. & *JWB37*, p. 449. & *JWB37*, p. 456. & *JWB37*, p. 457; *WW39*, p. 1784. & *WW39*, p. 2326.

[93] *JWB37*, p. 421. *WW39*, p. 838. & *WW39*, pp. 2093-4; *Jewish Chronicle*, 5/3/1937. & *WW39*, p. 1503; *Daily Express*, 18/11/1938; *Daily Telegraph*, 12/11/1938; *Evening Standard*, 21/12/1938. & *WW39*, p. 2159. & *JWB37*, p. 422.

French monarchy. But in England it plays a far greater part
than in any other. The Bar is one of the chief modes of entry
into the governing class for men not born into that class. Opportunities for enormous earnings, on a scale quite different
from what may be found in any other country, are open to the
English Lawyers' Guild. Every member of the Bar who is
elected to Parliament and remains there for more than quite a
brief period has a prescriptive right to live off the taxes when
he retires. There are innumerable posts kept for them, varying
in income (paid by the tax-payer) from £1,500 or £1,800 to
£20,000 a year. All the higher magistracy —and all the lower
magistracy except the petty jurisdiction of the village
squires—is drawn from members of the Bar

Since it is a further mark of the Aristocratic State that in
it there is no separation of powers, and that the Judiciary can
and does act on occasion as a part of the executive, the active
political force of the lawyers is far greater in England than in
any other country.[94]

Even if we limit ourselves only to religious Jews, we find a great number of them among the best-known barristers and solicitors. Among the former we note the following Jews: H. M. Abrahams, A. H. Berman, Sir Benjamin Cohen, G. Cohen, Sir Herbert Cohen, Dr. Samuel Daiches, Percy de
Worms, A. S. Diamond, Sir Leonard Franklin, Adolph Langdon, Sir George
Leon, Sir Daniel Levy, Cyril Moses Picciotto, W. Summerfield, G. Webber,
Sir Percy Harris, Philip Vos and R. F. Levy. Langdon holds important positions as the treasurer of the Inner Temple and the director of a legal seminary. G. Webber is known for his articles on administrative issues and international law, which are published in the legal periodicals *Law Times* and
Law Journal; W. Summerfield and Cyril Moses Picciotto are known for
their publication of legal textbooks. One only need look at the list of barristers' names to know how many Jews there are, even though it must be borne
in mind that many have already disguised themselves with the adoption of
traditional English surnames. Nevertheless one finds nine Levys, Levinsons,
or other variants which denote this priestly caste, and 17 Cohen or Cohn, to
cite just two examples.[95]

---

[94] Belloc: *Contemporary England*, pp. 34-5. Translator's note: QVOS.
[95] *JWB37*, pp. 398-511. & *JWB37*, p. 443; *WW39*, p. 1395. & *Jewish Chronicle*, 3/9/1937.
& *JWB37*, p. 459; *WW39*, p. 1823. & *JWB37*, p. 511, 505; *Jewish Chronicle*, 8/4/1938. &
The Law List 1938, pp. 56-7, 162-3. Translator's note: One can surmise that it is because
Cohen and Levy are high-status (priestly caste) surnames within Judaism that there was
more reluctance to disguise Jewish origin in those bearing those names, as evidently a
cost-benefit analysis must have pointed to an overall greater benefit to be gained from

The same can be seen in the list of London solicitors where, for example, there are 15 Cohens and the eight Levys (including variants of this surname). Sir Percy Simmons and Sir George Lewis belong to the law firms Simmons & Simmons and Lewis & Lewis, which are among the most important in Great Britain.[96]

The above overview has hopefully given the reader a certain knowledge of the Judaization or Jewish influence in politics, government administration and legal circles. In finance and economics, art and science, education and the press, the picture is the same everywhere. There is almost no aspect of English life in which the Jew is not dominant, and in which we do not find Jewish interests at the heart of everything.

Coal, Metals, Shipping, Petroleum

There are, above all else, certain Jewish families whose power and influence extend far beyond the confines of England.

We shall start with the Mond family, now the family of Lord Melchett, whose founder, Ludwig Mond, emigrated from Hesse to England in 1866 as a poor chemist. As the inventor of a certain soda process, he soon had a large factory to exploit his invention. He soon became one of the largest industrialists in England and held numerous positions. The writer Hector Bolitho, in his hagiographic profile of Mond, claimed that: 'For his workmen he had understanding and compassion.' This view should be considered in light of the following anecdotes, which Bolitho gives in the same text:

> He was humane without being sentimental. When a workman suddenly fell at his feet from a great height, Ludwig bent over him and said, 'My poor man, are you hurt?' The man stood up and said, 'No.' 'Then get on with your work' was Ludwig's only comment as he walked away. [...]
>
> Once, with a twinkle in his eye, he had said, in discussing some new machinery, that the machinery would cost two thousand pounds. 'When machinery wears out, I must replace it at great cost. But if six men wear out, I can sack them and get new ones'.[97]

We cannot share Bolitho's view, but instead take Ludwig Mond's words at face value, especially as they confirm the Jews' exploitation of working peo-

---

broadcasting high social status (and presumably intellectual status) within Judaism, over the risk of broadcasting Jewish origin.

[96] *The Law List 1938*, pp. 502-3, 603. & *JWB37*, pp. 497, 465.

[97] Bolitho: *Twelve Jews*, pp. 155-175. Translator's note: All QVOS (pp. 168, 165, 169 respectively).

ple, an exploitation which we thoroughly condemn. In 1909 Ludwig Mond died. His second son Alfred, who was swept into Parliament on the Liberal tide of 1906, who was appointed Minister of Health in 1922 and then raised to the Peerage in 1928, took the family's worldly success into the political realm.[98]

Some people who knew Alfred Mond described him as 'a cruel man.' Be that as it may, he ruthlessly expanded the power he had inherited from his father. In 1923, he founded the Amalgamated Anthracite Collieries, thereby gradually consolidating almost the entire coal mining industry in Wales, so that in his capacity as chairman of this group he came to control 85% of the coal in Wales. He also had extraordinary influence in the nickel industry.[99]

He was a director of the British Dyes Corporation, which rationalized a large part of the dye industry. In 1927 he managed to combine almost all British chemical factories into one group under the name Imperial Chemical Industries (ICI). The stamp duty on the founding agreement alone amounted to one million pounds. Thus one can imagine the power that Lord Melchett represented.

In his later years, he became an ardent Zionist and visited Palestine. During his stay there, Alfred Mond no longer saw himself as an English statesman, nor as a captain of industry. 'I do not consider myself as an Englishman. I am a Palestinian... my heart is in Eretz-Israel.' As he walked towards Tiberias after a visit to Migdal to meet some Jews who had gathered there to meet him, he turned to one of his companions and said, 'These are my people. This is my electorate. These are my people'.[100]

After his return from Palestine, he 'forced the cause of Zionism upon the officials.' He tried with all means at his disposal to get the British government to accede to his plans for the colonization of Palestine, but they were apparently suspicious of his fanatical zeal and strove to evade his pressure. He was gradually entrusted with the highest positions in Jewish organizations, becoming President of the English Zionist Federation, then Joint Chairman of the Council of the Jewish Agency, the body recognized by the League of Nations as being directly responsible for the progress of Zionism.

In 1929, he used all his arts of persuasion and influence to dissuade Lord Beaverbrook from his press campaign in the *Daily Express,* a newspaper which had almost the highest circulation figures in Great Britain. At that time, Lord Beaverbrook was still strongly opposed to the government's policy in Palestine. When in October 1930 the Zionists felt that the cause of the Jews there was not being promoted vigorously enough, they accused Alfred

---

[98] Bolitho: *Alfred Mond*, pp. 127, 146, 148.
[99] Bolitho: *Alfred Mond*, p. 364. Translator's note: QVOS. & pp. 244-5.
[100] Bolitho: *Alfred Mond*, pp. 327, 357, 359. & pp. 362-66. Translator's note: QVOS (p. 263).

Mond of 'not forcing the British Government to fulfil the promise of the Balfour Declaration.' Another case in which it is admitted from an authentic source that the Jews pressure governments.[101]

We should mention at this juncture that, in addition to the previously untouched family archives, our informant Bolitho had 83 people at his disposition—cabinet ministers, trade union leaders, chemists, secretaries, servants, friends and relations—when he was gathering material for his biography of Lord Melchett. The magnificently decorated book had a print run of only 200 copies, and it would probably be correct to assume that Bolitho wrote it for a fee and at the instigation of the Mond family.[102]

Alfred Mond passed away on 27 December 1930. His son Henry, currently one of the most powerful industrialists in the world, succeeded him in his position of power. He is chairman or a director of the following companies:[103]

Amalgamated Anthracite Collieries Ltd.
Barclays Bank Ltd.
Imperial Chemical Industries Ltd.
Industrial Finance and Investment Corporation Ltd.
International Nickel Company of Canada Ltd.
Mond Staffordshire Refining Co. Ltd.
Palestine Electric Corporation Ltd.
Power-Gas Corporation Ltd.
South Staffordshire Mond Gas Company Ltd.
Thames House Estate Ltd.[104]

The number of companies is not as significant as that of other financial and economic magnates, but several of his companies are among the most powerful in the world. For example, Imperial Chemical Industries Ltd. has a share capital of £95 million, and directly controls around 50 other companies as well as also having very significant interests in other companies. The Amalgamated Anthracite Collieries, whose lawyers are Oppenheimer and Nathan, controls around 85% of the total coal production in Wales and is the sole or main shareholder in a whole series of Welsh mines. The share capital of this company is £9,500,000.

The last thing we shall mention is the International Nickel Company of Canada Ltd. Its stock capital is approximately $90 million, and its balance

---

[101] Bolitho: *Alfred Mond*, pp 369-375. Translator's note: Both QVOS.
[102] Bolitho: *Alfred Mond*, Foreword. & Dedication. Translator's note: It is likely that Aldag consulted a first edition, which referenced this initial print run, a reference absent from subsequent editions.
[103] Bolitho: *Alfred Mond*, p. 382.
[104] *Directory of Directors 1938*, pp. 1154.

sheet as of 31 December 1936, showed assets of $153,696,746. International Nickel Company owns:

a) The entire capital of International Nickel Co. Inc. (Incorporated in Delaware), Ontario Refining Co. Ltd. and the Moon Nickel Co. Ltd.;

b) Approximately 100,000 acres (equivalent to approximately 160,000 *Morgen*) of mineral-bearing land, including approximately 15 copper and nickel mines in the District of Sudbury, Ontario;

c) Hydro-electric power plants, foundries, rolling mills, refineries, and research and testing laboratories in Canada, the United States and Great Britain.[105]

Lord Melchett is far from the only Jew in the coal and metal industries; we find numerous other Hebrews in these fields, of whom we shall name only a few. The de Pas family has major interests in the coal industry of the British Empire. They can found, among other places, on the board of directors of the following companies:

Amalgamated Collieries of South Africa Ltd.
Chandler's Limited
Coronation Collieries Ltd.
Springfield Collieries Ltd.
Vereeniging Estates Ltd.[106]

If we pick any one of these companies at random, we will see how incredibly interconnected it is with other companies. The chairman of Amalgamated Collieries is Theodore Marks, who, given his name, can be assumed to be Jewish until proven otherwise. The company was founded at the time to gain direct control of various important companies. Most of the authorized capital of two million pounds is in the hands of Vereeniging Estates Ltd. This company is chaired by Louis Marks, of whom the same can be said as what was said regarding Theodore Marks, and, among the directors, alongside de Pas, can be counted another Jew, Julius Weil. This company in turn includes numerous companies with large mining and other rights. The capital is £1,750,000.[107]

---

[105] *Stock Exchange Year Book 1938*, pp. 2798, 1421, 1437.
[106] *Directory of Directors 1938*, p. 455.
[107] *Stock Exchange Year Book 1938*, pp. 2958, 3149.

We would also like to mention two Jews with significant influence in the metal industry, namely A. M. Baer and Sir George Leon. The former is a director in:

Henry Gardner & Co.
Amalgamated Metal Corporation Ltd.
British Metal Corporation Ltd.
Metal Market and Exchange Company Ltd.[108]

Sir George Leon is also a director of Henry Gardner & Co. and of the Amalgamated Metal Corporation, a holding company with an authorized capital of £5,600,000. The assets consist mainly of all shares of British Metal Corporation Ltd., which has an authorized capital of £5,000,000 and which in turn controls Brametta S. A., registered in Switzerland, the British Metal Stockholders Trust Ltd., Huntingdon Heberlein & Co. Ltd., and partly controls National Alloys Ltd. and Light Alloys Ltd.[109]

A considerable influence of the Jews can also be seen in shipping. This particularly applies to the Ellerman family, whose founder was Sir John Ellerman, who died in July 1933. At his death he was considered one of the so-called 'Big Five' of shipping. His *Times* obituary [July 18, p. 9] described him as 'a financial genius' who directly controlled a total fleet of 1,500,000 tons gross. He also had strong interests in other shipping lines such as Cunard, and the Peninsular and Oriental Steam Navigation Company [P. & O.].

In addition to his dominant position in shipping, he also had great influence in the brewery industry and the press, which we shall discuss later. His estate was officially assessed at £36,684,994, which incurred inheritance tax of around £18 million. The main bulk and management of his assets passed to his son, the present Sir John Ellerman. The companies controlled by the father reported that generally nothing had changed on the death of the elder Sir John. Accordingly, the son continues to occupy his father's dominant position in the market. Today he is a director of the following companies:[110]

Audley Trust Ltd.
Brewery and Commercial Investment Trust Ltd.
Debenture Securities Investment Company Ltd.
Ellerman Property Trust Ltd.
Ellerman's Wilson Line Ltd.
London Publishing Co. Ltd.[111]

---

[108] *Directory of Directors 1938*, p. 67.
[109] *Directory of Directors 1938*, p. 1010; *Jewish Year Book 1937*, p. 461. & *Stock Exchange Year Book 1938*, p. 846. & p. 998.
[110] *Times*, 18/7/1933, 21/7/1933, 16/8/1933, 30/9/1936.
[111] *Directory of Directors 1938*, p. 522.

Apparently Sir John Ellerman is at least as capable a businessman as his father, having already increased his fortune, which had been reduced to £18 million by inheritance tax, to around £40 million over the course of five years. [112]

Another influential Jewish family, although not of the same importance as that previously mentioned, is the Instone (i.e. Einstein) family. There are three brothers, Sir Samuel, Captain Alfred, and Theodore. The first in particular was big in shipping, coal, and aviation. His death in November 1937 aroused great public sympathy. Sir Samuel Instone was chairman of the:

> Askern Coal and Iron Company Ltd.
> Bedwas Navigation Colliery Comp. Ltd.
> S. Instone and Co. Ltd., with a capital of £1.500.000.

and a director of the:

> British Benzol and Coal Distillation Ltd.
> Imperial Airways Ltd.
>> Imperial Airways (Continental) Ltd. (like our Lufthansa),
>> with five million pounds of authorized capital.

Today his brother Theodore is his successor in the first four companies, also as chairman or director, while Alfred acts as deputy chairman or director in the same companies. [113]

The Jewish Samuel family, now the family of Lord Bearsted, is dominant in the oil industry. Marcus Samuel, who initially ran a small business in Houndsditch, in the East End of London, must be seen as the founder of the family. His trade consisted mainly of painted shells, but later grew to include curios, general produce, and rice. As his wealth increased, his connections increased, and after a business trip to Japan he began shipping petroleum from Russia to the Far East, which proved to be a great success over the years. Samuel brought together the companies involved in this trade and, with financial help from the House of Rothschild, founded the now global

---

[112] *Daily Express*, 11/1/1939. Translator's note: According to his *Times* obituary of 18/7/1973 (p. 18), Ellerman (fils) was a reclusive figure whose main passion was zoology, and he co-authored the major works *Checklist of Palaearctic and Indian Mammals, 1758 to 1946* (1951) and *Southern African Mammals, 1758 to 1951* (1953). He was also a keen pianist and Gilbert and Sullivan expert. The *Times* also reports that he took a close personal interest in the family business but left the running of the business to others. He left no heirs to the baronetcy.

[113] *Jewish Year Book 1937*, p. 449; *Directory of Directors 1937*, p. 874, *idem. 1938*, p. 884; *Stock Exchange Year Book 1938*, p. 2802, 2811, 2870, 1421; *Times*, 10/11/1937, 11/11/1937.

and famous Shell Transport and Trading Company with a capital of £1,800,000. Later this trust had a fierce battle with the Royal Dutch Petroleum Co., but the battle ended with the merger of both companies.

Samuel was knighted in 1898 after two of his tugboats refloated the British warship HMS Victorious that had run aground in Port Said. In 1891 he was elected alderman of the London ward of Portsoken, a year later, Sheriff of the City of London, and from 1902-1903 he was Lord Mayor of London, after which he received the traditional baronetcy. In 1921 Samuel was elevated to the Peerage as Baron Bearsted of Maidstone and in 1925 was made a viscount. He died on 17 January 1927, surviving his wife by only a few hours. His son Walter inherited his title and all of his positions. Walter Samuel, 2nd Viscount Bearsted, is currently chairman or a director of the following important companies:[114]

M. Samuel & Co. Ltd.	Shell Company (Hellas) Ltd.
Alliance Assurance Co. Ltd.	Shell Company (Malta) Ltd.
Anglo-Mexican Petroleum Co. Ltd.	Shell Company of Australia Ltd.
Anglo-Saxon Petroleum Co. Ltd.	Shell Company of Bulgaria Ltd.
Asiatic Petroleum Co. Ltd.	Shell Company of Estonia Ltd.
Asiatic Petroleum Co. (Federated Malay States) Ltd.	Shell Company Klaipeda (Memel) Ltd.
Asiatic Petroleum Co. (India) Ltd.	Shell Company of Latvia Ltd.
Asiatic Petroleum Co. (North China) Ltd.	Shell Company of Lithuania Ltd.
Asiatic Petroleum Co. (Philippine Islands) Ltd.	Shell Company of New Zealand Ltd.
Asiatic Petroleum Co. (Siam) Ltd.	Shell Company of Nigeria Ltd.
Asiatic Petroleum Co. (South China) Ltd.	Shell Company of Portugal Ltd.
Asiatic Petroleum Co. (Straits Settlements) Ltd.	Shell Company of Turkey Ltd.
Bataafsche Petroleum Maatschappij	Shell Company of West Africa Ltd.
British Malayan Petroleum Co. Ltd.	Shell Company (Pacific Islands) Ltd.
Eagle Oil and Shipping Co. Ltd.	Shell Company (Porto Rico) Ltd.
Egyptian Engineering Stores S. A.	Shell Company (West Indies) Ltd.
Elba Tinplate Co. Ltd.	Shell-Mex Argentina Ltd.
Lloyds Bank Ltd.	Shell-Mex Chile Ltd.
London and Holyrood Trust Ltd.	Shell-Mex Uruguay Ltd.
London and National Property Co. Ltd.	Shell Overseas Exploration Co. Ltd.
Nineteen twenty-eight Investment Trust Ltd.	Shell Transport and Trading Co. Ltd.
Nineteen twenty-nine Investment Trust Ltd.	Société Anonyme Astra-Romana
Perham Investment Trust Ltd.	Société Anonyme des Pétroles Jupiter
St. Helens Estates Ltd.	Société Française Shell de Tunisie
Samuel Estates Ltd.	Société Shell de Maroc
Samuel Samuel and Co. Ltd.	Venezuelan Oil Concessions Ltd.
Sarawak Oilfields Ltd.	

---

[114] *Times*, 18/1/1927 p. 16. Translator's note: The obituary reveals how Samuel came from a relatively low position in life to reach his latter position of fortune and renown, and the reader cannot help but be impressed by his life story. The early (relative) obscurity and poverty is revealed by the 1891 incident of Samuel being elected Alderman of Portsoken, a Jewish community in London's East End, when he feared that he would not be accepted into the Aldermanic body, given that at the time he was so little known and his shell business so small.

Of all of these companies, the Shell Transport and Trading Company Ltd. alone can be seen as a global power, as it is a holding company for many other companies. Its authorized capital amounts to £43,000,000, but this should be considered small in relation to its assets. Two other Jews are directors of this company, namely Peter Montefiore Samuel and Sir Robert Waley Cohen, the latter in turn serving as chairman or a director of the following corporations:[115]

Agricultural Mortgage Co. of Palestine Ltd.	New Schibaieff Petroleum Co. Ltd.
Anglo-Egyptian Oilfields Ltd.	North Caucasian Oil Fields Ltd.
Anglo-Mexican Oil and Shipping Co. Ltd.	Palestine Corporation Ltd.
Anglo-Mexican Petroleum Co. Ltd.	Palestine Publishing Co. Ltd.
Anglo-Saxon Petroleum Co. Ltd.	Shell Company of Australia Ltd.
Asiatic Petroleum Co. (India) Ltd.	Shell Company of New Zealand Ltd.
Asiatic Petroleum Co. Ltd.	Shell Company of Portugal Ltd.
Baldwins Ltd.	Shell-Mex Argentina Ltd.
Bataafsche Petroleum Maatschappij	Shell-Mex Chile Ltd.
British Malayan Petroleum Co. Ltd.	Shell-Mex Uruguay Ltd.
Canadian Eagle Oil Co. Ltd.	Société Commerciale et Industrielle
Eagle Oil and Shipping Co. Ltd.	United British Oil Fields of Trinidad Ltd.
English and Scottish Investors Ltd.	

Of course, next to these Jewish giants in the oil industry, other greats, such as B. Maisel and Johanna Maisel, pale into insignificance. Both are directors of Maisels Petroleum Trust, as well as Orient Oil and Finance Co. Ltd. (£1,500,000 capital). Johanna is also a director of Romana Petroleum Co. Ltd. The two Maisels' interests focus mainly on Romanian oil.[116]

Finally, in our list of oil magnates, we would not wish to overlook Sir William Garthwaite, who, according to a leaflet by Arnold Leese, is said to be half-Jewish (the son of a Jewish mother and Aryan father) and married to a Jewess. The latter also applies to his son, whose wife is the daughter of the full Jew Lord Duveen. His family can therefore be viewed as almost fully Jewish. Sir William has interests in the following ventures:[117]

British Controlled Oilfields Ltd.
Central Area Exploitation Company (Venezuela) Ltd.
Lautaro Nitrate Company Ltd.
Oertz International Streamline Rudder Comp. Ltd.[118]

The number of companies is not as impressive as some of the others mentioned above, but some of them are nevertheless extremely important. Around two-thirds of the oil production in Central and South America,

---

[115] *Directory of Directors 1938*, pp. 1497, 341. *Stock Exchange Year Book 1938*, p. 3203. *Jewish Year Book 1937*, pp. 404, 417.
[116] *Directory of Directors 1938*, p. 1109; *Stock Exchange Year Book 1938*, p. 3196.
[117] *Who's Who 1939*, p. 1161; *Jewish Year Book 1937*, p. 423.
[118] *Directory of Directors 1938*, p. 622.

which feature among the most important producers in the world, are in the hands of British Controlled Oilfields. The majority of the shares are said to be owned by the British government. The authorized capital is $27,500,000.[119]

The Lautaro Nitrate Company controls a large proportion of nitrates in Chile and has an authorized capital of over two million pounds. Another director of this company goes by the name of Paul Wirtz, a name which is anything but English, and it is therefore doubtful that he is anything other than Jewish.[120]

The Judaization of the Insurance Industry

Jews also have a dominant position in insurance companies. Thus we find Lionel de Rothschild as chairman, Lord Bearsted and the half-Jewish Lord Rosebery as directors, and the Jew A. Levine as general manager of the Alliance Assurance Co. which has an authorized capital of £5,450,000. The Allied Assurance Co. has absorbed the following companies, among others:

> Royal Farmers and General Insurance Co.
> Provincial Insurance Co.
> Salop Fire Office
> Shropshire and North Wales Assurance Co. Ltd.
> Imperial Insurance Co. Ltd.
> Imperial Life Insurance Co.
> Provident Life Office
> Economic Life Assurance
> Alliance Marine and General Assurance Co. Ltd.[121]

This and another insurance company, the Guardian Eastern Insurance Company Ltd., are considered to be purely Jewish, both according to the Jews' own statements and in terms of their intended purpose. The following facts led to its founding:

For years, many insurance companies in England had refused to insure the Jews. Some companies had even gone so far as to deny any liability for damages in their general terms and conditions if Hebrews were involved. The Jews had and still have difficulties getting insurance from certain companies. In 1936, a Board of Trade official gave evidence on this subject before the Departmental Committee on Compulsory Insurance, and expressed

---

[119] *Stock Exchange Year Book 1938*, p. 3178; Denny, pp. 95-109.

[120] *Stock Exchange Year Book 1938*, p. 3167. Translator's note: Note that this final sentence can be found in the 1940 *Juden beherrschen England*, but not in the 1943 *Das Judentum in England*, so it may be that Aldag removed it in the interim, or it was omitted in error. It has been included here for the reader to decide on its merits.

[121] *Stock Exchange Year Book 1938*, p. 2615; *Jewish Year Book 1938*, p. 467.

his view that 'a great deal was to be said for putting an end to this species of vexatious and offensive discrimination.' His remarks were applauded by the chairman of the committee, the Jew Sir Felix Cassel.[122]

The Jews protested in meetings against this difference in treatment, and for this reason Sir Moses Montefiore had long ago founded the Alliance Assurance Company to enable his fellow Jews to take out insurance. The Guardian Eastern Insurance Company was founded for the same reason. The *Jewish Chronicle*, the official organ of the Jews in Britain, made repeated references to this issue and also to the fact that leading Jews, such as Nathan Laski, A. J. Belisha, Colonel Sir Herbert Jessel, S. J. Cohen, and Montagu Gluckstein, were the directors of this purely Jewish company. The company has a capital of £1,000,000, and the first three Jews of those listed are still directors of the company to this day.[123]

We also find Hebrews in leading positions everywhere else in the insurance industry. At least two Jews, Sir George Schuster and Sir Charles Seligman, are directors of the Commercial Union Assurance Co. Ltd., whose authorized capital is £3,750,000. Over time it has taken over or come to control numerous companies, which include:

Nottinghamshire and Midland Fire Insurance Co. Ltd.	Edinburgh Assurance Co. Ltd.
Straits Fire Insurance Co. Ltd.	National Insurance Co. of Great Britain
West of England Fire and Life Insurance Co.	Palatine Insurance Co. Ltd.
Colonial Assurance Co.	Union Assurance Soc. Ltd.
Accident Insurance Co. Ltd.	West of Scotland Insurance Office Ltd.
British General Insurance Co. Ltd.	Ocean Accident and Guarantee Corp. Ltd.

These companies include other companies that are impossible to list in their entirety. For example, one of the companies listed above, the British General Insurance Co. Ltd., has a decisive influence over the following companies:

Northern Equitable Insurance Co. Ltd.
Cosmopolitan Insurance Corporation Ltd.
London and Midland Insurance Co. Ltd.
British and European Insurance Co. Ltd.
National Accident Compensation Co.[124]

---

[122] *Jewish Chronicle*, 3/7/1936 p. 10; *Daily Express*, 29/9/1923; Banister, p. 134. Translator's note: QVOS from the JC article, which is a report of the official's comment, not the comment itself. The official was referring to the motor industry, and not only Jewish drivers would rendered ineligible, but also bookmakers, jockeys, actors and members of the RAF. The incidence of insured Jewish businesses burning down spontaneously had become so common that from the late 19th century onwards that the phrase 'Jewish lightning' had entered general parlance to describe such apparent 'acts of God'.
[123] *Jewish Chronicle*, 27/10/1922, pp. 13, 19-20; 3/11/1922, pp. 17-8. & *Stock Exchange Year Book 1938*, p. 2638.
[124] SEYB38, p. 2622.

The Jew H. R. Mosenthal is a director of the London and Lancashire Insurance Co., which in the British Empire alone controls 23 companies of a similar type and which has a capital of £5,000,000. The Jewish E. A. Mosenthal is a director of the Marine Insurance Co. Ltd., capitalized with £1,000,000, and Maurice Stern is an executive of the Norwich Union Life Insurance Company. The Jew Sir Ewart Levy holds a senior position in the State Assurance Co. Ltd. His ethnic kinsman, the aforementioned A. Levine, is, in addition to other business ventures, chairman or a director of the following companies:[125]

Aviation and General Insurance Co. Ltd.
National Boiler and General Insurance Co. Ltd.[126]

and has also made a name for himself in insurance. In 1937, he was president of the Chartered Insurance Institute. The aforementioned Jewish MP, Colonel Harry Day, is chairman of Metropolitan Re-Insurance Co. Ltd, and of the Mutual Property Life and General Insurance Co. He is also chairman of seven other companies.[127]

The Goschen family also plays a major role in insurance. The founder of the family came from Germany. The head of the family is now Viscount Goschen. His brother, Sir William Henry Goschen, is chairman of four insurance companies. One of Arnold Leese's pamphlets informs us that the family is Jewish. Lord Riddell also explicitly stated it in his *Diary*. However, we have doubts about this assertion, given that the earliest ancestor to whom the Göschen family (as they were known in Germany) can trace back their pedigree, is said to have been a 'worthy parish clergyman' of the Lutheran faith who lived in Saxony around 1609.[128]

Judaized Finance

The extent of Hebrew dominance in the area of finance is aptly shown by the following remark from Michelet, which we take from a recent publication from the Count of Saint-Aulaire:

---

[125] *SEYB38*, p. 2646; *DD38*, p. 1217. & *SEYB38*, p. 2650; *DD38*, p. 1217. & *SEYB38*, p. 2658; *DD38*, p. 1619. & *DD38*, p. 1015; *Jewish Chronicle*, 26/3/1937.

[126] *DD38*, p. 1014; *Jewish Year Book 1937*, pp. 462, 1938, 467; *Jewish Chronicle*, 9/12/1938.

[127] *DD38*, pp. 439-40.

[128] *DD38*, pp. 664-5; *Who's Who 1939*, pp. 1243-4. & Riddell, p. 7. & Elliot: Vol. I, p. 1. Translator's note: QVOS.

It is said that the Jews have no country of their own. They have. It is the London Stock Exchange.[129]

Just think of the power of the Rothschild banking house, whose origins and development we have already discussed. The 20th century has further encouraged its expansion, so that despite American competition, it has lost none of its global importance. The wealth of the house is indicated by the fact that in April 1938 the Rothschild family donated £10,000 to Jewish refugees and £50,000 in December of the same year.[130]

It is also worth mentioning the Sassoon family, or the 'Rothschilds of the East', as they are often called, who immigrated to England from Mesopotamia and India. Not only does this family hold a dominant position in various parts of Asia—opium is one of its main trades—but it has three important banks in the City of London, which, after the death of Sir Philip Sassoon, are now under the direction of his brother Sir Victor Sassoon. The influence of this family is hardly, if at all, inferior to that of Rothschild.[131]

---

[129] Translator's note: QVOS from *Geneva Versus Peace* (1937), p. 73.

[130] *Jewish Chronicle*, 8/4/1938, 2/12/1938.

[131] *Jewish Encyclopedia*, Vol. XI, pp. 66-68; *Who's Who 1939*, p. 2825; *SEYB38*, p. 628. Translator's note: The Sassoon dynasty built its vast fortune through the opium trade in India and China, where it became the leading opium importer, according to Jonathan Kaufman, author of *The Last Kings of Shanghai: The Rival Jewish Dynasties That Helped Create Modern China* (Viking, 2020). In an interview with the *Forward*, even apologist Kaufman admits that the Jews knew what they were doing to the country, saying: 'They knew it was bad. The Sassoons had to dismiss some of their Chinese employees because they were addicted to opium. Many of the Jewish families fought tooth and nail against banning opium. Opium was legal and used for medicinal purposes. Like people who sell cigarettes and alcohol, their feeling was that they were filling a need. They also looked upon the Chinese as being different from Westerners. They felt that the Chinese weren't like us, so selling opium to the Chinese was seen as something that could be done... the consequences for China were catastrophic.' [See: 'When Jews were kings (and opium lords) in Shanghai', Benjamin Ivey, *Forward*, 2 June 2020. https://forward.com/culture/442250/when-jews-were-kings-and-opium-lords-in-shanghai.] Note that Kaufman is being disingenuous here; foreign-grown opium had been illegal in China since 1729 and its use was controlled, but the Chinese authorities had been powerless to stop the illegal importation and trade, especially after military defeat to the British had led to a loss of sovereignty, and rule by British bayonet. This defeat came when the Chinese had finally tried to fight back against this growing devastation of their society by making opium possession illegal, seizing contraband opium in warehouses, and closing opium dens. This led to the British invading in 1839, which in turn led to China's defeat in the so-called Opium Wars, marking the start of the Chinese 'Century of Humiliation', the bitter remembrance of which will continue to have geopolitical repercussions in Chinese-Western relations for a long time to come. For more on how mass opium addiction ruined China (but made the Sassoons, as Kaufman asserts, multi-billionaires by today's standards), see Vassilev [in Translator's Bibliography].

Sir Elly Kadoorie and his late brother Sir Ellis Kadoorie played a major role in the business deals of the Far East, just as Sir Leonard Cohen's name also has a great resonance in the same region. Cohen is, among other things, a director of the Bengal & North Western Railway Co. Ltd. (capital £4,798,000) and the Rohilkund & Kumaon Railway Co. Ltd. (capital £800,000).[132]

The name Hambro should not be missing from the list of financial tycoons. The head of the family is Sir Eric Hambro, director of the Royal Exchange Assurance Co., who, along with other members of this family, can be found in many business ventures and who has great influence in the City.[133]

The family business, Hambros Bank Ltd., which enjoys a great reputation in the international financial world, recently celebrated its centenary. It was founded in 1839 by Charles Joachim Hambro, a son of the powerful Joseph Hambro, court banker to the three Scandinavian kingdoms. It was Charles who, by means of a loan, sustained the Danish throne through the turbulence of the Revolutions of 1848; he was then raised to the barony for his services.

The managing director of Hambros Bank is Charles Jocelyn Hambro, who is also on the Board of Directors of the Bank of England, as well as being a director of the Great Western Railway and Chairman of the English Delegates to the Joint Standing Committee of the Anglo-Swedish Trade Agreement. Since 1939 he has been head of the Scandinavian department in the British Ministry of Economic Warfare.

Another member of Hambros Bank is John Henry Hambro, who is also on the board of directors of Ecco (English Commercial Corporation Ltd.). Shortly after the end of the Great War, Hambros Bank merged with the British Bank of Northern Commerce, whose loans flowed into Norway, Denmark, Finland, etc. under the auspices of the League of Nations. Other members include Lieutenant-Colonel Harald Everard Hambro and Ronald Olaf Hambro, who also play a decisive role in the family bank.

The influence of the Hambro family also extends into mainland Europe, where we find its most famous member in the person of Norway's former President of the Parliament, Carl Joachim Hambro. His influence on the politics of this country has had a disastrous effect, and the Norwegian people are the ones who suffer, having to pay for the failed policies of their Jewish representative.

Werner Sombart, in his famous book *The Jews and Modern Capitalism* (1913), says the following regarding the Jewishness of the banking sector in England:

---

[132] *Who's Who 1939*, p. 635; *Jewish Year Book 1937*, p. 415.
[133] *Who's Who 1939*, pp. 1353-4; *Directory of Directors 1938*, p. 719; *Stock Exchange Year Book 1938*, p. 592; *Daily Express*, 21/1/1939; *Jewish Encyclopedia*, Vol. VI, p. 190.

> Here, as I am told on the best authority, of the 63 banks in the
> *Bankers' Almanack* for 1904, 33 were Jewish firms, or at least
> with a strong Jewish interest, and of these 33, 13 were first-
> class concerns.[134]

Of particular interest in this context is the role of Jews in the Bank of
England. Being able to make a definitive statement on this matter is particularly difficult due to the fact that this institution, which has long enjoyed
considerable legal privileges, is practically exempt from having to make anything public. There is therefore no official register that would serve as a point
of reference, but one must definitely discount the notion that the British government has majority control. Not even HM Treasury is represented on the
board, and one would not be wrong to assume that the Bank of England is
run predominantly by men who belong to international banking entities. To
what extent these are in turn controlled by Hebrews is impossible for us to
elucidate. In any case, together with the aforementioned Jew Hambro, a
member of the aforementioned Goschen family was also on the board of
directors until recently. It is unknown what role the Rothschilds play in the
Bank of England, but one often hears the claim that they control it.[135]

Lord Bearsted (surname Samuel), along with Colonel F. D. Samuel and
Peter Montefiore Samuel, is a director of the important banking house Sam-
uel & Co., whose capital of £2,000,000 cannot begin to reflect the influence
that this bank exercises on international finance. The same can be said of the
firm Samuel, Montagu & Co. (with its Jewish directors E. L. Franklin, L. S.
Montagu, S. E. Franklin, Lord Swaythling, and C. M. Franklin), as well as of
Japhet & Co., which has the Jewish Saemy Japhet as its chairman, and Paul
Lindenberg, Max Fontheim and Gottfried Loewenstein as directors.[136]

In this context, it is perhaps not without interest that the price of gold
for the world market is set every morning in the Rothschild Banking House
by the following five Jewish companies:

N. M. Rothschild & Sons
Marcus Samuel & Co.
Samuel, Montagu & Co.
S. Japhet & Co.
Mocatta & Goldsmid (official gold and silver bullion brokers to
    the Bank of England).[137]

---

[134] Sombart, p. 105. Translator's note: QVOS.
[135] Jarvie, pp. 1-36. & p. 36-40. Translator's note: Jarvie does not (cannot) go beyond
speculation in this regard, as he was informed by a BoE letter that the list of bank stockholders was known only to the stockholders themselves (p. 8).
[136] *Stock Exchange Year Book 1938*, p. 627. & pp. 609, 599.
[137] *Action*, 23/1/1937.

Also enjoying a wide scope of action is the Jewish firm Erlangers Ltd. (capital £2,000,000), which has Baron Emile d'Erlanger as its chairman, and Baron Frederic d'Erlanger and Leo F. A. d'Erlanger as his deputies. Individual members of this family have other major interests in:

Beira Railway Comp. Ltd. (chairman)	Harrods (Buenos Aires) Ltd. (director)
British South Africa Co. (vice-president)	Leach's Argentine Estates (deputy chair)
Channel Tunnel Comp. Ltd. (chairman)	South America Stores Ltd. (director)
Forestal Land, Timber and Railways Comp. Ltd. (chair)	British Airways Ltd. (director)
Pauling and Co. Ltd. (chairman)	Hillman's Airways Ltd. (director)
Rhodesia Railways Trust Ltd. (chairman)	Hellenic and General Trust Ltd. (director)
Sterling Trust Ltd. (chairman)	International Sleeping Car (director)
Chilian Stores Ltd. (director)	Share Trust Ltd. (director)

What can be said for this family also applies to the others mentioned above: they are all represented in many companies, and almost all of these individual companies, such as the British South Africa Co., are of great importance. In the aforesaid company, two other Jews, Sir Edmund Davis and Sir Ernest Oppenheimer, act as directors. We shall discuss this company at greater length in a subsequent chapter, but for now it is sufficient to say that it has a capital of £6,750,000 and that it practically controls entire British colonies.[138]

Another well-known banker is Sir Albert Stern of the Stern Brothers banking house. Sir Albert is a director of other companies such as:

Bank of Romania Ltd.
British French Discount Bank Ltd.
Midland Bank Ltd
Midland Bank Executor and Trustee Co. Ltd.
Ottoman Bank Ltd. (£10.000.000)
Steaua Romana
Steaua Romana Société Anonyme pour l'Industrie du Petrole.[139]

Sir Max Bonn also belongs to the ranks of great financiers, who, as well as involvement in three other companies, is also chairman or a director of:

Helbert, Wagg & Co. Ltd.
Bank of London and South America (£4.500.000)
Brazilian Trust and Loan Corporation Ltd.
Helbert, Wagg & Co. (New York) Ltd.[140]

---

[138] *Stock Exchange Year Book 1938*, pp. 2232-33.

[139] *DD38*, p. 1619; *SEYB38*, pp. 620, 632; *Jewish Chronicle*, 3/9/1937; *JYB37*, p. 504.

[140] *DD38*, p. 176; *SEYB38*, p. 555.

Sir Louis Sterling is another personage in this group of financiers, who, among other companies, has interests in:

National Industrial Credit Corporation Ltd.
Bankers Commercial Security Ltd.
Mercantile Credit Company Ltd.[141]

Sir. L. Franklin is a partner in the well-known bank of Keyser (A.) and Co. in the City. Other board-members of this bank are the Jews J. A. Franklin, G. L. Schlesinger, E. A. Franklin, and C. M. Keyser. The company has significant interests in many companies. Henry Kahn is chairman and director of ten companies of all kinds, and Sir Osmond Elim d'Avigdor-Goldsmid serves as chairman or a director of the following companies:[142]

Anglo-Chinese Finance and Trade Corporation Ltd.
C. R. E. Trust Ltd.
General Funds Investment Trust Ltd.
Land Revenues Trust Ltd.
Pekin Syndicate Ltd.
Chinese Central Railways Ltd.
Royal Insurance Comp. Ltd.[143]

Sir Sigismund Mendl, who served in the War Office Advisory Committee during the Great War, is also well known in the financial world. He is a director of the National Discount Company Ltd. in addition to six other companies. Within the National Discount Company (capital £2,700,000), Jews Francis Goldsmid and Sir Charles Seligman hold senior positions. Sir Sigismund Mendl's brother, Sir Charles Mendl, worked as a press attaché at the British Embassy in Paris.[144] Sir Charles Seligman is a partner in the famous Seligman Brothers bank; his other partners are D. E. Seligman, Leon Rueff, Louis Fleischmann, V. S. Seligman, D. A. Seligman, and R. J. Seligman. The company has a big influence in the economy.[145]

In the so-called 'Big Five' banks, there are also Jews in director-level positions:

---

[141] *DD38*, p. 1619; *Jewish Chronicle*, 30/4/1937, 3/9/1937.
[142] *SEYB38*, p. 600; *Jewish Year Book 1937*, pp. 431, 456. & *DD38*, p. 937; *Jewish Year Book 1937*, p. 459.
[143] *DD38*, p. 341; *Who's Who 1939*, p. 800.
[144] *Who's Who 1939*, p. 2179; *DD38*, p. 1157; *SEYB38*, p. 614.
[145] *Who's Who 1939*, p. 2865; *Jewish Year Book 1937*, p. 495; *SEYB38*, p. 628,

Sir Victor Schuster in the National Provincial Bank Ltd. (capital
£60,000,000)[146]
Lord Bearsted in Lloyds Bank Ltd. (capital £74,000,000)[147]
Sir Albert Stern in the Midland Bank Ltd. (capital
£45,200,000)[148]
Lord Goschen and Sir George Schuster in Westminster Bank
Ltd. (capital £33,000,000)[149]
Lord Melchett in Barclays Bank (capital £20,000,000).[150]

This list, which of course only represents a fraction of the Jews in finance, must suffice for our purposes. But we hope that we have convinced
the reader that the London Stock Exchange does indeed appear to be 'the
country of the Jew.'

The Gold and Diamond Industries

The situation in the gold and diamond industries is similar to the situation in
finance. Here too we can limit ourselves to listing a few of the leading Jews
in order to give the reader a basic idea of their far-reaching influence.
     Sir George W. Albu is chairman and managing director of General Min-
ing and Finance Corporation Ltd. He is also chairman or a board member of:

Barclays Bank (Dominion, Colonial and Overseas)
Durban Roodeport Deep Ltd.
East Rand Proprietary Mines Ltd.
Van Ryn Gold Mines Estate Ltd.
West Rand Consolidated Mines Ltd.
West Witwatersrand Areas Ltd.[151]

The General Mining and Finance Corporation, of which Leopold Albu
is the London managing director and chairman, has a capital of £1,500,000.
It has large interests in various other mines and other concerns. The capital
of Durban Roodeport Deep Ltd. is £1,200,000, that of East Rand Proprietary
Mines Ltd., £1,800,000, Van Ryn Gold Mines Estate Ltd., which has absorbed various other gold mines, has a capital of £250,000, while the capital
of West Rand Consolidated Mines Ltd. is £2,150,000. This last company has
in turn significant interests in Violet Consolidated Gold Mining Co. Ltd.,

---

[146] *SEYB38*, p. 615.
[147] *SEYB38*, p. 603.
[148] *SEYB38*, p. 607.
[149] *SEYB38*, p. 636.
[150] *SEYB38*, p. 567.
[151] *Directory of Directors 1938*, p. 16.

West Rand Mines Ltd. and a number of other mines. Members of the London Committee of the latter company include Leopold Albu, Julius Friedlander and C.S. Goldman.[152]

The aforementioned Leopold Albu, who is chairman or a director of a number of the same companies as Sir George Albu, also has significant interests in the following companies:

> International Russian Corporation Ltd.
> Phoenix Oil and Transport Co. Ltd.
> Phoenix Oil Products Ltd.[153]

The latter two possessing a capital of £4,500,000 and £650,000 respectively.[154]

Ludwig Ehrlich is chairman or a director of the following companies (note that this list is not exhaustive):

> Anglo Canadian Trustees Ltd.
> Associated Mining and Finance Co. Ltd.
> Blackwater Mines Ltd.
> Carmen Valley Gold Mines Ltd.
> Consolidated Gold Fields of New Zealand Ltd.
> H. E. Proprietary Ltd.
> Harmony Lands and Minerals Ltd., which owns, among other
>   things, 'The Harmony Estate', a property of some 186,492
>   acres, as well as mineral rights in other vast regions.[155]
> Luipaards Vlei Estate and Gold Mining Ltd.
> Palmarejo and Mexican Gold Fields Ltd.
> Siberian Syndicate Ltd.
> West Spaarwater Ltd., which has an authorized capital of
£2,000,000

And in the same capacity, Julius Friedlander acts in the following companies:

> Bellsbank Estate and Exploration Co. Ltd.
> East Rand Proprietary Mines Ltd. (capital: £1,800,000)[156]
> East Rietfontein Syndicate Ltd.
> Geduld Proprietary Mines Ltd. (capital: £1,500,000)[157]

---

[152] *SEYB38*, p. 3013. & p. 3000. & p. 3003. & p. 3147. & p. 3155.
[153] *Who's Who 1939*, p. 34; *Directory of Directors*, p. 16.
[154] *SEYB38*, p. 3199. & *SEYB38*, p. 3200.
[155] *SEYB38*, p. 2297.
[156] *SEYB38*, p. 3003.
[157] *SEYB38*, p. 3012.

Johannesburg Consolidated Investment Co., whose other directors include: G. J. Joel, H. J. Joel, Sir Robert N. Kotze and Gustav Imroth. We shall go into this company in more detail below.

M. A. C. S. Ltd.

South African Land and Exploration Co. Ltd., which has 15 holdings comprising 76,021 acres in various districts of the Transvaal, Natal and the Orange River Colony, as well as mineral rights for another 35 holdings comprising 137,952 acres.[158]

West Rand Consolidated Mines (capital: £2,150,000, see Albu).

Major Charles Sydney Goldman is chairman or a director of:

Central European Mines Ltd.

Consolidated Main Reef Mines and Estate Ltd. (capital: £1,247,602)[159]

General Mines Investment Ltd.

Gold Coast and Ashanti Stool Concessions Ltd.

Henckel von Donnersmarck Beuthen Estates Ltd.

New Modderfontein Gold Mining Co. Ltd. (capital: £1,400,000, with an average dividend of 112.25% per annum over the past ten years)[160]

Polish Timber Iron Car and Waggon Co. Ltd.

Southern European Metal Corporation Ltd.

West Rand Consolidated Mines (capital: £2,150,000, see Albu)

Witbank Colliery Ltd.[161]

Gustav Imroth, Director of the Johannesburg Consolidated Investment Co. Ltd. (share capital £4,345,000, discussed in more detail below), is also on the board of Government Goldmining Areas (Modderfontein) Consolidated Ltd., which, with a capital of £1,400,000, has paid an average annual dividend of 113% on shares between the years 1934-1938, and which is exempt from the usual profit tax levied on other Transvaal gold mines.[162]

Geoffrey Joel is a director of: De Beers Consolidated Mines, which has taken charge of 13 diamond mines and leased out others. Its assets include 50% of the capital of:[163]

---

[158] *SEYB38*, p. 3119.
[159] *SEYB38*, p. 2992.
[160] *SEYB38*, p. 3074.
[161] *Who's Who 1939*, p. 1283; *Directory of Directors 1938*, p. 655.
[162] *Directory of Directors 1938*, p. 879. & *SEYB38*, p. 3020.
[163] *Directory of Directors 1938*, p. 912. & *SEYB38*, p. 2997.

African Explosives and Industries Ltd., whose capital is £5,000,000 and which owns all the shares of Cape Explosives Works Ltd, as well as considerable land holdings in the Transvaal, Natal and Rhodesia.[164]

Premier (Transvaal) Diamond Mining Co. Ltd., which, among other things, paid the following dividends:

> 1923: 300%,
> 1924: 700%,
> 1925: 500%,
> 1926: 500%,
> 1927: 250%.[165]

De Beers continue to have significant interests in:

> Cape Coast Exploration Ltd. (£1,000,000)[166]
> Consolidated Diamond Mines of South West Africa Ltd.
>   (£4,500,000)[167]
> Diamond Corporation Ltd (£5,000,000)[168]
> New Jagersfontein Mining and Exploration Co. Ltd.
>   (£1,000,000)[169] as well as preferential rights (the right of first
>   refusal) on all diamond mines discovered on the lands of the
>   South West Africa Company and those of the aforementioned
>   British South Africa Company.

Geoffrey Joel is also director of:

> Johannesburg Consolidated Investment Co. Ltd (see Friedlander and
>   Imroth), whose share capital is £4,345,000 and which, in addition to
>   considerable real estate in Johannesburg, has extensive share interests
>   in the following companies:[170]
>   Consolidated Murchison (Transvaal) Gold Fields and
>   Development Co. Ltd.
>   East Champ d'Or Gold Mining Co. Ltd.
>   East Daggafontein Mines Ltd. (£1,350,000)[171]
>   Government Gold Mining Areas (Modderfontein) Cons. Ltd.

---

[164] *SEYB38*, p. 826.
[165] *SEYB38*, p. 3096.
[166] *SEYB38*, p. 2983.
[167] *SEYB38*, p. 2991.
[168] *SEYB38*, p. 1179.
[169] *SEYB38*, p. 3073.
[170] *SEYB38*, p. 3029.
[171] *SEYB38*, p. 3001.

**Langlaagte Estate and Gold Mining Co. Ltd. (£1,519,833)[172]
**New State Areas Ltd. (£1,514,037)[173]
Potgietersrust Platinum Ltd. (£1,962,500)[174]
Rand Leases (Vogelstruisfontein) Gold Mining Co. Ltd.
  (£1,500,000)[175]
**Randfontein Estates Gold Mining Co., Witwatersrand Ltd.
  (£4,063,553)[176]
South African Breweries Ltd. (£3,000,000)[177]
**Van Ryn Deep Ltd. (£1,196,892)[178]
Vogelstruisbult Gold Mining Areas Ltd. (£2,750,000)[179]
**Witwatersrand Gold Mining Co. Ltd., which also has diamond
  interests and partnerships in the Northern Rhodesian copper
  fields.

In the companies marked **, Geoffrey Joel is also listed as a director.

Harry J. Joel, in addition to being a director of a number of the companies listed under Geoffrey Joel, is also a director of Barnato Bros. Ltd. and a member of the London Committee of the following companies:[180]

Consolidated Collieries Ltd.
Ferreira Estate Co. Ltd.
New Springs Colliery Ltd.
Phoenix Colliery Ltd.
South African Carbide and By-Products Co. Ltd.

Meanwhile, J. B. Joel, who also has interests in many of the companies listed above, serves as chairman or a director of:[181]

Cape Explosives Works Ltd. (average annual dividend from
  1928-1938: 47.5%)[182]
Companhia de Diamantes de Angola (£2,000,000). The size of
  this company is clear from the fact that, among other things, it

---

[172] *SEYB38*, p. 3043.
[173] *SEYB38*, p. 3075.
[174] *SEYB38*, p. 3096.
[175] *SEYB38*, p. 3099.
[176] *SEYB38*, p. 3100.
[177] *SEYB38*, p. 756.
[178] *SEYB38*, p. 3147.
[179] *SEYB38*, p. 3150.
[180] *Directory of Directors 1938*, p. 912.
[181] *Directory of Directors 1938*, pp. 912-3.
[182] *SEYB38*, p. 1062.

has the sole right to carry out mining explorations in an area of around 390,000 square miles (around 600,000 sq. km) until 1971, and to exploit the diamond-bearing deposits discovered until then indefinitely. The company is exempt from Portuguese import duties on equipment and materials, as well as from export duties on diamonds.[183]

Nchanga Consolidated Copper Mines (authorized capital: £5,000,000).[184]

Rhodesian Anglo American Ltd. Authorized capital: £6,500,000, although the directors have the right to borrow up to twice the authorized share capital. If the remuneration paid to the directors—there are 12 of them—is less than 2.5% of the dividend paid for the year in question, they are entitled to the difference, which should not exceed £12,000 per annum. The company has interests in various other mining companies.[185]

Theatre Royal, Drury Lane.

We should not overlook Sir Robert Kotze, nor Gilbert Roy Lewis. As well as a number of the companies cited in connection with Joel, the former is a director of:[186]

East Geduld Mines Ltd. (£1,800,000)[187]

Geduld Proprietary Mines Ltd. (£1,500,000, average dividend of the period 1928-1938 about 50% per annum)[188]

Grootvlei Proprietary Mines Ltd. (£2,500,000)[189]

Legal and General Assurance Society Ltd. (£1,000,000)[190]

Marievale Consolidated Mines Ltd. (£2,250,000)[191]

New Jagersfontein Mining and Exploration Co. Ltd. (£1,000,000)[192]

---

[183] *SEYB38*, p. 2964. Translator's note: This company was more commonly known as Diamang, and it was Portugal's largest colonial company, formed by a consortium of international finance. It managed tens of thousands of employees in a territory equivalent to one third of mainland Portugal, and with its own army, it was described as 'a state within a state'.

[184] *SEYB38*, p. 3070.

[185] *SEYB38*, p. 3105.

[186] *Directory of Directors 1938*, p. 973. & *Directory of Directors 1938*, p. 1017.

[187] *SEYB38*, p. 3001.

[188] *SEYB38*, p. 3012.

[189] *SEYB38*, p. 3022.

[190] *SEYB38*, p. 2642.

[191] *SEYB38*, p. 3053.

[192] *SEYB38*, p. 3073.

While Gilbert Roy Lewis is Deputy Chairman of Lewis and Marks Ltd., and is a director or on the advisory board of the following companies:

African and European Investment Comp. Ltd. (£2,750,000)	Roberts Victor Diamonds Ltd.
Amalgamated Collieries of South Africa Ltd. (£2,000,000)	South Rand Exploration Co. Ltd.
Chandler's Ltd.	Springfield Collieries Ltd.
Coronation Collieries Ltd.	Swaziland Corporation (1924) Ltd.
Crown Diamond Mining and Exploration Co. Ltd.	Union Street Corporation (of South Africa) Ltd.
Grootvlei Proprietary Mines Ltd. (£2,500,000)	Vereeniging Brick and Tile Co. Ltd.
Lonely Reef Gold Mining Co. Ltd.	Vereeniging Estates Ltd.
New Central Witwatersrand Areas Ltd.	Vryheid Coronation Ltd.
New Machavie Gold Mining Co. Ltd.	West Spaarwater (£2,000,000).
Palmietkuil Gold Mining Co. Ltd. (£1,700,000)	

The Jews in Africa

While the aforementioned Hebrews strongly dominate the gold and diamond industries, we now come to the magnates who do not limit themselves to these sectors, but who are also leaders in trade, industry, agriculture, mining and finance in Africa. The partners and co-directors in the firm Lewis and Marks (capital £1,600,000) alongside the aforementioned Gilbert Roy Lewis, are Louis Marks, Theodore Marks, and J. M. Marks.[193]

Louis Marks is chairman or a director of: Bechuanaland Farms Ltd., a subsidiary of the African and European Investment Co. (£2,750,000), which has significant interests in: Crown Diamond Mining and Exploration Co. Ltd., Elandsfontein Platinum Ltd., as well as in various other companies, and including their own estates, it has:

> 441 estates comprising...857,443 acres,
> The mineral rights in 180 estates comprising...176,173 acres,
> And coal rights in 31 estates comprising...46,284 acres in Transvaal, Bechuanaland, Orange Free State etc., as well as 259 gold mining claims in the Boksburg District.
> Carolina Coal Mining Co. Ltd.
> Cattle Ranchers Ltd.
> Cobra Emeralds Ltd.
> Eastern Province Cement Ltd. (£1,011,288)
> Elandsfontein Platinum Ltd.
> Garner Motors Ltd.
> Largo Colliery (£2,000,000)
> Rand Refinery Ltd.
> South African Glass Union Ltd.
> South African Salt Works Ltd.

---

[193] *Directory of Directors 1938*, pp. 1121-3; *SEYB38*, p. 1511.

Stewarts and Lloyds of South Africa Ltd. (share capital £7,370,275), which owns all shares of 7 other firms, as well as major interests in another twelve.[194]

Union Line Co. Ltd.

Vaal River Salt Works Ltd.

Weltevreden Gold Mining Syndicate Ltd.

Witwatersrand Co-operative Smelting Works Ltd.

Witwatersrand Native Labor Association Ltd.

And in a number of the same companies as Gilbert R. Lewis, Theodore Marks and J. M. Marks are listed as directors, chairmen, and advisory board members in a total of 29 companies.

Sir Ernest Oppenheimer is chairman or a director of:[195]

African Cables (Proprietary) Ltd.	Holfontein (T. C. L.) Gold Mining Co. Ltd.
Anglo-American Corporation of South Africa Ltd. (£5,000,000)	Lace Proprietary Mines Ltd.
Anglo-American Investment Trust Ltd. (£2,500,000)	Libanon Gold Mining Co. Ltd. (£2,500,000)
Blyvooruitzicht Gold Mining Co. Ltd. (£2,950,000)	Rand Leases (Vogelstruisfontein) Gold Mining Co. Ltd.
Boart Products South Africa (Proprietary) Ltd.	Rand Selection Corporation Ltd. (£1,000,000)
Brakpan Mines Ltd. (£1,150,000; average dividend in 1928-1938: 48.6% annual)	Rhodesia Broken Hill Development Co. Ltd. (£3,250,000)
British South Africa Co. (which we shall discuss in more detail below)	Rietfontein (No. 11) Gold Mines Ltd. (£1,100,000)
Cape Coast Exploration Ltd. (£1,000,000)	Société Minière du Beccka
Consolidated Company Bultfontein Mine Ltd.	Spaarwater Gold Mining Co. Ltd. (£2,000,000)
Daggafontein Mines Ltd. (£1,750,000; average dividend 1934-1938: 41% annual)	Springs Mines Ltd. (£1,750,000)
Gold Coast Exploration Ltd.	West Rand Investment Trust Ltd. (capital: £4,000,000)
Griqualand West Diamond Mining Co. (£1,057,000)	West Springs Ltd. (£1,935,000)

Let us now take a closer look at the British South Africa Company, whose other directors include Baron Emile B. d'Erlanger and Sir Edmund Davis. This company's field of operations is in Rhodesia, namely:

a) Southern Rhodesia: in the provinces of Mashonaland and Matabeleland comprising some 149,000 square miles (approx. 242,000 sq km);

b) Northern Rhodesia: a merger of North East and North West Rhodesia comprising 291,000 square miles (473,000 sq km).

The entire area was previously managed by this company. However, when on 12 September 1923, Southern Rhodesia was officially declared a colony of the British Empire, and in 1924 the South Africa Company renounced administration of Northern Rhodesia, an agreement was made with the British government which, among other things, set out the following: that the company would surrender its rights and claims in Southern Rhodesia and transfer its buildings etc., which had been used for administrative purposes, as well as cede its land and monopoly rights, with the exception of the mineral rights in Northern Rhodesia to which it would continue to be entitled. In

---

[194] *SEYB38*, pp. 2955, 1741, 2958, 2925.
[195] *Directory of Directors 1938*, p. 1280.

exchange, on 1 January 1923, the company would receive a cash payment of £3,750,000 from the government and would continue to share in the net proceeds of land sales in North West Rhodesia until 1 April 1964. The British Crown would recognize all of the company's mineral rights in Northern and Southern Rhodesia and would grant the widest possible protection to its railway interests. The Crown would waive all claims against the company regarding the extraordinary military expenses incurred during the war. The company would retain all of its commercial and economic rights and assets, and no further claims would be made against it regarding the land used for its own commercial purposes or entrusted to third parties.

Under an agreement dated 29 June 1933, the government acquired the company's mineral rights in Southern Rhodesia for £2,000,000. The company's main activities now consist of:

> Mining rights throughout all of Northern Rhodesia;
> About 600,000 acres of land in the Bechuanaland Protectorate;
> Mineral rights in approx. 16,000 square miles of Nyasaland;
> Until 1964, a half-share in the net proceeds from government land sales in North West Rhodesia;
> Approximately 2,677,000 acres of property in North East Rhodesia;
> Additional land holdings of 110,107 acres in Southern Rhodesia;
> A significant portion of the Wankie Colliery Co. Ltd.;
> 80% of the shares of Rhodesia Railway Trust Ltd.;
> All shares of Rhodesian Land Bank Ltd; and
> Decisive influence in the Beira Railway Co. Ltd. The Rhodesian railway network, including Beira, extends over 2708 miles.[196]

Sir Ernest Oppenheimer is also involved in a number of the companies already listed in relation to Joel and Friedlander.

Sir Edmund Davis, who in the *Jewish Year Book* is referred to simply as an 'art collector,' is chairman or a director of the following companies:[197]

> Rhodesian Land, Cattle and Ranching Corporation, whose authorized capital is £1,000,000, and whose assets include an estate of approx. 2,771,662 acres in Southern Rhodesia.[198]
> African Chrome Mines Ltd.
> African Manganese Co. Ltd.
> Anglo-Continental Mines Co. Ltd.
> Baluchistan Chrome Co. Ltd.

---

[196] *SEYB38*, pp. 2232-3.
[197] *Directory of Directors 1938*, p. 432: *Jewish Year Book 1938*, p. 423.
[198] *SEYB38*, p. 2376.

Baluchistan Mining Syndicate Ltd.
Bechuanaland Exploration Co.
Charterland and General Exploration and Finance Co. Ltd.
Chinese Central Railways Ltd.
Chrome Co. Ltd.
Compagnie Tunisienne des Phosphates du Djebel Mdilla
Consolidated Mines Selection Co. Ltd.
East Africa Mining Areas Ltd.
East African Lands and Development Co. Ltd.
Etablissements Courmont
Fanti Consolidated Investment Co.
J. Picard and Co. Ltd.
Josiah Smale and Son Ltd.
Mufulira Copper Mines
Northern Rhodesia Power Corporation Ltd.
Otavi Mines and Railway Company
Raw Asbestos Distributors
Rhodesia Chrome Mines
Rhodesia Copper and General Exploration and Finance Co. Ltd.
Rhodesia Railway Ltd.
Rhodesian and General Asbestos Corporation Ltd.
Rhodesian Anglo-American Co. Ltd.
St. Swithin's Ores and Metals Ltd.
Shabani Railway Co. Ltd.
Société d'Enterprises Industrielles et Minières
South West Africa Co. Ltd. (capital £2,000,000)[199]
Southern Rhodesia Metals Ltd.
Turner and Newall, whose authorized capital is £7,250,000, is
 engaged principally in the manufacture of asbestos articles. It owns
 factories in eight different locations. Sixteen other companies have
 been merged into it and it also owns the entire capital of:
  Bell's United Asbestos Co. Ltd.
  Dominion Blue Asbestos Co. Ltd.
  Elands Valley Transport Co.
  New Amianthus Mines Ltd.
  Raw Asbestos Distributors
Turner Bros. Asbestos Co. Ltd.
United Exploration Co. Ltd.
Wankie Colliery Co. Ltd. (capital £1,100,000)[200]
Yangtse Valley Co. Ltd.

---

[199] *SEYB38*, p. 3122.
[200] *SEYB38*, p. 3152.

In addition, Sir Edmund Davis, along with Marks, Oppenheimer, Joel, etc., is involved in a whole series of other influential companies, which is beyond our purview to list individually.

It is difficult to imagine the extent to which all of these companies are closely connected and interlocked with each other. However, to attempt such an exposition here would go outside of the scope of this work. Nevertheless, we believe that our outline above should give the reader at least a small insight into the situation, which should lead him to a better understanding of certain realities. In this respect, it is worth mentioning a *Daily Express* article of 29 October 1938, which bears the headline: 'Business leaders call on Britain: Unite East African Territories!' The article reads: 'Twenty men who represents millions of British capital (!) have adopted the following resolution of the East African Chamber of Commerce: 1. Tanganyika must remain British, 2. Tanganyika, Kenya and Uganda must be made into a single customs union.'

The aforementioned list of Jewish magnates of finance, with huge interests in gold, diamonds, coal mines, plantations, and in all branches of industry and trade in Africa, could be considerably enlarged without great difficulty. To name just a few: Col. Benjamin Hansford, Sir Bernard Eckstein, Isidore W. Schlesinger, Sir Henry Strakosch, Edmond Weil, Julius Weil, Rene Weil, Samuel Weil, Leopold Weil, and Julius Sigimund Wetzlar.

The Weils are involved as directors, managing directors or chairmen in 13 different diamond, gold, and silver mining companies, which in turn have interests in numerous other companies. The same applies to Wetzlar with 17 companies, many of them million-dollar corporations with huge real estate holdings and a significant stake in another series of large companies. Eckstein, meanwhile, owns millions of acres in Brazil and Africa for which he has timber and mineral rights, and on which he has vast coffee and cotton plantations. Schlesinger is more diverse in his interests. He is, among other things, managing director of Tanganyika Forests and Lumber Co Ltd, which has 60,900 acres of forest in Tanganyika, of which 400 acres or more may be cut down annually. He is also Chairman of the African Consolidated Investments Corporation Ltd., which has an authorized capital of £2,250,000, and which directly controls the following companies:[201]

African Canning and Packing Corporation Ltd.
Anglo International Securities Corporation Ltd.
Colonial Banking and Trust Co. Ltd.
Golden Valley Citrus Estates Ltd.
Tanganyika Forests and Lumber Co.

---

[201] *Directory of Directors 1938*, p. 1801. & pp. 1810-1. & *SEYB38*, pp. 2309, 2359, 2399. & p. 1910.

As well as also holding significant interests in various other South African companies.[202] Schlesinger is also active in the areas of insurance, finance, theatre, etc. and is chairman of:

> African Life Assurance Society Ltd.
> African Theatres Ltd.
> Anglo-International Securities Corporation Ltd.
> British Consolidated Investments Corporation Ltd.
> Golden Valley Citrus Estates.
> O. K. Bazaars (1929) Ltd.

African Theatres Ltd. was founded to take over the theatres and cinemas of the African Theatres Trust Ltd. It also owns 78% of the capital of African Consolidated Theatres Ltd. The O. K. Bazaars (Bazaar and General Store Proprietors) company owns 14 department stores in South Africa, as well as half the shares of Parok Ltd.; it also controls Paramount Stores Ltd., Allied Drug Co. Ltd. (which in turn controls Publix Ltd.), the Grand Parade Buildings, O. K. Emporium Ltd. and other subsidiaries.[203]

The above exposition may also help to explain why the British press artificially sparked such great resistance to the German colonies being returned. In this context, it is interesting to read the following excerpt from a *Daily Express* article of 1 November 1938, which discusses the 'uncertainty about the colonies':

> A major uncertainty that absolutely requires clarification is the government's attitude towards the former German colonies. This is of particular interest for the investment of capital in the South African gold mining industry, as the current uncertainty makes it extremely difficult for the major mining financiers to carry out huge plans which may include raising £20,000,000 of new capital, needed for the exploration of the Far West Rand and other new gold fields...

Do we need any greater proof that the German colonies are welcome prey to the money-hungry Jews, a booty which they in no way wish to relinquish?

The Judaization of Film

We shall now take a look at the Judaization of the film industry, which has increasingly been put into the service of anti-German propaganda. It has

---

[202] *SEYB38*, p. 2192.
[203] *SEYB38*, pp. 2615, 826, 2201, 2227, 1307, 1672. *Directory of Directors 1938*, p. 1507.

been left more or less entirely up to the Jews and their friends what kind of films are produced, released and distributed. What is true is that before every film there is always a reproduction of an authorization certificate which bears the inscription: 'Passed by the British Board of Film Censors', which is sometimes undersigned by an MP, which works to create the impression that this is a state institution. In fact, this so-called censorship board is appointed and paid for by the film producers. It is up to the reader to decide to what extent its impartiality and independence is compromised by the film tycoons who pay for it.

At the same time, everything possible is done to make socialist and communist films available to the public. In 1926 the Film Society was founded. The two main people responsible for this, the full Jews Ivor Montagu, brother of Lord Swaythling, and Sidney Bernstein, were in contact with Serge Eisenstein, another Jew who for several years had been Moscow's chief film propagandist. Three years later, the London Workers' Film Society was founded, which released films containing dangerous communist propaganda. Here, too, Ivor Montagu is in a key executive position.[204]

The extent to which the film industry is dominated by Jews can best be seen by listing the film magnates and their interests. Of course, here too we shall have to limit ourselves to listing a few of the most well-known.

There is probably no need to go into detail about the Hungarian Jew Alexander Korda and his partner Erich Pommer. In addition to their joint company, London Film Productions, the latter also has his own Pommer Productions.

The three brothers Isidore, Mark, and Maurice Ostrer, sons of Jewish emigrants who came from Poland in the 1890s and who settled in the London East End district of Whitechapel, control hundreds of cinemas and music halls, while they also produce (or produced) films.[205]

Isidore Ostrer is president of:

Denman Picture Houses Ltd.
General Theatre Corporation Ltd.
Provincial Cinematograph Theatres Ltd.
Gaumont-British Picture Corporation Ltd.
Gaumont-British Distributors Ltd.
Lothbury Investment Corporation.[206]

---

[204] Lane, pp. 73-76. Translator's note: The entire chapter, 'Aliens and the Films', is recommended to researchers for Lane's far-sightedness, as it shows how, as early as the 1920s, Lane worked to try to persuade the government that cinema was being used by hostile forces to subvert and demoralize the mass psyche, at a time when the government was ideologically *laissez-faire*. & Lane, pp. 78-80.

[205] *Daily Express*, 9/1/1939.

[206] *Directory of Directors 1938*, p. 1286.

Mark Ostrer, of the Ostrer Brothers banking house, is chairman or a director
of the following companies:

Albany Ward Theatres Ltd.	National Electric Theatres Ltd.
Associated Provincial Picture Houses Ltd.	New Century Pictures Ltd.
B. B. Pictures (1920) Ltd.	Newington Electric Theatres Ltd.
Birmingham West End Cinema Ltd.	North of England Cinemas Ltd.
Classic Cinemas Ltd.	P. C. T. Construction Co. Ltd.
Davis Theatre (Croydon) Ltd.	Provincial Cinematograph Theatres Ltd.
Denman (London) Cinemas Ltd.	Royal Hotel, Edinburgh, Ltd.
Denman (Midlands) Cinemas Ltd.	Scala (Leeds) Ltd.
Gainsborough Pictures (1928) Ltd.	Sheffield Music Hall Comp. Ltd.
Haymarket Estates Ltd.	Tivoli Palace Ltd.
Leeds Picture Playhouse Ltd.	Trocadero Super-Cinema (Liverpool) Ltd.
Metropolis and Bradford Trust Co.	United Picture Theatres Ltd.
Moss Empires Ltd.	Victoria Palace Ltd.

He is also chairman or managing director of the companies already listed for
Isidore Ostrer.

The third brother, Maurice Ostrer, does not only have interests in most
of the aforementioned companies of Isidore and Mark Ostrer, but also has
interests in the following companies:

British Acoustic Films Ltd.	Gaumont-British Screen Services Ltd.
Bush Radio Ltd.	Gaumont Construction Co. Ltd.
Classic Cinemas Ltd.	Gaumont Super Cinemas Ltd.
Electrical Fono Films Ltd.	Glasgow Tivoli
Film Clearing Houses	Haymarket Capitol Ltd.
Gaumont-British Instructional Ltd.	Theatre Services Ltd.

To get a sense of the far-reaching influence that the aforementioned
corporations have, let us take a closer look at some of them. Without a doubt
the most important is the Gaumont-British Picture Corporation Ltd, which,
in addition to a number of its own cinemas, owns all the shares in the following companies:

Denman Picture Houses Ltd.
Gaumont-British Distributors Ltd.
Gaumont-British Picture Corporation of America Inc.
Gaumont Construction Co. Ltd.
Ideal Films Ltd.
Standard Films Co. Ltd.
Theatre (Grimsby) Ltd.
W. and F. Film Service Ltd.

As well as being the majority shareholder in:

British Acoustic Films Ltd.
Gaumont Super-Cinemas Ltd.
New Standard Film Co. Ltd.
Provincial Cinematograph Ltd.

Each one of these companies in turn controls a series of other film and cinema-theatre companies. The Gaumont-British Picture Corporation for its part acts as general administrator for all companies owned or controlled by the following companies:

General Theatre Corporation Ltd.
Moss Empires Ltd.
Denman Picture Houses Ltd.

This last company (Denman Picture Houses Ltd.) was founded in 1928 with the purpose of:
   a)   Acquiring ownership of the following companies:

Aighburt Picture House Ltd.	Grand Cinema Ltd.
Attractive Cinema (West Kensington) Ltd.	Kinematograph Properties Ltd.
Beresford Cinema Ltd.	Kings Hall (Penge) Ltd.
Broadway Variety Ltd.	Magnet Cinema (Wavertree) Ltd.
Consolidated Cinematograph Cos. Ltd.	New Cross Cinema Ltd.
Corona Cinema (Great Crosby) Ltd.	Popular Cinemas Ltd.
Dingle Picturedrome Ltd.	Thompson and Collins Enterprises Ltd.

   b)   Gaining the majority stake in various other companies.

Denman Pictures Houses Ltd. directly or indirectly controls 102 cinemas and also owns the majority stake in another 24 cinemas. Its authorized capital is £1,650,000.[207]
     The General Theatre Corporation, in which the three Ostrer brothers act as president, director, and managing director respectively, has decisive influence over eight different cinema companies or entertainment venues and has the majority stake in 59 cinemas or variety theatres.[208]
     The Provincial Cinematograph Theatres Ltd. owns, among other things, the entire capital of seven cinemas or cinema groups. It directly controls:

Associated Provincial Picture Houses Ltd.
City Cinema Ltd.
Dorking Regional Theatre Ltd.
Leeds Picture Playhouse Ltd.
P. C. T. Construction Co. Ltd.

---

[207] *SEYB38*, p. 1174.
[208] *SEYB38*, p. 1293.

Royal Hotel (Edinburgh) Co. Ltd.
Trocadero Super-Cinema (Liverpool) Ltd.

And manages the business of:

Regent (Stamford Hill) Ltd.
Scala (Ealing) Ltd.
Scala (Kilburn) Ltd.
Scala (Maida Vale) Ltd.
York Cinemas Ltd.

It also owns, either directly or through its subsidiaries, 108 theatres etc. Its capital amounts to £3,200,000.[209]

The Associated Provincial Picture Houses Ltd., directly controlled by the aforementioned Provincial Cinematograph Theatres Ltd., was set up with an authorized capital of £1,000,000 for the purpose of acquiring sites, contracts and site options in various cities for the purpose of erecting cinemas thereon. The company owns 18 cinemas, nine of which are also incorporate a coffee house. It also has significant interests in a number of other cinemas.[210]

The capital of P. C. T. Construction Co. Ltd., to pick just one from the multitude of companies controlled by the Provincial Cinematograph Theatres Ltd., is £1,750,000. Its main tasks are in the area of finance, and it is not difficult to guess that it also has a far-reaching influence.[211]

All in all, Gaumont-British currently controls around 350 cinemas in the UK, which are estimated to be visited by around three million people per week.[212] In early 1939, the newspapers were filled with big headlines about a £20,000,000 deal which involved plans to merge Gaumont-British with Odeon Theatres (Chairman: Oscar Deutsch, whom we shall soon discuss). Together, these two entities already control more than 500 theatres. If this deal were to go through, they would represent by far the largest group in the British cinema industry and would undoubtedly strengthen their position of power.[213]

The aforementioned Oscar Deutsch, who has been active during the current war as a member of the Territorial Army Public Interest Committee, to promote recruiting for the Anti-Aircraft Division in London, is a director of:

Copper Sheets (Sales) Ltd.
Decorative Crafts Ltd.
Deutsch and Brenner

---

[209] *SEYB38*, p. 1746.
[210] *SEYB38*, p. 886.
[211] *SEYB38*, p. 1687.
[212] Lane, p. 80.
[213] *Daily Express*, 7/1/1939, 9/1/1939.

> Entertainments and General Investment Corp. Ltd.
> London and Southern Cinemas Ltd.
> Odeon Theatres Ltd.
> Scophony Ltd.
> Sound and Cinema Equipment Ltd.
> United Artists Corporation Ltd.[214]

His influence in the cinema industry is also considerable. For example, Odeon Theatres Ltd—whose other directors include M. Silverstone and E. C. Simmons—has taken over the management of various companies with 84 cinemas, to which additional cinemas have since been added. Odeon, in turn, has direct control over London and Southern Super Cinemas Ltd., as well as Entertainments and General Investment Corporation Ltd., the latter of which owns, controls or manages 54 cinemas through its subsidiaries. Odeon also manages another 71 theatres for which it has purchase options. Its authorized capital is £6,000,000.[215]

The aforementioned London and Southern Super Cinemas Ltd.—whose deputy chairman and managing director is Arthur Cohen—owns, directly or through its subsidiaries, 15 cinemas in London, Greater London, and Middlesex, as well as having direct control of eight other cinema groups.[216]

It would go beyond the scope of this work to enumerate all of the Jewish threads that run through the English film industry and cinema operations. The names Alfred Levy, Sidney Bernstein, and Abrahams may serve as a point of reference for those who wish to delve into this matter in more detail.

The 'enormous significance' of cinema was recognized by the previous Chancellor of the Exchequer, Sir John Simon, at a dinner of the British Kinematograph Society, held at London's famous Trocadero Restaurant on 8 February 1939. The *Times* gives the following report of his address to those present:

> Proposing the toast of 'The Society', Sir John Simon said the enterprise in which its members were engaged was one of enormous significance and importance for the community and the State. He doubted very much whether there was any other

---

[214] *Directory of Directors 1938*, p. 459. Translator's note: Readers may be interested to know that in British Secret Service files made public in 2019, in 1940 MI5 was concerned that the Odeon cinema chain was a front for a Soviet spy ring, as the Soviet spy Arnold Deutsch (who recruited the Cambridge spy ring) was Oscar's cousin, and it was through Oscar that he, and other suspected Russian spies, obtained permission to remain in Britain. For more details see: https://www.dailymail.co.uk/news/article-7496559/MI5-thought-Odeon-cinema-chain-Russian-spies.html

[215]   *SEYB38*, p. 1675.

[216]   *SEYB38*, p. 1534.

way of informing and influencing public opinion which was likely in the future to be so important—important to the statesman, important to the publicist, important for the future of liberty and democracy, decency and taste and judgement.

To an increasing extent the cinema was forming and directing public taste and judgment. There was therefore a great responsibility resting upon the cinema industry that it should use its enormous influence in the most worthy way. That was one of the reasons why he rejoiced so heartily that they were developing an authoritative British cinema industry.[217]

The working conditions for cinema staff are apparently not particularly social, as can be seen from a leaflet distributed by the trade union concerned, on the occasion of a strike. This leaflet states that although it had been contractually agreed that employees would work for a maximum of 48 hours per week, the employers did not adhere to this agreement in any way—after first giving an overview of the profits achieved by the various cinema companies, as shown below:

> Gaumont-British Picture Corporation for the year 1937:
> > Net profits for the year from theatres... £561,701
> > Preferential dividend....................... £178,750
> Provincial Cinematograph Theatres Ltd:
> > A dividend of 10% was declared for the tenth
> > consecutive year.
> General Theatre Corporation:
> > An increase in profits of £61,072.

The trade-union leaflet then went on to demand a reduction in the 64-hour working week and a modest share of these dividends as a supplement to the workers' inadequate salary.[218]

Science and Education in Jewish Hands

If we now turn to the universities, to the related educational system, and to science in general, we can of course only deal with a few of the best-known Jews in this area, of whose ancestry we can be completely assured. Those we shall name are, with very few exceptions, denominational Jews.

---

[217] *Times*, 9/2/1939 p. 12. Translator's note: QVOS. The original article also has a non-exhaustive list of those present.
[218] Leaflet of the Electrical Trades Union, London Central Committee.

Lane's judgment from 1934 on the general influence of Jews in education is very revealing:

> We opened our educational institutions (many of them endowed by old benefactions and more recently subsidised by the British Exchequer) to all comers, irrespective of age or sex, race or creed. Age and sex matter little, but race and creed are fundamental. And now, alike among the teachers and the taught, an Alien influence boding ill for English traditions, customs and codes, has long since sprung into existence and is making its presence felt. None of these elements lose an opportunity to abuse the tolerance which we have accorded them; their influence and activities are devoted to the promulgation of disloyal, seditious, and revolutionary teachings. They are eternally seeking to replace patriotism and nationalism by Pacifism and Internationalism. Alien people are corrupting our young, and they constitute a dangerous and weakening element in our midst.
>
> Old foundations endowed for the purpose of teaching Christian children are passing into the hands of those who will use them as instruments by which the Alien shall benefit and the native shall suffer.[219]

Our research has confirmed this impression with solid proof. First of all, let us start with the two universities that are forever associated with science and education in Great Britain, those of the greatest renown: Oxford and Cambridge.

In the former we find, among others, Isaiah Berlin and Chaim Rabinovitch as examples of lecturers, Dr. J. Marshak as a statistician, Herbert Loewe as an Orientalist, M. Lutzki, who is an assistant in the Oriental Department of the Bodleian Library, Walter George Ettinghausen [Walter Eytan] as a lecturer in German, and Eduard Fraenkel as a professor of Latin. Arthur Goodhart is a law professor and a contributor to the Law Quarterly Review. Among other things, he published the book *Poland and the Minority Races* (1920). Ephraim Lipson, lecturer in economics, has written numerous works in this field. He is editor of the History of Europe series and was editor of the Economic History of Europe series from its inception until 1934. He is also a contributor to the *Transactions of the Royal Historical Society*, *English Historical Review* and *Fortnightly Review*. Redcliffe Salaman, Director of the Agricultural and Forestry Research Institute, has held many honorary positions, including membership of the Royal Society. He

---

[219]Lane, p. 151 ff. Translator's note: QVOS.

has done a great deal of pioneering research on potatoes and has contributed to various scientific journals such as *The Lancet*.[220]

At Oxford, we also find the zoologist Solly Zuckerman, who is also the author of various works. Sir Alfred Zimmern is the first Professor of International Politics (i.e. International Relations) in the world. He also written a series of books, which include the titles *The Third British Empire* and *The League of Nations and the Rule of Law*. Over the years, he has held many important positions, including Deputy Director of the League of Nations' Institute for Intellectual Co-operation, and Founder/Director of the Geneva School of International Studies. He was also a member of the Political Intelligence Department at the Foreign Office, and a staff inspector at the Board of Education. Cecil Roth and Daniel Meredith Bueno de Mesquita have recently been appointed to the University of Oxford, as Reader in Post-Biblical Jewish Studies and Research Fellow respectively.

Finally, we must also mention that in addition to those mentioned above, another 27 academic posts were filled after 1933 by emigrants from Germany, Austria, etc. They were appointed through the mediation of a society specifically set up for this purpose, the Society for the Protection of Science and Learning. The current president of this society is the Archbishop of York. In addition to well-known Jews, many personages from British public life are to be found on the management board, with nobility and knights being particularly well represented. This institution has been assigned the mission of accommodating Jewish (or Jewish-descended) scientists who have emigrated from Germany into new positions. Further on in this chapter, we will see to what extent this has been achieved in Great Britain.[221]

Apparently this large number of Jewish professors has already had an impact in political terms. From experience we ourselves know, and it has been confirmed to us again and again, that a large proportion of the students at Oxford, perhaps even the majority, have fallen for communism.

In Cambridge, we find almost the same tableau: Dr. L. Harris is Director of Food Laboratories who has published widely on biochemistry. His contributions to the journal *The Proceedings of the Royal Society* and others

---

[220] *Jewish Year Book 1937*, p. 407. Translator's note: Profiles for most of the people listed can be found on the Oxford Chabad Society's website: www.oxfordchabad.org/templates/ articlecco_cdo/aid/457389/jewish/Oxford-Jewish-Personalities.htm & *Jewish Year Book 1937*, p. 483. & p. 470. & p. 468. & p. 469. & p. 425. & p. 430. & p. 438. Translator's note: This book was the product of Goodhart's trip to Poland as part of the aforementioned joint US-UK commission sent to investigate the Polish pogrom allegations of 1919. & *Jewish Year Book 1937*, p. 467; *Who's Who 1939*, p. 1905. & *Jewish Year Book 1937*, p. 489; *Who's Who 1939*, p. 2804.

[221] *Who's Who 1939*, p. 3535. & Seton Hutchison, p. 17; *Who's Who 1939*, p. 3534. & *Jewish Chronicle*, 25/11/1938, p. 47. & *Annual Report of the Society for the Protection... 1934, 1935, 1937, 1938*.

are well known. R. Kahn is a lecturer in economics, Reuben Levy is a lecturer in Persian, and Hersch Lauterpacht is Whewell Professor of International Law. Charles S. Myers is a well-known psychologist with numerous publications and contributions to scientific journals. After 1933, 25 German Jews alone were accepted onto the teaching staff at Cambridge University. With such success, it is easy to see why the building of a synagogue in Cambridge became necessary.[222]

London has a particularly large number of Jews in its scientific institutions, which is known to be the case in all metropolises in Judaized countries. So we find L. P. Aaronson as a lecturer in economic science at the City of London College, M. Dainow as a lecturer in psychology, who has many well-known publications to his name, and S. Dainow as a reader in modern languages. Sir Percival David is a member of the Institute of Archeology and was Director of the world-famous Exhibition of Chinese Art in 1935-1936.[223]

H. Finer lectures on administrative law and is well known for publications such as *The British Civil Service* and *English Local Government*. M. Ginsberg is a professor of sociology and has also published numerous works in his field. He is, among other things, co-editor of the magazine *Social Review*. Jacob Isaacs is a reader in English language and literature. In addition to his publications, he has made a name for himself as editor of both *English Library Reprints* and *Contemporary Movements in European Literature,* and as a regular contributor to the *Times Literary Supplement*, the *Review of England*, the *Spectator* and others. Barnet Janner, MP for Whitechapel from 1931 to 1935, serves as president of the Students Representative Council and editor of the *University Magazine*. Herbert Jolowicz is a professor of Roman law and has been dean of the law faculty since 1937. In addition to well-known works, he is editor of the *Journal of the Society of Public Teachers of Law*. Harold Kisch is a surgeon at University College Hospital, while Harold Laski is Professor of Political Science and Education at the London School of Economics. Laski has held numerous important positions in both disciplines. His publications are well-known and he has made regular contributions to periodicals such as the *New Republic, Harvard Law Review, The*

---

[222] *Jewish Year Book 1937*, p. 442; *Who's Who 1939*, p. 1395. & *Jewish Year Book 1937*, p. 455. & p. 465. & *Jewish Chronicle*, 9/12/1938. Translator's note: The JC mentions Lauterpacht in the context of a speech he gave to the Cambridge University Jewish Society titled 'The Principle of Humanitarian Intervention.' He was a member of the British team at the Nuremberg Trials in 1946, helped to draft Israel's Declaration of Independence in 1948, and was knighted in 1956. & *Jewish Year Book 1937*, p. 476; *Who's Who 1939*, p. 2316. & *Annual Report of the Society for the Protection... 1938*, p. 14. & *Jewish Chronicle*, 30/4/1937; 29/10/1937. Translator's note: Interestingly, in the speech given by Dr. Salaman at the luncheon preceding the ceremony of the laying of the foundation stone (April issue), he discussed the Jews of medieval Cambridge, and mentioned their expulsion in 1275.

[223] *Jewish Year Book 1937*, p. 398. & p. 420. & p. 420; *Who's Who 1939*, p. 786.

Nation, and the *Manchester Guardian*. Hyman Levy is Professor of Mathematics at the Imperial College of Science and Technology; he has held many honorary positions in science. His numerous publications on mathematics and aeronautics, as well as his contributions to scientific journals, are very well respected.

At the same institution, L. Roth is a lecturer and at Acton Technical College, B. Simons is a full professor in the same discipline. Charles Seligman was Professor of Anthropology at the University of London. He published a large number of scientific works and regularly contributed articles to journals such as the *Journal of the Anthropological Institute*, *Geographical Journal*, the *Lancet*, and the *British Journal of Psychology*. In 1922, Charles Singer, Professor in the History of Medicine, was named President of the Third International Congress of the History of Medicine in London; it goes without saying that he also published numerous works. J. Wartzki is a lecturer in Oriental Languages, Samson Wright Professor of Psychology and Claude Spiers a lecturer in Chemistry. Dr. Salomon Birnbaum is a lecturer in Hebrew Palaeography at the School of Oriental Studies, University of London.

Finally, one of the best-known Jewish academics is Abraham Wolf, Professor of Logic and Scientific Method at University College London, who also lectures at the London School of Economics. Among his many achievements, he was co-editor of the 14th edition of the *Encyclopedia Britannica*, and editor of the History of the Sciences Library, and has authored many well-known works. He has also been President of the Examination Board for Academic Examinations in Scientific Fields.[224] No fewer than 59 German Jews were given university positions in London after 1933.[225]

Of course, the number of Jews at the smaller universities is correspondingly lower. Lewis Namier [born Ludwik Bernstein in Russian Poland] is Professor of Modern History at the University of Manchester. Among other things, he contributed to the 4th and 5th volumes of Major Temperley's *History of the Peace Conference of Paris*, which we ourselves have used as a reference, and during the Great War he held positions in the Propaganda Department (1915-17), the Political Intelligence Bureau of the Department of Information (1917-18) and the Political Intelligence Department of the Foreign Office (1918-20). From 1929 to 1931 he served as political secretary to the Jewish Agency for Palestine, and at the same time (1929-1933) was also a member of Records Committee of Parliament. At the same university,

---

[224] *JYB37* p. 428. & *JYB37* p. 435; *WW39*, p. 1203. & *JYB37* p. 450; *WW39*, p. 1633. & *JYB37* p. 453; *WW39*, p. 1655. & *JYB37* p. 454; *WW39*, p. 1692. & *JYB37* p. 457; *WW39*, p. 1784. & *JYB37* p. 460; *WW39*, p. 1831. & *JYB37* p. 465; *WW39*, p. 1882. & *JYB37* p. 487. & *JYB37* p. 498. & *JYB37* p. 496; *WW39*, p. 2865. & *JYB37* p. 498. *WW39*, p. 2927. & *JYB37* p. 509. & *JYB37* p. 517. & *JYB37* p. 503. & *Jewish Chronicle*, 21/10/1938. & *JYB37* p. 513; *WW39*, p. 3470.

[225] *Annual Report of the Society for the Protection... 1938*, p. 14.

Dr. W. Susman teaches in the Pathology Department, and R. Wilenski teaches Art History, having written many books on Modern Art as well as contributing articles to the *Observer*, *Apollo*, *The Studio* and others. Polanyi, of Hungarian origin, is a professor of Chemistry.

More recently, Adolf Loewe was hired as a lecturer in Modern Political Philosophy, David Blank as a lecturer in Jurisprudence, S. Abelson as the first medical assistant in the Faculty of Clinical Research, and Bruno Rossi—a recent immigrant from Italy—was appointed as Professor of Physics. The University of Manchester has accepted nine scholars from among the ranks of the newly arrived German Jews.[226]

Noah Morris is a lecturer in Medicine at the University of Glasgow, and five other Jewish emigrants from Germany have received teaching positions there.[227]

Selig Brodetsky, an ardent Zionist, is Professor of Applied Mathematics at Leeds University. He has written various books, as well as numerous articles for scientific journals. Myer Coplans is a well-known scholar in Bacteriology, who has written almost countless articles and books. Up until now, as far as can be determined, only one German Jewish scholar has been accommodated at Leeds.[228]

In Birmingham, we find Hugh Goitein as Professor of Commercial Law, Sophia Weitzmann as a lecturer in History, and eight other German Jews. H. Cohen is Professor of Medicine at Liverpool, Israel Levine, Head of the Philosophy Faculty and J. Sager Professor of Botany at the University of Exeter. J. Lipkin is Professor of Medicine at the University of Liverpool, R. Powell, lecturer in Jurisprudence at the University of Hull, L. Rosenhead, Professor of Applied Mathematics at Liverpool, and J. Yoffey lecturer in Anatomy at Cardiff University. Finally, it should be mentioned that, among the Universities that have accepted German Jews onto their teaching staff, Birmingham has accepted eight German Jews, Bristol four, Edinburgh seven and Glasgow five.[229]

---

[226] *JYB37* p. 477; *WW39*, p. 2320. & *JYB37* p. 505. & *JYB37* p. 513; *WW39*, p. 3412. & *Jewish Chronicle*, 18/11/1938; *WW39*, p. 3470. & *Jewish Chronicle*, 13/1/1939. & 11/11/1938. & *Annual Report of the Society for the Protection... 1938*, p. 14.

[227] *Jewish Year Book 1937*, p. 475. Translator's note: I am very aware that the author's use of *Emigrant/Emigranten* (as well as *auswandern* in its various forms) could be seen as problematic in this historical context (to say the least), but I have chosen to faithfully represent what was written, even at the expense of a potentially more accurate choice of word. It should also be borne in mind that this word choice may have been determined by the circumstances in which the book was written and published, in which a 'neutral' term was the only politically viable option.

[228] *Jewish Year Book 1937*, p. 409; *WW39*, p. 386. & *Jewish Year Book 1937*, p. 418; *WW39*, p. 677. & *Annual Report of the Society for the Protection... 1938*, p. 14.

[229] *Jewish Year Book 1937*, p. 436. & p. 511. & pp. 462, 489. & p. 467. & p. 482. & p. 486. & p. 517.

By November 1938, a total of 251 Jews from Germany had been accommodated at British academic and research institutions in Great Britain.
We are convinced that this number is now far greater, given the increased
emigration of Jews from 1939 onwards. It is therefore not surprising that the
ugliest propaganda campaigns against the Third Reich have come from the
academic institutions of England. Hence it will be no surprise to the reader
that the Chief Rabbi of London had an honorary degree of Doctor of Laws
conferred upon him by the Chancellor of the University of London, who is
the Earl of Athlone, the king's uncle.[230]

The Jews also have considerable influence over education in general.
Lane calls attention to the increasingly widespread foreign infiltration in this
area and the associated dangers for the population as a whole. Here too we
shall examine the veracity of his judgement, by focusing on individuals, their
positions and publications.[231]

So it is that we find well-known educators such as Joseph Bernberg and
V. Cohen with books such as *Economic Society* and *The Nineteenth Century*,
as well as Charles Fox, director of the Teacher Training Institute with his
books *Practical Psychology* and *The Mind and Its Body*. L. Franks, formerly
deputy mayor of the London district of Stoke Newington, is now headmaster
of a boys' school in Hackney. Sidney Golding is an English teacher at the
London County Council Hackney Institute. He is an English examiner at the
Air Ministry, and at the London University Civil Service Examinations. A.
Gould is headmaster of Park House School in Middlesex, and J. Hadida
headmaster of a boys' school in Mile End. Isaac Gourvitsch is also a teacher
at the Hackney Institute. A. Kahn is a former inspector at the Board of Education, Morris Lewis is a lecturer in Education at the University of Notting-
ham, Miss A. Marks is a school inspector and H. Salomons is headmaster of
a state school in Christian Street. J. Simons is a lecturer in Modern Languages at Portsmouth College. Sir Philip Magnus held a senior post in the
Board of Education, as did Sir Philip Hartog. The latter is the author of many
publications, e.g. *An Examination of Examinations*, *The Marks of Examin-
ers*, *The Purposes of Examination* and *The Writing of English*. He has also
published various articles in *Special Reports on Educational Subjects of the
Board of Education* and *Fortnightly Review*.

Mr. Maurice Wollman was elected a Member of the Royal Society of
Literature, an honor for his services to literature as seen in his two antholo-
gies, *Modern Poetry 1922-1934* and *Poems of Twenty Years*. Wollman was
formerly an Examiner in English for the Northern Universities Joint Ma-

---

[230] *Annual Report of the Society for the Protection...1938*, p. 14. & *Jewish Chronicle*,
2/12/1938.
[231] Lane, pp. 151-60.

triculation Board and has been working in this capacity at the University of London and at the Civil Service Commissioners since 1938.[232]

One can see from this short compilation that Jews can be found everywhere in leading positions in Education. At the same time, there are also a number of English people whose work has a markedly Jewish spirit. From 1924 to 1929, the Minister of Education was Lord Eustace Percy, son of the Duke of Northumberland. One can get a glimpse of his mentality from, for example, his book *Responsibilities of the League* (1919), in which he says, among other things:

> [B]ut her [Russia's] revolution has been no passing freak of Jewish fury and the belt of Slav nations which, with independence gained, stretches to the gates of Bavaria, to the Adriatic and to Adrianople, is no mere figment of ethnology. Absurd as the enthusiasms of our Western sovietmongers may be, Russia is to-day a field of political invention and a source of inspiration to millions outside her frontiers, and the future may well depend on the extent to which the imagination of the Western democracies can keep pace with hers.[233]

The extent to which Jews and their ideas are valued in institutional centers, and their doctrines preached to the youth, can be seen from the following incident:

When the Jew I. Ellis, O.B.E., J.P., Headmaster of Finnart House School, retired in October 1938, Sir Alexander Maxwell, Secretary of State for the Home Office, praised the outgoing head's service of 38 years as par-

---

[232] *Jewish Year Book 1937*, pp. 407, 417, 429. & p. 431. & p. 436. & p. 439. & p. 440. & p. 439. & p. 455. & pp. 470, 466. & p. 490. & p. 498. & p. 469. & p. 448; *Who's Who 1939*, p. 1407. & *Jewish Chronicle*, 27/1/1939.

[233] Percy, p. 150. Translator's note: QVOS. I feel that this quotation may have been somewhat misconstrued by Aldag, as Percy's recognition of Bolshevik Russia's energy is not necessarily an endorsement, but rather a simple statement of fact. Indeed, Percy goes on to candidly discuss the Jewish Question (pp. 150-5), and admits that, alongside Russia, 'the other great problem of the future is Jewish', due to the general Jewish tendency to refuse assimilation after emancipation. This refusal has left the Jew with the choice that 'he must either pull down the pillars of the whole national state system or he must create a territorial sovereignty of his own.' In this choice between 'Jewish Bolshevism' and 'Zionism', 'Eastern Jewry seems to hover uncertainly between the two.' However, Percy sees the great danger in European statesmen relying on Zionism as the way to make the Jews contented, wisely understanding that the Jewish 'spirit of revolt' will not be extinguished by giving them Palestine. Indeed, he sees the Zionist project as a violation of the Arab right to self-determination and a likely source of trouble for the future, as it appears to have been foisted on world leaders, who appear incapable of controlling its trajectory. He ends his thoughts on Zionism with: 'The only thing that can be predicted with certainty is that it will dominate the whole family of nations for many years to come.'

ticularly outstanding, and told those assembled, as the *Jewish Chronicle* reports: 'The Children's Department of the Home Office had always consulted him when they contemplated the launching of any new scheme.' Sir Alexander then turned to address the boys of the school:

> Addressing the boys, Sir Alexander told them how, as they would be growing up, England would be deciding whether it was going to be governed in accordance with tradition, whether people would be allowed to think for themselves, or whether they should be forced to think as the Government wished them to. At the first sight, the latter was an attractive doctrine. The dictators of Europe said they knew what was right, and anyone who disagreed did so at great peril. He reminded them of the prophets of Judah and Israel, who had rebuked the dictatorial kings, and whose words had become part of the tradition of the English and had helped, during the Reformation, in developing ideas of freedom.[234]

We would also not to wish overlook the field of medicine. To this end, the following are some of the most prominent Jews in this profession:

Abraham Abelson is a well-known specialist in internal medicine, and has written various works, such as *Measurement of Mental Ability*. Frederic Alexander works in the same specialty and is also a surgeon; he has likewise authored several publications. Dr. Harold Avery works at the Central Research Clinic and E. Baron works at the Prince of Wales Hospital. S. Blackman, a well-known radiologist, has authored numerous publications, and G. Cohen is, among other things, member of the Royal Society for Medicine. Dr. M. Cutner is known for his books and contributions to scientific journals. J. Emanuel was formerly Professor of Medicine at the University of Birmingham. V. Feldman is chief physician at the Essex County Sanatorium, and W. Feldman is a well-known gynecologist and pediatrician. M. Fenton is a dermatologist at Battersea General Hospital and N. Finzi is head of the radiology department at St. Bartholomew's Hospital. From Hugh Gainsborough there are numerous medical works and journal articles. D. H. [Dennis Herbert] Geffen is a British Medical Health Officer, recognized in public health; W. Geffen is, among other things, Deputy Chairman of the Kensington Medical Society; M. Goldblatt is a physiologist at St. Thomas' Hospital, and Dr. J. A. [Jacob Arthur] Gorsky is surgeon to A Division of the Metropolitan Police. Davis Haldin has written various works on skin diseases.

B. Homa and D. Krestin are well-known doctors of internal medicine, the latter a member of the Royal Society for Medicine. Martin Israel is As-

---

[234] *Jewish Chronicle*, 28/10/1938, p. 15. Translator's note: QVOS.

sistant Director of the Department of Clinical Research and Investigations and J. H. [Juda Hirsch] Quastel is Director of Research at the Cardiff City Mental Hospital. Bertram Nisse and G. Slot are big names in rheumatism, with both specialists having various publications in the field. The brothers Arnold and Maurice Sorsby rose to great prominence in the British medical world. Both are, among other things, surgeons in the City of London and have published numerous works, the former on eye diseases, the latter on deafness and ulcers. Arnold is a contributor to various scientific journals, such as the *Quarterly Journal of Medicine*, and Maurice is co-editor of the *Medical Forum* and the series *Pocket Monographs of Practical Medicine,* and *Short Histories of Medicine*. Simon Wigoder is a medical examiner for Royal London Assurance, and Eugene Wolff is a well-known pathologist. Both are authors of numerous scientific papers.[235]

This brief compilation of leading Jewish doctors may suffice for our purposes. It remains for future researchers to write a book about the Judaization of medicine in England. What has been said also applies to dentists, although we shall refrain from listing them. In this field and in the medical profession, however, currents are already emerging that warn of foreign infiltration, as has become evident through the immigration of Jewish doctors and dentists. At the annual meeting of the British medical profession in July 1938, extensive discussions took place about the fact that the more or less uncontrolled influx of immigrants could no longer be tolerated. The Jews and their friends, by contrast, considered this Jewish immigration to be a great advantage to public health and therefore demanded more assistance from the authorities to help these Jewish refugees settle, as was particularly expressed in the House of Lords by the Jewish Viscount Samuel and the Jewish Marquess of Reading.[236]

---

[235] *Jewish Year Book 1937*, p. 398. & p. 400. & pp. 402, 404. & p. 408, 413. & p. 419. & p. 424. & p. 428. & p. 428-9. & p. 433. & pp. 434-8. Translator's note: The BMJ obituaries for Dr. D. H. Geffen and Dr. Gorsky's BMJ obituary are available online at: https://www.bmj.com/content/2/5151/583.4 and https://www.ncbi.nlm.nih.gov/pmc/articles/PMC1959297 respectively. & p. 441. & p. 446, 458. & p. 450, 483. & p. 479, 498. & p. 501; *Who's Who 1939*, p. 2984. & *Jewish Year Book 1937*, pp. 513, 515.

[236] *Daily Telegraph*, 11/7/1938, 28/7/1938. Translator's note: See, for example, the 27 July 1938 debate 'Refugee Problems' in *Hansard* (House of Lords), Vol. 110, p. 1207 ff. For clues on why there were concerns about these new Jewish doctors see Chapter XI ('The Jew as a Physician') of Samuel Roth's 1934 *Jews Must Live*, which discusses the Jewish doctor's tendency towards profit-motive over patient care, leading to the financial exploitation of the most vulnerable. Eugen Dühring, in his 1881 *Die Judenfrage*, complained that the Judaisation of the medical profession in Germany had led to an unreasonable hike in fees, the removal of on-call duties, the removal of midwives in order to monopolise birth help, and the creation of new income streams such as vaccination (see page 189 of English edition, *Eugen Dühring on the Jews*). On these vaccines being made compulsory, Dühring was particularly scathing, blaming Jewish influence on medicine, the

An editorial in the *Daily Express* from 9 July 1938, entitled: 'Harleystrasse', shows the extent to which the Judaization of English medicine has already taken place. Doctors of renown and skill practice in Harley Street, which is now so full of German émigrés that the newspaper, to illustrate this fact most graphically, translated the word 'Street' into German. The newspaper states that at that time —which is to say, about four years ago— 187 German Jews had already set themselves up as doctors in Harley Street, and although the newcomers' plight is regrettable, such an influx of foreigners was nevertheless proving to be intolerable for the English doctors, especially given that the Home Office had already approved new licenses to practice for the month of August 1938. As is well known, the influx of German Jews increased significantly in 1939. Are there still English doctors in Harley Street?

It is impossible within the scope of this work to cover all branches of science, which is why we shall limit ourselves to noting only some of the most prominent Jews in various fields.

Professor Edward Neville de Costa Andrade, Quain Professor of Physics at University College, London, is one of the foremost physicists in the field of atomic research.[237]

Abraham Shalom Yahuda is active in the field of Oriental Studies. His publications have appeared in German, English and Spanish. R. Barnett is Assistant Curator of the Egyptian Department and Assyrian Antiquities at the British Museum, and J. Leveen holds the corresponding position in the Department of Oriental Books and Manuscripts at the same institution. Miss Phyllis Abrahams is on the British Academy Committee for a Dictionary of Medieval Latin. Samuel Alexander is a professor of Philosophy and has received almost countless honors and awards. Philip Guedalla is known for his historical publications. He was formerly a barrister and, among other things, legal advisor to the Contracts Department of the War Office and the Ministry of Munitions during the Great War. Levy Leonard is a member of the Royal Institute of Chemistry and of the Chemical Society, while P. E. Spielman is a noted chemist. Miss S. Rosenfeld contributes articles to numerous journals, such as *Review of English Studies*. Jacob Rich is a member of the Royal In-

---

press and the legislature for this new illiberal and un-German law (idem, p.71) and warns elsewhere in the book 'if things are not directed, the descendants of traders in old wardrobes, scraps and cattle bones must get to the very bones of the modern peoples after they have pocketed their wealth and lamed their minds through inoculation' (p. 194). See Translator's Bibliography for both sources.

[237] *Daily Telegraph*, 1/2/1939; *Jewish Year Book 1937*, p. 401. Translator's note: *The Telegraph* news snippet, titled '13 Times Energy of Radium—Striking Development', details Andrade's laboratory breakthrough regarding the properties of 'slow neutrons', an article which is amusing for its total opacity to the lay reader, who will have constituted 99.999% of the readership (myself included).

stitute of International Affairs and a former editor of the *Jewish Chronicle*. In addition to other publications, Alfred Ornstien is known as the editor of The *Property Companies' Year Book*. Also worthy of mention is Sir Henry Rothband, a civil servant who made a name for himself through his important work on social issues.[238]

Finally, we shall end with a mention of the Jew Sir Lionel Faudel Phillips —one of the leading import merchants in Great Britain—who, according to the British Council's own reports, has a preeminent position in this institution. The British Council is a largely state-backed organization which exists to spread British culture and values abroad, including the creation of cultural propaganda through appropriate events. It is no secret that its end goal is political.[239]

The Jew in Art and Literature

We now wish to give the reader a brief impression of the extent to which the British art world has also become Judaized. This issue has already been aptly and thoroughly discussed in an article of the April 1924 issue of *The Jewish Peril* magazine. It is not surprising that degenerate art was declared the latest leap in progress, which pointed the way to the creation of a new generation. Here too Jewish spirit triumphs. The most famous art galleries were in the hands of Jews, as seen particularly with the Leicester, Goupil, and National Galleries. It is almost redundant to mention that nothing has changed today. The fully Jewish Lord Joseph Duveen and the Rothenstein family are leading voices in this sphere. The former was the most influential figure at the National Gallery, the nation's largest collection of paintings. He occupied top positions at institutions including the Wallace Collection, the National Portrait Gallery, the Imperial Gallery of Art, and the Museum of Modern Art (MoMA) in New York. He also founded the British Artists Organization for the promotion of lesser-known artists, and was a member of the National Art Collections Fund. He received innumerable honorary posts and other awards, and wrote the book *Thirty Years of British Art*.[240]

The head of the Rothenstein family is Sir William Rothenstein. He was principal of the Royal College of Art from 1920 to 1935, a member of the Royal Fine Art Commission and a senior executive at the Tate Gallery. His

---

[238] *JYB37*, p. 517; *WW39*, p. 3516. & *JYB37*, pp. 403, 462, p. 399, p. 400; *WW39*, p. 37. & *JYB37*, p. 440; *WW39*, p. 1315. & *JYB37*, p. 503; *WW39*, p. 3001. & *JYB37*, pp. 485, 486; *WW39*, p. 2680. & *JYB37*, p. 480. & p. 487; *WW39*, p. 2763. Translator's note: Most notably, from 1915 onwards, Rothband campaigned for an employment scheme for disabled ex-servicemen. For his highly effective and admirable work, which made a big impact nationwide, Rothband was awarded a baronetcy in 1923.

[239] *Who's Who 1939*, p. 1029.

[240] *Jewish Year Book 1937*, p. 423; *Who's Who 1939*, p. 937.

paintings and drawings are found all over the world and his writings are numerous and well known. Sir William's eldest son John is now Director and Curator of the Tate Gallery. He had previously been Director of the Leeds City Art Gallery, and had held the same position at the City Art Gallery and the Ruskin Museum of Sheffield. He too has also published many works on art and artists, and writes for, among other publications, the *Times Literary Supplement*. Another son of Sir William, Michael Rothenstein, recently held a painting exhibition at the Matthiesen Gallery. Sir William Rothenstein's brother Albert has meanwhile taken the name of Albert Rutherston, and is no less prominent than the other members of the family. His paintings and drawings hang in the Tate Gallery, the British Museum, the Victoria and Albert Museum, and others. He has been the set designer for various theatres, and is the editor of the Contemporary British Artist Series.[241]

Solomon Joseph Solomon was a well-known portrait painter and, after the war, President of the Royal Society of British Artists. John Henry Amshewitz is also a portrait and fine art painter. His works can be found in the halls of the London Stock Exchange, Liverpool City Hall, South Africa House on Trafalgar Square, the Victoria and Albert Museum, etc. He became the chief cartoonist for the *Sunday Times*. Two other painters, Frank Lewis Emanuel and Herbert Arthur Horwitz, held exhibitions at the Royal Academy and the Salon de Paris, among others, and murals by Emanuel can be found in the London Stock Exchange.

Edmond Xavier Kapp is also a well-known artist whose paintings hang in the National Portrait Gallery, the British Museum, the Victoria and Albert Museum, the Peace Palace of the League of Nations in Geneva, etc. He also contributes serious articles to magazines and newspapers, including *Time and Tide*, the *New Statesman and Nation*, the *Manchester Guardian*, the *Daily Telegraph*, and the *Observer*. Mark Gertler belongs to the new English art movement, Joseph Mordecai is a well-known portrait painter, who has painted the portraits of King Edward VII and Lord Kitchener. His portrait of King Edward VII now hangs in St. James's Palace. Isaac Snowman has painted King George V and Queen Mary. One of the most ardent defenders of modern art in words, writing and images is Alfred Aaron Wolmark, who has held numerous painting exhibitions all over the world. Reuben Rubin is

---

[241] *Who's Who 1939*, p. 2763; Seton Hutchison, p. 18-9. & *Who's Who 1939*, p. 2763. & *Evening Standard*, 31/10/1938. Translator's note: The article notes that 'Sir William trained Michael from his earliest years to be an artist and craftsman. He took him away from school at the age of twelve and sent him to a trade school, where he learnt woodcarving, sculpture and architecture, and where most of his fellow-pupils were artisans learning to be ecclesiastical woodcarvers. He had his first commission at the age of sixteen.' It may have been this influence from his classmates that led Michael, in the newspaper's words, to prefer 'more allegorical and mystical subjects. Two of his pictures represent the Crucifixion in modern dress.' & Who's Who 1939, pp. 2791, 2763.

also a well-known painter who, in 1930 and 1938, held exhibitions at Tooth's Gallery.[242]

The most famous (and most controversial) sculptor and painter is Jacob Epstein, son of Polish Jews, born in New York in 1880. His first big commission appears to have been in 1907, when he was tasked with decorating the facade of the new British Medical Association buildings in the Strand. His finished work consisted of 18 sculpted human figures, whose unveiling aroused a wave of indignation regarding their moral and artistic merits. He was attacked by most of the press, as well as almost all of the religious and other social organizations. Among the few who defended him were the *Times* [see, for example, the *Times,* 24/6/1908, p. 14]. His artistic influences include Rodin, African sculpture, and Cubism, as, according to the artist, 'negro sculpture is governed by the same considerations that govern all sculpture.' However, in the words of John Betjeman, 'Epstein has chosen to get his inspiration from Jewry.' Another of his works, this time of Jesus Christ, was harshly criticized, as almost all of his works have been, and was branded blasphemous. Among his busts, two have been made of Ramsay MacDonald. Given the Jews' influence over the art world, it is not surprise that, as the *Jewish Chronicle* of 19 November 1937 reports, Epstein was chosen to be the representative British sculptor for the Venice biennial exhibition of 1938.[243]

After having cited some of the most famous Jews in painting and sculpture, we shall now take a brief look at the world of literature.

In terms of past luminaries, we need only recall the aforementioned Benjamin Disraeli and Grace Aguilar, although we should add to them Sir Francis Palgrave (1788-1861), son of the Jew Meir Cohen. In 1823, he embraced Christianity on marriage, and took the name of Palgrave [his wife's mother's maiden name] after receiving the requisite royal permission. Nine years later, he was raised to the knighthood. Besides many learned historical and antiquarian works, his pen has produced a wide variety of enjoyable

---

[242] *Jewish Year Book 1937*, p. 360. & p. 401; *WW39*, pp. 54-5. & *Jewish Year Book 1937*, p. 447. & p. 450; *WW39*, p. 1717. & *Jewish Year Book 1937*, p. 434; *WW39*, p. 1178. & *Jewish Year Book 1937*, p. 475. & p. 499. & p. 515; *WW39*, p. 3471. & *Jewish Chronicle*, 7/10/1938, p. 33.

[243] *Jewish Year Book 1937*, p. 425; *Who's Who 1939*, p. 988; *Jewish Peril*, April 1924; Bolitho: *Twelve Jews*, pp. 85-100. Translator's note: Note that the profile of Epstein found in Bolitho is actually authored by John Betjeman, from whom the above quotations are reproduced verbatim (pp. 100, 85, respectively). According to Betjeman, a staunch admirer of Epstein, the charges of blasphemy came from the fact that Epstein had dared to portray Christ (who was a subject of several Epstein statues) as 'a beardless Jew.' As with all of the Jewish artists featured in this chapter, I urge readers, in the words of T. E. Hulme (the greatest champion of Epstein's work, whose opinion is reproduced in Betjeman's study), 'to go and judge for themselves'.

literature, a bibliography of which would be too extensive to reproduce here.[244]

His four sons likewise made a name for themselves in different fields. Francis Turner Palgrave (1824-1897) was editor of the *Golden Treasury of English Songs and Lyrics,* and Professor of Poetry at the University of Oxford. William Gifford Palgrave (1826-1888) is known for his travel writing, particularly his two-volume *Personal Narrative of a Year's Journey through Central and Eastern Arabia,* and for his activity in the consular service. Sir Robert Harry Palgrave (1827-1919) produced the three-volume *Palgrave's Dictionary of Political Economy,* as well as being variously editor of *The Economist, The Banking Almanac* and *The Bankers' Magazine.* Sir Reginald Frances Palgrave (1829-1903) was a Clerk of the House of Commons.[245]

Israel Zangwill, who latterly became a Zionist leader, aside from writing fiction on purely Jewish themes also wrote novels and dramatic sketches of a more universal character. These latter works include *The Master, The Mantle of Elijah, Six Persons, Three Penny Bits, The Revolting Daughter,* and *The Memento of Death,* all of which appear to have won the acclaim of the British and American public. Most of his poetry was published under the title *Blind Children.*[246]

Finally, of the old generation we shall cite Solomon Lazarus Lee (1859-1926). While his forebears had changed their surname from Levy to Lee, Solomon did another name change to become Sidney Lee. He then became Sir Sidney Lee when he was raised to the baronetcy in 1911. Oxford-educated, he has written numerous works on Shakespeare, and he has dealt extensively with the problem of the guilt of Rodrigo Lopez, the model for Shakespeare's Shylock. His works on England's greatest poet have found wide diffusion. He is perhaps best known for his editorial work on the *Dictionary of National Biography.* For the first 21 volumes he worked as a contributor for the editor Leslie Stephen, for the next five volumes he was co-editor, and for volumes 27-63 (and the later supplements and index, which totaled 41 volumes) he was sole editor. He has written a book on Queen Victoria, among many others. King George V commissioned him to write a biography of his father, King Edward VII, putting all of the archives at his

---

[244] *Gentleman's Magazine* of 1861, part II, pp. 441-5; *Dictionary of National Biography,* vol. XV, pp. 107-8.

[245] *Dictionary of National Biography,* Vol. 15, pp. 109-10. *Jewish Encyclopedia,* Vol. 9, p. 505. Translator's note: The DNB entries for both father and second son William Gifford underscore the linguistic brilliance of this family. Francis Palgrave translated the poem 'Battles of the Frogs and Mice' from Latin to French at the age of eight, a work which was published by his proud stockbroker father, while William was a brilliant linguist who reportedly was able to speak colloquial Japanese within two months. Like his father, William became a Christian, in his case dying in the Catholic faith.

[246] *Jewish Encyclopedia,* vol. 12, pp. 633-635.

disposal. His other publications are so numerous that they cannot possibly be listed in their totality here. Sir Sidney died unmarried in 1926, and the ashes of the chairman of the Shakespeare Birthplace Trust were scattered in Stratford-upon-Avon in honor of his life's passion.[247]

Modern playwrights and writers include, among others, Major J. Brandon, F. Emanuel, L. Spero, and Ben Levy with many well-known works such as *The Devil, Evergreen, The Poet's Heart* etc. Solicitor Harold Rubinstein is particularly prolific. Since 1913, his plays have become well known, with titles including *Consequences, Exodus, Churchill, The Dickens of Gray's Inn,* and *Prelude to Tragedy.* He is also secretary to the League of British Dramatists. Marion Harry Spielmann is a leading writer and art critic. It is impossible to list here all his works and institutional positions. He has contributed to *Bryan's Dictionary of Painters* and the *Dictionary of National Biography,* and has collaborated on various editions of the Art entry of the *Encyclopedia Britannica.* He co-edited part of the New Art Library and for 17 years has been responsible for publishing the *Magazine of Art.* His articles in leading magazines and newspapers are difficult to count. His wife Mabel Henrietta Spielmann (née Samuel) does not enjoy such a level of fame, but her works, such as *The Rainbow Book,* are nevertheless recognized. Other Jews, namely Lily Tobias, Rose Woolf, S. Bensuan, Hannah Berman, Regina Block, and N. Burstein, have distinguished themselves with their work. Italian-born Humbert Wolfe (1885-1940), a senior official in the Ministry of Labor, has written dozens of volumes of poetry, prose, translations and satire, and more recently, the *National Service Handbook.* Louis Zangwill can also look back on the publication of numerous works, as can Gladys Stern. Her plays, such as *The Matriarch,* and *The Man Who Pays the Piper,* were very well received by London audiences.[248]

---

[247] *Jewish Encyclopedia,* Vol. VII, pp. 661-2; *Dictionary of National Biography,* Vol. 1922-1930, pp. 497-502 [?]; *Times,* 4/3/1926, 6/3/1926. Translator's note: Note that I am unsure of Aldag's DNB reference; the DNB website itself saying that Sidney Lee's DNB life was published in 1937. The *Times* obituary (4/3/1926, p. 9), also lists Lee's numerous honorary degrees, fellowships and trusteeships.

[248] *Jewish Year Book 1937,* pp. 409, 434, 464, 502; *WW39,* p. 1862. & *Jewish Year Book 1937,* p. 488; *WW39,* p. 2777. & *Jewish Year Book 1937,* p. 502; *WW39,* p. 3001. Translator's note: Note that Aldag, seeing the name 'Marion Spielmann' in the sources, erroneously but understandably assumed that the subject was female. Spielmann's full name has been inserted into the text and the mistake amended accordingly. & *Jewish Year Book 1937,* p. 502. Translator's note: The original text describes Mabel as Marion's 'namesake', Aldag not realizing that the shared surname was a result of the Spielmanns being a married couple. The text has likewise been updated for accuracy. & *Jewish Year Book 1937,* pp. 506, 517, 406, 408, 411. & *Jewish Year Book 1937,* p. 513; *WW39,* p. 3470. Translator's note: Although he has fallen into obscurity today, Humbert Wolfe was one of the best-selling poets of the interwar years. & *Jewish Year Book 1937,* p. 519; *WW39,* p. 3719.

It is also only fitting that we should mention the Sassoons, namely, Alfred, David, Flora and Siegfried. Of the four, the last in particular has become known for numerous works in poetry and prose, with notable examples being: *Memoirs of a Fox-Hunting Man*, *Vigils*, *The Old Century*, *Sherston's Progress* and *War Poems*. The war poetry is of a repugnance that can only be typical of a Jew. There is nothing in them of sacrifice for one's comrades, nor a sense of sacred cause in the duty of the front-line soldier. One only needs to read his poems 'Suicide in the Trenches', 'They', 'Return of the Heroes,' and 'The Hero' to get an understanding of his sentiments. We would not wish to deny the reader the opportunity of sampling one of his poems, in which the Jewish spirit is revealed:

The Hero

'Jack fell as he'd have wished,' the Mother said,
And folded up the letter that she'd read.
'The Colonel writes so nicely.' Something broke
In the tired voice that quavered to a choke.
She half looked up. 'We mothers are so proud
Of our dead soldiers.' Then her face was bowed.

    Quietly the Brother Officer went out.
He'd told the poor old dear some gallant lies
That she would nourish all her days, no doubt.
For while he coughed and mumbled, her weak eyes
Had shone with gentle triumph, brimmed with joy,
Because he'd been so brave, her glorious boy.

    He thought how 'Jack,' cold-footed, useless swine,
Had panicked down the trench that night the mine
Went up at Wicked Corner; how he'd tried
To get sent home; and how, at last, he died,
Blown to small bits. And no one seemed to care
Except that lonely woman with white hair.[249]

Finally, we would like to mention the art critic Reginald Wilenski, who was in the secret service during the Great War. His numerous books and essays, such as those in the *Observer*, the *Apollo*, and *The Studio*, have garnered widespread attention in England.[250]

[Translator's note: The original reference had 1937 for the Who's Who year, but this is likely to be an error.]

[249] Sassoon: 'The Hero.' p. 26. Translator's note: Poem reproduced verbatim from original source. The reader is invited to reflect upon both perspectives of the events of WW1, and decide which 'side' best reflects his own position.

[250] Seton Hutchison, p. 14; *Who's Who 1939*, p. 3412.

Nor is the field of music any exception when it comes to Jewish eminence. Gertrude Azulay is a professor at Trinity College of Music, author of *Youth's Own Book of Great Composers* and editor of *Adult Albums*. Gustav Pearlson is a member and examiner of the National College of Music, and the pianist Harriet Cohen, who is famous in music circles, was chosen to represent England at the Salzburg International Festival of 1924. Mark Hambourg is also famous in England as a pianist, and Lionel Tertis has made a name for himself for, among other things, his compositions for viola. Moses Baritz—recently deceased—was a renowned music critic and consultant to the Columbia Gramophone Company, as well as the author of many essays in various music magazines. He was also one of the founders of the Socialist Party of Great Britain. Sir Ronald Landon enjoys great fame as a conductor, composer and principal of the Guildhall School of Music. In 1918, he received special honors from the Freemasons. He has also written prolifically about music, and has worked as a music critic for the *Artist*, *The Onlooker*, and *The Tatler* periodicals, as well as being editor of *Musical News*, and of the musical section of the *News Chronicle*.[251]

The theatre industry is also subject to huge Jewish influence, as can easily be seen, for example, from the yearly review of Jews in theatre which the *Jewish Chronicle* published in their 11 September 1936 issue. Many plays performed in the past season were by Jewish authors, such as Heinrich Schnitzler, Sarah Gertrude Millin, Herni Bernstein, the aforementioned Humbert Wolfe, Ernst Toller, and the writing duo Bella and Samuel Spewack. The number of Jewish actors was also quite considerable. Henry Cass served as a stage director at the Old Vic, a theatre almost exclusively dedicated to Shakespearean productions. But the best proof of the Jews' control of the theatre stems from the fact that many theatres, and far from the worst or most insignificant ones, are in Jewish hands.

The Theatre Royal, Drury Lane has two Jewish directors: Jack Barnato Joel, the gold magnate, and Louis Dreyfus. Another theatre company, Associated Theatre Properties (London) Ltd., has Sir Harold Wernher as chairman, and A. Gumpert and M. S. Myers as directors. All three are Jews. This company owns the Apollo Theatre, the Cambridge Theatre, His Majesty's Theatre, the Shaftesbury Theatre, the Adelphi Theatre and the Gaiety Theatre. The company also controls Associated Catering Co. Ltd., which owns the rights to the catering/refreshment side of the theatre business, and the Theatrical and General Advertising Co. Ltd., which controls a large part of the advertising business and the associated marketing side of the theatre industry.[252]

---

[251] *Jewish Year Book 1937*, p. 403. & p. 480; *WW39*, pp. 633-4. & *Jewish Year Book 1937*, p. 441; *WW39*, p. 1353. & *Jewish Year Book 1937*, p. 506; *WW39*, p. 3143. & *Jewish Chronicle*, 8/4/1938. & *Jewish Year Book 1937*, p. 488; *WW39*, p. 2891.

[252] *SEYB38*, p. 1924; *Directory of Directors 1938*, p. 913. & *SEYB38*, p. 887.

Radio

In our study of the Judaization of the individual spheres of British life, we have yet to deal with the radio and the press. Both, along with the cinema, are crucial modern means of controlling a nation: their influence over public opinion is undeniable.

One of the first directors of the British Broadcasting Corporation, or BBC as it is called, was Godfrey Isaacs, familiar to us from the Marconi scandal. It is to the credit of Lieutenant-Colonel Arthur Henry Lane that he revealed how, right from the start of the BBC being founded, Jews and their socialist friends— e.g. Lord Sankey, the Archbishop of York and the Jewish Marxist-Zionist Professor Harold Laski—were in leading positions within the corporation. It is therefore unsurprising that the BBC has a taken on a certain character, which is symptomatic of their agenda. Individuals who are not committed to the Jewish agenda hardly get a chance to speak on the radio, and one looks in vain for the much-vaunted English freedom of speech.

Little or nothing is known about the actual staff. Lane once contacted the BBC in an attempt to find out this information, and his request was flatly denied.[253]

Even though the BBC's tendentious and deliberately mendacious attitude in its reporting often reveals a Jewish spirit and Jewish hatred towards the Third Reich, and even though its warm sympathy and advocacy for all Jewish concerns leave no doubt as to who is in control there, all that we have is circumstantial evidence.

As has often been the case, we once more resort to our tried-and-tested source of information, the *Jewish Chronicle*. At the back of every issue, this weekly magazine provides a schedule of the European broadcasters' radio programs for the following week.

The singular thing here is that only the broadcasts mentioned are those that are Jewish in character, i.e. that either involve Jewish music, art, or literature, or involve Jews. Since the compilation was made by the official organ of British Jewry, we have no reservations about accepting it as correct. In order to get an overview, we have carried out research on certain periods in 1936, 1937 and 1938. For the period from May 15 to October 23, 1936, i.e. 24 weeks, 242 such broadcasts were registered. A similar sample for the period from October 1 to December 31, 1937, i.e. 14 weeks, gave a total of 263 programs, compared to a total of 56 broadcasts across the entire European continent. The year 1938 shows a considerable increase, because for the period from October 14 to December 30, i.e. 12 weeks, the number of programs in England was 366, while on the continent it was only 16. Taking all

---

[253] Lane, pp. 84-95.

of this into account gives us a weekly average of 10 programs for 1936, 20 for 1937, and 30 for 1938.

Nothing could better illuminate the spirit of the BBC than these stark figures. Apparently the Jewish-themed broadcasts were significantly increased in 1939, because according to the first issue of the *Jewish Chronicle* for 1939 (the January 6 issue), the number of such broadcasts for the following week amounted to 40. Compared to these numbers, it is easy to see the paucity of such broadcasts on the entire European continent, despite the fact that, at this time, there were still many European states friendly to Jews. It is also worth noting that, from 24 June 1936 onwards, England even produced an exclusively Jewish program which, as well as to Great Britain, was broadcast to South Africa—a certainly appropriate country for such programming—on Wednesday evenings.[254]

The Press

There has surely never been a country in the world where the influence of the press is as great as it is in England, where newspapers are sold at a disproportionately low price and consequently have a huge circulation. There are newspapers with a daily circulation of two million or more copies per day. This does not mean that there are only two million readers of the newspapers in question, but undoubtedly many more, since there are always 'fellow readers' in the family or the circle of friends or workmates. It is quite possible, as expressed in a recent publication, that for a newspaper with a print-run of two million copies there are about seven million readers. In any case, given that Britain has a total population of around 46 million, one can appreciate the impact that newspapers with such sales figures must have.[255]

To this must be added the fact that the average Englishman is only too willing to believe what his newspaper tells him, and alternative views are either rejected outright as untrue, or at least treated with skepticism. It is dif-

---

[254] *Jewish Chronicle*, 8/5/1936, 19/6/1936. Translator's note: The show was called 'Almonds and Raisins' and was described as 'an all-Jewish revue' of music and sketch comedy, 'presented in English, with occasional interpolations in Yiddish.' The JC also goes on to say: 'Items have been typically chosen, which, while being typically Jewish, lack the vein of melancholy which largely permeates Jewish art. The entire present program is characterized by the spirit of youth, and all the performers are young people.' This suggests that there was an awareness among (undoubtedly Jewish) BBC staff of the need to boost morale among the Jewish population as the skies were darkening over Europe, and, because it was known that many Jews were avoiding certain types of media out of a fear of inducing anxiety or depression, a 'safety notice' was given in order for them to consider watching the show. This example also demonstrates how, even as early as the 1930s, state broadcasters knew the techniques which could be used to re-moralize (or conversely demoralize) certain demographics within the population.

[255] Soames, p. 57.

ficult to make him see that those who control a newspaper only report on what interests them and what serves their agenda. Soames rightly points out that in a newspaper which answers to people with financial interests in sawmills, the reader will learn nothing of the poor working conditions in these places. Thus, the reader does not notice the influence of certain interest groups, and believes he can look down with contempt on the press of authoritarian countries, which is supervised by the state. But here he overlooks the fundamental difference, which is that in England the newspapers are controlled by companies whose main purpose is making money, and whose influence over the masses comes almost exclusively from these press magnates' personal interests and ideology, whereas in an authoritarian state only the interests of the people are the deciding factor.[256]

This introduction to the topic should suffice to show the extraordinary importance of the press in England. It can well be supposed that the Jew has also recognized this and has made extensive use of it. Proving this exhaustively and scientifically is extremely difficult. Nevertheless, we believe we can give the reader a certain impression of this fact.

The newspaper industry is dominated by the following six major groups (with a few notable exceptions that shall be discussed later):

1. Odhams Press
2. Beaverbrook Group
3. Berry Group
4. News Chronicle Group
5. Daily Mail Group
6. Westminster Press

In all of these corporations we will either find Jews in leading positions or we feel their spirit.

The chairman and managing director of Odhams Press is the Jew Baron Southwood of Fernhurst, who was recently ennobled and who used to go by the name Julius Salter Elias. He is chairman of Illustrated Newspaper Ltd., which owns the following titles: *The Tatler*, *The Drapers Record*, *Men's Wear*, *The Bystander*, and *The Sphere*, the latter absorbing *The Graphic* in 1932. It also directly controls British National Newspapers, which it controls jointly with Inveresk Paper Co. Ltd., evidence of its close connection with the latter.[257]

Illustrated Newspaper Ltd. also has major interests in Illustrated London News & Sketch Ltd., which controls Sporting & Dramatic Publishing

---

[256] Belloc, in his prologue to Soames' book, p. IX. & Soames, pp. 63-4. & pp. 85-6. & Steed: *The Press*, p. 100.
[257] *Jewish Chronicle*, 3/9/1937, p. 48. & *SEYB38*, pp. 1419, 1442.

Ltd., the publisher of *Sporting & Dramatic News*. The chairman of both companies mentioned is also Baron Southwood, who is likewise chairman and managing director of Odhams Press Ltd., as well as director of Odhams Properties Ltd. The latter company (Odhams Properties Ltd.) was formed primarily to acquire the publishing rights to *The People* newspaper, which now has a circulation of over three million copies.[258]

In any case, Odhams Press Ltd. is by far Lord Southwood's largest holding, which was founded primarily to obtain all the rights to John Bull Ltd, which still publishes *John Bull* and *Everywoman's* today. This company also owns all shares of Coming Fashions Ltd., Dean & Son Ltd., English Newspapers Ltd., Gosnay Advertising Ltd., Kinematograph Publications Ltd., Press Printers Ltd., Melody Maker Ltd., N.R.P. & Co. Ltd., and Wyman's London Printing Co. Ltd.. It also controls Clarion Press Ltd., Odhams (Watford), Victoria House Printing Co. Ltd., Feathered World Ltd. and Willbank Publications Ltd. These numerous companies publish, among others, the following magazines:

1. *The Melody Maker*
2. *Cinematograph Weekly*
3. *Picturegoer*
4. *Electrical Trading*
5. *Weekly Illustrated*
6. *Passing Show*
7. *Ideal Home*
8. *Broadcaster*
9. *Sporting Life*
10. *20 Story Magazine*[259]

Finally, Odhams Press publishes the *Daily Herald*, which has a daily circulation of over two million. This newspaper is the official organ of the Marxist Labour Party. Another Jew, Alexander Easterman, was literary editor and deputy foreign editor on the staff of this newspaper until 1938, when he became chief foreign correspondent. He had previously served as foreign editor for the *Daily Express*. His contributions to the Zionist cause are significant.[260]

---

[258] *SEYB38*, p. 1419. & *SEYB38*, pp. 1675-6.

[259] *The Writers' and Artists' Year Book 1938*, pp. 62, 54, 81, 30, 110, 78, 48; Odhams, p. 45.

[260] *Jewish Year Book 1938*, p. 423. & p. 426. Translator's note: The Jewish Telegraphic Agency's 7/9/1983 obituary for Alexander Easterman reports that he resigned from the *Daily Express* after a disagreement with the publisher, Lord Beaverbrook, over the newspaper's editorial policy towards Hitler. Regarding Zionism, the same source reports that Easterman was made Political Secretary of the World Jewish Congress in the late 1930s, and became head of its International Affairs Department in 1941, later representing the WJC at the Belsen trials, at the Nuremberg trials, and at the UN.

We get a rough idea of the size of this newspaper company when we are told by its co-founder that, as early as 1934, it printed some 60 newspapers and employed ten thousand people. At the shareholders' meeting of 1 May 1934, Lord Southwood reported that trading turnover for the year was in excess of £8,500,000. Almost £2,000,000 had been paid in salaries and wages alone, and paper consumption for the year amounted to over 132,000 tons.[261]

The Beaverbrook Group includes:

1. *The Daily Express*, circulation approximately 2,500,000.
2. *Sunday Express*, circulation approximately 1,500,000.
3. *The Evening Standard*, circulation approximately 500,000.[262]

Lord Beaverbook, who practically owns this group and whom Winston Churchill temporarily appointed as Minister of Aircraft Production, is undoubtedly sympathetic to the Jews. He was close friends with the Jew Lord Melchett. On 7 March 1928, Lord Beaverbrook wrote in the *Daily Express* that 'it was not their faults but their virtues that made the Jews in England unpopular, suspicious and hated.' On 4 December 1930, he expressed his satisfaction that there was no anti-Semitism in England, and on 17 September 1930, we find similar thoughts in the *Daily Express*, if more emphatically philo-Semitic in tone: 'The commercial and intellectual abilities of the Jews,' wrote Lord Beaverbrook, 'are so outstanding in Britain because there is no ban or barrier against them. In our case, the Jewish question has been solved through the complete absorption of Jews into our diverse activities, and the nation is therefore richer and happier. In time, it will be realized on the continent that there is no other solution'.[263]

This should be enough to demonstrate the position of the chief executive of the Beaverbrook Group. Next to him we find Jews in leading positions. For example, R. D. Blumenfeld was formerly the editor of the *Daily*

---

[261] Odhams, p. 43-44

[262] *Daily Express*, 9/12/1938, Soames, p. 54.

[263] Bolitho: *Lord Melchett*, p. 337. Translator's note: Care should be taken with what powerful men will say to or about powerful rivals or adversaries in the interests of diplomacy, and always bearing in mind that an individual's views can change over time. Beaverbrook's comments over the years indicate that he understood the reality of Jewish power in Britain, the tendency for Jews to lie to further an agenda, and the potential for the Jews to get Britain into an unnecessary war with Germany. Indeed, it was Beaverbrook's perceived sympathy towards Hitler that caused Easterman to resign. The *Jerusalem Post* of 4/6/2008 also reports of Beaverbrook's 1942 conversation with his friend Joseph P. Kennedy Sr. (who opposed US entry into WW2 just as Beaverbrook had opposed Britain's entry), in which Kennedy complained to him of the Jews' over-representation in Washington, Beaverbrook himself was reported as saying, years later, that the United States 'was a subjugated nation to a Jewish minority' (ibid.).

Express, then became the chairman of the same newspaper. We recall that not long ago the Jew Alexander Easterman was the foreign editor of the *Daily Express*. Lord Castlerose, director of the group's three newspapers, wrote in the *Daily Express* of 30 May 1930: 'If he were a Jew, he would earn his money in America but spend it in England because there only the idiots are anti-Semites.'[264]

The Berry Group brings together around 30 newspapers. The main paper is the *Daily Telegraph*, with a circulation number that is very close to the two-million mark. The political stance of this newspaper is quite well known in Germany. It is one of the most anti-German newspapers in Britain, and its sympathy for the Jews knows no bounds. Lord Camrose can be considered the head of this group, which is almost exclusively in the hands of his family, which has the surname Berry. Lord Camrose himself probably has no Jewish blood in his veins, but the Berry family's close ties to the Hebrews are indisputable. One of its younger members has married a daughter of Rothschild.[265]

The News Chronicle Group includes the *News Chronicle,* with a circulation of around 1,500,000 copies, and the *Star,* with around 700,000. It also has various provincial newspapers. There can be little doubt that this group is under Jewish influence.[266]

Until November 1936 it was under the control of United Newspapers Ltd., whose chairman in 1926 was the Jew Lord Reading. United Newspapers Ltd. was in turn controlled by the Daily Chronicle Investment Corporation, which was in turn controlled by General Investors and Trustees Ltd. Three directors of the latter were Jews: Harry Kahn, Maurice Stern, and Felix Rose (formerly Rosenheim). According to *Action*, the shareholders of this company were almost exclusively Jews.[267]

In the meantime, however, a formal change has occurred in the *News Chronicle*'s financial obligations to the latter company because, in November 1936, United Newspaper Ltd.'s interests in this newspaper were transferred to the Daily News Ltd. We were unable to find any further information about the character of this group from official material. In any case, the *News Chronicle*'s pro-Jewish political stance, that sought to establish a popular front, has not changed in any way.

The Daily Mail Group includes, among other titles, the *Daily Mail*, with a circulation of almost two million copies, and the *Evening News,* with around 700,000. Until the beginning of 1939, these were the only two daily newspapers in London that championed friendship with Germany. But this only lasted as long as Lord Rothermere owned the majority of the shares,

---

[264] *Who's Who 1939*, p. 317. & p. 541.

[265] *Who's Who 1938*, p. 536. *SEYB38*, p. 847; *Action* 2/4/1936.

[266] Soames, p. 55.

[267] Jackson, p. 287. & *SEYB38*, pp. 1974, 1160-1. & *Action*, 12/3/1936. & *SEYB38*, p. 2717; *Jewish Year Book 1938*, pp. 459, 491.

which is no longer the case. Rather, the Daily Mail Group is now controlled by an anonymous person who stands behind a block of shares. His name cannot be identified because the shares are held in a bank trust. One suspects him to be Rothschild, Sieff, or Sir John Ellerman.[268]

As has already been discussed, Lord Rosebery is half-Jewish, and one of his daughters is married to the Marquess of Crewe, who also has Jewish blood in his veins. Lord Rosebery has interests in the Westminster Press, of which he is a director. This company owns all shares in Bradford District Newspaper Company Ltd., which has direct control over the following companies:[269]

Barrow News and Mail Ltd.	North of England Newspaper Co. Ltd.
Bedfordshire Standard Ltd.	Northern Press Ltd.
Bedfordshire Times Publishing Co. Ltd.	Nottingham Journal Ltd.
Birmingham Gazette Ltd.	Oxford Times Ltd.
City and Town Building Ltd.	Stamford Mercury Ltd.
Darlington and Stockton Times Newspaper Co. Ltd.	Swindon Press Ltd.
Durham County Advertiser and General Printing Co.	Westmorland Gazette Ltd.
Lancaster Guardian Ltd.	Wm. Dresser and Sons Ltd.
Lincolnshire Guardian Printing and Publishing Co. Ltd.	Wiltshire Gazette Ltd.[1]
Lincolnshire Newspaper Ltd.	

These companies publish a large number of titles. According to Grünbeck's list made at the beginning of 1936, they publish four morning newspapers, nine evening newspapers, a Sunday newspaper, 38 weekly newspapers and eight sports newspapers.[270]

Some of the newspapers outside these six groups also have considerable influence. This certainly applies to the *Times*. Some years ago, the late Jew Sir John Ellerman had a considerable stake in this newspaper, but he sold his shares on Lord Northcliffe's death in 1922. At the moment, no director nor large shareholder involved in the *Times* can be officially verified as Jewish. But we have recently come across so many articles in the *Times* that enthusiastically favor the Jews that we need hardly discuss this newspaper's obvious political stance.[271]

Until recently, the *Sunday Referee* belonged to the Jewish cinema magnate Isidore Ostrer. He himself has written various books on economic issues, particularly those relating to gold, while Maurice Ostrer, his brother, is chairman of Sunday Referee Publishing Co. Ltd. The *Sunday Referee* also used to have as its managing director a Jew named Mark Goulden. Until

---

[268] Soames, pp. 55-6.
[269] *Who's Who 1938*, p. 2918.
[270] Grünbeck, Vol. II, pp. 135-6. Translator's note: Reference unclear, as the source is absent from the bibliography.
[271] *Times*, 18/7/1933.

1929 he was chief editor of the *Eastern Morning News* and other newspapers; and then became editor of the *Yorkshire Evening News*.[272]

The current ownership structure of the *Daily Mirror* is quite opaque. The *Mirror* is a daily newspaper with a circulation of around a million copies. The *Evening Standard* of 11 October 1938 intimates that the Jew Israel Sieff has a considerable stake in it. The same issue reports that nearly 600,000 Ordinary shares [of a total of 5,600,000 Ordinary shares] are held by bank nominees. Perhaps, as the *Evening Standard* has speculated, these are Sieff's shares. Other Jews, such as Nathan Wolff and Mayerstein, are also mentioned in connected with its ownership. In any case, the Jew Sir John Ellerman has a significant stake in the *Daily Mirror,* with the same issue of the *Evening Standard* even going as far as to say that 'it is sometimes said that Sir John Ellerman controls the Daily Mirror', although the same article admits that he appears in the shareholders' list only as a joint holder of 153,725 shares. The *Evening Standard* of 19 September of the same year reveals this millionaire has a wide range of press investments. It has emerged that his top manager, Sir William Cox, has acquired 480,000 shares in Odhams Press. It is not clear whether this purchase was made for Sir John Ellerman, but whatever the case, he is likely to have a great deal of influence over the company through his managing director, especially since Sir William Cox is the company's vice-president.[273]

The magazine *The Leader* has a strong anti-German bias, which is probably not least due to the fact that H. Hyams, a leading Freemason and Jew, is listed as the co-editor. The owner of said magazine is Alfred Cosher Bates, likely also a Jew, who was involved in the scandal of the former minister J. H. [James Henry] Thomas.[274]

---

[272] *Directory of Directors 1938*, pp. 1286-7. & *Jewish Chronicle*, 3/7/1936, p. 17. & *Who's Who 1938*, p. 1323; *Jewish Year Book 1938*, p. 443.

[273] *Evening Standard*, 19/9/1938 and 11/10/1938; *Daily Express*, 11/1/1939, *The Britisher*, 15/9/1937. Translator's note: Given that the earlier *Evening Standard* news snippet also informs readers of Ellerman's gifts to London Zoo (of an egg-eating snake and two poisonous puff-adders), readers may speculate that the gaining of political influence over the English plebeian masses through investments in the tabloid press was the last thing on Ellerman's mind.

[274] *Jewish Chronicle*, 7/2/1936. Translator's note: The article states that Hyams is Grand Vice-President of the Achei Brith Order, and was its representative at the Grand Lodge. & *Action*, 16/1/1937. Translator's note: The scandal referred to took place in 1936. The Colonial Secretary, known commonly as Jimmy Thomas, was forced to resign from politics after it was revealed that he had been entertained by stock exchange speculators and had leaked confidential information regarding the tax changes planned in the budget. One of the people party to these secrets was his friend and business associate, Alfred Cosher Bates, whom the subsequent Judicial Tribunal discovered had given Thomas £15,000 for no satisfactory reason.

The influence of Jews on the actual content of the newspapers and magazines is particularly great. We have already extensively referred to the collaboration of numerous Jews in periodical content, but would also like to list a few more here.

David Magarshack is a former editor of *Foreign Affairs*, Israel Cohen is a well-known journalist and currently General Secretary of the Zionist Organization. He was formerly a correspondent for the *Glasgow Herald* and *Globe*, and at times a special correspondent for the *Times, Manchester Guardian, Westminster Gazette*, etc. He still writes articles for the *Quarterly Review, Fortnightly Review, Nineteenth Century, Contemporary, Times*, etc.[275]

In this context we would also like to mention one of Britain's most famous journalists, Herbert Sidebotham, whom we discussed earlier in this volume. He is not Jewish, but is very close to this race. He has achieved global prominence under his pseudonyms 'Candidus' in the *Daily Sketch*, 'A Student of Politics' in the *Daily Telegraph* and 'Scrutator' in the *Sunday Times*. His sympathies for the Jews are so strong that one could feasibly call him a Zionist, especially since he himself emphasizes his support for this cause. He has written various books on Palestine and the issues surrounding the Balfour Declaration. As early as 1916 he was a member of the original British Palestine Committee in Manchester and was a member of the Palestine Mandate Society.[276]

The Jew Leonard Woolf is known not only for his books but also for his work in the press. He was previously editor of the *International Review*, the international section of the *Contemporary Review*, the literary section of *The Nation*, and since 1931 he has been co-editor of the *Political Quarterly*. He also founded the Hogarth Press, a book publishing company, in 1917.[277]

Finally, the Jew Mortimer Epstein is editor of the *Annual Register* and the *Statesman's Year Book*.[278]

In addition to the evidence provided above, there is also the much larger, outwardly unseen influence of the Jews, which is based on financial interests or other Jewish means of power that are only recognizable to those in the know. We shall give but one example of this:

A few years ago, Lord Rothermere began to champion Sir Oswald Mosley's National Socialist movement in the newspaper he controlled at the time, the *Daily Mail*. After a few weeks, the Jews and their friends threatened—as a reliable source informs us—to pull their advertisements from the newspaper in question. Before long, Lord Rothermere had to choose be-

---

[275] *Jewish Year Book 1938*, p. 473. & p. 417-8; *Who's Who 1938*, pp. 671-2.

[276] *Who's Who 1939*, p. 2909. Translator's note: Sidebotham's books are listed in the Bibliography.

[277] *Jewish Year Book 1937*, p. 517; *Who's Who 1939*, p. 3490.

[278] *Who's Who 1939*, p. 988.

tween the death of his newspaper or abandoning his politics. He decided to keep his newspaper going.

In addition, a large number of publishers are either Jewish themselves or under Jewish influence. The former include, for example: Victor Gollancz, chairman and managing director of the large publishing house of the same name. He is also managing director of Mundanus Ltd. and chairman of Favil Press Ltd. His political outlook is best demonstrated by his founding of the Left Book Club. This association publishes a wide variety of discounted books, which are all of a Marxist tendency and are often directed against the Third Reich. The influence of these books on the population was and is so strong that nationalist circles felt compelled to form the Right Book Club as a counterweight.[279]

The well-known publishing company Tuck (Raphael and Sons) Ltd. is also almost exclusively Jewish. Hebrew Gustave Tuck is chairman and managing director, Sir Reginald Tuck and D. A. Tuck are listed as directors. The company also has branches in New York and Paris, and a capital of £500,000.[280]

Until recently, Sir Leon Levison was chairman of the well-known publishing house Marshall, Morgan, & Scott.[281]

There are also countless publishers who are friendly to Jews and who, partly out of fear of a boycott and partly out of sympathy, refuse to publish any book that is against the Jews and their system—something that we witnessed personally when a friend made efforts to get such a book published in Britain.

Jews Everywhere

Wherever we look in England, all we see is Jews. Jewish influence, Jewish interests, and Jewish control. We have already examined many areas of English life, but there are still others outstanding that we cannot deal with in detail here, so we will limit ourselves to a brief summary. Jews everywhere: that is the conclusion that we have come to as a result of our analysis of the situation.

Their influence is significant in the food industry, much of which is completely in their hands. Anyone who has ever been to London knows the big corporations:

Home and Colonial Stores Ltd.
Lipton Ltd.
Maypole Dairy Co. Ltd.
Allied Suppliers Ltd.

---

[279] *Jewish Year Book 1938*, p. 411; *Who's Who 1938*, p. 1297.
[280] *Jewish Year Book 1937*, p. 507; *Who's Who 1939*, p. 3222. *SEYB38*, p. 1953.
[281] *Who's Who 1938*, p. 1984.

And knows that there is no district, no suburb, no matter how remote, where one cannot find branches of these companies. Sir George Schuster—whom we have encountered several times—is listed as the chairman of these companies. The capital of Home & Colonial Stores Ltd. is £4,500,000. The company controls two other companies and owns all the shares in an additional two companies. The Maypole Dairy Co. Ltd., with a capital of £3,000,000, has three other companies under its control and over a thousand branches in its network.[282]

This sector also includes Lyons & Co. Ltd., which also has a huge number of branches, sometimes several on the same street. Lyons & Co. Ltd. is engaged in the distribution of certain foodstuffs and at the same time has tea rooms, restaurants and hotels. The capital is £9,925,000. The chairman is the aforementioned Sir Isidore Salmon, while other Jews such as Harry Salmon, Maurice Salmon, Julius Salmon, Major M. Glückstein, B. Glückstein, B. A. Salmon, I. M. Glückstein and S. J. Salmon are directors. The company should be considered a purely Jewish company, which also has direct control in Black & Green Ltd., James Hayes & Sons Ltd., and W. H. & F. J. Horniman & Co. Ltd. It should also be noted that Lyons & Co. Ltd. owns two of London's largest and most modern hotels: the Strand Palace Hotel and the Cumberland Hotel.[283]

The sugar refining industry is dominated by a single company—Tate & Lyle Ltd.—which has a near monopoly. The capital is £6,200,000. The president of this company, Sir Charles Lyle, may not be Jewish, but he is married to the Jewish Edith Levy. The son born from this union is now married to the daughter of the industrialist and MP Sir John Jarvis.[284]

The Jews also represent great power in the tobacco industry. Edward S. Baron is, for example, chairman of Carreras, Ltd., and although this company is not as large as Imperial Tobacco, it is still, nevertheless, very important. It has a capital of £3,825,000 and it controls:

Alexander Bogulavsky Ltd.
Baron Cigarette Machinery Co. Ltd.
R. J. Lea Ltd.
Ray and Co. Ltd.
City Tobacco Ltd.

---

[282] *Directory of Directors 1938*, p. 1509; *SEYB38*, pp. 1391, 1594.
[283] *SEYB38*, pp. 1548-9.
[284] *Who's Who 1939*, pp. 1962-3, 1657; *Directory of Directors 1938*, p. 904; *SEYB38*, pp. 1912-3.

Baron, as his donations to Jewish refugees indicate, is a particularly keen supporter of Hebrew causes.[285]

Among the directors of the world-famous company Lever Brothers and Unilever Ltd, we find the van den Bergh family. The three members of this family are A. van den Bergh, who is the deputy chairman, and J. P. and S. J. [Sidney James] van den Bergh, who are directors. A. van den Bergh donated £1,000 to the fund for Jewish refugees, and this name is often found among Jews. The company possesses a capital of £141,418,750 and has largely cornered the soap and margarine markets of the British Empire, Europe and other parts of the world.[286]

The Jew Lord Hirst holds a key position in the electricity industry. He is chairman of most of the following companies, and in those where he does not hold the chair, he is a director:

General Electric Co. Ltd.	Général Electric de France Ltd.
Anglo-Argentine Electric Co. Ltd.	Lemington Glass Works Ltd.
British Electrical and Allied Manufacturers Ass. (Inc.)	Madeira Electric Lighting Co. Ltd.
Electric Development and Securities Trust Ltd.	Palestine Electric Corporation Ltd.
Electricity Company of Macclesfield Ltd.	Pirelli-General Cable Works Ltd.
Frinton-on-Sea and District Electric Light and Power Co.	Steel Conduit Co. Ltd.
General Electric Company of China Ltd.	Travancore Minerals Co. Ltd.
General Electric Company of India Ltd.	

The importance of some of these enterprises can be seen from the fact that, to detail but two as examples: the General Electric Co. Ltd. has a capital of £9,600,000 and controls 16 companies in the mother country and overseas territories, while the Electric Development and Securities Trust Ltd. exercises control over twenty other companies.[287]

The Jews themselves admit that the fur, boot and shoe, furniture, and tailoring trades are exclusively in their hands. According to their own data, there are around 40,000 workers employed in the fur trade, 20,000 of them in London alone. There are many small entrepreneurs ('chamber-masters') who refine the furs (e.g. dressing and dyeing) and whose workers are paid

---

[285] *Jewish Year Book 1937*, p. 404; *Jewish Chronicle*, 9/12/1938, p. 13; *SEYB38*, pp. 1068-9. Translator's note: The JC article referred to concerns the charitable trust set up for by Bernhard Baron, founder of Carreras, Limited, of which Edward Baron (clearly a relative), is trustee. The article goes on to report that £43,000 had just been donated to various Jewish charities for the year, and that almost half a million pounds had been disbursed to Jewish organizations since the charitable trust had been set up.

[286] *Jewish Chronicle*, 9/12/1938 p. 18; *Jewish Year Book 1937*, p. 508. Translator's note: Supporting the author's thesis, the same JC issue shows that there was also a D. van den Bergh who similarly donated £1,000 to the same cause (Council for German Jewry), and page 16 of the same issue reveals that there was a G. van den Bergh on the Committee of the Jewish Colonization Society. The Huygens Institute for the History of the Netherlands confirms that the van den Berghs were indeed a Jewish family. See, for example: https://resources.huygens.knaw.nl/bwn1880-2000/lemmata/bwn3/bergh & *SEYB38*, p. 1508.

[287] *Directory of Directors 1938*, p. 805; *SEYB38*, pp. 1290-1, 2116.

starvation wages. It is impossible for the authorities in question to determine whether the 48-hour week, set by the Fur Trade Board, is being adhered to. According to the *Jewish Chronicle* report, there is one large manufacturer, 'unfortunately a Jew', who is regarded as being to a great degree responsible for these deplorable, anti-social evils. He is not a technically a manufacturer himself, but paradoxically enough, he is known as the largest manufacturing furrier in England, despite his name not appearing on the Trade Board list of manufacturing furriers. He sub-contracts the work to a large number of Jewish chamber-masters, and yet accepts no responsibility for the sweating that occurs, because under Trade Board regulations, only the owner of the workshop (i.e. the chamber-master) is responsible for conditions. This despite the fact that the chamber-master are clearly being exploited and not being paid sufficiently to maintain conditions.

In 1930 it was officially stated that almost a third of the workers employed in the fur industry received less than the minimum wage.[288] Similar conditions prevail in the boot and shoe industry. There are numerous factories in North London whose owners are almost exclusively Jewish. The working conditions are only tolerable if the companies belong to the Incorporated Federated Associations of Boot and Shoe Manufacturers of Great Britain and Ireland. However, many companies are outside this federation and the conditions in them are the most despicable.[289]

Conditions are also miserable in the furniture industry, which is also almost entirely in the hands of Jews. In London alone, it employs around 50,000 workers. As the *Jewish Chronicle* explains:

> In the furniture trade, the non-producing wholesaler, that is, the middleman, who appears to be so necessary in other trades, has almost disappeared, and his place has been taken by the large-scale manufacturer who sells his products direct to the retail distributors. This position of manufacturer has largely been taken over by the Jews, so far as London is concerned. There is among them great competition for trade, and, as they are not organized, the evils of unbridled competition occur. This reacts upon the worker, and as he is frequently un-

---

[288] *Jewish Chronicle*, 19/2/1937, p. 26-27. Translator's note: QVOS.

[289] *Jewish Chronicle*, 12/2/1937, p. 25-6. Translator's note: The report tells of effective slave labor conditions, child labor, anti-social working hours, of having to wade through pools of urine in the factory, of non-flushing toilets, the stench of excrement in the workplace, leaking roofs, poor ventilation, choked exhaust pipes on machines etc. etc. It should be said however, that the report states that in North London, where almost all of the shoe-manufacturers are Jews, all respect the unionized conditions, and that it is 'mainly the action of one specific Jewish manufacturer, who is not a member of the Federation, who is responsible for nine-tenths of the mud thrown at the Jews in North London'.

organized, he is unable to defend himself, and abuses occur. A Trade Union official told me that among some of the rank and file of the furniture workers there was a strong latent anti-Semitic feeling, and it is no mere coincidence that the Black-shirts are strongest in Bethnal Green and Shoreditch, districts which have always been the centers of the furniture trade. A large outward movement has taken place to districts like Tottenham, Ponder's End, Slough and Wembley, and again it is no mere coincidence that there is a strong anti-Jewish feeling around Angel Road, Tottenham, where Jewish manufacturers maintain large establishments employing 95 per cent. non-Jewish labor.

The truth is that some Jewish employers in the furniture trade have made anti-Semites of their employees because of the bad conditions of work.

It is asserted that Jewish masters take advantage of the lack of regulation by making their employees work abnormally long hours. Whilst this is as true of the non-Jewish employer as of the Jew, in the cabinet trade, because of the large number of Jewish masters, this assertion is used as a means of disseminating hatred of the Jews. It is true, however, only of non-Union Jewish firms. It cannot be denied that many do work their employees for from fifty to sixty hours a week, instead of forty-seven, as laid down by the agreement. It is equally true that many do not pay the usual 1s. 9d. per hour to cabinet-makers, chair-makers, machinists and wood-carvers, but pay 1s. per hour and, in extreme cases, less. It has been verified further that sanitary conditions in many cases leave very much to be desired. I must conclude that in the cabinet trade there are Jewish employers who are 'submissive to unconscionable practices,' and this acts to the detriment of Jewry. The enforcement of a seven-day week in a non-Jewish area, the removal of lavatory doors so that employees may not remain away from work for too long, may be practices that result in a healthy balance-sheet each year, **but they are just as certainly responsible for 'racial unrest' and the harming of innocent Jews through the hateful selfishness of a handful of greedy employers who are thereby traitors to Jewry.**[290]

---

[290] *Jewish Chronicle*, 5/2/1937 p. 24. Translator's note: QVOS and formatted (i.e. excerpts of text in bold) as per original source.

Recent investigations have shown that nothing has changed regarding these conditions. The National Amalgamated Furnishing Trades Association decided to address this problem and issued a press release, of which the following is an excerpt:

> Records will prove that an extraordinary proportion of those participating in Fascist propaganda have some occupational connection with the furniture trade.
>
> It is a known fact that furniture manufacture and distribution is controlled almost exclusively by Jewish employers; Fascist propagandists, because of the low wages and excessive hours of employment prevailing in factories, find such vicious exploitation a fertile ground for anti-Semitism.
>
> A small number of Jewish employers, out of a total of hundreds, have an honorable record for consistently maintaining the agreed standard of wages and conditions of employment in spite of almost overwhelming competition from the 'Sweat Den', and have worked with the Unions to establish reasonable wages and conditions for the workers; to these we convey our thanks and appreciation.
>
> The National Amalgamated Furnishing Trades Association is glad to learn of the response to the call for financial aid for the victims of the Nazi terror, but the pleasure is tempered with the knowledge that many of those who have given large sums to this deserving cause, nevertheless from the beginning of the year to the end, ruthlessly exploit labor in this country in the furniture trade.
>
> We feel entitled to declare that the £100 to £1,000 given to these charitable objects by this type of employer is in the nature of 'conscience money' or a blatant 'skin-saving' gesture.
>
> Can we be expected to give the credit of a charitable mind when we know that to provide these donors with 'fortunes in a brief period', thousands of furniture workers, Gentile and Jew, are forced to work for low wages and hours of labour far in excess of the forty-seven per week approved by local trade agreements.
>
> Numerous cases have occurred within recent months where men have been discharged from their employment because they were members of the Union—one firm in Edmonton, in order to circumvent a signed agreement, but a few months old, has, within the past fortnight, discharged their employees who refused to hand over their Trade Union membership cards—these incidents which have occurred in nu-

merous factories demonstrate the mockery of such employers pleading against atrocities and restriction of freedom of thought, and allows the contention often made, that if Fascism was not anti-Semitic, they would find their spiritual home in the ranks of the 'Storm Troopers'.

Absolute disregard of the customs of the country has been proved by the report of an independent investigator into working conditions in what these employers are pleased to call 'mass production' furniture factories—wages as much as 9d. per week below the agreed 'fair' rate, and hours of employment up to eighty per week, Sundays included.

It is not a matter of importance to the national life that work must go on in these factories seven days per week, but it is essential to the owners that the full 'pound of flesh' should be obtained from their employees, no matter that thousands of furniture workers, Gentile and Jewish, are compelled to queue up at the Employment Exchange or the offices of the Unemployment Assistance Board.

These conditions breed anti-Semitism and Fascism, and we can only assume that this type of furniture employer on whom the responsibility lies for the fertile ground on which the seeds of anti-Semitism is sown, will rely on the natural hostility of the people of this country against all forms of repression to preserve him from the fate afflicting the victims of Fascism on the Continent.

If avarice brought the reward which is its due, few people would trouble, but it is the decent people who would suffer from the rise of dictatorship, those who fertilized the growth by their exploitation would retreat to another refuge; and the worker, Jew and Gentile, would suffer alongside those who have a regard for liberty.

In cases where a statement of profits must, by law, be made available for public information, exorbitant sums are recorded as having been extracted from the business. Bonus shares, the device for reducing the percentage, is common. On the formation of the company, colossal amounts are paid for 'goodwill', yet it is not possible, we are told, for reasonable wages and conditions to be paid, and that the Unions and the Employers' Federation, which for generations have negotiated agreements, should lower the standard of conditions to the level of the 'Sweat Den', to give the owners the privilege of saying, 'we have now agreed to observe "fair" conditions of employment and wage'—we are of the opinion that we shall have public support when we reply 'disgorge some of your excessive profits'.[291]

The *Jewish Chronicle* then went on to report that representatives of both employers and workers had had a meeting in the Ministry of Labor, at which it was decided that a joint committee be set up to investigate the allegations of poor wages and working conditions, including eighty-hour working weeks, with a few to further action being taken. We hardly believe that any solution will be found, since these conditions have been known since the mass immigration of Jews around 1900, and, despite the occasional protest, nothing has been done about it.

At a subsequent meeting of the Board of Deputies of British Jews, a Mr. Diamond brought up the matter of the trade union's official statement and press conference. The *Jewish Chronicle* reported Mr. Diamond as saying that the statement was 'of a very ugly character indeed, and for the first time in this country a Trade Union had, in the course of complaining of the troubles that had arisen between it and the employers, raised the racial issue'.[292]

One of the big names in the furniture industry is Sir Benjamin Drage, director and technical advisor of the well-known furniture company Drage's Ltd.[293]

By the point that Jews were immigrating *en masse* at the dawn of the century, official investigations had already established that the Jews were the sole masters of the tailoring and clothing industry. Even then, the conditions for the workers, who were mainly employed from home, were seen as inhumane. To this day, nothing of this situation has changed. In many cases, home workers have only a single room for themselves and their often-large family to live in. In order to survive on starvation wages, they have to work all day and half the night. The number of people employed in this industry is estimated to be around 25,000. In the factories, the work spaces are anything but pleasant. Here too, in this branch of industry, there is cutthroat competition, and the biggest sufferer is once again the worker. The company owners

---

[291] *Jewish Chronicle*, 16/12/1938, p. 34. Translator's note: QVOS, and quoted more extensively than it was in the original study, due to its perceived historical importance. It should also be noted that the Amalgamated Union of Upholsterers asked the JC to publicize the fact that it was in no way connected with the press release, and the London Furniture Trades Federation similarly wished to distance themselves from the press conference which took place the same day as the press release. The Jewish People's Council also issued a response to the trade union's statement, in which it objected to its tone.

[292] *Jewish Chronicle*, 23/12/1938, p. 25. Translator's note: QVOS. Incidentally, the Board also brought up the fact that the great majority of manufacturers who were not represented at the Ministry of Labor meeting were Jewish. The Board also discussed the problem of (Jewish) 'price-cutting shops', which would sell groceries at cut-throat prices which was designed to drive their competitors out of business.

[293] *Jewish Year Book 1937*, p. 422; *SEYB38*, p. 1191.

make huge profits: for example, the *Jewish Chronicle* tells of the recent case of a Jewish strike picket who bought a coat from a shop in the West End of London, for two guineas [42 shillings], and paraded the street with it, advertising that it had been made in the East End for 9 shillings 6d. More and more factories are being built by Hebrews in the so-called 'rag trade'.[294]

Here, too, one Jew—Sir Montague Burton—is undeniably the leader. He is also a zealous Zionist, as well as chairman and managing director of:

> Burton (Montague) Ltd.
> Burton (Montague) Estates Ltd.
> Burton (Montague) Shop Properties Ltd.

The capital of the first company listed is £5,500,000. It has shops in almost every major town center in England, 621 in total. The factories are in Leeds and Walkden, Lancashire.[295]

The unscrupulous manner in which the Jews exploited their monopoly in the tailoring and clothing industry during the Great War is clear from their own writings. As the Jew Louis Golding wrote in his serialized essay *A Rationale of Anti-Semitism*:

> A certain Jewish 'master-tailor' abides in my memory. He was making vast profits in the manufacture of war-time khaki, and was announcing them on the top of a 'bus and in strident tones. Not one of his confections, he boasted, would keep its stitches for a month. 'It vos grand,' he swore, 'money for dirt'.[296]

Jews also hold a dominant position in the hairdressing trade, especially in London. Wages are also kept extremely low and employees are often forced to work a twelve-hour day, and in many cases even on Sundays. There are no measures for legal protection. Such Jewish exploitation is made possible by the so-called Hairdresser's and Barber's (Sunday Closing) Act of 1930. Although this law generally requires shops to be closed on Sundays, it provides an exception for Jews under certain conditions. A Jewish shop-

---

[294] *Jewish Chronicle*, 22/1/1937, pp. 25-26, 29/1/1937 pp. 20-21. Translator's note: The anecdote comes from the 29/1/1937 issue. & *Jewish Chronicle*, 5/10/1934 p. 18.

[295] *Jewish Year Book 1937*, p. 441; *SEYB38*, pp. 1041, 2235; *Jewish Chronicle*, 28/10/1938.

[296] *Jewish Chronicle*, 25/11/1921 (Supplement, iv). Anecdote also repeated verbatim in Banister, p. 138. Translator's note: QVOS. Golding (in the JC source) then goes on to say: 'The morality of the gentleman does not at the moment concern us, but the crass vulgarity which blinded him to the resentment his fellow-travelers might feel on the score that possibly their own sons and brothers would be clad in this deliberate and conscious shoddy, perturbed me.'

keeper is thus allowed to have his shop open on Sunday if he is closed on Saturday. Interestingly, this law met with a certain amount of resistance when it was debated in Parliament, when it was described as giving an unjustified preference to a religious community.

The Jews have taken unlawful advantage of this exemption by circumventing the law through the following maneuver: a Jew purchases two stores in different places under different names. One locale is open on Saturday and the other on Sunday. Employees are transferred from one place to another as needed, as the *Jewish Chronicle* reporter reveals to his readers: 'In one particular case, I am told, every Saturday night the staff take the chairs to a shop higher up the road, ready for Sunday morning.' People who refuse to work seven days are fired. Most of the time this doesn't happen because, as the *Jewish Chronicle* states, 'some masters have also kept wages low, saying that assistants can make them up by working on the extra day.'

The differential police treatment between Jews and non-Jews was also leading to resentment, warned the *Jewish Chronicle* reporter, and he gave the following example:

> I was told of an incident that occurred last year when Yom Kippur fell on a Saturday. The majority of Jewish hairdressers informed the Local Authority, in accordance with the Act, that they were going to open on Sunday for that particular week only. At Christmas time in the same year, it was to the advantage of non-Jewish hairdressers to remain open on Sunday. A number did so, were fined for breaking the Act, and one, indignant at what he considered to be the special treatment of the Jew, is now a member of the British Union of Fascists.

It was rightly pointed out in 1934 in the *Hairdresser's Weekly Journal* that such behavior would inevitably bring personalities like Hitler and Mosley to power, as the following reader's letter attests:

> 'Britisher', quite rightly ask: 'How many Sabbaths have the Jews? My answer to that query is that many of those Jewish hairdressers who have pressed to enforce Clause 3 have no Sabbath at all. They favoured that Clause not because they are religious, and wished to attend Synagogue and to rest. Nothing of the kind. They simply favour that Clause because they are much busier on Sunday than Saturday.
>
> Many of them have two shops, opening one on Sunday and one on Sunday [sic]. This is nothing else but hypocrisy, as those particular Jews never were law-abiding citizens in this or any other country. They are the black sheep of the Jewish race

and are the very ones who are creating Hitlers and Mosleys. I am a Jew myself and I do know how to appreciate the freedom the Jews are having in this country.[297]

We would like to emphasize once more that the above data on the fur, footwear, furniture, and hairdressing trades have been taken from a series of articles in the *Jewish Chronicle*. We made the decision to completely forego reports from anti-Jewish sources on the same topic, because we considered the admissions from the Jews themselves to be sufficiently eloquent.

Jews also play a major role in chain stores like Woolworths. Here we shall cite only one company as an example: Marks & Spencer. The chairman and managing director is Simon Marks, his deputy in these roles is J. M. Sieff, and directors include Norman Laski and Harry Sacher. The aforementioned Colonial Minister Leo Amery and the Marquess of Milford Haven are also directors. The attorneys are Arthur Benjamin and Cohen. The company's capital is £3,300,000, and 226 stores have been opened in the UK to date.[298]

The extent to which retail trade is in the hands of Jews can best be seen on Jewish holidays. A stroll through the commercial streets of London gives the best object lesson: on these days most shops are closed, or they are kept open with only a few Aryan workers. The well-known Harrods group is split into Harrods Ltd. and Harrods (Buenos Aires) Ltd. The common telegraphic address is but one indicator of how closely these two companies are connected to each other. The former includes the well-known giant department stores of Harrods, Dickins & Jones, D. H. Evans & Co. Ltd. and others. On the board of directors of Harrods (Buenos Aires) Ltd. sits the financially powerful Jew Baron d'Erlanger, who certainly also has a stake in Harrods Ltd., even if he does not make this known to the outside world. Incidentally, as Fraser points out, Harrods has three Jewish directors, the same three Jewish directors that on the board of D. H. Evans and Co.[299]

Jewish Influences and Their Effects

A brief survey of the above compiled material will not only prove the destructive influence of Judaism, but will also justify the conclusion that the whole of British life is to a large extent influenced, if not dominated, by the

---

[297] *Jewish Chronicle*, 26/2/1937; *Hairdresser's Weekly Journal*, 18/9/1934. Translator's note: All QVOS (the *Jewish Chronicle*, which reproduces the hairdressing journal's letter). As can be deduced, the JC reporter was concerned about the two-tier nature of the Act being a source of anti-Semitism, and states that as a result, 'a strong demand for the repeal of the Clause has arisen, among both Jews and non-Jews.'

[298] *Jewish Year Book 1937*, pp. 460, 471, 488, 497; *SEYB38*, pp. 1582-3.

[299] *Jewish Chronicle*, 22/1/1937, pp. 25-26, 29/1/1937 pp. 20-21. Translator's note: The anecdote comes from the 29/1/1937 issue. & *Jewish Chronicle*, 5/10/1934 p. 18.

Jews and their system. In politics, economics, culture, and all areas of public life, it is the same picture everywhere. It seems as if there is no corner of England left that Jews have not penetrated.

The question then arises as to where this state of things has already led England or will lead England in the future. Not even the friends of the Jews can deny that an alien element has come into the country with the Hebrews, which has to have had an impact in one way or another, not least because they will always remain a foreign body who will never be absorbed into the nation. A letter from 'B. Felz' to the *Jewish Chronicle* of 8 December 1911 (p. 38), proves that this understanding of things is no mere theory. Writing of the unhappy Jewish reaction to Mr. Chesterton's lecture at the West End Jewish Literary Society, Mr. Felz admits: 'The patriotism of the Jew is merely a cloak he assumes to please the Englishman, and so when Mr. Chesterton is shrewd enough to detect the Jew beneath the Englishman's clothing, the masqueraders become exceedingly angry.' The self-confessed 'Jew of the younger generation' also ends his letter by saying: 'I think it can be laid down as a general law, that the more Jews become Englishmen, the less they become Jews. That does not imply any moral censure; it is simply a statement of fact, and Jews who pretend that they can at once be patriotic Englishmen and good Jews are simply living lies.'

This in turn agrees with the words of the Jew M. Wodislawski, who declared: 'I am a British citizen, but first and foremost I am Jewish.' After the Great War, the Hebrews noted with satisfaction that between the Jews of the various countries there had never been a state of war or even hostility, and in the *Jewish Chronicle* of 26 August 1927, we read that 'the Jews are international. Denying this or pretending that it is not the case does not change this established fact'.[300] According to another Jewish admission:

> [I]t is a regrettable fact that the debauchers, the instigators of crimes and the people with all type of bad traits in business are generally Jews. If we could deny it, we would. We would even keep it a secret if we could. But we can neither deny it nor debate it away...[301]

What results have the Jewish spirit, when combined with Puritan and liberal principles, produced in England? In addition to many other negative externalities, of which more later, the entire system is perfectly revealed in the number of unemployed men and the problems that this causes.

---

[300] *Jewish World*, 1/1/1909. & 15/1/1919. Translator's note: The quotation in this form could not be found, and appears to the author's (accurate) gloss of the transcript of the speech given at the Zurich Conference on Jewish Rights by Rabbi Dr. Stephen S. Wise, President of the American Jewish Congress, pp. 17-18 of source.

[301] *British Guardian*, 23/5/1924.

Although the state of war mobilized a great deal of manpower for national defense and the war industry, the number of unemployed people—there were still over a million at the beginning of 1941—speaks an eloquent and at the same time disturbing language. Since the assistance that they receive is insufficient, the miserable conditions of these people must necessarily result in a slow physical and mental perishing. In his book *News of England*, writer Beverley Nichols describes the suffering everywhere, the decline of entire towns and the resulting collapse of those affected. He reports numerous cases in which young people between the ages of 16 and 18 have never worked, nor have ever seen their fathers work.[302]

The pauperization of the masses has reached such proportions over the past sixty years because employers in Puritan-Jewish England are only interested in making money, not in the wellbeing of the community. Even today there are unthinkably hellish working conditions in that land—inconceivable for members of the Third Reich—while companies paying annual dividends of 60% or even 100% are not uncommon. As examples, we shall cite Woolworths and Austin Motor Works, to name just two such companies.[303]

The systematic decline of agriculture, which incidentally had begun at the end of the 18th century and caused ever-more free peasant farmers to disappear from their own land, took on critical proportions with the introduction of Free Trade, which caused thousands upon thousands to give up their land, or to exchange work in the fields for new sources of income in the city. The resulting oversupply of manpower led to starvation wages and further unemployment with its well-known pernicious consequences.

There is no picture more shocking than the official statistics on recipients of government support. Until the outbreak of the Great War there was only one type of claimant in existence: those who received welfare support. After the introduction of unemployment benefit, there were two categories of claimant. It will certainly be possible that here and there people who receive an old-age pension will also receive welfare support, so that they will be better off than unemployment-benefit recipients in general. It should also be taken into account that among the latter, there are many people who are no longer able to work. There are also cases where a person, with the approval of the relevant authorities, receives both benefits, meaning that he or she is listed twice. But this is rare and is offset by the fact that others who are unemployed do not register for some reason and therefore do not appear in the official statistics.

In any case, it is clear that the people who are registered either for welfare support or unemployment benefit together represent the legion of undernourished paupers, a situation which will lead to the strength and vitality

---

[302] Nichols, p. 233 ff.
[303] SEYB38, pp. 891, 2065.

of the nation being ravaged as time goes on. The numbers for the different time periods are as follows:[304]

Year	Total U.K. Population	Unemployed, on Unemployment Benefit	Unemployed, on Welfare
1871	31,555,694		1,280,000 (approx.)
1881	34,952,204		1,000,000 (approx.)
1890	37,484,764		1,000,000 (approx.)
1900	41,164,297		1,000,000 (approx.)
1913	45,468,000		933,166
1927	45,388,000	1,145,000	1,803,702
1934	46,666,000	2,407,000	1,880,177
1938	47,485,000	1,800,000 (approx.)	1,484,359

This relatively great suffering of the population has had a particular impact on health. This has recently become most noticeable among schoolchildren, which has become a matter of serious concern at teachers' conferences. On other occasions, people have noted the problem, but without taking any practical measures to change the situation. It is true that in 1937 an organization was set up to try to improve the health of the population, but by the beginning of 1939 virtually nothing was heard of it. At a trade union assembly in 1937 it was pointed out that it would be impossible to improve children's health unless there was an improvement in their nutrition. Furthermore, it must be said that in the food industry everything is done to ensure that the seller makes the maximum profit, regardless of the quality or nutritional value of the food being sold. This has largely been achieved by offering consumers almost all vegetables, fruits, etc. in tinned form. Even potatoes come in tins, a fact that might make you laugh if the thinking it reveals were not so sad.

The quality of the beer and of other types of alcoholic beverages, the production of which is likewise based solely on the profit motive, is also detrimental to health. In England, there is a very high level of alcohol consumption, which in 1936 led to no fewer than 44,525 convictions for drunkenness. The visions that one often sees in London are also shocking: babies in prams being left outside the front door of the pub at night, while the mother inside tries to keep up with the men drinking.[305]

---

[304] McNair Wilson, p. 41 ff. & *Statistical Abstracts for the United Kingdom: 1939*, pp. 4, 5, 97, 132; *Accounts and Papers... 1902*, Vol. 62, pp. 257, 266-8; *Accounts and Papers ...1886*, Vol. 68, p. 187, 195-6.

[305] *Daily Telegraph*, 30/3/1937. & For more details, see Nichols, pp. 88-97.

One victim of the Jewish system is undoubtedly Great Britain's agriculture, which has been hit particularly hard. It was doomed to collapse when cheap foodstuffs flooded in from all parts of the world after the triumph of the Free Trade ideology, introduced by Peel but firmly and definitively anchored into the country by Disraeli. Although this increased exports— England's suppliers bought their finished goods from England—this trade did not benefit the nation, but only the Jews and their friends, who, making money both from imports and exports, profited twice from this system. In this way, the current conditions in agriculture have undoubtedly permitted a gradual increase in pure money power with its globalist plans. To be competitive, low wages for workers were a prerequisite, but this could only be achieved in conjunction with cheap food.

In that context, who cared about the harm or even destruction of the nation's agriculture? Who cared that thousands and thousands were driven off the land and living in abject poverty? This brought a new influx of labour into the cities, and the main goal sought by the money power—low wages— was achieved. In the first thirty years following the introduction of Free Trade, around 120,000 agricultural workers and their families left the countryside, of whom very few found decently paid jobs. Most became paupers or emigrated.[306]

According to the latest statistics, no fewer than 180,000 agricultural workers and their families have emigrated over the last ten years. Since 1921, 2,600,236 acres of once-productive land have fallen out of cultivation. In addition, the land that is still under cultivation is deteriorating more and more because the farmers, due to a lack of capital, are unable to buy the necessary equipment etc. that a modern farming business requires. For the same reason, most agricultural companies have neither silos nor other storage options, so they have to sell the harvest from the field itself as far as is possible. Since this creates an extraordinary oversupply on the markets, the already low prices fall still further and the farmer barely receives enough to pay his taxes. The situation in agriculture is therefore completely hopeless.[307]

A brilliantly-written work, supported by statistical evidence, has been published from the pen of the well-known agrarian Viscount Lymington, a former member of Parliament and a sincere friend of Germany even in these difficult days. No one was better qualified to take a stand on this burning issue, since he himself maintains a model estate. The title of this book, *Famine in England*, says it all, and we only wish that a German translation were published to show the difference in attitude between the Third Reich government and the British government towards agriculture. Purpose and space prohibit us from giving further details from Lord Lymington's book.

---

[306] McNair Wilson, p. 149. & *Daily Express*, 20/10/1938.
[307] *Daily Express*, 20/10/1938. & Nichols, p. 181. & Lymington, p. 120 ff.

That agriculture can no longer survive with what is has, was confirmed by an article in the *Daily Express* of 14 December 1938. The owner of a farm of about 120 hectares had to put £1,601 into it in one year. With the appointment of a new Minister of Agriculture, the peasantry hoped that their situation would improve, but we do not have faith that this will happen, as it would mean changing a state of affairs that has been in place for almost a century, and would require drastic measures, which is not really in the spirit of the English people, not to mention the resistance that it would receive from the money power led by the Jews. The option of paying subsidies to farmers is unlikely to prove viable given Britain's strained financial situation, especially since all circles hostile to agriculture would be against it.

Finally, the existence of the so-called Political and Economic Planning group (PEP), is likely to stand in the way of a movement of free upward development. Founded in 1931, this association has set up boards with great powers, in a type of self-regulation for the various sectors of the economy. Many sectors of agriculture have already been affected by this new regulatory system, e.g. there is a milk board and a potato board which specify exactly how much milk or how many potatoes a farmer can produce, and which also set the prices. These boards have given rise to the greatest bitterness in the agricultural sector, which complains of completely inadequate prices and intolerable injustices, as well as the disproportionate contributions that they have to pay to the PEP. An excess of milk produced that cannot be used on the farm has to be thrown away because farmers are not allowed to sell it. If there has been a bountiful potato harvest which exceeds the set amount that the farmer has been allotted to sell, he has no choice but to leave them in the field, where they often rot unless poor people go and secretly collect them. It has even happened that only certain grades of potatoes are allowed to be sold, which means that most of the rest are likely to spoil, while millions of people in the world's largest and richest empire do not have enough to eat.[308]

All of this is only possible because big capital works with the PEP group to become the ultimate master of the free peasantry. We know that this has been the aim of the Jews and their friends since ancient times, for they need the impoverishment of the masses in the cities, and control over the peasants in the countryside, in order to dictate their terms. Thus we see little hope for a revitalization of agriculture in England, especially since after the Great War the big landowners, knowing that crop prices were set to dip, sold large parts of their land to their tenant farmers, who to buy the land had to borrow money at high interest rates from the banks, and thus fell into the clutches of the Jews and their friends when agricultural prices took their inevitable tumble. 'The effect of the whole transaction,' Belloc wrote, 'was

---

[308] *Daily Express*, 12/10/1938, 28/10/1938, 5/11/1938, 18/11/1938, 19/11/1938, 22/11/1938, 23/11/1938, 30/11/1938, 15/12/1938.

that masses of English land had been transferred from the old great Land-lords to the banks, and that the men who actually tilled the soil and had adventured their small capital in the development of small farms, were left paying tribute to the money-lending machine which modern banking has become.' Belloc is likewise correct when he states: 'In the Commercial State the peasantry will be destroyed'.[309]

So today, as we witness the collapse of the British Empire, we must reflect on the contributory role played by the plutocracies' destruction of the free and independent peasant class, a goal sought by the Jews for centuries because this class was the least amenable to their influence. We remember with horror that this process once threatened to take hold in Germany, too, and we must therefore be doubly grateful that the targeted measures of the Reich farmers' leader Richard Walther Darré put an end to the capitalist exploitation of the German peasantry once and for all, and secured her the place she deserves. As a result, blood and soil have regained their rights, and if today we plan for the thousand-year Reich, the reality of this will be in no small measure assured by the protective regulations for agriculture put in place by a brilliant leadership.

What is remarkable is the fact that the PEP group has already made its way into various sectors of the general economy without the public knowing practically anything about it. The few who do know about it believe that this organization is a tool with which the Jews can directly control the economy in new ways with unprecedented success. The president of this all-powerful group is the Jew Israel Sieff, the vice-president and assistant managing director of the aforementioned Marks & Spencer, similar to Woolworths. He is also Honorary President of the Zionist Federation of Great Britain and Ireland. His political views can be described as radical left. It is even said, based on American publications, that he maintains close ties to the group of Jews—namely Jacob Schiff, Warburg and others—who provided the original financial support to the Bolsheviks and thus kept them in power.

Two other directors of the PEP group are the aforementioned Lord Melchett and Lord Eustace Percy. The former needs no further identification as a full Jew, but with regard to the latter, it should be mentioned that he has fallen completely into the Jews' orbit. During his time working as an attaché at the British Embassy in Washington, he was close friends with the Zionist Professor Felix Frankfurter, who has recently been appointed Associate Justice of the Supreme Court with the help of his patron Roosevelt. Another of the PEP's leading men, Kenneth Lindsay, described by Fry as Sieff's docile secretary, was formerly third chairman of the Labor Club at Oxford University and is known for his radical left-wing views. From this brief summary of

---

[309] Belloc: *Crisis*, pp. 152-3. Translator's note: QVOS. & Belloc: *Contemporary England*, p. 62 ff. Translator's note: QVOS.

some of the PEP group's leaders—at least the most influential and energetic —the reader will have a rough idea of the group's goals.[310]

Thus we can see that it is only a certain small group which benefits from the current Jewish system in England. In addition to the army of unemployed and an agriculture in decline, there are signs of degeneration everywhere else. The disused factories in Britain's industrial regions speak volumes. The slums of London, Glasgow, Manchester, Leeds, and other cities are hard to imagine: we find them unbearable.

A serious question is the mixing of the blood of the English with all possible races, which is becoming more and more noticeable. According to our estimate, there are, as we know, about 1.7 million Jews to some 44 million English [i.e. about 3.9%], and additional contingents of Hebrews are streaming into the country on a daily and weekly basis. Nothing is being done to prevent intermarriage; on the contrary, the nobility and ruling circles in particular bear eloquent witness to this racial profanation.[311]

In addition to the many Jews, there are thousands of Colored men, Negroes, Chinese, etc., in London, Cardiff, Liverpool, Manchester, Hull, and other cities, and it hardly causes a stir when they marry English girls, who then go on to give birth to numerous mixed-race children. The physical examination for military service is usually a good touchstone for a nation's general state of health, and as early as the turn of the century, 60% of the Englishmen who volunteered to enlist were found to be unfit. During the Great War, after the introduction of conscription, there was an even better opportunity to carry out checks in this regard, which produced an even more shocking result: 64-65% of men were unfit for field service. In 1918, Lloyd George told a special conference at Manchester Hippodrome that the results of the physical examinations were 'appalling. I hardly dare tell you the results'.[312]

---

[310] *Jewish Year Book 1938*, p. 502. Translator's note: According to his Jewish Telegraphic Agency obituary of 15/7/1972, Sieff also co-founded the World Jewish Congress, of which he became vice-president and chairman of its European executive. & *Unseen Net*, pp. 4-5; *Jewish Communal Register 1921* (New York); Steed: *Through Thirty Years*, Vol. II, p. 302. Translator's note: Steed affirms in his memoir that when it came to the securing the Bolsheviks power and international legitimacy, 'the prime movers were Jacob Schiff, Warburg, and other international financiers, who wished above all to bolster up the Jewish Bolshevists in order to secure a field for German and Jewish exploitation of Russia.' & *Unseen Net*: p. 4 ff.; *Jewish Daily Post*, 16/6/1935; Fry, p. 235 ff. Translator's note: 'Leslie Fry' was the pen name of Louise Chandor-Shishmareff.

[311] Ludovici: *Defense of Conservatism*, p. 231-2.

[312] Lane, pp. 43-52; Landa, p. 275 ff. Banister, pp. 126-9. Translator's note: Banister, in his book first published in 1923, states that 'Liverpool alone has found work for some 5,000 colored men' (p. 128), and attributes the 'rapidly increasingly negro element in the population' to 'the preference of Jewish employers for negro labor. Most of the negroes and other colored men here, and practically all those engaged in theatrical performances, have been imported by Jews.' (p. 41). Lane's chapter 'The Alien and Public Health' is

With regard to this fact, the question then arises as to whether the English people show any sign of degeneration. We are aware of the many different views on the topic. However, within the scope of our present study we cannot deal with this topic in detail, but must mainly limit ourselves to citing facts that are related to the Jewish Question.

Extremely interesting and instructive is the book *Man: An Indictment* by A. M. Ludovici, who with great clarity argues that degeneration has reached considerable proportions. He does not deny the bravery and value of the British soldier in the Great War, but rightly remarks that this is not evidence to the contrary, since animals are also capable of fighting, which proves nothing more than a reasonably strong survival instinct. But this cannot hide the fact that other necessary qualities, such as willpower, determination, self-discipline, etc., are becoming ever rarer among the British people. 'We have mass-thought and opinion imposed on the population, in the same way as are their standardized manufactured boots,' Ludovici writes, 'and any attempt at raising them from their hypnotic condition, by stating truths that are incompatible with their standardized intellectual pabulum, is to earn the reputation of insanity or crankiness.' We know that the Jews want precisely this situation for a country; under such circumstances, the programming, and (one might well say) the dumbing-down of the people is made easier with the help of the modern methods and means of propaganda.[313]

---

very recommended to researchers looking for on-the-ground truth about the third-world conditions that existed in the multicultural areas of 1930s England. & Ludovici: *Man* pp. 191-5. Translator's note: Quoted word as per original source (*Times* 13/9/1918, p. 8). Ludovici, himself a front-line officer in WW1, put the real percentage of unfit men as much higher, saying that 'I challenge any officer who was on the Western Front, whether in the artillery or infantry, to deny that the men we used to get as reinforcements, even as early as the autumn of 1916, were often among the poorest specimens of manhood we had ever seen—dull-witted, delicate, toothless, and often rheumatical. Thousands of these men are taking war-disability pensions today, who ought never to have crossed the water, who only crossed it in order to be invalided home again...' Lloyd George, in the speech quoted above, also told those assembled (referring to the army's fitness grades): 'You cannot maintain an A1 Empire with a C3 population' and admitted that he had been 'staggered' by the Minister of National Service's admission that at least a million men had been lost to the fighting ranks due to the systematic neglect of the nation's health. He also apologized to the doctors who, due to the shocking levels of unfitness not being believed by government officials, were made to re-examine men in the hope that there had been some kind of diagnostic error.

[313] Ludovici, pp. 141-181. & Ludovici, pp. 262-3. Translator's note: QVOS. Coincidentally, Ludovici's 1927 discussion of the mind-control effects of mass communication precedes the publication of Edward Bernays' book *Propaganda* by only a year. Winston Churchill, who himself knew how to manipulate the masses with rhetorical techniques, best summed up the elites' supremely arrogant view of the individual as an empty vessel to be filled with the opinions of his 'betters' when he said: 'There is no such thing as public opinion. There is only published opinion.'

How else to explain the fact that the parliamentary parties do not demand an unconditional solution to the calamitous misery that is so widespread in England? Old people struggle to find the barest necessities to live, the unemployed are demonstrating for the lack of a good square meal in a long time, and the farmers—the wellspring of a nation—have for decades been heading towards ruin. The MPs, whose electorate consists largely of these poor, passed a law increasing their annual allowances from £400 to £600, and yet the majority of them refused to grant a modest increase in the Old Age Pension. Abandoned by their rulers, these poor wretches have resigned themselves to their fate.[314]

While the people themselves are neglected, and many of their children, due to weakness and malnutrition, are unable to take part in the exercise classes that are so strongly recommended for health, while there are slums everywhere in the larger cities, and countless unemployed people whose lives are just wasting away, nothing is spared for when it comes to making clamorous propaganda for the Jewish cause.

Not only does the press, without exception, defend the cause of the 'poor displaced Jews', not only does the radio try to help through appeals for donations and numerous 'enlightening' lectures about these pitiable souls, ex-Prime Minister Stanley Baldwin and the Mayor of London, have, through their patronage, raised enormous sums for the Lord Baldwin Fund for Refugees, far in excess of the limit of 20 million shillings. Meanwhile, on the so-called Stage and Screen Day of Saturday, January 14, the theatres and cinemas donated 10% of their income to the same cause, resulting in a donation of over £31,000, and even the Sunday collections of the Church of England ended up giving over £52,000 to the Jews. Regardless of one's political views, an impartial person must be asking why the first concern is not with alleviating the needs of one's own people, why Baldwin does not speak for the native unemployed, why the theatres and cinemas do not donate money for the British poor and elderly, and why the government does not make millions available for a job creation scheme that would offer work and bread and would improve public housing, roads and other infrastructure. With a different set of priorities, the government could provide hospitals that are not, as they are now, dependent almost exclusively on voluntary donations, and which do not suffer a grave lack of beds, instruments and rooms to be able to treat the seriously ill.[315]

---

[314] *Daily Express*, 24/11/1938. & 5/12/1938. & 24/11/1938.

[315] *Times*, 1-10/2/1939; *Sunday Times*, 15/1/1939. Translator's note: The *Times* of 4/2/1939 reports of the fund nearing the £400,000 mark. & *Times*, 9/2/1939, p. 9. Translator's note: This article covers both the cinema/theatre and church initiatives. & *Evening Standard*, 31/12/1938. Translator's note: The front-page headline story 'London Conference Bid To Save the Hospitals', breaks down the dire financial situation of these institutions, and their huge reliance on charity from the public, which is clearly insufficient. The

Would sensible people put up with being pushed out of their positions by emigrants in order to swell the endless ranks of the unemployed? Despite all official denials, one hears continual stories of Englishmen having been fired in order to give jobs to immigrant Jews. It is not uncommon for companies to even be forced to do this by their Jewish business partners or clients, as they often make the conclusion of business dependent on it. If a company rejects such a request, it will not receive any orders, even if it has worked with the Hebrews for years. It is pure extortion, of course, but it has repeatedly proven to be effective.[316]

As for the influence and attitude of the Church, many people, including the writer Ludovici, are of the opinion that it has contributed significantly to the degeneration of the English people. However, we cannot deal with this topic in detail here, as we must limit ourselves to solely to the Church's attitude towards the Jewish Question.[317]

Dr. Cosmo Lang, who as the former Archbishop of Canterbury was head of the Church of England, could be found at many large protest meetings against the Third Reich's policies towards Jews. At a church conference in July 1938, he ordered that the following Sunday, July 17—the day for which the chief rabbi had scheduled prayers in every synagogue of the British Empire for the Jews in Germany—the Anglican, Roman Catholic, and Free Christian communities were to 'unite with their Jewish brothers in prayer for those who had to suffer so cruelly.' It was also he who ordered that the Sunday church collection be used for the benefit of the Jews.[318]

Dr. Temple, former Archbishop of York and current Archbishop of Canterbury, did not lag behind his fellow archbishop in his defense of the Jews: in October 1938 he delivered a lecture titled 'The World's Debt to Israel and its presentation in Education' at the Society of Jews and Christians in London, and four months earlier, in June 1938, he described the German

---

article expresses indignation that 'the vital health services the hospitals provide should be largely dependent on thousands of young men and girls cajoling coppers from passers-by in the streets.' It also describes how hospitals would routinely send donation requests to private individuals, for example, if a birth of a baby had been announced in the press, the parents would receive begging letters, some from children's hospitals, describing 'in the most harrowing fashion the diseases and distress of less fortunate babies'.

[316] *Daily Express*, 14/10/1938. & *Sunday Express*, 23/10/1938.

[317] Ludovici: *Man*, p. 212. Translator's note: In a manner of speaking, Ludovici did say this (at least if one interprets the statement 'Bolshevism is the outcome of Christian values, the true descendant of Christian tradition in Europe'), however his main argument is that it is the physical degeneration of the English people that has caused a concomitant decline in their religious sentiment and ethical preoccupations, not the other way round.

[318] *Star*, 11/7/1938; *Daily Telegraph*, 18/7/1938; *Voice of Britain*, p. 3-4.

measures against the Jews as 'the greatest outrage in living memory... incompatible with the fundamental principles of civilization'.[319]

Other high ecclesiastical dignitaries, such as the bishops of Chichester, Southwark, Durham, Ripon, Chelmsford, Ipswich, Manchester, London, Salisbury, Bristol and Bradford, also stood up on this issue. The Archbishop of York, along with the Bishop of Chichester, the Bishop of Bradford, and the Bishop of Bristol (as well as other prominent clerical and lay members of the Church of England), addressed an open letter to Mr. Neville Laski, K.C., chairman of the Board of Deputies, in which they strongly condemned Germany's anti-Jewish measures and described the German racial policy as 'wicked folly'.[320]

Dr. Matthews, Dean of St. Paul's Cathedral, said that 'as a Liberal and Christian it was incumbent upon him to protest against the persecution of Jews in various parts of the world and the attempt to carry that evil spirit into this country. Since the War, there had been a remarkable decay of compassion, and things that would have stirred their fathers, today left them cold and unmoved'.[321]

We could fill page after page with similar statements from church leaders, but we will limit ourselves solely to reproducing the official Jewish opinion of the Church's efforts to serve the Jewish cause, which we found in an editorial of the *Jewish Chronicle* dated 7 October 1938:

> The churches in particular, here, as in America, have taken a stand for justice towards Jewish and other minorities which is greatly heartening, though their weakening hold on the masses should not be overlooked.

One wonders why there is no influential voice anywhere to make it clear to the Church that it should first concern itself with the cause of the poor in England, raising its political voice and providing material assistance for its

---

[319] *Jewish Chronicle*, 28/10/1938, pp. 25, 28. Translator's note: Both the lecture title and quotation are QVOS.

[320] *Voice of Britain*, pp. 4-9; *Daily Telegraph*, 28/7/1938, p. 12; *Jewish Chronicle*, 9/12/1938; *Daily Telegraph*, 14-15/11/1938. & 19/12/1938, p. 9. Translator's note: QVOS.

[321] *Jewish Chronicle*, 30/4/1937 p. 20. Translator's note: Aldag's original text stated that Dr. Matthews 'claimed that "anti-Semitism means decadence",' however, this notion has obviously come from the (highly misleading) headline of the JC article, as a careful reading of the entire text shows that the phrase 'Anti-Semitism means decadence' refers to Dr. Moses Gaster's comment, while the sub-headline 'Warning by Dean of St. Paul's', in fact refers to a separate section of the article in which Dr. Matthews features. I have thus replaced Aldag's erroneous but understandable statement with what was actually reported for Dr. Matthew's speech. Incidentally, the actual comment from Dr. Gaster was that 'anti-Semitism was a sign of political, economic, and intellectual disintegration'.

own flock, before getting so involved with foreign Jews that it even makes church funds available to them.

For various writers, another symptom of decline is the fact that more money is spent on betting and gaming in England than in any other country in the world. In 1935, annual turnover across the various gambling groups was £400 million—half the normal English budget—of which around £300 million came from horse racing, but football betting is also growing in popularity. While the money gambled on the so-called Football Pool was £8 million in 1934, a year later it had reached £20 million, and in 1937 it had reached £30 million, which means that it has undoubtedly increased still further in the meantime. With a population of about 44 million, well over 30 million Football Pool letters are delivered by the General Post Office every week, which represents an income of around £140,000.

Everywhere you see 'penny arcades' filled with gaming machines, where men and women, young and old, try their luck. They are usually members of the lower classes, who would be better off investing their pennies in food than succumbing to the lure of the Jewish spirit of speculation, which, through temptingly low stakes, stimulates their passion for gambling, and lures one penny after another out of their pockets. The large amount spent on gambling and its ubiquitous presence is not a sign of economic wellbeing: one only has to observe the punters in the betting shops and at the gaming machines to realize that they are the poorest people.

Beverley Nichols, to whom we owe the figures above, describes how he observed with horror and deep concern 'crowds of men hurrying from the labor exchanges, to spend the first two shillings of their weekly dole on a postal order for a football coupon'—a considerable proportion of their reduced income.[322]

The statements made by the two writers Belloc and Ludovici, who both deal with the question of the Jewish danger to England, are interesting.

The former rightly points out that England is ruled more or less by a small number of rich people. Only the omnipresent merchant spirit made this possible, and led to wealth first asserting then consolidating its primacy. As a result, the joy of creating goods, what might be called craftsmanship, was lost, and then emerged the principle of abandoning production as a measure of wealth, as money became abstracted from the process of production. In a productive society, the superiority of the thing produced is the measure of success; in a commercial society, the amount of wealth accumulated by the dealer is the sole measure of success (the quality of the goods sold being irrelevant). Over time, this must necessarily lead to the ruin of the peasantry that creates the goods. Who should be surprised that England and the Jews are so closely tied that Israel not only has a warm friend and constant ally in

[322] Nichols, pp. 64-73. Translator's note: QVOS (p. 70).

England, but even an enthusiastic patron![323] This is the clear-eyed insight of a man who has closely studied England's problems for decades and who professes himself to be a friend of the Hebrews.

Ludovici pointed out these dangers to English life even more frankly in his various writings. He recognized how the Jew, due to the idiosyncrasies of his character, had to deconstruct all of the old English ideals because they were alien to him, and threatened to block the path of his trajectory towards control of the nation. All that remained was the rubble of the former values of the British people, and in their place the Jewish spirit with all of its detrimental consequences.[324]

In 1938, the well-known writer and clergyman William Ralph Inge told *Evening Standard* readers the following personal anecdotes:

> The other day I met a man who has given up a lucrative position in commerce because he could not stand the almost universal corruption and 'graft' which he found in business. Things have become much worse, he thought, in the last ten years.
>
> Another man told me that 'the word of an Englishman' is no longer a proverb for truthfulness and rectitude among foreign nations. In fact, our business men have now a rather bad reputation.[325]

The old British spirit as it was once known in the world, and which saw king and country as the highest ideals, must be in severe danger, as it had come to the point where, in 1938, the students of Oxford University had made the decision 'never to die for King and Country under any circumstances'.[326]

Left-wing radical influences have been mostly responsible for this attitude, triggered primarily by Jewish elements. It was they who advocated the spread of such ideas immediately after the end of the Great War. The Zionist leader Israel Zangwill became the spokesman for Bolshevism in Communist meetings as early as 1919. That year, as he explained to a largely Jewish audience in the Albert Hall, Great Britain should not oppose the Soviet Union, but rather it should conclude a pact of friendship with them. This is most forcefully demonstrated in the closing lines of his speech, latterly titled *Hands Off Russia*:

---

[323] Belloc: *Crisis*, p. 209 ff.; *Contemporary England*, pp. 5, 50 ff.

[324] Ludovici: *A Defense of Conservatism*, pp. 154-5. Translator's note: See also quotation corresponding to footnote 458 (England's Impotence). Ironically, Aldag makes this statement about Ludovici's frankness without appearing to realize that it was Ludovici who had penned the pseudonymous book *Jews and the Jews in England*, which was unsurprisingly Ludovici's most forthright work on the Jewish Question.

[325] *Evening Standard*, 4/11/1938 p. 7. Translator's note: QVOS.

[326] Zukerman, p. 75 ff.; *Daily Express*, 4/11/1938. Translator's note: QVOS (Zukerman, p. 78).

> Let us intervene in Russia not with arms or blockades, but
> with food and friendship! Let us leave Russia the right she has
> proclaimed for all—the right of self-determination.[327]

We learn from the *Morning Post* of 2 March 1920, that in a public
speech Zangwill described Bolshevism as a form of Christianity and raised
the question of why the workers of Great Britain did not fight for such ideals
of humanity.

When various Jews were accused of Bolshevik agitation, their like-
minded kinsmen sang Marxist songs in the courtroom.[328] There was a strong
Bolshevik tendency among the Jewish population, especially in the East End
of London. The following is an excerpt from an open letter written by a Jewish woman, which appeared in the *Morning Post* of March 10 and 11, 1919:

> It was the Jews who made the revolution possible in Russia.
> The Jewish youth joyfully devoted themselves to this work of
> destruction, which precedes a world reformation; they came to
> England to continue their work...

The newspapers regularly reported on the Jews stirring up unrest among the
working-class populations of London, Glasgow, and other industrial cities.
Most notably, it was the current Labor MP, Emanuel Shinwell, a former tai-
lor from Poland, who made a name for himself with his radical Marxist activities. While he was leading the agitation in Glasgow, his colleague Simon
Greenspon was the leading the riot in Belfast. But even in London, Jews
were identified as the main troublemakers.[329]

The close collaboration between Zionism and Marxism was later repeatedly mentioned in the press.[330] A report on the Comintern Congress held
in Moscow in 1928 stated, among other things, that: 'Mr. Cohen of Great
Britain "strongly recommended the use of subversive propaganda not only in
the British army, navy and air force, but also in the territorial army—the
English militia".'[331]

---

[327] *Morning Post*, 8/2/1919, 23/4/1919; Zangwill, p. 8. Translator's note: QVOS.

[328] *Morning Post*, 10/3/1919.

[329] *Morning Post*, 19/1/1919, 25/1/1919, 8/4/1919, 23/4/1919. Translator's note: Given the
level of Jewish influence on the British press at the time, it would be interesting to know to
what extent newspapers other than the *Morning Post* covered this activity and, if any did,
the language that was used. The *Standard*, which as we saw in chapter 6 was the other big
title that dared be critical of Jewish behavior during the 19th-century, had ceased publication in 1910, apparently leaving the *Morning Post* to be the lone nativist and anti-
establishment voice in the wilderness. & *Morning Post*, 30/1/1919, 31/1/1919, 1/2/1919,
5/2/1919.

[330] *Morning Post*, 7/10/1922.

[331] *Morning Post*, 20/9/1928.

We have witnessed the development of this situation ourselves. By silently digging under the foundations of society, under the radar of the authorities, the Jews fomented the growth of Bolshevism until they finally achieved their goal, and fraternization between the British and the Soviets is now complete.

And the Future?

Given the facts presented above, there can hardly be any doubt that London has become the center of world Jewry since the return of the Jews under Cromwell. It must therefore fall if the Jewish Question is to be solved globally, because not only does London still have the world trapped in a vast web of financial entanglements, but because England's hegemonic power has been put to serving Jewish interests. One only has to think of the Treaty of Versailles, which was dictated by the Jews or their straw men. Even the plague on humanity born from this, the League of Nations, is, as the Jews themselves boast, a Jewish invention. As late as 1937, the Count of Saint-Aulaire, the former French ambassador to London, wrote the following:

> [A]re we not paying too great an honor to freemasonry when we attribute to it the greatest share in the genesis of the League of Nations and in responsibility for its acts? Is not this secret society a society with limited responsibility, not only by reason of its mental weakness, but also because it is, above all else, the instrument of forces more secret still and more to be feared? Is it not unjustly accused of all the sins of Jewry? And if freemasonry is but an instrument, then President Wilson was but the instrument of an instrument.[332]

Apart from the numerous examples given of the existence of organized international Jewry, the Hebrews themselves have repeatedly given us confirmation of this fact. So let us cite them, in their own words. The *Jewish Chronicle* editorial of 7 October 1938, which appeared shortly after the Munich Agreement, stated:

> A Europe has emerged in which the democracy has been forced to retreat... One of two things may happen now. Either democrats will pull themselves together and stand with unity and vigour for their ideals, or else they will themselves, as Mr. Churchill warned, succumb to the policy of adopting Totalitarianism so as to defend themselves against the dictator States

---

[332] Saint-Aulaire, p. 73. QVOS.

with their own weapons. Both of these eventualities call for a stern reconsideration by Jews of the lines of activity they have adopted hitherto. They demand a new Jewish spirit, more positive action, and a more independent and self-reliant attitude. If, for instance, democrats are to stand up for their democratic souls, then the old idea that Jews may not align themselves as Jews with any system of political thought becomes, to say the least of it, ripe for immediate reconsideration. Apart from democracy, there is no hope for us.

If, on the other hand, the democracies are going to seek salvation by adopting the dictatorship ideologies and methods which have gone from one victory to another, then that situation, full of the gravest import for the Jewish people, will call equally loudly for a revision of the old ways. It will call, for example, for Jewish organization and unity of a kind not heretofore considered, let alone practiced. The notion that Jews must not come together resolutely for mutual protection may have to go by the board. It has never availed us much in past years. It has only been met with insensate talk about international Jewish action which has run to the most fantastic and criminal lengths. In a Europe in which democracy and all that implies are in eclipse, and the Jewish people are correspondingly in danger, Jews may well have to make an end of such hesitations, and come boldly out with the determination that they will resist unitedly the perils that beset them, and defend themselves against them as best as unarmed people may. Their enemies have now, for years, assailed the Jews, not in one country alone but in all. The Jews may now have to consider what steps they can unitedly take to beat off this world attack.

New and more positive ways will have to permeate and inspire Jewish action in all their relationships with other peoples, not excluding Zionism. The policy of *schnorring* for a crumb or two at this or that Foreign Office, and the attitude of 'yes-men' without a will or soul of their own, will no longer be adapted to the new power-politics era, if such an era there is to be. It will have to be superseded by Jewish initiative, Jewish independence, and a spirit of self-confidence.[333]

Another *Jewish Chronicle* article, dated 14 October 1938 [p.11, quoted verbatim], makes a similar appeal to British Jewry, for 'a readiness to lay our

---

[333] Translator's note: QVOS. It has been quoted more extensively here than in the original German text, in the interests of ensuring accuracy of meaning.

every atom of support on the altar of national defense'—further evidence that they see London and Great Britain as the center of their resistance. Later issues proclaim:

> the Jewish community in England, though numbering not more than 333,000 souls, is the most important and powerful in Europe... [T]his country is still the strongest bulwark of civil liberty, democracy, and tolerance...[334]
>
> The Jew in England is threatened, *qua* citizen, by the undeniable danger which confronts the country. But in that danger lurks also a dire threat to the democratic principle which is the major basis of Jewish security. That menace, too, is held over the general community. But for the Jew it is, if anything, especially grave. If Britain, the very citadel of democracy, should, Heaven forbid, be overthrown in a war, liberty would perish almost everywhere, and the fetters would be fastened more tightly even then now on Jews abroad, as well as on Jewish hands there which now are free. In the light of these threats, I hold that the burden of extra effort is unquestionably laid on Jewish citizens. If any of them are still hesitating about enrolling in the Territorial Defence Force, I would ask them how they can square their hesitancy with the deadly perils which I have briefly mentioned and which are simply beyond denial. How can they, how dare they, stand aloof from a cause in which the lives and liberties not only of the country which is their home, but the dearest and most vital interests of millions of their coreligionists abroad are at stake? [...]
>
> Without a strong Britain there is no hope for them [the Jews]—no future even for the National Home [Palestine], which cannot exist in isolation from this country, and would pass into German or Italian hands in the event of these nations' victory. I am confident that Jews will not betray their own future or their fellow-countrymen. But the time to prove it is now, and not when the dread issue is joined and the enemy is at the gates.[335]

From these publications, it seems that international Jewry, under the leadership of London, intends more than ever to take up the fight against its enemies.

---

[334] *Jewish Chronicle*, 28/10/1938 p. 32. Translator's note: QVOS. Note the kabbalistic number given for the Jewish population of England.
[335] *Jewish Chronicle*, 6/1/1939, p. 11. Translator's note: QVOS.

Is there any prospect of breaking the power of the Jews in the British Empire? We believe that W. H. Steed was wrong when he said: 'The Jewish question can only be solved by Jews.' Centuries have already passed in complete futility waiting for this to happen, which has meanwhile caused the world to forget about the reality of the problem.[336] Nor are we in agreement with Cobbett [Ludovici], who says that today's England is so completely dominated by the Jews that if they were eliminated, the entire political and economic structure of the state would collapse. Apart from that, Cobbett believes that the English nation has already become so impoverished and weakened by the Jews and their system that it is no longer able to muster the necessary energy to save itself:

> The age-long rake-off of the transformed ruling or possessing classes—whether Jews or Englishmen—who have considered profit rather than service, quick and clean sources of income rather than production, has left the people and their soil not only disintegrated but exhausted. Everywhere in plant, animal and human being there are signs of generations of ruthless exploitation, systematic devitalization. The people no longer even care for the greatness on which their ancestors squandered their blood and treasure.
>
> They are no longer interested in their own ascendancy, in maintaining their own strength against the world. So incapable have the majority become of any self-assertion or productive work requiring initiative and spirit that even the production of their own entertainment is a thing of the past, and the practice of passively receiving entertainment or of having some distracting or diverting process performed upon them, preferably while they are sitting in a chair, has become a national addiction and habit. Meanwhile, the whole of Western civilization marches swiftly on towards Communism...[337]

Even though there may be a kernel of truth in this, we do not believe that the decomposition has gone so far that everything is lost. There has surely been no other country in history who has fought against the Jews with greater tenacity and determination than England. Think of the anti-Jewish forces that arose in the year 1753, and from 1830 to 1858! It was not simply a matter of

---

[336] Steed: *Hapsburg*, p. 180. Translator's note: QVOS. However, it would be difficult for anyone to disagree with what Steed later states in the same paragraph: 'The Jewish problem is one of the great problems of the world, and no man, be he a writer, politician or diplomatist, can be considered mature until he has striven to face it squarely on its merits.'
[337] Cobbett, pp. 116-7. Translator's note: QVOS (inserted into the text for its perceived interest to the modern reader, as Ludovici's words ring truer than ever today).

discrepancies in religion, but also self-preserving, loyal English men defending themselves against foreign infiltration. Let us show this fact to Cobbett and say to him: 'Only the cause that is abandoned is truly lost.'

But not only do we have hope, we are even seeing signs that the traditional anti-Jewish spirit is reawakening in England. It is the immortal achievement of Adolf Hitler to have brought the Jewish problem back to the consciousness of not only the Germans, but also other peoples. The self-preservation instinct is beginning to emerge everywhere, including in England.

In a parliamentary debate on Racial, Religious and Political Minorities, Sir Samuel Hoare expressed his consternation that an anti-Jewish movement was emerging: 'I know it from my own experience that there is the making of a definite anti-Jewish movement. I do my best as Home Secretary to stamp upon an evil of that kind'.[338]

During a debate on the influx of aliens, the Conservative member of Parliament Howard Gritten asked the Home Secretary: 'In the matter of the admission of aliens to this country, may I ask the right hon. gentleman whether the Government intend to continue its special favors to its friends the Jews?' To which Sir Samuel replied: 'There are no special favors to any class of people'.[339]

Especially among the humble circles of the population, people are beginning to awaken more and more to the Jewish problem. People are complaining that foreigners are being given a great deal of help, without anything being done to alleviate the suffering among the British people themselves. The voices are not yet too loud, but they are at least strong enough to make the Jews sit up and take notice. The *Jewish Chronicle* of 7 October 1938 (p. 11) describes the general rise in anti-Semitism. 'I am bound to say that I have been startled and shocked by the evidences I have seen of the rise of a vocal, yes, and sometimes vicious, anti-Semitism in London,' the writer of the article in question admits, and goes on to say:

---

[338] *Daily Express*, 22/11/1938. Translator's note: QVOS (*Hansard*, House of Commons, 'Racial, Religious and Political Minorities' debate, 21 November 1938, Vol. 341, p. 1468).

[339] *Evening Standard*, 15/12/1938. Translator's note: QVOS. Readers may like to consult the original context of this exchange (*Hansard*, House of Commons, 'Aliens' debate, 15 December 1938, Vol. 342, p. 2172), and also refer to Gritten's previous exchange with Hoare, during the 'Refugees' debate of 8 December, 1938 (*Hansard*, HoC, Vol. 342, p. 1345), in which he asked, regarding the scheme to settle 50,000 Jewish children into Britain, if Hoare planned on obtaining the consent of the House before agreeing to the scheme. During the same debate, Gritten also asked: 'In view of the great numbers of unfortunate British unemployed, does the hon. Gentleman, his Department or the Government intend to put a limit or a period to the enormous influx of aliens to this country?' It was a question he repeated in the aforementioned debate a week later, and it is a question that is still being asked by the British people today, and which to date has not received a satisfactory answer.

One of the worst examples was told me a day or two ago by a friend. He was travelling on the top of a bus, and heard four men, soon reinforced by five others, enlarging on the supposed sins of 'the Jews.' One of them shouted that he would not fight unless six Jews were forced to go in front of him. When my friend interposed with the remark that 50,000 Jews fought in the last war, he was met with jeers and a volley of cynical laughter. 'Perhaps a hundred!' was the reply, 'and then only in defense'.[340]

The feeling of Jewish fear is also clearly revealed in a long essay in the *Jewish Chronicle* of 28 October 1938, which has the telling headline: 'Shadow of the Swastika: Nazism Creeping Into England.' Meanwhile, attempts are being made to convince the British public that anti-Semitism in Britain 'was no native growth', but had been 'sown and watered in Germany until it was ripe to be transplanted' and it only 'flourished in a soil of ignorance and prejudice.' A Jewish Defense Committee is supposed to provide educational publications and expose the 'lies' of anti-Jewish circles. Trained speakers are sent into the streets with 'an answer to every Fascist calumny'.[341]

Understandably, it is in the Hebrews' own interest to nip burgeoning anti-Semitism in the bud. Nevertheless, individual consciousness is growing, and with it the anti-Jewish movement. The majority of the English people are not yet aware of the Jewish danger. They will see it when they eventually have to settle their huge score with the tribe of Judah and its system.

Conclusion

A procession of events and personalities have gone by in the preceding chapters, laying bare the frightening extent to which England has been Judaized. It shall remain an open question whether the mixing of the best racial strata of England with the dangerous parasite people is an accident of circumstance or intentional. We do not wish to examine here whether the English nobility,

---

[340] Translator's note: I have inserted the start of this anecdote, not with the same intention as the original writer, which was to illustrate the falsity of English belief around Jewish participation in WWI, but because the most telling part of the tale—the first Englishman's comment—appears to indicate that the common Englishman of the time instinctively understood that there was a political and mediatic push to get the country, and Englishmen like him, into a war to fight and die for Jewish interests. This understanding of events may also have been strengthened by the bill posters that were stuck on shop windows around London bearing messages such as 'Britons—fight for Britons only' (see the *Jewish Chronicle*, 18 November 1938, p. 42).

[341] *Jewish Chronicle*, 18/11/1938, p. 13. Translator's note: QVOS. & *Jewish Chronicle*, 18/11/1938, pp. 40-1; 25/11/1938, pp. 14-15. Translator's note: QVOS.

the truly distinctive ruling class of Britain, unconsciously or with apparently intelligent foresight absorbed into itself the dangerous, plutocratic and immensely powerful representatives of Judaism in the belief that they could thereby neutralize them. Nor shall we seek to discover whether English Jewry consciously merged with the English nobility in order, in turn, to neutralize the power of this otherwise potentially threatening ruling class. Whether by accident or by design, the end result is the same, even if we tend more towards the idea of premeditation on both sides. The only important thing is the result of this insane policy.

Based on the material presented in this study, despite the fact that it is only a summary outline of the topic, the reality of the Judaization of English life can no longer be dismissed. Although the lists of names and organizations, positions of power, and personal, political and financial interconnections may seem superfluous to some, it is nevertheless necessary in order to give the reader an idea of the endless sources of Jewish influence and their means for intervention in English life.

England is the stronghold and center of international Jewry because in England the Jewish element was able to conquer the most important and decisive positions in the nation. The Jew truly rules in England and if necessary, will avail himself of some form of intermediary authority with which to camouflage and conceal his power. What is, then, the fate of England? The wealth and power of the Empire have not been able to prevent one diplomatic defeat after another in recent years, nor has it been able to prevent the fracturing of the state, the withering away of millions of unemployed, or the healthy peasantry, once the pride and backbone of the nation, being destroyed, leaving the English nation with a seemingly urban destiny.

Demographically, the situation of the island kingdom is anything but positive: instead of implementing a targeted and intelligent population policy to counteract the loss of the best English blood to the Empire, the senseless mixing with the Jewish element, as destructive physically as it is psychologically, has created further sources of weakness. We shall not prophesy here. History will pronounce its merciless but just verdict.

For the second time in history, Germany is at war with England. We Germans know who our 'English enemy' is.

Judah may believe that it has achieved its goal. But we know how to thwart its plans.

The English fate is indissolubly linked to the Jewish fate. Both are inextricably intertwined. This fact will determine the future of England.

www.ingramcontent.com/pod-product-compliance
Lightning Source LLC
Chambersburg PA
CBHW030904120626
46554CB00001B/2